O. HOOD PHILLIPS & JACKSON: CONSTITUTIONAL AND ADMINISTRATIVE LAW

Eighth Edition

BY

THE LATE O. HOOD PHILLIPS
Q.C., D.C.L., M.A.(OXON.), J.P.

*Formerly Emeritus Professor of Jurisprudence
and sometime Dean of the Faculty of Law
in the University of Birmingham*

AND

PAUL JACKSON
LL.D. (LIVERPOOL), B.C.L. (OXON.), M.A. (DUBLIN)

Emeritus Professor of Law, University of Reading

AND

PATRICIA LEOPOLD
LL.B (Belfast), LL.M (Exeter)

Senior Lecturer in Law, University of Reading

LONDON
SWEET & MAXWELL
2001

First edition . . *1952*
Second edition . . *1957*
Third edition . . *1962*
Fourth edition . . *1967*
Fifth edition . . *1973*
Sixth edition . . *1978*
Seventh edition . . *1987*
Eighth edition . . *2001*

Published in 2001 by
Sweet & Maxwell Limited of
100, Avenue Road, London NW3 3PE
http://www.sweetandmaxwell.co.uk
Typeset by Interactive Sciences Ltd, Gloucester
Printed in England by MPG Books Ltd, Bodmin, Cornwall

A CIP catalogue record for this book
is available from the British Library

ISBN 0421 574801
ISBN ISE EDITION 0421 576502

No natural forests were destroyed to make this product,
only farmed timber was used and re-planted.

O. HOOD PHILLIPS & JACKSON:
CONSTITUTIONAL
AND ADMINISTRATIVE LAW

AUSTRALIA
LBC Information Services Sydney
Sydney

CANADA and USA
Carswell
Toronto, Ontario

NEW ZEALAND
Brooker's
Auckland

SINGAPORE and MALAYSIA
Sweet & Maxwell Asia
Singapore and Kuala Lumpur

PREFACE TO THE EIGHTH EDITION

Introducing the preface to the third edition of this work, in 1962, Owen Hood Phillips commented that Britain had lost an Empire and gained a Council on Tribunals. Had he lived to see this edition he might have been tempted to say that Britain has lost a Constitution and gained a Dome. It is not only, however, the changes of the last four years that have necessitated the rewriting of much of the text of earlier editions. Parliament and the courts have legislated and deliberated over the whole period since 1987 with a vigour which has left almost no chapter untouched.

In Part I, there is a new chapter on Devolution and the chapter on The United Kingdom and Europe has been extensively rewritten. In Part II, all six chapters dealing with Parliament have similarly been largely rewritten. In Part III, the changes have been, perhaps, less dramatic although the chapters on the Cabinet and the Prime Minister and Central Government Departments and Civil Service have had to take account of important developments. The two chapters which formerly dealt with the Armed Forces and Emergencies have been replaced by one which deals with both topics and the Security Services and Terrorism. Part IV—Justice and Police—has required considerable revision while the Human Rights Act 1998 has necessitated a new chapter in Part V and, an expansion in the chapters dealing with individual freedoms. Other statutory developments have led to a further chapter in this Part, Official Secrecy and the Right to Know.

The chapter on Offences Against the State has, on the other hand, disappeared and its contents distributed elsewhere—treason, for example, to the chapter on the Monarchy, terrorism to the newly expanded chapter, already mentioned, on the Armed Forces and other topics while Official Secrets and DA Notices belong appropriately to the new chapter referred to above.

The disappearance of the chapter on Local Government marks, however, the abandonment of any attempt to deal with this increasingly specialised and highly technical subject, apart from a brief survey in Chapter 2. We believe this change reflects the reality that the law of local government no longer forms a part of the great majority of courses on Constitutional (or Public) Law.

In Part VI, apart from this omission of a long established topic, the chapter on Public Corporations tries to reflect the change from nationalisation to privatisation and Chapter 29 reflects the renewed awareness of the importance of Delegated Legislation and the controversies that can surround it.

Despite the changes and the re-writing we hope that this is still in a recognisable way, an edition of *Hood Phillips*. We have tried to keep in mind its extensive use (and citation) in countries outside the United Kingdom and those readers whose interest in constitutional law—and the history of the British Constitution—are not confined to the pressing needs of an imminent university examination.

We are again indebted to our colleagues for answering patiently our many queries in areas where we wished to draw on their expertise, to Mr Ian Sainsbury of the University Library who continues to demonstrate the superiority of the human brain to the most modern computerised retrieval systems, and to Mrs Julie Jones for her patient and efficient assistance in converting indecipherable writing into a legible word-processed text.

Once again too we must thank Sweet and Maxwell for a forbearance which must far exceed that which publishers routinely show to errant authors. We are grateful also for the suggestion that we contribute a tribute to the memory of Owen Hood Phillips.

At various points in the text we have tried to incorporate references to events occurring after the June 2001 Election and reports of some recent cases. That in turn may have led to inconsistencies in the text. We apologise for any confusion so caused.

PJ

PML

OWEN HOOD PHILLIPS, Q.C., D.C.L.
1907–1986

Owen Hood Phillips was born at Portsmouth on September 30, 1907, the younger son of a Surgeon Captain in the Royal Navy. He read law at Oxford and always retained an affection for his old college, Merton. His distinguished academic career began at King's College London, where he returned as Reader after two years as lecturer at Trinity College, Dublin. He gained first hand experience of the workings of government during World War II when he served as a civil servant in the Ministries of Labour and Aircraft production.

In 1946 he was appointed Barber Professor of Jurisprudence at the University of Birmingham. He devoted much of the rest of his life to establishing the place of Birmingham among the leading law schools—a position helped by his own reputation, based not merely on his writings but for example on his role as constitutional adviser in 1953 to 1954 to the Singapore Constitutional Commission and again as a delegate to the Malta Constitutional Conference in 1955 and 1958.

His earliest writing had been done in the time spared from "my work in a Government Department, and not seldom it was accompanied by the sound of air-raids, flying bombs or rockets". He always had in mind not merely those taking examinations in law but also "the 'intelligent layman' whose intelligence is manifested by his avoiding examinations in law altogether".

In the current climate it is interesting to note that his *Reform of the Constitution* appeared as long ago as 1970 and anticipated many of the issues which subsequently became fashionable. After a lifetime of legal textbooks and articles in the Law Quarterly Review and Public Law he indulged an abiding fascination by publishing in 1972, *Shakespeare and the Lawyers*.

From 1975, when he retired, to his death in 1986, he retained his interest in the law and was able to devote more time, in company with his wife Lucy, to gardening, travelling and entertaining, while taking up the reading of *A la recherche du temps perdu*. His dry wit and slightly quizzical view of the world never deserted him—even in his last days in hospital.

One of us had the privilege of working with him for many years, both of us had the pleasure of knowing him. His memory will remain vivid to generations of his pupils and former colleagues even as he becomes merely a name on the cover of a book to students of this century.

CONTENTS

	page
Preface to Eighth Edition	*v*
Tribute to O. Hood Phillips	*vii*
Table of Cases	*xxvii*
Table of European Cases	*lxxxiii*
Table of Statutes	*lxxxix*
Table of Foreign Statutes	*cxxiii*
Table of European Legislation	*cxxiv*
Table of European Convention on Human Rights 1950	*cxxv*

PART I: GENERAL PART

1. THE NATURE OF CONSTITUTIONAL AND ADMINISTRATIVE LAW

	para
Law	1–002
The state	1–004
The constitution of a state	1–005
Fundamental laws and judicial review of legislation	1–009
The scope of constitutional law	1–012
Administrative law	1–013
Public law	1–014
The functions of government	1–015
Doctrine of the separation of powers	1–017
Fundamental rights	1–019

2. GENERAL CHARACTERISTICS OF THE BRITISH CONSTITUTION

Unitary constitution: the United Kingdom	2–001
Unwritten constitution	2–006
Flexible constitution	2–011
Legislative supremacy of Parliament	2–012
Constitutional or limited Monarchy	2–013
Responsible parliamentary government	2–014
Importance of constitutional conventions	2–017
Independence of the judiciary from the executive	2–018
No strict separation of powers	2–020
No distinct system of administrative law	2–023
The rule of law	2–025
The British Constitution and human rights	2–034
Local government	2–035

3. PARLIAMENTARY SUPREMACY 1: HISTORY AND NATURE

I. HISTORIAL INTRODUCTION	3–001
The King as lawmaker	3–002
The Judges and a Higher Law	3–011

II. THE NATURE OF PARLIAMENTARY SUPREMACY   3–013

    Examples of subject-matter   3–018
    Practical limitations   3–022

4. *PARLIAMENTARY SUPREMACY II: PROBLEM OF SELF-LIMITATION*

The problem of self-limitation   4–001

  I. SUBJECT-MATTER OF LEGISLATION   4–002

    Repeal or amendment   4–002
    Acts of Union   4–005
    Grants of Independence   4–011
    European Communities Act 1972   4–016
    European Convention on Human Rights   4–024

  II. "MANNER AND FORM" OF LEGISLATION   4–025

    Authentication of Acts of Parliament   4–026
    Courts not concerned with procedure in Parliament 4–028
    Contrary arguments   4–030
    Parliament Acts   4–035
    Regency Acts   4–038
    Conclusion   4–039

5. *DEVOLUTION AND REGIONALISM*

  Introduction   5–001

  I. DEVOLUTIOIN   5–002

    Background to the 1998 devolution statutes   5–007
    The 1998 Provisions for Devolution   5–012
    Similarities in the three devolution schemes   5–013

  II. SCOTLAND   5–020

    The Executive   5–022
    The Parliament   5–024

  III. NORTHERN IRELAND   5–029

    The Executive   5–031
    The Assembly   5–033

IV. WALES   5–036

V. ENGLAND   5–042

VI. DEVOLUTION AND INTRA-GOVERNMENT RELATIONS   5–047

The future of devolution and the unitary constitution   5–050

6. THE UNITED KINGDOM AND EUROPE

I. INTRODUCTION   6–001

The Institutions   6–003
The Sources of Community Law   6–011
Supremacy and Direct Applicability   6–012

II. THE UNITED KINGDOM LEGISLATION   6–015

European Communities Act 1972   6–016
European Elections   6–019

III. COMMUNITY LAW AS A SOURCE OF DOMESTIC LAW   6–021

Enforceable Community rights   6–022
Reference to the European Court of Justice   6–023
Secondary legislation   6–027

IV. PARLIAMENT AND COMMUNITY LAW

Scrutiny by committees   6–029

V. THE IMPACT OF COMMUNITY LAW   6–034

7. CONSTITUTIONAL CONVENTIONS

I. THE NATURE AND PURPOSE OF CONSTITUTIONAL
   CONVENTIONS   7–001

Nature of constitutional conventions   7–001
Judicial recognition of conventions   7–005
Purpose of constitutional conventions   7–008
How and when do conventions become established?   7–010
Why are conventions observed?   7–011

II. CLASSIFICATION AND ILLUSTRATIONS OF CONSTITUTIONAL
    CONVENTIONS   7–014

1. Conventions relating to the exercise of the royal prerogative and the working of the Cabinet system   7–015
2. Conventions relating to the relations between the Lords
   and Commons, and proceedings in Parliament   7–018

3. Conventions regulating the relations between the United
   Kingdom and other members of the Commonwealth   7–019

PART II: PARLIAMENT

8. THE HIGH COURT OF PARLIAMENT

I. HISTORICAL INTRODUCTION   8–001

Judicial functions   8–003
Committees and Tribunal of Inquiry   8–003

II. THE MEETING OF PARLIAMENT   8–009

Royal prerogative in relation to Parliament   8–010
Frequency of duration and parliaments   8–013
Summons of a new Parliament   8–015
Meeting of a new Parliament   8–016
Beginning of a new session   8–017

III. THE PREROGATIVE OF DISSOLUTION   8–018

The Queen, the Prime Minister and the Commons   8–018
Exceptional situations   8–022

IV. THE LORDS AND COMMONS IN CONFLICT   8–029

Earlier conflicts   8–029
Events leading to the Parliament Act 1911   8–030
Events leading to the Parliament Act 1949   8–032
The Parliament Acts 1911 and 1949   8–034
The 1968 reform proposals   8–038
The 2000 reform proposals   8–039

9. THE HOUSE OF LORDS

Introduction   9–001
Historical introduction   9–002

I. COMPOSITION OF THE HOUSE OF LORDS   9–007

Lords Spiritual   9–008
"Elected" Hereditary peers   9–009
Life peers and life peeresses   9–010
Lords of Appeal in Ordinary   9–012
Disqualification from membership of the House   9–013
Standing Orders relating to attendance   9–014
Officers of the House   9–015

II. Modern Functions of the House of Lords 9–020

III. Reform of the House of Lords 9–034

Historical Background 9–034
The House of Lords Act 1999 and the Royal Commission on
the Reform of the House of Lords 9–035
The roles and functions of the reformed second chamber 9–037
Composition of the "new second chamber" 9–038
Resources 9–043

IV. The House of Lords as the Final Court of Appeal 9–044

Before the Appellate Jurisdiction Act 1876 9–044
From the Appellate Jurisdiction Act 1876 9–047
The Appellate Committee and Judicial Committee of the
House of Lords as Constitutional Courts 9–052

10. THE HOUSE OF COMMONS

I. Membership of the House of Commons 10–001

Historical Introduction 10–001
Miscellaneous existing disqualifications 10–005
The House of Commons Disqualification Act 1975 10–006
Payment of Members 10–015
The Speaker 10–016
House of Commons staff 10–025
Government and Opposition Whips 10–029

II. Parliamentary Franchise and Elections 10–025

Modern history of the parliamentary franchise 10–025
Qualifications for the franchise 10–026

III. Political Parties, the Electoral Commission and
Boundary Reviews 10–037

Reform of the law relating to political parties and election
campaigns 10–037
Political Parties 10–038
The Electoral Commission 10–042

IV. The Election Campaign 10–046

Conduct of elections 10–046
Election expenses 10–049
The Media and elections 10–055
The ballot 10–057
The voting system 10–058
Disputed elections 10–061
Referendums 10–063

11. PARLIAMENTARY PROCEDURE

    I. THE NATURE OF PARLIAMENTARY PROCEDURE   11–001

        Content   11–002
        Historical development   11–003
        Sources of parliamentary procedure   11–004

    II. PROCEDURE IN THE COMMONS   11–006

        Order of business   11–006
        Rules of debate   11–007
        Limiting and organising debate   11–011
        The working methods of the House   11–015

    III. PROCEDURE ON LEGISLATION   11–018

        Introduction   11–018
        Drafting of Bills   11–019
        Classification of Bills   11–020
        Ordinary procedure on Public Bills   11–022
        Procedure in the Lords   11–030
        Royal Assent   11–031
        Carry Over of Bills   11–032
        Post Legislative Scrutiny   11–033
        Private Members' Bills   11–034
        Procedure on Private Bills   11–036

12. NATIONAL FINANCE AND SCRUTINY OF THE ADMINISTRATION

    I. NATIONAL FINANCE   12–001

        Introduction   12–001
        The Crown and the Commons   12–002
        The annual cycle of finance   12–004
        Public expenditure   12–005
        Public Revenue   12–012
        Securing the legality of public expenditure   12–017

    II. THE SCRUTINY OF THE ADMINISTRATION   12–021

        Questions   12–022
        Debates   12–027
        Select Committees   12–029

13. PARLIAMENTARY PRIVILEGE

    The nature of parliamentary privilege   13–001

    I. THE PRIVILEGES OF THE COMMONS   13–004

        1. Freedom of speech and debate   13–005
        2. Freedom from arrest   13–016

3. Right of the House to regulate its own composition   13–017
4. Exclusive right to regulate its own proceedings   13–018
5. Parliament's disciplinary and penal powers   13–020

II. THE PRIVILEGES OF THE LORDS   13–026

Privileges of the House   13–026

III. MEMBERS' CONDUCT AND MEMBERS' INTERESTS   13–028

PART III: THE CENTRAL GOVERNMENT

14. THE MONARCHY

Title to the Throne   14–002
Accession   14–003
Coronation   14–004
Abdication   14–005
Royal Style and Titles   14–006
The Royal Family   14–007
Regency Acts 1937–1953   14–008
The Sovereign's Private Secretary   14–011
Treason   14–012
Treason-felony   14–021
Attempt to alarm or injure the Sovereign   14–022
Proposals for reforming the law of treason   14–023

15. THE ROYAL PREROGATIVE

I. GENERAL NATURE OF THE PROERGATIVE   15–001

Historical introduction   15–002
Classification of the prerogative   15–007
Personal prerogatives   15–009
Effect of statute on the prerogative   15–010

III. THE PREROGATIVE IN DOMESTIC AREAS   15–012

1. Executive prerogatives   15–012
2. Judicial prerogatives   15–018
3. Legislative prerogatives   15–019

IV. THE PREROGATIVES IN FOREIGN AFFAIRS   15–021

Acts of state   15–021
Passports   15–027
Treaties   15–028
Sovereign Immunity and Diplomatic representation   15–032

16. THE PRIVY COUNCIL

I. THE COUNCIL AS AN INSTRUMENT OF GOVERNMENT   16–001

Historical introduction   16–001
The Privy Council at the present day: the composition of the
    Privy Council   16–003
Functions of the Privy Council   16–004
Meetings of the Privy Council   16–007
Committees of the Council   16–008

II. THE JUDICIAL FUNCTIONS OF THE PRIVY COUNCIL   16–009

Historical introduction   16–009
The Judicial Committee—composition   16–010
Jurisdiction   16–011
A new role   16–012
Procedure   16–013
Special reference   16–014

17. THE CABINET AND THE PRIME MINISTER

I. DEVELOPMENT OF THE CABINET   17–001

Origins in the Privy Council   17–001
Opposition of Parliament   17–002
Growth of political ideas relating to the Cabinet   17–003

II. THE CABINET   17–005

Functions of the Cabinet   17–005
Composition of the Cabinet   17–007
Shadow Cabinet   17–010
Cabinet Committees   17–011
The Cabinet Office   17–014
Ministerial responsibility and accountability   17–016

III. THE PRIME MINISTER   17–025

Formal position   17–025
Functions of the Prime Minister   17–026
Choice of Prime Minister   17–028
Should a Prime Minister be a peer?   17–033
Prime Ministerial government   17–034

18. CENTRAL GOVERNMENT DEPARTMENTS AND CIVIL SERVICE

I. CENTRAL GOVERNMENT DEPARTMENTS   18–001

Offices of state   18–001
The Ministry   18–004
Organisation of Government Departments   18–005
The Treasury   18–007

Lord Chancellor's Department 18–009
Law Officers' Departments 18–010
Home Office 18–014
Foreign and Commonwealth Office 18–015
Privy Council Office 18–016
Scottish Office 18–017
Welsh Office 18–018
Northern Ireland Office 18–019
Other government departments 18–020

II. THE CIVIL SERVICE 18–021

Organisation and Management of the Civil Service 18–022
Next Steps Agencies 18–023
Who is a civil servant? 18–025
The legal status of civil servants 18–026
Conduct and Discipline 18–029
Political activities of civil servants 18–031

19. THE ARMED FORCES: EMERGENCIES: THE SECURITY SERVICES
AND TERRORISM

I. THE ARMED FORCES 19–002

Introduction 19–002
Legal position of member of the armed forces 19–004
Military law 19–009
Courts-martial 19–010
Jurisdiction of the High Court 19–014
Visiting Forces 19–017

II. EMERGENCY POWERS OF THE EXECUTIVE 19–019

Common Law Powers to Deal with an Emergency 19–019
Statutory Powers to Deal with an Emergency: In Time of
Peace 19–026
Statutory Powers to Deal with an Emergency: In Time of
War 19–031
Emergency powers and personal freedom 19–034

III. THE SECURITY SERVICES 19–038

IV. TERRORISM 19–041

PART IV: JUSTICE AND POLICE

20. THE ADMINISTRATION OF JUSTICE

I. PREROGATIVE AND ADMINISTRATION OF JUSTICE 20–002

The prerogative of mercy 20–004
Appointment of judges 20–006

II. The Courts   20–007

    Initiation of proceedings   20–012
    Trial by Jury   20–017

III. The Judiciary   20–025

    Judicial independence   20–025
    Judicial impartiality   20–036
    Judicial immunity   20–041

IV. Contempt of Court   20–043

    Civil contempt   20–045
    Criminal contempt   20–047
    Jurisdiction to punish contempts   20–053

21. THE POLICE

History of the police   21–002
Centralising and nationalising trends in policing   21–005
Main functions of the police   21–006
Legal status of police officers   21–009
Police Accountability   21–012
Complaints against police officers   21–021

PART V: RIGHTS AND DUTIES OF THE INDIVIDUAL

22. RIGHTS AND DUTIES GENERALLY

I. Introduction   22–001

    Rights of the individual under the United Kingdom Con-
      stitution   22–002
    International Covenants   22–004
    The European Convention   22–005
    The European Convention before the Human Rights Act
      1998   22–007
    Community Law   22–014

II. The Human Rights Act 1998   22–015

    The Scheme of the Act   22–015
    The Convention Rights   22–028
    Applying the Act   22–050

23. NATIONALITY, CITIZENSHIP, IMMIGRATION AND EXTRADITION

I. Introduction   23–001

    Nationality and allegiance   23–001
    The Act of 1914   23–002

British Nationality Act 1948   23–003

II. THE BRITISH NATIONALITY ACT 1984   23–005

Introduction   23–005
Categories of citizenship   23–006
British citizenship   23–007
British Dependent Territories Citizenship   23–013
British Overseas Citizenship   23–014
British subjects   23–015
British Protected Persons   23–016
British Nationals (Overseas)   23–017

III. ALIENS AND CITIZENSHIP OF THE UNION   23–018

Aliens   23–019
Citizenship of the Union   23–022

IV. IMMIGRATION, ASYLUM AND DEPORTATION   23–023

Immigration   23–024
Asylum   23–031
Deportation   23–034
Appeals and Judicial Review   23–035

V. EXTRADITION   23–041

Introduction   23–014
Extradition Act 1989   23–042
Backing of warrants   23–048

24. FREEDOM OF PERSON AND PROPERTY

I. FREEDOM OF THE PERSON   24–001

General principles   24–001
Police powers   24–003
Bail   24–023
Binding over   24–026
Other types of deprivation of liberty of the person   24–028
Writ of habeas corpus   24–034

II. FREEDOM OF PROPERTY   24–041

The Englishman's castle   24–041
Police Powers of entry and search   24–043
Customs, revenue and other officials   24–050

25. FREEDOM OF EXPRESSION

Introduction   25–001

I. DEFAMATION, LIBEL AND BLASPHEMY 25–003

Defamation 25–003
Libel 25–006
Blasphemy 25–007

II. OFFENCES AGAINST THE STATE, PUBLIC ORDER 25–009

Sedition 25–009
Incitement to racial hatred 25–010
Terrorism 25–011

III. CONTEMPT OF COURT 25–012

Unintentional interference by prejudicial publications 25–013
Deliberate interference with particular proceedings 25–014
Reporting of Judicial Proceedings 25–015
Contempt and refusal to reveal sources of information 25–016

IV. LIBERTY OF THE PRESS 25–018

Privacy and the press 25–019
Confidentiality and public interest 25–020
Disclosure of sources of information 25–022
Press Complaints Commission 25–023

V. OBSCENITY, INDECENCY AND CENSORSHIP 25–024

Obscene publications 25–024
Regulating the media and entertainment 25–032
The Broadcasting Standards Commission 25–036

26. FREEDOM OF EXPRESSION: OFFICIAL SECRECY AND THE RIGHT TO KNOW

I. OFFICIAL SECRETS 26–003

The Official Secrets Act 1911 26–003
The Official Secrets Act 1920 26–004
The Official Secrets Act 1989 26–005
"D.A." Notices 26–011
Breach of Confidence 26–012

II. STATE SURVEILLANCE 26–013

III. FREEDOM OF INFORMATION AND OPEN GOVERNMENT 26–024

The Data Protection Act 1998 26–025
Environmental Information Regulations 1992 (as amended 1998) 26–027
Local Government 26–028
The Freedom of Information Act 2000 26–029

The Public Interest Disclosure Act 1998   26–032

27. *FREEDOM OF ASSEMBLY AND ASSOCIATION*

Introduction   27–001

   I. FREEDOM OF ASSEMBLY   27–002

Public meetings, assemblies and demonstrations   27–002
The place of assembly   27–003
Restrictions on meetings, assemblies and demonstrations   27–006
Common law powers to prevent and provide for the dispersal
   of meetings, assemblies and demonstrations   27–007
The Public Order Act 1986   27–011
Public Order Offences   27–018
Some general statutory offences and common law provi-
   sions   27–027
Meetings addressed by a member of a proscribed organisa-
   tion   27–032
Picketing   27–033
Sporting events   27–036

   II. FREEDOM OF ASSOCIATION   27–038

Proscribed organisations   27–039
The wearing of "political" uniforms   27–040

PART VI: ADMINISTRATIVE LAW

INTRODUCTION TO PART VI

28. *PUBLIC CORPORATIONS AND REGULATORY BODIES*

   I. NATURE AND PURPOSE OF PUBLIC CORPORATIONS   28–001

     (i) Managerial—industrial or commercial   28–002
     (ii) Managerial—social services   28–003
     (iii) Regulatory and advisory   28–004

   II. LEGAL POSITION OF PUBLIC CORPORATIONS   28–007

Appointment and powers   28–008
Liability to judicial proceedings   28–009

   III. PRIVATISATION   28–013

   IV. REGULATING THE REGULATORS   28–016

29. *DELEGATED LEGISLATION*

   I. NATURE AND PURPOSE OF DELEGATED LEGISLATION   29–002

Forms of delegated legislation   29–003
Quasi legislation   29–004

Statutory Instruments 29–005
The reasons for delegated legislation 29–006
Concerns with types of delegated powers 29–011

II. PARLIAMENTARY SAFEGUARDS FOR DELEGATED LEGISLATION 29–017

1. At the pre-legislative stage 29–018
2. Laying before Parliament 29–019
3. Scrutinising committees 29–024
4. Special types of Delegated Legislation 29–030
5. Other controls in Parliament 29–035
6. Publication 29–036
7. Prior consultation 29–038

30. ADMINISTRATIVE JURISDICTION

Introduction 30–001

I. TRIBUNALS 30–004

Reasons for creating special tribunals 30–005
Examples of statutory tribunals 30–011
Domestic tribunals 30–017
Tribunals and Inquiries Act 1992 30–018
Reasons to be given for decisions 30–023

II. MINISTERIAL DECISIONS AND INQUIRIES 30–024

Inquiries 30–025

31. JUDICIAL CONTROL OF PUBLIC AUTHORITIES: I. LIABILITY

I. PUBLIC LAW: EXCESS OR ABUSE OF POWERS 31–002

Judicial control of powers 31–002
Ultra Vires rules 31–003
Abuse of power 31–008
Unreasonableness 31–011
Natural justice: procedural impropriety 31–013
Sub-delegation of powers 31–019
Estoppel 31–020

II. PRIVATE LAW: ORDINARY JUDICIAL CONTROL 31–021

Liability in contract 31–022
Liability for nuisance 31–023
Liability for negligence 31–024
Failure to perform statutory duties 31–025

32. JUDICIAL CONTROL OF PUBLIC AUTHORITIES: II. REMEDIES

    I. SUPERVISORY JURISDICTION OF THE HIGH COURT   32–002

        A. REMEDIES

            1. Certiorari (Quashing Order)   32–004
            2. Prohibition (Prohibiting Order)   32–007
            3. Mandamus (Mandatory Order)   32–009
            4. Injunction and Declaration   32–010

        B. SUFFICIENT INTEREST   32–011

        C. THE SCOPE OF JUDICIAL REVIEW   32–012

        D. THE AVAILABILITY OF OTHER REMEDIES   32–013

        E. DISCRETIONARY   32–014

    II. STATUTORY RIGHTS OF APPEAL   32–016

    III. EXCLUSION OR RESTRICTION OF THE JURISDICTION OF THE
         COURTS   32–017

    IV. PRIVATE LAW REMEDIES AGAINST PUBLIC AUTHORITIES   32–022

            1. Action for damages   32–022
            2. Injunction and specific performance   32–023
            3. Action for declaration   32–024

33. CROWN PROCEEDINGS

    I. LIABILITY OF THE CROWN   33–001

        Introduction   33–001
        Crown Proceedings Act 1947   33–003
        Right to sue the Crown in contract, etc.   33–004
        Liability of the Crown in tort   33–008
        Provisions relating to the armed forces   33–012
        Acts done under prerogative or statutory powers   33–014
        The Queen in her private capacity   33–015
        Estoppel   33–016

    II. CIVIL PROCEEDINGS BY AND AGAINST THE CROWN   33–017

        Jurisdiction and procedure   33–017
        Judgments and execution   33–020
        Discovery and interrogatories   33–021
        Crown Privilege and Public Interest Immunity   33–022

34. NON-JUDICIAL REMEDIES

    Introduction   34–001

I. THE COUNCIL ON TRIBUNALS   34–002

Work of the Council on Tribunals   34–003

II. PARLIAMENTARY COMMISSIONER FOR ADMINISTRATION AND
    OTHERS   34–005

Maladministration   34–005
Parliamentary Commissioner for Administration   34–006
Appointment   34–007
Investigation of complaints   34–008
Departments and authorities covered   34–009
Devolution   34–010
Reports by Commissioner   34–011
Select Committee on the Parliamentary Commissioner for
    Administration   34–012
Judicial Review   34–013
Reform   34–014
Health Service Commissioners   34–015
Commissioners for local administration   34–016
Conclusion   34–018

PART IV: THE COMMONWEALTH

35. DEPENDENT TERRITORIES

I. THE BRITISH ISLANDS   35–001

Isle of Man   35–002
The Channel Islands   35–003

II. TERRITORIES OF THE COMMONWEALTH   35–004

The British Empire   35–004
Her Majesty's dominions   35–005
British possessions   35–006
British colonies   35–007
British protectorate   35–008
British trust territories   35–009
Dependent territories   35–010
Dependencies   35–011
The Commonwealth   35–012
Independent members of the Commonwealth   35–013

III. BRITISH COLONIES   35–014

Introduction   35–014
Legislation by the United Kingdom Parliament   35–018
Legislation by the Crown   35–019
Powers of Colonial Legislatures   35–022
Composition of colonial legislatures   35–028

The powers of the Governor   35–029
Executive council and ministers   35–030
Development of internal self-government   35–031
Future developments   35–032

36. INDEPENDENCE WITHIN THE COMMONWEALTH

I. THE DOMINIONS AND THE STATUTE OF WESTMINSTER   36–001

Development of Dominion statutes   36–001
The Statute of Westminster 1931   36–003
Repugnance of Dominion legislation to United Kingdom
  statutes   36–004
Extraterritorial operation of Dominion legislation   36–005
Extension of United Kingdom legislation to the Dominions   36–006
Application to Canada   36–007
Application to Australia   36–009
Application to New Zealand   36–012

II. THE COMMONWEALTH AT PRESENT DAY   36–013

Grant of independence   36–013
Independence constitutions   36–017
Full membership of the Commonwealth   36–019
The Monarchy in the Commonwealth   36–021
Republics in the Commonwealth   36–024
Citizenship   36–025
Consultation and co-operation   36–026

37. APPEALS TO THE PRIVY COUNCIL

I. APPEALS FROM DEPENDENT TERRITORIES   37–001

Privy Council Precedents   37–002
1. Appeals by "right of grant"   37–003
2. Appeals by "special leave" of the Privy Council   37–006

II. APPEALS FROM INDEPENDENT COMMONWEALTH COUNTRIES   37–009

Appeals and Statute of Westminster   37–009
Privy Council precedents   37–011
Waning jurisdiction of the Privy Council   37–012
Suggested Commonwealth Court of Appeal   37–016

                                                              page

INDEX   *819*

TABLE OF CASES

56 Denton Road, Twickenham, Re [1953] Ch. 51; [1952] 2 All E.R. 799, Ch D ... 33–016
A. (A Mental Patient) v. Scottish Ministers; D (A Mental Patient) v. Scottish
   Ministers; R (A Mental Patient) v. Scottish Ministers 2001 S.C. 1; 2000
   S.L.T. 873, 1 Div 5–015
A. (Children) (Conjoined Twins: Medical Treatment) (No.1), Re; sub nom. A
   (Children) (Conjoined Twins: Surgical Separation), Re [2001] 2 W.L.R.
   480; [2000] 4 All E.R. 961, CA 22–031, 22–050
A. v. United Kingdom [1998] 2 F.L.R. 959; [1998] 3 F.C.R. 597; (1999) 27
   E.H.R.R. 611, ECHR 22–032
ADT v. United Kingdom [2000] 2 F.L.R. 697; 9 B.H.R.C. 112; [2000] Crim. L.R.
   1009; [2000] Fam. Law 797; The Times, August 8, 2000, ECHR 22–039
Abas v. Netherlands [1997] E.H.R.L.R. 418 24–053
Abbott v. Queen, The [1977] A.C. 755; [1976] 3 W.L.R. 462, PC 37–011
Abdulaziz v. United Kingdom (A/94); Cabales v. United Kingdom (9473/81);
   Balkandali v. United Kingdom (9474/81) (1985) 7 E.H.R.R. 471, ECHR;
   affirming in part (1984) 6 E.H.R.R. 28, Eur Comm HR 22–013, 22–026, 22–039
Abeyesekera v. Jayatilake [1932] A.C. 260, PC 35–021
Abrams v. United States (1919) 250 U.S. 616 25–001
Abse v. Smith [1986] Q.B. 536; [1986] 2 W.L.R. 322, CA 2–021, 2–028
Adams v. Adams (Att.-Gen. intervening) [1971] P. 188; [1970] 3 W.L.R. 934,
   PDAD 18–011, 35–025
Adams v. Naylor [1946] A.C. 543, HL; affirming [1944] K.B. 750, CA 33–002
Adams v. War Office [1955] 1 W.L.R. 1116; [1955] 3 All E.R. 245, QBD 33–012
Adan v. Secretary of State for the Home Department; sub nom. R. v. Secretary
   of State for the Home Department, ex p. Adan [1999] 1 A.C. 293; [1998] 2
   W.L.R. 702, HL 23–031, 23–032
Addis v. Crocker [1961] 1 Q.B. 11; [1960] 3 W.L.R. 339, CA 20–042
Adegbenro v. Akintola [1963] A.C. 614; [1963] 3 W.L.R. 63, PC 7–007, 8–024
Administrator of Austrian Property v. Russian Bank for Foreign Trade (1931) 48
   T.L.R. 37, CA 15–019, 23–020
Aero Zipp Fasteners v. YKK Fasteners (UK) Ltd [1973] C.M.L.R. 819; [1973]
   F.S.R. 580, Ch D 4–021
Agricultural Horticultural and Forestry Industry Training Board v. Aylesbury
   Mushrooms Ltd [1972] 1 All E.R. 280; The Times, October 23, 1971,
   QBD 31–005
Ahmad v. Inner London Education Authority [1978] Q.B. 36; [1977] 3 W.L.R.
   396, CA 22–008, 22–010, 22–040
Ahmed v. United Kingdom [1999] I.R.L.R. 188; (2000) 29 E.H.R.R. 1; 5
   B.H.R.C. 111; [1998] H.R.C.D. 823 .... 18–031, 27–038
Air Canada v. Secretary of State for Trade (No.2) [1983] 2 A.C. 394; [1983] 2
   W.L.R. 494, HL 7–005, 33–023, 33–026, 33–027
Air India v. Wiggins [1980] 1 W.L.R. 815; [1980] 2 All E.R. 593, HL 3–020
Airedale NHS Trust v. Bland [1993] A.C. 789; [1993] 2 W.L.R. 316, HL 22–031,
                                                                                            22–050
Airey v. Ireland (No.1) (A/32) (1979–80) 2 E.H.R.R. 305, ECHR 20–012, 22–028,
                                                                                            22–030
Akar v. Att.-Gen. of Sierra Leone [1970] A.C. 853; [1969] 3 W.L.R. 970, PC 4–035
Al Nahkel for Contracting and Trading Ltd v. Lowe [1986] Q.B. 235; [1986] 2
   W.L.R. 317, QBD 15–015
Alconi Ltd v. Republic of Colombia [1984] A.C. 580 15–032
Alderson v. Booth [1969] 2 Q.B. 216; [1969] 2 W.L.R. 1252, DC 24–010

Alfred Crompton Amusement Machines Ltd v. Customs and Excise Commissioners (No.2) [1974] A.C. 405; [1973] 3 W.L.R. 268, HL 33–023
Ali (Mohammed Muktar) v. Queen, The [1992] 2 A.C. 93; [1992] 2 W.L.R. 357, PC 37–013
Allen v. Flood [1898] A.C. 1 9–051
Allen v. Gulf Oil Refining Ltd [1981] A.C. 1001; [1981] 2 W.L.R. 188, HL ... 31–023
Allen v. Thorn Electrical Industries Ltd; Griffin v. Metropolitan Police District Receiver [1968] 1 Q.B. 487; [1967] 3 W.L.R. 858, CA 2–033
Alleyne-Forte v. Att.-Gen. of Trinidad and Tobago [1998] 1 W.L.R. 68; [1998] R.T.R. 75; (1997) 141 S.J.L.B. 238, PC 37–013
Allgemeine Gold und Silberscheideanstalt v. Customs and Excise Commissioners [1980] Q.B. 390; [1980] 2 W.L.R. 555; [1980] 1 C.M.L.R. 488, CA; [1978] 2 C.M.L.R. 292, QBD 6–039
Allingham v. Minister of Agriculture and Fisheries [1948] 1 All E.R. 780; 64 T.L.R. 290, DC 31–019
Amalgamated Society of Engineers v. Adelaide Steamship Co (1920) 28 C.L.R. 129 35–005
Amalgamated Society of Railway Servants v. Osbourne [1910] A.C. 87, HL ... 10–015
Amand v. Secretary of State for the Home Department; *sub nom* Amand v. Home Secretary & Minister of Defence of Royal Netherlands Government [1943] A.C. 147, HL; affirming [1942] 2 K.B. 26, CA 24–039
Ambard v. Att.-Gen. for Trinidad and Tobago [1936] A.C. 322, PC 20–047
Amendment of the Constitution of Canada, Re (1982) 125 D.L.R. (3d) 1 ..... 7–004, 7–006
American Express v. British Airways Board [1983] 1 W.L.R. 701; [1983] 1 All E.R. 557, QBD 28–002
An Bord Bainne Co-operative Ltd (Irish Dairy Board) v. Milk Marketing Board [1984] 2 C.M.L.R. 584; (1984) 81 L.S.G. 2223, CA 6–037
Ancell & Ancell v. McDermott [1993] 4 All E.R. 355; [1993] R.T.R. 235, CA 31–024
Anderson v. Gorrie [1895] 1 Q.B. 668, CA 20–041
Anderson v. United Kingdom [1998] EHRLR 27–013
Anderson, Ex.p (1861) 3 El & El 487 24–040
Anisminic v. Foreign Compensation Commission (No.2) [1969] 2 A.C. 147; [1969] 2 W.L.R. 163, HL 8–036, 31–007, 32–018, 32–019
Annalisa Carbonari v. Universita degli Studi di Bologna [1999] E.C.R. 1103 6–013
Anns v. Merton LBC [1978] A.C. 728; [1977] 2 W.L.R. 1024, HL 31–024
Anton Piller KG v. Manufacturing Processes Ltd [1976] Ch. 55; [1976] 2 W.L.R. 162, CA 24–052
Application des Gaz SA v. Falks Veritas Ltd [1974] Ch. 381; [1974] 3 W.L.R. 235, CA 6–012, 6–037
Argyll (Duchess) v. Argyll (Duke) [1967] Ch. 302; [1965] 2 W.L.R. 790, Ch D ... 17–023
Armour v Liverpool Corporation [1939] Ch. 422, Ch D 32–022
Arnold v. King, The [1914] A.C. 644, PC 37–008
Arrowsmith v. Jenkins [1963] 2 Q.B. 561; [1963] 2 W.L.R. 856, DC 27–001, 27–028
Arrowsmith v. United Kingdom (1980) 3 E.H.R.R. 218 22–040
Arsenal Football Club Ltd v Smith; Arsenal Football Club Ltd v Ende [1979] A.C. 1; [1977] 2 W.L.R. 974, HL 32–011, 32–016
Arthur J.S. Hall & Co v. Simons; *sub nom.* Harris v. Scholfield Roberts & Hall; Barratt v. Ansell (t/a as Woolf Seddon) [2000] 3 W.L.R. 543; [2000] 3 All E.R. 673, HL 20–005, 20–042
Artico v. Italy (A/37) (1981) 3 E.H.R.R. 1, ECHR 22–028
Ashbury v. Ellis [1893] A.C. 339, PC 35–026
Ashby v. White (1703) Ld. Raym. 938 ... 2–008, 9–045, 10–036, 10–061, 13–003, 33–010
Askoy v. Turkey (1996) 23 E.H.R.R. 553 22–032
Associated Newspapers Ltd v. Dingle; *sub nom.* Dingle v. Associated Newspapers Ltd [1960] 2 Q.B. 405; [1960] 2 W.L.R. 430, QBD 13–011, 13–014

Associated Provincial Picture Houses Ltd v. Wednesbury Corporation [1948] 1
K.B. 223; [1947] 2 All E.R. 680, CA .. 22–023, 31–002, 31–011, 31–012, 33–022
Astley v. Younge (1759) 2 Burr. 807 20–042
Atkins v. DPP (1989) 89 Cr.App.Rep. 199, DC 27–024
Atkins v. DPP; *sub nom.* DPP v. Atkins [2000] 1 W.L.R. 1427; [2000] 2 All E.R.
425, QBD 25–030
Atkinson v. United States Government; *sub nom.* R. v. Brixton Prison Governor,
ex p. Atkinson [1971] A.C. 197; [1969] 3 W.L.R. 1074, HL 23–045
Att.-Gen. v. Associated Newspapers Ltd [1994] 2 A.C. 238; [1994] 2 W.L.R.
277, HL 20–048
Att.-Gen. v. Bastow [1957] 1 Q.B. 514; [1957] 2 W.L.R. 340, QBD 32–023
Att.-Gen. v. BBC; *sub nom.* Dible v. BBC [1981] A.C. 303; [1980] 3 W.L.R. 109,
HL 15–029, 20–007, 20–043, 22–008, 22–020, 30–001
Att.-Gen. v. Brotherton; *sub nom.* Yorkshire Derwent v. Brotherton [1992] 1 A.C.
425; [1991] 3 W.L.R. 1126, HL 4–037
Att.-Gen. v. Butterworth; *sub nom.* Attorney General's Application, Re [1963] 1
Q.B. 696; [1962] 3 W.L.R. 819, CA 20–049
Att.-Gen. v. Clough [1963] 1 Q.B. 773; [1963] 2 W.L.R. 343, QBD 8–007, 25–016
Att.-Gen. v. Connolly [1947] I.R. 213, HC (Irl) 20–047
Att.-Gen. v. De Keyser's Royal Hotel Ltd, Re *sub nom.* De Keyser's Royal Hotel
Ltd v. King, The [1920] A.C. 508, HL; affirming [1919] 2 Ch. 197, CA 15–002,
15–003, 15–004, 15–004, 15–004, 15–010, 24–054, 33–005,
33–014
Att.-Gen. v. Donaldson (1842) 10 M. & W. 117 15–019
Att.-Gen. v. English [1983] 1 A.C. 116; [1982] 3 W.L.R. 278, HL 25–013
Att.-Gen. v. Fulham Corporation [1921] 1 Ch. 440 31–004
Att.-Gen. v. Great Southern and Western Railway Co. [1925] A.C. 754, HL;
reversing [1924] 2 K.B. 450, CA 33–007, 35–005, 36–023
Att.-Gen. v. Guardian Newspapers Ltd (No.1); *sub nom.* Spycatcher: Guardian/
Observer Discharge [1987] 1 W.L.R. 1248; [1987] 3 All E.R. 316, HL 25–001,
25–020
Att.-Gen. v. Guardian Newspapers Ltd (No.2) [1990] 1 A.C. 109; [1988] 3
W.L.R. 776, HL 25–020, 26–024
Att.-Gen. v. Guardian Newspapers Ltd [1999] E.M.L.R. 904; *The Independent,*
July 30, 1999, QBD 25–013
Att.-Gen. v. Hislop [1991] 1 Q.B. 514; [1991] 2 W.L.R. 219, CA 25–014
Att.-Gen. v. Independent Television News Ltd [1995] 2 All E.R. 370; [1995] 1
Cr. App. R. 204, QBD 25–013
Att.-Gen. v. Jonathan Cape Ltd; Att.-Gen. v. Times Newspapers Ltd [1976] Q.B.
752; [1975] 3 W.L.R. 606, QBD 7–005, 17–007, 17–023, 25–001, 25–020
Att.-Gen. v. Jones [2000] 1 Q.B. 66; [1999] 3 W.L.R. 444, QBD 10–005, 13–017
Att.-Gen. v. Leveller Magazine Ltd [1979] A.C. 440; [1979] 2 W.L.R. 247, HL ... 20–043,
20–048
Att.-Gen. v. M.G.N. Ltd; *sub nom.* Mirror Group Newspapers, Re [1997] 1 All
E.R. 456; [1997] E.M.L.R. 284, QBD 25–013
Att.-Gen. v. Mulholland; Att.-Gen. v. Foster [1963] 2 Q.B. 477; [1963] 2 W.L.R.
658, CA 8–007
Att.-Gen. v. News (ʋ Newspapers Ltd [1987] Q.B. 1; [1986] 3 W.L.R. 365,
CA 25–013
Att.-Gen. v. News Grou, ʋwspapers Ltd [1989] Q.B. 110; [1988] 3 W.L.R.
163; [1988] 2 All E.. QBD 25–014
Att.-Gen. v. Newspaper Pub' ʰinₑ ᴾlᶜ [1988] Ch. 333; [1987] 3 W.L.R. 942,
CA 25–020
Att.-Gen. v. Nissan; *sub nom* N.ₛ Att.-Gen. [1970] A.C. 179; [1969] 2
W.L.R. 926.HL 15–021, 15–022, 15–024, 15–025, 32–021

Att.-Gen. v. Prince Ernest Augustus of Hanover; *sub nom.* Prince Earnest of
    Hanover v. Att.-Gen. [1957] A.C. 436; [1957] 2 W.L.R. 1, HL 4–002, 23–001
Att.-Gen. v. Punch Ltd [2001] 2 All E.R. 655 *The Times,* March 30, 2001 25–014
Att.-Gen. v. Royal Society for the Prevention of Cruelty to Animals *The Times,*
    June 22, 1985, DC 20–049
Att.-Gen. v. Smith [1958] 2 Q.B. 173; [1958] 3 W.L.R. 81, QBD 32–023
Att.-Gen. v. Stewart (1815) 2 Mer. 143 35–017
Att.-Gen. v. Times Newspapers [1974] A.C. 273 .... 25–012, 25–014
Att.-Gen. v. Times Newspapers Ltd *The Times,* February 12, 1983, Div.Ct 25–013
Att.-Gen. v. Times Newspapers Ltd; *sub nom.* Att.-Gen. v. Observer and Guard-
    ian Newspapers [1992] 1 A.C. 191; [1991] 2 W.L.R. 994, HL 20–043, 25–020
Att.-Gen. v. Unger [1998] 1 Cr. App. R. 308; [1998] E.M.L.R. 280, QBD 25–013
Att.-Gen. v. Wilts United Dairies (1922) 37 T.L.R. 884; 91 L.J.K.B. 897 .... 2–008, 3–010,
                                           12–003, 19–040, 19–041, 24–053, 29–012, 31–005
Att.-Gen. v. Wimbledon House Estate Co [1904] 2 Ch. 34, Ch D 32–023
Att.-Gen. for Canada v. Att.-Gen. for Ontario (Appeal No.100 of 1936) [1937]
    A.C. 326, PC 15–028
Att.-Gen. for Ceylon v. Silva (AD) [1953] A.C. 461; [1953] 2 W.L.R. 1185, PC 15–020
Att.-Gen. for New South Wales v. Perpetual Trustee Co Ltd [1955] A.C. 457;
    [1955] 2 W.L.R. 707, PC 18–026, 21–009
Att.-Gen. for New South Wales v. Trethowan [1932] A.C. 526, PC; (1931) 44
    C.L.R. 394, High Ct Austr. 4–032, 35–024
Att.-Gen. for Northern Ireland's Reference (No.1 of 1975) [1977] A.C. 105 19–006,
                                                   19–031, 19–032, 20–032
Att.-Gen. of British Columbia v. Att.-Gen of Canada (1889) 14 App.Cas. 295 37–007
Att.-Gen. of Canada v. Cain; Att.-Gen. of Canada v. Gilhula [1906] A.C. 542,
    PC 23–021, 35–026
Att.-Gen. of Ceylon v. Kumarasinghege Don John Perera [1953] A.C. 200;
    [1953] 2 W.L.R. 238, PC 37–008
Att.-Gen. of Fiji v. DPP [1983] 2 A.C. 672; [1983] 2 W.L.R. 275, PC 37–013
Att.-Gen. of Hong Kong v. Lee Kwong-Kut; Att.-Gen. of Hong Kong v. Lo Chak
    Man [1993] A.C. 951; [1993] 3 W.L.R. 329, PC 22–052, 37–013
Att.-Gen. of Hong Kong v. Ng Yuen Shiu [1983] 2 A.C. 629; [1983] 2 W.L.R.
    735, PC 31–018
Att.-Gen. of Jamaica v Williams [1998] A.C. 351; [1997] 3 W.L.R. 389, PC ... 37–013
Att.-Gen. of New Zealand v. Horton [1999] 1 W.L.R. 1195; (1999) 143 S.J.L.B.
    149, PC 37–012
Att.-Gen. of Ontario v. Att.-Gen. of Canada [1947] A.C. 127; [1947] 1 All E.R.
    137, PC 37–006, 37–010
Att.-Gen. of St. Christopher, Nevis and Anguilla v. Reynolds [1980] A.C. 637;
    [1980] 2 W.L.R. 171, PC 19–046, 32–021
Att.-Gen. of the Duchy of Lancaster v. G.E. Overton (Farms) Ltd [1981] Ch. 333;
    [1980] 3 W.L.R. 869, Ch D 15–004, 15–013
Att.-Gen. of the Gambia v. Momodou Jobe [1984] A.C. 689; [1984] 3 W.L.R.
    174, PC 37–013
Att.-Gen. of the Gambia v. N'Jie [1961] A.C. 617; [1961] 2 W.L.R. 845, PC 37–007
Att.-Gen. of Trinidad and Tobago v. Whiteman [1991] 2 A.C. 240; [1991] 2
    W.L.R. 1200, PC 22–019, 37–013
Att.-Gen. of Victoria, Re (1866) 3 Moo.P.C. (N.S.) 527 37–007
Att.-Gen. to the Prince of Wales v. Collom [1916] 2 K.B. 193, KBD 33–016
Att.-Gen's Reference (No.3 of 1977) [1978] 1 W.L.R. 1123, CA 25–026
Att.-Gen's Reference (No.5 of 1980) [1980] 3 All. E.R. 816 25–026
Att.-Gen's Reference (No.3 of 2000) [2001] Crim. L.R. 645 21–006
Attygalle v. King, The [1936] A.C. 338, PC 37–008
Australian Consolidated Press Ltd v. Uren (Thomas) [1969] 1 A.C. 590; [1967]
    3 W.L.R. 1338, PC 37–001, 37–002, 37–011

Australian Woollen Mills v. Australia [1956] 1 W.L.R. 11; [1955] 3 All E.R. 711,
PC 33–006
Aydin v. Turkey (1998) 25 E.H.R.R. 251; 3 B.H.R.C. 300, ECHR 22–032
Ayr Harbour Trustees v. Oswald (1883) L.R. 8 App. Cas. 623, HL 31–022
Azam v. Secretary of State for the Home Department; sub nom. R. v. Governor
of Pentonville Prison, ex p. Azam [1974] A.C. 18; [1973] 2 W.L.R. 1058,
HL 3–018, 23–028, 23–040

B (A Minor) (Adoption by Parent), Re; sub nom. B (A Minor) (Adoption:
Jurisdiction), Re [1975] Fam. 127; [1975] 2 W.L.R. 569, Fam Div 31–015
Bache v. Essex County Council [2000] 2 All E.R. 847; [2000] I.C.R. 313; The
Times, February 2, 2000, CA 30–020
Badry v. DPP of Mauritius [1983] 2 A.C. 297; [1983] 2 W.L.R. 161, PC 20–047,
37–008
Bailey v. Williamson (1873) L.R. 8 Q.B. 118 .... 27–004, 29–023
Bain v. Fothergill (1874) L.R. 7 H.L. 158 9–046
Bainbridge v. Postmaster-General [1906] 1 K.B. 178, CA 18–025, 33–0
Baldwin & Francis Ltd v. Patents Appeal Tribunal [1959] A.C. 663; [1959] 2
W.L.R. 826, HL 32–004, 32–005
Balfour v. Foreign and Commonwealth Office [1994] 1 W.L.R. 681; [1994] 2 All
E.R. 588, CA 33–027
Balogh v. St. Albans Crown Court [1975] Q.B. 73; [1974] 3 W.L.R. 314, CA 20–044,
20–050
Bank of England v. Vagliano Brothers; sub nom. Vagliano Brothers v. Bank of
England [1891] A.C. 107, HL; reversing (1889) L.R. 23 Q.B.D. 243, CA 4–022
Bank voor Handel en Scheepvaart NV v. Administrator of Hungarian Property
See Bank voor Handel en Scheepvaart NV v. Slatford (No.2) [1954] A.C.
584; [1954] 2 W.L.R. 867, HL 15–020, 23–020, 33–010
Bankers' Case (1700) 14 St.Tr. 1 33–005
Barclays Bank International Ltd v. Queen, The [1974] Q.B. 823; [1973] 3 W.L.R.
627, QBD 33–018
Barnard v. National Dock Labour Board [1953] 2 Q.B. 18; [1953] 2 W.L.R. 995,
CA 31–019
Barnardiston v. Soame (1674) 6 St. Tr. 1063; (1689) 6 St. Tr. 1119 10–061
Barnardo v. Ford; sub nom. R. v. Barnardo; Gossage's Case, Re [1892] A.C. 326,
HL; affirming (1890) L.R. 24 Q.B.D. 283, CA 24–037
Barnato, Re; sub nom. Joel v. Sanges [1949] Ch. 258; [1949] 1 All E.R. 515,
CA 32–024
Barnett v. French [1981] 1 W.L.R. 848; (1981) 72 Cr. App. R. 272, DC 33–002
Barraclough v. Brown [1897] A.C. 615, HL 32–013
Barrett v. Enfield LBC [1999] 3 W.L.R. 79; [1999] 3 All E.R. 193; [1999] L.G.R.
473, HL 31–024
Barrett v. Ministry of Defence [1995] 1 W.L.R. 1217; [1995] 3 All E.R. 87, CA 33–013
Barritt v. Att.-Gen [1971] 1 W.L.R. 1713; [1971] 3 All E.R. 1183, PDAD 20–040
Barrow's Case 91811) 14 East 346; Foster, 158 19–004
Bastable v. Little [1907] 1 K.B. 59, KBD 24–022
Bate's Case (Case of Impositions) (1606) Lane 22; 2 St. Tr. 371 .... 3–008, 15–002
Bateman's Trusts, Re (1873) L.R. 15 Eq. 355 35–005
Bayer AG v. Winter (No.1) [1986] 1 W.L.R. 497; [1986] 1 All E.R. 733, CA 15–015
Beach v. Freeson [1972] 1 Q.B. 14; [1971] 2 W.L.R. 805, QBD 13–006
Beatty v. Gillbanks (1882) 9 Q.B. 308; (1882) 15 Cox C.C. 138 .... 24–041, 27–008
Belfast Corporation v. Daly [1963] N.I. 78 31–012
Belgian Linguistic Case (1968) 1 E.H.R.R. 252 .... 22–044, 22–047
Belgische Radio en Televisie v. SABAM [1974] E.C.R. 51 6–012
Bell v. DPP of Jamaica [1985] A.C. 937; [1985] 3 W.L.R. 73, PC 37–013
Bell v. Secretary of State for Defence [1986] Q.B. 322; [1986] 2 W.L.R. 248 33–012

Belsfield Court Construction Co Ltd v. Pywell [1970] 2 Q.B. 47; [1969] , W L.R. 1051, QBD 32–005
Bendenoun v. France (A/284) (1994) 18 E.H.R.R. 54, ECHR 24–053
Benham v. United Kingdom (1996) 22 E.H.R.R. 293; The Times, June 24, 1996, ECHR 24–001
Bennett v. Chappell [1966] Ch. 391; [1965] 3 W.L.R. 829, CA 32–024
Bentley (Derek William), Re [2001] 1 Cr.App.R. 307 .... 20–004, 20–005
Bentley v. Brudzinski (1982) 75 Cr. App. R. 217; [1982] Crim. L.R. 825, DC 24–019, 24–022
Bethel v. Douglas [1995] 1 W.L.R. 794; [1995] 3 All E.R. 801, PC 15–010
Bibby v. Chief Constable of Essex Police (2000) 164 J.P. 297; [2000] R.A. 384, CA 24–008
Bilston Corporation v. Wolverhampton Corporation [1942] Ch. 391, Ch D 4–033
Birdi v. Secretary of State for Home Affairs (1975) 119 S.J. 322; The Times, February 12, 1975, CA 22–009
Birkdale District Electric Supply Co Ltd v. Southport Corporation [1926] A.C. 355, HL; affirming [1925] Ch. 794, CA 31–022
Blackburn v. Att.-Gen [1972] C.M.L.R. 882, CA 4–011, 4–012, 4–017
Blackburn v. Att.-Gen. [1971] 1 W.L.R. 1037; [1971] 2 All E.R. 1380, CA 15–029
Blackburn v. Bowering [1994] 1 W.L.R. 1324; [1994] 3 All E.R. 380, CA 24–020
Black-Clawson International Ltd v. Papierwerke Waldhof-Ashaffenburg AG [1975] A.C. 591; [1975] 2 W.L.R. 513, HL 4–037
Blackpool Corporation v. Locker [1948] 1 K.B. 349; [1948] 1 All E.R. 85, CA 31–020
Blankard v. Galdy (1693) 2 Salk. 411 .... 35–015, 35–017
Blathwayt v. Baron Cawley [1976] A.C. 397; [1975] 3 W.L.R. 684, HL 22–010
Blomquist v. Att.-Gen. of the Commonwealth of Dominica [1987] A.C. 489; [1987] 2 W.L.R. 1185 37–013
Boakes v. Postmaster-General The Times, October 27, 1962, CA 28–012
Board of Education v. Rice; sub nom. R. v. Board of Education [1911] A.C. 179, HL; affirming [1910] 2 K.B. 165 .... 31–017, 31–018, 32–004, 32–009
Board of Trade v. Temperley Steam Shipping Co. Ltd (1927) 27 Ll. L. Rep. 230, CA; affirming (1926) 26 Ll. L. Rep. 76, KBD 33–006
Bombay & Persia Steam Navigation Co. v. Shipping Controller (1921) 7 Ll. L. Rep. 226, CA; affirming [1920] 3 K.B. 402, KBD 33–018
Bombay & Persia Steam Navigation Co. Ltd v. Maclay See Bombay & Persia Steam Navigation Co v. Shipping Controller
Bombay Province v. Bombay Municipal Corporation [1947] A.C. 58; 62 T.L.R. 643, PC 15–019
Bonnard v. Perryman [1891] 2 Ch. 269 22–018
Boodram v. Baptiste [1999] 1 W.L.R. 1709; The Times, June 1, 1999, PC 37–013
Booth & Co. v. National Enterprise Board (NEB) [1978] 3 All E.R. 624,QBD 28–008
Boots Chemists (New Zealand) Ltd v. Chemists Service Guild of New Zealand Inc. [1968] A.C. 457; [1967] 3 W.L.R. 1121, PC 37–012
Bourgoin SA v. Ministry of Agriculture Fisheries and Food [1986] Q.B. 716; [1985] 3 W.L.R. 1027, CA 6–037
Bousefield v. North Yorkshire CC [1982] 44 P. & C.R. 203, Ch D (See also Tillmire Common, Re) 32–024
Bowles v. Bank of England [1913] 1 Ch. 57, Ch D 2–026, 7–013, 12–003, 12–014, 31–005
Bowman v. Secular Society Ltd; sub nom. Secular Society Ltd v. Bowman; Bowman, Re [1917] A.C. 406, HL; affirming [1915] 2 Ch. 447, CA 25–007
Bowman v. United Kingdom (1998) 26 E.H.R.R. 1; 4 B.H.R.C. 25, ECHR 10–051, 22–049
Bozano v. France (1987) 9 E.H.R.R. 297; The Times, January 7, 1987; ECHR 23–041
Bradford Corporation v. Myers [1916] 1 A.C. 242, CA 31–022
Bradlaugh v. Clarke (1883) 8 App.Cas. 354 9–045

Bradlaugh v. Gossett (1884) 12 QBD 271 .... 10–002, 13–006, 13–007, 13–018
Brannigan and McBride v. UK (1999) 17 E.H.R.R. 539 19–054
Brasserie du Pecheur SA v. Germany (C46/93); R. v. Secretary of State for
    Transport, ex p. Factortame Ltd (No.4) (C48/93) [1996] Q.B. 404; [1996] 2
    W.L.R. 506; [1996] E.C.R. I–1029, ECJ 6–014
Brassey's Settlement, Re [1955] 1 All E.R. 577; [1955] 1 W.L.R. 192ᶜh D 35–011
Brazier v. Ministry of Defence [1965] 1 Lloyd's Rep. 26, QBD 33–011
Brazil v. Chief Constable of Surrey [1983] 1 W.L.R. 1155, CA 24–019, 24–022
Bribery Commissioner v. Ranasinghe [1965] A.C. 172; [1964] 2 W.L.R. 1301,
    PC 3–014, 4–001, 4–034, 35–022, 36–018
Bright v. Attorney General [1971] 2 Lloyd's Rep. 68; [1971] R.T.R. 253, CA 33–011
Brighton Corporation v. Packham (1908) 72 J.P. 318 27–004
Brind v. United Kingdom (1994) 77–ADR. 42 25–033
British Airports Authority v. Ashton [1983] 1 W.L.R. 1079; [1983] 3 All E.R. 6,
    DC 31–012
British Airways Board v. Laker Airways Ltd; sub nom. Laker Airways Ltd v.
    Secretary of State for Trade and Industry [1985] A.C. 58; [1984] 3 W.L.R.
    413, HL; reversing [1984] Q.B. 142; [1983] 3 W.L.R. 544, CA 3–021, 15–023,
                                                    15–029, 22–007, 31–002, 31–008
British Broadcasting Corporation v. Johns [1965] Ch. 32; [1964] 2 W.L.R. 1071,
    CA 15–004, 28–010
British Coal Corporation v. King, The [1935] A.C. 500, PC 4–011, 7–005, 16–013,
                                                    35–026, 37–006, 37–010, 37–011
British Medical Association v. Greater Glasgow Health Board [1989] A.C. 1211;
    [1989] 2 W.L.R. 660, HL 33–017
British Oxygen Co Ltd v. Board of Trade See British Oxygen Co Ltd v. Minister
    of Technology
British Oxygen Co Ltd v. Minister of Technology; sub nom. British Oxygen Co
    Ltd v Board of Trade [1971] A.C. 610; [1970] 3 W.L.R. 488, HL 31–010
British Railways Board v. Pickin; sub nom. Pickin v. British Railways Board
    [1974] A.C. 765; [1974] 2 W.L.R. 208, HL 3–012, 3–016, 3–017, 4–029, 7–018,
                                                    11–040, 13–003, 13–018
British Steel Corporation v. Granada Television Ltd [1981] A.C. 1096; [1980] 3
    W.L.R. 774, HL 25–016, 25–018, 25–020
Broadmayne, The [1916] P. 64, CA 15–016
Brocklebank v. King, The [1925] 1 K.B. 52; (1924) 19 Ll. L. Rep. 375, CA ... 33–005
Brogan v. United Kingdom (A/145–B) (1989) 11 E.H.R.R. 117; The Times,
    November 30, 1988, E.C.H.R. 19–054, 22–013, 22–027, 24–001
Bromley LBC v. Greater London Council [1983] 1 A.C. 768; [1982] 2 W.L.R.
    92, HL 3–023, 31–004, 31–008
Broome v. Cassell & Co (No.1) [1972] A.C. 1027; [1972] 2 W.L.R. 645, HL 22–010
Broome v. DPP; sub nom. Hunt v. DPP [1974] A.C. 587; [1974] 2 W.L.R. 58,
    HL 27–033, 27–034
Brown v. Lord Advocate 1984 S.L.T. 146, OH 33–012
Brown v. Stott [2001] 2 W.L.R. 817; [2001] 2 All E.R. 97, PC 22–053
Browne v. Queen, The [1999] 3 W.L.R. 1158, PC 2–021, 37–013
Browning v. War Office [1963] 1 Q.B. 750; [1963] 2 W.L.R. 52, CA 33–011
Bryan v. United Kingdom (A/335–A) (1996) 21 E.H.R.R. 342; [1996] 1 P.L.R.
    47, ECHR 22–036, 30–027
Buchanan (James) & Co Ltd v. Babco Forwarding & Shipping (UK) Ltd [1978]
    A.C. 141; [1977] 3 W.L.R. 907, HL 15–029
Buck v. Att.-Gen. [1965] Ch. 745; [1965] 2 W.L.R. 1033, CA 36–017
Budd v. Anderson [1943] K.B. 642 19–044
Bullard v. Croyden Hospital Group Management Committee [1953] 1 Q.B. 511;
    [1953] 2 W.L.R. 470, QBD 28–011
Bulmer v. Bollinger [1974] Ch. 401; [1974] 3 W.L.R. 202, CA 6–023

Burden v. Rigler [1911] 1 K.B. 337, KBD 27–001, 27–004, 27–029
Burdett v. Abbot (1811) 14 East 1 13–007
Burdett v. Abbot (1812) 4 Taunt 401 19–005
Burmah Oil Co v. Lord Advocate [1965] A.C. 75; [1964] 2 W.L.R. 1231, HL ... 2–027,
    3–018, 9–024, 15–003, 15–004, 15–017, 15–025, 15–026, 19–032,
    19–047, 33–013, 33–014, 33–026
Burnley BC v. England (1978) 76 L.G.R. 393; 77 L.G.R. 227 31–012
Buron v. Denman (1848) 2 Ex. 167 15–024
Burt v. Governor-General [1992] 3 N.Z.L.R. 672 20–004
Burton v. British Railways Board (C19/81) [1982] Q.B. 1080; [1982] 3 W.L.R.
    387; [1982] E.C.R. 554, ECJ; [1981] I.R.L.R. 16, EAT 6–026
Bush v. Green [1985] 1 W.L.R. 1143; [1985] 3 All E.R. 721, CA 20–053
Bushell v. Secretary of State for the Environment [1981] A.C. 75; [1980] 3
    W.L.R. 22, HL 30–026, 30–028
Bushell's Case (1670) 6 St. Tr. 999; (1677) Vaughan 135 20–042
Buttes Gas and Oil Co. v. Hammer (No.3); Occidental Petroleum Corporation v.
    Buttes Gas and Oil Co. (No.2) [1982] A.C. 888; [1981] 3 W.L.R. 787, HL 15–021,
    33–026
Buxoo v. Queen, The [1988] 1 W.L.R. 820; (1988) 132 S.J. 967, PC 37–008
Buxton v. Minister of Housing and Local Government [1961] 1 Q.B. 278; [1960]
    3 W.L.R. 866, QBD 32–016, 34–003

C. (A Minor) (Wardship: Contempt), Re [1986] 1 F.L.R. 578; [1986] Fam. Law
    187, CA 20–045
CILFIT v. Italian Ministry of Health (C283/81) [1982] E.C.R. 3415; [1983] 1
    C.M.L.R. 472, ECJ 6–024
Caballero v. United Kingdom (2000) 30 E.H.R.R. 643; [2000] Crim. L.R. 587,
    ECHR 24–023
Cain v. Doyle (1946) 72 C.L.R. 409 15–020
Calder (John) Publications Ltd v. Powell [1965] 1 Q.B. 509; [1965] 2 W.L.R.
    138, DC 25–025
Calder v. Bull (1798) 3 Dall. 386 15–017
Calder v. Halket (1839) Moo. P.C. 28 20–041
Caldwell v. McLaren (1883) 9 App.Cas. 295 37–007
Calvin's Case (1608) 8 Co. Rep. 1a ... 14–003, 15–002, 23–001, 35–004, 35–015, 35–017
Camelot Group Plc v. Centaur Communications Ltd [1999] Q.B. 124; [1998] 2
    W.L.R. 379, CA 25–017
Campbell v. Hall (1774) 1 Cowp. 204; Lofft 655 .... 2–008, 35–004, 35–017, 35–021
Campbell v. Tameside MBC [1982] Q.B. 1065; [1982] 3 W.L.R. 74, CA 33–024
Campbell v. United Kingdom (A/233A) (1993) 15 E.H.R.R. 137; The Times,
    April 1, 1992, ECHR 24–032
Campbell AG (Arcam) v. Worcestershire CC (1963) 61 L.G.R. 321 15–019
Campbell and Cosans v. United Kingdom (No.2) (A/48) (1982) 4 E.H.R.R. 293,
    ECHR 22–012, 22–032, 22–047
Campbell and Fell v. United Kingdom (1984) 7 E.H.R.R. 165 ... 20–026, 22–036, 22–037,
    24–032
Caparo Industries Plc v. Dickman [1990] 2 A.C. 605; [1990] 2 W.L.R. 358, HL ... 31–024
Cape Breton, Re (1846) 5 Moo. P.C. 259 36–026
Capital and Counties Bank v. Henty (1882) L.R. 7 App. Cas. 741, HL 25–003
Capon v. DPP [1998] Crim.L.R. 870 27–014
Carl Zeiss Stiftung v. Rayner and Keeler Ltd (No.2) [1967] 1 A.C. 853; [1966]
    3 W.L.R. 125, HL 15–005, 15–032
Carltona Ltd v. Commissioners of Works [1943] 2 All E.R. 560 .... 7–005, 18–024,
    23–034, 31–003, 31–019
Carr v. Fracis Times & Co [1902] A.C. 176, HL 15–024
Carus Wilson's Case (1845) 7 Q.B. 984 24–040

Case of Armes (1597) Pop. 121 19–028
Case of Ecclesiastical Persons (1601) 4 Co. Rep. 14b 15–019
Case of Monopolies (1602) 11 Co.Rep. 84b 15–004, 31–003, 33–014
Case of Proclamations (1610) 12 Co.Rep.74; 2 St. Tr.723 .... 2–008, 3–003, 4–016,
15–002, 15–019, 15–029, 22–011, 31–003, 33–014
Case of Prohibitions (Prohibitions del Roy) (1607) 12 Co. Rep.63 .... 2–010, 20–002
Case of the Duchy of Lancaster (1562) Plowd.212 15–002
Case of the King's Prerogative in Saltpetre (1607) 12 Co.Rep. 12 .... 15–002, 15–016
Case of the Sheriff of Middlesex, Re (1840) 11 Ad. & E. 273 .... 3–001, 13–003
Castioni, Re [1891] 1 Q.B. 149, QBD 23–044, 24–034
Central Control Board (Liquer Traffic) v. Cannon Brewery Co Ltd [1919] A.C.
744, HL; affirming [1918] 2 Ch. 101, CA 28–010
Central Independent Television Plc, Re [1991] 1 W.L.R. 4; [1991] 1 All E.R.
347, CA 25–015
Ceylon University v. Fernando [1960] 1 W.L.R. 223; [1960] 1 All E.R. 631, PC 32–024
Chaffers v. Goldsmid [1894] 1 Q.B. 186 11–006
Chahal v. United Kingdom (1997) 23 E.H.R.R. 413, ECHR 22–012, 22–033, 22–034,
22–043, 23–034, 23–036, 23–037, 23–047, 30–002
Chambers v. DPP [1995] Crim. L.R. 896; [1995] C.O.D. 321, QBD 27–025
Chandler v. DPP; sub nom. R. v. Chandler [1964] A.C. 763; [1962] 3 W.L.R. 694,
HL 15–005, 15–013, 19–004, 26–003
Chang Hang Kiu v. Piggott [1909] A.C. 312, PC 37–008
Chappell v. United Kingdom (A/152) (1990) 12 E.H.R.R. 1; [1989] 1 F.S.R. 617,
ECHR 24–052
Charles v. Trinidad and Tobago [2000] 1 W.L.R. 384; The Times, May 27, 1999,
PC 37–013
Chassagnou v. France (2000) 29 E.H.R.R. 615; 7 B.H.R.C. 151, ECHR ... 22–042, 22–046
Cheall v. Association of Professional, Executive, Clerical and Computer Staff
(APEX) [1983] 2 A.C. 180; [1983] 2 W.L.R. 679, HL 22–008
Cheall v. United Kingdom 42 D.R. 178 22–042
Cheney v. Conn; sub nom. Cheney v. Inland Revenue Commissioners [1968] 1
W.L.R. 242; [1968] 1 All E.R. 779, Ch D 3–015, 3–016, 3–026, 15–029
Cheng v. Governor of Pentonville Prison; sub nom. R. v. Governor of Pentonville
Prison, ex p. Cheng [1973] A.C. 931; [1973] 2 W.L.R. 746, HL 23–044
Chester v. Bateson [1920] 1 K.B. 829, KBD 19–041, 20–013, 29–014, 31–005
China Navigation Co. v. Att.-Gen. [1932] 2 K.B. 197; (1932) 43 Ll. L. Rep. 37,
CA 15–012, 15–013
Chivers & Sons Ltd v. Air Ministry [1955] 1 Ch. 585 22–055
Chloride Industrial Batteries Ltd v. F & W Freight Ltd [1989] 1 W.L.R. 823;
[1989] 3 All E.R. 86, CA 35–003
Chokolingo v. Att.-Gen. of Trinidad and Tobago [1981] 1 W.L.R. 106; [1981] 1
All E.R. 244, PC 2–021
Choudhury, Ex.p See R. v. Bow Street Magistrates' Court, ex p. Choudhury
Christian v. Corrin (1716) 1 P. Wms. 329 35–002
Christians against Racism and Fascism v. United Kingdom (1980) 21 D.R. 138 ... 27–017
Chung Chi Cheung v. King, The [1939] A.C. 160; (1938) 62 Ll. L. Rep. 151,
PC 3–026
Chung Chuck v. King, The [1930] A.C. 244, PC 37–003
Church of Scientology of California v. Customs and Excise Commissioners
[1981] 1 All E.R. 1035; [1981] S.T.C. 65, CA 6–024
Church of Scientology of California v. Johnson-Smith [1972] 1 Q.B. 522; [1971]
3 W.L.R. 434, QBD 13–014
Churchill v. Foot The Times, January 28, 1968 33–010
Churchman v. Joint Shop Stewards' Committee [1972] 1 W.L.R. 1094; [1972] 3
All E.R. 603, CA 20–046
Churchward v. R. (1865) L.R. 1 Q.B. 173; 6 B. & S. 807 33–006

Cinnamond v. British Airports Authority [1980] 1 W.L.R. 582; [1980] 2 All E.R.
  368, CA 31–012
City of London v. Wood (1710) 12 Mod. 669 3–011
Civilian War Claimants' Association v. King, The [1932] A.C. 14, HL 15–022
Clarke v. Chadburn [1985] 1 W.L.R. 78; [1985] 1 All E.R. 211, Ch D 20–046
Clay Cross (Quarry Services) Ltd v. Fletcher; sub nom. Fletcher v. Clay Cross
  (Quarry Services) Ltd [1978] 1 W.L.R. 1429; [1979] 1 All E.R. 474, CA 4–022
Clayton v. Heffron (1960) 105 C.L.R. 214 .... 4–032, 4–033
Clifford, Re; O'Sullivan, Re [1921] 2 A.C. 570, HL (UK-Irl) 19–035, 32–007
Cocks v. Thanet DC [1983] 2 A.C. 286; [1982] 3 W.L.R. 1121, HL 32–010
Coffin v. Coffin (1808) 4 Mass.1 13–007
Coffin v. Smith (1980) 71 Cr. App. R. 221, DC 24–022, 27–007
Collco Dealings Ltd v. Inland Revenue Commissioners (No.2); sub nom. Inland
  Revenue Commissioners v. Collco Dealings Ltd [1962] A.C. 1; [1961] 2
  W.L.R. 401, HL 3–026
Collector of Land Revenue South West District Penang v. Kam Giu Paik [1986]
  1 W.L.R. 412 31–005
Collins v. Henry Whiteway & Co Ltd [1927] 2 K.B. 378, KBD 25–003
Collins v. Minister of the Interior [1957] (1) A.D. 552 3–014
Collins v. Wilcock [1984] 1 W.L.R. 1172; [1984] 3 All E.R. 374, DC 24–019, 24–022
Commercial and Estates Co of Egypt v. Board of Trade [1925] 1 K.B. 271;
  (1924) 19 Ll. L. Rep. 275, CA 15–017, 33–005
Commercial Cable Co v. Newfoundland [1916] 2 A.C. 610, PC 33–007
Commission of the European Communities v. United Kingdom (C207/83); sub
  nom. Origin Marking of Retail Goods, Re (C207/83) [1985] E.C.R. 1201;
  [1985] 2 C.M.L.R. 259, ECJ 6–035
Commission of the European Communities v. United Kingdom See Excise
  Duties on Wine (No.2), Re (C170/78)
Commission of the European Communities v. United Kingdom See Tachographs,
  Re (128/78)
Commissioners of Crown Lands v. Page See Crown Lands Commissioners v.
  Page
Commissioners of Customs and Excise v. Cure and Deeley Ltd [1962] 1 Q.B.
  340; [1961] 3 W.L.R. 798, QBD 31–003, 31–005
Commonwealth of Australia v. Kidman (1926) 32 A.L.R. 1, PC 33–007
Complaint against Liverpool City Council, Re [1977] 1 W.L.R. 995; [1977] 2 All
  E.R. 650, DC 34–017
Condron v. United Kingdom (35718/97) (No.2) (2001) 31 E.H.R.R. 1; [2000]
  Crim. L.R. 679, ECHR 24–017
Conegate Ltd v. Customs and Excise Commissioners (121/85) [1987] Q.B. 254;
  [1987] 2 W.L.R. 39, ECJ (4th Chamber) 6–036, 6–037
Coney v. Choyce; Ludden v. Choyce [1975] 1 W.L.R. 422; [1975] 1 All E.R. 979,
  Ch D 31–006
Congreve v. Home Office [1976] Q.B. 629; [1976] 2 W.L.R. 291, CA 3–010, 31–008
Conservative and Unionist Office v. Burrell [1982] 1 W.L.R. 522; [1982] 2 All
  E.R. 1, CA 2–016
Conway v. Rimmer [1968] A.C. 910; [1968] 2 W.L.R. 998, HL 26–024, 33–022,
                                                                                                        33–023
Cook v. Alexander [1974] Q.B. 279; [1973] 3 W.L.R. 617, CA 13–012
Cook v. Sprigg [1899] A.C. 572, PC 15–022, 15–026
Coomber v. Berkshire Justices (1883) L.R. 9 App. Cas. 61, HL 15–020, 21–009
Cooper v. Hawkins [1904] 2 K.B. 164 .... 15–019, 33–010
Cooper v. Wandsworth Board of Works (1863) 14 C.B. N.S. 180 .... 32–001, 32–022
Co-operative Agricola Zootecrucia S, Antonio v. Amministrazione delle finanze
  dello Stato [1996] E.C.R. I–4373 6–013

Co-operative Committee on Japanese Canadians v. Att.-Gen. for Canada [1974]
  A.C. 87, PC 3–026
Copyright Owners Reproduction Society v. EMI (Australia) Pty Ltd (1958) 100
  C.L.R. 597 .... 4–013, 36–006
Cordell v. Second Clanfield Properties Ltd [1969] 2 Ch. 9; [1968] 3 W.L.R. 864,
  Ch D 2–010
Corke, Re [1954] 1 W.L.R. 899; [1954] 2 All E.R. 440, DC 24–037
Corporation of Manchester v. Markland [1934] 2 K.B. 101 31–024
Cossey v. United Kingdom (A/184); sub nom. C. v. United Kingdom [1991] 2
  F.L.R. 492; [1993] 2 F.C.R. 97; (1991) 13 E.H.R.R. 622, ECHR 22–042
Costello-Roberts v. United Kingdom (A/247–C) [1994] 1 F.C.R. 65; (1995) 19
  E.H.R.R. 112, ECHR 22–032
Council of Civil Service Unions (CCSU) v. Minister for the Civil Service
  (G.C.H.Q. Case) [1985] A.C. 374; [1984] 1 W.L.R. 1174, HL 6–039, 15–003,
                        15–004, 15–005, 15–023, 15–029, 16–005, 18–026, 18–027,
                        19–004, 19–047, 20–004, 22–007, 27–038, 31–002, 31–003,
                                                        31–012, 31–018, 32–021
Countrywide Banking Corporation Ltd v. Dean (Liquidator of CB Sizzlers Ltd)
  [1998] A.C. 338; [1998] 2 W.L.R. 441 37–012
Cowan v. Condon; sub nom. Cowan v. Commissioner of Police of the Metropolis
  [2000] 1 W.L.R. 254; [2000] 1 All E.R. 504, CA 24–044
Cowie v. Remfrey (1846) 5 Moo.P.C. 232 16–013
Cox v. Army Council; sub nom. R. v. Cox [1963] A.C. 48; [1962] 2 W.L.R. 950,
  HL 19–019
Cox v. Green [1966] Ch. 216; [1966] 2 W.L.R. 369, Ch D 32–024
Cox v. Hakes (1890) 15 App.Cas. 506, HL 24–038, 24–039
Cozens v. Brutus [1973] A.C. 854; [1972] 3 W.L.R. 521, HL 27–023
Crampton v. Varna Railway (1872) 7 Ch.App. 562 32–023
Crawford, Re (1849) 13 Q.B. 613 24–040
Croft v. Dunphy [1933] A.C. 156; (1932) 43 Ll. L. Rep. 435, PC 35–022, 35–026
Crook v. Corporation of Seaford (1871) L.R. 6 Ch. 551 32–023
Crown Estates Commissioners v. Wordsworth (1982) 44 P. & C.R. 302; (1982)
  264 E.G. 439, CA 15–019
Crown Lands Commissioner v. Page sub nom. Commissioners of Crown Lands
  v. Page [1960] 2 Q.B. 274; [1960] 3 W.L.R. 446, CA 15–007, 33–006
Cruz Varas v. Sweden; sub nom. Varas Cruz v. Sweden (1992) 14 E.H.R.R. 1;
  The Times, May 8, 1991, ECHR 22–033
Cudgen Rutile (No.2) Pty Ltd v. Chalk [1975] A.C. 520; [1975] 2 W.L.R. 1, PC ... 31–022,
                                                                              33–006
Cunningham, Re (1967) 86. W.N. (Pt 2) (N.S.W.(323 36–009
Curl's Case (1727) Stra. 788 25–024
Cussons (New Zealand) Pty Ltd v. Unilever Plc [1998] A.C. 328; [1998] 2
  W.L.R. 95 , PC 37–012
Cutler v. Wandsworth Stadium Ltd [1949] A.C. 398; [1949] 1 All E.R. 544,
  HL 31–025

D. v. National Society for the Prevention of Cruelty to Children (NSPCC) [1978]
  A.C. 171; [1977] 2 W.L.R. 201, HL 33–023, 33–024
Daimler Co v. Continental Tyre and Rubber Co (Great Britain) Ltd; [1916] 2
  A.C. 307, HL; reversing [1915] 1 K.B. 893, CA 23–020
Damodhar Gordhan v. Deoram Kanji (1876) 1 App.Cas. 352, PC 15–031
Danby's Case (1679) 11 St.Tr. 599 20–004
Darcy v. Allen (Case of Monopolies) (1602) 11 Co.Rep. 84b 3–007
Darnel's Case (the Five Knights' Case) (1627) 3 St. Tr. 1 .... 3–008, 15–002, 24–034
Davey Paxman & Co Ltd v. Post Office The Times, November 16, 1954 3–010

Davies v Presbyterian Church of Wales [1986] 1 W.L.R. 323; [1986] 1 All E.R.
  705, HL 32–016
Davis v. Carew-Pole [1956] 1 W.L.R. 833; [1956] 2 All E.R. 524, QBD 32–024
Davis v. Shaughnessy [1932] A.C. 106, PC 37–006
Davison v. Farmer (1851) 6 Ex. 242 35–002
Davy v. Spelthorne BC [1984] A.C. 262; [1983] 3 W.L.R. 742, HL 1–014, 32–022
Dawkins v. Lord F. Paulet (1869) L.R. 5 Q.B. 94 .... 19–025, 20–041
Dawkins v. Lord Rokeby (1866) 4 F. & F. 806 .... 19–025, 20–041, 20–042, 25–003
Day v. Savadge (1615) Hobart 85 3–011
Daymond v. Plymouth CC See Daymond v. South West Water Authority
Daymond v. South West Water Authority; sub nom. Daymond v. Plymouth City
  Council [1976] A.C. 609; [1975] 3 W.L.R. 865, HL 31–005
De Dohse v. R. (1886) 3 T.L.R. 114, HL 18–026
D'Emden v. Pedder (1904) 1 C.L.R. 91 35–022
De Freitas v. Benny [1976] A.C. 239; [1975] 3 W.L.R. 388, PC 20–004, 37–013
De Freitas v. Permanent Secretary of Ministry of Agriculture, Fisheries, Lands
  and Housing [1999] 1 A.C. 69; [1998] 3 W.L.R. 675, PC 37–013
De Jager v. Att.-Gen. of Natal [1907] A.C. 326 14–012
De Lasala v. De Lasala [1980] A.C. 546; [1979] 3 W.L.R. 390, PC 37–002
De Morgan v. Director General of Social Welfare [1998] A.C. 275; [1998] 2
  W.L.R. 427, PC 37–010
De Morgan v. Metropolitan Board of Works (1880) 5 Q.B.D. 155 27–004
Dean of St. Asaph's Case 25–018
Dean v. Dean [1987] 1 F.L.R. 517; [1987] 1 F.C.R. 96 ;(1987) 17 Fam. Law 200,
  CA 20–044
Debtor (Order in Aid No.1 of 1979), Re; sub nom. Debtor ex p. Viscount of the
  Royal Court of Jersey, Re [1981] Ch. 384; [1980] 3 W.L.R. 758, Ch D ... 35–003
Debtor Ex.p Viscount of the Royal Court of Jersey, Re See Debtor (Order in Aid
  No.1 of 1979), Re
Defrenne v. Sabena (No.2) (C43/75); sub nom. Defrenne v. SA Belge d'Exploita-
  tion de la Navigation Aerienne (SABENA) (C43/75) [1981] 1 All E.R. 122;
  [1976] E.C.R. 455, ECJ 6–012
Demicoli v. Malta (A/210) (1992) 14 E.H.R.R. 47; The Times, October 15, 1991,
  ECHR 13–023
Denning v. Secretary of State for India (1920) 37 T.L.R. 138 18–026
Department of Transport v. Egoroff [1955] A.C. 667; [1955] 2 W.L.R. 632,
  CA 15–019
Department of Transport v. North West Water Authority [1984] A.C. 336; [1983]
  3 W.L.R. 707, HL 31–023
Derbyshire CC v. Times Newspapers Ltd [1993] A.C. 534; [1993] 2 W.L.R. 449,
  HL 22–002, 22–008, 22–041, 25–001, 25–003
Desmond v. Thorn [1983] 1 W.L.R. 163; [1982] 3 All E.R. 268, QBD 25–006
DF Marais v. General Officer Commanding the Lines of Communication; sub
  nom. DF Marais, Ex.p [1902] A.C. 109, PC 19–034, 19–035
DF Marais, Ex.p See DF Marais v. General Officer Commanding the Lines of
  Communication
Diamond v. Minter [1941] 1 All E.R. 390 23–042
Dibble v. Ingleton; sub nom. Ingleton v. Dibble [1972] 1 Q.B. 480; [1972] 2
  W.L.R. 163, DC 24–021
Dickinson v. Del Solar [1930] 1 K.B. 376; (1929) 34 Ll. L. Rep. 445, KBD ... 15–033
Dillet, Re (1887) 12 App.Cas. 549 .... 37–007, 37–008
Dillon v. Balfour (1887) 20 L.R. Ir.600 13–005
Dimes v. Grand Junction Canal (1852) 3 H.L. Cas. 759 .... 20–038, 30–014
Dingle v. Associated Newspapers Ltd See Associated Newspaper Ltd v. Din-
  gle

DPP v. A & BC Chewing Gum Ltd [1968] 1 Q.B. 159; [1967] 3 W.L.R. 493,
QBD 25–025
DPP v. Channel Four Television Co Ltd [1993] 2 All E.R. 517; [1993] Crim. L.R.
277, QBD 20–044, 20–045
DPP v. Fidler [1992] 1 W.L.R. 91; (1992) 94 Cr. App. R. 286, DC 27–033
DPP v. Hancock; DPP v. Tuttle [1995] Crim. L.R. 139; [1995] C.O.D. 32,
QBD 27–026
DPP v. Hawkins; sub nom. Crown Prosecution Service v. Hawkins [1988] 1
W.L.R. 1166; [1988] 3 All E.R. 673, QBD 24–010
DPP v. Hutchinson [1990] 2 A.C. 783; [1990] 3 W.L.R. 196, HL 31–006
DPP v. Jones (Margaret) [1999] 2 A.C. 240; [1999] 2 W.L.R. 625; [1999] 2 All
E.R. 257, HL .. 1–019, 9–052, 22–042, 27–001, 27–004, 27–013, 27–028, 27–033
DPP v. Jordan; sub nom. R. v. Jordan; R. v. Staniforth [1977] A.C. 699; [1976]
3 W.L.R. 887, HL 25–026
DPP v. Luft; DPP v. Duffield; Duffield v. DPP [1977] A.C. 962; [1976] 3 W.L.R.
32, HL 10–051
DPP v. Morrow; sub nom. Morrow v. DPP [1994] Crim. L.R. 58; The Independ-
ent, April 13, 1993, QBD 27–025
DPP v. Orum [1989] 1 W.L.R. 88; [1988] 3 All E.R. 449, QBD 27–026
DPP v. Tokai [1996] A.C. 856; [1996] 3 W.L.R. 149, PC 37–013
DPP v. Walsh [1981] I.R. 412 20–047
DPP v. Whyte; sub nom. Corbin v. Whyte [1972] A.C. 849; [1972] 3 W.L.R. 410,
HL 25–025, 25–031
DPP for Northern Ireland v. Lynch [1975] A.C. 653; [1975] 2 W.L.R. 641, HL 37–011
District Registrar v. Lord Chancellor, ex p. Lightfoot; sub nom. Lightfoot v. Lord
Chancellor [2000] Q.B. 597; [2000] 2 W.L.R. 318; [1999] 4 All E.R. 583,
CA 1–019, 22–002
Docherty v. South Tyneside Borough, The Times, July 3, 1982 31–010
Doe d. Thomas v. Acklam (1824) 2 B. & C. 778 4–014
Dombo Beheer BV v. The Netherlands (A/274–A) (1994) 18 E.H.R.R. 213,
ECHR 22–037
Donnelly v. Jackman [1970] 1 W.L.R. 562; [1970] 1 All E.R. 987, DC 24–019
Douglas v. Hello! Ltd [2001] 2 W.L.R. 992; [2001] 2 All E.R. 289; The Times,
January 16, 2000, CA 22–054, 25–019
Dow Jones Publishing Co v. Att.-Gen. of Singapore [1989] 1 W.L.R. 1308, PC ... 37–010
Dowty Boulton Paul Ltd v. Wolverhampton Corporation (No.1) [1971] 1 W.L.R.
204; [1971] 2 All E.R. 277, Ch D 31–022, 33–006
Dr. Bentley's Case (1723) 31–016
Dr. Bonham,s Case (1610) 8 Co.Rep. 114 3–011
Dr. Foster's Case (1615) 11 Co.Rep. 56b 4–002
Drake v. Chief Adjudication Officer (C150/85) [1987] Q.B. 166; [1986] 3 W.L.R.
1005; [1986] 3 All E.R. 65, ECJ (4th Chamber) 6–037
D'Souza v. DPP [1992] 1 W.L.R. 1073; [1992] 4 All E.R. 545, HL 24–043
Dudfield v. Ministry of Works (1964) 108 S.J. 118 18–027
Dudgeon v. United Kingdom (7525/76) (1981) 3 E.H.R.R. 40, Eur Comm HR 22–013,
22–039
Dudley Metropolitan Borough Council v. Debenhams Plc (1995) 159 J.P. 18;
(1994) 158 J.P.N. 746, QBD 24–050
Duff Development Co. v. Government of Kelantan [1924] A.C. 797, HL 15–005,
15–023, 35–008
Dugdale v. Kraft Foods Ltd [1976] 1 W.L.R. 1288; [1977] 1 All E.R. 454; [1977]
I.C.R. 48, EAT 30–010
Duke of Brunswick v. King of Hanover (1844) 6 Beav. 1 23–001
Duke v. GEC Reliance Ltd; sub nom. Duke v. Reliance Systems Ltd [1988] A.C.
618; [1988] 2 W.L.R. 359, HL 4–022, 6–013

Duke v. Reliance Systems Ltd *See* Duke v. GEC Reliance Ltd
Duncan v. Cammell Laird & Co Ltd (Discovery) [1942] A.C. 624; [1942] 1 All
E.R. 587, HL 33–022
Duncan v. Jones [1936] 1 K.B. 218, KBD 27–009, 27–030
Dunkley v. Evans [1981] 1 W.L.R. 1522; [1981] 3 All E.R. 285, QBD 31–006
Dunkley v Queen, The [1995] 1 A.C. 419; [1994] 3 W.L.R. 1124, PC 37–013
Dunlop v. Woollahra Municipal Council [1982] A.C. 158; [1981] 2 W.L.R. 693,
PC 32–022
Dunn v. MacDonald [1896] 1 Q.B. 555 18–026
Dunn v. Queen, The [1896] 1 Q.B. 116, CA 18–026
Duport Steels Ltd v. Sirs [1980] 1 W.L.R. 142; [1980] 1 All E.R. 529, HL ... 2–021, 2–028
Dyson v. Att.-Gen. (No.1) [1911] 1 K.B. 410, CA 17–019, 20–032, 33–017, 33–018

Earl Fitzwilliam's Wentworth Estates Co. v. Minister of Housing and Local
Government [1952] A.C. 362; [1952] 1 All E.R. 509, HL; affirming [1951]
2 K.B. 284, CA 31–009
Earl of Antrim's Petition, Re [1967] 1 A.C. 691 10–005
Earl of Leicester v. Wells-next-the-Sea Urban DC [1973] Ch. 110; [1972] 3
W.L.R. 486, Ch D 31–022
Earl of Shrewbury's Case (1611) 9 Co.Rep. 42a 20–029
Earldom of Annandale and Hartfell [1986] A.C. 319; [1986] 2 W.L.R. 43 9–004,
13–026
East India Co. v. Campbell 91749) Ves.Sen. 246 23–042
East Suffolk Rivers Catchment Board v. Kent [1941] A.C. 74, HL 31–024
Edgington v. Swindon Corporation [1939] 1 K.B. 86, KBD 31–023
Edinburgh and Dalkeith Railway v. Wauchope (1842) 8 Cl. & F.710 ..... 3–016, 3–017,
4–009, 7–018, 11–040
Edwards v. Bairstow [1956] A.C. 14; [1955] 3 W.L.R. 410, HL 32–016
Eichengruen v. Mond [1940] Ch. 785, CA 23–020
Eleko v. Office Administering Nigeria (No.1) [1928] A.C. 459, PC 24–038
Eleko v. Office Administering Nigeria (No.2) [1931] A.C. 662, PC 15–024
Ellen Street Estates Ltd v. Minister of Health [1934] 1 K.B. 590, CA 3–015, 4–004,
4–028
Elliott v. Southwark LBC [1976] 1 W.L.R. 499; [1976] 2 All E.R. 781, CA 30–023
Ellis v. Dubowski [1921] 3 K.B. 621, KBD 25–038, 31–019
Ellis v. Home Office [1953] 2 Q.B. 135; [1953] 3 W.L.R. 105, CA 33–009
Elphinstone v. Bedreechund (1830) 1 Knapp 316 19–035
Empson v. Smith [1966] 1 Q.B. 426; [1965] 3 W.L.R. 380, CA
Enever v. King, The (1906) 3 C.L.R. 969 21–009
Enfield LBC v. Mahoney [1983] 1 W.L.R. 749; [1983] 2 All E.R. 901, CA 20–046
Engel v. The Netherlands (No.1) (A/22) (1979–80) 1 E.H.R.R. 647, ECHR 22–036
Engelke v. Musmann; *sub nom.* Musmann v. Engelke [1928] A.C. 433, HL;
reversing [1928] 1 K.B. 90, CA 15–005, 15–023
Entick v. Carrington (1765) 19 St. Tr. 1029 .... 2–008, 2–026, 24–041, 24–046
Errington v. Minister of Health [1935] 1 K.B. 249, CA 31–013, 32–004
Eshugbayi (Eleko) v. Government of Nigeria (Office Administration) *See* Eleko
v. Office Administering Nigeria (No.1) and (No.2)
Esquimalt and Nanaimo Railway Co v. Wilson [1920] A.C. 358, PC 33–018
Essex CC v. Ministry of Housing and Local Government (Stansted Airport
Inquiry) (1967) 18 P. & C.R. 531 30–024
Evans, Re; *sub nom.* R. v. Governor of Brixton Prison, ex p. Evans [1994] 1
W.L.R. 1006; [1994] 3 All E.R. 449, HL 23–046
Excise Duties on Wine (No.2), Re (C170/78); *sub nom.* Commission of the
European Communities v. United Kingdom (C170/78) [1983] E.C.R. 2265;
[1983] 3 C.M.L.R. 512, ECJ 6–026

F. (Mental Patient: Sterilisation), Re *See* F. v. West Berkshire Health Authority

F. v. West Berkshire Health Authority; *sub nom.* F. (Mental Patient: Sterilisation), Re [1990] 2 A.C. 1; [1989] 2 W.L.R. 1025, HL 15–015

Fabrigas v. Mostyn 20 St.Tr. 175; (1773) 1 Cowp. 161 35–017

Fairmount Investments v. Secretary of State for the Environment [1976] 1 W.L.R. 1255; [1976] 2 All E.R. 865, HL 30–025

Faithful v. Admiralty *The Times,* January 24, 1964; The Guardian, January 24, 1964 18–027

Falkland Islands Co v. R. (1863) 1 Moo.P.C. (N.S.) 299 37–003

Farrell v. Secretary of State for Defence [1980] 1 W.L.R. 172; [1980] 1 All E.R. 166, HL 19–032

Fatuma Binti Mohammed Bin Salim Bakhshuwen v. Mohammed Bin Salim Bakhshuwen [1952] A.C. 1, PC 37–002

Fayed v. Al-Tajir [1998] Q.B. 712 15–021

Fayed v. United Kingdom (A294–B) (1994) 18 E.H.R.R. 393; The Times, October 11, 1994, ECHR 20–041

Feather v. Queen, The (18650 6 B.& S. 257 33–017

Featherstone, Re (1953) 37 Cr. App. R. 146, DC 24–034

Felton v. Callis [1969] 1 Q.B. 200; [1968] 3 W.L.R. 951, QBD 15–015

Ferdinand, Ex-Tsar of Bulgaria, Re *See* Ferdinand, Re

Ferdinand, Re; *sub nom.* Ferdinand (Ex-Tsar of Bulgaria), Re [1921] 1 Ch. 107, CA 15–022

Ferguson v. Earl of Kinnoull (1842) 9 Cl. & F. 251, HL 20–041

Ferguson v. Home Office *The Times,* October 8, 1977 33–009

Fernandez, Ex.p (1862) 19 C.B. (N.S.) 3 20–043

Findlay, Re [1985] A.C. 318; [1984] 3 W.L.R. 1159, HL 31–018

Findlay v. United Kingdom (1997) 24 E.H.R.R. 221; *The Times,* February 27, 1997, ECHR 19–021, 22–012, 22–036

Finnegan v. Clowney Youth Training Programme Ltd [1990] 2 A.C. 407; [1990] 2 W.L.R. 1035, HL 4–022, 6–013

Fisher v. Minister of Public Safety and Immigration (No.2) [2000] 1 A.C. 434; [1999] 2 W.L.R. 349, PC 37–013, 37–014

Fisher v. Oldham Corporation [1930] 2 K.B. 364, KBD 21–009, 21–011

Fitzgerald v. Muldoon [1976] 1 N.Z.L.R. 615 .... 3–013, 36–013

Fitzpatrick v. Sterling Housing Association Ltd [2001] 1 A.C. 27; [1999] 3 W.L.R. 1113, HL; reversing [1998] Ch. 304; [1998] 2 W.L.R. 225 ..... 2–026, 22–039

Fletcher v. Peck (1810) 6 Cranch 87 1–010

Fletcher's Application, Re [1970] 2 All E.R. 527 (Note), CA 34–008, 34–013

Forbes v. Cochrane (1824) 2 B. & C. 448 24–034

Ford v. Metropolitan Police District Receiver [1921] 2 K.B. 344 27–019

Foreman v. Corporation of Canterbury (1871) L.R. 6 Q.B. 214 31–024

Forester v. Secretary of State for India (1872) L.R.Ind.App 15–022

Foster v. British Gas Plc (C188/89) [1991] 1 Q.B. 405; [1991] 2 W.L.R. 258; [1990] E.C.R. I–3313, ECJ 6–013

Foster v. British Gas Plc [1991] 2 A.C. 306; [1991] 2 W.L.R. 1075, HL 26–003

Fothergill v. Monarch Airlines Ltd [1981] A.C. 251; [1980] 3 W.L.R. 209, HL 15–029

Foulkes v. Chief Constable of the Merseyside Police [1998] 3 All E.R. 705; [1998] 2 F.L.R. 789, CA 24–008, 24–022, 27–009

Fox, Ex.p (1793) 5 St.Tr. 276 19–003

Fox v. Stirk and Bristol Eletoral Registration Officer; *sub nom.* Ricketts v. City of Cambridge Electoral Registration Officer; Ricketts v. Registration Officer for the City of Cambridge [1970] 2 Q.B. 463; [1970] 3 W.L.R. 147, CA 10–028

Francome v. Mirror Group Newspapers Ltd [1984] 1 W.L.R. 892; [1984] 2 All E.R. 408, CA 2–028, 18–029, 25–020

Francovich v. Italian Republic (C6/90); Bonifacti v. Italy (C9/90) [1991] E.C.R.
    I–5357; [1993] 2 C.M.L.R. 66, ECJ 6–014, 6–038
Frankland and Moore v. Queen, The [1987] A.C. 576; [1987] 2 W.L.R. 1251,
    PC 35–002, 37–001, 37–011
Franklin v. Att.-Gen. (No.2) See Franklin v. Queen, The (No.2)
Franklin v. Att.-Gen. [1974] Q.B. 185; [1973] 2 W.L.R. 225, QBD 33–018
Franklin v. Queen, The (No.2) [1974] Q.B. 205; [1973] 3 W.L.R. 636, CA 33–018
Fraser v. Balfour (1918) 34 T.L.R. 502 19–024
Fraser v. Hamilton (1917) 33 T.L.R. 431 19–024
Fratelli Variola v. Italian Minister of Finance [1973] E.C.R. 981 6–012
Free Church of Scotland (General Assembley) v. Lord Overtoun; Macalister v.
    Young [1904] A.C. 515, HL 9–051, 22–024
Freeman v. Home Office [1984] Q.B. 524; [1984] 2 W.L.R. 802, CA 33–009
French Kier Developments Ltd v. Secretary of State for the Environment [1977]
    1 All E.R. 296; (1977) 244 E.G. 967, QBD 30–023, 30–028
Freshwater Biological Association v. Ministry of Defence The Times, December
    14, 1970 33–010
Fryer v. Bernard (1724) 2 P.W. 262 16–009
Funke v. France (A/256–A) [1993] 1 C.M.L.R. 897; (1993) 16 E.H.R.R. 297,
    ECHR 24–048, 26–018
Furniss v. Dawson [1984] A.C. 474; [1984] 2 W.L.R. 226, HL 3–006

Gallagher v. Post Office [1970] 3 All E.R. 712; 9 K.I.R. 78, Ch D 28–009
Garden Cottage Foods Ltd v. Milk Marketing Board [1984] A.C. 130; [1983] 3
    W.L.R. 143, HL 6–037
Garland v. British Rail Engineering Ltd (No.2); Roberts v. Cleveland AHA;
    MacGregor Wallcoverings v. Turton [1983] 2 A.C. 751; [1982] 2 W.L.R.
    918, HL 4–021, 6–025
Gaskin v. Liverpool City Council [1980] 1 W.L.R. 1549; 124 S.J. 498, CA 33–024,
                                                                                    33–026
Gaskin v. United Kingdom (A/160) [1990] 1 F.L.R. 167; (1990) 12 E.H.R.R. 36,
    ECHR 22–039, 33–024
Gay News and Lemon v. United Kingdom (1983) 5 E.H.R.R. 123 ...... 22–037, 25–008
Geddis v. Proprietors of Bann Reservoir (1878) L.R. 3 App. Cas. 430, HL 31–024
Geelong Harbor Trust Commissioners v. Gibbs Bright & Co (A Firm) (The
    Octavian) [1974] A.C. 810; [1974] 2 W.L.R. 507, PC 37–010
General Medical Council v. British Broadcasting Corporation [1998] 1 W.L.R.
    1573; [1998] 3 All E.R. 426, CA 20–007
General Medical Council v. Spackman; sub nom. R. v General Medical Council
    ex p. Spackman [1943] A.C. 627, HL; affirming [1942] 2 K.B. 261, CA 31–013,
                                                                                    32–005
Gentel v. Rapps [1902] 1 K.B. 160, KBD 31–006
Ghani v. Jones [1970] 1 Q.B. 693; [1969] 3 W.L.R. 1158, CA 15–027
Gibson v. East India Co (1839) 5 Bing.N.C. 262 18–027
Gibson v. Lord Advocate 1975 S.C. 136; 1975 S.L.T. 134; [1975] 1 C.M.L.R.
    563, OH 1–014, 4–007, 6–037
Gidley v. Lord Palmerston (1822) 3 Brod. & B. 275 18–026
Gilbert v. Trinity House Corporation (1886) 17 Q.B.D. 795 28–010
Gillick v. West Norfolk Area Health Authority [1986] A.C. 112; [1985] 3 W.L.R.
    830, HL 29–004, 32–010, 33–018
Gitonas v. Greece (1998) 26 E.H.R.R. 691, ECHR 10–002
Givaudan & Co v. Minister of Housing and Local Government [1967] 1 W.L.R.
    250 30–023
Glasewska v. Sweden (1986) 45 D.R. 300 22–049
Glasgow Corporation v. Central Land Board 1956 S.C. (HL) 1; 1956 S.L.T. 41 ... 15–001;
                                                                                    28–010, 33–022

Glynn v. Keele University [1971] 1 W.L.R. 487; [1971] 2 All E.R. 89, Ch D 32–015
Godden v. Hales (1686) 11 St. Tr. 1166; 2 Showers 275 .... 3–005, 4–002
Golden Chemical Products, Re [1976] Ch. 300; [1976] 3 W.L.R. 1, Ch D 31–019
Golder v. United Kingdom (1975) 1 E.H.R.R. 524 .... 22–013, 22–028, 22–036, 24–032
Goldsmith v. Pressdram Ltd *The Times,* November 23, 1976, CA; affirming
   [1977] Q.B. 83, QBD 25–006
Goodwin v. Fortescue (1604) 2 St. Tr. 91 10–061
Goodwin v. United Kingdom (1996) 22 E.H.R.R. 123; 1 B.H.R.C. 81, ECHR 25–002,
   25–017, 25–022
Goose v. Wilson Sandford & Co (No.1) (1998) 95(12) L.S.G. 27; (1998) 142
   S.J.L.B. 92; *The Times,* February 19, 1998, CA 20–031
Gorris v. Scott (1874) L.R. 9 Ex. 125, Exchequer Div 31–025
Gorton Local Board v. Prison Commissioners (1887) 15–019
Goswami, ex p; *sub nom.* R. v. Brixton Prison Governor, ex p. Goswami [1967]
   Crim. L.R. 234; 116 N.L.J. 1712; (1966) 111 S.J. 17, DC 24–025
Gough v. Chief Constable of Derbyshire *The Times*, July 19, 2001 .... 6–022, 22–053
Gould v. Stuart [1896] A.C. 575, PC 18–026
Gouriet v. Union of Post Office Workers; *sub nom.* Att.-Gen. v. Gouriet [1978]
   A.C. 435; [1977] 3 W.L.R. 300, HL 18–011, 31–008, 32–023, 33–018
Government of Canada v. Aronson; *sub nom.* DPP v. Aronson [1990] 1 A.C. 579;
   [1989] 3 W.L.R. 436, HL 23–043
Government of Denmark v. Nielsen *See* Nielsen, Re
Grad v. Finanzamt Traunstein (C9/70) [1970] E.C.R. 825; [1971] C.M.L.R. 1,
   ECJ 6–011
Grant v. Gould (1792) 2 H.Bl. 98 .... 19–005, 19–024
Grant v. Secretary of State for India 91877) 2 C.P.D. 445 19–004
Grant's Will Trusts, Re; *sub nom.* Harris v. Anderson [1980] 1 W.L.R. 360;
   [1979] 3 All E.R. 359, Ch D 2–016
Green v. DPP (1991) 155 J.P. 816; [1991] Crim. L.R. 782, DC 24–021
Green v. Moore (No.1) [1982] Q.B. 1044; [1982] 2 W.L.R. 671, DC .. 24–019, 24–022
Greene v. Secretary of State for Home Affairs [1962] A.C. 284 .... 19–045, 24–034
Greene, Re (1941) 57 T.L.R. 533 24–037
Greenshields v. Magistrates' of Edinburgh (1711) 2–003, 9–044
Greenwell v. Prison Commissioners (1951) 101 L.J. 486, CC 33–009
Gregory v. Camden LBC [1966] 1 W.L.R. 899; [1966] 2 All E.R. 196, QBD 32–011
Gregory, Re [1901] A.C. 128, PC 37–007
Grice v. Dudley Corporation [1958] Ch. 329; [1957] 3 W.L.R. 314, Ch D 31–009
Grieve v. Douglas-Home 1965 S.C. 315; 1965 S.L.T. 186, Election Petitions
   Ct 10–049
Groppera Radio AG v. Switzerland (A/173) (1990) 12 E.H.R.R. 321; *The Times,*
   April 16, 1990, ECHR 10–056
Grosvenor Hotel, London, Re (No.1) [1964] Ch. 464; [1964] 2 W.L.R. 184,
   CA 33–027
Grosvenor Hotel, London, Re (No.2) [1965] Ch. 1210; [1964] 3 W.L.R. 992,
   CA 33–022
Grove v. Eastern Gas Board [1952] 1 K.B. 77; [1951] 2 All E.R. 1051, CA 24–051
Groves v. Lord Wimborne [1898] 2 Q.B. 402, CA 31–025
Grunwick Processing Laboratories Ltd v. Advisory, Conciliation and Arbitration
   Service (ACAS) *sub nom.* Advisory, Conciliation and Arbitration Service v.
   Grunwick [1978] A.C. 655; [1978] 2 W.L.R. 277, HL 31–008
Guzzardi v. Italy (A/39) (1981) 3 E.H.R.R. 333, ECHR 24–028

HK (An Infant), Re; *sub nom.* K(H) (An Infant), Re [1967] 2 Q.B. 617; [1967]
   2 W.L.R. 962, QBD 23–038
HTV v. Price Commission [1976] I.C.R. 170; 120 S.J. 298, CA 31–020
Hadkinson v. Hadkinson [1952] P. 285; [1952] 2 All E.R. 567, CA 20–045

Hagen v. Fratelli D. & G. Moretti SNC; *sub nom.* Hagen v. D & G Moretti SNC
[1980] 3 C.M.L.R. 253; [1980] F.S.R. 517, CA 6–024
Haggard v. Pelisier Frères [1892] A.C. 61 20–041
Hales v. R (1918) 34 T.L.R. 589, CA 18–026
Halford v. United Kingdom [1997] I.R.L.R. 471; (1997) 24 E.H.R.R. 523,
ECHR 22–039, 26–014
Hall v. Hall (1944) 88 S.J. 383, (Hereford CC) 3–015, 14–002
Hamer v. United Kingdom (7114/75) (1982) 4 E.H.R.R. 139, Eur Comm HR ...... –22–042
Hamilton v. Al Fayed [2001] A.C. 395; [2000] 2 W.L.R. 609; [2000] 2 All E.R.
224, HL; affirming [1999] 3 All E.R. 317, CA 13–006, 13–015, 13–018
Hammersmith and City Railway Co v. Brand (1869) L.R. 4 H.L. 171; (1866–67)
L.R. 2 Q.B. 223, QB 31–023
Hammersmith BC v. Boundary Commission *The Times,* December 15, 1954 3–016,
4–033
Hammond v. Howell (1677) 2 Mod. 219 20–041
Hampshire CC v. Shonleigh Nominees Ltd [1970] 1 W.L.R. 865; [1970] 2 All
E.R. 144, Ch D 32–024
Handyside v. United Kingdom (A/24) (1979–80) 1 E.H.R.R. 737, ECHR 22–029,
22–030, 25–002, 25–024, 27–001
Hanson v. Radcliffe Urban DC [1922] 2 Ch. 490, CA 31–009
Harley Development Inc. v. Inland Revenue Commissioner [1996] 1 W.L.R. 727;
[1996] S.T.C. 440, PC 32–013
Harman and Hewitt v. United Kingdom [1989] 14 E.H.R.R. 657 19–048
Harman v. United Kingdom (1985) 7 E.H.R.R. 146 20–046
Harold Stephen & Co Ltd v. Post Office [1977] 1 W.L.R. 1172; [1978] 1 All E.R.
939, CA 7–003, 28–008, 28–012
Harper v. Secretary of State for the Home Secretary; *sub nom.* Merricks v.
Heathcoat Amory [1955] Ch. 238; [1955] 2 W.L.R. 316, CA 4–033
Harris v. Donges; *sub nom.* Harris v. Minister of the Interior [1952] 1 T.L.R.
1245; 1952 (2) S.A. 428 .... 3–014, 4–028, 4–030
Harris v. Minister of the Interior *See* Harris v. Donges
Harris v. Sheffield United Football Club; *sub nom.* Sheffield United Football
Club v. South Yorkshire Police Authority [1988] Q.B. 77; [1987] 3 W.L.R.
305, CA 21–008, 21–015
Hart v. O'Connor [1985] A.C. 1000; [1985] 3 W.L.R. 214, PC 37–011
Hashman and Harrup v. United Kingdom (2000) 30 E.H.R.R. 241 ...... 22–029, 24–027
Hasselblad (GB) Ltd v. Orbinson [1985] Q.B. 475; [1985] 2 W.L.R. 1, CA 25–003
Hastings, Re (No.1) [1958] 1 W.L.R. 372; [1958] 1 All E.R. 707, DC 24–038
Hastings, Re (No.2) [1959] 1 Q.B. 358; [1958] 3 W.L.R. 768, DC 24–038
Hastings, Re (No.3) [1959] 1 All E.R. 698, DC 24–038
Hauptzollamt Bremen-Freihafen v. Waren-Import Gesellschaft Krohn & Co
[1970] E.C.R. 451 6–012
Haxey's Case (397) Rot. Parl., iii, 434 13–005
Hearson v. Churchill [1892] 2 Q.B. 144 19–005
Heath v. Pryn (1670) 1 Vent. 14 4–027
Heaton's Transport Co v. Transport and General Workers Union [1973] A.C. 15;
[1972] 3 W.L.R. 431, HL 20–038
Heddon v. Evans (1919) 35 T.L.R. 642 .... 19–024, 20–041
Hellewell v. Chief Constable of Derbyshire [1995] 1 W.L.R. 804; [1995] 4 All
E.R. 473, QBD 22–054, 25–019
Herbert Berry Associates Ltd v. Inland Revenue Commissioners; *sub nom.*
Herbert berry Associates Ltd (In Liquidation), Re [1977] 1 W.L.R. 1437;
[1978] 1 All E.R. 161, HL 15–010
Herring v. Templeman [1973] 3 All E.R. 569; 72 L.G.R. 162, CA 32–006
Hibernian Property Co Ltd v. Secretary of State for the Environment 72 L.G.R.
350; (1973) 27 P. & C.R. 197, QBD 30–025

Higgs v. Minister of National Security [2000] 2 A.C. 228; [2000] 2 W.L.R.
1368 37–014
Hill v. Chief Constable of West Yorkshire [1989] A.C. 53; [1988] 2 W.L.R. 1049,
HL 21–011, 31–024
Hills v. Ellis [1983] Q.B. 680; [1983] 2 W.L.R. 234, DC 24–021
Hinchliffe v. Sheldon [1955] 1 W.L.R. 1207; [1955] 3 All E.R. 406, DC 24–021
Hinds v. Queen, The; DPP v. Jackson [1977] A.C. 195; [1976] 2 W.L.R. 366, PC ... 2–021,
36–018, 37–013
Hinds, Ex p. (No.2); sub nom. Hinds, Re The Times, February 15, 1961, HL;
affirming [1961] 1 W.L.R. 325, DC 24–034
Hipperson v. Newbury Electoral Officer [1985] Q.B. 1060; [1985] 3 W.L.R. 61,
CA 10–028, 10–036
Hirst v. Chief Constable of West Yorkshire (1987) 85 Cr. App. R. 143; (1987)
151 J.P. 304, QBD 27–001, 27–028
Hoani Te Heuheu Tukino v. Aotea District Moari Land Board [1941] A.C. 308,
PC 35–016
Hodge v. Att.-Gen. (1839) 3 Y. & Co. Ex. 342 33–018
Hodge v. R. (1883) 9 App Cas 117 .... 4–037, 35–022
Hodgson v. Carlisle Board of Health (1857) 8 E. & B. 116 15–020
Hoekstra v. H.M. Advocate (No.2) 2000 J.C. 387; 2000 S.L.T. 602, HCJ Appeal 9–051,
20–039
Hoekstra v. H.M. Advocate (No.3) 2000 J.C. 391; 2000 S.L.T. 605; The Times,
April 14, 2000 22–051
Hoekstra v. H.M. Advocate (No.5) [2001] 1 A.C. 216; [2000] 3 W.L.R. 1817;
2001 S.L.T. 28, PC 5–015, 20–039
Hoffman La Roche v. Secretary of State for Trade and Industry [1975] A.C.
295 .... 31–005, 33–018
Holmes, Re (1861) 2 John & H. 527 35–005
Home Office v. Dorset Yacht Co Ltd [1970] A.C. 1004; [1970] 2 W.L.R. 1140,
HL 33–009
Home Office v. Harman; sub nom. Harman v. Home Office [1983] 1 A.C. 280;
[1982] 2 W.L.R. 338, HL; affirming [1981] Q.B. 534, CA 20–040, 20–044,
20–046, 22–008, 25–001
Hood v. United Kingdom (2000) 29 E.H.R.R. 365; The Times, March 11, 1999,
ECHR 19–022, 22–012
Hoop, The 91799) 1 C.Rob. 196 23–020
Horseferry Road Stipendiary Magistrate, ex p. Siadatan; sub nom. R. v. Metro-
politan Magistrate, ex p. Siadatan [1991] 1 Q.B. 260; [1990] 3 W.L.R. 1006,
QBD 27–024
Horvath v. Secretary of State for the Home Department [2000] 3 W.L.R. 379;
[2000] 3 All E.R. 577, HL 23–032
Hotel and Catering Industry Training Board v. Automobile Proprietary [1969] 1
W.L.R. 697; [1969] 2 All E.R. 582, HL 31–005
Hottentot Venus' Case (1810) 13 East 195 24–034
Houlden v. Smith (1850) 14 Q.B. 841 20–041
Houston v. BBC 1995 S.C. 433; 1995 S.L.T. 1305, 1 Div 10–056
Howell v. Falmouth Boat Construction Co Ltd [1951] A.C. 837; [1951] 2 All
E.R. 278, HL 33–016
Hubbard v. Pitt [1976] Q.B. 142; [1975] 3 W.L.R. 201, CA 27–001
Hughes v. Department of Health and Social Services [1985] A.C. 776; [1985] 2
W.L.R. 866, HL 18–026, 31–018
Hughes and Vale Pty Ltd v. Gair (1954) 90 C.L.R. 203 .... 4–032, 4–033
Hull v. McKenna [1926] I.R. 402 .... 16–013, 37–016
Hunt, Re; sub nom. Hunt v. Allied Bakeries (No.3) [1959] 2 Q.B. 69; [1959] 2
W.L.R. 686, CA 20–042

Hunter v. Canary Wharf Ltd [1997] A.C. 655; [1997] 2 W.L.R. 684, HL 27–031
Hussain v. United Kingdom; Singh v. United Kingdom (1996) 22 E.H.R.R. 1; 1
  B.H.R.C. 119, ECHR 22–034, 24–032
Hutton v. Bright (1852) 3 H.L.C. 341 9–046
Hutton v. Upfill (1850) 2 H.L.C. 674 9–046
Hyde Park Residence Ltd v. Secretary of State for the Environment, Transport
  and the Regions (2000) 80 P. & C.R. 419; [2000] 1 P.L.R. 85; *The Times,*
  March 14, 2000, CA 29–013

I v. DPP [2001] 2 W.L.R. 765 27–016
Ibrahim v. King, The [1914] A.C. 599, PC 37–008
Ibralebbe v. Queen, The [1964] A.C. 900; [1964] 2 W.L.R. 76, PC 4–031, 16–012,
                                                                            37–010, 37–011
Ibralebbe v. R. *See* Ibralebbe v. Queen, The
Immigration and Naturalisation Service v. Chadha (1983) 51 U.S. Law Week
  4907 1–018
Imperial Tobacco Ltd v. Attorney General [1981] A.C. 718; [1980] 2 W.L.R.
  466, HL 32–010
Imports of Potatoes, Re (C231/78); *sub nom.* Commission of the European
  Communities v. United Kingdom (C231/78) [1979] E.C.R. 1447; [1979] 2
  C.M.L.R. 427, ECJ 6–036
Imports of Poultry Meat, Re (C40/82); *sub nom.* Commission of the European
  Communities v, United Kingdom (C40/82) [1982] E.C.R. 2793; [1982] 3
  C.M.L.R. 497, ECJ 6–036
In re Burke [2001] 1 A.C. 422, HL 23–045
Inland Revenue Commission v. Hambrook [1956] 2 Q.B. 641; [1956] 3 W.L.R.
  643, CA 18–026, 18–027
Inland Revenue Commissioner (New Zealand) v. Wattie [1999] 1 W.L.R. 873;
  [1998] S.T.C. 1160, PC 37–012
Inland Revenue Commissioners v. Collco Dealings Ltd *See* Collco Dealings Ltd
  v. Inland Revenue Commissioners (No.2)
Inland Revenue Commissioners v. Rossminster Ltd *See* R. v. Inland Revenue
  Commissioners, ex p. Rossminster Ltd
Inquiry under the Company Securities (Insider Dealing) Act 1985, Re [1988]
  A.C. 660; [1988] 2 W.L.R. 33, HL 25–016
Institute of Patent Agents v. Lockwood [1894] A.C. 347 .... 3–016, 31–005, 32–017
International Railway v. Niagara Parks Commission [1941] A.C. 328, PC;
  reversing [1940] O.R. 33, CA (Ont); affirming 28–010
Internationale Handelsgesellschaft v. Einfuhr– und Vorratsstelle fur Getreide und
  Futtermittel (11/70) [1970] E.C.R. 1125; [1972] C.M.L.R. 255, ECJ 6–011, 6–039
Intpro Properties (UK) Ltd v. Sauvel [1983] Q.B. 1019; [1983] 1 W.L.R. 1, QBD ... 15–032
Ireland v. United Kingdom (1978) 2 E.H.R.R. 25 .... 22–005, 22–027, 22–032
Isaacs & Sons v. Cook [1952] 2 K.B. 391 25–003
Isaacson v. Durant (Stephney Election Petition) (1886) 17 Q.B.D. 54 .... 2–003, 23–001
Ismail, Re [1999] 1 A.C. 320; [1998] 3 W.L.R. 495, HL 23–043
Iveagh (Earl) v. Minister of Housing and Local Government [1964] 1 Q.B. 395;
  [1963] 3 W.L.R. 974, CA 30–023

JH Rayner (Mincing Lane) Ltd v. Department of Trade and Industry [1990] 2
  A.C. 418; [1989] 3 W.L.R. 969, HL 15–005
James v. Minister of Pensions [1947] K.B. 867; [1947] 2 All E.R. 432, KBD 30–009
James v. United Kingdom (A/98) (1986) 8 E.H.R.R. 123; [1986] R.V.R. 139,
  ECHR 22–046, 24–054
Janson v. Driefontein Consolidated Mines Ltd; West Rand Central Gold Mines
  Co Ltd v. De Rougemont; *sub nom.* Driefontein Consolidated Gold Mines
  Ltd v. Janson [1902] A.C. 484, HL; affirming [1901] 2 K.B. 419, CA 23–020

Jenkes (1676) 6 St.Tr. 1190 24–035
Jenkins v. Att.-Gen. (1971) 115 S.J. 674; *The Times,* August 14, 1971 15–015
Jenkins v. Kingsgate (Clothing Productions) Ltd (C96/80) [1981] 1 W.L.R. 972;
   [1981] E.C.R. 911, ECJ; [1981] 1 W.L.R. 1485, EAT 6–026
Jepson and Dyas-Elliot v. Labour Party [1996] I.R.L.R. 116, IT 10–059
John v. DPP [1985] 1 W.L.R. 657; [1985] Crim. L.R. 304, PC 37–013
John v. Express Newspapers [2000] 1 W.L.R. 1931; [2000] 3 All E.R. 257, CA ... 25–017
John Lewis & Co Ltd v. Tims; *sub nom.* Tims v. John Lewis & Co [1952] A.C.
   676; [1952] 1 W.L.R. 1132, HL 24–011
Johnson v. Phillips [1976] 1 W.L.R. 65; [1975] 3 All E.R. 682, QBD 25–019, 24–021
Johnson v. Sargant [1918] 1 K.B. 101, KBD 29–036
Johnson v. United Kingdom (1999) 27 E.H.R.R. 296; (1998) 40 B.M.L.R. 1,
   ECHR 24–030
Johnston v. Chief Constable of the Royal Ulster Constabulary (C222/84) [1987]
   Q.B. 129; [1986] 3 W.L.R. 1038; [1986] 3 All E.R. 135, ECJ 6–037, 6–040,
                                                                             22–014
Johnstone v. Pedlar [1921] 2 A.C. 262, HL (UK-Irl); affirming [1920] 2 I.R. 450,
   CA (UK-Irl) 2–008, 15–025, 23–019
Johnstone v. Sutton (1786) 1 T.R. 493 .... 19–025, 19–026
Jones, Dec'd, Re [1981] Fam.7 19–005
Jones v. Department of Employment [1989] Q.B. 1; [1988] 2 W.L.R. 493, CA 33–010
Jones v. Robson [1901] 1 Q.B. 673, QBD 29–036
Jones v. Secretary of State for Social Services [1972] A.C. 944; [1972] 2 W.L.R.
   210, HL 3–016
Jordan v. Burgoyne [1963] 2 Q.B. 744; [1963] 2 W.L.R. 1045, DC 27–023
Jordan v. United Kingdom *The Times,* May 18, 2001, ECHR 22–031
Joseph v. Ministry of Defence *The Times,* March 4, 1980, CA 33–009
Joyce v. DPP [1946] A.C. 347, HL; affirming [1945] W.N. 220, CCA 2–010, 14–016,
                                                                             15–027
Justices of Lancashire v. Stretford Overseers (1858) E.B. & E. 225 15–020

Kahan v. Pakistan Federation [1951] 2 K.B. 1003; [1951] 2 T.L.R. 697, CA ... 15–023
Kahn v. United Kingdom [2000] Crim.L.R. 684 24–018
Kariapper v. Wijesinha [1968] A.C. 717; [1967] 3 W.L.R. 1460, PC 4–031, 8–006
Kaur v. Lord Advocate 1980 S.C. 319; 1981 S.L.T. 322; [1980] 3 C.M.L.R. 79,
   OH 22–010, 22–011
Kavanagh v. Chief Constable of Devon and Cornwall [1974] Q.B. 624; [1974] 2
   W.L.R. 762, CA 30–010
Kaya v. Turkey (1999) 28 E.H.R.R. 1; [1998] H.R.C.D. 291, ECHR 22–031
Kaye v. Robertson [1991] F.S.R. 62; *The Times,* March 21, 1990, CA 25–019
Keane v. Governor of Brixton Prison; *sub nom.* R. v. Governor of Brixton Prison,
   ex p. Keane; R. v. Brixton Prison Governor, ex p. Keane [1972] A.C. 204;
   [1971] 2 W.L.R. 1243, HL 23–048
Keenan, Re [1972] 1 Q.B. 533; [1971] 3 W.L.R. 844, CA 24–037
Keighley v. Bell (1866) 4. F. & F. 763 .... 19–006, 19–008
Kenny v. Cosgrave [1926] I.R. 517 18–026
Kenny v. National Insurance Officer (1/78) [1978] E.C.R. 1489; [1978] 3
   C.M.L.R. 651, ECJ 6–026
Kensington Income Tax General Commissioners v. Aramayo [1916] 1 A.C. 215,
   HL; affirming [1914] 3 K.B. 429, CA 32–008
Kensington LBC v. Wells (1973) 72 L.G.R. 289, CA 32–013
Kent v. Metropolitan Police Commissioner *The Times,* May 15, 1981 27–017
Kenyatta v. Queen, The [1954] 1 W.L.R. 1053; 98 S.J. 508, PC 37–008
Kerr v. DPP (1994) 158 J.P. 1048; [1995] Crim. L.R. 394, QBD 24–022
Khan v. United Kingdom [2000] Crim.L.R. 684, ECHR 22–039, 26–017
Khoo Hooi Leong v. Khoo Chong Yeok [1930] A.C. 346, PC 35–017

Kielley v. Carson (1842) 4 Moo.P.C. 63 .... 13–020, 35–020
Kimber v. Press Association (1893) 62 L.J.Q.B. 152 .... 20–040, 25–003
King v. Liverpool City Council [1986] 1 W.L.R. 890; [1986] 3 All E.R. 544, CA ... 33–009
King v. Sussex Justices, ex p. McCarthy *See* R. v. Sussex Justices, ex p.
    McCarthy
King, The v. Hendon Rural DC, ex p. Chorley [1933] 2 K.B. 696, KBD 32–005
King's College, Cambridge v. Eton College P. Wms. 53 3–005
Kioa v. West (1985) 62 A.L.R. 321 31–018
Kirklees MBC v. Wickes Building Supplies Ltd [1993] A.C. 227; [1992] 3
    W.L.R. 170, HL 33–018
Kirmani v. Captain Cook Cruises Pty. Ltd (No.2), ex p. Att.-Gen. of Queensland
    (1984) 58 A.L.R. 108 36–011
Kjeldsen, Busk Madsen and Pedersen v. Denmark (1976) 1 E.H.R.R. 711 22–047
Klass v. Germany (A/28) (1979–80) 2 E.H.R.R. 214, ECHR 22–025, 22–043
Knowles v. King, The [1930] A.C. 366, PC 37–008
Knuller (Publishing, Printing and Promotions) Ltd v. DPP *sub nom.* R. v. Knuller
    (Publishing, Printing and Promotions) Ltd [1973] A.C. 435; [1972] 3
    W.L.R. 143, HL 7–002, 25–028
Kodeeswaran Chelliah v. Att.-Gen. of Ceylon [1970] A.C. 1111; [1970] 2
    W.L.R. 456, PC 18–026, 18–027
Kokkinakis v. Greece (1994) 17 E.H.R.R. 397; *The Times,* June 11, 1993,
    ECHR 22–041
Kruse v. Johnson; *sub nom.* Knise v. Johnson [1898] 2 Q.B. 91, QBD 23–038, 31–012
Kruslin v. France (1990) 12 E.H.R.R. 547; *The Times,* May 3, 1990, ECHR ... 22–029
Kuwait Airways Corporation v. Iraqi Airways Co (No.1) [1995] 1 W.L.R. 1147;
    [1995] 3 All E.R. 694, HL 15–032
Kynaston v. Secretary of State for the Home Affairs (1981) 73 Cr. App. R. 281;
    [1982] Crim. L.R. 117, CA 22–007

Labrador Boundary Dispute, Re (1927) 137 L.T. 187 36–026
Lake v. King (1668) 1 Wms Saund. 131 13–011
Laker Airways Ltd v. Department of Trade [1977] Q.B. 643; [1977] 2 W.L.R.
    234, CA 15–003, 15–004, 15–010, 28–008, 31–005, 33–016
Lane v. Cotton (1701) 1 Ld. Raym 646 .... 18–025, 33–002, 33–008
Lansbury v. Riley [1914] 3 K.B. 229, KBD 24–026
Lasky, Jaggard and Brown v. United Kingdom [1997] 24 E.H.R.R. 39 22–039
Law v. Llewellyn [1906] 1 K.B. 487, CA 20–041
Law v. National Greyhound Racing Club [1983] 1 W.L.R. 1302; [1983] 3 All
    E.R. 300, CA 32–012
Lawless v. Ireland (1961) 1 E.H.R.R. 15 .... 22–005, 22–023, 22–045
Lawlor, Re (1978) 66 Cr. App. R. 75, DC 23–048
Le Mesurier v. Le Mesurier [1895] A.C. 517, PC 37–007
Leach v. Money (1756) 3 Burr. 1962; 19 St.Tr. 1001 .... 24–007, 25–009
Leaman v. R. [1920] 3 K.B. 663 19–004
Lee v. Bude & Torrington Railway (1871) L.R. 6 C.P. 576 .... 3–012, 3–016
Lee v. Lee's Air Farming Ltd [1961] A.C. 12; [1960] 3 W.L.R. 758; [1960] 3 All
    E.R. 420, PC 37–012
Lee v. Walker [1985] Q.B. 1191; [1985] 3 W.L.R. 170; [1985] 1 All E.R. 781,
    CA 20–045
Leech v. Deputy Governor of Parkhurst Prison *See* R v. Deputy Governor of
    Parkhurst Prison, ex p. Leech
Lemon v. United Kingdom *See* Gay News and Lemon v. United Kingdom
Letellier v. France (A/207) (1992) 14 E.H.R.R. 83, ECHR 24–023, 24–024
Lever (Finance) Ltd v. Westminster Corporation [1971] 1 Q.B. 222; [1970] 3
    W.L.R. 732, CA 31–020
Levine v. Morris [1970] 1 W.L.R. 71; [1970] 1 All E.R. 144, CA 33–011

Lewis v. Att.-Gen. of Jamaica [2000] 3 W.L.R. 1785; 9 B.H.R.C. 121, PC 20–004, 37–014

Lewis v. Cattle [1938] 2 K.B. 454, KBD 21–009, 31–010

Lewis v. Cox [1985] Q.B. 509; [1984] 3 W.L.R. 875, DC 24–021

Liberal Party v. United Kingdom (8765/79) (1980) 4 E.H.R.R. 106, Eur Comm HR 10–058

Liberal Party, R. and P. v. United Kingdom (1980) 21 D.R. 211 22–049

Liebmann, Ex.p See R. v. Vine Street Police Station Superintendent, ex p. Liebmann

Lincoln v. Daniels [1962] 1 Q.B. 237; [1961] 3 W.L.R. 866, CA 20–042

Lindley v. Rutter [1981] Q.B. 128; [1980] 3 W.L.R. 660, DC 24–022

Lingen v. Austria (1986) 8 E.H.R.R. 407 25–002

Linnett v. Coles [1987] Q.B. 555; [1986] 3 W.L.R. 843, CA 24–034

Lion Laboratories Ltd v. Evans [1985] Q.B. 526; [1984] 3 W.L.R. 539, CA 25–020

Lipkin Gorman v. Cass The Times, May 29, 1985 15–015

Lippiat v. Electoral Registration Officer March 21, 1996 10–028

Liquidators of the Maritime Bank of Canada v. Receiver General of New Brunswick [1892] A.C. 437, PC 35–029

Lithgow v. United Kingdom (A/102) (1986) 8 E.H.R.R. 329; The Times, July 7, 1986, ECHR 22–046, 24–054

Litster v. Forth Dry Dock & Engineering Co Ltd; sub nom. Forth Estuary Engineering v. Litster [1990] 1 A.C. 546; [1989] 2 W.L.R. 634, HL 4–022, 6–013, 22–020

Littrell v. United States of America (No.2) [1995] 1 W.L.R. 82; [1994] 4 All E.R. 203, CA 15–030, 19–028

Liversidge v. Anderson [1942] A.C. 206, HL 3–016, 7–005, 17–019, 19–044, 19–045, 19–046, 24–001, 31–019

Liyanage v. Queen, The [1967] 1 A.C. 259; [1966] 2 W.L.R. 682, PC ... 2–021, 4–034, 37–013

Liyanage v. R See Liyanage v. Queen, The

Llandudno UDC v. Woods [1899] 2 Ch. 705, Ch D 27–004

Lloyd v. McMahon [1987] A.C. 625; [1987] 2 W.L.R. 821, HL 31–016

Locabail (UK) Ltd v. Bayfield Properties Ltd [2000] Q.B. 451; [2000] 2 W.L.R. 870, CA 20–038, 31–014

Local Government Board v. Arlidge See R. v. Local Government Board, ex p.Arlidge

Lodge v. DPP The Times, October 26, 1988, DC 27–026

Lodwick v. Saunders [1985] 1 W.L.R. 382; [1985] 1 All E.R. 577, DC 24–022

London & Clydeside Estates Ltd v. Aberdeen DC [1980] 1 W.L.R. 182; [1979] 3 All E.R. 876, HL 31–006

London County Council v. Bermondsey Bioscope Ltd [1911] 1 K.B. 445, KBD 25–038

London County Territorial and Auxiliary Forces Association v. Nichols; London County Territorial and Auxiliary Forces Association v. Parker [1949] 1 K.B. 35; [1948] 2 All E.R. 432, CA 15–020

London County Territorial and Auxiliary Forces Association v. Nichols [1949] 1 K.B. 35; [1948] 2 All E.R. 432, CA 33–16

Lonrho Exports Ltd v. Export Credits Guarantee Department [1999] Ch. 158; [1998] 3 W.L.R. 394, Ch D 15–028

Lonrho Ltd v. Shell Petroleum Co Ltd (No.1) [1980] 1 W.L.R. 627; 124 S.J. 412, HL 33–024

Lord Bishop of Natal, Re (1865) 3 Moo.P.C. (N.S.) 115 35–020

Lord Bruce of Donnington v. G. Aspden (C208/80) [1981] E.C.R. 2205; [1981] 3 C.M.L.R. 506, ECJ 6–026

Lord Gray's Motion, Re [2000] 2 W.L.R. 664; 2000 S.C. (H.L.) 46, HL 9–009

Lord Kinross, Re [1905] A.C. 468, HL 9–045

Lord Luke of Pavenham v. Minister of Housing and Local Government [1968]
    1 Q.B. 172; [1967] 3 W.L.R. 801, CA 30–028
Lord Mayhew's Motion, Re [2000] 2 W.L.R. 719, HL 9–009
Lowdens v. Keaveney [1903] Ir.R. 82 27–031
Lowe's Wills Trusts, Re *sub nom.* More v. Attorney General; Trusts of the Will
    of Lowe, Re [1973] 1 W.L.R. 882; [1973] 2 All E.R. 1136; 117 S.J. 489,
    CA 15–013
Lucas v. Lucas; Lucas v. High Commissioner for India [1943] P. 68, PDAD ... 18–027
Lynch v. DPP for Northern Ireland *See* DPP for Northern Ireland v. Lynch
Lynch v. Fitzgerald [1938] I.R. 382 19–030

M (Minors) (Breach of Contact Order: Committal), Re [1999] Fam. 263; [1999]
    2 W.L.R. 810; [1999] 2 All E.R. 56, CA 20–044
M, Re *See* M. v. Home Office
M. v. Home Office; *sub nom.* M, Re [1994] 1 A.C. 377; [1993] 3 W.L.R. 433,
    HL 4–023, 15–007, 20–045, 33–017
McAliskey v. BBC [1980] N.I. 44 10–055
Macarthys Ltd v. Smith [1981] Q.B. 180; [1980] 3 W.L.R. 929, CA 6–025
McBean v. Parker [1983] Crim. L.R. 399, DC 24–022
Macbeath v. Haldimand (1786) 1 T.R. 172, KB 33–007
McC (A Minor), Re; *sub nom.* McCann v. Mullan [1985] A.C. 528; [1984] 3
    W.L.R. 1227, HL 2–008, 2–019, 20–041
McCann, Farrell and Savage v. United Kingdom (A/324) (1996) 21 E.H.R.R. 97;
    The Times, October 9, 1995 22–031
McCarey v. Associated Newspapers Ltd [1965] 2 Q.B. 86, CA reversing [1964]
    1 W.L.R. 855, QBD 25–003
McCartan Turkington Breen v. Times Newspapers Ltd; *sub nom.* Turkington v.
    Times Newspapers Ltd [2001] 2 A.C. 277; [2000] 3 W.L.R. 1670; [2000] 4
    All E.R. 913, HL 25–005
McCarthy & Stone (Developments) Ltd v. Richmond upon Thames LBC; *sub
    nom.* R. v. Richmond upon Thames LBC., ex p. McCarthy & Sone (Devel-
    opments) Ltd [1992] 2 A.C. 48; [1991] 3 W.L.R. 941, HL 3–010, 29–012
McCawley v. King, The [1920] A.C. 691, PC 4–031, 35–025, 36–009
McCawley v. R. *See* McCawley v. King, The
MacCormick v. Lord Advocate 1953 S.C. 396; 1953 S.L.T. 255, 1 Div 2–003, 4–008,
                                                                                        4–009, 36–021
McEldowney (AP) v. Forde [1971] A.C. 632; [1969] 3 W.L.R. 179, HL 19–045,
                                                                                        19–053, 31–005
McFadden, Re *The Times,* March, 13, 1982 23–049
McGonnell v. United Kingdom (2000) 30 E.H.R.R. 289; 8 B.H.R.C. 56; *The
    Times,* February 22, 2000, ECHR 2–021, 9–017, 9–051, 20–036, 22–036, 22–051
MacGregor v. Lord Advocate 1921 S.C. 847 15–001
McInnes v. Onslow Fane [1978] 1 W.L.R. 1520; [1978] 3 All E.R. 211, Ch D 31–018
Mackay v. Att.-Gen. for British Columbia [1922] 1 A.C. 457, PC 33–007
Mackay v. Marks [1916] 2 I.R. 241 31–005
McKee v. Chief Constable for Northern Ireland [1984] 1 W.L.R. 1358; [1985] 1
    All E.R. 1, HL 19–046
McKendrick v. Sinclair 1972 S.C. (HL) 25; 1972 S.L.T. 110, HL 15–004
McKenzie v. McKenzie [1971] P. 33; [1970] 3 W.L.R. 472, CA 30–020
Macleod v. Att.-Gen. of New South Wales [1891] A.C. 455, PC 35–026, 36–005
McLeod v. Commissioner of the Police of the Metropolis [1994] 4 All E.R. 553,
    CA 24–043, 27–003
McLeod v. United Kingdom [1998] 2 F.L.R. 1048; [1999] 1 F.C.R. 193; (1999)
    27 E.H.R.R. 493, ECHR 24–043, 27–003, 27–008
McLorie v. Oxford [1982] Q.B. 1290; [1982] 3 W.L.R. 423, DC 24–022, 24–041

MacMahon v. Department of Education and Science [1983] Ch. 227; [1982] 3
W.L.R. 1129, Ch D 6–024, 6–035
MacManaway, Re; House of Commons (Clergy Disqualification) Act (1801), Re
[1951] A.C. 161; 66 T.L.R. (Pt. 2) 808, PC 10–005, 10–013, 13–017, 16–014
McWhirter v. Att.-Gen. [1972] C.M.L.R. 882, CA 2–011, 3–026, 4–017
McWhirter v. Independent Broadcasting Authority; sub nom. McWhirter's
Application, Re [1973] Q.B. 629; [1973] 2 W.L.R. 344, CA 25–035
Madras Electric Supply Corporation Ltd v. Boarland [1955] A.C. 667; [1955] 2
W.L.R. 632, HL 15–020
Madrazo v. Willes (1820) 3 B. & Ald. 353 33–008
Madzimbamuto v. Lardner-Burke [1969] 1 A.C. 645; [1968] 3 W.L.R. 1229, PC 4–013,
7–003, 14–018, 35–025
Mahon v. Air New Zealand [1984] A.C. 808; [1984] 3 W.L.R. 884, PC 2–024,
Makanjuola v. Metropolitan Police Commissioner [1992] 3 All E.R. 617, CA;
affirming in part (1990) 2 Admin. L.R. 214 .... 21–011, 33–025, 33–028
Malins v. Post Office [1975] I.C.R. 60 28–012
Malone v. Commissioner of Police of the Metropolis (No.2) [1979] Ch. 344;
[1979] 2 W.L.R. 700, Ch D 2–027, 15–004, 22–007, 22–054, 26–014
Malone v. United Kingdom (1985) 7 E.H.R.R. 14 .... 22–012, 22–029, 22–039, 26–014,
26–016
Manchester CC v. Greater Manchester CC (1980) 78 L.G.R. 560 31–004
Manchester Corporation v. Farnworth [1930] A.C. 171, HL; affirming [1929] 1
K.B. 533, CA 31–023
Manchester Corporation v. Manchester Palace of Varieties [1955] P. 133; [1955]
2 W.L.R. 440, Ct of Chivalry 18–002
Mandla v. Lee [1983] 2 A.C. 548; [1983] 2 W.L.R. 620, HL 25–010
Manitoba Fisheries Ltd v. Queen, The (1978) 88 D.L.R. (3d) 462, Sup Ct (Can) ... 15–010,
24–054
Manley-Casimir v. Att.-Gen. for Jersey The Times, February 12, 1965 35–003
Manuel v. Att.-Gen; Noltcho v. Att.-Gen. [1983] Ch. 77; [1982] 3 W.L.R. 821,
CA 3–013, 4–012, 4–014, 36–007, 36–008, 36–015, 36–017
Marbury v. Madison (1803) 1 Cranch 137 1–010
Marck v. Belgium (1979) 2 E.H.R.R. 330 22–040
Marks v. Commonwealth of Australia (1964) 111 C.L.R. 548 19–005
Marks v. Frogley [1898] 1 Q.B. 888, CA; reversing [1898] 1 Q.B. 396, QBD 19–025
Marleasing SA v. La Comercial Internacional de Alimentacion SA (C106/89)
[1990] E.C.R. I–4135; [1993] B.C.C. 421, ECJ (6th Chamber) 6–013
Marriage v. East Norfolk River Catchment Board [1950] 1 K.B. 284; [1949] 2
All E.R. 1021, CA 31–023
Marrinan v. Vibart [1963] 1 Q.B. 528; [1962] 3 W.L.R. 912, CA 20–042
Marsh v. Arscott (1982) 75 Cr. App. R. 211; [1982] Crim. L.R. 827, QBD 27–023
Marshall v. BBC [1979] 1 W.L.R. 1071; [1979] 3 All E.R. 80, CA 10–055
Marshall v. Southampton and South West Hampshire Area Health Authority
(No.1) (C152/84) [1986] Q.B. 401; [1986] 2 W.L.R. 780; [1986] E.C.R.
723 6–013
Martin v. O'Sullivan [1984] S.T.C. 258; 57 T.C. 709, CA; affirming [1982]
S.T.C. 416 .... 3–016, 10–0–14
Maryon-Wilson's Estate, Re [1912] 1 Ch. 55, CA 35–011
Masterson v. Holder [1986] 1 W.L.R. 1017; [1986] 3 All E.R. 39, DC 27–023
Matadeen v. Pointu [1999] 1 A.C. 98; [1998] 3 W.L.R. 18, PC 37–013
Mathieu-Mohin v. Belgium (A/113) (1988) 10 E.H.R.R. 1, ECHR 10–026, 22–049
Mattueof's Case (1709) 10 Mod.Rep. 4 15–032
Maynard v. Osmond [1977] Q.B. 240; [1976] 3 W.L.R. 711, CA 31–012
Meaden v. Wood [1985] Crim. L.R. 678; The Times, April 30, 1985,DC 31–019
Medway v. Doublelock Ltd [1978] 1 W.L.R. 710; [1978] 1 All E.R. 1261,
Ch D 33–023

Mellenger v. New Brunswick Development Corporation; *sub nom.* Mellinger v.
New Brunswick Development Corporation [1971] 1 W.L.R. 604; [1971] 2
All E.R. 593, CA 15–023, 28–010, 35–005, 35–013
Mellstrom v. Garner [1970] 1 W.L.R. 603; [1970] 2 All E.R. 9, CA 32–024
Memorandum (1722) 2 P. Wms. 74 .... 35–016, 35–017
Mepstead v. DPP [1996] Crim.L.R. 111 .... 24–019, 24–022
Merchandise Transport v. British Transport Commission (No.1) [1962] 2 Q.B.
173; [1961] 3 W.L.R. 1358, CA 30–009
Mercury Communications Ltd v. Director General of Telecommunications
[1996] 1 W.L.R. 48; [1996] 1 All E.R. 575, HL 28–017
Merkur Island Shipping Corporation v. Laughton [1983] 2 A.C. 570; [1983] 2
W.L.R. 778, HL 2–027
Merricks v. Heathcoat-Amory and the Minister of Agriculture, Fisheries and
Food [1955] Ch. 567; [1955] 3 W.L.R. 56, Ch D 4–033, 33–017
Merricks v. Nott-Bower [1965] 1 Q.B. 57; [1964] 2 W.L.R. 702, CA 33–022
Mersey Docks and Harbour Board Trustees v. Cameron (1865) 11 H.L. Cas.
443 15–020
Mersey Docks and Harbour Board Trustees v. Gibbs (1866) L.R. 1 H.L. 93 9–051,
15–020, 28–009, 31–024, 32–022
Metropolitan Asylum District Managers v. Hill (1881) 6 App. Cas. 193, HL 31–023,
32–022
Metropolitan Properties Co (FGC) Ltd v. Lannon [1969] 1 Q.B. 577; [1968] 3
W.L.R. 694, CA 30–010, 31–015
Meunier, Re [1894] 2 Q.B. 415, QBD 19–050, 23–044
Middleton v. Croft (1743) Cas. T. Hard. 326 (Eccles. Ct) 4–026, 15–014
Midland Cold Storage Ltd v. Turner [1972] 3 All E.R. 773; [1972] I.C.R. 230,
NIRC 20–046
Midland Railway Co v. Pye (1861) 10 CBNS 179 22–037
Mighell v. Sultan of Johore [1894] 1 Q.B. 149, CA 15–005, 15–023, 35–008
Miller (TA) Ltd v. Ministry of Housing and Local Government [1968] 1 W.L.R.
992; [1968] 2 All E.R. 633, CA 30–010
Miller v. Knox (1838) 4 Bing N.C. 574 19–030
Ming Pao Newspapers Ltd v. Att.-Gen. of Hong Kong [1996] A.C. 907; [1996]
3 W.L.R. 272, PC 37–013
Minister of Agriculture and Fisheries v. Matthews [1950] 1 K.B. 148; [1949] 2
All E.R. 724, KBD 31–020
Minister of Home Affairs (Bermuda) v. Fisher [1980] A.C. 319; [1979] 2 W.L.R.
889, PC 22–009, 37–013
Minister of Supply v. British Thomson-Houston Co Ltd [1943] K.B. 478, CA 33–007
Ministry of Agriculture, Fisheries and Food v. Jenkins [1963] 2 Q.B. 317; [1963]
2 W.L.R. 906, CA 15–019
Minquiers and Ecrehos Case I.C.J. Reports (1953) p. 47 35–003
Minta v. Secretary of State for the Home Department; *sub nom.* R. v. Secretary
of State for the Home Department, ex p. Minta [1992] Imm. A.R. 380; *The
Times,* April 14, 1992, CA; affirming *The Times,* June 24, 1991, QBD 23–026
Mitchell v. Queen, The [1999] 1 W.L.R. 1679, PC 37–013
Mitchell v. R. [1896] 1 Q.B. 121 19–004
Mohammad Yakub Khan v. R (1947) 63 T.L.R. 94 37–008
Mohammed v. Trinidad and Tobago [1999] 2 A.C. 111; [1999] 2 W.L.R. 552,
PC 24–018
Mohammed-Holgate v. Duke [1984] A.C. 437; [1984] 2 W.L.R. 660, CA 21–007,
24–009
Molyneaux, Ex.p [1986] 1 W.L.R. 331; (1986) 83 L.S.G. 1314, QBD 5–008
Montgomery v. HM Advocate; Coulter v. HM Advocate [2001] 2 W.L.R. 779;
2001 S.C. 1, PC 22–053
Moore v. Green (No.2) [1983] 1 All E.R. 663, DC 24–019, 24–022

Moore v. United Kingdom; Gordon v. United Kingdom (2000) 29 E.H.R.R. 728,
　ECHR 22–012
Morgan v. Att.-Gen. [1965] N.Z.L.R. 134 33–009
Morgan v. Att.-Gen. of Trinidad and Tobago [1988] 1 W.L.R. 297; (1988) 132
　S.J. 264, PC 37–013
Morris v. Beardmore [1981] A.C. 446; [1980] 3 W.L.R. 283, HL 1–019, 21–007,
　　　　　　　　　　　　　　　　　　　　　　　　　　　　　　24–041
Morris v. Crown Office; *sub nom.* Morris v. Master of the Crown Office [1970]
　2 Q.B. 114; [1970] 2 W.L.R. 792, CA 20–050
Morrow v. DPP *See* DPP v. Morrow
Mortensen v. Peters (1906) 8 F. (J.C.) 93 .... 3–016, 3–027
Moss v. McLachlan (1985) 149 J.P. 167; [1985] I.R.L.R. 76, DC 27–009, 27–010
Mulcahy v. Ministry of Defence [1997] 1 W.L.R. 294, HL 33–013
Mulvenna v. Admiralty 1926 S.C. 842; 1926 S.L.T. 568, 1 Div 18–027
Municipal Council of Sydney v. Campbell [1925] A.C. 338, PC 31–009
Municipality of Pictou v. Geldert [1893] A.C. 524, PC 35–016
Munster v. Lamb (1883) 11 Q.B.D. 588 20–042
Mure v. Kaye (1811) 4 Taunt 43 23–042
Murphy (J.) & Sons Ltd v. Secretary of State for the Environment [1973] 1
　W.L.R. 560; [1973] 2 All E.R. 26, QBD 30–028
Murphy, Re [1991] 5 N.I.J.B. 72, QBD 27–016
Murray v. United Kingdom (1990) 22 E.H.R.R. 29 24–016
Musgrave v. Pulido (1879) 5 App.Cas. 102, PC 15–022, 15–025
Musgrove v. Chun Teeong Toy [1891] A.C. 491 .... 15–024, 23–019
Mutasa v. Att.-Gen. [1980] Q.B. 114; [1979] 3 W.L.R. 792, QBD 15–012, 35–014
Mwenya, Ex.p [1960] 1 Q.B. 241; [1959] 3 W.L.R. 767, CA 15–024, 24–040, 35–008

NHS Trust A v. M; NHS Trust B v. H [2001] 2 W.L.R. 942; [2001] 1 All E.R.
　801, Fam. Div 22–050
Nabob of the Carnatic v. East India Co (1793) 2 Ves. 56 15–022
Nadan v King, The [1926] A.C. 482, PC 37–006
Nakkuda Ali v. Jayaratne *See* Nakkuda Ali v. MF de S Jayaratne
Nakkuda Ali v. MF de S Jayaratne; *sub nom.* Ali v. Jayaratne [1951] A.C. 66; 66
　T.L.R. (Pt 2) 214, PC 19–045
National & Provincial Building Society v. United Kingdom; Leeds Permanent
　Building Society; Yorkshire Building Society v. United Kingdom [1997]
　S.T.C. 1466; (1998) 25 E.H.R.R. 127, ECHR 22–047
National Coal Board v. Galley [1958] 1 W.L.R. 16; [1958] 1 All E.R. 91, CA 28–010
National Union of General and Municipal Workers v. Gillian [1946] K.B. 81,
　CA 3–016
Navigators and General Insurance Co v. Ringrose [1962] 1 W.L.R. 173; [1962]
　1 All E.R. 97, Ca 35–003
Ndlwana v. Hofmeyr [1937] A.D. 229 4–011
Neilson v. Laugharne [1981] Q.B. 736; [1981] 2 W.L.R. 537, CA 33–025
Neimietz v. Germany (A/251–B) (1992) 24–048
Nelsovil Ltd v. Minister of Housing and Local Government [1962] 1 W.L.R. 404;
　[1962] 1 All E.R. 423, DC 30–024
Netz v. Chuter Ede [1946] Ch. 224, Ch D 15–024, 23–021
Neumeister v. Austria (No.1) (A/8) (1979–80) 1 E.H.R.R. 91, ECHR 24–023, 24–024,
　　　　　　　　　　　　　　　　　　　　　　　　　　　　　　24–025
New South Wales v. Bardolph (1934) 52 C.L.R. 455 33–007
New York Times Co v. United States (1971) 403 U.S. 713 26–024
New Zealand Loan & Mercantile Agency Co Ltd v. Morrison [1898] A.C. 349,
　PC 35–016
Newbery v. Queen, The [1965] 7 F.L.R. 34 .... 35–016, 35–021

Newcastle Breweries v. King, The (1920) 2 Ll. L. Rep. 236; [1920] 1 K.B. 854,
  KBD 24–054
News Group Newspapers Ltd v. Society of Graphical and Allied Trades
  (SOGAT) 1982 [1986] I.C.R. 716; [1986] I.R.L.R. 227, CA; [1986] I.R.L.R.
  337, HC 27–031, 27–034
Nicholas v. Parsonage; *sub nom.* Nicholas v. DPP [1987] R.T.R. 199; [1987]
  Crim. L.R. 474, DC 24–022
Nicholson v. Secretary of State for Energy (1977) 76 L.G.R. 693 30–010
Nicol v. DPP; Selvanayagam v. DPP (1996) 160 J.P. 155; [1996] Crim. L.R. 318,
  QBD 27–008; 27–009
Nielsen, Re; *sub nom.* Denmark v. Nielsen [1984] A.C. 606; [1984] 2 W.L.R.
  737, HL 23–043
Ningkan (Stephen Kalong) v. Malaysia [1970] A.C. 379; [1969] 2 W.L.R. 365,
  PC 7–007, 37–012
Nissan v. Att.-Gen. *See* Att.-Gen. v. Nissan
Nobrega v. Att.-Gen. of Guyana (1967) 10 W.I.R. 187, CA 18–026, 18–027
Nold v. Commission of the European Communities (C4/73) [1975] E.C.R. 985;
  [1974] E.C.R. 491; [1974] 2 C.M.L.R. 338, ECJ 6–011, 6–039
Nordsee v. Reederei Mond (102/81) [1982] E.C.R. 1095; [1982] Com. L.R. 154,
  ECJ 6–026
Norweb Plc v. Dixon [1995] 1 W.L.R. 636; [1995] 3 All E.R. 952, QBD 31–022
Norwich Pharmacal Co v. Customs and Excise Commissioners [1974] A.C. 133;
  [1973] 3 W.L.R. 164, HL 33–023
Nottingham Area No.1 Hospital Management Committee v. Owen [1958] 1 Q.B.
  50; [1957] 3 W.L.R. 707, QBD 28–011
Nyali Ltd v. Att.-Gen. [1957] A.C. 253; [1956] 3 W.L.R. 341, HL 35–008

O'Brien v. Sim-Chem [1980] 1 W.L.R. 1011; [1980] 3 All E.R. 132, HL 4–022
O'Connell v. Queen, The (1844) 11 Cl. & Fin. 155 9–045
O'Hara v. Chief Constable of the Royal Ulster Constabulary [1997] A.C. 286;
  [1997] 2 W.L.R. 1; [1997] 1 All E.R. 129, HL 21–009, 24–009
O'Kelly v. Harvey (1883) 14 L.R.Ir. 105 27–009
O'Kelly v. Trust House Forte Plc [1984] Q.B. 90; [1983] 3 W.L.R. 605, CA ... 32–016
O'Loughlin v. Chief Constable of Essex [1998] 1 W.L.R. 374; *The Times,*
  December 12, 1997, CA 24–041, 24–043
O'Moran v. DPP; Whelan v. DPP [1975] Q.B. 864; [1975] 2 W.L.R. 413, DC 19–053,
                                                                                    27–040
O'Reilly v. Mackman; Millbanks v. Secretary of State for the Home Department;
  Derbyshire v. Mackman; Dougan v. Mackman; Millbanks v. Home Office
  [1983] 2 A.C. 237; [1982] 3 W.L.R. 1096, HL ... 2–024, 31–001, 31–018, 32–006,
                                                                        32–010, 32–024
Observer and Guardian v. United Kingdom (A/216); Sunday Times v. United
  Kingdom (Spycatcher) (A/217) (1992) 14 E.H.R.R. 153; *The Times,*
  November 27, 1991, ECHR 25–021, 26–010
Odlum v. Stratton (1946) 33–022
Officier van Justitie v. Kolpinghuis Nijmegen BV (C80/86) [1987] E.C.R. 3969;
  [1989] 2 C.M.L.R. 18, ECJ (6th Chamber) 6–014
Ong Ah Chuan v. Public Prosecutor; Koh Chai Cheng v. Public Prosecutor
  [1981] A.C. 648; [1980] 3 W.L.R. 855, PC 31–013
Open Door Counselling v. Ireland; Dublin Well Woman Centre v. Ireland
  (A/246) (1993) 15 E.H.R.R. 244; *The Times,* November 5, 1992, ECHR 22–025
Oriental Bank Corporation, Ex.p The Crown, Re (1885) L.R. 28 Ch. D. 643, Ch
  D 35–005
Orsolina Leonesio v. Minister for Agriculture and Forestry of the Italian Repub-
  lic [1972] E.C.R. 287 6–012

Oskar v. Government of the Commonwealth of Australia [1988] A.C. 366;
[1988] 1 All E.R. 183, HL 23–047
Osman v. Ferguson [1993] 4 All E.R. 344, CA 21–011, 31–024
Osman v. United Kingdom [1999] 1 F.L.R. 193; (2000) 29 E.H.R.R. 245; [1999]
Fam. Law 86, ECHR 22–031, 22–036, 31–024
Otto-Preminger-Institut v. Austria (1994) 19 E.H.R.R. 34 .... 22–030, 22–041
Owner of SS Raphael v. Brandy [1911] A.C. 413, HL; affirming [1911] 1 K.B.
376, CA 18–028
Owners of the Tramontana v. Ministry of Defence and Martin [1969] 2 Lloyd's
Rep. 94, PDAD 33–011

Paddington Corporation v. Att.-Gen. *sub nom.* Boyce v. Paddington Corporation
[1906] A.C. 1, HL; reversing [1903] 2 Ch. 556, CA; reversing [1903] 1 Ch.
109, Ch D 32–001, 32–023
Padfield v. Ministry of Agriculture, Fisheries and Food [1968] A.C. 997; [1968]
2 W.L.R. 924, HL 3–010, 7–005, 31–008, 32–009, 33–018
Pan American World Airways Inc's Application, Re; *sub nom.* Lockerbie Air
Disaster, Re [1992] Q.B. 854; [1992] 3 W.L.R. 191, CA 15–007
Panesar v. Nestlé Co [1980] I.C.R. 144; [1980] I.R.L.R. 64, CA 22–008
Paola Faccini Dori v. Recreb Srl [1994] E.C.R. 1–3325; [1994] 1 C.M.L.R.
665 6–013
Papworth v. Coventry [1967] 1 W.L.R. 663; [1967] 2 All E.R. 41, DC 27–005
Paris Adult Theatre v. Slaton (1973) 413 U.S. 49 25–001
Parkin v. Norman; Valentine v. Lilley [1983] Q.B. 92; [1982] 3 W.L.R. 523,
DC 27–023
Parliamentary Election for Bristol South-East, Re [1964] 2 Q.B. 257; [1961] 3
W.L.R. 577, Election Ct 9–002, 9–005, 10–005, 10–047, 10–062
Parliamentary Privilege Act 1770, Re [1958] A.C. 331; [1958] 2 W.L.R. 912,
PC 13–003, 16–014
Parochial Church Council of Aston Cantlow and Wilmeste with Billesley War-
wickshire v. Wallbank *The Times*, June 15, 2000, CA 22–055
Pasmore v. Oswaldtwistle Urban DC (No.2) [1898] A.C. 387, HL; affirming
[1897] 1 Q.B. 625, CA 32–013
Paton v. United Kingdom (8416/78) (1981) 3 E.H.R.R. 408, Eur Comm HR ... 22–031
Paty's Case (1704) 2 Ld. Ryam 1105 .... 10–061, 13–03
Pawlett v. Att.-Gen. (1668) Hardr. 465 33–018
Payne v. Payne *The Times,* March 9, 2001, CA 22–054
Peacock v. Bell (1666) 1 Wms. Saund. 74 20–041
Peacock v. London Weekend Television Ltd (1986) 150 J.P. 71; (1986) 150 J.P.N.
47, CA 25–013
Pearce v. Secretary of State for Defence [1988] A.C. 755; [1988] 2 W.L.R. 1027,
HL 33–012
Pearlman v. Harrow School Governors [1979] Q.B. 56; [1978] 3 W.L.R. 736,
CA 31–007, 32–004
Peden International Transport v. Lord Mancroft [1989] P.L. 398 13–027
Pedro v. Diss [1981] 2 All E.R. 59; (1981) 72 Cr. App. R. 193, DC 24–019
Peninsular and Oriental Steam Navigation Co v. Kingston [1903] A.C. 471, PC 35–026
People v. Croswell (1804) 3 Johns (N.Y.) 337 25–018
Pepper v. Hart [1993] A.C. 593; [1992] 3 W.L.R. 1032, HL 4–022, 4–036, 4–037,
13–014, 22–019, 26–003
Percy v. DPP [1995] 1 W.L.R. 1382; [1995] 3 All E.R. 124, DC 27–008, 27–009
Percy v. Glasgow Corporation [1922] 2 A.C. 299, HL 32–022
Peterkin v. Chief Constable of Cheshire *The Times*, November 16, 1999 27–010
Petition of Right, A, Re [1915] 3 K.B. 649, CA 15–004
Pfizer v. Ministry of Health [1965] A.C. 512; [1965] 2 W.L.R. 387, HL 3–007, 28–011,
33–011

Pharmaceutical Society of Great Britain v. Dickson [1970] A.C. 403; [1968] 3
  W.L.R. 286, HL 32–024
Phillip v. DPP of Trinidad and Tobago [1992] 1 A.C. 545; [1992] 2 W.L.R. 211,
  PC 24–034
Phillips v. Eyre (1870) L.R. 6 Q.B. 1 .... 15–017, 19–028, 35–023
Pickering v. Liverpool Daily Post and Echo Newspapers Plc; sub nom. P. v.
  Liverpool Daily Post and Echo [1991] 2 A.C. 370; [1991] 2 W.L.R. 513,
  HL 20–007
Pickin v. British Railways Board See British Railways Board v. Pickin
Pickstone v. Freemans Plc [1989] A.C. 66; [1988] 3 W.L.R. 265, HL 4–022, 6–013
Pickwell v. Camden LBC [1983] Q.B. 962; [1983] 2 W.L.R. 583; [1983] 1 All
  E.R. 602, QBD 31–004, 31–011
Picton v. Cullen [1900] 2 I.R. 612 18–028
Piddington v. Bates; sub nom. Robson v. Ribton-Turner [1961] 1 W.L.R. 162;
  [1960] 3 All E.R. 660, QBD 27–009, 27–033, 27–034
Pierce v. Bemis (The Lusitania) [1986] Q.B. 384; [1986] 2 W.L.R. 501, QBD 15–013
Piermont v. France (A/314) (1995) 20 E.H.R.R. 301, ECHR 22–045
Piersack v. Belgium (A/53) (1983) 5 E.H.R.R. 169, ECHR 26–018
Piracy Jure Gentium, Re; Reference under the Judicial Committee Act 1833, Re
  [1934] A.C. 586; (1934) 49 Ll. L. Rep. 411, PC 16–014
Plattform Artzte fur das Leben v. Austria (1991) 13 E.H.R.R. 204 ...... 22–030, 27–008
Plimmer v Wellington Corporation (1884) L.R. 9 App. Cas. 699, PC 33–016
Polites v. The Commonwealth (1945) 70 C.L.R. 60 (High Ct. Australia)   3–026
Politi SAS v. Italian Minister of Finance (C43/71) [1971] E.C.R. 1039; [1973]
  C.M.L.R. 60, ECJ   6–012
Poplar Housing and Regeneration Community Association Ltd v. Donoghue The
  Times, June 21, 2000, CA 22–054
Port Louis Corporation v. Att.-Gen. of Mauritius [1965] A.C. 1111; [1965] 3
  W.L.R. 67, PC 31–006
Porter v. Freudenberg; Krelinger v. S Samuel & Rosenfeld sub nom. Merten's
  Patents, Re [1915] 1 K.B. 857, CA 23–020
Post Office v. Estuary Radio Ltd [1968] 2 Q.B. 740; [1967] 1 W.L.R. 1396, CA   3–020,
                                                                                   15–031
Post Office v. Mears Construction [1979] 2 All E.R. 813, QBD 28–002
Powell v. Apollo Co (1885) 10 App.Cas. 282 35–022
Powell v. May [1946] K.B. 330, KBD 31–006
Powell v. United Kingdom; Rayner v. United Kingdom (1990) 12 E.H.R.R. 355;
  The Times, February 22, 1990, ECHR 22–039
Poyser and Mills' Arbitration, Re; sub nom. Poyser v. Mills [1964] 2 Q.B. 467;
  [1963] 2 W.L.R. 1309, QBD 30–023
Practice Direction (CA: Tape Recorders) [1981] 1 W.L.R. 1526; [1981] 3 All
  E.R. 848, CA 20–050
Practice Direction (Contempt: Reporting Restrictions) [1982] 1 W.L.R. 1475;
  [1983] 1 All E.R. 64, CA 25–015
Practice Direction (HL: Petitions for Leave to Appeal) [1979] 1 W.L.R. 497;
  [1979] 2 All E.R. 359, HL   9–049
Practice Note (Jury: Juror: Excuse) [1988] 3 All E.R. 177 20–020
Practice Note (Jury: Stand By: Jury Checks) [1988] 3 All E.R. 1086; (1989) 88
  Cr. App. R. 123 20–020
Practice Note (Justices Clerks) [1953] 1 W.L.R. 1416; [1953] 2 All E.R. 1306,
  QBD 31–015
Prasad v. Wolverhampton BC [1983] Ch. 333 20–008
Pratt v. Att.-Gen. of Jamaica [1994] 2 A.C. 1; [1993] 3 W.L.R. 995, PC 37–013
Prebble v. Television New Zealand Ltd [1995] 1 A.C. 321; [1994] 3 W.L.R. 970,
  PC 13–003, 13–014, 13–018
Preiss v. General Dental Council The Times, August 14, 2001, PC 22–053

Pretore di Salo v. Persons Unknown (C14/86); *sub nom.* Criminal Proceedings
   against a Person or Person Unkown (C14/86) [1987] E.C.R. 2545; [1989] 1
   C.M.L.R. 71, ECJ (5th Chamber) 6–014
Price v. United Kingdom *The Times*, August 13, 2001, ECHR 22–032
Pride of Derby and Derbyshire Angling Association Ltd v. British Celanese Ltd
   [1953] Ch. 149; [1953] 2 W.L.R. 58, CA 31–023, 32–023
Prince v. Gagnon (1882) 8 App.Cas. 103 37–007
Prince v. Secretary of State for Scotland; *sub nom.* Prince v. Younger 1985 S.C.
   8; 1985 S.L.T. 74, OH 6–019
Prince's Case (1606) 8 Co.Rep. 1a 4–026, 4–027, 15–015
Prometheus, The (1948–49) 82 Ll. L. Rep. 859, CA; affirming (1948–49) 82 Ll.
   L. Rep. 172, PDAD 18–026
Pubblico Ministero v. Ratti (148/78) [1979] E.C.R. 1629; [1980] 1 C.M.L.R. 96,
   ECJ 6–013
Punton v. Ministry of Pensions and National Insurance (No.2) [1964] 1 W.L.R.
   226; [1964] 1 All E.R. 448, CA 32–024
Puttick v. Att.-Gen. [1980] Fam. 1; [1979] 3 W.L.R. 542, Fam Div 23–009
Pyx Granite Co Ltd v. Ministry of Housing and Local Government [1960] A.C.
   260; [1959] 3 W.L.R. 346, HL 32–013

Queen Caroline's Claim (1821) 1 St. Tr. (N.S.) 949 7–002
Queen, The v. Price (1854) 8 Moo.P.C. 203 37–007
Quietlynn Ltd v. Southend BC (C23/89) [1991] 1 Q.B. 454; [1991] 2 W.L.R.
   611; [1990] 3 All E.R. 207; [1990] E.C.R. I–3059, ECJ (6th Chamber) ... 6–036
Quigley, Re [1983] 8 N.I.J.B. 24–036, 24–037
Quigley v. Chief Constable of the Royal Ulster Constabulary [1983] 5 N.I.J.B;
   [1983] NI 238, CA (NI) 23–040, 24–037
Quin v. King, The *The Times,* November 8, 1951 35–003

R. v. A. (Joinder of Appropriate Minister) [2001] 1 W.L.R. 789; The Times,
   March 21, 2001; The Independent, March 27, 2001, HL 22–016
R. v. Ahlers [1915] 1 K.B. 616, CA 14–016
R. v. Allen (1862) 1 B. & S. 850 20–003
R. v. Allen [1921] 2 I.R. 241 19–035
R. v. Altrincham Justices, ex p. Pennington (Norman); R v Altrincham Justices, ex
   p. Pennington (Arthur Charles) [1975] Q.B. 549; [1975] 2 W.L.R. 450, DC ... 31–015
R. v. Anderson; R. v. Oz Publications Ltd [1972] 1 Q.B. 304; [1971] 3 W.L.R.
   939, CA (Crim Div) 25–025, 25–029
R. v. Andrews [1999] Crim. L.R. 156; (1998) 95(43) L.S.G. 32; The Times,
   October 15, 1998 20–020
R. v. Argent [1997] 2 Cr. App. R. 27; (1997) 161 J.P. 190, CA (Crim Div) 24–017
R. v. Army Board of Defence Council, ex p. Anderson [1992] Q.B. 169; [1991]
   3 W.L.R. 42, DC 31–017
R. v. Arrowsmith [1975] Q.B. 678 25–009
R. v. Arundel Justices, ex p. Westminster Press Ltd [1985] 1 W.L.R. 708 20–048
R. v. Askew (1768) 4 Burr. 2186 32–009
R. v. Aston University Senate, ex p. Roffey [1969] 2 Q.B. 538; [1969] 2 W.L.R.
   1418, DC 32–006
R. v. Atkins *See* Atkins v. DPP
R. v. Attwood (1617) Cro.Jac. 421 25–007
R. v. BBC, ex p. Referendum Party [1997] E.M.L.R. 605; (1997) 9 Admin. L.R.
   553, QBD 10–056
R. v. Barnsley MBC, ex p. Hook [1976] 1 W.L.R. 1052; [1976] 3 All E.R. 452,
   CA 6–039, 32–005
R. v. Baron de Clifford *The Times,* December 13, 1935 8–006

R. v. Beck, ex p. Daily Telegraph [1993] 2 All E.R. 177; (1992) 94 Cr. App. R.
  376, CA 25–015
R. v. Bedwellty Urban DC, ex p. Price [1934] 1 K.B. 333, KBD 32–009
R. v. Benjafield [2001] 2 All E.R. 609; [2001] Crim. L.R. 245; *The Times,*
  December 28, 2000, CA (Crim Div) 22–053
R. v. Bertrand (1867) L.R. 1 P.C. 520 .... 37–003, 37–008
R. v. Bingham [1973] Q.B. 870; [1973] 2 W.L.R. 520, CA (Crim Div) 26–004
R. v. Bisset [1980] 1 W.L.R. 335; (1980) 70 Cr. App. R. 46, CMAC 3–005, 19–022
R. v. Board of Control, ex p. Rutty; *sub nom.* Rutty, Re [1956] 2 Q.B. 109; [1956]
  2 W.L.R. 822, DC 24–034
R. v. Board of Trade, ex p. St Martin Preserving Co. Ltd [1965] 1 Q.B. 603;
  [1964] 3 W.L.R. 262, QBD 32–009
R. v. Board of Visitors of Dartmoor Prison, ex p. Smith [1987] Q.B. 106; [1986]
  3 W.L.R. 61, CA 32–007, 32–012
R. v. Board of Visitors of Hull Prison, ex p. St. Germain (No.1); R. v. Board of
  Visitors of Wandsworth Prion, ex p. Rosa [1979] Q.B. 425; [1979] 2 W.L.R.
  42, CA 24–032
R. v. Board of Visitors of the Maze Prison, ex p. Hone [1988] A.C. 379; [1988]
  2 W.L.R. 177, HL 31–017
R. v. Bottrill, ex p. Kuechenmeister [1947] K.B. 41; [1946] 2 All E.R. 434, CA 15–005,
                                                                                      15–023, 23–021
R. v. Bouchereau (C30/77) [1978] Q.B. 732; [1978] 2 W.L.R. 251, ECJ 6–026, 6–035,
                                                                                      23–023
R. v. Boundary Commission, ex p. Foot [1983] Q.B. 600 10–045
R. v. Bournemouth Justices, ex p. Grey *The Times,* May 31, 1986 33–024
R. v. Bournewood Community and Mental Health NHS Trust, ex p. L; *sub nom.*
  L, Re [1999] 1 A.C. 458; [1998] 3 W.L.R. 107, HL 24–034
R. v. Bow Street Magistrates' Court, ex p. Choudhury [1991] 1 Q.B. 429; [1990]
  3 W.L.R. 986, QBD 22–041, 25–007, 25–009
R. v. Bow Street Metrploitan Stipendiary Magistrate, ex p. Government of
  U.S.A. [2000] 2 A.C. 216, HL 23–043, 23–045
R. v. Bow Street Metropolitan Stipendiary Magistrate, ex p. Noncy P Ltd [1990]
  1 Q.B. 123; 89 Cr.App. R. 121, CA 6–037
R. v. Bow Street Metropolitan Stipendiary Magistrate, ex p. Pinochet Ugarte
  (No.1); *sub nom.* R. v. Evans, ex p. Pinochet Ugarte (No.1) [2000] 1 A.C.
  61; [1998] 3 W.L.R. 1456, HL 1–020, 15–032
R. v. Bow Street Metropolitan Stipendiary Magistrate, ex p. Pinochet Ugarte
  (No.2); *sub nom.* Pinochet Ugarte (No.2), Re; R. v. Evans, ex p. Pinochet
  Ugarte (No.2); R. v. Bartle, ex p. Pinochet Ugarte (No.2) [2000] 1 A.C. 119;
  [1999] 2 W.L.R. 272, HL 20–038, 22–051, 31–014
R. v. Bow Street Metropolitan Stipendiary Magistrate, ex p. Pinochet Ugarte
  (No.3) [2000] 1 A.C. 147; [1999] 2 W.L.R. 827, HL 1–020, 3–026, 15–021,
                                                                      22–004, 23–043, 23–044
R. v. Bowden [2001] Q.B. 88; [2000] 2 W.L.R. 1083; [2000] 2 All E.R. 418, CA ... 25–030
R. v. Bracknell Forrest DC *See* R. (on the application of Johns) v. Bracknell
  Forest DC
R. v. Brailsford [1905] 2 K.B. 730, KBD 15–027
R. v. British Airports Authority ex p. Wheatley [1983] R.T.R. 466; 81 L.G.R.
  794, CA 31–012
R. v. Britten [1969] 1 W.L.R. 151; [1969] 1 All E.R. 517, CA(Crim Div) 26–003
R. v. Brixton Prison Governor, ex p. Ahsan [1969] 2 Q.B. 222; [1969] 2 W.L.R.
  618, DC 24–034, 24–036
R. v. Broadcasting Complaints Commission, ex p. BBC (1995) [1995] E.M.L.R.
  241; (1995) 7 Admin. L.R. 575, QBD 25–036
R. v. Broadcasting Complaints Commission ex p. Owen [1985] Q.B. 1153;
  [1985] 2 W.L.R. 1025, DC 31–009

R. v. Broadcasting Standards Commission, ex p. BBC [2000] 3 W.L.R. 1327;
[2000] 3 All E.R. 989, CA 25–036
R. v. Broadfoot (1743) 18 St.Tr. 1323; Foster, *Crown Law*, p.154 19–003
R. v. Broadmoor Special Hospital Authority, ex p. S [1998] C.O.D. 199; (1998)
95(8) L.S.G. 32, CA; affirming *The Times,* November 5, 1997, QBD 24–029
R. v. Bromley LBC, ex p. Lambeth LBC *The Times,* June 16, 1984, DC 32–010
R. v. Brown (1841) C. & Mar. 314 19–031
R. v. Brown (1977) 64 Cr. App. R. 231; [1977] R.T.R. 160, CA 24–006
R. v. Burah (1878)3 App Cas. 889 4–037
R. v. Burdett (1820) 4 B. & Aid. 95 25–018
R. v. Burdett (1821) 4 B. & Ald. 314 25–009
R. v. Burns [1982] Crim.L.R. 522 20–021
R. v. Burns 16 Cox 355 25–009
R. v. Calder & Boyars Ltd [1969] 1 Q.B. 151; [1968] 3 W.L.R. 974, CA (Crim
Div).. 25–025
R. v. Calderwood, ex p. Manchester Corporation *The Times,* February 27, 1974,
DC 32–009
R. (Carroll and Another) v. Secretary of State for the Home Department *The
Times*, August 16, 2001, HL 22–053
R. v. Casement [1917] 1 K.B. 98 .... 2–010, 14–015
R. v. Cassel [1916] 1 K.B. 595 10–005
R. v. Central Criminal Court, ex p. Adegbesan [1986] 1 W.L.R. 1292; [1986] 3
All E.R. 113, DC 24–047
R. v. Central Criminal Court, ex p. Francis and Francis [1989] A.C. 346; [1988]
3 W.L.R. 989, HL 24–047
R. v. Central Criminal Court, ex p. Raymond [1986] 1 W.L.R. 710; [1986] 2 All
E.R. 379, QBD 32–004, 32–012
R. v. Chancellor of Cambridge University (1716) 1 Str. 557 31–016
R. v. Chancellor of St. Edmundsbury and Ipswich Diocese, ex p. White [1948]
1 K.B. 195; [1947] 2 All E.R. 170, CA 22–024, 32–006
R. v. Chandler (No.2); *sub nom.* Chandler v. Commissioner of Police of the
Metropolis [1964] Crim. L.R. 404, HL [1964] 2 Q.B. 322 20–020
R. v. Cheltenham Justices ex p. Secretary of State for Trade [1977] 1 W.L.R. 95;
[1977] 1 All E.R. 460, QBD 33–023
R. v. Chesterfield Justices, ex p. Bramley [2000] Q.B. 576; [2000] 2 W.L.R. 409,
QBD 24–045, 24–046, 24–047
R. v. Chief Adjudication Officer, ex p. Bland *The Times,* February 6, 1985, DC ... 32–013
R. v. Chief Constable of Devon and Cornwall, ex p. Central Electricity Generat-
ing Board [1982] Q.B. 458; [1981] 3 W.L.R. 867, CA 21–008, 27–008
R. v. Chief Constable of Kent, ex p. L; R. v. DPP, ex p. B [1993] 1 All E.R. 756;
(1991) 93 Cr. App. R. 416, DC 20–015
R. v. Chief Constable of the Merseyside Police, ex p. Calveley [1986] Q.B. 424;
[1986] 2 W.L.R. 144 32–013
R. v. Chief Constable of South Wales, ex p. Merrick [1994] 1 W.L.R. 663; [1994]
2 All E.R. 560; [1994] Crim. L.R. 852, QBD 24–016
R. v. Chief Constable of Sussex, ex p. International Trader's Ferry Ltd [1999] 2
A.C. 418; [1998] 3 W.L.R. 1260, HL 6–036, 21–008
R. v. Chief Constable of the West Midlands ex p. Wiley [1995] 1 A.C. 274;
[1994] 3 W.L.R. 433, HL 33–025, 33–028
R. v. Chief Constable of Warwickshire, ex p. Fitzpatrick [1999] 1 W.L.R. 564;
[1998] 2 All E.R. 65, QBD 24–047
R. v. Chief Immigration Officer, Gatwick Airport, ex p. Kharrazi [1980] 1 W.L.R.
1396; [1980] 3 All E.R. 373, CA 23–038
R. v. Chief Immigration Officer, Heathrow Airport, ex p. Salamat Bibi [1976] 1
W.L.R. 979; [1976] 3 All E.R. 843, CA 22–010, 29–004, 36–021

R. v. Chief Rabbi of the United Hebrew Congregations of Great Britain and the Commonwealth, ex p. Wachmann; *sub nom.* R. v. Jacobovits, ex p. Wachmann [1992] 1 W.L.R. 1036; [1993] 2 All E.R. 249, QBD 22–024

R. v. Chief Registrar of Friendly Societies, ex p. New Cross Building Society [1984] Q.B. 227; [1984] 2 W.L.R. 370, CA 20–040, 31–011

R. v. Chiswick Police Superintendent, ex p. Sacksteder [1918] 1 K.B. 578, CA 23–034

R. v. Civil Service Appeal Board, ex p. Bruce [1988] 3 All E.R. 686; [1988] I.C.R. 649, DC 18–029

R. v. Clark [1964] 2 Q.B. 315; [1963] 3 W.L.R. 1067, CCA 27–031

R. v. Clayton; R. v. Halsey [1962] 1 W.L.R. 1184, HL; [1963] 1 Q.B. 163, CCA 25–025

R. v. Clerkenwell Magistrates' Court, ex p. Telegraph Plc [1993] Q.B. 462; [1993] 2 W.L.R. 233; [1993] 2 All E.R. 183, DC 25–015

R. v. Commandant of Knockaloe Camp (1917) 117 LT 627 23–021

R. v. Commissioner of the Metropolis *The Times,* March 7, 1980, CA 21–007

R. v. Commissioner of Police of the Metropolis, ex p. Blackburn (No.1) [1968] 2 Q.B. 118; [1968] 2 W.L.R. 893, CA 21–007

R. v. Commissioner of Police of the Metropolis, ex p. Blackburn (No.2) [1968] 2 Q.B. 150; [1968] 2 W.L.R. 1204, CA 20–047

R. v. Commissioner of Police of the Metropolis, ex p. Blackburn [1973] Q.B. 241; [1973] 2 W.L.R. 43, CA 21–007

R. v. Commissioner of Police of the Metropolis, ex p. Hammond; *sub nom.* Commissioner of Police of the Metropolis v. Hammond [1965] A.C. 810; [1964] 3 W.L.R. 1, HL 24–039

R. v. Comptroller General of Patents, Designs and Trade Marks ex p. Gist-Brocades [1986] 1 W.L.R. 51; (1985) 129 S.J. 889, HL 6–025

R. v. Condron [1997] 1 W.L.R. 827; [1997] 1 Cr. App. R. 185, CA 24–017

R. v. County Quarter Sessions Appeals Committee, ex p. M.P.C. [1948] 1 K.B. 260 24–008

R. v. Cowle (1759) 2 Burr. 834 .... 24–040, 32–002

R. v. Criminal Injuries Board, ex p. A [1999] 2 A.C. 330; [1999] 2 W.L.R. 974, HL 31–007, 32–003

R. v. Criminal Injuries Compensation Board, ex p. Lain [1967] 2 Q.B. 864; [1967] 3 W.L.R. 348, QBD 15–011, 22–024, 32–006

R. v. Cripps, ex p. Muldoon; *sub nom.* R. v. Commissioner Cripps QC, ex p. Muldoon [1984] Q.B. 686; [1984] 3 W.L.R. 53, CA 10–062, 20–007, 32–004

R. v. Cuming, ex p. Hall (1887) 19 Q.B.D. 13 19–005

R. v. Cunninghame Graham and Burns (1888) 16 Cox C.C. 420 27–004

R. v. Customs and Excise Commissioners, ex p. Hedges & Butler Ltd [1986] 2 All E.R. 164, DC 31–005

R. v. Dairy Produce Quota Tribunal for England and Wales, ex p. Caswell [1990] 2 A.C. 738; [1990] 2 W.L.R. 1320, HL 32–003

R. v. Damaree (1709) 15 St. Tr. 521 14–014

R. v. Deevey [1977] Crim.L.R. 550 22–010

R. v. Denbigh Justices, ex p. Williams; R. v. Denbigh Justices, ex p. Evans [1974] Q.B. 759; [1974] 3 W.L.R. 45, QBD 20–040

R. v. Deputy Governor of Parkhurst Prison, ex p. Hague; *sub nom.* Hague v. Deputy Governor of Parkhurst Prison [1992] 1 A.C. 58; [1991] 3 W.L.R. 340, HL 22–022, 22–032, 24–031

R. v. Deputy Governor of Parkhurst Prison, ex p. Leech; *sub nom* Leech v. Deputy Governor of Parkhurst Prison [1988] A.C. 533; [1988] 2 W.L.R. 290, HL 24–032

R. v. Deputy Industrial Injuries Commissioner, ex p. Moore [1965] 1 Q.B. 456; [1965] 2 W.L.R. 89, CA 30–010

R. v. DPP, ex p. Kebilene; *sub nom.* R. v. DPP, ex p. Kebelene [2000] 2 A.C. 326; [1999] 3 W.L.R. 972, HL 19–055, 22–023, 22–052, 32–004

R. v. DPP, ex p. Manning [2001] Q.B. 330; [2000] 3 W.L.R. 463, QBD 20–015

R. v. Director of Serious Fraud Office, ex p. Smith; *sub nom.* Smith v. Director
of Serious Fraud Office [1993] A.C. 1; [1992] 3 W.L.R. 66; [1992] 3 All
E.R. 456, HL 24–017
R. v. Disciplinary Committee of the Jockey Club, ex p. Aga Khan [1993] 1
W.L.R. 909; [1993] 2 All E.R. 853, CA 22–024, 32–012
R. v. Dixon [1993] Crim. L.R. 579, CA 27–021
R. v. Drybones (1969) 9 D.L.R. (3d) (Supreme Ct. Cananda) 4–031
R. v. Dunsheath, ex p. Meredith [1951] 1 K.B. 127; [1950] 2 All E.R. 741, DC 32–009
R. v. Durkin [1953] 2 Q.B. 364; [1953] 3 W.L.R. 479, CMAC 19–009
R. v. Dytham [1979] Q.B. 722; [1979] 3 W.L.R. 467, CA 21–007
R. v. Earl of Crewe, ex p. Sekgome [1910] 2 K.B. 576, CA 15–024
R. v. East Kerrier Justices, ex p. Mundy [1952] 2 Q.B. 719; [1952] 2 All E.R.
144, DC 31–015
R. v. East Norfolk Local Valuation Court, ex p. Martin [1951] 1 All E.R. 743;
115 J.P. 248, DC 32–004
R. v. Editor of the New Statesman, ex p. DPP (1928) 44 T.L.R. 301 20–047
R. v. Eeet [1983] Crim. L.R. 806, Crown Ct 24–022
R. v. Effik [1995] 1 A.C. 309; [1994] 3 W.L.R. 583, HL 26–014
R. v. Election Court, ex p. Sheppard; *sub nom.* R. v. Harwood (Election Court),
ex p. Sheppard [1975] 1 W.L.R. 1319; [1975] 2 All E.R. 723, QBD 10–062
R. v. Electricity Commissioners [1924] 1 K.B. 171 .... 3–016, 32–004, 32–007
R. v. Elliott, Hollis and Valentine (1629) 3 St. Tr. 294 .... 13–005, 13–007
R. v. Entry Clearance Officer (Bombay), ex p. Amin; *sub nom.* Amin v. Entry
Clearance Officer (Bombay) [1983] 2 A.C. 818; [1983] 3 W.L.R. 258, HL ... 23–039
R. v. Epping (Waltham Abbey) Justices, ex p. Burlinson [1948] 1 K.B. 79; [1947]
2 All E.R. 537, KBD 31–023
R. v. Eyre (1868) Finlayson, 73 19–034
R. v. Fellows; R. v. Arnold [1997] 2 All E.R. 548; [1997] 1 Cr. App. R. 244, CA
(Crim Div) 25–026
R. v. Fineberg [1958] N.Z.L.R. 119 4–031
R. v. Fineberg [1968] N.Z.L.R. 443 35–022
R. v. Forbes (1865) 10 Cox C.C. 362 24–020
R. v. Ford [1989] Q.B. 868; [1989] 3 W.L.R. 762; [1989] 3 All E.R. 445, CA 20–020
R. v. Forde (1985) 81 Cr. App. R. 19; (1985) 149 J.P. 458; [1985] Crim. L.R. 323,
CA 24–019
R. v. Foster [1985] Q.B. 115; [1984] 3 W.L.R. 401, CA 20–004
R. v. Fulham, Hammersmith and Kensington Rent Tribunal, ex p. Zerek [1951]
2 K.B. 1; [1951] 1 All E.R. 482, DC 32–004, 32–005
R. v. Gaming Board for Great Britain, ex p. Benaim [1970] 2 Q.B. 417; [1970]
2 W.L.R. 1009, CA 31–016
R. v. Garth [1986] A.C. 268; [1986] 2 W.L.R. 80, HL 19–023
R. v. General Medical Council, ex p. Gee *See* Gee v. General Medical Council;
sub nom. R. v. General Medical Council, ex p. Gee [1987] 1 W.L.R. 564;
[1987] 2 All E.R. 193, HL; affirming [1986] 1 W.L.R. 1247, CA; reversing
[1986] 1 W.L.R. 226, QBD 30–017, 32–012
R. v. Goldstein [1983] 1 W.L.R. 151; [1983] 1 All E.R. 434, HL; [1982] 1 W.L.R.
804, CA (Crim Div) 6–018
R. v. Gordon-Finlayson, ex p. An Officer [1941] 1 K.B. 171, KBD 19–020
R. v. Gott (1922) 16 Cr.App.R. 87, CA 25–007
R. v. Gough [1993] A.C. 646; [1993] 2 W.L.R. 883, HL 20–021, 20–038, 31–014
R. v. Governor of Belmarsh Prison, ex p. Gilligan [2001] 1 A.C. 84; [1999] 3
W.L.R. 1244, HL 23–049
R. v. Governor of Brixton Prison, ex p. Caborn-Waterfield; *sub nom.* Caborn-
Waterfield [1960] 2 Q.B. 498; [1960] 2 W.L.R. 792, QBD 24–034
R. v. Governor of Brixton Prison, ex p. Kahan [1989] Q.B. 716; [1989] 2 W.L.R.
721, QBD 23–045

R. v. Governor of Brixton Prison, ex p. Kolczynski; *sub nom.* Kolczynski, Re [1955] 1 Q.B. 540; [1955] 2 W.L.R. 116 23–044

R. v. Governor of Brixton Prison, ex p. Naranjan Singh; *sub nom.* Naranjan Singh, Re [1962] 1 Q.B. 211; [1961] 2 W.L.R. 980, QBD 24–034

R. v. Governor of Brixton Prison, ex p. Sadri [1962] 1 W.L.R. 1304; [1962] 3 All E.R. 747, QBD 24–034

R. v. Governor of Brixton Prison, ex p. Soblen (No.1); *sub nom.* R. v. Secretary of State for Home Affairs, ex p. Soblen [1963] 1 Q.B. 829; [1962] 3 W.L.R. 1145, CA 24–034, 24–037

R. v. Governor of Brixton Prison, ex p. Soblen (No.2) [1963] 2 Q.B. 243, CA; affirming [1962] 3 W.L.R. 1154, QBD 23–034, 23–041

R. v. Governor of Brixton Prison, ex p. Walsh [1985] A.C. 154; [1984] 3 W.L.R. 205, HL 24–034

R. v. Governor of Canterbury Prison, ex p. Craig; *sub nom.* Craig, Re [1991] 2 Q.B. 195; [1990] 3 W.L.R. 127, QBD 24–024

R. v. Governor of Durham Prison, ex p. Carlisle [1979] Crim.L.R. 175, DC 23–048

R. v. Governor of Durham Prison, ex p. Singh [1984] 1 W.L.R. 704; [1984] 1 All E.R. 983, QBD 24–033, 24–034

R. v. Governor of Pentonville Prison, ex p. Alves; *sub nom.* Alves v. DPP; Alves, Re [1993] A.C. 284; [1992] 3 W.L.R. 844, HL 23–046

R. v. Governor of Pentonville Prison, ex p. Azam *See* Azam v. Secretary of State for the Home Department

R. v. Governor of Pentonville Prison, ex p. Budlong; *sub nom.* Habeas Corpus Applications of Budlong and Kember, Re [1980] 1 W.L.R. 1110; [1980] 1 All E.R. 701, QBD 23–041

R. v. Governor of Pentonville Prison, ex p. Healy (1984) 128 S.J. 498; *The Times,* May 11, 1984, DC 23–041

R. v. Governor of Pentonville Prison, ex p. Osman (No.3); *sub nom.* Osman (No.3), Re [1990] 1 W.L.R. 878; [1990] 1 All E.R. 999, DC 24–034

R. v. Governor of Pentonville, ex p. Sinclair; *sub nom.* Sinclair v. DPP; Sinclair v. USA [1991] 2 A.C. 64; [1991] 2 W.L.R. 1028, HL 23–046

R. v. Governor of Richmond Remand Centre, ex p. Ashgar; *sub nom.* R. v. Chief Immigration Officer, ex p. Ashgar [1971] 1 W.L.R. 129; (1970) 115 S.J. 14, DC 24–034

R. v. Governor of Risley Remand Centre, ex p. Hassan; *sub nom.* Hassan, Re [1976] 1 W.L.R. 971; [1976] 2 All E.R. 123; 120 S.J. 333, DC 24–034

R. v. Governor of Risley Remand Centre, ex p. Marks [1984] Crim. L.R. 238, DC 23–048

R. v. Governor of Winson Green, ex p. Littlejohn [1975] 1 W.L.R. 893; [1975] 3 All E.R. 208, DC 23–044

R. v. Graham-Campbell, ex p. Herbert [1935] 1 K.B. 594, KBD 13–019, 15–019, 32–009

R. v. Greater Birmingham Appeal Tribunal ex p. Simper [1974] Q.B. 543; [1973] 2 W.L.R. 709, CA 31–008

R. v. Greater London Council, ex p. Blackburn [1976] 1 W.L.R. 550; [1976] 3 All E.R. 184, CA 25–038

R. v. Greater London Council, ex p. Burgess [1978] I.C.R. 991; [1978] I.R.L.R. 261, DC 22–008

R. v. Greenway [1998] P.L. 357 13–009

R. v. Griffin (1989) 88 Cr. App. R. 63; [1988] Crim. L.R. 680, CA 20–044

R. v. Guildhall Magitrates' Court, ex p. Primlaks Holding Co. [1990] 1 Q.B. 261; [1989] 2 W.L.R. 841, DC 24–046

R. v. Hackney, Islington and Stoke Newington Rent Tribunal, ex p. Keats [1951] 2 K.B. 15 (Note); [1950] 2 All E.R. 138, DC 31–007

R. v. Halliday, ex p. Zadig [1917] A.C. 260, HL; affirming [1916] 1 K.B. 738, CA 19–045

R. v. Hampden (Case of Ship-Money) (1637) 3 St. Tr. 825 ..... 3–009, 15–002, 15–016, 19–003

R. v. Hardy (11794) 24 St. Tr. 199 14–018

R. v. Hebron (1989) 11 Cr. App. R. (S.) 226; [1989] Crim. L.R. 839, CA 27–020

R. v. Henn [1981] A.C. 850; [1980] 2 C.M.L.R. 229, HL 6–024, 6–025, 6–036, 6–037

R. v. Hicklin (1868) L.R. 3 Q.B. 360, QB 25–024

R. v. Higher Education Funding Council, ex p. Institute of Dental Surgery [1994] 1 W.L.R. 242; [1994] 1 All E.R. 651, QBD 31–016

R. v. Hillingdon LBC, ex p. Puhlhofer [1986] A.C. 484; [1986] 2 W.L.R. 259, HL 32–014

R. v. Hillingdon LBC, ex p. Royco Homes [1974] Q.B. 720; [1974] 2 W.L.R. 805, QBD 31–008

R. v. HM Coroner for Greater Manchester, ex p. Tal [1985] Q.B. 67; [1984] 3 W.L.R. 643, QBD 32–004, 32–006

R. v. HM Queen in Council, ex p. Vijayatunga [1990] 2 Q.B. 444; [1989] 3 W.L.R. 13, CA 16–008

R. v. HM Treasury, ex p. Smedley; sub nom. R. v. Economic Secretary to the Treasury, ex p . Smedley [1985] Q.B. 657; [1985] 2 W.L.R. 576, CA 6–016, 7–004, 32–011

R. v. Holmes, ex p. Sherman; sub nom. Sherman and Apps, Re [1981] 2 All E.R. 612; (1981) 72 Cr. App. R. 266, DC 24–034

R. v. Home Secretary, ex p. Soblen See R. v. Governor of Brixton Prison, ex p. Soblen (No.1)

R. v. Horne Took (1794) 25 St. Tr. 1 14–018

R. v. Horseferry Road Justices, ex p. Independent Broadcasting Authority [1987] Q.B. 54; [1986] 3 W.L.R. 132, QBD 25–034, 31–025, 32–007

R. v. Horseferry Road Magistrates Court, ex p. Bennett (No.1); sub nom. Bennett v. Horseferry Road Magistrates Court [1994] 1 A.C. 42; [1993] 3 W.L.R. 90, HL 2–027

R. v. Housing Appeal Tribunal [1920] 3 K.B. 334, KBD 32–009

R. v. Howell [1982] Q.B. 416; [1981] 3 W.L.R. 501; [1981] 3 All E.R. 383, CA ... 24–008, 24–022, 27–008

R. v. Hull University Visitor, ex p. Page See R. v. Lord President of the Privy Council ex p. Page

R. v. Hurst (Judge Sir Donald), ex p. Smith [1960] 2 Q.B. 133; [1960] 2 W.L.R. 961, QBD 32–004

R. v. Immigration Appeal Tribunal, e xp. Ali Ajmal [1982] Imm. A.R. 102, CA 22–007

R. v. Immigration Appeal Tribunal, ex p. Alexander; sub nom. Alexander v. Immigration Appeal Tribunal [1982] 1 W.L.R. 1076; [1982] 2 All E.R. 766, HL 29–004

R. v. Immigration Appeal Tribunal, ex p. Begum The Times, July 24, 1986 ...... 23–038, 29–004, 31–012

R. v. Immigration Appeal Tribunal, ex p. Joyles [1972] 1 W.L.R. 1390; [1972] 3 All E.R. 213, DC 29–033

R. v. Immigration Appeal Tribunal, ex p. Secretary of State for the Home Department [1990] 1 W.L.R. 1126; [1990] 3 All E.R. 652, CA 23–019

R. v. Immigration Appeal Tribunal, ex p. Shah [1999] 2 A.C. 629; [1999] 2 W.L.R. 1015, HL 23–032, 29–021

R. v. Immigration Appeal Tribunal, ex p. Singh (Bakhtaur) [1986] 1 W.L.R. 910; [1986] 2 All E.R. 721, HL 23–024, 23–038, 29–004

R. v. Independent Broadcasting Authority, ex p. Whitehouse Times, April 4, 1985, CA; reversing (1984) 81 L.S.G. 1992, DC 25–035

R. v. Inland Revenue Commissioners, ex p. National Federation of Self Employed and Small Businesses Ltd [1982] A.C. 617; [1981] 2 W.L.R. 722, HL 3–006, 22–025, 32–011

R. v. Inland Revenue Commissioners, ex p. Preston [1985] A.C. 835; [1985] 2
W.L.R. 836, HL 31–019, 31–020, 32–013
R. v. Inland Revenue Commissioners, ex p. Rossminster Ltd; *sub nom.* Inland
Revenue Commissioners v. Rossminster Ltd; Rossminster and Tucker, Re
[1980] A.C. 952; [1980] 2 W.L.R. 1, HL 19–045, 24–051
R. v. Inner London Education Authority ex p. Westminster City Council [1986]
1 W.L.R. 28; [1986] 1 All E.R. 19, QBD 31–009
R. v. Inner London Education Authority, ex p. Hinde; R. v. Inner London
Education Authority, ex p. Duverley [1985] 1 C.M.L.R. 716; 83 L.G.R. 695;
The Times, November 19, 1984, QBD 6–035
R. v. International Stock Exchange of the United Kingdom, ex p. Else (1982) Ltd
[1993] Q.B. 534; [1993] 2 W.L.R. 70; [1993] 1 All E.R. 420, CA 6–023
R. v. Intervention Board for Agricultural Produce, ex p. E.D. & F. Man (Sugar)
Ltd [1986] 2 All E.R. 115; [1985] E.C.R. 2889, ECJ (5th Chamber) 31–002
R. v. James (1839) 8 C. & P. 131 19–008
R. v. Jefferson [1994] 1 All E.R. 270; (1994) 99 Cr. App. R. 13, CA 27–019
R. v. Jones (Yvonne) [1978] 3 All E.R. 1098; (1978) 67 Cr. App. R. 166, CA 24–022
R. v. Jones; R. v. Whicher [1999] 2 Cr. App. R. 253; (2000) 2 L.G.L.R. 157, CA
(Crim Div) 10–049
R. v. Jordan [1967] Crim. L.R. 483, DC 2–011, 3–015, 22–041
R. v. Jordan and Tyndall [1963] Crim. L.R. 124, CCA 27–040
R. v. Judge Fraser Harris, ex p. Law Society [1955] 1 Q.B. 287 32–009
R. v. Kelly [1982] A.C. 665; [1981] 3 W.L.R. 387, HL 3–021
R. v. Kennett (1781) 5 C. & P. 282 19–029
R. v. Kent Justices (1890) 24 Q.B.D 181 15–020
R. v. Kent Justices, ex p. Lye [1967] 2 Q.B. 153; [1967] 2 W.L.R. 765, DC 3–020,
15–031
R. v. Kent Police Authority, ex p. Godden; *sub nom.* Godden. Re [1971] 2 Q.B.
662; [1971] 3 W.L.R. 416, CA 32–008
R. v. Ketter [1940] 1 K.B. 787, CCA 15–024, 35–008
R. v. Khan [1997] A.C. 558; [1996] 3 W.L.R. 162, HL 19–048, 24–041, 26–017
R. v. Knightsbridge Crown Court, ex p. Aspinall Curzon Ltd *The Times,* Decem-
ber 16, 1982 32–006
R. v. Knightsbridge Crown Court, ex p. International Sporting Club (London)
[1982] Q.B. 304; [1981] 3 W.L.R. 640, QBD 32–006
R. v. Knuller (Publishing, Printing and Promotions) Ltd *See* Knuller (Publishing,
Printing and Promotions) Ltd v. DPP
R. v. Lambert *The Times,* July 6, 2001, HL 22–050
R. v. Lambeth Justices, ex p. Yusufu; *sub nom.* R. v. Governor of Brixton Prison,
ex p. Yusufu [1985] Crim. L.R. 510, DC 15–032
R. v. Lander [1919] N.Z.L.R. 305, Ct of Appeal, New Zealand 36–026
R. v. Latif; R. v. Shahzad [1996] 1 W.L.R. 104; [1996] 1 All E.R. 353, HL 21–006
R. v. Legal Aid Board, ex p. Kaim Todner; *sub nom.* R. v. Legal Aid Board, ex
p. T (A Firm of Solicitors) [1999] Q.B. 966; [1998] 3 W.L.R. 925; [1998]
3 All E.R. 541, CA 20–048
R. v. Legislative Committee of the Church Assembly ex p. Haynes-Smith [1928]
1 K.B. 411, KBD 32–004, 32–006, 32–007
R. v. Leigh [1897] 1 Q.B. 132 31–008
R. v. Leman Street Police Station Inspector, ex p. Venicoff [1920] 3 K.B. 72,
KBD 23–034
R. v. Lemon; *sub nom.* Whitehouse v. Lemon [1979] A.C. 617; [1979] 2 W.L.R.
281, HL 22–008, 25–001, 25–007
R. v. Liverpool Corporation, ex p. Liverpool Taxi Fleet Operators Association
[1972] 2 Q.B. 299; [1972] 2 W.L.R. 1262, CA 31–018, 31–020, 32–007

R. v. Local Commissioner for Administration for the North and East Area of England ex p. Bradford City Council [1979] Q.B. 287; [1979] 2 W.L.R. 1, CA 34–016

R. v. Local Government Board, ex p. Arlidge; *sub nom.* Local Government Board v. Arlidge [1915] A.C. 120, HL; reversing [1914] 1 K.B. 160, CA 2–031, 3–016, 31–016

R. v. London CC, ex p. Corrie [1918] 1 K.B. 68, KBD 31–010

R. v. London CC, ex p. Entertainments Protection Association [1931] 2 K.B. 215, CA 32–005

R. v. Lord Chancellor, ex p. Lightfoot [2000] 2 Q.B. 597, CA 22–002

R. v. Lord Chancellor, ex p. Whitham [1998] Q.B. 575; [1998] 2 W.L.R. 849; [1997] 2 All E.R. 779, QBD 1–019, 20–013, 22–002

R. v. Lord Chancellor's Department, ex p. Nangle [1992] 1 All E.R. 897; [1991] I.C.R. 743, DC 18–029

R. v. Lord President of the Privy Council ex p. Page; *sub nom.* R. v. Hull University Visitor, ex p. Page [1993] A.C. 682; [1993] 3 W.L.R. 1112, HL 31–007

R. v. Lord Saville of Newgate, ex p. Anonymous Soldiers [2000] 1 W.L.R. 1855; [1999] 4 All E.R. 860, CA 8–007, 8–008

R. v. Lords Commissioners of the Treasury (1872) L.R. 7 Q.B. 387, QB 32–009

R. v. Lower Munslow Justices, ex p. Pudge [1950] 2 All E.R. 756; 114 J.P. 509, KBD 31–015

R. v. Lynch [1903] 1 K.B. 444 .... 14–015, 15–023, 23–011

R. v. Machin [1980] 1 W.L.R. 763; [1980] 3 All E.R. 151, CA 20–044

R. v. Mahroof (1989) 88 Cr. App. R. 317, CA 27–020

R. v. Managers of South Western Hospital, ex p. M [1993] Q.B. 683; [1993] 3 W.L.R. 376, QBD 24–034

R. v. Manchester City Justices, ex p. Davies [1989] Q.B. 631; [1988] 3 W.L.R. 1357, CA 20–042

R. v. Manchester Overseers (1854) 3 E.& B. 336 15–020

R. v. Mansfield Justices, ex p. Sharkey [1985] Q.B. 613; [1984] 3 W.L.R. 1328, DC 24–025

R. v. Martin [1956] 2 Q.B. 272; [1956] 2 W.L.R. 975, CCC 3–020

R. v. Martin [1998] A.C. 917; [1998] 2 W.L.R. 1, HL 19–009

R. v. Mason [1981] Q.B. 881; [1980] 3 W.L.R. 617, CA 20–021

R. v. McCann (1990) 92 Cr.App.R. 239 20–021

R. v. McIlkenny [1992] 2 All E.R. 417; (1991) 93 Cr. App. R. 287, CA (Crim Div) 20–004, 20–029

R. v. McKenzie; R. v. Davis [1979] Crim. L.R. 164, Crown Ct (Bristol) 24–022

R. v. Medical Appeal Tribunal, ex p. Gilmore [1957] 1 Q.B. 574; [1957] 2 W.L.R. 498, CA 32–004, 32–005, 32–017

R. v. Medical Appeal Tribunal, ex p. Hubble [1959] 2 Q.B. 408; [1959] 3 W.L.R. 456, CA; affirming [1958] 2 Q.B. 228, DC 30–010

R. v. Minister of Health, ex p. Davis [1929] 1 K.B. 619, CA 32–008

R. v. Minister of Health, ex p. Yaffe; *sub nom.* Minister of Health v. King, The [1931] A.C. 494, HL; reversing [1930] 2 K.B. 98, CA ... 31–006, 32–008, 32–018

R. v. Ministry of Defence, ex p. Smith [1996] Q.B. 517; [1996] 2 W.L.R. 305, CA 15–005, 22–007, 22–028, 22–039

R. v Monopolies and Mergers Commission, ex p. Argyll Group Plc [1986] 1 W.L.R. 763; [1986] 2 All E.R. 257, CA 32–015

R. v. Montgomery [1995] 2 All E.R. 28; [1995] 2 Cr. App. R. 23, CA 20–050

R. v. Murphy (1986) 5 N.S.W.L.R. 18 13–014

R. v. Mylius *The Times,* February 2, 1911 18–011

R. v. Nat Bell Liquors Ltd [1922] 2 A.C. 128, PC 31–007, 32–005

R. v. National Coal Board, ex p. National Union of Mineworkers [1986] I.C.R. 791 32–012

R. v. National Insurance Commissioner, ex p. Warry; *sub nom.* R. v. National
Insurance Commissioner, ex p. Insurance Officer (C41/77) [1978] Q.B. 607;
[1978] 3 W.L.R. 99, ECJ 6–025
R. v. National Joint Council for the Craft of Dental Technicians (Disputes
Committee), ex p. Neate [1953] 1 Q.B. 704; [1953] 2 W.L.R. 342, DC 32–006,
32–012
R. v. Nazari [1980] 1 W.L.R. 1366; [1980] 3 All E.R. 880, CA (Crim Div) 23–034
R. v. Nelson and Brand (1867) Special Report, pp.99–100 .... 19–033, 19–033
R. v. Newbury Justices, ex p. du Pont (1983) 78 Cr.App.R 255, DC 20–053
R. v. Newmarket Assessment Committee, ex p. Allen Newport Ltd [1945] 2 All
E.R. 371 30–010
R. v. North and East Devon HA, ex p. Coughlan [2001] Q.B. 213; [2000] 2
W.L.R. 622, CA 31–019
R. v. North Worcestershire Assessment Committee, ex p. Hadley [1929] 2 K.B.
397, KBD 32–008
R. v. Northumberland Compensation Appeal Tribunal ex p. Shaw [1952] 1 K.B.
338; [1952] 1 All E.R. 122, CA 32–004, 32–005
R. v. Oakes [1959] 2 Q.B. 350; [1959] 2 W.L.R. 694, CCA 26–004
R. v. Offen (No.2) [2001] 1 W.L.R. 253; [2001] 2 All E.R. 154; [2001] 1 Cr. App.
R. 24, CA (Crim Div) 20–035, 22–050
R. v. Ogden, ex p. Long Ashton Rural DC [1963] 1 W.L.R. 274; [1963] 1 All
E.R. 574, DC 32–009
R. v. Oldham Justices, ex p. Cawley [1997] Q.B. 1; [1996] 2 W.L.R. 681, QBD ... 24–034
R. v. Oxford, ex p. Levey (1987) 151 L.G. Rev. 371, CA; affirming *The Times,*
December 18, 1985, DC 21–008
R. v. Paddington and St Marylebone Rent Tribunal, ex p. Bell London and
Provincial Properties Ltd [1949] 1 K.B. 666; [1949] 1 All E.R. 720, KBD 31–009,
32–004, 32–008
R. v. Page [1954] 1 Q.B. 170; [1953] 3 W.L.R. 895, CMAC 19–020
R. v. Panel on Take-Overs and Mergers, ex p. Datafin Plc [1987] Q.B. 815;
[1987] 2 W.L.R. 699, CA 22–024, 32–006, 32–012
R. v. Paris; R. v. Abdullahi; R. v. Miller (1993) 97 Cr. App. R. 99; [1994] Crim.
L.R. 361, CA 24–018
R. v. Parliamentary Commissioner for Administration ex p. Balchin [1998] 1
P.L.R. 1; [1997] J.P.L. 917 34–013
R. v. Parliamentary Commissioner for Administration ex p. Dyer [1994] 1
W.L.R. 621; [1994] 1 All E.R. 375, DC 34–013
R. v. Parliamentary Commissioner for Standards, ex p. Al Fayed [1998] 1 W.L.R.
669; [1998] 1 All E.R. 93, CA 13–018
R. v. Patents Appeal Tribunal, ex p. Swift & Co. [1962] 2 Q.B. 647; [1962] 2
W.L.R. 897, DC 32–005
R. v. Pennington (1985) 81 Cr. App. R. 217; (1985) 149 J.P. 615, CA 20–020
R. v. Picton (1804–10) 30 St.Tr. 225 35–017
R. v. Pieck [1981] Q.B. 571; [1981] 2 W.L.R. 960; [1981] E.C.R. 2171, ECJ (1st
Chamber) 6–026, 6–035
R. v. Pigg [1983] 1 W.L.R. 6; [1983] 1 All E.R. 56, HL
R. v. Pinney (1832) B & Ad. 947 .... 19–029, 19–031
R. v. Pitt (1762) 3 Burr. 1335 13–025
R. v. Plymouth Justices, ex p. Rogers [1982] Q.B. 863; [1982] 3 W.L.R. 1, QBD 6–024,
6–026
R. v. Ponting [1985] Crim. L.R. 318, CCC 18–030, 26–003
R. v. Portobello Barracks Commanding Officer, ex p. Erskine Childers [1923]
I.R. 5 19–035
R. v. Post Office, ex p. Byrne [1975] I.C.R. 221; 119 S.J. 341, DC 32–006
R. v. Post Office, ex. p. Association of Scientific, Technical and Managerial
Staffs [1981] 1 All E.R. 139; [1981] I.C.R. 76, CA 31–006

R. v. Powell (1994) 98 Cr. App. R. 224; *The Times,* June 3, 1993, CA 20–050
R. v. Queen's County Justices [1908] 2 I.R. 285 31–014
R. v. RA Manchester Legal Aid Committee, ex p. Brand & Co. [1952] 2 Q.B.
    413; [1952] 1 All E.R. 480 .... 32–004, 32–005
R. v. Race Relations Board, ex p. Selvarajan [1975] 1 W.L.R. 1686; [1976] 1 All
    E.R. 12, CA 31–019
R. v. Radio Authority, ex p. Bull [1998] Q.B. 294; [1997] 3 W.L.R. 1094; [1997]
    2 All E.R. 561, CA 10–056
R. v. Reading Justices, ex p. South West Meat Ltd (No.2) [1992] Crim. L.R. 672;
    The Independent, December 13, 1991, QBD 24–047
R. v. Registrar of Companies, ex p. Central Bank of India *See* R. v. Registrar of
    Companies, ex p. Esal (Commodities) Ltd (In Liquidation)
R. v. Registrar of Companies, ex p. Esal (Commodities) Ltd (In Liquidation); *sub*
    nom. R. v. Registrar of Companies, ex p. Central Bank of India [1986] Q.B.
    1114; [1986] 2 W.L.R. 177, CA 32–020
R. v. Rhuddlan Justices, ex p. HTV Ltd [1986] Crim. L.R. 329, DC 25–015
R. v. Richards, ex p. Fitzpatrick and Browne 91955) 92 C.L.R. 157 13–020
R. v. Roble [1997] Crim. L.R. 449, CA 24–017
R. v. Rothwell [1993] Crim. L.R. 626, CA (Crim Div) 27–019
R. v. Rule [1937] 2 K.B. 375, CCA 13–006
R. v. Sabri [1965] Crim. L.R. 102; 108 S.J. 922; *The Guardian,* November 10,
    1964, CCA 23–005
R. v. St. Edmundsbury and Ipswich Diocese (Chancellor), ex p. White [1948] 1
    K.B. 195; [1947] 2 All E.R. 170, CA 2–010
R. v. St. Edmundsbury BC, ex p. Investors Ltd [1985] 1 W.L.R. 1168 31–006
R. v. Samuel [1988] Q.B. 615; [1988] 2 W.L.R. 920; (1988) 87 Cr. App. R. 232,
    CA (Crim Div) 24–016
R. v. Sandbach Justices, ex p. Williams; *sub nom.* R. v. Sandbach, ex p. Williams
    [1935] 2 K.B. 192; (1935) 99 J.P. 51, KBD 2–008
R. v. Saunders (C175/78) [1980] Q.B. 72; [1979] 3 W.L.R. 359, ECJ 6–021
R. v. Secchi [1975] 1 C.M.L.R. 383; [1976] Crim. L.R. 392, MC 6–035
R. v. Secretary of State for Employment, ex p. Equal Opportunities Commission
    [1991] 1 A.C. 1, HL 4–023, 22–016
R. v. Secretary of State for Employment, ex p. Equal Opportunities Commission
    [1995] 1 A.C. 1; [1994] 2 W.L.R. 409, HL 9–052, 22–025
R. v. Secretary of State for Foreign Affairs, ex p. Greenberg [1947] 2 All E.R.
    550, KBD 24–040
R. v. Secretary of State for Foreign and Commonwealth Affairs, ex p. Indian
    Association of Alberta [1982] Q.B. 892; [1982] 2 W.L.R. 641, CA 15–007,
    35–005, 36–008, 36–015, 36–017
R. v. Secretary of State for Foreign and Commonwealth Affairs, ex p. Lord Rees-
    Mogg [1994] Q.B. 552; [1994] 2 W.L.R. 115, QBD 6–015
R. v. Secretary of State for Foreign and Commonwealth Affairs, ex p. Ross-
    Clunis; *sub nom.* Ross-Clunis v. Secretary of State for Foreign an Com-
    monwealth Affairs [1991] 2 A.C. 439; [1991] 3 W.L.R. 146, HL 23–005
R. v. Secretary of State for Foreign and Commonwealth Affairs, ex p. Trawnik
    The Times, February 21, 1986, CA; affirming (1985) 82 L.S.G. 2739, DC 15–005,
    33–003
R. v. Secretary of State for Foreign and Commonwealth Affairs, ex p. World
    Development Movement Ltd [1995] 1 W.L.R. 386; [1995] 1 All E.R. 611,
    QBD 12–031, 13–014, 22–025, 32–011, 32–012
R. v. Secretary of State for Health, ex p. United States Tobacco International Inc.
    [1992] Q.B. 353; [1991] 3 W.L.R. 529, DC 29–038
R. v. Secretary of State for Home Affairs, ex p. Budd [1942] 2 K.B. 14, CA 19–045
R. v. Secretary of State for Home Affairs, ex p. Château Thierry (Duke) [1917]
    1 K.B. 922, CA; reversing [1917] 1 K.B. 552, KBD 23–005

R. v. Secretary of State for Home Affairs, ex p. Lees [1941] 1 K.B. 72, CA 19–044, 19–045

R. v. Secretary of State for Home Affairs, ex p. Santillo (131/79) (No.1); *sub nom.* R. v. Secretary of State for Home Affairs, ex p. Santillo [1981] Q.B. 778; [1981] 2 All E.R. 897; [1980] 2 C.M.L.R. 308, ECJ 6–025, 23–023

R. v. Secretary of State for Home Department, ex p. Thakrar; *sub nom.* R. v. Immigration Officer at Heathrow Airport, ex p. Thakrar [1974] Q.B. 684; [1974] 2 W.L.R. 593, CA 3–027

R. v. Secretary of State for Social Security, ex p. Joint Council for the Welfare of Immigrants [1997] 1 W.L.R. 275; [1996] 4 All E.R. 385, CA 22–025, 23–033, 29–013

R. v. Secretary of State for Social Services, ex p. Association of Metropolitan Authorities [1986] 1 W.L.R. 1; [1986] 1 All E.R. 164, QBD 31–006, 32–015

R. v. Secretary of State for Social Services, ex p. Bosmore Medical Supplies Ltd *The Times,* December 16, 1985 6–024

R. v. Secretary of State for Social Services, ex p. Britnell [1991] 1 W.L.R. 198; [1991] 2 All E.R. 726, HL 29–013

R. v. Secretary of State for Social Services, ex p. Camden LBC 29–023

R. v. Secretary of State for Social Services, ex p. Child Poverty Action Group [1990] 2 Q.B. 540; [1989] 3 W.L.R. 1116; [1989] 1 All E.R. 1047, CA ... 22–025, 32–012

R. v. Secretary of State for Social Services, ex p. Connolly [1986] 1 W.L.R. 421; [1986] 1 All E.R. 998, CA 32–013

R. v. Secretary of State for Social Services, ex p. Sherwin (1996) 32 B.M.L.R. 1, QBD 18–024

R. v. Secretary of State for the Environment ex p. Brent LBC [1982] Q.B. 593; [1982] 2 W.L.R. 693, DC 31–010

R. v. Secretary of State for the Environment, ex p. Greenwich LBC *The Times,* December 19, 1985, CA 29–019

R. v. Secretary of State for the Environment, ex p. Norwich County Council [1982] Q.B. 808; [1982] 2 W.L.R. 580, CA 32–021

R. v. Secretary of State for the Environment , ex p. Nottinghamshire CC [1986] A.C. 240; [1986] 2 W.L.R. 1 .... 31–002, 31–005

R. v. Secretary of State for the Environment, ex p. Ostler [1977] Q.B. 122; [1976] 3 W.L.R. 288, CA 32–019

R. v. Secretary of State for the Environment, ex p. Ward [1984] 1 W.L.R. 834; [1984] 2 All E.R. 556, QBD 32–013, 32–015

R. v. Secretary of State for the Environment, Transport and the Regions, ex p. Alconbury *The Times,* January 24, 2001 24–054

R. v. Secretary of State for the Environment, Transport and the Regions, ex p. Holdings and Barnes Plc *See* R. (on the application of Holding & Barnes Plc) v, Secretary of State for the Environment, Transport and the Regions

R. v. Secretary of State for the Home Affairs, ex p.; *sub nom.* Dannenberg v. Secretary of State for Home Affairs [1984] Q.B. 766; [1984] 2 W.L.R. 855, CA 6–035, 23–023

R. v. Secretary of State for the Home Department *The Times,* May 24, 2001 ... 29–021

R. v. Secretary of State for the Home Department, ex p. Akhtar [1981] Q.B. 46; [1980] 3 W.L.R. 302, CA 23–011

R. v. Secretary of State for the Home Department, ex p. Anderson; *sub nom.* R. v. Governor of Wormwood Schrubs Prison, ex p. Anderson [1984] Q.B. 778; [1984] 2 W.L.R. 725, QBD 20–013, 24–032

R. v. Secretary of State for the Home Department, ex p. Anderson; *sub nom.* R. v. Governor of Wormwood Scrubs Prison, ex p. Anderson [1984] Q.B. 778; [1984] 2 W.L.R. 725, QBD 31–005

R. v. Secretary of State for the Home Department, ex p. Bennett *The Times,* August 18, 1986, CA 29–004, 31–010

R. v. Secretary of State for the Home Department, ex p. Bentley [1994] Q.B. 349;
[1994] 2 W.L.R. 101, DC 20–004, 37–013

R. v. Secretary of State for the Home Department ex p. Benwell [1985] Q.B. 554;
[1984] 3 W.L.R. 843, QBD 31–011

R. v. Secretary of State for the Home Department, ex p. Bhajan Singh [1976]
Q.B. 198; [1975] 3 W.L.R. 225, CA 22–009, 22–010

R. v. Secretary of State for the Home Department, ex p. Bhurosah (Shadeo)
[1968] 1 Q.B. 266; [1967] 3 W.L.R. 1259, CA 35–005

R. v. Secretary of State for the Home Department, ex p. Brind [1991] 1 A.C. 696;
[1991] 2 W.L.R. 588, HL 13–014, 22–011, 25–001, 25–035, 28–008, 31–002

R. v. Secretary of State for the Home Department, ex p. Bogdaycay 23–039

R. v. Secretary of State for the Home Department, ex p. Cheblak [1991] 1 W.L.R.
890; [1991] 2 All E.R. 319, CA 23–040, 24–034

R. v. Secretary of State for the Home Department, ex p. Daley [2001] 2 W.L.R.
1622 24–032

R. v. Secretary of State for the Home Department, ex p. Doody [1994] 1 A.C.
531; [1993] 3 W.L.R. 154, HL 24–032, 31–016

R. v. Secretary of State for the Home Department, ex p. Fayed (No.1) [1998] 1
W.L.R. 763; [1997] 1 All E.R. 228, CA 23–008, 31–016

R. v. Secretary of State for the Home Department, ex p. Fernandes [1981]
Imm.A.R. 1; *The Times,* November 21, 1980 22–008

R. v. Secretary of State for the Home Department, ex p. Fire Brigades Union
[1995] 2 A.C. 513; [1995] 2 W.L.R. 464, HL 2–022, 3–016, 15–011, 29–016

R. v. Secretary of State for the Home Department, ex p. Hindley [1998] Q.B.
751; [1998] 2 W.L.R. 505, QBD 13–014

R. v. Secretary of State for the Home Department, ex p. Hindley [2000] 2 W.L.R.
730; [2000] 2 All E.R. 385, HL 31–018

R. v. Secretary of State for the Home Department, ex p. Hosenball [1977] 1
W.L.R. 766; [1977] 3 All E.R. 452, CA 7–005, 22–010, 23–034, 29–004

R. v. Secretary of State for the Home Department, ex p. Khan (Asif) [1984] 1
W.L.R. 537 23–008

R. v. Secretary of State for the Home Department, ex p. Khan (Asif Mahmood)
[1984] 1 W.L.R. 1337; [1985] 1 All E.R. 40, CA 31–019

R. v. Secretary of State for the Home Department, ex p. Khawaja; Khazrai v.
Immigration Officer, London (Heathrow) Airport [1982] Imm. A.R. 9,
IAT 23–028, 23–029, 23–038, 23–040, 24–036

R. v. Secretary of State for the Home Department, ex p. Kirkwood [1984] 1
W.L.R. 913; [1984] 2 All E.R. 390, QBD 22–008

R. v. Secretary of State for the Home Department, ex p. Ku; *sub nom.* R. v.
Secretary of State for the Home Department, ex p. Kuet [1995] Q.B. 364;
[1995] 2 W.L.R. 589, CA 23–029

R. v. Secretary of State for the Home Department, ex p. Leech (No.2) [1994]
Q.B. 198; [1993] 3 W.L.R. 1125, CA 1–019, 22–002, 24–031, 24–032

R. v. Secretary of State for the Home Department, ex p. Manning *See* R. v. DPP,
ex p. Manning

R. v. Secretary of State for the Home Department, ex p. McAvoy [1984] 1
W.L.R. 1408; [1984] 3 All E.R. 417, QBD 18–014, 22–032, 24–031, 32–012

R. v. Secretary of State for the Home Department, ex p. McWhirter (1969) 119
N.L.J. 926; *The Times,* October 21, 1969, DC 10–045

R. v. Secretary of State for the Home Department, ex p. Minta *See* Minta v.
Secretary of State for the Home Department

R. v. Secretary of State for the Home Department, ex p. Muboyayi [1992] Q.B.
244; [1991] 3 W.L.R. 442, CA 23–040, 24–034

R. v. Secretary of State for the Home Department, ex p. Northumbria Police
Authority [1989] Q.B. 26; [1988] 2 W.L.R. 590, CA; reversing in part
[1987] 2 W.L.R. 998, QBD 15–010, 15–012, 21–001, 21–003, 21–019

R. v. Secretary of State for the Home Department, ex p. Oladehinde [1991] 1
    A.C. 254; [1990] 3 W.L.R. 797, HL 18–024, 23–034, 31–019
R. v. Secretary of State for the Home Department, ex p. Phansopkar [1976] Q.B.
    606; [1975] 3 W.L.R. 322, CA 22–009
R. v. Secretary of State for the Home Department, ex p. Pierson; *sub nom.*
    Pierson v. Secretary of State for the Home Department [1998] A.C. 539;
    [1997] 3 W.L.R. 492; [1997] 3 All. E.R. 577, HL 2–022, 24–032
R. v. Secretary of State for the Home Department, ex p. Puttick [1981] Q.B. 767;
    [1981] 2 W.L.R. 440, QBD 23–009
R. v. Secretary of State for the Home Department, ex p. Ruddock [1987] 1
    W.L.R. 1482; [1987] 2 All E.R. 518, QBD 1–019, 15–005, 22–002
R. v. Secretary of State for the Home Department, ex p. Sahota [1999] Q.B. 597;
    [1998] 2 W.L.R. 626, CA 6–021
R. v. Secretary of State for the Home Department, ex p. Santillo (No.2) [1981]
    Q.B. 778; [1981] 2 W.L.R. 362, CA 6–035
R. v. Secretary of State for the Home Department, ex p. Simms; *sub nom.* R. v.
    Secretary of State for the Home Department, ex p. Main [2000] 2 A.C. 115;
    [1999] 3 W.L.R. 328, HL 1–019, 2–022, 20–005, 22–002, 24–032, 25–001
R. v. Secretary of State for the Home Department, ex p. Sivakumaran [1988]
    A.C. 958; [1988] 1 All E.R. 193, HL 23–032, 23–039
R. v. Secretary of State for the Home Department, ex p. Swati [1986] 1 W.L.R.
    477; [1986] 1 All E.R. 717, CA 23–038, 29–004, 32–013, 32–014
R. v. Secretary of State for the Home Department, ex p. Ullah *The Times,* June
    27, 2001, CA 23–008
R. v. Secretary of State for the Home Department, ex p. Venables; R. v. Secretary
    of State for the Home Department, ex p. Thompson [1998] A.C. 407; [1997]
    3 W.L.R. 23; [1997] 3 All E.R. 97, HL 24–032, 37–013
R. v. Secretary of State for the Home Department, ex p. Zamir *See* Zamir v.
    Secretary of State for the Home Department
R. v. Secretary of State for Trade and Industry, ex p. Ford (Ian Kynaston) (1984)
    4 Tr. L. 150, DC 31–006
R. v. Secretary of State for Transport, ex p. Factortame Ltd [1990] 2 A.C. 85;
    [1989] 2 W.L.R. 997, HL 4–023, 6–009, 22–016, 33–017
R. v. Secretary of State for Transport, ex p. Factortame Ltd (No.2) [1990] E.C.R.
    I–2433; [1990] 3 C.M.L.R. 375, ECJ; [1991] 1 A.C. 603, HL 6–009, 9–052,
                                                                                                  33–018
R. v. Secretary of State for Transport, ex p. Factortame Ltd (No.5) [2000] 1 A.C.
    524; [1999] 3 W.L.R. 1062, HL 6–014, 6–038
R. v. Secretary of State for Transport, ex p. Gwent CC [1988] Q.B. 429; [1987]
    2 W.L.R. 961; [1987] 1 All E.R. 161, CA 30–026
R. v. Secretary of State for Transport, ex p. Pegasus Holdings (London) Ltd
    [1988] 1 W.L.R. 990; [1989] 2 All E.R. 481, ,QBD 31–002
R. v. Secretary of State for Transport, ex p. Philippine Airlines *The Times,*
    October 17, 1984, CA 31–006
R. v. Secretary of State for War [1891] 2 Q.B. 326, CA 32–009
R. v. Self [1992] 1 W.L.R. 657; [1992] 3 All E.R. 476; (1992) 95 Cr. App. R. 42,
    CA 24–009
R. v. Selvage; R. v. Morgan [1982] Q.B. 372; [1981] 3 W.L.R. 811, CA (Crim
    Div) 20–044
R. v. Sheer Metalcraft [1954] 1 Q.B. 586; [1954] 2 W.L.R. 777, QBD 29–037
R. v. Sheffield Crown Court, ex p. Brownlow [1980] Q.B. 530; [1980] 2 W.L.R.
    892, CA (Crim Div) 20–021
R. v. Shepherd (1841) 1 Q.B. 170 15–020
R. v. Shipley (1783) 21 St.Tr. 847 25–018
R. v. Singleton [1995] 1 Cr. App. R. 431; [1995] Crim. L.R. 236, CA 24–047

R. v. Skinner (Edward George) [1968] 2 Q.B. 700; [1968] 3 W.L.R. 408, CA
(Crim Div) 31–019
R. v. Skirving; R. v. Grossman [1985] Q.B. 819; [1985] 2 W.L.R. 1001, CA ... 25–025
R. v. Smith [1900] Cape of Good Hope Supreme Ct. 561 19–007
R. v. Smith [1910] 1 K.B. 17, CCA 29–036
R. v. Smurthwaite; R. v. Gill [1994] 1 All E.R. 898; (1994) 98 Cr. App. R. 437,
CA (Crim Div) 21–006
R. v. Socialist Worker Printers and Publishers Ltd., ex p. Attorney-General
[1975] Q.B. 637; [1974] 3 W.L.R. 801, DC 20–048
R. v. Soothill, ex p. Ashdown *The Times,* April 2, 1955, DC 32–009
R. v. Southampton Justices, ex p. Green [1976] Q.B. 11; [1975] 3 W.L.R. 277,
CA 32–005
R. v. Southwark Crown Court, ex p. Bowles; *sub nom.* R. v. Guildford Crown
Court, ex p. DPP [1998] A.C. 641; [1998] 2 W.L.R. 715, HL 24–047
R. v. Speaker, ex p. McGuinness [1997] N.I. 359 .... 10–019, 13–018
R. v. Spear; R. v. Hastie; R. v. Boyd [2001] EWCA Crim 2; (2001) 98(12) L.S.G.
43; *The Times,* January 30, 2001 19–022
R. v. Special Commissioners of Income Tax ex p. Stipplechoice Ltd (No.1)
[1985] 2 All E.R. 465; [1985] S.T.C. 248, CA 32–011
R. v. Spencer; R. v. Smails [1987] A.C. 128; [1986] 3 W.L.R. 348, HL 20–020
R. v. Speyer [1916] 2 K.B. 858 10–005
R. v. Staniforth; R. v. Jordan *See* DPP v. Jordan
R. v. Stewart (1857) 8 E. & B. 360 15–020
R. v. Sussex Justices ex p. McCarthy; *sub nom.* R. v Sussex JJ, ex p. McCarthy
[1924] 1 K.B. 256, KBD 31–015
R. v. Tarrant [1998] Crim. L.R. 342; The Times, December 29, 1997, CA (Crim
Div) 20–020
R. v. Thames Justices, ex p. Brindle [1975] 1 W.L.R. 1400 19–027
R. v. Thames Magistrates Court, ex p. Polemis (The Corinthic); *sub nom.* R. v.
Thames Justices, ex p. Polemis [1974] 1 W.L.R. 1371; [1974] 2 All E.R.
1219, QBD 31–016
R. v. Thistlewood (1820) 33 St. Tr. 681 14–013
R. v. Thompson (C7/78) (No.1) [1980] Q.B. 229; [1980] 2 W.L.R. 521; (1979)
69 Cr. App. R. 22, ECJ 6–025, 6–039
R. v. Torbay Licensing Justices ex p. White [1980] 2 All E.R. 25, DC 31–010
R. v. Tottenham and District Rent Tribunal, ex p. Northfield (Highgate) [1957] 1
Q.B. 103; [1956] 3 W.L.R. 462, DC 32–008
R. v. Tottenham Magistrates' Court, ex p. Williams [1982] 2 All E.R. 705,
QBD 19–027
R. v. Trainer (1864) 4 F. & F. 105 19–008
R. v. Tronoh Mines Ltd; R. v. Barrenger; R. v. Times Publishing Co. [1952] 1 All
E.R. 697; [1952] 1 T.L.R. 461, CCC 10–049
R. v. Tubbs (1776) Cowp. 512 19–003
R. v. Tucker [1952] 2 All E.R. 1074; (1952) 36 Cr. App. R. 192, CMAC 19–008,
19–023
R. v. University of Liverpool, ex p. Caesar-Gordon [1991] 1 Q.B. 124 24–032
R. v. Vaughan (1769) 4 Burr. 2494 35–017
R. v. Vine Street Police Station Superintendent, ex p. Liebmann [1916] 1 K.B.
268, KBD 23–021
R. v. Wear Valley DC, ex p. Binks [1985] 2 All E.R. 699, QBD 31–018
R. v. Wells Street Stipendiary Magistrate, ex p. Deakin [1980] A.C. 477; [1979]
2 W.L.R. 665, HL 22–008, 25–006
R. v. West Glamorgan CC, ex p. Gheissary *The Times,* December 18, 1985 31–020
R. v. West Yorkshire Coroner, ex p. Smith (No.1) [1983] Q.B. 335; [1982] 3
W.L.R. 920, CA 3–020

R. v. West Yorkshire Coroner, ex p. Smith (No.2) [1985] Q.B. 1096; [1985] 2
W.L.R. 332; [1985] 1 All E.R. 100, DC 20–053, 22–020
R. v. Wicks [1936] 1 All E.R. 384 25–006
R. v. Wilkes (1768) Wilson 322; 916780 4 Burr. 2829 18–011
R. v. Williams (Gladstone) [1987] 3 All E.R. 411; (1984) 78 Cr. App. R. 276, CA
(Crim Div) 24–020
R. v. Wormwood Scrubs Prison (Governor), ex p. Boydell [1948] 2 K.B. 193;
[1948] 1 All E.R. 438, DC 19–026
R. v. Worthington-Evans, ex p. Madan [1959] 2 Q.B. 145; [1959] 2 W.L.R. 908,
DC 32–004
R. v. Young [1995] Q.B. 324; [1995] 2 W.L.R. 430, CA 20–048
R. (Alconbury Developments Ltd) v. Secretary of State for the Environment,
Transport and Regions [2000] 2 W.L.R. 1389, HL 22–053, 24–054, 30–002
R. (C) v. Mental Health Review Tribunal *The Times*, July 11, 2001, CA 22–050
R. v. (Daly) v. Secretary of State for the Home Department [2001] 2 W.L.R.
1622, HL 22–054
R. (Garde) v. Strickland [1921] 2 I.R. 313 19–035
R. (H) v. Mental Health Tribunal North and East London Region [2001]
H.R.L.R. 752, CA 22–050, 24–030, 29–034
R. (Hume) v. Londonderry Justices [1972] N.I. 91 2–027
R. (O'Brien) v. Military Governor, N.D.U. Interment Camp [1924] 1 I.R. 32 ... 19–035
R. (on the application of Holding & Barnes Plc) v. Secretary of State for the
Environment, Transport and the Regions; *sub nom.* R. v. Secretary of State
for the Environment, Transport and the Regions, ex p. Holdings & Barnes
Plc [2001] UKHL 23; *The Times,* May 10, 2001, HL 22–053, 30–002
R. (on the application of Javed) v. Secretary of State for the Home Department
[2001] 3 W.L.R. 323 29–021
R. (on the application of Johns) v. Bracknell Forest DC; *sub nom.* R. (on the
application of Johns) v. Bracknell Forest BC *The Daily Telegraph,* February
13, 2001, QBD (Admin Ct) 22–054
R. (on the application of M.) v. Commissioner of Police for the Metropolis *The
Times*, August 17, 2001 24–016
R. (on the application of Montana) v. Secretary of State for the Home Depart-
ment; *sub nom.* R. v. Secretary of State for the Home Department, ex p.
Montana [2001] 1 W.L.R. 552; [2001] 1 F.L.R. 449; *The Times,* December
5, 2000, CA 22–054, 23–009
R. (Professional Contractors Group Ltd) v. Inland Revenue Commissioners; *sub
nom.* R. v. Inland Revenue Commissioners, ex p. Professional Contractors
Group Ltd [2001] EWHC Admin 236; [2001] S.T.C. 629; *The Times,* April
5, 2001, QBD (Admin Ct) 22–055
R. (Zeqiri) v. Secretary of State for the Home Department *The Times*, March 16,
2001, CA 23–038
R. & W. Paul Ltd v. Wheat Commission [1917] A.C. 139 31–006
Racal Communications Ltd, Re; *sub nom.* Company (No.00996 of 1979), Re
[1981] A.C. 374; [1980] 3 W.L.R. 181, HL 31–007
Racz v. Home Office [1994] 2 A.C. 45; [1994] 2 W.L.R. 23, HL 32–022
Ragho Prasad v. Queen, The [1981] 1 W.L.R. 469; [1981] 1 All E.R. 319, PC 37–008
Rai v. United Kingdom (1995) 82–ADR. 134 27–004
Raine (Nicola), Re; *The Times,* May 5, 1982, DC 24–037
Rainey v. Greater Glasgow Health Board [1987] A.C. 224; [1986] 3 W.L.R.
1017, HL 4–022
Raleigh v. Goschen [1893] 1 Ch. 73 .... 7–003, 33–008, 33–020
Ranaweera v. Ramachandran [1970] A.C. 962; [1970] 2 W.L.R. 500, PC 33–010
Ras Behari Lal v. King-Emperor, The (1933) 60 Ind.App. 354 37–008
Raymond v. Att.-Gen. [1982] Q.B. 839; [1982] 2 W.L.R. 849, CA 7–005, 17–019,
20–015

Raymond v. Honey [1983] 1 A.C. 1; [1982] 2 W.L.R. 465, HL 24–031
Reckley v. Minister of Public Safety and Immigration (No.2) [1996] A.C. 239,
    PC 20–004
Reckley v. Minister of Public Safety and Immigration (No.2) [1996] A.C. 527;
    [1996] 2 W.L.R. 281, PC 37–013, 37–014
Rederiaktiebolaget Amphitrite v. King, The [1921] 3 K.B. 500; (1921) 8 Ll. L.
    Rep. 443, KBD 31–022, 33–006, 33–014
Rediffusion (Hong Kong) Ltd v. Att.-Gen. of Hong Kong [1970] A.C. 1136;
    [1970] 2 W.L.R. 1264, PC 4–033, 35–023
Redmond-Bate v. DPP (1999) 163 J.P. 789; [2000] H.R.L.R. 249; The Times,
    July 28, 1999, QBD 27–009, 27–030
Rees v. United Kingdom (1986) 9 E.H.R.R. 56 22–042
Reference under the Government of Ireland Act 1920, Re [1936] A.C. 352 16–012
Reilly v. King, The [1932] S.C.R. 597; [1934] A.C. 176, PC 18–028
Renouf v. Att.-Gen. for Jersey [1936] A.C. 445, PC 35–003
Republic of Bolivia Exploration Syndicate Ltd, Re [1914] 1 Ch. 139 15–033
Restrictions on Imports of Lamb (No.1), Re (C232/78); sub nom. Commission of
    the European Communities v. France (C232/78) [1979] E.C.R. 2729; [1980]
    1 C.M.L.R. 418, ECJ 6–036
Reynolds v. Times Newspapers Ltd [2001] 2 A.C. 127 [1999] 3 W.L.R. 1010;
    [1999] 4 All E.R. 609, HL 9–052, 25–001, 25–005
Rhyl Urban DC v. Rhyl Amusements Ltd [1959] 1 W.L.R. 465; [1959] 1 All E.R.
    257, Ch D 31–020, 31–022
Riach v. Lord Advocate 1932 S.L.T. 20, 1 Div 18–026
Ribitsch v. Austria (A/336) (1996) 21 E.H.R.R. 573, ECHR 22–032, 24–010
Rice v. Connolly [1966] 2 Q.B. 414; [1966] 3 W.L.R. 17, DC 24–021
Ricketts v. Cox (1982) 74 Cr. App. R. 298; [1982] Crim. L.R. 184, DC 24–021
Ricketts v. Queen, The [1998] 1 W.L.R. 1016; (1998) 142 S.J.L.B. 63, PC 37–013
Ridge v. Baldwin (No.1) [1964] A.C. 40; [1963] 2 W.L.R. 935, HL 2–008, 2–024,
                                                                                                19–045, 31–017, 32–004
Riel v. R (1880) 10 App.Cas. 675 35–022
Rigby v. Chief Constable of Northamptonshire [1985] 1 W.L.R. 1242; [1985] 2
    All E.R. 985, QBD 21–011, 33–010
Ringer, Ex p. (1909) 25 T.L.R. 718, DC 32–020
Riordan v. War Office [1961] 1 W.L.R. 210; [1960] 3 All E.R. 774 (Note), CA 18–026,
                                                                                                18–028
Ripon (Highfield) Housing ConfirmationOrder 1938, Re; sub nom. White and
    Collins v. Minister of Health [1939] 2 K.B. 838, CA 31–007
Riverside Mental Health NSA Trust v. Fox [1999] F.L.R. 614, CA 33–018
Roberts v. Chief Constable of Cheshire Police; sub nom. Roberts v. Jones (Chief
    Constable of Cheshire) [1999] 1 W.L.R. 662; [1999] 2 All E.R. 326, CA 24–012
Robertson v. Minister of Pensions [1949] 1 K.B. 227; [1948] 2 All E.R. 767,
    KBD 18–028, 33–006, 33–016
Robertson v. Secretary of State for the Environment [1976] 1 W.L.R. 371,
    QBD 17–025
Robins v. National Trust Co. Ltd [1927] A.C. 515, PC 37–002
Robins & Son Ltd v. Minister of Health; sub nom. Brighton (Everton Place Area)
    Housing Order 1937, Re; [1939] 1 K.B. 520, CA 31–009
Robinson (Frank) v. Queen, The [1985] A.C. 956; [1985] 3 W.L.R. 84, PC 37–013
Robson v. Hallett [1967] 2 Q.B. 939; [1967] 3 W.L.R. 28, QBD 24–022
Rodriguez v. Speyer Bros. [1919] A.C. 59, HL 23–020
Rodwell v. Thomas [1944] K.B. 596, KBD 15–013, 18–026
Rogers v. Secretary of State for the Home Department [1973] A.C. 388; [1972]
    3 W.L.R. 279, HL 33–023
Rondel v. Worsley; sub nom. Rondel v. W [1969] 1 A.C. 191; [1967] 3 W.L.R.
    1666, HL 20–042

Ronnfeldt v. Phillips (1918) 35 T.L.R. 46 19–041
Rookes v. Barnard (No.1) [1964] A.C. 1129; [1964] 2 W.L.R. 269, HL 37–011
Rootkin v. Kent CC [1981] 1 W.L.R. 1186; [1981] 2 All E.R. 227, CA 31–020
Rost v. Edwards [1990] 2 Q.B. 460; [1990] 2 W.L.R. 1280, QBD 13–006
Rover International Ltd v. Cannon Film Sales Ltd (No.2) [1987] 1 W.L.R. 1597;
    [1987] 3 All E.R. 986, Ch D 35–003
Royal Aquarium Society v. Parkinson [1892] 1 Q.B. 431, CA 25–003
Royal College of Nursing v. Department of Health and Social Security [1981]
    A.C. 800; [1981] 2 W.L.R. 279, HL 29–004
Royal Government of Greece v. Brixton Prison Governor; sub nom. R. v. Brixton
    Prison Governor, ex p. Kotronis [1971] A.C. 250; [1969] 3 W.L.R. 1107,
    HL 23–045
Royal Hong Kong Jockey Club v. Miers [1983] 1 W.L.R. 1049; (1983) 80 L.S.G.
    2215, PC 37–004
Royster v. Cavey [1947] K.B. 204; [1946] 2 All E.R. 642, CA 33–002, 33–010
Rustomjee v. R. (1876) 2 Q.B.D. 69 .... 15–022, 15–029
Ryan's Case (1936) 52 L.Q.R. 241 4–032
Rylands v. Fletcher; sub nom. Fletcher v. Rylands (1868) L.R. 3 H.L. 330, HL
    (1866) L.R. 1 Ex. 265, Exchequer Div 9–045, 33–010

S (A Barrister), Re [1970] 1 Q.B. 160; [1969] 2 W.L.R. 708, Visitors (Inns of
    Ct) 31–019
S.W. v. United Kingdom (1995) 21 E.H.R.R. 363 22–037
Sagnata Investments Ltd v. Norwich Corporation; sub nom. Norwich Corpora-
    tion v. Sagnata Investments Ltd [1971] 2 Q.B. 614; [1971] 3 W.L.R. 133 31–010
Salaman v. Secretary of State for India [1906] 1 K.B. 613, CA 15–022
Salomon v. Customs and Excise Commissioners; sub nom. Previously published
    as Solomon v. Customs and Excise Commissioners [1967] 2 Q.B. 116;
    [1966] 3 W.L.R. 1223, CA 3–026, 22–011
Sammut v. Strickland [1938] A.C. 678, PC 35–017, 35–021
Sammy v. Birkbeck College The Times, May 20, 1965, CA; affirming (1964) 108
    S.J. 897; The Times, November 3, 1964 32–009
Samuel, Sir Stuart, Re [1913] A.C. 514, PC 16–014
Sander v. United Kingdom 8 B.H.R.C. 279; [2000] Crim. L.R. 767, ECHR 20–021
Sanders v. Chichester The Times, December 2, 1994 10–041
Sanders v. Punch Ltd [1998] 1 W.L.R. 986; [1998] 1 All E.R. 234, Ch D 25–017
Sandhu, Re The Times, May 10, 1985, HL 6–024
Sarpon, The [1916] P. 306 15–016
Saunders v. United Kingdom [1998] 1 B.C.L.C. 362; [1997] B.C.C. 872; (1997)
    23 E.H.R.R. 313, ECHR 20–043, 24–014, 24–017
Sayce v. Ameer Ruler Sadig Mohammed Abbasi Bahawalpur State [1952] 2 Q.B.
    390; [1952] 2 All E.R. 64, CA 15–023
S-C (Mental Patient: Habeas Corpus), Re; sub nom. Simpson-Cleghorn, Re
    [1996] Q.B. 599; [1996] 2 W.L.R. 146, CA 24–034
Scanfuture UK Ltd v. Secretary of State for Trade and Industry; sub nom.
    Scanfuture UK Ltd v. Bird [2001] I.R.L.R. 416; The Times, April 26, 2001,
    EAT 20–026, 22–052, 30–002, 30–013
Schaffenius v. Goldberg [1916] 1 K.B. 284, CA 23–019
Schenk v. Switzerland (A/140) (1991) 13 E.H.R.R. 242; The Times, August 2,
    1988, ECHR 24–018
Schering Chemicals Ltd v. Falkman [1982] Q.B. 1; [1981] 2 W.L.R. 848, CA 22–008
Schmidt, Re; sub nom. Schmidt v. Germany; R. v. Secretary of State for the
    Home Department, ex p. Schmidt [1995] 1 A.C. 339; [1994] 3 W.L.R. 228,
    HL 23–047, 24–024
Schmidt v. Secretary of State for Home Affairs [1969] 2 Ch. 149; [1969] 2
    W.L.R. 337, CA 23–019, 23–027, 31–018

Schtraks v. Government of Israel; *sub nom.* R. v. Governor of Brixton Prison, ex
p. Schtraks; Schtraks (Shalom), Re [1964] A.C. 556; [1962] 3 W.L.R. 1013,
HL 23–044
Science Research Council v. Nasse [1980] A.C. 1028; [1979] 3 W.L.R. 762,
HL 33–024
Scott v. Scott [1913] A.C. 417, HL; reversing [1912] P. 241, CA 20–040, 20–044
Scottish National Party v. Scottish Television Plc 1998 S.L.T. 1395; 1997 G.W.D.
20–932, OH 10–056
Seaman v. Netherclift (1876) 2 C.P.D. 53 20–042
Search for Work in Ireland, Re (CU 13/77) [1978] 2 C.M.L.R. 174, NI Comm 6–026
Secretary of State for Defence v. Guardian Newspapers Ltd [1985] A.C. 339;
[1984] 3 W.L.R. 986, HL 25–016
Secretary of State for Education and Science v. Tameside MBC; *sub nom.*
Secretary of State for Education and Science v. Metropolitan Borough of
Tameside [1977] A.C. 1014; [1976] 3 W.L.R. 641, HL 3–023, 31–011, 32–021
Secretary of State for India v. Kamachee Boye Sahaba (1859) 13 Moo.P.C. 22 15–022
Secretary of State for the Home Department v. O'Brien; *sub nom.* Secretary of
State for Home Affairs v. O'Brien [1923] A.C. 603, HL; affirming ... 24–034, 24–038
Secretary of State for the Home Department, ex p. Montana *See* R. (on the
application of Montana) v. Secretary of State for the Home Department
Secretary of State for Trade and Industry v. Langridge [1991] Ch. 402; [1991] 2
W.L.R. 1343, CA 31–006
Selcuk v. Turkey; Asker v. Turkey (1998) 26 E.H.R.R. 477; [1998] H.R.C.D.
475, ECHR 22–032
Selwyn, Ex.p (1872) 36 J.P. 54 .... 3–015, 4–005
Seven Bishops' Case (1688) 12 St Tr. 371 3–004
Shaaban bin Hussien v. Chong Fook Kam [1970] A.C. 942; [1970] 2 W.L.R. 441,
PC 37–012
Shahid Iqbal, Re, [1979] 1 W.L.R. 425; [1979] 1 All E.R. 675, CA affirming
[1979] Q.B. 264, DC 24–036
Shaw v. DPP; *sub nom.* R. v. Shaw [1962] A.C. 220; [1961] 2 W.L.R. 897, HL 22–037,
25–028
Shaw v. Shaw [1979] Fam. 62; [1979] 3 W.L.R. 24, Fam Div 15–032
Shaw Savill and Albion Co. Ltd v. Australia (1940) 66 C.L.R. 344, HC (Aus)
Sheffield v. United Kingdom; Horsham v. United Kingdom [1998] 2 F.L.R. 928;
[1998] 3 F.C.R. 141; (1999) 27 E.H.R.R. 163, ECHR 22–042
Sheilch v. Chief Constable of Greater Manchester Police [1989] 2 W.L.R.
1102 21–009
Shenton v. Smith [1895] A.C. 229, PC 18–026
Sherdley v. Sherdley [1988] A.C. 213; [1987] 2 W.L.R. 1071, HL; reversing
[1986] 1 W.L.R. 732 2–021
Shields v. E. Coomes (Holdings) Ltd; *sub nom.* E. Coomes (Holdings) Ltd v.
Shields [1978] 1 W.L.R. 1408; [1979] 1 All E.R. 456, CA 4–022
Shipton, Re; *sub nom.* Arbitration between Anderson & Co. and Harrison
Brothers & Co. Re [1915] 3 K.B. 676, KBD 15–016
Shirley v. Fagg (1675) 6 St. Tr. 1122 9–044
Short v. Poole Corporation [1926] Ch. 66, CA 31–008
Sidebotham, Ex.p (1880) L.R. 14 Ch. D. 458, CA 32–016
Sigurjonsson v. Iceland (A/264) (1993) 16 E.H.R.R. 462; *The Times,* July 27,
1993, ECHR 22–042
Sillars v. Smith 1982 S.L.T. 539; 1982 S.C.C.R. 367, HCJ Appeal 3–016, 4–009
Silver v. United Kingdom (A/161) (1983) 5 E.H.R.R. 347, ECHR; affirming
(1981) 3 E.H.R.R. 475, Eur Comm HR 22–029, 22–043, 24–032
Sim v. Stretch [1936] 2 All E.R. 1237; (1936) 53 T.L.R. 669, HL 25–003
Simcock v. Rhodes (1978) 66 Cr. App. R. 192; [1977] Crim. L.R. 751, DC 27–023

Simmonds v. Newell; *sub nom.* Defiant Cycle Co. v. Newell [1953] 1 W.L.R.
826; [1953] 2 All E.R. 38, DC 29–037
Simpson v. Att.-Gen. [1955] N.Z.L.R. 271, CA 7–003
Simpsons Motor Sales (London) Ltd v. Hendon Corporation [1964] A.C. 1088;
[1963] 2 W.L.R. 1187, HL; affirming [1963] Ch. 57, CA 31–004
Sir H. Blount's Case (1737) 1 Atk. 296 19–019
Sirros v. Moore [1975] Q.B. 118; [1974] 3 W.L.R. 459, CA 2–019, 20–042
Sisters of Charity of Rockingham v. King, The [1922] 2 A.C. 315, PC 24–054
Skilton v. Epsom and Ewell UDC [1937] 1 K.B. 112, CA 31–024
Skinner v. East India Company (1666) St. Tr. 710 9–044
Slave Grace (1827) 2 Hag.Adm. 94 24–034
Sloan (Henry James) v. General Medical Council; *sub nom.* Sloan v. General
Medical Council [1970] 1 W.L.R. 1130; [1970] 2 All E.R. 686, PC 31–016
Smalley, Re [1985] A.C. 622; [1985] 2 W.L.R. 538, HL 32–004
Smith v. Birmingham Guardians (1857) 7 E. & B. 483 15–020
Smith v. Director of the Serious Fraud Office *See* R. v. Director of Serious Fraud
Office, ex p. Smith
Smith v. East Elloe Rural DC [1956] A.C. 736; [1956] 2 W.L.R. 888, HL 32–016,
32–018, 32–019
Smith v. London Transport Executive [1951] A.C. 555; [1951] 1 All E.R. 667,
HL 28–008, 31–019
Smith v. Moss [1940] 1 K.B. 424, KBD 33–009
Smith v. Pywell (1959) 178 E.G. 1009 32–017
Smith v. United Kingdom; Grady v. United Kingdom; Beckett v. United King-
dom; Lustig-Prean v. United Kingdom [1999] I.R.L.R. 734; (2000) 29
E.H.R.R. 493, ECHR 22–039, 22–043
Snoxell v. Vauxhall Motors; Charles Early & Marriott (Witney) Ltd v. Smith
[1978] Q.B. 11; [1977] 3 W.L.R. 189, EAT 6–012
Sobhuza II v. Miller [1926] A.C. 518, PC 15–024
Societe United Docks v. Government of Mauritius; Marine Workers Union v.
Mauritius Marine Authority [1985] A.C. 585; [1985] 2 W.L.R. 114, PC ... 15–017,
37–013
Sodor and Man (Bishop) v. Derby (Earl) (1751) 2 Ves. Sen. 337 35–002
Soering v. United Kingdom (A/161) (1989) 11 E.H.R.R. 439; *The Times,* July 8,
1989, ECHR 22–033, 23–047
Somersett v. Steuart (1772) 20 St.Tr. 1 24–034
South East Asia Fire Bricks Sdn. Bhd. v. Non-Metallic Mineral Products Manu-
facturing Employees Union [1981] A.C. 363; [1980] 3 W.L.R. 318, PC 31–007,
32–017
South West Water Authority v. Rumbles [1984] 1 W.L.R. 800, CA 31–005
Southend-on-Sea Corporation v. Hodgson (Wickford) (1978) 77 L.G.R. 185,
CA 31–020
Sovfracht (VO) v, Van Udens Scheepvaart en Agentuur Maatschappij (NV
Gebr); *sub nom.* NV Gerb Van Udens Scheepvaart en Agentuur Maatsc-
chappij v. V/O Sovfracht [1943] A.C. 203; (1942) 74 Ll. L. Rep. 59, HL 23–020
Spackman v. Plumstead District Board of Works (1885) L.R. 10 App. Cas. 229,
HL 31–013
Sparks v. Edward Ash Ltd [1943] K.B. 223, CA 31–012
Special Commissioners of Income Tax v. Pemsel (1889) 21 Q.B.D. 313 32–009
Spencer v. United Kingdom [1998] 25 E.H.R.R. C.D. 105 25–023
Sporrong and Lonnroth v. Sweden (A/52) (1983) 5 E.H.R.R. 35, ECHR 22–046
Springer v. Doorly (1950) L.R.B.G. 10; (1950) L.Q.R. 299 29–023
Stanbury v. Exeter Corporation [1905] 2 K.B. 838, KBD 33–010
Staple Dairy Products v. Intervention Board for Agricultural Produce (C84/81)
[1982] E.C.R. 1763; [1984] 1 C.M.L.R. 238, ECJ 2–027
Starey v. Graham [1899] 1 Q.B. 406 29–023

Starrs v. Procuator Fiscal Linlithgow *See* Starrs v. Ruxton
Starrs v. Ruxton; *sub nom.* Ruxton v. Starrs; Starrs v. Procurator Fiscal (Linlithgow) 2000 J.C. 208; 2000 S.L.T. 42, HCJ Appeal 5–026, 20–026, 22–051
Startin v. Solihull MBC [1979] R.T.R. 228 31–012
Steaua Romana, The and Oltenia, The [1944] P. 43, PDAD 33–006
Steel v. United Kingdom (1999) 28 E.H.R.R. 603; 5 B.H.R.C. 339, ECHR 24–008, 24–026, 24–027, 27–001
Steele Ford & Newton v. Crown Prosecution Service (No.2); *sub nom.* Holden & Co v. Crown Prosecution Service (No.2) [1994] 1 A.C. 22; [1993] 2 W.L.R. 934; (1993) 97 Cr. App. R. 376 3–010
Steeples v. Derbyshire CC [1985] 1 W.L.R. 256; [1984] 3 All E.R. 468, QBD 31–006, 32–011, 32–016
Stefan v. General Medical Council (No.1) [1999] 1 W.L.R. 1293; [2000] H.R.L.R. 1, PC 31–016
Stewart v. Secretary of State for Scotland 1998 S.C. (H.L.) 81; 1998 S.L.T. 385, HL 20–030
Stockdale v. Hansard (1839) 9 Ad. & E. 1 .... 2–008, 3–001, 3–016, 13–003, 13–011
Stoke on Trent City Council v. B & Q Plc (C169/91) [1993] A.C. 900; [1993] 1 All E.R. 481; [1992] E.C.R. I–6635; [1993] 1 C.M.L.R. 426 6–036
Storer v. British Gas Plc; *sub nom.* Storer v. BG Plc (formerly British Gas Plc) [2000] 1 W.L.R. 1237; [2000] 2 All E.R. 440, CA 20–040
Stott v. Brown *See* Brown v. Stott
Stourton v. Stourton [1963] P.302; [1963] 2 W.L.R. 397, PDAD 13–016, 13–027
Stovin v. Wise and Norfolk CC [1996] A.C. 923; [1996] 3 W.L.R. 388, HL 31–024
Stran Greek Refineries & Stratis Andreadis v. Greece (A/301–B) (1995) 19 E.H.R.R. 293, ECHR 22–046
Strode's Case (1513) 13–005
Stroud v. Bradbury [1952] 2 All E.R. 76; 116 J.P. 386, DC 24–051
Suarez (No.1), Re; *sub nom.* Suarez v. Suarez [1918] 1 Ch. 176, CA 15–033
Sultan of Johore v. Abubakar Tunku Aris Bendahar [1952] A.C. 218, PC 15–023, 35–008
Sun Fire Office v. Hart (1889) 14 App.Cas. 98 37–007
Sunday Times v. United Kingdom (No.1) (A/30) (1979–80) 2 E.H.R.R. 245; (1979) 76 L.S.G. 328, ECHR 20–043, 22–012, 25–002, 25–012, 25–013, 25–016
Sunday Times v. United Kingdom (Spycatcher) (No.2) (A/217) (1992) 14 E.H.R.R. 229, ECHR 25–002, 25–021
Sussex Peerage Case (1844) 11 Cl. & F. 85 14–007
Sutton v. Att.-Gen. (1923) 39 T.L.R. 294 18–027
Swinney v. Chief Constable of Northumbria (No.1) [1997] Q.B. 464; [1996] 3 W.L.R. 968, CA 31–024
Swiss-Israel Trade Bank v. Government of Malta [1972] 1 Lloyd's Rep. 497, QBD 15–030
Syce v. Harrison [1981] Crim. L.R. 110; [1980] Crim. L.R. 649, DC 24–022
Sylvester's Case (1702) 7 Mod. 150 23–019
Szalatnay-Stacho v. Fink [1947] K.B. 1; [1946] 2 All E.R. 231, CA 25–003

T. v. Immigration Officer *See* T. v. Secretary of State for the Home Department
T. v. Secretary of State for the Home Department; *sub nom.* R. v. Secretary of State for the Home Department, ex p. T; T. v. Immigration Officer [1996] A.C. 742; [1996] 2 W.L.R. 766, HL 23–032, 23–044
T. v. United Kingdom; V v. United Kingdom [2000] 2 All E.R. 1024 (Note); (2000) 30 E.H.R.R. 121, ECHR 22–034
Tachographs, Re (128/78); *sub nom.* Commission of the European Communities v. United Kingdom [1979] E.C.R. 419; [1979] R.T.R. 321, ECJ 6–026
Taffe v. Downes (1813) 3 Moo. P.C. 20–041

Tai Hing Cotton Mill Ltd v. Liu Chong Hing Bank Ltd (No.1) [1986] A.C. 80;
[1985] 3 W.L.R. 317, PC 37–011
Tamlin v. Hannaford [1950] 1 K.B. 18; (1949) 65 T.L.R. 422, CA 15–019, 28–010,
33–010
Taylor v. Att.-Gen. of Queensland (1917) 23 C.L.R. 457 35–025
Taylor v. Brighton Corporation [1947] K.B. 736; [1947] 1 All E.R. 864, CA 31–012
Taylor v. Co-operative Retail Services Ltd [1982] I.C.R. 600; [1982] I.R.L.R.
354, CA 22–008
Taylor v. Director of the Serious Fraud Office; *sub nom.* Taylor v. Serious Fraud
Office [1999] 2 A.C. 177; [1998] 3 W.L.R. 1040, HL 20–042
Teh Cheng Poh (alias Char Meh) v. Public Prosecutor, Malaysia [1980] A.C. 458;
[1979] 2 W.L.R. 623, PC 37–012
Teixiera de Castro v. Portugal (1998) 28 E.H.R.R. 101 .... 24–018, 26–019
Teodoro Wagner Miet v. Fondo de Garantia Salarial [1993] E,C.R. 6911; [1995]
2 C.M.L.R. 49 6–013
Terrell v. Secretary of State for the Colonies [1953] 2 Q.B. 482; [1953] 3 W.L.R.
331, QBD 18–026, 18–027, 18–028
Territorial and Auxiliary Forces Association v. Nichols *See* London County
Territorial and Auxiliary Forces Association v. Nichols
Theophile v. Solicitor-General; *sub nom.* Debtor (No. 355 of 1947), Re [1950]
A.C. 186; [1950] 1 All E.R. 405, HL 3–026
Thomas, Ex.p [1956] Crim. L.R. 119, DC 24–025
Thomas v. Att.-Gen. of Trinidad and Tobago [1982] A.C. 113; [1981] 3 W.L.R.
601, PC 18–026
Thomas v. Baptiste [2000] 2 A.C. 1; [1999] 3 W.L.R. 249, PC 37–013
Thomas v. National Union of Mineworkers [1985] I.R.L.R. 136 .... 27–031, 27–034
Thomas v. Queen, The (1875) L.R. 10 Q.B. 31 33–005
Thomas v. Queen, The [1980] A.C. 125, PC 37–012
Thomas v. R. (1875) L.R. 10 Q.B. 31 33–007
Thomas v. Sawkins [1935] 2 K.B. 249, KBD 2–010, 24–043, 27–003
Thomas v. Sorrell (1674) Vaughan 330 .... 3–005, 20–004
Thomas v. Sutters [1900] 1 Ch. 10, CA 31–006
Thomas v. University of Bradford; *sub nom.* Thomas v. Bradford University
[1987] A.C. 795; [1987] 2 W.L.R. 677, HL 16–008
Thornhill v. Att.-Gen. of Trinidad and Tobago [1981] A.C. 61; [1980] 2 W.L.R.
510, PC 37–013
Thornton v. Police [1962] A.C. 339; [1962] 2 W.L.R. 1141, PC 23–005
Three Rivers DC v. Governor and Company of the Bank of England [2001]
UKHL 16; [2001] 2 All E.R. 513; *The Times,* March 23, 2001, HL ... 28–002, 32–022
Thurn and Taxis (Princess) v. Moffitt [1915] 1 Ch. 58, Ch D 23–019
Thynne v. United Kingdom (A/190); Wilson v. United Kingdom; Gunnell v.
United Kingdom (1991) 13 E.H.R.R. 666; The Times, December 10, 1990,
ECHR 22–034, 24–032
Tillmire Common, Re [1982] 2 All E.R. 615; (1982) 79 L.S.G. 1292, Ch D (*See*
Bousefield v. North Yorkshire CC) 32–024
Tilonko v. Att.-Gen. of Natal (Court Martial) [1907] A.C. 93, PC 19–034, 37–008
Tilonko v. Att.-Gen. of Natal [1907] A.C. 461, PC 37–008
Tinnelly & Sons Ltd v. United Kingdom; McElduff v. United Kingdom (1999) 27
E.H.R.R. 249; 4 B.H.R.C. 393, ECHR 20–041
Tito v. Waddell (No.2); Tito v. Att.-Gen. [1977] Ch. 106; [1977] 3 W.L.R. 972,
Ch D 15–012, 33–018, 35–014, 35–016
Tobin v. Queen, The (1864) C.B. (N.S.) 310 33–005
Tomasi v. France (A241–A) (1993) 15 E.H.R.R. 1, ECHR 22–032

Town Investments Ltd v. Department of the Environment; *sub nom.* London County Freehold and Leasehold Properties v. Department of the Environment; HEPC (Mayfair Properties) v. Department of the Environment [1978] A.C. 359; [1977] 2 W.L.R. 450, HL 15–007, 18–025, 33–008
Tracomin SA v. Sudan Oil Seeds Co Ltd [1983] 1 W.L.R. 1026; [1983] 3 All E.R. 137, CA 3–018, 22–037
Transocean Marine Paint Association v. Commission of the European Communities (C17/74) [1974] E.C.R. 1063, ECJ 6–039
Trapp v. Mackie [1979] 1 W.L.R. 377; [1979] 1 All E.R. 489, HL 20–042, 25–003
Trawnik v. Gordon Lennox; *sub nom.* Trawnik v. Ministry of Defence [1985] 2 All E.R. 368, CA; reversing [1984] 2 All E.R. 791, Ch D 18–011, 22–007, 33–003
Trendtex Trading Corporation v. Central Bank of Nigeria [1977] Q.B. 529; [1977] 2 W.L.R. 356, CA 3–026, 28–010
Trethowan v. Peden (1931) 44 C.L.R. 394 4–032
Trethowan's Case 44 C.L.R. 426 .... 4–032, 4–033
Triefus Co Ltd v. Post Office [1957] 2 Q.B. 352; [1957] 3 W.L.R. 1, CA 28–002
Triggs v. Staines Urban DC [1969] 1 Ch. 10; [1968] 2 W.L.R. 1433, Ch D 31–022
Tucker (A Bankrupt), ex p. Tucker, Re [1990] Ch. 148; [1988] 2 W.L.R. 748, CA; reversing [1987] 1 W.L.R. 928, Ch D 3–020
Tunbridge Wells Corporation v. Baird; *sub nom.* Baird v. Tunbridge Wells Corporation [1896] A.C. 434, HL; affirming [1894] 2 Q.B. 867, CA 27–004
Twine v. Bean's Express 62 T.L.R. 458; (1946) 175 L.T. 131 33–009
Tyler v. United Kingdom (1978) 2 E.H.R.R. 1 35–001
Tynan v. Balmer; *sub nom.* Tynan v. Chief Constable of Liverpool [1967] 1 Q.B. 91; [1966] 2 W.L.R. 1181, QBD 27–033, 27–034
Tyrer v. United Kingdom (1978) 2 E.H.R.R. 1 .... 22–006, 22–013, 22–028, 22–032

Underhill v. Ministry of Food [1950] 1 All E.R. 591; 66 T.L.R. (Pt. 1) 730 33–018
Union Government Minister of Lands v. Whittaker's Estate [1916] App.D.(S.A.) 203 35–017
United Kingdom Association Professional Engineers (UKAPE) v. Advisory, Conciliation and Arbitration Service (ACAS) [1981] A.C. 424; [1980] 2 W.L.R. 254, HL; reversing [1979] 1 W.L.R. 570, CA 22–008
United States v. Caltex (1952) 344 U.S. 149 15–017
United States v. McCaffery [1984] 1 W.L.R. 867; [1984] 2 All E.R. 570, HL 23–043
Universal Thermosensors Ltd v. Hibben [1992] 1 W.L.R. 840; [1992] 3 All E.R. 257, Ch D 24–052
Universities of Oxford and Cambridge v. Eyre and Spottiswoode [1964] Ch. 736; [1963] 3 W.L.R. 645, Ch D 15–015
University Council of the Vidyodaya University of Ceylon v. Silva [1965] 1 W.L.R. 77; [1964] 3 All E.R. 865, PC 32–006
Utah Construction & Engineering Pty Ltd v. Pataky [1966] A.C. 629; [1966] 2 W.L.R. 197, PC 31–005

Valsamis v. Greece (1997) 24 E.H.R.R. 294; [1998] E.L.R. 430, ECHR 22–047
Van Duyn v. Home Office (C41/74) [1975] Ch. 358; [1975] 2 W.L.R. 760; [1974] E.C.R. 1337 .... 6–013, 6–025, 6–035, 23–023
Van Gend en Loos [1963] E.C.R.1 .... 6–012, 6–013
Van Marle v. Netherlands (1986) 8 E.H.R.R. 483, ECHR 22–046
Vaudin v. Hamon [1974] A.C. 569; [1973] 3 W.L.R. 257, PC 35–003
Vauxhall Estates Ltd v. Liverpool Corporation [1932] 1 K.B. 733, KBD 3–015, 4–004
Venables v. News Group Newspapers; Thompson v. News Group Newspapers Ltd [2001] 2 W.L.R. 1038; [2001] 1 All E.R. 908, Fam Div 25–019
Venicoff, Ex.p *See* R. v. Leman Street Police Station Inspector, ex p. Venicoff
Verrall v. Great Yarmouth BC [1981] Q.B. 202; [1980] 3 W.L.R. 258, CA 25–001
Vertue v. Lord Clive (1769) 6 Burr. 2472 19–005

Vestey v. Inland Revenue Commissioners (No.2) [1980] A.C. 1148; [1979] 3
    W.L.R. 915, HL; affirming [1979] Ch. 177 3–006
Vicar of Writtle v. Essex CC 77 L.G.R. 656 33–009
Vidyodaya University of Ceylon v. Silva *See* University Council of the Vidyo-
    daya University of Ceylon v. Silva
Vignon v. DPP [1997] Crim.L.R. 289, DC 27–026
Vine v. National Dock Labour Board [1957] A.C. 488; [1957] 2 W.L.R. 106,
    HL 31–019, 32–001
Viscount Canterbury v. Att.-Gen. (1843) 1 Phillips 306; (1843) 12 L.J. Ch. 281 ... 33–005
Viscountess Rhondda's Claim [1922] 2 A.C. 339, HL 4–037, 9–002, 9–004
Von Colson and Kamann v. Land Nordrhein-Westfahlen (C14/83); Harz v.
    Deutsche Tradax GmbH (C79/83) [1984] E.C.R. 1891; [1986] 2 C.M.L.R.
    430, ECJ 6–013

W v. Essex CC [2000] 2 W.L.R. 601; [2000] 2 All E.R. 237, HL; reversing in part
    [1999] Fam. 90, CA 31–022
Waddington v. Miah; R. v. Miah; Waddington v. Miah [1974] 1 W.L.R. 683;
    [1974] 2 All E.R. 377, HL 3–018, 22–009, 22–020, 22–037
Walker v. Baird [1892] A.C. 491, PC 15–025, 33–008
Walker v. Queen, The [1994] 2 A.C. 36; [1993] 3 W.L.R. 1017, PC 37–010
Walker v. UNISON 1995 S.L.T. 1226; 1995 S.C.L.R. 786, OH 10–049
Wallace v. Commissioners Tax, Bombay (1948) 75 I.A. 86, PC 35–026
Walsall Overseers v. London and North Western Railway (1879) 4 App.Cas. 30,
    HL 32–005
Walsh v. Barlow [1985] 1 W.L.R. 90 31–006
Walters v. W.H. Smith & Son Ltd [1914] 1 K.B. 595, KBD 24–009
Walwin Ltd v. West Sussex CC [1975] 3 All E.R. 604; 74 L.G.R. 177, Ch D 15–010
Wan Ping Nam v. Minister of Justice of German Federal Republic 1972 J.C. 43;
    1972 S.L.T. 220, HCJ 23–047
Wandsworth LBC v. Winder (No.1) [1985] A.C. 461; [1984] 3 W.L.R. 1254,
    HL 32–001
Wang v. Inland Revenue Commissioner [1994] 1 W.L.R. 1286; [1995] 1 All E.R.
    637, PC 31–006, 31–014
Warren v. Smith (Magdalen College Case) (1615) 11 Co.Rep. 66b 15–019, 20–003
Wason v. Walter (1868) L.R. 4 Q.B. 73 .... 2–008, 13–005, 13–012, 25–004
Waterfalls Town Management Board v. Minister of Housing [1956] Rhod. &
    Ny.L.R. 691 33–006
Webb v. EMO Air Cargo (UK) Ltd (No.2) [1995] 1 W.L.R. 1454; [1995] 4 All
    E.R. 577, HL 4–022, 6–013
Webb v. Minister of Housing and Local Government [1965] 1 W.L.R. 755;
    [1965] 2 All E.R. 193, CA 31–008, 31–009
Weber, Ex.p [1916] 1 A.C. 421, HL; affirming [1916] 1 K.B. 280 (Note), CA 23–021
Weber's Trustees v. Riemer 1947 S.L.T. 295; 1947 S.L.T. (Notes) 30, OH 23–020
Webster v. Southwark LBC [1983] Q.B. 698; [1983] 2 W.L.R. 217, QBD 10–048
Wednesbury Corporation v. Ministry of Housing and Local Government (No.2)
    [1966] 2 Q.B. 275 .... 30–025, 33–022
Weeks v. United Kingdom (A/114) (1988) 10 E.H.R.R. 293; *The Times,* March
    5, 1987, ECHR 22–034, 24–032
Welch v. United Kingdom (A/307–A) (1995) 20 E.H.R.R. 247; The Times,
    February 15, 1995, ECHR 22–037
Wells v. Minister of Housing and Local Government [1967] 1 W.L.R. 1000;
    [1967] 2 All E.R. 1041, DC 31–020
Wells v. Williams (1697) 1 Ld.Raym. 282 .... 23–019, 23–020
Welsh v. Chief Constable of Merseyside [1993] 1 All E.R. 692, QBD 33–010
Wemhoff v. Germany (A/7) (1979–80) 1 E.H.R.R. 55, ECHR 24–023
Wensleydale Peerage Case (1856) 5 H.L.C. 958 .... 9–012, 9–046, 13–026, 15–004

Wershof v. Commissioner of the Police of the Metropolis [1978] 3 All E.R. 540;
(1979) 68 Cr. App. R. 82, QBD 24–022
West Rand Central Gold Mining Co v. King, The [1905] 2 K.B. 391, KBD 15–022
Western Fish Products Ltd v. Penwith DC [1981] 2 All E.R. 204; 77 L.G.R. 185,
CA 31–020
Westinghouse Electric Corporation Uranium Contract Litigation MDL Docket
235 (No.2), Re; *sub nom.* Rio Tinto Zinc Corporation v. Westinghouse
Electric Corporation (Nos.1 and 2) [1978] A.C. 547; [1978] 2 W.L.R. 81,
HL 6–022, 15–023
Westminster Bank v. Minister of Housing and Local Government [1971] A.C.
508; [1970] 2 W.L.R. 645, HL 31–008
Westminster City Council, Re [1983] 1 A.C. 768 31–004
Westminster Corporation v. L & N.W. Railway [1905] A.C. 426, HL 31–009, 31–011
Westwood v. Post Office [1974] A.C. 1; [1973] 3 W.L.R. 287, HL reversing *The
Times,* November 24, 1972, CA 28–009
Wheeler v. Leicester City Council [1985] A.C. 1054; [1985] 3 W.L.R. 335, HL ... 31–019
Whicker v. Hume (1858) 7 H.L.C. 124, HL 35–016
White and Collins v. Minister of Health *See* Ripon (Highfield) Housing Con-
firmation Order 1938, Re
White v. Kuzych; *sub nom.* Kuzych v. White [1951] A.C. 585; [1951] 2 All E.R.
435 31–013
White v. Morley [1899] 2 Q.B. 30 31–006
Whitehouse v. Bogdanov *The Times,* March 19, 1982 25–037
Whitehouse v. Gay News Ltd and Lemon *See* R. v. Lemon
Whitfield v. Le Despencer (1778) 2 Cowp. 754 28–002
Wi Matua's Will [1908] A.C. 448 15–019
Wick and Dennis' Case (1589) 1 Leo. 190 33–020
Wickhambrook Parochial Church Council v. Croxford [1935] 2 K.B. 417, CA 22–055
Wilkes v. Lord Halifax (1769) 19 St.Tr. 1407 24–007
Wilkes v. Wood (1763) 19 St.Tr. 1153 .... 24–046, 25–009
Willcock v. Muckle [1951] 2 K.B. 844; [1951] 2 All E.R. 367, KBD 19–047
William Cory & Son Ltd v. London Corporation [1951] 2 K.B. 476; [1951] 2 All
E.R. 85, CA 31–022
Williams v. Home Office (No.2) [1982] 2 All E.R. 564, CA; affirming [1981] 1
All E.R. 1211, QBD 24–031, 32–024, 33–025
Williams v. Howarth [1905] A.C. 551, PC 35–005
Willion v. Berkley (1561) Plowd. 223 15–019
Willmott v. Atack [1977] Q.B. 498; [1976] 3 W.L.R. 753, QBD 24–021
Wilson v. Independent Broadcasting Authority 1979 S.C. 351; 1979 S.L.T. 279,
OH 10–056
Winder v. DPP (1996) 160 J.P. 713; (1996) 160 J.P.N. 786, QBD 27–014
Windsor and Maidenhead RBC v. Brandrose Investments [1983] 1 W.L.R. 509;
[1983] 1 All E.R. 818, CA 31–022
Winfat Enterprise (Hong Kong) Co Ltd v. Att.-Gen. of Hong Kong [1985] A.C.
733; [1985] 2 W.L.R. 786, PC 31–018, 35–015
Wingham, Re [1949] P. 187 19–005
Wingrove v. United Kingdom (1997) 24 E.H.R.R. 1; 1 B.H.R.C. 509, ECHR 22–041,
25–002, 25–008
Winterwerp v. The Netherlands (A/33) (1979–80) 2 E.H.R.R. 387, ECHR 22–034,
24–028
Wirral Estates v. Shaw; *sub nom.* Wirral Estates Ltd v. Shaw [1932] 2 K.B. 247,
CA 15–020
Wise v. Dunning [1902] 1 K.B. 167, KBD 27–009
Wolfe Tone's Case (1798) 27 St.Tr. 613 .... 19–029, 19–035
Wolfgram v. Germany (1986) 46 D.R. 213 22–026
Woodhall, Ex.p, Re; *sub nom.* Woodhall, ex p. (1888) L.R. 20 Q.B.D. 832, CA ... 24–039

Woollett v. Minister of Agriculture and Fisheries [1955] 1 Q.B. 103; [1954] 3
    W.L.R. 776, CA 31–019
Worringham v. Lloyd's Bank Ltd; Humphreys v. Lloyds Bank Ltd [1981] 1
    W.L.R. 950; [1981] 2 All E.R. 434, ECJ 6–025
Worthington v. Robinson (1897) 75 L.T. 446 18–026
Wright v. Fitzgerald (1799) 27 St.Tr. 759 19–029
Wring, Re; Cook, Re; sub nom. Practice Note (DC: Habeas Corpus) [1960] 1
    W.L.R. 138; [1960] 1 All E.R. 536 (Note), DC 24–034, 24–037

X. v. Commissioner of Police of the Metropolis [1985] 1 W.L.R. 420; [1985] 1
    All E.R. 890, Ch D 21–006
X. v. United Kingdom (1981) 23 D.R. 228 22–048
X. v. United Kingdom (1981) 4 E.H.R.R. 188 .... 22–034, 30–002
X. (HA) v. Y. [1988] 2 All E.R. 648; [1988] R.P.C. 379, QBD 25–020
X. (Minors) v. Bedfordshire CC [1995] 2 A.C. 633; [1995] 3 W.L.R. 152, HL 31–024,
                                                                                              31–025
X Ltd v. Morgan-Grampian (Publishers) Ltd [1991] 1 A.C. 1; [1990] 2 W.L.R.
    1000, HL 2–026, 20–045, 25–016
X, Y and Z v. United Kingdom [1997] 2 F.L.R. 892; [1997] 3 F.C.R. 341; (1997)
    24 E.H.R.R. 143, ECHR 22–039

Yaassen-Gobbels v. Beambtenfonds voor het Mijnbedrijf [1966] E.C.R. 261 6–026
York Corporation v. Henry Leetham & Sons Ltd [1924] 1 Ch. 557, Ch D 31–022
Young v. United Kingdom (A/44); James v. United Kingdom; Webster v. United
    Kingdom [1982] E.C.C. 264; [1981] I.R.L.R. 408; (1982) 4 E.H.R.R. 38,
    ECHR 22–042
Youngstown Sheet & Tube Co v. Sawyer 343 U.S. 579 1–018
Youssoupoff v. Metro-Goldwyn-Mayer Pictures Ltd (1934) 50 T.L.R. 581; 99
    A.L.R. 964, CA 25–003
Yoxford and Darsham Farmers' Association Ltd v. Llewellin (1946) 62 T.L.R.
    347 19–041

Zacharia v. Republic of Cyprus; sub nom. Zacharia, Re [1963] A.C. 634; [1962]
    2 W.L.R. 1163, HL 24–034
Zamir v. Secretary of State for the Home Department; sub nom. R. v. Secretary
    of State for the Home Department, ex p. Zamir [1980] A.C. 930; [1980] 3
    W.L.R. 249, HL 23–028
Zamora, The (No.1) [1916] 2 A.C. 77, PC; reversing [1916] P. 27, PDAD 3–026,
                                                                       15–023, 22–020, 31–003

TABLE OF EUROPEAN CASES

A. v. United Kingdom (1999) 27 E.H.R.R. 611; [1998] 2 F.L.R. 959, ECHR 22–032
ADT v. United Kingdom [2000] 2 F.L.R. 697; *The Times*, August 8, 2000, ECHR 22–039
Abas v. The Netherlands [1997] E.H.R.L.R. 418 24–053
Abdulaziz, Cabales and Balkandali v. United Kingdom (1985) 7 E.H.R.R. 471, ECHR 22–013, 22–026, 22–039
Ahmad v. Inner London Education Authority (No. 8160/78) (1982) 4 E.H.R.R. 126; (1981) 22 D.R. 27, ECHR 22–010, 22–040
Ahmad and Others v. United Kingdom (2000) 29 E.H.R.R. 1, ECHR 27–038
Airey v. Ireland (1979) 2 E.H.R.R. 305 .... 24–019, 22–028, 22–030
Anderson and Others v. United Kingdom [1998] E.H.R.L.R. 218 27–013
Andrea Francovich v. Italian Republic [1991] E.C.R. 5357; [1993] 2 C.M.L.R. 66 6–014
Annalisa Carbonari v. Universita degli Studi di Bologna [1999] E.C.R. 1103 6–013
Arrowsmith v. United Kingdom (1980) 3 E.H.R.R. 218, ECHR 22–040
Artico v. Italy (1981) 3 E.H.R.R. 1, ECHR 22–28
Askoy v. Turkey (1996) 23 E.H.R.R. 553, ECHR 22–032
Aydin v. Turkey (1997) 25 E.H.R.R. 251, ECHR 22–032

Belgian Linguistics case (1968) 1 E.H.R.R. 252, ECHR 22–044, 22–047
Belgissche Radio en Televisie v. SABAM [1974] E.C.R. 51 6–012
Bendenoun v. France (No. 12547/86) (1994) 18 E.H.R.R. 54, ECJ 24–053
Benham v. United Kingdom (1996) 22 E.H.R.R. 293, ECHR 24–001
Bowman v. United Kingdom (1998) 26 E.H.R.R. 1; 4 B.H.R.C. 25, ECHR 10–051, 20–049
Bozano v. France (No. 5/985/91/138) (1987) 9 E.H.R.R. 297, ECHR 23–041
Brannigan and McBride v. United Kingdom (1994) 17 E.H.R.R. 539, ECHR 19–055
Brasserie du Pecheur SA v. Germany (C46/93); R. v. Secretary of State for Transport ex p. Factortame (No. 4) (C48/93) [1996] E.C.R. I–1929; [1996] 1 C.M.L.R. 889, ECJ 6–014
Brogan v. United Kingdom (1989) 11 E.H.R.R. 117, ECHR 19–055, 22–013, 22–027, 24–001
Bryan v. United Kingdom (A/335 A) (1996) 21 E.H.R.R. 342; [1996] 1 P.L.R. 47, ECHR 22–036, 30–027
Burton v. British Railways Board (No. 2) (No. 19/81) [1981] I.R.L.R. 17; [1982] Q.B. 1080, ECJ 6–026

Caballero v. United Kingdom (2000) 30 E.H.R.R. 643; [2000] Crim. L.R. 587, ECHR 24–023
Cambell v. United Kingdom (C–13590/88) (1993) 15 E.H.R.R. 137, ECHR 24–032
Cambell and Cosans v. United Kingdom (1982) 4 E.H.R.R. 293, ECHR 22–012, 22–032, 22–047
Cambell and Fell v. United Kingdom (1984) 7 E.H.R.R. 165, ECHR 20–026, 22–036, 22–037, 24–032
Chahal v. United Kingdom (1997) 23 E.H.R.R. 413; (1997) 1 B.H.R.C. 405, ECHR 22–012, 22–033, 22–034, 22–043, 23–034, 23–036, 30–002
Chappell v. United Kingdom (No. 17/1981/140/194) (1989) 12 E.H.R.R. 1, ECHR 24–052
Chassagnou v. France (2000) 29 E.H.R.R. 615; 7 B.H.R.C. 151, ECHR ... 22–042, 22–046
Cheall v. United Kingdom (1985) 42 D.R. 178 22–042
Choudhury v. United Kingdom, app.17439/90 25–007

Christians against Racism and Fascism v. United Kingdom (1980) 21 D.R. 138 ... 27–017
C.I.L.F.I.T. v. Italian Minstry of Health [1983] 1 C.M.L.R. 472 6–024
Condron v. United Kingdom [2000] Crim. L.R. 679, ECHR 24–017
Co-operative Agricola Zootecrucia S. Antonio and Others v. Amministrazione
 delle finanze dello Stato [1996] E.C.R. I–43736–013
Cossey v. United Kingdom (C–16/1989/176/232) (1990) 13 E.H.R.R. 622;
 [1991] 2 F.L.R. 292, ECHR 22–042
Costello-Roberts v. United Kingdom (C–89/1991/ 341/414) (1995) 19 E.H.R.R.
 112; [1994] 1 F.C.R. 65, ECHR 22–032
Council for Civil Service Unions v. United Kingdom (1988) 10 E.H.R.R. 269,
 ECHR 27–038
Cruz Varas v. Sweden (C–15576/89) (1991) 14 E.H.R.R. 1, ECHR 22–033

Defrenne v. Sabena (No. 2) [1976] E.C.R. 455 6–012
Demicoli v. Malta (C–13057/87) (1992) 14 E.H.R.R. 47, ECHR 13–023
Dombo Beheer BV v. The Netherlands (No. 14448/88) (1994) 18 E.H.R.R. 213,
 ECHR 22–037
Drake v.Chief Adjudication Officer (No. 150/85) [1986] 3 All E.R. 65; [1986] 2
 W.L.R. 1005, ECJ 6–038
Dudgeon v. United Kingdom (1981) 4 E.H.R.R. 149, ECHR 22–013, 22–039

E.C. Commission v. United Kingdom [1979] E.C.R. 419 6–026
E.C. Commission v. United Kingdom [1982] I.R.L.R. 33; [1982] I.C.R. 578 ... 6–038
E.C. Commission v. United Kingdom [1983] E.C.R. 2265 6–026
E.C. Commission v. United Kingdom [1985] 2 C.M.L.R. 259 6–035
Engel v. The Netherlands (1976) 1 E.H.R.R. 647, ECHR 22–036

Fayed v. United Kingdom (No. 17101/90) (1994) 18 E.H.R.R. 393, ECHR 20–041
Findlay v. United Kingdom (1997) 24 E.H.R.R. 221, ECHR 19–021, 22–012, 22–036
Foster v. British Gas (C–188/89) [1990] E.C.R. I–3313; [1991] 2 W.L.R. 258,
 ECJ 6–013
Fratelli Variola v. Italian Minister of Finance [1973] E.C.R. 891 6–012
Funke v. France A 256–A (No. 10828/84) (1993) 16 E.H.R.R. 297, ECHR 24–048,
 26–018

Gaskin v. United Kingdom (No. 2/1988/146/200) (1990) 12 E.H.R.R. 36; [1990]
 1 F.L.R. 167, ECHR 22–039, 33–024
Gay News and Lemon v. United Kingdom (1983) 5 E.H.R.R. 123, ECHR 22–037,
 25–007
Giltonas v. Greece (1998) 26 E.H.R.R. 691 10–002
Golder v. United Kingdom (1975) 1 E.H.H.R. 524, ECHR 22–013, 22–028, 22–036,
 24–032
Goodwin v. United Kingdom (1996) 22 E.H.R.R. 123; (1996) 1 B.H.R.C. 81,
 ECHR 25–002, 25–017, 25–022
Grad v. Finanzamt Traunstein [1970] E.C.R. 825 6–011
Groppera Radio A v. Switzerland (No. 14/1988/158/214), Series A, vol. 173
 (1990); *The Times*, April 6, 1990, ECHR 10–056
Guzzardi v. Italy (1980) 13 E.H.R.R. 333, ECHR 24–028

Hagen v. Fratelli D. and Morretts S.N.C. [1980] 3 C.M.L.R. 253 6–024
Halford v. United Kingdom (1997) 24 E.H.R.R. 523; [1997] I.R.L.R. 471,
 ECHR 22–039, 26–014
Hamer v. United Kingdom (1979) 4 E.H.R.R. 139, ECHR 22–042
Handyside v. United Kingdom (1976) 1 E.H.R.R. 737 .... 22–029, 22–030, 25–002,
 25–024, 27–001

Hanptzollamt Bremen-Freihafen v. Waren-Import Gesellschaft Krohn & Co. [1970] E.C.R. 451 6–012
Harman v. United Kingdom (1985) 7 E.H.R.R. 146, ECHR 20–046
Hashman and Harrup v. United Kingdom (2000) 30 E.H.R.R. 241; 8 B.H.R.C.104, ECHR 22–029, 24–027
Hood v. United Kingdom (2000) 29 E.H.H.R. 365; *The Times*, March 11, 1999, ECHR 19–022
Hussain v. United Kingdom (1996) 22 E.H.R.R. 1; (1996) 1 B.H.R.C 119, ECHR 22–034, 24–032

Imports of Potatoes, Re: E.C. Commission v. United Kingdom [1979] 2 C.M.L.R. 427, ECJ 6–036
Imports of Poultry, Re: E.C. Commission v. France [1982] 3 C.M.L.R. 497, ECJ 6–036
Internationale Handelsgesellschaft [1970] E.C.R. 1125; [1972] C.M.L.R. 112 6–011
Ireland v. United Kingdom (1978) 2 E.H.R.R. 25, ECHR 22–005, 22–032

James v. United Kingdom (1986) 8 E.H.R.R. 123, ECHR 24–054
Johnson v. United Kingdom (1999) 27 E.H.R.R. 296; (1998) 40 B.M.L.R. 1, ECHR 24–030
Johnston v. Chief Constable of the R.U.C. [1987] Q.B. 129; [1986] 3 All E.R. 135; [1986] E.C.R. 1651, ECJ 6–038, 6.040

Kaya v. Turkey (1999) 28 E.H.R.R. 1; [1998] H.R.C.D. 291, ECHR 22–031
Kenny v. National Insurance Officer [1978] E.C.R. 1489; [1978] 3 C.M.L.R. 651, ECJ 6–026
Khan v. United Kingdom [2000] Crim. L.R. 684; 8 B.H.R.C. 310, ECHR 22–039, 24–018
Kjeldsen, Busk Madsen and Pederson v. Denmark (1976) 1 E.H.R.R. 711, ECHR 22–047
Klass v. Germany [1979] 2 E.H.R.R. 214, ECHR 22–025, 22–043
Kokkinakis v. Greece (No. 14307/88) (1994) 17 E.H.R.R. 397, ECHR 22–041
Kruslin v. France (1990) 12 E.H.R.R. 547, ECHR 22–029

Lasky, Jaggard and Brown v. United Kingdom [1997] 24 E.H.R.R. 39, ECHR 22–039
Lawless v. Ireland [1961] 1 E.H.R.R. 15, ECHR 22–005, 22–023, 22–045
Lemon v. United Kingdom (1982) 24 E.H.R.R. C.D. 75, ECHR 25–002, 25–008
Letellier v. France (C–12369/86) (1991) 14 E.H.R.R. 83, ECHR 24–023
Liberal Party, R. and P. v. United Kingdom (1980) 4 E.H.R.R. 106; (1980) 21 D.R. 211, ECHR 10–058, 22–049
Lingen v. Austria (1986) 8 E.H.R.R. 407, ECHR 25–002
Lithgow v. United Kingdom (No. 2/1984/74/112–118) (1986) 8 E.H.R.R. 329, ECHR 22–046, 24–054
Lord Bruce of Donnington v. G. Aspden [1981] E.C.R. 2205 6–026

McCann, Farrell and Savage v. United Kingdom (1996) 21 E.H.R.R. 97, ECHR 22–031
McGonnell v. United Kingdom (2000) 30 E.H.H.R. 289; *The Times*, February 22, 2000, ECHR 2–021, 20–036, 22–036, 22–051
McLeod v. United Kingdom (1999) 27 E.H.R.R. 493; [1998] 2 F.L.R. 1048, ECHR 24–043, 27–003, 27–008
Malone v. United Kingdom (1985) 7 E.H.R.R. 14, ECHR 22–012, 22–029, 22–039, 26–014, 26–016
Marck v. Belgium (1979) 2 E.H.R.R. 330, ECHR 22–040
Marleasing SA v. La Comercial Internacional de Alimentacion SA [1990] E.C.R. 4135; [1992] 1 C.M.L.R. [1992] 1 C.M.L.R. 305 6–013

Marshall v. Southampton and South West Hampshire Area Health Authority
[1986] E.C.R. 723, [1986] 2 W.L.R. 780, ECJ 6–013
Mathieu-Mohin v. Belgium (1988) 10 E.H.R.R. 1, ECHR 10–026, 20–049
Moore and Gordon v. United Kingdom (2000) 29 E.H.R.R. 728, ECHR 22–013

National and Provincial Building Society, The, Leeds Permanent Building Soci-
ety, The and the Yorkshire Building Society v. United Kingdom (1997) 25
E.H.R.R.R. 127; [1997] S.T.C. 1466, ECHR 22–047
National Union of Belgian Police v. Belgium (1975) 1 E.H.R.R. 578, ECHR 27–038
Neimietz v. Germany A 251–B (1992) 16 E.H.R.R. 97, ECHR 24–048
Neumeister v. Austria (No. 1) A/8 (1968) 1 E.H.R.R. 55, ECHR 24–023, 24–024,
                                                                                           24–025
Nold v. E.C. Commission [1974] E.C.R. 491; [1974] 2 C.M.L.R. 338 ..... 6–011, 6–039
Nordsee v. Reederei Mond (No. 102/81) [1982] Com. L.R. 154; [1982] E.C.R.
1095, ECJ 6–026

Observer and Guardian v. United Kingdom (1992) 14 E.H.R.R. 153, ECHR 25–021,
                                                                                           26–010
Open Door Counselling and Dublin Well Woman v. Ireland (C–14234/88 and
C–14235/ /88) (1993) 15 E.H.R.R. 244, ECHR 22–025
Orsolina Leonesio v. Minister for Agriculture and Forestry of the Italian Repub-
lic [1972] E.C.R. 287 6–012
Osman v. United Kingdom [1999] Fam. L.R. 86; [1999] 1 F.L.R. 193; (2000) 29
E.H.R.R. 245, ECHR 22–031, 31–024
Otto-Preminger-Institut v. Austria (No. 134070/87) (1994) 19 E.H.R.R. 34,
ECHR 22–030, 22–041

Paola Faccini Dori v. Recreb Srl [1994] E.C.R. I–3325; [1994] 1 C.M.L.R. 665 ... 6–013
Paton v. United Kingdom (1980) 3 E.H.R.R. 409, ECHR 22–031
Piermont v. France (1995) 20 E.H.R.R. 301, ECHR 22–045
Piersack v. Belgium A/53 (1983) 5 E.H.R.R. 169, ECHR 26–018
Plattform Ärtzte für das Leben v. Austria (1991) 13 E.H.R.R. 204, ECHR 22–030,
                                                                                           27–008
Politi S.A.S. v. Italian Minister of Finance [1971] E.C.R. 1039 6–012
Powell and Rayner v. United Kingdom A/172 (1990) 12 E.H.R.R. 355, ECHR 22–039
Pubblico Ministero v. Ratti [1979] E.C.R. 1629; [1980] C.M.L.R. 96, ECJ 6–013

Quietlynn Ltd v. Southend B.C. (C–23/89) [1990] E.C.R.1–3059; [1990] 3
C.M.L.R. 55; [1990] 2 AU E.R. 207, ECJ 6–036

R. v. Bouchereau [1978] Q.B. 732; [1978] 2 W.L.R. 250, ECJ 6–026
R. v. Pieck (No. 157/79) [1981] E.C.R. 2171; [1981] 2 W.L.R. 960, ECJ 6–026, 6–035
R. v. Saunders (No. 175/78) [1980] Q.B. 72; [1979] 3 W.L.R. 359, ECJ 6–021
Rai and Others v. United Kingdom (1995) 82–A D.R. 134 27–004
Rees v. United Kingdom (No. 2/1985/88/135) (1986) 9 E.H.R.R. 56; [1987] 2
F.L.R. 111, ECHR 22–042
Restrictions on Imports of Lamb, Re: E.C. Commission v. France [1980] 1
C.M.L.R. 418, ECJ 6–036
Ribbitsch v. Austria (1986) 8 E.H.R.R. 45, ECHR 24–010
Ribitsch v. Austria A/336 (1996) 21 E.H.R.R. 573, ECHR 22–032

S.W. v. United Kingdom (1995) 21 E.H.R.R. 363, ECHR 22–037
Saunders v. United Kingdom (1997) 23 E.H.R.R. 313; (1997) 2 B.H.R.C. 358,
ECHR 20–043, 24–014, 24–017
Selçuk and Asker v. Turkey (1998) 26 E.H.R.R. 477; [1998] H.R.C.D. 475,
ECHR 22–032

Sheffield and Horsham v. United Kingdom (1998) 27 E.H.R.R. 163; [1998] 2
F.L.R. 928, ECHR 22–042
Sigurjonsson v. Iceland (C–24/1992/369/433) (1993) 16 E.H.R.R. 462, ECHR 22–042
Silver v. United Kingdom (1983) 5 E.H.R.R. 347; (1980) 3 E.H.R.R. 475,
ECHR 22–029, 22–043
Smith and Grady v. United Kingdom (2000) 29 E.H.R.R. 493; [1999] I.R.L.R.
734, ECHR 22–039, 22–043
Soering v. United Kingdom (1989) 11 E.H.R.R. 439, ECHR 22–033, 23–047
Spencer v. United Kingdom [1998] 25 E.H.R.R. C.D. 105 25–023
Sporrong and Lönnroth v. Sweden (1983) 5 E.H.R.R. 35, ECHR 22–046
Steel v. United Kingdom (1998) 28 E.H.R.R. 603; 5 B.H.R.C. 339, ECHR 24–008,
24–027, 27–001
Stran Greek Refineries & Stratus Andreadis v. Greece (1995) 19 E.H.R.R. 293,
ECHR 22–046
Sunday Times v. United Kingdom [1979] 2 E.H.R.R. 245, ECHR 20–043, 22–012,
25–002, 25–012, 25–013, 25–016
Sunday Times v. United Kingdom (No. 2) (1992) 14 E.H.R.R. 229, ECHR 25–002,
25–021

T. and V. v. United Kingdom (2000) 30 E.H.R.R. 121; 7 B.H.R.C. 659, ECHR 22–034
Teixiera de Castro v. Portugal (1999) 28 E.H.R.R. 1; (1998) 28 E.H.R.R. 101; 4
B.H.R.C. 533, ECHR 24–018, 26–019
Teodoro Wagner Miet v. Fondo de Garantia Salarial [1993] E.C.R. 6911; [1995]
2 C.M.L.R. 49 6–013
Thynne, Wilson and Gunnell v. United Kingdom (1991) 13 E.H.R.R. 666,
ECHR 22–034
Tinnelly and Sons Ltd v. United Kingdom (1999) 27 E.H.R.R. 249; 4 B.H.R.C.
393, ECHR 20–041
Tomasi v. France (C–12850/87) (1993) 15 E.H.R.R. 1, ECHR 22–032
Transocean Marine Paint Association v. E.C. Commission (No. 17/74) [1974]
E.C.R. 1063, ECJ 6–039
Tyrer v. United Kingdom (1978) Series A, No. 26; (1979–80) 2 E.H.R.R. 1,
ECHR 22–013, 22–032, 35–001

Valsamis v. Greece (1996) 24 E.H.R.R. 294, ECHR 22–047
Van Duyn v. Home Office [1974] E.C.R. 1337; [1975] Ch. 385; [1975] 1
C.M.L.R. 1 .... 6–013, 6–025, 6–035, 23–023
Van Gend Loos [1963] E.C.R. 1 .... 6–012, 6–013
Van Marle and Others v. The Netherlands (1986) 8 E.H.R.R. 491, ECHR 22–046
Von Colson and Kamann v. Land Nordrhein-Westfahlen [1984] E.C.R. 1891;
[1986] 2 C.M.L.R. 430 6–013

Welch v. United Kingdom (1995) 20 E.H.R.R. 247, ECHR 22–037
Weeks v. United Kingdom (No. 3/1985/89/136) (1988) 10 E.H.R.R. 293,
ECHR 22–034, 24–032
Wemhoff v. Germany (1968) 1 E.H.R.R. 155, ECHR 24–023
Wingrove v. United Kingdom (1997) 24 E.H.R.R. 1; (1997) 1 B.H.R.C 509,
ECHR 22–041, 25–002, 25–008
Winterwerp v. The Netherlands (1979) 2 E.H.R.R. 387, ECHR 22–034, 24–028
Wolfgram v. Germany (1986) 46 D.R. 213 22–026

X v. United Kingdom (1981) 4 E.H.R.R. 188; (1981) 23 D.R. 228, ECHR 22–034,
22–049, 30–002
X and the Association of Z v. United Kingdom,1971 Commission Decision 10–056

Yaassen-Gobbels v. Beambtenfonds voor het Mijnbedrijf [1966] E.C.R. 261 6–026

Young, James and Webster v. United Kingdom (1982) 4 E.H.R.R. 38; [1983]
      I.R.L.R. 35, ECHR 22–042

TABLE OF STATUTES

1181	Assize of Arms	21–002
1215	Magna Carta 1–019, 2–007,	
	3–008, 19–040	
1284	Statutum Walliae (12	
	Edw.1)	2–002
1285	Statute of Westminster	21–002
	Statute of Winchester (12	
	Edw.1, c.2)	20–019
1351	Statute of Treason (25	
	Edw. 3, c.2) 14–007,	
	14–012, 14–018	
1361	Justices of the Peace Act	
	(34 Edw.3, c.1) 20–009,	
	24–026	
1495	Treason Act (11 Hen.7,	
	c.1) 4–002, 14–018	
1533	Clergy Act (25 Hen.8,	
	c.16)	15–014
1534	Act of Supremacy (26	
	Hen.8, c.1)	15–014
1536	Laws in Wales Act (28	
	Hen.8, c.3)	2–002
1539	Statute of Proclamations	
	(31 Hen.8, c.8) 3–003,	
	29–012	
1540	Judges Act	20–047
1541	Royal Assent by Commis-	
	sion Act (33 Hen.8,	
	c.21)	8–011
1543	Treason Act (35 Hen.8,	
	c.2)	14–019
1554	Treason Act (1 & 2 Ph. &	
	M,. c.10)	14–020
1609	Naturalisation Act (7 Ja.1,	
	c.2)	4–002
1627	Petition of Right (3 Cha.	
	1, c.1) 19–034, 24–034	
1660	Parliament Act (12 Cha.2,	
	c.1) 3–013, 4–027	
	Tenures Abolition Act (12	
	Cha.2, c.24)	3–009
1662	Licensing Act (14 Cha.2,	
	c.4)	25–018
1664	Triennial Act (16 Cha.2,	
	c.1)	8–013
1679	Habeas Corpus Act (31	
	Cha.2, c.1) 24–034,	
	24–035	
1688	Bills of Rights (1 Will. &	
	Mar. Sess. 2, c.2) 2–007,	
	2–041, 3–005, 3–008,	
	3–009, 13–002, 13–005,	
	15–004, 18–002, 19–002,	
	24–025, 24–053	
	Mutiny Act (1 Will. &	
	Mar., c.5)	19–020
	Coronation Oath Act (1	
	Will. & Mar,. c.6) ...	14–004
1689	Crown and Parliament	
	Recognition Act (2	
	Will. & Mar., c.1) 2–007,	
	3–013	
1694	Meeting of Parliament Act	
	(6 & 7 Will. & Mar.,	
	c.2) 4–030, 7–016	
	s.1	8–013
	s.2	8–013
	s.3	8–013
1695	Treason Act (7 & 8 Will.	
	3, c.3)	14–020
	Parliamentary Elections	
	Act (7 & 8 Will.3,	
	c.25)	10–005
1700	Act of Settlement (12 &	
	13 Will. 3, c.2) 2–007,	
	2–018, 3–015, 9–013,	
	10–003, 14–002, 14–005,	
	17–002, 20–029, 23–019	
	s.6	10–003
1702	Treason Act (1 Anne, st.2,	
	c.21)	14–018
1706	Union with Scotland Act	
	(6 Anne c.11) 2–003,	
	2–004, 2–007, 4–007,	
	4–010, 5–021, 5–049,	
	9–044, 14–003	
1707	Act of Union with Eng-	
	land Act 4–010, 5–021,	
	5–049	
	Succession to the Crown	
	Act (6 Anne c.41) 8–014,	
	10–003, 14–018, 17–002	
	s.24	10–003
	s.25	10–003
	Union with Scotland	
	(Amendment) Act (6	
	Anne c.41)	16–003
1708	Diplomatic Privileges Act	
	(7 Anne c.12)	15–032

1708 Treason Act (7 Anne c.21) 14–018
1711 Church Patronage (Scotland) Act (10 Anne c.21) 4–007
1715 Septennial Act (1 Geo. 1, st.2, c.38) 4–002, 4–030, 8–036
1750 The Calendar (New Style) Act (c.23) 2–007
1765 Isle of Man Purchase Act (5 Geo.3, c.26) 35–002
1766 American Colonies Act (6 Geo. 3, c.12) 3–013
1770 Parliamentary Privilege Act (10 Geo.3, c.50) 13–003
1772 Royal Marriages Act (12 Geo. 3, c.11) 14–005, 14–007
1778 Taxation of Colonies Act (18 Geo. 3, c.12) 4–001
1782 House of Commons (Disqualification) Act (22 Geo.3, c.45) 10–004
Truce with America Act (22 Geo. 3, c.46) 4–014
Colonial Leave of Absence Act (22 Geo.3, c.75) 35–023
1783 Trade with America Act (22 Geo. 3, c.26) 4–014
Trade with America Act (23 Geo. 3, c.39) 4–014
America Loyalists Act (22 Geo. 3, c.80) 4–014
1790 Speaker of the House of Commons Act (30 Geo.3, c.10) 10–019
1793 Aliens Act (33 Geo.3, c.4) 23–019
1795 Treason Act (36 Geo.3, c.7) 14–018, 14–021
1797 Incitement to Mutiny Act 25–009
Meeting of Parliament Act (37 Geo.3, c.127) 8–090, 8–012
1800 Act Union with Ireland Act (39 & 40 Geo.3., c.67) ... 2–004, 4–005, 5–008, 9–044, 16–003
Crown Private Estates Act (39 & 40 Geo.3, c.80) 15–009

1801 House of Commons (Disqualification) Act (41 Geo.3, c.42) 10–004
House of Commons (Clergy Disqualification) Act (41 Geo.3, c.63) 10–005
1814 Treason Act (54 Geo.3, c.146) 14–019
1816 Habeas Corpus Act (56 Geo.3, c.100) 24–036
1817 Treason Act (57 Geo.3, c.6) 14–019
1824 Clerk of the Parliaments Act (c.82)
s.2 9–019
1825 Duke of Atholl's Rights, Isle of Man Act (6 Geo.4, c.34) 35–002
1829 Metropolitan Police Act (10 Geo.4, c.7) 21–002, 21–007
s.52 27–005
Roman Catholic Relief Act (10 Geo.4, c.7) ... 10–002
s.9 10–005
1832 Representation of the People Act (2 & 3 Will. 4, c. 45) 7–018, 8–025, 10–025, 11–003, 12–022, 13–011, 17–004
1833 Corrupt and Illegal Practices Act 10–049
Judicial Committee Act (3 & 4 Will.4, c.41) 10–013, 16–010, 16–013, 37–006, 37–009, 37–010
s.3 10–013
s.4 .... 10–013, 16–014
1834 Poor Law Amendment Act (4 & 5 Will. 4, c.76) 2–036
1835 Municipal Corporations Act (5 & 6 Will. 4, c.76) 2–036, 21–002
1839 City of London Police 21–002
Metropolitan Police Act (2 & 3 Vict., c.47)
s.66 24–019
Rural Police Act (2 & 3 Vict., c.93) 21–002
1840 Parliamentary Papers Act (3 & 4 Vict., c.9) 13–011
s.1 .... 13–013, 25–003

1840   Parliamentary   Papers
      Act—*cont.*
      s.2 .... 13–011, 25–003
      s.3 ..... 13–011, 13–013, 25–005
      s.4 13–011
1842   Treason Act (c. 51) 14–022
1843   Settlements of Coast of
      Africa and Falkland
      Islands Act (6 & &
      Vict., c.13) 35–020
      Theatres Act (6 & 7 Vict.,
      c.68) 25–037
      Foreign Jurisdiction Act
      (6 & 7 Vict., c.94) 4–025,
                                 35–008
      Libel Act (6 & 7 Vict.,
      c.96)
      s.6 25–006
1844   Bank Charter Act (c.32)
      s.11 28–002
      Judicial Committee Act (7
      & 8 Vict, c.69) 37–006,
                       37–009, 37–010
1846   Fatal Accidents Act (7 & 8
      Vict., c.101) 33–011
      Baths and Wash-houses
      Act (9 & 10 Vict.,
      c.74) 31–004
1848   Treason Felony Act (11 &
      12 Vict., c.12) 14–021
1853   Universities (Scotland)
      Act (16 & 17 Vict.,
      c.89) 4–007
1855   Deputy Speaker Act (18 &
      19 Vict., c.84) 10–022
1856   County and Borough Po-
      lice (19 & 20 Vict.,
      c.69) 21–002
1857   Probate Act (20 & 21
      Vict., c.77) 3–015
      Obscene Publications Act
      (20 & 21 Vict.,
      c.83) 25–024
1858   Chancery Amendment Act
      (21 & 22 Vict.,
      c.27) 20–018
      Jews Relief Act (21 & 22
      Vict., c.49) 10–002
1860   West Coast of Africa and
      Falkland Islands Act
      (23 & 24 Vict.,
      c.121) 35–020
      Petitions of Right Act (23
      & 24 Vict., c.34) 33–007,
            33–015, 33–018, 33–019

1861   Offences Against the Per-
      son Act (24 & 25
      Vict., c.100)
      s.9 3–021
      s.57 3–021
1862   Crown Private Estates Act
      (25 & 26 Vict.,
      c.37) 15–009
1865   Crown Suits Act (28 & 29
      Vict., c.104) 33–018
      Colonial Laws Validity
      Act (28 & 29 Vict.,
      c.63) 4–033, 35–021,
           35–023, 35–026, 36–003,
           36–004, 36–016, 37–006,
                             37–009
      s.1 35–024
      s.2 .... 35–023, 36–014
      s.3 35–023
      s.4 35–024
      s.5 .... 4–025, 4–032, 4–033,
           35–024, 36–011, 36–012
1866   Exchequer and Audit De-
      partments Act (29 &
      30 Vict., c.39) 11–005,
                             12–018
1867   Representation of the Peo-
      ple Act (30 & 31
      Vict., c. 102) 8–014,
                             10–025
      British North America Act
      (30 & 31 Vict., c.3) ... 7–006,
                  36–001, 36–007
      War Department Stores
      Act (30 & 31 Vict.,
      c.128) 33–004, 33–007
      Prorogation Act (30 & 31
      Vict., c.81) 8–012
1868   Parliamentary Elections
      Act (31 & 32 Vict.,
      c.125) 10–048, 10–049,
           10–062, 11–005, 13–017
      Documentary Evidence
      Act (31 & 32 Vict.,
      c.32) 29–022
      Promissory Oaths Act (31
      & 32 Vict., c.72) 10–002,
                             20–026
1869   Pensioners Civil Disabili-
      ties Relief Act (32 &
      33 Vict., c.15) 10–003
      Newspapers, Printers and
      Reading Rooms Re-
      peal Act (32 & 33
      Vict., c.24) 25–018

1869   Irish Church Disestablish-
         ment Act (32 & 33
         Vict., c.42) 3–015, 4–005
       High Constables Act (32
         & 33 Vict., c.47) 21–002
       Debtors Act (32 & 33
         Vict., c.62) ... 13–016, 24–036
1870   Naturalisation Act (33 &
         34 Vict., c.14) 23–001,
                         23–002, 23–011
       Forfeiture Act (33 & 34
         Vict., c.23) ... 9–013, 10–005,
                                  14–019
       Extradition Act (33 & 34
         Vict., c.52) 23–042,
                         23–043, 23–047
         s.2 23–045
         s.16 23–046
         Sched. 1 23–043
       Meeting of Parliament Act
         (33 & 34 Vict., c.81) ... 8–090,
                                  8–012
1872   Parliamentary and Munic-
         ipal Elections Act (35
         & 36 Vict., c.61 10–057
1873   Crown Private Estates Act
         (36 & 37 Vict.,
         c.61) 15–009
       Supreme Court of Judica-
         ture Act (36 & 37
         Vict., c.66) 20–009
         s.5 20–029
1875   Conspiracy and Protection
         of Property Act (38
         & 39 Vict., c.86)
         s.7 .... 27–033, 27–034
1876   Customs   Consolidation
         Act (39 & 40 Vict.,
         c.36)
         s.42 .... 6–036, 25–029
       Appellate Jurisdiction Act
         (39 & 40 Vict., c.59) ... 9–012,
                     9–044, 9–046, 9–047,
                     9–047, 16–010, 20–026,
                                  23–037
         s.3 9–047
         s.4 9–047
         s.5 9–047
         s.6 .... 2–018, 9–047, 20–029
         s.8 9–047
         s.9 9–047
1877   Colonial Stock Act (40 &
         41 Vict., c.59) 33–018

1878   Baths   and   Wash-house
         Act (c.14) 31–004
       Bishoprics Act (41 & 42
         Vict., c.68) 9–008
1879   Parliamentary   Elections
         and Corrupt Practices
         Act (42 & 43 Vict.,
         c.75) 10–061
1881   Newspaper Libel and Reg-
         istration Act (44 &
         45 Vict., c.60) 25–018
         s.8 25–018
       Fugitive Offenders Act
         (44   &   45   Vict.,
         c.69) 23–042
       Army Act (44 & 45 Vict.,
         c.75) 19–002,
                                  19–020
1882   Municipal   Corporations
         Act (45 & 46 Vict.,
         c.50)
         s.191(4) 31–017
1883   Explosive Substances Act
         (46   &   47   Vict.,
         c.3) 20–014
       Corrupt and Illegal Prac-
         tices Act (46 & 47
         Vict., c.33) 10–048
1884   Colonial   Prisoners   Re-
         moval Act (c.31) 35–029
       Representation of the Peo-
         ple Act (48 & 49
         Vict., c.3) 10–025
       Great Seal Act (47 & 47
         Vict., c.30) 8–023, 18–002
1886   Riot (Damage) Act (49 &
         50 Vict., c.38) 27–019
1887   Corners Act (50 & 51
         Vict., c. 46) 15–013
       British Settlements Act
         (50   &   51   Vict.,
         c.54) 35–020
       Appellate Jurisdiction Act
         (50 & 51 Vict., c.70) ... 9–012,
                                  16–010
1888   Local   Government   Act
         (51   &   52   Vict.,
         c.41) 2–036
       Oaths Act (51 & 52 Vict.,
         c.46) 10–002
       Law of Libel Amendment
         Act (51 & 52 Vict.,
         c.64) 25–003
         s.8 25–018
1889   Corrupt and Illegal Prac-
         tices Act 5–019

1889 Herring Fishery (Scotland) Act (c.52 & 53 Vict., c.23) 3–027
1890 Inland Revenue Regulation Act (c.21) 18–008
Colonial Courts of Admiralty Act (53 & 54 Vict., c.27) 37–001
Anglo-German Agreement Act (53 & 54 Vict., c.32) 4–014
Foreign Jurisdiction Act (53 & 54 Vict., c.32) ... 3–021, 35–008, 37–002
1892 Foreign Marriage Act (55 & 56 Vict., c.23) 29–014
1893 Rules Publication Act (56 & 57 Vict., c.73) 29–036
s.1 29–036
s.3 29–036
1894 Merchant Shipping Act (57 & 58 Vict., c.60)
s.515 27–019
s.735 36–010
s.636 36–010
s.686(1) 3–021
Local Government Act (56 & 57 Vict., c.73) 2–036
1895 Judicial Committee Amendment Act (58 & 59 Vict., c.44) 16–010
1900 Commonwealth of Australia Constitution Act (63 & 64 Vict., c.12) 36–009
ss.1–8 36–009
s.9 36–009
s.128 36–009
1901 Demise of the Crown Act (11 Edw. 7, c.5) 16–003
1903 Poor Prisoner's Defence Act (3 Edw. 7, c.38) 20–016
1904 Wireless Telegraphy Act (4 Edw. 7, c.24) 3–010
1905 Aliens Act (c.13) 23–023
1906 Street Betting Act (6 Edw. 7, c.43) 31–006
Workmen's Compensation Act (c.58) 18–028
1907 Criminal Appeal Act (7 Edw. 7, c.23) 9–049
1908 Appellate Jurisdiction Act (8 Edw. 7, c.51) 16–010

1908 Public Meeting Act (8 Edw. 7, c.66) 27–029
1910 Accession Declaration Act (10 Edw. 7&1 Geo.5, c.29) 14–003
Finance Act (10 Edw. 7 & 1 Geo. 5, c.35) 33–018
1911 Parliament Act (1 & 2 Geo. 5, c. 13) .. 2–007, 2–012, 4–035, 4–036, 7–018, 8–013, 8–019, 8–030, 8–031, 8–034, 8–035, 8–036, 9–024, 9–025, 9–027, 9–034, 10–018, 11–005, 12–009, 12–015, 29–001, 32–019
s.1(1) 8–034
(2) 12–015
s.2 8–038
(1) 8–035, 8–037
s.3 8–036
s.4 8–036
s.5 .... 8–036, 8–038
s.5 8–037
s.6 .... 8–036, 12–003
s.7 4–002
Copyright Act (1 & 2 Geo.5, c.46) 4–013
Official Secrets Act (1 & 2 Geo. 5, c.46) 20–014, 26–003
s.1 26–003
(2) 26–003
s.2 .... 26–003, 26–005
(1) 26–003
s.3 26–003
s.7 26–004
1913 Provisional Collection Act (3 & 4 Geo. 5, c.3) 7–013, 12–014
Foreign Jurisdiction Act (c.16) 3–021
Aliens Restrictions (Amendment) Act 1919 (9 & 10 Geo. 5, c.92) 23–019
1914 Re-election of Ministers Act (c.2) 10–003
British Nationality and Status of Aliens Act (c.4 & 5 Geo. 5, c.17) 23–002, 23–019
Defence of the Realm (Consolidation) Act (c.5 Geo. 5, c.63) 3–010, 19–041, 29–010

1914 Bankruptcy Act (4 & 5
         Geo. 5, c.59)
         s.122 35–003
      Government of Ireland
         Act (4 & 5 Geo. 5,
         c.90) 9–025
      Welsh Church Act (4 & 5
         Geo. 5, c.91) 9–025,
                                        10–005
1915 Defence of the Realm Act
         (c.5 & 6 Geo. 5,
         c.8) 29–010
1916 Parliament and Local
         Elections Act (6 & 7
         Geo. 5, c.44) 3–018
      Prevention of Corruption
         Act (6 & 7 Geo. 5,
         c.64) 5–019
1917 Parliament and Local
         Elections Act (7 & 8
         Geo. 5, c. 13) 3–018
1917 Chequers Estate Act (7 &
         8 Geo. 5, c.55) 17–025
1918 Parliament and Local
         Elections Act (8 & 9
         Geo. 5, c.22) 3–018
      Parliament (Qualification
         of Women) Act (8 &
         9 Geo. 5, c.47) 10–002
      Representation of the Peo-
         ple Act (7 & 8 Geo.
         5, c.64) 10–025
1919 Re-election of Ministers
         Act (9 & 10 Geo. 5,
         c.2)
         s.2 17–008
      Ministry of Transport Act
         (9 & 10 Geo. 5,
         c.50) 33–007
      Acquisition of Land (As-
         sessment of Compen-
         sation) Act (9 & 10
         Geo. 5, c.57)
         s.7(1) 4–004
      Church of England As-
         sembly (Powers) Act
         (9 & 10 Geo. 5, c.
         76) 15–014, 29–003
      Ministry of Agriculture
         and Fisheries Act
         (c.91) 18–003
      Aliens   Restrictions
         (Amendment) Act (9
         & 10 Geo. 5, c.92) 23–019
         s.3 25–009

1920 Indemnity Act (10 & 11
         Geo. 5, c.48) 19–040
      Emergency Powers Act
         (10 & 11 Geo. 5,
         c.55) 19–036, 19–037,
                    29–003, 29–010, 29–021
         s.1 19–036
         (1) 19–035
         s.2(1) 19–035
         (2) 19–035
         (3) 19–035
      Government of Ireland
         Act (10 & 11 Geo. 5,
         c.67) ... 2–004, 5–003, 5–013,
                                        5–030
      Official Secrets Act (10 &
         11 Geo. 5, c.75) 26–004
         s.1(1) 26–004
         s.2 26–004
         (1) 26–003
         s.3 26–005
         s.4 26–005
         s.7(4) 26–004
1921 Tribunals of Inquiry (Evi-
         dence) Act (11 & 12
         Geo. 5, c.7) ... 8–007, 8–008,
                           20–033, 30–016
1922 Irish Free State (Constitu-
         tion) Act (13 Geo. 5,
         c.1) 16–003
      Irish Free State (Agree-
         ment) (12 & 13 Geo.
         5, c.4) 2–004, 4–005
1925 War Charges (Validity)
         Act (15 & 16 Geo. 5,
         c.6) 3–010, 3–018
      Anglo-Italian (East Afri-
         can Territories) Act
         (15 & 16 Geo. 5,
         c.9) 15–031
      Housing Act (15 & 16
         Geo. 5, c.14) 4–004
      Administration of Estates
         Act (15 & 16 Geo. 5,
         c.23) 15–013
      Supreme Court of Judica-
         ture (Consolidation)
         Act (15 & 16 Geo. 5,
         c.23)
         s.12(1) 20–029
      Criminal Justice Act (15
         & 16 Geo. 5, c.86)
         s.41 20–050
1926 Re-election of Ministers
         Act (16 & 17 Geo. 5,
         c.19) 10–003

1926 Judicial Proceedings (Regulation of Reports) Act (16 & 17 Geo. 5, c.61) 20–040
1927 Prayer Book Measure 32–007
1928 Copyright Order Confirmation (Mechanical Instruments: Royalties) Act (18 & 19 Geo. 5, c.Iii) 4–013
Representation of the People (Equal Franchise) Act (18 & 19 Geo. 5, c.12) 10–025
1929 Local Government Act (19 & 20 Geo. 5, c.17) 2–036
1930 Housing Act (20 & 21 Geo. 5, c. 39) 4–004
Poor Law Act (20 & 21 Geo. 5, c.17) 2–036
British North American Act (20 & 21 Geo. 5, c.26) 36–007
1931 House of Commons Disqualification (Declaration of Law) Act (21 & 22 Geo. 5, c. 13) 10–004
Statute of Westminster (22 & 23 Geo. 5, c.4) 2–007, 4–011, 7–019, 14–006, 35–003, 35–013, 36–003, 36–013, 36–015, 37–009, 37–010
s.1 36–008
ss.2–6 .... 36–009, 36–012
s.2 .... **36–004**, 36–010, 36–014, 37–010
(2) 4–013
s.3 .... 35–026, 36–005, 36–010, 36–014, 37–010
s.4 .... 4–011, 4–012, 4–013, 7–019, 36–006, 36–008, 36–010, 36–011, 36–014
s.5 .... 36–009, 36–010
s.6 36–009
s.7 36–007
(3) 36–007
s.8 .... 36–009, 36–012
s.9 36–009
(1) 36–009
(2) 36–011
(3) 36–006, 36–010, 36–011

1931 Statute of Westminster —cont.
s.10(2) 36–011
s.11 36–003
Architects (Registration) Act (21 & 22 Geo. 5, c.33) 30–017
1933 Administration of Justice (Miscellaneous Provisions) Act (23 & 24 Geo. 5, c.36) 32–002
Local Government Act (23 & 24 Geo. 5, c.51) 2–036
1934 Law Reform (Miscellaneous Provisions) Act (24 & 25 Geo. 5, c.41)
s.1 33–011
Incitement to Disaffection Act (24 & 25 Geo. 5, c.56) 25–009
s.1 25–009
s.2 25–009
1935 Government of India Act (26 Geo. 5 & 1 Edw. 8, c.2) 35–026
Law Reform (Married Women and Tortfeasors) Act (25 & 26 Geo. 5, c. 5, c.30) ... 33–011
1936 Declaration of Abdication Act (1 Edw. 8 & 1 Geo. 6, c.3) 14–002, 14–005, 36–006
Public Order (1 Edw. 8 & 1 Geo. 6, c.6) 27–029
s.1 .... 14–003, 27–040
s.2 27–040
s.5 .... 27–022, 27–023
(1) 27–025
(2) 27–024
Public Health Act (26 Geo. 5 & 1 Edw. 8, c.49) 24–051, 28–011
Private Legislation Procedure (Scotland) Act (26 Geo. 5 & 1 Edw. 8, c.52) 11–036
1937 Regency Act (1 Edw. 8 & 1 Geo. 6, c.16) 4–038, 14–008, 14–009, 14–010
Ministers of the Crown Act (1 Edw. 8 & 1 Geo. 6, c.38) ... 2–016, 7–007, 7–018, 10–004, 17–025
s.4 7–007

1937 Physical Training and
        Recreation Act (1
        Edw. 8 & 1 Geo. 5,
        c.46) 17–025
     Factories Act (1 Edw. 8 &
        1 Geo. 6, c.67) 33–002
1938 Administration of Justice
        (Miscellaneous Pro-
        visions) Act (1 & 2
        Geo. 6, c.63) 32–002,
                                      32–022
1939 Emergency Powers (De-
        fence) Act (2 & 3
        Geo. 6, c.62) 19–042,
        19–044, 19–047, 29–010,
                                      33–003
     s.1(3) 29–015
     s.2 .... 3–010, 19–041
     s.22 29–012
     Import, Export and Cus-
        toms Powers (De-
        fence) Act (c.69) 19–047,
                                      29–010
1940 Emergency Powers (De-
        fence) Act (3 & 4
        Geo. 6, c.20) 19–043,
                                      19–047
     Truck Act (3 & 4 Geo. 6,
        c.38) 3–018
     Emergency Powers (De-
        fence) Act (No. 2) (3
        & 4 Geo. 6, c.45) 3–018,
        19–042, 19–043
     Finance (No. 2) Act (3 &
        4 Geo. 6, c.48) 31–005
1941 Prolongation of Parlia-
        ment Act (5 & 6 Geo.
        6, c.37) 3–018
1942 Minister of Works and
        Planning   Act
        (c.23) 18–003
1943 Parliament (Elections and
        Meeting) Act (6 & 7
        Geo. 6, c.25) .. 8–090, 8–012
     Prolongation of Parlia-
        ment Act (6 & 7 Geo.
        6, c.46) 3–018
1944 Law Officers Act (7 & 8
        Geo. 6, c.25) 18–013
     Education Act (7 & 8 Geo.
        6, c. 31)
     s.68 .... 22–010, 32–020
     National Fire Service Reg-
        ulations (Indemnity)
        Act (7 & 8 Geo. 6,
        c.35) 29–022

1944 Prolongation of Parlia-
        ment Act (7 & 8 Geo.
        6, c.45) 3–018
     Ministry of National In-
        surance Act (c.46) ... 18–003
1945 Representation of the Peo-
        ple Act (8 & 9 Geo.
        6, c.5) 10–025
     British Settlements Act (9
        & 10 Geo. 6, c.7) 35–020
     Statutory Orders (Special
        Procedure) Act (9 &
        10 Geo. 5, c.18) 11–036,
                          29–003, 30–025
     Law Reform (Contribu-
        tory Negligence) Act
        (8 & 9 Geo. 6,
        c.28) 33–011
     Requisitioned Land and
        War Works Act (8 &
        9 Geo. 6, c.43) 19–050
1946 Ministry of Defence
        Act 18–003
     Bank of England Act (9 &
        10 Geo. 6, c.27) 28–002
     Statutory Instruments Act
        (9 & 10 Geo. 6,
        c.36) 29–004, 29–019,
                                      29–036
     s.1 29–036
     s.2 .... 29–036, 29–037
     s.3(1) 29–036
         (2) 29–036, 29–037
     s.4 29–022
         (1) 29–022
         (2) 29–036
     s.5 .... 29–020, 29–022
     s.6 29–020
     s.7(3) 29–022
     s.8 29–037
     Coal Industry Nationalisa-
        tion Act (9 & 10 Geo.
        6, c.59) 28–002
     s.3(1) 28–007
     Atomic Energy Act (9 &
        10 Geo. 6, c.68) 33–011
     New Towns Act (9 & 10
        Geo. 6, c.68) 28–003
     National Health Service
        Act (9 & 10 Geo. 6,
        c.81) 28–011
     s.13 28–011
     Cable and Wireless Act (9
        & 10 Geo. 6, c.82) 28–002

1947 Ceylon Independence Act
(11 & 12 Geo. 6,
c.7) 4–014, 36–013
Indian Independence Act
(10 & 11 Geo. 6,
c.30) 4–014, 36–013,
36–014, 36–015, 37–010
Crown Proceedings Act
(10 & 11 Geo. 6,
c.44) ... 1–002, 2–007, 2–030,
11–022, 15–008, 15–009,
15–010, 15–017, 15–019,
18–010, 18–025, 19–004,
20–002, 20–003, 22–007,
28–002, 28–009, 28–012,
33–001, 33–003, 33–011,
33–017, 33–018, 33–022
Pt I 33–011, 33–017
s.1 .... 33–004, 33–019
s.2 33–010
(1) 33–008, 33–009
(2) 33–010
(5) 33–010
s.3 .... 3–007, 33–011
s.4 33–011
s.9 28–002
s.10 .. 32–019, 33–011, 33–011,
33–013
s.10a 33–013
s.10(1) 33–012
(2) 33–011
s.11 .... 33–009, 33–014
s.13 ... 33–004, 33–017, 33–019
s.14 33–019
s.15 33–017
s.17 .... 15–007, 33–017
s.21(1) 24–034, 33–017
s.22 33–017
s.23 33–018
s.24 33–019
s.25 33–020
s.26 33–020
s.27(1) 18–027
s.28 33–022
(1) 33–021, 33–022
s.29(1) 33–019
s.32 15–009
s.38(2) 33–010, 33–017
(3) 33–015
s.40 32–019
(1) 33–015, 33–019
(2) 33–003, 33–010
(c) 2–001
(3) 33–003

1947 Crown Proceedings Act
—cont.
s.52 2–001
s.53 33–003
Transport Act (10 & 11
Geo. 6, c.49) 28–002,
28–010
Town and Country Plan-
ning Act (10 & 11
Geo. 6, c.51) 28–010
Electricity Act (10 & 11
Geo. 6, c.54) 28–002
1948 Requisitioned Land and
War Works Act (11
& 12 Geo. 6, c.17) 19–050
National Assistance Act
(11 & 12 Geo. 6,
c.29)
s.47 24–028
Companies Act (11 & 12
Geo. 6, c.38) 32–019
British Nationality Act (11
& 12 Geo. 6, c.56) ... 15–022,
15–024, 23–002, 23–003,
23–004, 23–005, 23–011,
23–015
Pt I 23–003
Pt II 23–003
s.1 .... 15–026, **23–003**
s.2 .... **23–003**
s.3 .... **23–003**
s.4 23–004
s.5 23–004
s.12 23–004
Laying of Documents be-
fore Parliament (In-
terpretation) Act (11
& 12 Geo. 6, c.59) 2–007,
29–022
Representation of the People Act (11 & 12
Geo. 6, c.65) 10–025
Gas Act (11 & 12 Geo. 6,
c.67) 24–051, 28–002
1949 Parliament Act (12, 13 &
14 Geo. 6, c.103) 2–007,
2–012, 4–035, 4–036,
6–020, 7–018, 8–032,
8–033, 8–034, 8–035,
8–036, 8–038, 9–024,
9–025, 9–027, 9–034,
10–018, 11–005, 29–001
Ireland Act (12, 13 & 14
Geo. 6, c.41) ... 2–005, 3–018,
10–005, 36–003, 36–020
s.1(2) 4–005

1949 Ireland Act—*cont.*
    s.2 23–018
    s.5(1) 22–018
    Lands Tribunal Act (12, 13 & 14 Geo. 6, c.42) 32–015
    Wireless Telegraphy Act (12, 13 & 14 Geo. 6, c.54) 26–017, 30–016
    Airways Corporation Act (12, 13 & 14 Geo. 6, c.57) 28–002
    Legal Aid and Advice Act (12, 13 & 14 Geo. 6, c.57) 18–009, 20–013
    British North America (12, 13 & 14 Geo. 6, c.81) Act 4–012, 36–007
    India (Consequential Provisions) Act (12, 13 & 14 Geo. 6, c.92) 36–024
1950 Foreign Compensation Act (14 Geo. 6, c.12) 15–022, 30–016
    s.4 32–017
1951 Courts-Martial (Appeals) Act (14 & 15 Geo. 6, c.46) 19–023
    Price Control and Orders (Indemnity) Act (14 & 15 Geo. 6, c.59) 29–022
1952 Diplomatic Immunities (Commonwealth Countries and Republic of Ireland) Act (15 & 16 Geo. 6 & 1 Eliz. 2, c.18) 36–026
    Cinematography Act (15 & 16 Geo. 6 & 1 Eliz. 2, c.28) 25–038
    Crown Lessees (Protection of Sub-Tenants) Act (15 & 16 Geo. 6 & 1 Eliz. 2, c.40) 28–010
    Customs and Excise Act (15 & 16 Geo. 6 & 1 Eliz. 2, c.44) 6–036
    Prison Act (15 & 16 Geo. 6 & 1 Eliz. 2, c.52) ... 24–031
    s.12 24–031
    Defamation Act (15 & 16 Geo. 6 & 1 Eliz.2, c.66) 25–003, 33–011

1952 Visiting Forces Act (15 & 16 Geo. 6 & 1 Eliz. 2, c.67) 15–033, 19–026
    Pt I 19–026
    Pt II 19–026
    s.9 19–027
1953 Regency Act (2 & 3 Eliz. 2, c.1) 4–038, 14–008, 14–010
    Post Office Act (1 & 2 Eliz. 2, c. 36)
    s.11 25–029
    Royal Titles Act (1 & 2 Eliz. 2, c.9) 4–008
    Prevention of Crime Act (1 & 2 Eliz. 2, c.36) ... 27–031
1954 Law Reform (Limitation of Actions) Act (2 & 3 Eliz. 2) 15–019
    Wireless Telegraphy (Validation of Charges) Act (3 & 4 Eliz. 2, c.2) 3–010, 3–018
    Rights of Entry (Gas and Electricity Boards) Act (c.21) 24–051
    Atomic Energy Authority Act (2 & 3 Eliz. 2, c.32) 28–011
    Pharmacy Act (2 & 3 Eliz. 2, c.61) 30–017
1955 Locos Islands Act (3 & 4 Eliz. 2, c.5) 4–011
    Army Act (3 & 4 Eliz. 2, c.18) 19–023
    s.134 19–023
    Aliens Employment Act (4 & 5 Eliz. 2,c.18) ... 23–019
    Air Force (c.19)
    ss.24–31 19–023
1956 Magistrates' Courts (Appeals from Binding-Over Orders) Act (4 & 5 Eliz. 2, c.44) 24–028
    Copy Right Act (4 & 5 Eliz. 2, c.74) 4–013
1957 Coroners Court Act 15–013
    Ghana Independence Act (5 & 6 Eliz. 2, c.6) 4–014
    House of Commons Disqualification Act (5 & 6 Eliz. 2, c.20) 10–004
    Solicitors Act (5 & 6 Eliz. 2, c.27) 20–042
    Electricity Act (5 & 6 Eliz. 2, c.48)

1957 Electricity Act—*cont.*
s.38 28–011
Geneva Conventions Act
(5 & 6 Eliz. 2,
c.52) 3–015
Naval Discipline Act (5 &
6 Eliz. 2, c.53) 19–003
ss.2–4 19–023
ss.9–10 19–023
s.42 19–023
Federation of Malaya In-
dependence Act
(c.60)
s.3 37–012
1958 Life Peerages Act (6 & 7
Eliz. 2, c.21) ... 9–011, 9–015
Land Powers (Defence)
Act (6 & 7 Eliz. 2,
c.30) 19–050
Public Records Act (6 & 7
Eliz. 2, c.51) 17–023
Tribunals and Inquiries
Act (6 & 7 Eliz. 2,
c.66) 30–018, 32–004,
34–002
s.9 32–015
s.11 32–016
Sched. 1 32–015
1959 Defamation Act
s.9 13–013
Highways Act (7 & 8 Eliz.
2, c. 25) .. 27–028, 30–026A,
32–018
Judicial Pensions Act (8 &
9 Eliz. 2, c.9) 20–029
Chevening Estate Act (7
& 8 Eliz. 2, c.49) 17–025
Town and Country Plan-
ning Act (7 & 8 Eliz.
2, c.53)
s.33 .... 30–018, 30–026
Obscene Publications Act
(7 & 8 Eliz. 2, c.66) 6–036,
25–025, 25–026, 25–028,
25–029, 25–033, 25–038
s.1 25–025
s.2(4) 25–028
s.3 25–027
s.4 25–026
1960 Ghana (Consequential
Provisions Act (8 & 9
Eliz. 2, c.41) 36–016
Finance Act (8 & 9 Eliz. 2,
c.44)
s.39(5) 3–018

1960 Cyprus Act (8 & 9 Eliz. 2,
c.52)
s.2(1) 35–010
Administration of Justice
Act (c.65) 20–044
s.1 24–039
s.14 .... 24–037, 24–038
s.15 24–039
1961 Crown Estates Act (9 &
10 Eliz. 2, c.55) 15–013
1962 Commonwealth Immi-
grants Act (10 & 11
Eliz. 2, c.21) 23–005,
23–023
South Africa Act (10 & 11
Eliz. 2, c.23) 36–020
Transport Act (10 & 11
Eliz. 2, c.46) 24–042
s.3(1) 28–007
(4) 28–007
1963 Ecclesiastical Jurisdiction
Measure (No.1) 22–024
Purchase Tax Act (c.9)
s.27(2) 31–005
London Government Act
(c.33) 2–037
Malaysia Act (c.35)
s.5 37–013
Peerage Act (c.48) 9–005,
17–033
s.3 10–005
s.5 10–035
Kenya Independence Act
(c.54)
s.6 37–013
1964 Defence (Transfer of
Functions) Act
(c.15) 18–001, 18–003
s.2 15–008
Industrial Training Act
(c.16)
s.1(4) 31–005
Continental Shelf Act
(c.29) 3–020
Emergency Powers Act
(c.38) 19–036, 19–037
s.1 19–037
s.2 .... 19–037, 29–042
Malawi Independence Act
(c.46)
s.5 37–013
Police Act (c.48) 15–010,
21–002, 21–003, 21–016,
21–018, 21–021
s.14 19–032
s.41 21–019

1964 Police Act—*cont.*
    s.45(4) 28–006
    s.48 21–011
    s.51 .... 24–019, 33–010
      (3) 24–021
    Emergency Laws (Re-enactment and Repeals) Act (c.60) 19–043
    British North America Act (c.73) 4–001
    Obscene Publications Act (c.74)
    s.1 25–025
    Statute Law Revision Act (c.79) 3–013
    Diplomatic Privileges Act (c.81) 15–032, 36–026
1965 Ministerial Salaries and Members' Pensions Act (Northern Ireland)(c.18) 7–018
    War Damage Act (c.18) ... 3–019
                              15–017
    Law Commissions Act (c.22) 9–017
    Finance Act (c.25) 3–015
    Carriage of Goods by Road Act (c.37) 35–003
    Statutory Orders (Special Procedure) Act (c.43) 11–038, 29–003
    Backing of Warrants (Republic of Ireland) Act (c.45) 23–041, 23–048, 23–049
    s.1(1) 23–048
      (2) 23–048
      (3) 23–048
    s.2 23–048
    s.3 23–049
    New Towns Act (c.49) 28–003
    s.35(3) 28–011
    Commons Registration Act (c.64) ... 30–016, 32–023
    Murder (Abolition of Death Penalty) Act (c.71) 22–045
    Race Relations Act (c.73) ... 3–015, 25–010
    Southern Rhodesia Act (c.76) 35–025
1966 Church of England Convocations Act (c.2) ... 15–014
    Tribunals and Inquiries Act (c.43) 30–018

1966 Prices and Incomes Act (c.53) 13–019
1967 West Indies Act (c.4) 36–016
    General Rate Act (c.9)
    s.69 32–010
    Parliamentary Commissioner Act (c.13) 7–016
    s.8(4) 17–007
    s.10 25–003
      (5) 13–002
    Sched. 2 34–009
    Sched. 3 34–009
    Royal Assent (c.23) 2–007, 4–026, 8–011, 11–031
    Marine, etc., Broadcasting (Offences) Act (c.41) 3–020
    Public Records Act (c.44) 17–023
    Criminal Law Act (c.58) ... 9–013, 10–005, 14–020, 22–031
    s.3 .... 19–032, 24–010
    Sched. 3 10–005
    Antarctic Treaty Act (c.65) 3–020
    Welsh Language Act (c.66) 3–020
    Fugitive Offenders Act (c.68) 23–042, 23–047
    s.3(1)(c) 23–043
    Wireless Telegraphy Act (c.72) 26–017
1968 Provisional Collection of Taxes Act (c.2) 2–026, 11–005, 12–003, 29–012
    Administration of Justice Act (c.5)
    s.1(1)(a) 9–012
    Commonwealth Immigrants Act (c.9) 23–005
    National Loans Act (c.13) 12–012
    Consular Relations Act (c.18) 15–032, 15–033
    Courts-Martial (Appeals) Act (c.20) 19–023
    Agriculture (Miscellaneous Provisions) Act (c.34)
    s.3 29–019
1968 International Organisations Act (c.48) 15–033
1968 Caravan Sites Act (c.52) 32–012

1968	Theatres Act (c.54)	25–037
	s.1(4)	25–037
	s.2	25–037
	s.3	25–037
	s.4	25–003
	s.7(1)	25–037
	s.8	25–037
	Theft Act (c.60)	20–014
	Domestic and Appellate Proceedings (Restriction of Publicity) Act (c.63)	20–040
	Gaming Act (c.65)	
	s.43(2)	24–044
	Medicines Act (c.67)	30–017
	Transport Act (c.73)	
	s.106(1)	28–007
1969	Parliamentary Commissioner (Northern Ireland) Act (c.10)	34–010
	Genocide Act (c.12)	23–043
	Representation of the People Act (c.15)	
	s.1	10–025
	Foreign Compensation Act (c.20)	
	s.3	32–017
	Immigration Appeals Act (c.21)	
	s.24(2)	29–036
	Family Reform Act (c.46)	10–005
	Post Office Act (c.48)	2–030, 28–001, 28–012
	s.9(4)	28–007
	s.29	28–002, 28–012
	s.30	28–012
	Statute Law (Repeals) Act (c.52)	2–007
	Children and Young Persons Act (c.54)	33–024
1970	Income and Corporation Taxes Act (c.9)	12–013
	Taxes Management Act (c.9)	12–013
	s.2	24–051, 30–016
	s.4	30–016
	Equal Pay Act (c.41)	4–022
1971	Rolls-Royce (Purchase) Act (c.9)	28–002, 28–014
	Courts Act (c.23)	9–0–17, 18–009, 20–009
	s.4	20–030
	ss.16	20–026
	s.17	20–026, 20–030
	(4)	20–030

1971	Courts Act—*cont.*	
	s.21(3)	20–030
	(6)	20–030
	Coinage Act (c.24)	15–015
	Misuse of Drugs Act (c.38)	30–017
	s.23(1)	24–043
	(2)	24–004, 24–019
	Wild Creatures and Forest Law Act (c.47)	15–015
	Statute Law (Repeals) Act (c.52)	10–005
	Sheriff Courts (Scotland) Act (c.58)	20–026
	s.12	20–030
	Tribunals and Inquiries Act (c.62) ..	28–005, 30–018, 30–027, 32–004
	Diplomatic and Other Privileges Act (c.64)	
	s.4	15–033
	Civil Aviation Act (c.75)	15–011
	Immigration Act (c.77)	3–027, 6–025, 6–026, 6–035, 22–007, 22–009, 23–005, 23–007, 23–018, 23–019, 23–023, 23–024, 23–028, 23–037, 23–037, 23–038, 23–039, 24–033, 29–004, 32–012, 36–025
	s.1	23–025
	s.2	23–025
	s.3	23–026, 23–036, 29–019
	(2)	23–024
	(5)	23–034
	(6)	23–034, 23–036
	(9)	23–026
	s.5	23–034
	s.7	23–034
	s.8	23–026
	s.10	23–026
	s.16	23–028
	s.19	23–024
	s.24	23–028
	s.33	23–028
	(1)	23–028
	(5)	23–019
	Sched. 2	23–028
	Town and Country Planning Regulations (London) Indemnity Act (c.78)	29–022
1972	Island of Rockall (c.2)	3–020
	Civil List Act (c.7)	15–013
	s.6	15–013

1972 Northern   Ireland   Act
         (c.10) 3–019, 19–040
      Northern Ireland (Tempo-
         rary Provisions) Act
         (c.22) 2–005, 4–005,
                                   11–022
      Finance Act (c.41) 12–003
      s.54(8) 33–020
      Housing   Finance   Act
         (c.47) 3–018
      Parliamentary and Other
         Pensions   Act
         (c.48) 17–025
      s.26 17–025
      National   Health   Service
         (Scotland)   Act
         (c.58) 34–015
      Gas Act (c.60) 24–051, 28–002
      European   Communities
         Act (c.68) 3–020, 4–004,
                            4–016, 4–020, 4–030,
                            4–034, 4–039, 5–021,
                            5–030, 6–012, 6–015,
                            6–016, 6–027, 15–029,
                            15–030, 22–016
      s.1(3) 6–016
      s.2 .... 4–021, 6–019, 29–011
         (1) 4–007, 4–016, 6–017,
                                   6–021
         (2) 4–016, 5–023, 5–037,
                  6–017, 6–018, 6–021, 6–022,
                  6–038, 12–006, 23–026
         (3) 6–016
         (4) 4–016, 4–020, 4–021,
                            4–022, 29–013
      s.3 .... 4–016, 4–023, 6–018
      s.5 12–012
      s.11 3–020
      Sched. 2 .... 6–017, 6–018,
                                   29–011
      Local   Government   Act
         (c.70) 2–036
      s.235(1) 29–003
      s.254(2) 29–013
      Criminal   Justice   Act
         (c.71) 27–002
      s.36 20–032
      Northern Ireland (Border
         Poll) Act (c.77) 1–016
1973 Administration of Justice
         Act (c.15) 20–029
      Northern Ireland (Consti-
         tution) Act (c.36) 1–016,
                                   4–005
      s.1 4–005
      s.32(3) 16–003

1973 National   Health   Service
         Re-organisation Act
         (c.32) 34–015
      Fair Trading Act (c.41) 28–004,
                                   30–016
      Pakistan Act (c.48) 36–020
      Bangladesh Act (c.49) 36–020
      Northern Ireland (Emer-
         gency   Provisions)
         Act (c.53) 19–039
      Government   Trading
         Funds Act (c.63) 18–023
1974 Local   Government   Act
         (c.7) 34–016
      s.32(3) 34–017
      s.34(3) 34–017
      Contingencies Fund Act
         (c.18) 12–003
      Juries Act (c.23) ... 20–019, 20–022
      s.1 .... 20–018, 24–031
      s.2(5) 20–019
      s.12(6) 20–020
      s.17 .... 20–017, 20–018
      Sched. 1, Pt II 24–031
      Lord Chancellor (Tenure
         of Office and Dis-
         charge of Ecclesiasti-
         cal Functions) Act
         (c.25) 9–015
      Northern   Ireland   Act
         (c.28) 4–005, 29–002
      Pakistan Act (c.34) 36–020
      Health   and   Safety   at
         Work,   etc.   Act
         (c.37) 10–023, 13–019,
                  28–006, 29–004, 30–013
      s.10 28–006
      s.11 28–006
      s.16 .... 28–006, 29–004
      s.17 29–004
      s.18 28–006
      s.20 24–051
      s.48 15–019
      s.72 15–019
      Consumer   Credit   Act
         (c.39) 28–004, 30–016
      s.1 28–005
      s.3 28–005
      s.4 28–005
      Prevention of Terrorism
         (Temporary   Provi-
         sions) Act (c.55) 14–051,
                                   23–048

1975 Social Security Act
(c.14) 3–016
House of Commons Dis-
qualification Act
(c.24) 10–006, 10–007,
10–009, 10–062, 17–007,
17–008, 17–025, 20–037
s.1 10–007
(2) 10–008
(4) 10–009
s.2 10–010
s.6 10–012
s.7 .... 10–013, 10–047
s.8 10–014
s.10 10–014
Sched. 1
Pt I 10–007
Pt II 10–007
Pt III 10–007
Pt IV 10–011
Pt VI 10–008, 10–011
Ministers of the Crown
Act (c.26) .. 17–007, 18–001,
18–003
s.5(5) 18–003
Ministerial and Other Sal-
aries Act (c.27) 2–016,
9–016, 10–010, 10–011,
10–024, 17–007, 17–025,
18–004
s.1 10–019
s.2 10–018
Sched. 1, Pt V 18–004
Referendum Act (c.33) 1–016,
4–019
Farriers (Registration Act
(c.35) 30– 017
British Leyland Act
(c.43) 28–002
Criminal Jurisdiction Act
(c.59) 23–048, 23–049
Sex Discrimination Act
(c.65) 6–025, 10–059,
28–006, 29–013
Housing Finance (Special
Provisions) Act
(c.67) 3–018
Industry Act (c.68)
s.7(1) 28–007
Employment Protection
Act (c.71)
s.6 29–004
Civil List Act (c.82) 15–013
1976 Prevention of Terrorism
(Temporary Provi-
sions) Act (c.8) 14–051

1976 Statute Law (Repeals) Act
(c.16)
Pt VII 36–024
Police Act (c.46) 21–021,
29–004
s.83 29–004
s.87 29–004
Parliamentary and other
Pensions and Salaries
Act (c.48)
s.6 .... 12–018, 34–007
Armed Forces Act
(c.52) 19–008
Bail Act (c.63) 24–024
s.4 24–024
s.5(3) 24–024
s.5B 24–024
s.9 24–024
Sched. 1 24–024
Pt I 24–024
Pt IIA 24–024
Race Relations Act
(c.74) 28–006
Energy Act (c.76) 19–038
s.1 19–038
Dock Work Regulation
Act (c.79) 9–027
Rent (Agriculture) Act
(c.80) 4–027
Fishery Limits Act
(c.86) 3–020
1977 Aircraft and Shipping In-
dustries Act (c.3) 9–027,
28–002
Social Security (Miscellaneous Provisions)
Act (c.5)
s.14(8) 3–018
Rent (Agriculture)
Amendment Act
(c.17) 4–027
Farriers (Registration
(Amendment) Act
(c.31) 30–017
Patents Act (c.37) 3–007
ss.55–59 .... 3–007, 33–011
Criminal Law Act (c.45) ... 15–013,
24–042, 25–039
s.1 27–038
s.5(3) 25–028
s.6 .... 24–042, 24–043
s.7 .... 24–042, 24–043
s.8 .... 24–042, 24–043
s.9 24–042
s.10 24–043
s.12A 24–042

1977 Criminal Law Act—*cont.*
          s.38 23–041
          s.53 25–026
      Housing (Homeless Per-
          sons) Act (c.48) 32–013
      National Health Service
          Act (c.49) 28–003
1978 Commonwealth Develop-
          ment   Corporation
          Act (c.2) 28–006, 36–028
      Northern Ireland (Emer-
          gency   Provisions)
          Act (c.5) 19–040
          s.19(1) 19–040
      Wales Act (c. 52) .. 1–016, 5–004,
                                   5–006
      European Assembly Elec-
          tions Act (c.10) 6–015,
                                   6–019
          s.6 6–019
          (1) 6–020, 15–030
      Solomon   Islands   Act
          (c.15) 23–016
      Internationally Protected
          Persons Act (c.17) 3–021,
                          23–043, 23–044
      Oaths Act (c.19) ... 10–002, 16–003
      Judicature (Northern Ire-
          land) Act (c.23) 20–010
          s.12 20–026
          s.13(1) 20–029
      Suppression of Terrorism
          Act (c.26) 3–021, 14–050,
                 23–043, 23–044, 23–048
      Interpretation Act (c.30)
          s.5 .... 2–001, 35–001, 36–003
          s.25 36–004
          Sched. 1 .... 2–002, 35–001,
                                   36–003
      State   Immunity   Act
          (c.33) 1–013, 15–023,
                                   15–032
          s.3 15–032
          s.4 15–032
          s.5 15–032
          s.6 15–032
          s.7 15–032
          s.10 15–032
          s.13 15–032
          s.16 15–032
          s.20 15–033
      House of Commons (Ad-
          ministration)   Act
          (c.36) 10–023
      Protection of Children Act
          (c.37) 25–030

1978 Scotland Act (c.51) 1–016,
                    5–004, 5–006, 5–015,
                                   5–021
          s.28(7) 5–014
          s.35 5–014
          s.58 5–014
1979 Customs and Excise Man-
          agement Act (c.2) 24–050
          s.27 24–050
          s.49 25–029
          s.77 24–050
          s.112 24–050
          s.113 24–050
          s.152(d) 2–022
          s.161 24–050
      Customs and Excise Man-
          agement Act (c.2) 18–008
      Estate   Agents   Act
          (c.38) 30–016
      Crown   Agents   Act
          (c.43) 28–006
          s.1(5) 28–011
          Sched. 3 28–006
      Justices of the Peace Act
          (c.55) 18–002
          s.7(2) 20–030
1980 Reserve   Forces   Act
          (c.9) 19–003
      Protection of Trading In-
          terests Act (c.11) 3–021
      National Health Service
          (Invalid   Direction)
          Act (c.15) 3–018
      British   Aerospace   Act
          (c.26) 28–013
      Magistrates' Courts Act
          (c.43) 20–009
          s.1 24–007
          (4) 24–007
          ss.17A–17C 20–017
          s.41 24–024
          s.43B 24–024
          s.71 20–040
          s.115 24–027
          s.117 24–024
          s.143 29–010
      Housing Act (c.51)
          s.73 15–019
          s.23(1) 32–020
      Imprisonment (Temporary
          Provisions)   Act
          (c.57) 2–022
      Limitation Act (c.58)
          s.37 33–018
          Sched. 1, Pt II 33–018

1980   Civil   Aviation   Act
     (c.60) 28–002, 28–013
     Criminal   Justice   (Scot-
     land) Act (c.62) 4–009,
                              27–036
     Local   Government   Plan-
     ning   and   Land   Act
     (c.65)
     s.184 34–017
     Highways Act (c.66) 30–002
     s.16 30–025
     s.106 30–025
     s.137 .... 27–004, 27–028
1981   International   Organisa-
     tions Act (c.9)
     Parliamentary   Commis-
     sioner   (Consular
     Complaints)   Act
     (c.11) 34–009
     Representation of the Peo-
     ple Act (c.34) 10–047
     s.1 .... 3–018, 10–002, 24–031
     British   Telecommunica-
     tions Act (c.38) 2–020,
                      28–001, 28–013
     s.3 28–013
     s.23 2–030
     s.29 2–030
     s.59 7–003
     s.79 28–014
     Indecent   Displays   (Con-
     trol) Act (c.42) 25–030
     s.1(5) 25–030
     Atomic Energy (Miscella-
     neous   Provisions)
     Act (c.48) 28–014
     Contempt   of   Court   Act
     (c.49) 20–040, 20–043,
           20–052, 22–012, 25–012,
                   25–013, 25–014
     s.2 25–013
     (2) 25–013
     s.3 25–013
     s.4 25–015
     s.5 25–013
     s.6(c) 20–051, 25–014
     s.7 .... 20–044, 25–013
     s.9 20–050
     s.10 ... 20–050, 25–016, 25–022
     s.11 20–048
     s.12 20–053
     s.14 20–045
     s.15 20–045
     Sched. 1 25–013

1981   Supreme Court Act (c.54) ... 2–007,
                              20–026
     s.1(2) 9–018
     s.5(1)(a) 9–018
     s.8 20–048
     s.9 20–029
     s.11 2–018
     (2) 20–029
     (8) 20–029
     s.12 20–029
     (7) 20–029
     s.14(4A) 20–045
     s.29(3) 32–004
     s.31 .... 2–024, 32–001,
                   32–002, 33–017
     (1)(c) 32–022
     (6) 32–003
     s.42 20–013
     s.62 20–018
     s.86 29–003
     British   Nationality   Act
     (c.61) 2–007, 14–015,
           15–022, 15–024, 15–026,
           22–054, 23–005, 23–006,
           23–007, 23–014, 23–018,
           23–028, 35–001, 35–007
     s.1 .... 15–022, 23–007
     (3) 23–007
     (4) 23–007
     s.2 23–007
     (1)(d) 23–025
     (2) 23–025
     s.3 ..... 23–009, 23–026, 35–013
     (3) 23–007
     s.4 .... 23–009, 23–015
     s.5 .... 23–009, 35–007
     s.6 23–008
     (1) 23–008
     (2) 23–008
     s.7 23–009
     s.8 23–009
     s.9 23–009
     s.11(2) 23–007
     s.12 23–011
     (4) 14–015
     s.15 35–007
     s.24 14–015
     s.29 14–015
     s.30 ... 14–015, 15–022, 15–026
     s.31 ... 15–022, 15–026, 23–006
     s.37 ... 10–026, 15–022, 23–006
     s.38 .... 23–016, 35–008
     s.39 .... 23–025, 23–007
     (2) 23–007
     s.40 23–011
     s.44 .... 23–008, 32–008

1981 British Nationality Act
      —cont.
      s.44(1) 32–018
         (2) 32–018
         (3) 32–018
      s.50(1) 23–006, 23–007,
                    35–008, 35–010
         (2) 23–007
      s.52(6) 9–013
      Sched. 1 23–008
      Sched. 6 35–010
      Sched. 7 .... 9–013, 10–005
      Local Government, Plan-
         ning and Land Act
         (c.65) 28–003
      Acquisition of Land Act
         (c.67) 22–053, 30–002,
                    30–025, 32–015
      s.13 30–025
      Broadcasting Act (c.68)
      s.4(3) 31–025
      Wildlife and Countryside
         Act (c.69)
      s.24 28–006
      s.37 29–003
1982 Canada Act (c.11) ... 3–013, 4–012,
                    35–013, 36–008, 36–015,
                    36–022
      Preamble 36–008
      s.1 36–008
      s.2 .... 4–011, 36–008
      Taking of Hostages Act
         (c.28) 3–021, 14–050,
                    23–044, 23–045
      Local Government (Mis-
         cellaneous   Provi-
         sions) Act (c.30)
      s.3 25–030
      s.17 24–051
      s.27 24–051
      Sched. 3 25–030
      Government Finance Act
         (c.32) 28–006
      s.26 28–006
      s.27 28–006
      Cinematograph (Amend-
         ment) Act (c.33) 25–038
      Aviation   Security   Act
         (c.36) 3–020, 14–050,
                    23–042
      Legal Aid Act (c.44) 20–016
      Civic Government (Scot-
         land) Act (c.45)
      s.62 27–015
      s.65 27–015

1982 Employment Act (c.46)
      s.2 3–018
      Criminal   Justice   Act
         (c.48) 6–018
      s.38 29–010
      Administration of Justice
         Act (c.53)
      s.62 20–019
      s.70 20–010
      Sched. 8 20–010
      Commonwealth Develop-
         ment   Corporation
         Act (c.54) 36–028
1983 Representation of the Peo-
         ple Act (c.2) 2–016,
                    10–005, 10–026, 10–046,
                    23–006
      Pt III 10–062
      s.1 10–026
      s.3 10–034
         (1) 24–031
         A 10–031
      s.4 10–027
         (2) 10–028
      s.5 10–028
         (2) 10–028
         (3) 10–028
      s.6 10–028
      s.7 10–031
      s.7A 10–032
      s.7B 10–032
      s.7C 10–032
      s.10 10–036
      ss.14–17 19–006
      s.23 .... 8–014, 22–049
      s.24 10–036
      s.56 10–036
      s.57 10–036
      s.60 .... 10–036, 10–048
      s.61 10–036
      s.63 10–036
      s.71A 10–048
      s.73 10–053
         (4) 10–052
      s.75 .. 10–049, 10–051, 10–053,
                    10–054
         (c)(i) 10–055
         (ii) 10–051
      s.76 .. 10–049, 10–050, 10–051,
                    10–053
      s.81 10–053
      s.82 10–053
      ss.85–87 10–054
      s.90A 10–050
      s.90B 10–050
      s.90C 10–050

1983 Representation of the Peo-
         ple Act—*cont.*
       s.92 3–020
       s.93 10–055
       s.95 10–048
       ss.95–97 27–005
       s.106 10–048
       ss.109–112 10–048
       ss.113–115 10–048
       s.118 .... 10–046, 10–049
       s.144 .... 10–062, 3–018
       s.159(1) 10–005
           (2) 10–005
       s.173 10–036
       s.202(1) 10–026
       Sched. 1 8–015
       Pt II, r.12 10–047
       Pt III 22–049
     British Nationality (Falk-
         land   Islands)   Act
         (c.6) 23–009, 35–007
     Currency Act (c.9) 15–015
     Mental Health Act (c.20) ... 9–013,
           13–027, 24–029, 24–030,
                 30–002, 30–006
       s.2 24–029
       s.3 24–029
       s.35 24–029
       s.36 24–029
       s.38 24–029
       s.41 24–029
       s.47 .... 24–029, 24–32
       ss.72–74 22–034
       s.73 24–030
       s.74 24–030
       s.139 24–030
           (1) 24–030
       s.141 10–005
     Coroner's   Juries   Act
         (c.31) 20–019
     National   Audit   Act
         (c.44) 11–005, 12–017
       s.1 .... 12–018, 17–025
       s.6(1) 12–018
           (2) 12–018
       s.7(1) 12–018
       s.8 12–018
     County Courts (Penalties
         for Contempt) Act
         (c.45) 20–045, 20–053
     Medical Act (c.54) 16–012,
                                 30–017
       s.36 30–017
       s.40 30–017
1984 Intelligence   Services
         Act 24–003

1984 Prevention of Terrorism
         (Temporary   Provi-
         sions) Act (c.8) 14–051,
             22–026, 22–027, 24–001
     Town and Country Plan-
         ning Act (c.10) 15–019
     Telecommunications   Act
         (c.12 .... 28–014)
       s.43(1)(a) 25–029
       s.94 28–015
     Somerset   House   Act
         (c.21) 18–002
     Public Health (Control of
         Disease)   Act
         (c.22) 24–029
       s.10 24–029
       s.13 24–029
       s.16 24–029
       s.37 24–029
       s.38 24–029
     Dentists Act (c.24) 16–012
       s.27 30–017
       s.29 30–017
     County   Courts   Act
         (c.28) 20–009
       s.66(3) 20–018
       s.118 20–053
     Juries   (Disqualification)
         Act (c.34) 20–019
     Data   Protection   Act
         (c.35) 26–025
       s.7 26–026
     Video   Recordings   Act
         (c.39) 25–039
       s.1 25–039
       s.2(1) 25–039
           (2) 25–039
       s.4 25–039
       A 25–039
           (2) 25–039
       s.7 25–039
       s.88 25–039
     Finance Act (c.43)
       s.8 3–018
     Health and Social Security
         Act (c.48)
       s.5 30–020
       Sched. 3 30–020
     Building Act (c.55) 29–008
       s.1 29–008
       s.12 31–019
       s.13 31–019
       s.14 29–008
       s.95 24–051

nance Factories a Military Services Act
(c.59) 28–013
e and Criminal Evidence Act (c.60) 21–003,
21–009, 21–010, 21–021,
24–001, 24–003, 24–004,
24–014, 24–021, 24–046,
25–022
Pt II 24–043, 24–050
Pt IV 24–012
Pt V 24–012
s.1 .... 24–004, 24–005
(3) 24–019
(4) 24–019
(8)(b) 24–044
(8A) 24–004
(9)(a) 24–004
s.2 24–004
s.3 24–004
s.4 ..... 24–004, 24–005, 27–010
s.5 24–005
s.8 .... 24–046, 24–47
s.9 .... 24–048, 24–050
s.10 .... 24–044, 24–047
(2) 24–048
s.11 24–048
s.12 24–048
s.15 .... 24–047, 24–050
(1) 24–048
s.16 .... 24–047, 24–050
s.17 .. 24–043, 24–044, 24–050,
27–003
(1)(b) 24–043
(5)–(6) 24–043
s.18 ... 24–012, 24–044, 24–050
(1)(a) 24–044
(2) 24–045
(5)(b) 24–044
s.19 24–045
(6) 24–045
s.22 24–045
s.23 24–044
s.24 ... 24–008, 27–020, 27–021
(2) 25–010
(5) 24–009
s.25 .. 24–008, 24–009, 24–022,
27–024, 27–028, 27–029
(1) 24–019
(3) 27–007
s.26 .... 24–010, 27–029
(2) 24–010
(5) 24–008
s.27(4) 24–014
s.28 24–010
s.29 24–012

1984 Police and Criminal Evidence Act—cont.
s.30 .... 24–011, 24–012
s.32 .... 24–044, 24–050
(1) 24–019
(2)(b) 24–011, 24–044
(3) 24–044
(4) 24–011
(6) 24–044
s.35 24–012
(1) 24–011
s.36 21–010
s.37(2) 24–012
s.38(6) 24–024
s.40 .... 24–012, 24–024
s.41 24–012
s.42 .... 21–010, 24–012
s.47(8) 24–024
s.54 24–013
(4) 24–019
(5) 24–013
s.55 .... 24–014, 24–019
s.56 24–013
s.58 24–013
(1) 24–016
(2) 24–016
(8) 24–016
s.59 20–016
s.61 24–015
(4)(a) 24–019
(b) 24–019
s.62 24–014
(10) 24–014
(1A) 24–014
s.63 24–014
B 24–015
C 24–015
s.65 24–014
s.66 29–004
s.67 29–004
s.76 24–018
s.78 .... 24–018, 24–045
s.114 24–050
s.116 24–009
s.117 .. 24–010, 24–014, 24–019
Sched. 1 24–048
Sched. 7 27–029
1985 Election (Northern Ireland) Act (c.2) 10–048
Brunei and Maldives Act
(c.3) 36–016
Milk (Cessation of Production) Act (c.4)
s.2 24–051

1985 Companies Act (c.6) 10–039,
                    24–017, 28–014
     Pt XA 10–038
     s.401 32–019
     New Towns and Urban
          Development Cor-
          poration Act (c.5) 28–003
     London Regional Trans-
          port (Amendment)
          Act (c.10) 3–018
     Cinemas Act (c.13) 25–038
     s.1(3) 25–038
     Hong Kong Act (c.15) 23–006,
                    23–013, 23–017, 35–015
     Prosecution of Offences
          Act (c.23) .. 18–013, 20–005,
                    20–014, 24–003
     s.2 20–014
     s.6 20–014
     s.10 20–015
     s.23 20–015
     s.24 20–015
     Local Government (Ac-
          cess to Information)
          Act (c.43) 26–028
     Representation of the Peo-
          ple Act (c.50) 10–025,
                                        10–046
     ss.1–3 10–030
     ss.5–9 .... 10–034, 10–036
     s.13 10–047
     s.20 8–015
     Sched. 4 10–035
     Local Government Act
          (c.51) 2–037
     Appropriation Act (c.55)
          Sched. B, Pt. 15 2–016
     Interception of Communi-
          cations Act (c.56) 2–027,
                    19–050, 22–012, 24–003,
                    26–014, 26–022
     s.1 26–014
     (3) 26–014
     (6) 26–014
     s.2 26–015
     s.3 26–014
     s.4 26–014
     s.5 ..... 26–014, 26–015, 26–016
     (5) 26–015
     s.6 26–015
     s.7 32–018
     (8) 32–018
     s.9 26–015
     ss.11–12 26–015
     s.14 26–015
     ss.15–18 26–015

1985 Interception of Communi-
          cations Act—cont.
     s.23 26–016
     s.24 26–016
     s.81 26–015
     Sporting Events (Control
          of Alcohol, etc.)
          (c.57) 27–036
     European Communities
          (Finance) Act
          (c.64) 6–016
     Housing Act (c.68)
     ss.58–78 32–013
     s.164 32–020
1986 Australia Act (c.2) 4–011,
                    35–013, 36–010, 36–015,
                                        36–022
     s.1 36–010
     s.2 36–010
     s.3 36–010
     s.4 36–010
     s.5 36–010
     s.6 36–011
     s.7 36–011
     s.8 36–011
     s.9 36–011
     s.10 36–011
     s.11 36–011
     s.12 36–011
     s.15 36–011
     s.51 36–010
     Local Government Act
          (c.10)
     s.28 9–023
     Airports Act (c.31) 28–013
     Drug Trafficking Act
          (c.32) 24–048
     Gas Act (c.44) 24–051, 28–013
     Insolvency Act (c.45) 13–016
     s.427 .... 9–014, 10–005
     Social Security Act
          (c.50) 34–011
     Parliamentary Constituen-
          cies Act (c.56) 5–045,
                                        10–044
     s.3(5) 10–045
     s.3A 10–045
     s.4 10–044
     Education (No.2) Act
          (c.61) 22–012, 27–005
     Public Order Act (c.64) 2–031,
                    21–010, 20–014, 24–008,
                    27–006, 27–009, 27–011,
                    27–018, 27–022, 27–031,
                                        27–035

1986	Public Order Act—*cont.*	
	Pt I	27–019
	Pt III	25–010
	Pt IV	27–037
	s.1	27–019, 27–021
	(2)	27–019
	(3)	27–019
	(5)	27–019
	A	27–036
	s.2	27–019, 27–020, 27–021, 27–035
	(2)	27–020
	s.3	27–019, 27–021
	(1)	27–021
	(2)	27–021
	(3)	27–021
	(5)	27–021
	(7)	27–023
	s.4	7–002, 27–019, 27–022, 27–023, 27–024, 27–025, 27–026, 27–035
	(1)	27–023
	(2)	27–024
	(3)	27–024
	s.4A	27–022, 27–024, 27–025, 27–026, 27–035
	(1)	27–025
	(2)	27–024, 27–025
	(3)	27–025
	s.5	27–022, 27–023, 27–024, 27–025, 27–026, 27–035
	(1)	27–026
	(2)	27–025
	(3)	27–025
	(4)	27–026
	s.6(1)	27–019
	(2)	27–020, 27–021
	(3)	27–023
	(4)	27–026
	(5)	27–020
	s.7	27–036
	(1)	27–019
	(3)	27–025
	s.8	27–019, 27–021
	s.10	27–019
	(1)	27–019
	(3)	27–019
	s.11	27–015, 27–035
	(1)	27–015
	(2)	27–015
	(3)	27–015
	(8)	27–015
	(9)	27–015
	s.12	21–010, 27–004, 27–015, 27–016
	(1)	27–015, 27–016

1986	Public Order Act—*cont.*	
	s.12(2)	27–015
	(3)	27–016
	(4)	27–016
	(5)	27–016
	(6)	27–016
	s.13	27–016, 27–017
	(1)	27–016
	(2)	27–016
	(7)	27–016
	(8)	27–016
	(9)	27–016
	(10)	27–016
	s.14	21–010, 27–002, 27–003, 27–012, 27–035
	(1)	27–012
	(2)	27–012
	(3)	27–012
	(4)	27–012
	(5)	27–012
	(6)	27–012
	s.14A	27–004, 27–012, 27–013, 27–035
	(1)	27–012
	(2)	27–012
	(6)	27–012
	(9)	27–012
	s.14B	27–012, 27–013, 27–035
	s.14C	27–012, 27–013, 27–035
	s.15	27–015
	s.16	27–002, 27–015
	s.17	25–010
	s.18	25–010
	(1)	27–023
	(5)	25–010
	s.19	25–010
	(1)	27–023
	s.20	25–010, 25–037
	(1)	27–023
	s.21	25–010
	(1)	27–023
	s.22	25–010
	s.23	25–010
	(1)	27–023
	s.24	24–048, 25–010
	s.25	25–010
	s.26(1)	25–010
	(2)	25–010
	s.27(1)	25–010
	s.28	25–010
	s.30	27–037
	s.31(4)	27–022
	(5)	27–022
	s.37	27–037

1987   Immigration (Carriers' Li-
     ability) Act (c.24)   23–033
     Crown   Proceedings
     (Armed Forces) Act
     (c.25)   33–011
     s.1   33–013
     s.2   33–013
     Access to Personal Files
     Act (c.37)   26–025
     Criminal   Justice   Act
     (c.38)   18–013
     Family   Reform   Act
     (c.42)   22–054
     Parliamentary and other
     Pensions   Act
     (c.45)   10–015
1988   Coroners Act   20–018
     Local   Government   Act
     (c.9)   28–013
     Immigration Act (c.14)
     s.3   23–026
     s.7 ....   23–023, 23–026
     Criminal   Justice   Act
     (c.33) 15–011, 20–019,
                24–048, 24–054
     s.118(1)   20–021
     s.134 ... 3–026, 15–033, 22–004
     (1)   23–044
     s.139   24–004
     s.139B   24–004
     s.153   24–024
     Legal Act (c.34)
     s.29   20–044
     Finance Act (c.39)
     s.156   12–006
     Education   Reform   Act
     (c.40)
     s.205   16–008
     Copyright, Designs and
     Patents Act (c.48)
     s.167(2)   10–019
     Road Traffic Act (c.52)
     s.6   24–044
     s.38   29–004
     s.163   24–004
     s.172   22–053
1989   Prevention of Terrorism
     (Temporary   Provi-
     sions) Act (c.4)   14–051,
                    27–039
     s.13A   24–005
     s.13B   24–005
     s.16A 14–055, 22–052,
                    22–053
     s.16B 22–052, 22–053

1989   Security   Service   Act
     (c.5) 19–048, 19–049,
                19–050, 26–014
     Water Act (c.15)   28–013
     Representation of the Peo-
     ple Act (c.28)   10–025
     Electricity Act (c.29)   24–051,
                    28–013
     Extradition Act (c.33)   14–050,
          23–041, 23–042, 23–043,
          23–044, 23–045, 23–046
     Pt III   23–042
     s.1   23–045
     s.2   23–043
     s.3   23–045
     s.5   23–045
     s.6 ..... 23–044, **23–045,** 23–048
     (1)(a)   23–045
     s.7   23–046
     s.8(1)(b)   23–046
     s.9   23–046
     s.11   23–047
     (3)   23–047
     s.12   23–047
     s.22   23–044
     s.23   23–044
     s.24   23–044
     s.25   23–045
     Sched. 1 ....   23–042, 23–045,
                    23–046
     para. 4   23–046
     Football   Spectators   Act
     (c.37)
     Sched. 1   27–037
     Statute Law (Repeals) Act
     (c.43)   37–012
     Children Act (c.52)   22–054
1990   Education (Student Loans)
     Act (c.6)   29–011
     Town and Country Plan-
     ning Act (c.8) 22–053,
                30–002, 32–015
     s.35   30–025
     Sched. 6   30–024
     Pakistan Act (c.14)   36–020
     Food Safety Act (c.16)   13–019
     Computer   Misuse   Act
     (c.18)
     s.15   23–043
     National   Health   Service
     and Community Care
     Act (c.19)   28–003
     Access to Health Records
     Act (c.23)   26–025
     Social   Security   Act
     (c.27)   34–018

1990 Government Trading Act
         (c.30) 18–023
      Aviation and Maritime Se-
         curity Act (c.31) 14–050
      British Nationality (Hong
         Kong) (c.34) 23–017,
                                       35–015
      Human Fertilisation and
         Embryology   Act
         (c.37) 28–006
      s.8 28–006
      s.9 28–006
      Courts and Legal Services
         Act (c.41) 9–012, 20–009,
            20–013, 20–026, 29–013,
                                       34–018
      s.41 30–016
      s.110 20–034
      Broadcasting Act (c.42) ... 10–055,
                         11–033, 25–034
      Pt I 10–055
      Pt II 10–055
      s.1 25–034
      s.6 25–034
         (1)(b) 25–035
         (c) 25–035
         (e) 25–034
      s.8(2) 10–056
      s.10(1) 25–035
         (2) 25–035
      s.36 10–056
      s.84 25–034
      s.92 10–055
         (2)(a)(i) 10–056
      s.94(1) 25–035
         (2) 25–025
      s.152 25–036
      s.162(1)(b) 25–025
      s.166 25–003
      s.203(1) 13–013
      Sched. 20, para.1 13–013
      Import and Export Control
         Act (c.45) .. 19–047, 29–010,
                                       29–022
1991 War Crimes Act (c.13) 4–036,
                                        9–025
      Football (Offences) Act
         (c.19) 27–036
      s.2 27–036
      s.3 27–036
      s.4 27–036
      Northern Ireland (Emer-
         gency   Provisions)
         Act (c.24) 19–040

1991 Child   Support   Act
         (c.48) 29–011
      Ports Act (c.52) 28–013
      Criminal   Justice   Act
         (c.53) 9–012, 24–031
      s.34 22–034
      Deer Act (c.54)
      s.12 24–044
      Water   Industry   Act
         (c.56) 28–013
      s.208 28–014
      Land Drainage Act (c.59)
      s.66 29–003
1992 Boundaries Commissions
         Act 10–044
      Parliamentary Corporate
         Bodies Act (c.27) 10–020
      Social Security Contribu-
         tion and Benefits Act
         (c.4) 23–033
      Competition and Services
         (Utilities)   Act
         (c.43) 28–014
      Civil Service (Manage-
         ment of Functions)
         Act (c.61) .. 18–022, 18–024,
                                       18–029
      Social Security Admini-
         stration Act (c.5) 23–033,
                                       30–012
      Transport and Works Act
         (c.42) 11–038, 22–053,
                          29–003, 30–002
      s.12 32–016
      Museums   and Galleries
         Act (c.44) 17–025
      Trade Union and Labour
         Relations (Consoli-
         dation) Act (c.52)
      s.203 27–034
      s.220 .... 27–033, 27–034
      s.241 27–033
      Tribunals and Inquiries
         Act (c.53) ... 30–001, 30–018
      s.1 34–002
      s.6 30–019
      s.7 30–019
      s.9 30–026
      s.11 .... 30–021, 32–015
      s.12 30–022
      Sched. 1 .... 30–019, 34–002
1993 Judicial Pensions and Re-
         tirement Act (c.8) 20–029
      s.11(8) 20–029
      Osteopaths Act (c.21) 11–035,
                                       16–012

1993 Asylum and Immigration
          Appeals Act (c.23) ... 23–023,
                                   23–033
      s.2 23–031
      Bail (Amendment) Act
          (c.26)
      s.1 24–024
      European Communities
          (Amendment) Act
          (c.32) 6–015, 7–017
      s.2 15–030
      Welsh Language Act
          (c.38) 2–002
      Railways Act (c.43) 28–013,
                                   28–015
      s.118 28–015
      s.119 28–015
      Health Service Commis-
          sioners Act (c.46) 34–015
      Pensions Scheme Act
          (c.48)
      ss.145–151 34–018
1994 Intelligence Services Act
          (c.13) 19–048, 19–049,
                          19–050, 26–014
      s.1 21–005
      s.2 21–005
      Chiropractors Act
          (c.17) 16–012
      Social Security (Incapac-
          ity for Work) Act
          (c.18) 29–038
      Value Added Tax (c.23) 6–017,
                                   12–012
      s.2 29–012
      s.82 30–016
      Sched. 11 24–050
      Sched. 12 30–016
      Police and Magistrates
          Courts Act (c.29) 9–017,
          21–003, 21–012, 21–013,
                                   21–019
      s.37(f) 21–024
      Pt IV 18–009
      Criminal Justice and Pub-
          lic Order Act (c.33) ... 20–019,
          24–003, 24–008, 24–009,
          24–014, 24–017, 24–024,
          25–025, 25–039, 27–006,
          27–011, 27–013, 27–018,
                                   27–031
      s.25 .... 24–023, 24–024
      s.26 24–024
      s.27 24–024
      s.34 24–017
          (2) 24–017

1994 Criminal Justice and Pub-
          lic Order Act—cont.
      ss.34–37 24–016
      ss.34–39 24–011
      s.35 24–017
      s.36 24–017
      s.37 24–017
      s.51 20–044
      s.59(1) 24–014
          (2) 24–011
      s.60 24–005
      s.61 .... 24–042, 27–014
      ss.63–66 27–003
      s.68 .... 27–004, 27–014
      s.69 .... 27–004, 27–014
      s.70 27–012
      ss.72–74 24–042
      s.84 25–030
      s.88 25–039
      s.90 25–039
      s.92 25–029
      s.154 27–022
      s.155 25–010
      Sched. 9 25–025
      Drug Trafficking Act
          (c.37) 24–048, 24–054
      Deregulation and Con-
          tracting Out Act
          (c.40) 11–005, 28–013,
          29–017, 29–018, 29–031,
                                   29–033
      Pt I 29–013, 29–031
      s.1(1) 29–031
          (3) 29–033
1995 South Africa Act (c.3) 36–020
      Proceeds of Crime Act
          (c.11) 24–048
      Jobseekers Act (c.18) 29–011
      Crown Agents Act
          (c.24) 28–006, 28–013
      Environment Act (c.25) ... 28–006
      Criminal Appeal Act
          (c.35) 20–005
      s.13 20–005
      s.16 20–004
      Gas Act (c.45) 24–051
1996 Health Service Commis-
          sioners (Amendment)
          Act (c.5) 34–015
      Northern Ireland (Entry to
          Negotiations) Act
          (c.11) 1–016
      s.89 21–008
      Reserve Forces Act
          (c.14) 19–003

1996   Police Act (c.16) 21–003,
                                      21–012
         Pt IV 21–021
         s.3 21–013
             (2) 21–013
         s.4 21–013
         s.5B 21–013
         s.6 21–013
             (1) 21–013
             (4) 21–013
         s.7 21–013
         s.8 21–013
             (2)(d) 21–013
             (3) 21–015
         s.9 21–014
         s.9A 21–014
         s.9B 21–013
         s.9E 21–013
         s.10 .... 21–009, 21–014
             (2) 21–014
         s.11 21–013
             (3) 21–013
         s.12 21–013
         s.15 21–015
         s.20 21–020
         s.20A 21–020
         s.22 21–015
         s.23 21–015
         s.24 21–015
             (2) 21–015
         s.25 21–015
         s.32 21–016
         s.33 21–016
         s.36 21–016
         s.37 .... 21–013, 21–017
         s.38 21–017
         s.40 21–013
         s.42 21–018
         s.43 21–014
         s.44 21–018
         s.45 21–018
         s.46 21–018
         s.47 21–018
         s.48 21–018
         s.49 21–018
         s.50 .... 21–018, 21–024
         s.54 21–019
         s.55 21–019
         s.57 21–019
         s.66 21–021
         s.67 21–021
             (4) 21–021
         s.68 21–021
         s.69 21–021
         s.70 21–021
         s.71 21–021

1996   Police Act—cont.
         s.72 21–022
         s.74 21–022
         s.75 21–022
         s.76 21–022
         s.77 21–023
         s.78 21–022
         s.79 21–023
         s.84 21–024
         s.88 21–011
         s.89 .. 21–008, 24–019, 24–022,
                                      27–007
             (1) 24–021
             (2) 24–019, 24–021
         s.93(1) 21–014
         s.96 21–020
         Sched. 2 21–013
         Sched. 2A 21–013
         Sched. 3 21–013
         Sched. 5 21–021
       Employment   Tribunals
           Act (c.17) ... 30–006, 30–013
         s.6(1) 30–020
         s.20 30–002
       Employment Rights Pro-
           tection Act (c.18) 19–004
         s.43 26–032
         ss.43C–43H 26–032
         ss.103A–105(6A) 26–032
         s.194 10–023
       Northern Ireland (Emer-
           gency   Provisions)
           Act (c.22) ... 19–040, 27–039
       Treasure Act (c.24) 15–013
       Criminal Procedure and
           Investigations   Act
           (c.25) 20–017, 24–003,
                                      33–038
       Offensive Weapons Act
           (c.26) 24–009, 27–031
         s.4 24–004
       Commonwealth Develop-
           ment   Corporation
           Act (c.28) 28–006
       Defamation Act (c.31) 20–018
         s.1(3)(d) 13–013
         s.4 25–003
         s.13 .. 13–002, 13–003, 13–015,
                                      25–003
             (4) 13–006, 13–015
             (5) 13–008
         s.14 .... 20–040, 25–003
         s.15 .... 13–012, 13–013
             (2) 25–004
             (3) 25–004
         Sched. 1 25–004

1996 Defamation Act—*cont.*
      Pt I 25–004
      para. 1 25–004
      para. 2 25–004
      para.3 25–004
      para.4 25–004
      para.5 25–004
      para.6 25–004
      para.7 25–004
      para. 9 25–005
      para.12 25–005
      para.12(2) 25–005
      para.13 25–005
      para.14 25–005
      Pt II 25–004, 25–005
      Security   Service   Act
        (c.35) 19–048, 21–005
      Hong Kong (War Wives
        and   Widows)   Act
        (c.41) 23–017, 35–015
      Armed   Forces   Act
        (c.46) 19–022, 22–012,
                                      22–036
      Asylum and Immigration
        Act (c.49)
        s.2 23–031
      Housing Act (c.52) 22–054
      Statutory   Instruments
        (Production and Sale)
        Act (c.54) 29–036
      Broadcasting Act (c.55) ... 25–034
        s.107 25–036
        s.108 25–036
        s.111 25–036
        s.119 25–036
        s.120 25–036
        s.264 25–036
      Education Act (c.56)
        s.333 30–016
        s.476 30–016
        s.479 30–016
      Public   Order   (Amend-
        ment) Act (c.59) 27–026
1997 Civil   Procedure   Act
        (c.12)
        s.1 29–003
        s.2 29–003
        s.7 24–052
      British Nationality (Hong
        Kong) Act (c.20) 11–035,
                             23–017, 35–015
      Knives Act (c.21)
        s.8 24–005

1997 Justices of the Peace Act
        (c.25) 20–009, 20–026,
                                      20–030
      s.5 20–026
      ss.10A-D 20–009
      s.10A 20–030
      s.21 20–026
      s.26 20–030
      Protection from Harass-
        ment Act (c.40) 24–009,
                             27–004, 27–033
      Crime   (Sentences)   Act
        (c.43) 9–012, 20–017,
                             20–035, 24–031, 24–032
      s.2 .... 20–035, 22–050
      Police Act (c.50) 19–047,
                  19–048, 21–005, 21–015,
                             26–019, 26–023
      Pt III 24–003, 24–041,
                  24–049, 26–017, 26–018
      s.91 .. 24–041, 24–049, 25–009,
                             26–018, 26–023
      s.92 .... 24–041, 26–018
      s.93 24–049
        (2) 26–018
        (4) 26–018
        (5) 26–018
      s.95 26–018
      s.96 26–018
      s.97 16–019
      ss.97–100 26–018,
                                      26–019
      Referendums   (Scotland
        and   Wales)   Act
        (c.61) 1–016
      Plant   Varieties   Act
        (c.66) 30–016
      Special Immigration Ap-
        peals   Commission
        Act (c.68) .. 22–012, 23–034,
                             23–035, 23–036
        s.4 23–037
        s.5(2) 23–037
        s.5(3) 23–037
        ss.74–78 23–037
        s.79 23–037
1998 Government of Scotland
        Act 18–017
      School   Standards   and
        Framework   Act
        (c.31) 22–012, 22–032,
                                      30–016
        Sched. 18 30–016

1998 School Standard and
        Framework Act
        —*cont.*
    Sched. 24 30–016
    Sched. 25 30–016
    Public Processions
        (Northern Ireland)
        Act (c.2) 27–015
    Greater London Authority
        Referendum Act
        (c.3) 1–016
    Employment Rights (Dis-
        pute Resolution) Act
        (c.8) 30–013
    Bank of England (c.11) ... 12–016
        s.11(a)–(b) 12–016, 28–002
    Northern Ireland (Elec-
        tions) (c.12) 5–011
    Social Security Act
        (c.14) 30–012
    Audit Commission Act
        (c.18) 28–006
    European Communities
        (Amendment) Act
        (c.21)
    s.2 .... 6–020, 15–030
    Public Interest Disclosure
        Act (c.23) .. 11–037, 18–030,
                        26–003, 26–031
    Data Protection Act
        (c.29) 7–016, 24–002,
                26–025, 26–026, 26–030
    Pt IV 26–026
    s.1 26–025
    s.2 26–025
    s.3 26–026
    s.10 26–026
    s.11 26–026
    s.13 26–025
    s.14 26–026
    s.27 17–007
    s.28 26–026
    s.29 26–026
    s.30 26–026
    s.31 26–026
    s.32 .... 26–025, 26–026
    s.33 26–026
    s.63(2) 15–007
    Sched.1 26–025
    Crime and Disorder Act
        (c.37) 14–018, 14–023,
                        27–022
    s.36 .... 14–019, 22–045

1998 Crime and Disorder Act
        —*cont.*
    s.25 24–005
    s.28 27–022
    s.56 24–024
    s.119 20–015
    Sched. 8 20–015
    Government of Wales
        (c.38) 2–003,
                5–014, 5–015, 5–039,
                16–012, 20–008
    s.1(2) 5–038
    s.2 9–052
    s.18(12) 5–035
    s.22 5–037
    s.27 5–037
    s.28 5–037
    s.29 5–037
    s.30 5–035
    s.31 5–035
        (4) 5–036
    s.34 5–038
        (2) 18–022
    s.35 5–038
    s.53 5–040
    s.54 5–039
    s.56 5–028,
                        5–040, 5–041
    s.57 5–041
    s.62 5–040
    ss.64–68 5–036
    s.72 5–019
    ss.74–75 5–019
    ss.77–78 5–019
    s.79 5–019
    s.106 5–037
    s.107 .... 5–016, 5–038
    s.108 5–037
    s.111 34–010
    s.113 5–038
    s.114 5–038
    s.115 5–038
    s.121 5–038
    s.126 5–038
    Sched. 2 5–037
    Sched. 3, Pt II 22–047
    Sched. 4 5–037
    Competition Act (c.41) 6–038,
                        30–016

1998 Human Rights Act (c.42) 1–019,
1–020, 2–021, 2–027,
2–034, 4–023, 4–039,
5–016, 5–021, 5–030,
6–001, 7–017, 9–028,
9–036, 9–041, 9–051,
9–052, 11–005, 13–003,
14–052, 18–009, 19–043,
20–015, 20–029, 20–031,
20–032, 20–033, 20–039,
20–043, 22–002, 22–011,
22–012, 22–015, 22–019,
22–023, 22–030, 22–042,
22–050, 22–052, 22–055,
23–023, 23–033, 23–037,
23–047, 24–032, 24–041,
25–019, 26–014, 26–019,
26–021, 27–001, 27–002,
27–026, 27–030, 28–017,
30–002, 30–026A, 31–002
s.1 .... 22–015, 22–026
(2) 22–047
s.2 ..... 22–015, 22–023, 22–043
s.3 .... 3–018, 4–024, 22–015,
22–016, 22–020, 22–021, 22–052,
24–001
(1) 27–027
(7) 22–016
s.5 .... 22–016, 27–027
s.6 .... 22–015, 22–016, 22–017,
22–021, 22–023, 22–025, 25–023
(1) 22–024, 24–001
(3) 22–016, 22–022,
22–023, 22–025
(a) 22–023
(b) 22–023, 22–024
(4) 22–023
ss.7–9 22–019
s.7 .... 22–017, 22–025
(1) 22–025
(a) 26–023
(7) 22–017, 22–025
s.8 22–017
(2) 22–035
(4) 22–017
s.9 22–017
(3) 22–035
s.10 .... 22–016, 29–034
(2) 29–013
(6) 22–024
s.11 22–019
s.12 .. 22–018, 25–019, 25–021,
25–023
(2) 22–018
(3) 22–018
(4) 22–018, 25–021

1998 Human Rights Act—cont.
s.13 .... 22–018, 22–024
s.15 22–047
s.16 24–001
s.19 ... 11–025, 14–051, 22–017
s.21 29–001
(1) 5–016, 22–024,
29–001
(5) 22–045
Sched.1 .... 22–015, 22–017
Sched.2 .... 22–016, 29–034
Regional Development
Agencies Act
(c.45) 5–042
s.4 5–042
s.8 5–043
Scotland Act (c.46) 5–014,
5–015, 5–016, 5–020,
5–021, 10–044, 16–012,
20–001, 20–008, 22–051
Pt IV 5–018
ss.23–26 5–019
s.28 5–021
(1) 4–010
s.29 5–021
s.30(2) 5–021
s.31(1)–(2) 5–026
s.33 .... 5–015, 5–026
s.35 .... 5–023, 5–026
s.37 .... 4–010, 5–049
s.39 5–019
ss.41–42 5–019
s.43 5–019
s.44 .... 5–022, 5–028
s.45(2) 5–022
s.51(2) 18–022
s.52 5–023
(5) 5–023
s.53 5–023
s.53(2) 5–023
s.56 5–023
s.57 .... 5–016, 5–023
s.58 5–023
s.63 5–023
s.86 5–045
s.95 20–026
s.103 5–023
Sched. 4 5–021
Sched. 5
Pt. I 5–021
Pt II 5–021
Sched. 6 22–053
Scotland Act (c.46) 29–001
s.91 34–010

1998 Northern Ireland Act
(c.47) 5–015, 5–030,
16–012, 20–008, 39–001
Pt I 5–011
Pt II 5–011
s.1 5–029
s.3 5–011
s.5(6) 5–014
s.6 5–016
s.7 5–030
s.8(b) 5–030
s.10 5–034
s.11 .... 5–015, 5–034
s.13(4) 5–034
s.14 5–034
s.15(4) 5–014
s.20(2) 5–031
s.22 5–030
s.23 5–032
s.24 .... 5–016, 5–030
s.25 5–303
s.26 .... 5–014, 5–030
s.29 5–033
s.30 5–035
s.43 5–019
ss.44–46 5–019
s.48 5–034
s.50 5–019
ss.68–70 5–034
s.78 34–010
Sched. 1 10–063
Sched. 2 5–030
Sched. 2.12 5–013
Sched.3 5–030
Sched.4 5–035
Registration of Political
Parties Act (c.48) 2–016,
10–038, 10–056
Pt III 10–038
Pt IV 10–038
1999 Mental Health (Public
Safety and Appeals)
(Scotland) Act 5–015
European Parliamentary
Elections Act (c.1) 4–036,
6–015, 6–020, 9–025,
10–059
Health Act (c.8)
s.60 30–017
Sched. 3 30–017
Water Industry Act (c.9) ... 28–013

1999 Commonwealth Development Corporation
Act (c.20) 36–028
Football (Offences and
Disorder) Act
(c.21) 27–037
Access to Justice Act
(c.22) 20–009, 20–013,
20–026, 20–030, 20–044
Youth Justice and Crimi-
nal Evidence Act
(c.23) 9–028, 20–048
s.44 20–040
s.58 24–016
s.59 20–043
Sched. 3 20–043
Pollution Prevention and
Control Act (c.24) 29–015,
29–038
Local Government Act
(c.27) 2–037, 28–013
Pt I 21–019
Greater London Authority
Act (c.29) 2–037, 10–059,
21–004, 21–012, 21–015,
21–016, 21–020
Pt VI 21–004
s.24(1) 21–013
Welfare Reform and Pen-
sions Act (c.30)
s.82 29–012
Immigration and Asylum
Act (c.33) .. 23–026, 23–031,
23–034, 23–035, 23–036,
24–033
Pt II 23–034
Pt IV 23–035, 24–033
Pt V 23–034, 23–036
Pt VI 23–033
Pt VII 23–033
s.10 23–030
s.11 .... 23–031, 23–031
s.12 23–031
(1)(a)–(b) 23–031
s.32 23–033
s.37 23–033
s.42 23–033
s.56 23–036
s.57 23–036
s.59 23–036
s.60 23–036
s.63 23–036
s.65 ... 23–030, 23–031, 23–033
s.66 23–030
s.69 23–036
(5) 23–030

1999 Immigration and Asylum
        Act—*cont.*
    s.71 23–031
    s.72(2)(a) 23–031
    s.83 23–033
    s.84 23–033
    s.87 23–033
    s.90 23–026
    s.95 23–033
    ss.99–100 23–033
    s.101 23–033
    s.115 23–033
    s.121(a)–(b) 23–031
    s.124(4)–(5) 23–031
    s.145 23–033
    Sched. 1 23–033
    Sched. 2 23–036
    Sched. 3 23–036
    Sched. 14 23–036
    House   of   Lords   Act
        (c.34) .. 9–001, 9–002, 9–005,
            9–009, 9–013, 9–014,
            9–035, 10–005, 13–026,
                            17–033
    s.2 9–009
    s.3 .... 9–005, 10–035
    s.5(1) 9–003
    s.6 14–007
2000 Bail   Judicial   Appoint-
        ments, etc. (Scotland)
        Act (asp 9) ... 5–027, 20–026
    Crown Prosecution Serv-
        ice Inspectorate Act
        (c.10) 20–015
    Disqualification Act 10–007
    Northern   Ireland   Act
        (c.1) 5–011
    Representation of the Peo-
        ple Act (c.2) 10–025,
            10–026, 10–027, 10–028,
            10–031, 10–032, 10–036
    s.10 10–043
    Sched. 2 10–030
    Sched. 4 10–034
    Armed Forces Discipline
        Act (c.4) 19–021, 22–012
    Financial   Services   and
        Markets Act (c.8) 34–018
    s.1 28–005
    s.2 28–005
    s.118 28–005
    s.119 28–005
    s.123 28–005
    s.132 30–016

2000 Terrorism Act (c.11) 14–050,
            14–051, 14–054, 22–026,
            24–001, 24–048, 24–049,
            24–054, 25–011, 27–039
    Pt II 14–052, 14–053
    Pt III 14–053
    Pt V 14–052, 14–053
    Pt IV 14–053
    Pt VII 14–055
    s.1 ..... 14–051, 14–053, 25–011
        (1) 14–051
            (b) 14–052
            (c) 14–052
        (2) 14–051, 14–052,
                        22–026, 22–027
        (3) 14–052
        (4) 14–052
        (5) 14–052
    s.2 22–028
        (1) 22–027
    s.3 .... 14–052, 22–027
        (4) 25–011
        (5) 25–011
    s.4 14–052
    s.6 14–052
    s.9 14–052
    s.10 14–052
    s.11 14–053
    s.12 .... 14–052, 14–053
        (4) 14–055
    s.13 14–053
    s.14 ... 14–053, 22–026, 22–027
    ss.15–18 .... 14–052, 14–053
    s.16 .... 14–053, 22–026
    s.18 14–045
    s.19 .... 25–011, 25–022
        (3) 25–011, 25–022
    s.23 14–054
    s.25 14–053
    ss.26–31 14–053
    s.30 14–052
    s.32 14–053
    ss.36–36 24–049
    s.37 14–053
    s.39(5)(a) 15–055
    s.40 14–052
    s.41 14–053
        (3) 14–054
    s.42 14–054
    s.43 14–054
    ss.44–46 24–005
    s.44 14–054
    s.54 .... 14–052, 14–054
        (4) 14–055
    ss.56–63 14–052
    s.57 .... 14–054, 14–055

2000 Terrorism Act—*cont.*
s.57(2) 14–055
s.58 14–054
(3) 14–055
ss.59–61 14–054
s.59 14–054
s.62 14–055
s.63 14–054
ss.62–64 14–050
s.77 14–055
s.103 14–055
s.112 14–055
s.118 .... 14–054, 14–055
Sched. 2 .... 14–052, 25–011
Sched. 3 14–052
Sched. 5 14–053
para.3 24–049
Finance Act (c.17)
s.149 24–051
s.150 24–051
Government Resources
and Accounts Act
(c.20) 12–007
Learning and Skills Act
(c.21) 28–006
Local Government Act
(c.22) 32–037, 4–016
ss.68–74 34–016
s.90 28–006
s.92 34–017
Regulation of Investiga-
tory Powers Act
(c.23) 5–014, 19–048,
22–012, 24–002, 24–003,
24–041, 26–018, 26–019,
26–021
Pt I 26–014, 26–023
Pt II 26–014, 26–023
s.1 26–014
s.5 26–009
s.17 26–023
s.22(2) 16–019
s.26(2) 26–019
(3) 26–019
s.27 26–019
s.28 16–019
(2) 16–019
(3) 16–019
s.29 16–019
(2) 16–019
(3) 16–019
s.32(3) 26–019
(6) 26–019
ss.33–34 16–019
s.35 26–019
s.36 26–019

2000 Regulation of Investigatory Powers Act
—*cont.*
s.37 26–019
s.41 26–019
s.42 26–019
s.44 26–019
s.47 26–019
ss.50–52 26–020
s 53 26–020
s.57 26–021
s.58 26–021
(7) 26–021
s.59 .... 26–021, 26–023
s.61 26–021
s.60 26–023
s.62 26–023
s.63 26–023
s.65(2)(d) 26–023
ss.66–69 26–023
s.67 26–023
(8) 26–023
s.71 26–019
Sched. 1 16–019
Football (Disorder) Act
(c.25) 27–037
Postal Services Act
(c.26) 28–012, 28–014
s.1 .... 28–011, 28–014
s.4(1) 28–012
s.62 28–014
s.90 28–012
s.91 28–012
s.93 28–012
s.101 28–015
Utilities Act (c.27) 28–014,
28–015
s.1 28–011
s.3 28–015
s.4 28–015
s.9 28–015
s.13 28–015
Health Service Commis-
sioners (Amendment)
Act (c.28) 34–015
Police (Northern Ireland)
Act (c.32) 21–003
Race Relations (Amend-
ment) Act (c.34) 5–014,
21–011, 28–006
Freedom of Information
Act (c.36) 9–017, 26–003,
26–023, 26–025, 26–029,
30–016
Pt II 26–030
Pt VI 26–031

2000 Freedom of Information
Act—*cont.*
Pt V 26–031
s.1 .... 26–029, 26–030
  (3) 26–029
s.2 26–030
s.3 26–029
s.7 26–029
s.12 26–029
s.13 26–029
s.14 26–029
s.18 26–031
s.19 .... 26–030, 26–031
s.20 .... 26–030, 26–031
s.21 .... 26–030, 26–031
s.22 .... 26–030, 26–031
s.23 26–030
s.24 26–030
s.25 26–030
s.26 26–030
s.27 26–030
s.28 26–030
s.29 26–030
s.30 26–030
s.31 26–030
s.32 26–030
s.33 26–030
s.34 26–030
s.36 26–030
s.37 26–030
s.38 26–030
s.39 26–030
s.40 26–030
s.41 26–030
s.42 26–030
s.43 26–030
s.44 26–030
s.45 .... 26–030, 26–031
s.46 .... 26–030, 26–031
s.48 26–031
s.49 26–031
s.50 26–031
s.51 26–031
s.52 26–031
s.53 26–031
s.54 26–031
s.55 26–031
s.59 26–031
s.60 26–030
s.74 26–027
Sched. 1 26–029
Sched. 3 26–031
Countryside and Rights of
Way Act (c.37)
s.73 28–006

2000 Transport Act (c.38) 28–004,
28–013
s.41 28–014
s.201 29–003
Political Parties, Elections
and Referendums Act
(c.41) 10–025, 10–037,
10–041, 10–046, 10–048,
10–049, 10–063
Pt I 10–042
Pt II 10–041, 10–047
Pt III 10–039, 10–041
Pt IV 10–039, 10–041
Pt VII 10–062, 10–063
s.1 10–018
s.3 10–042
s.5 10–043
s.6 10–043
s.7 10–043
s.8 10–043
s.9 10–043
s.10 10–043
s.11 .... 10–043, 10–056
s.13 10–043
ss.14–17 10–043
s.16 10–045
s.18 10–043
s.19 10–043
s.20 10–043
s.22 .... 10–041, 10–047
  (3) 10–041
  (5) 10–041
s.24 10–041
s.26 .... 10–039, 10–041
s.28(4) 10–041
s.29(2) 10–041
s.36 10–039
s.41 10–039
s.42 10–039
s.43 10–039
s.47 10–039
ss.50–53 10–039
s.52 10–039
  (2)(b) 10–039
s.54 10–039
s.56 10–039
s.62 10–039
s.63 10–039
s.88 10–054
s.94 10–054
s.95 10–054
s.104 10–063
s.105 10–063
s.108 10–063
ss.108–110 10–036
s.125 10–036

2000 Political Parties, Elections
         and   Referendums
         Act—*cont.*
      s.130 .... 10–048, 10–050
      s.131 .... 10–051, 22–049
      s.132 10–050
      s.134 10–050
      s.135 10–046
      s.136 .... 10–005, 10–036
      s.139 10–038
      s.141 10–030
      s.144 10–055
      s.155 29–010
      Sched. 3 .... 10–043, 10–045
      Sched. 8 10–053
      Sched. 9 .... 10–052, 10–053
      Sched. 10 10–054
      Sched. 11 10–054

2000 Political Parties, Elections
         and   Referendums
         Act—*cont.*
      Sched. 13 10–063
      Sched. 16 .... 10–048, 10–050
      Sched. 19 10–038
      Disqualification   Act
         (c.42) 10–007
      Sexual Offences (Amend-
         ment) Act (c.44) 5–014,
                                        9–025
2001 Regulatory Reform Act
         (c.6) 29–033
      Criminal Justice and Po-
         lice Act (c.16) 24–002
      s.42 24–004
      Armed   Forces   Act
         (c.19) 19–022
      s.23 19–024

TABLE OF FOREIGN STATUTES

Australia
1867   Constitution Act 35–025

Canada
1921   Canadian Nationals Act ... 36–025
1946   Canadian   Citizenship
          Act 36–025
1982   Constitution Act 36–008

Isle of Man
1916   Acts of Tynwald (Emer-
          gency Promulgation)
          Act 35–002
          s. 3 35–002
1961   Isle of Man Constitution
          Act 35–002
1971   Isle of Man Constitution
          Act 35–002
1991   Statute   Law   Revision
          Act 35–002

New Zealand
1947   New Zealand Constitution
          (Amendment) Act 36–012

1956   Electoral Act 4–031
          s. 189 4–031
1961   Crimes Act
          s. 406(6) 37–012
1973   New Zealand Constitution
          Amendment Act 36–012
1996   Constitution Act 36–013
          s. 15(1) 36–013
          (2) 36–013
          s. 25 36–013

Republic of Ireland
1782   Habeas   Corpus   Act
          (Ireland) 24–040
1948   Republic of Ireland Act 36–003

South Africa
1934   Status of the Union Act 4–014,
                                              36–003
1951   Separate   Representation
          of Voters Act 3–014

United States of America
1946   Administrative   Procedure
          Act 29–017

1951 Treaty establishing the
European Coal and
SteelCommunity
(ECSC), Paris 6–001,
6–002

1957 Treaty establishing the
European Atomic
EnergyCommunity
(EURATOM),
Rome 6–001

EC .Treaty (Treaty of
Rome) 4–017, 4–019,
6–001,6–006, 6–037,
6–039
Art. 4[D] 6–003
Art.6[F] 6–011
Art. 7[4] 6–003, 6–010
Art. 11[5a] 6–006
Art. 12 6–012
Art. 18(1)[8a] 6–036
Art. 28[30] 6–025, 6–036,
6–036
Art. 30[36] 6–025, 6–036
Art. 36 21–008
Art. 39[48] 6–013, 6–025,
6–035, 23–022
Art. 43[52] 23–022
Art. 81[85] 6–037
Art. 82[86] 6–037
Art. 85 6–012
Art. 86 6–012
Art. 119 6–012
Art. 141[119] 6–025, 6–038,
6–039
Art. 177 6–009
Art. 189 6–012
Art. 190[138] 6–019
Art. 190(4)[138(3)] 6–019
Art. 201[144] 6–004
Art. 202[145] 6–005
Art. 203[146] 6–005
Art. 205(1)[148(1)] 6–005
Art. 211[155] 6–007
Art. 213[157] 6–007
Art. 216[158] 6–007
Art. 220[164] 6–008, 6–009,
6–011

1957 EC Treaty—cont.
Art. 221[165] 6–008, 6–009
Art. 222[166] 6–008, 6–009
Art. 223 6–008
Art. 225[168a] 6–008, 6–009
Art. 225a 6–009
Art. 226[169] 6–007, 6–008,
6–026
Art. 227[170] 6–007, 6–008,
6–026
Art. 234[177] 6–009, 6–013,
6–017, 6–019, 6–023,
6–024,6–026, 6–038
Art. 236[173] 6–008
Art. 247[186] 6–010
Art. 248[188c] 6–010
Art. 249[189] 6–011, 6–012,
6–013
Art. 288[215] 6–011
Art. 310[238] 35–001

1972 Accession Treaty 4–017, 6–002
1992 Treaty on European Union
(TEU) (Maastricht
Treaty) 4–017, 6–002,
6–006, 6–015, 6–027,
6–028, 6–030, 6–036
Title V 6–028, 6–030
Title VI 6–027, 6–030
Art. 17(1)[8] ... 23–018, 23–022
Art. 21[8d] 34–018
Art. 23(2)[J.13(2)] 6–006
Art. 40[K.12] 6–006
Art. 195[138e] 34–018
Art. 251 6–028
Protocol 13 6–027
1997 Treaty of Amsterdam 6–003,
6–015, 6–020, 6–027

Directives
Dir. 64/221 6–035
Dir. 75/117 Equal
Pay Directive ... 6–038
Dir. 95/46 26–025
Dir. 97/66 Tele-
coms Data Pro-
tection
Directive 24–002

TABLE OF EUROPEAN CONVENTION ON HUMAN RIGHTS 1950

European Convention on Human
  Rights 1950 ... 1–020, 3–028, 4–018,
          5–016, 5–030, 5–034,
      6–001,6–011, 6–039, 19–052,
      20–039, 20–041, 20–042, 20–047,
      20–048,22–011, 22–014, 22–015,
      24–001, 24–009, 24–012, 24–022,
      24–024,24–027, 24–032, 24–048,
      24–049, 24–050, 24–051, 25–013,
      25–015,25–018, 26–007, 26–010,
      26–014, 26–016, 26–018, 26–019,
      26–021, 27–003, 27–008, 27–009,
              29–001, 35–001
Art. 1 .... 22–030, 22–046, 22–047,
                     25–001
Art. 2 .... 22–026, 22–027, 22–031,
        22–047, 22–050, 24–001
  (2) 24–010
Art. 3 .... 10–002, 19–050, 20–035,
      22–012, 22–013, 22–027,22–028,
      22–032, 22–033, 24–010, 24–014,
           24–015, 24–028
Art. 4(1) 22–027, 22–033
Art. 5 .... 5–015, 19–055, 20–035,
      22–009, 22–012, 22–013, 22–033,
      22–034, 22–050, 23–034, 24–001,
      24–023, 24–027, 24–028,24–029,
          24–030, 24–034
  (1) 22–034, 24–001, 24–008
  (c) 24–005, 24–008
  (f) 23–041, 24–001, 24–033
  (3) 19–055, 22–007, 22–027,
        22–028, 24–001,24–023
  (4) 22–034, 23–036, 24–033
  (5) 22–035, 22–045
  (e) 24–028
Art. 6 ... 2–021, 6–040, 13–022, 13–023,
    19–022, 19–053, 20–012, 20–021,
    20–025, 20–026, 20–043, 20–045,
    20–048, 22–005,22–007, 22–009,
    22–021, 22–028, 22–035, 22–036,
    22–037, 22–043,22–044, 22–045,
    22–050, 22–051, 22–052, 22–053,
    23–034, 23–001,24–008, 24–014,
    24–016, 24–017, 24–018, 24–023,
    24–024, 24–053,24–054, 26–019,
      26–023, 30–026, 30–027
  (1) 13–003, 20–036, 20–040,
      22–036, 22–051,22–053
  (2) 19–055, 22–020, 22–037,
      22–052, 22–053

European Convention on Human
  Rights 1950—*cont.*
Art. 6(3)(c) 20–012, 20–044
Art. 7 .... 13–022, 22–009, 22–027,
        22–037, 24–054
  (2) 22–038
Arts 8–11 22–039,
Art. 8 .... 19–055, 20–048, 22–007,
      22–009, 22–010, 22–013,22–021,
      22–028, 22–037, 22–039, 22–040,
      22–047, 22–054, 23–034,24–001,
      24–014, 24–015, 24–018, 24–041,
      24–042, 24–048, 24–049,24–052,
      24–054, 25–019, 25–023, 26–015,
           26–017
  (2) 24–042, 26–013
Art. 9 .... 22–008, 22–010, 22–023,
      22–028, 22–040, 22–041,22–047,
          25–007, 25–008
Art. 10 .... 10–026, 20–040, 20–043,
      22–008, 22–012, 22–020, 22–023,
      22–028, 22–040, 22–041, 22–042,
      22–045, 22–047, 20–049, 24–008,
      24–027, 25–002, 25–005, 25–008,
      25–011, 25–012, 25–013, 25–017,
      25–019, 25–021, 26–010, 26–024,
      27–001, 27–002, 27–003, 27–007,
          27–023, 27–032
  (1) 10–056, 25–002, 25–033
  (2) 10–056, 24–027, 25–003,
    25–010, 25–021, 25–024, 25–033,
      27–001, 27–008, 27–038
Art. 11 .... 22–008, 22–028, 22–042,
    24–048, 25–011, 27–001, 27–002,
    27–003, 27–004, 27–007, 27–010,
    27–016, 27–023, 27–031, 27–032,
         27–034, 27–038
  (2) 27–001, 27–004, 27–012,
      27–013, 27–016,27–038
Art. 12 .... 22–009, 22–029, 22–042
Art. 13 .... 6–040, 22–009, 22–012,
    22–017, 22–043, 23–034, 23–036
Art. 14 .... 22–007, 22–039, 22–040,
    22–044, 22–047, 22–054, 24–001,
            24–004
Art. 15 .... 19–051, 22–013, 22–026
  (3) 22–027
Art. 16 22–045
Art. 17 .... 19–051, 22–045, 25–010
Art. 18 22–045

European Convention on Human
    Rights 1950—*cont.*
Art. 22 22–006
Art. 25 22–006
Art. 27(2) 22–006
Art. 34 .... 22–006, 22–017, 22–025
Art. 41 22–017
Art. 48 22–006
Protocol 1 22–045

European Convention on Human
    Rights 1950—*cont.*
Art. 1 .... 22–028, 22–046, 22–055,
                                    24–054
Art. 2 .... 22–012, 22–026, 22–032,
                            22–040,22–047
Art. 3 .... 10–026, 10–057, 10–058,
                                    22–049
Protocol 6 ..... 22–031, 22–033, 22–045
Protocol 11 22–006

PART I

GENERAL PART

CHAPTER I

THE NATURE OF CONSTITUTIONAL AND ADMINISTRATIVE LAW

The constitutional law of a state is the law relating to the constitution of that **1–001** state. It is therefore desirable at the outset to discuss briefly the terms "Law," "State" and "Constitution."

Law

Many attempts have been made to define this apparently simple term, and for **1–002** these the reader is referred to books on legal theory which English writers commonly call jurisprudence. We are concerned with state law (municipal law), and it will be sufficient for our present purpose to define the law of a state as consisting of those rules of conduct which are enforced by the duly constituted courts of that state. This would not be an adequate definition for the student of jurisprudence, or the science of law in general; for it does not explain whence the courts derive their authority to lay down the law, nor why the courts in administering justice look to certain sources and not to others, and look to those sources in a certain order and in a certain way. To say that the law is the law because the courts declare it to be so would be like defining an acid as that which turns litmus paper red. Litmus paper provides a convenient working test whereby the chemist determines whether a given liquid is acid or alkali, but it does not explain what acids and alkalis are in themselves. Similarly, enforcement by the courts is a sort of litmus test which may be used to distinguish between legal and non-legal rules of conduct. Enforcement by the courts does not necessarily mean specific enforcement, but usually takes the form of punishment or some other treatment (in criminal law), or an order to pay damages or to deliver up property (in civil law).

This criterion is admittedly imperfect when applied to constitutional and administrative law. In the first place, many decisions in English administrative law are made by tribunals other than the ordinary courts. These tribunals, however, are created by Acts of Parliament; their jurisdiction, composition and powers are defined by statute, and their decisions—whether subject to appeal to the courts or not—are recognised and enforced by the courts. Again, law cannot be enforced against the government, though it can be enforced against members of the government individually. Nor can law be enforced against Parliament or either House of Parliament, although the courts may make a declaration as to the law in relation to either of the Houses, and law may be enforced against members of either House personally. Actions in tort or contract may be brought against a government department representing the Crown, but the judgment cannot be enforced by execution.[1] The law is not enforceable against the Queen in her personal capacity, but this is not of practical importance. Statutory "duties" may be declared by Parliament to be unenforceable in the courts, such as was the duty of the Post Office to provide a postal service under section 59 of the British Telecommunications Act 1981[1a]; and the performance of certain functions by the

---

[1] Crown Proceedings Act 1947.
[1a] For the current position under the Postal Services Act 2000 see *post* para. 28–012.

Speaker under the Parliament Acts may not be questioned in the courts. Moreover "the law and custom of Parliament," although it is recognised by the ordinary courts, is enforced by the Houses of Parliament through their officers, and is both historically and analytically a distinct branch of British constitutional law.[2]

1–003   Some writers, however, find the essential element of legal rules to be their recognition as obligatory, by legislative and executive as well as by judicial officers.[3] But the question remains, what would happen (or what ought to happen) if a given rule were broken? We still need the formal distinction between rules which the courts enforce and rules which they do not enforce. If constitutional conventions were called laws, then we should have to distinguish between judicially-enforced laws and non-judicially-enforced laws.[4]

Legal rules, with these modifications, are thus distinguished from rules of public morality which are not enforced by the courts, although they may in some cases, *e.g.* constitutional conventions (such as the responsibility of members to Parliament), be recognised as existing by the courts. Although constitutional conventions are not laws as here defined, a study of them is essential to the understanding of a constitution—especially the British Constitution—and a description of the more important conventions is always included in books on British constitutional law.[5]

Legal rules are also distinguished from rules of private morality or ethics which are not enforced by the courts, *e.g.* the moral obligation to carry out a freely made bargain which is not unlawful but which for some reason (such as absence of consideration) lacks legal sanction. The contents of ethics and law overlap to a great extent, *e.g.* murder, theft and slander; but there are many rules of ethics which the law does not seek to enforce, such as the commandment to honour our parents; and many legal rules which are not intrinsically moral, such as the husband's general liability to pay tax on his wife's income.

Law includes not only the sum total of particular laws, whether statutory or otherwise, but also the complex interrelations between those laws, as well as the technique—judicial precedent, statutory interpretation and so on—by which the law is administered.

The state
1–004   This is another very difficult term to define, and a full discussion of this question also falls within the province of jurisprudence or political theory. It is a concept that plays little part in the constitutional law of the United Kingdom, its place being taken by that of the Crown.[6] For present purposes, however, we may define a state as an independent political society occupying a defined territory, the members of which are united together for the purpose of resisting external force and the preservation of internal order. No independent political society can be termed a state unless it professes to exercise both these functions; but no modern state of any importance contents itself with this narrow range of activity. As civilisation becomes more complex, population increases and social conscience

---

[2] See Chap. 13; and for Standing Orders, Chap. 11.
[3] See *e.g.* A. L. Goodhart, *English Law and the Moral Law* (1955), pp. 46–65.
[4] See further, O. Hood Phillips, "Constitutional Conventions: A Conventional Reply" (1964) 8 J.S.P.T.L. 60; and *post*, Chap. 7.
[5] See Chap. 7; also Chaps 8, 17 and 36.
[6] See M. Loughlin, "The State, the Crown and the Law" in *The Nature of the Crown*, eds M. Sunkin and S. Payne (1999, Oxford).

arises, the needs of the governed call for increased attention; taxes have to be levied to meet these needs; justice must be administered, commerce regulated, educational facilities and many other social services provided.

A fully developed modern state is expected to deal with a vast mass of social problems, either by direct activity or by supervision or regulation. In order to carry out these functions, the state must have agents or organs through which to operate. The appointment or establishment of these agents or organs, the general nature of their functions and powers, their relations *inter se* and between them and the private citizen, form a large part of the constitution of a state.

The constitution of a state[7]

The word "constitution" is used in two different senses, the abstract and the concrete. The constitution of a state in the abstract sense is the system of laws, customs and conventions which define the composition and powers of organs of the state, and regulate the relations of the various state organs to one another and to the private citizen. A "constitution" in the concrete sense is the document in which the most important laws of the constitution are authoritatively ordained. A country, such as our own, which has no "written" constitution as explained below, has no constitution in the concrete sense of the word.[8] It should be clear from the context which meaning is being employed.

1–005

Written and unwritten constitutions[9]

A constitution is said to be "written" when the most important constitutional laws are specifically *enacted*. Probably all states, except the United Kingdom and Israel[10] now have mainly written or enacted constitutions. New Zealand, until recently, had a largely unwritten constitution. The New Zealand Parliament, however, enacted a Constitution Act in 1996.[11] Those who attain power in a state, whether as a result of revolution (*e.g.* France), war of independence (*e.g.* United States), federation or confederation of existing units (*e.g.* Switzerland), or emergence of a new independent nation (*e.g.* former British colonies and protectorates), put into the form of legislative enactment the manner in which the state is to be organised, government carried on and justice administered, and this arrangement is commonly approved by a referendum of the electorate. The most important laws constituting the basis of the state are specified in one formal document or a series of formal documents which are binding on the courts and all persons concerned.

1–006

It is not practicable for a written constitution to contain more than a selection of constitutional laws. It is invariably supplemented, within the limits prescribed in the constitution, by amendments passed in the prescribed manner; by organic laws, and other legislation passed in the ordinary way from time to time to fill in gaps; usually also by judicial decisions interpreting the written documents; and

---

[7] See Colin Munro, "What is a Constitution?" [1983] P.L. 563.

[8] Or indeed, in any sense according to F.F. Ridley, "There is No British Constitution," (1988) 41 Parl. Affairs, 340.

[9] The distinction is criticised as misleading and inexact by C. Munro, *Studies in Constitutional Law* (2nd ed., 1999, Butterworths).

[10] H. E. Baker, *The Legal System of Israel* (2nd ed., 1968); E. Likhovski, *Israel's Parliament* (1972): there are "basic laws," but no constitution has been drawn up yet.

[11] *post*, para. 36–012.

by customs and conventions regulating the working of the machinery of government.[12] Organic laws are a special class of laws for the passing of which a constitution prescribes some special procedure, but which do not amount to constitutional amendments.

Flexible and rigid constitutions

1–007   A more significant classification of the types of constitution is that into "flexible" and "rigid," metaphors given currency by Bryce.[13] A *flexible* constitution was defined by Dicey as "one under which every law of every description can legally be changed with the same ease and in the same manner by one and the same body." Dicey defined a *rigid* constitution as "one under which certain laws generally known as constitutional or fundamental laws cannot be changed in the same manner as ordinary laws."[14] The distinction is of great importance in relation to constitutional amendment.

Where the constitution is rigid, certain provisions are distinguished from others in that some *special procedure* is necessary for their alteration, if they are legally alterable at all. Most European and American constitutions are rigid. The method of amending "fundamental" or "constitutional" laws varies in different constitutions: it may be the legislature sitting in a special way (as in France) or with a prescribed majority or a prescribed quorum (as in Belgium), the convention of a special constituent body (as in the United States), the consultation of the component members of a composite state (as in the United States and Swiss Federations), or a referendum of the electorate (as in Switzerland and Australia). Amendment of the United States Constitution, for example, requires either initiation by two-thirds of both Houses of Congress and ratification by the legislatures of three-fourths of the states (the usual method), or initiation by two-thirds of the states and ratification by conventions in three-fourths of the states (*e.g.* repealing 18th Amendment on prohibition).

1–008   A subdivision of rigid constitutions can be drawn according to whether the special amending procedure is within the sole power of the legislature, or whether some outside agency has to be brought in. In the latter case the constitution may be said to be supreme over the legislature.

Sometimes a constitution or part of it may not be legally alterable at all, as certain articles of the Constitution of the German Federal Republic (1949), the "basic articles" of the Constitution of the Republic of Cyprus (1960) and the representation of a state in the United States Senate (unless that state consents); or it may be unalterable before a certain time, *e.g.* certain provisions of the United States Constitution before 1808. In such cases any alteration would legally amount to revolution.

It is unnecessary and it may be confusing to draw a distinction, as Dicey does in the first definition quoted, between the relative ease and difficulty of amending a law; this is not a distinction of which lawyers can take account, for it depends on political and psychological factors. It may be more difficult to pass a British

---

[12] Wheare, *Modern Constitutions*, Chaps 3, 7 and 8. See *e.g.* Munro, *The Constitution and Government of the United States* (4th ed.), pp. 76–88; Dawson, *The Government of Canada*, pp. 69–72; H. W. Horwill, *Usages of the American Constitution* (1925).

[13] *Studies in History and Jurisprudence*, Vol. 1, Essay 3. Other descriptive names considered by Bryce were moving and stationary, or fluid and solid (crystallised); *op. cit.* pp. 131–132. Lord Birkenhead L.C. preferred "controlled" and "uncontrolled": *McCawley v. The King* [1920] A.C. 691, PC. *cf.* Wheare. *op. cit.* Chap. 6.

[14] Dicey, *Law of the Constitution* (10th ed.), pp. 126 *et seq.*, and 146–150.

statute amending the law relating to the sale of intoxicating liquors or the opening of shops on Sunday than to pass a French statute reducing the period of office of the President of the Republic from seven to five years.

Unwritten constitutions are in practice flexible, but written constitutions are not necessarily rigid. The constitutions of the Australian states for example are written and largely flexible.

Fundamental laws and judicial review of legislation

Those who frame a rigid constitution seem to be placed in a dilemma. They **1–009** may give the power to interpret the constitution and to declare legislation invalid *ex post facto* as being repugnant thereto, to the ordinary courts, or to a special constitutional court. Here the final and supreme power would appear to be vested in the courts, which would usually be contrary to the intention of the framers of the constitution. Why should judges, whose function is primarily judicial, set up their own views in opposition to the will of a popularly elected legislative assembly? Two answers may be suggested: first, the judges may be appointed by the executive which initiates legislation and presumably keeps in touch with public opinion; or, alternatively, the "will of the people" is supposed to be embodied in the constitution in a more permanent way than it is represented in the legislative assembly of the day.

On the other hand, if the legislature itself is given authority to interpret the constitution, what guarantee is there that it will ever hold itself to be wrong? In other words, how can the constitution in this case be rigid at all? Dicey saw this difficulty and stated the paradox that the "fundamental laws" in the continental type of "rigid" constitution placing restrictions on the authority of the ordinary legislature, without giving power of judicial review, so far from being laws of a particularly sacrosanct character are found on analysis not to be laws at all. When the courts are not given and have not assumed authority to declare legislation unconstitutional, the constitutional restrictions on legislative activity—though in fact they may be carefully observed—appear on Dicey's view to be merely constitutional conventions resting on the force of public opinion.[15]

It is comparatively rare for the courts to have jurisdiction to review legislation **1–010** ("constitutional adjudication") except in federal states, such as Switzerland[16] and the federal members of the Commonwealth, where some check is necessary to preserve the respective rights of the federation and its component members.[17] The United States is the classic example of a federation in which each state as well as the federation has a completely rigid constitution. Here the state courts have jurisdiction to declare state legislation repugnant to the state constitution; and the federal courts have jurisdiction to declare provisions of state constitutions, state legislation and federal legislation repugnant to the Federal Constitution. It is not strictly accurate to say that the courts declare legislation void: when cases are brought before them judicially, they may declare that an alleged right or power does not exist or that an alleged wrong has been committed because a certain statute relied on is unconstitutional. Under the influence of Chief Justice

---

[15] *cf.* Bryce, *op. cit.* pp. 193–198.
[16] C. Hughes, *The Federal Constitution of Switzerland*; Geoffrey Sawer, *Modern Federalism* (1969), Chap. 10.
[17] Judicial review obtains in dependent territories of the Commonwealth, however, because their legislatures are regarded as subordinate to the British Parliament; *post*, Chap. 35.

Marshall the American Supreme Court first assumed the power of declaring Federal legislation unconstitutional in *Marbury v. Madison* (1803),[18] and the power of declaring state legislation repugnant to the Federal Constitution in *Fletcher v. Peck* (1810).[19] It may be added by way of further justification that, not only is the United States a federation, but the executive is not responsible to the legislature and so there is not the same reason for the will of the legislature to prevail. The Republic of Ireland, on the other hand, is a unitary state, with an executive legally as well as conventionally responsible to the legislature, whose Constitution gives the Supreme Court and High Court some power of review.[20]

The modern alternative to review of legislation by the ordinary courts is not necessarily the complete absence of any review of constitutionality. A special constitutional court may be set up for such cases, as in the Constitutions of the Republic of Cyprus (1960), West Germany, and Italy.

1–011   Another device is to establish a constitutional council to which Bills may be referred *before* being submitted to the Head of State for his assent. Thus the Constitution of the Fifth French Republic (1958) provides for a *Conseil Constitutionnel* composed of former Presidents of the Republic and nine other members, three being appointed by each of the President of the Republic, the President of the National Assembly and the President of the Senate. Before organic laws are promulgated, the Council must examine them to ensure that they do not conflict with the constitution. The President of the Republic, the Prime Minister or the President of either House may also submit ordinary laws to the Council before they are promulgated. If a provision is declared unconstitutional it cannot be promulgated or come into force. There is no appeal against decisions of the Constitutional Council, which are binding on all public, administrative and judicial authorities. This device differs from judicial review in that the *Conseil* is not a court, and judicial review operates *ex post facto*.

The Constitutions of the Irish Republic and India expressly recognise the distinction between fundamental rights safeguarded by the courts against amendment otherwise than by the appropriate procedure, and "directive principles of social (or state) policy" for the general guidance of the legislature but which are not cognisable by any court. Such directive principles of state policy are morally binding on the legislature, but can scarcely be called laws.

The scope of constitutional law

1–012   The constitutional law of a state is the law relating to its constitution. Where the constitution is written, even though it may have to be supplemented by other materials, it is fairly easy to distinguish the constitutional law of a state from the rest of its legal system; but where, as in Britain, the constitution is unwritten, it is largely a matter of convenience what topics one includes in constitutional law, and there is no strict scientific distinction between that and the rest of the law. Thus the United Kingdom constitution can well be said to be marked by three

---

[18] 1 Cranch 137.
[19] 6 Cranch 87.
[20] By Article 26 the Supreme Court may rule on the constitutional validity of legislation before it receives the President's assent.

By Article 34.3.2, both the High Court and Supreme Court have jurisdiction to declare unconstitutional legislation after it has been enacted.

striking features: it is indeterminate, indistinct, and unentrenched.[21] It follows from what has been said that constitutional law deals, in general, with the distribution and exercise of the functions of government, and the relations of the government authorities to each other and to the individual citizen. It includes the rules—though the nature of these is difficult to define—which identify the law-making authorities themselves, *e.g.* the legislature and the courts.[22]

More specifically, constitutional law embraces that part of a country's laws which relates to the following topics, among others: the method of choosing the Head of State, whether king or president; his powers and prerogatives; the constitution of the legislature; its powers and the privileges of its members; if there are two Chambers, the relations between them; the status of Ministers and the position of the civil servants who act under them; the armed forces and the power to control them; the relations between the central government and local authorities; treaty-making power; citizenship; the raising and spending of public money; the general system of courts, and the tenure and immunities of judges; civil liberties and their limitations; the parliamentary franchise and electoral boundaries; and the procedure (if any) for amending the constitution.

Administrative law

A distinction is commonly drawn in continental countries between constitu- **1–013**
tional law and administrative law, but because English law is not codified or officially systematised English jurists have found difficulty in determining the distinction. Sir Ivor Jennings contended that administrative law, like other branches of law, ought to be defined according to its subject-matter, namely, public administration. Administrative law then determines the organisation, powers and duties of administrative authorities.[23]

What specially distinguishes administrative authorities from private individuals is the extent of their powers. An important aspect of administrative law is the control exercised by courts or tribunals over those powers, especially in relation to the rights of citizens. The remedy of the citizen may be left to the jurisdiction of the ordinary courts, or the matter may be regulated by special rules and adjudicated by special courts or by administrative tribunals. A system of administrative courts or tribunals is not essential for the existence of administrative law, as is shown by the experience of Belgium, which did not set up a *Conseil d'Etat* until 1946; but the fact that France has long possessed special administrative tribunals—notably the *Conseil d'Etat*—which in appropriate cases oust the jurisdiction of the ordinary civil courts, has no doubt helped towards the systematisation of administrative law in that country.[24]

Where there is a written constitution, as in France and the United States, it is easier to demarcate administrative law from constitutional law, although neither the French *droit administratif* nor American administrative law is codified. Where the constitution is unwritten, as in this country, it is largely a matter of convenience where the line is drawn.[25]

---

[21] S. E. Finer, Vernon Bogdanor, Bernard Rudden, *Comparing Constitutions* (1995, Oxford) p. 40.
[22] See H. L. A. Hart, *The Concept of Law* (2nd ed., 1994) Chap. VI.
[23] Jennings, *The Law and the Constitution* (5th ed.), p. 217.
[24] L. N. Brown and J. Bell, *French Administrative Law* (5th ed., 1998).
[25] *Post*, Chap. 2; and Pt VI. For a statutory recognition of the term "administrative law" see the State Immunity Act 1978, s.3(2).

Public law

1–014   A convenient descriptive term for both constitutional law and administrative law is public law. Many legal systems, influenced by Roman Law,[26] draw a clear distinction between public law and private law. Public law matters may be dealt with in separate courts. The rights and remedies of parties may depend on whether a claim raises a question of public law or private law. As Lord Wilberforce has explained,

> "The expressions 'private law' and 'public law' have recently been imported into the law of England from countries which, unlike our own, have separate systems concerning public law and private law. No doubt they are convenient expressions for descriptive purposes. In this country they must be used with caution ... The principle remains intact that public authorities and public servants are, unless clearly exempted, answerable in the ordinary courts for wrongs done to individuals."[27]

The reasons for this development and its significance will be discussed later.[28]

The functions of government

1–015   Montesquieu in *L'Esprit des Lois* (1748),[29] following attempts by Aristotle[30] and Locke,[31] divided the powers of government into: (i) the legislative power; (ii) the executive power in matters pertaining to the law of nations, and (iii) the power of judging; and so we get the first statement of the modern classification to which we are now accustomed, *viz*: (i) legislative, (ii) executive, and (iii) judicial.

We may attempt a general description of the various governmental functions in the modern state on the following lines:

(i) *The legislative function* is the making of new law, and the alteration or repeal of existing law. Legislation is the formulation of law by the appropriate organ of the state, in such a manner that the actual words used are themselves part of the law: the words not only contain the law, but in a sense they constitute the law. Legislation may take the form of the decree of a personal ruler, whether king or dictator; or it may be issued by an autocratic body or by a democratic assembly wholly or partly elected by the people. Without a legislative body of some sort a state could not provide law readily enough to meet modern conditions.

Two methods of direct lawmaking are found in some states: the *referendum* by which certain measures have to be submitted for approval to the electorate before being enacted by the legislature; and the *initiative* by which certain kinds of

---

[26] Public law was that part of the law which concerned the State; private law that which concerned individuals; D.1.1.1.2; *Institutions* 1.1.4. (In this sense criminal law must be regarded as part of public law.) A similar distinction had been drawn by Aristotle, *Rhet* i.13.3. Scots law distinguishes public right and private right (Stair, *Institutions* 1.1.23). See, Article XVIII of the Union with Scotland Act; *Gibson v. Lord Advocate* 1975 S.L.T. 134; *post*, para. 4–007.

[27] *Davy v. Spelthorne B.C.* [1984] A.C. 262. The difficulties of transposing the concepts to the English legal system are discussed in J.W.F. Allison, *A Continental Distinction in the Common Law* (2000).

[28] *post*, Part VI, Introduction.

[29] Bk XI, Chap. 6.

[30] Aristotle, Vol. IV (transl. Jowett).

[31] John Locke, *Second Treatise of Civil Government* (1690) Chap. 12.

measures may be proposed by a specified number of the electors for enactment.[32] The referendum is usually a method for amending federal constitutions.[33]

(ii) *The executive or administrative function* is the general and detailed carrying on of government according to law, including the framing of policy and the choice of the manner in which the law may be made to render that policy possible. In recent times, especially since the industrialisation of most civilised countries, the scope of this function has become extremely wide. It now involves the provision and administration or regulation of a vast system of social services—public health, housing, assistance for the sick and unemployed, welfare of individual workers, education, transport and so on—as well as the supervision of defence, order and justice, and the finance required therefore, which were the original tasks of organised government.

(iii) *The judicial function* consists in the interpretation of the law and its application by rule or discretion to the facts of particular cases. This involves the ascertainment of facts in dispute according to the law of evidence. The organs which the state sets up to exercise the judicial function are called courts of law or courts of justice.

Although the above classification of the functions and corresponding powers **1–016** of government, based on a material or functional analysis, may be useful in helping to arrange the facts and to think about the problems of government, the categories are inclined to become blurred when it is attempted to apply them to the details of a particular constitution. Some hold that the true distinction lies not in the nature of the powers themselves, but rather in the procedure by which they are exercised. Thus legislation involves a formal and instantaneous act designed to establish general rules by which all disputes shall be settled; administration is a continuing and mainly informal process aimed at preventing disputes in classes of cases and does not create rights by establishing precedents; adjudication presupposes an existing dispute in a particular case, is governed by strict rules of procedure and evidence and tends to create rights by establishing precedents.

Others hold that the distinction is organic or formal. Thus administration consists of the operations, whatever their intrinsic nature may be, which are performed by administrators; and administrators are all state officials who are neither legislators nor judges.[34] This last doctrine seems to be as difficult to apply as the functional or material conception of governmental functions. Thus in the Constitution of the Fifth French Republic not only has the Parliament other powers than the strictly legislative, but the law-making power is divided between the Parliament (*loi*) and the government (*règlement*), so that the Parliament may only make laws dealing with matters enumerated in article 34, while all others matters fall within the province of ministerial regulation.[35]

---

[32] Wheare, *op. cit.* Chap. 6; A. B. Keith, *British Cabinet System* (2nd ed., Gibbs), pp. 256–260; H. J. Laski, *Introduction to Politics*, pp. 66–68; Philip Goodhart. *Referendum* (1971).

[33] It has, however, become increasingly popular in the United Kingdom since 1972: Northern Ireland (Border Poll) Act 1972; Referendum Act 1975; Scotland Act 1978; Wales Act 1978; Referendums (Scotland and Wales) Act 1997; Greater London Authority Referendum Act 1998. Legislation relating to Northern Ireland has made standing provision for the use of referendums; Northern Ireland (Constitution) Act 1973; Northern Ireland (Entry to Negotiations) Act 1996; Northern Ireland Act 1998.

[34] Jennings, *op. cit.* pp. 24–25. For a contrast between the conceptual and the functional approach, see Griffith and Street, *Principles of Administrative Law.* (4th ed., 1967).

[35] B. Nicholas, "Loi, Règlement and Judicial Review in the Fifth Republic" [1970] P.L. 251.

Doctrine of the separation of powers[36]

1–017   The doctrine of "the separation of powers" as usually understood is derived from Montesquieu,[37] whose elaboration of it was based on a study of Locke's writings[38] and an imperfect understanding of the eighteenth-century English Constitution. Montesquieu was concerned with the preservation of political liberty. "Political liberty is to be found," he says, "only when there is no abuse of power. But constant experience shows us that every man invested with power is liable to abuse it, and to carry his authority as far as it will go. . . . To prevent this abuse, it is necessary from the nature of things that one power should be a check on another. . . . When the legislative and executive powers are united in the same person or body . . . there can be no liberty. . . . Again, there is no liberty if the judicial power is not separated from the legislative and the executive. . . . There would be an end of everything if the same person or body, whether of the nobles or of the people, were to exercise all three powers."

A complete separation of powers, in the sense of a distribution of the three functions of government among three independent sets of organs with no overlapping or co-ordination, would (even if theoretically possible) bring government to a standstill. What the doctrine must be taken to advocate is the prevention of tyranny by the conferment of too much power on any one person or body, and the check of one power by another. There is an echo of this in Blackstone's *Commentaries* (1765): "In all tyrannical Governments . . . the right of making and of enforcing the laws is vested in one and the same man, or the same body of men; and wheresoever these two powers are united together there can be no liberty"; and this doctrine was taken over by the fathers of the American Constitution.

The question whether the separation of powers (*i.e.* the distribution of the various powers of government among different organs), in so far as is practicable, is desirable, and (if so) to what extent, is a problem of political theory and must be distinguished from the question which alone concerns the constitutional lawyer, namely, whether and to what extent such a separation actually exists in any given constitution. As a matter of fact the doctrine has not received much acceptance either in its country of origin or in other European countries. Governmental powers are co-ordinated by the effective part of the executive—the Council of Ministers or Cabinet—which is created by, but in fact controls, the legislature in which its members sit. The executive in some democratic countries is made responsible to the legislature; but in totalitarian states the executive has acquired complete domination over both the legislature and the judiciary. The doctrine may be said to have received its main application in democratic countries by securing the independence of the courts from the control of the executive.[39]

1–018   The United States Constitution goes further than any other in applying the doctrine. Thus the federal executive power is vested in the President, the federal legislative power is vested in Congress, and the federal judicial power is vested

---

[36] W. B. Glyn, *The Meaning of the Separation of Powers* (1965); M. J. C. Vile, *Constitutionalism and the Separation of Powers* (1967); G. Marshall, *Constitutional Theory* (1971), Chap. 5. Colin Munro, "The Separation of Powers" [1981] P.L.19; Munro, *Studies in Constitutional Law* pp. 295–307.

[37] *L'Esprit des Lois*, Chap. XI, pp. 3–6.

[38] Locke, *Second Treatise of Civil Government* Chaps. 12–13.

[39] The doctrine of the separation of powers in its earlier history had no true application to judicial matters, and had nothing to do with the independence of judges: C. M. McIlwain. *Constitutionalism: Ancient and Modern* (1940) (revised ed., 1947), pp. 141–142.

in the Supreme Court. The President and his Cabinet are not members of Congress (except that the Vice-President presides over the Senate), and they are not responsible to Congress. The President holds office for a fixed term and he is not necessarily of the same political party as the majority in either House of Congress. The President and Cabinet cannot initiate Bills or secure their passage through Congress, but he may recommend legislation in a message to Congress. But the separation of powers is by no means complete, the three branches of government being connected by a system of "checks and balances." Madison's theory was that one branch must not have the whole of another branch vested in it, nor obtain control over another branch. The chief danger in a republic with a representative legislature was, he thought, that the legislature (rather than the executive) would encroach on the other departments.[40] Thus the President may veto measures passed by Congress, though his veto may be overridden by a two-thirds vote of both Houses. The President has the power to negotiate treaties, but they must be ratified by a two-thirds vote of the Senate. The Supreme Court, asserting the continued significance of the separation of powers, has held that Congress has no power to veto executive acts of the President.[41] The Senate may refuse to confirm certain appointments made by the President, notably that of judges of the Supreme Court; and the judges of that court, although appointed for life, may be removed by impeachment. The power of judicial review of legislation was assumed by the Supreme Court, and was not expressly conferred— although it may perhaps be implied—by the constitution. The three branches of government are therefore interrelated; they act as checks on each other. The problem that may have to be faced before long is whether the draftsmen of the constitution, in their zeal to prevent too great a concentration of power, did not provide restraints that unduly hamper the working of government.[42]

Fundamental Rights

Rights which are regarded as possessed by human beings prior to their recognition by a legal system—or despite their denial by a legal system—can conveniently be described as human rights or natural rights. Formulations of natural rights date from the second half of the eighteenth century, the revolutionary period in America and France.[43] Both countries borrowed largely from English experience and thought, especially as embodied in the writings of Locke[44] and, in the case of America, Coke's commentary on Magna Carta and Blackstone's *Commentaries* (1765). For Blackstone the absolute rights of Englishmen were the rights of personal security, personal liberty and private property.

Such rights when recognised in a constitution and guaranteed protection against curtailment (except by legislation passed by special procedure) can be distinguished as "fundamental rights." In this sense the British Constitution does not recognise "fundamental rights." Nonetheless, the courts increasingly refer to rights as "fundamental" or "constitutional" which because of their importance

1–019

---

[40] *The Federalist*, Nos. 47 and 48 (1788).
[41] *Immigration and Naturalisation Service v. Chadha* (1983) 51 *U.S. Law Week* 4907; B. Schwartz, (1984) 100 L.Q.R.9.
[42] See, *e.g. Youngstown Sheet & Tube Co. v. Sawyer*, 343 U.S. 579 (1952) (the "Steel Seizure Case"): B. Schwartz, *American Constitutional Law*, Chap. 7.
[43] See further D'Entreves, *Natural Law* (2nd ed., 1970) especially Chapter 4.
[44] *Two Treatises of Civil Government* (1690); see Bk. II, "Of Civil Government."

cannot be restricted except by clear words in an Act of Parliament.[45] The enactment of the Human Rights Act 1998 and the ensuing duty of public authorities to act in a way compatible with Convention rights will, almost inevitably, encourage further use of such terminology.[46]

Many modern constitutions incorporate certain "fundamental rights" such as personal freedom, equality before the law, freedom of property, free elections, freedom of speech, freedom of conscience and worship, freedom of contract, the right of assembly, the right of association and family rights. They are always restricted, expressly or impliedly, by some such concepts as "public order" or "due process of law"; and the courts may or may not have jurisdiction to review legislation that infringes such rights.

1–020   The American Declaration of Independence (1776) states that all men are created equal, and among their inalienable rights are life, liberty and the pursuit of happiness. The American "Bill of Rights" consists of 10 amendments added in 1791 to the Federal Constitution of 1787.[47] These rights include free exercise of religion, freedom of speech and the press, peaceable assembly, petition for redress of grievances (1st Amendment); security of persons, houses, papers and effects from unreasonable searches and seizures (2nd Amendment); no deprivation of life, liberty or property without due process of law[48] (5th Amendment); and freedom from excessive bail or fines and from cruel or unusual punishments (8th Amendment). The American Constitution had already provided that the writ of habeas corpus should not be suspended, that no *ex post facto* law should be passed, and that the trial of all crimes, except in cases of impeachment, should be by jury.[49] Later amendments abolished slavery, and preserved the franchise from discrimination on grounds of race, colour or sex. The constitutions of individual American states also contain Bills of Rights.

A Declaration of the Rights of Man was prefaced to the French Constitution of 1791, and was confirmed by the preambles to the Constitutions of 1946 and 1958.

A Universal Declaration of Human Rights was adopted by the General Assembly of the United Nations in 1948, and this was followed by the European Convention for the Protection of Human Rights and Fundamental Freedoms drawn up at Rome in 1950. The Convention came into force in 1953 but did not have legal effect inside the United Kingdom until the coming into effect of the Human Rights Act 1998.[50]

The United Nations has subsequently adopted Conventions on Refugees (1951), Slavery (1956), the Elimination of Racial Discrimination (1965); Civil and Political Rights (1966) and Against Torture and other Cruel, Inhuman or Degrading Treatment or Punishment (1984). The impact of such international

---

[45] *Morris v. Beardmore* [1981] A.C. 446, HL (privacy of the home); *R. v. Secretary of State for the Home Department ex p. Ruddock* [1987] 2 All E.R. 518 (right of access to the courts); *R. v. Lord Chancellor ex p. Witham* [1998] Q.B. 575 (Div. Ct) (right of access to the courts). *Dist. R. v. Lord Chancellor ex p. Lightfoot* [2000] CA; *R. v. Home Secretary of State ex p. Leech (No 2)* [1994] Q.B. 198, CA; *R. v. Secretary of State for the Home Department ex p. Simms* [2000] 2 A.C., HL (rights of prisoners); *D.P.P. v. Jones* [1999] A.C. 240, HL (public right of peaceful assembly: Lord Irvine, at pp. 253–255.)

[46] See, *post* p. 115.

[47] A Bill of Rights was intentionally excluded from the original United States Constitution for the reasons given by Hamilton in *The Federalist*, No. 88.

[48] "Due process of law" may be traced back to (1354) 28 Edw. III, c.3.

[49] The Statute of Provisors 1351–52, c.4, required for a criminal charge indictment or presentment of good and lawful people of the neighbourhood.

[50] See *post*, Chap. 22.

declarations on domestic law was dramatically shown in *R. v. Bow Street Magistrate ex p. Pinochet (No. 3)*[51] where the House of Lords held that the immunity of a former head of state from criminal proceedings in the courts of the United Kingdom did not, after the coming into effect of the 1984 Convention against Torture, apply to charges based on allegations of torture.

---

[51] [2000] 1 A.C. 147. The House consisted of a Committee of seven Law Lords. The original decision of the House that General Pinochet was not entitled to immunity, reported [2000] 1 A.C. 61, had been set aside in a subsequent hearing on the ground of the close connection between a member of the House and one of the organisations involved in the appeal: [2000] 1 A.C. 119; *post*, para. 31–013 *et seq.*

CHAPTER 2

GENERAL CHARACTERISTICS OF THE BRITISH CONSTITUTION

Unitary constitution: the United Kingdom

2–001   The United Kingdom constitution was traditionally described as unitary as opposed to federal or confederal. Devolution and other constitutional reforms introduced since the election of 1997 have led, however, to the suggestion that the constitution should now be described as quasi-federal.[1] The United Kingdom is a union of England, Wales, Scotland and Northern Ireland.[2] The state for the purpose of international relations is the United Kingdom, although it is often popularly but inaccurately referred to as "Britain," "Great Britain" or "England." The words "United Kingdom," when used in a statute or public document, mean Great Britain and Northern Ireland, unless the contrary intention appears.[3]

Wales[4]

2–002   The *Statutum Walliae*, passed in 1284 after Edward I had defeated Llewelyn ap Griffith, declared that Wales was incorporated into the Kingdom of England. Henry VIII completed the introduction of the English legal and administrative system into Wales. This union was effected by annexation rather than treaty. The Laws in Wales Act 1536 united Wales with England, and gave to Welshmen all the laws, rights and privileges of Englishmen. Welsh constituencies received representation in the English Parliament. An Act of 1542 covered land tenure, courts and administration of justice. References to "England" in Acts of Parliament passed between 1746 and 1967 include Wales.[5] The judicial systems of England and Wales were amalgamated in 1830.

The Government of Wales Act 1998 devolved limited powers of government to the Welsh Assembly which it established.[6]

Scotland[7]

2–003   Scotland and England were separate kingdoms with their own rulers until 1603, when James VI of Scotland succeeded Elizabeth I as James I of England.

---

[1] R. Hazell, "Reinventing the Constitution" [1999] P.L. 84.

[2] The status of the Isle of Man and the Channel Islands is discussed in Chap. 35.

[3] Interpretation Act 1978, s.5 and Sched. 1. For an express intention to the contrary see the Crown Proceedings Act 1947 where references to the United Kingdom (*e.g.* in s.40(2)(c)) have to be read in the light of s.52.

[4] See William Rees. *The Union of England and Wales* (University of Wales Press, 1938); J. F. Rees, *Studies in Welsh History* (Cardiff, 1947); *Welsh Studies in Public Law* (J. A. Andrews ed. 1970).

[5] Wales and Berwick Act 1746; Welsh Language Act 1967. It may be objected that this statute—like many others—has a singularly inapt short title; H. W. R. Wade, *Constitutional Fundamentals* (1980), p. 19. For the further promotion of the Welsh language, see the Welsh Language Act 1993.

[6] See *post*, Chap 5.

[7] See T. B. Smith, *Scotland: The Development of its Laws and Constitution* (1962); J. D. B. Mitchell, *Constitutional Law* (2nd ed., 1968); *The British Commonwealth: Development of its Laws and Constitution: 1 The United Kingdom*, pp. 603 *et seq.*; T. B. Smith, "The Union of 1707 as Fundamental Law" (1957) P.L. 99; G. M. Trevelyan, *Ramillies and the Union with Scotland*, Chaps 12–14; D. Daiches, *Scotland and the Union* (1977); D. N. MacCormick, "Does the United Kingdom have a Constitution?" (1978) 29 N.I.L.Q.I.

The name "Great Britain" was suggested by Francis Bacon: "Brief Discourse Touching the Happy Union of the Kingdoms of England and Scotland."

This was merely a personal union, and was followed in 1707 by a union of the two Kingdoms into a United Kingdom of Great Britain.[8] The Treaty was ratified by both the English and Scottish Parliaments, which ceased to exist on the transference of their powers to the Parliament of Great Britain. The Union with Scotland Act 1706 provided for the succession of the Crown of Great Britain in accordance with the English Act of Settlement. There was to be a Parliament of Great Britain. Any law in force in either Kingdom inconsistant with the terms of the Union was to be void. Conventions of constitutional government were coming into being in England, but there was no constitutional tradition in Scotland and so the development of conventions after the Union continued on the English lines.[9] Scots law was to continue in force unless altered by the Parliament of Great Britain. Public law might be assimilated, but Scots private law was not be changed "except for evident utility of the subjects within Scotland." The preservation of the established Presbyterian Church in Scotland ("Church of Scotland") is an essential term of the Union.[10] Scotland has its own system of courts, with final appeal in civil, but not criminal, cases to the House of Lords.[11] The Scotland Act 1998 created a Scottish Parliament with somewhat wider powers than those of the Welsh Assembly.[12]

Northern Ireland[13]

For centuries before 1800 Ireland had been a subordinate Kingdom of the English (British) Crown. It had a Parliament of its own on the English model, though how far it was subordinate to the English (British) Parliament was a matter of controversy. Ireland also had a system of courts on the English model, but again doubts were expressed from time to time whether final appeal lay to the English or the Irish House of Lords. The executive in Ireland was definitely under the control of the English Government through the Lord-Lieutenant. The Union with Ireland Act 1800 united the two Kingdoms of Great Britain and Ireland into the United Kingdom of Great Britain and Ireland, under provisions similar to the Union of 1707. Again a personal union was turned into a legislative union. However, the union with Ireland, unlike that with Scotland, was not based on a treaty negotiated by commissioners representing each country, but was brought about by Acts of the British and Irish Parliaments following parallel resolutions passed by each Parliament in response to messages from the Crown.

2–004

---

[8] There was also a personal union of Great Britain and Hanover from 1714 to 1837, and the Act of Settlement 1700 provided that England should not be obliged to engage in any war for the defence of Hanover without the consent of Parliament. As to allegiance, see *Isaacson v. Durant (Stepney Election Petition)* (1886) 17 Q.B.D. 54.

[9] *cf. MacCormick v. Lord Advocate* 1953 S.C. 396; *post*, para. 4–008.

[10] See R. King Murray, "The Constitutional Position of the Church of Scotland" [1958] P.L. 155. And see further, *post*, para. 4–007.

[11] *Greenshields v. Magistrates of Edinburgh*, Robertson, App. 12. See Dicey and Rait, *Thoughts on the Union between England and Scotland*, pp. 194–195; Turberville, *The House of Lords in the Eighteenth Century*, pp. 94–95, 139–141. *cf.* Scottish Episcopalians Act 1711.

[12] See, *post* Chap. 5.

[13] See H. Calvert, *Constitutional Law in Northern Ireland* (1968); *The British Commonwealth: Development of its Laws and Constitutions: I The United Kingdom* (1955), pp. 411 *et seq.* (by L. A. Sheridan); A. S. Queckett. *The Constitution of Northern Ireland* (1928–46); V. T. H. Delaney, *The Administration of Justice in Ireland* (2nd ed., 1965); Claire Palley. "The Evolution, Disintegration and Possible Reconstruction of the Northern Ireland Constitution (1972)," 1 *Anglo-American Law Review* 368.

The greater part of Ireland ceased to form part of the United Kingdom in 1922[14] and after a period of "Dominion status" similar to that of Canada at the time, it became in 1949 an independent republic outside the Commonwealth.[15] Northern Ireland, consisting of six[16] of the nine counties of Ulster, remained within the United Kingdom, and for half a century from 1920 considerable legislative and executive powers were devolved on it, so that it had its own subordinate Parliament and government departments.[17] The Province also had (and still has) its own system of courts, with final appeal in both civil and criminal cases to the House of Lords.

2–005   In 1972 the existing constitutional arrangements were suspended by the Northern Ireland (Temporary Provisions) Act 1972. A Secretary of State for Northern Ireland became responsible for governing the Province. Subsequent constitutional developments are discussed in Chapter 5 (Devolution).

Unwritten constitution

2–006   The British Constitution is described as "unwritten"[18] because it is not embodied, wholly or mainly, in any enactment or formally related series of enactments.[19] At the time of the Norman conquest, constitutions were of a customary nature. After the civil war of the seventeenth century, Cromwell drew up an Instrument of Government (1653)[20]—the only written constitution the English[21] have had; but this came to an end in 1660 with the restoration of the monarchy. Suggestions for a written constitution for the United Kingdom put forward on wide grounds[22] have attracted little general support hitherto, as distinct from support for the proposal of a Bill of Rights. The constitutional reforms effected since 1997 have not involved the adoption of a written constitution but have on the contrary, relied for their efficacy on the unwritten rule of the supremacy of Parliament.

The laws of the British constitution comprise three kinds of rules: statute law, common law, and custom (especially parliamentary custom). To these we must add constitutional conventions if we are to understand modern developments and the manner in which the constitution works. The sources of the legal rules are the same as for private law, namely, statutes, judicial precedents, customs and books of authority, except that under the third head we must include parliamentary custom. Treaties are not in themselves sources of municipal (*i.e.* national) law, as they are in some countries.

---

[14] Irish Free State (Agreement) Act 1922.

[15] Ireland Act 1949.

[16] Antrim, Armagh, Down, Fermanagh, Londonderry and Tyrone.

[17] Government of Ireland Act 1920, as amended from time to time.

[18] Or "not written," "part-written," "uncodified" or "evolutionary": L. Wolf-Phillips, *Comparative Constitutions* (1972), pp. 46–47; E. Barendt, *An Introduction to Constitutional Law* (1998), pp. 32–34.

[19] *ante*, para. 1–005.

[20] S. R. Gardiner, *Constitutional Documents of the Puritan Revolution, 1625–1660* (3rd ed., 1906), p. 405.

[21] Cromwell also incorporated Scotland and Ireland into the Protectorate.

[22] *e.g.* Lord Hailsham, *The Dilemma of Democracy* (1978); O. Hood Phillips, *Reform of the Constitution* (1970); *British Government in an Era of Reform* (ed. W. V. Stankiewicz, 1976), pp. 78–93. Lord Scarman, "Constitutional Reform, A Legal Possibility?" (Holds-worth Club Address 1979); D. C. M. Yardley, "Constitutional Reform in the United Kingdom" [1980] Cur.Leg.Prob. 147.

Statutes

These consist of Acts of Parliament and subordinate legislation. **2–007**
Some of the principles and detailed rules of the British Constitution are contained in formally unrelated Acts of Parliament, such as the Act of Settlement 1700; the Parliament Acts 1911 and 1949; the Crown Proceedings Act 1947; the Supreme Court Act 1981 and the British Nationality Act 1981. Laws intended to bind both Houses of Parliament are put into the form of Acts, *e.g.* Provisional Collection of Taxes Acts, the Laying of Documents before Parliament (Interpretation) Act 1948 and the Royal Assent Act 1967. There are also a few important documents of a quasi legislative nature, such as Magna Carta 1215 (and subsequent reissues and confirmations by King and Parliament[23]), and the Bill of Rights 1688 (passed by a "convention" Parliament, but deemed to have the force of statute)[24] and at least two Acts of Parliament which have a peculiar status—the Union with Scotland Act 1706,[25] based on a treaty negotiated by the English and Scottish Parliaments, and the Statute of Westminster 1931, based on conventions agreed between the United Kingdom and the British Dominions at that time.

Subordinate legislation consists mainly of legislation made by persons or bodies to whom the power has been delegated by Parliament. Parliament confers on the Queen in Council the power to legislate by Orders in Council, a method which is useful for filling in the more important details giving effect to the principles of the enabling Act, and also valuable in times of emergency when Parliament may not be in session. Legislative powers are also frequently delegated by Parliament to individual Ministers, local government authorities and public corporations. Delegated legislation issued by Ministers usually takes the form of orders, rules or regulations, and these in appropriate cases are mostly published as Statutory Instruments. Delegated legislation made by local authorities is known as byelaws, and is published by the local authority concerned.

Judicial precedents

Many of the principles of British constitutional law are to be inferred from **2–008** decisions of the courts in particular cases, such as the extent of the liberties of the citizen, determined in disputes between individuals and the executive. Such cases arise incidentally, as it were, in the ordinary course of litigation. They will most commonly be found in the decisions of the Queen's Bench Division (previously the Court of King's Bench), which not only grants damages for breach of legal rights but also has a special jurisdiction in proceedings for habeas corpus, certiorari, prohibition and mandamus; in the decisions of the Court of Appeal and

---

[23] The version of Magna Carta that became law for subsequent times was that of Henry III (1225); and the authoritative text was that of (1297) 25 Edward I, later understood as expounded by Coke in his Second Institute. Obsolete provisions—not including Cap. 14 (forbidding excessive fines) and Cap. 29 (Caps. 39 and 40 of 1215)—were repealed in the nineteenth century by Statute Law Revision Acts. See *The Great Charter* (Griswold ed., 1965, New York) Alec Samuels, "Magna Carta as living law" (1969) 20 N.I.L.Q. 49. Confirmations by Edward I (1297) and Edward III (1324) were largely repealed by the Statute Law (Repeals) Act 1969.

[24] Crown and Parliament Recognition Act 1689. The statute now known as the Bill of Rights was passed in 1688 in a session of the new reign beginning on February 13. The Calendar (New Style) Act 1750 adopted belatedly the Gregorian calendar and laid down that for the future each year should begin on January 1, not March 25 as formerly. Hence, retrospectively, February 13, 1688 can be regarded as February 13, 1689. Famously also, 11 days were suppressed, September 3, 1752 becoming September 14.

[25] The argument that some of the terms of the Union with Scotland constitute fundamental rules of the British Constitution is discussed later; para. 4–006.

the House of Lords on appeal therefrom, and the Judicial Committee of the Privy Council in appeals from British overseas territories.[26]

Examples of judicial precedents laying down important principles of constitutional law, chosen from hundreds of cases that might be cited, are: *Ashby v. White* (1703)[27] (*ubi jus ibi remedium*); *Att.-Gen. v. Wilts United Dairies* (1922)[28] (no power to levy money without authority of Parliament); *Campbell v. Hall*[29] (no prerogative power to legislate for colony with representative assembly); *Entick v. Carrington*[30] (general warrant illegal); *Johnstone v. Pedler*[31] ("act of state" no defence in tort as regards act committed in relation to a friendly alien in this country); *Case of Proclamations*[32] (the King cannot create offences by proclamation); *Stockdale v. Hansard*[33] (Commons cannot change law by claiming new privileges); *Wason v. Walter*[34] (defence of qualified privilege extends to unauthorised reports of parliamentary debates); *Ridge v. Baldwin*[35] (*audi alteram partem*); *In re Mc.C (A Minor)*[36] (immunity of judges; privileged position of superior courts).

Custom

2–009   A custom in private law is a rule of conduct which has not been adjudicated upon by the courts, but which would be recognised and enforced by the courts if the matter came before them. It is based on usage, but in order that it may be recognised by the courts as law, a custom must be: (i) regarded by those subject to it as obligatory; (ii) certain; (iii) reasonable; (iv) of immemorial antiquity; and (v) it must have been in existence continuously. These are the main tests which English courts apply to an alleged local custom, and they would presumably apply the same tests to an alleged general custom not hitherto adjudicated upon. The traditional doctrine was that the common law of England consisted of the general "customs of the realm." It is true to a certain extent that the early common law consisted of general immemorial customs; but it is almost certain that general customs are no longer a creative source of English private law, as they have all become embodied by judicial recognition and enforcement in the system of case law or else have been displaced by legislation.

Custom (largely feudal in origin) has been a source of important parts of our constitutional law, for example, the royal prerogative and parliamentary privilege.[37] As Plucknett said: "Feudal custom includes the relationship of Crown and nobles until the moment when this body of custom separates and becomes, first, the law of the prerogative, and then later still combines with the custom of the King's High Court of Parliament to form modern constitutional law."[38] The royal

---

[26] The influence of equity on constitutional law has been comparatively slight, although the remedies of injunction and declaration were equitable in origin: see Hanbury, "Equity in Public Law" in *Essays in Equity*, p. 80.

[27] Ld.Raym. 938.

[28] 91 L.J.K.B. 897; *post* para. 3–010 and para. 29–012.

[29] (1774) 1 Cowp. 204; Lofft 655.

[30] (1765) 19 St.Tr. 1029, 1066.

[31] [1921] 2 A.C. 262.

[32] (1610) 12 Co.Rep. 74.

[33] (1839) 9 Ad. & E. 1.

[34] (1868) L.R. 4 Q.B. 73.

[35] [1964] A.C. 40, HL.

[36] [1985] A.C. 528, HL.

[37] But much of parliamentary privilege is not of "immemorial antiquity": Parliament itself may be said to have originated with Edward I.

[38] T. F. T. Plucknett, *A Concise History of the Common Law* (5th ed.), p. 309.

prerogative is now regarded as part of the common law. The law and custom of Parliament, including parliamentary privilege, is a special kind of customary law—recognised, but not developed, by the ordinary courts—which is not of immemorial antiquity. There may still be some customary constitutional laws which have not had occasion to be recognised by the courts but which would be so recognised if the question came before them, for example, such rules (not being statutory or merely conventional) as prescribe the forms according to which acts of the Crown are to be performed. If so, customs of this kind would hardly require immemorial antiquity, but would rest rather on the necessity of there being some form (such as sealing and counter-signature) by which the Crown's acts can be authenticated.

Books of authority

The general rule applied by English courts is that textbooks, however eminent **2–010** their authors, and whether or not they were judges, are not authoritative.[39] Between later authors and some of the earlier writers, however, there is a difference of authority so great as virtually to amount to a difference in kind. Some of the earlier textbooks are treated by the courts as authoritative statements of the law of their time, and therefore of present law if it is not shown to have been changed, which may be quoted and relied on in court on the authority of their authors. The statements of such writers are presumed to be evidence of judicial decisions that have been lost, and they are therefore accepted if not contrary to reason. This is chiefly to be explained by the difficulty of ascertaining the law of early times, and of course it only applies in the absence of statutes and reported decisions on the point. Whether a textbook will be treated as authoritative in this special sense is determined by the tradition of the legal profession and the practice of the courts, and depends on such factors as the reputation of the author and the date when the book was written.

Among the books of authority that are most important as sources of English constitutional law are Fitzherbert's *Abridgment* (1516), Brooke's *Abridgment* (1568), Glanvill's *Tractatus de Legibus et Consuetudinibus Angliae* (*c.* 1189), Bracton's treatise of the same name (*c.* 1250),[40] Littleton's *Tenures* (*c.* 1470), Fitzherbert's *Natura Brevium* (1543), Coke's *Institutes of the Laws of England* (1628–1644), Hale's *History of the Pleas of the Crown* (published in 1736, 60 years after the author's death),[41] Hawkins' *Pleas of the Crown* (1716), Foster's *Crown Cases* (1762),[42] and Blackstone's *Commentaries on the Laws of England* (1765–1769).[43] Of these Blackstone's *Commentaries*, being the most general and elementary as well as the most recent, have not such a high authority on points of detail as Hale, Hawkins and Foster.

Flexible constitution

The British Constitution is described as "flexible" because any principle or **2–011** rule of the constitution can be altered by the same body and in the same manner as any other law. In other words, there is no formal distinction between laws that

---

[39] *Cordell v. Second Clanfield Properties Ltd* [1969] 2 Ch. 9, 16 *per* Megarry J.
[40] See *Case of Prohibitions (Prohibitions del Roy)* (1607) 12 Co.Rep. 63.
[41] See *R. v. Casement* [1917] 1 K.B. 98, 141–142.
[42] See *Joyce v. Director of Public Prosecutions* [1946] A.C. 347.
[43] "It is too late, in 1935, to attempt to show that Blackstone was wrong": *R. v. Sandbach* [1935] 2 K.B. 192, 197 *per* Humphreys J. See also *Thomas v. Sawkins* [1935] 2 K.B. 249; *R. v. St. Edmundsbury and Ipswich Diocese (Chancellor)* [1948] 1 K.B. 195.

are specifically "constitutional" or "fundamental" and that are not. The body which has the power to alter the constitution, or any other rules of law, is the Queen in Parliament, and the procedure is the same as for any other legislation. The legislature is supreme over the Constitution. There are no laws that cannot be repealed or altered in this way, that is to say, none that are "entrenched."[44] The flexibility of the British Constitution is a corollary of the fact that there is no written constitution or "higher law" binding on Parliament, and the consequent legislative supremacy of Parliament. The courts therefore have no power to "review" parliamentary legislation and to declare it unconstitutional.[45]

It follows also that the distinction drawn between British constitutional law and administrative law or other branches of English law, and the selection of the contents of each, are matters of convenience, guidance being sought from tradition and comparison with other constitutions.

Legislative supremacy of Parliament[46]

2–012   The most important characteristic of British constitutional law is the legislative supremacy (sometimes called "sovereignty") of the United Kingdom Parliament. Positively this means that Parliament can legally pass any kind of law whatsoever: negatively it means that there is no person or body whose legislative power competes with it or overrides it. We may call it the one fundamental law of the British Constitution,[47] which may itself be unalterable by Parliament.[48]

Constitutional or limited Monarchy

2–013   The British political system is in form monarchical. But it is a limited or "constitutional" monarchy, as opposed to an absolute or strong monarchy.[49] That is to say, the governmental powers which as a matter of legal form are vested in the Queen are in practice exercised according to the laws, customs and conventions of the constitution; and they are exercised either by the Queen on the advice of her Ministers or by the Ministers in her name.[50] This principle applies both to the Queen's common law ("prerogative") powers[51] and to her statutory powers. It is a product of English political history from the seventeenth century, when the monarch ceased to govern either himself directly or through delegates limited only by the law. The modern principle is secured by means of constitutional conventions.[52] "Constitutionalism" involves both legal limits to arbitrary power and also political responsibility of the government to the governed.[53]

---

[44] cf. McWhirter v. Att.-Gen. [1972] C.M.L.R. 882, CA (summons for declaration that accession to EEC would be contrary to the Bill of Rights, struck out as an abuse of the process of the court); R. v. Jordan [1967] Crim.L.R. 483 (Race Relations Act restricts "freedom of speech").

[45] A written and entrenched constitution for this country is advocated in Lord Hailsham, The Dilemma of Democracy (1978) and O. Hood Phillips, Reform of the Constitution (1970).

[46] See further, Chaps 3 and 4.

[47] Taken with the Parliament Acts 1911 and 1949 and the convention that the Queen will not refuse the Royal Assent to Bills, this virtually means the supremacy of a majority of the House of Commons. "That is really all the British Constitution that there is": Kenneth Pickhorn, M.P. (1956) 550 H.C.Deb., col. 1821.

[48] post, Chap. 4.

[49] O. Hood Phillips, "A Hundred Years of Constitutional Monarchy," (1978) 75 L.S. Gaz. 64.

[50] post, para. 36–021 for the position with regard to the Queen as Head of the Commonwealth.

[51] post, Chap. 15.

[52] post, para. 2–017 and Chap. 7.

[53] McIlwain, op.cit. p. 146.

Responsible parliamentary government

Parliamentary government

Parliament itself does not govern, nor is it capable of doing so. The expression **2–014** "parliamentary government" is somewhat misleading, and means government by the executive in and through Parliament. Parliament exercises supreme control over all branches of government. Besides its supreme law making power, Parliament supervises the general conduct of the executive. It makes and unmakes state offices and government departments, controls their finances, asks questions concerning the carrying out of their duties, and debates motions of confidence. Parliament also reorganises the system of courts, though it does not in practice interfere with the conduct of litigation. All this is a matter partly of law, partly of custom and partly of convention.

Responsible government

Ministers are responsible to Parliament—more particularly to the House of **2–015** Commons. They defend their conduct there, and continuance in office depends on retaining the confidence of the Commons. This is mainly a matter of constitutional convention.[54] The key to responsible parliamentary government lies in the Cabinet system, which ensures that Ministers are members of the legislature, that they must retain the confidence of the Commons, and that they can appeal to the electorate to return an assembly that will support their policy.

Responsible parliamentary government of this kind may be found in a republican régime, as in India. It is in marked contrast to the presidential system that exists, for example, in the United States, where the executive power is vested in the President, who is not a member of Congress and whose continuance in office does not depend on the support of the House of Representatives.[55]

Representative government

It is implied in what has been said of the British Constitution that the **2–016** legislature "represents" the people in a general way. Responsible government involves representative government, though the converse is not necessarily true. A general election nowadays is in effect the election of a prime minister, the leader of a political party with a certain programme. Political parties are a development since 1688. They rest almost entirely on convention or merely political fact, though their existence was assumed by the Ministers of the Crown Act 1937, which defined the Leader of the Opposition and granted him a salary.[56]

Representative government presupposes that the electors are free to organise themselves in political parties, and (within the limits imposed by the requirements of public order and peaceful change) to express their views and to criticise the government. The party system is inevitable in a democratic country, since men disagree about political ends and means. It is "a convenient device to enable

---

[54] See *post*, Chaps. 7 and 17.
[55] In addition to the "executive" type of President (*e.g.* USA) and the "parliamentary" type of President (*e.g.* India), there are other varieties of the presidential system, *e.g.* in South America and Africa.
[56] See now, Ministerial and other Salaries Act 1975. For a further reference see House of Commons (Administration) Act 1978, s.1(4).

the majority to have their way and the minority to have their say."[57] Party organisation exists both in the constituencies and in Parliament. Parties are voluntary associations, subject to the general law.[58] Increasingly, however, they are becoming subject to specific legal regulation.[59] Although, as George Tierney said, it is the duty of the Opposition[60] to oppose, the responsible aspect of the party system is brought out in the expression "His Majesty's Opposition," which was coined—originally as a joke—by J. C. Hobhouse early in the last century.

Following the Report of the Houghton Committee[61] public funds have been made available to opposition political parties, according to a formula which takes account of the number of seats held by each party and the number of votes cast.[62]

Representative government is now assisted also by secret ballot, universal adult suffrage,[63] independent Boundary Commissions, and a strict limitation of the powers of the House of Lords as against the House of Commons.[64]

In contrast to other forms of political system the British system is described as a liberal democracy. It is a qualified democracy for the activity of government is limited; society is recognised as being pluralistic, that is to say, government is not in the interest of any one group or groups but in the common interest; the majority opinion prevails but minorities are given a chance to become the majority.[65]

Importance of constitutional conventions[66]

2–017   The word "conventions," as used by constitutional lawyers, refers to rules of political practice which are regarded as binding by those whom they concern—especially the Sovereign and statesmen—but which would not be *enforced* by the courts if the matter came before them. The lack of judicial enforcement distinguishes conventions from laws in the strict sense. This is an important formal distinction for the lawyer, though the politician may not be so interested in the distinction. Privileges enforced by each House are also excluded from the definition of conventions.

---

[57] S. D. Bailey, *The British Party System* (Hansard Society, 1952), p. xii. For the political parties, see also Sir Ivor Jennings, *Party Politics*, Vol. II; *The Growth of Parties* (1961); I. Bulmer-Thomas, *The Growth of the British Party System* (1965); Robert McKenzie, *British Political Parties* (2nd ed., 1963); C. S. Emden, *The People and the Constitution* (2nd ed.); S. E. Finer, *The Changing British Party System, 1945–1979* (1980); V. Bogdanor, *People and the Party System and Multi Party Politics and the Constitution* (1983).

[58] See *Conservative and Unionist Office v. Burrell* [1982] 1 W.L.R. 522, CA; *Re Grant's Will Trusts* [1980] 1 W.L.R. 360.

[59] Registration of Political Parties Act 1998 which provide for a register of party names and emblems and amends the Representation of the People Act 1983 which allowed a reference to candidates' party affiliations on the ballot paper. See now, Political Parties Elections and Referendums Act 2000.

[60] *post*, para. 7–018.

[61] *Report of Committee on Financial Aid to Political Parties* (1976) Cmnd. 6601.

[62] The legal authority for such payments is to be found in the annual Appropriation Act (*infra* p. 220), *e.g.* Appropriation Act 1985, Sched. (B) Pt 15, Class XIII, Vote 2.

[63] *post*, Chap. 10. Direct "participation" of the people at the national level is not practicable, even if it were thought desirable; see Bernard Crick, " 'Them and Us': Public Impotence and Government Power" [1968] P.L. 8; and see Crick, *In Defence of Politics* (1962; Pelican, 1964), Chap. 3 ("A Defence of Politics Against Democracy").

[64] *post*, Chap. 28.

[65] S. E. Finer, *Comparative Government* (1970).

[66] See further, *post*, Chap. 7.

Conventions are found to a greater or less extent in most countries that have written constitutions. This is so not only in the Commonwealth countries[67] but also, for example, in the United States. There the method of electing the President and the manner of choosing the President's Cabinet are governed largely by convention.[68] What is characteristic of the British Constitution is the extremely important part played by conventions. Not only do the British have no written constitution, but they have been reluctant to stereotype their rules of government in the form of statutes. Many important political developments have been effected since 1688 without recourse to legal forms at all. It is constitutional conventions that describe and explain how the constitution works, how it lives and grows. Their general purpose is to adapt structure to function. In this way the strong monarchy of 1688 has become a limited monarchy with responsible parliamentary government.

Independence of the judiciary from the executive[69]

The justices of the Royal courts, which grew up in Norman and Plantagenet **2–018** times, were the King's servants: down to the time of the Stuarts they usually held office during the King's pleasure and, like other Crown servants, could be dismissed by the King at will.[70] This fact doubtless affected some of the judicial decisions given in the reigns of James I and Charles I. After the revolution of 1688, judges of superior courts were appointed "during good behaviour," but there was doubt whether at common law this referred merely to good behaviour in relation to the King. Eventually the Act of Settlement 1700 provided that "Judges commissions be made *quamdiu se bene gesserint*, and their salaries ascertained and established, but upon the address of both Houses of Parliament it may be lawful to remove them." The first and third of those provisions have been substantially re-enacted by the Judicature Acts and are now to be found in the Supreme Court Act 1981, s.11. The security of tenure of Lords of Appeal is protected by section 6 of the Appellate Jurisdiction Act 1876. Their effect is that judges of the *superior* British courts may not be removed except for misbehaviour in their office or (probably) conviction of some serious offence. Removal is by the Crown. Removal may be on an Address by both Houses of Parliament, but it is not certain whether such an Address is necessary.[71]

There are now statutory retiring ages for all judges (except the Lord Chancellor) and magistrates. Circuit judges and magistrates are removable at the instance of the Lord Chancellor on the grounds of incapacity or misbehaviour under various statutes.[72]

The provision as regards the ascertainment and establishment of salaries is **2–019** secured by the practice of passing permanent Acts[73] defining judicial salaries and charging them on the Consolidated Fund. The executive, therefore, cannot bring pressure to bear on the judges by threatening to reduce their salaries, nor do their

---

[67] On Conventions in Australia, see George Winterton, *Parliament, The Executive and the Governor General* (1983).

[68] W. B. Munro, *The Government of the United States* (4th ed., 1936) pp. 80–83.

[69] See further, *post*, Chap. 20.

[70] Blackstone discusses the independence of the judiciary in a chapter on the King's Prerogative: Bl. Com. I. 269.

[71] See S. Shetreet, *Judges on Trial* (1976) and *post*, Chap. 20.

[72] *post*, Chap. 20.

[73] Strictly, there are no *permanent* Acts, *i.e.* Acts which Parliament cannot repeal or amend. The expression here refers to Acts passed for an indefinite period, as contrasted with Acts passed for some definite period, *e.g.* Annual Acts.

salaries come up for annual review (with opportunity for discussion of their conduct) by the House of Commons as do most estimates of public expenditure.

As the body of Ministers or "the Government" has in practice come to play the part in public affairs formerly played by the Sovereign, the modern significance of the independence of the judges is that they are free from control or influence by the Government in the administration of justice. Even the Houses of Parliament do not seek to interfere in the conduct of current litigation; not only are the judges' salaries charged on the Consolidated Fund, but it is a parliamentary custom that questions should not be asked in the House about the decisions of the courts in particular cases.

A different, though relevant, principle is the immunity of judges from legal proceedings taken against them in respect of the discharge of their judicial functions, in order that the law may be administered freely and without fear or favour.[74]

No strict separation of powers

2–020   There is not, and never has been, a strict separation of powers in the English constitution in the sense that legislative, executive and judicial powers are assigned respectively to different organs, nor have checks and balances between them been devised as a result of theoretical analysis.[75] Development of our public institutions has been mainly empirical.

The Crown has always been an element in the exercise of all three kinds of powers—executive (the Queen's government, Her Majesty's ministers), legislative (the Queen in Parliament, throne in the House of Lords, royal assent to Bills), and judicial (Royal Courts of Justice, Her Majesty's judges, indictment in the name of the Queen). The Cabinet and other ministers are members of the legislature. Most notably, the Lord Chancellor presides over the Second Chamber, is the head of the judiciary and is a Cabinet Minister. (Recent developments have cast the spotlight on the compatibility of his judicial role with his other functions.[76]) The Home Secretary exercises the prerogative of mercy, and the Attorney-General may enter a *nolle prosequi* to a prosecution on indictment. Ministers and government departments have powers of delegated legislation, while ministers and administrative tribunals have power to make decisions affecting private rights, and local government authorities may make byelaws for the good rule and government of their area.

The Houses of Parliament do not act exclusively as parts of a legislature but also set up select committees of inquiry and committees to scrutinise the administration. The House of Lords, besides being the Second Chamber, acts in another capacity as the final court of appeal. Early Parliaments, indeed, were concerned as much with judicial matters and the receiving of petitions and remedying of grievances as with actual law making.[77]

Courts must have some executive powers to prevent interference with their proceedings and to secure enforcement of their decisions. Final appeal from certain overseas courts, as well as in certain kinds of cases in this country, lies to

---

[74] *Sirros v. Moore* [1975] Q.B. 118, CA; *Re McC (A Minor)* [1985] A.C. 528, HL.

[75] For the eighteenth century, Holdsworth finds Montesquieu's analysis inadequate and misleading: *History of English Law*, Vol. X. pp. 713–724.

[76] There has been concern expressed about the Lord Chancellor sitting particularly in cases involving devolution issues: *post* paras 18–009, 22–036 and 22–051.

[77] *post*, pp. 123–124.

the Judicial Committee of the Privy Council, technically an advisory executive organ of the Crown.

The absence of judicial review of Acts of Parliament may look like a separation of powers, though it is not based on a theory of that kind but expresses the doctrine of the sovereignty of Parliament. **2–021**

From that doctrine it follows that while the power of making law belongs to Parliament, the duty of the judges is to apply it—interpreting it where necessary—whatever their views about the wisdom, justness or morality of the legislation at issue. Nor are the courts concerned, in interpreting the law, with the wishes and views of the Government[78] or the likelihood of the Government finding the courts' interpretation unwelcome.[79] It is doubtful whether it is helpful or necessary to attribute that clear distinction of roles to a theory of the separation of powers, as Lord Diplock did in *Duport Steels Ltd v. Sirs*.[80] There has been concern expressed about the Lord Chancellor sitting in cases involving devolution issues. The Human Rights Act 1998 is particularly relevant in the light of the decision of the European Court of Human Rights in *McGonnell v. U.K.*[81] (Position of Deputy Bailiff of Guernsey as judge and member of the legislature: breach of Art. 6 E.C.H.R.)

The "basic concept of separation of legislative, executive and judicial power as it had been developed in the unwritten constitution of the United Kingdom" was also relied on by Lord Diplock as a guide to the interpretation of the constitution of Jamaica in *Hinds v. The Queen*.[82] In that case the Privy Council held that vesting the power to vary sentences in certain cases in a Review Board, the majority of members of which were not judges, was an unconstitutional attempt to vest judicial powers in a body not entitled to exercise such powers. A written constitution may enshrine the doctrine of the separation of powers, explicitly or by implication. To borrow it from the United Kingdom seems, however, dangerous: a country where not merely the Home Secretary[83] but even the Commissioners of the Customs and Excise[84] can release prisoners from jail. By contrast in *Liyanage v. R*[85] the Privy Council, in striking down legislation as an improper interference with the judicial power rejected any analogy drawn from the British Constitution. "The British constitution is unwritten whereas in the case of Ceylon their lordships have to interpret a written document from which alone the legislature derives its legislative power."[86]

In *R. v. Home Secretary ex p. Fire Brigades Union*[87] Lord Mustill referred to "the peculiarly British conception of the separation of powers". Lord Steyn has said that the constitutional principle of the separation of powers becomes important when the government has a massive majority in the House of Commons and parliamentary scrutiny of the acts and intentions of the executive is not always as **2–022**

---

[78] *Abse v. Smith* [1986] Q.B. 536, 554 *per* Sir John Donaldson M.R.

[79] *Sherdley v. Sherdley* [1986] 1 W.L.R. 732, 736 *per* Sir John Donaldson M.R.

[80] [1980] 1 W.L.R. 142, 157. Similarly, *Chokolongo v. Att.-Gen. of Trinidad and Tobago* [1981] 1 W.L.R. 106, 110 *per* Lord Diplock.

[81] *The Times*, February 22, 2000.

[82] [1977] A.C. 195, followed in *Browne v. The Queen* [1999] 3 W.L.R. 1158, P.C.

[83] See, for example, Imprisonment (Temporary Provisions) Act 1980; a statute which passed through all its stages in both Houses and received the Royal Assent within a mere two days.

[84] Customs and Excise Management Act 1979, s.152(d); note, [1984] P.L. 2.

[85] [1967] 1 A.C. 259, 288 *per* Lord Pearce. See G. Marshall, *Constitutional Theory*, p. 120. ("The strong and surprising adoption of the separation of powers doctrine").

[86] See further, O. Hood Phillips, "A constitutional myth: separation of powers" (1977) 93 L.Q.R. 11.

[87] [1995] 2 A.C. 513.

careful as it ought to be.[88] One writer has found something of a puzzle between judicial support for the view that the constitution is firmly based on the separation of powers and the weight of academic judgement to the opposite effect.[89]

Where the judges are interpreting ambiguous written constitutions there is, of course, nothing to prevent them using the principle of the separation of powers to aid them in their task. In the case of the United Kingdom, too, resort to the separation of powers provides a justification for interpreting legislation. It fits in with the current approach, illustrated in cases on prisoners' rights and the powers of the Home Secretary,[90] that statutes must be read in the context of basic principles of common law. But all that is rather different from a constitution where the rights of the courts are beyond the powers of the legislature and the executive, where the executive, by law, is subject to the control of the legislature.[91]

No distinct system of administrative law

2–023   Administrative law, as we have seen,[92] determines the organisation, powers and duties of administrative authorities. It is the law relating to public administration. English and Scots law contain both general principles and detailed rules relating to the structure of administrative authorities, their functions and powers, and the supervision of the relations between them and the private citizen. Administrative authorities include Ministers and central government departments, local government authorities, public corporations, and their officers and servants. There are numerous statutes establishing their structure, and conferring the powers (including powers of delegated legislation and administrative jurisdiction) necessary for the exercise of their functions relating to such matters as public health, education, transport, planning, housing, national insurance, electricity supply and so on. Administrative Tribunals deal with a wide range of matters ranging from social welfare and employment to mental health and immigration, from which appeal may lie to the courts on questions of law. But until recently it could not be said that there was a *system* of administrative law in this country—and there is still no *system* of administrative courts.

The topics covered by administrative law in the United Kingdom have to be picked out, as a matter of choice, from the general body of our constitutional law. They comprise, roughly, the topics covered by Part VI of this book. The rest of our constitutional law would then deal with the monarchy and the royal prerogative, the conduct of foreign affairs, and control of the armed forces and the civil service; Parliament; nationality, citizenship aliens and immigration; offences against the State and public order; the general principles relating to the rights of the individual; the administration of justice; and the Commonwealth.

This view has slowly gained ground among academic lawyers. At first, English writing on administrative law tended to deal mainly with the delegation to the

---

[88] "The Role of the Bar, The Judge and The Jury," [1999] P.L. 51, citing his earlier article, "The Weakest and Least Dangerous Department of Government," [1997] P.L. 84.

[89] Munro, *Studies in Constitutional Law* (2nd ed, 1999), p. 306.

[90] *R. v. Home Secretary ex p. Pierson* [1998] A.C. 539, HL; *R. v. Home Secretary ex p. Simms* [2000] 2 A.C. 115, HL.

[91] "The separation of powers, at least as formulated by Montesquieu, has never really been taken seriously in the United Kingdom"; E. Barendt, *An Introduction to Constitutional Law* (1998) p. 34.

[92] *ante*, para. 1–013.

executive of legislative and judicial powers,[93] not because administrative law is confined to these topics but largely because the great influence of Dicey[94] made them controversial ground and they revealed tendencies that were resented by the more conservative and individualist members of the legal profession.[95] Dicey's attitude was due not only to his political predilections in favour of individual liberty as against government "interference," but also to a misunderstanding of the French *droit administratif* which led to the false conclusion that there could be no administrative law without a separate system of administrative courts.[96]

In *Ridge v. Baldwin*[97] Lord Reid said: "We do not have a developed system of administrative law—perhaps because until fairly recently we did not need it." Developments since then[98] have been such that Lord Diplock has claimed that **2–024**

> "The extension of judicial control of the administrative process has provided over the last 30 years the most striking feature of the development of the common law in those countries of whose legal systems it provides the source; and although it is a development that has although it is a development that has already gone a long way towards providing a system of administrative law as comprehensive in its content as the droit administratif of countries of the civil law, albeit differing in procedural approach, it is a development that is still continuing."[99]

Important elements in that development were the introduction in 1977[1] of a new, simplified procedure (application for judicial review) by which to challenge the legality of administrative acts and the decision of the House of Lords in 1983[2] that actions involving administrative bodies must now be categorised as raising questions of "public law" or "private law." In the former case the new procedure must be used. Only where questions of private law are involved can a plaintiff sue a public authority without having recourse to the application for judicial review. There may not yet be a separate *system* of Administrative Law but there are now separate procedures for enforcing public rights and private rights.

The rule of law

Introductory

The "rule of law" is an ambiguous expression, and may mean different things for different writers.[3] Only when it is clear in what sense the phrase is being used **2–025**

---

[93] *e.g.* Carr, *Delegated Legislation; Concerning English Administrative Law; Robson, Justice and Administrative Law* (3rd ed.); Allen, *Law and Orders* (3rd ed.); *Administrative Jurisdiction*.

[94] Dicey, *Law of Constitution* (10th ed. 1959), Chap. 12.

[95] See Lord Hewart, *The New Despotism*; Cmnd. 4060 (1932), *Report of the Committee on Ministers' Powers*.

[96] See, however, Dicey's article, *"Droit Administratif* in Modern French Law" (1901) 17 L.Q.R. 302, on changes in French administrative law after 1872. Dicey did not deny the existence of any administrative law in England, but the existence of anything like the French *droit administratif* as he understood it.

[97] [1964] A.C. 40, HL.

[98] See *post*, Part VI, Introduction.

[99] *Mahon v. Air New Zealand* [1984] A.C. 808.

[1] The reform was initially effected by amendments to the Rules of the Supreme Court. Subsequently legislative effect was given to the new procedure (contained in R.S.C. Ord. 53) by the Supreme Court Act 1981, s.31.

[2] *O'Reilly v. Mackman* [1983] 2 A.C. 237.

[3] *The Rule of Law, Ideal or Ideology* (ed. Hutchinson and Monahan) (1987).

is there any value in asking whether the rule of law exists in a particular legal system.

Historically, the phrase was, perhaps, first used with reference to a belief in the existence of law possessing higher authority—whether divine or natural—than that of the law promulgated by human rulers which imposed limits on their powers. It was probably in this sense that Aristotle expressed the view that "the rule of the law is preferable to that of any individual."[4] Bracton, writing in the thirteenth century adopted the theory generally held in the Middle Ages that the world was governed by law, human or divine; and held that "the King himself ought not be subject to man but subject to God and to the law, because the law makes him king."[5] The same view is also expressed in the Year Books of the fourteenth and fifteenth centuries.[6] Such superior law governed kings as well as subjects and set limits to the prerogative. On that ground Fortescue, in the middle of the fifteenth century, based his argument that there could be no taxation without the consent of Parliament.[7] During the conflict between King and Parliament in the reigns of the early Stuarts, the doctrine propounded by Coke was the superiority of the traditional common law over King and executive; but the common lawyers (including Coke in his later life) were in alliance with Parliament, and this theory had to be combined with the new doctrine of the supremacy of Parliament. What was supreme, therefore, was the law for the time being; that is to say, the common law subject to such changes as King in Parliament might make from time to time.[8] This view eventually prevailed with the revolution of 1688, although the law now regarded as supreme was not the common law (subject to parliamentary change) in the narrow sense, but the whole of English law, both statute law and case law, in whatever courts it was administered.

2–026   Thus it could be said that the British Constitution does not know of any rule of law since no superior law puts limits to what Parliament may legislate.[9] Suggestions by writers and (extrajudicially) by certain judges that there are limits to what Parliament may enact and hence is subject to the rule of law are purely speculative.[10] In this sense it would be appropriate to describe those legal systems which recognise a judicial power to hold legislation unconstitutional as being subject to the rule of law.

Although the courts have no power to hold legislation unconstitutional they interpret it on the assumption that Parliament did not intend to breach fundamental principles of the common law; "I must . . . be faithful to Parliament's sovereign will. Nevertheless, I am entitled to presume that Parliament always intends to conform to the rule of law as a constitutional principle and accordingly

[4] *Politics*, Vol. III, P. 16. He goes on to define law as "reason unaffected by desire." Commentators point out that Aristotle is not necessarily expressing his own view in this chapter; he may be reporting views held by others.
[5] "Ipse autem rex non debet esse sub homine sed sub Deo et sub lege, quia lex facit regem": *De Legibus et Consuetudinibus Angliae*, f. 5 b.
[6] See *Report of Committee on Ministers' Powers* Cmnd. 4060, (1932) pp. 71–72.
[7] *De Laudibus Legum Angliae*, Chap. 18; *The Governance of England*, Chap. 3.
[8] Holdsworth, *History of English Law*, Vol. II, pp. 441–442; Vol. X, pp. 647–649. See also F. W. Gough, *Fundamental Law in English Constitutional History* (1955); *cf.* Roscoe Pound, *The Development of Constitutional Guarantees of Liberty* (1957); McIlwain, *The High Court of Parliament*, Chap. 2.
[9] See *post* para. 4–006 *et seq.*, for possible limits arising from the Union with Scotland, membership of the European Union, and adherence to the European Convention on Human Rights.
[10] T. R. S. Allen, *Law, Liberty and Justice* (1993); Sir John Laws, "Law and Democracy", [1995] P.L. 72; Lord Woolf, "Droit Public-English Style" [1995] P.L. 57.

to respect the constitutional rights of the individual to enjoy equality under the law."[11] In *X Ltd v. Morgan-Grampian (Publishers) Ltd* Lord Bridge said that the rule of law rests on twin foundations: the sovereignty of the Queen in Parliament in making the law and the sovereignty of the Queen's courts in interpreting and applying the law.[12]

A second sense in which the phrase may be used is that the Crown (or Executive) must be able to demonstrate a lawful authority for its actions, whether common law, statutory or prerogative. A search warrant is not lawful merely because issued by a Secretary of State: *Entick v. Carrington*.[13] Taxation can be levied only by, or under, an Act of Parliament; hence the Crown cannot lawfully demand taxes on the basis of a resolution of the House of Commons.[14] Thus the rule of law can be said to be a characteristic of the British Constitution which precludes arbitrary action on the part of the Crown or members of the Government.[15]

The importance of this limit on the activities of the Executive must not be over-estimated. It does not have to show express authority for every action; "England . . . is not a country where everything is forbidden except what is expressly permitted: it is a country where everything is permitted except what is expressly forbidden"; *Malone v. Metropolitan Police Commissioner*.[16] In the absence of statutory provisions or judicial precedent to the contrary, the Home Secretary was not precluded from authorising the tapping of private telephones.[17] The enactment of the Human Rights Act 1998 will, of course, restrict Executive powers in those areas falling within the scope of Convention rights. Where statutory authority is required, the Government can generally secure the passing by Parliament of such laws as it wants.[18] **2–027**

In many instances governments, of whatever political hue, prefer to achieve their objectives by "extra-legal" means, rather than introduce legislation with the possible embarrassment of Parliamentary criticism and, subsequently, the risk of challenge in the Courts. Employers are "persuaded" to follow government guidelines on pay, under the threat of losing grants and government contracts.[19] A "voluntary" system of censorship relating to matters of defence and security insulates decisions taken by the responsible officials from any form of review.[20] In some instances particular sections of the community may be prepared to reach

---

[11] *Fitzpatrick v. Stirling Housing Association* [1998] Ch. 304, 337 *per* Ward L.J.

[12] [1991] 1 A.C. 1, 48.

[13] (1765) 19 St. Tr. 1029, 1066. See, too, discussion of the "right" of a condemned prisoner to insist on being executed: Maitland, *The Constitutional History of England*, p. 476; P. Brett "Conditional Pardons and the Commutation of Death Sentences," (1957) 20 M.L.R. 131; R. F. V. Heuston, *Essays in Constitutional Law* (2nd ed. 1964) pp. 69–70.

[14] *Bowles v. Bank of England* [1913] 1 Ch. 57. *cf.* Provisional Collection of Taxes Act 1968.

[15] See *infra* Chap. 33 for the supervisory jurisdiction of the High Court under which decisions of Ministers may be invalidated if they have failed to exercise their discretionary powers properly.

[16] [1979] Ch. 344, 357 *per* Sir Robert Megarry V.-C. A more robust approach was taken by the House of Lords in *R. v. Horseferry Road Magistrates Court ex p Bennett* [1994] 1 A.C. 42. (Accused tricked into returning to United Kingdom. Criminal proceedings stayed: rule of law requires courts to refuse to countenance unworthy conduct.)

[17] But see now, Interception of Communications Act 1985; and the Regulation of Investigatory Powers Act 2000; *post*, para. 26–014.

[18] For example, *Burmah Oil Co v. Lord Advocate* was followed by the War Damage Act 1965; *R. (Hume) v. Londonderry Justices* [1972] N.I. 91 by the Northern Ireland Act 1972.

[19] G. Ganz, [1978] P.L. 333.

[20] E. Barendt, "Prior Restraints on Speech" [1985] P.L. 253, 273. See also E. Barendt, *Freedom of Speech* (1985), p. 1135. (Informal rules regulating publication of ministers' memoirs).

informal agreements with a government in order to avoid being subjected to what they fear will be still stricter control by legislation.[21]

The rule of law may, again, be used to refer to those formal characteristics which rules of a legal system must possess before citizens can take them into account in determining their future conduct.[22] The law must, for example, as far as possible, be clear; "Absence of clarity is destructive of the rule of law."[23] Retrospective legislation is, generally, to be avoided.[24]

2–028   A system of law which complied with the "rule of law" in the two senses just discussed might, nonetheless, be a system which most people would regard as grossly unjust. The Executive might wield only powers given to it by law; the individual laws of the system might be admirably clear and possess every other desirable formal quality but their aim might be, for example, to maintain one group in power in that state and to deny, on racial or religious grounds, all rights to members of other groups. It is for this reason that some writers and jurists have used the phrase "rule of law" to refer to a minimum material or substantive element in a legal system. Perhaps the most important example of this approach is to be found in the *Declaration of Delhi*, 1959[25] according to which the rule of law implies, *inter alia*:—a right to representative and responsible government; certain minimum standards or principles for the law, including those contained in the Universal Declaration and the European Convention, in particular, freedom of religious belief, assembly and association, and the absence of retroactive penal laws; that a citizen who is wronged should have a remedy against the state or government; the certainty of the criminal law, the presumption of innocence, reasonable rules relating to arrest, accusation and detention pending trial, the giving of notice and provision for legal advice, public trial, right of appeal, and absence of cruel or unusual punishments; the independence of the judiciary.

Admirable though the sentiments contained in the *Delhi Declaration* may be, it can be argued that to equate them with the rule of law is confusing and misleading; indeed, in the words of one writer is a "perversion of the doctrine."[26] The objection to attempting to equate the phrase with a particular set of political beliefs is that it involves the use of a term which seems to imply the objective existence of certain qualities in the structure of a legal system as a covert political slogan to give approval to a particular system which the speaker or writer considers satisfactory.

Yet another sense in which "rule of law" may be used is to refer to the general duty binding "all citizens in a Parliamentary democracy to obey the law, unless

---

[21] Richard Lewis, "Insurers' Agreements not to enforce strict legal rights: Bargaining with Government and the Shadow of the Law." (1985) 48 M.L.R. 275.

[22] J. Raz, "The Rule of Law and Its Virtue" (1977) 93 L.Q.R. 195.

[23] *Merkur Island Shipping Corpn v. Laughton* [1983] 2 A.C. 570, *per* Lord Diplock.

[24] *Infra*, p. 55. In *R. v. Kirk* [1985] 1 All E.R. 453 the European Court described non-retroactivity of criminal legislation as a general principle of law observed by the Court and common to all the legal orders of member states. See also Article 7 of the European Convention of Human Rights. (Retroactive legislation is not, however, entirely precluded in the European Community: *Staple Dairy Products v. Intervention Board for Agricultural Produce* [1984] 1 C.M.L.R. 238.)

[25] "Declaration of Delhi" (1959) 2 Jo.Int.Com. of Jurists; pp. 7–32 "The Rule of Law in a Free Society" in *Report of International Congress of Jurists* (New Delhi, 1959). See further, N. S. Marsh, "The Rule of Law as a Supra- National Concept" in *Oxford Essays in Jurisprudence* (ed. A. G. Guest 1961), Chap. 9; N. S. Marsh, "Civil Liberties in Europe" (1959) 75 L.Q.R. 530; A. H. Robertson, *Human Rights in the World* (1972).

[26] Raz. See note 17, at p. 196. See also T. D. Weldon, *The Vocabulary of Politics op. cit.* (1953), p. 61.

and until it can be changed by due process."[27] A similar duty binds the judge: unless he applies the law laid down by Parliament, whatever his own views, "public confidence in the political impartiality of the judiciary, which is essential to the continuance of the rule of law" will be endangered.[28]

The "untrammelled power" of the courts to regulate their own proceedings in cases where they are not regulated by ancient usage or statute has been claimed to be essential for "the maintenance of the rule of law": *Abse v. Smith*.[29]

For students of the British Constitution however the rule of law pre-eminently means Dicey's doctrine of the rule of law.

Dicey's doctrine of the rule of law

Dicey first published his *Law of the Constitution*, based on lectures he gave as **2–029** Vinerian Professor of English Law at Oxford, in 1885. His purpose was to deal "only with two or three guiding principles which pervade the modern constitution of England."[30] The three distinguishing characteristics of the English Constitution that he chose to explain and illustrate were "the Sovereignty of Parliament, the Rule of Law, and the Conventions of the Constitution."[31] A large part of the book was devoted to an exposition of his doctrine of the "rule of law,"[32] and this has had a profound influence among those who think and write about the constitution, as well as those who work it.

For Dicey the expression "the rule of law" included three distinct though kindred conceptions:

(i) The absence of arbitrary power. No man is above the law. No man is punishable except for a distinct breach of law, established in the ordinary legal manner before the ordinary courts.

(ii) Equality before the law. Every man, whatever his rank or condition, is subject to the ordinary law and the jurisdiction of the ordinary tribunals. This Dicey contrasted with the French *droit administratif*, under which the responsibility of public officers for their official acts is decided by a distinct system of administrative courts.

(iii) The general principles of the British Constitution—especially the liberties of the individual, such as personal liberty, freedom of speech and public meeting—are the result of judicial decisions in particular cases. The constitution is judge-made.

---

[27] *Francome v. Mirror Group Newspapers Ltd* [1984] 1 W.L.R. 892, 897 *per* Sir John Donaldson M.R. The Master of the Rolls recognised that in some cases the citizen might feel a moral obligation to disobey the law—on which see Geoffrey Marshall, *Constitutional Theory* Chap. IX.

[28] *Duport Steels v. Sirs* [1980] 1 W.L.R. 142, 157 *per* Lord Diplock.

[29] [1986] Q.B. 536, 555 *per* May L.J.

[30] Preface to first edition (1885). A recent biography and analysis of Dicey's work and thought is R. A. Cosgrove, *The Rule of Law: Albert Venn Dicey* (1981).

[31] Dicey, *Law of the Constitution* (8th ed., 1914), p. xvii.

[32] Dicey, *Law of the Constitution* (10th ed. 1959), Part II. H. W. Arndt, "The Origins of Dicey's Concept of 'The Rule of Law' (1957) 31 A.L.J. 117, points out that Dicey elaborated and expanded the ideas of W. E. Hearn in *The Government of England* (1867), to which Dicey made a general reference in the Preface to his first edition. Dicey first used the phrase in 1875; "Stubbs' Constitutional History of Great Britain," *Nation* 20 (March 4, 1875) 154; Cosgrove, *op. cit.* p. 67.

2–030   Dicey's doctrine has been chiefly criticised with regard to the notion of equality before the law and the topic of administrative law.[33]

The first principle ("No man is punishable," etc.) applies generally in criminal law. Criminal courts usually have a wide discretion with regard to punishment, but this favours the citizen as it is a discretion downwards from a statutory maximum. The principle excludes, as a general rule, preventive detention, compulsory acquisition of goods and direct enforcement of administrative decisions, although preventive detention by order of the Home Secretary was authorised by Parliament during the two World Wars.

Whether discretionary powers conferred on Ministers by Parliament should be described as "arbitrary" or not is, largely, a matter of judgment. To the extent that Dicey objected to any discretion being conferred on ministers he was, it has been pointed out, attempting to turn particular political and economic theories into a constitutional doctrine. Certainly, the granting of wide powers to ministers is now a settled feature of legislation.[34]

To the doctrine that all persons have equal rights and duties before the law, however, so many exceptions have now to be made that the statement is of doubtful value. Ministers and other public authorities have many powers that the ordinary person has not got. Thus local authorities have statutory power under certain conditions to buy land compulsorily, and the police have special powers of arrest and search by common law and statute, and ministers have wide powers of delegated legislation. Immunity from the general law of tort may attach to acts done "in contemplation or furtherance of a trade dispute."[35] Rights and obligations of the individual are now decided in many cases not by the ordinary courts but by special or administrative tribunals. Judges and ambassadors have immunity from being sued in the courts, although the immunity of judges actually favours "the rule of law" to the extent that it helps secure the independence of the Judiciary from control by the Executive. In one important respect we are paradoxically nearer to Dicey's "rule of law" than when he wrote, for the common law immunity in tort of the Crown (in effect, the government) was largely removed by the Crown Proceedings Act 1947.[36] Nonetheless the government retains legal immunities and privileges not possessed by the private citizen.[37]

2–031   With regard to administrative law,[38] its existence does not necessarily involve special administrative courts, as is shown by the fact that Belgium before 1946

---

[33] See, *e.g.* E. C. S. Wade in Dicey, *Law of the Constitution* (10th ed.), pp. xcvi–cli; Jennings, *op. cit.* Chap. 2, s.1 and Appendix II; "In Praise of Dicey" (1935) 13 *Public Administration* 123; B. Schwartz, *French Administrative Law and the Common-Law World,* Chap. 10. For a re-appraisal of Dicey's doctrine, see F. H. Lawson, "Dicey Revisited" (1959), *Political Studies*, Vol. VII, pp. 109, 207. See also P. P. Craig, *Public Law and Democracy in the United Kingdom and the United States of America* (Oxford, 1990).

[34] Quite exceptional powers may be delegated to ministers in times of emergency: see *post,* Chap. 19.

[35] The width of the immunity tends to vary with the political complexion of the government. For the present position see *Harvey on Industrial Relations and Employment Law,* Vol. 2, Pt. M.

[36] An anomalous exception was the exemption of the Post Office and its employees under s. 9 of that Act, which was substantially re-enacted in the Post Office Act 1969. See now the British Telecommunications Act 1981, s.23 (immunity of British Telecom) and s.29 (immunity of Post Office).

[37] G. Zellick, "Government beyond Law" [1985] P.L. 283.

[38] Dicey, *op. cit.* Chap. 12; *cf.* A. V. Dicey, "*Droit Administratif* in Modern French Law" (1901) 17 L.Q.R. 302; "The Development of Administrative Law in England" (1915) 31 L.Q.R. 148 (based on the case of *Local Government Board v. Arlidge* [1915] A.C. 120).

had a *droit administratif* without such separate courts. The essence of administrative law is that different principles should apply in relation to the official acts of public authorities and officers. These are not confined to liability to pay compensation for injury caused to private individuals. In any event, *droit administratif* is looked upon by the French as a protection for the individual, not as a privilege for public officials.[39] If French administrative law provides compensation for excess or abuse of power *ex post facto*, English administrative law might be said to seek to deter public officials from exceeding their powers in the first instance.

Whatever Dicey's initial distrust of a separate system of administrative law it should be remembered that the development of such a system has been claimed as one of the judicial achievements of the last thirty years.[40]

It is not easy to see how Dicey's treatment of the "rights of the subject" in British constitutional law is related to the other parts of his doctrine. It is true that the rights of the individual are mostly to be inferred from judicial decisions[41] and are therefore part of the common law, especially if such enactments as the Bill of Rights 1688 be regarded mainly as declaratory. That such rights are *part* of the ordinary law is a necessary consequence of the fact that the British Constitution is unwritten; but the fundamental principle both in the ordinary English law and in British constitutional law is the legislative supremacy of Parliament, so that it cannot be said with exactness that either the principles or the decisions are *derived* from the others.

In so far as Dicey's general statement of the rule of law may be taken to   **2–032** involve the existence in the English Constitution of certain principles almost amounting to fundamental laws, his doctrine is logically inconsistent with the legislative suspremacy of Parliament. Dicey attempted to reconcile the two notions by saying that parliamentary sovereignty favors the rule of law because the will of Parliament can be expressed only in the form of an Act, which must be interpreted by the courts; and that the rule of law favours parliamentary sovereignty, as any additional discretionary powers that the government needs can only be obtained from Parliament.[42] His doctrine is a political theory, in some of its aspects connected with the doctrine of the separation of powers. From another point of view it implies moral restrictions on the legislative activity of Parliament, its juridical nature resembling the "directive principles of state policy" found in the Constitutions of the Republic of Ireland and India.

Conclusion

Despite the supremacy of Parliament, theories of the rule of law may be   **2–033** significant in at least three ways. First they may influence legislators. The substantive law at any given time may approximate to the "rule of law," but this only at the will of Parliament. Secondly, their principles may provide canons of interpretation which give an indication of how the law will be applied and legislation interpreted. English courts lean in favour of the liberty of the citizen, especially of his person: they interpret strictly statutes which purport to diminish that liberty, and presume that Parliament does not intend to restrict private rights

[39] L. Neville Brown and J. Bell, *French Administrative Law*, (5th ed., 1998, Chap. 11).
[40] *ante*, para. 2–024.
[41] But statutes have curtailed some (*e.g.* Public Order Act 1986) and modified others (*e.g.* Habeas Corpus Acts). See further, *post*, Chaps 24–26.
[42] Dicey, *op. cit.* Chap. 13.

in the absence of clear words to the contrary.[43] But Parliament could pass an Act requiring the judges to interpret social legislation freely in favour of the administration. Thirdly, the rule of law may be a rule of evidence: everyone is prima facie equal before the law. A person, whether an executive officer or not, may have peculiar rights, powers, privileges or immunities; but, if so, he must prove them. In this sense, the government is subject to law.

The British Constitution and human rights[44]

2–034   The British Constitution contains no fundamental rights in the strict sense. Being unwritten and flexible, the constitution in any of its parts can be changed in the same way as any other part, namely, by ordinary Act of Parliament. The legislative supremacy of Parliament means that there is no legal limit to the extent to which Parliament can abridge or abolish rights that in other countries may be regarded as "fundamental."[45] The practical checks are the influence of public opinion, the vigilance of the Opposition, and the restrictive interpretation of the courts. Traditionally, the rights of the individual in English law are the *residue* of freedom that is left after legislative and executive powers have been defined, and their extent can only be determined by examining the restrictions placed on the activity of the individual and the enjoyment of his property.[46]

This attitude, however, will have to give way to the recognition by the Human Rights Act 1998 of Convention rights and the duty of public authorities not to act incompatibly with such rights.[47]

Local government[48]

2–035   The present structure of local government authorities in England and Wales is based on recent legislation although counties, boroughs and parishes as units for various purposes are ancient. In the shire, hundred and vill is found the key to the present organisation of rural areas for local government purposes—the county, the district and the civil parish. An antithesis between centralisation and decentralisation runs through the history of the organisation of English government. In the early Middle Ages, both before and after the Norman Conquest, the chief royal officer for the control of local government was the sheriff of the county or shire, subject to the supervision of the King's Council. The general administration was carried on in the county court, the assembly of the freeholders of the county over which the sheriff presided.

Over a period of centuries the sheriff gradually lost nearly all his functions, so that Maitland could say in 1885 that the whole history of English justice and police might be described as "the decline and fall of the sheriff."[49] After various experiments, the local administration of justice was given in the middle of the

[43] See, *e.g. Allen v. Thorn Electrical Industries Ltd* [1968] 1 Q.B. 487, CA. This aspect of the importance of the rule of law is developed by T. R. S. Allen "Legislative Supremacy and The Rule of Law" [1985] C.L.J. 111.
[44] See further, *post*, Chap. 22.
[45] But see dicta cited *ante*, para. 1–019.
[46] See *post*, Chaps 22–27.
[47] *post* Chap. 22.
[48] Redlich and Hirst, *History of Local Government in England* (ed. B. Keith-Lucas, 2nd ed., 1970); W. A. Robson, *The Development of Local Government* (3rd ed., 1954); S. Webb, *The Evolution of Local Government* (1951); Holdsworth, *History of English Law*, Vol. X, pp. 126–339; *A Century of Municipal Progress 1835–1935* (ed. Laski, Jennings and Robson, 1935); K. B. S. Smellie, *A Hundred Years of Local Government* (2nd ed., 1950).
[49] *Justice and Police* (1885), p. 69. For the modern sheriff, see *The High Sheriff* (*The Times*, 1961).

fourteenth century to justices of the peace. For nearly 500 years, that is, until the year 1834, the control of local government outside the boroughs was mainly in the hands of these justices of the peace, for besides the judicial functions in which they displaced the sheriffs and the county and hundred courts, a long series of statutes cast on them numerous administrative duties concerning such matters as highways, poor relief, wages and licensing.[50] The justices themselves were controlled by the King's Council until the Star Chamber was abolished in 1640. For the next 200 years local government was, subject to the legislative power of Parliament, almost autonomous: practically the only control was exercised by the courts in applying the doctrine of *ultra vires* and issuing prerogative writs.

The period from the Middle Ages down to the early nineteenth century also saw a great growth in the size and number of towns, and to the justices of the peace as local government authorities we must add the boroughs. Further, the statutory institution of ad hoc bodies for specific purposes, which began with the Statute of Sewers 1531, was increasingly adopted in the eighteenth century for such purposes as the poor law, turnpike roads and urban sanitation.

Modern local government, characterised by *locally elected councils*, was inaugurated by the Poor Law Amendment Act 1834 and the Municipal Corporations Act 1835. The former Act reorganised the administration of the poor law which, apart from police, had hitherto been the most important function of local government. The Municipal Corporations Act provided for an elected borough council in place of an oligarchy of co-opted burgesses. The process of creating elected councils was continued by the introduction, first, of county councils and county borough councils in 1888,[51] and then of urban district councils, rural district councils and parish councils in 1894.[52] Ad hoc authorities continued to be created during the nineteenth century for highways, schools and sanitation, but they gradually disappeared. The general principle in modern times was to have one local authority for all services in its area, and this was largely brought about by 1930.[53] The Local Government Act 1933 consolidated the legislation relating to the structure of local government outside London, and remained the basis of the law until the coming into effect of the Local Government Act 1972. **2–036**

The government of London has always stood apart from the general system, owing to the maintenance of the ancient privileges of the City of London and the great size and population of Greater London.

The City of London Corporation is a body corporate by prescription, its full style according to a statute of 1690 being "The Mayor and Commonalty and Citizens of the City of London". The Corporation was not affected by the Municipal Corporations Acts 1835–1882, but it is governed—mostly in accordance with royal charters granted from time to time—by three courts. The City of London is a common law corporation with some financial resources that are not subject to statutory control.

Local government outside the City was from 1899 based on the London County Council and the metropolitan borough councils.[54] In 1963 the Greater London Council was created[55]—and abolished in 1985.[56] An authority for the **2–037**

---

[50] Sir Carleton Allen, *The Queen's Peace*, Chap. 5.
[51] Local Government Act 1888.
[52] Local Government Act 1894.
[53] Local Government Act 1929; Poor Law Act 1930.
[54] Local Government Act 1999.
[55] London Government Act 1963.
[56] Local Government Act 1985.

whole of London was re-established by the Greater London Authority Act 1999 which also introduced the novelty of a directly elected mayor.

In the case of the country at large the present government's philosophy of raising the standards of local government finds expression in the Local Government Act 2000. Provisions are made generally for the election of mayors and elaborate arrangements have been enacted to ensure that members of local authorities comply with codes of conduct which describe the standards expected of members of local authorities.[57]

---

[57] For the powers of local authorities and their relationship with central government see S.H. Bailey, *Cross, Local Government Law* (9th ed., 1996); M. Loughlin, *Local Government in the Modern State* (1986); M. Loughlin, "Restructuring of Central-Local Government Relations", *The Changing Constitution* (ed. J. Jowell and D. Oliver, 4th ed., 2000, Oxford), Chap. 6.

CHAPTER 3

PARLIAMENTARY SUPREMACY I: HISTORY AND NATURE

I. HISTORICAL INTRODUCTION

In the nineteenth century the prevailing juristic theory in this country was **3–001** Austin's doctrine of sovereignty, which supposed that in every mature legal system there was some person or body—the "Sovereign"[1]—vested with unlimited power to make law.[2] Austin himself did not apply his own doctrine consistently to the British Constitution. Dicey's treatment, in which he ascribed sovereignty to the United Kingdom Parliament, was more consistent.[3]

The doctrine of sovereignty in the theory of municipal law as opposed to international law, however, is now out of fashion, and the continued use of the term "sovereignty" in the present context tends to prejudice discussion of the lawmaking power of the United Kingdom Parliament, with which legislature we are here concerned. A body may have supreme (highest) power without necessarily being sovereign (unlimited) in Austin's sense, nor do we need to assert or imply here that there must be a sovereign authority in every legal system.

The establishment of parliamentary supremacy was a product of the revolution of 1688.[4] Before then the chief rivals were, first, the King or King in Council, and then the common law courts. Later the House of Commons acting by resolution occasionally threatened a breach in the authority of the Parliament as a whole.[5]

---

[1] The doctrine of sovereignty was derived by Austin from Bodin, Hobbes, Blackstone and Bentham. Coke's description of the "transcendant and absolute" power and jurisdiction of Parliament for making of laws in proceeding by bill (4 Inst. 36) was thought by Sir Ivor Jennings to refer to the jurisdiction of the High Court of Parliament (*The Law and the Constitution* (5th ed., 1959), App. III). Sir Thomas Smith's discussion in *De Republica Anglorum* (1589), Bk. 2, Chap. 1 (Alston ed.), of the "absolute" power of Parliament probably referred to Parliament as the highest court, "absolute" here meaning "not subject to appeal." In the Middle Ages the King ruled (subject to custom and advice) and was called the Sovereign, but "the Sovereign" as applied to the modern constitutional monarch is a courtesy title.

[2] John Austin, *The Province of Jurisprudence Determined* (1832). There are many editions and commentaries, notably H. L. A. Hart's edition (1954) and Jethro Brown's *The Austinian Theory of Law* (1906). Most English textbooks on jurisprudence contain criticisms of Austin's theory; and see H. L. A. Hart, *The Concept of Law* (2nd ed., 1994). Bentham's work, inadequately published until recently, would no doubt be known to Austin; see H. L. A. Hart, "Bentham on Sovereignty" (1967) 2 Ir. Jur. (N.S.) 327; J. H. Burns, "Bentham on Sovereignty: an Exploration" in *Bentham and Legal Theory* (M. H. ed. James, p. 133 (re-printed from (1973) 24 N.I.L.Q.).

[3] *Law of the Constitution*, (10th ed., 1959) Chaps 1–3, *cf.* E. C. S. Wade's Introduction, pp. xxxiv–xcvi. Dicey suggests indeed that Austin's general theory of sovereignty was a deduction from the position of the British Parliament.

[4] The historical development of the doctrine, drawing on numerous pre-1688 instances, is described in J. Goldsworthy, *The Sovereignty of Parliament* (1999) which refutes the suggestion that the concept of Parliamentary supremacy owes its origin to Dicey.

[5] *Stockdale v. Hansard* (1839) 9 Ad. & E. 1; *Case of the Sheriff of Middlesex* (1840) 11 Ad. & E. 273; *post*, Chap. 13.

The King as lawmaker

3–002   Parliament emerged as an effective body in the fourteenth century.[6] In the reign of Henry VI the Lords and Commons framed the statutes and the King assented in much the same fashion as at the present day. Nevertheless it would seem that the King continued to legislate on matters of lesser or temporary importance. Whether there was a significant distinction between the terms "statute" and "ordinance," the former applying to Parliament and the latter to royal legislation, has long been a matter of controversy, but Plucknett thought these terms were synonymous.[7]

Proclamations

3–003   The Statute of Proclamations 1539,[8] which gave the King power, with the advice of the Council, to make proclamations that would have the force of statutes, was of very limited scope and short-lived. Intended for emergencies, it provided that proclamations might not impose the death penalty (except for cases of heresy), take away a subject's property or conflict with existing statutes, customs or common law. This Act was repealed in the first year of Edward VI.[9] Notwithstanding its repeal, Mary and Elizabeth I continued to make and enforce proclamations concerning imports and also certain religious matters.

In the reign of James I the Commons complained of the abuse of proclamations. The opinion of Chief Justice Coke and four of his colleagues was sought and given in the *Case of Proclamations* (1610),[10] when James I wanted to prohibit by proclamation the building of new houses in London in order to check the over-growth of the capital, and the manufacture of starch from wheat so as to preserve wheat for human consumption. The opinion was to the effect that no new offence can be created by proclamation; the only prerogative possessed by the Crown is that which is conferred by the law of the land; but that to prevent offences the King can by proclamation warn his subjects against breaches of the existing law, in which case a breach would be the more serious.

The suspending and dispensing powers

3–004   By virtue of the *suspending* power the King claimed to postpone indefinitely the general operation of a given statute; by virtue of the *dispensing* power he relieved particular offenders or classes of offenders from the statutory penalties they had incurred. In the reign of Henry VII it was held that the King could at common law dispense with *mala prohibita* but not *mala in se*.[11] Subject to this restriction, both the suspending and dispensing powers were accepted as part of the prerogative in the sixteenth and seventeenth centuries. The Stuarts used these prerogatives to subvert established laws. James II issued a proclamation that a

---

[6] See E. B. Fryde and E. Miller (eds.) *Historical Studies of the English Parliament: Origins to 1399* (1970); Sir Goronwy Edwards *The Second Century of the English Parliament* (1979); R. G. Davies and J. H. Denton (eds), *The English Parliament in the Middle Ages* (1981).

[7] T. F. T. Plucknett, *Statutes and their Interpretation in the Fourteenth Century*, p. 34. See also S. E. Thorne, *Introduction to a Discourse upon the Exposition and Understanding of Statutes* (Huntington Library, 1942); H. G. Richardson and G. O. Sayles, *Law and Legislation from Aethelberht to Magna Carta* (1966); "The Early Statutes" (1934) 50 L.Q.R. 201, 540.

[8] 31 Hen. VIII, c. 8. The Act was debated by Parliament for 15 days, the Commons rejecting the first Bill sent down by the Lords.

[9] (1547) 1 Edw. VI, c. 12.

[10] 12 Co.Rep. 74; 2 St.Tr. 723.

[11] Y.B.Mich. 11 Hen. VII, no. 35 (1495) *per* Fineux C.J.; see Holdsworth, *History of English Law*, Vol. VI, pp. 218–219.

Declaration of Indulgence, suspending the operation of all laws against Roman Catholics, should be read in all the churches; but in the *Seven Bishops' Case* (1688)[12] the Primate and six bishops were acquitted by a jury on a charge of seditious libel for signing a petition claiming that to read the declaration would be illegal and against their conscience. The right of the subject to petition the King was also confirmed.

In *Thomas v. Sorrell* (1674)[13] the plaintiff claimed a penalty for selling wine **3–005** without a licence contrary to a statute of 12 Charles II. The jury returned a special verdict that they had found a patent of 9 James I incorporating the Vintners Company and granting them permission to sell wine without a licence, *non obstante* an Act of 7 Edward VI forbidding such sale. The judges decided that the King might dispense with an individual breach of a penal statute by which no man was injured, or with the continuous breach of a penal statute enacted for the King's benefit. In *Godden v. Hales* (1686)[14] a collusive action was brought to test the King's *dispensing* power. Sir Edward Hales accepted appointment as colonel of a regiment, and was sued for a penalty for neglecting to take the oaths of supremacy and allegiance and to receive the Sacrament according to the Test Act of 25 Charles II. Hales pleaded a dispensation of James II. The court held that the dispensation barred the right of action, as the King had a prerogative to dispense with penal statutes in particular cases for reasons of which the King was the sole judge.

The Bill of Rights 1688 declared: "That the pretended power of *suspending* of laws or the execution of laws by regal authority without consent of Parliament is illegal; that the pretended power of *dispensing* with laws or the execution of laws by regal authority *as it hath been assumed and exercised of late* is illegal."[15] Projected legislation, stating in what cases dispensation should be legal, was never passed.[16] It is by virtue of the words "as it hath been assumed and exercised of late" in relation to the dispensing power that the prerogative right to pardon was retained. These words were also relied on as legalising a dispensation granted by Elizabeth I in 1566 in the *Eton College* case (1815)[17] where, owing to their insertion, a fellow of Eton College was allowed to hold a living in conjunction with his fellowship.

The prohibition on the suspending and dispensing powers might be thought to **3–006** give rise to doubts about the legality of the practice of the Inland Revenue of making extra-statutory concessions to tax payers. The practice is not new and certainly existed in the nineteenth century. By 1944 it was so well established that a list of agreed concessions was published.[18] Sir Stafford Cripps said in 1947 that such concessions had come into existence "without any particular legal authority under any Act of Parliament but by the Inland Revenue under my authority."[19] Judicial concern about the powers claimed by the Revenue was

---

[12] 12 St.Tr. 371.

[13] Vaughan 330.

[14] 11 St.Tr. 1166; 2 Shower 275.

[15] For attempts to suspend legislation in New Zealand, see W. A. McKean, "The Suspending Power Exhumed," [1978] P.L.7. P. Joseph, "Doing Things the Stuart Way: 1688 and All That", [1991] P.L. 29. An example of a dispensing power conferred by statute is to be found in s.134 of the Army Act 1955 under which a superior officer may "condone" an offence committed by a soldier; see *R. v. Bisset* [1980] 1 W.L.R. 335 (Ct–M.A.C.); *post*, para. 19–022.

[16] Holdsworth, *op. cit.* Vol. VI, pp. 215–225, 240–241.

[17] *King's College, Cambridge v. Eton College*, P.Wms. 53; Broom, *Constitutional Law*, p. 503.

[18] The latest list was published in 1985: see N. L. J. May 31, 1985, p. 534.

[19] See D. W. Williams, "Extra Statutory Concessions" [1979] B.T.R. 137, 140.

voiced in *Vestey v. I.R.C. (No 2)*.[20] In that case a taxpayer claimed that the construction of the relevant statute urged by the Revenue could not be correct because, *inter alia*, of the absurdly wide liability it would impose on beneficiaries under a trust. The Revenue's response that there was no risk of any individual being harshly treated; in its discretion particular beneficiaries would be assessed for reasonable sums. Walton J. and the House of Lords held that the beneficiaries were not liable to tax under the statute. Walton J. went on to indicate very clearly his belief that the power of dispensing claimed by the Revenue was contrary to the Bill of Rights. In the House of Lords Lord Wilberforce similarly emphatically repudiated any such power, although the Commissioners must act with administrative common sense, so that they were under no duty to expend a large sum of taxpayers' money in attempting to collect a small amount of tax, and they could bring humanity to bear in hard cases.[21] The problem arose in another way in *Furniss v. Dawson*[22] where the House of Lords abandoned the principles laid down in earlier cases and, in wide and vague terms, indicated that elaborate schemes designed to minimise tax liability might in future be at risk of being set aside at the instance of the Revenue. To allay alarm the Inland Revenue issued a draft statement of practice indicating what schemes would continue to be acceptable. As the result of concern expressed that the Revenue was claiming a dispensing power, the statement was withdrawn—and a similar one, in the form of a written answer to a parliamentary question, was issued by the Chief Secretary to the Treasury.[23]

Monopolies

3–007   Formerly the granting of monopolies by the monarch was presumed to inflict a hardship on the public. In the *Case of Monopolies* (1602)[24] Darcy, a servant of Elizabeth I and grantee of the sole rights of importing and making playing-cards, sued Allein for interfering with his grant. The court held that the grant was a monopoly and void, and that the Queen could not exercise her dispensing power to confer private gain on an individual contrary to statutes of Edward III and Edward IV, which imposed a penalty on the importation of certain goods and were enacted for the public good. The grant of monopolies is now governed by Patent Acts.[25]

Taxation

3–008   It was supposed to have been settled by Magna Carta and by legislation in the reigns of Edward I and Edward III that taxation beyond the levying of customary feudal aids required the consent of Parliament. One of the central themes of English constitutional history was the gaining of control of taxation and national finance in general by Parliament, and in particular the Commons; for this control meant that the King was not able to govern for more than short periods without

---

[20] [1979] Ch. 177; [1980] A.C. 1148.
[21] Administrative commonsense is exemplified in *R. v. I.R.C. ex p. National Federation of Self Employed and Small Businesses Ltd* [1980] A.C. 952. ("Amnesty" to Fleet St. casuals).
[22] [1984] A.C. 474.
[23] Dawn Oliver, "Tax Planning and Administrative Discretion" [1984] P.L. 389. The case for the legality of the Revenue's practice of making concessions is argued by John Alder, "The Legality of Extra-Statutory Concessions," 180 N.L.J. 1980, 180.
[24] *Darcy v. Allein*, 11 Co.Rep. 84b. For the background of this case, see D. R. Seaborne Davies, "Further Light on the Case of Monopolies" (1932) 48 L.Q.R. 394.
[25] The Crown's right to make use of patents is preserved by the Crown Proceedings Act 1947, s.3 (see *Pfizer v. Ministry of Health* [1965] A.C. 512.) and the Patent Act 1977, ss 55–59.

summoning Parliament, and Parliament could insist on grievances being remedied before it granted the King supply. This applied at least to *direct* taxation. With regard to *indirect* taxation different considerations might apply. Down to the early seventeenth century import duties, for example, were regarded rather as licences or concessions than as taxes and, further, the royal prerogative relating to foreign affairs—and hence the regulation of foreign trade in the national interest—was relevant. Issue was joined in two famous cases in the reigns of James I (the "Case of Impositions") and Charles I (the "Case of Ship-Money").

In *Bate's Case (Case of Impositions)* (1606)[26] Bate, a Levant merchant, refused to pay a duty imposed by letters patent of James I on the import of currants, contending that the imposition was contrary to a statute of Edward III which declared that such taxation required the consent of Parliament. The Court of Exchequer gave judgment unanimously for the King. Their reasons were that foreign affairs, and therefore foreign commerce, were within the absolute power of the King; as the King could prohibit the importation of goods, still more could he tax imported goods; and the court must accept the King's statement that the purpose of the tax was to regulate foreign trade. Coke and Popham C.JJ. thought this decision was right.[27] The judgment has been condemned by some modern historians, but it may well have been warranted by the law of that time in so far as it rested on the prerogative power to regulate foreign trade. This power, however, was liable to be abused, and danger also lay in dicta treating the matter as a question of revenue within the "absolute" (*i.e.* inalienable) powers of the Crown. It was in the debate on impositions in 1610, says Holdsworth,[28] that the supremacy of the King in Parliament over the King out of Parliament was first asserted by James Whitelocke.

The Petition of Right 1628 was occasioned largely by *Darnel's Case (The Five Knights' Case)* (1627),[29] where the defendants were imprisoned for refusing to pay a forced loan. The Petition of Right was assented to by Charles I, and has always been regarded as having statutory force although largely superseded by the Bill of Rights. It forbad tallages, aids, forced loans, benevolences, taxes and suchlike charges "without common consent by Act of Parliament."[30]

While this document was still fresh in men's minds, Charles I (after consulting the judges) imposed under the Great Seal a direct tax known as ship-money, to be used to furnish ships for the navy. The tax was charged first on the seaport towns, which had the primary responsibility for finding ships and men for the national defence, and then on the inland counties. In *R. v. Hampden (Case of Ship-Money)* (1637)[31] proceedings were taken against John Hampden, a Buckinghamshire gentleman, for refusing to pay the amount of £1 assessed on him. The majority of the judges in the Court of Exchequer Chamber gave judgment for

3–009

---

[26] 2 St.Tr. 371. See further Holdsworth, *History of English Law*, Vol. VI, pp. 42–48; G. D. G. Hall, "Impositions and the Courts 1554–1606" (1953) 69 L.Q.R. 200.

[27] 12 Co.Rep. 33.

[28] *Some Lessons from our Legal History*, pp. 124–125.

[29] 3 St.Tr. 1.

[30] Tallages were imposts set by the King as landlord on his own demesne lands, aids were free-will offerings by tenants to their lord in time of need, and benevolences were extorted free-will offerings. These methods of raising money were not invented by the Stuarts, but were known in the fourteenth and fifteenth centuries.

[31] 3 St.Tr. 825. See further Holdsworth, *History of English Law*, Vol. VI, pp. 48–54; D. L. Keir, "The Case of Ship-Money" (1936) 52 L.Q.R. 546.

the King. The gist of their decision was that the King's prerogative to defend the realm in time of danger overrode the general principle that taxation required the consent of Parliament, and that the King was sole judge both of the existence of an emergency and also of the steps to be taken to meet the danger. It is difficult to criticise this decision in the light of the law at that time. The precedents were conflicting, and Hampden's counsel did not place much reliance on the Petition of Right. The verdict of most historians has been against the correctness of the decision, which they put down to the subservience of the judges to the King. Even if the decision was right in law, it had implications that were politically dangerous. The judgment itself was declared void by the Long Parliament in 1641.

The eventual solution was political rather than legal, for the revolution of 1688 meant that Parliament henceforth controlled the King. The Bill of Rights 1688 accordingly settled the matter for the future, as regards both direct and indirect taxation, by declaring that "levying money for or to the use of the Crown by pretence of prerogative without consent of Parliament for longer time or in other manner than the same is or shall be granted is illegal." It may be noted that the Tenures Abolition Act 1660 had confirmed the abolition of military tenures, and no revenue was derived from that source after 1645.[32]

3–010   An attempt by the government (which in modern times represents the Crown) to levy money without express statutory authority was *Att.-Gen. v. Wilts United Dairies.*[33] The Attorney-General sought to recover £15,000 from Wilts United Dairies, representing a fee of 2d. a gallon on milk purchased by them under licence from the Food Controller, which was granted under statutory orders made in virtue of Regulations issued under the Defence of the Realm (Consolidation) Act 1914. The House of Lords unanimously upheld the decision of the Court of Appeal that the charge was *ultra vires* as a levy of money for the use of the Crown without the authority of Parliament. Lord Buckmaster stated that neither the Act creating the Ministry of Food, nor the Regulations issued under the Defence of the Realm Act, directly or by inference enabled the Food Controller to levy payment. The charges to the extent of £18,000,000 were validated retrospectively by the War Charges (Validity) Act 1925.[34]

In 1954 it was discovered that the Post Office had for many years been inadvertently charging licences for wireless sets without the power to do so, since no regulations with the consent of the Treasury had been issued as required by the Wireless Telegraphy Act 1904. The Post Office repaid the plaintiff's licence and costs,[35] and the charge for wireless licences was validated retrospectively by the Wireless Telegraphy (Validation of Charges) Act 1954. In *Congreve v. Home Office*[36] the Home Secretary gave notice of his intention to increase the fees for television licences. Some licence holders, in order to forestall the increase, took out new licences at the existing rate before their licence had expired. The Home

---

[32] For the "sovereignty" of Parliament in the eighteenth century, see Holdsworth, *op. cit.* Vol. X, pp. 526–531.

[33] (1922) 37 T.L.R. 884; 91 L.J.K.B. 897. The same principle requires local authorities to be able to show explicit legislative authorisation for the imposition of charges for services: *McCarthy and Stone (Developments) Ltd v. Richmond on Thames L.B.C.* [1992] 2 A.C. 48, HL.

[34] Parliament can, of course, expressly delegate the power to levy such charges, and did so in the Second World War by the Emergency Powers (Defence) Act 1939, s.2.

[35] *Davey Paxman & Co Ltd v. Post Office* (action settled) *The Times*, November 16, 1954.

[36] [1976] Q.B. 629.

Secretary, who had a statutory discretion to revoke television licences, proposed to revoke such overlapping licences unless the increased fee was paid. The Court of Appeal held that the Minister's discretion must be exercised reasonably,[37] and that this was an attempt to levy money without authority of Parliament.[38]

Parliament's exclusive control over finance has also been recognised and applied to require explicit statutory authority to justify an order relating to the expenditure of public money.[39]

The Judges and a Higher Law[40]

Medieval judges, though appointed by the King, had inherent authority to declare and apply the law, which was mainly feudal and customary, even against the King[41]; and they could develop the law, within the limits set by a narrow range of sources, to meet new situations. But judges had no jurisdiction to change the direction of the law by introducing novel provisions or to abolish law already established: these functions fell within the province of legislation. A fundamentally new and written constitution like that of the United States would be required to give British courts coordinate authority with that of the legislature, involving jurisdiction to review primary legislation and to test its validity against the supreme law of the constitution. Judges cannot confer such authority on themselves.

3–011

There are dicta in the common law courts, however, down to the seventeenth century to the effect that there is a law of nature or reason superior even to Acts of Parliament. The most celebrated example is *Dr Bonham's Case*,[42] in which Coke C.J. presided over the King's Bench. The question was whether Dr Bonham was liable to pay a fine, half to the Crown and half to the Royal College of Physicians, under the charter of the College which had been confirmed by Act of Parliament. The Court gave judgment for Bonham on the ground that the College had no jurisdiction over those practising outside London; but Coke's report of the judgment goes on to say that "when an Act of Parliament is against common right and reason, or repugnant, or impossible to be performed, the common law will control it, and adjudge such act to be void." This statement was obiter, and is also inconsistent with what Coke says in his *Institutes*.[43]

In *Day v. Savadge*[44] the question was whether Day, as a freeman of the City of London, was exempt from wharfage duty on a bag of nutmegs. On behalf of the Corporation it was contended that by a statute of 7 Ric. II disputes as to the

---

[37] *Padfield v. Ministry of Agriculture, Fisheries and Food* [1968] A.C. 997, HL. The Parliamentary Commissioner had strongly criticised the Home Secretary's action: *Seventh Report of Parliamentary Commissioner for Administration*, Sess. 1974–75. p. 680.

[38] Citing *Att.-Gen. v. Wilts. United Dairies, supra*. The Home Secretary later obtained statutory power to alter television licence fees without advance notice.

[39] *Steele Ford & Newton v. Crown Prosecution Service* (1993) 97 Cr.App.R. 376, HL.

[40] J. W. Gough, *Fundamental Law in English Constitutional History*; Roscoe Pound, *The Development of Guarantees of Liberty* (1957); E. S. Corwin, *The "Higher Law" Background of American Constitutional Law* (reprint 1955).

[41] Bracton, *De Legibus et consuetudinibus Angliae*, f. 5b.

[42] (1610) 8 Co.Rep. 114, 118; *cf.* T. F. T. Plucknett, "Bonham's Case and Judicial Review" (1926) 40 *Harvard Law Review* 30; S. E. Thorne, "Dr Bonham's Case" (1938) 54 L.Q.R. 543.

[43] 4 Inst. 36. Coke as a Law Officer supported the prerogative, as a judge the supremacy of the common law (which he equated with reason), and as a parliamentarian the sovereignty of Parliament.

[44] (1615) Hobart 85, 97.

customs of the City were to be decided on the basis of a certificate of the mayor and aldermen. Hobart C.J., giving the judgment of the Court of Common Pleas, held that the custom in this case was to be tried by jury and not by certificate, and added obiter: "even an act of parliament, made against natural equity, as to make a man judge in his own case, is void in itself; for *jura naturae sunt immutabilia*, and they are *leges legum*." This dictum may be taken as illustrating a logical impossibility or moral limitation, or merely as traditional rhetoric. Again in *City of London v. Wood*,[45] where the Court of Common Pleas gave judgment for Wood on a writ of error from the Mayor's Court in an action for the recovery of a forfeiture to the City of London under a byelaw made by virtue of an Act of Parliament, Holt C.J. is reported to have approved Coke's dictum in *Dr Bonham's Case*, saying: "an Act of Parliament can do no wrong, though it may do several things that look pretty odd," and adding that an Act of Parliament may not make adultery lawful, though it may dissolve the marriage of A and his wife and make her the wife of B.

3–012   These cases concerned the privileges of corporations under royal charters confirmed by Parliament, and the dicta may be taken to express a presumption of interpretation that Parliament does not intend to confer on a corporation or its officers jurisdiction to determine its own legal rights in disputes between the corporation and other persons. Blackstone's statement that no human laws are of any validity if contrary to the "law of nature"[46] was a relic of traditional rhetoric. On the type of case cited above he is more explicit. If Parliament gave a man power to try all causes arising in his manor, Blackstone explains,[47] the courts would construe this as not intending to extend to causes in which he himself is a party; but if Parliament should clearly and expressly enact that he might try his own causes as well as those of other persons, no court would have power to defeat the intent of the legislature.

The modern view was expressed by Willes J. in *Lee v. Bude & Torrington Ry.*[48]:

"It was once said that if an Act of Parliament were to create a man judge in his own cause, the court might disregard it. That dictum, however, stands as a warning rather than an authority to be followed. ... Are we to act as regents over what is done by Parliament with the consent of the Queen, lords and commons? I deny that any such authority exists."

In *Pickin v. British Railways Board*[49] Lord Reid said:

"In earlier times many learned lawyers seem to have believed that an Act of Parliament could be disregarded in so far as it was contrary to the law of God or the law of nature or natural justice but since the supremacy of Parliament was finally demonstrated by the revolution of 1688 any such idea has become obsolete."

---

[45] (1710) 12 Mod. 669, 687–688. This report is, however, considered to be unreliable.
[46] Bl.Comm., I, 41.
[47] Bl.Comm., I, 91.
[48] (1871) L.R. 6 C.P. 576, 582.
[49] [1974] A.C. 765, 782.

More recently there has been a revival of interest in theories of limits to Parliamentary supremacy by reference to the Rule of Law or a framework of constitutional principles[50]—suggestions firmly rebutted by the Lord Chancellor, Lord Irvine.[51]

II. The Nature of Parliamentary Supremacy[52]

The "Legislative Supremacy of Parliament" means that Parliament (*i.e.* the   **3–013** Queen, Lords and Commons in Parliament assembled) can pass laws on any topic affecting any persons, and that there are no "fundamental" laws which Parliament cannot amend or repeal in the same way as ordinary legislation. Dicey[53] was following the tradition of Coke[54] and Blackstone[55] when he said that Parliament has "the right to make or unmake any law whatever," and further that "no person or body is recognised by the law of England as having the right to override or set aside the legislation of Parliament." Once a document is recognised as being an Act of Parliament, no English court can refuse to obey it or question its validity; *Manuel v. Att.-Gen.*[56] *per* Sir Robert Megarry V.C. In that case, presented with the text of the Canada Act 1982, the learned Vice Chancellor held himself obliged to recognise its validity once satisfied that it had been passed by the House of Commons and the House of Lords; had received the Royal Assent and there was no suggestion that the copy was not a true copy of the Act.[57]

Legislative supremacy as thus defined is a legal concept. The supremacy of Parliament, being recognised and acted on by the courts, is a principle of the common law. It may indeed be called the one fundamental law of the British Constitution, for it is peculiar in that it could not be altered by ordinary statute, but only by some fundamental change of attitude on the part of the courts resulting from what would technically be a revolution. Parliament could not, of course, confer this authority on itself. Thus the first Acts passed by the Convention Parliaments of 1660[58] and 1689,[59] legalising their own authority, confirmed the result of revolutions; and the American Colonies Act 1766,[60] asserting the

---

[50] Lord Woolf, "Droit Public—English Style," [1995] P.L. 57; Sir John Laws, "Law and Democracy" [1995] P.L. 72.

[51] "Judges and Decision Makers" [1996] P.L. 59. For an extended refutation of modern, revisionist theories, see J. Goldsworthy, *The Sovereignty of Parliament* (1999).

[52] Dicey, *Law of the Constitution* (10th ed.), Chaps. 1–3; H. W. R. Wade, "The Basis of Legal Sovereignty" [1955] C.L.J. 172, and review in [1954] C.L.J. 265; O. Hood Phillips, *Reform of the Constitution* (1970), Chaps. 1 and 7.

[53] Dicey, *op. cit.* pp. 39–40; quoted by Wild C.J. in *Fitzgerald v. Muldoon* [1976] 1 N.Z.L.R. 615, 622.

[54] 4 Inst. 36.

[55] Bl.Comm., I, 160–162.

[56] [1983] Ch.77, 86. The reference to an English court is explicable by the fact that the learned Vice–Chancellor is an English judge and was clearly not meant to imply that a different rule applies in Scotland: but see *post*, para. 4–008.

[57] On the definition of Act of Parliament, see *post*, para. 4–025 *et seq.*

[58] Parliament Act 1660.

[59] Crown and Parliament Recognition Act 1689.

[60] Repealed by the Statute Law Revision Act 1964.

full power and authority of Parliament to make laws binding on the American colonies, was merely declaratory.

3–014   On the other hand a state may be a sovereign state and yet have a legislature which is not unlimited and courts with jurisdiction to review its legislation. Thus the 1947 Constitution of Ceylon (an independent sovereign state within the Commonwealth) required for its amendment the Speaker's certificate that not less than two-thirds of the members of the House of Representatives voted in favour. It was held by the Privy Council in *Bribery Commissioner v. Rana-singhe*[61] that the Bribery Tribunal by which the respondent had been convicted was not lawfully appointed, because the Act under which it was appointed was passed by the ordinary legislative procedure, whereas it required a constitutional amendment relating to the appointment of judicial officers. This is also the principle that emerges from the South African case *Harris v. Minister of the Interior* ("the Cape coloured voters case"),[62] in so far as that case is relevant to the present context. The question in issue was the validity of the Separate Representation of Voters Act 1951, which was passed by the two Houses sitting separately and thus infringed section 152 of the South Africa Act 1909, which Act formed the basis of the Constitution. This section provided that no repeal or alteration of section 35 (qualification of Cape coloured voters) should be valid unless the Bill was passed by both Houses sitting together and the third reading was agreed to by not less than two-thirds of the members of both Houses. It was held by the Appellate Division of the Supreme Court of South Africa that the Separate Representation of Voters Act was invalid as the South Africa Act was a superior law to the Union Parliament, which it created. Whether the Union Parliament was called a "sovereign" legislature was a matter of definition: the Parliament functioning bicamerally was restricted in certain respects, but anything it could not do in that way could be done by a two- thirds majority in the Parliament functioning unicamerally.[63]

The legislative supremacy of the British Parliament, as well as being a legal concept, is also the result of political history and is ultimately based on fact, that is, general recognition by the people and the courts. It is therefore at the same time a legal and a political principle.[64]

3–015   The doctrine of the legislative supremacy of Parliament has been so firmly established that it has scarcely been challenged in the courts. When Canon Selwyn made an application questioning the validity of the Royal Assent to the Irish Church Disestablishment Act 1869 as being inconsistent with the Coronation Oath and the Act of Settlement, Cockburn C.J. and Blackburn J. in refusing the application said: "There is no judicial body in the country by which the validity of an act of parliament can be questioned. An act of the legislature is superior in authority to any court of law . . . , and no court could pronounce a judgment as to the validity of an act of parliament" (*ex p. Selwyn*).[65] In *Vauxhall*

---

[61] [1965] A.C. 172. Ceylon is now called Sri Lanka and has a new constitution.

[62] [1952] (2) A.D. 428; *sub nom. Harris v. Dönges* [1952] 1 T.L.R. 1245. See D. V. Cowen, *Parliamentary Sovereignty and the Entrenched Sections of the South Africa Act* (1951).

[63] The desired legislation was eventually passed by changing the composition of the Senate; see *Collins v. Minister of the Interior* [1957] (1) A.D. 552.

[64] Professor H. L. A. Hart calls it "the ultimate rule of recognition," which may be regarded both as an external statement of fact and as an internal criterion of validity; *The Concept of Law*, pp. 107–108.

[65] (1872) 36 J.P. 54.

Estates Ltd v. Liverpool Corporation[66] and *Ellen Street Estates Ltd v. Minister of Health*[67] counsel unsuccessfully argued that a later Act could not repeal the provisions of an earlier Act, with which it was inconsistent, except by express words. That contention, said Scrutton L.J. in the latter case, "is absolutely contrary to the constitutional position." In *Hall v. Hall*[68] the plaintiff claimed that the Probate Act 1857, on which the defendant based the title to a house, had not really received the Royal Assent as he challenged the Royal Succession from the days of James II. The county court judge said he could not ignore a statute that had been acted on for more than eighty years, and that in any event Parliament could validate all titles by passing an Indemnity Act.

In *R. v. Jordan*[69] J, who had been sentenced to imprisonment for offences under the Race Relations Act 1965, applied for legal aid to enable him to apply for habeas corpus on the ground that the Race Relations Act was invalid as being in curtailment of free speech. The Divisional Court, dismissing the application, held that Parliament was supreme and there was no power in the courts to question the validity of an Act of Parliament, adding that the ground of the application was completely unarguable. In *Cheney v. Conn*[70] a taxpayer contended that the Finance Act 1964 conflicted with the Geneva Conventions incorporated in the Geneva Conventions Act 1957, and that it was contrary to international law that part of his tax should go to the construction of nuclear weapons. Ungoed-Thomas J. held that there was no conflict between the two Acts; the Finance Act prevailed over international convenions, which are an executive act of the Crown; and that what Parliament enacts cannot be unlawful.

In *Martin v. O'Sullivan*[71] Nourse J. and the Court of Appeal refused to **3–016** consider a claim that proceedings in the House of Commons during the passage of the bill which became the Social Security Act 1975 were invalid because the members of the House were all disqualified from sitting. There was, according to the judges, a fundamental answer to this case, namely, that a court could only look at the parliamentary roll of statutes and if it appeared that an Act had passed both Houses of Parliament and had received the Royal Assent it could look no further.

In an appeal to the House of Lords in *Edinburgh and Dalkeith Ry v. Wauchope*,[72] where it had been suggested in the Scottish court below that a private Act might not be applicable against a person whose rights were affected but who had not been given prior notice, Lord Campbell pronounced the following dictum: "All that a Court of Justice can do is to look to the Parliament roll: if from that it should appear that a Bill has passed both Houses and received the Royal Assent, no Court of Justice can enquire into the mode in which it was introduced into Parliament, nor into what was done previous to its introduction, or what passed in Parliament during its progress in its various stages through both Houses." In another case concerning a private Act, *Lee v. Bude and Torrington*

---

[66] [1932] 1 K.B. 733 (D.C.) *post*, para. 4–004.
[67] [1934] 1 K.B. 590 (C.A.) *post*, para. 4–004.
[68] (1944) 88 S.J. 383 (Hereford C.C.). The judgment as reported appears to beg the question.
[69] [1967] Crim.L.R. 483; 9 J.P.Supp. 48.
[70] [1968] 1 W.L.R. 242.
[71] [1982] S.T.C. 416; [1984] S.T.C. 258, CA.
[72] (1842) 8 Cl. & F. 710; cited and followed, *Sillars v. Smith* 1982 S.L.T. 539; *post*, para. 4–009.

Ry.,[73] Willes J. said: "Acts of Parliament are the law of the land and we do not sit as a Court of Appeal from Parliament."[74]

3–017   The matter was fully reviewed again in relation to a private Act of Parliament by the House of Lords in *Pickin v. British Railways Board*,[75] where Pickin pleaded that the British Railways Act 1968 (c. xxxiv) contained a false recital, that the Board had misled Parliament by obtaining the Act *ex parte* as an unopposed Bill, and that it was therefore ineffective to deprive him of his land. Their Lordships held unanimously that the courts could not go behind private Acts to show that a provision should not be enforced, or examine proceedings in Parliament to show that the Board by fraudulently misleading Parliament, caused him loss. Lord Reid said that the law was correctly stated by Lord Campbell in *Edinburgh v. Dalkeith Ry v. Wauchope*[76]: although that was *obiter* [*semble*, as regards public Acts] no one since 1842 had doubted it. The court had no concern with the manner in which Parliament, or its officers in carrying out its standing orders, performed their functions.

Examples of subject-matter

3–018   Examples of the positive aspect of the legislative supremacy of Parliament as regards subject-matter are the Septennial Act 1715, extending the maximum duration of the existing and future Parliaments from three to seven years; the Parliament Acts 1911 and 1949, restricting the power of the House of Lords to withhold its assent to public Bills (especially money Bills), and reducing the maximum duration of a Parliament to five years; the prolongation of its own life

---

[73] (1871) L.R. & C.P. 576.

[74] Other judicial dicta that may be cited are: "The supremacy of Parliament. . . . That sovereign power can make and unmake the law": *per* Lord Denman C.J. in *Stockdale v. Hansard* (1839) 9 Ad. & E. 1; "Whereas . . . you may canvass a rule and determine whether or not it was within the power of those who made it, you cannot canvass in that way the provisions of an Act of Parliament": *per* Lord Herschell L.C. in *Institute of Patent Agents v. Lockwood* [1894] A.C. 347, 359; "For us an Act of Parliament duly passed by Lords and Commons and assented to by the King, is supreme and we are bound to give effect to its terms." *per* Lord Dunedin (Lord Justice General) in *Mortensen v. Peters* (1906) 8 F.(J.C.) 93, 100; "Parliament is omnipotent": *per* Vaughan Williams L.J. in *R. v. Local Government Board, ex p. Arlidge* [1914] 1 K.B. 160, 175–176; "Nothing we do or say could in any degree affect the complete power of the legislature by Act of Parliament to carry out the present scheme, or any other scheme": *per* Atkin L.J. in *R. v. Electricity Commissioners* [1924] 1 K.B. 171; "Parliament is supreme. It can enact extraordinary powers of interfering with personal liberty. If an Act of Parliament . . . is alleged to limit or curtail the liberty of the subject or vest in the executive extraordinary powers of detaining a subject, the only question is what is the precise extent of the powers given"; *per* Lord Wright in *Liversidge v. Anderson* [1942] A.C. 206; "Parliament has absolute sovereignty and can make what legal creatures if it likes"; *per* Scott L.J. in *National Union of General and Municipal Workers v. Gillian* [1946] 1 K.B. 81; "Parliament could do anything . . . being omnipotent": *per* Harman J. in *Hammersmith Borough Council v. Boundary Commission, The Times*, December 15, 1954. "The supremacy of Parliament . . . it is not for the Court to say that a parliamentary enactment, the highest law in this country, is illegal"; *per* Ungoed—Thomas J. in *Cheney v. Conn* [1968] 1 W.L.R. 242, 247; "That central feature of our constitution, the sovereignty of Parliament." *per* Lord Simon of Glaisdale in *Jones v. Secretary of State for Social Services* [1972] A.C. 944: "The supremacy of Parliament was finally demonstrated by the revolution of 1688"; *per* Lord Reid; "parliamentary democracy. Its peculiar feature in constitutional law is the sovereignty of Parliament," *per* Lord Simon of Glaisdale.: *Pickin v. British Railways Board, supra.* "Parliament has a legally unchallengeable right to make whatever law it thinks right"; *R. v. Home Secretary ex p. Fire Brigades Union* [1995] 2 A.C. 513 *per* Lord Mustill.

[75] [1974] A.C. 765. See P. Wallington, "Sovereignty Regained" (1974) 37 M.L.R. 686; and Chap. 11, *post*, for procedure in Private Bills.

[76] *Supra.*

by annual Acts to eight years by the Parliament that passed the Act of 1911,[77] and annual prolongations during the last war of the life of the Parliament that was elected in 1935[78]; the Act of Settlement 1700, which regulated the succession to the throne on the failure of Queen Anne's issue, and His Majesty's Declaration of Abdication Act 1936, which varied that succession; the Union with Scotland Act 1706, by which the English Parliament extinguished itself and transferred its authority to the new Parliament of Great Britain; the Government of Ireland Act 1920 and the Irish Free State Agreement Act 1922, dissolving the union between Great Britain and Ireland (which had been created by the Union with Ireland Act 1800), setting up a subordinate legislature in Northern Ireland[79] and giving Dominion status to the Irish Free State[80]; the Defence of the Realm Acts and Emergency Powers (Defence) Acts of the two World Wars, conferring extremely wide—though temporary—powers on the government.[81] Parliament may legislate with retroactive effect if it wishes. Although it is presumed that legislation is not intended to be retrospective[82] "If Parliament wishes to enact retrospectively it can do so, provided it uses sufficiently plain words. The intention to legislate retrospectively need not be expressed provided that there is a very clear implication to that effect."[83] Acts of Indemnity may legalise, for example, acts which when they were done were illegal, such as the Housing Finance (Special Provisions) Act 1975, removing further surcharges arising out of the failure of the Clay Cross councillors to implement the Housing Finance Act 1972 and terminating any local electoral disqualification arising from such surcharges.[84] Invalid delegated legislation may be retrospectively validated.[85] Other notable examples of retrospective legislation are the War Damage Act 1965,[86] and the Northern Ireland Act 1972 legalising retrospectively to 1920 the use of troops in Northern Ireland for certain civilian purposes.[87]

The absence of "fundamental" laws means, as we have seen in Chapter 2, that the courts have no jurisdiction to declare an Act of Parliament void as being *ultra vires* or "unconstitutional."

---

[77] Parliament and Local Elections Acts 1916, 1917 and 1918.

[78] Prolongation of Parliament Acts 1941, 1942, 1943 and 1944.

[79] *ante* p. 18.

[80] Recognised as the independent Republic of Ireland by the Ireland Act 1949.

[81] See especially, Emergency Powers (Defence) No. 2 Act 1940, authorising Defence Regulations to make provision "for requiring persons to place themselves, their services and their property at the disposal of His Majesty."

[82] *Waddington v. Miah* [1974] 1 W.L.R. 683, HL.

[83] *Tracomin S.A. v. Sudan Oil Seeds Co. Ltd* [1983] 1 W.L.R. 1026, 1030 *per* Sir John Donaldson M.A. See also *Azam v. Secretary of State for the Home Dept.* [1974] A.C. 18. The interpretation of legislation which retrospectively imposed criminal liability would in appropriate proceedings, be subject to the rule laid down in section 3 of the Human Rights Act 1998; *post* 22–016 (Art. 7 prevents retrospective criminal legislation).

[84] J. E. Trice, "Rule of Law: Clay Cross," *New Law Journal*, April 4, 1974.

[85] National Health Service (Invalid Direction) Act 1980.

[86] Reversing the decision of the House of Lords as regards war damage in *Burmah Oil Co v. Lord Advocate* [1965] A.C. 75.

[87] Other examples of retrospective legislation include Marriage Validation Acts, the War Charges (Validity) Act 1925, the Truck Act 1940, the Charitable Trusts (Validation) Act 1954, the Wireless Telegraphy (Validation of Charges) Act 1954, the Finance Act 1960, s.39(5) ("the foregoing provisions of this section shall be deemed always to have had effect"); Finance Act 1984, s.8 (increase of surtax rates for 1972–1973). The Social Security (Miscellaneous Provisions) Act 1977, s.14(8); noted [1979] P.L.58. The Representation of the People Act 1981, s.1, the Employment Act 1982, s.2 and the London Regional Transport (Amendment) Act 1985.

Composition

3–019   Parliament is also free to alter its own composition. The composition of the House of Commons may be affected by redistribution of seats, alteration of the franchise or changes in the disqualifications for membership. The composition of the House of Lords has been affected by extending the qualification of Scottish peers, and the creation of life peerages and Lords of Appeal. Parliament could confine membership of the House of Lords to life peers. Indeed, Parliament could abolish the House of Lords, perhaps without its own consent under the provisions of the Parliament Act[88] and it could abolish the monarchy, though that would require the Royal Assent. It would be idle to speculate on the abolition of the House of Commons, as such an event postulates a completely different kind of constitution.

Persons and areas

3–020   With regard to persons and areas, since Parliament is the Parliament of the United Kingdom its Acts are presumed to apply to the United Kingdom and not to extend further. If an Act is not intended to apply to Wales,[89] Scotland or Northern Ireland, or if it is intended to apply outside the United Kingdom, *e.g.* to a colony, this must be expressly stated.[90] Thus the European Communities Act 1972 includes the United Kingdom, together with (for certain purposes) the Channel Islands, the Isle of Man and Gibraltar. Parliament can define the country's territory,[91] fishery limits,[92] and continental shelf.[93] It can penalise offences of an international or Community character,[94] the broadcasting of election propaganda from abroad,[95] the operation of private radio stations outside territorial waters,[96] and the destruction of animals and plants in Antarctica.[97]

The general principle, however, is expressed in the words of Donaldson L.J. in *R. v. West Yorkshire Coroner ex p. Smith*,[98]

> "Every Parliamentary draftsman writes on paper which bears the legend, albeit in invisible ink, 'This Act shall not have extra-territorial effect save to the extent that it expressly so provides.' The court knows this and they read it into every statute."

The presumption against a parliamentary intention to make acts done abroad by aliens triable as criminal offences by British courts is particularly strong.[99] The presumption in the case of a British subject is less strong.[1]

---

[88] But see Peter Mirfield, "Can the House of Lords Lawfully be Abolished?" (1979) 95 L.Q.R. 36; George Winterton, "Is the House of Lords Immortal?" (1979) 95 L.Q.R. 386.

[89] References to "England" in Acts of Parliament after 1967 no longer include Wales: Welsh Language Act 1967.

[90] *R. v. Martin* [1956] 2 Q.B. 272, *per* Devlin J.

[91] Island of Rockall Act 1972.

[92] Fishery Limits Act 1976, extending British fishing limits to 200 miles from the territorial sea baselines of the United Kingdom.

[93] Continental Shelf Act 1964.

[94] Aviation Security Act 1982; European Communities Act 1972, s.11.

[95] Representation of the People Act 1983, s.92.

[96] Marine etc. Broadcasting (Offences) Act 1967; passed as a consequence of *R. v. Kent Justices, ex p. Lye* [1967] 2 K.B. 153 (D.C.); *Post Office v. Estuary Radio* [1967] 1 W.L.R. 1396, CA.

[97] Antarctic Treaty Act 1967. Acts of this kind are usually based on international treaties.

[98] [1983] Q.B. 335.

[99] *Air India v. Wiggins* [1980] 1 W.L.R. 815, HL.

[1] *Re Tucker* [1987] 1 W.L.R. 928 (Bankruptcy proceedings).

For obvious reasons Parliament does not generally attempt to legislate with **3–021** regard to acts done in foreign territory.[2] Under the Foreign Jurisdiction Acts 1890–1913, however, the Crown has power to make laws for overseas territories over which it has acquired jurisdiction. Criminal jurisdiction may be exercised over British citizens for acts committed abroad, for example, in the cases of murder, manslaughter and bigamy, under the Offences Against the Person Act 1861, ss.9 and 57 and in the case of any crime under the Merchant Shipping Act 1894, s.686(1).[3] Increasingly it is necessary to have resort to legislation with extra-territorial effect to deal with terrorism and give effect to international conventions aimed at its eradication.[4] An unusual example of legislation with extra-territorial effect is the Protection of Trading Interests Act 1980 under which British firms trading abroad may be guilty of criminal offences if, contrary to a direction of the Secretary of State, they comply with instructions from foreign courts or officials when to do so would in the Secretary of State's view damage the trading interests of the United Kingdom.[5]

The application of legislation passed by the British Parliament to independent members of the Commonwealth is discussed later in Chapter 37.

Practical limitations

There are in practice, of course, factors which limit Parliament's ability to pass **3–022** any laws it likes, or, rather, which limit the choice of measures that the government puts before Parliament for approval. These factors are the concern of the political scientist rather than the student of constitutional law, but it is convenient to mention some of the more important ones briefly here.

The mandate or party manifesto

The government is expected to carry out the policy (if any) indicated at the last **3–023** general election and is not expected to act contrary to that policy, according to the general and rather vague doctrine of the "mandate," which seems to have been invented in the latter part of the nineteenth century. But a government acts for the whole people, not only those who voted for their party. Ministers are servants of the Crown and members of Parliament are not delegates. The government must remain flexible and deal with emergencies, so that it may be its duty to ignore or even to act against the mandate. In any case, a government that has been in power for some time must meet changing circumstances in all fields of the national life such as defence and the state of the economy, and is not expected to mark time because it has exhausted its "mandate," which may have been expressed in very general terms and which few electors (except professional politicians) read. In Sir Ivor Jennings's words: "The doctrine of the mandate is part of the political cant. It is a stick used by the Opposition to beat the Government. ... The doctrine is, however, of importance. Though it must necessarily be vague and its operation a matter of dispute, it is recognised to exist."[6] (*A fortiori* a local

---

[2] With regard to independent members of the Commonwealth see *post*, Chap. 36.

[3] *R. v. Kelly* [1982] A.C. 665.

[4] Aviation Security Act 1982; Suppression of Terrorism Act 1978; Internationally Protected Persons Act 1978; Taking of Hostages Act 1982.

[5] See further, *British Airways Bd v. Laker Airways Ltd* [1985] A.C. 58.

[6] Jennings, *Cabinet Government* (3rd ed.), p. 505. See also C. S. Emden, *The People and the Constitution* (2nd ed.); G. H. L. Le May, "Parliament, the Constitution and the 'Doctrine of the Mandate' " (1957) 74 *South African Law Journal* 33.

authority cannot rely on the terms of its manifesto to avoid exercising discretionary powers vested in it in a reasonable manner.[7])

Public opinion

3–024   Parliament must also take account of the even vaguer concept of "public opinion." Public opinion expresses itself through the press, radio, television, trade unions, industrialists, local councillors, party organisations and in countless other ways. The manner in which it is interpreted by the government and other members of Parliament must obviously affect Parliament's activities, including the passing of legislation. The moral ideas and ideals of the community, especially as expressed through the leaders of the Churches, make their influence felt. The strength of the Opposition—although *ex hypothesi* a minority in the Commons—is a variable factor, but in our system of parliamentary government the official Opposition must always be taken into account. The government's legislative proposals must stand up to debate, the debates will be reported in the media or be available in *Hansard*, and the government must remember that within a few years at most it will have to face another general election.

Consultation of organised interests

3–025   In modern times the government does not in practice introduce legislation affecting well-defined sections of the community without first consulting organisations of the groups specially concerned or interested ("pressure groups"). In matters affecting industry or trade, for example, the Minister proposing to initiate legislation would consult the employers' associations, chambers of commerce and the trade unions, notably the officers of the Trade Unions Congress and the Confederation of British Industry. The National Farmers Union would be consulted in matters affecting agriculture. Any reorganisation of local government would involve discussions with the associations representing the different kinds of local authorities. Professional associations would expect to be consulted in any matter that concerned their professions. Thus the introduction of the National Health Service would have been impossible without the co-operation of the General Medical Council, and reforms in legal procedure would involve discussions with the Bar Council and the Law Society. Societies promoting causes, such as the Howard League for Penal Reform and the R.S.P.C.A., would also be consulted where appropriate.[8]

There is no general legal duty to consult. Still less is the Minister bound to accept the advice given, which will often be conflicting anyway. The practice is to discuss the general principles of the proposed legislation, rather than the draft Bill.[9]

International Law

3–026   The customary principles of International law are said to be part of the law of England,[10] but treaties do not automatically become part of English law.[11] Thus, according to the majority view in *R. v. Bow Street Magistrate ex p. Pinochet (No*

---

[7] *Bromley L.B.C. v. G.L.C.* [1983] 1 A.C. 768. But *cf. Secretary of State for Education and Science v. Tameside M.B.C.* [1977] A.C. 1014, HL.

[8] See F. E. Finer, *Anonymous Empire* (2nd ed.).

[9] Sir Ivor Jennings, *Parliament* (2nd ed.), Chap. 7.

[10] For a discussion of the doctrines of "incorporation" and "transformation," see *per* Lord Denning M.R. in *Trendtex Trading Corp. v. Central Bank of Nigeria* [1977] Q.B. 529, CA.

[11] *McWhirter v. Att.-Gen.* [1972] C.M.L.R. 882; CA *per* Lord Denning M.R. *post*, para. 15–028.

3),[12] the jurisdiction of the English courts rested on the Criminal Justice Act 1988, s.134, not on the United Kingdom's adherence to the International Convention against Torture and other Cruel, Inhuman or Degrading Treatment or Punishment 1984. International law as such does not bind Parliament, although the activities of Parliament are in fact restrained by considerations of international law and the comity of nations.[13] There is a presumption that Parliament does not intend to legislate contrary to the principles of international law, and a statute would be interpreted as far as possible so as not to conflict with them[14]; but the legal power of Parliament to make laws contrary thereto remains,[15] and redress would have to be sought by diplomatic action and not through the courts. Where a statute is clear and unambiguous the "comity of nations" is irrelevant (*per* Lord Porter in *Theophile v. Solicitor-General*[16]), its provisions must be followed even if they are contrary to international law (*per* Viscount Simonds in *I.R.C. v. Collco Dealings Ltd*),[17] for the sovereign power of Parliament extends even to breaking treaties (*per* Diplock L.J. in *Salomon v. Customs and Excise Commissioners*[18]).

This principle is well illustrated by the case of *Mortensen v. Peters*.[19] Mortensen, a Danish citizen and captain of a Norwegian trawler, was convicted by the High Court of Justiciary of infringing the Herring Fishery (Scotland) Act 1889, which forbad trawling in the Moray Firth, although the acts done took place outside the three-mile limit. Diplomatic representations were made to the Foreign Office, and the Crown remitted the fine, although it recognised that the Court was right to apply the Act of Parliament. Shortly afterwards an Act was passed[20] providing that prosecutions should not be brought under the Act of 1889 for trawling outside the three-mile limit, but that fish caught by prohibited methods might not be landed or sold in the United Kingdom. And in *R. v. Secretary of State for Home Department, ex p. Thakrar*,[21] where an Asian British protected person, who had been expelled from Uganda, claimed the right to enter the United Kingdom, the Court of Appeal held that any rule of international law requiring a state to receive its nationals expelled by another State was expressly excluded by the Immigration Act 1971.

3–027

Community Law and Human Rights

The impact of Community Law on the traditional doctrine of parliamentary supremacy will be discussed in Chapters 4 and 7. The position of the European Convention on Human Rights will be discussed in Chapter 22.

3–028

---

[12] [2000] 1 A.C. 147, HL.

[13] See *Cheney v. Conn* [1968] 1 W.L.R. 242, *ante*, p. 52, *Chung Chi Cheung v. The Kingd* [1939] A.C. 160, 167–168, PC *per* Lord Atkin; Holdsworth, "The Relation of English Law to International Law" *Essays in Law and History*, p. 260; *History of English Law*, Vol. XIV, pp. 22–33.

[14] *The Zamora* [1916] A.C. 77, PC; *Co-operative Committee on Japanese Canadians v. Att.-Gen. for Canada* [1974] A.C. 87, 104, PC; *cf. Polites v. The Commonwealth* (1945) 70 C.L.R. 60 (High Ct. Austr.).

[15] *cf. Sovereignty within the Law*, by Arthur Larson, C. Wilfred Jenks and Others (1966).

[16] [1950] A.C. 186, 195.

[17] [1962] A.C. 1, HL.

[18] [1967] 2 Q.B. 116, CA.

[19] (1906), 8 F 93, *per* Lord Dunedin, Lord-Justice General. The ship was in fact British owned, but was given a foreign master and registration with a view to evading the Scottish fishery regulations.

[20] Trawling in Prohibited Areas Prevention Act 1909.

[21] [1974] Q.B. 684: anyway, such a rule between states could not be invoked by an individual.

CHAPTER 4

PARLIAMENTARY SUPREMACY II: PROBLEM OF SELF-LIMITATION[1]

The problem of self-limitation

4–001   The problem raised in this chapter is that known to logicians as self-referring or reflexive propositions. The view put forward here is that it is impracticable for a legislature to limit itself as to the laws it shall make[2] or repeal unless it is empowered, expressly or impliedly, so to limit itself by some "higher law," that is, some (logically and historically) prior law *not laid down by itself*.[3] If our courts were to recognise any limitation on the power of Parliament to pass statutes applicable within the United Kingdom, dealing with (say) the constitutional status of Northern Ireland or Community law or civil rights, there would have to be some juridical reason for such decision. In British constitutional law, what could be such a reason?

One of three possible higher laws might be suggested: (i) a supreme Constitution, that is, a written Constitution (not enacted by Parliament itself) containing provisions entrenched against alteration by (ordinary) Act of Parliament; (ii) the primacy of International law, including Community treaties, or (iii) natural law. However, we have seen in Chapter 2 that the first (a written Constitution with entrenched provisions) does not exist. As Lord Pearce said in *Bribery Commissioner v. Ranasinghe*[4]: "in the Constitution of the United Kingdom there is no governing instrument which prescribes the lawmaking powers and the forms which are essential to those powers." In Chapter 3 we have seen that judicial authority is strongly against the second (primacy of International law, including treaties), and there is no judicial decision in favour of the third (natural law).

The question may be illustrated in relation, first, to the subject-matter of legislation, and, secondly, to the "manner and form" of legislation.

---

[1] Dicey *Law of the Constitution* (10th ed.), pp. 64–70; Anson, *Law and Custom of the Constitution*, Vol. 1 (5th ed. Gwyer), pp. 7–8; H. W. R. Wade, "The Basis of *Legal Sovereignty* [1955] C.L.J. 172, and review in [1954] C.L.J. 265; Hood Phillips, *Reform of the Constitution* (1970), pp. 151–156; "Self-Limitation by the United Kingdom Parliament" (1975) 2 *Hastings Constitutional Law Quarterly*, 443.

cf. Sir Ivor Jennings, *The Law and the Constitution* (5th ed.), Chap. 4; D. V. Cowen, "Legislature and Judiciary: Reflections on the Constitutional Issues in South Africa" (1952) 15 M.L.R. 282; (1953) 16 M.L.R. 273; B. Beinart, Parliament and the Courts" [1954] *South African Law Review* 135; G. Marshall, *Parliamentary Sovereignty and the Commonwealth* (1957), Chap. 4, and *Constitutional Theory* (1971) Chap. 3; R. F. V. Heuston, *Essays in Constitutional Law* (2nd ed., 1964), Chap. 1; J. D. B. Mitchell, *Constitutional Law* (2nd ed., 1968), Chap. 4; George Winterton, "The British Grundnorm: Parliamentary Supremacy Re-examined" (1976) 92 L.Q.R. 591.

[2] The Taxation of Colonies Act 1778, for removing all doubts and apprehensions, provided, that after the passing of the Act Parliament would not impose any taxes on the colonies in North America and the West Indies, except such duties as might be expedient for the regulation of commerce and for the use of the colony concerned.

[3] See Alf Ross, "On Self-Reference and a Puzzle of Constitutional Law" (1969) 78 *Mind*; Hans Kelsen, *General Theory of Law and State* (1945), pp. 124–128. *cf.* H. L. A. Hart, *The Concept of Law* (2nd ed., 1994) p. 149 *et seq.* distinguishing between *continuing* omnipotence (sovereignty) and *self-embracing* omnipotence (sovereignty): "it is clear that the presently accepted rule is one of continuing sovereignty so that Parliament cannot protect its statutes from repeal."

[4] [1965] A.C. 172, PC.

I. SUBJECT-MATTER OF LEGISLATION

Repeal or amendment

The Treason Act 1495, which was passed to protect subjects who had served   **4–002**
a *de facto* king from being impeached or attainted for treason under some future
de jure king, either by the course of law or by Act of Parliament, provided that
if any such Act of Attainder were to be passed, it should be void and of no effect.
Bacon wrote[5] that the latter provision was illusory. "For a supreme and absolute
power cannot conclude itself, neither can that which is in its nature revocable be
made fixed"; and Coke wrote[6] that the Act would be applicable to ordinary
prosecutions for treason, but would not restrain any parliamentary attainder.
Henry VIII procured an Act in 1536[7] enabling future kings to revoke any Acts
passed while they were under the age of 24 years. This Act was repealed in the
first year of Edward VI,[8] when he was 10 years old, the royal assent being given
by the Protector, Somerset, and the Council consisting of Henry's executors.

Coke introduces a section of his *Institutes* with the heading: "Acts against the
power of the Parliament subsequent bind not . . . for it is a matter in the law of
the Parliament, *quod leges posteriores priores contrarias abrogant.*"[9] In *Godden
v. Hales*[10] Herbert C.J. said: "if an Act of Parliament had a clause in it that it
should never be repealed, yet without question, the same power that made it may
repeal it." It is true that Parliament apparently thought it necessary in 1705 to
pass two Acts[11] in order to naturalise Princess Sophia, Electress of Hanover (who
was abroad), without her having to take the oath of allegiance at Westminster as
required by the Naturalisation Act 1609; but it is submitted that one Act would
have been sufficient, the Act of 1609 being regarded not as binding Parliament
itself until repealed or amended but as being directed towards petitioners and
officials. The Meeting of Parliament 1694 provided: "That from henceforth no
Parliament whatsoever . . . shall have any continuance longer than for three
years only at the farthest." Yet at the time of the Jacobite rising Parliament
enacted in the Septennial Act 1715[12]; "That this present Parliament and all
Parliaments that shall at any time henceforth be called assembled or held shall
and may have continuance for seven years and no longer" unless sooner dissolved by the Crown. This extension of the life of the existing Parliament as well
as future Parliaments did in fact meet considerable opposition in both Houses,
and the controversy over it outside Parliament continued for many years.

Blackstone, who quoted Coke's statement (*supra*), says[13]: "Acts of Parliament   **4–003**
derogatory from the power of subsequent parliaments bind not. . . . Because the

---

[5] *History of Henry VII* (1622), p. 133.
[6] Co. Inst. 43.
[7] 28 Hen. VIII, c.17.
[8] 1 Edw. VI, c. 11. The repealing Act still allowed the king to revoke statutes passed while he was
under 24 years of age, but such revocation was not to have retrospective effect.
[9] 2 Co. Inst. 685: "Later laws abrogate prior laws that are contrary to them"; and *Dr Foster's Case*
(1615), 11 Co.Rep. 56b, 62b.
[10] (1686) 11 St.Tr. 1165, 1197.
[11] 4 & 5 Anne, c. 14 and c. 16. See *Att.-Gen. v. Prince Ernest Augustus of Hanover* [1957] A.C. 436,
per Viscount Simonds.
[12] Amended by Parliament Act 1911, s.7, reducing the maximum life of Parliament to five years.
[13] 1 Bl. Comm. 90–91.

legislature being in truth the sovereign power, is always of equal, always of absolute authority: it acknowledges no superior upon earth, which the prior legislature must have been, if its ordinances could bind a subsequent parliament. And upon the same principle Cicero, in his letters to Atticus, treats with a proper contempt these restraining clauses, which endeavour to tie up the hands of succeeding legislators. 'When you repeal the law itself,' says he, 'you at the same time repeal the prohibitory clause, which guards against such repeal.' " Dicey[14] followed this tradition. Many readers have formed the view that it is an exception to what these writers called the "sovereignty" of Parliament; but the apparent paradox is verbal only, as will be seen if the proposition is expressed the other way round: "Parliament is not bound by its predecessors." Indeed the marginal note in Coke's *Institutes* reads: "Subsequent Parliaments cannot be restrained by the former."

As has been suggested in the previous chapter, it is preferable to use the expression "legislative supremacy" rather than "sovereignty" in relation to Parliament's lawmaking power. In either event the power of *express* repeal is so well established that it has never been contested in the courts. "It is good constitutional doctrine," said Lord Reid extrajudicially,[15] "that Parliament cannot bind its successors."

4–004   There are two cases, however, in which it has been argued by counsel that a provision in an earlier Act precluded *implied* repeal in a later Act. The Acquisition of Land (Assessment of Compensation) Act 1919, s.7(1), stated: "The provisions of the Act or order by which the land is authorised to be acquired . . . shall . . . have effect subject to this Act, and so far as inconsistent with this Act those provisions shall cease to have or shall not have effect. . . . " The marginal note (which is not binding) to section 7 reads: "Effect of Act on existing enactments." In *Vauxhall Estates Ltd v. Liverpool Corporation*[16] the plaintiffs claimed that compensation for land compulsorily acquired from them should be assessed on the basis of the Act of 1919 and not on the less favourable terms provided by the Housing Act 1925. The Divisional Court held that even if the Act of 1919 could be construed as intended to govern future as well as existing Acts assessing compensation, which construction was doubtful, yet the relevant provisions must be regarded as impliedly overridden by the inconsistent provisions of the Act of 1925. In *Ellen Street Estates Ltd v. Minister of Health*[17] a similar argument on the relation between the provisions for compensation contained in the Act of 1919 and the Housing Act 1925 and 1930 was raised in the Court of Appeal. Here the decision that the Housing Acts impliedly repealed the Act of 1919 in so far as they were inconsistent with it was part of the ratio. "The Legislature cannot, according to our constitution," said Maugham L.J., "bind itself as to the form of subsequent legislation, and it is impossible for Parliament to enact that in a subsequent statute dealing with the same subject-matter there can be no implied repeal. If in a subsequent Act Parliament chooses to make it plain that the earlier statute is being to some extent repealed, effect must be given to that intention just because it is the will of the Legislature."

---

[14] *loc. cit.*
[15] "The Judge as Law Maker" (1972) 12 J.S.P.T.L. 22, 25.
[16] [1932] 1 K.B. 733.
[17] [1934] 1 K.B. 590; approving *Vauxhall Estates Ltd v. Liverpool Corporation supra*, *cf.* F.M. Auburn, "Trends in Comparative Constitutional Law" (1972) 35 M.L.R. 129.

Three topics call for special treatment in this context, namely, Acts of Union, Independence Acts conferring independence on countries that formerly came under the authority of Parliament, and the European Communities Act 1972.

Acts of Union

Union with Ireland

The Union with Ireland was negotiated by commissioners,[18] and based on Acts **4–005** of the British and Irish Parliaments[19] in response to messages from the Crown. The Union with Ireland Act 1800, passed by the British Parliament, provided that the Kingdoms of Great Britain and Ireland should be united "for ever" into one Kingdom, by the name of the United Kingdom of Great Britain and Ireland; and that the United Kingdom should be represented in one and the same Parliament. It further provided that the government and doctrine of the United Church of England and Ireland should be and should remain "for ever" assimilated to those of the existing Church of England, and that the continuance of the United Church should be deemed "an essential and fundamental part" of the Union of the two Kingdoms. Nevertheless, the Church of Ireland was disestablished by the Irish Church Act 1869,[20] some 50 years before the political Union itself was partly dissolved by the creation of the Irish Free State. Although there was much opposition in this country to the disestablishment of the Church of Ireland, it does not seem to have been based on the theory that the union of the Churches was legally indissoluble. Similarly, the difficulties preceding the separation of the Irish Free State from the United Kingdom by the Irish Free State (Constitution) Act 1922 were political and not legal.

When the secession of Eire (the Republic of Ireland) from the Commonwealth was recognised by the United Kingdom Parliament in the Ireland Act 1949 the following declaration was inserted in section 1(2): "It is hereby declared that Northern Ireland remains part of His Majesty's dominions and of the United Kingdom, and it is hereby affirmed that in no event will Northern Ireland or any part thereof cease to be part of His Majesty's dominions and of the United Kingdom without the consent of the Parliament of Northern Ireland."

This provision was confirmed by the Northern Ireland (Temporary) Provisions Act 1972, which suspended the Parliament of Northern Ireland. Then the Northern Ireland Constitution Act 1973 abolished the Northern Ireland Parliament and replaced it by an Assembly, declaring and affirming in section 1 that in no event would Northern Ireland or any part thereof cease to be part of His Majesty's dominions and of the United Kingdom without the consent of the majority of the people of Northern Ireland voting in a poll held for this purpose.[21] The Northern Ireland Act 1974 then abolished the Assembly, provided for the holding of a constitutional Convention (now extinct), and preserved the declaration in the 1973 Act with the provision for a referendum.[22] It appears that: (i) if the requirement in the 1949 Act for the consent of the Northern Ireland Parliament

---

[18] There was no formal treaty between Great Britain and Ireland.
[19] Union with Ireland Act 1800.
[20] *ex p. Selwyn* (1872) 36 J.P. 54; *ante*, para. 3–015
[21] A referendum was held in Northern Ireland in 1973 and a large majority of those voting favoured staying in the United Kingdom.
[22] The subsequent legislative history of Northern Ireland is dealt with in Chap. 5.

were binding on the United Kingdom Parliament, the provisions of the 1973 Act could not have been passed in the proper form; (ii) if the declaration in the 1949 Act were binding on Parliament, there would be no need to confirm it in 1972; and (iii) if the declaration in the 1973 Act were binding there would be no need to confirm it in 1974.

These declarations, it is submitted, should be regarded as expressions of intention and establishing a constitutional convention, based on agreement and analogous to that applying to self-governing colonies.[23]

Union with Scotland[24]

4–006   The Union was preceded by a treaty negotiated by the Parliaments of England and Scotland through commissioners. The Articles of Union were ratified first by the Scottish Parliament ("Estates") which also passed Acts for securing the Presbyterian Church government and concerning the election of Scottish representatives to the Parliament of Great Britain, which Acts were to be part of the terms of the Union. Then the English Parliament ratified the terms approved by the Scottish Estates, together with an Act for the security of the Church of England. While Englishmen refer to the English Act of Union, Scotsmen tend to refer to the "Treaty."

4–007   The Union with Scotland Act 1706, passed by the English Parliament, provided that the two Kingdoms of England and Scotland should for ever after be united into one Kingdom by the name of Great Britain (Art. I); the United Kingdom of Great Britain should "be represented by one and the same Parliament" to be styled the Parliament of Great Britain (Art. III); that (subject to a common public law) Scots law was to remain as before but alterable by the Parliament of Great Britain, except that no alterations should be made "in laws which concern private right except for evident utility of the subjects within Scotland" (Art. XVIII). Article XIX preserved the Court of Session and Court of Justiciary as superior Scottish courts in all time coming, subject to regulations made by the Parliament of Great Britain for better administration of justice. The Act incorporated an Act for securing the Protestant religion and Presbyterian Church governments in Scotland, paragraph 2 of which required professors of Scottish universities to subscribe to the Confession of Faith (a religious test), and paragraph 4 of which states that this Act with the establishment therein contained "shall be held and observed in all time coming as a fundamental and essential condition of any treaty or union to be concluded betwixt the two Kingdoms without any alteration thereof or derogation thereto in any sort for ever."

It was clearly intended that the Union itself should be permanent, and that certain provisions—concerning, or mainly concerning, the Scottish Church—

---

[23] cf. Lord MacDermott, "The Decline of the Rule of Law" (1972) 23 N.I.L.Q. 474, 493, who suggests that the constitutional Acts relating to (Northern) Ireland from 1800 may together constitute a fundamental law, and it is arguable that the United Kingdom Parliament has no power to alienate the allegiance or reduce the status of the people of Northern Ireland. And see H. Calvert's "very tentative" arguments in *Constitutional Law of Northern Ireland* (1968), Chap. 1.

[24] Dicey and Rait, *Thoughts on the Union between England and Scotland* (1920) G.M. Trevelyan, *Ramillies and the Union with Scotland*, Chaps. 12–14. cf. T.B. Smith in *The British Commonwealth*, Vol. 1, Pt II, *Scotland*, pp. 641–650; "The Union of 1707 as Fundamental Law" [1957] P.L. 99; *British Justice: The Scottish Contribution* (1961), pp. 201–213. J.D.B. Mitchell, "Sovereignty of Parliament—Yet Again" (1963) 79 L.Q.R. 196; Lord Kilbrandon, "A Background to Constitutional Reform" (Holdsworth Club, University of Birmingham, 1975).

should be unalterable. The Church Patronage (Scotland) Act 1711,[25] repealing a Scottish Act and restoring lay patronage in Scotland, has been described as "the chief and almost the only example of an Act of the British Parliament passed in violation of the Act of Union," and is said to have been "opposed to the spirit, and probably the letter, of the Act of Union."[26] As early as 1713 a Bill to repeal the Union Act was introduced and nearly passed in the House of Lords.[27] The provision requiring professors at Scottish universities to subscribe to the Confession of Faith was repealed by the Universities (Scotland) Act 1853. With regard to changes in Scots private law, it is not certain whether Parliament or the Scottish courts are supposed to have the power to determine whether they are for the "evident utility" of Scottish citizens.

In *Gibson v. Lord Advocate*[28] G. sought a declaration that section 2(1) of the European Communities Act 1972 was contrary to Article XVIII of the Act of Union, and therefore null and void, in so far as it purported to enact as part of the law of Scotland certain Community Regulations providing for equal treatment of Member States with regard to fishing in maritime waters. He argued that, immediately before the Act of Union, Scottish subjects had exclusive fishing rights in Scottish coastal waters; that the laws conferring these rights concerned "private right," and that the Community Regulations were not "for the evident utility of the subjects within Scotland." Lord Keith dismissed the action on the grounds, first, that the action was incompetent in seeking consideration of the utility of an Act of Parliament and, secondly, that Community Regulations operate in the field of public and not private law. His Lordship stated that the question whether an Act purporting to alter a particular aspect of Scots private law was for "evident utility" of the subjects within Scotland (Art. XVIII) is not justiciable in the courts; but he reserved his opinion on the question whether the court would have jurisdiction where an Act purported to abolish the Court of Session or the Church of Scotland, or to substitute English law for the whole body of Scots private law.

The most significant question is whether Parliament has power to repeal or **4–008** radically amend the provisions relating to the Presbyterian Church in Scotland. The orthodox view, at any rate among English writers, is that at the Union the English and Scottish Parliaments extinguished themselves and at the same time transferred their powers to the new Parliament of Great Britain, and it is assumed that the Parliament of Great Britain inherited and developed the characteristics of the English Parliament, including sovereignty.[29] If so, this means that the United Kingdom Parliament, although morally bound by the terms of the Union with regard to the Scottish Church, might legally repudiate them.[30] In the Scottish

---

[25] 10 Anne, c. 21.

[26] Dicey and Rait, *op. cit.* pp. 280–281.

[27] Dicey and Rait, *op. cit.* pp. 298–300.

[28] 1975 S.L.T. 134; [1975] 1 C.M.L.R. 563 (Outer House, Court of Session); *post*, para. 6–038. And see J.M. Thomson "Community Law, the Act of Union, and the Supremacy of Parliament" (1976) 92 L.Q.R. 36; A.W. Bradley, "Scots Private Law—'Evident Utility,' " in *Devolution* (Essays, ed. H. Calvert, 1975), p. 101.

[29] It is commonly said that the Scottish Parliament was not recognised as having sovereignty; but *cf.* Erskine, *Inst.* i, 1, 19; Bk. 1, Tit. IV, 61.

[30] So Blackstone, *Commentaries*, Introduction, para. 4 note; Austin, *The Province of Jurisprudence Determined* (ed. Hart) Lecture 6, pp. 256–257; Maitland, *Constitutional History*, p. 332. Dicey and Rait, *op. cit.* 252–254 thought that the declaration concerning the Scottish Church, though not a legal limitation represented a moral restriction and a warning.

courts, however, doubt has been expressed whether this view is sound. *Mac-Cormick v. Lord Advocate*[31] (the "Royal Numeral Case") arose out of the official use in Scotland of the title "Elizabeth II," which was adopted by royal proclamation under a power conferred by the Royal Titles Act 1953. The Court of Session held that the Treaty did not prohibit the use of the numeral, and that the petitioners had no legal title or interest to sue. Either of these reasons would have been sufficient for the decision, but the Court added obiter that it was not satisfied that the Royal Titles Act would be conclusive if it had been repugnant to the Treaty, although in any event the court would have no jurisdiction to review a governmental act of this kind. "The principle of the unlimited sovereignty of Parliament," said Lord Cooper, "is a distinctively English principle which has no counterpart in Scottish constitutional law. . . . I have difficulty in seeing why it should have been supposed that the new Parliament of Great Britain must inherit all the peculiar characteristics of the English Parliament but none of the Scottish Parliament, as if all that happened in 1707 was that Scottish representatives were admitted to the Parliament of England." Here we have Scottish obiter dicta to the effect that Parliament is bound by the fundamental terms of the Treaty (or Act of Union), although the effect of the dicta is considerably reduced by the admission "that there is neither precedent or authority of any kind for the view that the domestic courts of either Scotland or England" have jurisdiction to review governmental acts done under unconstitutional legislation, and *a fortiori* (presumably) to review the unconstitutional legislation itself.

4–009   In *Sillars v. Smith*,[32] where the validity of the Criminal Justice (Scotland) Act 1980 was challenged, the Lord Justice-Clerk (Wheatley) cited both *Edinburgh and Dalkeith Ry Co v. Wauchope*[33] and *MacCormick v. Lord Advocate* before concluding that the appellants' plea should be rejected, "based as it is on a submission that the Act of 1980 which had gone through all the parliamentary processes and received the Royal Assent is invalid."

But to hold that Parliament is bound by certain articles of the Union—whatever that may mean in the absence of a judicial power of review—raises difficulties that appear to be insoluble in legal terms. It implies that there is a fundamental law to which Parliament is subordinate. Then what happens if this subordinate Parliament infringes the fundamental law? To say that the Union would be terminated involves the assumption that England and Scotland are still separately identifiable nations. If Parliament cannot alter these fundamental terms, who can? There might come a time when the Presbyterian Church was no longer a majority church in Scotland. How can the wishes of the Scottish people be known? The Members of Parliament for Scottish constituencies are a minority in the Commons and they are not necessarily Scotsmen. There is no provision in the Treaty for appointing commissioners to negotiate a revision, or for holding a plebiscite in Scotland. As a matter of legal theory the conclusion must be that the doctrine of sovereignty or legislative supremacy has developed since the Union as a characteristic of the United Kingdom Parliament.[34] It is highly probable that the House of Lords in its judicial capacity would hold this view if the matter

---

[31] 1953 S.C. 396; 1953 S.L.T. 255. See T.B. Smith, "Two Scots Cases" (1953) 69 L.Q.R. 512–516.
[32] 1982 S.L.T. 539.
[33] (1842) 8 Cl. & F. 710.
[34] D.G.T. Williams, "The Constitution of the United Kingdom," [1972B] C.L.J. 266, 270.

came before it, although there is no appeal from Scottish courts to the House of Lords in criminal cases.[35]

The power of the United Kingdom Parliament to make law for Scotland is **4–010** expressly preserved by section 28(7) of the Scotland Act 1998 and section 37 provides that the Union with Scotland Act 1706 and the Union with England Act 1707 have effect subject to the 1998 Act. Logically those provisions cannot give the United Kingdom Parliament powers that did not already possess. They demonstrate, however, the view of Parliament that there are no existing limitations. It remains to be seen if the question should arise what view the courts would take.

Grants of Independence

Statute of Westminster 1931

Another problem (though scarcely of practical importance) is whether Parlia- **4–011** ment can continue to legislate for members (or former members) of the Commonwealth which have been granted independence. After the growth of conventions relating to self-governing colonies, the next legislative stage was section 4 of the Statute of Westminster 1931. This provides that an Act of the United Kingdom Parliament passed thereafter shall not extend, or be deemed to extend, to a Dominion (as therein defined) as part of the law of that Dominion unless it is expressly declared in the Act concerned that that Dominion[36] has requested, and consented to, its enactment. The definition of "Dominion" for this purpose now covers Canada, Australia and New Zealand.[37] This provision enacted what was already an established convention, which was also recited in the preamble to the Statute. It is a statement of Parliament's intention, and also a direction to the courts, which are concerned only with the presence or absence of a declaration in the Act of a Dominion's request and consent. The Statute did not purport to terminate Parliament's power to legislate for the Dominions altogether. It was contemplated that such request and consent might still be forthcoming in particular cases, as happened, for example, in connection with Australian and New Zealand emergency powers during the war and with the Cocos Islands Act 1955, which transferred the Cocos Islands to Australia. Further, reservations were made with regard to the power of constitutional amendment in some of the Dominions, which they would otherwise have had under section 2, so that in 1964 Parliament amended the Canadian Constitution

---

[35] Professor T.B. Smith ([1957] P.L. 99) argues that the twofold ratification constituted both a treaty *jure gentium* and a fundamental law for the Union, whereas the Acts of Parliament of each country bound the subjects within that country alone as ordinary legislation. The Treaty *qua* Treaty ceased to exist by merger of the parties at the Union. What is left, Professor Smith contends, is the "fundamental law" which cannot be altered except by (technical) revolution. On the question of judicial review, he admits that a private individual would seldom have a title to sue, and the Lord Advocate would presumably agree with the government of which he was a member.

Lord Kilbrandon, in "A background to Constitutional Reform," *loc. cit.* says the Treaty is now defunct since the independent countries of England and Scotland have ceased to exist, and its functions have been superseded by the Union Acts of the two Parliaments. If it is wrong to accept the unlimited sovereignty of the Parliament of Great Britain, he asks, where is the lawful machinery for putting the matter right?

[36] The request and consent required are those of the government of the Dominion concerned, and in the case of Australia those of its Parliament also.

[37] The Statute originally applied also to Newfoundland (now a province of Canada), and to South Africa and the Irish Free State (later Eire or the Republic of Ireland), which are no longer within the Commonwealth.

at Canada's request.[38] (Canada's legislative dependence on the United Kingdom was formally determined by the Canada Act 1982, s.2.[39])

Lord Sankey L.C. in *British Coal Corporation v. The King*[40] said obiter that as a matter of "abstract law" Parliament could repeal this Statute either expressly or by passing legislation inconsistent with it; but he added, "that is theory and has no relation to realities." More recently, in *Blackburn v. Attorney-General*[41] Lord Denning M.R. went so far as to say obiter; "We have all been brought up to believe that, in legal theory, one Parliament cannot bind another and that no Act is irreversible. But legal theory does not always march alongside political reality. Take the Statute of Westminster 1931, which takes away the power of Parliament to legislate for the Dominions. Can anyone imagine that Parliament could or would reverse that Statute? Take the Acts which have granted independence to the Dominions and territories overseas. Can anyone imagine that Parliament could or would reverse these laws and take away their independence? Most clearly not. Freedom once given cannot be taken away.[42] Legal theory must give way to practical politics." But Salmon L.J. was content to remark; "As to Parliament, in the present state of the law, it can enact, amend and repeal any legislation it pleases."

4-012   The meaning and effect of section 4 of the Statute of Westminster was considered in *Manuel v. Attorney General*.[43] The plaintiffs sued on behalf of themselves and certain Indian "bands." They sought declarations to the effect that the United Kingdom Parliament had no power to amend the Canadian Constitution so as to prejudice the Indian Nations of Canada without their consent, and that the Canada Act 1982 was therefore *ultra vires*. Indian rights had been confirmed by a Royal Proclamation made in 1763, subsequently confirmed under a number of "treaties" made with the Indian bands and entrenched under the British North American Acts. The plaintiffs argued that the amendment of certain entrenched Indian rights still required United Kingdom legislation even after the British North America (No. 2) Act 1949 conferred on the Canadian Parliament a limited power of constitutional amendment. At first instance Sir Robert Megarry V.-C. held that once he was satisfied that the document before him was an Act of Parliament it was his duty to apply it. The Vice-Chancellor went on to consider the dictum of Lord Denning in *Blackburn v. Attorney General*, quoted in the previous paragraph. He commented that it was clear from the context that Lord Denning was using the word "could" in the sense of "could effectively," and not "could as a matter of abstract law." His Lordship added:

"I have grave doubts about the theory of the transfer of sovereignty as affecting the competence of Parliament. In my view it is a fundamental of the English constitution that Parliament is supreme. As a matter of law the courts of England recognise Parliament as being omnipotent in all save the power to destroy its omnipotence. On the authority of Parliament the courts of a

[38] British North America Act 1964, empowering the Canadian Parliament to legislate with regard to old age pensions.

[39] *post*, para. 36–008. See also, *post* para. 36–010 for the Australian Act 1986.

[40] [1935] A.C. 500, 520; the case concerned Canadian legislation passed before the Statute of Westminster.

[41] [1972] C.M.L.R. 882, CA.

[42] An echo of the words of Stratford A.C.J. in *Ndlwana v. Hofmeyr* [1937] A.D. 229, 237, "Freedom once conferred cannot be revoked."

[43] [1983] Ch. 77. See O. Hood Phillips, "Statute of Westminster in the Courts" (1983) 99 L.Q.R. 342.

territory may be released from their legal duty to obey Parliament, but that does not trench on the acceptance by the English courts of all that Parliament does. Nor must validity in law be confused with practical enforceability."[44]

In the Court of Appeal, Slade L.J., delivering the judgment of the Court, held that the Canada Act 1982 complied with the requirements of section 4 which

"does not provide that no Act of the United Kingdom Parliament shall extend to a Dominion as part of the law of that Dominion unless the Dominion has in fact requested and consented to the enactment thereof. The condition that must be satisfied is a quite different one, namely, that it must be 'expressly declared in that Act that that Dominion has requested, and consented to, the enactment thereof.' ... If an Act of Parliament contains an express declaration in the precise form required by section 4, such declaration is in our opinion conclusive as far as section 4 is concerned."[45]

The Court of Appeal did not therefore have to consider the effect of a failure to comply with the provisions of section 4.

If section 4 of the Statute of Westminster is regarded primarily as a rule of **4–013** construction addressed to the courts,[46] it seems probable that British courts (if the question could be brought before them) would continue to regard Parliament as unrestricted by it, at least as far as the monarchies are concerned.[47] Section 4 refers to alteration of *the law of a Dominion*, not to alteration of *the law in this country*. As Lord Reid stated with reference to the Statute of Westminster in *Madzimbamuto v. Lardner-Burke*[48]: "It is often said it would be unconstitutional for the United Kingdom Parliament to do certain things, meaning that the moral, political and other reasons against doing them are so strong that most people would regard it as highly improper if Parliament did these things. But that does not mean that it is beyond the power of Parliament to do such things. If Parliament chose to do any of them the courts could not hold the Act of Parliament invalid." However, the courts of the country (former "Dominion") concerned (in so far as they could not construe such Act as not being intended to infringe the section) would presumably decline to apply an offending British statute, and an appeal to the Privy Council could be prevented or nullified by local legislation where such appeals have not already been abolished. And appeals from that country to the Privy Council would very soon be abolished. Such a divergence of judicial decisions in other parts of the Commonwealth from decisions in this country would be a reflection in the courts of a (technical) revolution that had already taken place in the political sphere.[49]

It has been suggested above that the local court would, if possible, construe an Act of Parliament as not being intended to apply to the Dominion, unless passed at its request and with its consent. This is borne out by *Copyright Owners*

[44] [1983] Ch. 77, 89.

[45] At p. 106.

[46] See K. C. Wheare, *The Statute of Westminster and Dominion Status* (5th ed.), Chap. 6, s.3. And see further *post*, Chap. 36.

[47] A republic is not one of Her Majesty's dominions, and it may be that on this ground an Act of Parliament would not be construed as extending to it.

[48] [1969] 1 A.C. 645, 723, PC.

[49] s.2(2) of the Statute of Westminster allows the Dominions to pass laws repugnant to United Kingdom legislation, but to say that this would enable the Dominions to nullify a repeal of the Statute begs the question.

Reproduction Society v. E.M.I. (Australia) Pty Ltd,[50] where the High Court of Australia held that Copyright Acts of 1928 and 1956 did not apply to Australia. Dixon C.J. said that even before 1931 there was a strong convention that the United Kingdom Parliament would not legislate for a Dominion without its consent: there was therefore in Australian courts a rule of construction that, in the absence of evidence of such consent, a United Kingdom Act was not intended to apply to that Dominion.

Independence Acts

4–014   The "Dominion status" of 1931, by the further development of constitutional conventions in relation to the countries concerned, has in effect become independence within the Commonwealth. The grant of independence to a number of former dependent territories from 1947 onwards has been done by separate Acts of Parliament. As regards legislative powers, the Independence Acts for Ceylon (1947) and Ghana (1957) followed the Statute of Westminster,[51] but the Act for Nigeria (1960) and those that followed did not contemplate that the country concerned would in future request the United Kingdom to legislate for it. The post-war Independence Acts have gone further than the Statute of Westminster by expressly divesting the United Kingdom Government of any responsibility for the government of those countries.

A distinction might be drawn between the mere transfer of the *legislative* powers of Parliament under the Statute of Westminster and the transfer also of the *governmental* powers of the United Kingdom under the post-war Independence Acts. Where in relation to a particular territory the sovereignty of the Crown as head of the United Kingdom Government has been transferred to a sovereign state, or in such a way as to make the transferred a sovereign state—recognised as such by other countries, and becoming a member of the United Nations—it seems absurd to say that Parliament can still legislate for such territory. Could Parliament cancel the cession of Heligoland to Germany,[52] or even repudiate the independence of the United States.[53] Nonetheless in the words of Sir Robert Megarry V.-C.

> "Plainly once statute has granted independence to a country the repeal of the statute will not make the country dependent once more; what is done is done, and is not undone by revoking the authority to do it. Heligoland did not in 1953 again become British. But if Parliament then passes an Act applying to such a country I cannot see why that Act should not be in the same position

[50] (1958) 100 C.L.R. 597. The Acts concerned were the Copyright Order Confirmation (Mechanical Instruments: Royalties) Act 1928, and the Copyright Act 1956. The draftsmen of the 1956 Act indicated that the repeal of the Copyright Act 1911 was not intended to affect the law of any country other than the United Kingdom. And see H.R. Gray, "The Sovereignty of the Imperial Parliament" (1960) 23 M.L.R. 647.

[51] The Indian Independence Act 1947 followed the Status of the Union Act 1934 (South Africa) in providing that Acts of the United Kingdom Parliament would not extend thereto unless adopted by its own legislature.

[52] Anglo-German Agreement Act 1890. This Act was repealed by the Statute Law Revision Act 1953.

[53] An Act of 1782 (22 Geo. III, c.46) authorised the Crown to negotiate a truce with America, and by the Treaty of Paris 1783, signed between Great Britain and the United States, Britain acknowledged the United States to be free, sovereign and independent states; and relinquished all claims to the government of the same. Statutes of 1782 relating to trade with America and American loyalists (23 Geo. III, c. 26, 39, 80) implied that the United States were no longer British colonies: *Doe* d. *Thomas v. Acklam* (1824) 2 B. & C. 778.

as an Act applying to what has always been a foreign country, namely, an Act which the English courts will recognise and apply but one which the other country will in all probability ignore ... "[54]

The distinction between the method used in 1931 and the method used after **4–015** 1947, however, is probably no longer significant. When the courts recognise the political fact that territory formerly under the authority of Parliament has become independent of that authority, then Parliament can no longer alter the law in that territory; although it may pass laws in relation to persons or acts in such territory as in any other "foreign" country, which may be enforceable in the courts of this country.[55]

The legislative supremacy of Parliament, then, is a concept of British public law. It is recognised by the Courts of the United Kingdom[56] and its dependencies,[57] and is enforced by these courts in relation to persons and property which are or which come within their jurisdiction.

European Communities Act 1972

The Treaties whereby the United Kingdom agreed to join the European **4–016** Communities (the "Common Market") were executive acts, affecting the relations between the United Kingdom and the other member States. In order to provide for the consequent changes of law in this country an Act of Parliament was necessary.[58] This was the European Communities Act 1972, which is discussed more fully in Chapter 6. Its main provisions are briefly as follows. Section 2(1) gives effect to rights and obligations created by or arising under the Treaties, *i.e.* created by the Treaties themselves and by existing and future Community Regulations which take effect directly as law in the Member States. (Enforceable Community Rights). With regard to future Community Regulations this was a constitutional innovation, introducing a new and special kind of secondary legislation.[59] Section 2(2) confers a limited power to give effect by Statutory Instrument to Community Directives. Section 2(4) provides, in effect, that delegated legislation made under section 2(2) may make any such provision as might be made by Act of Parliament, and that existing and future enactments are to be construed and have effect subject to the provisions of section 2. It should be emphasised that the Act contains no provision purporting to exclude or limit the power of Parliament to repeal or amend the Act itself. Section 3 provides that for the purpose of legal proceedings, the meaning of the Treaties and the validity or meaning of any Community Instrument are questions of law which, if not referred to the European Court of Justice at Luxembourg for a preliminary ruling, are to be determined in accordance with the principles laid down by that Court. The general effect of the European Communities Act is to override *existing* domestic law so far as is inconsistent therewith, and to impose a presumption of interpretation that *future* statute law is to be read subject to Community law for the time being in force. Parliament is expected to refrain from passing legislation inconsistent with Community law.

---

[54] *Manuel v. Att.-Gen.* [1983] Ch. 77, 88.
[55] *ante*, para. 3–020.
[56] But as to Scotland, *cf. ante*, para. 4–006.
[57] *i.e.* colonies and other dependencies from whose courts appeal lies to the Privy Council.
[58] *Case of Proclamations* (1610) 12 Co.Rep. 74; Bill of Rights 1688, Art. 4.
[59] *post*, Chap. 6.

4–017   It was widely objected that Parliament, by passing the European Communities
Act, would surrender a large part of its "sovereignty" to the Community institutions, and that as there is no time limit in the Treaties Parliament would be
binding itself for ever. In *Blackburn v. Attorney-General*[60] the plaintiff sought a
declaration that the government, by signing the Treaty of Rome, would surrender
in part the sovereignty of Parliament and would surrender it for ever, which
would be in breach of law. The Court of Appeal decided that the statement of
claim disclosed no cause of action and should be struck out. The Treaty of
Accession to the EEC was a prerogative act, and the question with regard to
Parliament was hypothetical. Lord Denning M.R. after stating that "in theory Mr
Blackburn is quite right in saying that no Parliament can bind another, and that
any Parliament can reverse what a previous Parliament has done," added:
"nevertheless so far as this court is concerned, I think we will wait till that day
comes;" but he did so (it is submitted) not because he doubted the soundness of
Mr Blackburn's proposition, but because courts do not answer hypothetical
questions that have not yet arisen. In *McWhirter v. Attorney-General*[61] the Court
of Appeal held that the plaintiff might not argue that joining the EEC would be
contrary to the Bill of Rights, which declared that full powers of government are
vested in the Crown. The exercise of the prerogative could not be impugned in
the courts, either before or after a treaty is signed. "Even though the Treaty of
Rome has been signed," said Lord Denning M.R. "it has no effect, so far as these
Courts are concerned, until it is made an Act of Parliament. Once it is implemented by an Act of Parliament, these Courts must go by the Act of Parliament."
A similar lack of success attended the efforts of Lord Rees-Mogg to challenge
provisions of the Maastricht Treaty, despite the Court of Appeal agreeing that he
had raised interesting issues.[62]

4–018   Successive Lord Chancellors, both in the House of Lords and extra-judicially,
denied either that Parliament would surrender its sovereignty or that the Act
would be irreversible—Lord Kilmuir and Lord Dilhorne in the House of Lords
in 1962, Lord Gardiner in the House of Lords in 1967, and Lord Hailsham of St
Marylebone in 1971.[63] Lord Gardiner[64] pointed out that the United Kingdom had
accepted restraints on its legislative power to take account of obligations arising
out of such treaties as the United Nations Charter, the European Convention on
Human Rights, NATO and GATT. The treaty obligations are reciprocal: all the
members remain sovereign States: the United Kingdom would take part in the
making of new Regulations (which in practice is done unanimously),[65] and also
in the judicial work of the EEC tribunals. Lord Hailsham[66] further pointed out
that there were "stacks" of treaties designed to last for an indefinite period, some
designed to last for ever, and most peace treaties fall under one of these heads.
He saw membership of the Community not as a derogation from sovereignty, but
as sovereignty plus the advantages of membership. Lord Gardiner also said:

---

[60] [1971] 1 W.L.R. 1037, CA.
[61] [1972] C.M.L.R. 882, CA.
[62] [1994] Q.B. 552, CA.
[63] H.L.Deb., Vol. 322, cols. 195–208.
[64] H.L.Deb. cols. 1202–1204 (May 8, 1967).
[65] The unanimity principle is used in important matters, and could not be abrogated without the
agreement of the United Kingdom, whose Ministers depend on Parliamentary support: see letter from
Lord Gladwyn to *The Times*, January 9, 1975.
[66] At the Mansion House: *The Times*, July 14, 1971, Lord Hailsham also said: "either Dilhorne or
Kilmuir got every leading lawyer . . . to discuss this very question and they came to the same
conclusion": *The Listener*, July 13, 1972, p. 40.

"Under the British constitutional doctrine of Parliamentary sovereignty no Parliament can preclude its successors from changing the law. . . . There is in theory no constitutional means available to us to make it certain that no future Parliament would enact legislation in conflict with Community law"; but he added that repeal of the Act would be a breach of *international obligations*, unless it was justified by exceptional circumstances and had the approval of the other member States.[67]

Again, Lord Diplock has expressed the opinion extrajudicially that: "If the **4–019** Queen in Parliament was to make laws which were in conflict with this country's obligations under the Treaty of Rome, those laws and not the conflicting provisions of the Treaty would be given effect to as the domestic law of the United Kingdom."[68] And Lord Justice Scarman (as he then was) has written: "The European Communities Act preserves, of course, the *de jure* sovereignty of Parliament. Community law has the force of law because Parliament says so. . . . The European Communities Act cannot be read as limiting the sovereignty of Parliament. No British court could, I suggest, go so far as to hold that Parliament today had limited the freedom of action of Parliament tomorrow without a constitutional reform that is in fact beyond the power of Parliament by statute to effect."[69]

The attitude of leading statesmen and responsible political parties is also relevant in considering the fundamentals of the Constitution. Mr Harold Wilson, then Leader of the Opposition, is reported to have said in a speech at Born in February 1972[70] that a future Labour Government would withdraw from the EEC if it could not satisfactorily renegotiate the terms for British membership: it would recognise "the British constitutional doctrine that one Parliament cannot bind its successors." Again, in February 1974, he announced that if Labour won the pending general election (which it did) it would renegotiate the terms of Britain's entry (*sic*) into the EEC, and if these negotiations did not succeed then the existing treaty obligations would not be regarded as binding.[71] It was publicly known that the Labour Government, formed in 1974, was sharply divided on the question of Britain's continued membership of the EEC. Renegotiation of the terms of membership attracted little attention, but in order to preserve the unity of their party in the Commons, the Government (advocating continued membership) adopted the unprecedented and controversial device of a referendum.[72] The passing of the Referendum Act 1975, under the authority of which the referendum was held,[73] implied that the Government and members of Parliament generally presumed that, if the result of the referendum in the United Kingdom as a whole went against continued membership, this country would withdraw from the EEC and Parliament would pass legislation repealing the European

---

[67] See note 64, *ante.*

[68] "The Common Market and the Common Law" (1972) 6 *Law Teacher,* 3, 5.

[69] "The Law of Establishment in the European Economic Community" (1973) 24 N.I.L.Q. 61, 70–72.

[70] *The Times,* February 5, 1972.

[71] *The Times,* February 13, 1974.

[72] *Referendum on United Kingdom Membership of the European Community* Cmnd. 5925 (1975).

[73] The question was: "Do you think that the United Kingdom should stay in the European Community (the Common Market)?" Votes were counted in England and Wales by counties, in Scotland by regions and in Northern Ireland as a whole. Courts were precluded from entertaining any proceedings for questioning the numbers of ballot papers counted or answers given in the referendum. And see R. E. M. Irving, "The United Kingdom Referendum, June 1975" (1975) 1 *European Law Review* 3.

Communities Act and disentangling our domestic law from Community law. The Government conceded that Parliament would not be bound by the result of the referendum, but indicated that the Government itself would abide by it. In the event a large majority in England and smaller majorities in Scotland, Wales and Northern Ireland voted in favour of the United Kingdom remaining in the EEC.

Conflict between United Kingdom law and Community law

4–020   Two provisions of the European Communities Act 1972 deal with the relationship between Community Law and the domestic law of the United Kingdom. Section 2(4) provides:

> "The provision that may be made under subsection (2) above includes, subject to Schedule 2 to this Act, any such provision (of any such extent) as might be made by Act of Parliament, and any enactment passed or to be passed, other than one contained in this Part of this Act, shall be construed and have effect subject to the foregoing provisions of this section, but, except as may be provided by any Act passed after this Act, Schedule 2 shall have effect in connection with the powers conferred by this and the following sections of this Act to make Orders in Council and regulations."

Section 3(1) provides:

> "For the purposes of all legal proceedings any question as to the meaning or effect of any of the Treaties, or as to the validity, meaning or effect of any Community instrument, shall be treated as a question of law (and, if not referred to the European Court be for determination as such in accordance with the principles laid down by and any relevant decision of the European Court."

Section 2(4) is a complex piece of draftsmanship which is best regarded as consisting of three parts. The first (from the beginning to "as might be made by Act of Parliament") deals with the making of delegated legislation to implement Community obligations (under section 2(2)), and provides that such subordinate legislation has the effect of an Act of Parliament or that it may not merely change the common law but may amend or repeal Acts of Parliament. The third part (from the words "but, except as may be provided" to the end) protects Schedule 2 from amendment by delegated legislation made under the Act. Thus it imposes a limit to the wide powers conferred by the first part of the subsection.

4–021   The second part of the subsection—and any enactment passed or to be passed, other than one contained in this Part of this Act, shall be construed and have effect subject to the foregoing provisions of this section—can only be described as obscure. It would not be surprising if it were dealing only with delegated legislation; the other two parts of the subsection are, unarguably, so confined.[74] If "enactment to be passed" includes future Acts of Parliament, as is generally assumed, what becomes of the reference to "in this Part of this Act." Is "enactment" being used to mean both statute and section? No explanation of these cryptic words is entirely satisfactory. Probably the least unsatisfactory is that they lay down a rule of construction or a presumption of interpretation in the

---

[74] See J. M. Thomson, "The Supremacy of European Community Law?" [1976] S.L.T. 273.

absence of a clear express intention in a later Act.[75] With regard to existing legislation, section 2 confers power to make such amendments as may be necessary to give effect to Community law. With regard to future legislation, subsection (4) expresses a rule of construction that would have to give way in a British court to a contrary expressed intention.[76] Parliament did not even purport to entrench this provision which, at most, attempts[77] or, better, pretends to secure the supremacy of Community law.

In *Garland v. British Rail Engineering Ltd*[78] Lord Diplock, with whom the other members of the House concurred, clearly treated section 2(4) as establishing a rule of interpretation. He envisaged that an English (*semble*, Scottish also) court would have to apply "an express, positive statement in an Act of Parliament passed after January 1, that a particular provision is intended to be made in breach of an obligation assumed by the United Kingdom under a Community Treaty." The only question was what, if anything, short of an express, positive statement would justify a court in the United Kingdom applying domestic law which conflicted with Community law.

It might be thought that there is little likelihood of *implied* conflicts[79] because **4–022** of the presumption of construction contained in section 2(4) and the judicial ingenuity exercisable in the construction of statutes. This has been exhibited in a number of cases relating to equal pay legislation.[80] In *O'Brien v. Sim-Chem*[81] the House of Lords managed to reach a conclusion compatible with Community law while unable to explain how it reached that conclusion. Lord Russell, who delivered the only speech, could do little more than say that he was happy "to echo the words of Lord Bramwell in *Bank of England v. Vagliano Brothers* [1891] A.C. 107, 138: 'This beats me' and jettison the words in dispute as making no contribution to the manifest intention of Parliament."

In *Pickstone v. Freemans plc*[82] the House of Lords felt entitled, in order to interpret regulations made under the Equal Pay Act 1970, to take account of

---

[75] There is no problem about conflict between United Kingdom statutes passed before January 1, 1973 and Community Law. The European Communities Act itself resolves any such conflict in favour of Community law: sub. ss.2(1) and 2(2). In such cases it is true to say that the Act "enacted that relevant Common Market law should be applied in this country, and should, where there is a conflict, override English law." *per* Graham J. in *Aero Zipp Fasteners v. Y.K.K. Fasteners (U.K.) Ltd* [1973] C.M.L.R. 819, 820. (Interpretation of pre-1973 rules of court).

[76] The words "shall be construed" surely supply the answer to the argument that s.2(4) cannot be "a mere rule of construction"; de Smith, *Constitutional and Administrative Law* (5th ed. 1985), p. 91.

[77] H.W.R. Wade, *Constitutional Fundamentals* (1980) pp. 25–27 and 31–34.

[78] [1983] 2 A.C. 751, 771. See further, O. Hood Phillips, "A Garland for the Lords: Parliament and Community Law Again," (1982) 98 L.Q.R. 524.

[79] Any unintended conflicts could be remedied by amending Acts, either *ad hoc* or (if such conflicts should become frequent) by an annual Communities Act: H.W.R. Wade, "Sovereignty and the European Communities" (1972) 88 L.Q.R. 1. See also F.A. Trindale, "Parliamentary Sovereignty and the Primacy of European Community Law" (1972) 35 M.L.R. 375. See also, on implied repeal and conflict, Evelyn Ellis, "Supremacy of Parliament and European Law" (1980) 96 L.Q.R. 511; "Parliamentary Supremacy After a Decade of EEC Membership," (1982) 7 *Holdsworth Law Review* 105.

[80] See, for example, *Shields v. E. Coomes (Holdings) Ltd* [1978] 1 W.L.R. 1408; *Clay Cross (Quarry Services) Ltd v. Fletcher* [1978] 1 W.L.R. 1429; *Rainey v. Greater Glasgow Health Board*, HL [1987] A.C. 224.

[81] [1980] 1 W.L.R. 1011, 1017; noted (1981) 97 L.Q.R. 5.

[82] [1989] A.C. 66, HL.

Parliament's intention, as ascertained from Hansard that the regulations were intended to give effect to Community law.[83] In *Litster v. Forth Dry Dock & Engineering Co Ltd*[84] the House felt able to give to regulations, meant to implement a European Directive, the required meaning by implying into the regulations some additional words. In *Webb v. EMO Air Cargo (U.K.) Ltd (No. 2)*[85] the House of Lords recognised that it must construe United Kingdom legislation consistently with the provisions of a Directive even where the legislation was made before the Directive.[86]

4–023   As will be seen in Chapter 6, the House of Lords has gone beyond construing United legislation so as to make it consistent with Community law to holding that even an Act of Parliament which is inconsistent with Community law must be disregarded by the courts in litigation having a Community element: *R. v. Secretary of State for Transport, ex p. Factortame Ltd*[87]; *R. v. Secretary of State for Employment ex p. Equal Opportunities Commission.*[88] In neither case, it should be noted, did the relevant legislation *explicitly* contradict Community law. Thus the House of Lords could claim to be following the wishes of Parliament as laid down in the European Communities Act 1972 section 3 that it should decide cases involving Community law in accordance with the principles laid down by the European court, one of which is the primacy of Community law over inconsistent municipal law.[89]

European Convention on Human Rights

4–024   The unique relationship between Community law and domestic law was recognised in the White Paper[90] which preceded the Human Rights Act 1998 and in the legislation itself. The White Paper referred to the importance which the Government attached to Parliamentary sovereignty and to the absence from the European Convention on Human Rights of any requirement that signatory States accord priority to its provisions over their domestic law, unlike the position in the case of Community law. This view finds expression in the Human Rights Act 1998 under which the superior courts may make a finding that legislation is incompatible with the Convention but it is up to Parliament to amend such legislation.[91] There is no judicial power to set aside legislation. And most courts can—and must—minimise conflicts between domestic law and Convention rights by giving effect to domestic legislation "so far as it is possible to do so" in a way which is compatible with Convention rights. (Section 3)

---

[83] Thus anticipating the decision in *Pepper v. Hart* [1993] A.C. 593.

[84] [1990] 1 A.C. 546.

[85] [1995] 1 W.L.R. 1454.

[86] See later, para. 6–013 for Community law on the interpretation of municipal law by municipal courts. *Duke v. Reliance Systems Ltd* [1988] A.C. 618 and *Finnegan v. Clowney Youth Training Programme Ltd* [1990] 2 A.C. 407, where the House of Lords refused to apply interpretative ingenuity, are discussed later, *post* para. 6–013.

[87] [1990] 2 A.C. 85; [1991] 1 A.C. 603. It is one of the curiosities of legal history that litigation of such significance should have been later revealed to have been based on a mistaken view of English law: *Re M.* [1994] 1 A.C. 377, HL.

[88] [1991] 1 A.C. 1.

[89] See *post* para. 6–012. By simply asserting the supremacy of Community law Lord Bridge, in *Factortame* avoided any reference to the doctrine of implied repeal of legislation by a later Act: see *ante* para. 4–004.

[90] (1997) CM 3782.

[91] ss.4 and 10. *post*, Chap. 22.

II. "MANNER AND FORM" OF LEGISLATION

The next question is whether Parliament can bind its successors as to the   **4–025**
"manner and form"[92] of legislation, that is, as regards its own procedure.

Authentication of Acts of Parliament

There must be some rules logically prior to Parliament by which an act can be   **4–026**
recognised as the act of Parliament.[93] This is not a matter of limiting Parliament,
but of identifying its enactments. The principle applies to all legislatures, and is
not a problem relating specifically to "sovereignty." For many centuries, except
during the revolutionary Commonwealth period in the seventeenth century,
"Parliament" has meant the Monarch, the Lords and Commons in Parliament
assembled. "There is no Act of Parliament," says Coke,[94] "but must have the
consent of the Lords, the Commons and the Royal Assent of the King, and as it
appeareth by Records and our Books, whatsoever passeth in Parliament by this
threefold consent, hath the force of an Act of Parliament." And in *Middleton v.
Croft*[95] Lord Hardwicke L.C., said: "As to the general nature, and fundamentals
of our constitution, no new law can bind the people of this land, but what is made
by the King and Parliament; nor any law made by the King alone, nor by the
King with consent of any particular number or body of men." It has been a
custom since the reign of Edward III for the Lords and Commons to deliberate
separately,[96] but Parliament's formal acts until 1967 were always done by one
body in the Parliament chambers.[97] An Act of Parliament then, is a measure
enacted by these three elements acting together in a way customarily prescribed
by themselves, namely, by a simple majority of the members present and voting
in each House separately, and assented to by the Queen. The legislative formula
for ordinary Acts of Parliament has long been established as follows: "Be it
enacted by the Queen's most Excellent Majesty, by and with the advice and
consent of the Lords Spiritual and Temporal, and Commons, in this present
Parliament assembled, and by the authority of the same, as follows. ... "[98] It
will be noticed that this formula does not refer to the Houses of Lords and
Commons.

The chief original sources for Acts of Parliament before 1849 are the Statute
Rolls and Parliament Rolls, consisting of inrollments in Chancery and proceedings in Parliament. We also have most of the original Acts since Henry VII, *i.e.*
the drafts from which the Clerk of the Parliaments made up the inrollments.
Since 1849 the Queen's printer has made two vellum prints authenticated by the
proper officer of each House, one of which is kept in the House of Lords and the
other deposited in the Public Record Office. Except in rare cases of doubt, printed

---

[92] The expression is taken from the Colonial Laws Validity Act 1865, s.5 and ultimately from the
Foreign Jurisdiction Act 1843.

[93] These rules are both common law and fact.

[94] 4 Inst. 25. And see *The Prince's Case, post.*

[95] (1743) Cas. T. Hard. 326 (Eccls. Ct.).

[96] A. F. Pollard, *Evolution of Parliament* (2nd ed.), pp. 120–123.

[97] Pollard, *op. cit.* p. 123. And see Chitty, *Prerogatives of the Crown*, p. 75: "That which constitutes
law is the concurring assent of all the branches of the legislature, wherever it may originate, whatever
may happen to be the form of it." For the giving of the Royal Assent, and the Royal Assent Act 1967,
see *post*, para. 8–011.

[98] Different formulae are used for Finance and Appropriation Acts, private Acts, and Acts passed
under the special procedure of the Parliament Acts.

copies of the statutes are sufficient—the King's (Queen's) printer's copies for Acts passed since 1713, and Statutes of the Realm for statutes passed down to that year.

4–027   It appears from *The Prince's Case*[99] that it was sometimes difficult to determine the authenticity of earlier Acts, and that a charter (recited as coming from the King and apparently having the authority of Parliament) would be accepted as an Act of Parliament if it was entered on the Parliament Roll and had always been allowed as an Act. In *Heath v. Pryn*[1] counsel challenged the Parliament Act 1660 on the ground that the Lords and Commons were not summoned by the King's writ, but the Court of King's Bench said: "the Act being made by the King, Lords and Commons they ought not now to pry into any defects of the circumstances of calling them together." The recital of the assent of the Monarch, Lords and Commons is generally taken to be conclusive, and it is doubted whether a *litigant* would be allowed to attempt to prove that one of these assents had not in fact been given. On the other hand, *either House* may have the privilege of asserting by reference to its journals that it had not agreed to the Bill, or that amendments proposed by one House had not been agreed by the other. A House of Lords amendment to the Bill that became the Rent (Agriculture) Act 1976 was agreed to by the Commons under the guillotine procedure without discussion: but through the inadvertence of the House of Lords officials who prepare Bills for the Royal assent, the amendment was not inserted. Parliament consequently passed the Rent (Agriculture) Amendment Act 1977 in order to give effect to the amendment.

Although the question of the authentication of Acts is sometimes brought into discussions about the legislative supremacy of Parliament, it is more appropriately described by Erskine May as "Subsidiary Points in connection with Legislative Procedure."[2] Under the Parliament Acts, however, the Speaker's certificate is stated to be conclusive.[3]

Courts not concerned with procedure in Parliament

4–028   Centlivres C.J. in *Harris v. Minister of the Interior*[4] suggested that a Bill passed by both Houses of British Parliament sitting together would not be an Act of Parliament, as otherwise a Conservative Prime Minister who had lost his majority in the Commons could get a Bill passed by the Lords and Commons sitting together. But Centlivres C.J. took as his example a particular case which would be constitutionally objectionable. It may be replied, conversely, that it would be absurd for a court to deny validity to an Act passed unanimously by both Houses sitting together. There seems to be no strictly legal objection to the Lords and Commons debating and voting in a joint sitting. The matter seems now to be one of the Commons' privileges and of constitutional convention. If it is one of the Lords' privileges also, both Houses would have to agree before a joint sitting could be held. It is submitted that the courts would not wish to involve themselves in these procedural matters.

---

[99] (1606) 8 Co.Rep. la., 13b, 18a–19b, 20b, 28a. The Court included Lord Ellesmere L.C., Coke C.J. and Fleming C.B.

[1] (1670) 1 Vent. 14.

[2] Erskine May *Parliamentary Practice* (22nd ed. 1997) p. 571. See Craies, *Statute Law* (7th ed. 1971), pp. 37–38.

[3] *cf. post*, p. 144.

[4] (1952) (2) S.A. (A.D.) 428, 470. And see R. T. E. Latham, "The Law of the Commonwealth," in *Survey of British Commonwealth Affairs*, Vol. 1, ed. Hancock, pp. 523–524.

The decision of the Court of Appeal in *Ellen Street Estates Ltd v. Minister of Health*[5] is a precedent for saying that Parliament cannot bind its successors as to the form of subsequent legislation by providing that there shall be no *implied* repeal of an Act.

The judgment of the House of Lords in *Pickin v. British Railways Board*[6] may **4–029** be relied on in relation to public as well as private Acts (although as to public Acts the considered statement was strictly *obiter*), to the effect that the courts will not concern themselves with the *procedure* by which a Bill passed through either House. Suppose that when a Labour Government was in office Parliament had passed an Industrial Relations Act which contained a provision that it might not be repealed or amended unless the Bill for that purpose was approved by the votes of not fewer than two-thirds of the members of the House of Commons.[7] It is submitted that if Parliament under a future Conservative Government passed an Act purporting to repeal or amend that earlier Act, the courts would hold the subsequent Act valid even though it could be shown that it had received fewer than two-thirds of the votes of the members of the Commons. Similarly, with an Act to alter the status of Northern Ireland as part of the United Kingdom which was passed without first holding a referendum.[8]

It is submitted that the courts would regard these as procedural matters. This does not mean that if Parliament made such statutory provisions they would be "void." Steps taken under them to hold a national referendum or a plebiscite in Northern Ireland would be lawful. What we are saying is that the same Parliament, or a subsequent Parliament (probably of a different political complexion), could repeal these provisions or simply ignore them. There is no reason why a later Act should be accorded less authority than an earlier one.

Contrary arguments

It has been argued by Sir Ivor Jennings[9] and others that the requirement of a **4–030** referendum or the approval of some outside body such as the Parliament of Northern Ireland would constitute, not a procedural requirement, but a change in the *composition* of Parliament (which for this purpose would include the electorate or the Northern Ireland Parliament, as the case might be) and so be binding on the legislature. This view, if followed through to its logical conclusion, would lead to absurd results, for by the law and custom of Parliament all the elements constituting Parliament must be summoned to Westminister by Royal Writs to deliberate, vote and hear the Royal Assent. The application of this argument to the repeal of the European Communities Act 1972, implementing withdrawal of the United Kingdom from the EEC, would require us to regard the governments or legislatures, or even the electorates, of the other Member States (although aliens) as forming part of the composition of Parliament of this purpose. Again, a change in the composition of Parliament has been classified as a matter of

---

[5] [1934] 1 K.B. 590; *ante*, para. 4–004.
[6] [1974] A.C. 765; *ante*, para. 3–017.
[7] Such a provision would require a government to have the unusual majority of more than 200 in the Commons.
[8] *ante*, para. 3–018.
[9] *e.g.* Jennings, *Constitutional Laws of the Commonwealth* (1957), pp. 124–125; R. F. V. Heuston, *Essays in Constitutional Law* (2nd ed., 1964); and see Jennings, *The Law and the Constitution* (5th ed., 1959), pp. 151–163.

procedure rather than subject-matter, and so (it is argued) binding on Parliament.[10] But if this were so the members of the Commons elected for three years under the Triennial Act 1694[11] who took part in passing the Septennial Act 1715 would not have been qualified to sit for the extra four years, with incalculable consequences for the validity of subsequent legislation.

Alternatively it has been argued by followers of D.V. Cowen[12] that a requirement such as a special majority of (say) two-thirds in either House or both Houses would constitute a *redefinition* of "Parliament" for this purpose, so in that case "Parliament" would mean the Queen, Lords and the Commons approving by a majority of not less than two-thirds. This *"redefinition,"* it should be noticed, would be done not by some higher law as in the South African case of *Harris v. Minister of the Interior*[13] but by Parliament itself. To say that Parliament (while retaining its existing composition) can redefine *itself* in this way begs the question. It is a fiction or formula designed to avoid classifying the matter as "procedural," and so not within the ambit of the courts. The argument applied to the Triennial Act would mean that Parliament in 1694 redefined itself in such a way that a future Parliament was not competent to legislate after three years. In so far as this argument differs from the "composition" argument, also, it would lead to the consequence that the word "Parliament" as applied to the United Kingdom Parliament could have an indefinite number of meanings.

4–031   The unicameral New Zealand Parliament is similarly not limited by a higher law,[14] and an "uncontrolled"[15] constitution can be amended by implication by an ordinary statute.[16] The Electoral Act passed by the New Zealand Parliament in 1956 included section 189 which states that certain provisions relating to such matters as the life of Parliament, the franchise and secret ballot, may not be repealed or amended except by a majority of 75 per cent. of all the members of the House of Representatives or by a simple majority of votes in a referendum. Section 189 did not itself require this special procedure for its own repeal or amendment. It has been argued, first, that in any event in order to alter these electoral provisions it would be necessary to repeal section 189 (*semble* by a simple majority); but, secondly, that section 189 is probably binding on the New Zealand Parliament as a "redefinition" of the legislature for this purpose.[17] Most New Zealand lawyers and politicians at the time, however, admitted that the sanction provided by section 189 was merely moral and conventional,[18] and it is submitted that this is the correct view. The reason why the legislature did not try to "entrench" section 189 itself was that it recognised that such an attempt would be ineffectual.

[10] G. Marshall, *Constitutional Theory*, p. 42; G. Winterton, *The British Grundnorm: Parliamentary Supremacy Re-examined, loc. cit.*
[11] Now entitled the Meeting of Parliament Act.
[12] D. V. Cowen, *Parliamentary Sovereignty and the Entrenched Sections of the South Africa* (1957).
[13] D. V. Cowen's original argument referred to the meanings of "Parliament" in different sections of the constituent South Africa Act.
[14] New Zealand Constitution Amendment Act 1973 (NZ). *cf.* the dictim of Moller J. at first instance in *R. v. Fineberg* [1958] N.Z.L.R. 119.
[15] See *McCawley v. R.* [1920] A.C. 691, PC *per* Lord Birkenhead L.C.
[16] *Kariapper v. Wijesinha* [1968] A.C. 717, PC; *cf. Ibralebbe v. R.* [1964] A.C. 900, PC; no implied repeal of entrenched provisions. And *cf. R. v. Drybones* (1969) 9 D.L.R. (3d) (S.C. Canada) on Canadian Bill of Rights.
[17] See *e.g.* Aikman, *New Zealand, its Laws and Constitution* (2nd ed. Robson), pp. 66–69.
[18] See *e.g.* K.J. Scott, *The New Zealand Constitution* (1962), pp. 6–9.

The arguments concerning "manner and form" or "redefinition" in relation to **4–032** the United Kingdom Parliament have also prayed in aid cases concerning legislatures that are subordinate to a higher law, or "controlled" constitutions. The first and best known of these is *Attorney-General for New South Wales v. Trethowan*.[19] The New South Wales legislature had passed an Act in 1929 providing that no Bill to abolish the Legislative Council (the Upper House) should be presented to the Governor for his assent unless it had been approved at a referendum, and that this provision should also apply to any Bill to repeal or amend the Act. After a change of government in 1930 two Bills were introduced, one to repeal the Act of 1929 and the other to abolish the Legislative Council. The Privy Council held that if they received the Governor's assent without being approved at a referendum the Acts would be void, because they would not have been passed in the "manner and form" required by the law in force in New South Wales. It is clear from the judgment of the Privy Council, and has been confirmed since by the Australian High Court,[20] that the decision in *Trethowan*'s case was based on the ground that New South Wales (although no longer a "colony") was still subject to the Colonial Laws Validity Act 1865, which recognises the lawmaking power of a representative colonial legislature provided that its laws are passed "in such manner and form as may from time to time be required by an Act of Parliament . . . or colonial law for the time being in force in the said Colony." "The answer depends," said Lord Sankey L.C. in that case, "entirely upon the consideration of the meaning and effect of section 5 of the Act of 1865." The limitation placed on itself by the New South Wales legislature in 1929 was therefore binding on it in 1930 *by virtue of the Colonial Laws Validity Act*, a "higher law" passed by a legislature to which it was legally subordinate. The case is no authority whatsoever for saying that the United Kingdom Parliament can bind itself in this way.

The application of the "manner and form" argument to the United Kingdom **4–033** Parliament appears to have been initiated by an obiter dictum of Dixon J., as he then was, in the Australian High Court in *Trethowan*'s case.[21] His lordship suggested that if the United Kingdom Parliament passed legislation concerning the abolition of the House of Lords similar to that passed by the New South Wales legislature in 1929, it would be unlawful to present a repealing or abolition Bill for the Royal Assent; and if it was found possible (*sic*) to raise the question for judicial decision the court would be bound to pronounce it unlawful to do so; further that, if such Bill did receive the Royal Assent without being submitted to a referendum, the courts might (*sic*) be called upon to consider whether the

[19] [1932] A.C. 526, PC on appeal from the High Court of Australia in *Trethowan v. Peden* (1931) 44 C.L.R. 394. The case could have been argued on the question whether an injunction would lie to prevent the Bills from being presented to the Governor for the Royal Assent, but the Australian High Court allowed special leave to appeal to the Privy Council only on the question of "manner and form." The use of the case in this context is largely due to the fact that it was "a recent decision" when Jennings published the first edition of his *The Law and the Constitution* in 1933. See also O. Hood Phillips, "Ryan's Case" (1936) 52 L.Q.R. 241.

[20] *Clayton v. Heffron* (1960) 105 C.L.R. 214; G. Sawer in [1961] P.L. 131. Dixon C.J. and the majority of the court said the case had no analogy to *Trethowan*, where there was a definite statutory prohibition against presenting the Bill to the Governor: here the ground was that the procedure was not correctly followed. And see *per* Dixon C.J. in *Hughes and Vale Pty. Ltd v. Gair* (1954) 90 C.L.R. 203. *cf.* W. Friedmann, "Trethowan's Case, Parliamentary Sovereignty and the Limits of Legal Change" (1950) 24 A.L.J. 103.

[21] 44 C.L.R. 426. The dictum seems to have been inspired by counsel's argument.

supreme legislative power in respect of the matter had in truth been exercised in the manner required for its authentic expression and by the elements in which it had come to reside. He concluded that the answer was "not clear." In a later Australian case,[22] however, Dixon C.J. (as he had become) said that in Australian law an injunction ought not to be granted in connection with the legislative process,[23] that therefore *Trethowan's* case was probably wrongly decided, and the remedy was judicial review after the Royal Assent had been given. He implied that it was unlikely that such a case could be brought before the courts in the United Kingdom. The disinclination of English courts to intervene by injunction in the process of private Bill or delegated legislation is shown in several decisions.[24] *A fortiori* they are unlikely to intervene in the process of public Bill legislation, which is a matter within the cognisance of Parliament.[25] In *Harper v. Home Secretary*,[26] where an injunction was refused to restrain the Home Secretary from presenting a draft electoral boundaries order (approved by both Houses) to the Privy Council, Lord Evershed M.R. pointed out that *Tretho-wan's* case was concerned with a strictly limited legislature, and said: "That seems to me quite a different case from the present. We are here in no sense concerned with a Parliament or legislature having limited legislative functions according to the constitution."

In *Rediffusion (Hong Kong) Ltd v. Attorney-General of Hong Kong*[27] the Privy Council held that no declaration or injunction lay to restrain the colonial legislature of Hong Kong from debating, passing and presenting to the Governor a copyright Bill, although it might, if enacted by the Governor's assent, be void under the Colonial Laws Validity Act 1865, s.5, as being repugnant to United Kingdom statute. The principle of this decision would clearly rule out declaration or injunction as ways of preventing the presentation of a Bill to the Queen for the Royal Assent.

4–034   What we have said about cases concerning subordinate legislatures applies also to two appeals to the Privy Council from Ceylon, which are sometimes cited in this context. The reason for the invalidity of the Bribery Tribunal in *Bribery Commissioner v. Ranasinghe*[28] and of the special court in *Liyanage v. R.*,[29] was

---

[22] *Hughes & Vale Pty. Ltd v. Gair* (1954) 90 C.L.R. 203.

[23] It might be regarded as a breach of privilege: *Clayton v. Heffron* (1960) 105 C.L.R. 214.

[24] *Bilston Corporation v. Wolverhampton Corporation* [1942] 1 Ch. 391 (statutory obligation not to oppose application for private Bill); *Hammersmith Borough Council v. Boundary Commission for England, The Times*, December 15, 1954 (forwarding of Boundary Commission's report to Home Secretary); *Merricks v. Heathcoat-Amory* [1955] Ch. 567 (ministerial marketing scheme); *Harper v. Home Secretary* [1955] Ch. 238, CA. And see W. S. Holdsworth (1943) 59 L.Q.R. 2 (denying jurisdiction of courts in such cases); Z. Cowen, "The Injunction and Parliamentary Process" (1955) 71 L.Q.R. 336.

[25] On injunctions against minister of the Crown, and the Crown Proceedings Act 1947, s.21, see *Re M* [1994] 1 A.C. 377, HL, *post*, para. 33–017.

[26] [1955] Ch. 238, *ante*.

[27] [1970] A.C. 1136; O. Hood Phillips, "Judicial Intervention in the Legislative Process" (1971) 87 L.Q.R. 321. *cf.* G. Sawer, "Injunction, Parliamentary Process, and the Restriction of Parliamentary Competence" (1944) 60 L.Q.R. 83: suppose an Act expressly authorises the citizen and the courts to intervene by injunction.

[28] [1965] A.C. 172. *cf.* G. Marshall, "Parliamentary Sovereignty: A Recent Development" (1966–67) 12 McGill L.J. 523.

[29] [1967] 1 A.C. 259.

that the setting up of these judicial institutions had not been done by the special legislative procedure of constitutional amendment required by the written[30] Constitution of Ceylon, although that country was a sovereign state. In the *Ranasinghe* case Lord Pearce said that there was no analogy to the British Constitution, which has no instrument governing the forms of the lawmaking power.[31]

Attempts have been made to suggest drafting formulae by which Parliament might bind itself, but none of them would be effective to prevent repeal or amendment by a later Act.[32] (The European Communities Act 1972 does not, it should be remembered, contain any provision purporting to bind future Parliaments.)

Parliament Acts[33]

Public Acts (with one specific exception) may, in certain circumstances, be **4–035** passed by the Queen and the Commons without the consent of the Lords under the Parliament Acts 1911 and 1949. It has been argued that by the Parliament Acts Parliament has bound itself for the future as to the manner and form of legislation, or that for this purpose "Parliament" now consists of the Queen and the Commons. It is submitted that both arguments are unsound. In the first place, the Parliament Acts do not limit the powers of Parliament. All Bills (including Money Bills) must be sent to the Lords, and the Lords have the opportunity of agreeing to them all if they wish. What the Parliament Acts do is to alter the usual procedure for public Bills by limiting the time during which the Lords may deliberate: after that time a Bill may be sent for the Royal Assent although the Lords have not agreed to it. This is an alternative permissive procedure, which only comes into play after the prescribed period if the Lords do not consent to a Bill in the form approved by the Commons. Again, the five-year maximum life of Parliament is effective in that, if Parliament is not dissolved by prerogative by the end of five years, it would be dissolved automatically by the Parliament Act 1911; but Parliament can during the five-year period pass an Act in the ordinary way extending or reducing its life.[34]

Secondly, the Parliament Acts do not alter the composition of Parliament.[35] When an Act is passed by the Queen and the Commons under the provisions of the Parliament Acts, the enacting formula must state that this is done in accordance with the provisions of those Acts (which include the sending of the Bill to

[30] The Ceylon Constitution of 1947 was not merely "written," but contained entrenched clauses subject to judicial review.

[31] "The cases cited by the 'manner and form' school do not, in the end, seem very helpful"; Munro *Studies in Constitutional Law* (2nd ed.), p. 160.

[32] *e.g.* Keir and Lawson, *Cases in Constitutional Law* (4th ed., 1954), p. 7: an Act providing that no Bill to repeal it should have effect unless approved by a referendum (passage omitted from later editions); J. L. Montrose, *Precedent in English Law and other Essays* (1968) and J. D. B. Mitchell, *Constitutional Law* (2nd ed., 1968), p. 89, cite the National Insurance Act 1965, s.116, which reproduced certain departmental regulations but provided that their validity might be determined as though they remained delegated legislation. Montrose, *op. cit.* pp. 283–284, also suggested the application of Interpretation Acts and the maxim *generalia specialibus non derogant* as possible limitations on the doctrine that Parliament cannot bind itself.

[33] See further, *post*, Chap. 8.

[34] Parliament in fact extended its life during both World Wars.

[35] *cf.* Jennings, *Constitutional Laws of the Commonwealth* (1957), pp. 124–125.

the Lords),[36] and so it may best be regarded as a kind of subordinate or delegated legislation.[37]

Indeed, we may doubt whether the measure calling itself "the Parliament Act 1949" is valid.[38] The Parliament Act 1911, of course, received the consent of the House of Lords; but the "Parliament Act 1949"—designed to reduce still further the period during which the Lords might delay a public Bill other than a Money Bill—did not receive the consent of the Lords but purported to be passed in accordance with the provisions of the Parliament Act 1911. It therefore offended against the general principle of logic and law that delegates (the Queen and Commons) cannot enlarge the authority delegated to them. We are not, of course, arguing—as it is impossible in English law to argue—that an Act of Parliament is invalid; what we are questioning is whether the measure called "the Parliament Act 1949" bears the character of an Act of Parliament. In other words we are contending that the Parliament Act 1911, as an enabling Act, cannot itself be amended by subordinate legislation of the Queen and Commons.[39]

4–036   No Act purported to be passed without the consent of the Lords "in accordance with the provisions of the Parliament Acts 1911 and 1949" until the War Crimes Act 1991, followed within a few years by the European Parliamentary Elections Act 1999. At one stage it appeared that opposition from hereditary peers might lead to reliance on "the Parliament Acts 1911 and 1949" in order to secure the passing of the House of Lords Bill but ultimately the House of Lords Act 1999 became law with the consent of the Upper House. The 1949 Act was, however, invoked recently to secure the enactment of the Sexual Offences Amendment Act 2000 which reduces the age of homosexual consent from 18 to 16.

The validity of the War Crimes Act 1991 was, apparently, unsuccessfully challenged in the trial of *Serafinowicz* but there is no reported judgment on the issue and, it is believed, counsel did not raise the question in the trial of *Sawoniuk*.

It has been suggested that the argument raised in earlier editions has been undermined by the decision of the House of Lords in *Pepper v. Hart*.[40] It is true that an examination of Hansard reveals the belief of government ministers that the procedures of the 1911 Act could be used to amend the 1911 Act itself. But it is equally clear that section 4 of the Act—which required legislation passed without the consent of the House of Lords to be introduced by the special words of enactment which explicitly refer to the 1911 Act—was introduced by peers who did not wish to see its procedures used to further reduce the powers of the House.

4–037   The decision in *Pepper v. Hart* seemed self evidently correct when the Inland Revenue sought to tax an individual on a basis which had been explicitly repudiated by the relevant minister when the legislation was being debated. But can a minister by making wide claims for what he wants to achieve bind later

---

[36] A number of procedural provisions must be complied with, as to which the Speaker's certificate is stated to be conclusive: Parliament Act 1911, s.3. *cf. Akar v. Att.-Gen. of Sierra Leone* [1970] A.C. 853, PC.

[37] H. W. R. Wade [1954] C.L.J. 265; [1955] C.L.J. 193.

[38] Hood Phillips, *Reform of the Constitution*, pp. 18–19, 91–93; letter from O. Hood Phillips to *The Times*, July 15, 1968; Graham Zellick, "Is the Parliament Act *Ultra Vires?*" (1969) 119 New L.J. 716.

[39] *R. v. Burah* (1878) 3 App Cas 889 and *Hodge v. R.* (1883) 9 App Cas 117 are, it is suggested, not inconsistent with this proposition.

[40] [1993] A.C. 593.

courts to accept his interpretation of a statute—or even to accept an interpretation which gives him or the House of Commons powers which the law says they do not have.[41] *Pepper v. Hart* will need further elaboration in later litigation if it is not to have very unfortunate consequences.[42]

It has also been argued that giving the words of section 2 of the 1911 Act their ordinary and natural meaning—the first rule of statutory interpretation—they are sufficiently wide to extend to later amendments of the 1911 Act, such as the legislation of 1949. To that it can be replied that it is equally fundamental that legislation is not to be taken to make any alteration in the common law beyond what it expressly so does.[43]

In recognition of the controversy surrounding the Parliament Act 1949, Lord Donaldson of Lymington, a former Master of the Rolls, introduced into the House of Lords in November 2000, the Parliament Acts (Amendment) Bill. The purpose of the Bill, which did not become law, was to confirm the status of the 1949 Act and the Acts which, at that time had been passed under its terms and to ensure that the provisions of the 1911 and 1949 Acts could not be used for the future to affect the constitution or powers of the House of Lords and could not themselves be amended except by Act of Parliament passed in the conventional way.

Regency Acts[44]

The Regency Acts 1937–53 provide that if the Sovereign is under 18 years of **4–038** age, the royal functions shall be exercised by a Regent appointed under the provisions of the Acts. The Regent may assent to Bills, except Bills altering the succession to the throne or repealing the Acts securing the Scottish Church. It is clear that the Regent and the two Houses could not repeal these exceptions, not because Parliament has bound its successors, but because legislation passed with the Regent's assent is a kind of subordinate or delegated legislation which must keep within the limits prescribed by the Regency Acts. On the other hand, it seems that a Sovereign under the age of eighteen could assent to Bills, including Bills excepted from the Regent's authority and Bills to repeal or amend the Regency Acts themselves,[45] for a Sovereign is never an infant at common law and Parliament is not bound by the procedure provided by the Regency Acts. This does not mean that these provisions of the Regency Acts are "void." They are valid and effective so long as they remain unrepealed in that, if a Regent is appointed, Bills assented to by him (subject to the two exceptions) will be recognised as valid statutes.

---

[41] Obviously a court will not be bound under the Human Rights Act 1998 by a minister's statement under s.19 that the provisions of legislation are compatible with the Convention rights.

[42] For a searching critique, see D. Robertson, *Judicial Discretion in the House of Lords* (1998) Chap. 5. "To take the opinion whether of a minister or an official or a committee as to the intended meaning in particular applications of a clause or phrase would be a stunting of the law and not a healthy development"; *per* Lord Wilberforce, *Black-Clawson International Ltd v. Papierwerke Waldhof-Ashaffenburg A.G.* [1975] A.C. 591 at p. 630.

[43] *Black-Clawson International Ltd v. Papierwerke Waldhof-Ashaffenburg A.G.* [1975] A.C. 591 at p. 614 *per* Lord Reid; *A.G. v. Brotherton* [1992] 1 A.C. 425 at p. 439 *per* Lord Oliver. For an application of the principle, no doubt unattractive to modern susceptibilities, see *Viscountess Rhondda's Claim* [1922] 2 A.C. 33.

[44] See further, *post*, Chap. 4.

[45] H. W. R. Wade [1955] C.L.J. 193n.

Conclusion

4–039   It appears that the only way by which the legislature of this country could become legally limited would be for the United Kingdom Parliament to extinguish itself, after surrendering its powers to a new written constitution,[46] with entrenched provisions (*e.g.* as to abolition of the Second Chamber, the life of Parliament, membership of EEC, and a Bill of Rights) and judicial review—a constitution limiting the powers of the new legislature *and to which the new legislature would owe its existence.* The new constitution could either be drafted by the existing Parliament, or its drafting could be entrusted to a constituent assembly, the new constitution perhaps receiving the extra moral sanction of an inaugural referendum. In either case there would be a *breach of continuity* between the old and the new constitutions.[47]

It is, of course, true that Parliament is unlikely to repeal the European Communities Act 1972 or the Human Rights Act 1998. Devolution is, no doubt, here to stay. But predictions about what Parliament might wish to do or, in political terms, might or might not be able to do, are irrelevant to the importance of the legal doctrine of Parliamentary Supremacy. It is because of that doctrine that when Parliament wishes to do something it can, safe from challenge in the courts and from the need to follow particular procedures.

---

[46] *cf.* A. V. Dicey. *England's Case against Home Rule* (3rd ed., 1887), pp. 241–245; could Parliament merely transfer its powers to another legislature?

[47] Hood Phillips, *Reform of the Constitution*, pp. 156 *et seq.* For another suggestion, see Lord Hailsham, *The Dilemma of Democracy*, Chap. 36.

CHAPTER 5

DEVOLUTION AND REGIONALISM

Introduction

In chapter 2 we saw how the United Kingdom evolved from a union of **5–001**
England, Wales, Scotland and Ireland. As a consequence of this history the
United Kingdom had a unitary constitution in which political and legal powers
were centralised to a remarkable extent. However, within this system there was
a measure of devolution of administrative powers to Scotland, and to a lesser
extent to Wales. From 1921 to 1972 Northern Ireland enjoyed an extensive
degree of devolution with legislative and executive powers devolved to the
Province's Parliament and government. The extend to which there was devolution within the United Kingdom before 1999 will first be considered.

I. DEVOLUTION

The term devolution[1] refers to the delegation of central government powers **5–002**
without the relinquishment of supremacy by the central legislature. Devolution
may be legislative or administrative or both, and in its more advanced forms
involves the exercise of powers by persons or bodies who, although acting on
authority delegated by the Westminster Parliament, are not directly answerable to
it or to the central government.[2] Devolution is said not to affect the unity of the
United Kingdom or the power of Westminster to legislate (even in devolved
matters) for all or any part of the United Kingdom, or to repeal or amend the
devolution arrangements themselves. It should be distinguished from "decentralisation", which is a method whereby some central government powers of decision-making are exercised by officials of the central government located in
various regions,[3] and federalism. In a federal system supremacy is *divided*
between the federal legislature and government on the one hand and the legislatures and governments of the constituent units on the other, and the basic terms
of a federal constitution (notably the distribution of powers) are *entrenched* so
that they cannot be amended at the sole discretion of the federation or of any
province or combination of provinces.[4]

Northern Ireland[5]

From 1921 to 1972 the Northern Ireland Parliament and government had **5–003**
powers under the Government of Ireland Act 1920 to make laws "for the peace
order and good government of Northern Ireland", only matters such as foreign

---

[1] For the background see: (1973) Cmnd. 5460, *Report of Royal Commission on the Constitution*
(Kilbrandon); Cmnd. 5460–61, *Memorandum of Dissent*: (1974) Cmnd. 5732, *Democracy and
Devolution: Proposals for Scotland and Wales*; (1975) Cmnd. 6348, *Our Changing Democracy:
Devolution to Scotland and Wales*; (1976) Cmnd. 6585, *Devolution to Scotland and Wales: Supplementary Statement*; (1977) Cmnd. 6890, *Devolution: Financing the Devolved Services.*
[2] Cmnd. 5460, p. 165.
[3] Cmnd. 6348, pp. 55–56.
[4] Cmnd. 5460, pp. 152–154.
[5] See C. McCrudden, "Northern Ireland and the British Constitution", in *The Changing Constitution*,
(J. Jowell and D. Oliver eds, 3rd ed., 1994); B. Hadfield, "The Northern Ireland Constitution", in
Northern Ireland: Politics and the Constitution (B. Hadfield ed., 1992).

relations, defence and nationality were reserved to Westminster. Local Northern Ireland ministries and departments were established in the usual areas of government, and in this period Northern Ireland passed its own laws and had its own system of administration and its own civil service. The Home Office was the United Kingdom department with responsibility for Northern Ireland, but it had no presence in Northern Ireland and had little direct knowledge of what was happening there. Although Westminster had retained ultimate legislative power, a convention developed that it did not concern itself with matters formally devolved to Northern Ireland. Devolution as envisaged by the Government of Ireland Act 1920 came to an end in 1972; that it did so was not a defect in the concept of devolution,[6] but a reflection on a system which failed to take account of the divisions within the Province, allowed one party which represented the majority of the people in Northern Ireland to ignore the interests of any other group, and too great a willingness by successive United Kingdom governments not to intervene.

Scotland[7] and Wales

5–004   Although the central administration of Scotland had been the exclusive responsibility of the British Government since 1707, and the Westminster Parliament the sole source of legislation for Scotland, the distinctive Scottish legal system and Scots law were guaranteed by the Treaty of Union 1707. In 1885 a Scottish Office headed by a Minister with a seat in the cabinet, was created. The office was upgraded to Secretary of State in 1937, and in 1939 the main base of the Scottish Office became Edinburgh. Gradually executive powers were devolved to the Scottish Office, which was able to devise, execute and administer the policies of the United Kingdom government in a Scottish context. In addition the different legal system required statutes that applied only to Scotland to be made by Westminster. Scotland then had a system of administrative devolution.

Wales also had administrative devolution, but it had developed at a slower pace than in Scotland. By 1945 fifteen government departments had Welsh sections with offices in Wales, but it was not until 1964 that the Welsh Office and a Secretary of State for Wales were created, although a Minister of State for Welsh Affairs had been established in 1951. Initially the Secretary of State for Wales had limited powers, with powers being extended gradually. Unlike Scotland, Wales did not have its own laws and legal system, and there was no need to legislate separately for Wales, except for legislation connected with such matters as Welsh language, culture and heritage.

The Scotland Act 1978 and the Wales Act 1978

5–005   Nationalism in Scotland and Wales first became a considerable electoral factor at the general election of 1966, when the Nationalist parties received the votes of 20 per cent of the electors in those countries. A Royal Commission on the Constitution was set up in 1969. Its terms of reference were "to examine the present functions of the central legislature and government in relation to the several countries, nations and regions of the United Kingdom; and to consider . . . whether any changes are desirable . . . in the present constitutional and economic relationships . . . " Although the terms of reference were wide enough to cover almost any aspect of the Constitution, the Commission limited its review

---

[6] See the Kilbrandon Report, (see *ante* note 1) para. 548.
[7] See the Stair Encyclopedia, *The Laws of Scotland*, vol. 5.

almost entirely to the question of national feelings and devolution. The terms of reference insisted on the preservation of the political and economic unity of the United Kingdom. The Kilbrandon Commission issued majority and minority reports in 1973.[8] The Government did not accept either report in its entirety, but held further discussions and issued several White Papers. In particular the Government pointed out that there were few parallels anywhere for dividing between two levels of government powers and functions long exercised centrally in a unitary state, and that after devolution to Scotland and Wales each part of the United Kingdom would have a different form of government.

The impetus to introduce legislation devolving power to Scottish and Welsh **5–006** assemblies was the parlous position of Mr Callaghan's minority government from 1976 onwards and his wish to secure political allies wherever they could be found. Initially one bill to deal with both countries was introduced in the 1976–77 Session of Parliament but was abandoned after the government's defeat when it attempted to introduce a guillotine motion. Two separate bills were introduced in the 1977–78 Session, which after a long parliamentary struggle became the Scotland Act 1978 and the Wales Act 1978. The Scotland Act provided for a directly elected Assembly with legislative and executive powers, the Wales Act for an Assembly with executive powers only. The devolution legislation required the Acts to be approved in referendums; it also required the approval of 40 per cent of those entitled to vote before the provisions would come into effect. This threshold was not achieved in either country, and the legislation was repealed.

Background to the 1998 devolution statutes

Scotland and Wales[9]

From 1978 to 1992 the pressures for devolution to Scotland and Wales mainly **5–007** came from outside government and parliament; the then Conservative government was committed to the preservation of the Union, and opposed to devolution. The Scottish Constitutional Convention—a pressure group established in 1989— helped to pave the way for devolution by the publication of reports and proposals.[10] In the 1992 general election both the Labour Party and the Liberal Democratic Party were in favour of devolution to Scotland and Wales. The Conservative Party, re-elected in 1992, remained opposed to devolution, and instead introduced a series of procedural reforms designed to enhance the treatment of Scottish and Welsh business in Parliament, improve aspects of the Scottish and Welsh Offices and increase executive devolution.[11] Throughout the period of Conservative government, the Conservative Party had little electoral support in Scotland and Wales. This difference between the electoral preferences of the people in Scotland and Wales, and the political composition of

[8] *op. cit.* note 1. Of 16 Commission members, eight favoured a scheme of legislative as well as executive devolution to Scotland, six favoured a similar scheme of devolution to Wales, and eight members were in favour of coordinating and advisory Regional Councils for England, partly indirectly elected by the local authorities and partly nominated.

[9] See James Mitchell, "The Creation of the Scottish Parliament: Journey without End", (1999) 52 Parl. Affairs 651; Laura McAllister, "The Road to Cardiff Bay: The Process of Establishing the National Assembly for Wales", (1999) 52 Parl. Affairs. 635.

[10] *Towards Scotland's Parliament* (1990), *Scotland's Parliament, Scotland's Right* (1995).

[11] *Scotland in the union: a partnership for good*, Cm. 2225 (1993); see Patricia Leopold Chap. XIII "Autonomy and the British Constitution", in *Autonomy: Applications and Implications* (Markku Suksi ed., 1998).

the government at Westminster, increased the demands in Scotland and Wales for devolution. In 1997 Labour won the general election with a commitment to institute a wide range of constitutional reforms. White Papers on Scottish and Welsh devolution were published in July 1997[12] in which devolution was placed in the wider context of a series of constitutional reforms which would decentralise power, open up government, reform Parliament and increase individual rights. The Referendums (Scotland and Wales) Act 1997 was passed to give voters in each country the opportunity to decide if the government should go ahead and introduce legislation for devolution based on the respective White Papers. In a 60 per cent turnout, 74.3 per cent of those voting agreed that there should be a Scottish Parliament; a week later, in a 51 per cent turnout, 50.3 per cent of those voting supported the creation of a Welsh Assembly. The 1979 referendums had required 40 per cent of the electorate to support the devolution legislation, there was no such threshold in the 1997 Act, and the on the basis of the referendum results the Scotland Bill and the Government of Wales Bill were published. Both Bills received the Royal Assent in 1998, and the first elections were held in May 1999.

Northern Ireland

5–008   The establishment of lasting new provisions for the government of Northern Ireland had been the aim of successive governments for many years. United Kingdom governments came to recognise that solutions to the problems of Northern Ireland had to involve the Republic of Ireland, and in 1981 both governments agreed to establish an Anglo-Irish Inter-government Council. In 1985 the Governments of the United Kingdom and the Republic of Ireland concluded the Anglo-Irish Agreement which established within the framework of the Inter-Government Council, an Inter-governmental Conference. This would consider, on a regular basis, matters relating to Northern Ireland and relations between the two parts of the island of Ireland. The Agreement specified the matters to be considered: political matters; security and related matters; legal matters, including the administration of justice and the promotion of cross-border co-operation. The Agreement was unsuccessfully challenged by four Unionist Members of Parliament on the basis *inter alia* that it would fetter the statutory functions of the Secretary of State for Northern Ireland, that it handed over partial sovereignty to the Irish Republic and would be in breach of the Union with Ireland Act 1800.[13] Although the Anglo-Irish Agreement committed the British Government to the restoration of devolution to Northern Ireland, the opposition of the Unionists to the Agreement meant that no progress was made.

5–009   In 1993 behind the scenes talks between several of the political parties in Northern Ireland progressed sufficiently to allow the "peace process" to be given official recognition and encouragement. The Downing Street Declaration[14] between the British and Irish governments recognised and renewed the position of Northern Ireland as part of the United Kingdom so long as that was the wish of the majority of the people of Northern Ireland. It also stated that the British government had no "selfish, strategic or economic interest in Northern Ireland", thereby indicating the neutrality of the British government in the future constitutional position of Northern Ireland. Although ceasefires were announced in 1994,

[12] *Scotland's Parliament*, Cm. 3658, *A Voice for Wales* (Cm. 3718).
[13] *ex p. Molyneaux* [1986] 1 W.L.R. 331.
[14] Cm. 2442 (1993).

it proved impossible to convene multi-party talks. The governments of the United Kingdom and Ireland continued to work towards a constitutional settlement, and in 1995 a series of Frameworks documents were agreed. These documents outlined proposals for a power-sharing model of devolution which would include both the main communities in Northern Ireland, and address the relationship between the two parts of Ireland and that between Ireland and the United Kingdom. In 1995 unsuccessful attempts were made to encourage the holding of multi-party talks by the establishment of an international body chaired by a former U.S. Senator, George Mitchell. Unionist opposition to the Frameworks proposals, the slim majority of the Conservative Government, and the ending of the ceasefire put back the hopes of a constitutional settlement for Northern Ireland. The election of a Labour Government did not mark any change of policy on Northern Ireland, but the Government's clear commitment to general constitutional reform and sound majority in the House of Commons provided the necessary impetus to make new progress. Multi-party negotiations—which with the renewal of its cease-fire included Sinn Fein—under the chairmanship of Mr George Mitchell started and concluded on Good Friday 1998 with the Belfast Agreement.[15] The Belfast Agreement was supplemented by agreements between the British and Irish governments on its implementation.[16]

There are several aspects to the Belfast Agreement. First it provided that **5–010** Northern Ireland would remain part of the United Kingdom and would not cease to do so unless the people of Northern Ireland voted otherwise in a border poll; the claim to jurisdiction over all of Ireland provided in the constitution of the Republic of Ireland was to be repealed. Secondly the Agreement provided in three strands the institutional framework for devolution, each strand representing one of the sets of relationships that exist in Northern Ireland. Strand One required the establishment of an elected Assembly with legislative powers and an Executive. Strand Two provided for the establishment of a North-South Ministerial Council to deal with matters of mutual interest to the Assembly and the Irish Government.[17] Strand Three created the British-Irish Council.[18] Finally the Agreement addressed a variety of issues of concern to both sides of the community: the establishment of a Human Rights Commission and an Equality Council; an Independent Commission on Decommissioning, and a commitment to the disarmament of the paramilitary organisations; policing; security; prisoner releases and the criminal justice system. In May 1998 referendums on the Belfast Agreement were held in Northern Ireland and the Republic of Ireland. In a 80.98 per cent turnout, 71.2 per cent of those who voted approved the agreement in Northern Ireland, and in a 55.47 per cent turnout, 94 per cent of those who voted did so in the Republic of Ireland.

The procedure for the introduction of the Northern Ireland Assembly began **5–011** with transitional arrangements found in the Northern Ireland (Elections) Act 1998. This resulted in elections in June 1998 for the "new Northern Ireland Assembly", which was to become the Northern Ireland Assembly once an Order in Council was made implementing Parts I and III of the Northern Ireland Act

---

[15] *The Agreement reached in multi-party negotiations* Cm. 4292 (1998).
[16] *Agreement Establishing Implementing Bodies* Cm. 4293 (1998); *Agreement Establishing a North-South Ministerial Council* Cm. 4294 (1998); *Agreement Establishing a British-Irish Council* Cm. 4296 (1998).
[17] *post* para. 5–047
[18] *post* para. 5–048

1998—the Act which implemented the Belfast Agreement.[19] Until that time Northern Ireland remained subject to direct rule from Westminster, and the elected "new Assembly" was to start work establishing committees, standing orders etc. in anticipation of the implementation of the 1998 Act. The Devolution Order in Council was to be made, "If it appeared to the Secretary of State that sufficient progress has been made in implementing the Belfast Agreement" (section 3 of the Northern Ireland Act 1998). Mr George Mitchell returned to attempt to persuade the various parties to implement the Belfast Agreement, the apparent success of this process lead to the necessary Devolution Order being made in December 1999. It was short lived; devolution was suspended 10 weeks later[20] but was restored again in May 2000.[21]

The 1998 Provisions for Devolution[22]

5–012   The devolution schemes for Scotland, Northern Ireland and Wales were devised to meet the perceived different needs and circumstances of each country. "The union state, which was never entirely uniform, may be seen to be more disparate than before. Political factors have produced an asymmetrical state, where Westminster and Whitehall have different relationships with each of the constituent parts of the United Kingdom."[23] However there are certain similarities between the different devolution schemes, and these will be outlined before considering each scheme individually.

Similarities in the three devolution schemes

The electoral systems

5–013   In all three countries there is one legislative chamber and elections are by proportional representation (PR). The relevant devolution legislation provides precise details of how elections are to be conducted. Supervision of electoral systems is given to the relevant Secretary of State for each country, and in the case of Northern Ireland elections are an "excepted matter".[24] Systems of PR were established to encourage multi-party "government" in the devolved administrations.

The system for Scotland and Wales gives voters two votes. The first is a vote for a constituency member elected by the traditional first past the post method; 73 Members of the Scottish Parliament (M.S.P.) and 40 Members of the Welsh Assembly are elected this way. The second vote is for members to represent the regions, which are based on the European Parliament election regions. Scotland has eight regions each returning seven members, Wales five, each returning four members. These additional regional members are elected by the d'Hondt[25]

---

[19] The aspects of the Belfast Agreement which dealt with policing and prisoner releases were dealt with in separate legislative provisions.

[20] Northern Ireland Act 2000.

[21] See Rick Wilford and Robin Wilson, "A 'Bare Knuckle Ride': Northern Ireland", in *The State and the Nations: The First Years of Devolution in the United Kingdom* (R. Hazell ed., 2000).

[22] See Vernon Bogdanor, *Devolution in the United Kingdom* (1999); Alan Ward, "Devolution: Labour's Strange Constitutional 'Design' ", in *The Changing Constitution* (Jowell and Oliver eds, 4th ed., 2000); Noreen Burrows *Devolution* (2000).

[23] Colin Munro *Studies in Constitutional Law* (2nd ed., 1999) at p. 44.

[24] Schedule 2.12 to the Northern Ireland Act 1998; this means that powers over elections can not be transferred to the Northern Ireland Assembly. Elections by PR had been provided in the Government of Ireland Act 1920, but was not an excepted matter, and was abandoned by the Northern Ireland Parliament in 1929.

[25] Named after its inventor.

system of proportional representation whereby each elector casts his vote for a particular party list[26] and seats are allocated by reference to the votes cast for each party in the region. As Scotland elects 56 of its 129 members by this system compared to 20 of the 60 members in the Welsh Assembly, representation in the Scottish Parliament is likely to be more proportional to the votes cast than is the case in Wales.

A different system of PR was adopted for the Northern Ireland Assembly: the single transferable vote, whereby voters mark their preference numerically against their chosen candidates, the application of a formula establishes the quotas required to elect the necessary number of representatives. The 18 Westminster constituencies for Northern Ireland each return six members to the Assembly.

Subordination to Westminster

It is a characteristic of a devolved system that powers are delegated by the **5–014** centre to the regions without relinquishment of sovereignty.[27] The 1997 White Paper stated that: "The United Kingdom Parliament is and will remain sovereign in all matters."[28] Acts passed by the Scottish Parliament and by the Northern Ireland Assembly are not sovereign, and may be set aside by the courts if they exceed the institution's legislative competence. The Scotland Act[29] and the Northern Ireland Act[30] both make it clear that the Westminster Parliament retains power to legislate for both countries, not only on matters specifically reserved to Westminster, but also on devolved matters. Since Westminster remains the principal law maker for Wales there was no need for a similar provision in the Government of Wales Act. The precise details of the relationships between each of the new institutions and Westminster (and Whitehall) were not provided in the relevant statutes, but are found in a variety of non-binding written agreements. Included in this is a convention which states that Westminster will not normally legislate with regard to devolved matters without the consent of the relevant devolved institution.[31] In the first two years of devolution, 14 Bills that fell within the legislative powers of the Scottish Parliament were passed by Westminster.[32] So far as Scotland is concerned, the constitutional theory of the legislative supremacy of Westminster will have to be considered in the light of the political reality that it is the Scottish Parliament that legislates and speaks for Scotland. During the 1920–1972 period of devolution to Northern Ireland Westminster found it difficult to exercise its supremacy over Northern Ireland, despite the fact that the Unionist dominated Parliament saw devolution as second best to full integration into the United Kingdom, and did not wish to provoke conflict with the British government. It will be even more difficult in the case of Scotland

---

[26] It is also possible to vote for a particular candidate on a party list, *cf.* the system for the elections to the European Parliament. For an explanation of the different types of voting system see Munro *Studies in Constitutional Law* (1999), Chap. 4.

[27] *Kilbrandon Report* (see *ante* note 1) para. 543.

[28] Cm. 3658, para. 42.

[29] s.28(7) provides that Scotland's legislative power "does not affect the power of the United kingdom to make laws for Scotland." The Secretary of State for Scotland has powers to override the Scottish Parliament (s.35) and Executive (s.58).

[30] ss.5(6), 15(4), 26.

[31] *Memorandum of Understanding and Supplementary Agreement*, (1999) Cm. 444, para. 13; see also H.C. 148 (1998–99), and see *post* para. 5–047.

[32] Including the Race Relations (Amendment) Act 2000, the Regulation of Investigatory Powers Act 2000 and the Sexual Offences (Amendment) Act 2000. In each case the consent of the Scottish Parliament was sought and given.

where independence is an option; a dispute with the government of the United
Kingdom could make this option more attractive to many in Scotland.

There also remain Secretaries for State for each of the countries, who have
responsibilities for promoting the devolution settlement, ensuring effective working relationships between the Government and the devolved administrations, and
helping to resolve any disputes which may arise.[33] This representation of Scotland, Wales and Northern Ireland at Cabinet level, gives them advantages over
the English regions. The different devolution arrangements for each devolved
administration mean that each Secretary of State has different roles within these
responsibilities. For example the Secretary of State for Wales has a particular role
to safeguard Welsh interests when legislation is going through Westminster; the
Secretary of State for Scotland has powers to prevent or require action by the
Scottish Executive to ensure compatibility with international obligations[34]; it is
the Secretary of State for Northern Ireland who submits Bills for the Royal
Assent. The future role of the territorial Secretaries of State is unclear; it has been
suggested that if the separate offices continue, then devolution will have
failed.[35]

Devolution issues

5–015   Devolution issues are described in all three Acts as questions concerning the
lawful exercise of power under respectively, the Scotland Act, the Government
of Wales Act and the Northern Ireland Act.[36] Each Act defines the term by listing
the questions that are to be regarded as devolution issues for the purposes of that
Act.[37] In short these are questions concerned with whether the relevant body has
acted within its statutory powers, or infringed a European Convention right[38] or
European Community law. Special judicial procedures are provided to resolve
these questions. All three Acts provide the same scheme for lower courts to refer
devolution issues to higher courts and for further appeals in respect of such
decisions. The Judicial Committee of the Privy Council[39] has final jurisdiction in
such matters. A question on legislative competence may be referred to the Privy
Council while a Bill is going through its legislative procedures.[40] The relevant
law officers within their jurisdictions have to be notified of any devolution issue
proceedings to which they are not a party, and can require devolution proceedings
to which they are a party to be referred to the Judicial Committee. There is a wide
variation in the roles and powers of the law officers with respect to devolution
issues in the three jurisdictions, reflecting differences in the existence, roles and
powers of the law officers in each country.[41]

---

[33] *Memorandum of Understanding* Cm. 4444 (1999) p. 1. See also *the Procedural Consequences of
Devolution* H.C. 147 (1998–99).

[34] As does the Secretary of State for Northern Ireland.

[35] R. Hazell (ed.), *Constitutional Futures* (1999, Oxford University Press), p. 137.

[36] See *Hoekstra v. H.M. Advocate* [2001] A.C. 216; 2001 S.L.T. 28 where the Privy Council
considered the meaning of a devolution issue.

[37] See Scotland Act 1998, sched. 6, Northern Ireland Act 1998, sched. 10, Government of Wales Act
1998, sched. 8.

[38] The first Act passed by the Scottish Parliament, the Mental Health (Public Safety and Appeals)
(Scotland) Act 1999, was unsuccessfully challenged in the Court of Session as being contrary to Art.
5 E.C.H.R.; *A v. The Scottish Ministers* 2001 S.C. 1.

[39] See *post* Chap. 16.

[40] Scotland Act 1998, s.33 and Northern Ireland Act 1998, s.11.

[41] See Burrows, *Devolution* (2000), Chap. 6.

Human rights

The devolved bodies are bound by the E.C.H.R. by the Human Rights Act **5–016** 1998; Acts made by the Scottish Parliament and Northern Irish Assembly are regarded as subordinate legislation for the purpose of the Human Rights Act (s.21(1)), enabling Acts which are incompatible with Convention rights to be quashed by a higher court. The Human Rights Act applied to the devolved bodies before it came into effect for the rest of the United Kingdom.

The obligation to comply with Convention rights is reinforced by the devolution legislation which also provides that the devolved bodies should apply E.C.H.R. rights; acting in a way that appears to be incompatible with Convention rights will raise a devolution issue. The Scotland Act, s.29 and the Northern Ireland Act, s.6 provide that legislation that is incompatible with Convention rights is outside the legislative competence of the relevant institution. Sections 57 and 24 respectively prohibit members of the respective Executives from making subordinate legislation that is incompatible with Convention rights.[42] Section 107 of the Government of Wales Act provides similar restrictions on the more limited law-making powers of the Welsh Assembly; however the Assembly will not have acted *ultra vires* if it makes secondary legislation which is incompatible with Convention rights where this is required by United Kingdom primary legislation. Since there is no legal restriction to prevent Westminster legislating contrary to the Human Rights Act, nor is there any obligation on it legislating in response to a declaration of incompatibility,[43] it is possible that there could be legal provisions in England and Wales, that would not be permissable in Scotland or Northern Ireland.

The Northern Ireland Act provides for additional human rights protections not found elsewhere in the United Kingdom. A Minister or Northern Ireland Department may not make subordinate legislation, or do any act which discriminates against a person or class of persons on the grounds of religious belief or political opinion (section 24(1)(c)); a statutory Human Rights Commission is established to "keep under review the adequacy and effectiveness in Northern Ireland of law and practice relating to the protection of human rights" (sections 68 and 69). There is widespread support in the Scottish Parliament for the establishment of a similar Commission there.

Cabinet style of government

In all three countries an executive is drawn from the elected members, but the **5–017** formation and powers of the executives is very different. Borrows describes them as " 'designer cabinets', tailored to suit very different constitutional settlements."[44] As will be seen,[45] the method of selecting the Executives is laid down in some detail in the relevant statutes, as is the basis of the relationship between the Executives and the elected bodies; the exact relationships will be determined by the development of constitutional conventions. The very different types of cabinet government mean that the convention of collective responsibility with its characteristics of unanimity, confidentiality and the need for the confidence of the legislature which have developed with respect cabinet government for the United

---

[42] As defined by the Human Rights Act 1998, see *post* Chap. 22.
[43] See *post* Chap. 22.
[44] At p. 104.
[45] *post* paras 5–022, 5–031 and 5–040.

Kingdom, cannot apply in the same way to the cabinets in the devolved institutions.[46]

Funding

5–018   The funding arrangements for all three countries is basically the same as pre-devolution. Block grants of money are paid to each administration by Westminster. The sums are uprated annually in accordance with the Barnett Formula,[47] which allocates increased funds on a pro rata basis to increases in England. This formula has tended to contribute to higher public expenditure per head in Scotland, Wales and Northern Ireland compared to poorer regions of England and the Barnett formula was subject to inquiry in advance of devolution.[48] However, the application of the Barnett Formula means that the actual money available to Scotland, Wales and Northern Ireland depends on how United Kingdom Ministers in the spending departments such as education and health (largely devolved), protect their budgets against claims for funding by departments such as defence and foreign relations (not devolved). United Kingdom government policy decisions will effect the level of the block grant, irrespective of how the Barnett Formula works in the allocation of funds. The Barnett Formula is an administrative measure and was not given statutory force by the devolution legislation; it can be changed or replaced by the United Kingdom Government, as it was in July 2000 when, contrary to the formula, the assigned budget for Wales was increased. Each administration determines for itself how to spend the money assigned in the block grant. In all three devolved schemes there are statutory provisions for the scrutiny of accounts.

Only Scotland is not totally dependent on Westminster for its revenue. One of the questions in the 1997 referendum was whether the Scottish Parliament should have tax varying powers; 65.5 per cent of those who voted were in favour of such powers, which are found in Part IV the Scotland Act. This allows the Scottish Parliament with respect to Scottish tax payers to increase or decrease the basic rate of income tax set by the United Kingdom Parliament by a maximum of 3 per cent. If the Scottish Parliament decreases the tax rate, a payment has to be made to the Inland Revenue to account for the shortfall.

Members' Interests and conduct and privileges

5–019   The devolution legislation adopts a mixture of statutory and non-statutory provisions to regulate this, based on the experience at Westminster. The establishment of a public Register of Members' Interests and a prohibition on paid advocacy is found in the devolution legislation.[49] It is for the devolved institutions within this statutory framework to establish rules and procedures, and in certain circumstances it will be a criminal offence to fail to comply with the rules. Codes of Conduct for members and Ministers, overseen by a committee on Standards and Privileges, have been agreed and published in all three countries. A more restricted freedom of speech than that found at Westminster[50] is provided in the devolution legislation.[51] All three devolved legislatures have statutory

---

[46] See Burrows *Devolution* (2000), Chap. 4.

[47] Named after the former Chief Secretary to the Treasury, this formula has been used since the late 1970s.

[48] See H.C. 341 (1997–98), H.C. 619 (1998–99).

[49] s.39 Scotland Act; s.43 Northern Ireland Act; s.72 Government of Wales Act.

[50] *post* Chap. 13.

[51] ss.41, 42 Scotland Act; s.50 Northern Ireland Act; ss.77, 78 Government of Wales Act. The provision are not identical in the three statutes, but have broadly the same effect.

powers to call for witnesses and documents in connection with matters within the competence of the relevant body. Unlike the position at Westminster, there is provision in certain circumstances for the prosecution of un-cooperative witnesses—including members of the legislature.[52] The devolution legislation specifically provides that each of the legislatures is a public body for the purposes of the Prevention of Corruption Acts 1889 to 1916.[53] This ensures that the statute law on the corrupt making or acceptance of payments in connection with a public body's business applies, something that is unclear with respect to Westminster.[54]

II. SCOTLAND

The Scotland Act 1998 provides for both a Scottish Executive and a Parliament. **5–020** Of the three schemes of devolution, the Scottish one is closest to that found at Westminster, although the 1998 Act allows for the Scottish Parliament to regulate itself by means of Standing Orders. In advance of the first elections a cross party Consultative Steering Group was established to make recommendations on the procedure and working of the new Parliament.[55] After the first election these recommendations were the basis for the establishment of Standing Orders on for example, the making of legislation, and the committee structure.

Devolved and legislative competence
The functions of the Scottish Parliament and the Scottish Executive are only **5–021** those within their "devolved competencies". This means that both bodies have to act within the powers as provided by the 1998 Act. The powers of the Executive are in effect circumscribed by the powers of the Parliament.[56] However, unlike the Scotland Act 1978 where specifically defined legislative and executive competencies were transferred to the new Scottish bodies leaving all other powers to be exercised by Westminster and United Kingdom ministers, the 1998 legislation lists those matters reserved for Westminster and United Kingdom ministers, leaving the rest for the Scottish bodies. The Scottish Parliament has a general power to make laws, known as Acts of the Scottish Parliament (section 28),[57] "within its legislative competence" (section 29), which means that Acts must not:

(i) Modify those "protected provisions" listed in Schedule 4. These include aspects of the Acts of Union, 1706, 1707; the Human Rights Act 1998; parts of the European Communities Act 1972, and most of the Scotland Act 1998.

(ii) Concern "reserved matters" listed in Schedule 5. Part I of the schedule provides five general reserved matters: the constitution, political parties, foreign affairs, public service, defence, and treason. Part II provides

---

[52] ss. 23–26 Scotland Act; ss. 44–46 Northern Ireland Act; ss. 74–75 Government of Wales Act.
[53] s.43 Scotland Act; s.79 Government of Wales Act.
[54] See Joint Committee on Parliamentary Privilege Report, H.L. Paper 43, H.C. 214 (1998–99), Chap. 3, and *post* Chap. 13.
[55] *Shaping Scotland's Parliament* (H.M.S.O., 1998).
[56] Unless the Executive is acting on the basis of additional powers transferred to it by Order in Council or on an agency basis.
[57] See Burrows *Devolution* (2000), pp. 57–65 for a discussion on whether Acts of the Scottish Parliament and Northern Ireland Assembly are a species of primary legislation or a species of subordinate legislation.

specific reservations with eleven broad heads, under each of which are listed the particular items which are not within the competence of the Scottish Parliament and Executive. The broad heads are: financial and economic matters, home affairs, trade and industry, energy, transport, social security, regulation of the professions, employment, health and medicine, media and culture and miscellaneous. There is provision for the modification by Order in Council of reserved matters (section 30(2)), so enabling an increase in the powers of the Scottish Parliament and Executive.

(iii) Be incompatible with European Convention rights or European Community law.

(iv) Have extra-territorial effect.

(v) Remove the Lord Advocate as head of the system of criminal prosecution in Scotland.

The fields in which the Scottish Parliament and Executive have powers include: the health service,[58] local government—including expenditure and the financing of local government, education and training, housing, transport, sport, the legal system including law and order, farming, fishing, forestry, the arts, the countryside and economic development. The Scottish Parliament has a limited tax varying power,[59] it has to approve a Scottish budget and can debate any matter of national or international importance, irrespective of whether the subject matter is devolved or reserved.

The Executive

Appointment and dismissal and composition

5–022   Section 44 of the Scotland Act states that the Scottish Executive comprises the First Minister, other ministers appointed by Her Majesty on his recommendation, and the Scottish Law Officers (the Lord Advocate and the Solicitor General for Scotland, who may, but need not be, M.S.P.s).[60] The First Minister is appointed by Her Majesty from among M.S.P.s. Her Majesty's discretion may be regarded as limited by section 45 which requires the Scottish Parliament to nominate a First Minister from its members, who will then be recommended by the Presiding Officer[61] to Her Majesty for appointment.[62] The First Minister is required to have his Ministerial recommendations approved by the Scottish Parliament (section 47(2)), so establishing the notion that the Executive is responsible to Parliament. Ministers may resign from office, or be removed by the First Minister. If the Scottish Parliament resolves by simple majority that it has no confidence in the

---

[58] Apart from those matters reserved to Westminster which include abortion; embryology, surrogacy and genetics; medicines, medical supplies and poisons (sched. 5 Pt II Head J).

[59] *ante.* para. 5–018.

[60] The press release in which the first Executive was named referred to it as "the Cabinet"; more recently the First Minister has referred to it as the "government". Its composition is as provided by s.44, apart from the exclusion of the Solicitor General.

[61] The Presiding Officer (and his two deputies) have similar roles to the Speaker of the House of Commons, but with additional statutory functions and powers.

[62] The Scotland Act does not specifically require an election, but where, as has happened, there are several nominations there was an election.

Executive it must resign immediately (section 45(2)), but a general election will only follow if a replacement Executive cannot be established.

In the 1999 elections no one party had an overall majority. A "Partnership for Scotland" was agreed between the Labour Party and the Scottish Liberal Democrats, and the political composition of the Executive reflected this agreement. The ministerial team of 19 is much larger than the ministerial team found in the Scottish Office prior to devolution.

Executive Functions

The Scotland Act transfers to Scottish Ministers functions previously exercised by Ministers of the Crown that are within "devolved competence",[63] including the exercise of the prerogative and any functions conferred on a Minister of the Crown by any statute in force before devolution came into effect (section 53(2)).[64] The Scottish Executive therefore exercises devolved executive powers on behalf of the Crown. In due course, additional statutory functions will be conferred on Scottish Ministers by Acts of the Scottish Parliament (section 52). Executive functions are vested in the Scottish Ministers collectively but, with the exception of the specific powers of the First Minister and the Lord Advocate, can be exercised by any member of the Scottish Executive (section 52(5)). There are specified exceptions to the general transfer of functions provided in section 53. Section 56 lists certain functions (shared powers) which although transferred to Scottish Ministers can be also exercised by Ministers of the Crown; section 57 extends shared powers to the power of Scottish Ministers under section 2(2) of the European Communities Act 1972 to implement Community law obligations.[65]

5–023

The Sovereign retains direct executive powers to appoint and remove Ministers, to dissolve the Parliament and require a general election to be held and to give the Royal Assent to Bills passed by the Scottish Parliament. Several powers remain with the government of the United Kingdom including: elections; the power to prevent or require action in connection with international obligations (sections 35, 58); payment of money into the Scottish Consolidated Fund; the entitlement of the Attorney General to initiate and participate in devolution proceedings; powers of Her Majesty in Council to alter Parliament's legislative competence, and transfer additional ministerial function to Scottish Ministers.

It is for the Scottish Executive to decide the policy and legislative programme to be followed, and a four year plan was published in September 1999.

The Parliament

Committees in the Scottish Parliament

The Scottish Parliament works extensively through committees, although unlike the devolution legislation for Wales and Northern Ireland, detailed provisions on committees are not included in the Scotland Act. The establishment of

5–024

---

[63] See *ante* para. 5–021.
[64] s.63 allows for additional powers to be transferred to Scottish Ministers by Order in Council; s.108 provides authority to transfer powers from Scottish Ministers to a Minister of the Crown.
[65] See *post* para. 6–018. The *Concordat on Co-ordination of E.U. Policy Issues* attempts to set out the role of the Scottish Executive in European matters, see Cm. 4444 (1999) paras. 17, 19, and *post* para. 5–049.

certain committees is mandatory: Procedures; Standards; Finance; Audit; European; Subordinate legislation; Equal Opportunities and Public Petitions. In addition the Scottish Parliament has general powers to establish subject committees.[66] Eight have been established: Education, Culture and Sport, Enterprise and Lifelong Learning, Health and Community Care, Justice and Home Affairs, Social Inclusion, Transport and the Environment. These subject committees have several roles: to assist in the scrutiny and revision of legislation; to scrutinise the Executive; to conduct inquiries as required by the Parliament; initiate legislation; scrutinise financial proposals. The volume of work imposed on these committees could put a strain on their ability to work effectively.

Legislative procedures in Scotland

5–025   The Scottish Parliament may pass both primary and secondary legislation for Scotland. As the Parliament is unicameral its procedures must ensure that there is proper scrutiny of both types of legislation.

Primary legislation

5–026   Standing Orders require pre-legislative consultation with bodies or parties who would be concerned with the proposed legislation. On introducing a Bill the relevant Minister must provide:

(i) written statements from both the member of the Executive in charge of the Bill and the Presiding Officer that in his or her view it is within the legislative competence of the Parliament (section 31(1),(2));

(ii) a financial memorandum giving estimates of the administrative and other costs, and indicating where those cost will fall;

(iii) explanatory notes summarising what the Bill will do;

(iv) a policy memorandum setting out the policy objectives of the Bill, the alternative approaches considered and discounted, the consultation undertaken, effect of the legislation on equal opportunities, human rights sustainable development, etc.

Section 36 requires a Bill to pass through three stages, but leaves the details to be provided by Standing Orders.[67] In Stage one the general principles of the Bill are considered, this will usually involve a Bill being referred to one or more subject committee; the final debate and vote will be before the whole Parliament. In stage two the Bill is subjected to detailed scrutiny, either by a committee or by a committee of the whole Parliament, amendments may be introduced at this stage and at the third stage, when the Parliament will vote on whether the Bill should be passed.

A Bill will be presented for the Royal Assent by the Presiding Officer, provided it has not been referred to the Privy Council. Section 33 provides that, within a four week period of a Bill being passed, the Advocate General (a member of the Scottish Executive), the Lord Advocate or the Attorney General

---

[66] These are the equivalent of statutory committees in Northern Ireland; in Wales subject committees are included within the general heading of statutory committees.

[67] Standing Orders of the Scottish Parliament provide for a slightly different procedure for seven different types of Public Bills: Member's Bill (the equivalent of a Private Member's Bill at Westminster); Committee Bill; Budget Bills, Consolidation Bills, Statute Law Revision or Repeal Bills; Emergency Bills. There is also a separate procedure for Private Bills.

(both United Kingdom ministers) may refer a question of the legislative competence of the Parliament to pass the Bill to the Judicial Committee of the Privy Council. In addition the Secretary of State for Scotland may intervene to prohibit the Presiding Officer from presenting a Bill for the Royal Assent where he has reasonable grounds to believe that it would be incompatible with any international obligation or the interests of defence or national security or would have an adverse effect on the law as it applies to reserved matters (section 35). This gives a United Kingdom Minister of the Crown a power to prevent the enactment of legislation by the Scottish Parliament.

Since May 1999 a variety of Acts have been passed, including two based on long standing recommendations of the Scottish Law Commission, examples of the benefit of devolution. The Bail, Judicial Appointments, etc. (Scotland) Act 2000 was passed to ensure compatibility with the E.C.H.R. of several aspects of Scots law and procedure including: procedures for the granting of bail; the terms of appointment of temporary sheriffs, following the decision of the High Court of Justiciary in *Starrs and Chambers v. Procurator Fiscal Linlithgow*[68]; and the court duties of Justices of the Peace.

Secondary Legislation

A Subordinate Legislation Committee considers all instruments laid before Parliament on a variety of procedural aspects. An instrument is then referred to the lead committee, the committee within whose remit the subject matter of the instrument falls; this committee must report within 40 days whether the instrument should be approved or annulled.   **5–027**

The scrutiny functions of the Scottish Parliament

The Scottish Parliament holds the Executive to account[69] in much the same way as at Westminster: by debate, parliamentary questions[70] and committees including subject committees which shadow the portfolios of the Scottish Ministers. A Code of Conduct for Scottish Ministers adopted in July 1999 is similar to that found at Westminster. It states that Ministers have a duty to account and be held to account for the policies, decisions and actions taken within their field of responsibility. A Code of Practice on Access to Scottish Executive Information will eventually be replaced by a Scottish Freedom of Information Act.   **5–028**

The Scottish Parliament may only force an election before the end of its four year term if such a move has the support of two thirds of its members, or if a vacancy arises in the officer of First Minister and no member is able to win sufficient support to form a new government within 28 days (section 4).

III. NORTHERN IRELAND

The very different background to the devolution settlement for Northern Ireland is seen in section 1 of the Northern Ireland Act 1998. This declares that Northern Ireland remains part of the United Kingdom, and provides that it will not cease to be so without the consent of the people of Northern Ireland voting   **5–029**

---

[68] [2000] S.L.T. 42, this decision also lead to moves by the Scottish Executive to establish an independent Judicial Appointments Commission.

[69] The word "accountable" does not appear in s.44 of the Scotland Act which establishes the Scottish Executive *cf.* s.56 of the Government of Wales Act, which establishes the Welsh Executive Committee.

[70] Provided for in Standing Orders; in the first four months of the Scottish Parliament's existence more questions were put down than in a year at Westminster.

in a poll for that purpose. It marks a new beginning for devolution in the Province by repealing the Government of Ireland Act 1920.[71]

Devolved and Legislative Competence

5–030   A general legislative power is devolved to the Northern Ireland Assembly, but this power is subject to greater restraints than is the case in Scotland. Three types of powers are defined in the Northern Ireland Act: "transferred matters", "excepted matters" and "reserved matters." The Northern Ireland Assembly and Northern Ireland Executive have functions in relation to "transferred matters", which are all matters which are not "excepted" or "reserved". Excepted matters are set out in Schedule 2, and are matters which, in effect, will never be transferred to the Northern Ireland institutions; these include: Crown matters, Parliament, international relations, defence, treason, elections, national security, nuclear energy and the Northern Ireland Constitution including parts of the 1998 Act.[72] A much longer list of reserved matters is laid down in Schedule 3 including Crown property, post office and postal services, criminal law, courts, firearms and explosives, telecommunications, measurements, surrogacy, data protection and consumer safety. An item on the reserved list is potentially within the legislative competence of the Assembly but only with the consent of the Secretary of State for Northern Ireland (section 8(b)). However, as in Scotland, the Assembly even with respect to transferred matters, must act within its legislative competence,[73] which means that Acts must not:

(i) have extra-territorial application;

(ii) deal with an "excepted matter" other than in an ancillary way;

(iii) be incompatible with E.C.H.R. rights or European Community law;

(iv) discriminate against any person or class of persons on the ground of religious belief or political opinion[74];

(v) modify an "entrenched enactment".[75]

The legislative powers of the Northern Ireland Assembly include agriculture, environment, education, health,[76] social services, culture and the arts. Unlike the position in Scotland, employment, the civil service[77] and social security[78] are within the powers of the Assembly. Powers have been transferred to the Executive within those areas that fall within the legislative competence of the Assembly[79]; additional powers can be conferred by a Act of the Assembly (section 22).

[71] See Brigid Hadfield, "The Belfast Agreement, Sovereignty and the State of the Union", [1998] P.L. 599.

[72] "Excepted matters" under the Northern Ireland Act are similar to "reserved matters" under the Scotland Act.

[73] Similar restrictions apply to limit the powers of Northern Ireland Ministers and their Departments.

[74] There is no such limitation on the Scottish Parliament or Executive.

[75] *viz.* most of the European Communities Act 1972, the Human Rights Act 1998 and various sections of the Northern Ireland Act 1998 (s.7).

[76] Apart from those matters reserved to Westminster which include embryology, surrogacy and genetics.

[77] Northern Ireland has always had its own civil service, it is possible that Scotland and Wales will eventually seek their own civil service.

[78] Benefit rates must remain the same as elsewhere in the United Kingdom.

[79] Subject to similar restrictions ss.24, 25, 26.

The Executive

Appointment, dismissal and composition

The particular problems of Northern Ireland have led to a complex procedure **5–031** for the establishment of the Northern Ireland Executive which aims to move Northern Ireland towards power-sharing. The Assembly elects the First and Deputy First Ministers as a team,[80] and both are designated as chairmen of the Northern Ireland Executive Committee (section 20(2)). They are required to act jointly when exercising their functions which include nominating Ministers to the North-South and British-Irish Councils, exercising certain prerogative powers of the Crown in Northern Ireland and deciding on the number and functions of, the Northern Ireland Ministers.[81] The latter decision has to be approved by the Assembly. Unlike the position in Scotland and Wales, the First Minister and his deputy have no powers to nominate, appoint or dismiss other members of the Executive Committee. Ministers to fill the positions have to be elected by the Assembly using the d'Hondt system of proportional representation which is designed to give the parties ministerial posts in proportion to their strength in the Assembly, but not necessarily the posts of their choice. The Executive Committee so established is a multi-party body which will require cross-community support[82] from the Assembly; it is not bound by collective responsibility and neither the First Minister nor his deputy have any power to discipline the Executive as a whole.

The establishment of the first Northern Ireland Executive Committee was a long drawn out affair, with the Assembly and the Executive committee suspended for a time. It was not until May 2000 that devolution was reinstated, but without the participation of two Democratic Unionist Ministers.[83]

Executive Functions

Executive power in Northern Ireland continues to be vested in Her Majesty, **5–032** but with respect to transferred matters it will exercised on Her Majesty's behalf by Northern Ireland Ministers and Departments (section 23). The Executive Committee, composed of the various Ministers, has the functions set out in Strand One of the Belfast Agreement. It was part of this Agreement that Ministers should agree a Programme for Government; the first draft programme was eventually agreed in October 2000, as was a draft budget which reflected the regional priorities of Northern Ireland. A Code of Conduct for Ministers, similar to the one which applies to United Kingdom Ministers, was agreed in March 1999.

The United Kingdom Government retains a number of powers to legislate for the Assembly by Order in Council, *e.g.* to amend the list of reserved and excepted matters following a request from the Assembly.

---

[80] Each successful candidate must have the support of a majority of the Assembly and the support of both the majority of Unionist and Nationalist members.

[81] Up to a statutory maximum of 10.

[82] A variety of decisions in the Assembly can only be taken if there is "cross-community support." Members are required when signing the Assembly roll to designate themselves as "unionist", "nationalist" or other. Calculations as to whether a measure has cross-community support are based on these designations.

[83] See *ante* para. 5–011.

The Assembly

Committees in the Assembly

5–033   The 1998 Act provides for statutory committees to "advise and assist each Minister in the formulation of policy" (section 29). The d'Hondt method of election is used to ensure that the committees represent the Assembly composition, making them another feature of power sharing within the Assembly. These committees have several different roles: to scrutinise and revise legislation in the course of its passage through the Assembly; to assist in the formulation of policy; to initiate legislation; and to hold the Executive to account.

Legislative procedure in the Assembly

5–034   The Northern Ireland Assembly can pass both primary and subordinate legislation. Procedure for both is broadly the same as that in Scotland,[84] with the following differences with respect to primary legislation:

(i) at the pre-legislative stage, the Civic Forum[85] has to be consulted on social, economic and cultural matters;

(ii) the Presiding Officer[86] must scrutinise a Bill on its introduction to the Assembly and before its final stage to ensure it is within the legislative competence of the Assembly; if he considers that a Bill is concerned with an excepted matter in an ancillary fashion, or with a reserved matter, he has to refer it to the Secretary of State to determine if the legislative process can continue (section 10);

(iii) the Presiding Officer must send a copy of every Bill to the Northern Ireland Human Rights Commission[87] which can advise as to the compatibility of the Bill with human rights, including the E.C.H.R. (section 13(4));

(iv) a committee established by the Assembly has power to examine Bills to ensure their conformity with equality and human rights requirements;

(v) only the Attorney-General of Northern Ireland (a United Kingdom government minister)[88] within a four week period of a Bill being passed may make a reference to the Privy Council on any question of the legislative competence of the Assembly (section 11);

(vi) the Secretary of State for Northern Ireland submits Bills for the Royal Assent and has a discretion not to do so in certain circumstances (section 14).

Only three Acts were passed by the Assembly in 1999–2000, two further Bills that were going through the Assembly when it was suspended were brought into force by the Secretary of State acting under section 48 of the 1998 Act.

---

[84] Statutory committees can delegate their responsibilities in relation to the procedural scrutiny of subordinate legislation to an officer of the Assembly known as the Examiner of Statutory Rules.
[85] Established under Strand One of the Belfast Agreement, it has 60 members, and includes representatives of business, agriculture, the churches, voluntary bodies etc.
[86] A similar position to that found in Scotland, *ante* note 61.
[87] See ss. 68–70, and *ante* para. 5–016, it replaces the previous Standing Advisory Committee on Human Rights.
[88] There is no equivalent to the Scottish Lord Advocate in Northern Ireland. From 1921–1972 Northern Ireland had its own Attorney-General.

The scrutiny functions of the Northern Ireland Assembly

Ministers are required by statute to: "be accountable . . . through the Assem- **5–035**
bly, for the activities within their responsibilities, (and) their stewardship of public
funds . . . ; (and to) ensure all reasonable requests for information from the
Assembly . . . are complied with."[89] The Assembly has the same means of holding
the Executive to account as in Scotland: debates, question time and committees.

An additional unique type of accountability to the Assembly is found in the
powers of the Assembly to police "the pledge of office",[90] to which all serving
Ministers must subscribe. This, *inter alia*, commits Ministers to democratic and
non-violent government and to serve all the people of Northern Ireland equally.
The Assembly can resolve that it has no confidence in a Minister either because he
is not committed to non-violence and exclusively peaceful and democratic means
or he has failed to observe any other of the terms of the pledge of office.[91] If
carried, such a resolution (which requires cross-community support; section 30)
would exclude a Minister from office for a 12 month period. The Assembly may
on similar grounds resolve that it has no confidence in a particular party.[92]

IV. WALES

The National Assembly

The National Assembly for Wales is elected for a four year term with no **5–036**
provision for early dissolution; such provision was unnecessary as it is not a
legislative body able to refuse to pass government Bills, all powers to make
primary legislation remain with Westminster. The Secretary of State for Wales is
required to "carry out such consultation (with the Assembly) about the government's legislative programme for the session as appears to him to be appropriate" (section 31).[93] This requires him to attend and participate in the
Assembly's proceedings at least once each parliamentary session. The National
Assembly may consider and make representations to the United Kingdom government about any matter affecting Wales (section 33), which the Assembly has
interpreted as a right to propose Bills and suggest amendments to Bills before
Westminster; there is no obligation on the Government to take such representations into account.[94]

The National Assembly was established to replace the Secretary of State for
Wales in the administration of Wales and in the enactment of subordinate
legislation, known as Assembly Orders,[95] as well as the issuing of circulars
setting out policy statements and giving guidance on the carrying out of statutory

[89] See Sched. 4 of the 1998 Act which includes this obligation in the Ministerial Code of Conduct.
[90] See Sched. 4 to the 1998 Act.
[91] Which includes compliance with the Ministerial Code of Conduct.
[92] A motion to this effect may be moved by any 30 members of the Assembly, by the First and Deputy
Ministers acting together, or the Presiding Officer acting on instructions from the Secretary of State
ss.18(12) and 30).
[93] He need not consult about a Bill if he considers that there are considerations which make it
inappropriate for him to do so (s.31(4)).
[94] The relationship between the Assembly and the Secretary of State for Wales has been further
explained in a Protocol adopted in January 2000; *Devolution—A Dynamic, Settled Process* (Institute
for Welsh Affairs).
[95] Standing Orders provide for the procedures for the enactment of subordinate legislation, subject to
the requirements of ss.64–68 of the Government of Wales Act 1998.

powers. In consequence Assembly Members are members of both the executive and the legislature in Wales.

Powers and functions of the National Assembly

5–037   *Devolved and legislative competence* The Assembly has such specific powers and functions as are transferred, conferred or imposed on it by the 1998 Act or any other Act (section 22). Before these powers could be exercised the Secretary of State for Wales, by Order in Council, had to transfer the ministerial functions laid down in Schedule 2 of the 1998 Act to the National Assembly. The necessary Order[96] came into effect in July 1999, and the National Assembly has had conferred on it powers in the fields of: agriculture, forestry, fisheries and food; culture (including museums, galleries and libraries); economic development; education and training; the environment; health and the health services; highways; housing; industry; local government; social services; sport and recreation; tourism; town and country planning; transport, water and flood defence; and the Welsh language. Additional powers will be transferred to the National Assembly as new legislation is enacted by Westminster. The extent and expansion of its powers depends on the extent to which the Westminster parliament is willing to delegate further discretionary powers to it.

The National Assembly has powers to transfer to itself by statutory instrument all or any of the functions of any of the Welsh health authorities (section 27). It also has a variety of powers with respect to those Welsh public bodies listed in schedule 4, including the Further Education Funding Council for Wales, the Welsh Tourist Board and the Sports Council for Wales (section 28). It may in certain circumstances make regulations under section 2(2) of the European Communities Act 1972 (section 29).

The functions exercised by the Assembly or the members of the Assembly Cabinet[97] are only exercisable within the scope of the powers transferred to or conferred on them. There are specific limitations on its legislative powers with respect to European Community obligations (section 106), human rights (section 107) and international obligations (section 108).

5–038   *Additional functions* The Assembly is expected to contribute to the economic growth of Wales by setting a new economic agenda for Wales, while promoting sustainable development (section 121).[98] It is also required to sustain and promote local government in Wales (section 113), promote the interests of voluntary organisations (section 114) and consult with business organisations (section 115). It is a national debating and investigatory forum for Wales and Welsh affairs and may to cause inquires to be held in any matter relevant to its functions (section 35).

The 1998 Act established the National Assembly as a "body corporate" (section 1(2)), and all Assembly staff are members of the home civil service (section 34). The Assembly has instituted steps to give its civil servants greater independence and to move away from body corporate status. The Assembly is required, so far as is possible, to treat the English and Welsh languages equally;

---

[96] (S.I. 1999 No. 672); Sched. 1 of the Order lists Acts of the Westminster Parliament which delegated powers to Ministers of the Crown, which so far as they relate to Wales are transferred to the National Assembly.

[97] *post* para. 5–040.

[98] See also s.126 on reforms to the Welsh Development Agency.

members may speak in either language and simultaneous translation is provided for speeches made in Welsh.

The Committee structure

The Welsh Assembly runs under a committee structure. The 1998 Act requires **5–039** the Assembly to establish an executive committee, subject committees, a subordinate legislation scrutiny committee, an audit committee and regional committees.[99]

The Executive Committee

Although the Welsh Assembly is the executive in Wales, the equivalent to a **5–040** cabinet is found in the form of the Executive Committee. Its members are the Assembly First Secretary, the chair of the Executive Committee, and the Assembly Secretaries (section 56). The 1998 Act allows the Assembly to provide its own title for this committee and it has decided that it should be called the Cabinet and its members known as Ministers headed by a First Minister, the nomenclature which will be adopted here. The First Minister is elected by the National Assembly[1] and he notifies the Assembly of the Ministerial appointments he has made (section 53).[2] The Assembly has no role in the appointment or dismissal of the other Ministers.[3] The First Minister has discretion as to the how to allocate the fields of responsibilities devolved to the Assembly to his Ministers. The Assembly can delegate the powers and functions transferred to it to any committee of the Assembly,[4] or to the First Minister (section 62).

The Welsh Cabinet is of a different type to that found at Westminster, and the Ministers are not ministers in the same way as at Westminster or in Scotland and Northern Ireland; it exercises its functions on behalf of the Assembly and in co-operation with it and Ministers do not have powers by virtue of their office. The more powers and functions that are delegated to the Cabinet and its Ministers, the more the Welsh Cabinet will begin to function like its Westminster equivalent.

The First Minister is accountable to the Assembly for the Assembly Cabinet as a whole, and each Minister is accountable to the Assembly for the exercise of those parts of the Assembly's functions allocated to him (section 56). The Assembly is required to include provisions in its standing orders to allow for questions to the members of the Assembly Cabinet. Assembly committees play an important role in enforcing accountability.

In the 1999 election the Labour Party emerged as the largest party, but without **5–041** overall control of the National Assembly. It decided to form a minority administration, but in February 2000, a vote of no confidence in the First Minister resulted in his resignation. The election of a new First Minister, Rhodri Morgan resulted in a informal relationship with Plaid Cymru and the publication of a policy document which was in part supported by Plaid Cymru. In October 2000

---

[99] Additional committees may be established as the Assembly considers appropriate (s.54), *e.g.* a committee on Equal Opportunities and on European Affairs.

[1] If the First Minister resigns, or loses the confidence of the Assembly, a replacement has to be elected by the Assembly; the other Ministers remain in office. In February 2000, Alun Michael resigned as First Minister shortly before a vote of no confidence was carried by 31 votes to 27.

[2] Standing Orders provide a maximum of nine Ministers including the First Minister.

[3] It can pass a motion of censure on a Minister as it did by 30 votes to 27 in respect of the Agriculture Secretary in October 1999; she remained in office until dismissed by the First Minister in July 2000.

[4] Which can further delegate the power to the Minister or a sub-committee (s.62).

a more formal coalition between Labour and the Liberal Democratic Party—which was give two seats in the Cabinet—emerged with the publication of a Partnership Agreement.

Subject committees with responsibilities for the fields in which the Assembly have functions are elected by the Assembly, (section 57). The Minister for that field or fields is a member of the relevant committee, but does not chair it. The roles of these committees include:

(i) holding the administration to account by calling for papers and witnesses to appear before them;

(ii) policy-making both with respect to the work of the Welsh Assembly and by responding to, developing and amending Westminster legislative proposals;

(iii) considering such draft secondary legislation as the Deputy Presiding Officers decide should be referred to them;

(iv) reviewing expenditure and advising on budget allocation.

There is a *subordinate legislation committee* which scrutinises all subordinate legislation that comes before the Assembly to ensure that it is not defective and that all the necessary procedures have been complied with. *The Audit Committee* is responsible for ensuring that the Assembly's resources are used properly and efficiently. It examines and reports on the reports of the accounts of the Assembly prepared by the Auditor General for Wales. It may take evidence on behalf of the House of Commons' Public Accounts Committee, which can continue to investigate public expenditure in Wales. *Regional Committees* for each of the four regions of Wales have to meet in their regions at least twice a year and advise the Assembly on matters affecting the relevant region.

V. ENGLAND

5–042   England is the only country in the United Kingdom without its own particular institutions.[5] A separate regional parliament and government for England would put England in the same position as Scotland, Wales and Northern Ireland. This solution would be a move towards a federation in which England, by virtue of its size, would be dominant and become a rival to Westminster. It was for these reasons that in 1973 the Kilbrandon Commission concluded that a United Kingdom federation of four countries with a federal Parliament and four provincial Parliaments was unrealistic.[6] A variation would be to exclude Scottish, Welsh and Northern Irish M.P.s from taking part in "English business" at Westminster, creating an English parliament within Westminster.[7] The problem with this solution is that it ignores the fact that any issue involving the expenditure of public money is of concern to all of the United Kingdom, since the level of the block grant to the devolved administrations is dependant on the level of expenditure in England.[8] The least radical solution would be to introduce a

---

[5] This raises the role of Scottish M.P.s in the passing of legislation that will not apply to Scotland, see *post* para. 5–045.

[6] Cmnd. 5460.

[7] See H.C. 185 (1998–99) for a discussion of this proposal; it is a proposal which appears to have the support of the Conservative Party. See Robert Hazell, "The English question: can Westminster be a proxy for an English Parliament?" [2001] P.L. 268.

[8] *ante* para. 5–018.

variety of procedural reforms within Westminster.[9] The alternative would be to create a series of regional assemblies for the various regions of England.[10] Although no moves have been made towards any of these solutions, the Regional Development Agencies Act 1998 could be regarded as a first step towards regional devolution within England.

The Regional Development Agencies Act 1998 provides for the creation of eight new Regional Development Agencies which came into effect from April 1999.[11] The purposes of these agencies is: to further economic development and regeneration; to promote business, employment and the development of the skills required in the relevant area; and where relevant to an area, to contribute to sustainable development in the United Kingdom (section 4).[12] Broad powers are conferred on the Agencies to do whatever they think is necessary to achieve these purposes (section 3). The Agencies are established as non-department public bodies, to operate independently from government (section 3). However, the Secretary of State has extensive statutory powers with respect to the Agencies including the power to appoint members, alter the extent of a region, make grants, issue guidance and directions. The ability of the RDAs to implement the roles assigned to them was initially constrained by their budgets and restrictions on how they spend the money allocated to them.[13]

The RDA Act provides the potential for a statutory relationship to develop between RDAs and Regional Chambers. Regional Chambers are non-statutory bodies which have been set up as voluntary associations of local councillors and representatives from businesses, trade unions, voluntary organisations etc. All eight English regions have established such Chambers, most calling such bodies "assemblies". Where the Secretary of State is of the opinion that a Chamber is suitable[14] he may designate it as the Regional Chamber for the region (section 8), thereby requiring the RDA in the exercise of its functions, to consult and have regard to the views expressed by the Chamber. Section 18 enables the Secretary of State to extend the roles of the Chambers by developing a line of accountability between a RDA and a Regional Chamber. How this will work will depend on the directions given by the Secretary of State which could include directing that the RDA should supply the Chamber with certain specified information and answer questions about the information supplied by it to the Chamber. The fact that the Chambers are unelected and lack statutory authority limits the extend to which they can develop meaningful powers. The pressure for regional assemblies in England is uneven with the regional bodies in the north of England taking most of the initiatives.

5–043

Government Offices

In 1994 Government Offices were established in each of the eight English regions with the task of providing better integration of government activity. The work of these regional offices should be strengthened by the establishment in April 2000 of a Regional Coordination Unit, headed by a government minister.

5–044

---

[9] *post* para. 5–046.

[10] One of the problems with this solution is that there are not always obvious regions within England.

[11] Provision was made for a ninth Agency in London, which was established in April 2000 as part of the Greater London Authority.

[12] See the White Paper, *Building Partnerships for Prosperity*, Cm. 3814 (1997).

[13] Combined RDA budgets should rise by £500m per year by 2003–4.

[14] The basic criteria were laid down in the White Paper (Cm. 3814 (1997)); further guidance was issued in September 1998.

It remains to be seen whether these initiatives (and proposals to establish formal relationships between regional Government Offices with RDAs) will strengthen central government in the regions rather than encourage regionalism.

Westminster and England, Scotland, Wales and Northern Ireland

5–045   No immediate change was made in the number of M.P.s sent to Westminster by Scotland, Wales or Northern Ireland. Section 86 of the Scotland Act 1998 by amending the rules for the redistribution of seats in the Parliamentary Constituencies Act 1986, allows for a reduction in the number of Scottish seats in the House of Commons[15]; this reduction is to be put into effect after the next review by the Boundary Commission for Scotland, sometime between 2002 and 2006. No similar provisions are found in the legislation for Wales or Northern Ireland.[16]

A matter that has not been resolved is what has come to be known as the "West Lothian Question",[17] or more accurately the English Question. Since M.P.s representing English, Welsh or Northern Ireland constituencies have no votes on legislation passed by the Scottish Parliament, why should M.P.s representing Scottish constituencies at Westminster be allowed to vote on legislation which applies to England and Wales, but not to Scotland? No solution has been put forward to this question by the Government. Possible solutions were discussed above.[18]

5–046   Prior to devolution Scotland, Wales and Northern Ireland each had a Grand Committee in the House of Commons. These committees, in particular the Scottish Grand Committee, had their roles enhanced in 1994–95 to enable them to hold ministers to account and debate matters of concern to the relevant country. The Procedure Committee has concluded that post-devolution such committees should be abolished.[19] There was no equivalent committee for England—a Committee on Regional Affairs had been established and abandoned in the mid 1970s. The standing orders to update and re-establish this committee were approved by the Commons in April 2000 and it met once, the day before the House was dissolved in May 2001. The committee had 15 members representing English constituencies, and its meetings could be attended by any English M.P.; its role was to consider any matter relating to regional affairs in England which might be referred to it.[20] If re-established, it could become a forum for English regional issues. Westminster Hall sessions[21] could provide another opportunity to debate matters pertaining to England.

---

[15] See *post* Chap. 10. At present there are 72 Scottish constituencies, which is likely to be reduced to about 58. Schedule 1 to the Scotland Act requires constituencies for the Scottish Parliament to be the same as the Westminster constituencies; unless the Scotland Act is amended, a reduction in the number of Westminster constituencies would result in a reduction in the size of the Scottish Parliament.

[16] From 1922 to 1979 Northern Ireland sent 12 M.P.s to Westminster; as a consequence of the abolition of the Northern Ireland Parliament and the imposition of direct rule this was eventually raised to 17 in 1979, and subsequently to 18.

[17] Named after the constituency then represented by Mr Tam Dalyell who raised issue in the 1970s.

[18] *ante* para. 5–042.

[19] H.C. 376 (1998–99).

[20] S.O. 117.

[21] *post* para. 11–017.

VI. Devolution and Intra-Government Relations[22]

The relationship between the devolved institutions and the United Kingdom is **5–047** one that is being worked out using a mixture of informal and formal machinery. The *Memorandum of Understanding*[23] and supplementary agreements provide the basis for these relationships. It established the Joint Ministerial Committee and set out five principles to govern intra-governmental relations post devolution: good communication; co-operation; exchange of scientific, technical and policy information; confidentiality; accountability. At the informal level there are the daily contacts between the relevant Whitehall department and the relevant departments in the devolved administrations. The relationships between departments are found in concordats, some of which were published at the same time as the *Memorandum of Understanding*[24] one clear purpose of these concordats is to avoid litigation. In addition Devolution Guidance Notes are published from time to time by the Cabinet Office.[25]

At the formal level the *Joint Ministerial Committee* (JMC) was established to provide central co-ordination of the overall relationship between the United Kingdom government and the devolved institutions. It is a meeting of the Prime Minister and his deputy, the Scottish and Northern Irish First Ministers and Deputy First Ministers, the Welsh First Minister and one other Minister and the territorial Secretaries of State, and has to meet in plenary session once a year. It may also meet in a functional format with representatives of the relevant Ministers of, for example, health or education, or in a bilateral format where there is a dispute between the United Kingdom Government and a devolved administration. The chair is always taken by a United Kingdom Government Minister.

The Belfast Agreement committed the parties to the creation of institutions on an all Ireland basis and on a United Kingdom and Irish basis. The *North-South Ministerial Council* is a meeting of Ministers from the Republic of Ireland and Northern Ireland with the purpose of developing "consultation, cooperation and action within the island of Ireland."[26] Its terms of reference laid down in the Belfast agreement are that it is to: exchange information, discuss and consult; use best endeavours to reach agreement on the adoption of common policies; take decisions on policies for implementation separately in each jurisdiction; take decisions on policies and actions for cross-border bodies. It has met regularly since power was devolved to Northern Ireland.

The *British-Irish Council* was created to provide for "harmonious and mutu- **5–048** ally beneficial development of the totally of relationships among the people of these islands."[27] It includes representatives from the British and Irish governments, the devolved administrations, the Isle of Man and the Channel Islands. It meets twice a year in plenary format, and can meet in functional format at any

---

[22] See R. Cornes, "Intergovernmental Relations in a Devolved United Kingdom: Making Devolution Work", in *Constitutional Futures: a history of the next ten years* (R. Hazell ed., 1999); R. Hazell "Intergovernmental Relations: Whitehall Rules OK?" in *The State and the Nations* (R. Hazell, ed., 2000). J. Poirer, "The Functions of Intergovermental Agreements: Post-Devolution Concordats in a Comparative Perspective", [2001] P.L. 134

[23] Cm. 4444 (1999). It is stated that this is a statement of political intent and not a binding agreement.

[24] The four published with the *Memorandum* were on Coordination of E.U. Policy Issues; Financial Assistance to Industry; International Relations and Statistics.

[25] *e.g.* on the roles of the territorial Secretaries of State; post devolution primary legislation affecting Scotland and Wales.

[26] Cm. 4294 (1999).

[27] Belfast Agreement.

other time. In the first meeting drugs, social exclusion, environment, transport and the knowledge economy were discussed. The *British-Irish Intergovernmental Conference* is a standing Conference of the British and Irish governments designed to promote bilateral co-operation on matters of mutual interest. Its main focus is likely to be security matters.

5–049   An area where there is potential for conflict between the devolved administrations and the United Kingdom government is European policy.[28] Matters such as agriculture, transport and the environment have been devolved, but these are matters which are also subject to E.U. law. It is the United Kingdom government which is responsible for representing the interests of the devolved administrations as well as that of the United Kingdom as a whole. The devolved bodies have to observe European law, and may be required to implement directives: providing a concurrent power of implementation with Westminster. This is one of the most complicated parts of the devolved relationship, and was the subject of one of the first concordats. The concordat provides for full information to be provided to the devolved administrations and for consultations to allow the latter to have input into the government negotiating line. It is possible for ministers from the devolved administrations to be part of the United Kingdom delegation to the Council of Ministers. The JMC meeting in European format may be used to discuss and resolve European matters; European matters may also be discussed in the three institutions established under the Belfast Agreement. All three devolved administrations have opened offices in Brussels, but they are required to act in a manner consistent with the responsibilities of the United Kingdom government for European matters.

The future of devolution and the unitary constitution[29]

5–050   Devolution in Northern Ireland is subject to pressures unlike those found in the other countries: policing, decommissioning, violence, sectarianism. Even without these problems it has been suggested that the devolution settlement is based on a "democratic constitution unlike any other attempted", which asks the Northern Ireland politicians to "make something work that on its face is unworkable".[30] Direct rule of the Province from Westminster may return.

Devolution for Scotland and to a lesser extent for Wales, was in part to prevent demands for separatism and to preserve the Union. The different schemes for Scotland and Wales not only reflected the differences in administrative devolution to the two countries before 1998, they also reflected the perceived lack of substantial support for devolution in Wales. The scheme of only giving executive devolution to Wales may be temporary. The workings of the Welsh National Assembly are being considered by a Review Group from the Assembly, and an independent review of the Assembly's powers has been instituted. How quickly pressure is put on Westminster to provide Wales with something similar to that found in Scotland, may depend on how United Kingdom governments respond to Welsh interests in preparing their legislative programmes. Scotland, despite its Parliament with legislative powers, may also ask for more powers. Should Scotland wish to seek independence it could not do so unilaterally: the Scottish Parliament cannot amend the Scotland Act, the matter would be for negotiation with the rest of the United Kingdom. Unlike Northern Ireland, where the devolution legislation provides for the right of the people of Northern Ireland to

---

[28] Geoffrey Clark, "Scottish Devolution and the European Union" [1999] P.L. 504.

[29] Borrows, Chap. 7 "The future of Devolution?" in *Devolution* (2000).

[30] Alan Ward, in *The Changing Constitution* (Jowell and Oliver eds, 4th ed., 2000) pp. 133, 134.

leave the union if and when a majority so wishes, leaving the union is not formally part of the 1998 constitutional settlement with Scotland.[31]

Devolution is accommodated within the unitary British state. It has resulted in **5–051** the limitation of the power of the central state, while still maintaining the sovereignty of the Westminster Parliament.[32] What has been achieved has some of the characteristics of a federation[33]: the Judicial Committee of the Privy Council as a new constitutional court; a formal division of legislative powers between Westminster and Scotland and Northern Ireland respectively; the use of referendums politically, if not legally, to entrench the arrangements; institutional machinery to consider inter-governmental relations. There are several ways in which the devolution arrangements are quite different from those found in a federation: the statutes establishing the devolved systems are subject to the legislative control of Westminster[34]; the schemes for devolution are different in all three countries; England has no institutions exercising devolved powers and United Kingdom Ministers represent the interest of England and the United Kingdom in inter-governmental discussions with representatives of the devolved bodies; financially the devolved administrations are dependant on the centre for funding. The United Kingdom has not become a federal system, but it is moving in at least a quasi-federal direction.

---

[31] The Union with Scotland Act 1706 and the Union with England Act 1707 remain in force and have effect subject to the Scotland Act 1998 (s.37).

[32] *ante* para. 5–014.

[33] See A.V. Dicey, *Introduction to the Law of the Constitution*, 10th ed. (1959) p. 144.

[34] Although it is arguable that with respect to Scotland this is of greater legal than political significance, see *ante* para. 5–014.

CHAPTER 6

THE UNITED KINGDOM AND EUROPE

I. INTRODUCTION

6–001   In Western Europe, in the years following the end of the Second World War, statesmen's actions and policies were guided by their memories of the atrocities of the recently defeated Nazi regime in Germany and the growing threat posed by the Red Army in the East of Europe and powerful Communist parties, loyal to the Soviets, in the Western democracies, particularly in Italy and France. The newly adopted written constitutions of the European democracies recognised the fundamental value of human rights and the status of international law as superior to municipal law. These developments led to a European-wide recognition of the importance of certain basic human rights in the European Convention for the Protection of Human Rights and Fundamental Freedom, 1950. This Convention, in the drafting of which British lawyers played a leading role, was ratified by the United Kingdom in 1951. The subsequent history of the Convention in British courts and the coming into force of the Human Rights Act 1998 in October 2000 are considered later in Chapter 22.

The Convention on Human Rights was adopted by the Council of Europe, a widely based body, established in 1949, to safeguard and realise the ideals and principles which represent their common heritage. At the same time, however, a smaller group of six nations—France, the German Federal Republic,[1] Italy, Belgium, Holland and Luxembourg—set about establishing close economic and commercial links which would both strengthen the individual members but also remove the possibility of war between them from the future. It is these early plans which explain the use in the plural of the phrase "European Communities" and despite the subsequent creation of a European Union, these bodies retain their separate, if attenuated existence. In 1951 the six created the European Coal and Steel Community by the Treaty of Paris; in 1957 the European Atomic Energy Community and the European Economic Community were established by two Treaties of Rome. The United Kingdom, after a period of scepticism, applied to join the Communities in 1961, when Mr Macmillan was Prime Minister and Mr Heath led the negotiations on behalf of the Government. This attempt to join was frustrated in 1963 by France. Mr Wilson's Government renewed the application in 1967, and negotiations were continued after the general election of 1970 by Mr Heath's Government. With the approval of Parliament a Treaty of Accession was signed at Brussels in 1972, to take effect from January 1, 1973. At the same time Denmark and the Republic of Ireland become members. Subsequently Greece, Spain, Portugal, Austria, Finland and Sweden have become members. Norway has twice successfully applied for membership but on both occasions

---

[1] *i.e.* West Germany with its capital at Bonn. East Germany was a satellite of Russia and Berlin was administered by a commission representing the four (former) allies—the United States, the United Kingdom, France and Russia—until the unification of Germany in 1989, following the dismantling of the Berlin Wall.

(1972 and 1995) the Norwegian voters have rejected membership in a referendum. At present a large number of other states, many formerly part of the Russian Communist Empire, are in the process of attempting to join the Communities.[2]

Important amendments to the provisions of the original treaties were effected **6–002** by the agreement known as the Single European Act which was signed in 1986 and entered into force in 1987.

In 1993 even more extensive amendments and developments were effected by the Treaty of European Union (the Maastricht Treaty) which, *inter alia* created the European Union. Further important reforms were effected by the Treaty of Amsterdam which came into effect in 1999. At the time of writing negotiations on further changes, particularly to cope with the accession of new members, have been concluded and will lead, when ratified to a Treaty of Nice.

The constitutional significance of the United Kingdom membership of the Communities and the Union rests in the unique relationship between our domestic law and the law emanating from the Treaty of Rome which established the European Economic Community (renamed the European Community by the Maastricht Treaty). From the beginning of the Coal and Steel Community in 1951 the members envisaged an organisation where, contrary to the traditional principles of international law, decisions of community bodies would have a supra-national authority inside the territories of the Member States. The relationship of national and community law would be one of *monism*, not *dualism*. It is this feature of Community law which presents problems for all Member States but particularly for the United Kingdom which has never accorded any authority to treaty law unless made part of domestic law by legislation.[3]

Before, however, considering this issue it is convenient to outline briefly at this stage the structure and institutions of the Union and allied communities, the sources of Community law and the special characteristics of the legal orders created by the treaties.[4]

The Institutions

Article 7[4] of the European Community Treaty, as amended and renumbered,[5] **6–003** provides that the tasks entrusted to the Community shall be carried out by a European Parliament, a Council, a Commission, a Court of Justice and a Court of Auditors. Each institution shall act within the limits of the powers conferred upon it by the Treaty. The Council and the Commission are assisted by an Economic and Social Committee and a Committee of the Regions, acting in an advisory capacity.

---

[2] Bulgaria, the Czech Republic, Hungary, Poland, Romania, Slovakia, Slovenia, Estonia, Latvia, Lithuania, Cyprus, Malta and Turkey.

[3] *ante*, para. 3–026 and *post*, para. 15–028 *et seq.*

[4] See further, A. Arnull, A. Dashwood, M. Ross and D. Wyatt, *Wyatt and Dashwood's European Union Law* (4th ed., 2000, Sweet & Maxwell); S. Weatherill and P. Beaumont, *European Union Law* (3rd ed., 1999, Penguin); T. C. Hartley, *Foundations of European Community Law* (4th ed., 2000, Oxford); L. Collins, *European Community Law in the United Kingdom* (5th ed., 2001).

[5] The Treaty on European Union formally effected the change of name from European Economic Community. The Treaty of Amsterdam renumbered the Articles of the EC Treaty, the new number being given here first and the old number in brackets. The old numbers will still be found in judgments and literature pre-dating the Treaty of Amsterdam. Although there continue to exist distinct communities they operate through one set of institutions which exercise, as appropriate, the relevant powers under the particular constituting treaty.

Article 4[D] of the Treaty on European Union gives formal recognition to the existence of the European Council—a regular meeting of ministers which had developed a *de facto* existence outside the provisions of the various treaties. The European Council brings together the Heads of State or of Government of the Member States and the President of the Commission. The European Council meets at least twice a year under the chairmanship of the Head of State or of Government which holds the Presidency of the Council. It submits a report to the European Parliament after each of its meetings and a yearly written report on the progress achieved by the Union.

The European Parliament

6–004   For the first 30 years of its life the European Parliament was correctly referred to as the Assembly and, until elections held in 1979, its members were chosen by the legislatures of the Member States from among their own members. The new title, which dates from the coming into effect of the Single European Act, reflects its changing role as a body, directly elected by voters of the Member States and its growing powers. At present the Parliament has 626 members. The representation by state ranges from 99 (Germany) to 6 (Luxembourg).[6] Inevitably, to put any limit on overall size, while allowing effective representation for the smaller states, the smaller states, in terms of votes required to elect a member, are over represented compared to the larger.

The Treaty of Nice envisages an expansion in numbers to 738. To accommodate the new members will require a reduction in the representation of the existing members—except for Luxembourg which retains six members and Germany whose continued 99 will reflect its pre-eminent position in terms of population, while France, Italy and the United Kingdom for example will each lose 13 members. Spain will lose 12 members and with 52 members will have equal representation to Poland, the largest of the aspiring entrants.[7]

The Parliament now has extensive powers in various fields: it participates in the law-making processes of the Communities; it shares budgetary powers with the Council and has powers of supervision over the Commission with the ultimate power of a motion of censure over the Commission as a whole: Art. 201 [144]. In March 1999 the then Commission resigned *en masse* after a critical report on its conduct without the Parliament moving to a formal vote of censure. Whatever lessons can or should be drawn from that surprising event, it clearly means that the Parliament can no longer be disregarded in the workings of the Communities.

The Council

6–005   This body, which must be distinguished from the European Council, was established by the founding treaties. The Council consists of a representative of each Member State at ministerial level, authorised to commit the government of that Member State: Art. 203 [146]. The importance of the Council is clear from the terms of Art. 202 [145] which provides that the Council is to ensure co-ordination of the general economic policies of the Member States and to make decisions.

---

[6] France, Italy and the United Kingdom each has 87 members; Spain, 64; Holland, 31; Belgium, Greece and Portugal, 25 each; Denmark and Finland, 16 each; Ireland, 15; Sweden, 22;
[7] Of the other existing members Belgium, Greece and Portugal will have 20 members each, Sweden 18; Denmark and Finland, 13 each; Ireland, 12.

Article 205(1)[148(1)] provides that the Council may reach decisions by a majority vote of its members, except where otherwise provided in the Treaty. In most cases where a decision can be reached by a majority the Treaty requires a "qualified majority", that is by 62 votes out of 87. For this purpose each member state has a number of votes, weighted to represent its population: Luxembourg has two votes, France 10.[8] Germany also has 10 although since reunification its population is greater than that of France or any other member state. Its wish to see this distinction reflected in voting power led to difficulties in the negotiations leading to the Treaty of Nice. But in Europe there is a solution to every difficulty. In the new enlarged Council France and Germany will continue to have the same voting power: 29. But a qualified majority will require not merely a certain number of votes (255) but also that that majority represents countries whose combined population amounts to 62 per cent of the population of the Communities—thus giving added importance to the German vote while retaining numerical equality between France and Germany.[9]

Another source of dissension at Nice was the extension of qualified majority voting to issues which had hitherto required unanimity.   **6–006**

Earlier disputes, even where the Treaties provided for decision-making by qualified majority, revealed an insight into the political reality behind the language of the texts. In 1966 the Members of the Council adopted the Luxembourg Compromise in which they agreed that where a member state regarded a decision as involving an important national interest the Council, instead of proceeding by qualified majority, would attempt to reach a solution acceptable to all members. The legal status of the compromise was regarded as open to doubt and the members did not agree on exactly what had been settled by it.[10] However, provisions similar in terms to the Compromise now appear in the Community Treaty and the Treaty on European Union.[11]

The Commission

Article 211 [155] defines the role of the Commission as ensuring the proper   **6–007** functioning and development of the common market.

Article 213 [157] provides that the Commission consists of 20 members. The Commissioners must be chosen on the grounds of their general competence and their independence must be beyond doubt. They must act in the general interest of the Community and be completely independent in the performance of their duties. Nonetheless the Member States insist on ensuring that each has a national on the Commission (in the case of the smaller states) and two nationals (in the case of Germany, France, Italy, Spain and the United Kingdom). The nomination of the President (chosen by common accord of the governments of the Member States: Art. 216 [158]) and of the Commissioners (chosen by the government of the President-designate) are subject to approval by the European Parliament.

[8] Italy and the United Kingdom have 10 votes; Spain 8; Belgium, Greece, Holland and Portugal, 5; Austria and Sweden, 4; Denmark, Ireland and Finland, 3.

[9] The proposed new voting arrangements for the other existing members: Italy and the United Kingdom, 29 votes each; Spain, 27; Belgium, Greece, Holland and Portugal, 13; Austria and Sweden, 10; Denmark, Ireland and Finland, 7. Of the proposed entrants, Poland will receive 27 votes, while at the other extreme 4 votes are proposed for Cyprus and Latvia, 3 for Malta.

[10] The United Kingdom invoked the Compromise unsuccessfully in 1982; Germany, successfully, in 1985.

[11] Art. 11 [5a] EC Treaty (initiatives on closer co-operation in the Community sphere); Art. 40 [K. 12] TEU (closer co-operation in the fields of Justice and Home Affairs); Art. 23(2) [J.13(2)] TEU (common foreign and security policy).

Commissioners are appointed for a term of five years, which is renewable and their decisions are reached by a simple majority.

As the number of Member States increases reforms will obviously be required to the method of nominating Commissioners if the body is not to become too large to function effectively. At Nice a maximum number of 27 Commissioners was envisaged. The larger states would give up their right to nominate two commissioners from 2005 and a rotation system will keep the size of the Commission to the agreed maximum.

The Commission has a wide range of important powers and duties. Article 211 [155] provides that it shall ensure the application of the provisions of the Treaty. It may make recommendations to the Council relating to the making of new law and is responsible for carrying out the policies given legal effect by decisions of the Council. Article 226 [169] confers a power to ensure compliance with the terms of the Treaty by Member States and, if necessary, institute proceedings before the Court of Justice.[12]

The Court[13]

6–008   The Court of Justice at present consists of 15 judges (Art. 221 [165]), assisted by 8 Advocates-General (Art. 222 [166]).[14] The Court may sit in plenary session or in Chambers, consisting of three or five judges. Article 223 provides that the judges and advocates-general must possess the qualifications required for appointment to the highest judicial offices in their respective countries or be jurisconsults of recognised competence. The further requirement that appointment (for a term of six years) shall be by common accord of the governments of the Member States has enabled the Member States to ensure that each has one of its nationals appointed to the Court. (The five largest states always provide an advocate general).

The increasing work load of the Court with the resulting delays in dealing with case led to the establishment of a Court of First Instance in 1988 by the Council, exercising powers conferred on it by the Single European Act and now to be found in Art. 225 [168a] of the Treaty. As with the Court of Justice, membership equals the number of Member States and there is one national from each state. The Court of First Instance also sits in Chambers of three or five judges which may delegate the power to hear a case to a single judge. Appeal on a point of law lies to the Court of Justice.

Article 220 [164] gives the Court of Justice the duty to ensure that in the interpretation and application of the Treaty the law is observed. The Court does this through two distinct heads of jurisdiction. Direct Actions are those in which the Court applies Community law to actions before it involving the Member States and the organs of the Community.[15] It is this type of jurisdiction alone which is possessed by the Court of First Instance.

6–009   Under Article 234 [177] the Court of Justice (but not the Court of First Instance) may give preliminary rulings on questions of community law referred

---

[12] The Commission also has a role in proceedings under Article 227 [170] where proceedings are instituted by a member state.

[13] A. Arnull, *The European Union and its Court of Justice* (Oxford, 1999); L. Neville Brown and T. Kennedy, *Brown and Jacobs, The Court of Justice of the European Communities* (5th ed., Sweet & Maxwell, 2000).

[14] See Brown and Kennedy, *op. cit.*, Chap. 4.

[15] *e.g.* Article 226 [169] (actions brought by Commission); Article 227 [170] (actions brought by member states); Article 236 [173] (judicial review of Community acts).

to it by municipal courts. This provision is designed to ensure uniformity of application of community law by municipal courts. It is not an appellate procedure. Thus in the *Factortame* litigation the *existence* of jurisdiction to award interim relief for an alleged breach of a community right was referred to the Court of Justice by the House of Lords.[16] The *exercise* of that jurisdiction, once the Court of Justice had found that it existed, was for the national Court, that is the House of Lords.[17] Similarly, the Court of Justice in a reference relating to the deportation of community nationals laid down the principle—that not every criminal conviction justified deportation: the conduct in question must constitute a genuine and serious threat to public order—but whether the facts of the particular case fell within that principle was for the national court to determine.[18] The full significance of Article 234 [177] will become obvious later in this Chapter.

The Treaty of Nice will make some important changes to the provisions of the EC Treaty which relate to the two Courts. Article 221[165] will be amended to provide that the Court of Justice will consist of one judge per Member State. The number of Advocates General may be increased from 8 on the request of the Court by a unanimous vote of the Council: Article 222[166]. The Court of First Instance will comprise at least one judge per Member State, the number of judges to be determined by the Statute of the Court of Justice. The Statute may also provide for the Court to be assisted by Advocates General: Article 225[168a]. An innovation, designed to deal with the increasing work load of the two courts is contained in the new Article 225a which provides for the creation of judicial panels to hear cases at first instance in specific areas, with a right of appeal on law only, if so provided, on law and fact, to the Court of First Instance. Finally Article 220 [164] is amended to include a reference to the Court of First Instance in respect of the obligation to ensure the observation of the law in the interpretation and application of the Treaty and to provide for the creation of judicial panels under the new Article 225a.

The Court of Auditors

The Court of Auditors has been included in Article 7[4] as one of the five **6–010** Community Institutions since the Treaty of Maastricht although it had been established in 1975, succeeding to the role and duties of the Audit Board. At present the Court consists of 15 members; under the Treaty of Nice it will consist of one national from each Member State: Article 247 [1886]. The Court of Auditors is responsible for examining Community accounts and reporting to the European Parliament on them: Article 248 [188c].

The Sources of Community Law

Community Law is derived from a number of sources. First, obviously, the **6–011** provisions of relevant treaties, as they are interpreted by the Court of Justice.

---

[16] *R. v. Secretary of State for Transport ex p. Factortame Ltd* [1990] 2 A.C. 85, HL.

[17] *R. v. Secretary of State for Transport ex p. Factortame Ltd* [1990] E.C.R.I.-2433; [1990] 3 C.M.L.R. 375 (E.C.J.); [1991] 1 A.C. 603, HL.

[18] [1981] Q.B. 778, Div.Ct. and CA; [1980] 2 C.M.L.R. 308, ECJ Templeman L.J. commented, "The Divisional Court was obliged to turn its back on reality and to propound certain questions to the European Court of Justice. Immersed in the cloudy generality of its functions under article 177 of the EEC Treaty, the European Court was also obliged to ignore reality but furnished replies which enable this court now to approach the moment of truth"; [1981] Q.B. 778, 797. See A. Arnull, *The European Union and its Court of Justice* (Oxford, 1999) pp. 49–69.

Secondly, law made in accordance with the provisions of those treaties.[19] In particular Article 249 [189] of the Community Treaty provides for the making of regulations and directives which are, in effect, legislation and, as will be seen, may confer rights on individuals in municipal courts and result in liability on the part of Member States to litigants for breach of community law. The same Article recognises a power to make decisions which are binding on those to whom they are addressed. Decisions may, according to the Court of Justice, confer rights on third parties.[20] Thirdly, the Court of Justice, in discharging its duty to "ensure that in the interpretation and application of this Treaty the law is observed", (Article 220 [164]), has called upon general principles of law which it has identified as inherent in the Treaty or common to the laws of Member States,[21] Explicit references to this source can be found for example in Article 288 [215] of the EC Treaty which directs the Court to decide questions relating to the non-contractual liability of the Community "in accordance with the general principles common to the laws of the Member States" and Article 6[F] of Treaty on European Union which provides that the Union shall respect fundamental rights as guaranteed by the European Convention for the Protection of Human Rights . . . *and as they result* from the constitutional traditions common to the Member States as general principles of Community law. (It could be said that the Court had anticipated this statement by its own decisions in cases such as *Internationale Handelsgesellschaft*[22] and *Nold v. Commission*.[23])

Supremacy and Direct Applicability

6–012   In Chapter 4 we saw that the European Court regards community law as superior to any conflicting domestic legislation and that the House of Lords has applied this approach even to the terms of legislation enacted after the European Communities Act 1972.[24] Here it remains to consider another fundamental characteristic of the legal order developed by the Court of Justice, its capacity to create rights which individuals can enforce in municipal courts, without the need for municipal legislation, a characteristic referred to as direct effectiveness.[25] (Regulations are *directly applicable* in all Member States, in the language of Article 249 [189]; it will be in any particular case a matter of applying the tests outlined in the following paragraphs to establish whether a particular litigant can establish under a Regulation a directly effective right which can be protected in a municipal court.)

Direct effectiveness may be *vertical*, that is applicable between individual litigants and Member States and public bodies forming part of the state, or *horizontal* that is applicable between private litigants. Both types of effectiveness have been found applicable in the case of treaty provisions and regulations. In the case of directives, effective is limited to *vertical* effectiveness.

---

[19] "One of the most striking characteristics of the legal order established by the Treaty is the competence vested in the Community institutions to enact legislation for the purposes of carrying out the objectives of the Treaty;" Wyatt and Dashwood's European Union Law (4th ed., 2000, Sweet & Maxwell), p. 83.

[20] *Grad v. Finanzamt Traunstein* [1970] E.C.R. 825.

[21] J. A. Usher, *General Principles of EC Law* (Longman, 1998); T. Tridimas, *The General Principles of EC Law* (Oxford, 1999). See further, Pt V of this Chapter.

[22] [1970] E.C.R. 1125; [1972] C.M.L.R. 112.

[23] [1974] E.C.R. 491; [1974] 2 C.M.L.R. 338. See Tridimas, *op.cit.*, Chap. 6 and *post* Chap. 22.

[24] *ante* para. 4–020 *et seq.*

[25] Chap. 4.

To be directly effective, a rule of Community law—whether a provision of the EEC Treaty or of a Regulation or Directive or Decision made under the Treaty—must be clear and unconditional; capable of being implemented without legislative intervention by the Member States and by its nature indicate that it does not only concern the Member States in their relations *inter se*. In the *Van Gend en Loos* case[26] the European Court held that Article 12 of the Treaty which forbade the introduction of new customs duties or any increase in existing duties, had vertical direct effect so that an individual could rely on its terms in a natural court against a public body, the Dutch Inland Revenue Administration. In *Belgische Radio en Televisie v. SABAM*[27] the European Court gave horizontal direct effect to Articles 85 and 86 of the Treaty which forbid practices which unduly reduce competition or amount to an abuse of a dominant trading position. In *Defrenne v. Sabena (No. 2)*[28] the European court held that the principle of equal pay for equal work, laid down by Article 119 had vertical direct effect.[29] Regulations are explicitly recognised under Article 189 as being directly applicable. Direct vertical effectiveness was attributed by the European Court to two Regulations providing for the payment of premiums in respect of slaughtered dairy cows in *Orsolina Leonesio v. Minister for Agriculture and Forestry of the Italian Republic*.[30] The nature of Regulations, as explained by the Court,[31] is such that there can be no doubt that they are also capable of having vertical direct effect.

The distinction between vertical and horizontal effectiveness assumes a particular importance in the case of Directives since Article 249 [189] provides that directives are binding upon Member States as to the result to be achieved but leave to the national authorities the choice of form and methods. At first sight it might be thought hard to argue that a directive could satisfy the tests of clarity, certainty and lack of necessity for municipal legislation laid down in *Van Gend en Loos*.   **6–013**

The possibility of *vertical* direct effect was, however, recognised by the Court of Justice in *Van Duyn v. Home Office*.[32] The right to rely on a sufficiently clear and unequivocal term in a directive arises when a Member State has failed to implement the directive in its municipal law by the end of the period prescribed or has failed to implement it correctly.[33] The Court has refused, on the other hand, to recognise horizontal direct effect.[34] Nonetheless pressure continues to extend the effectiveness of directives at the instance of litigants to and in a

---

[26] [1963] E.C.R. 1.

[27] [1974] E.C.R. 51; cited by the Court of Appeal in *Application des Gaz S.A. v. Falks Veritas Ltd* [1974] Ch. 381.

[28] [1976] E.C.R. 455. See *Snoxell and Davies v. Vauxhall Motors* [1978] Q.B. 11.

[29] The Court ruled that direct effect was to be limited to the future so its decision could not open the floodgates to claims based on facts occurring before its judgment in that case.

[30] [1972] E.C.R. 287.

[31] *Hanptzollamt Bremen-Freihafen v. Waren-Import Gesellschaft Krohn & Co* [1970] E.C.R. 451; *Politi S.A.S. v. Italian Minister of Finance* [1971] E.C.R. 1039; *Fratelli Variola v. Italian Minister of Finance* [1973] E.C.R. 981.

[32] [1974] E.C.R. 1337; [1975] Ch. 338. (Directive on free movement of workers, implementing Art. 39[48] on the free movement of workers). A decision noteworthy also as the first reference by an English Court under Art. 234[177].

[33] *Co-operative Agricola Zootecrucia S. Antonio and Others v. Amministrazione delle finanze dello Stato* [1996] E.C.R. I-4373.

[34] *Ratti* [1979] E.C.R. 1629; *Marshall v. Southampton and South West Hampshire Area Health Authority* [1986] E.C.R. 723; *Foster v. British Gas* [1990] E.C.R. I- 3313; *Paola Faccini Dori v. Recreb Srl* [1994] E.C.R. I- 3325.

number of cases the Court has seemed to come close to allowing something very like horizontal effect.[35]

An indirect effect has been accorded by the Court of Justice to the provisions of directives even although not themselves directly effective by the adoption of the principle in a number of decisions that national courts must interpret national law—and in particular national law introduced to give effect to non-directly effective provisions of a directive—in the light of the wording and purpose of the directive. The principle applies to legislation whether the provisions in question were adopted before or after the directive. Since the principle is one of inter-pretation or construction it follows that in some cases the national legislations cannot be made to be consistent with the terms of the directive, in which case the principles explained in the following paragraph become relevant.[36] Despite dicta not always entirely consistent with *Marleasing* the House of Lords has probably moved to a position in accordance with that decision.[37]

6–014   The duty to interpret national law consistently with the provisions of directives is subject to the general principles of community law and thus in the area of criminal liability for breach of directive provisions the municipal courts must respect the principles of legal certainty and non-retroactivity.[38]

The principles so far discussed prevent national legal systems legislating in a way which is incompatible with community law: they do not, however, provide a remedy for a litigant whose community right has been initially infringed, or indeed merely ignored by a failure to legislate. That gap was filled by the decision in *Andrea Francovich v. Italian Republic*[39] which recognised a liability in damages on the part of states for failure to comply with their obligation to implement community law. In that case Italy had failed, within the time limit specified to implement the terms of a directive. In the later cases of *Brasserie du Pecheur S.A. v. Germany*, and *R. v. Secretary of State for Transport ex p. Factortame Ltd (No. 4)*[40] the Court applied the principle to the situation where a breach of Community law arose from the provisions of municipal law. Again the Court recognised a right to damages. In both situations the rule of Community law relied on must be intended to confer rights on individuals. There must be a direct causal link between the breach and the damage sustained. Where the Member State has a discretion in adopting national rules the alleged breach must arise from a manifest disregarding of the limits of its discretion. Although the

---

[35] Lackhoff and Nyssens, "Direct Effect of directives in triangular situations", (1998) 23 E.L.Rev. 397; C. Hilson and T.A. Downes, "Making Sense of Rights: Community Rights in E.C. Law" (1999) 24 E.L. Rev. 121; S. Prechal, "Does direct effect still matter?" (2000) 37(5) C.M.L. Rev. 1047.
[36] *Von Colson and Kamann v. Land Nordrhein-Westfahlen* [1984] E.C.R. 1891; [1986] 2 C.M.L.R. 430; *Marleasing SA v. La Comercial Internacional de Alimentacion SA* [1990] E.C.R. 4135; [1992] 1 C.M.L.R. 305; *Teodoro Wagner Miet v. Fondo de Garantia Salarial* [1993] E.C.R. 6911; [1995] 2 C.M.L.R. 49; *Paola Faccini Dori v. Recreb Srl* [1994] E.C.R. 3325; [1994] 1 C.M.L.R. 665; *Annalisa Carbonari v. Università degli Studi di Bologna* [1999] E.C.R. 1103.
[37] *Duke v. Reliance Systems Ltd* [1988] A.C. 618; *Pickstone v. Freemans plc* [1989] A.C. 66; *Litster v. Forth Dry Dock & Engineering Co Ltd* [1990] 1 A.C. 546; *Finnegan v. Clowney Youth Training Programme Ltd* [1990] 2 A.C. 407; *Webb v. EMO Air Cargo (U.K.) Ltd* [1992] 4 All E.R. 929.
[38] *Officier van Justitie v. Kolpinghuis Nijmegen BV* [1987] E.C.R. 3639; [1989] 2 C.M.L.R. 18; *Pretore di Salò v. Persons Unknown* [1987] E.C.R. 2565; [1989] 1 C.M.L.R. 71.
[39] [1991] E.C.R. 5357; [1993] 2 C.M.L.R. 66.
[40] [1996] E.C.R. I-1929; J. Steiner, "From direct effects to *Francovich*: shifting means of enforce-ment of Community law", (1993) 18 E.L. Rev. 3. See further, T. Tridimas, *The General Principles of EC Law* (Oxford, 1999), Chap. 9.

right to damages arises under Community law the calculation of damages is a matter for the relevant legal system.[41]

The House of Lords considered these cases in *R. v. Secretary of State for Transport ex p. Factortame Ltd (No. 5)*[42] where it held that Spanish fishermen were entitled to damages for losses which they might be shown to have suffered as a consequence of the enactment of the Merchant Shipping Act 1988 which was in breach of their community rights. The House held that the breach of Community law was "sufficiently serious" to fall within the rule enunciated by the Court of Justice because the legislation was deliberately adopted. What was done by the Government was not done inadvertently. Although the Government had legal advice that it might not be in breach of Community law the legislation was clearly discriminatory on the grounds of nationality. The consequences to those affected were inevitably going to be extremely serious. The Commission had warned that the legislation was in its view, in breach of Community law. Although the view of the Commission is not binding, a government which disregards it does so at its own risk.

II. THE UNITED KINGDOM LEGISLATION

Effect has been given inside the United Kingdom to the treaties establishing   **6–015** and regulating the European Communities and European Union by the European Communities Act 1972 and a series of later Acts.[43] The difficulties surrounding the passing of the European Communities (Amendment) Act 1993, to give effect to certain provisions of the Treaty on European Union (the Maastricht Treaty) almost brought down Mr Major's government and raised in stark terms the contrast between ratification by the royal prerogative and Parliamentary approval by legislation.[44] Ultimately the Government secured the passage of the tortuously worded Act after resorting to a vote of confidence. Elections to the European Assembly were provided for by the European Assembly Act 1978 and to the European Parliament by the European Parliamentary Elections Act 1999.

European Communities Act 1972

Section 1 is a deceptive section which appears to do no more than provide a   **6–016** short title for the Act (sub s.1) and define certain terms such as "the Communities" and "the Treaties" which are used later in the Act (subsection 2). "The

---

[41] P. P. Craig, "The Community, The State and Damages Liability" (1997) 113 L.Q.R. 67; T. A. Downes, "Trawling for a remedy: State liability under Community law", (1997) 17 L.S. 286.
[42] [2000] 1 A.C. 524.
[43] *e.g.* European Communities (Greek Accession) Act 1979; European Communities (Spanish and Portuguese Accession) Act 1985; European Communities (Amendment) Act 1986, (to give effect to the Single European Act); European Communities (Amendment) Act 1993, (consequent on the Treaty of Maastricht); European Communities (Amendment) Act 1998 (consequent on the Treaty of Amsterdam).
[44] For an attempt to prevent ratification in the courts: *R. v. Foreign Secretary ex p. Rees-Mogg* [1994] Q.B. 552. See G. Marshall, "The Maastricht Proceedings", [1993] P.L. 402; R. Rawlings, "Legal Politics: The United Kingdom and Ratification of the Treaty on European Union", [1994] P.L. 254 and 367.

Treaties" include various specifically named treaties[45] and *inter alia* any treaty ancillary to any of "the Treaties" entered into by the United Kingdom. Additions to "the Treaties", as defined, may be made by Order in Council, subject to the approval by resolution of both Houses of Parliament, if the treaty was entered into by the United Kingdom after January 22, 1972. (subsection 3) The significance of that subsection became clear in *R. v. H.M. Treasury, ex p. Smedley*,[46] where the applicant sought to challenge the legality of a draft Order in Council which purported to recognise as an ancillary treaty an agreement to make payments to cover expenditure required under the budget which had been agreed by the Community. The importance of such recognition is to be found in section 2(3) of the 1972 Act which provides the Treasury with authority to charge on and issue out of the Consolidated Fund or, as the case may be, the National Loans Fund, the amounts required to meet any obligation created or arising under "the Treaties". From which it follows that once an international agreement has been declared to be one of the Community Treaties the Treasury is, without further authority, entitled to make any payments called for by that agreement. Although the Court of Appeal could not express a view on a draft Order in Council, it indicated that an Order in Council in the terms of the draft would have been *intra vires*. Sir John Donaldson M.R. thought that the concept of one treaty being "ancillary" to another was not one of precision and it was no doubt for that reason, amongst others, that Parliament has provided in section 1(3) of the 1972 Act for a system whereby an Order in Council should be conclusive of what treaties were to be regarded as Community treaties. The Master of the Rolls added that in his view nothing could be more ancillary to the Community treaties than the provision of funds to enable the Community to fulfil its essential functions. Slade L.J. similarly thought that the phrase was deliberately "an imprecise expression of wide and somewhat uncertain import".

6–017   *Section 2(1)* provides that all such rights and obligations from time-to-time created or arising under the Treaties, and all such remedies and procedures from time to time provided for by or under the Treaties, as in accordance with the Treaties are without further enactment to be given legal effect or used in the United Kingdom shall be recognised and be available in law, and be enforced, and followed accordingly; and the expression "enforceable community right" shall refer to one to which this subsection applies. This subsection provides for the recognition and enforcement in the United Kingdom of directly effective Community rights and obligations enjoyed by or imposed on Member States or private individuals. This means Community law as interpreted in accordance with the Treaties. It covers rights and obligations created by the Treaties themselves, by existing and future Community *Regulations* and by *Directives*. It is a constitutional innovation to give effect to *future* Community Regulations and Directives which thus constitute a new source of law in this country. The expression "remedies and procedures" appears to provide for references under Article 234[177] to the European Court of Justice. Community law that is not directly applicable is dealt with elsewhere in the Act, notably in section 2(2) and Schedule 2, or in other Acts such as the Value Added Tax Act 1994.

---

[45] Including those introduced by subsequent legislation included in note 43 above.
[46] [1985] Q.B. 657, CA. For statutory provisions relating to the United Kingdom's financial obligations to the Community see the European Communities (Finance) Act 1985 and the European Communities (Finance) Act 1995.

Section 2(2) confers power by Order in Council or ministerial regulation   **6–018**
(subject to Schedule 2) to give effect to existing and future community laws that
are not directly effective or applicable, especially Community *Directives* (which
set out the objects to be achieved while leaving it to each member state to choose
the method of achieving them). This power includes power to deal with supplementary matters, probably including references to the European Court of Justice.
The person exercising any statutory power or duty is empowered to have regard
to the objects of the Community and to any rights and obligations of the United
Kingdom under the Treaties.[47]
Schedule 2 provides that the power to make subordinate legislation under
section 2(2) does not include power:

(a) to impose of increase taxation; or

(b) to legislate with retroactive effect; or

(c) to confer power of sub-delegation,[48] except rules of court; or

(d) to create any new criminal offence punishable with imprisonment for
more than two years or (on summary conviction) three months, or with a
fine up to the maximum figure on level 5 or *per* day at level 3.[49]

The power of subordinate legislation conferred is to be exercised by statutory
instrument; and any such statutory instrument, if made without a draft having
been approved by each House, is subject to annulment by resolution of either
House.
Section 3, which was discussed in Chapter 4, provides for the reference to the
European Court of questions relating to Community law and directs the courts of
the United Kingdom to determine disputes involving Community law according
to the principles laid down by the European Court. Any question of the meaning
of a provision of European law is to be treated as a question of law, that is it is
to be determined by the judge, not the jury, and in the light of argument from
counsel not on the basis of evidence by expert witnesses.[50]

European Elections

The first legislative provision for elections necessitated by membership of the   **6–019**
Communities took the form of the European Assembly Election Act 1978.
Although it has largely been overtaken by events it remains of interest because
of the unsuccessful litigation which it provoked and the provisions of section
6.
Apart from Northern Ireland where three members representing one constituency were to be returned by the single transferable vote system, the method
of voting in England, Wales and Scotland was the traditional British simple
majority—or first past the post system.

---

[47] In practice delegated legislation giving effect to Community law is often made under general
enabling provisions in other statutes.
[48] Sub-paragraph (c) does not apply to a power to legislate conferred otherwise than under s.2(2), or
to a power to give administrative directions.
[49] Criminal Justice Act 1982.
[50] See *R. v. Goldstein* [1982] 1 W.L.R. 804, CA.

The legality of this system under Community law was challenged in *Prince v. Secretary of State for Scotland*[51] in which a group of S.D.P. Liberal Alliance voters applied to the Court of Session for a declarator "that the pursuers had an 'enforceable Community right' in terms of section 2 of the European Communities Act 1972, to a system of election which is not discriminatory and which gives equal weight to all votes cast so far as practicable in the forthcoming election for members of the European Parliament." The pursuers' argument was that the European Elections Act 1978, in so far as it did not provide for proportional representation, was *ultra vires* the Treaty of Rome. While Article 190(4) [138(3)] of the Treaty had envisaged that the Council would lay down a uniform system of voting throughout the Community, no scheme had been adopted as a result of the United Kingdom's veto. However, Article 138(3) had nevertheless provided that direct elections were to be "by universal suffrage". Like other provisions of the Treaty, Article 190[138] fell to be interpreted in accordance with fundamental principles of Community law which included the right of equality or non-discrimination. The right to equality of voting was thus "an enforceable community right" in terms of the European Communities Act 1972: this had been infringed by the 1978 Act, which, by endorsing the first-past-the-post system, was unequal and discriminating. As important issues of Community law were inevitably involved in their declaratory conclusions, the pursuers maintained that a reference to the European Court of Justice was necessary under Article 234[177]. In refusing the reference, Lord Cameron held that on the pleadings as they stood, a reference would be premature because no attempt had been made to formulate with sufficient precision the questions which were to be put to the European Court of Justice, which, in his Lordship's view did *not* exist "for the purpose of determining academic questions". Moreover, there were serious issues in the case which were still uncertain and had to be clarified before a reference could be made. For example, there were doubts whether the pursuers had title to sue merely because they were on the electoral lists, whether Article 190[138]—which *prima facie* gives no rights to individuals—could be the basis of enforceable Community rights and, finally, whether the principle of equality in Community law could be invoked outside commercial matters.

6–020   Section 6 provided that no treaty which was intended to increase the powers of the Assembly should be ratified by the United Kingdom unless it had been approved by an Act of Parliament. Normally treaties are ratified by the Crown (or executive) although legislation is required subsequently if they are to have effect within the United Kingdom. In this instance the Executive is precluded from even concluding an agreement without legislative approval.[52]

Thus, following section 6, the European Communities (Amendment) Act 1998 contains, in section 2, a provision that, for the purposes of section 6, the Treaty of Amsterdam is approved.

The method of election of United Kingdom representatives to the European Parliament is currently governed by the European Parliamentary Elections Act 1999 which, having failed to secure the consent of the House of Lords, was enacted under the Parliament Act 1949.[53] The United Kingdom is divided into electoral regions. In Northern Ireland, which constitutes one region, voting is by the single transferable vote system but in the regions of Scotland, Wales and

---

[51] [1985] S.L.T. 74.
[52] See further, *post* para. 15–030.
[53] See *ante* para. 4–036.

England, voting is by a list system which, in effect, puts the choice of representatives in the hands of the party apparatchiks who drew up each party list.

III. Community Law as a Source of Domestic Law

Community law is a direct source of law in this country in the case of matters **6–021** having a "European element",[54] if it is "directly applicable" to individuals, and if such law is either self-executing or implemented under section 2(2) of the European Communities Act 1972 or by any other Act of Parliament.

Enforceable Community rights
Section 2(1) of the 1972 Act gives effect in British courts to rights and **6–022** obligations which, under Community law, are to have effect within Member States without further enactment. Provisions which are not directly applicable or effective are not part of the law of the United Kingdom until legislation has made them so under section 2(2). Hence it is not true to say that Community law is part of domestic law "lock, stock and barrel" as Lord Denning M.R. said in *Re Westinghouse Uranium Contract*.[55] Whether a rule of Community law requires domestic legislation to become part of the law of the Member States or is law *proprio vigore* is itself a matter of Community law. In the case of the litigant seeking to rely on Community law in a British court, it is necessary to show that the rule in question creates a directly enforceable individual right (direct effect). Rules of Community law may, however, be directly applicable within Member States without creating individual rights.

Reference to the European Court of Justice[56]
As we saw earlier, Article 234 [177] of the EC Treaty gives the European **6–023** Court of Justice jurisdiction to give preliminary rulings on Community law at the request of the courts of Member States. This Article provides that:

(1) The European Court has jurisdiction to give preliminary rulings concerning:

  (a) the interpretation of the Treaty;
  (b) the validity and interpretation of acts of Community institutions;
  (c) the interpretation of the statutes [*i.e.* constitutions] of bodies established by the Council.

(2) Any court or tribunal of a Member State *may*, if it considers that a decision thereon is necessary to enable it to give judgment, request the Court to give a ruling.

---

[54] *R. v. Saunders* [1980] Q.B. 72, E.C.J. (Freedom of movement of workers: Art. 39 [48] inapplicable to purely domestic provisions of criminal law which do not involve discrimination between nationals of different Member States). *R. v. Secretary of State for the Home Dept, ex p. Sahota* [1999] Q.B. 597, CA. See also *Gough v. Chief Constable of Derbyshire, The Times* July 19, 2001, CA. (Banning order under Football Spectators Act 1989 not in breach of E.C. law: Member State entitled to restrict citizens from leaving its territory on public policy grounds). See Arnull *op cit.* pp. 321–324.
[55] [1978] A.C. 547, 564.
[56] *Wyatt and Dashwood, op. cit.* Chap. 11.

(3) A court or tribunal of a Member State [in which such a question arises] against those whose decision there is no judicial remedy under national law, *shall* bring the matter before the European Court.[57]

Where the national court has a discretion under (2), the principles on which a British court should exercise that discretion were indicated by Lord Denning M.R. in *Bulmer v. Bollinger*.[58] The question was whether English firms might continue to describe their products as "champagne cider" and "champagne perry," or whether under Community law the word "champagne" might be used only for wine produced in the Champagne district of France. The French company wanted the English judge to refer the question to the European Court for preliminary rulings, but the Court of Appeal held that an English judge or court below the House of Lords has a complete discretion whether to refer to the European Court a question of the interpretation of the Treaty. Lord Denning M.R. said that:

(a) the decision of the question must be *necessary* to enable the English court to give judgment;

(b) the decision of the question must be *conclusive* of the case;

(c) if the court decides a decision is *necessary* it must still in the exercise of its discretion consider such circumstances as the delay involved, the difficulty and importance of the point, the expense, and the burden on the European Court. In order to exercise its discretion properly the court should decide the facts before considering whether to make a reference to the European court.

Lord Denning M.R.'s guidelines have been criticised as unduly restrictive, in particular his requirement that the point in question is conclusive of the case only if whichever way it is decided by the European Court, it will determine the outcome of the case. It may be that a point decided in one way would be conclusive of a case: judges should surely be entitled to seek a ruling from the European Court in such circumstances. Doubts were also expressed about Lord Denning M.R.'s suggestion that it is not necessary to refer a question where the law is clear and the national court has merely to apply the law (the *acte clair* doctrine).[59]

More recently, in *R. v. Stock Exchange ex p. Else (1982) Ltd*[60] Sir Thomas Bingham M.R. suggested domestic courts should refer questions for preliminary rulings unless they were completely confident that they could resolve the issue themselves and went on to caution against such confidence in an unfamiliar fields. "If the national court has any real doubt it should ordinarily refer."

---

[57] Schedule 1 to the Civil Procedure Rules continues in effect the provisions of the former R.S.C., Ord. 114 which deals with references by the High Court to the European Court and appeals from the High Court in such cases to the Court of Appeal. Rules of Court have also been made with regard to references to the European Court in criminal appeals, and from the Crown Court and County Courts.

[58] *H.P. Bulmer v. J. Bollinger SA* [1974] Ch. 401.

[59] A. Dashwood and A. M. Arnull, "English Courts and Art. 177 of the E.E.C. Treaty", (1984) 4 Y.E.L. 255, 263.

[60] [1993] 2 W.L.R. 70, 76; [1993] 1 All E.R. 420, 426, CA.

The European Court itself had the opportunity to consider the meaning of **6–024**
Article 234 [177] in *C.I.L.F.I.T. v. Italian Ministry of Health*,[61] where it was
asked to consider the meaning of the third paragraph of the Article (which relates
to a national court against whose decision there is no judicial remedy under
national law). The European Court concluded that there is no duty to refer a
question where the question is irrelevant, that is if the answer to that question,
regardless of what it may be, cannot affect the outcome of the case. Secondly,
there is no duty to refer a question which is materially similar to one already
decided by the Court.[62] Thirdly, there is no need to refer where there is no real
doubt about the law. (The *acte clair* doctrine.) Before, however, a national court
comes to the conclusion that such is the case, it must be convinced that the matter
is equally obvious to the courts of the other Member States and to the Court of
Justice.[63] A *fortiori*, it might be thought, a court with a discretion to refer
questions to the European Court will be entitled not to do so in these three
cases.

The third paragraph of Article 177 applies not only to the House of Lords,
from whose decisions there can never be an appeal, but to any court in the United
Kingdom against whose decision in particular proceedings there is no further
judicial remedy. There may be doubt as to what constitutes a judicial remedy.
Thus a tribunal against whose decision there is no appeal may be said to fall
within the third paragraph although in certain circumstances its decision could be
set aside on an application for judicial review.[64] Similarly the Court of Appeal
should perhaps be included within the third paragraph if, for any reason, no
further appeal is available.[65]

The desirability of establishing the facts of a case before referring a question
to the European Court is, as a matter of general principle, obvious and has been
emphasised in *R. v. Henn*.[66] It is not, however, an invariable rule: *R. v. Plymouth
Justices ex p. Rogers*.[67] In both cases, too, emphasis was placed on the need for
caution on the part of magistrates and judges at first instance in referring cases
to the European Court.[68] Appellate courts are better placed to assess the need for
a reference and to formulate questions.

References by United Kingdom courts and tribunals

The first reference from the House of Lords was in *R. v. Henn*[69] where the   **6–025**
appellants had been convicted of offences in connection with importing obscene
or indecent articles. The House asked the European Court whether a statutory
prohibition on the importing of a type of article constituted a "quantative
restriction on imports" within Article 28 [30] and, if so, whether it could none the
less be justifiable within Article 30 [36] as a restriction imposed on the "grounds
of public morality, public policy or public security." In *Garland v. British Rail*

[61] [1983] 1 C.M.L.R. 472.
[62] See, for example, *R. v. Secretary of State for Social Services, ex p. Bosmore Medical Supplies Ltd,
The Times*, December 16, 1985.
[63] See, for example, *Re Sandhu The Times*, May 10, 1985, HL.
[64] *post*, Chaps 31 and 32.
[65] *Hagen v. Fratelli D. and G. Morretts S.N.C.* [1980] 3 C.M.L.R. 253, 255 *per* Buckley L.J.
[66] [1981] A.C. 580, HC. See too, *Church of Scientology of California v. Customs and Excise Cmrs.*
[1981] 1 All E.R. 1035, CA.
[67] [1982] Q.B. 863.
[68] A caution demonstrated, for example, by Dillon J. in *MacMahon v. Department of Education and
Science* [1983] Ch. 227.
[69] [1981] A.C. 580; *post*, para. 6–036.

Engineering[70] the House of Lords sought the opinion of the European Court on the meaning of "pay" in Article 141 [119], before construing the Sex Discrimination Act 1975. References from the Court of Appeal (Civil Division) have also often been concerned with equal pay and sex discrimination: *e.g. Macarthys v. Smith*[71]; *Worringham v. Lloyds Bank Ltd*[72] The Court of Appeal (Criminal Division) in *R. v. Thompson*[73] inquired whether the prohibition on the quantitative restriction of imports under Article 28 [30] applied to gold and silver coins; and, if it did, whether a restriction on the importing of such coins might be justified on the grounds of public policy under Article 30 [36].

The deportation of EC nationals convicted of criminal offences gave rise to a reference by the Divisional Court in *R. v. Secretary of State for Home Affairs, ex p. Santillo*.[74] In *R. v. National Insurance Commissioner, ex p. Warry*[75] the Divisional Court in proceedings for judicial review of a decision of the National Insurance Commissioner referred a question relating to entitlement to social security benefits to the European Court.

Reference to the European Court of Justice from the High Court is illustrated by *Van Duyn v. Home Office*.[76] Miss D, of Dutch nationality, had been offered employment as secretary with the Church of Scientology at a college in England, but the immigration officer refused her leave to enter under the Immigration Act 1971 (exclusion conducive to the public good), and the question arose whether this infringed Article 39 [48] of the EC Treaty (freedom of movement of workers). The Vice-Chancellor held:

(i) that issues of fact and of national law should in general be determined before reference is made to the European Court; and

(ii) that the question of whether Article 39[48] of the Treaty of Rome confers on individuals *rights* enforceable in the courts of Member States should properly be determined by reference to the European Court before trial of the action. His Lordship therefore stayed the proceedings and requested a preliminary ruling from the European Court which ruled that:

(a) Article 39 [48] and the Council Directive on the movement and residence of foreign nationals confer on individuals rights (qualified by the Directive) which national courts must protect; but

(b) a member state may impose restrictions justified on grounds of public policy, and may take into account the conduct of the individual concerned and his association with some organisation considered by the State as socially harmful, even though it is not an unlawful association and no similar restriction is placed on its own nationals against taking employment with that organisation.

---

[70] [1983] 2 A.C. 751; *ante*, para. 4–021. Patent law was the subject of the reference in *R. v. Comptroller Patents ex p. Gist-Brocades* [1986] 1 W.L.R. 51, HL.
[71] [1981] Q.B. 180.
[72] [1981] 1 W.L.R. 950; [1982] 1 W.L.R. 841.
[73] [1980] Q.B. 229; 69 Cr.App.R. 22.
[74] [1981] Q.B. 778, DC and CA; [1980] 2 C.M.L.R. 308; *supra* para. 6–009.
[75] [1978] Q.B. 607.
[76] [1974] 1 W.L.R. 1107; subsequent proceedings [1975] Ch. 385; [1975] 1 C.M.L.R. 1.

The Employment Appeal Tribunal has referred various questions to the European Court relating to pay and discrimination.[77]   **6–026**

The application of the criminal law in magistrates' courts may have a European element and require reference being made to the European Court, for instance with regard to the deportation of EEC nationals (*R. v. Bouchereau*,[78]) offences under the Immigration Act 1971 (*R. v. Pieck*[79]) or the enforcement of United Kingdom fishing legislation (*R. v. Plymouth Justices, ex p. Rogers*[80]).

Tribunals, as well as courts, are within the terms of Article 234 [177].[81] References have been made by the National Insurance Commissioner[82] and the Special Commissioners for Income Tax.[83]

The jurisdiction of the European Court to give preliminary rulings on points of Community law at the request of national courts and tribunals must not be confused with its jurisdiction directly to enforce Community law. The Commission or a member state may bring an action in the Court against any state which is alleged to be in breach of its Treaty obligations (EC Treaty Articles 226 [169] and 227 [170]). A State which is found to be in breach of Treaty obligation is under a duty to take the necessary measures to comply with the judgment of the Court. The Commission, for example, after lengthy negotiations with the United Kingdom about the latter's failure to implement a Regulation relating to the use of tachographs in lorries finally brought proceedings in the European Court. A judgment against the United Kingdom[84] resulted in domestic legislation to give effect to Community law. Similarly the United Kingdom only took steps to reduce the discriminatory levels of excise duty on imported wines after the Commission had successfully brought proceedings in the European Court.[85]

It is difficult to calculate exactly the number of cases brought against individual Member States, and figures may be misleading unless it is remembered different states have joined the Communities at different times. Nonetheless, the figure for the United Kingdom of 47 compares favourably with 384 for Italy, 238 for Belgium and 220 for France.[86]

Secondary legislation

The European Communities Act 1972 did not give effect to a static body of   **6–027** rules—as is usually the case when a statute makes a treaty part of the law of the United Kingdom. The law of the Community continues to grow, through decisions of the European Court and legislation in the form of Regulations, Decisions and Directives. Much of this law, indeed, may correctly be regarded as too fundamental and broad in scope to be fairly described as secondary.[87] Accession

---

[77] See *Jenkins v. Kingsgate (Clothing Productions) Ltd* [1981] 1 W.L.R. 972; [1981] 1 W.L.R. 1485; *Burton v. British Railways Board* [1981] I.R.L.R. 17; [1982] Q.B. 1080; [1983] I.C.R. 544.

[78] [1978] Q.B. 732.

[79] [1981] E.C.R. 2171 (Reference from Pontypridd Magistrates' Court).

[80] [1982] Q.B. 863.

[81] The Court of Justice has held Art. 234 [177] applies to tribunals established by law, *e.g. Vaassen-Göbbels v. Beambtenfonds voor het Mijnbedrijf* [1966] E.C.R. 261 (Dutch Social Security Tribunal) but not to an arbitrator, appointed by parties to a contract: *Nordsee v. Reederei Mond* [1982] E.C.R. 1095.

[82] (Since 1980, the Social Security Commissioners). See *Kenny v. National Insurance Officer* [1978] E.C.R. 1489; *Re Search for Work in Ireland* [1978] 2 C.M.L.R. 174.

[83] *Lord Bruce of Donnington v. G. Aspden* [1981] E.C.R. 2205.

[84] *Commission v. United Kingdom* [1979] E.C.R. 419.

[85] *Commission v. United Kingdom* [1983] E.C.R. 2265.

[86] Based on figures up to the end of 1999, as calculated by Brown and Kennedy, *op. cit.*, p. 424.

[87] Brown and Kennedy, *op. cit.* p. 7.

to the Treaties and their enactment in the European Communities Act 1972 means that bodies outside the United Kingdom may by their decisions and legislation affect domestic law. Both Houses of Parliament have responded to the issues raised by this new situation in ways discussed in the following section while the Treaty on European Union attempted to deal more generally with the issue of enhancing the role of national legislatures as part of an attempt to address what is coyly described as the problem of the democratic deficit in the structure of the Communities and Union.

IV. PARLIAMENT AND COMMUNITY LAW

Parliament's role in the making of secondary Community legislation by Community institutions is, at best, indirect. To provide a more effective method of scrutinising proposals for new Community legislation than debates and questions to Ministers, both Houses established specialist committees. Political, institutional and economic developments in the Communities since 1972, in particular the establishment of the European Union which created the potential for new categories of document in addition to proposals for legislation, have resulted in both Houses reforming and extending their systems of scrutiny of European business by committee.

Reforms to enhance the role of national parliaments were also provided by the TEU, but this did not become effective until a new Protocol[88] was agreed in the Treaty of Amsterdam 1998. This required a six week period to elapse between a legislative proposal under Title VI of the TEU being made available to the Commission, Parliament and Council and a decision by the Council to adopt an act of common position on the basis of that proposal. This was to allow time for national parliaments to scrutinise European business. The opening of a National Parliament Office in Brussels has enabled national parliaments to find out in advance of formal proposals what is happening, it should also assist collaboration with other national parliaments.

The Scrutiny Reserve

6–028   Underpinning the provisions to be discussed for parliamentary scrutiny of proposed European legislation and other types of proposal provided for under the TEU, is the understanding, found in resolutions of both Houses,[89] that Ministers will not agree to such proposals while they are still being considered by Parliament. The purpose of these resolutions is to enable Parliament to attempt to influence the position the Government will take in negotiations with the other Member States. The current resolutions are those of November 17, 1998 in the House of Commons,[90] and December 6, 1999 in the House of Lords.[91] These resolutions take account of the increased use of the co-decision procedure provided in the TEU and consequent use of Conciliation Committees to deal with

---

[88] The Protocol on National Parliaments (Protocol 13).
[89] The first resolution was passed in 1980, before that date the understanding was based on undertakings given by successive Governments.
[90] H.C.Deb. Vol. 319, cols. 778–779, November 17, 1998.
[91] H.L.Deb. Vol. 607, cols. 1019–1020. This is similar, but not identical to the House of Commons resolution; until this resolution the Lord had relied on an informal understanding to the same effect as the Commons' resolution.

disputes between the Council and the European Parliament (Article 251). Ministers should not agree to any compromise proposal that may emerge from the Conciliation Committee while that agreement is still subject to scrutiny or awaiting consideration by the House. The Scrutiny. Reserve also applies to agreements under Titles V (Common Foreign and Security Policy) or VI (Co-operation in Justice and Home Affairs) of the TEU.

The Scrutiny Reserve may apply during parliamentary recesses when the Scrutiny Committee does not meet. Ministers may give agreement to a proposal still awaiting scrutiny or consideration by the House in certain circumstances:

(i) if the proposal is confidential, routine, trivial or is substantially the same as a proposal on which scrutiny has been completed;

(ii) if the Scrutiny Committee indicates that the Minister can do so;

(iii) if the Minister has special reasons for doing so.

In the latter case the Minister is required to explain his reasons to the Committee and the House as soon as possible. The Scrutiny Reserve could be made more authoritative by putting it in statutory form.

Scrutiny by committees

The two Houses have slightly different types of committee which complement each other: the Lords' committee conducts in depth analysis of a few significant European proposals, while the Commons' committee assesses all proposals. There is provision for concurrent meetings of the committees, but this power is rarely formally exercised. **6–029**

The House of Commons

The system of scrutiny by a specialist committee on European legislation devised after accession was reformed in 1990 and again in 1998.[92] Originally the Committee in the House of Commons was concerned only with specific proposals for European legislation. The TEU gave rise to new categories of documents to be agreed under the two new "pillars" of the E.U., which did not fall within the Committee's original terms of reference. **6–030**

The European Scrutiny Committee[93] is a Select Committee of 16 members entitled to appoint specialist advisers and call for witnesses and evidence. Its terms of reference allow it to examine E.U. documents and:

(i) report its opinion on the legal and political importance of such documents;

(ii) make recommendations for further consideration of any such document by one of the European Standing Committees[94];

(iii) to consider any issue arising upon such document or related matters.

---

[92] Following recommendations by the Select Committee on Modernisation, H.C. 791 (1997–98); see also H.C. 51 (1995–96), H.C. 77 (1996–97).
[93] Originally known as the European Legislation Committee.
[94] *post* para. 6–031.

The term European document is widely defined to include: proposals under the Community treaties, documents published for submission to the European Council, the Council, the European Central Bank; proposals further to Titles V and VI of the Treaty of European Union for submission to the Council. As well as the E.U. documents the committee receives explanatory memorandum prepared by the relevant Government Department and can seek further information from Departments.

6–031   *European Standing Committee* There are three European Standing Committees[95] each consisting of 13 members; any MP may take part in the proceedings of one of these Committees, but may not take part in any vote in the Committee. Each Standing Committee is responsible for several government departments, and when recommending that a European document requires further consideration, the European Scrutiny Committee specifies the Standing Committee to which a document should be referred. Government Ministers appear before these committees to answer questions for a maximum of one and a half hours, and the committee will debate the matter for a further one and a half hours and if appropriate agree on a motion, *e.g.* that the Minister does not agree to the proposed legislation. A motion in similar, but not necessarily identical terms, will be moved without debate in the House a few days later.[96]

The House of Lords

6–032   *The European Union Committee* has a membership of 20, but works through subcommittees which co-opt Lords not on the Committee. In consequence around 70 Lords are involved in the work of the Committee and its six sub-committees. The sub-committees deal with: economic and financial affairs, trade and external relations; energy, industry and transport; environment, public health and consumer protection; agriculture, fisheries and food; law and institutions[97]; social affairs, education and home affairs. The terms of reference of the committee are to consider E.U. documents[98] and other matters relating to the E.U. Although the committee and its sub-committees examine some E.U. documents, their more frequent role is to make detailed enquiries into subjects chosen by the sub-committee from within their field of activity, *e.g.* the Euro, reforming E.C. competition procedures, fraud, e-Commerce. This is a very active committee, whose reports are highly regarded throughout Europe, and are capable of influencing European policy development.[99]

Debates

6–033   The Government publishes White Papers every six months on Community developments which can form the basis for debates in either House. Since 1989 debates on European documents have been held in the European Standing Committees rather than on the floor of the House.

---

[95] Increased from two to three in November 1998.
[96] It is for the government to decide the wording of the motion to be moved.
[97] This committee is always chaired by a Law Lord.
[98] This is widely defined in virtually the same terms as in the House of Commons, see para. 6–030.
[99] See the evidence published by the Select Committee on the Committee Work of the House H.L. 35 (1991–92).

V. The Impact of Community Law

In earlier parts of this chapter the relationship between Community law and the   **6–034**
laws of the United Kingdom was discussed with particular reference to the ways
in which Community law becomes enforceable as part of domestic law. In this
part it is intended to look, in outline, at the substantive effect of Community law
in those areas where it has already played a particularly important role and where
it may be important in the future.[1]

From *Van Duyn v. The Home Office*[2] onwards, the right of freedom of
movement of workers (Article 39 [48]) has been involved in many cases before
the domestic courts. EEC workers may not be refused admission to the United
Kingdom except within the limits laid down by Directive 64/221, which allows
states to exclude an individual on grounds of public policy or of public security
but only on the basis of the individual's personal conduct. In *R. v. Bouchereau*[3]
the European Court considered the circumstances in which an EC national could
be deported after a criminal conviction, and concluded that deportation was only
justified where the infringement of the law posed a genuine and sufficiently
serious threat affecting one of the fundamental interests of society which went
beyond the threat to public order which is inherent in any crime.

In *R. v. Secretary of State for the Home Department, ex. p. Dannenberg*[4] the
Court of Appeal pointed out that Community law now requires that reasons must
be given when a judge recommends that an EEC national should be deported. To
attempt to impose on an EC national who is entitled to enter the United Kingdom
a time limit on his stay under the Immigration Act 1971 is a breach of Community law: *R. v. Pieck*.[5] Rules requiring a qualifying period of residence before an
EC national is eligible to apply for a local education award were held to
constitute discrimination in breach of Article 39 [48] in *MacMahon v. Department of Education and Science*.[6]

Serious impediments to the free movement of goods, in the sense of the normal   **6–035**
range of imports and exports, are likely to be challenged directly in the European
Court. Thus restrictions by the United Kingdom on the importing of potatoes[7]
and poultry[8] were referred to the Court by the Commission, as were restrictions
by France on imports of lamb from the United Kingdom.[9] A rather different
example of the United Kingdom being found to be in breach of Article 28 [30]

---

[1] Other examples, of course, can be found in the discussion of the conflict between community law
and U.K. law in Chap. 4.
[2] [1974] E.C.R. 187; [1975] Ch. 358. See further A. Arnull, *The European Union and its Court of
Justice* (Oxford, 1999), Chaps 8 and 10. Non-workers, such as students, have progressively been
given rights by a series of directives and citizenship of the Union (Art. 18(1)[8a], created by the
Maastricht Treaty) involves a general right to move and reside within the territories of Member
States: Wyatt and Dashwood's European Union Law (4th ed., 2000, Sweet & Maxwell), Chap.
16.
[3] [1978] Q.B. 732. *cf. R. v. Secchi* [1975] 1 C.M.L.R. 383 (Met. Magistrate): (Italian in London not
a worker; even if he were, convictions for theft and indecency justified recommendation for
deportation).
[4] [1984] Q.B. 766. See further on the compatibility of U.K. deportation law with EEC law, *R. v.
Secretary of State for the Home Department, ex p. Santillo* [1981] Q.B. 778.
[5] [1981] E.C.R. 2171.
[6] [1983] Ch. 227. See also *R. v. ILEA, ex p. Hinde, The Times*, November 19, 1984.
[7] *Re Imports of Potatoes. E.C. Commission v. U.K.* [1979] 2 C.M.L.R. 427, E.C.J.
[8] *Re Imports of Poultry Meat: E.C. Commission v. France* [1982] 3 C.M.L.R. 497, E.C.J.
[9] *Re Restrictions on Imports of Lamb: E.C. Commission v. France* [1980] 1 C.M.L.R. 418, E.C.J.

is provided by *Commission v. U.K.*[10] where the Court held that a Statutory Instrument which required certain categories of goods sold by retailers to be marked with an indication of the countries of origin was a quantitative restriction on the movement of goods. It is not entirely surprising that resort to Article 28 [30] in domestic courts should be made in cases where, at first sight, Community law has little relevance. In *R. v. Henn*,[11] for example, the only hope of the accused importers was to argue that the United Kingdom's prohibition on the importing of obscene or indecent articles was contrary to Community law. The European Court held that such a prohibition could be justified in the light of Article 30 [36] which refers to "public morality, public policy or public security," and that the question of public morality was to be determined by each state in accordance with its own scale of values. The Court did not discuss the fact that the test of obscenity or indecency applied to imported books[12] was wider than the test applied for example, under the Obscene Publications Act 1959, to books published in England, although Advocate General Mr J. P. Warner referred to the complexities of the laws of the United Kingdom which arise: first because the laws of the different parts of the United Kingdom, namely England and Wales, Scotland, Northern Ireland, and the Isle of Man, are different, and, in each case, derived from a variety of sources rather than from any coherent scheme; and secondly because nowhere in the United Kingdom is pornography treated quite as strictly internally as on its importation.

The importers of various articles of an erotic nature were however more successful in *Conegate Ltd v. Customs and Excise Commissioners.*[13] The European Court held that the United Kingdom was not entitled to prohibit the import of goods under Article 30 [36] where the manufacture of such goods was not prohibited in its own territory under its domestic law.

Article 28 [30] has also been invoked in cases challenging the compatibility of Sunday trading laws with community law[14] and the licensing provisions imposed on sex shops.[15]

In *R. v. Chief constable of Sussex ex p. International Trader's Ferry Ltd*[16] it was unsuccessfully argued that the failure of the Sussex Police to provide sufficient resources to enable the applicants to carry on their trade in the face of protests by animal rights groups was in breach of Article 28 [30] as constituting a measure amounting to a restriction on the freedom of movement of goods. The House of Lords expressed doubt whether a decision by a police force constituted a "measure" within the terms of the Article but concluded that if it did it was within the terms of the proviso contained in Article 30 [36].

6–036   The first judicial consideration of the effect of the EC Treaty on English law involved Articles 81 [85] and 82 [86] which are designed to ensure free competition: *Application des Gaz S.A. v. Falks Veritas.*[17] Later cases in which these Articles have been relied on have shown the difficulties that may arise in finding

[10] [1985] 2 C.M.L.R. 259, E.C.J.
[11] [1981] A.C. 580.
[12] Customs Consolidation Act 1876, s.42; Customs and Excise Act 1952, s.304.
[13] [1987] 2 W.L.R. 39, *Conegate* was distinguished and *Henn* applied in *R. v. Bow Street Metropoitan Stipendiary Magistrate ex p. Noncy p Ltd* [1990] 1 Q.B. 123; 89 Cr. App. R. 121, CA.
[14] *Stoke on Trent City Council v. B & Q* [1993] A.C. 900; [1992] E.C.R.I–6635; [1993] 1 C.M.L.R. 426. See further, Arnull, *op. cit.* p. 282 *et seq.*
[15] *Quietlynn Ltd v. Southend B.C.* [1990] E.C.P.I.–3059; [1990] 3 C.M.L.R. 55; [1990] 3 AU E.R. 207.
[16] [1999] 2 A.C. 418, HL.
[17] [1974] Ch. 381, CA.

the appropriate domestic remedy to protect a Community right. In *Garden Cottage Foods Ltd v. Milk Marketing Board*[18] the appellants sought an injunction to prevent the Board from acting in a way which constituted a breach of Article 82 [86]. The House of Lords took the view that an injunction ought not to have been granted on the facts and also, contrary to the view expressed in the Court of Appeal, indicated that contravention of Article 82 [86] could be remedied by an award of damages by analogy to a breach of statutory duty. It has, however, been argued that there is considerable doubt about the appropriate remedy under Community law for a breach of Article 82 [86] and that the House of Lords should have referred the issue to the European Court.[19]

In *Bourgoin S.A. v. Ministry of Agriculture Fisheries and Food*[20] the Court of Appeal was concerned with the remedies available where a ministerial order had been held by the European Court to be in breach of Article 28 [30] of the Treaty. Parker L.J., who delivered the judgment of the majority, held that a *mere* breach of the Treaty was remediable by judicial review, declaring the minister's order to be invalid and ordering the officials concerned to permit the landing of the goods. The *Golden Cottage Foods* case, in the opinion of the learned Lord Justice, established that there is a right to damages where there has been a breach of law which also amounts to an abuse of power. In *An Bord Bainne Co-operative Ltd (Irish Dairy Board) v. Milk Marketing Board*[21] the English Courts had to decide whether rights arising under competition provisions of the EEC Treaty fell within the sphere of private law or public law for the purpose of determining the appropriate forms of procedure and remedies[22]: the Court of Appeal decided that the rights were private law rights and the plaintiff could, by writ, seek damages for their breach. (The desirability of seeking the view of the European Court was, again, not raised).

Dicta in these cases in relation to the availability of damages for breach of community rights by domestic law must, of course, now be read in the light of the decisions of the Court of Justice discussed earlier, *Francovich and Brasserie du Pecheur*[23] and the application of those decisions by the House of Lords in *R. v. Secretary of State for Transport ex p. Factortame Ltd (No. 5)*.[24] **6–037**

Article 141 [119], as was obvious from the earlier discussion of references to the European Court under Article 234 [177], has been a fruitful source of litigation. In a number of cases initiated by the Commission the United Kingdom has been held by the Court to be in breach of its obligations under Community law relating to equality between the sexes. Following the decision of the Court in *E.C. Commission v. U.K.*[25] that the provisions of the Equal Pay Act 1970 failed to comply with the EEC Equal Pay Directive (75)/117), the United Kingdom Statute was amended by the Equal Pay (Amendment) Regulations, under section 2(2) of the European Communities Act 1972.[26] That is the procedure which in

[18] [1984] 3 W.L.R. 143, HL.
[19] M. Friend and J. Shaw, "Damages for Abuse of Dominant Position" (1984) 100 L.Q.R. 188.
[20] [1986] Q.B. 716.
[21] [1984] 2 C.M.L.R. 584. The Competition Act 1998 was passed to bring domestic law into accord with EC law.
[22] *post*, Chap. 33.
[23] *ante*, para. 6–014.
[24] [2000] 1 A.C. 524; *ante*, para. 6–014.
[25] [1982] I.R.L.R. 33, [1982] I.C.R. 578. See too *Drake v. Chief Adjudication Officer* [1986] 3 All E.R. 65, E.C.J.; *Johnston v. Chief Constable of the R.U.C.* [1986] 3 All E.R. 135, E.C.J.
[26] Equal Pay (Amendment) Regulations 1983, (S.I. 1983 No. 1794).

practice is likely generally to be followed where there is a discrepancy or conflict between domestic and Community law.

A problem peculiar to Scots law was raised in *Gibson v. Lord Advocate*.[27] G. sought a declaration that section 2(1) of the European Communities Act 1972 was contrary to Article XVIII of the Union Act, and therefore null and void, so far as it purported to enact as part of the law of Scotland certain Community Regulations providing for equal treatment of member states with regard to fishing in maritime waters. He argued that immediately before the Act of Union, Scottish subjects had exclusive fishing rights in Scottish coastal waters; that the laws conferring these rights "concerned private right," and that the Community Regulations were not "for the evident utility of the subjects within Scotland." Lord Keith dismissed the action, not only on the ground that action was incompetent in seeking consideration of the utility of an Act of Parliament[28] but also on the ground that Community Regulations operate in the field of public law and not private law.

6–038   In assessing the possible future significance of Community law it must be remembered that apart from the provisions of the Treaties and subsequent secondary legislation, the European Court has developed a concept of general principles of Community law with which it supplements and completes the written texts which it has to interpret and apply.[29] Thus the principles known in common law countries as "natural justice" have been applied by the European Court as general principles of law.[30] From the provisions of Article 141 [119] and other Articles the Court has fashioned a general concept of "equality." The principle of "proportionality" which has been referred to by the Court on a number of occasions has been cited by Lord Diplock in *Council of Civil Service Unions v. Minister for Civil Service*[31] as a possible new ground on which ministerial and administrative decisions may be subject to review under domestic law. The recognition by the Court that the general principles of law include respect for fundamental human rights[32] provides a point of contact between the EC and the European Convention on Human Rights.[33]

It remains to be seen to what extent the Court will be encouraged in this approach by the adoption at the Intergovernmental Conference at Nice of a Charter of Fundamental Rights. The Charter's legal standing is unclear. It is not part of the Treaty of Nice or attached to it in any way. Article 51 of the Charter states, however, that the institutions of the EU shall respect the rights, observe the principle and promote the application of the Charter in accordance with their respective powers.

An attempt to make use of this link was unsuccessful. In *Allgemeine Gold und Silberscheideanstalt v. Cmrs. of Customs & Excise*[34] where the German plaintiffs

---

[27] [1975] 1 C.M.L.R. 563; 1975 S.L.T. 136.

[28] *ante*, para. 4–007.

[29] *ante*, para. 6–011.

[30] *Transocean Marine Paint Association v. E.C. Commission* [1974] E.C.R. 1063.

[31] [1985] A.C. 374; *post*, para. 31–002. *cf. R. v. Barnsley Metropolitan Borough Council, ex p. Hook* [1976] 1 W.L.R. 1052 where Lord Denning M.R. suggested that judicial review was applicable on the ground of natural justice where an administrative body had imposed a punishment out of proportion to the offence.

[32] *Internationale Handelsgesellschaft* [1970] E.C.R. 1125, 1134; *Nold v. E.C. Commission* [1973] E.C.R. 491.

[33] *ante*, para. 6–011 and *post*, para. 22–014.

[34] [1978] 2 C.M.L.R. 292; [1980] 1 C.M.L.R. 488, CA. This case was the sequel to *R. v. Thompson* [1980] Q.B. 229; *ante*, para. 6–025.

claimed that the forfeiture of smuggled krugerrands was contrary to the European Convention and therefore contrary to Community law. Donaldson J. held that, while the EEC Treaty might have been drafted against a background of the recognition of human rights, it did not incorporate them by unwritten, implied Articles. The proper remedy, if the plaintiffs thought that the United Kingdom legislation infringed the European Convention on Human Rights, was to complain to the European Court of Human Rights. The Court of Appeal affirmed Donaldson J., without adverting to the matter of the European Convention, although Lord Denning M.R. remarked briskly that there is no rule of International law which prohibits the forfeiture of smuggled goods.

In *Johnston v. Chief Constable of the R.U.C.*,[35] however, the applicant, on a **6–039** reference to the Court of Justice, by an Employment Tribunal, was successful in challenging the legality of a conclusive certificate issued by the Secretary of State which purported to exclude her statutory right of access to a tribunal on the ground of national security. The right of access to a judicial body was a general principle of law which underlies the constitutional traditions common to member states. The Court referred to Articles 6 and 13 of the European Convention on Human Rights and stated that the principles on which that Convention is based must be taken into consideration in Community law.

---

[35] [1987] Q.B. 129, ECJ.

CHAPTER 7

CONSTITUTIONAL CONVENTIONS[1]

I. THE NATURE AND PURPOSE OF CONSTITUTIONAL CONVENTIONS

Nature of constitutional conventions

7–001   Some study of constitutional conventions is necessary in order to understand the working of the British Constitution. In drawing the distinction between the laws and conventions of the Constitution, Dicey was anticipated by a number of nineteenth-century writers, notably by E. A. Freeman in his *Growth of the English Constitution* (1872)[2]; but the significance of conventions in the working of the British Constitution, and therefore the importance of their study for an understanding of our constitution, were brought out by the emphasis Dicey placed upon them. Dicey's discussion of the distinction between the laws and conventions of the Constitution was not designed to exclude the latter from the purview of law students. On the contrary, his purpose was to insist that the student of constitutional law ought not to neglect to study the conventions as well.

Conventions are sometimes called "unwritten laws," but this is very confusing because according to the generally accepted doctrine they are not laws at all. "Unwritten law" in our system is a term properly applied to the common law. Again conventions are sometimes called "customs." This is liable to cause confusion with customary law, which not only is law in the strict sense but requires for its validity (as conventions do not) immemorial antiquity.

The working definition of constitutional conventions suggested here is: *rules of political practice which are regarded as binding by those to whom they apply, but which are not laws as they are not enforced by the courts or by the Houses of Parliament.*

This definition *distinguishes* constitutional conventions from:

7–002   (i) *mere practice, usage, habit or fact*, which is not regarded as obligatory, such as the existence of political parties (fact) or the habit of Chancellors of the Exchequer in carrying from Downing Street to the House of Commons a dispatch case supposed to contain his "Budget" speech. If the persons concerned are not aware that they are under an obligation to act in a certain way, there is no convention. On the other hand, the opinion that they are bound is not conclusive

---

[1] See Dicey, *Law of the Constitution* (10th ed.), Chaps 14 and 15; *cf.* Professor E. C. S. Wade's *Introduction*, pp. cli–cxci; R. A. Cosgrove, *The Rule of Law, Albert Venn Dicey, Victorian Jurist* (1981), pp. 87–90. Sir Ivor Jennings, *The Law and the Constitution* (5th ed.), Chap. 3; *Cabinet Government* (3rd ed.), Chap. 1; *Parliament* (2nd ed.), Chap. 3; G. Marshall and G. C. Moodie, *Some Problems of the Constitution* (5th ed.), Chap. 2; K. C. Wheare, *Modern Constitutions* (1951), Chap. 8; *The Constitutional Structure of the Commonwealth* (1960); S. A. de Smith. *The New Commonwealth and its Constitutions* (1964), Chaps 1–3; O. Hood Phillips, "Constitutional Conventions: A Conventional Reply" (1964) 8 J.S.P.T.L. 60; C. R. Munro, "Laws and Conventions Distinguished" (1975) 91 L.Q.R. 218; "Dicey on Constitutional Conventions." [1985] P.L. 637; G. H. L. Le May, *The Victorian Constitution* (1979); G. Marshall, *Constitutional Conventions* (1984). T. R. S. Allen, *Law, Liberty, and Justice* (1993, Oxford).
[2] O. Hood Phillips, "Constitutional Conventions: Dicey's Predecessors" (1966) 29 M.L.R. 137.

as they may be mistaken. The precise content of some conventions is uncertain, since they must be flexible enough to meet changing circumstances; and as that which is not certain cannot be obligatory, it is sometimes difficult to distinguish between obligatory rules and non-obligatory practice, such as the consultation of outside interests when social welfare legislation is being drafted.[3]

(ii) *non-political rules, i.e.* rules of conduct which are not referable to the needs of constitutional government, *e.g.* ethical or moral rules, or the almost invariable custom of crowning the Queen Consort, which has no constitutional significance.[4]

(iii) *judicial rules of practice such as the rules of precedent.* In *R. v. Knuller (Publishing, Printing and Promotions) Ltd,*[5] Lord Simon of Glaisdale referred to the current practice under which the House of Lords does not consider itself as bound by its own previous decisions as "one of those conventions which are so significant a feature of the British constitution, as Professor Dicey showed in his famous work." Whatever the status of the rules of judicial precedent, particularly in the House of Lords,[6] to describe them as conventions is probably more misleading than helpful.

(iv) *rules enforced by the courts, i.e. laws.* Judicial enforcement does not   **7–003**
necessarily, or indeed usually, imply specific enforcement. In public law it usually involves an action for damages, declaration or injuction, habeas corpus or judicial review of administrative action; or it may involve a criminal prosecution or a defence to a criminal charge.[7] Sir Ivor Jennings,[8] while admitting that there was this formal distinction between laws and conventions, contended that there was no distinction of substance. The distinction may perhaps be comparatively unimportant for the political scientist or the politician, but it is surely of vital importance for lawyers.[9] Mitchell criticised the distinction on the ground that there may be laws with no judicial sanction.[10] It is true, as Jennings pointed out, that laws cannot be enforced against the government as a body or against either House of Parliament; but they can be enforced against individual Ministers personally,[11] or (subject to parliamentary privilege, which is itself part of the law) against individual members of either House; and judgment may be delivered (though not executed) against a government department.[12] It is also true, as Mitchell pointed out, that Parliament sometimes imposes "duties" on public authorities while going on to say that such duties are not to be enforced by

---

[3] See E. C. S. Wade in Dicey, *op. cit.* at pp. cliv–clv.
[4] In *Queen Caroline's Claim* (1821) 1 St.Tr.(N.S.) 949, the Privy Council held that the Queen Consort has no legal right to be crowned.
[5] [1973] A.C. 435, 484.
[6] See Sir Rupert Cross, *Precedent in English Law* (4th ed., 1991), pp. 109 *et. seq.*
[7] In *Madzimbamuto v. Lardner-Burke* [1969] 1 A.C. 645 the Privy Council held that the convention under which the United Kingdom Parliament did not legislate for Southern Rhodesia without the consent of the government of that colony, although important as a convention, had no effect in limiting the powers of the United Kingdom Parliament.
[8] Jennings, *Law and the Constitution* (5th ed.), p. 117.
[9] The distinction between legal and non-legal rules is recognised outside the field of constitutional law, *e.g.* (formerly) the Judges' Rules, the *Highway Code* and Codes of Practice made under various statutes.
[10] J. D. B. Mitchell, *Constitutional Law* (2nd ed. 1968), pp. 34–39.
[11] *Raleigh v. Goschen* [1893] 1 Ch. 73.
[12] Crown Proceedings Act 1947.

judicial proceedings. For example section 59 of the British Telecommunications Act 1981, provides "(1) It shall be the duty of the Post Office . . . to provide . . . such services for the conveyance of letters as satisfy all reasonable demands for them. . . . (4) Nothing in this section shall be construed as imposing upon the Post Office, either directly or indirectly, any form of duty or liability enforceable by proceedings before any court."[13] On analysis it appears that from a legal point of view such "duties" are properly classed as powers.[14] The statutory requirement that a Governor-General shall direct the issue of writs has been construed to be directory, not mandatory[15]; and the requirement that a Minister shall lay certain instruments before Parliament would probably be interpreted in the same way.[16]

7–004 (v) *rules enforced by the Houses of Parliament* through their officers, *e.g.* the Speaker and the Serjeant-at-Arms, notably parliamentary procedure and privilege (part of "the law and custom of Parliament," which is itself part of the common law in the wide sense). These may, however, overlap constitutional conventions. Thus some parts of parliamentary practice constitute conventions, such as the protection of minorities in debate and the party composition of committees. Standing Orders are often said to be examples of constitutional conventions; but on analysis they will be found to consist partly of law, partly of mere practice, and only to a small extent of convention.[17]

It is also useful to distinguish "conventions" from such distinct, if allied, concepts as "'traditions,' 'principles' and 'doctrines.' "[18] The purpose of conventions may be seen as to give effect to these traditions, principles or values.[19] In *R. v. H.M. Treasury, ex p. Smedley,*[20] for example, Sir John Donaldson M.R. referred to the relationship between Parliament and the judiciary in terms of conventions:

"Although the United Kingdom has no written constitution, it is a constitutional convention of the highest importance that the legislature and the judicature are separate and independent of one another, subject to certain ultimate rights of Parliament over the judicature."

The independence of the judiciary might be described as a *principle* of the Constitution since 1668, enshrined in successive statutory provisions guaranteeing judicial security of tenure.[21]

Judicial recognition of conventions

7–005 The fact that the courts do not *enforce* constitutional conventions does not mean that the courts do not incidentally recognise their existence. They may be

[13] subs. (4) means what it says: *Harold Stephen & Co Ltd v. Post Office* [1977] 1.W.L.R. 1172, CA; *per* Lord Denning M.R. at p. 1177.

[14] Although s.58 enumerates "powers" of the Post Office. The non-performance of "duties" would concern the ultimate authority of the Minister under the Act. For the current position under the Postal Services Act 2000, see *post*, para. 28–012.

[15] *Simpson v. Att.-Gen.* [1955] N.Z.L.R. 271, CA of New Zealand.

[16] *post*, para. 29–023.

[17] *post*, Chap. 11.

[18] Geoffrey Marshall, *Constitutional Conventions* (1984), p. 3.

[19] *Reference re Amendment of the Constitution of Canada* (1982) 125 D.L.R. (3d) 1, 84, *per* Martland, Ritchie, Dickson, Beek, Chouinard, Lamer J.J.

[20] [1985] Q.B. 657, 666.

[21] *post*, para. 20–025.

relied on as an aid to statutory interpretation or to justify non-intervention by the courts in ministerial decisions in areas in which the courts feel that they cannot or should not become involved. Thus the responsibility of the Home Secretary to Parliament was one of the reasons for the decision of the House of Lords in *Liversidge v. Anderson*.[22] The Judicial Committee of the Privy Council in *British Coal Corporation v. The King*[23] mentioned the conventions regulating what was then called Dominion status, and also the convention that the Crown invariably accepts the Judicial Committee's advice. In *Carltona Ltd v. Commissioners of Works*[24] Lord Greene M.R. referred to the convention of a Minister's responsibility to Parliament for the acts of his officials; in *Att.-Gen. v. Jonathan Cape Ltd*,[25] Lord Widgery C.J. referred to the doctrine of joint responsibility within the Cabinet, Cabinet meetings, the Secretary to the Cabinet and the Prime Minister; and in *ex p. Hosenball*,[26] Lord Denning M.R. referred to the responsibility of the Home Secretary to Parliament for the exercise of his power to deport persons on grounds or national security. In *Air Canada v. Secretary of State for Trade*[27] there were a number of references to the convention which prohibits ministers of one party from having access to the papers of their predecessors of other parties without the agreement of the previous administration.

The case *Re Amendment of the Constitution of Canada*[28] that came before the   **7–006**
Supreme Court of Canada in 1981 is of great interest as being a unique discussion of constitutional conventions by a Commonwealth court of the highest standing, especially since a case of this kind could never come before British courts who have no jurisdiction to determine such matters.[29] The Canadian Supreme Court was hearing an appeal from various provincial courts exercising their statutory jurisdiction to consider references from the Executive on matters which included questions that otherwise might not be justiciable. In addition to the legal question whether the consent of the Provinces was required before the Canadian Parliament could request the United Kingdom to amend the Canadian Constitution

---

[22] [1942] A.C. 206; but the Home Secretary was also required by statutory regulation to report monthly to Parliament. Ministerial responsibility was also referred to in *Padfield v. Minister of Agriculture, Fisheries and Food* [1968] A.C. 997, by Lord Reid, and in *Raymond v. Attorney-General* [1982] Q.B. 839, by Sir Sebag Shaw.

[23] [1935] A.C. 500; W. Ivor Jennings, "The Statute of Westminster and Appeals" (1936) 52 L.Q.R. 173.

[24] [1943] 2 All E.R. 560.

[25] [1976] Q.B. 752; refusing an injunction to restrain publication of Vol. 1 of Richard Crossman, *Diaries of a Cabinet Minister*.

[26] *R. v. Secretary of State for Home Department, ex p. Hosenball* [1977] 1 W.L.R. 766, DC, 776, CA.

[27] [1983] A.C. 394, HL. See further, Lord Hunt of Tanworth, "Access to a Previous Government's Papers" [1982] P.L. 514. Mr Callaghan was reported in *The Times*, July 14, 1986 to have agreed to allow Conservative Ministers to examine the papers on which the Labour Government in 1977 had decided to buy the Nimrod airborne early warning system; *post* para. 17–022.

[28] (1981) 125 D.L.R. (3d) 1. And see O. Hood Phillips, "Constitutional Conventions in the Supreme Court of Canada" (1982) 98 L.Q.R. 194. *cf.* Rodney Brazier and St. John Robilliard, "Constitutional Conventions: The Canadian Supreme Court's Views Reviewed" [1982] P.L. 28: they go too far in saying "the question of the existence, but not of the precise limits of a convention is now unquestionably a justiciable issue." The jurisdiction of the Canadian Supreme Court in this context was based on certain special provincial statutes, and in any event that Court's opinions, though persuasive, are not binding in this country.

[29] The Judicial Committee of the Privy Council might possibly be called upon to give an opinion on such a matter in relation to the constitution of some other Commonwealth country from which appeals to it have not been abolished.

(British North America Act 1867, as amended), the Supreme Court accepted appellate jurisdiction to determine whether such consent was required by constitutional convention and, if so, whether the convention had been observed in that case. Both the existence and content of the alleged convention being disputed, the Supreme Court's decision involved an analysis of the general nature of constitutional conventions. A majority held in the first place that a constitutional convention cannot crystallise into law. They said[30]:

> "No instance of an explicit recognition of a convention as having matured into a rule of law was produced. The very nature of a convention, as political in inception and as depending on a persistent course of political recognition by those for whose benefit and to whose detriment (if any) the convention developed over a considerable period of time, is inconsistent with its legal enforcement. . . . The attempted assimilation of the growth of a convention to the growth of the common law is misconceived. The latter is the product of judicial effort, based on justiciable issues which attained legal formulation and are subject to modification and even reversal by the courts which gave them their birth. . . . No such parental role is played by the courts with respect to conventions."

Conventions, said their Lordships, are not enforced by the courts: if there is a conflict between conventions and law the courts must enforce the law. The sanctions for conventions are political, though the violation of conventions is "unconstitutional." The Supreme Court approved Jennings's criteria for establishing the existence of a convention (*supra*). However, Jennings says "it is sometimes enough to show that a rule has received general acceptance," and goes on to speak of the assertions of "persons of authority," whereas their Lordships apparently took the view that it is the actors who must have treated the rule as binding.[31] The majority admitted a lack of precision in the convention asserted, but came to the conclusion that "at least a substantial measure" of provincial agreement was necessary, a requirement which was not satisfied in this case. A minority (including Laskin C.J.) had no doubt that the consent of all the Provinces was required, taking the view, which it is submitted is preferable, that a convention must be sufficiently definite to be understandable and understood. They said further that conventions have the unquestioned acceptance not only of the politicians but of the public at large. The precedents on this view were far from conclusive.

7–007 Legislation may recognise or presuppose conventions. Thus the Ministers of the Crown Act 1937 implied a knowledge of the existence of the Prime Minister, the Leader of the Opposition and the Cabinet; and later statutes dealing with salaries and pensions acknowledge the existence of leaders of the Opposition and Chief Whips in both Houses.[32] The preamble to the Statute of Westminster 1931 recites several conventions of inter-Commonwealth relations.

---

[30] At p. 22.
[31] Marshall, *op. cit.* note 18 pp. 11–12, on the obligatory nature of conventions distinguishes between "positive morality" (subjective test) and "critical morality" (objective test), preferring the latter but not stating definitely whose opinion is to be taken.
[32] See now, Ministerial and other Salaries Act 1975. *post*, para. 10–024.

Conventions are capable of being formulated in statute, *e.g.* the Statue of Westminster 1931, s.4, and they have been incorporated (with or without justiciable effect) in various Commonwealth constitutions.[33]

Devolution has resulted in the role of the Prime Minister in the appointment of the Lord President and Lord Justice Clerk being given statutory recognition, presumably to prevent any possible dispute over the respective rights of himself and the First Minister.[34]

The laws of the constitution could stand alone, although the constitution would then be antiquated and static; but the conventions would be meaningless without their legal context. Every constitutional convention is closely related to some law or laws, which it implies. The conventions forming the Cabinet system, for example, presuppose the laws relating to such matters as the Queen's royal prerogative, the office and powers of Ministers (except the Prime Minister), the constitution of government departments, and the composition of Parliament. There are thus layers, as it were, of laws, conventions and facts (political practice); and any one situation may be governed by a number of layers of this kind, perhaps including a statute which implies the existence of a convention.

On the other hand, constitutional conventions are subject to the processes of growth and transformation. As Baldwin said in the House of Commons at the time of the "agreement to differ" in 1932: "The historian can probably tell you perfectly clearly what the constitutional practice of the country was at any given period in the past, but it would be very difficult for a living writer to tell you at any given period in his lifetime what the constitution of the country is in all respects, and for this reason, that at almost any given moment of our lifetime, there may be one practice called 'Constitutional' which is falling into desuetude and there may be another practice which is creeping into use but which is not yet called 'Constitutional.' "[35]

Purpose of constitutional conventions

Conventions are a means of bringing about constitutional development without formal changes in the law.[36] This they often do by regulating the exercise of a discretionary power conferred on the Crown by the law. It must not be supposed that conventions are peculiar to unwritten constitutions. They are found to a greater or less extent in written constitutions as well. Canada and Australia,[37] for example, observe the main British constitutional conventions, and many conventions have been developed in the United States relating to such matters as the method of electing the President, his choice and use of a Cabinet, and "senatorial courtesy" in making appointments to office.[38] This informal method of change is more adaptable than a series of statutes or constitutional amendments. The

7–008

---

[33] *Adegbenro v. Akintola* [1963] A.C. 614, PC *per* Viscount Radcliffe; *cf. Ningkan v. Government of Malaysia* [1970] A.C. 379; see de Smith *The New Commonwealth and its Constitution* (1964), pp. 51–52, 88–90. K.J. Keith, "The Courts and the Conventions of the Constitution" (1967) 16 I.C.L.Q. 542. (British constitutional conventions were not expressly incorporated but were used by the courts to help to interpret the Nigerian constitution); C. Sampford and D. Wood, "Codification of Constitutional Conventions in Australia," [1987] P.L. 231.

[34] Scotland Act 1998, s.95(1).

[35] H.C. Deb., Vol. 261, ser. 5, col. 515 (1932).

[36] Conventions therefore change in accordance with the underlying ideas of government: see Holdsworth, "The Conventions of the Eighteenth-Century Constitution" (1932) 17 *Iowa Law Review* 161.

[37] George Winterton, *Parliament, the Executive and the Governor-General* (Melbourne, 1983).

[38] H. W. Horwill, *The Usages of the American Constitution* (1925).

general tendency is towards democracy, due regard being had to the protection of minorities and their right to be heard.

The ultimate object of most conventions is that public affairs should be conducted in accordance with the wishes of the majority of the electors. The reason why the Ministry must be chosen from the party or parties enjoying a majority in the Commons is that, on the assumption that the majority of the Commons reflect the views of the majority of the electors,[39] a Ministry so selected will be most likely to give effect to the will of the nation as a whole. And this is also the reason why the Queen should act on the advice of Ministers, why Ministers should resign if they lose the confidence of Commons, and why the House of Commons should have a political ascendancy over the House of Lords, especially in matters of finance.

To ensure that the power of government shall be exercised in accordance with the popular will, that will must be ascertained from those best qualified to know it, namely, the elected representatives of the people; hence the convention requiring Parliament to be summoned annually. If the Government no longer retains the confidence of the House of Commons the Prime Minister should ask for a dissolution of Parliament,[40] in order to enable the electorate, through a new Parliament, to obtain a new Ministry more in accordance with its views.

7–009   In this way the legal framework of 1688—a strong monarchy limited in certain specific ways—has become a "constitutional" monarchy, that is to say, a democratic political system with a hereditary Head of State practically bereft of governmental powers and distinguished from the head of the Government (Prime Minister). To meet current political ideas and social needs, conventions have facilitated the growth of the Cabinet system; changed the emphasis on the functions of Parliament, which is now largely occupied in representing the views of the electors by criticising the government's activities and debating their measures; and developed the autonomy of other Commonwealth countries.

Conventions also make the legal constitution work by providing means for co-operation in the practice of government. In particular, the Cabinet system co-ordinates the work of the various government departments among themselves, and promotes co-operation between the departments and Parliament and between the Ministry and the Queen. Similarly, the conventions governing inter-Commonwealth relations enable the members of the Commonwealth, although independent, to co-operate to a great extent in their defence and foreign policy.

How and when do conventions become established?

7–010   It is wrong to suppose that constitutional conventions are analogous to customary law in that they must necessarily have existed a long time, or even from time immemorial. A moment's thought will show that this cannot be so, for the conventions of our constitution mostly date from a time later than the Revolution of 1688, and in most cases a good deal later. Many conventions are indeed based on usage, although this is not necessarily of long standing. Some conventions, however—especially among those concerned with Commonwealth relations—are based on agreement,[41] and we know exactly when and how they were formulated.

---

[39] Owing to our "first past the post" electoral system, a majority in the Commons may, however, represent a minority of the voters and a smaller minority of the electorate.

[40] In some circumstances it may be appropriate for the Ministry to resign; *post*, para. 8–019.

[41] This is the sense in which international lawyers speak of "conventions."

It is not easy to say precisely how or when conventions based on usage come into existence. Every act by the Queen or a responsible statesman is a "precedent"[42] in the sense of an example which may or may not be followed in subsequent similar cases, but it does not necessarily create a binding rule. For that it must be generally accepted as creating a rule by those in authority. A long series of precedents all pointing in the same direction is very good evidence of a convention, but this is not possible in the case of recent precedents. Thus the fact that no monarch has refused the Royal Assent to a Bill since Queen Anne clearly points to the existence of a convention that the Royal Assent should not be refused; but can we say that the Queen may in no circumstances refuse the Prime Minister's request to dissolve Parliament?

Sir Ivor Jennings suggested two requirements for the creation of a convention: (i) general acceptance as obligatory, and (ii) a reason or purpose referable to the existing requirements of constitutional government. Thus one precedent might create a convention whereas a long series of precedents might not. Owing to Cabinet secrecy, posthumous biographies and prejudiced autobiographies, it is often difficult to find out whether the actors thought they were obeying a binding rule.[43]

Why are conventions observed?

What is it that induces obedience to these extra-legal or conventional rules? **7–011** The answer seems to be that obedience is yielded to the conventions because of the consequences that would plainly ensue if they were disregarded. Thus if Parliament were not summoned annually the army and air force could not lawfully be maintained, an important part of the public revenue, namely income tax, could not be lawfully raised, and even less could be lawfully spent.[44] If the Queen appointed as Prime Minister someone who did not enjoy the confidence of the majority of the Commons, he and his colleagues could be defeated in the lower House. If a government after such defeat in the House declined to resign or ask for a dissolution, the Commons could paralyse the business of government by withholding supplies or refusing to agree to the continuance in force of the Army and Air Force Acts. Even if a government succeeded in carrying on for a time in disregard of Parliament, it would cease to be in touch with the will of the electors and would forfeit their favour, assuming this had not been already lost by the recourse to extra-parliamentary government.

Some conventions are not always observed if special circumstances warrant a departure from established practice, but if they were not regularly observed they would not be, or would cease to be, conventions.[45] It is the reason or purpose for which they stand that both leads to their development and secures their observance. The "agreement to differ" in 1932, whereby certain Liberal members of the Cabinet were permitted by their colleagues to disagree openly on the majority's fiscal policy, was alleged to be justified by the necessity of preserving the National (Coalition) Government in view of the "economic crisis"; but it did not

---

[42] The word "precedent" is not, of course, used here in the technical sense of a legal (judicial) precedent.

[43] *Cabinet Government* (3rd ed.), pp. 5–13.

[44] That is, so long as the practice, itself also a convention, continues of authorising these matters by annual Acts or statutory provisions having force for one year only.

[45] F. D. Roosevelt broke the American convention against standing for the office of President for a third term. He was elected and later re-elected for a fourth term; but an amendment to the Constitution has since been passed limiting the tenure of office to two terms.

work, and the recalcitrant members soon resigned office.[46] The convention of the collective responsibility of Ministers has shown signs of weakening in the last few years, notably during the EEC referendum campaign in 1975 when the Prime Minister (Mr Wilson) allowed Ministers to speak against this country's staying in the Community, though this concession did not extend to speaking in Parliament.[47] One Minister who did speak in the Commons against the Government White Paper advocating continued membership of the EEC, was dismissed from office.[48]

7–012   Dicey rejected the answer that observance of constitutional conventions is secured by "public opinion," on the ground that it begs the question, which is, why does public opinion appear to be sufficiently strong to ensure the observance of the conventions?[49] In the past, respect for conventions was established by the threat of impeachment, greatly influenced by public opinion; but a stronger sanction was needed, and impeachment has in practice become obsolete as being unnecessary in view of the development of ministerial responsibility to Parliament. Dicey concluded that the sanction of constitutional conventions is to be found in the fact that a person who persisted in the breach of convention would inevitably be led into a breach of the law "sooner or later"—in one place he says "immediately." Thus if Parliament were not summoned in any one year, so that the annual Finance and Appropriation and Army Acts[50] expired, the collection of much of the national revenue (especially income tax), the expenditure of most of the public funds and the maintenance of a standing army and enforcement of military discipline would be illegal under the Bill of Rights.

Dicey dealt, however, only with one group of conventions, though admittedly the most important, namely, those that regulate the relations between the executive and Parliament, especially those between the government and the House of Commons. No breach of law would follow if Standing Orders relating to the rights of minorities were not followed in conducting the business of either House, nor (by English law) if the United Kingdom Parliament legislated for an independent member of the Commonwealth without its consent, nor (assuming it to be a constitutional convention, as distinct from the practice of the court, that they should not) if lay peers took part in an appeal before the House of Lords.

7–013   Further, certain qualifications must be made even in the case of those conventions to which Dicey's argument applies. If a government that was committing breaches of convention retained the confidence of the Commons it could procure the alteration of the law, as it did with the Provisional Collection of Taxes Act 1913, following the decision of *Bowles v. The Bank of England*[51] or the passage of an Act of Indemnity, thus indicating that the convention in question was considered undesirable or to have lost its purpose. Even if the government lost the confidence of the Commons, it might remain in office for some months without breaking the law owing to the time-lag between the lapsing of the Finance Act (fixing the standard rate of income tax and authorising most of the

---

[46] Keith Middlemas and John Barnes, *Baldwin* (1969) Chap. 24.
[47] See David L. Ellis, "Collective Ministerial Responsibility and Collective Solidarity", [1980] P.L. 367; *post* para. 17–019.
[48] *post*, para. 17–019.
[49] Dicey, *op. cit.* note 1; Chap. 15.
[50] His argument is not affected by the modern procedure whereby the Army and Air Force and Naval Discipline Acts are continued in force for 12 months at a time by Orders in Council subject to affirmative resolution of both Houses: Armed Forces Act 1976.
[51] [1913] 1 Ch. 57.

expenditure) and the Army Act and the beginning of the next financial year when the Commons must be asked for fresh supplies.

For the reasons stated above, however, it is submitted that it is not necessary to go as far as Dicey. The question why conventions are observed is a political or psychological question. One might equally ask what motives induce people to obey the law, since fear of the legal sanction only operates on some of the people some of the time.[52] As a matter of fact, statesmen probably observe the conventions because they wish the machinery of government to go on[53] and because they hope to retain the favour of the electorate.[54]

II. Classification and Illustration of Constitutional Conventions

This section should be prefaced by a reminder that it is not practicable either **7–014** to enumerate all the conventions applicable to the working of the British Constitution or to define most of them with any great precision. Subject to this caution, it is proper to ask what non-legal rules we would feel constrained to put into a written constitution if it was decided to have one?[55]

Constitutional conventions may be classified into three main groups:

(1) relating to the exercise of the royal prerogative and the working of the Cabinet system;

(2) regulating the relations between the Lords and Commons, and proceedings in Parliament; and

(3) regulating the relations between the United Kingdom and the independent members of the Commonwealth.

The first group is the most important, and forms the main theme of Dicey's discussion (*ante*). The second group has lost much of its importance as convention since the passing of the Parliament Acts. The third group has developed almost entirely since Dicey's day.

It is difficult to say to what extent conventions, in the sense in which we have defined them, exist in English local government, *e.g.* as to the election of chairmen of council and its committees, having regard to the state of the parties on the council. The practice varies greatly from one local authority to another, and is often not consistent over a period within the same authority. Further, political scientists who have examined this question tend to ignore the distinction between rules regarded as obligatory and mere practice.[56]

---

[52] See Bryce, *Studies in History and Jurisprudence*, Vol. II, Essay IX.

[53] Marshall and Moodie, *op. cit.* suggest that the sanction for the observance of conventions is that a breach of convention is likely to lead to a *change* of law.

[54] Reciprocity is the chief sanction of Parliamentary conventions; each Government is likely in time to be in opposition.

[55] Mr Trudeau, Prime Minister of Canada, made a partial attempt to do this in 1969; *The Constitution and the People of Canada* (Ottawa), pp. 64 *et seq.*

[56] See R. S. B. Knowles, "Local Government Practices—or Conventions?" (1958) 122 J.P. 856; E. S. Walker, "Conventions in Local Government" (1959) 123 J.P. 234; H. Maddick and E. P. Pritchard, "The Conventions of Local Authorities in the West Midlands" (1958) *Public Administration* 145; (1959), *Public Administration* 135.

1. Conventions relating to the exercise of the royal prerogative and the working of the Cabinet system

7–015   The Sovereign could legally declare war or make peace; dissolve Parliament at any time, and need not summon another for three years; she could refuse her assent to measures passed by both Houses of Parliament; she could at any time dismiss her Ministers and appoint others, and so on. The exercise of these powers, however, is either restricted altogether or regulated by conventions, of which the following are some of the most important.

(i) The Queen must invite the leader of the party or group commanding a majority of the House of Commons to form a Ministry. The person so called on is the "Prime Minister." In law the Prime Minister until recently did not exist, and even now is only referred to incidentally in statutes relating to salaries and pensions.[57]

(ii) The Queen must appoint as her other Ministers such persons as the Prime Minister advises her to appoint. Ministers should have seats in either the House of Commons or the House of Lords. The latter convention is illustrated by the appointment by Mr Harold Wilson of Mr Cousins and Mr Gordon Walker to ministerial posts after the Labour victory in the general election in October 1964. Neither was a Member of Parliament: Mr Cousins was a trade union official, and Mr Walker (who was appointed Foreign Secretary) had actually been defeated at Smethwick in the recent election. In January 1965 they stood as candidates in by-elections facilitated by the grant of life peerages to two Labour M.P.s. Mr Cousins was elected, but Mr Walker was again defeated and resigned office next day. (By law the Queen can appoint and dismiss Ministers at her pleasure).[58]

7–016   (iii) The body of Ministers so appointed become the "Government," and an inner ring of them is called the "Cabinet."[59] Cabinet Ministers are always made Privy Councillors, if not such already. The Cabinet is entirely the product of convention, and is unknown to the law except for a few incidental references in statutes relating to Ministerial salaries, the Parliamentary Commissioner Act 1967 and the Data Protection Act 1998.

(iv) The Queen is bound to exercise her legal powers in accordance with the advice tendered to her by the Cabinet through the Prime Minister. She has the right to be kept informed and to express her views on the questions at issue, but not to override ministerial advice. This advice is expected to be unanimous.

(v) The Queen must assent to every Bill passed by the Houses of Parliament, or passed by the House of Commons only in accordance with the provisions of the Parliament Acts. A sovereign has not refused assent to a Bill since Queen Anne refused her assent to the Scottish Militia Bill in 1707, and the exercise of this prerogative today would be unconstitutional.[60] (No Bill has the force of law until the Queen gives her assent, but there is no law requiring her to give it.)

---

[57] *post*, para. 17–025; Even so, to get the salary or pension the Prime Minister must hold, or have held, the legal office of First Lord of the Treasury.

[58] See also *post* para. 17–008 for the case of Lord Young of Graffham, elevated to the House of Lords in 1984 and appointed Minister without Portfolio before becoming, in 1985, Secretary of State for Employment. Gus Macdonald was appointed Scottish Office Minister for Business and Industry in August 1998, four months before he could take a seat in the House of Lords as Lord Macdonald.

[59] It has been suggested that it has also become a convention that the Opposition leaders should form a Shadow Cabinet; D. R. Turner, *The Shadow Cabinet in British Politics*, (1969).

[60] The Prime Minister might perhaps advise the Queen to refuse assent to a Private Bill passed by both Houses but to which the government objected; and possibly to a Public Bill if there has been a change of circumstances or a mistake has been found in the text; though in the latter case an amending Act would more likely be the appropriate procedure.

(vi) Parliament must be summoned to meet at least once each year. The observance of this convention is secured by the practice (probably itself also a convention) of limiting to one year at a time the statutory authority covering the raising and spending of part of the revenue and the maintenance of the Army and Air Force. (By the Meeting of Parliament Act 1694 Parliament must be summoned at least once in three years.)

(vii) The Government is entitled to continue in office only so long as it enjoys **7–017** the confidence of a majority in the House of Commons. The Prime Minister is bound to advise the Sovereign to dissolve Parliament, or to tender the resignation of himself and his ministerial colleagues, if the government is defeated on the floor of the House of Commons on a motion of confidence or of no confidence. Owing to party discipline, the defeat of a Government with a party majority in the Commons on a motion of this kind is rare in modern times. Mr Wilson's government was defeated in the Commons in March 1976 on its policy of cutting public expenditure, but it won a motion of confidence next day. When Mr Callaghan's government was defeated on a guillotine motion relating to the Scotland and Wales Bill in February 1977, this was not regarded by either side as a question of confidence. Similarly in May 1978 the Government was defeated twice in three days in Committee on amendments to the Finance Bill but did not—and was not expected—to resign.[61] A Government may, conversely, expressly make an issue one of confidence in order to bring its recalcitrant backbenchers into line, as for example Mr Major did, in order to secure the passage of legislation necessary to give effect to the Treaty of Maastricht.[62]

(viii) The Ministers are collectively responsible to Parliament for the general conduct of the affairs of the country. This collective responsibility requires that on a major question Ministers should be of one mind and voice. If any Minister does not agree with the policy of the majority in the Cabinet, he should resign or, if the matter is a minor one or he is not a member of the Cabinet, at least keep quiet about it.[63] On two occasions the convention has been formally waived, the "agreement to differ" in 1932 when members of the National government Cabinet were free to express conflicting views publicly on the economic crises then facing the country and the EEC Referendum campaign in 1976.[64] Where a decision is taken to postpone a decision—as currently, for example, whether (or when) to adopt the euro as the currency in place of the pound—collective responsibility is put under particular pressure as attempts are made to read into ministerial speeches indications of agreement—with or dissent from the officially agreed decision.[65]

(ix) Ministers are also individually responsible to Parliament for the administration of their departments.[66] A Minister must be prepared to answer questions in the House concerning matters for which he is administratively responsible, and

---

[61] *cf.* a defeat in the House on Budget resolutions which would lead to resignation. *Post*, para. 12–014. Motions other than motions of confidence or no confidence may be treated as matters of confidence, and rather more latitude is allowed to a minority government *i.e.* one that does not hold a party majority in the House. See further, pp. 150–152, See Philip Norton, "Government Defeats in the House of Commons: Myth and Reality," [1978] P.L. 360.

[62] European Communities (Amendment) Act 1993; *post* para. 15–030.

[63] *post*, para. 17–020.

[64] *ante.*, para. 4–019.

[65] The present position is that when the Cabinet is satisfied that a sufficient degree of "convergence," as measured by five economic tests, exists between the economies of the United Kingdom and the euro economies, a referendum will be held to decide the issue.

[66] *post*, para. 12–024.

if a vote of censure is passed against him he must resign his office. Standing Orders of the House of Commons assume the existence of the former convention by prescribing days and times for questions. (By law, Ministers are individually responsible to the Sovereign.)

(x) Ministers are expected to disembarrass themselves of any company directorships or shareholdings that would be likely, or might appear, to conflict with their official duties.[67]

(xi) A government should not advise the Crown to declare war, make peace or conclude a treaty unless there is ample ground for supposing that the majority of the Commons approve of the policy. (By law the power to make war and peace and to enter into international treaties is vested in the Queen, who is not bound to consult advisers[68] or Parliament, though the Bill of Rights prevents her from imposing taxation to meet financial commitments.)

2. Conventions regulating the relations between the Lords and Commons, and proceedings in Parliament

7–018   The House of Commons being the representative assembly, its will ought ultimately to prevail in cases of conflict with the House of Lords, which is mainly hereditary and partly nominated. Since medieval times the Commons have claimed the right to control national finance, that is, the levying of taxation and the supervision of the expenditure of public money.

Each House must have power to control the conduct of its own proceedings free from outside interference, and in course of time the Houses have evolved rules and customs, privileges and practice regulating legislative procedure and the conduct of debate.

The following are some of the most important conventions in this group:

(i) In cases of conflict the Lords should ultimately yield to the Commons.[69] (Perhaps the Parliament Acts 1911 and 1949—by defining the period during which the Lords may delay public Bills, other than a Bill to extend the maximum duration of Parliament—have rendered this convention unnecessary.) Until the Parliament Act 1911 was passed it was legitimate for a Ministry, when an important measure was rejected by the Lords, to advise the Sovereign as a last resort to create a sufficient number of peers to ensure its passage in the Upper House. The Treaty of Utrecht was ratified by this method in 1712; and the Reform Act 1832 and the Parliament Act 1911 were passed by the threat of recourse to it. (The Parliament Act 1911 made recourse to this expedient for the future unnecessary and perhaps improper.)

(ii) Proposals involving the expenditure of public money may only be introduced on behalf of the Crown by a Minister in the House of Commons. Standing Orders provide that a financial resolution shall only be proposed by a Minister on behalf of the Crown. There may be elements here of parliamentary custom and privilege, as well as constitutional convention. (The Parliament Act 1911 assumes, without expressly stating, that Money Bills will be introduced in the Commons.)

(iii) The business of the House of Commons is arranged informally "behind the Speaker's Chair" between the Prime Minister or Leader of the House and the

---

[67] See the *Ministerial Code*, the formal guide to conduct for ministers.

[68] Foreign countries, however, might well be unwilling to enter into a treaty that was not authenticated by the signature or seal of some senior Minister.

[69] See *post* paras 7–022 to 7–023 for a discussion of recent instances of serious embarrassment caused to the Government by the rejection and amendment of legislation by the House of Lords.

Leader of the Opposition. The last is a product of convention more recent than the Prime Minister, and fulfils the function of a sparring partner. Charles James Fox is generally regarded as the first Leader of the Opposition, when the younger Pitt became Prime Minister in 1783. (The Ministers of the Crown Act 1937 first gave the Leader of the Opposition a salary payable out of the Consolidated Fund; and the Ministerial Salaries and Members' Pensions Act 1965 gave salaries to the Leader of the Opposition in the House of Lords and the Chief Opposition Whips in both Houses.[70] These salaries are charged on the Consolidated Fund.) A member may, so far as his Chief Whip is concerned, safely absent himself from a debate if he obtains a "pair" from among members of the other party.

(iv) The majority in Parliament must not stifle minorities. It is a duty of the Speaker to protect minorities in debate, and so far as possible he calls on speakers from alternate parties.

(v) The political parties are represented in parliamentary committees in proportion to the number of their adherents in the House. (The Ministers of the Crown Act 1937 indirectly recognised the existence of political parties in its definition of the Leader of the Opposition.)

(vi) Peers who do not hold or have not held high judicial office do not take part when the House of Lords is sitting in its judicial capacity. (The Appellate Jurisdiction Acts provide for the appointment of a certain number of Lords of Appeal in Ordinary, but there is no law that lay peers may not sit as well.) This rule is perhaps rather one of parliamentary practice or the practice of the court than a "convention," as it is not of a political nature referable to the needs of constitutional government.[71]

(vii) We may say that there is a convention that the Houses of Parliament will not entertain, or pass, a private Bill without providing for adequate notice to be given to persons affected and allowing them an opportunity to state objections. The Standing Orders relating to private business, which are alterable in detail, presuppose this convention.[72]

3. Conventions regulating the relations between the United Kingdom and other members of the Commonwealth

A number of conventions have grown up, or have been formulated, regulating **7–019** the relations between the United Kingdom and the independent members of the Commonwealth, providing methods of co-operation and communication among the members of the Commonwealth and concerning negotiations between them and foreign countries. Many of these conventions were formulated as resolutions of Imperial Conferences between the wars, though that did not give them legal effect. The following are some of the most important of this group of conventions:

(i) The Parliament of the United Kingdom may not legislate for a former dependent territory that is now an independent member of the Commonwealth except at its request and with its consent. (This convention is recited in the preamble to the Statute of Westminster 1931, and enacted as section 4 of that Act. It has also been enacted in various Independence Acts.)

(ii) Any alteration in the law touching the succession to the throne or the Royal Style and Titles requires the assent of the Parliaments of Canada, Australia

---

[70] These provisions are now contained in more recent legislation.
[71] See further, *post*, para. 7–045.
[72] *cf. Edinburgh and Dalkeith Ry. v. Wauchope* (1842) 8 Cl. & F. 710, HL; *Pickin v. British Railways Board* [1974] A.C. 765, HL.

and New Zealand as well as of the Parliament of the United Kingdom. (This convention is recited in the preamble to the Statute of Westminster 1931.) The same convention may apply to other members of the Commonwealth of which Her Majesty is Queen.

(iii) The Queen in appointing the Governor-General of an independent Commonwealth country acts on the advice of the Prime Minister of that country.

(iv) The Governor-General is the representative of the Queen, not of the British Government, and acts on the advice of the government of the Commonwealth country concerned.

(v) The governments of the United Kingdom and the independent members of the Commonwealth keep each other informed with regard to the negotiation of treaties and the conduct of foreign affairs, and one of them can commit the others to active participation without their consent.

The Crown or the Governor-General would not be bound by English law to observe these last three conventions, but such conventions may be enacted in the constitutions of Commonwealth countries. Convention (iii) and (iv) are not applicable to Commonwealth countries that have become republics, and is doubtful whether convention (ii) is applicable to them.[73]

---

[73] See further, *post*, Chap. 36.

PART II

PARLIAMENT

CHAPTER 8

"THE HIGH COURT OF PARLIAMENT"[1]

I. HISTORICAL INTRODUCTION

In origin Parliament was not primarily a lawmaking body, nor are its functions **8–001** exclusively legislative at the present day. A "parliament" was a council summoned to discuss some important matter, and the name is still appropriate to its present activity of debating policy and questioning and criticising the government. The title given it in the Book of Common Prayer, "the High Court of Parliament," reminds us that Parliament was, and still is, a court—the highest court in the land. The word "court" (*curia*) has a number of meanings. It may mean the place where the Sovereign is, a body of judges appointed to administer the law, or a place where justice is administered. Coke, in his treatment of the jurisdiction of the courts, deals first with "The High and most Honourable Court of Parliament,"[2] and says that "the Lords in their House have power of Judicature, and both Houses together have power of Judicature."[3]

The distant precursor of Parliament was the *Curia Regis*, in which the judicial, executive and legislative powers were fused. Its remotest ancestor, the Witenagemot, also exercised all three functions of government. In the early Middle Ages ⟨...⟩ ff from the council, and the latter may be said to ⟨...⟩ n of Richard II. Appeal by writ of error ⟨...⟩ se of Lords. Adjudication was one of ⟨...⟩ ents, notably those of Edward I.[4] The ⟨...⟩ ard II in 1311) ordained that the King ⟨...⟩ ar in which pleas that had been delayed ⟨...⟩ l be recorded and determined.

⟨...⟩ ot the assembly he had in mind should **8–002** ⟨...⟩ ould be passed, or taxation discussed, ⟨...⟩ e medieval Parliament was not "demo- ⟨...⟩ at three factors combined to produce

⟨...⟩ processes of administration and law by ⟨...⟩ ng difficulties;

[1] The leading reference book on the topics discussed in Chaps 8–13 is Erskine May's *Treatise on the Law, Privileges, Proceedings and Usage of Parliament*, hereafter cited as Erskine May, *Parliamentary Practice*. The first edition appeared in 1844; the 22nd (current) edition in 1997. Although a valuable work of reference it is not itself authoritative nor is it necessarily always correct: Mr Robin Maxwell Hyslop M.P., letter to *Daily Telegraph* January 10, 1984. See also Griffith and Ryle, *Parliament* (R. Blackburn and A. Kenyon eds., 2nd ed., 2001).

[2] 4 Inst. 3,4.

[3] 4 Inst. 15.

[4] Maitland, *Memoranda de Parliamento* (1893); McIlwain, *The High Court of Parliament* (1910), Chap. 3; Baldwin, *The King's Council during the Middle Ages*, Chaps 1 and 12; Pollard, *Evolution of Parliament* (2nd ed., 1926), Chap. 2; Pike, *Constitutional History of the House of Lords* (1894), Chap. 4.

(ii) the desire of the barons to control the government by establishing a method of proper consultation; and

(iii) the popular desire to get abuses removed and grievances remedied through ready access to an institution which could grant the highest justice.[5]

Judicial functions

8–003   Before treating of the legislative functions of Parliament, which today are at least of equal importance to its general supervision of the government of the country, we may preserve a historical sense by glancing at its remaining judicial functions. These include:

(1) The appellate jurisdiction of the House of Lords, both civil and criminal.

(2) The judicial functions of the Lords and Commons within the sphere of their privileges.[6]

(3) The jurisdiction of the Lords and the Commons in committees dealing with private Bills.[7]

(4) The judicial functions of the Lords with regard to claims to ancient peerages.[8]

These are discussed later in their appropriate chapters. Here we will mention impeachment and attainder (now in practice obsolete) and trial of peers (abolished)[9] to which we add a note on Committees and Tribunals of Inquiry.

Impeachment

8–004   Impeachment was a judicial proceeding against any person, whether lord or commoner, accused of state offences beyond the reach of the law, or which no other authority in the state would prosecute. The Commons were the accusers, and the Lords were judges both of fact and law.

The first recorded case of impeachment occurred in 1376, when two lords and four commoners were charged with removing the staple from Calais, lending the King money at usurious interest, and buying Crown debts for small sums and then paying themselves in full out of the Treasury. There were no impeachments between that of the Duke of Suffolk for treason in 1449 and that of Sir Giles Mompesson in 1621 for fraud, violence and oppression. In the same year Bacon was impeached for bribery in the office of Lord Chancellor: the large fine was remitted and the King set him at liberty, but he was banned from public office for the rest of his life.[10] Most impeachments took place in the early 1640s.

8–005   The Act of Settlement 1700 provides that no pardon under the Great Seal shall be pleadable to an impeachment by the Commons. This provision arose out of

---

[5] G. O. Sayles, *The King's Parliament of England* (1975) covers the period 1258–1377.
[6] *post*, para. 13–020.
[7] *post*, para. 11–038.
[8] *post*, para. 9–004. This function remains, as the House of Lords Act 1999 does not affect the existence or continuation of hereditary titles.
[9] For the history of impeachment, attainder and trial of peers, see Stephen, *History of the Criminal Law* (1883), Vol. 1, Chap. 5.
[10] See Clifford Hall, "Francis Bacon: The 'Wisest, Brightest, Meanest of Mankind'?" (1976) 7 *Cambrian Law Review*, 38.

Danby's Case.[11] Danby was impeached in connection with a letter written by him to the English ambassador at Versailles with the approval of Charles II, who wrote on the letter: "This letter is writ by my Order—C.R." The last two cases of impeachment were those of Warren Hastings, Governor-General of India,[12] and Lord Melville, formerly treasurer to the Admiralty.[13] Both were acquitted.

The Joint Committee on Parliamentary Privilege said of impeachment "that the circumstances in which impeachment has taken place are now so remote from the present that the procedure may be considered obsolete."[14]

Acts of Attainder[15]

An Act of Attainder, though it served the same purpose as impeachment, was **8–006** strictly a legislative and not a judicial act. It was an Act of Parliament finding a person guilty of an offence, usually a political one of a rather insubstantial kind, and inflicting a punishment on him. The subject of the proceedings was allowed to defend himself by counsel and witnesses before both Houses. One of the first Acts of Attainder of which we know was that of the Duke of Clarence in 1477, and from about that time until James I's reign this procedure was commonly used instead of impeachment. Attainder was later used occasionally down to 1715. It has not been used since the early eighteenth century when Cabinet government was beginning to develop. We may therefore describe it also as obsolete.[16]

Committees and Tribunals of Inquiry

A Select Committee of Inquiry may be set up by either House to investigate **8–007** any matter of public interest, and such a committee may include persons who are not Members of Parliament. This method was first used in 1689 to investigate the conduct of the war in Ireland, but Parliament is a political body and voting tends to be on party lines. Dissatisfaction with the way in which a parliamentary committee had investigated the Marconi scandal[17] and a realisation that political scandals cannot be investigated by politicians led to the enactment of the Tribunals of Inquiry (Evidence) Act 1921.

This provides that on a resolution of both Houses on a matter of urgent public importance, a Tribunal of Inquiry may be appointed by the Queen or a Secretary of State with all the powers of the High Court as regards examination of witnesses and production of documents. The procedure provided by the statute is

---

[11] (1679) 11 St.Tr. 599.

[12] Impeachment of Warren Hastings (1787) Lords' Journals Vol. XXXVII, p. 678; (1795) Lords' Journals, Vol. XL, p. 388; P. J. Marshall, *The Impeachment of Warren Hastings* (1965).

[13] Impeachment of Lord Melville (1805) 29 St.Tr. 549.

[14] H.L. Paper 43-I, H.C. 214 (1998–99), para. 18, where details of the procedure for impeachment can be found. Two previous House of Commons Committees had recommended the abolition of impeachment: H.C. 34 (1967–68), H.C. 417 (1976–77). As was seen in 1999, impeachment remains important in the U.S.A.

[15] Lord Justice Somervell, "Acts of Attainder" (1951) 67 L.Q.R. 306. And see *Kariapper v. Wijesinha* [1968] A.C. 717.

[16] Also obsolete, but this time by virtue of statutory abolition (Criminal Justice Act 1948), is the so-called privilege of peers to be tried by the House of Lords for treason or felony, or misprision of either. This could be traced back to the *judicium parium* of Magna Carta, c.39, though the law did not become settled until well after 1215. If Parliament was sitting the House was presided over by the Lord Chancellor as the Lord High Steward. If Parliament was not sitting, the Lord High Steward acted as judge, sitting with a jury of peers. The last trial of a peer before the House of Lords was that of Baron de Clifford for manslaughter in 1935 (*R. v. Baron de Clifford, The Times*, December 13, 1935, pp. 15–16; *Proceedings on the Trial of Lord de Clifford*, H.M.S.O, 1936).

[17] Which involved allegations of corrupt financial speculation by members of the government, the select committee split along party lines, see H.C. 152 and 217 (1913).

essentially inquisitorial. If a person refuses to answer relevant and essential questions or to produce documents, the matter may be referred to the High Court to be dealt with as contempt of court.[18] From 1921 to 1982 twenty one such tribunals were set up[19]; no further Tribunals were established until 1996. In the intervening period a variety of statutory and non-statutory judicial inquiries were established. A characteristic of most of these inquiries, including those under the 1921 Act is that they are chaired by a judge.[20] Since 1996 several tribunals have been established including include the Cullen Tribunal into the Dunblane massacre[21]; the Waterhouse Tribunal to investigate allegations of child abuse in North Wales[22]; and the Saville Tribunal into the events of "Bloody Sunday" in Londonderry, the second tribunal to be established to investigate these events.[23]

8–008   Concern about the working methods of Tribunal of Inquiry and alternative non-statutory inquiries such as the 1963 Denning inquiry into the Profumo affair[24] led to the Salmon Royal Commission investigation. The Salmon Report considered whether the 1921 procedure which could expose people to unfair public scrutiny and where there were no strict rules of evidence, no right of appeal, no right to legal representation, and no opportunity to meet allegations made by witnesses "was so objectionable in principle that the Act should be repealed." It decided that the inquisitorial powers of tribunal should be retained, but only for matters of vital public importance where there was something in the nature of a nation-wide crisis of confidence. In addition it recommended certain safeguards, the six "cardinal principles" which would introduce adversarial procedures into the essentially inquisitorial procedure provide for in the 1921 Act. These included allowing witnesses before such tribunals to be legally represented and to be examined by his own counsel and to test evidence by cross-examination.[25] The difficulty of achieving a balance between ascertaining the "truth" and providing a procedure that is fair to individuals implicated in the

---

[18] This power was invoked at the Vassall spy inquiry in 1963, when two journalists refused to reveal the source of their information, one being sentenced to six months' imprisonment and the other to three months. *Att.-Gen. v. Clough* [1963] Q.B. 773 (Lord Parker C.J.): Clough never in fact served his sentence as the source revealed itself and he confirmed it: *Att.-Gen. v. Mulholland* and *Att.-Gen. v. Foster* [1963] 2 Q.B. 477, CA.

[19] These included: the Lynskey Tribunal to inquire into allegations of bribery and corruption arising out of the use of "contact men" to approach Ministers, Cmd. 7616 (1949); the Tribunal set up to inquire into the Aberfan disaster, H.C. 553 (1966–67); allegations of irregularities by the Crown Agents were investigated by a Tribunal of Inquiry under Croom Johnson J. which was set up in 1978 and reported in 1982, H.C. 364 (1981–82).

[20] See Drewry [1996] P.L. 368.

[21] Cm. 3386.

[22] H.C. (1999–2000)

[23] The first was the Widgery Tribunal 1972. See Brigid Hadfield "*R v. Lord Saville of Newgate, ex p. anonymous soldiers*: What is the Purpose of a Tribunal of Inquiry?", [1999] P.L. 663.

[24] Cmnd. 2152 (1963), where Lord Denning had been unhappy with his role as "detective, inquisitor, advocate and judge".

[25] *Royal Commission Tribunals of Inquiry* (1966) Cmnd. 3121.; *Report of Interdepartmental Committee on Tribunals of Inquiry and Contempt* (Salmon L.J.) (1969) Cmnd. 4078. The response of the government, *Tribunals of Inquiry set up under the Tribunals of Inquiry (Evidence) Act 1921*, (1973) Cmnd. 5313, was to accept the recommendations, but also to suggest that there could be circumstances when they would be observed in spirit but not in letter (para. 17). See also G. W. Keeton, *Trial by Tribunal* (1960); Z. Segal, "Tribunals of Inquiry: A British Invention Ignored in Britain." [1984] P.L. 206; Helen Grant, "Commissions of Inquiry—Is there a Right to be Legally Represented?", [2001] P.L. 377.

matter being investigated remains.[26] Most non-statutory tribunals after the Salmon Report adhered to its "cardinal principles"; an exception was the Scott inquiry into the "arms for Iraq"[27] affair where these principles were disregarded on the basis that they would be "inoperable and ineffective and inefficient".[28] In the light of the Scott inquiry the Council on Tribunals conducted a review of inquiry procedures based on recommendations in the Scott Report, and concluded that it would be impracticable to attempt to devise a single set of rules for every inquiry.[29]

The choice of the type of inquiry to investigate events which will inevitably have "political" elements is difficult.[30] The Scott inquiry was set up partly because a select committee investigation has been unable to conduct a proper investigation into what had happened. This has led to the suggestion that Parliament or one of its select committees should be able to establish a Parliamentary Commission, on the National Audit Office model, to "establish factual information on complex subjects".[31] Such a move would be a return to the pre-1921 type of Parliamentary investigation.

II. THE MEETING OF PARLIAMENT

A "parliament" lasts from the summons of the legislature until its sittings are terminated by dissolution or lapse of time. During a single parliament there may be a number of sessions—before 1914 generally not more than one a year, since 1918 usually two a year. A session is usually terminated by prorogation; it may also be terminated by the dissolution of Parliament and the calling of a general election. Within a session there are a number of sittings separated from each other by *adjournments*, which can be brought about by motion of each House. Either House may adjourn its sittings for any given number of hours, days, weeks, or months; but the Crown has a statutory power to issue a proclamation ordering resumption of business when both Houses stand adjourned for more than 14 days.[32]

8–009

---

[26] Some of the problems are illustrated in the litigation that arose out of the Saville Inquiry into "Bloody Sunday", *R v. Lord Saville of Newgate and others, ex p. B.O.U.V.* [1999] 4 All E.R. 860. It was held that a tribunal set up under the 1921 Act could not reach a decision that interfered with fundamental rights of individuals in the absences of compelling justification. In consequence the decision of the tribunal not to allow soldiers involved in "Bloody Sunday" in 1972 to anonymity had failed to take sufficient notice of the risk to the lives of the soldiers, and was unreasonable. See Hadfield, *op. cit.* note 23.

[27] *Inquiry into the Export of Defence Equipment and Dual-Use Goods to Iraq and Related Prosecutions*, H.C. 115 (1995–96). Sir Richard was given the option to request the inquiry to be converted into a 1921 Act inquiry.

[28] Evidence by Scott L.J. to the Public Service Committee, *Ministerial Accountability and Responsibility*, H.C. 313–III (1995–96) Q. 322; for criticisms of the procedure used see Lord Howe, "Procedure at the Scott Inquiry", [1996] P.L. 445.

[29] Published in H.L. Deb.Vol. 575, W.A. 149–150.

[30] See Wintrobe, "Inquiries after Scott: the return of the tribunal of inquiry", [1997] P.L. 18; "Parliamentary arithmetic and other political factors, as well as the nature of the controversy itself, can all influence the decisions about the modes of investigation and resolution." (At p. 29).

[31] *Export Licensing and B.M.A.R.C.*, H.C. 87 (1995–96), para. 172–3; *Ministerial Accountability and Responsibility*, H.C. 313 (1995–6).

[32] Meeting of Parliament Acts 1797 and 1870, Parliament (Elections and Meetings) Act 1942; in addition each House confers on its Speaker powers to recall Parliament during an adjournment if it is in the public interest to do so.

The exercise of the royal prerogative is necessary to summon, to prorogue or (before the expiration of the statutory period) to dissolve Parliament. The royal proclamation that dissolves one
Parliament also summons the next.

Royal prerogative in relation to Parliament

Sovereign's presence in Parliament

8–010   The Sovereign, although in constitutional theory present in the High Court of Parliament as in other courts, does not now in practice visit Parliament in person, except to read the speech from the Throne in the Lords' Chamber at the opening of a new Parliament or session. Other royal functions performed in whole Parliament, such as prorogation, dissolution or giving the Royal Assent to Bills, are now done by royal proclamation or commission under the Great Seal.[33]

A convention to ensure freedom of debate forbids the Sovereign to be present in either House sitting separately. As regards the Commons, the Sovereign was not present in the Middle Ages, but occasional intrusions were made in the seventeenth century. The Lords, on the other hand, were the Great Council and the Sovereign's presence was necessary in early times; but the practice of attending was dying out in the Stuart period and ceased on the death of Queen Anne.

Royal Assent to legislation

8–011   The Queen may still give the Royal Assent in person in Parliament, but this has not been done since 1854. The Royal Assent Act 1967 provides that the Royal Assent, signified by letters patent under the Great Seal signed with Her Majesty's own hand, may also be: (a) pronounced by commissioners in the presence of both Houses in the House of Lords in the manner customary since George III's reign[34]; or (b) notified to each House separately by the Speaker of that House. The latter method was new and avoids interrupting the proceedings of the Commons by a summons from Black Rod. The customary method (a) is still used at the time of prorogation.

When the Royal Assent is given to a public or private Bill the words "La Reine le veult" are pronounced by the Clerk of the Parliaments, and for a Money Bill the following: "La Reine remercie ses bons sujets, accepte leur benevolence, et ainsi le veult." If the Queen were to refuse her assent, which would now be unconstitutional, the tactful formula, "La Reine s'avisera" (The Queen will think about it) would be used.

Prorogation

8–012   The exercise of the prerogative of prorogation terminates a *session* of Parliament.[35] It is effected by command of the Queen—acting by convention on the advice, formerly, of the Cabinet but, it seems, in practice in modern times on the

---

[33] Since the reign of Charles II Parliament has only once, in 1818, been dissolved by the sovereign in person.

[34] Under the Royal Assent by Commission Act 1541, which was repealed by the 1967 Act.

[35] Normally a week earlier a press notice will have been issued by the Prime Minister's staff to the media giving the dates of the dissolution, the election and the first day of the new Parliament. Since 1966 it has not been the practice to make an announcement first to the House of Commons; see Blackburn, *The Electoral System In Britain* (1995) pp. 33–37.

advice of the Prime Minister[36]—such command being signified to both Houses either by the Lord Chancellor (in the Queen's presence or by commission) or by proclamation. In either case the date for the new session is stated, but statutes enable the Crown by proclamation to accelerate or defer the next meeting of a Parliament that stands prorogued.[37] The interval between two sessions is called a recess.

The former rule that the progress of Bills is stopped by prorogation has been modified. Both House commonly pass resolutions allowing private and hybrid bills to be proceeded with in the next session. In 1997 the House of Commons agreed that in certain circumstances an ad hoc motion could be passed to allow a public bill to be carried over to the next session,[38] this was not envisaged to happen very frequently. It is sometimes the case that a Minister is content to drop a Bill and to bring in an approved version later.

Prorogation may be preceded by the signification of the Royal Assent to Bills that have passed both Houses.

Frequency and duration and parliaments

It is a prerogative of the Crown to convene Parliament. In early times **8–013** Sovereigns generally pleased themselves when they would do so. Statutes have limited this prerogative.[39] Section 1 of the Meeting of Parliament Act 1694 which provides that a Parliament should be held once at least in three years, is still in force. Section 2 provides that within three years after the determination of every Parliament, legal writs shall be issued by directions of the Sovereign for calling another new Parliament. In effect this means that by law a general election need only be held within three years of the dissolution of Parliament, that is every eight years. Meanwhile the Bill of Rights 1688 had declared (section 13) that for the redress of all grievances and for the amending, strengthening and preserving of all laws, Parliament ought to be held "frequently." The real security, however, for the frequent—indeed annual—meeting of Parliament consists (as we saw in Chapter 7) in the practice of passing annual Finance Acts and annual orders continuing the Army and Air Force and Naval Discipline Acts. In modern times it is necessary to keep Parliament in almost constant session, not only to legislate but to supervise the government of the country, to say nothing of dealing with emergencies.

The power to dissolve Parliament is another prerogative of the Crown. By statute a parliament may also be terminated by lapse of time.[40] This is now regulated by the Parliament Act 1911, which provides (section 7) that the maximum life of a Parliament shall be five years. This period can, of course, be extended by Act of Parliament,[41] but it has only been done in wartime and the

---

[36] *post* para. 8–025.
[37] Meeting of Parliament Act 1797; Prorogation Act 1867; Meeting of Parliament Act 1870; Parliament (Elections and Meeting) Act 1943.
[38] The first Bill to be carried over was the Financial Services and Markets Bill in 1999. See *post* para. 11–032.
[39] Starting with the first Triennial Act which enacted that a Parliament should be held in every third year, itself repealed by the Triennial Act 1664.
[40] The Meeting of Parliament Act 1694, s.3 provided that no Parliament should last for more than three years. This provision was repealed at the time of the Scottish rising by the Septennial Act 1715, which provided that the existing and future Parliaments could continue for a period not exceeding seven years.
[41] Such a bill may not be passed without the consent of the Lords under the provisions of the Parliament Act 1911; see *post* paras 8–022 to 8–028.

practice has been to extend the period for one year at a time. Thus the Parliament that passed the Parliament Act 1911 survived until after the Armistice in 1918, and the Parliament elected in 1935 lasted until 1945.

Parliament and the demise of the Crown

8–014   Formerly Parliament expired when the Sovereign died, but this inconvenient rule was abolished by various statutes. On the demise of the Crown, Parliament (if sitting) is to proceed to act, and if prorogued or adjourned is to meet immediately without the usual form of summons.[42] The duration of an existing Parliament is not affected by a demise of the Crown.[43] All members of both Houses must take the oath of allegiance to the new Sovereign. When a demise of the Crown occurs after a proclamation summoning a new Parliament has been given it shall have no effect except that if the demise occurs before the date of the poll, the meeting of Parliament shall be delayed by 14 days.[44]

Summons of a new Parliament

8–015   When the Queen accepts the advice of the Prime Minister to dissolve,[45] a proclamation is published dissolving the existing Parliament and fixing the date for the meeting of the new Parliament. The proclamation also announces the making of an Order in Council directing the Lord Chancellor to issue the necessary writs. The Clerk of the Crown in Chancery then prepares Writs of Summons, which are sent to the temporal peers and the Lords Spiritual. The judges are also summoned to attend and advise, but (unless they are peers) they do not attend, though they may be asked to advise the House of Lords sitting as the final court of appeal. Writs of Elections are issued to the returning officers instructing them to cause election to be made of a member to serve in Parliament for the constituency mentioned, and to return the name to the Crown Office.[46]

Meeting of a new Parliament

8–016   On the appointed day each House assembles in its own chamber until the Gentleman Usher of the Black Rod (Black Rod) requires attendance of the Commons at the bar of the Lords. As many members as space permits and as have the inclination, then proceed with the Assistant Clerk of the Parliaments (Clerk to the House of Commons) to the "bar," a line which is deemed to mark the boundary of the Lords' Chamber. Unless the Sovereign is present, the commission for opening Parliament is then read by the Lord Chancellor. The Commons are then bidden by him to retire and proceed to the election of a Speaker. The election of Speaker ends the day.

Next day the new Speaker proceeds with the Commons to the bar of the House of Lords. He announces his election, which is confirmed by the Lord Chancellor in the name of the Sovereign. It is not certain whether the Sovereign's approval is required by law; but it is always sought and has only once been refused, by Charles II in the case of Sir Edward Seymour in 1678. After this the Speaker claims certain ancient privileges of the House. The Sovereign, if present, reads the Queen's speech. If she is absent her speech is read by the Lord Chancellor. It is drafted by the Cabinet, and outlines the government's policy with regard to

[42] Succession to the Crown Act 1707.
[43] Representation of the People Act 1867.
[44] Representation of the People Act 1985, s.20.
[45] *post.* paras 8–022 to 8–028.
[46] Representation of the People Act 1983, s.23 and Sched. 1.

foreign affairs and legislation. After this the Commons retire, and each member of either House proves his right to membership. Then members of both Houses take the statutory oath or affirmation of allegiance.

Beginning of a new session

At the beginning of each session when the Speaker returns from the Lords to **8–017** the House of Commons, a Bill for the Suppression of Clandestine Outlawries[47] is formally read the first time. This practice preserves the right of the House to initiate Bills not foreshadowed in the Queen's Speech, and in particular the ancient right of the Commons to air grievances before granting the Sovereign supplies. The Speaker then reads a copy of the Queen's Speech to the House, and a loyal address of thanks to Her Majesty for the speech is moved and seconded. On that question amendments may be moved, and the general debate on the address which takes place, is an opportunity for a debate on government policy. Out of courtesy to the Sovereign, the motion is agreed to without a division, though any amendments proposed may be voted on.

A similar debate on the Queen's Speech, in the form of a loyal address, takes place in the House of Lords after the formal first reading of the Select Vestries Bill.

III. THE PREROGATIVE OF DISSOLUTION[48]

The Queen, the Prime Minister and the Commons

One of the most important of the prerogative powers in connection with **8–018** Parliament is that to dissolve Parliament. However the significance of this power rests on the conventions which surround its exercise. Although in law the Queen may dissolve Parliament when she likes, her conduct would be unconstitutional (*i.e.* contrary to convention) if she did so without or against the advice of her Ministers. In what circumstances it is constitutionally proper for the Prime Minister (or the Cabinet) to refuse to advise a dissolution, and whether the Queen is necessarily bound by convention to dissolve when advised to do so, are questions discussed in the following paragraphs.

The conventions governing the exercise of the prerogative power to dissolve **8–019** Parliament are in normal circumstances the following:

(a) The Sovereign should dissolve Parliament when requested by the Prime Minister to do so.

(b) The Sovereign should not dissolve Parliament unless requested by the Prime Minister to do so.

---

[47] See G. Chowdharay-Best, "The Clandestine Outlawries and Select Vestries Bills" (1974) 124 New L.J. 230.

[48] Sir Ivor Jennings, *Cabinet Government* (3rd ed., 1959), pp. 412–428, and App. III; J.P. Mackintosh, *The British Cabinet* (3rd ed., 1977); B.S. Markesinis, *The Theory and Practice of Dissolution of Parliament* (1972); Anson, *Law and Custom of the Constitution* (1922 5th ed. Gwyer). Vol. I, pp. 325–330; Dicey *Law of the Constitution* (1959 10th ed.), pp. 432–437. See also B.E. Carter, *The Office of Prime Minister* (1956), pp. 273–294; E.A. Forsey, *The Royal Power of Dissolution of Parliament in the British Commonwealth* (1943); H.V. Evatt, *The King and His Dominion Governors* (1935).

(c) The Prime Minister has the power to choose the time of dissolution, within the five-year period prescribed by the Parliament Act 1911.[49] A convention appears to have developed in the years from the 1920s to the 1950s that the Prime Minister does not have to have the approval of the Cabinet before doing so.[50] This power of timing is a weapon of great political importance in the hands of the government, and especially of the Prime Minister.[51]

(d) If the Government party is defeated at a general election, the Prime Minister should tender the resignation of the Government at once, at least where another party has an overall majority, and the Opposition will take over. At one time, before the party unity was as definite as it is now, it was the practice to await defeat in the Commons. If there is in the future a return to a system where no one party has a clear majority this former practice may revive.[52]

(e) If the government is defeated in the House of Commons on a motion of confidence or a motion of no confidence, the Prime Minister must either ask for a dissolution or tender the resignation of himself and his ministerial colleagues. Such occasions are rare; only three times in the last century was a government dismissed in this way, the most recent being in 1979.[53] Where there is a dissolution, which is the usual course, Ministers retain office during the ensuing general election. The Address on the Queen's Speech and the general Budget resolution would be regarded as matters of confidence.[54] In practice also, before a debate on a major item of government policy the Prime Minister may indicate—largely for the information of his followers—that he intends to regard the pending vote as one of confidence. This may be resorted to by a Prime Minister who wishes to overcome dissidents in the party by the implied threat of a general election if government policy is not supported. On several occasions Mr Major, when faced with opposition from his own party on European Union policy, indicated that the passage of a piece of European legislation was a matter of confidence.[55]

8–020   A government with a clear majority in the House of Commons can usually be assured of the confidence of the House, governments with a very small majority or a minority government may be in a different position. It is no longer the case

---

[49] The alternative would be to have five fixed-term parliaments, see O. Hood Phillips, *Reform of the Constitution* (1970), p. 52; Blackburn, *The Electoral System in Britain* (1995), p. 49–65.

[50] See Lord Blake, *The Office of Prime Minister* (1975) p. 59, who explains how this developed due to a misunderstanding of the precedents. See also Geoffrey Marshall *Constitutional Conventions* (1984) pp. 48–53, who doubts the view that Cabinet approval is not required.

[51] Accounts of how this decision is taken can be found in the autobiographies of Prime Ministers and other leading members of political parties.

[52] After the February 1974 general election neither the Conservative nor Labour party had a majority in the Commons, although Labour had the most seats. Only after Mr Heath, the Conservative Prime Minister at the time of the election, had failed to persuade the Liberals to join a coalition did he resign and Mr Wilson, the leader of the Labour party, succeed him as Prime Minister.

[53] When the motion of no confidence in the then Labour government was carried by 311 votes to 310. H.C. Deb. vol. 965 cols. 461–590 (March 28, 1979).

[54] As happened with Mr Baldwin in 1929.

[55] *e.g.*, November 1992 on the European Communities (Amendment) Bill and in November 1994 on the European Communities (Finance) Bill.

(if it ever was)[56] that defeat in the division lobbies on a major matter calls in question a government's right to continue to govern.[57] In March 1974 Mr Wilson, who presided over a minority government, stated in the House that if the Government were defeated in the Commons it would consider its position and make a definitive statement after due consideration; but the Government would not be forced to go to the country except in a situation where members voted knowing the full consequences of their vote. He added that a snap division, or even a defeat on quite major matters, would not immediately lead to the Government's asking for a dissolution or resigning.[58] After the October 1974 election Labour were returned with a very small majority, and became a minority government in 1976. In the course of the next five years the Government were defeated forty-two times losing several Bills and, contrary to its wishes, having to accept amendments to other Bills.[59] However, it was not defeated in a confidence motion until March 1979.

Opposition parties do not necessarily want to force a general election at any given time. They may be short of electioneering funds or may think their electoral chances will improve later on. Defeats in by-elections do not require a government to resign unless they wipe out its majority in the Commons, though Balfour resigned in 1905 when Parliament was not in session as the loss of a series of by-elections indicated that his party no longer enjoyed the support of the electorate.

Defeats of a government in a committee of the Commons, which are not rare **8–021** when the government has a small majority, can usually be reversed later on the floor of the House. A minority government may lose its majority membership of committees, where its Bills are subject to amendment. When the Labour Government lost its overall majority in the Commons in the early part of 1976 there was controversy as to the meaning of the Standing Order that directs the Selection Committee to have regard to the composition of the House. Labour members argued that the principle of a Bill is approved by the Commons on second reading, and therefore the government should be assured that it can get its Bills through Committee; but they gave way and agreed to equal numbers of Labour and Conservative members together with third-party representative.

Exceptional situations

The question arises whether there are any exceptional circumstances in which **8–022** the Sovereign may: (i) dissolve Parliament without, or against, the advice of the Prime Minister; (ii) dismiss a Ministry that refuses to advise a dissolution; or (iii) refuse a dissolution when advised by the Prime Minister to dissolve.

1. Dissolution without or against advice

There is no instance in this country, since the Restoration, of a Sovereign **8–023** attempting to dissolve Parliament without or against the advice of the Ministry. It seems that, apart from convention, the Queen cannot now in practice dissolve

---

[56] See Philip Norton, "The House of Commons and the Constitution: The Challenges of the 1970s" (1981) *Parliamentary Affairs*, 253.

[57] See further Philip Norton "Government Defeats in the House of Commons: Myth and Reality" [1978] P.L. 360, *Dissention in the House of Commons 1974–1979* (1980); S. E. Finer, *Five Constitutions* (1979), pp. 68–69.

[58] H.C. Deb.Vol. 870, cols. 70–71 (March 12, 1974). The Government was defeated 17 times before the second election of 1974 was held.

[59] Even Mrs Thatcher's governments with safe majorities had to abandon legislation because of lack of support in the Commons, *e.g.* the Shops Bill 1986.

Parliament without or against the advice of her Ministers. Dissolution involves an Order in Council made at a meeting of the Privy Council convened by the Lord President of the Council; and the issue of a proclamation and writs of summons under the Great Seal, which is kept by the Lord Chancellor.[60] She might dissolve Parliament orally in the House of Lords, but proclamations and writs would still be required for the holding of elections and the summoning of the new Parliament. The Queen may take the initiative in proposing a dissolution, and then if the Ministers agree with her they adopt her policy as their own; but if Ministers refuse to advise a dissolution, they could only be dismissed.

2. Dismissal of a government that refuses to advise a dissolution

8–024   The last occasion in this country when a Ministry was dismissed was that of the North-Fox Coalition in 1783. During the Irish Home Rule controversy of 1913, Dicey expressed the opinion that the King might dismiss a Ministry that refused to advise a dissolution if he had reason to think that their policy, although supported by the House of Commons, was not approved by the electorate. On the other hand, although there might be an argument for dissolution if the Sovereign thought the Government had lost its majority in the country,[61] it is very doubtful whether she is sufficiently in touch with public opinion to judge the attitude of the electorate or to anticipate its decision on all items of the government's policy. Only most exceptional circumstances would justify the dismissal of a Ministry, such as unconstitutional conduct like introducing Bills for unnecessary or definite prolongations of the life of Parliament, gerry-mandering of constituencies or fundamental modifications of the electoral system in the interests of one party,[62] or if the government were unable to obtain supply from the Commons.[63]

Dismissal of a Ministry would be a last resort, for the evil to be expected from inaction by the Sovereign would have to be weighed against the evil of bringing the Crown into the political arena. And the Sovereign would have to be satisfied, presumably from the advice of the Leader of the Opposition (which normally cannot be sought unless the Government resigns) that an alternative Government was willing to take office.

3. Refusal of dissolution

8–025   Down to the early nineteenth century the defeat of the government at a general election was regarded as a rebuff to the Sovereign. Since the Reform Act 1832 the prestige of the Sovereign has been dissociated from the fate of governments and there has been no instance of refusal to dissolve the British Parliament.

---

[60] Great Seal Act 1884; a warrant under the Royal Sign Manual countersigned by the Lord Chancellor, or by a Secretary of State or two Treasury Commissioners, is necessary and sufficient authority for passing any instrument under the Great Seal; but the authority of the Lord Chancellor alone is sufficient in cases where that was so before the Act.

[61] Cf. *Adegbenro v. Akintola* [1963] A.C. 614, PC. For the background of this case, see B.O. Nwabueze, *Constitutionalism in the Emergent States* (1973), pp. 74–75.

[62] Jennings, *op. cit.* p. 412.

[63] The dismissal by the Governor-General of Australia of the Prime Minister (Mr Gough Whitlam) in November 1975 is an instructive precedent, but it must be studied in the light of the Senate's legal power to refuse to grant supply. See D.P. O'Connell, "The Dissolution of the Australian Parliament: 11, November 1975," (1976) 57 *The Parliamentarian*, 1–14. The Leader of the Opposition was invited to form a caretaker government (no appointments and no legislation) on the understanding that, when the Senate had approved the grant of supply, he would forthwith advise a dissolution.

George V is said to have refused (at least temporarily) to dissolve Parliament in 1910 and the Cabinet decided to resign; but he later agreed to a dissolution.[64] In 1918 the King only agreed to Lloyd George's request for a dissolution with justifiable reluctance: it is not certain whether Lloyd George would have resigned if the request had been refused.[65]

The question whether the Sovereign could still constitutionally refuse to dissolve Parliament when advised by Ministers to do so was raised in 1923–24 and 1950, and again early in 1974. In 1923 Ramsay MacDonald was appointed Prime Minister of a minority Labour Government which could only count on a majority in the House of Commons so long as it retained the support of a sufficient number of Liberals. Lord Cave, the Lord Chancellor in the previous administration, advised George V's private secretary, Lord Stamfordham, that if no constitutional reason exists for the request of a dissolution the Sovereign may properly refuse the request, provided he is assured that other Ministers are prepared to carry on the government. He went on to say that if a statesman is asked to form a government and makes it a condition of accepting office that the Sovereign will grant a dissolution in the event of a new government being defeated in the House of Commons, the Sovereign is under no obligation to give such a promise, and he should not give such an assurance unless it is the only way of securing that the government of the country will be carried on.[66]

Asquith (a former Liberal Prime Minister) said that "the Crown is not bound **8–026** to take the advice of a particular Minister to put its subjects to the tumult and turmoil of a series of general elections so long as it can find other Ministers who are prepared to give contrary advice. The notion that a Minister who cannot command a majority in the House of Commons . . . is invested with the right to demand a dissolution is as subversive of constitutional usage as it would, in my opinion, be pernicious to the paramount interests of the nation at large." When the minority Labour Government was defeated in the Commons in 1924, George V did not want to grant a dissolution but did so after consulting Conservative and Liberal leaders, who were unwilling to combine in the existing House. Lord Attlee thought that the King might legitimately have refused a dissolution to Ramsay MacDonald, but he added: "I fancy it was thought impolitic to refuse the request of the first Labour Prime Minister."[67] The view that a Sovereign is not bound to grant a dissolution when asked for, provided that he can obtain other Ministers to take responsibility for the royal refusal, was supported by Keith, who added: "The right to a dissolution is not a right to a series of dissolutions. The King could not, because a Ministry had appealed and lost an election, give them forthwith another without seeming to be endeavouring to wear out the resistance of the electors to the royal will."[68]

Refusal of a dissolution would be proper if, but only if, there was general agreement inside and outside the House of Commons that a general election should be delayed pending further developments of the situation, for where the view of the people can be gathered without a dissolution it would be absurd to insist upon it. As Anson said, the uniform practice for more than a century that

---

[64] Jennings, *op. cit.* p. 425.
[65] *ibid.* p. 425.
[66] R.F.V. Heuston, *Lives of the Lord Chancellors 1885–1940* (1964), pp. 432–435.
[67] "The Role of the Monarchy," *The Observer*, August 23, 1959.
[68] Keith, *op. cit.* p. 301.

the Sovereign should not refuse a dissolution when advised by her Ministers to dissolve has been largely due to the observance of another convention, namely, that dissolutions should not be improperly advised.

8–027   The other view is that the Sovereign's right to withhold a dissolution has become obsolete, and that the convention that she must in all circumstances accept the advice of the Prime Minister provides her with a clear and simple rule about which there can be no mistake.[69] Sir Ivor Jennings denied that it is a convention that a dissolution may not be refused, since Victoria, Edward VII, George V and their Prime Ministers all thought there was a right to refuse a dissolution[70]; but he thought that while the Queen's personal prerogative is maintained in theory, there are hardly any circumstances in which it could be exercised in practice. He pointed out, however, that this assumed a continuance of the two-party system. "If the major parties break up," he wrote,[71] "the whole balance of the Constitution alters; and then, possibly, the Queen's prerogative becomes important." Some writers who adopt the "new" doctrine which deprives the Queen of any discretion, would make an exception where a Prime Minister requests a second dissolution immediately after being defeated at a general election, provided that an alternative government could be formed.[72]

The former opinion, which allows a limited personal prerogative to the Sovereign, appears to be the better one. It is more in consonance with the traditions of British parliamentary government, and it has tended to be adopted in other Commonwealth countries. It was supported by Viscount Simon (a former Lord Chancellor) in April 1950[73] when the Labour Government had been returned with a majority of only six in the Commons. Attlee, who was Prime Minister in 1950, later expressed the opinion that if the Government had been defeated in the House at that time, George VI would have been within his rights in sending for the Leader of the Opposition if he thought a working majority in the House could have been obtained by him.[74]

8–028   The reason for the general convention that the Sovereign is bound by the advice of her Ministers is not applicable if they do not represent the wishes of the electorate (or the Commons). Among the factors that would have to be taken into account before the Sovereign could properly refuse a dissolution would be the time that had elapsed since the last dissolution, whether the last dissolution took place at the instance of the present Opposition, whether the question in issue is of great political importance, the supply position,[75] whether Parliament is nearing the end of its maximum term, whether the Prime Minister is in a minority in the Cabinet,[76] and whether there is a minority government.[77]

---

[69] Lord Chorley, letter to *The Times*, April 26, 1950.
[70] *Law and the Constitution* (1959 5th ed.), p. 135.
[71] *Cabinet Government* (1959 3rd ed.), pp. 427–428.
[72] G. Marshall and G.C. Moodie, *op. cit.*
[73] Letters to *The Times*, April 24 and 27, 1950, and see Wheeler-Bennett, *King George VI*, (1958) pp. 771–775.
[74] "The Role of the Monarchy," *loc. cit.*
[75] The grant of a dissolution must be dependent on supply having been voted to the Crown for the period that would elapse before the meeting of the new Parliament.
[76] Lord Blake in a letter to *The Times*, October 25, 1974.
[77] Markesinis, *op. cit.* thinks the practice shows that the Crown cannot refuse a dissolution to a majority government, but it may refuse a dissolution to a minority government (whether defeated or not) provided an alternative government can be formed.

IV. THE LORDS AND COMMONS IN CONFLICT[78]

Earlier conflicts

Until 1911 the United Kingdom was fully bicameral, except in respect of the **8–029** Commons' financial privileges. In the reign of Charles II the Commons passed resolutions denying the right of the Lords to introduce or amend Money Bills. They did not specifically deny the right of the Lords to reject a Money Bill, a right which the Lords continued formally to claim, although before 1860 they exercised it extremely rarely. In 1832 there was a serious controversy over the Reform Bill. William IV, much against his inclination, supported Lord Grey by threatening to use the prerogative power of creating sufficient peers to carry the measure in the House of Lords.[79]

In 1860 the Lords exercised their legal right of rejecting Money Bills by throwing out a measure for the repeal of the paper duty. Three resolutions to the following effect were carried in the Commons:

(1) that the right of granting aid and supplies to the Crown is in the Commons alone;

(2) that, although the Lords could legally reject Money Bills, yet the exercise of that power was regarded by the lower House with peculiar jealousy;

(3) that the Commons had the power so to impose and remit taxation and to frame Bills of Supply that the right of the Commons as to the matter, manner, measure and time might be maintained inviolate.[80]

In the following year, Gladstone being then Chancellor of the Exchequer, the opposition of the peers was overridden by tacking the provision regarding paper duties on to a general financial measure for the services of the year. The House of Lords, therefore, had to face the alternative of passing the provision they disliked, or of rejecting the whole financial provision for the year. They shrank from the latter alternative.

In 1869 the Irish Church Disestablishment Bill was strongly opposed by the Lords, in spite of the clearly expressed wishes of the electorate, but the difficulty was surmounted by Lord Cairns's influence. Another memorable dispute concerned the rejection in 1872 of a Bill to abolish the purchase of Army commissions. The warrant authorising the purchase of commissions was cancelled by exercise of the prerogative, and so the Government attained their object without a direct conflict between the two Houses. There was considerable friction between the two Houses when the Lords at first rejected the Representation of the People Bill in 1884, but mutual concessions were made by Salisbury and Gladstone. The next dispute was over Gladstone's second Home Rule Bill in 1893, but as the Lords were in this instance supported by the electorate their position was for the time being maintained.

---

[78] This section is confined to conflicts over legislation and finance.

[79] A power exercised by Queen Anne in 1712 by the creation of 12 Tory peers to ensure a majority in the House of Lords for approval of the terms of the Peace Treaty of Utrecht; however the commercial treaty between England and France was rejected by Parliament.

[80] C.S. Emden, *Selected Speeches on the Constitution*, Vol. I, pp. 141–142.

Events leading to the Parliament Act 1911[81]

8–030   In 1909–06 the Liberals were returned to power with a gigantic majority, only to find that their principle measures continued to be rejected or drastically amended by the upper House. In 1907 the Commons passed a resolution to the effect that the power of the Lords to alter or reject Bills passed by the Commons should be so restricted that the will of the Commons should prevail within the lifetime of a single Parliament. This resolution as explained by Campbell-Bannerman, the Prime Minister, afterwards with some expansion formed the basis of the Parliament Act 1911. In 1908–1909 Liberal measures—notably the Licensing Bill—were again thrown out by the Lords.

The climax was reached in 1909 when the Finance Bill, containing Lloyd George's Budget, was thrown out in its entirety. The Commons resolved that this action was "a breach of the Constitution, and a usurpation of the rights of the Commons." Edward VII refused to promise Asquith, the Prime Minister, to create enough peers to swamp the Lords until the government's financial policy had been endorsed by the electorate. Parliament was dissolved. In the general election of January 1910 the government lost many seats, but retained its majority with the help of Irish Nationalist and Labour members. The Lords then passed the Finance Bill, which had been reintroduced by the Commons. The Parliament Bill was introduced in the Commons in April; but Edward VII died, and a conference of party leaders was formed to try to reach a settlement and to preserve King George V from a constitutional crisis at the beginning of his reign. Lord Landsdowne, leader of the Conservative peers, proposed that when an important constitutional Bill dealing with such matters as the Crown or the Protestant succession thereto, or establishing a national legislature in Ireland, Scotland, Wales or England, has been rejected three times by the House of Lords, the matter should be decided by referendum. Balfour, the Conservative leader, moved a clause requiring a referendum also for Bills affecting the Parliamentary franchise, the distribution of Parliamentary seats, or the constitution and power of either House of Parliament or relations between the two Houses.[82] Another suggestion was that deadlock over non-financial Bills should be resolved at a joint sitting of both Houses, with the Speaker of the Commons as chairman. Other Lords' amendments would exclude from the operation of the Parliament Bill certain fundamental or constitutional matters, including Irish Home Rule.

8–031   The conference broke down, mainly on the application of the Bill to Home Rule, and in November the Cabinet advised another dissolution. It is now clear that the second general election was embarked on in deference to the wishes of Edward VII expressed shortly before his death. The Cabinet also asked the new King to promise to create a sufficient number of peers to pass the Parliament Bill, and advised that his intention should not be published unless and until the actual occasion should arise. About 400 additional peers[83] would have been needed. The King felt that he had no alternative but to assent to the advice of the Cabinet.

The following general election made little difference to the position of the parties. The Lords proposed a number of amendments to the Parliament Bill

---

[81] See Anson, *Law and Custom of the Constitution* (5th ed. Gwyer), Vol. I pp. 304–308; Jennings, *Parliament* (2nd ed.), pp. 408 *et seq.*; Harold Nicolson, *King George V*, pp. 102–104, 125–139, 148–158; Kenneth Rose and Roy Jenkins, *Mr Balfour's Poodle* (1954).

[82] See Philip Goodhart, M.P., *Referendum* (1971), Chap. 2.

[83] The provisional list of nominees later published shows that most of them had no male issue, so that the number of new hereditary peerages would in fact not have been large.

which the Commons rejected, and in the summer of 1911 the Prime Minister divulged the King's promise to create a sufficient number of peers to force the Bill through the Lords. The Parliament Bill was eventually passed by the Lords in August 1911 with the help of a large number of abstentions, a majority of 17 (131–114) voting against the Lords insisting on their amendments.

The Parliament Act 1911 in effect abolished the Lords' power to reject Money Bills (as therein defined); and substituted for their power to reject other public Bills a power to delay them (with one important exception) for two years spread over three sessions. The important exception was a Bill to extend the life of Parliament.

Events leading to the Parliament Act 1949[84]

In the general election of 1945 the Labour Party said that they would not allow the House of Lords to thwart the will of the people, but they did not ask for a mandate for its abolition or reform. There was a mandate for the nationalisation of certain industries, not including iron and steel. The House of Lords did not reject the Labour Government's nationalisation measures in 1945–47: they suggested a number of useful technical amendments, but did not insist on any amendments to which the Commons did not agree. It seemed likely, however, that the Lords would reject the Iron and Steel Bill.   **8–032**

In 1947 the Commons passed a Parliament Bill (in the form which eventually became the Parliament Act 1949) designed to reduce the period of the Lords' delaying power in the case of public Bills other than Money Bills from two years to one year, spread over two sessions instead of three. The object of introducing this Bill at that stage was to ensure the passing of the Iron and Steel Bill, and perhaps further nationalisation measures, in spite of the opposition of the Lords in the fourth year of the existing Parliament. The Conservative majority in the Lords opposed the Parliament Bill on the grounds that (*inter alia*) it did not reform the membership of the upper House, the nation had expressed no desire for it, and it would go far to expose the country to the dangers of single chamber government.

A Conference of Party Leaders, representative of the three main parties in each House was convened in 1948.[85] It was agreed that the discussion should treat the composition and powers of the House of Lords as interdependent, but as far as concerned powers the terms of reference were limited to the delaying power. The Conservative leaders regarded 12 months from the third reading in the Commons as the shortest period acceptable. The Labour leaders regarded the maximum period acceptable as nine months from the third reading in the Commons or one year from the second reading, whichever might be the longer in a particular case. The difference between the parties was more than a matter of three months, for it revealed a cleavage of opinion as to the purpose of the delaying power. The Labour view was that each House should have a proper time for the consideration of amendments to Bills proposed by the other. In effect this meant that the Commons should have time to think again. The Conservative view was that in the event of serious controversy between the two Houses on a measure on which the view of the electorate is doubtful, a sufficient time should elapse to enable the electorate to be properly informed of the issues involved and for public opinion to crystallise and express itself. This does not necessarily involve a general   **8–033**

---

[84] See Jennings, *op. cit.* pp. 428–434. For arguments as to the validity of the 1949 Act see *ante*. paras 4–035 to 4–036.
[85] (1948) Cmnd. 7380.

election. The Conference therefore broke down, and the Lords then rejected the Parliament Bill at its second reading. The Bill was eventually passed in 1949 without the consent of the Lords under the provisions of the Parliament Act 1911, it being necessary to introduce an extra short session for the purpose.

The Parliament Act 1949 was remarkable as being an important constitutional measure that included a retroactive provision (the proviso to section 1) extending to Bills introduced before the Parliament Bill itself.[86] The 1949 Act made no change with regard to Money Bills as the Lords could scarcely be allowed a shorter period to consider them than the month allowed by the 1911 Act.

The Parliament Acts 1911 and 1949[87]

8–034   The provisions of the 1911 Act, as amended in 1949, are to the following effect: After reciting (*inter alia*) that it was eventually intended to substitute for the existing House of Lords a second chamber constituted on a popular instead of a hereditary basis, it is provided that:

Section 1

(1) If a Money Bill, having been passed by the Commons and sent to the House of Lords[88] at least one month before the end of the session, is not passed by the Lords without amendment within one month after it has been sent up, the Bill, unless the Commons direct to the contrary, shall be presented to the Sovereign and become an Act of Parliament on the Royal Assent being signified, notwithstanding that the House of Lords have not consented to the Bill.[89]

(2) A Money Bill means a public Bill which, in the opinion of the Speaker of the House of Commons, contains only provisions dealing with the following topics:

> imposition, repeal, remission, alteration or regulation of taxation (not including local rates);
> imposition for any financial purposes of charges on the Consolidated Fund or the National Loans Fund, or on money provided by Parliament, or the variation of such charges;
> supply;
> appropriation, receipt, custody, issue or audit of accounts of public money;
> raising or guarantee of any loan (not including loans by local authorities) or the repayment thereof; or
> subordinate matters incidental to the above topics or any of them.

(3) There shall be endorsed on a Money Bill when sent up to the Lords, and when presented to the Sovereign for assent, a certificate signed by the

---

[86] The Iron and Steel Bill was not in fact forced through under these provisions, a compromise was reached whereby the proposed corporation would not be appointed until after the next general election, which the government lost.

[87] For the use made of the Parliament Act procedure see *post* paras 9–024 to 9–027.

[88] A Money Bill as defined in Standing Orders, which definition is wider than that in the Parliament Act 1911, must be introduced into the House of Commons in accordance with the privileges of the Commons and constitutional convention.

[89] The Parliament Acts assume separate sittings of the House of Lords and the House of Commons.

Speaker that the Bill is a Money Bill. Before so certifying the Speaker is to consult, if practicable, two members to be appointed from the Chairmen's Panel[90] at the beginning of the session by the Committee of Selection.

Section 2

(1) If any public Bill[91] (other than a Money Bill or a Bill containing any provision to extend the maximum duration of Parliament beyond five years)[92] is passed by the Commons in two[93] successive sessions (whether of the same Parliament or not),[94] and, having been sent to the Lords at least one month before the end of the session, is rejected by the Lords in each of those sessions, that Bill shall, on the second[95] rejection by the Lords, unless the Commons direct to the contrary, be presented to the Sovereign for the Royal Assent and thereupon become an Act of Parliament without the consent of the Lords. But the foregoing provision is not to take effect unless one year[96] has elapsed between the date of second reading[97] in the first of the sessions in the Commons and the date of its passing the Commons in the second[98] session.[99]   **8–035**

(2) When a Bill is presented to the Sovereign for assent under this section, the signed certificate of the Speaker[1] that the requirements of this section have been complied with shall be endorsed thereon.

(3) A Bill shall be deemed to be rejected by the Lords if it is not passed by them without amendment or with amendments agreed to by both Houses.

(4) A Bill shall be deemed to be the same Bill as a former Bill sent up to the Lords in the preceding session if, when sent to the Lords, it is identical with the former Bill or contains only such alterations as are certified by the Speaker to be necessary owing to lapse of time since the date of the former Bill, or to represent amendments made by the Lords in the former Bill in the preceding session and agreed to by the Commons.

The Commons may, if they choose, in the second[2] session suggest further amendments without inserting them in the Bill, and such suggested amendments, if agreed to by the Lords, shall be treated as amendments agreed to by both   **8–036**

---

[90] Composed of the Chairmen of Standing Committees of the Commons.
[91] Not including a Bill for confirming a Provisional Order, s.5.
[92] This exclusion from the Parliament Act 1911 was the only Lords' amendment agreed at a late stage of the proceedings on the Bill.
[93] Amendment made by the Parliament Act 1949.
[94] Prescribing more than one session enables both Houses to think again: a compromise is possible, or the Bill may be dropped.
[95] Amendment made by the Parliament Act 1949.
[96] *ibid.*
[97] The Parliament Acts assume the practice of having three readings.
[98] Amendment made by the Parliament Act 1949.
[99] A minimum time limit is also prescribed because the government could arrange one-day sessions.
[1] It has been suggested that it would be more satisfactory if a certificate of such importance were issued by a Joint Committee of the two Houses or a High Court judge.
[2] Amendment made by the Parliament Act 1949.

Houses; but the exercise of this power by the Commons shall not affect the operation of this section in the event of rejection of the Bill by the Lords.

Section 3.

The Speaker's certificate "*shall be conclusive for all purposes,[3] and shall not be questioned in any court of law.*"[4] It may be noticed that the Parliament Acts do not describe the Speaker's functions thereunder as "duties."[5]

Section 4.

When a Bill is sent up for the Royal Assent without the consent of the Lords the enacting formula is as follows:

"Be it enacted by the Queen's most excellent Majesty, *by and with the advice and consent of the Commons in this present Parliament assembled, in accordance with the provisions of the Parliament Act 1911 and 1949, and by the authority of the same, as follows.*"

Section 5.

"Public Bill" does not include a Bill for confirming a Provision Order.[6]

Section 6.

"Nothing in this Act shall diminish or qualify the existing rights and privileges of the House of Commons."[7]

Section 7.

"Five years shall be substituted for seven years as the time fixed for the maximum duration of Parliament under the Septennial Act 1715."

Measures not covered by the Parliament Acts

8–037 These include:

(i) a Bill to extend the maximum duration of Parliament (section 2(1));

(ii) Bills to confirm Provisional Orders (section 5);

(iii) Finance and other Supply Bills not certified as "Money Bills";

(iv) private Bills;

(v) Statutory Instruments[8] or other subordinate legislation; and

---

[3] This expression could cover the Lords and the Sovereign.

[4] In *Anisminic v. Foreign Compensation Commission* [1969] 2 A.C. 147 the House of Lords decided that where a statute states that an instrument such as an order or certificate shall be "conclusive evidence" or words to that effect, this implies that the instrument has been properly made, and does not extend to some purported order or certificate which was beyond the power of the maker to make. This principle could be applied to a certificate signed by the Speaker in misconstruction of the power conferred on him by the Parliament Act 1911.

[5] *cf. ante*, para. 7–003.

[6] "Public bill" is not otherwise defined by the Parliament Acts.

[7] This preserves the various privileges of the Commons, especially in relation to financial measures, *e.g.* that they should only be introduced in the lower House, and that the Lords should not amend a Money Bill. See *post*, para. 12–003.

[8] If the Lords reject a Statutory Instrument the Minister can introduce a new version, which the Lords are not likely to reject, *e.g.* Statutory Order imposing further economic sanctions on Rhodesia in 1968.

(vi) Bills introduced into the Lords.[9]

The 1968 reform proposals[10]

The main proposal in the abortive Parliament (No. 2) Bill 1968, would have **8–038**
reduced the period of delay to six months from the day on which the House of
Lords disagreed in the case of a public Bill sent up by the Commons, other than
a Money Bill, a Bill to extend the maximum duration of Parliament or a Bill to
confirm a Provisional Order. A resolution of the Commons to present such a Bill
for the Royal Assent without the Lords' consent would not have been affected by
prorogation or dissolution. Sections 2 and 5 of the Parliament Act 1911 and the
whole of the Parliament Act 1949 would have been repealed.

The 2000 reform proposals[11]

The Wakeham Report concluded that the balance between the two Houses **8–039**
which had evolved over many decades should not be radically disturbed.[12] It
supported neither a return to the fully bicameral nature of the pre-1911 Parliament, nor the removal of the Lords' suspensory veto over most primary legislation whereby it could no longer require the Government to justify a legislative
proposal to the Commons for a second time. One change recommended in the
Report was to amend the Parliament Acts to exclude the possibility of their being
further amended by the use of the Parliament Act procedures. The purpose of
such an amendment would be to give the Lords a veto over any attempt to
constrain its existing powers in respect of primary legislation; it would also
reinforce the Lords' veto over any Bill to extend the life of a Parliament.

---

[9] This limitation can be side-stepped. If a Government wishes to use the Parliament Act procedure in
respect of a Bill introduced in the Lords, then it can introduce a virtually identical Bill in the
Commons and sent it to the Lords before the end of the first session, as was done with the Criminal
Justice (Mode of Trial) No. 2 Bill 2000, after the Lords had passed a wrecking amendment to the first
Bill. The No. 2 Bill was eventually dropped by the Government.
[10] For the proposals relating to the composition of the House of Lords, see *post* para. 9–038.
[11] Report of the Royal Commission on the Reform of the House of Lords, (the Wakeham Report), "A
House for the Future", Cm. 4534. See *post* paras 9–035 to 9–043 for further details of the proposals
made in the Report.
[12] See *post* paras 9–024 to 9–027 for a discussion of the use made of the Parliament Act procedure.

CHAPTER 9

THE HOUSE OF LORDS[1]

Introduction

9–001   The composition and powers of the House of Lords has been a continuing matter of debate over the last 100 years. The election of a Labour Government in 1997 with a manifesto commitment to reform the Lords resulted in the enactment of the House of Lords Act 1999, the first stage of a promised extensive reform of the second chamber. In advance of the enactment of this Act the Government published a White Paper,[2] and established a Royal Commission to make recommendations on the role, functions and composition of a reformed second chamber. The Royal Commission reported in January 2000,[3] and its recommendations have been debated in both Houses.[4] The Queen's Speech in June 2001 stated that, following consultations, legislation would be introduced to implement the second phase of reform.

Historical introduction

9–002   The origin of the House of Lords is to be found in the Great Council (*magnum concilium*) of Norman times, and even in the earlier Witenagemot.[5] The *magnum concilium* of the Norman and early Plantagenet Kings was a council of the chief men of the nation, summoned by the King because of their wealth or skill. Wealth and power went with the holding of land, which was in the main hereditary. The next development is the notion of "peerage." A person who had received a summons to Parliament and had taken his seat, acquired not only a right to be summoned in future but a hereditary right to be summoned which descended to his heirs.

The older method of creating peerages was by writ of summons to Parliament, followed by the person summoned taking his seat. Baronies were created in this way in the reign of Edward I. A peerage by writ, as it was called, descended to the heirs general, *i.e.* male and female, lineal and collateral. The usual method of creating peerages in more recent times was by letters patent, which gave the grantee a right to a summons. A peerage by patent descends in accordance with the limitation in the patent, which is generally (though not invariably) to the lineal heirs male. Hereditary peerages[6] were of England and Scotland (created before the Union of England and Scotland), of Great Britain (created after the Union with Scotland and before the Union with Ireland) and of the United Kingdom (created since the Union with Ireland). Few hereditary peerages were

---

[1] Erskine May, *Parliamentary Practice* (22nd ed., 1997) Chaps 21, 25.

[2] "Modernising Parliament: Reforming the House of Lords", Cm. 4183, hereafter the 1999 White Paper.

[3] Royal Commission on the Reform of the House of Lords, *A House for the Future*, Cm. 4534, hereafter in this Chap. referred to as the Royal Commission.

[4] H.L.Deb. vol. 610, cols. 911–1036 (March 7, 2000); H.C.Deb. Vol. 352 (June 19, 2000).

[5] See Pike, *Constitutional History of the House of Lords*, (1894), especially Chap. 4, for further details.

[6] A person entitled to attend Parliament was under no obligation to apply for a writ of summons if he did not wish to do so, and it was the custom that a writ was only issued to a consenting party; *Re Parliamentary election for Bristol South-East* [1964] 2 Q.B. 257.

created in recent years.[7] Hereditary peeresses in their own right were only allowed to sit and vote in the House of Lords by virtue of section 6 of the Peerage Act 1963.[8]

The most recent development is the House of Lords Act 1999. By section 5(1) **9–003** of this Act, writs of summons in the right of a hereditary peerage have no effect after the 1998–1999 session as section 1 of the Act excludes holders of hereditary peerages from membership of the House of Lords.[9] The House of Lords Act 1999 does not affect the institution of the peerage itself. The heirs of peerages will inherit their titles according to the existing rules of succession, but they will not inherit a seat in Parliament.

Peerage claims

The House of Lords, acting on the advice of its Committee for Privileges,[10] **9–004** could itself and of its own motion determine the validity of the creation of a new peerage and the question whether the grantee was entitled to a writ of summons. The House also had the privilege of deciding whether anyone other than the original grantee was entitled to sit.[11] Claims to peerages which are in abeyance[12] or where the title is disputed will continue to be made by petition to the Crown, and the practice whereby such matters, after a preliminary ruling by the Lord Chancellor, are referred by the House of Lords to the Committee of Privileges will also continue to apply. Lapse of time is no legal bar to a peerage claim.[13] As a consequence of the House of Lords Act, future peerage claims will be concerned only with entitlement to the title.

Disclaimer of hereditary peerages

The main object of the Peerage Act 1963 was to permit the disclaimer of **9–005** hereditary peerages[14] with the result that the person concerned was relieved of the disqualification from voting for and being elected to the House of Commons. Section 1 allowed the holder of a hereditary peerage (other than an Irish peerage)[15] to disclaim the peerage for his life.[16] The effect of the House of Lords Act 1999 is that those hereditary peers who are no longer members of that House may vote in elections for, and be elected to, the House of Commons without the

---

[7] In January 1999 there were 759 hereditary peers, of whom nine were of first creation.

[8] *Viscountess Rhondda's Claim* [1922] 2 A.C. 339.

[9] With the exception of those excepted from section 1 by the Standing Orders of the House, see *post* para. 9–09. In addition to the nine hereditary peers of first creation in the House in 1999, six other hereditary peers were offered life peerages. The Committee of Privileges in the House of Lords was invited to consider whether the House of Lords Bill, if enacted, would affect the right of hereditary peers who had answered their writ of summons before the House of Lords Bill received the Royal Assent. The unanimous view of the Committee was that the Bill would remove the right of hereditary peers to sit and vote: H.L. Paper 106 (1998–99).

[10] The Committee for Privileges consists of 16 peers and four Lords of Appeal.

[11] *Viscountess Rhondda's Claim* [1922] 2 A.C. 339.

[12] *e.g.* because it descended to two or more females in the same degree.

[13] In *Earldom of Annadale and Hartfell* [1986] A.C. 319, an earldom was revived after 193 years.

[14] Report of Joint Committee on House of Lords Reform (1962) H.L. 23 and H.C. 38; *Re Parliamentary Election for Bristol South-East* [1964] 2 Q.B. 257. The Peerage Act did not deal with courtesy titles, which are matters of the Queen's pleasure and not of law.

[15] Irish peers have not been represented in the Lords since the death of the last representative peer of Ireland in 1961. See Lord Dunboyne, "Irish Representative Peers", [1967] P.L. 314.

[16] Those who succeeded to a peerage after the 1963 Act generally had a year in which to disclaim. However, anyone who was a member of the House of Commons had only one month from succession in which to disclaim; similarly a candidate for election to the House of Commons who succeeded to a peerage had, if he was elected to that House, one month in which to disclaim.

need to relinquish their peerages. The provisions of the Peerage Act remain in force for the benefit of those peers who wish for other reasons to disclaim their title for life.

Disclaimer of a peerage is irrevocable. A peer who disclaims is divested of the peerage and any offices or privileges attaching thereto. Disclaimer does not affect any rights of property (section 3). The anomaly that the Act makes disclaimer of a peerage operate for life only and does not affect succession on death, is less significant since the House of Lords Act 1999.

The future of the peerage

9–006   The Royal Commission recommended that those who become members of the reformed second chamber would not receive a peerage, and that the automatic link between a peerage and membership of the second chamber should be broken.[17] This would not prevent a Prime Minister from recommending an award of a peerage in recognition of a person's merit and achievements; such an honour would not be a bar to subsequent membership of the reformed second chamber.

I. COMPOSITION OF THE HOUSE OF LORDS[18]

9–007   The composition of the House of Lords changed with effect from the start of the 1999–2000 session. This composition has been described as "transitional" and is likely to be further altered.

Lords Spiritual[19]

9–008   The 26 Lords Spiritual now consist by statute of the Archbishops of Canterbury and York, the Bishops of London, Durham and Winchester, and 21 other diocesan bishops of the Church of England in order of seniority of appointment.[20] They are summoned on their "faith and love." In the Middle Ages archbishops and bishops could attend Parliament both as holders of important offices of state and as tenants-in-chief or holders of baronies. Their presence was not due to any theory of the "three estates" of clergy, barons and commons.[21] Until the Reformation the Lords Spiritual formed a large part, sometimes a majority, of the House of Lords. It was not certain at the time of Elizabeth I, when Acts of Supremacy and Uniformity were passed, whether a Bill that was opposed unanimously by the Lords Spiritual was valid.[22] The bishops were excluded during the Commonwealth period. Although in modern times the presence of the Bishops became associated with the establishment of the Church of England, in law the two are quite separate.[23]

---

[17] Royal Commission *op. cit* Recommendation 127.

[18] For an account written before the 1999 reforms see N. Baldwin, Chap. 2 in *The House of Lords its Parliamentary and Judicial Roles* (B. Dickson and P. Carmichael, eds, 1999).

[19] The Lords Spiritual are not peers.

[20] The number was fixed by the Bishoprics Act 1878. Although the See of Sodor and Man forms part of the Province of York the Bishop of Sodor and Man is not entitled to set in the Upper House as one of the Lords Spiritual, the Isle of Man not forming part of the United Kingdom.

[21] "Those who pray, those who fight, those who work": Maitland, *Constitutional History* (1908), p. 75.

[22] Maitland, "The Reformation," in *Cambridge Modern History*, Vol. II, p. 571.

[23] 1999 White Paper.

"Elected" Hereditary peers

Prior to the House of Lords Act 1999, the bulk of the Lords Temporal[24] **9–009** consisted of the holders of hereditary peerages. The 1999 Act removed the right of hereditary peers to sit and vote in the House of Lords.[25] However, to take account of the fact that no final decision on the composition of the Lords would be made or implemented before the hereditary peers were removed from the House, the original House of Lord Bill was amended (the "Weatherill amendment") to allow a small number of hereditary peers to sit temporarily in what has become known as the "transitional House". By section 2 of the 1999 Act no more than 90 people[26] can be excepted from the exclusion of hereditary peers provided for in section 1, and standing orders of the House can make provision for these exceptions. The standing orders provide several categories of excepted peers to be elected by their peers with the number to be elected in each category. In the case of each category only the hereditary peers from the party concerned can vote. The categories provided are: Labour peers (2), Conservative peers (42), Liberal Democrat (3), Cross-benchers (28).[27] In addition 15 peers are to be elected by the whole House from those ready to serve as, for example, Deputy Speaker. The standing orders make provision for the elections procedure and for by-elections.[28] It is envisaged that elected hereditary peers would be statutorily excluded from whatever is the final form of the composition of the House of Lords.[29]

Life peers and life peeresses[30]

In order to increase the number of those who could be expected in the **9–010** circumstances of the day to attend and take part in debates regularly—especially those who were not Conservatives—the Life Peerages Act 1958 gave Her Majesty power by letters patent to confer on any person (man or woman) a peerage for life, entitling him or her to rank as a baron and (unless disqualified by law) to receive writs of summons to attend the House of Lords and to sit and vote therein. No limit was set to the number of life peers, and it is for the Prime Minister of the day to decide on how many life peerage nominations are to be made to the Queen, and to who to recommend to receive them.[31] It is the decision

---

[24] In January 1999 there were 750 hereditary peers, of whom nearly 200 never attended. In the 1997–98 session 20 per cent of hereditary peers attended more than two-thirds of the House's sessions, and 67 per cent less than one-third. The equivalent figures for life peers was 40 per cent and 34 per cent. See 1999 White Paper, p. 14.

[25] For a discussion of the reasons for the 1999 reforms see the White Paper, in particular Chap. 5. The Committee of Privileges in the House of Lords considered two motions challenging different aspects of the Bill: *Lord Gray's Motion* [2000] W.L.R. 664, H.L. Paper 108 (1998–99); *Lord Mayhew's Motion* [2000] 2 W.L.R. 719, H.L. Paper 106 (1998–99).

[26] Anyone excepted as holder of the office of Earl Marshall or as performing the office of Lord Great Chamberlain, does not count towards the 90 (s.2(2)), this means that in effect 92 of the hereditary peers remain in the House of Lords.

[27] That is those members of the House who are independent and do not take a party whip.

[28] Ballot papers had the names of all the candidates for each party or group. Peers were required to vote for exactly the number of vacancies in the relevant party or group marking against each name the figure 1, 2, 3, etc. to indicate preference. Every vote had equal value and the candidates with the largest number of votes were elected. Preferences were only taken into account if there was a tie.

[29] The "Wetherill 92" remain in the Lords by virtue of a S.O. and primary legislation would not in fact be needed to remove them.

[30] O. Hood Phillips, "Lords and Ladies for Life" (1958) 1 *Oxford Lawyer* 21.

[31] Peerages may be created for a variety of different reasons, *e.g.* "working peers", Queens's Birthday List, Dissolution Honours List. See R. Brazier *Constitutional Practice* (3rd ed. 1999) Chap. 11, pp. 238–240 for details of the different lists.

of the Prime Minister as to how many peers from each party are appointed at any time. In March 2001 there were 564 life peers who had been appointed under the 1958 Act.[32]

The Appointments Commission

9–011   This Commission was established in 2000[33] and is a non-statutory,[34] advisory, non-departmental public body composed of seven members; one member representing each of the three main political parties the remainder,[35] including the chairman, to be politically impartial. The main role of the Commission is to take over from the Prime Minister the function of nominating sufficient Cross bench peers at least to fill any vacancies among this group. It is required to publish criteria for suitability for nomination and to actively invite nominations by the general public and encourage nominations from professional associations, charities and other public bodies that it judges appropriate. The White Paper stated that the Prime Minister would not be entitled to refuse a nomination the Commission had approved, and could only influence nominations in exceptional circumstances, such as those endangering the security of the realm.[36] At least until there is further reform of the composition of the Lords, nominations for peerages from the political parties will continue to be made by the parties to the Prime Minister who will decide the number of vacancies each party may fill.

The Commission takes over the functions of the Political Honours Scrutiny Committee in vetting the suitability of all nominations to life peerages.[37] In particular it will scrutinise candidates on the grounds of propriety in relation to political donations.[38]

Lords of Appeal in Ordinary

9–012   In the middle of the nineteenth century attention was drawn to the death of qualified lawyers in the House of Lords, which in one of its capacities is the highest court of appeal. The only solution, if the appellate jurisdiction of the House of Lords was to be retained, was to make a limited number of judges Lords of Parliament for life, or at least during their tenure of office; and, as at common law a peer could not be created for a term of years, and as the House had ruled that a peer for life would not be allowed by parliamentary custom to take his seat,[39] two Lords of Appeal in Ordinary were introduced by the Appellate Jurisdiction Act 1876. Their maximum number has been gradually increased to 12.[40]

---

[32] The party affiliation of these peers in March 2001 was Conservative 175, Labour 194, Liberal Democrat 57, Cross bench 132. From the 1997 election to June 2000, Mr Blair created 202 peers, the highest annual rate of peerage creation since 1958.

[33] It creation was proposed in the 1999 White Paper, p. 33. It made its first nominations in June 2001.

[34] In announcing the establishment of the Appointments Commission the Government indicated that in the final reform of the Lords, it would become statutory.

[35] Appointed by the Prime Minister.

[36] 1999 White Paper, p. 33, para. 12.

[37] One of the last decisions by this committee was the approval in March 2000 of a peerage for the Conservative Michael Ashcroft, allegedly on the unprecedented condition that he returned to residence in the United Kingdom from Belise.

[38] As recommended in the Fifth Report of the Committee on Standards in Public Life: "*The Funding of Political Parties in the United Kingdom*" Cm. 4057.

[39] *Wensleydale Peerage Case* (1856), 5 H.L.C. 958. An account of this case is given in Pike, *op. cit.* pp. 372–384.

[40] Administration of Justice Act 1968, s.1(1)(a).

As members of the upper House, the "Law Lords" (including retired Lords of Appeal[41] and judges who are peers) take part in debates on legislation affecting the law and the courts. This is not just limited to assisting the House with technical points of law; on several occasions in recent years it has involved strong political argument in opposition to aspects of proposed legislative reform.[42] There has been a convention since the 1920s that when the Law Lords speak on controversial non-legal matters they do so in a personal capacity.[43]

Disqualification from membership of the House

In addition to hereditary peers disqualified under the 1999 Act, the following are disqualified from sitting and voting in the House of Lords: **9–013**

(i) a person convicted of treason is disqualified till the expiry of his sentence of imprisonment or the receipt of a royal pardon[44];

(ii) bankrupts; the disqualification ceases on the bankruptcy being discharged[45];

(iii) a member who has been expelled by sentence of the House acting in its judicial capacity (*i.e.* on impeachment), unless pardoned by the Crown.[46]

Aliens[47] and persons under 21 years of age (Standing Order No. 2, 1685) are also disqualified from membership of the House; since the 1999 Act these disqualifications will merely serve as limitations as to those who can be given life peerages.[48]

Standing Orders relating to attendance

The House has power to enforce attendance, although this has not been exercised since 1841; but it is not within the power of the House to exclude members who habitually do not attend.[49] At the time of the passing of the Life Peerages Act 1958, Standing Order No. 20 was amended so as to provide that "Lords are to attend the sittings of the House or, if they cannot do so, obtain leave   **9–014**

---

[41] Lords of Appeal in Ordinary were at first Lords of Parliament during tenure of office only, but since the Appellate Jurisdiction Act 1887 they are entitled to sit in the House for life with the dignity of baron. They sit as Crossbench peers. The Royal Commission recommended, in line with its general recommendations on retirement age in the reformed second chamber, that they should retire at 75, (Royal Commission Recommendation 58).

[42] Examples include attacks on what became the Courts and Legal Services Act 1990, the Criminal Justice Act 1991, and the Crime (Sentences) Act 1997. For further details see J. A. G. Griffith, *The Politics of the Judiciary* (5th ed., 1997); *cf.* the 1999 White Paper which states that "by convention (the Law Lords) do not become involved in politically contentious issues." p. 39.

[43] Robert Stevens, *Law and Politics: The House of Lords as a Judicial Body, 1800–1976* (1979), p. 308.

[44] Forfeiture Act 1870, as amended by the Criminal Law Act 1967.

[45] Insolvency Act 1986, s.427.

[46] The House of Lords as a legislative chamber cannot disqualify one of its members. On the application of the Mental Health Act 1983 to Peers, see *post*, para. 13–027.

[47] Act of Settlement 1701, s.3. This disqualification does not extend to Commonwealth citizens or citizens of the Republic of Ireland: British Nationality Act 1981; s.52(6) and Sched. 7.

[48] The Royal Commission, recommended that there should be no minimum age for the reformed chamber (Royal Commission Recommendation 73).

[49] Report by the Select Committee: *The Powers of the House in Relation to the Attendance of its Members* (1956) H.L. 7.

of absence." This reform was designed to discourage sporadic forays by "back-woodsmen" hereditary peers. Leave of absence could be given for a session, or the remainder of a session or the remainder of the Parliament. If a Lord having been granted leave of absence wishes to attend during the period, he is expected to give at least one month's notice, after which the leave comes to an end. Prior to the 1999 Act, 56 hereditary and seven life peers had leave of absence.[50] Leave of absence is unlikely to be significant in the future; in March 2001 three life peers were on leave of absence. The average attendance has increased in recent years and in 1999–2000 was about 350.[51]

In general, members of the House of Lords do not receive salaries,[52] but since 1957 have been entitled to claim certain allowances and expenses on a daily basis, plus travelling expenses.

Officers of the House

The Lord Chancellor[53]

9–015   The Speaker of the House of Lords is the Lord High Chancellor of Great Britain, who is Keeper of the Great Seal.[54] He may not leave the country without first notifying the Queen in order that Commissioners may be appointed to affix the Great Seal in his absence. He has been called the Keeper of the Queen's Conscience since the time of Elizabeth I. The Lord Chancellor (Tenure of Office and Discharge of Ecclesiastical Functions) Act 1974, however, for the avoidance of doubt, declares that the office of Lord Chancellor is tenable by an adherent to the Roman Catholic faith.[55]

The Lord Chancellor presides over the House from "the Woolsack," a seat traditionally stuffed with wool, the emblem of England's medieval prosperity. The Speaker of the Lords need not be a peer, the Woolsack being notionally outside the limits of the Chamber.[56] As the officer who issues the writs for parliamentary elections and summoning of peers he is present *ex officio*. Because the Lord Chancellor is appointed by the Crown and not elected, the House of Lords never delegated to him authority to keep order, to control the order of speeches or to rebuke recalcitrant members. These powers are exercised by the House itself, usually under guidance from the Leader of the House, and in debate peers address the House and not the occupant of the Woolsack. The Lord Chancellor in debate speaks as a politically minded peer, standing a few feet

[50] In addition 67 hereditary peers could not attend as they had not sought a Writ of Summons. The figures for leave of absence have been higher in the past.

[51] See N. D. J. Baldwin, "The Membership of the House" in *The House of Lords at work* (D. Shell and D. Beamish, eds, 1993) for a study of attendance in the 1988–9 session.

[52] For, *e.g.* the Leader of the Opposition in the Lords, the Lord Chairman of Committees, and the Lords of Appeal in Ordinary all receive salaries.

[53] See Lord Schuster, "The Office of the Lord Chancellor" (1949) 10 C.L.J. 175; R.F.V. Heuston, *Lives of the Lord Chancellors* Vols. I (1964) and II (1987); Lord McKay, "The Chancellor in the 1990s", (1991) 44 C.L.P. 241; Diana Woodhouse, "The Office of Lord Chancellor", [1998] P.L. 617.

[54] He receives a salary payable as Speaker of the House of Lords, and a judicial salary which is charged on the Consolidated Fund.

[55] If the office is held by a Roman Catholic the Privy Council may provide for his ecclesiastical functions and patronage of livings to be performed by the Prime Minister or any other Minister. He is the patron of some hundreds of benefices in the Church of England.

[56] Before the reign of George III the Speaker of the Lords was sometimes a commoner called Lord Keeper (of the Great Seal), *e.g.* Sir Nicolas Bacon (1558) and his son Sir Francis Bacon (1617).

away from the Woolsack.[57] On a division he votes first, and has no casting vote. When the House is in Committee the Lord Chancellor speaks from the Government front bench.

The Lord Chancellor is the senior legal and constitutional adviser of the government, a Minister of the Crown and almost invariably a member of the Cabinet. His role as a member of the executive is "more or less significant, depending on the Lord Chancellor himself, the Prime minister, and the government's legislative programme."[58] Today the appointment of Lord Chancellor has been described as "in effect that of a minister of Justice".[59] In his executive role the present Lord Chancellor, Lord Irving, not only has responsibility for the administration of justice, but also for the implementation of the Government's constitutional reform programme.   **9–016**

The Lord Chancellor plays the leading part in the appointment, or recommending the appointment of judges, magistrates and legally qualified chairmen of statutory tribunals in England. For reasons of history rather than principle, he has responsibility for the Land Registry, the Public Record Office and the Public Trust Office,[60] and has general responsibility for court records. He also certifies, in cases of doubt, who is the Leader of the Opposition in the House of Lords for the purpose of the latter's salary.[61]

The Lord Chancellor has the prime responsibility under the Law Commissions Act 1965[62] for keeping law reform and the revision of statute law under constant review, especially by appointing and considering the reports of the Law Commission. It was after the Courts Act 1971 came into force that the Lord Chancellor and his department assumed one of its major roles and responsibilities. All higher courts and the county courts in England and Wales are directly administered by the Lord Chancellor's Department through the Courts Service.[63] In 1991 responsibility for magistrates' courts was also transferred to him.[64] The Freedom of Information Act 2000[65] requires the Lord Chancellor to issue a code of practice setting out practices which he considers public authorities (and other authorities whose records are subject to the Public Records Act 1958) should follow in relation to the keeping, management and destruction of their records.   **9–017**

The Lord Chancellor is the head of the judiciary in England and Wales,[66] presiding over the House of Lords sitting as the final court of appeal (the Appellate Committee), and over the Judicial Committee of the Privy Council when he is present. It is the Lord Chancellor who determines the composition of the relevant Committee, but in practice this is delegated to the Senior Law Lord. He therefore performs legislative, executive and judicial functions of great

---

[57] He moves two paces to the left of the Woolsack, which brings him to the place assigned to him by Henry VIII.
[58] Diana Woodhouse, *op. cit.* at p. 618.
[59] http://www.open.gov.uk/lcd/lc-const.htm. However some of the functions and duties that would normally fall to a Minister of Justice are exercised by the Attorney General or the Home Secretary, see *post*/paras 18–010, 18–014.
[60] Which became an executive agency in 1994.
[61] Ministerial and other Salaries Act 1975.
[62] The Home Secretary is concerned with reform of the criminal law.
[63] It became a separate executive agency in 1995.
[64] See now the Police and Magistrates' Court Act 1994, which provides for these courts to be locally administered, although the Lord Chancellor is accountable to Parliament for their operation.
[65] *post* para. 26–029.
[66] In Northern Ireland, the Lord Chief Justice is President of the High Court and the Court of Appeal. The Head of the judiciary in Scotland is the Lord President (and Lord Justice General).

importance. Although the Lord Chancellor may not frequently sit in the Appellate Committee[67] the question arises whether it is appropriate for him to do so at all, particularly in the light of the role the Appellate Committee could have in hearing cases on the Human Rights Act 1998 where there is a government interest, or the Judicial Committee on devolution disputes.[68] His position has been made less tenable by the decision of the European Court of Human Rights in *McGonnell v. United Kingdom*[69] that it was a violation of Article 6 for someone to sit as a judge who had other legislative or executive roles.

9–018   The Lord Chancellor is also President of the Supreme Court, an *ex-officio* judge of the Court of Appeal and President of the Chancery Division of the High Court.[70] He does not in practice sit in these latter courts, the senior judge of the Chancery Division now being called Vice-Chancellor; but he is responsible for regulating their business through the Rule Committee. Unlike other senior judges, the Lord Chancellor does not have security of tenure, nor does he necessarily have previous judicial experience before his appointment.[71]

The *Chairman of Committees*, who holds office for the session, is appointed by the House from its members, and takes the Chair when the House is in Committee, and is Deputy Speaker of the House. He also superintends all matters relating to private Bills and certain subordinate legislation. In addition a number of Lords are appointed as Deputy Chairman of Committees.

The other officers of the House are permanent officers[72] who have no party affiliations and whose duty is to the House, not to the Government of the day. The terms of service of the permanent staff are similar to those of civil servants but they are servants of Parliament not of the Crown. From 1976 to 1993 the staff of the House of Lords were covered by "analogous treatment" rather than directly by the various pieces of employment statute law that had included an express application to the staff of the Commons. Since 1993 they have been included within the various statutory protections.[73]

9–019   The offices of *Gentlemen Usher of the Black Rod and Serjeant-at-Arms of the House of Lords* were amalgamated in 1971. The holder executes warrants of commitment or attachment under the rules of the House, carries the black wand surmounted by a golden lion which is used as the Mace of the Lords, and desires

---

[67] See Lord Hailsham *A Sparrow's Flight* (1990), where he contrasts his judicial role with that of his father who was Lord Chancellor earlier in the twentieth century. See A. Bradney, "The Judicial Role of the Lord Chancellor", Chap. 8 in *The House of Lords its Parliamentary and Judicial Roles* (B. Dickson and P. Carmichael, eds, 1999).

[68] See *post* para. 26–029.

[69] (2000) E.H.R.R. 289. The Royal Court of Guernsey in hearing a planning appeal was presided over by the Bailiff of Guernsey, who was a professional judge, President of the legislature and head of Guernsey's administration. The Lord Chancellor has stated that he will use his discretion not to sit in devolution or human rights cases where he considered it would be "inappropriate or improper" to do so, H.L.Deb., Vol.593, Oct 20, 1998, *W.A.* 138; see the statement by the Lord Chancellor on the *McGonnell* case, H.L.Deb. Vol. 610 Col. 656, Thursday March 2, 2000. Dawn Oliver, "The Lord Chancellor, the Judicial Committee of the Privy Council and Devolution", [1999] P.L. 1.; Richard Corns, "*McGonnell v. United Kingdom*, the Lord Chancellor and the Law Lords", [2000] P.L. 166.

[70] Supreme Court Act 1981, s.1(2) and s.5(1)(a).

[71] It is also the case that before appointment the Lord Chancellor need not have been an active politician.

[72] For further details of the officers discussed below and other officers of the House see Erskine May *Parliamentary Practice* (22nd ed. 1997), Chap. 12.

[73] See G. Lock, "Statute law and case law applicable to Parliament", Chap. IV in *The Law and Parliament* (Oliver and Drewry, eds, 1998), p. 59.

the attendance of the Commons when necessary. He is responsible for accommodation, service and security in the House of Lords area of the Palace of Westminster.

The *Clerk of the Parliaments* is appointed by the Crown, and is removable only on an address from the House.[74] He is head of the Parliament Office, which consists of the permanent staff of the House. The minutes and journals of the House are prepared under his direction, he gives advise to Members of the House on order and procedure and pronounces the Royal Assent to Bills.

II. MODERN FUNCTIONS OF THE HOUSE OF LORDS[75]

Most legislatures contain—in addition to a representative assembly directly **9–020** elected by popular vote—a Second Chamber, upper House or Senate, elected indirectly or by some different method, or nominated.

This in spite of the apparent dilemma propounded by the Abbe Sieyes, that if a Second Chamber dissents from the First, it is mischievous, while if it agrees it is superfluous. In a federation a Second Chamber is regarded as essential in order to preserve the rights of the individual states. In a unitary state a Second Chamber is generally thought desirable in order to admit into the legislature persons with special kinds of experience or representing ethnic, religious or other minorities, and also to provide opportunity for second thoughts about policy and legislation. As this country has no written constitution, if we had a unicameral legislature our governmental system and laws would be at the mercy of a majority of one in the House of Commons, and moreover the House of Commons could prolong its own life indefinitely.

The functions and powers of the House of Lords in recent years may be considered under nine headings.[76] Most of these functions would continue or be strengthened under proposals by the Royal Commission, and these will be considered below. Additional functions proposed by the Royal Commission will be examined later.

(1) *Pre-legislative scrutiny*

The scrutiny of draft Bills by parliamentary committees is a new function for **9–021** both Houses of Parliament. Joint committees consisting of members of both Houses were appointed in 1998–99 to consider draft legislation on the Financial Services and Markets Bill, and the Local Government (Organisation and Standards) Bill. The Lords and the Commons each established a select committee to consider the draft Freedom of Information Bill 1999.

---

[74] Clerk of Parliaments Act 1824, s.2.
[75] B. Hadfield, "Whether or Whither the House of Lords" (1984) 35 N.I.L.Q. 313; Erskine May *Parliamentary Practice* (22nd ed. 1997), Chap. 21; "Organisation and conduct of business in the House of Lords." D. Shell, *The House of Lords* (1992); *The House of Lords at work* (D. Shell and D. Beamish, eds, 1993); *The House of Lords, its Parliamentary and Judicial Roles*, (B. Dickson and P. Carmichael, eds, 1999); Griffith and Ryle, *Parliament: Functions, Practice, and Procedure*, (2nd ed., 2001), edited by R. Blackburn and A. Keynon.
[76] Broadly derived from the Bryce Conference 1917–18, Cd. 9038 and the White Paper of 1968 on Reform of the House of Lords; Cmnd. 3799.

(2) Revision of Public Bills sent from the Commons

9–022   The House of Lords spends over half its time revising Bills from the Commons. The importance of this function arises from the lack of time available in the Commons to debate legislative proposals. In some cases where, for example, discussion has been curtailed by the guillotine, clauses may not have been discussed at all in the lower House. The lack of procedural restraints in the Lords, a more leisurely timetable than in the Commons, and a less partisan approach assist the Lords in its task of revising legislation. An average of two thousand amendments to Bills are moved each year, the majority of which are tabled by the government so it is not surprising that the majority of the Lord's amendments are accepted by the Commons.[77] However this global figure disguises the fact that on average half of the government's Bills are not amended at all.[78] The Lords has reformed its procedures to further enhance its ability properly to perform this task of revision.[79]

Not all amendments put forward in the Lords by a government are accepted, and defeats were inflicted on the Conservative Government during the period 1979–1997. In most cases the Government accepted the defeat or at least the principle involved despite its Commons majority.[80] In 1980, for example, the Duke of Norfolk led the successful opposition to a clause in the Education Bill which allowed local education authorities to impose transport charges for children travelling to school in rural areas. In 1984 the House forced the Government to compromise on its plans for transitional arrangements pending the abolition of the Greater London Council and the metropolitan councils contained in the Local Government (Interim Provisions) Bill. However the House of Lords was not in the end successful in changing the Local Government Finance Bill 1988, which replaced domestic rates by a "community charge" or "poll tax." The Bill had been challenged in the Commons with the government majority falling to 25, despite a majority of over 100 in the House. Despite continued opposition in the Lords, it was passed with the second highest turnout in the history of the Lords.[81] The House of Lords was unable to require the Commons and the Government to look again at a pieces of legislation that had been widely perceived to be unfair, and which in the event was repealed (on the initiative of a Conservative Government) in 1992.

9–023   Defeats averaged 12 per year between 1993 and 1996,[82] and have increased since the 1997 election of a Labour Government. The government was defeated 39 times in its first year of office,[83] 29 times in its second year and 27 times in its third year. In 1999–2000 during the first six months of the "transitional"

---

[77] See Michale Rush, "The House of Lords: The Political Context" Chap. 2 in *The House of Lords its Parliamentary and Judicial Roles* (B. Dickson and P. Carmichael, eds 1999), *op. cit.*

[78] See D. Shell, *op. cit.* p. 143–144., and Drewry and Brock, "Government Legislation: An Overview", Chap. 3 in *The House of Lords at work* (D. Shell and B. Beamish, eds 1993) *op. cit.*

[79] For example by the use of Public Bills Committees and the creation of a Delegated Powers and Deregulation Committee, *post.* para. 29–018.

[80] D. Shell, "The House of Lords and the Thatcher Government" (1985) 38, *Parliamentary Affairs* 16. See H.L.Deb., vol. 566, col. 90, October 1995, for details of government defeats in the House of Lords from 1970–1995.

[81] The Conservative majority was boosted by the attendance of over 100 peers who were irregular attenders, that is not members of the "working House."

[82] M. Rush, Chap. 1 in *The House of Lords its Parliamentary and Judicial Roles* (B. Dickson and P. Carmichael, eds 1999) *op. cit.* Between 1979 and 1990 of the 155 defeats suffered by the Government, 148 of them were on legislation; see D. Shell, *op. cit.*

[83] Five of which were on the European Parliamentary Elections Bill. This was a longer than average parliamentary year.

House, the Government suffered 15 defeats on legislation. The Government abandoned its attempt to include in the Local Government Bill 2000 the repeal of section 28 of the Local Government Act 1986 (the section which prevents local authorities from promoting homosexuality). In 1999 a wrecking amendment to the Criminal Justice (Mode of Trial) Bill 2000 caused the Government to withdraw the Bill before it had even been to the Commons.[84]

Difficulties arise when, from the point of view of the Government, revision becomes interference with the will of the people as expressed in the Commons. In the last resort the Lords cannot prevent the enactment of a Bill which it has insisted in amending contrary to the will of the Commons, but only delay its enactment.

(3) *The delaying of legislation*

Although of constitutional importance, the power possessed by the Lords to delay the enactment of legislation has been less significant than its role in revising legislation. The power of the House of Lords to delay legislation is regulated by constitutional convention and the Parliament Acts 1911 and 1949.[85] The Salisbury Convention was enunciated in 1945 when there was a Labour Government but few Labour peers in the House of Lords.[86] The convention as it developed provided that a government Bill which gives effect to a manifesto commitment would not be opposed at either the second or third reading; it may also apply to prevent "wrecking amendments", that is those which would destroy or alter a Bill beyond recognition.[87] This convention has reduced conflict between the two Houses during periods of Labour Government, and allowed a government without a majority in the Lords to secure its business. In the debate on the War Damage Bill 1965 the Marquess of Salisbury, a Conservative elder statesman, suggested that the House of Lords should only insist on its amendments: (i) if the question raises issues important enough to justify such drastic action; and (ii) if the issue is one which can be readily understood by the people and on which the Lords can expect their support, an issue on which the House of Lords would really be acting as the watchdog of the people.[88] In 1969 the Conservative Opposition moved a number of "wrecking" amendments in Committee to a Redistribution of Seats Bill, which they regarded as gerrymandering and therefore unconstitutional, and the amendments were passed by a majority greater than the number of hereditary peers present. The Lords then rejected a revised Bill, which the Government dropped.

9–024

Differences between the two Houses can normally be resolved without recourse to the Parliament Acts. When the House of Lords sends back a Bill with

9–025

---

[84] A Number 2 Bill was then introduced into the Commons, but this was also eventually withdrawn.

[85] For details see *ante* para. 8–03.

[86] It built on an earlier version of the mandate developed by the Third Marquess of Salisbury in the late 19th century.

[87] See Lord Carrington, *Reflect on Things Past: the Memoirs of Lord Carrington* (1988) p. 77–78; and the statement by Viscount Cranborne in H.L. Deb. Vol. 593, col. 1162 (15 Oct. 1998). The wrecking amendment to the Criminal Justice (Mode of Trial) Bill 1999 was said not to fall within the convention as the Bill had not been a manifesto commitment.

[88] H.L. Deb., Vol. 266, Cols. 784–785 (1965). Thus the Lords did not insist on their amendment to the War Damage Bill 1965, the purpose of which was to nullify the decision of the House of Lords as to war damage in *Burmah Oil Co v. Lord Advocate* [1965] A.C. 75.

amendments, a Committee of the House of Commons (if it disagrees with the amendments) sends the amended Bill back with a statement of its reasons for so doing, and a settlement is often reached by conferences between party leaders.

The Royal Commission suggested that although the Parliament Act procedure has been little used, it was probable that: "decisions—by both the Government and the House of Lords—about the handling of the most contentious Bills over the past 88 years have been influenced by the existence of the Parliament Acts. The threat of using, or the ability to override, the House of Lords' power of veto has influenced attitudes towards individual amendments to Bills as well as their overall principle."[89] Apart from the 1949 Act itself, only two other Acts have received the Royal Assent in accordance with the provisions of the Parliament Act 1911,[90] and three under the Parliament Act 1949: the War Crimes Act 1991 the European Elections Act 1999 and the Sexual Offences (Amendment) Act 2000.[91]

9–026   The War Crimes Act applies retrospectively to crimes committed during the second world war. As a Bill it was rejected by the Lords partly because of the difficulties of successful prosecutions after such a gap in time, and also because of its retrospective effect. In the Lords it was argued that the Salisbury Convention did not apply because the Bill was concerned with a moral issue, and had not been mentioned in the manifesto. Within the Lords views were divided as to which would do most damage to the future of the House: to reject it contrary to the will of the elected Commons or pass it contrary to the majority view in the Lords that it was a bad measure. The War Crimes Bill was passed by the Commons on a free vote, and the Opposition Labour Party supported the Government on the basis that the will of the Commons should prevail. This was the first Bill rejected by the Lords where the second and third readings in the Commons had had cross-party support, and the first use by a Conservative Government of the Parliament Act procedures.[92]

The European Elections Bill provided for a system of proportional representation for the election of United Kingdom members of the European Parliament. The system proposed gave voters a choice between parties but not between candidates; the Lords, contrary to the views of the Commons, insisted on its amendments which would have introduced a form of open list which would have allowed electors to vote for individual candidates, and the Bill was lost at the end of the 1997–98 session. The Bill was reintroduced in the new session, and voted down by the Lords at the second reading. It was then presented for the Royal Assent under the Parliament Acts, in time for its implementation for the 1999 European elections.

9–027   The threat of the use of its formal delaying power is potentially more important when a minority government is in office, since it is more difficult for such a government to claim an electoral mandate for its policies. During the minority Labour governments from February to October 1974 and from 1976–1979, the Lords did not use its delaying powers, but extensively amended legislation

---

[89] *op. cit.* Royal Commission para. 4.4.
[90] The Government of Ireland Act 1914 and the Welsh Church Act 1914, both of which were suspended by the outbreak of war. The former was eventually superseded by the Government of Ireland Act 1920; the latter became law with some modifications in 1919.
[91] Which lowered the age of consent for males in homosexual relationships from 18 to 16.
[92] G. Ganz, "The War Crimes Act 1991—Why No Constitutional Crisis?", (1992) 55 M.L.R. 87.

although usually giving way after the Bill was introduced in the Commons for a second time.[93]

The Royal Commission considered that it was important that the second chamber should be able to challenge a Government's legislative proposals and to force it to justify them to the Commons for a second time, taking account of cogent objections from the second chamber to the legislation. It concluded that other methods of resolving disputes between the two chambers of Parliament, such as the use of a referendum or a joint session of both chambers, offered no significant advantage over the continuation of the current position. It recommended that the suspensory veto arrangement which had emerged from the Parliament Acts 1911, 1949, should continue.[94]

(4) *The initiation of public legislation and private members' bills*

One role of the House of Lords has been described as the initiation of "non-controversial" legislation.[95] It is true that law reform measures and consolidation bills, bills giving effect to international agreements to which the United Kingdom has become a party and other issues which do not involve matters of party political controversy will start their legislative passage in the House of Lords. However for reasons of administrative convenience, namely to ensure that the volume of legislation passing through both Houses is evenly spread throughout the session, a variety of Bills, some of which are potentially controversial, are now introduced in the Lords. Recent examples include the Human Rights Act 1998, and the Youth and Criminal Evidence Act 1999.   **9–028**

There has been a fall in the number of Private Members' Bills introduced by peers, in part caused by pressure of time on the Lords. About two per session receive the Royal Assent; it is usual for Private Members' Bills originating from the Commons to be passed by the Lords.[96]

(5) *Scrutiny of private bills*[97]

(6) *Scrutiny of delegated legislation*[98]

In October 1994 the House of Lords affirmed its unfettered freedom to vote on any subordinate legislation submitted to it for its consideration.[99] In February 2000 the Greater London Authority (Election Expenses) Order came before the Lords and was rejected.[1] On the same day a motion for an Address for the annulment of the Greater London Authority (Election Rules) was agreed to, the first time the House had rejected a measure that required negative approval, that is a measure that would become law *unless* the Lords voted against it.   **9–029**

---

[93] See for, *e.g.* the Aircraft and Shipbuilding Industries Act 1977 and the Dock Work Regulation Act 1976.

[94] *op. cit.* Royal Commission paras. 4.3–4.12.

[95] See, *e.g.* Bryce Conference *op. cit.* and the 1968 White Paper, *op. cit.*

[96] See Natzler and Millar, "Private Members' Bills", Chap. 6 in *The House of Lords at work* (D. Shell and D. Beamish, eds 1993).

[97] *post*, para. 11–038.

[98] *post*. para. 29–018. The Royal Commission proposed a variety of reforms designed to improve the role played by the second chamber in the parliamentary scrutiny of Statutory Instruments.

[99] H.L. Deb. Vol. 558, col. 356, October 20, 1994.

[1] The first affirmative order to be rejected by the House since the Southern Rhodesia (United Nations Sanctions) Order 1968.

(7) Scrutiny of the Executive[2]

9-030   *Debates* in the Lords do not affect the fate of governments,[3] the practice being to "move for papers" and then to withdraw the motion rather than press it to a vote.

As in the Commons, *Question Time* is when the House is at its fullest and most lively. Questions to Ministers are of less significance than in the House of Commons. There are few ministers in the Upper House[4] and their Lordships do not have to concern themselves with the problems of constituents. The demand to ask questions has meant that it is rare for space to be available less than three or four weeks ahead, in consequence most questions are not current by the time they come up. Four oral questions (Starred Questions) only may be asked each day for half an hour at the start of business. Questions may be tabled up to a month ahead, and are allocated on a "first come first served" basis. To enable topical questions to be asked there are two topical starred questions each week on Wednesday and Thursday. The questions to be asked are determined by lot from questions tabled the previous Tuesday. Unstarred questions may also be put at the end of the day's business and may result in mini debates for one to one and a half hours. In addition over 4000 written questions were asked in 1999, compared to 2653 in 1997.

To enable Ministers to give important news first to Parliament, both Houses make provision for Ministers to make *Statements*. Most statements originate in the Commons, and by current practice it is for the Leader of the House to decide whether to have such a statement repeated in the Lords. After a statement 20 minutes are available for questioning the Minister.

European Union Matters The chief mechanism by which Parliament can scrutinise and control developments in the European Union is by bringing Ministers to account for decisions to which they contribute in the Council of Ministers. In the House of Lords this is the task of the *European Union Committee*.[5] The Royal Commission praised the work of this Committee and recommended that additional staff and resources should be made available to it.[6] It also recommended that a regular time should be set aside for dealing with Questions for Oral Answer on E.U. matters, (Recommendation 51).

(8) Full and free discussion of large and important questions

9-031   The House of Lords, by virtue of the wide and varied background of its members, particularly since the introduction of life peerages, and its freedom from the constraints of party discipline provides a place where controversial issues of any kind may be debated. Most Wednesdays are for general debates, with one Wednesday a month being set aside for two short debates, the topics being chosen by ballot from those put forward by backbench peers. About one-

---

[2] See also para. 29–018 on the House of Lords Delegated Powers and Deregulation Committee which plays a role in scrutinising executive powers.
[3] The House of Lords defeated the Government on a motion of confidence in January 1968 concerning the withdrawal of forces east of Suez and defence cuts. This had no practical effect.
[4] The Royal Commission suggested that a new mechanism should be developed which would require Commons Ministers to make statements to and deal with questions from members of the second chamber, (Recommendation 45). One possibility suggested was a Committee of the whole of the second chamber meeting off the floor of the chamber, (Royal Commission para. 8.8).
[5] The work of this committee is discussed in *ante* para. 6–032.
[6] Royal Commission Recommendations 46, 47. In Chap. 8 it made a variety of recommendations designed to improve scrutiny of E.U. business and for forging links between M.E.P.s and Westminster.

fifth of the time of the House is devoted to general debate. Ad hoc committees of the House, such as those which considered a proposed Bill of Rights,[7] Murder and Life Imprisonment,[8] Medical Ethics, and the Public Service,[9] contribute to this aspect of the work of the House of Lords. In March 2001 the House agreed to establish a Stem Cell Research Committee to consider and report on the issues connected with human cloning and stem cell research. Public opinion can be informed and educated by debate and the taking of evidence in these committees. Government can assess by public reaction the desirability of legislation on controversial matters where considerations of policy and principle are likely to take second place to a fear of offending vocal pressure groups. There was unanimous support from the Royal Commission for a continuation of the role of the reformed second chamber in providing a distinctive forum for national debate.

(9) *Select Committees*[10]

The House of Lords has the power to appoint select committees to examine any matter which in the opinion of the House, requires investigation. Until the 1970s such committees were concerned with the running of the House, but from that time the House began to use select committees to scrutinise public policy. In addition to ad hoc select committees (above) and the committees on E.U. law and on Delegated Powers and Deregulation, one of the most important committee is that on Science and Technology, first appointed in 1979 following the disbandment of the Science and Technology Committee in the Commons. Recent inquiries have looked at the management of nuclear waste,[11] and the scientific and medical evidence concerning cannabis.[12] This committee's reports are highly regarded at home and abroad, due "to a considerable extent to the expertise available to the House of Lords when Committee members are selected".[13] On the recommendation of the House of Lords Liason Committee[14] two additional committees were established in 2001: a Constitutional Committee to examine the constitutional implications of all public bills that come before the House and to keep under review the operation of the constitution, and an Economic Committee, to consider economic affairs.

9–032

The Lords have several other functions that are not of political importance. They are hereditary advisers of the Crown and have in theory the right of individual audience with the Sovereign; but this right is not now exercised except by Ministers who are Privy Councillors. Being part of the High Court of Parliament, the House of Lords retains certain judicial functions: it is the court of final appeal, it has the privilege of determining who is entitled to sit and vote in the House, it has the power to enforce its privileges and to punish for contempt, and it would try impeachments if they were still brought.

9–033

---

[7] (1978) H.L. 176.
[8] (1988–9) H.L. 78.
[9] (1997–8) H.L. 55.
[10] Cliff Grantham, Chap. 10 in *The House of Lords at work* (D. Shell and D. Beamish, eds, 1993) *op. cit.*
[11] Third Report, H.L. 41 (1998–99).
[12] Ninth Report, H.L. 151 (1997–98).
[13] Royal Commission, para. 8.29.
[14] H.L. 81 (1999–2000).

III. Reform of the House of Lords[15]

Historical Background

9–034   Reform of the House of Lords was considered by several committees in the twentieth century. A Select Committee chaired by Lord Rosebery reported in 1908 but was not acted upon. The need to reform the composition of the House of Lords was recognised in the preamble to the Parliament Act 1911 which recited that Parliament intended eventually "to substitute for the House of Lords as it at present exists a Second Chamber constituted on a popular instead of hereditary basis." This was followed by the Bryce Report in 1918, Cabinet Committee reports in 1922 and 1927 and a variety of Private Members' Bills over the next 10 years. During the passage of what became the Parliament Act 1949, discussions were held between the parties on reform of the both the powers and composition of the Lords, but the talks broke down on the period of delay the Lords could impose. Although a variety of reforms were made in the 1950s and 1960s it was not until 1966, when the Labour Party in its manifesto pledged to reform the House of Lords, that further moves were made. In 1967–8 inter-party talks were held on the reform of both the powers and composition of the House of Lords, and although they were broken off by the government[16] a White Paper based on the earlier discussions was issued.[17] The Parliament (No. 2) Bill was introduced by the Labour Government in 1968 with the substantial agreement of the leaders of each side in both Houses. However, an alliance of backbenchers from the two main parties ensured its defeat. In the 1970s the Labour Party supported the abolition of the House of Lords. Although in 1978 a Conservative committee under the chairmanship of Lord Home made proposals to reform the Lords, further reform of the Lords was not pursued in the subsequent years of Conservative government. Since 1992 the Labour Party policy has been to reform rather than abolish the Lords, and its 1997 Manifesto contained a pledge to do so in two stages.

The House of Lords Act 1999 and the Royal Commission on the Reform of the House of Lords

9–035   In January 1999 the Government published a White Paper, *Modernising Parliament: Reforming the House of Lords*[18] which set out the Government's step by step approach to reform of the Lords. The first stage was the enactment of the House of Lords Act 1999, which provided for the removal of the hereditary peers, and the establishment of a "transitional House". To facilitate stage two, the Government established a Royal Commission to make recommendations on the role and functions of a second chamber, and on the method or methods of

---

[15] Constitution Unit: *The Reform of the House of Lords*, (1996); *The Checks and Balances in Single Chamber Parliaments: A Comparative Study*, (1998); *The Rebalancing the Lords* (1998). Bogdanor *Power and the People-A Guide to Constitutional Reform* (1997); Richard and Welfare, *Unfinished Business, Reforming the Lords* (1999); *Constitutional Reform-The Labour Government's Constitutional Reform Agenda* (Blackburn and Plant, eds, 1999). Bogdonor, "Reform of the House of Lords: A Sceptical View." (1999) 70 *Political Quarterly*, pp. 382–374; McLean, "Mr Asquith's Unfinished Business," (1999) 70 *Political Quarterly*, pp. 382–389; Shell, "The Future of the Second Chamber", (1999) 70 *Political Quarterly*, pp. 390–395.
[16] After the Lords at the suggestion of the Conservative Opposition leadership, rejected the Southern Rhodesia (United Nations Sanctions) Order 1968.
[17] Cmnd. 3799, (1968).
[18] Cm. 4183, (1999).

composition required to enable it to fulfil its role and functions. The report of this Commission was to be considered by a joint committee of both Houses, but no such committee was set up, and it appears that the establishment of such a committee is unlikely. It remains to be seen how the Government plans to give effect to the consultation promised in the 2001 Queen's Speech on the legislative implementation of the second stage of reform.

The Royal Commission recommendations[19]
The term of reference for the Royal Commission required it to have regard to the position of the Commons as the pre-eminent chamber of Parliament, and to take account of devolution, the Human Rights Act and relations with the European Union.   **9–036**

The roles and functions of the reformed second chamber
The Royal Commission stated that a new second chamber should have four main roles: **9–037**

(i) It should bring a range of different perspectives to bear on the development of public policy.

(ii) It should be broadly representative of British society with a membership that reflected the various regions, vocations, cultures, ethnic groups, professions and religions found in Britain.

(iii) It should be one of the main "checks and balances" within the constitution, complementary to the House of Commons in identifying points of concern and able to require the Government and the House of Commons to "think again".

(iv) It should provide a voice for the nations and regions of the United Kingdom at the centre of public affairs.

The Royal Commission did not consider that would be any need for a radical change in the balance of powers between the two Houses of Parliament.[20] In addition to the functions considered above (in respect of several of which Royal Commission recommendations for improvements were noted) the Royal Commission suggested that the new second chamber should have an enhanced role in protecting the constitution. This would not require the second chamber to have additional powers, rather two new committees would be established: a Constitutional Committee (with a number of sub-committees) to scrutinise the constitutional implications of all legislation and to keep the operation of the constitution under review, and a Human Rights Committee to scrutinise all Bills and Statutory Instruments for human rights implications.[21] A second new role, reflecting a change in its composition, would be to give a voice at the centre of national affairs to the nations and regions of the United Kingdom. Finally it proposed the establishment of a Treaty Select Committee to scrutinise the 25 to 40 treaties laid before Parliament each year under the Ponsonby Rule. This Committee would

---

[19] Shell, "Reforming the House of Lords: the Report and overseas comparisons", [2000] P.L. 193; Meg Russell, *Reforming the House of Lords: Lessons from Overseas*, (2000).
[20] See *ante*, para. 8–039.
[21] The Constitution Committee was established in February 2001, and a Joint Committee on Human Rights in January 2001.

establish whether a Treaty raised issues which merited debate or reconsideration before ratification.[22] All these proposals could be implemented without legislation or other reforms of the House. These proposals have implications for the size of a reformed second chamber, since they would increase its workload.

Composition of the "new second chamber"

9–038   The Royal Commission considered that before it could make recommendations on composition, it needed to decide what characteristics the second chamber's members, individually and collectively, should possess. It concluded that it required three characteristics:

> (i) It should be authoritative: able to scrutinise the executive, hold the Government to account and shape legislation, but not be in a position to challenge the ultimate authority which the House of Commons derives by virtue of being directly elected. The view of the Royal Commission was that it was an error to suppose that a second chamber's authority could only stem from democratic election, and suggested that authority could come from the characteristics of the membership of the reformed second chamber.

> (ii) It should be sufficiently confident to use its powers in the most effective and appropriate manner; it was the view of the Royal Commission that throughout the twentieth century the House of Lords had been inhibited by both its lack of authority and lack of confidence.

> (iii) It should be broadly representative of British society as a whole, and as such could provide an alternative source of authority for the second chamber without threatening the democratic authority of the House of Commons.

The Royal Commission considered and rejected both a wholly (or largely) directly elected second chamber, and a chamber indirectly elected from the devolved institutions, local government electoral colleges or British Members of the European Parliament. It also rejected a chamber randomly selected or co-opted. Instead it recommended a chamber of around 550[23] consisting (in addition to the Bishops and Law Lords) of appointed and regional members all serving terms of three electoral cycles or 15 years.[24] It proposed that a fifth of the members should be cross-benchers.[25] It did not recommend the appropriate title for members of the new chamber, nor for the chamber itself, suggesting that, "the situation should be left to evolve".[26]

[22] Royal Commission Recommendation 56. The Liason Committee has recommended that the House should wait and see how new arrangements in the Commons for the scrutiny of treaties develops, H.L. 30 (2000–01).

[23] The actual size and political balance of the chamber would be determined by the Appointments Commission *ante* para. 9–011, thus removing a significant power from the Prime Minister of the day.

[24] By limiting the length of time any member could sit in the second chamber, the Royal Commission sought to avoid the chamber becoming elderly, and avoid awkward imbalances between the parties which could be difficult for the Appointments Commission to correct. Former members of the second chamber would not be entitled to stand for election to the House of Commons until 10 years after the end of their term of membership.

[25] This was thought be to enough to ensure that no single political party could achieve a working majority.

[26] Royal Commission, para. 18.11.

Appointed members would make up the bulk of the new chamber. These **9–039** members would no longer be appointed by the Monarch on the recommendation of the Prime Minister, since that system left "too much power in the hands of the Prime Minister of the day".[27] Members would be appointed directly by a statutory, independent *Appointments Commission*[28] which would have a general duty to appoint members and be empowered to appoint individual members on its own authority. In consequence all members of the second chamber, whether appointed, regional, Lords of Appeal in Ordinary or representative of the Church of England would be appointed by this body.[29] The remit of the Appointments Commission would be to create a second chamber which was broadly representative of British society on a range of stated dimensions and which possessed the characteristics outlined above. It would be for this Commission to exercise its own judgment in selecting appropriate numbers of appointees affiliated to political parties. Such individuals normally, but not necessarily, would be nominated by the parties, but the Commission would look for characteristics which justify their appointment on wider grounds.[30] The Commission would be required to achieve and maintain on overall balance between those members affiliated to political parties (both regional and directly appointed members) which matched the distribution of votes between the parties at the most recent general election.[31]

The Commission would be expected to publish, and regularly update, a statement indicating the broad characteristics it would expect of members of the new second chamber, and actively seek nominations.[32] It would vet nominations for propriety and high-level security checks should be undertaken on all short-listed candidates.[33] It would be required to make an annual report to Parliament which would be the main means whereby it would be held to account.[34]

Regional members should make up a significant minority of the new cham- **9–040** ber,[35] chosen on a basis which reflected the balance of political opinion within each of the nations and regions of the United Kingdom. This is the only section of the reformed House which the Royal Commission recommended should be elected, but it was unable to agree on the method of selection, and put forward three possible models, all based on the large constituencies used in connection with the European elections.[36]

Representation of religious faiths. The Royal Commission was in favour of religious faiths being represented in the chamber, but recommended that the concept of religious representation should be broadened to embrace Christian denominations other than the Church of England, and should include other faith communities.[37] It proposed that the Appointments Commission should ensure

---

[27] Royal Commission *op. cit.* para. 32.
[28] See *ante* para. 9–011 for the non-statutory Appointments Commission established in 2000.
[29] However it would have no discretion over the appointment of the latter three categories of members, and could not substitute its own judgment (Royal Commission Recommendation 82).
[30] *op. cit.* Royal Commission Recommendation 98.
[31] *op. cit.* Royal Commission Recommendation 70.
[32] *op. cit.* Royal Commission Recommendation 94–97.
[33] *op. cit.* Royal Commission Recommendation 99.
[34] *op. cit.* Royal Commission paras. 13.21–13.23.
[35] The Royal Commission was split on the numbers, the majority favouring a total of 87, but other possible figures were 65 and 195.
[36] *op. cit.* Royal Commission pp. 121–129.
[37] *op. cit.* Royal Commission Recommendation 108.

that at least five members of the second chamber should be broadly representative of the different non-Christian faith communities,[38] and that the total representation of the various Christian denominations throughout the United Kingdom should be 26. In consequence it recommended that the Church of England should have 16 representatives, the other 10 being allocated by the Appointments Committee to members of other Christian denominations in England, Scotland, Wales and Northern Ireland.[39]

9–041   *The Lords of Appeal in Ordinary* would continue to be members of the reformed second chamber, but would as with all members of the reformed second chamber be required to retire at 75. The Royal Commission noted that the Devolution Acts and the Human Rights Act increased the risk of legislation being justiciable in the future. To ensure that those exercising judicial functions could be seen to be impartial it recommended that the Lords of Appeal should publish a statement of principles which they intend to observe when debating and voting in the second chamber.[40]

9–042   *The existing life peers* provided a problem for the Royal Commission. By a majority it recommended that legislation should be enacted to allow those life peers who had been appointed before the publication of the Report and who so wished,[41] to be deemed to have been appointed to the reformed second chamber for life. Those appointed after the publication of the Report and before the second stage of reform, would be deemed to have been appointed for 15 years.

Resources

9–043   To ensure that the new second chamber could fulfil the functions envisaged for it, the Royal Commission recognised that the financial arrangements which applied to members had to be economically viable for those outside the south east of England and without a separate source of income.[42] It recommended that the system should continue whereby financial support should be linked to attendance in Parliament, but did not make any specific recommendation, suggesting that it should be for the Senior Salaries Review Body to consider the appropriate payment.[43] It also recommended additional office and secretarial resources should be made available to the second chamber corporately, rather than to individual members.[44]

The overall result of the reforms proposed by the Royal Commission would, in its view, result in a second chamber that was both more democratic and more representative that the present House of Lords. More democratic because the membership as a whole would reflect the balance of political opinion within the country; more representative because it would contain members from all parts of

[38] *op. cit.* Royal Commission Recommendation 109.
[39] It left it to the Church of England to determine how its reduced number of representatives should be identified.
[40] *op. cit.* Royal Commission Recommendation 59.
[41] Those who did not so wish should be allowed to retire form the second chamber (Royal Commission Recommendation 104). The Royal Commission suggested that within 20 years of the commencement of the legislation necessary to implement the Report, only a handful of members would remain in the second chamber by virtue of a life peerage.
[42] To take account of this, it recommended that the rules on the payment of expenses in respect of travel and overnight costs should be reconsidered to ensure that it was economically viable for those who live outside London to regularly attend Parliament (Royal Commission Recommendation 126).
[43] *op. cit.* Royal Commission Recommendations 119–123. It also recommended that Chairmen of significant committees should receive a salary in respect of their additional duties.
[44] *op. cit.* Royal Commission Recommendation 125.

the country and from all walks of life, broadly equal numbers of men and women and representatives of all the country's main ethnic and religious communities.[45]

IV. THE HOUSE OF LORDS AS THE FINAL COURT OF APPEAL[46]

Before the Appellate Jurisdiction Act 1876[47]

The early doctrine was that ultimate jurisdiction in the administration of justice **9–044** lay with "the King in his Council in Parliament," and in the fifteenth century it was held[48] that this jurisdiction in error belonged not to Parliament as a whole, but to the House of Lords which had been part of the Council. Error from the equitable jurisdiction of the Court of Chancery was not established until the case of *Shirley v. Fagg*.[49]

Since the dispute with the Commons over the case of *Skinner v. East India Company*[50] the Lords have not attempted to exercise an original jurisdiction in civil cases. The only criminal jurisdiction exercised at first instance by the House of Lords was the trial of peers for treason and felony, and trial on impeachment.[51]

The House of Lords assumed appellate jurisdiction in civil cases from Scottish courts (the Court of Session) soon after the Union, although this jurisdiction was not expressly conferred by the Union with Scotland Act 1707. The earliest case to attract public attention was *Greenshields v. Magistrates of Edinburgh* in 1711.[52]

The Union with Ireland Act 1800 conferred on the House of Lords appellate jurisdiction in civil cases from Irish courts.

Lay peers in the House

Few of the Lords had adequate legal qualifications, and the House discouraged **9–045** reports of its proceedings,[53] so that the House of Lords was scarcely regarded as a regular and ordinary court of justice before the end of the eighteenth century.[54] The last reported occasion on which lay peers attempted to take part in the strictly judicial proceedings of the House was *O'Connell v. The Queen*[55] on a writ of

---

[45] *op. cit.* Royal Commission para. 11.41.
[46] Le Sueur and Cornes, "What Do the Top courts Do?", (2000) 53 Current Legal Problems p. 53.
[47] Holdsworth, *History of English Law*, I, Bk, i, Chap. 4.
[48] (1485) Y.B. 1 Hen. VII, P. pl. 5.
[49] (1675) 6 St.Tr. 1122.
[50] (1666) St.Tr. 710.
[51] *ante*, Chap. 7.
[52] Robertson 12; Dicey and Rait, *Thoughts on the Union Between England and Scotland*, (1920), pp. 194–195; A.D. Gibb, *Law from Over the Border*, pp. 9–11; A.S. Turberville, *The House of Lords in the Eighteenth Century*, pp. 94–95, 139–141.
[53] Regular reports of House of Lords cases began with the authorised reports of Dow (1812–1818).
[54] Pollock's Preface to Volume 1 of the Revised Reports; Turberville, *op. cit.*; "The House of Lords as a Court of Law, 1784–1837" [1946] 52 L.Q.R. 189.
[55] (1844) 11 Cl. & Fin. 155, 421–426. The legally qualified peers present were Lord Lyndhurst L.C., and Lords Brougham, Campbell, Cottenham and Denman. The lay peers present included Lord Wharncliffe, the Earl of Stradbroke, the Marquess of Clanricarde and the Earl of Verulam. Clarke and Finelly cite previous examples of lay peers taking part in judicial decisions in 1695, 1697, 1703 (*Ashby v. White*), 1769, 1773, 1775 and 1783.

error from the Court of Queen's Bench in Ireland, in which the conviction of Daniel O'Connell for criminal conspiracy was quashed. This case may be said to have established the convention or practice that lay members do not take part when the House of Lords is setting as a court of appeal. The Lord Chancellor, Lord Lyndhurst, ignored the votes of the lay peers. A discussion followed, during which the legally qualified peers emphasised the argument that a peer who had not heard the whole proceedings should not vote. The lay peers eventually withdrew on the ground that only those qualified should vote. It appears, however, that Earl Spencer, a layman, sat in about 1860[56]; and that the second Lord Denman (son of the Chief Justice and a barrister of fifty years' standing) sat throughout, spoke and voted in *Bradlaugh v. Clarke*,[57] his vote (which was ignored) not affecting the result.[58]

Three is the quorum under Standing Orders of the House of Lords in both its legislative and judicial capacities, and it appears that the leading case of *Rylands v. Fletcher*[59] was heard by Lord Cairns L.C. with one other legally qualified peer (Lord Colonsay, former President of the Court of Session) and a lay peer—probably a Lord Spiritual—within call to form a quorum.[60]

9–046   There was wide criticism in the last century both of the House of Lords as a court of appeal and of the system of two-tier appeals. The attempt by virtue of the prerogative to create Baron Parke[61] a life peer with the right to sit and vote in the House of Lords had failed.[62] Lord Selborne, Liberal Chancellor, introduced the Supreme Court of Judicature Bill 1873, which in its original form would have given the final appeal in English cases to a new Court of Appeal while retaining the Lords' jurisdiction in Scottish and Irish cases. The opposition to the abolition of the House of Lords' jurisdiction was largely due to the fear that this would undermine the remaining powers of the hereditary House. Also, the Scots and Irish would not want their appeals to go to an English Court of Appeal. This Act, as amended to retain the Lords' jurisdiction, came into force at the beginning of 1876.[63]

From the Appellate Jurisdiction Act 1876[64]

9–047   Meanwhile a Bill introduced by the Conservative Chancellor, Lord Cairns, met most of the criticisms that had been made of the House of Lords as an appellate court. This became the Appellate Jurisdiction Act 1876. It provided for appeals in civil cases to be heard by the House of Lords from the new English Court of

---

[56] See *Re Lord Kinross* [1905] A.C. 468, 476.

[57] (1883) 8 App.Cas. 354.

[58] Lord du Parcq. "The Final Court of Appeal" (1949) C.L.P. 4–6; *cf.* R.E. Megarry in (1949) 65 L.Q.R. 22–24, Lord Denman is not mentioned in the law report: Megarry, *Miscellany-at-law* (1955), pp. 11–13. Lord Denman also attempted to vote in *Bain v. Fothergill* (1874) L.R. 7 H.L. 158, but his vote was not counted. It has been questioned whether lay peers sat in *Hutton v. Upfill* (1850) 2 H.L.C. 674, 647n., and *Hutton v. Bright* (1852) 3 H.L.C. 341.

[59] (1868) L.R. 3 H.L. 330.

[60] R. F. V. Heuston, "Who was the Third Lord in *Rylands v. Fletcher*?" (1970) 86 L.Q.R. 160.

[61] He was not a peer, but a baron (*i.e.* judge) of the Court of Exchequer.

[62] *Wensleydale Peerage Case* (1856) H.L.C. 958.

[63] Supreme Court of Judicature Acts 1873–1875.

[64] See L. Blom-Cooper Q.C. and G. Drewry, *Final Appeal: A Study of the House of Lords in its Judicial Capacity* (1972), and Chap. 6 "The Appellate Function" in *The House of Lords, its Parliamentary and Judicial Roles* (B. Dickson and P. Carmichael eds 1999). Robert Stevens, *Law and Politics: The House of Lords as Judicial Body 1800–1976* (1979); Alan Paterson, *The Law Lords* (1982); Dickson, Chap. 7 "The Lords of Appeal and their Work 1967–1996", in *The House of Lords its Parliamentary and Judicial Roles* (B. Dickson and P. Carmichael, eds 1999) *op. cit.*

Appeal, in addition to appeals from the courts of Scotland and Ireland (section 3).

The Act of 1876 created salaried Lords of Appeal in Ordinary, who must either have held high judicial office for at least two years or be practising barristers of not less than 15 years' standing (section 6). Their number, at first two, has been gradually increased by subsequent statutes. It provided that there should be present at the hearing of an appeal at least three of the following Lords of Appeal: (1) the Lord Chancellor, (2) the Lords of Appeal in Ordinary, and (3) such peers of Parliament as hold or have held "high judicial office" as therein defined. The last group includes ex-Lord Chancellors (section 5). In important cases the court usually consists of five members.

The Act further provided that the House of Lords may hear appeals during any prorogation of Parliament (section 8), and that arrangements may be made for the hearing of appeals by the Lords of Appeal in the name of the House of Lords during a dissolution of Parliament (section 9). The origin of the court is preserved, however, in the form to be used on an appeal, viz. a petition to the House of Lords praying that the matter may be reviewed before Her Majesty the Queen in her Court in Parliament (section 4). The Lords give their opinions in the form of speeches, and an appeal is won or lost on a vote in the House.

One effect of the Appellate Jurisdiction Act 1876 was to increase the importance of the House of Lords as a court of English common law. Previously it had been more important for Scottish appeals, while English appeals had usually been cases in equity.[65]   **9–049**

Appeals to the House of Lords in criminal cases, as distinct from jurisdiction on writ of error, were not introduced until the Criminal Appeal Act 1907, which created the Court of Criminal Appeal. Criminal appeals since 1966 lie from the criminal division of the Court of Appeal.

Appeals from Irish courts since 1922 are confined to Northern Ireland, but include criminal cases.

Lord Cairns had suggested a Judicial Committee of the House of Lords, sitting throughout the year in a separate courtroom. This did not occur until a change of practice at the end of the last war. The court used to sit in the House of Lords debating chamber when the House was not sitting for legislative business.[66] In 1948, the noise of the re-building consequent to the damage suffered to the Palace of Westminster during the war interrupted proceedings, and it was decided to move the judicial sittings from the temporary Chamber of the House, to a quieter committee room upstairs. For this purpose the Law Lords were constituted into an Appellate Committee consisting usually of five Law Lords.[67] This arrangement was so successful that it became permanent in 1951, and in 1960 authority was given for the creation of a second Appellate Committee to sit

---

[65] Robert Stevens, "The Final Appeal: Reform of the House of Lords and Privy Council, 1867–1876" (1964) 80 L.Q.R. 343.

[66] The House used to start non-judicial business at a quarter to four, when judicial business had concluded.

[67] Petitions for leave to appeal are referred to an Appeal Committee, consisting of three Law Lords: Practice Direction House of Lords: Petitions: Leave to Appeal) [1979] 1 W.L.R. 497. Since 1988 their decision is taken on the basis of written submissions only. The work of this Committee is substantial, with a steady increase in the last thirty years in the number of petitions and days on which the Committee sits; see B. Dickson Chap. 7 in *The House of Lords its Parliament and Judicial Roles* (B. Dickson and P. Carmichael, eds 1999) *op. cit.*

concurrently if necessary.[68] Standing Orders allow for the House to be recalled specifically for judicial business, and today Law Lords sit throughout the law terms.

9–050 The Lord Chancellor presides if present. However, the creation of the Judicial Committee enabled the Lords to start the transaction of public earlier in the afternoon, and this, in addition to the more recent increased work load of the Lord Chancellor's Department, has mean that the Lord Chancellor infrequently sits judicially. In his absence hearings are presided over, since 1984 by one of two Law Lords nominated by him for that purpose.

The decision of an Appellate Committee is reported to the House in the Chamber (usually on a Thursday afternoon) a reminder that it is the Court of Parliament that hears and determines appeals. However it has been the practice since 1962 that the opinions of the Lords of Appeal are no longer, as a general rule, delivered orally in the House. Their Lordships confine themselves to stating that, for the reasons given in their opinions, they would allow or dismiss the appeal. The question is then put from the Woolsack by the presiding Law Lord and the answer made.[69] The opinions of the Committee are of no binding force until agreed by the House. Copies of the opinions are available for counsel an hour beforehand. This practice is similar to that employed by the Judicial Committee of the Privy Council and saves time for both judges and counsel.

9–051 In cases of difficulty their Lordships may summon the judges of the Queen's Bench Division[70] for advice, but this has only been done four times since the creation of Lords of Appeal in Ordinary in 1876. The advice of the judges was usually accepted as in *Mersey Docks and Harbour Board v. Gibbs*,[71] but not always, as in *Allen v. Flood*,[72] this being the last English case in which the judges were summoned. The last occasion in a Scottish appeal was *Free Church of Scotland (General Assembly) v. Lord Overtoun*.[73]

The dual role of the Law Lords as members of the legislature and judiciary may require reconsideration in the light of the Human Rights Act, and in particular the decision of the European Court of Human Rights in *McGonnell v. United Kingdom*.[74] The prior involvement of any Law Lord in debates on Bills with human rights implications, or with potential application to Scotland, could give rise to alleged breaches of Art. 6,[75] should that judge sit in any subsequent case concerned with that legislation.[76]

---

[68] The tradition of hearing appeals in the Chamber of the House has not totally disappeared. At the end of the summer recess, before the resumption of the parliamentary session, for a period of one week the Law Lords hear appeals in the Chamber of the House.

[69] The Law Lords have allowed the broadcasting of the proceedings whereby they report their opinions to the House. In two of the recent Pinochet case their Lordships, for the first time, gave oral summaries of their written speeches; Rozenberg, "The *Pinochet* case and cameras in court", [1999] P.L. 178–184.

[70] The House had no authority to summon Chancery judges unless they were peers.

[71] (1866) L.R. 1 H.L. 93.

[72] [1898] A.C. 1. See further, R.F.V. Heuston, "Judicial Prospography," (1986) 102 L.Q.R. 90.

[73] [1904] A.C. 515.

[74] (2000) E.H.R.R. 289.

[75] Which provided for "a fair and public hearing ... by an independent and impartial tribunal. . ."

[76] In *Hoekstra v. H.M. Advocate*, [2000] A.C. 216, 2001 S.L.T. 28, an Appeal Court decision was quashed because one of the judges had made adverse comments about the E.C.H.R. in a Scottish newspaper.

The Appellate Committee and Judicial Committee of the House of Lords as Constitutional Courts?[77]

The Appellate Committee and Judicial Committee are generalist courts, which may as part of their case load deal with "constitutional" issues.[78] It could be argued that the United Kingdom's membership of the European Communities has given the House of Lords a role as a constitutional court, but it is one it shares with other U.K. courts. However, cases such as *R. v. Secretary of State for Transport, ex p. Factortame (No. 2)*[79] and *R. v. Secretary of State for Employment, ex p. the Equal Opportunities Commission*,[80] where the House of Lords accepted that where European Community law issues arise, the legislative supremacy of the United Kingdom is subject to an exception, have given an important lead to lower courts. This general constitutional role will increase with the coming into force of the Human Rights Act 1998, as all courts have to take account of E.C.H.R. case law (section 2), and again the lead given by the Lords will be important. The Judicial Committee of the Privy Council has in effect become the Constitutional Court for Scotland and Northern Ireland. A "devolution issue" may be resolved by direct reference to the Privy Council.[81] It will play a similar role for Wales, also having jurisdiction to decide devolution issues, but since the Welsh Assembly has no primary legislative powers it is probably less accurate to describe it in this context as a constitutional court for Wales.

9–052

---

[77] Robertson, "The House of Lords as a Political and Constitutional Court: Lessons from the Pinochet case", Chap. 2 in *The Pinochet Case: a Legal and Constitutional Analysis* (D. Woodhouse ed. 2000).

[78] *e.g. D.P.P. v. Jones* [1999] 2 A.C. 240 on freedom of assembly, *Reynolds v. Times Newspapers Ltd* [1999] 3 W.L.R. 1010, on freedom of speech.

[79] [1991] 1 A.C. 603, HL

[80] [1995] 1 A.C. 603, HL, and see Patricia Maxwell, "The House of Lords as a Constitutional Court-The Implications of ex parte E.O.C.", Chap. 10 in *The House of Lords its Parliament and Judicial Role* (B. Dickson and P. Carmichael, eds 1999) *op. cit.*

[81] See para. 5–015.

Chapter 10

THE HOUSE OF COMMONS

I. Membership of the House of Commons

Historical introduction[1]

10–001   Simon de Montfort, leader of the rebel forces against Henry III, may be called the founder of the House of Commons, though not the founder of Parliament. His innovation in 1265 was to summon not only the knights for each shire—there were precedents for this—but also two burgesses from each borough. This action was not based on any theory of representative government (which originated in ecclesiastical organisations before the thirteenth century), but in order to counter-act the power of the King.

Edward I revived the idea of summoning the knights and burgesses in 1275 primarily, it is supposed, for financial purposes. Parliament was in a formative stage in his reign, and some of his most important statutes were passed in the absence of the Commons. There was still no clear distinction between Council and Parliament. The Commons became more regularly established during the reign of Edward III, although as a body they were not of much influence before the end of the fourteenth century. The division of Parliament into two Houses may be said to have taken place in the reign of Edward III. Petitions involving judicial decisions were dealt with by the Council and the courts. The elected knights and the burgesses were concerned with common petitions and requests by the King for aids. In time they came to form a House of Commons, meeting in the Chapter House of Westminster Abbey, appointing a Speaker to reply in the parliament chamber to the King's requests and demanding that their common petitions be made statutes.[2]

The knights were elected in the county court by the freeholders. The borough franchise varied according to the customs and privileges of the various boroughs. For centuries members of the House of Commons consisted of knights and burgesses so elected.

10–002   Since 1774 a candidate for a parliamentary election need not have any connection with his constituency. In 1858 the property qualification was abol-ished. From the time of Elizabeth I penal statutes against papists, Protestant dissenters and others, and the requirement of a parliamentary oath that could conscientiously be taken only by Anglicans, virtually excluded non-Anglicans from Parliament for many years. Civil disabilities against dissenters were removed in 1828, and Roman Catholics were admitted to Parliament by the Roman Catholic Relief Act 1829. The oath was later made acceptable to Jews.[3] Quakers and others who objected to taking an oath were allowed to make an

---

[1] For a survey and guide to the literature, see Taswell-Langmead, *English Constitutional History* (11th ed. Plucknett), Chap. 6.
[2] A. F. Pollard, *The Evolution of Parliament* (2nd ed.), pp. 117–128.
[3] Jews Relief Act 1858.

affirmation.[4] Women were admitted to the House of Commons in 1918.[5] There has never been a statute prescribing the legal requirements for eligibility to stand for Parliament or to be a M.P. Instead there are a range of provisions, statutory, common law and by the law and custom of Parliament, which provide a variety of disqualifications from membership of the House of Commons.[6] With one exception,[7] these disqualifications do not prevent an individual standing for election, but can be invoked to prevent him from taking his seat in the House.[8]

Offices or places of profit from or under the Crown, and pensions at the pleasure of the Crown

The Act of Settlement 1700, s.6, would have provided that "no person who has **10–003** an office or place of profit under the King, or receives a pension from the crown, shall be capable of serving as a member of the House of Commons," but this provision was repealed before it came into force. The Succession to the Crown Act 1707, passed at the time of the union with Scotland, provided by section 24 that no person who held any office or place of profit under the Crown created after 1705,[9] and no person having any pension from the Crown during pleasure, should be capable of being elected or of sitting or voting as a member of the House of Commons. Section 25 provided that if a member of the House of Commons accepted any office of profit from the Crown, his election should become void but he should be capable of being re-elected. One who sat and voted as a member when disqualified was liable to pay a heavy fine at the suit of a common informer, although it seems that no common informer actions were ever brought for this purpose. Section 25, requiring re-election of a member on appointment to office, should probably be taken to apply only to offices existing in 1705.[10] By 1957 the disqualification in respect to those who held pensions from the Crown only applied to a very few persons, who held their pension "during pleasure", or (according to the Pensioners Civil Disabilities Relief Act 1869) for any term or number of years.

By the end of the eighteenth century three principles were established:

(i) certain non-ministerial offices were incompatible with membership of the House of Commons;

(ii) the control of the government over the House through members who were office-holders must be limited; but

(iii) a certain number of Ministers must be members of the House in order that Parliament could control the executive.

---

[4] Promissory Oaths Act 1868; Oaths Act 1888 (atheists). *Cf. Bradlaugh v. Gossett* (1884) 12 Q.B.D. 271. The current legislation is to be found in the Oaths Act 1978.
[5] Parliament (Qualification of Women) Act 1918.
[6] *post* para. 10–005.
[7] Representation of the People Act 1981, s.1.
[8] The disqualifications have to be compatible with Art. 3 E.C.H.R., but states have considerable latitude to establish rules for disqualifications: *Gitonas v. Greece* (1998) 26 E.H.R.R. 691.
[9] The date of an intervening Act, the Succession to the Crown Act 1705, which was repealed in order to take account of the Union.
[10] While s.24 refers to offices or places held under the Crown, s.25 specifies offices accepted from the Crown, which are probably limited to appointments made directly by the Crown and not through the medium of a Minister, *i.e.* senior ministerial offices and Household offices.

A series of statutes after 1707 therefore converted the distinction between the holders of "old" offices (qualified) and "new" offices (disqualified) into a distinction between the holders of political offices (qualified within limits) and non-political offices (disqualified), by disqualifying or suppressing many old offices of a non-ministerial nature and providing for the eligibility of the ministerial heads of newly created departments, subject to the necessity for re-election if already members.[11]

Number of Ministers in the House of Commons

10–004   A limit was set to the number of Ministers and Secretaries of State, respectively, who might sit in the House of Commons. The Ministers of the Crown Act 1937 abolished the distinction in this respect between Secretaries of State and other Ministers, but limited the total number who might sit in the Commons. There remained a residual number of Ministers who were excluded, and who therefore by convention had to sit in the House of Lords.[12]

Government contractors, i.e. persons who held contracts for or on account of the public service, were disqualified by the House of Commons (Disqualification) Acts 1782 and 1801, the purpose being to exclude those who contracted to supply goods to government departments and who might therefore be under the influence of the government. Actions by common informers were brought under these Acts for the penalty of £500 a day for sitting and voting while so disqualified. The House of Commons Disqualification (Declaration of Law) Act 1931 declared that the scope of the Acts was confined to contracts for furnishing or providing money to be remitted abroad, and wares and merchandise to be used in the service of the public.

The House of Commons Disqualification Act 1957[13] repealed the enactments disqualifying the holders of offices or places of profit under the Crown and of persons holding pensions from the Crown, and instead disqualified the holders of specified offices. The disqualification of government contractors was also removed by the Act of 1957, since there was no evidence of corruption in the previous 100 years and it was impracticable to remove anomalies. The right of common informers to sue was abolished and replaced with a right to seek a declaration from the Privy Council.

Miscellaneous existing disqualifications

10–005   There are several disqualifications from membership which are not affected by the House of Commons Disqualification Act:

1. *Aliens,*[14] *i.e.* persons who are not British subjects or Commonwealth citizens, and are not citizens of the Republic of Ireland.[15]

---

[11] Certain offices to which a member was appointed continued to vacate the seat but allowed re-election, until the requirement of re-election was finally abolished in 1926: Re-election of Ministers Act 1919 and 1926. Gladstone inadvertently vacated his seat in 1859 by accepting the post of Lord High Commissioner of the Ionian Islands: Sir Philip Magnus, *Gladstone,* p. 135.

[12] *cf.* later House of Commons Disqualification Acts and Ministers of the Crown Acts.

[13] Repealed and substantially re-enacted by the House of Commons Disqualification Act 1975; *post,* para. 10–006.

[14] *R. v. Cassel* [1916] 1 K.B. 595; *R. v. Speyer* [1916] 2 K.B. 858.

[15] Ireland Act 1949. British Nationality Act 1981, Sched. 7.

2. *Persons under 21 years of age.*[16]

3. *Persons suffering from mental illness.* "Lunatics" and "idiots" were disqualified at common law. The Mental Health Act 1983 s.141, now provides that the Speaker must be notified when a member is detained as a person suffering from mental illness. The Speaker must then obtain a medical report. If the detention is confirmed by this report, and the member is still detailed as a mental patient according to a second medical report six months later, his seat is vacated.

4. *Peers and peeresses,* were disqualified by the law and custom of Parliament.[17] Until the House of Lords Act 1999, the only exception were Irish peers[18]; those hereditary peers who are excluded from the House of Lords by the 1999 Act, are eligible for election to the Commons (section 3(1)).

5. *Clergy* Until the enactment of the House of Commons (Removal of Clergy) Disqualification Act 2001, a variety of clergy were disqualified from membership of the House of Commons.[19] The 2001 Act removes any disqualification from membership of the House of Commons as a consequence of a person having been ordained or being a Minister of a religious domination. The only disqualification that remains is if a person is a Lord Spiritual.[20]

6. *Treason.* A person convicted of treason is disqualified till the expiry of his sentence of imprisonment or the receipt of a royal pardon.[21]

7. *Other crimes.* A consequence of the Criminal Law Act 1967 was that convicted persons were not disqualified from membership of the House, but the House might pass a motion to expel such persons.[22] This gap in the law[23] was remedied by the Representation of the People Act 1981, s.1, which disqualifies for membership of the Commons anyone found guilty of an offence, whether before or after the passing of the Act, whether in

---

[16] Parliamentary Elections Act 1695; Family Law Reform Act 1969. It appears that before 1832 several infants sat in the Commons "by connivance," including Charles James Fox and Lord John Russell. See P. Norton "The Qualifying Age for Candidature in British Elections" [1980] P.L. 55.

[17] Report from the Committee of Privileges: *Petition concerning Mr Anthony Neil Wedgwood Benn* (1961) H.C. No. 142; *Re Parliamentary Election for Bristol South-East* [1964] 2 Q.B. 257. Wives and eldest sons of peers, who had courtesy titles, could sit.

[18] Peerage Act 1963, s.5 (non-representative Irish peers); *Re Earl of Antrim's Petition* [1967] 1 A.C. 691; Statute Law (Repeals) Act 1971.

[19] House of Commons (Clergy Disqualification) Act 1801, was passed to keep out the Rev. Horne Tooke. It disqualified clergy of the Church of England and the Church of Ireland, see *Re Macmanaway* [1951] A.C. 161, P.C.), and Ministers of the Church of Scotland. Clergy of the Church in Wales were not disqualified (Welsh Church Act 1914). The Roman Catholic Relief Act 1829 disqualified Roman Catholic priests.

[20] s.1(2), for the background see the Home Affairs Select Committee report, *Electoral Law and Administration* H.C. 768 (1997–98).

[21] Forfeiture Act 1870, as amended by the Criminal Law Act 1967, Sched. 3.

[22] This is rare now, but was used more frequently in the eighteenth and nineteenth centuries. Miss Bernadette Devlin M.P., who served six months' imprisonment in Northern Ireland in 1969 for encouraging petrol bomb attacks against the police was not expelled. No action was taken against Mr Terry Fields M.P. who in 1991 was imprisoned for 60 days for failing to pay his poll tax. See generally the report of the Select Committee of Privileges, *On the Rights of Honourable Members detained in Prison*, H.C. 185 (1970–71).

[23] Prior to 1967 those convicted of a felony and sentenced to more than 12 months imprisonment were statutorily disqualified from membership of the House.

the United Kingdom or elsewhere, and sentenced to be imprisoned or detained indefinitely or for more than one year.[24] If a member becomes disqualified under the terms of the Act his seat is vacated.

8. *Bankrupts*. Formerly, in England and Wales disqualification lasted for five years after discharge. Disqualification now ceases on discharge.[25]

9. *Corrupt and illegal practices*. Various statutes constituted certain kinds of conduct at parliamentary elections "corrupt" or "illegal" practices. These provisions are now to be found in the Representation of the People Act 1983.[26] The consequences so far as disqualification from sitting in the House of Commons is concerned are:

(a) If a candidate who has been elected is reported by an election court personally guilty, or guilty by his agents, of any corrupt or illegal practice, his election is void (section 159(1)).

(b) A candidate is also incapable of being elected for the constituency concerned: (i) for 10 years if reported personally guilty of a corrupt practice; (ii) for seven years if reported guilty by his agents of a corrupt practice or personally guilty of an illegal practice; and (iii) during the Parliament for which the election was held if reported guilty by his agents of an illegal practice (section 159(2)).

(c) A candidate reported by an election court personally guilty of a corrupt or an illegal practice is incapable for five years of being elected to the House of Commons, and if already elected shall vacate his seat (section 160).

(d) A person convicted of a corrupt or an illegal practice on indictment or by an election court is subject to the incapacities mentioned in (c) above (section 173).[27]

The House of Commons Disqualification Act 1975

10–006   From time to time Indemnity Acts were passed to indemnify members who had become disqualified unwittingly through holding certain offices or places of profit from or under the Crown,[28] and usually the election was validated also. Eventually the House of Commons Disqualification Act 1957 was passed, dealing with a particular range of problems, but not forming an exhaustive code of disqualification from membership.[29] There are a variety of grounds for the disqualifications: the impracticability of combining certain jobs, such as a member of the armed forces, with that of M.P.; a recognition of the need to keep certain functions separate and politically impartial, such as the judicial offices; the belief that it is incompatible to hold both a position of paid government employment and be a member of the House of Commons; and the fact that

[24] The statute was given retrospective effect to invalidate the election in April 1981 for the Constituency of Fermanagh and South Tyrone of a prisoner serving a long term of imprisonment for various firearms offences. See C.P. Walker, "Prisoners in Parliament: Another View," [1982] P.L. 389.

[25] Insolvency Act 1986, s.427.

[26] *post* para. 10–048.

[27] Section 136 of the Political Parties Elections and Referendums Act 2000, substituted a new s.173, and added illegal practice as a basis for requiring the vacation of a seat. It also provided for a stay of vacation of a seat pending an appeal; see *Attorney-General v. Jones* [2000] Q.B. 66 which illustrates the confusion in the previous law.

[28] See *ante*, para. 10–003

[29] See *ante*, para. 10–005 as to aliens, minors, etc.

certain positions of control in companies in receipt of government money are nominated by Ministers.[30]

The main provisions of the Consolidating Act of 1975 are as follows:

Section 1. Disqualification of holders of certain (non-ministerial) offices and places

A person is disqualified for membership of the House of Commons if he falls into any of the following categories: **10–007**

(1) (za) *Lords Spiritual.* As a consequence of the House of Commons (Removal of Clergy Disqualification) Act 2001, Lords Spiritual have been added to the list of those disqualified; a bishop who is not a Lords Spiritual member of the House of Lords is not disqualified.

(a) *Judicial offices.* The holders of the judicial offices specified in Part I of Schedule 1. These include judges of the Supreme Court, circuit judges and stipendiary magistrates, but not justices of the peace.

(b) *Civil service.* Civil servants, whether established or not, and whether whole or part time. Service regulations require that if a civil servant becomes a candidate for parliamentary election, he must resign his office.

(c) *Armed forces.* Members of the regular armed forces of the Crown. Service regulations forbid members of the regular forces from standing for Parliament. It was discovered that this regulation provided a means of getting service engagements terminated, so in 1963 the Home Secretary appointed an advisory committee. This committee reports to the appropriate Service Minister whether it is satisfied that an application to terminate a service agreement and stand for parliament is bona fide.

(d) *Police forces.* Members (*i.e.* full-time constables) of any police force maintained by a police authority.

(e) *Foreign legislatures.* Members of the legislature of any country outside the Commonwealth apart from members of the legislatures of the Republic of Ireland.[31] Members of such legislatures would generally be disqualified as aliens, but this provision disqualifies those with dual nationality.

(f) *Commissions and Tribunals,* etc. All the members of commissions, tribunals, and other bodies specified in Part II of Schedule 1. These include the boards of a variety of statutory bodies whose members are appointed by the Crown, *e.g.* the various electricity boards, the Development Agencies, the Gaming Board, the National Rivers Authority, the Lands Tribunal, the Council on Tribunals, and the Law Commissions. The list is constantly being extended or modified by statute.

---

[30] In contrast, the rules on paid employment for M.P.s by the private sector is regulated by Parliament itself, and not by statute, see *post* paras 13–028 to 13–034.
[31] See the Disqualification Act 2000 which amends the 1975 Act.

Certain other offices. The holders of various offices specified in Part III of Schedule 1, including British ambassadors and high commissioners, electoral commissioners, the Comptroller and Auditor-General, judge-advocates, Parliamentary Commissioner, chairmen of many statutory tribunals and councils, governors of the British Broadcasting Corporation, and registration officers at elections. These are disqualified either because they are appointed by the Crown or because their office is incompatible with membership of the House of Commons.

Section 1(2). Offices disqualifying for particular constituencies

10–008   The holder of any office described in Part IV of Schedule 1 is disqualified from membership for any constituency specified in the Schedule in relation to that office. A lord-lieutenant or sheriff, for example, is disqualified in relation to any constituency in the area for which he is appointed.

Section 1(4). Effect of section 1 (holders of certain offices)

10–009   A person is not disqualified for membership of the House of Commons by reason of holding any office or place of profit except as provided in the Act. Conversely, a person is not disqualified for appointment to any office or place by reason of his being a member of that House.[32]

Schedule 1 containing the list of offices mentioned above may be amended by Order in Council, following a resolution of the House of Commons—a remarkable example of delegated legislation which allows a government Minister in effect to enfranchise or disqualify the holders of a variety of officers on the basis of vague criteria. Her Majesty's printer is required to print copies of the Act with Schedule 1 as amended from time to time by Order in Council or other Acts (s.5).[33]

Section 2. Ministerial offices[34]

10–010   Not more than 95 holders of the ministerial offices specified in Schedule 2 may sit and vote at any one time in the House of Commons. It is now permissible for all senior Ministers, except the Lord Chancellor, to sit in the Commons.[35]

Section 4. Stewardship of the Chiltern Hundreds, etc

10–011   It was established by the early seventeenth century that a member could not resign his seat. If a member wished to relinquish his seat, therefore, it has been the practice since about 1750 to apply to the Chancellor of the Exchequer for the Stewardship of the Chiltern Hundreds. The office has for long been a sinecure, but it is technically an "office of profit under the Crown" and therefore under the previous law disqualified the holder from further membership of the Commons.

---

[32] The latter provision negatives what is called "reverse disqualification".

[33] The most recent reprint of the Act and schedules (the 15th) was in 1997, after the House agreed to government resolutions which disqualified an additional 3,400 office holders, and released 250 others. Acts of Parliament which create new official bodies usually make provision for the insertion of the new bodies into the relevant part of the schedule of the 1975 Act.

[34] These statutory provisions should be distinguished from the convention that Ministers shall disembarrass themselves of any company directorships or shareholdings which would be likely, or which might appear, to conflict with their official duties.

[35] The maximum number of persons whose salaries may be paid as holders of ministerial office is prescribed by the Ministers and other Salaries Act 1975.

In order to preserve this interesting historical relic, the Act provides that the Stewardship of the Chiltern Hundreds and three similar offices, for which application is made to the Chancellor of the Exchequer, shall be treated as included among the disqualifying offices listed in Part IV of Schedule 1.[36]

Section 6. Effect of disqualification, and provision for relief

If a person disqualified for membership is elected, his election is void; and if a member of the House becomes disqualified his seat is vacated. If, however, the disqualification has been removed the House may, if it appears proper to do so, direct that the disqualification shall be disregarded; but such order is not to affect proceedings on an election petition or the determination of an election court.[37]   **10–012**

Section 7. Jurisdiction of Privy Council as to disqualification

Any person who claims that a person purporting to be a member of the House of Commons is disqualified by the Act may apply to Her Majesty in Council for a declaration to that effect. The application is referred to the Judicial Committee in the same way as an appeal from a court under the Judicial Committee Act 1833, s.3. As regards disqualification-under the Act, this is an alternative method to an election petition,[38] though without the time limit. The Judicial Committee may direct an issue of fact to be tried in the High Court,[39] whose decision shall be final. A declaration may not be made, however, if an election petition is pending or has been tried, or if the House of Commons has directed that the disqualification shall be disregarded. It should be noticed that the House itself may resolve that a case be referred by the Crown to the Judicial Committee under section 4 of the Judicial Committee Act 1833 for an advisory opinion on a point of law, and this could include any legal disqualification, whether arising under the House of Commons Disqualification Act or not.[40]   **10–013**

Section 8. Relaxation of obligation to accept office

No member of the House of Commons or candidate for a parliamentary election may be *required* to accept any office which would disqualify him from membership. This relaxation does not apply to any obligation, statutory or otherwise, to serve in the armed forces of the Crown. It appears that the office of sheriff is the only other office which is by custom regarded as obligatory. Sheriffs were formerly required to remain in the county during this year of office, and therefore could not sit in the House.[41] In 1626 Charles I excluded Coke and four other members by "pricking" them sheriffs against their will,[42] but the Commons resolved in 1675 that it was a breach of privilege to appoint a member of the House as sheriff.[43] Section 8 was inserted *ex abundante cautela*, in case the   **10–014**

---

[36] There are four offices, enabling four members to resign in quick succession, *viz*. Steward or Bailiff of the Chiltern Hundreds, and Steward or Bailiff of the Manor of Northstead. The Chancellor of the Exchequer usually grants them alternately.

[37] *Post* para. 10–061.

[38] *Post*, para. 10–062.

[39] Or the Court of Session or the High Court in Northern Ireland.

[40] *e.g. Re MacManaway* [1951] A.C. 161, PC.

[41] 4 Co.Inst.48.

[42] Holdsworth, *History of English Law*, 1923–64, V, pp. 448–449.

[43] Wittke, *Parliamentary Privilege*, p. 38.

government should be able to exclude members of the Opposition by appointing them to disqualifying offices.

A candidate's consent to nomination at a parliamentary election must contain a statement that he is aware of the provisions of the Act, and that, to the best of his knowledge and belief, he is not disqualified from membership of the House of Commons (section 10).

The Act of 1957 repealed all provisions whereby common informers could sue for penalties in respect of parliamentary disqualifications. Apart from the procedure laid down in section 7 (*supra*) the Courts will not examine whether a member of Parliament is disqualified from sitting.[44]

Payment of Members

10–015   In medieval times knights, citizens and burgesses received a few shillings a day from their constituencies. This right was balanced by statutory penalties for non-attendance, which are now obsolete. Although called wages, these payments were intended as expenses, and they too became obsolete with the fall in the value of money.

As a result of the decision in *Amalgamated Society of Railway Servants v. Osborne*[45] declaring that a "political levy" by trades unions on their members was illegal, so that trades unions could not pay salaries to M.P.s whom they sponsored, the House of Commons resolved that members who were not Ministers should receive a salary under the annual Appropriation Act payable out of the Consolidated Fund. In addition since 1967 members have been entitled to an Office Cost Allowance toward the cost of office expenses and secretarial and research expenditure. Since 1971 a Member may claim an additional cost allowance in respect of the need to stay overnight in London.[46]

In order to avoid, or minimise, the embarrassment of members of Parliament having to determine their own salaries, in 1970 that duty was entrusted to Top (now Senior) Salaries Review Body which conducts regular reviews of the salaries of those working in the higher levels of the public service. From 1983–1993 members' salaries were linked with those of Grade 6 civil servants, and updated in accordance with the linkage. In 1993 the House resolved that members should be paid a set yearly salary to be increased annually. In 1996 the government asked the Senior Salaries Review Body to conduct a full review of parliamentary pay and salaries,[47] and in the light of this report the House resolved in 1996 that annual salary should be £43,000 to be increased annually (without the need for parliamentary decision) from April 1997 by the average percentage by which senior civil servant pay had increased in the previous year.[48] Various

---

[44] *Martin v. O'Sullivan* [1984] S.T.C. 258. (Challenge to qualifications of the entire House of Commons).

[45] [1910] A.C. 87, HL.

[46] The maximum annual Office Cost Allowance in 1999 was £49,232, that for overnight expenses was £12,717; M.P.s for inner London seats get a London supplement of £1,406. All these figures are to be increased in subsequent years by the March Retail Price Index. Members are also entitled to claim travelling expenses, and since 1998 a bicycle allowance. After the 2001 election, Members voted to increase these allowances and their salaries (note 48).

[47] Cm. 3330.

[48] In 2000 the salary was £49,822, the Senior Salaries Review Body in 2001 recommended that the figure should be increased. Ministers and other office holders, such as the Leader of the Opposition and the Speaker receive an additional salary.

statutes, of which the latest is the Parliamentary and other Pensions Act 1987, provide for the payment of pensions to former members of Parliament.

The Speaker[49]

10–016

The practice of the Commons having a spokesman arose gradually in the Middle Ages. The first two members who may be regarded as holding a definite office as Speaker were Sir Peter de la Mere and Sir Thomas Hungerford in the years 1376 and 1377. The Commons appear always to have elected their Speaker. For some time he also attended the King's Council, and his position as liaison between the Commons and the King was for long a dangerous one.

The Speaker is elected by the Commons from their own number at the beginning of each new Parliament. The Speaker of the previous Parliament is usually re-elected unanimously, if he is still a member and willing to stand. Re-election by the House has not been opposed since 1835. Where a vacancy occurs there is consultation with government and opposition, including back benchers. The custom had been that the Speaker is always chosen from a Government supporter, but this custom was not followed with the election of Miss Betty Boothroyd M.P. as Speaker in 1992. To indicate more clearly that the Speaker is chosen by the House as a whole and is not a Government appointment, the election procedure was changed in 1972[50] to allow for the chair to be taken by the "Father of the House" (the senior Member in years of service), who calls on a senior Government back bench Members to propose the motion that some other Member "do take the Chair of the House as Speaker"; this is normally seconded by a senior Opposition back bench Member.[51] If the election of a new Speaker is opposed, this is done on the basis of an amendment to the motion namely to leave out the name of the first candidate and insert the name of another candidate; the House has to decide on all candidates whose names are put forward as amendments to the motion before it considers the candidate first proposed. The assumption behind this procedure was that the "usual channels" would operate behind the scenes to present the House with a single candidate, or at least no more than two candidates. The procedure was known to have "inherent weaknesses"[52] and, as became obvious in October 2000, it was not intended to deal with a situation in which a multiplicity of candidates stood for election. The Procedure Committee has recommended that the 1972 system for electing the Speaker should be replaced by a ballot-based system, and this was accepted by the House in March 2001.[53] It is a convention that the Sovereign should be asked for, and should give, consent to the choice of Speaker.

A Speaker takes no active part in a parliamentary election campaign and stands as "the Speaker seeking re-election", since he belongs to no party. On some occasions the Speaker is returned to Parliament unopposed, but this is not always the case.[54] In order that a constituency may not be virtually disfranchised, it has

10–017

---

[49] See Dasent, *Speakers of the House of Commons* (1911), Erskine May, *Parliamentary Practice* (22nd ed., 1997); Sir Ivor Jennings, *Parliament* (2nd ed.), pp. 63 *et seq.*; Selwyn Lloyd, *Mr Speaker, Sir* (1976).

[50] See H.C. 111 (1971–72) for the background to this change.

[51] Where a Speaker has indicated that he or she wishes to retire while still a member of the House, the retiring Speaker may remain in the chair until his successor has been selected.

[52] See H.C. 386 (1995–96) para. 22.

[53] H.C. 40 (2000–2001).

[54] In a return to previous practice no major party contested the election of the Speaker in the 1997 or 2001 general elections.

been suggested that the Speaker should have a fictitious constituency or none at all, so that on a member's election as Speaker there would be a by-election in the constituency which returned him to Parliament. On the other hand, it would be incorrect to say that the Speaker's constituency is disfranchised, because the member who fills that office continues to look after the interests of his constituents.

The Speaker is the channel of communication between the Commons and the Queen, and between the Commons and the Lords. Hence his title of "Speaker" or spokesman. On his appointment he claims from the Sovereign certain "ancient and undoubted" privileges of the House at the beginning of each Parliament.[55]

10–018   Rulings from the Chair rather than Standing Orders are of importance in the maintenance of parliamentary procedure and order. The Speaker has various discretionary powers for example to restrict debate by selecting amendments and, in certain circumstances to direct members to restrict the length of their speeches.

The Speaker presides over the House, except when it is in Committee. When in the chair he maintains order, and guides the House on all questions of privilege and practice. He is expected to be impartial between political parties, and especially to protect the rights of minorities in the House and to ensure that they have their say. The Speaker does not take part in debate. He does not vote unless there is a tie, in which case, according to the ruling of Speaker Addington (1796), "the Speaker should always vote for further discussion where this is possible." Thus he will usually give his casting vote in favour of the introduction of a Bill, against amendments to a Bill at the report stage, against Lords' amendments to a Bill sent up by the Commons and against a guillotine motion.

The Speaker gives advice and rulings on procedure; signs warrants of committal for contempt, and reprimands members and strangers for misconduct; and signs warrants for the issue of writs for by-elections. The Speaker has the duty under the Parliament Acts 1911 and 1949 of certifying "Money Bills," and giving his certificate that the procedure for overriding the House of Lords has been complied with. If it were doubtful which was the largest party in opposition to the government in the House of Commons, or who was the leader in the House of such party, the Speaker would issue a certificate for this purpose, which would be binding and conclusive.[56] The Speaker has other statutory powers and duties including Chairman of the Speaker's Committee,[57] and the certification of the mental illness of a member.

10–019   On behalf of the House the Speaker exercises its functions as owner of parliamentary copyright.[58] Other administrative duties include the control of the House's accommodation and services. In *R. v. The Speaker, Ex p. Mc Guinness*[59] judicial review of the Speaker's decision[60] that those who refused to take the oath of allegiance, or to affirm allegiance were not entitled access to the facilities and services for M.P.s was refused.

---

[55] *Post*, Chap. 13.
[56] Ministerial and other Salaries Act 1975, s.2.
[57] See s.2 and sched. 2 of the Political Parties, Elections and Referendums Act 2000. This committee reports to the House of Commons on the work of the Electoral Commission, *post* para. 10–042.
[58] Copyright, Designs and Patents Act 1988, s.167(2).
[59] [1997] N.I. 359.
[60] H.C. Deb. Vol. 294, col.35–36, (1997–98).

The Speaker has an official residence. His salary is charged on and payable out of the Consolidated Fund.[61] This means that it is payable by permanent legislation, and does not come up for annual review and perhaps debate. On a dissolution of Parliament the Speaker retains office until a Speaker is chosen by the new Parliament. In precedence he ranks next after the Lord President of the Council. When he retires, it is customary to bestow on him a peerage and a statutory pension.

The Clerk of the House is head of the Parliament Office and is appointed by the Crown by letters patent. He has custody of all the records of the House, makes entries of what takes place in the House, and from these materials prepares the Journals. He endorses Bills sent up to the Lords. Under the Parliamentary Corporate Bodies Act 1992 he is the Corporate Officer of the House and as such is empowered to hold property and make contracts on behalf of the House of Commons.[62]
10–020

The Serjeant-at-Arms is appointed by the Crown by letters patent under the Great Seal. The present practice is for the Queen to discuss the appointment informally with the Speaker, who sounds the feelings of the party leaders. The Lancastrian Kings first appointed one of the Sergeants-at-Arms (originally royal bodyguards) to attend the Commons, and the Commons came to use him to protect their privileges because through him they could arrest or imprison offenders without having to take proceedings in the courts. During session he attends, with the mace,[63] the Speaker when the latter enters and leaves the House.
10–021

It is the duty of the Serjeant-at-Arms to carry out directions for maintaining order, and to arrest strangers who have no business in the House. With the mace in his hands he can arrest without warrant anyone who obstructs the Speaker's procession. He executes the Speaker's warrants for contempt, and when ordered to do so brings persons in custody before the bar of the House. He or his assistants serve processes of the House. When a person is arrested by order of the House, the Serjeant-at-Arms keeps the prisoner in his custody until arrangements are made for his bestowal elsewhere. The Metropolitan Police on duty in the precincts come under his orders when the House is in session. As housekeeper of the House he has charge of its committee rooms and other buildings, and supervises amongst others the Communications Directory which provides services to the House.

The Chairman of Ways and Means is a member elected at the beginning of each Parliament to preside over committees of the whole House. He maintains order in Committee and can "name" members, but where a suspension is necessary the Speaker reoccupies the chair. The closure can be applied by the Chairman in Committee.
10–022

The Chairman of Ways and Means also acts as Deputy Speaker, and by the Deputy Speaker Act 1855 he can exercise the Speaker's statutory functions. In both capacities he is expected to show the same political impartiality as the Speaker. He also has important duties in conjunction with the Chairman of

---

[61] Ministerial and other Salaries Act 1975, s.1. This is the culmination of a series of statutes going back to the Speaker of the House of Commons Act 1790.
[62] For the difficulties caused by this change to parliamentary law and practice see the evidence to the Parliamentary Privilege Joint Committee, H.L. Paper 50–i, ii, v, H.C. 401–i, ii, v, (1997–98).
[63] The mace, at first both a weapon and the Serjeant's emblem of office, has come to be regarded as the symbol of the authority of the House; but during prorogation the Serjeant-at-Arms reverts to being a member of the royal household, and the mace is returned to the Lord Chamberlain.

Committees of the House of Lords relating to private Bills. There are two Deputy Chairmen of Ways and Means, who may also act as Deputy Speaker. Neither the Chairman nor the Deputy Chairmen of Ways and Means speaks or votes except in an official capacity.

House of Commons staff

10–023   The appointment and terms of employment of the staff who work in the various departments of the House of Commons—for example, the Department of Administration and Finance, the Department of the Library, the Department of the Official Report of the House of Commons—is subject to the control of the House of Commons Commission, a body established by statute in 1978.[64] The Commission is the employer of all House departmental staff, with the exception of the Speaker's personal staff. Further administrative changes were made in 1991 in the light of the Ibbs Report.[65] The Commission now has responsibility for the personnel and financial management of the House for staff and Members of the House.[66] In 1999 a further review was carried out, and the Braithwaite Report[67] recommended further reforms.

In addition to staff appointed by the Commission the Speaker appoints his own personal staff. Staff appointed by the Commission and the Speaker's personal staff are entitled to the individual employment rights to which workers generally are entitled.[68]

Government and Opposition Whips[69]

10–024   The Government Whips consist of the Chief Whip (the Parliamentary Secretary to the Treasury), the Deputy Chief Whip (the first junior Lord of the Treasury) and the Junior Whips (the other four junior Lords of the Treasury, and the Treasurer, Comptroller and Vice-Chamberlain of the Household). The Government Chief Whip is responsible to the Prime Minister and Leader of the House for fitting the government's programme of business into the time available during the session. He and the Chief Whips of the other parties constitute the "usual channels" through which business communications pass between the parties.

It is the duty of the Whips, whether acting for the government or not, to see that their parties are fully represented at important divisions and to arrange "pairs." They also keep their leaders informed of the state of feeling in the party. Again, they act as intermediaries between the leaders of the party and the constituency organisations, and can often influence the local association in its choice of candidate. The Chief Opposition Whip and Assistant Opposition Whip, nominated by the Leader of the Opposition, and the Assistant Government Whip, have statutory salaries.[70]

---

[64] House of Commons (Administration) Act 1978. The Commission consists of the Speaker, the Leader of the House of Commons, a member of the House nominated by the Leader of the Opposition and three other members of the House, appointed by the House, not being Ministers of the Crown.

[65] Report on House of Commons Services H.C. 38 (1990–91).

[66] Excluding the salaries and allowances of Members.

[67] *House of Commons Review of Management and Services* H.C. 745 (1998–99).

[68] Employment Rights Act 1996, s.194. However the Health and Safety at Work Act 1974 does not apply to either House of Parliament, see Geoffrey Lock Chap. IV "Statute law and case law applicable to Parliament", in *The Law and Parliament* edited by Dawn Oliver and Gavin Drewry (1998).

[69] "Whip," originally "whipper-in," is a term derived from the hunting field.

[70] Ministerial and other Salaries Act 1975.

II. PARLIAMENTARY FRANCHISE AND ELECTIONS

Modern history of the parliamentary franchise[71]

The modern history of the parliamentary franchise begins with the Representa-   **10–025**
tion of the People Act 1832 ("the Reform Act") which extended the franchise by
means of property qualifications from the landed gentry and borough caucuses to
the middle classes. The indirect consequences of this Act and its successors were
immense. The Commons became the predominant element in the government of
the country, the Crown became detached from politics, and governments recognised that they depended on the will of the electorate.[72]

The Representation of the People Act 1867, by introducing certain occupation
and lodger qualifications in the boroughs, gave the vote to many urban workers.
The Representation of the People Act 1884 extended the lodger and householder
qualifications to counties, thus giving the vote to many agricultural workers.
The Representation of the People Act 1918 introduced adult male suffrage, and
for the first time gave the vote to women, but only at the age of 30.[73] The Act
provided for both a residence and a business premises qualification. The Representation of the People Act 1945 assimilated the local government franchise to
the parliamentary franchise in so far as every parliamentary elector was to have
the local government franchise. The Representation of the People Act 1948 laid
down that no elector should have more than one vote at a general election,
abolished the business premises qualification and the university franchise and
provided that each constituency should henceforth elect only one member.
The Representation of the People Act 1969, s.1, lowered the minimum age of
voting from 21 to 18 years. The Representation of the People Acts 1985, 1989
extended voting rights to expatriates in certain circumstances. The Representation of the People Act 2000 (RPA 2000) reformed the system of registration of
voters and made new provisions for voting at parliamentary and local elections.
Further extensive reforms to many aspects of the law relating to elections are
found in the Political Parties, Elections and Referendums Act 2000 (PPER Act
2000).

The following account is mainly concerned with the House of Commons.[74]

Qualifications for the franchise

The law and administration on the franchise and elections has to be looked at   **10–026**
in the light of Article 10 (freedom of expression) and Protocol 1, Article 3 of the
European Convention of Human Rights. The latter requires the holding of "free
elections at reasonable intervals by secret ballot, under conditions which will
ensure the free expression of the people in the choice of the legislature".[75]

---

[71] Sir Ivor Jennings, *Party Politics I: Appeal to the People* (1960); D.E. Butler, *The Electoral System in Britain since 1918* (2nd ed., 1963); Robert Blackburn, *The Electoral System in Britain* (1995).
[72] The proportion of the electorate to the population was raised from 3 to 4 per cent by the Act of 1832, from 18 to 47 per cent by the Act of 1918, and to 65 per cent by the Act of 1928.
[73] Women received the vote at the age of 21 by the Representation of the People (Equal Franchise) Act 1928.
[74] See Chap. 5 for elections to the Scottish Parliament and the Welsh and Northern Ireland Assemblies.
[75] The leading case is *Mathieu-Mohin v. Belgium* (1987) 10 E.H.R.R. 1, where the European Court of Human Rights stated that Protocol 1 required equal treatment of all citizens in the exercise of their right to vote and stand for election, but that this did not preclude the imposition of conditions on those rights. States had a wide margin of appreciation in this sphere.

The Representation of the People Act 1983, s.1[76] provides that a person, in order to qualify as a parliamentary elector in any constituency, must:

(a) be registered in the register of parliamentary electors for that constituency;

(b) not be subject to any legal incapacity to vote (age apart);

(c) be either a Commonwealth citizen[77] or a citizen of the Republic of Ireland; and

(d) be of voting age (that is, 18 years or over) on the date of the poll.[78]

No one may vote more than once in the same constituency at any parliamentary election or in more than one constituency.

Registration[79]

10–027   The RPA 2000 Act made fundamental changes to the system of electoral registration by introducing a scheme of a "rolling" electoral register to enable electors to be added to, and deleted from, the register at any time of the year. Registration is no longer dependant on residence on a single annual qualification date; a person may be eligible to be registered as an elector at any point in the year. Throughout the Act entitlement to register is based on the "relevant date", which is the date on which an application for registration is made. This reform should assist in keeping the register up to date.

Residence

10–028   Some guidance is given to the courts by section 5 of the 1983 Act[80] which provides, in particular, that regard shall be had to the purpose and other circumstances, as well as to the fact, of a person's presence at, or absence from, the address in question.[81] This guidance has been expanded by the RPA 2000 to take account of those who have no settled address. Section 5(2) provides that a person "staying at a place otherwise than on a permanent basis" may "in all the circumstances" be taken to be at that time resident there, if he has no home elsewhere. The Court of Appeal has adopted a broad matter of fact approach to residence which would seem to be in accordance with the requirements of Protocol 1, Article 3. In *Hipperstone v. Newbury Electoral Officer*[82] it held that the occupation of tents, vehicles and other makeshift accommodation by women in the vicinity of a United States Air force Base at Greenham Common was

---

[76] As substituted by the Representation of the People Act 2000, which made extensive alterations to the 1983 Act.

[77] British Nationality Act 1981, s.37.

[78] For the purposes of the Representation of the People Acts a person attains a given age at the commencement of the relevant anniversary of his birthday, Representation of the People Act 1983, s.202(1).

[79] s.4 of the 1983 Act, as substituted by the RPA 2000.

[80] As substituted by the RPA 2000, but virtually the same as that provided in the 1983 Act.

[81] s.5(3) expressly deals with various examples of temporary absence, and s.6 provides that a merchant seaman's absence shall not prevent him being regarded as resident at the address where, but for his duties, he would normally live or at any hostel or club which provides accommodation for merchant seamen at which he commonly stays in the course of his employment.

[82] [1985] Q.B. 1060. See also *Fox v. Stirk and Bristol Electoral Registration Officer; Ricketts v. Cambridge City Electoral Registration Officer* [1970] 2 Q.B. 463, CA (Students living in college or hall of residence—or, presumably, in lodgings—entitled to be registered in that constituency.)

sufficient to entitle the women to register as voters. It was irrelevant that their living accommodation was such that under other legislation they might be described as homeless: "To import considerations based upon the standard of accommodation into qualification for the franchise would be to put the clock back to the days when the franchise depended upon a property qualification."[83] The Court also held that for the purpose of qualifying for the franchise it was irrelevant that the women might be trespassers or even guilty of criminal offences as a result of living where they had chosen to.

In England, Wales and Scotland it is only necessary to establish residence on the relevant date. In Northern Ireland a voter must establish residence in Northern Ireland for the whole of the period of three months ending on the relevant date.[84]

Special rules have been laid down for five classes of voters:

(1) *Service voters* (sections 14–17) Until the RPA 2000 service voters could only **10–029** vote if a "service declaration" had been made. Any of the following persons has the right, on making a service declaration, to be entered on the register as a service voter in the constituency in which he or she would have been residing if he were not abroad:

(a)   a member of the forces;

(b)   any other person employed in the service of the Crown in a post outside the United Kingdom;

(c)   an employee of the British Council in a post outside the United Kingdom;

(d)   the wife or husband of a member of the forces;

(e)   the wife or husband of a person within (b) or (c) who is residing outside the United Kingdom to be with her husband (or his wife).

The RPA 2000 enables those with a service qualification to register in the same way as other voters (provided they meet the residence criterion) or as an overseas elector.

(2) *Overseas electors*[85] A British citizen, otherwise entitled to vote in a parlia- **10–030** mentary election, may do so even though not resident in the United Kingdom provided that he satisfies the definition of overseas elector and has made an overseas elector's declaration. An overseas elector must:

(a)   be resident outside the United Kingdom;

(b)   have been included on a register in respect of residence in a particular constituency; and

---

[83] At p. 1072, *per* Sir John Donaldson. See the unreported decision of the County Court in *Lippiat v. Electoral Registration Officer*, March 21, 1996. (A homeless man was entitled to use a day centre as his address for residence.)
[84] Representation of the People Act 1983, s.4(2), as substituted by the 2000 Act.
[85] Representation of the People Act 1985, ss.1–3, as substituted by Sched. 2 of the RPA 2000, as amended by s.141 of the PPER 2000.

(c) the date by which residence was determined for inclusion in the register is not more than 15 years earlier than the relevant date of the register in which the elector wishes to be included as an overseas elector.

10–031   (3) *Mental patients* Section 3A of the 1993 Act (as inserted by the RPA 2000) disqualifies those who are detained in mental institutions as a result of criminal activity. Other patients (whether detained or voluntary) may register in relation to their residence in the mental institution, provided the period likely to be spent there is sufficient to satisfy the residence requirement.[86] Alternatively, a mental patient may register at an address where he is resident, other than the mental hospital in which he is a patient or, if there is no such place, make a declaration of local connection (see below).

10–032   (4) *Persons Remanded in Custody*[87] Provisions similar to those which apply to persons in mental hospitals apply to remand prisoners.

10–033   (5) *Those with a National Residence*[88] Patients in mental hospitals (other than those detained as a consequence of criminal activity) and remand prisoners who are not resident at some address other than the institution where they are being detained, may make a *"declaration of local connection"*. This method of registration (which is also available to the homeless) enables a person to be registered as an elector either at an address where he would be residing if he was not detained, or at an address where he has resided. In the case of a homeless person "the address of, or which is nearest to, a place in the United Kingdom where he commonly spends a substantial part of his time (whether during the day or at night)" will suffice. A person who makes such a declaration will be regarded as resident at that address for the purpose of section 4.

Manner of voting
10–034   Voters who, for various reasons are unable to attend in person at the appropriate polling station may apply to be treated as "absent voters" and exercise their franchise by proxies. All registered electors are eligible to apply for a postal vote.[89] Special assistance has to be made to provide assistance with voting for persons with disabilities.

Disqualifications from the franchise
10–035   The following are subject to legal incapacity from voting, either under the Act of 1983 or under the pre-existing law:

(i) Aliens

(ii) Minors (under 18 years of age).

(iii) Peers, except Irish peers,[90] and those hereditary peers who are no longer entitled to sit in the House of Lords.[91]

---

[86] Representation of the People Act 1983, s.7, as substituted by the RPA 2000.
[87] Representation of the People Act 1983, s.7A, as inserted by the RPA 2000.
[88] s.7B, 7C of the 1983 Act as inserted by the RPA 2000.
[89] ss.5–9 of the 1985 Act as substituted by Schedule 4 of the RPA 2000.
[90] Peerage Act 1963, s.5.
[91] House of Lords Act 1999, s.3. There is little doubt that the Lords Spiritual are ineligible to vote; see P. Hughes and S. Palmer, "Voting Bishops", [1983] P.L. 393.

(iv) Convicted persons while detained in penal institutions or unlawfully at large, having escaped from confinement.[92]

(v) A person who has been reported by an election court personally guilty, or who has been convicted of a corrupt practice is disqualified for five years from voting at any parliamentary election. In the case of an illegal practice the five-year disqualification is limited to that constituency.[93]

Returning and registration officers

The returning officers are the sheriffs of counties, the chairmen of district **10–036** councils and the mayors of London boroughs.[94] Most of their duties, however, are delegated to the registration officers of districts and London boroughs, who are disqualified from membership of the House of Commons.

The principal duty of the registration officer is to maintain a register of parliamentary electors for each constituency in his area, and a register of local government electors, and to publish a new version of the register at least once a year.[95] He must further keep lists of voters entitled to vote by post or proxy.[96] The duty to maintain an electoral register for each constituency is fulfilled by an annual canvass of the area for which he is responsible. It is his duty to determine any application by a person to be registered or any objection to any registration. Appeal lies to the County Court and then to the Court Appeal from whose decision there is no appeal.[97]

Returning officers, registration officers, presiding officers and others who commit breaches of their official duties are liable for penalties under section 63 of the Representation of the People Act 1983 but no action for damages now lies against them: *cf. Ashby v. White*.[98]

III. POLITICAL PARTIES, THE ELECTORAL COMMISSION AND BOUNDARY REVIEWS

Reform of the law relating to political parties and election campaigns

In 1997 the Labour Government extended the terms of reference of the **10–037** Committee on Standards in Public Life (the Neil Committee) to include political party funding. In March 1998 the Home Office sought the advise of the Neil Committee on several specific topics connected with elections including: foreign funding of political parties, rules on disclosure of donations to political parties,

---

[92] Representation of the People Act 1983, s.3, as amended by the Representation of the People Act 1985, Sched. 4. This section was unsuccessfully challenged as a breach of human rights in *R. (on the application of Pearson and another) v. Secretary of State for the Home Department and others* [2001] H.R.L.R. 39.

[93] Representation of the People Act 1983, ss.60, 61 and s.173 as substituted by s.136 of the PPER Act 2000. For corrupt and illegal practices, see *post* para. 10–048.

[94] Representation of the People Act 1983, s.24. Separate provisions apply to Scotland and Northern Ireland.

[95] Section 9 of the 1993 Act as inserted by the RPA 2000. These registers are to be combined, as far as practicable, with "L" marked against the names of persons registered as local government electors only.

[96] Representation of the People Act 1985, ss.5–9, as substituted by schedule 4 of the RPA 2000.

[97] Representation of the People Act 1983, s.10 and s.56 (see s.57 for Scottish Appeals). The procedure, in England, is exemplified by *Hipperson v. Newbury Electoral Officer* [1985] Q.B. 1060.

[98] (1703) 2 Ld. Raym. 938.

and rules on election expenditure. In 1998 the Neil Committee published its Fifth report, *The Funding of Political Parties*[99] in which it made wide ranging recommendations, not only on funding, but also on the regulation of electoral and referendum campaigns, and on the desirability of establishing of an Electoral Commission[1] to oversee aspects of electoral law and procedure. The Government responded positively in a White Paper[2] including a draft Bill, which became the Political Parties Elections and Referendums Act 2000 (PPER Act).

Political Parties

10–038   Political parties are voluntary organisations which play an important part in the democratic process: they enable citizens to play a role in policy-making, and are the principle means for the representation of electors in both national and local government. Until the PPER Act, the law played little part in regulating political parties. The Registration of Political Parties Act 1998 had introduced requirements for the registration of political parties, but there was little legal provision on the funding of political parties.[3] The Neil Committee[4] noted that the absence of any legal requirement on political parties to reveal the sources of their income raised concerns that powerful businesses could (anonymously) attempt to "buy" influence with a political party. It was concerned at the possibility that political parties were receiving anonymous and/or foreign donations, and recommended that such donations should be banned. It also recommended that details of donations should be recorded and reported to the Electoral Commission. These recommendations are implemented in Parts III and IV of the Act.

Funding of political parties

10–039   The new arrangements build on the existing requirements that political parties should be registered.[5] Before a party can be registered it must adopt a scheme, approved by the Electoral Commission, which sets out arrangements for regulating its financial affairs (section 26). Registered political parties are required to keep accounts showing income and expenditure and to provide the Commission with an annual statement of their accounts in accordance with regulations laid down by the Commission (sections 41–42). The Commission may prescribe different requirements according to the gross income of the party, allowing in effect for reduced regulation for parties with a small turnover. Where a registered party's annual income or expenditure exceeds £250,000, the accounts must be audited by a qualified auditor (section 43). A failure to comply with the statutory requirement for accounting is a criminal offence (section 47).

Donations are defined widely to include gifts of money or other property; subscriptions; loans, property or services at less than commercial value; sponsorship (sections 50–53). Certain payments and services are specifically excluded from the definition including grants for security at party conferences, party political broadcasts and services provided by an individual voluntarily in his own time (section 52). Donations may only be accepted if they are by "permissable

---

[99] Cm. 4057.

[1] *Post* para. 10–042.

[2] Cm 4413 (1999).

[3] The Companies Act 1985 had required companies making a donation to a party to declare this. The PPER Act s.139 and sched. 19 inserts a new Part XA into the Companies Act which imposes much stricter controls on political donations.

[4] See too H.C. 301, (1993–94).

[5] *Post* para. 10–041.

donors" and the identity of the donor is known; a party has 30 days from receipt of a donation to be satisfied that the donation is one that it can accept within the rules, if not it must be returned to the donor (section 56). Permissable donors are defined so as to prevent the foreign funding of political parties and include: an individual registered on the electoral register; a company registered in the United Kingdom and incorporated in the European Union and which carries on business in the United Kingdom; a registered political party; a trade union (section 54). Parties have to keep details of all donations over £200,[6] and the party treasurer has to prepare a quarterly donation report for the Commission recording donations of £5,000 or more, or which over a period of time amounts to £5,000 or more. Where a donation has been recorded, any further donations from that source of over £1,000 must be recorded (section 62). During election periods weekly donation reports are required (section 63). These rules, which impose extensive responsibilities on party treasurers, are enforced by a combination of civil and criminal penalties. Section 36 allows the Commission to provide financial and other assistance for "existing registered parties"[7] to enable them to comply with Parts III and IV of the Act.

The Neill Committee recognised that its proposals could reduce the money available to political parties and also recommended that the existing scheme of state aid (Short money) to opposition political parties in parliament[8] to assist them in carry out their parliamentary duties, should be reviewed with a view to substantially increasing the sums made available. The payment of Short money is governed by resolution of the House; in May 1999 the House agreed to increase the overall sum payable to a maximum of £5,012,182; a 270 per cent increase. It also altered the basis upon which payment was made; there is some concern that the use to which this money can be put, as the term "parliament business", is unclear.[9]

10–040

The Registration of Political Parties

Part II of the PPER Act 2000 re-enacts with modifications the Registration of Political Parties Act 1998. Section 22 requires political parties who wish to nominate candidates for a "relevant election"[10] to be registered with the Electoral Commission.[11] To register, a political party has to submit an application to the Commission specifying *inter alia*[12] the party's registered name and, if wished, up to three emblems to be used by the party on ballot papers. An application may be refused where, for example, the name (or emblem) is the same as that of a party already registered or would be likely to cause confusion with a party already registered (sections 28(4) and 29(2)). The requirement to register names and emblems was a response to a decision of an Election Court

10–041

---

[6] s.52(2)(b). Neill had suggested over £50. To avoid donors using multiple small donations to avoid s.50, s.68 requires a donor who makes small donations totalling more than £5,000 in a year, to report this to the Commission; a failure to do so is an offence.
[7] *i.e.* those already registered under the 1998 Act.
[8] Introduced into the House of Commons in 1975 and named after the then Leader of the House; introduced into the House of Lords in 1996, and known there as "Cranborne" money.
[9] See H.C. 293 (2000–2001), paras 40–53.
[10] *viz*: elections to Westminster; the European and Scottish Parliaments; the Welsh and Northern Irish Assemblies; local government elections (s.22(5)).
[11] Special provision is made for Independent candidates and the Speaker seeking re-election (s.22(3)).
[12] See sched. 4 PPER Act.

that the nomination and ballot papers of a candidate calling himself a "Literal Democrat" were valid.[13] The PPER Act imposes controls on the income and expenditure of political parties and in consequence the new rules on registration are more detailed than before. Each registered party has to have a registered leader, nominating officer and treasurer (section 24); the latter officer is responsible for ensuring that the party concerned complies with the statutory controls on income and expenditure found in Parts III and IV of the Act. A party will not be registered unless the Electoral Commission approves its scheme setting out arrangements regulating the financial affairs of the party (section 26). The Electoral Commission maintains two registers: a Great Britain register and a Northern Ireland register.

The Electoral Commission

10–042   Electoral law and administration had become increasingly complicated. The number of elected bodies had increased as had the type of voting system and the use being made of referendums. Another change in the last thirty years was in the nature and practice of election campaigning; there will continue to be changes with the use of electronic media. There was increasing support from academics,[14] and both the Neill Committee[15] and the Jenkins Commission[16] for the establishment of an independent Electoral Commission to oversee various aspects of the regulation of elections and political parties. Part I of the PPER Act provides for the appointment of an Electoral Commission for the United Kingdom. This is established as a body corporate, independent of government and accountable to Parliament, its members are appointed by the Queen, but with the agreement of the Speaker of the House of Commons and after consultation with the leaders of the parties represented in the Commons (section 3).

10–043   The general functions of the Electoral Commission are: to publish reports on all elections and referendums in the United Kingdom (section 5); to take over from the Home Office the practice of reviewing matters relating to elections etc including for, *e.g.* boundary changes and the registration of political parties (section 6); the right to be consulted by the Home Secretary before the exercise of certain delegated powers to change aspects of electoral law (section 7); the power to recommend to the Home Secretary that he should exercise certain functions (section 8); to be involved in decisions to establish and test pilot schemes for local elections, as provided by section 10 of the RPA 2000 (section 9); to provide advise and assistance to registration and returning officers with respect to their statutory functions (section 10); to promote public awareness about the electoral systems and the systems of national and local government and the E.U. institutions (section 13). The Electoral Commission is also responsible for maintaining registers of political parties, recognised third parties,[17] permitted

---

[13] *Sanders v. Chichester, The Times*, December 2, (1994).
[14] See David Butler *The Case for an Electoral Commission—Keeping Election Law Up-to-Date*, (Hansard Society, 1998); The Constitution Unit, (*Establishing an Electoral Commission* 1997); Robert Blackburn *The Electoral System in Britain*, (1995).
[15] Cm. 4057, Chap. 11.
[16] Set up to recommend an alternative voting system for the House of Commons, Cm. 4090 (1998). The Home Affairs Select Committee H.C. 768 (1997–98), also supported the establishment of an Electoral Commission.
[17] See *post* para. 10–054.

participants in a referendum,[18] and those making political donations.[19] Broadcasters are required to have regard to the Commission's views on party political broadcasts before making rules on such broadcasts (section 11).

The Commission is to establish Boundary Committees for England, Scotland, Wales and Northern Ireland, and transfer to them the functions of the existing Boundary Commissions.[20] The Commission eventually will take over certain of the functions previously exercised by the Boundary Commissions (sections 14–17 and Schedule 3). This is unlikely to happen before 2005. The functions of the Local Government Commission for England—the body responsible for reviewing local electoral boundaries—should be transferred to the Electoral Commission by 2002 (section 18).[21] The Electoral Commission was established in October 2000.

Constituencies and boundaries

Four permanent and independent Boundary Commissions for England, Scotland, Wales and Northern Ireland were set up in 1944. By the Parliamentary Constituencies Act 1986[22] the Commissions were to keep under review the representation in the House of Commons[23] of the part of the United Kingdom with which they are concerned and to submit reports to the Home Secretary as to the redistribution of seats at intervals of not less than eight or more than twelve years.[24] The criteria to be applied as far as practicable include numerical equality of voters between constituencies, respect for the boundaries of natural local communities, the distance to be travelled between parts of a single constituency, and the balance between the several parts of the United Kingdom. The number of constituencies allotted is not substantially greater or less than 613 for Great Britain (including at least 71 for Scotland and 35 for Wales) and 17 for Northern Ireland. The number is 659 at present. Parliamentary constituencies are still divided into county and district constituencies. Every constituency is to return a single member. The electorate of each constituency is to be as near as practicable to its "electoral quota," which is about 60,000 at present; but Scotland and Wales, containing large rural areas, are over-represented. There is provision in the Scotland Act 1998 for a future reduction in the number of Scottish seats in the House of Commons.

Boundary Commission reports are to be laid before Parliament by the Secretary of State as soon as may be, together with a draft Order in Council giving effect (with or without modifications) to their recommendation. If the draft Order is approved by resolution of each House, the Secretary of State must submit it to Her Majesty in Council, and the Order will take effect on the dissolution of

10–044

---

[18] See *post* para. 10–063.

[19] See *post* para. 10–039.

[20] This was not one of the Neil's Committee's recommendations, it thought that to give it this responsibility would overload the Commission.

[21] Provision is also made for the Scottish Ministers (s.19) and the National Assembly for Wales (s.20) to transfer the functions of the relevant local government commissions to the Electoral Commission.

[22] As amended by the Boundaries Commissioners Act 1992.

[23] The Boundary Commissions are also responsible under devolution legislation for the review of the regional boundaries for the constituencies for the devolved legislatures.

[24] A failure to submit a report within the appropriate time limit will not invalidate the report for the purpose of any enactment, s.3(2A) Parliamentary constituencies Act 1986, as amended by the Boundary Commission Act 1992.

Parliament. Section 4 of the Act of 1986 provides that the validity of an Order in Council when made may not be called in question in any legal proceedings.

10–045   Once section 16 of the PPER 2000 is implemented, the functions of the Boundary Commissions will be absorbed by the Electoral Commission, which can require the relevant Boundary Committee[25] to carry out a review and submit it to the Commission. The Electoral Commission will make recommendations to Parliament based on those reviews; it will no longer be possible for the Secretary of State to modify recommendations on boundary reviews; he is required to lay before Parliament the draft of an Order in Council giving effect to the Commission's recommendations.[26] These reductions in the powers of the Secretary of State should be seen in the context of cases where Ministers have either attempted to avoid implementing Boundary Commission reports,[27] or attempted to prevent a report being submitted to the Home Secretary.[28]

IV THE ELECTION CAMPAIGN

Conduct of elections

10–046   The conduct of elections is governed mainly by the Representation of the People Acts 1983 and 1985, and the Political Parties, Elections and Referendums Act 2000. The latter Act makes extensive and fundamental changes to the conduct of elections and regulates aspects of the campaign that had not previously been regulated.

Candidates[29]

10–047   A candidate must submit a nomination paper to the returning officer within the prescribed time between a dissolution of Parliament and polling day. The nomination must be signed by the proposer and seconder, and eight other electors. The nomination paper may only include a description which associates the candidate with a political party where that party has been registered under Part II of the PPER Act 2000; the description has to be authorised by a certificate issued by or on behalf of the registered nominating officer of the party (section 22). To be valid the nomination form must be accompanied by the deposit of £500 which is forfeited if the candidate fails to obtain one twentieth of the votes cast (section 13 of the 1985 Act).

The returning officer may declare that a nomination paper is invalid if it fails to satisfy the rules relating to signatures and deposit, if the nomination paper is in breach of the rules on the registration of political parties, or if the candidate is disqualified by the Representation of the People Act 1981, (*i.e.* is serving a sentence of imprisonment of more than one year, or of an indefinite period).[30] A candidate disqualified from membership of the House of Commons, on any ground other than that contained in the 1981 Act, may be nominated and stand for election. The validity of his election must be subsequently challenged in the

---

[25] *ante* para. 10–043.
[26] ss. 3(5), 3A and 4 of 1986 Act, as amended by Sched. 3 of the PPER Act 2000.
[27] *R. v. Home Secretary, ex p. McWhirter, The Times*, October 21, 1969, DC.
[28] *R. v. Boundary Commission ex p. Foot* [1983] Q.B. 600.
[29] See s.118 of the 1983 Act as amended by s.135 of the PPER Act which amends the definition of candidate to ensure that it includes sitting M.P.s.
[30] Representation of the People Act 1983, Sched. 1, Pt. II, r. 12.

Election Court,[31] as for example, happened in the case of Viscount Stansgate (Tony Benn)[32] or by way of reference to the Privy Council under the House of Commons Disqualification Act 1975, s.7.

A candidate is required to have an election agent, though he may be his own **10–048** agent. Stringent limits are set on the permissible amount of election expenses, and the purposes for which they may be incurred.[33] Election expenses must be paid through the election agent, and they must be declared to the returning officer together with bills or receipts and published. The PPER Act introduces a new requirement, that returns to election expenses must include details of donations of £50 or more.[34] Every candidate is entitled for the purpose of holding public meetings to the use of a suitable room in a school within the constituency.[35]

Corrupt practices include personation, bribery, treating and undue influence.[36] These were ill-defined offences at common law. Corrupt practices continued after the Reform Act 1832, and a significant improvement only came with the Parliamentary Elections Act 1868 and the Corrupt and Illegal Practices Act 1883.[37]

Illegal practices include false statements as to candidates (1983 Act, s.106); corruptly inducing a person's withdrawal from candidature (1983 Act, s.106); use of unauthorised premises; payment for exhibition of election notices, except to a commercial advertising agent; not printing the name and address of the printer on election publications; employment of paid canvassers; and any other payments contrary to, or in excess of, those allowed by the Acts.[38]

Election Expenses

Introduction

Until the enactment of the PPER Act, the legislation on election expenditure **10–049** reflected the Corrupt and Illegal Practices Act 1833, which was passed at a time when elections were fought mainly at constituency level and national campaigns were rare. The 1833 Act had set a limit to election expenses, and it, and the Parliamentary Elections Act 1868 virtually eliminated bribery, treating and undue influence. Section 76 of the Representation of the People Act 1983 set stringent limits on the permissable amount of spending by individual candidates and the purposes for which expenditure may be incurred. The items that counted towards election expense were largely the same as those found in the 1833 Act.[39]

---

[31] *post* paras 10–061 to 10–062.

[32] *Re Parliamentary Election for Bristol South East* [1964] 2 Q.B. 257.

[33] *Post* para. 10–049.

[34] s.130 and Sched. 16 of the PPER Act.

[35] Representation of the people Act 1983, s.95. *Webster v. Southwark L.B.C.* [1983] Q.B. 698 (Writ of sequestration to enforce right of National Front candidate).

[36] Representation of the People Act 1983, ss.60, 113–115.

[37] Cornelius O'Leary, *The Elimination of Corrupt Practices in British Elections*, 1868–1911 (1962). In Northern Ireland personation is still regarded as a problem that requires the taking of special measures. By the Election (Northern Ireland) Act 1985, an elector may not vote unless he is able to identify himself by production of one of the documents specified in the Act, *e.g.* a driving licence or passport. See the Second Report from the Northern Ireland Affairs Committee, "*Electoral Malpractice in Northern Ireland*", H.C. 316, (1997–98).

[38] Representation of the People Act 1983, ss 109–112. S.71A was added by s.130 PPER Act, it creates a new offence with respect to the giving of donations to persons other than the candidate or his agent.

[39] As defined by s.118 of the 1983 Act and sched. 3, where for example telegrams counted as an election expense, but mobile telephones were not listed. The PPER Act repeals this part of Sched. 3.

Confusion in the existing law as to what was an election expense was illustrated by *R. v. Jones*[40] where a successful candidate's conviction for falsifying election expenses was quashed; Lord Bingham referred to an "intermediate area, (where) questions of judgment may arise".

As a consequence of the decision in *R. v. Tronoh Mines Ltd*,[41] general nation-wide advertising was not subject to statutory limits. Here advertisements had been issued by the sugar industry against nationalisation, McNair J. held that the relevant section of the Act of 1949[42] was not intended to prohibit expenditure on advertisements supporting the interests of a particular party generally in all constituencies.[43] The earlier case of *Grieve v. Douglas-Home*[44] also supported the distinction between national and constituency expenditure.

The law by not regulating national expenditure by the political parties failed to take account of the fact that general elections could only be won by extensive expenditure, mainly on advertisements. The Neill Committee in its Fifth report[45] noted that the total national expenditure by the Labour and Conservative parties at the 1997 general election was about £60m., 90 per cent of which was on national expenditure. It proposed widespread changes to the law on constituency and national expenditure on elections; it also proposed that third party expenditure, such as that in *Tronoh Mines*, should be limited and controlled.

Constituency spending

10–050   This is regulated by imposing a financial limit on a candidate's permitted election expenses at constituency level (section 76 of the 1983 Act as amended by section 132 PPER Act), and by defining what is covered by "electoral expenses". The PPER Act introduces new provisions to provide controls on donations to candidates for the purpose of meeting election expenses, breaches of this provision is an illegal practice (section 130 and Schedule 16).[46] The financial limit to election expenses can be varied by the Secretary of State by order to vary the figures to take account of a change in the value of money.[47] The absence of national expenditure by the parties at by-elections results in more constituency spending, which since 1989 has been recognised in higher limits for election expenses in by-elections.[48]

The definition of election expenses has been clarified and expanded by the PPER Act to include any expense incurred by or on behalf of a candidate in respect of the acquisition or use of any property or the provision of any goods, services or facilities for the purpose of a candidate's election. Provision is also made for the calculation of the value of property, services etc. provided free of charge or at a discount (section 134 which inserts new sections 90A, 90B and 90C into the 1983 Act).

---

[40] [1999] 2 Cr. App. Rep. 253.
[41] [1952] 1 All E.R. 697.
[42] Which for all material purposes is the same as s.75 of the 1983 Act.
[43] *Walker v. UNISON* 1995 S.L.T.
[44] 1965 S.L.T. 186 (Scottish Election Court).
[45] Cm 4057 (1998), Chap. 10.
[46] See *ante* para. 10–048.
[47] In 2001 the amount was set at £5,483 plus a capitation fee for the number of entries in the register of electors, this worked out at an average of about £9,000 per candidate.
[48] In 1997 the figure for by-elections was approximately £36,000 per candidate, s.132 of the PPER Act increases this to £100,000 maximum per candidate.

Third party constituency expenditure

10–051 Section 75 of the 1983 Act prohibits unauthorised expenditure,[49] *inter alia*, on account of advertisements or publications "with a view to promoting or procuring the election of a candidate at the parliamentary election in the constituency". The purpose of this section is to ensure equality between candidates by preventing the statutory limits laid down in section 76 being ignored by, for example, supporters of the candidate or pressure groups. Section 75 has also been used to prosecute those who incur expenditure by seeking to discourage voters from voting for particular candidates.[50]

National campaign expenditure[51]

10–052 The PPER Act introduces for the first time controls on campaign expenditure by political parties. It does this by imposing financial limits on the total campaign expenditure permitted by registered political parties "for election purposes"[52] and by defining what is meant by campaign expenditure. It also imposes accounting and administrative responsibilities on the treasurer of a political party in connection with these rules and restrictions.

Schedule 9 provides the total campaign expenditure permitted in a parliamentary general election.[53] The maximum amount a party may spend is based on the number of constituencies contested. An allowance of £30,000 is made for each constituency, up to a maximum in relation to England of £810,000, in relation to Scotland of £120,000 and in relation to Wales of £60,000.[54] Special provisions are made for different totals when the period during which a general election is pending overlaps with an election to the European Parliament or an election to a devolved legislature.

10–053 Campaign expenses includes direct expenditure such as party political broadcasts, advertisements, unsolicited materials addressed to electors, the party manifesto, market research, rallies, transport, etc. (schedule 8) and expenditure on benefits in kind—property, services and facilities (section 73). Campaign expenditure is calculated with reference to "the relevant campaign period" which is defined in Schedule 9.[55] With respect to general elections it is a period of 365 days before the date of the poll.[56] Apportionments are allowed to take account of a party's normal running costs in the campaign period. A Code of Practice to assist in identifying and calculating campaign expenditure is provided by the Electoral Commission.

---

[49] That is expenditure in excess of £500 incurred by anyone other than the candidate, his agent or those authorised by the agent, s.75(1)(c)(ii). The sum was increased from £5 to £500 by s.131 of the PPER Act to comply with the decision of the E.C.H.R. in *Bowman v. United Kingdom* (1998) 26 E.H.R.R. 1.

[50] *D.P.P. v. Luft* [1977] A.C. 962; C. Munro, "Elections and Expenditure" [1976] P.L. 300.

[51] Pt V of the PPER Act.

[52] Which is defined by s.73(4) as "promoting or procuring electoral success for the party at any relevant election". It does not apply to expenses incurred with a view to enhancing a particular candidate as these are covered by the 1983 Act.

[53] It also provides for limits on campaign expenditure for elections to the European and Scottish Parliaments, and the Welsh and Northern Irish Assemblies.

[54] No maximum is provided in relation to Northern Ireland.

[55] Sched. 9 includes details of what is a "relevant period" for elections to the European Parliament, the Scottish Parliament, and the Welsh and Northern Irish Assemblies. It also provides guidance for when there are elections to more than one of these bodies at the same time, or close together.

[56] This part of the Act came into force on February 16, 2001; the Government promised that there would be "transitional limits" if a general election was called before February 2002.

The registered Treasurer of a party has responsibilities similar to that of a candidate's agent to ensure that the rules on national campaign expenditure are obeyed: no campaign expenditure can be incurred (section 75), or payment made in respect of such expenditure (section 76) without his authority. Section 82 requires him within four months of the election, to make a return to the Electoral Commission with details of campaign expenditure[57]; this return will be made available for public inspection. A variety of offences are created in relation to a failure to comply with these sections.

Third party campaign expenditure[58]

10–054   The PPER Act applies restriction to national election expenditure[59] by individuals and organisations other than by registered political parties. These controls have a similar purpose to those found in section 75 of the 1983 Act with respect to constituency expenditure by third parties.[60] This part of the Act applies to "controlled expenditure" by third parties, that is expenses in connection with election materials available to the public at large designed to promote or procure the election of a particular registered party or a particular category of candidate. The controls imposed also apply to expenditure in kind, that is property, goods and services (sections 85–87).

The Act makes different provisions for two types of third party: recognised third parties, and those that are not recognised. To become a recognised third party an individual, a registered company or an unincorporated association has to submit a notification to the Electoral Commission (section 88)[61]; this gives such parties higher limits for controlled expenditure, but increased responsibilities— similar to those imposed on political parties—to account for expenditure to the Commission (section 94 and schedules 10 and 11).[62] Third parties who are not recognised commit an offence if, during the regulated period before an election, they incur controlled expenditure in excess of £10,000 for England, and £5,000 for each of Scotland, Wales and Northern Ireland (section 94).

The Media and elections

10–055   The statutory restrictions on election expenses in individual constituencies do not apply to the publication of any matter relating to the election in newspapers or other periodicals or in broadcasts made by the BBC or any of the other specified broadcasters.[63] Section 93 of the 1983 Act had in effect allowed a candidate who did not wish to take part in a broadcast about a constituency pending a parliamentary or local election to prevent such a broadcast going ahead without his participation.[64] This has been repealed by section 144 of the PPER Act and replaced with a section requiring each broadcasting authority to adopt a code of practice on the broadcasting of local items during an election period. It is an illegal practice to broadcast from outside the United Kingdom in connection

---

[57] If such expenditure exceeds £250,000, there must be a report on the return by a qualified auditor (s.81).

[58] Pt VI PPER Act.

[59] The controls also apply to elections to the European and Scottish Parliaments, and the Welsh and Northern Irish Assemblies.

[60] *ante* para. 10–051.

[61] The Electoral Commission keeps a register of all third party notifications made to it under s.88.

[62] Donations to recognised third parties are controlled by s.95 and sched. 11.

[63] Representation of the People Act 1983, s.75(1)(c)(i), as amended by the Broadcasting Act 1990, 1996. Pts I and III of the 1990 Act, as amended by the 1996 Act, list those licensed to broadcast.

[64] See *McAliskey v. BBC* [1980] N.I. 44; *Marshall v. BBC* [1979] 1 W.L.R. 1071.

with a parliamentary or local election otherwise than as arranged by the BBC or one of the other licensed broadcasters.[65]

There is a statutory duty on the Independent Television Commission (ITC) to **10–056** ensure that news programmes presented by licensed television services are accurate and impartial, and that due impartiality is preserved in political pro- grammes. Rules on party political broadcasts have been drawn up by the relevant broadcasting authority.[66] The BBC accepts similar standards and makes provi- sion for political broadcasts as part of its role as a public service broadcaster, although it has no statutory obligation to do so. At the time of elections in particular parties are sensitive to the possibility of partiality in programmes. The Court of Session in *Scottish National Party v. Scottish Television plc*[67] indicated that in deciding such issues impartiality had to be considered in the light of the service as a whole over a range of programmes and over a period of time. The courts would only interfere with the discretion of the broadcasters if the decision was unlawful.[68] Political parties, candidates and interest groups cannot advertise politically on radio or television, or buy air time for political purposes.[69] It is possible that this ban on political advertising could be regarded as a breach of Article 10(1) of the E.C.H.R., unless it can be justified under Article 10(2).[70] There are no such restrictions on press or poster advertising. Broadcasting authorities allocate free air-time to political parties for party political and election broadcasts.[71] For the majority of broadcasters this is a voluntary undertaking.[72] Up to the 1997 general election the allocation of broadcasting time between the political parties was undertaken by a non-statutory body, the Committee on Party Political Broadcasting,[73] which mediated between the parties and the broad- casters. In the 1997 election all parties which fielded 50 or more candidates were given air-time.[74] The BBC and ITC decided in June 1997 that in future they would deal directly with the political parties and not through the Committee on Party Broadcasting. The broadcasting authorities indicated a desire to reform party political broadcasting; there was particular concern that single issue parties

---

[65] s.92 as amended by the Broadcasting Act 1990.

[66] Broadcasting Act 1990 s.6(i)(b)(c), for radio see s.90(i)(b).

[67] 1997 G.W.D. 20–932, Outer House.

[68] *cf. Huston v. BBC* 1995 S.L.T. 1305 where the BBC in Scotland was barred from transmitting a long interview with the Prime Minister three days before local elections; and *Wilson v. Independent Broadcasting Authority* 1979 S.C. 351 where before the 1979 devolution referendum a series of party political broadcasts, three in favour and one against devolution, were barred.

[69] Broadcasting Act 1990, s.8(2) applies to television advertisements, s.92(2)(a)(i) to radio broad- casts. In *R. v. Radio Authority ex p. Bull* [1997] 2 All E.R. 561, the Court of Appeal held that decision of the Radio Authority to reject advertisements from Amnesty International was not unreasonable since its objects were "mainly political".

[70] *i.e.* the restriction would have to be shown to pursue a legitimate aim which is necessary in a democratic society, *cf. X and the Association of Z v. United Kingdom* a decision of the Commission in 1971, and the decision of the European Court of Human Rights in *Groppera Radio AG v. Switzerland* Series A vol. 173 (1990).

[71] Only those political parties registered under the Political Parties Registration Act 1998, are eligible for, but not entitled to, such broadcasts (s.14).

[72] Only Channels 3, 4, and 5 are required to do so, Broadcasting Act 1990, s.36.

[73] The committee consisted of officials from the broadcasting authorities and representatives of the various parties.

[74] The reasonableness of the allocation criteria was unsuccessfully challenged in *R. v. BBC and Independent Television Commission ex p. Referendum Party* [1997] E.M.L.S. 605, (1997) 9 Admin. L.R. 553.

would field candidates just to gain access to national television.[75] The broadcasters have agreed that in future the threshold for a party election broadcast would be that at least one sixth of all seats had to be contested.[76] The PPER Act s.11 requires broadcasters to consider any views put forward by the Electoral Commission before making any rules or determining a policy with respect to party political broadcasts. Party political broadcasting by any party not registered under the PPER Act is prohibited (section 37).

The ballot

10–057   The Parliamentary and Municipal Elections Act 1872, commonly known as the "Ballot Act," made the vitally important innovation of substituting a secret ballot (by placing a cross on a ballot paper in a polling booth) for open election at the hustings. These provisions are now contained in the Representation of the People Act 1983. Each voter's ballot paper has a number printed on the back, which number is also printed on the counterfoil as it may be necessary in later judicial proceedings to discover whether there has been personation or plural voting; but such strict precautions as are humanly possible are made to ensure that no unauthorised person can ascertain, by a comparison of the ballot paper with the counterfoil, for which candidate a given elector voted.[77]

A description of the candidate, not exceeding six words, is allowed if desired in the nomination paper and on the ballot paper to enable a candidate's party to be shown. The candidate's party emblem may also be included.[78]

The voting system[79]

10–058   The system of voting at parliamentary elections in the United Kingdom is commonly called "first past the post" (F.P.T.P.), whereby voting takes place in single-member constituencies and the candidate with the highest number of votes is declared elected. But:

(i) the successful candidate is often elected with fewer than 50 per cent of the votes cast;

(ii) the representation of the parties in the House of Commons does not accurately reflect their strength among the electorate, the party with most votes usually getting a disproportionably large number of seats, while small parties (*e.g.* the Liberals Democrats) are under-represented[80]; and

(iii) the result of general election usually depends on the results in a small number of marginal constituencies.

---

[75] See the Consultation Paper on the Reform of Party Political Broadcasting, 1998.

[76] For a general election this would be 110 candidates. Special arrangements apply where a broadcaster can separate transmission in England, Scotland and Wales, and a party meets the threshold for one part of Great Britain only. Northern Ireland has separate arrangements.

[77] It is arguable that this procedure is in breach of the requirement of a secret ballot as provided by Protocol 1, Art. 3, E.C.H.R..

[78] In both cases this is only permissable if the party and emblem have been registered with the Electoral Commission.

[79] See Enid Lakeman, *Twelve Democracies: Electoral Systems in the European Community*, (4th ed, 1991).

[80] In the 1997 General Election the Labour Party obtained 44.4% of the votes polled and 64.4% of the seats. The Liberal Democrats obtained 17.2% of the votes and 7.0% of the seats. The figures were similar in the 2001 election.

The British system is also adopted by India, the United States, Canada, and until recently, New Zealand.[81] There are a variety of proportional representation systems in European countries, many of which use a Regional List System (RLS) with multi-member constituencies. Article 3 of the First Protocol of the E.C.H.R. which requires free elections under conditions "which will ensure the free expression of the opinion of the people", does not require any particular voting system. A claim by the Liberal Party that the "first past the post" system used at United Kingdom parliamentary elections was unfair was rejected by the European Commission on Human Rights.[82]

For elections other than to the House of Commons, there are now a variety of **10–059** different voting systems, most of which have been introduced since the 1997 election.[83] Elections to European Parliament are by R.L.S. based on multi-member electoral regions.[84] The parties determine the order of candidates on the list,[85] and each voter has one vote which may be cast for a party list or an independent candidate. Seats are allocated according to a formula which ensures some proportionality between the total votes cast for a party in an electoral region and the seats won.[86] The compilation of party lists for European and other elections which use this method of selection has required the parties to re-examine their selection procedure for candidates. It is unclear whether the adoption of a system of selection that positively discriminates in favour of women is in breach of the Sex Discrimination Act 1975 or the Equal Pay Directive.[87]

Elections to the Scottish Parliament and the Welsh National Assembly are by the Additional Member System (A.M.S.), a combination of F.P.T.P. and R.L.S.[88] The Supplemental Vote system, which allows voters two votes was used for elections for the Mayor of London, while elections to the Greater London Authority was by F.P.T.P. for constituency members and a constituency list using the A.M.S. system.[89] Finally, in Northern Ireland the Single Transferable Vote, which requires multi-member constituencies, is used for elections to the Assembly,[90] the European Parliament and for local government elections. A characteristic of several of these systems is that voters have a choice between parties rather than between candidates, which raises questions as to independence and local

---

[81] In 1996 New Zealand held its first elections under a Mixed Member Proportional (M.M.P.) system. Under this system F.P.T.P. is used for constituency seats, the remainder are settled by the M.M.P. system, which is a variation of the Party List System.

[82] *Liberal Party v. United Kingdom* (1980) 4 E.H.R.R. 106.

[83] Northern Ireland has had the Single Transferable Vote (STV) system for a variety of elections since 1972.

[84] The European Parliamentary Elections Act 1999, for the legislative history of this Act see *ante* para. 9–026. Scotland and Wales each form a single electoral region, with Scotland having eight M.E.P.s and Wales five. England is divided into nine regions having between four and 11 M.E.P.s. Northern Ireland is one region with three M.E.P.s, but using the STV system of voting.

[85] The list is described as "closed" as it cannot be altered by voters.

[86] The d'Hondt formula, which is said to favour larger parties. This formula is also to be used to calculate the additional seats for the Scottish Parliament and the Welsh National Assembly.

[87] Although an industrial tribunal in *Jepson and Dyas-Elliot v. The Labour Party and others* [1996] I.R.L.R. 116 decided that woman only shortlists were in breach of the 1975 Act, there remains doubt as to whether the 1975 Act applies to the selection of Parliamentary candidates. See Howard Davis, "All-Women Shortlists in the Labour Party", [1995] P.L. 207. The 2001 Queen's Speech promised legislation to allow political parties to make positive moves to increase the representation of women in public life.

[88] See *ante* Chap. 5.

[89] Greater London Authority Act 1999

[90] *Ante* Chap. 5.

commitment of elected members who owe their election to their position on the party list.

10–060   It is possible that there could be another type of voting system in the United Kingdom. Further to its 1997 manifesto promise, the Government set up the Jenkins Commission as an independent commission to recommend an alternative voting system for the House of Commons.[91] In its report[92] it reviewed several alternative systems, as well as the variety of voting systems now in existence in the United Kingdom. As an alternative to the F.P.T.P. system it proposed a new variation on proportional representation a: "two-vote mixed system, which can be described as either limited A.M.S. or A.V. Top-up". Under this system each elector would have two votes. One vote would be to elect, by A.V., a M.P. for an individual constituencies; 80 to 85 per cent of M.P.s would be elected in this way. The second vote would be used to vote for either a party or a candidate.[93] For this second vote the United Kingdom would be divided into top-up areas— "preserved" counties and equivalently sized metropolitan districts in England and the regions used for the additional members for the Scottish Parliament and the Welsh Assembly. A referendum may be held to determine whether to accept these proposals, or whether to continue with the F.P.T.F. scheme.

Disputed elections

10–061   The King and Council originally settled election disputes, but as early as the reign of Richard II the Commons began to remonstrate against this practice. James I in the proclamation summoning his first Parliament specifically forbad the choice of bankrupts and outlaws. Sir Francis Goodwin was elected (against his will) for Buckinghamshire, but the Clerk of the Crown refused to receive the return on the ground that Goodwin was an outlaw, and Sir John Fortescue, a Privy Councillor, was elected in his place. The case of *Goodwin v. Fortescue* (1604)[94] followed, the real struggle being in the background between the Commons and the King. The Commons disputed Goodwin's outlawry, and contended that in any event outlawry did not disqualify him. The King and the Commons consented to submit the dispute to the judges, but no such reference took place. Finally, James admitted the right of the Commons to judge disputed election returns.[95] The Commons' privilege was confirmed by the Court of Exchequer Chamber and the House of Lords during the protracted litigation in *Barnardiston v. Soame* (1674–1689).[96]

After *Goodwin v. Fortescue* disputed elections were tried first for a time by Select Committees of the House, then by a committee of the whole House, the decisions tending to be made on party lines, and from 1770 by Select Committees under the provisions of various statutes. Eventually the Parliamentary Elections Act 1868, passed after the very corrupt general election of 1865, handed jurisdiction in disputed elections over to the Court of Commons Pleas, proper safeguards being added to secure to the Commons their privileges. By the Parliamentary

[91] Previous reports on the electoral system include the Royal Commission on Electoral Systems 1910, Cd 5136, and Speaker's Conferences in 1944, Cmd 6534, and 1968, Cmnd 3550.

[92] *Independent Commission on the Voting System*, Cm 4090, 1998.

[93] *i.e.* it would be an open not a closed list system.

[94] 2 St.Tr. 91.

[95] The Commons later claimed the privilege of settling the rights of electors, and this gave rise to the celebrated cases of *Ashby v. White* (1703) 2 Ld. Raym. 938 and *Paty's Case* (1704) 2 Ld. Raym. 1105.

[96] (1674) 6 St.Tr. 1063, 1092; (1689) 6 St.Tr. 1119.

Elections and Corrupt Practices Act 1879 this jurisdiction was, with similar safeguards, committed to two judges of the High Court.

Election court

These provisions are now re-enacted in Part III of the Representation of the   **10–062**
People Act 1983. An election petition[97] may be presented by:

(a) a person who voted or had the right to vote;

(b) a person claiming to have had the right to be elected or returned; or

(c) a person alleging that he was a candidate.[98]

The election court consists, in England, of two judges of the Queen's Bench Division, acting without a jury. They have the powers of the High Court, and may sit in the constituency for which the election was held. Discovery and interrogatories are allowed. If the person elected is found to be disqualified, and if the electors knew the facts on which his disqualification was based, the election court may declare the candidate with the next highest number of votes to have been elected.[99] If the circumstances warrant, an election may simply be held to be void.[1]

Appeal lies on a question of law with the leave of the High Court to the Court of Appeal, whose decision is final, the Commons not being willing that such questions should be decided by the House of Lords.[2] The election court certifies its finding to the Speaker. Section 144 of the 1983 Act provides that the House shall order the certificate and report to be entered in their Journals, and shall give the necessary direction for confirming or altering the return, or for issuing a writ for a new election, as the case may be.[3]

Referendums[4]

The use of a referendum has become a more frequent feature of the British   **10–063**
political system; from 1973–1998 there were eight referendums in the United Kingdom to which the new provisions would have applied had they been in force at the time. The Neil Committee recommended that referendums should be subject to statutory controls, and supervised by an Electoral Commission.[5] The PPER Act does not provide a statutory authority for the calling of a referendum;

---

[97] Such petitions were common in Victorian times, but are rare today. A recent example of a successful petition was in respect of the election for Winchester in 1997. Here the Election Court held that there had been a breach of the Election Rules and declared the election void.

[98] *Cf.* application to the Judicial Committee of the Privy Council for a declaration under the House of Commons Disqualification Act 1975, s.7; *ante*, para. 10–013.

[99] See *Re Parliamentary Election for Bristol South-East* [1964] 2 Q.B. 247.

[1] It is uncertain whether it is possible to seek judicial review of a decision by an Election court *cf.* *R. v. Election Court ex p. Sheppard* [1975] 2 All E.R. 725 and *R. v. Cripps ex p. Muldoon* [1984] Q.B. 68.

[2] Corresponding provisions in the cases of Scotland and Northern Ireland confer jurisdiction on two judges of the Court of Session and the High Court or the Court of Appeal of Northern Ireland.

[3] The Commons have the privilege, however, of deciding whether a person who has been duly elected shall be allowed to sit in the House, *post*, para. 13–017.

[4] Pt VII of the PPER Act.

[5] In 1996, the Naire Commission on the Conduct of Referendums (Home Office) recommended the creation of an independent commission to regulate referendums.

primary legislation will be required on each occasion.[6] The Electoral Commission is to consider the proposed wording of a referendum question and publish a statement on the intelligibility of the question asked (section 104). Part VII and Schedule 13 introduce similar types of regulation with respect to "permitted participants" (section 105) in a referendum campaign as apply to political parties in an election campaign: controls on donations, expenditure, making of returns, etc. It also provides that a permitted participant may apply to the Commission to be designated as an organisation to whom financial assistance is available from the Commission (sections 108–110). This followed the Neil Committee recommendations that there should be core funding for "Yes" and "No" campaigns in each referendum. Section 125 restricts central and local government from publishing or distributing promotional materials in relation to a referendum for 28 days before the date of the poll. Referendum campaign broadcasting is limited to those organisations designated by the Commission under section 108.

---

[6] The only standing statutory authority for the holding of a referendum is found in Sched. 1 of the Northern Ireland Act 1998.

CHAPTER 11

PARLIAMENTARY PROCEDURE[1]

I. THE NATURE OF PARLIAMENTARY PROCEDURE

The functions of Members of Parliament are not only, or indeed primarily, **11–001** legislation (including taxation) but cover the discussion of policy and current affairs, and—especially in the Commons—the supervision of national finance and scrutiny of the administration. This chapter deals with parliamentary procedure generally, and the ordinary legislative process; while the next chapter covers national finance and scrutiny of the administration. The emphasis, for obvious reasons, is on the House of Commons.

Content

The content of parliamentary procedure may be divided into the following **11–002** parts:

1. *Forms of proceedings, e.g.* the various stages in the passing of a Bill the process of debate by motion, question and division; the methods by which the Commons control the administration in supply, questions to Ministers and motions for the adjournment.

2. *Machinery,* including the officers of each House (especially the Speaker of the Commons), committees and "Whips."

3. *Rules of procedure in the strict sense, i.e.* directions which govern the working of the forms of proceedings and the machinery of each House; *e.g.* the rule that a public Bill may be presented without an Order of the House; the rule that the principle of a Bill is decided on the second reading; and the rules regulating the powers and duties of the Speaker in the conduct of debate and the maintenance of order.

4. *Parliamentary conventions, i.e.* rules not enforced by the Chair but by the public opinion of the House; for example, the rule that the Government will reply to reports made by Select Committees which touch on the actions of a government department.

Rules of procedure vary considerably in importance, that is to say, in the extent to which they are essential or useful to the exercise of their functions by each House. At one end of the scale is the Standing Order of the House of Commons that expenditure must be proposed by the Crown, which is of great constitutional

---

[1] See Erskine May, *Parliamentary Practice* (22nd ed., 1997). See also K. Bradshaw and D. Pring, *Parliament and Congress* (1972); Bernard Crick, *The Reform of Parliament* (2nd ed., 1968); J.A.G. Griffith, *Parliamentary Scrutiny of Government Bills* (1974); Walkland and Ryle, *The Commons Today* (1981); Chap. 4, *Parliament in the 1980s* (Philip Norton ed., 1985); P. Riddell *Parliament under Pressure (2000)*; Griffith and Ryle, *Parliament, Functions Practice and Procedure* (2nd. ed. Blackburn and Kenyon ed., 2000). Report of the Hansard Society Commission on Parliamentary Scrutiny, *The Challenge for Parliament* (2001).

importance; at the other end come rules, such as that the "Ayes" divide to the right and the "Noes" to the left, where it does not matter what the rule is so long as there is one.

Historical development

11–003   The forms and rules show traces of their origin in various stages of historical development. So far as the development of the Commons procedure is concerned, Lord Campion (a former Clerk of the House of Commons) suggested the following periods:

   (i) From the establishment of Parliament to the beginning of the Commons Journals, during which period constitutional forms came to be settled (c. 1300–1547).

   (ii) The period of "ancient usage," from the beginning of the Journals to the Restoration (1547–1660).

   (iii) The period of later "parliamentary practice," from the Restoration to the great Reform Act (1660–1832).

   (iv) The period of modern Standing Orders (from 1833 to the present day).

Sources of parliamentary procedure

11–004   The sources of parliamentary procedure may be classified as follows:

   (i) *Practice, i.e.* the unwritten part of procedure;

   (ii) *Standing Orders*; also Sessional Orders and ad hoc resolutions;

   (iii) *Rulings from the Chair, i.e.* by the Speaker or Chairman of Committees;

   (iv) *Acts of Parliament* regulating certain aspects of the procedure of both Houses.

The greater part of the procedure of the House of Commons is unwritten and has to be collected from the Journal[2] (made from the Votes and Proceedings[3]), reports of debates and personal experience. Standing Orders are merely appendant to the unwritten part, which they presuppose.[4] The well-known rules that a Bill is "read" three times, and that certain kinds of amendments may be moved on the second or third reading, are not contained in Standing Orders but are part of unwritten practice. In ascertaining what is the practice of the House reliance is placed on precedents as recorded in the Journals. The practice before 1832 was evolved mainly in order to facilitate and encourage debate.

Standing Orders are passed in the ordinary way by resolution of the House; but it is expressly provided that they shall last beyond the end of the session, otherwise they would be terminated by prorogation. The main purpose of Standing Orders relating to public business is to enable more business to be done by

---

[2] The permanent official record of the proceedings of the House, compiled from the minute books of the Clerks at the table, and published annually.
[3] The daily record of the proceedings of the House.
[4] The Standing Orders referred to here, and elsewhere, are those of December 17, 1998, H.C. 7 (1998–99).

speeding up debate.[5] Sessional Orders are passed for the session only, and ad hoc Orders or resolutions for the particular occasion; the former are often experimental and both are used to regulate the order of business. A Standing Order or a Sessional Order can be set aside by an Order of the same kind, and either can be suspended by an ad hoc Order. An express Order of any kind overrides a rule of practice.

The function of the Speaker or Chairman in giving rulings is mainly interpretative and declaratory, and involves the application of practice and Standing Orders in particular circumstances as they arise. **11–005**

Acts of Parliament modifying parliamentary procedure are few. They are passed in order to bind both Houses, so that one House cannot change the rule without the other. Some of the more important examples are the Exchequer and Audit Departments Act 1866, the Parliamentary Elections Act 1868,[6] the Parliament Acts 1911 and 1949, the Provisional Collection of Taxes Act 1968, the National Audit Act 1983, the Deregulation and Contracting Out Act 1994 and the Human Rights Act 1998. Acts of Parliament, of course, have overriding authority over the Orders of both Houses or either of them.

The House of Lords procedure contains a larger proportion of Standing Orders. Their purpose is rather to declare practice than to accelerate business. About a quarter of the Lords Standing Orders relate to privileges.

The rules relating to private business (*i.e.* private Bills) are mainly contained in a separate set of Standing Orders of each House.

II. PROCEDURE IN THE COMMONS

Order of business

The working arrangements of the House have been altered in recent years in an attempt to make parliament more efficient and more effective.[7] The principle changes[8] have been: an increase in morning sittings[9]; an attempt to reduce sittings after 10.00p.m.[10]; a reduction in Friday sittings to enable M.P.s to return to their constituencies[11]; and the introduction, initially as an experiment, of additional sittings in Westminister Hall on the days when the House is sitting.[12] **11–006**

---

[5] See Ilbert, *Parliament* (3rd ed., Carr), pp. 117–118. *Cf.* Lord Chorley, "Bringing the Legislative Process into Contempt" [1968] P.L. 52, 54; "the caterpillar speed of the legislative process is really one of its outstanding values."

[6] Now the Representation of the People Act 1983, Pt. III.

[7] The 2001 Hansard Society Report *op.cit.* note 1, suggested that recent reforms had made Parliament more efficient, but not more effective (at 1.52).

[8] Implementing recommendations from the Select Committee, *Sittings of the House* H.C. 20 (1991–92), (the Jopling Report), and aspects of the First Report from the Select Committee on Modernisation of the House of Commons, *The Parliamentary Calendar*, H.C. 60, (1998–99).

[9] For several years the House sat on a Wednesday morning at 9.30, and after a short adjournment at 2 p.m., met again at 2.30. This morning sitting was removed as part of the House's experiment with Westminister Hall sittings introduced in 1999, see *post* para. 11–017. As an experiment agreed in 1998, it meets on Thursday from 11.30 a.m. to 7.30 p.m.

[10] Since 1995 there has been much less use of S.O. No. 15, which allows a Minister to move to suspend the "ten o'clock rule" for any business.

[11] Ten Fridays are designated as "constituency Fridays", in addition three are dropped when the House rises on a Thursday for a recess.

[12] The House accepted the proposal for Westminister Hall sittings in May 1999, following a report from the Modernisation Committee, Second Report, *Sittings of the House in Westminister Hall* H.C. 194 (1998–99).

The usual order of business on Monday, Tuesday, Thursday[13] and Wednesday after 2.30p.m. is:

(1) prayers;

(2) business taken immediately after prayers, *e.g.* motions for new writs, and private business;

(3) questions for oral answer, and private notice questions[14];

(4) business taken after questions, *e.g.* ministerial statements, proposals to move the adjournment under S.O. No. 24 (urgency motions), consideration of Lords' amendments, raising matters of privilege;

(5) business taken "at the commencement of public business," *e.g.* presentation (first reading) of public Bills, and government motions regulating the business of the House;

(6) consideration of report of Committee of Standards and Privileges;

(7) public business, *i.e.* mainly "Orders of the Day" (including the stages of public Bills and Committees of the whole House) and notices of motion;

(8) certain business motions by Ministers;

(9) business exempted from the 10-o'clock rule (including Finance, Consolidated Fund, and Appropriation Bills);

(10) presentation of public petition[15];

(11) adjournment motions.

If the House has not previously adjourned, then for ordinary business it sits until half an hour after the motion for the adjournment has been proposed: 10.00pm on Monday, Tuesday and Wednesday, 7.00pm on Thursday and 2.30pm on Friday. For business exempted from the normal adjournment rule it will sit until the conclusion of exempted business. Sittings on Saturday are rare,[16] and on Sunday are confined to emergencies.

Rules of debate

11–007   The rules of debate that have been developed over the years are designed to ensure orderly conduct, the dignity of the House and the right of a minority to be heard. A debate is always on a motion, *e.g.* "that the Bill be read a second time"; and every matter is determined on a question put by the Speaker and resolved by the House in the affirmative or negative. A member who wishes to speak must rise in his place and "catch the Speaker's eye." The House leaves to the Speaker a broad discretion over whom to call in a debate, generally this means calling alternative members from either side of the House. The House agreed in 1998

---

[13] Some items are omitted on Thursdays and Fridays.

[14] See *post*, para. 12–022, Chap. 11

[15] It is an ancient liberty of the citizen to petition Parliament to remedy some grievance; *Chaffers v. Goldsmid* [1894] 1 Q.B. 186, However, few petitions are presented nowadays and they are no longer debated in the House, so that they have lost their importance. Their place may be said to have been taken by members' questions.

[16] The House met on a Saturday during the Falklands conflict, see H.C. Deb., Vol. 21, col. 633 (April 3, 1982).

that the Speaker no longer need observer the former practice whereby Privy Councillors[17] had priority in being called. A Member may only speak once in the House to the same question, except to raise points of order or to correct misrepresentations of fact. All remarks must be addressed to the Chair.[18]

There are rules to ensure relevancy and to avoid repetition. The House has agreed that in certain circumstances the Speaker has a discretion to limit back-bench speakers to a time limit, usually between eight and fifteen minutes (excluding interventions) either for an entire debate or between certain times during a debate.[19] This marks a change in the rules of the House and is designed to maximise the number of Members who may speak in a debate. The House has its own rules on the content of speeches. For example, no reference may be made to legal actions that fall under the House's *sub judice* convention,[20] nor may the name of the Queen be mentioned either disrespectfully or in order to influence the House.[21] No treasonable or seditious words are allowed, nor may a person speak to obstruct business. Members must not be referred to by name, but as "the Hon Member for Camford," etc.[22] nor may any offensive expressions against Members be used or personal charges made. If a Member refuses to withdraw an objectionable remark, he may be suspended. No allusion may be made to a debate of the same session on any question not at the time under discussion. A Member may refer to notes but must not read his speech. It is a rule of the House that a Member who has a relevant[23] pecuniary interest or benefit, whether direct or indirect, in a question must declare his interest if he speaks, and must not vote on it.[24] This rule applies to all proceedings of the House and Select Committees including communications between Members, and with Ministers or civil servants; tabling any written notice such as the asking of questions; Early Day Motions and introducing a "ten-minute rule bill".

Urgency motions

Under Standing Order No. 24 a Member who has given proper notice to the Speaker may, at the commencement of public business, propose in an application lasting not more than three minutes, to move the adjournment of the House on "a specified and important matter that should have urgent consideration." If the Speaker rules that the matter is proper to be discussed under the Standing Order—having regard to the extent to which it concerns the administrative

11–008

[17] Who, as present and former Cabinet Ministers, had an advantage at the expense of back-benchers.

[18] In most assemblies this is an excellent rule as an aid in maintaining order. It is in contrast to the practice in the House of Lords, where it is evidently not needed and peers address the House.

[19] S.O. No. 47.

[20] Resolutions of July 23, 1963 and June 28, 1972.

[21] Disraeli when Prime Minister, with Queen Victoria's approval, obtained the permission of the House in 1876 to use the Queen's name in debate, in order to rebut a statement made in a public speech that the Queen had asked two previous Prime Ministers for the title of Empress of India: Robert Blake, *Disraeli* (1966), p. 563. Following a reference to the views of the Queen in the course of a debate in the Lords on succession to the Crown, the House of Lords Procedure Committee recommended, and the House accepted, that the rule should continue but that there could be exceptions, H.L. 106 (1997–98).

[22] To aid Members the annunciators now display both the constituency and the name of the Member who has the floor.

[23] The test is, if a pecuniary interest might reasonably be thought by others to influence a Member's speech.

[24] Members are also required to register their interests for inclusion in the Registrar of Members' Interests, and to comply with the Code of Conduct which includes a section on the declaration of interests, see *post* para. 13–034.

responsibilities of Ministers and the possibility of the matter being brought before the House in time by other means—and the House gives leave, the motion is usually debated at the commencement of public business next day, but exceptionally at 7 p.m. on the same day. The Speaker does not have to give reasons for his decision. The present content of this Standing Order dates mainly from 1967, when it was changed in an attempt to enable such debates to take place more frequently than had been the case. However in recent sessions applications have been unsuccessful, and there were no such debates from the 1992–93 session to the 2000–2001 session.[25]

Reform

The 2001 Hansard Society Report suggested that a Steering Committee composed of representatives of all parties, should be established to organise the business of the House of Commons and manage the parliamentary timetable.

Suspension of Member[26]

11–009   When a member contumaciously declines to accept a ruling of the Speaker, *e.g.* by refusing to "withdraw" an offensive remark, or is guilty of misbehaviour or flagrantly breaks the rules of the House, the Speaker may be asked to "name" him. The question is then put that the Member be suspended from the service of the House, and if the motion is carried he is suspended on the first occasion until the fifth day, on the second occasion in the same session until the twentieth day, and on a subsequent occasion until further order or until the end of the session. A suspended Member must withdraw from the precincts of the House, and since 1998, will lose his parliamentary salary for the period of suspension.[27]

Divisions

11–010   When the Speaker closes a debate by "putting the question," he first senses the feeling of the House by asking members to say "Aye" or "No," but in any important matter the Members challenge the Speaker's opinion and he orders a division. Electric bells are rung, the lobbies are cleared, and after two minutes the Speaker puts the question again. Unless the division is then "called off" the members now present divide by filing through the two lobbies, their names being checked and the numbers counted by two Members nominated to act as tellers for each lobby. The figures are then read out to the Speaker by the senior teller for the majority.

The quorum of 40 for a division, including the Speaker, was established in 1641. If a division reveals that fewer than that number of Members are present the business under discussion stands adjourned and the House proceeds to the next business.[28]

Limiting and organising debate

11–011   A government may expect its Bills to go through parliament in a reasonable time, but should also expect that legislation to have been properly discussed and

---

[25] The Select committee on Procedure, H.C. 282 (1966–67) thought about five emergency debates each session would be about right.

[26] S.O. Nos. 43, 44, 45.

[27] S.O. No. 45A.

[28] There is no requirement for a quoram for the transaction of the business of the House; the House may not be counted at any time (S.O. No. 41(2)).

where appropriate changed by parliament. To enable these often conflicting aims to be achieved a variety of devises and procedures are available.

Closure[29]

This is a device for bringing to an end a debate or a speech[30] at any time. A member moves "that the question be now put," and if the Speaker or Chairman accepts the motion and it is carried in a division, not fewer than 100 Members voting in its support, further debate on the subject must cease. The Speaker has a discretion to refuse the closure where he considers that the rights of the minority would be infringed, or that the motion is an abuse of the rules of the House. The closure appears to being used less frequently now than in the past.

11–012

Programming of Legislation[31]

There have always been attempts by government and opposition to agree an informal voluntary timetable for the parliamentary stages of a Bill.[32] The benefits of this have often been outweighed by the opposition fear that to do so will remove from it the weapon of delaying legislation. Where voluntary timetabling has not been possible, then the alternative has the use of allocation of time motions. In the 1997–8 session a new procedure was introduced whereby programme motions were agreed for some or all stages of 10 Bills.[33] These motions were moved after the second reading and provided details of the Committee to be used for the Committee stage, the date for the Committee to report[34] and the time for the remaining stages of the Bill.

These details were worked out by agreement between the Whips, but in the light of representations from all sides of the House, including backbenchers. This new procedure is regarded by the Modernisation Committee as a qualified success; the main defect has been inadequate discussion of aspects of some Bills, and the Committee has made proposals to improve the position.[35] A programmed Bill cannot be guillotined in respect of the stages which have been programmed.

11–013

Guillotine

The most extreme of the methods available to a government to curtail debate and ensure the passage of legislation is an "allocation of time" order (or Guillotine). To ensure that the remaining proceedings on a public Bill in the House or Committee are speeded up, a Minister may move either (a) that specified dates and days be allocated to the various stages of the Bill, or (b) that the Committee shall report the Bill to the House by a certain date, leaving the details to the Business Committee of the House or a business sub-committee of

11–014

---

[29] S.O. No. 36, 37.

[30] S.O. No. 29.

[31] The First Report of the Select Committee on Modernisation of the House of Commons, *The Legislative Process*, H.C. 190 (1997–98); the Chairmen's Panel Report H.C. 296 (1997–98).

[32] This is a closed process with details known only to the Whips concerned. From 1994 until 1997, following the Jopling Report, H.C. 20 (1991–92) voluntary timetabling became a regular practice. Its success was probably due to the uncontroversial legislation introduced in this period.

[33] Including the Scotland Bill, the Human Rights Bill and the Crime and Disorder Bill; a total of 15 bills were programmed in the period May 1997 to June 2000.

[34] The committee appoints a sub committee to decide how to allocate the available time to the various clauses of the Bill.

[35] Second Report from the Modernisation Committee, *Programming Legislation and Timing of Votes*, H.C. 589 (1999–2000).

the Committee. An allocation of time order is not usually moved until after the second reading of a Bill, and only when it appears that it is making little progress in Committee. Each guillotine motion is debated for a maximum of three hours, and is nearly always subject to a division.[36] A consequence of a guillotine motion is that when the "guillotine" falls large sections of a Bill may have received little or no scrutiny. Guillotine motions have been used on all types of Bills including those of constitutional importance.[37]

The working methods of the House

11–015   Much of the work of the House clearly is performed in the chamber of the House of Commons, but there are two additions important methods of working: committees, which have a long history in the House; and Westminister Hall sittings which were introduced as an experiment in 1999.

Committees of the Commons[38]

11–016   The Commons have long made use of committees for various purposes. Sometimes a matter was committed to a single Privy Councillor, more often the committee was a Committee of the whole House. The main function of Standing Committees has been to consider and amend public Bills, thus doing what the House could do if it had time. Select Committees do the kind of things that the House as a whole could not easily do. Committees of the Commons may be classified as follows:

1. *Committees of the whole House, i.e.* the House itself sitting with a Chairman instead of the Speaker.[39] This procedure is used for: Bills of "first class constitutional importance",[40] to ensure that all Members have the maximum opportunity to debate and move amendments to such bills; unopposed private members' bills; uncontroversial bills where the committee stage will be short[41]; and where an emergency situation requires the rapid enactment of legislation.[42]

2. *Standing Committees.* Standing Orders provide for the appointment of as many Standing Committees as may be necessary for the consideration of public Bills, and other business committee or referred to a Standing Committee. They consist of 16 to 50 members nominated by the Committee of Selection which is required to have regard to the qualifications of Members, and also to the composition of the House. Their most important function is to consider Bills which, having been read a second time, stand committed to a Standing Committee. It is possible to have a "Special Standing Committees" for the Committee

---

[36] The House accepted, without a division, a guillotine for the Scotland Bill 1998 since it was considered by a Committee of the Whole House.

[37] The Referendums (Scotland and Wales) Bill 1997, and the European Communities (Amendment) Bill 1997 were both guillotined, but they had their committee stage on a Committee of the Whole House. A total of 18 Bills were guillotined in the period May 1997 to June 2000.

[38] For a comparison with the committee system of the United States Congress, see K. Bradshaw and D. Pring, *Parliament and Congress* (1972) Chap. 5, especially pp. 258–262.

[39] The Serjeant-at-Arms places the mace on brackets beneath the table. The Chairman does not sit in the Speaker's chair, but on a chair "at the table" which is ordinarily occupied by the Clerk of the House.

[40] *e.g.,* Northern Ireland (Sentencing) Bill 1998, Scotland Bill 1998, Government of Wales Bill 1998. There is no definition of what this phrase means.

[41] *e.g.,* Landmines Bill 1998, also Consolidation Bills.

[42] *e.g.,* Criminal Justice (Terrorism and Conspiracy) Bill 1998; Parliament was recalled during the summer recess to pass this Bill, which went through all its parliamentary stages in two days.

stage of a Bill.[43] Other examples of Standing Committees are the European Standing Committees, Second Reading Committee, Regional Affairs,[44] and Delegated Legislation.

3. *Select Committees*. These are Committees composed of a number of Members specially named, and appointed from time to time or regularly re-appointed to consider or deal with particular matters. Select Committees have their powers and authority delegated to them by the House of Commons, including the power to send for "persons, papers and records."[45]

There are several types of Select Committee. They include:

(i) Select Committees for considering public Bills (rarely employed), or to make a detailed study of some topic before the preparation of legislation, *e.g.* direct elections to the European Assembly (1976)

(ii) Select Committees on private Bills;

(iii) Sessional Committees re-appointed at the beginning of every session, either under Standing Order or an Order renewed each session, to consider all subjects of a particular nature, or such of them as are referred to it, or to perform other functions of a permanent nature, *e.g.* the Selection Committee, the Standing Orders Committee, the Public Accounts Committee, the Committee on Standards and Privileges, the Select Committee on the Parliamentary Commissioner, Broadcasting, the Liaison Committee, the European Scrutiny Committee, The Deregulation Committee, the Finance and Services Committee and the Select Committee on Procedure.

(iv) Departmental Select Committees established for the first time in 1979. Their main purpose is to scrutinise the administration. The functions of these committees and the Committee of Public Accounts will be examined in the next chapter.

(v) *Ad hoc* Select Committees set up to consider specific matters of concern to the House, *e.g.* Select Committee on Standards in Public Life (1994), Select Committee on Modernisation of the House of Commons (1997).

4. *Joint Committees, i.e.* a Select Committee of the Commons sitting with a Select Committee of the Lords, an equal number being chosen from each House. The Chairman may be a Member of either House. Joint Committees are set up from time to time to deal with non-political questions that equally concern both Houses, *e.g.* since 1973 there has been a Joint Committee on Statutory Instruments which undertakes the technical scrutiny of Statutory Instruments, and some private Bills are dealt with in this way. There is also a joint Standing Committee to consider Consolidation Bills. This Committee reviews the form, drafting and amendment of such legislation, and the practice in preparation of legislation for presentation to Parliament.[46] In 1997 a Joint Committee on Tax

---

[43] S.O. No. 91; see *post* para. 11–026.
[44] A committee on Regional Affairs was established in 1975, but soon fell into disuse. In April 2000 a new committee based on the structure of the European Standing Committee was established. It is designed, in the aftermath of devolution, to provide a forum for M.P.s who sit for English constituencies. It met once in May 2001.
[45] For details see *post* para. 12–030.
[46] S.O. No. 140.

Simplification Bills (S.O. No. 60) was established to consider the committee stage of such Bills. There is also a Joint Standing Committee to consider Statute Law Revision Bills, Human Rights and Bills to give effect to Law Commission proposals. A Joint Committee on the next stage of the reform of the House of Lords had been promised, but now seems unlikely.

Westminster Hall Sittings

11–017   General agreement that there were matters which the House should debate, but did not have time to do so, lead to the experiment of Westminister Hall sittings. This refers to the House sitting in another location, on the same days as the House sits, but not necessarily at the same time.[47] For a trial period, the room in which these sittings take place is arranged as a wide hemicycle, to facilitate the non-confrontational style of debate that it is hoped to encourage. This experiment is seen primarily to provide additional time for private Members to raise matters on adjournment debates, the discussion of select committee reports, and for novel kinds of business to be debated in the House, *e.g.* regional affairs, Law Commission proposals, foreign affairs debates focussed on particular regions of the world.

III. Procedure on Legislation[48]

Introduction

11–018   For some time there has been concern about the way the legislative process works: how legislation is prepared, drafted, passed through Parliament and published; and of the final product—the statute.[49] Parliament and Government have responded to these concerns: the Inland Revenue and H.M. Customs have embarked on programmes to rewrite legislation and one of the early decisions of the new 1997 parliament was to establish a Select Committee on the Modernisation of the House of Commons. The first report of this committee was on the legislative process[50]; other reports connected with this followed,[51] and the House of Commons has implemented most aspects of these reports in an attempt to improve the legislative process. The Standing Orders of the House allow for a variety of different options to be adopted for the passage of legislation, but advantage has not always been taken of this flexibility.

Drafting of Bills

11–019   Nearly all government Bills are drafted by Parliamentary Counsel to the Treasury, a staff of barristers or solicitors in the Treasury whose office was constituted in 1869. Parliamentary Counsel also advise on amendments proposed during the passage of a Bill.

---

[47] It was envisaged that there would be a maximum of six sittings a week, in total about 18 hours. There is a quorum of four for these sittings. Average attendance is between 10 and 12.

[48] Miers and Page, *Legislation* (1990); Bennion, *Statute Law* (1990).

[49] See in particular, *Making The Law*, the Report of the Hansard Society Commission *The Legislative Process*, November 1992. Earlier reports included the Heap Report, *Statute Law Deficiencies* (1970), and the Renton Report *The Preparation of Legislation* Cmnd 6053 (1975). The Hon Dame Mary Arden, "Modernising Legislation", [1998] P.L. 65.

[50] H.C. 190 (1997–98)

[51] Fourth Report, *Conduct in the Chamber* H.C. (1997–98)

To enable better understanding of the content and purpose of proposed legislation, and to encourage pre legislative scrutiny, a recent practice has been for drafts of proposed Bills to be published for public consultation[52] and possible consideration by *ad hoc* select or joint committee or departmental select committee.[53] A further recent move has been to make publically available the Explanatory Notes prepared by Parliamentary Counsel on Bills and their clauses.

Classification of Bills

A project of law during its passage through Parliament is called a Bill, and its subdivisions are called clauses. Bills are classified into three kinds: **11–020**

1. *Public Bills, i.e.* measures affecting the community at large or altering the general law. A public Bill applies by description to all persons subject to the authority of Parliament or to certain classes of such persons. Strictly, all public Bills are introduced by Members in their capacity as members; but in ordinary language those introduced by Ministers are called "government Bills," and those introduced by private (or unofficial) members are called "private Members' Bills." Government Bills are far the most numerous, and are assured of the general support of the government's majority. Little time is allotted to private members' Bills,[54] which must be carefully distinguished from private Bills (*post*).

2. *Private Bills, i.e.* measures dealing with local or personal matters, such as a Bill giving special powers to a local authority or altering a settlement. They apply to particular persons or groups who are named or otherwise identified (*e.g.* by locality). They are promoted by petition by interested persons or bodies outside Parliament and are governed by special procedure under separate Standing Orders.[55]

3. *Hybrid Bills, i.e.* Bills which, although they are introduced as public Bills (mostly by the Government, but occasionally by private members), affect a particular private interest in a manner different from the private interest of other persons or bodies of the same category or class, in such a way that if they were private Bills preliminary notices to persons affected would have to be given under the Standing Orders. They are governed by a special procedure before second reading similar to that on private Bills, but which obviates the necessity of allowing objectors to appear one by one before the House. The classification is difficult in some cases[56]: thus the Bill to nationalise the Bank of England, the London Passenger Transport Bill and the Cable and Wireless Bill were held to be hybrid Bills; but the Bills to nationalise gas, electricity and the coal industry were regarded as public Bills. More recently Bills to provide for the construction of a Channel tunnel rail link and for Cardiff Bay barrage were introduced under the procedure for hybrid Bills.

---

[52] As already happened with the majority of Law Commission legislative proposals. A further reform has been to announce in the Queens' Speech legislative proposals for future parliamentary sessions.

[53] *e.g.* the draft Bill on freedom of information was considered by the Select Committee on Public Administration, the draft Bill on food standards was considered by an *ad hoc* select committee and the Social Security Committee conducted pre-legislative scrutiny on the draft Bill on pension sharing on divorce.

[54] *post*, para. 11–034.

[55] *post*, para. 11–038.

[56] The matter may be referred to the Examiners, two officials appointed by the House of Lords and the Speaker.

11–021   It appears that the Commons can suspend their Standing Orders relating to hybrid Bills, but that the Lords could still classify the Bill as hybrid.

Ordinary procedure on Public Bills[57]

11–022   Most kinds of public Bills may originate either in the Commons or the Lords, but there are certain classes of Bills, such as Money Bills and Bills dealing with the representation of the people, which by parliamentary custom or constitutional convention may originate only in the Commons. A relaxation of the privileges of the House of Commons in 1972 has made it possible for financial Bills to be introduced in the House of Lords.[58] In practice more Bills originate in the Commons than in the Lords, although the latter method is convenient for non-controversial topics that either require little discussion, such as the National Heritage Act 1996 or that require technical discussion on non-party lines, such as the Crown Proceedings Act 1947. Consolidation measures are another type of Bill which may originate in the House of Lords, for example the Justice of the Peace Act 1996. In recent years more controversial legislation such as the Human Rights Act 1998 and the Crime and Disorder Act 1998 were introduced in the House of Lords. Where an Act of Parliament is required urgently, Bills may be introduced concurrently in both Houses for example the Northern Ireland (Temporary Provisions) Act 1972.

Introduction of Bills

11–023   A member, whether a Minister or unofficial member, introduces a Bill by presenting it at the table or by motion for leave to introduce it, in either case after giving notice. The former method is usual, as the latter may lead to a debate.

     The five stages through which a Bill passes in the legislative process in the Houses are: (i) first reading, (ii) second reading, (iii) committee stage, (iv) report (or consideration of amendments) stage, and (v) third reading.

(i) *First reading*

11–024   The Bill is ordinarily presented in "dummy," *i.e.* a sheet of paper on which is the name of the Member, and the title of the Bill. The "first reading" is purely formal. The Clerk at the table reads the title only. The Bill is then deemed to have been read a first time, and is ordered to be printed.[59]

(ii) *Second reading*

11–025   Section 19 of the Human Rights Act 1998[60] requires the Minister in charge of a Bill in either House before the second reading of a Bill to make a statement to the effect that in his view the provisions of the Bill are compatible with the Convention rights, a written statement to this effect must also be published. If such a "statement of compatibility" is not possible, then a statement to this effect must be made and the Minister must explain why the government nevertheless

---

[57] For Money Bills and Financial clauses. see *post*, Chap. 12.

[58] S.O. No. 80.

[59] The Modernisation Committee has suggested that some Bills could be sent to an *ad hoc* First Reading Select Committee after the first reading (H.C. 90 (1997–98)). Departmental Select Committees can look at the implications of a Bill and make a report, see First Report from the Welsh Affairs Committee, H.C. 186 (1995–96) on the implications of the Nursery Education and Grant Maintained Schools Bill 1996, on nursery education in Wales.

[60] See *post*, para. 20–015.

wishes to proceed with the Bill. A negative statement should alert Parliament to the need for particular scrutiny of a Bill.

The member in charge of the Bill moves that it "be now read a second time." The Bill is not actually read, but its main principles are discussed. If no one objects to the Bill, it can be "read" a second time when unopposed business is taken. If it is opposed,[61] it can only come on on one of the days fixed for taking opposed Bills.

A Minister, having given 10 days' notice, may propose that a public Bill be referred to a Second Reading Committee[62] to make a recommendation to the House whether it should or should not be read a second time. If this committee so recommends, the formal question is put to the House without further debate. This procedure, designed to save time, has been little used, other than for Law Commission Bills which stand automatically referred to it, and minor Bills originating in the Lords. It is suitable for Bills which are not "measures involving large questions of policy nor likely to give rise to differences on party lines",[63] and may be used unless at least 20 members object.[64]

(iii) *Committee stage*

The great majority of Bills[65] which pass the second reading will stand committed **11–026** to a particular Standing Committee, unless the House otherwise orders. The other options are: a Committee of the Whole House[66]; splitting the committee stage between a Committee of the Whole House and a Standing Committee[67]; a Joint Committee of the two Houses; an *ad hoc* Select Committee, which at present is only used for the quinquennial Armed Forces Bill; a Special Standing Committee. The latter is able to hold four select committee meetings during the 28 days from the date of the committal of a Bill, and to use up to three morning sittings to take oral evidence from affected outside interests, after which it will reverts to being a "normal" Standing Committee. Despite evidence that this procedure has been successful, it has been little used.[68] A Minister may move a motion that a Consolidation Bill be not committed, and if this is agreed, it will have no committee stage.

The committee stage is the time for discussing details and proposing amendments. The Bill is taken clause by clause, and amendments are moved in the order in which they come in the clause. In the committee stage the procedure is less formal than in the House; a motion need not be seconded, and a member may speak more than once on the same question. When the clauses are finished new

---

[61] In 1772 a Bill was rejected, thrown about and kicked out of the House; Anson, *Law and Custom of the Constitution*, Vol. I (5th ed. 1922, Gwyer), p. 272.

[62] This is a Standing Committee nominated for the consideration of each Bill referred to it.

[63] H.C. Deb. Vol. 251, Col. 1464, December 19, 1994.

[64] It was used for two uncontroversial Bills in 1997: the Birds (Registration Charges) Bill, and the Policemen and Firemen Pensions Bill. Prior to devolution, Bills relating exclusively to Scotland, Wales or Northern Ireland could be referred to the appropriate Grand Committee.

[65] The exceptions are Consolidated Fund and Appropriation Bills (*post* Chap. 12), and tax simplification bills, which stand committed to the Joint Committee on Tax Simplification Bills.

[66] *ante* para. 11–016.

[67] *e.g.* six clauses of the Government of Wales Bill 1998 were taken on the floor of the House, the remainder in a Standing Committee.

[68] See H. J. Beynon [1982] P.L. 193. The Modernisation Committee in its first report (H.C. 190 (1997–98)) recommended procedural changes to encourage greater use of this type of committee, and the Immigration and Asylum Bill 1998 was referred to a special standing committee, the first Bill since 1994 to be so referred.

clauses and postponed clauses are considered. After that the schedules, if any, are taken.

11–027 *Selection of amendments.*[69] In order to save time, Standing Orders give to the Speaker on the report stage, or a Chairman of Committee, the power to select certain new clauses or amendments for discussion. The rest are voted on without debate. A previous announcement is made concerning the selection of amendments.

1–028 (iv) *Report stage.* The Bill as amended in Committee is then "reported" to the House. It may, with certain restrictions, be further amended as in Committee. It is not unusual for the Government to table numerous amendments at this stage, some representing undertakings given in Committee. If voluntary timetabling fails and the Speaker exercises his power of selection of amendments (*ante*), his reason for not "calling" a particular amendment will often be that it has been fully discussed in Committee.[70] When a Bill has been dealt with by a Committee of the Whole House and has not been amended, there is no report stage, it will progress straight to the Third Reading.

11–029 (v) *Third reading.* After the Bill has been considered on report, it is put down for "third reading." If there is a debate on third reading, it is on general principles and only verbal amendments can be moved.[71] The Bill as a whole can be opposed in principle by the same method as at second reading. If the motion "that the Bill be now read a third time" is carried—which it almost certainly will be if it is a government Bill—the Bill is deemed to have passed the House. It is now sent up to the House of Lords, endorsed with the words "*Soit baille aux Seigneurs*" (let it be sent to the Lords).

Procedure in the Lords[72]

11–030 The procedure on legislation in the House of Lords resembles generally the procedure in the Commons, although it has greater flexibility.[73] As soon as possible after the first reading all Public Bills, except Consolidation and Supply Bills, are considered by the Delegated Powers and Deregulation Committee.[74] This committee considers whether any Bill inappropriately delegates legislative power, or whether there is an inappropriate degree of parliamentary scrutiny in respect of the exercise of a delegated power. After the second reading it is possible to refer any bill to a Special Public Bill Committee, however this procedure is virtually limited to Bills originating from the Law Commission. Special Public Bill Committees have 28 days in which to take oral and written evidence on bills before considering them in the usual way.[75] The committee

---

[69] S.O. No. 32.

[70] The criteria for the selection of amendments at Report stage were listed by Mr Speaker King in a memorandum to the Procedure Committee (1966–67) H.C. 539 p. 87.

[71] The Bill may, however, be recommended to a committee to allow the introduction of amendments, this is very rare.

[72] For the procedure under the Parliament Acts see *ante*, para. 8–034.

[73] The Lords debated its procedure on May 10, 2000, H.L.Deb. Col. 1574–1657; a review of its procedure seems likely in the near future.

[74] This committee had its origins in a committee set up in 1992; its terms of reference were expanded and it became an established sessional committee from the beginning of the 1994–95 session. C.M.G. Himsworth "The delegated powers scrutiny committee", [1995] P.L. 34.

[75] Henry Brooke, "Special Public Bill Committees", [1995] P.L. 351.

stage of most Public Bills is taken in a Committee of the Whole House, alternatively they may be committed to a Grand Committee of the House. The main difference is that no divisions can be taken in a Grand Committee and amendments may only be agreed to if there is no dissent.[76] The main legislative role of the Lords is revision, and the majority of amendments are moved by Ministers. An important difference between the two Houses is that no closure or guillotine is available in the House of Lords.

If the Lords propose amendments to a Bill sent up by the Commons, the Bill is endorsed "*A ceste bille avecque des amendemens les Seigneurs sont assentus*" and returned to the Commons for consideration. The Commons may assent to the amendments ("*A ces amendemens les Communes sont assentus*"), or dissent from them, or further amend them ("*Ceste bille est remise aux Seigneurs avecque des raisons*").

Royal Assent

When a Bill has been passed by both Houses, or passed by the Commons **11–031** under the Parliament Acts, it is ready to receive the Royal Assent. The normal procedure is for Royal Assent by notification as provided by the Royal Assent Act 1967.[77]

Carry Over of Bills

Until 1997, the normal requirement for public Bills was that they had to go **11–032** through all their parliamentary stages in a single parliamentary session.[78] Any Bill which failed to do so had to be introduced as for the first time in the next session. Bills introduced late in a session, or which unexpectedly were more complicated or controversial that originally thought, could have their parliamentary stages rushed, and not receive proper scrutiny. In 1997 the House of Commons agreed[79] that where a Bill had not gone through the House in which it originated, and there was agreement through "the usual channels" that a Bill was suitable for carry over, then a specific *ad hoc* motion could be put forward to allow for this.[80] A Government guarantee was given that a Bill would only be carried over to meet the general convenience of the House, and that Special Standing Committees would be used when a Bill was carried over.

Post Legislative Scrutiny

One of the criteria for a reformed legislative system identified by the Moder- **11–033** nisation Committee was the monitoring of legislation that has come into force. To a limited extent this has been done by the departmentally related select committees.[81] The House has accepted that this type of activity could be further encouraged, and that in appropriate cases *ad hoc* Select Committees could be established to look at a particular piece of legislation.

---

[76] From its introduction in 1995 to 1999, 18 Government Bills have had their committee stage in a Grand Committee, few agreed amendments were made on these Bills, see Minuites of Evidence p. 38–49, Second Report of the Modernisation Committee, H.C. 194 (1998–99).

[77] *See ante* para. 8–011

[78] Hybrid and private Bills may be carried over from one session to the next.

[79] Approving the Third Report of the Modernisation Report, H.C. 543 (1997–8). A similar suggestion had been made in 1929 by a Joint Committee *Suspension of Bills in Session*, H.C. 105 (1928–29).

[80] The first Bill to be carried over was the Financial Services and Markets Bill, which was carried over at committee stage.

[81] *e.g.* the Second Report from the National Heritage Committee, *The Future of the BBC*, H.C. 77 (1993–4), which looked at the Broadcasting Act 1990.

Private Members' Bills[82]

11–034   Public Bills may be introduced by private Members. Private Members do not introduce Bills authorising expenditure, because these require a financial resolution with a recommendation from the Crown. However where a Private Members' Bill proposes an incidental charge on the public revenue, and the Bill has Government support, a Minister may move the necessary resolution.[83] Otherwise private members are free as regards subject-matter. There are a number of procedures under which private Members may initiate Bills.

The Ballot[84]

There are always more private Members wishing to introduce Bills than there is Parliamentary time available. At the beginning of each session a Ballot is held and the 20 successful members have priority to introduce a Bill in the time made available.[85] Many of these Members have no particular subject in mind for a Bill and will have suggestions made to them by pressure groups and others. The Government may offer "Whips" Bills to such Members, that is Bills which for some reason the Government does not wish to include in its legislative programme, but would support if put through as a Private Members' Bill.[86]

Ten Minute Rule[87]

A private Member who has not won a place in the ballot can take advantage of the "Ten Minute Rule," whereby motions for leave to introduce Bills may be set down at the commencement of public business on Tuesdays and Wednesdays. Members must give three weeks' notice of such a motion. After the mover has briefly explained the objects of the Bill, another member is allowed to make a short speech in opposition, and the question is then put without further debate. This procedure gives early publicity to controversial measures. Bills under this rule are limited to one a day, and a member is limited to one such notice in a period of 15 sitting days.

Standing Order No. 57

This is the way the majority of Government Bills are presented, and it can be used by private Members.

11–035   The difficulty with Private Members' Bills is to find sufficient time to go through their various parliamentary stages. Private Members' Bills have precedence over Government Bills on 13 Fridays in the session.[88] Members who were successful in the ballot have priority on the first seven of these Fridays and for this reason success in the ballot is the most likely way to success with a Private Members' Bill. To assist members to get Private Members' Bills through their second reading, provided 10 days' notice is given, a sponsoring member can

---

[82] See Peter G. Richards *Private Members Legislation* in *The Commons Today* (Walkland and Ryle eds, 1981 Chap. 6).
[83] S.O. No. 50.
[84] S.O. No. 14.
[85] The Government agreed in 1972 to grant up to £200 towards drafting expenses of members gaining the first 10 places in the ballot. The sum of £200 has never been revised.
[86] In recent years there has been an increase in these types of Bills, which have the best chanch of success.
[87] S.O. No. 23.
[88] S.O. No. 14.

move a motion to refer a Bill to a Second Reading Committee.[89] This can only be done on or after the seventh private members' Friday and one objection can defeat the motion. A major hurdle to a Bill getting its second reading or completing its Report stage, is securing the Closure of the debate. If the debate is still progressing when it is time for the House to adjourn, the Closure has to be successfully moved and this will require 100 Members voting in favour of the motion. The chance of a Private Members' Bill reaching the final stage—or even an advanced stage—by the end of the session (when uncompleted Bills usually expire) is generally remote, unless the Government give it their active support.[90] About 15 Private Members' Bills become Acts each session.[91] Even Bills which fail to become law may have succeeded in drawing attention to a subject and even persuaded the Government to introduce legislation on the matter.

Procedure on Private Bills[92]

Private Bills are initiated not by Members of Parliament within the House, but by petition from persons or bodies ("promoters") outside Parliament. The procedure on private Bills is complicated and governed by a special set of Standing Orders; it is also slow and time consuming. Private Bills were common in the eighteenth and nineteenth centuries in respect of the construction of railways and canals (local Bills), and to provide for divorce, family estates and naturalisation of aliens (personal Bills). In modern times local authorities and statutory undertakers sought private Bills to increase their powers to enable them to better fulfil their functions. Until the 1980's, there had been a decline in private Bills, partly due to the increase in the areas covered by Public General Acts, and because new more convenient statutory procedures were introduced to enable the making of Provisional Orders which in turn were superseded by Special Procedure Orders.[93] A resurgence in private legislation in the 1980's in respect of "works" (railways, bridges, harbours and river barrages), with the consequent increase in pressure on parliamentary time, led to the establishment of a Joint Committee on Private Bill Procedure. This committee made extensive recommendations to effect changes to the way in which works projects should be authorised,[94] were enacted in the Transport and Works Act 1992. This in effect means that, except in highly exceptional circumstances, works projects no longer require a private Bill, but can be authorised by a ministerial order. In consequence there has been a considerable reduction in the number of private Bills coming before Parliament.

11–036

In respect of those private Bills that are still required Standing Orders require that full notice shall be given, so that persons affected may come in and oppose. A private Bill is usually introduced by being presented at the table by the Clerk

11–037

[89] Only one Bill, in 1989, has successfully used this procedure.

[90] See A.P. Herbert, *The Ayes Have it: Independent Members* (1937); P.A. Bromhead, *Private Members' Bills in the British Parliament* (1956). It has been suggested that there should be a steering committee, or that private members' Bills should be given priority according to the amount of support they obtain.

[91] *e.g.* Osteopaths Act 1993, British Nationality (Hong Kong) Act 1997, Public Interest Disclosure Act 1998.

[92] *op. cit.*, May, *Parliamentary Practice*, Part III. This sketch does not apply to Scottish Bills, for which a special procedure was provided by the Private Legislation Procedure (Scotland) Act 1936. Where the subject matter of a private Bill in within the competence of the Scottish Parliament, this will now be the appropriate forum.

[93] Statutory Orders (Special Procedure) Acts 1945, 1965. Special Procedure Orders are now only required where certain categories of land are subject to compulsory acquisition.

[94] H.L. Paper No. 97, H.C. 625 (1987–88).

of the Private Bill Office. It is then deemed to have been read a first time. Intricate questions frequently arise as to the *locus standi* of various parties to appear and be heard before the Select Committee. The second reading is the first opportunity the House has to discuss the general principles of the Bill. The Bill usually passes the second reading unopposed or with directions to the Committee to delete or insert certain provisions. When the Bill has passed the second reading it goes either to the Committee on Unopposed Bills or, if opposed at this stage, to a Select Committee. The Select Committee proceeds to hear counsel and witnesses for and against the objects of the Bill, and if it finds that a sufficient case for legislation has been made out, declares the preamble proved. The clauses are then gone through before the contending parties, evidence is taken and arguments of counsel heard, and amendments, if necessary, are made. The Bill, as amended in Committee, is then reported to the House. After third reading, the Bill is sent to the other House.

11–038   In *Pickin v. British Railways Board*[95] the House of Lords held unanimously that the plaintiff was not entitled to challenge the private Act obtained by the Railways Board on the ground that the House had been deceived by the preamble reciting that plans and a list of persons affected had been duly delivered to the appropriate local authority, so that the Bill went before the Committee on Unopposed Bills.

Although private Bills are by Standing Orders subject to a number of formalities that do not apply to other Bills, when they come before either House they are read the same number of times and treated at each stage in a similar way to public Bills. If passed by both Houses, a private Bill receives the Royal Assent in the same way as a public Bill, except that a different form of words is used: *Soit fait comme il est desire*.

---

[95] [1974] A.C. 765; approving *Edinburgh and Dalkeith Ry v. Wauchope* (1842) 8 Cl. & F. 710, HL; see P. Wallington (1974) 37 M.L.R. 686.

CHAPTER 12

NATIONAL FINANCE AND SCRUTINY OF THE ADMINISTRATION

I. NATIONAL FINANCE[1]

Introduction

Governments require powers of raising and spending money. In the British system the regulation of national finance is governed by rules of financial procedure concerning the relationship between the Crown and the House of Commons. The functions of the Commons are to authorise most types of public expenditure (supply services) and most taxation; and to satisfy itself that the expenditure it approved has been properly spent.

12–001

The Crown and the Commons

Erskine May says:

12–002

"It was a central feature in the historical development of parliamentary influence and power that the Sovereign was obliged to obtain the consent of Parliament ... to the levying of taxes to meet the expenditure of the State. But the role of Parliament in respect of State expenditure and taxation has never been one of initiation: it was for the Sovereign to demand money and for the Commons to respond to the demand."[2] The basis constitutional principle remains that: "the Crown demands money, the Commons grant it, and the Lords assent to the grant."[3]

Five general principles should here be noticed:

12–003

(1) A proposal affecting supply for the public service or a charge on the public revenue must be recommended by a Minister (royal recommendation) ("the Crown demands money"). This common law principle is now in part embodied in Standing Order No. 48 which dates back to 1713. It demonstrates the control which the Government has over expenditure and taxation since it prevents back-bench M.P.'s from proposing additional expenditure or taxation.

(2) A proposal to raise or spend public money must be introduced in the House of Commons ("the Commons grant it"). This is part of the custom of Parliament and one of the privileges of the Commons, asserted by resolutions of 1671 and 1678, confirmed in 1860 and 1910 and implied by the Parliament Act 1911. So in the Queen's Speech on the opening, prorogation or dissolution of Parliament, the Commons are separately

---

[1] Erskine May, *Parliamentary Practice* (22nd ed., 1997), Chaps. 29–33; K. Bradshaw and D. Pring, *Parliament and Congress* (1972); Griffiths and Ryle, *Parliament: Functions, Practice and Procedures* (2nd. ed, R. Blackburn and A. Kenyon eds., 2000) Report of the Hansard Society Commission on Parliamentary Scrutiny, *The Challenge for Parliament* (2001), Chap. 5 and Appendix 6.
[2] May, *op. cit.* p. 733
[3] *loc. cit.*

addressed when estimates or supply are mentioned; and the principle appears in the enacting formulae of the annual Finance and Appropriation Acts.

(3) Charges, whether for the raising[4] or spending of money, must be authorised by legislation originating in the Commons. This rule is subject to statutory modifications.[5]

(4) Charges for the raising or spending of money must first be considered by the Commons in the form of a resolution which, when passed, will authorise the charge to be included in a Bill. Consolidated Fund Bills are brought in upon supply resolutions; finance and other taxing bills are brought in upon Ways and Means resolutions.

(5) The Lords may not *alter* Bills of aids and supplies ("the Lords assent to the grant"), although in theory they may reject them, as any other kind of Bill (subject now to the Parliament Acts). Such Bills include (a) supply to the Crown, becoming a Consolidated Fund Bill, or (b) taxation (Finance Bill). This is similarly a privilege of the Commons, included in the resolutions of 1671 and 1668. Section 6 of the Parliament Act 1911, preserving the Commons' privileges, allows the Commons to choose whether to proceed on the Lords' amendments under the procedure of the Act[6] or under their privileges: in the latter case they may waive their privileges and accept the Lords' amendments.

The annual cycle of finance

12–004   Each financial year, which runs from April 1 to March 31, is treated separately, and money voted for one financial year cannot be applied to a subsequent year. Although, as will be seen, some expenditure and revenue is given permanent statutory authority, most is subject to annual control by Parliament. Since the financial year does not coincide with the parliamentary session, Parliament in any one session will consider provisions relating to more than one financial year. The annual cycle of finance will be considered first with regard to expenditure (supply) and then with regard to revenue (ways and means).

Public expenditure

12–005   Public expenditure may be of two types: supply services or Consolidated Fund services. The bulk of public expenditure is on the supply services which include the armed forces, the civil service and the general requirements of government departments. These services are described as charges paid out of "moneys provided by Parliament" and are subject to the annual control of Parliament under its supply procedure, and require statutory authorisation. Consolidated Fund services are charges on the "public revenue" or "public funds" and permanent Acts give continuing authorisation to pay these services out of the Consolidated Fund or National Loans Fund. This means that Parliament does not have to give annual authorisation for their payment. These services include

---

[4] Art. 4, Bill of Rights 1688 " . . . the levying of money for or to the use of the Crown without grant of Parliament is illegal.": *Att.-Gen. v. Wilts United Dairies* (1921) 37 T.L.R. 884; *Bowles v. Bank of England* [1913] 1 Ch. 57.

[5] Provisional Collection of Taxes Act 1968, *post*, para. 12–014; Finance Act 1972; Contingencies Fund Act 1974.

[6] The definition of "Money Bill" in the Parliament Act 1911 is narrower than that for the purposes of Commons procedure.

payment of interest on the national debt; the Queen's Civil List; the salaries of judges of the superior courts, the Speaker, the Comptroller and Auditor General and the Parliamentary Commissioner for Administration; and payments to meet European Community obligations.[7]

The estimates and other supply information for Parliament[8]

Every autumn government departments prepare estimates of their expenditure **12–006** for the next financial year, based on the policy for each department which has been decided by the responsible Minister with the approval of the Cabinet. The overall Government plans for public spending will have been conduced earlier through the Public Expenditure Survey. The Estimates are submitted to the Treasury,[9] which scrutinises them in the interests of economy within the limits of government policy. In particular it will check that they are within the Government's "cash limits,"[10] which will have been published with the Budget. Cash limits set a limited amount of cash which the Government proposes to spend on certain services during the financial year. The Cabinet, which is the umpire in any dispute between the departments and the Treasury, finally settles the Estimates, which are presented to the Commons in the spring.[11] Since 1991 each government department has also published a Departmental Report on its expenditure plans and the policy objectives they are designed to meet; these contain much of the information formerly included in the Estimates.[12] At the same time the Treasury publishes a document entitled "Public Expenditure Statistical Analysis", which provides, for example tables on trends in public expenditure, central government and local authority expenditure and expenditure analysis. Details of public expenditure plans for several years ahead are published with Chancellor's Budget Report.[13] There is no definition of public expenditure agreed to by Parliament, and the figure given is to some extent an arbitrary total dependent on the definition adopted by the Government. However, whatever precise definition is used, it covers a much wider spectrum of public spending than that found in the annual supply estimates. In particular it will include[14] local authority expenditure,[15] the Consolidated Fund Standing Services, and National Insurance benefits, none of which is subject to the Estimates procedure. The House is aware of the long term context in which public expenditure is planned, but its role is limited to the approval of the annual estimates.

[7] European Community Act, s.2(3).

[8] The Finance Act 1998, s.156 places a statutory obligation on the Treasury to lay before Parliament four documents: a Financial Statement and Budget Report; an Economic and Financial Strategy Report; a Debt Management Report; and a Pre-Budget Report.

[9] *post,* para. 18–07.

[10] Cash limits are not subject to separate parliamentary approval, but they are assimilated in the estimates so that Parliament is aware whether or not an estimate is subject to a cash limit. In 1998–99 of 103 main estimates, 84 were cash limited.

[11] Although the form of the estimates is responsibility of the Treasury as the chief financial department, by established usage important changes in the customary form of the estimates should be first approved by the Committee of Public Accounts and the Treasury Select Committee, acting on behalf of the House.

[12] The justification for expenditure, and tables on long-term capital projects are also included in the Departmental Reports.

[13] A motion to approve the Government's public expenditure plans as outlined in the Budget is submitted to the House immediately after the Finance Bill has been brought in. This is political in content and has no legal effect.

[14] Expenditure from the Contingencies Fund is not included as public expenditure, since no expenditure from it is planned.

[15] The single largest item of non-supply expenditure, usually representing about 25 per cent.

12–007   At present the Estimates only set out the cash sums that it is calculated will be required during the forthcoming financial year to pay for the relevant public services; they do not show the value of assets held or the liabilities outstanding from the previous financial year or those to be spread over future years.[16] The Estimates are divided into "classes" each of which corresponds to a separate programme as laid down in the Government's annual Public Expenditure Survey. Classes are divided into units of appropriation known as "votes", one or two for each department, on which it is theoretically possible for the House to take a separate decision. The Estimates provide the basis for Parliament to authorise specific expenditure by Appropriation Act, and for audit by the Comptroller and Auditor-General.[17] The Estimates have an important role in the system by which the House exercises formal control over Government expenditure, but they are an inadequate basis for debate on the Government's expenditure plans.

The financial information available to the House of Commons has increased in recent years, but it is questionable if the House or its committees, are able to make the best use of this information.

Supply business

12–008   From the earliest days of Parliament the granting of supply was the basis of the power of the Commons over the executive. Gradually this control became formal only. Despite reforms in 1982 the Procedure Committee in 1999 said of the House's power over expenditure that: "if not a constitutional myth, (it is) very close to one."[18]

The House's consideration of the Estimates is divided into two categories: those that are debated on "Estimate Days", and the remainder (the majority) which are formally approved. Three full days are set aside each session for the consideration of such of the estimates as are selected for discussion by the Liaison Committee, which considers bids from individual Select Committees for discussion of the Estimates from its department.[19] In accordance with the constitutional requirement that it is for the Crown to initiate the financial work of the House, it will be for a Minister formally to move the motion on which the debate will take place. Amendments to the motion can only be to reduce and not to increase the total sum demanded, if such an amendment were to be passed it would be tantamount to a vote of no confidence. No estimate has been rejected for over a century. The House is not actually able to influence the Estimates and the Estimates selected by the Liaison Committee for discussion are more often chosen as vehicles for debates on select committee reports, than on the actual

---

[16] This is in the process of changing, with a move to a system of resource or accrual based accounting. The new system is designed "to give a more comprehensive picture of departments' programmes by linking resources consumed with outputs produced as far as possible, by covering all departmental spending, and by inclusion of information on assets and liabilities." Fourth Report of the Treasury and Civil Service Committee, H.C. 212 (1994–95) The first resource bases estimates should be presented for the year 2001–2. Legal provision is made for this change in the Government Resources and Accounts Act 2000; see Hollingsworth and White, "Public finance reform: The Government Resources and Accounts Act 2000", [2001] P.L. 50.

[17] See *post* para. 12–018

[18] Sixth Report, *Procedure for Debate on the Government's Expenditure Plans*, H.C. 295, (1998–99), p. vi.

[19] S.O.No. 54. The timing of the three days is flexible, the only requirement is that they are taken before August 5.

Estimates.[20] At 10.00 p.m. on each Estimate Day a vote is taken on the selected estimates and any proposed amendments.

Under S.O. 55 those estimates not selected for debate on an Estimates Day will **12–009** be dealt with *en block* three times a year under the Supply guillotine, that is a vote will be taken without any prior debate. The deadlines set out in the S.O. for the House to vote on certain estimates ensures that the Government gets the money it needs when it needs it.[21]

In accordance with principle 4 (*supra*), the estimates once approved by the Commons must be embodied in legislation. This is finally provided for in the annual Appropriation Act which authorises the issue of money from the Consolidated Fund and appropriates in detail the application of the amounts voted to the departments. This is usually passed in July or August. However money is usually required by departments before this date. Interim statutes called Consolidated Fund Acts are therefore passed from time to time, providing votes on account to cover expenditure in the period from April 1 to the time when the Appropriation Act will be passed. These Acts also provide for supplementary estimates to cover unforeseen expenditure in the current financial year and even "excess votes" to provide for excess expenditure incurred by a department in the previous financial year. The Appropriation Act, which is itself a final Consolidated Fund Act, deals with the balances of money voted but so far undisposed of, and confirms retrospectively the appropriations made by the Consolidated Fund Acts. Proceedings on Consolidated Fund and Appropriation Bills is formal, that is without debate; if such a Bill is not certified as a "money bill" for the purposes of the Parliament Act 1911,[22] its proceedings through the Lords is also formal. The effect of passing these Acts is to authorise the Treasury to issue money out of the Consolidated Fund to pay for the various public services.

Despite the formal, legal significance of the Appropriation Act, it must be remembered that a great deal of public expenditure falls out-side its terms. Nor does it reflect governmental commitments for the future, so that it has been said that the figures contained in the Act are "in economic terms ... all but meaningless."[23]

The Contingencies Fund[24]

An exception to the rule that Parliament must vote money for a service before **12–010** expenditure is incurred, is found in the Contingencies Fund. Money can be advanced out of this fund on the authority of the Treasury up to a total of two per cent of the previous year's total estimates provisions.[25] This fund can be used to finance urgent expenditure which is in the public interest, but there is no statutory

---

[20] The Procedure Committee in its report, *Resource Accounting and Budgeting* H.C. 438 (1997–98) noted that in the previous five years only two Estimate Days had been devoted to actual departmental estimates or expenditure plans, para. 11. In the same report the Clerk of the House stated that since 1987 only four amendments to reduce Estimates had been put to the House, p. 76.

[21] The Procedure Committee in its report, *Procedure for Debate on the Government's Expenditure Plans* H.C. 295 (1998–99), has proposed that in the light of the information now available to the House and in particular to departmental select committees, the range of motions to be debated on Estimate Days should be widened to allow debate on the long term expenditure plans of a department.

[22] See *ante* para. 8–034.

[23] Daintith. "The Law in Short Term Economic Policy" (1976) 92 L.Q.R. 62, 71.

[24] McEldowney, "The Contingencies Fund and the Parliament Scrutiny of Public Finance" [1988] P.L. 232.

[25] Contingencies Fund Act 1974.

definition of what this may be. The use of this fund is regulated by the Treasury. Any money paid from this fund has to be repaid, and Parliament will be asked to vote the necessary supply to enable this to happen.

The Role of Departmental Select Committees

12–011   As has been seen role of the Commons in Supply procedure is weak, but the constitutional requirement that the Crown must seek the authority of the Commons for Supply gives Parliament the authority to question and to demand information from government. One of the main ways this could be achieved is through the departmental select committees which are able to examine the expenditure, administration and policy of the principal government departments and associated public bodies.[26] However, there is no obligation on these committees to examine expenditure, or to take any action on the departmental estimates that are sent to them. Each committee also receives the relevant annual Departmental Reports which contain details of the performance of each department in the previous year, its future expenditure plans and the precise policy objectives these are designed to meet. The Departmental Reports are more likely to be examined by the departmental select committees than the estimates, and some committees take evidence and make reports on departmental expenditure plans.[27] The most significant examination of expenditure plans is by the Treasury Select Committee.

Public revenue

12–012   The national revenue is not solely derived from taxation. The Exchequer derives a certain revenue from the Crown lands, in respect of which and other hereditary Crown revenues Parliament pays over to the Queen a fixed annual sum called the Civil List. The Government will also raise money by borrowing which need only be approved by the Commons in a general way.[28] In modern times, however, the great bulk of revenue is supplied to the Crown by Parliament for the government of the country. It is the practice to impose some taxes by "permanent Acts" which remain in force until repealed or amended, *e.g.* stamp duties and capital transfer tax, value added tax,[29] and to impose others by annual Acts, which remain in force for one year only. Thus the annual Finance Act sets out the rates of income tax, customs and excise duties.[30] These taxes and duties are known as "charges upon the people." All the national revenue of whatever kind goes into the Bank of England, where it is credited to the Exchequer account and

---

[26] S.O. No. 152, see further *post* para. 12–029.

[27] The Procedure Committee H.C. 295 (1998–99) has proposed that a S.O. should provide that when laid the main estimates and other associated documentation should be automatically referred to the relevant select committee, which would have to report back to the House within a specified time. The increased work imposed on such committee would require additional resources and in particular specialist advisers for the select committees.

[28] The First Report from the Select Committee on Procedure (Finance) (1983) suggested that the House of Commons should concern itself with both the form and amount of public borrowing. (1972–83; H.C. 241); this has not been accepted by any government.

[29] Value Added Tax Act 1994. The Treasury may by order increase (by no more than 25%) or decrease the rate of VAT.

[30] These are also subject to E.C. law; see European Communities Act 1972 (ECA), s.5 which grants a power to the Treasury to use delegated legislation to alter customs duties in furtherance of a Community obligation.

is called the Consolidated Fund.[31] Withdrawals must be authorised by statute,[32] and are subject to control by the Comptroller and Auditor General.[33]

Ways and means business

Taxes which are authorised for one year only,[34] such as the rates of income tax **12–013** and corporation tax, require annual Parliamentary approval for their continuation. This is also the case for an increase in a permanent tax, such as customs and excise duties, the imposition of a new tax or the extension of the incidence of an existing tax. Proposals for the rates of these taxes are contained in the Chancellor of the Exchequer's financial statement of the year, or Budget, which is presented near the beginning of the financial year.[35] A Pre-Budget Report stating the Government's assessment of the economy and outlining the aims of the forth-coming Budget will have been published in the previous autumn to encourage informed debate.[36] In addition to tax rates, the Budget contains a financial review of the previous year, an estimate of probable expenditure for the next year and a statement of the Government's general financial and economic policy.[37] The Budget is considered in some detail by the Treasury Select Committee; the other departmental committees may also do so. The Treasury Committee report on the Budget will be published in time for the second reading of the Finance Bill.

Budget resolutions

Before the Finance Bill which will give effect to Budget changes can be **12–014** brought in, the House must approve the Ways and Means resolutions upon which the Bill will be founded.[38] In the case of the Budget this happens in two stages. Immediately after the Chancellor's speech the necessary detailed budget resolu-tions to allow the continued collection of income and capital transfer tax and for changes in the rates of these taxes or in the rates of any of the permanent taxes or duties, will be introduced. These resolutions will then be provisionally passed by the House. Since there will not at that stage have been an opportunity to debate these resolutions, they will have to be further approved by the House within ten days. This will be in the course of the subsequent four day general debate on all the budget resolutions, at the end of which the House will vote on the resolutions and, if agreed, the Finance Bill will be ordered to be brought in. For more than a century before the case of *Bowles v. Bank of England*[39] it had

---

[31] Established in 1787 by the younger Pitt. Before that date the various taxes were charged arbitrarily on particular sources of revenue. The National Loans Act 1968 established the National Loans Fund and some of the functions and revenues from the Consolidated Fund were transferred to it, in particular all government borrowing transactions go through the National Loans Fund.

[32] Either a Consolidated Fund Act or an Appropriation Act.

[33] See *post* para. 12–018.

[34] Permanent authority for the machinery for collecting these taxes is contained in, for example, Income and Corporation Taxes Act 1970 (as amended) and Taxes Management Act 1970 (as amended).

[35] The timing of the Budget has varied over the years, from 1993–96 it was in the autumn, the new Labour government reverted to the practice adopted prior to 1993 of a spring budget.

[36] This innovation was welcomed by the Treasury Committee. H.C., 647 (1997–98). The Environ-mental Audit Committee has taken evidence on each of the Government's Pre-Budget Reports and on the Budget itself, and issued reports, see, *e.g. The 1999 Budget: Environmental Implications* H.C. 325 (1998–99).

[37] One of the Budget papers is the *Financial Statement and Budget Report*, which is printed as a House of Commons Paper. As well as summarising the Budget tax measures, this contains an analysis of financial strategy and planned developments in the economy.

[38] Rule 4 *ante*. para. 12–003.

[39] [1913] 1 Ch. 57.

been the practice to anticipate the passing of legislation by collecting certain taxes on the authority of the resolutions. In that case Parker J. declared the practice of deducting tax without the authority of an Act of Parliament to be a violation of the Bill of Rights 1688. The decision resulted in immediate legislation[40] to give temporary statutory effect to the proposals contained in the resolutions. The position is now governed by the Provisional Collection of Taxes Act 1968.[41] This Act requires the resolutions to be confirmed by the second reading of the Bill relating to the tax within 25 days of the House approving the resolutions. It also provides that their statutory effect shall continue only until August 5, if passed in the previous March or April, or May 5, if passed in the previous November or December or for four months if passed at any other time. This then gives the Government a deadline for the passage of its Finance Act.

The Finance Bill

12–015   Debates on the second reading of the Finance Bill usually cover a general review of national finance. Amendments may be put forward, but they may not increase the amount or extend the area of incidence of a tax as already authorised in the resolutions.[42] The Committee stage is divided between a committee of the whole House and a standing committee.[43] The Report stage is similar to that for other Bills, and the Third Reading is usually combined with the second day of the Report stage.

The Finance Bill is not usually a "Money Bill" for the purposes of the Parliament Act 1911 since it often includes provisions dealing with subjects other than those enumerated in section 1(2) of the Parliament Act. Therefore, subject to the special privileges of the Commons in relation to finance, it will proceed through the Lords in the usual way. Since the Lords do not seek to amend the Finance Bill it normally passes through all its stages in a single day.

The Royal Assent is given in the form: *La Reine remercie ses bons sujets, accepte leur be'ne'volence et ainsi le veult.*

The Bank of England

12–016   In 1997 the new Labour Chancellor of the Exchequer announced that the Bank of England would in future act independently of Government in the setting of interest rates, and that legislation would be introduced to provide for this. The Bank of England Act 1998 provides for the establishment of a committee of the Bank, the Monetary Policy Committee (MPC), which is to: "maintain price stability, and subject to that to support the economic policies of Her Majesty's Government, including its objectives for growth and employment" (section 11(a),(b)). The Treasury Select Committee has had particular responsibility for holding the MPC to account. This has included taking evidence from members of the MPC and although there is no statutory requirement to do so, it has conducted confirmation hearings for all the members of the MPC.

Securing the legality of public expenditure

12–017   In addition to approving the raising and spending of public money, Parliament must ensure that the sums of public money voted by it, and no more, have been

---

[40] Provisional Collection of Taxes Act 1913.

[41] Which has been amended by subsequent Finance Acts.

[42] It is possible to propose a decrease in a tax, and in 1994 the Government was forced to abandon its proposal to impose additional VAT on domestic fuel.

[43] This standing committee has between 30 to 40 members, compared to other standing committees on Bills which have 15 or 20 members.

spent for the purposes for which they were granted. This scrutiny of the legality of public expenditure is carried out by a Select Committee, the Committee of Public Accounts, which bases its work on reports made by the Comptroller and Auditor General (C. & A.G.). This structure for an external audit of public accounts was established at the end of the nineteenth century,[44] and in substance remained little changed until 1983 when the National Audit Act (NAA) was passed, which helped to ensure that the C. & A.G. was more independent of government.[45]

The Comptroller and Auditor General[46]

The C. & A.G. is an officer of the House of Commons, appointed by the **12–018** Crown on an address by the House of Commons which is moved by the Prime Minister with the agreement of the Chairman of the Public Accounts Committee.[47] His independence of the executive and Parliament is ensured in several ways: his salary is charged on the Consolidated Fund[48]; he holds office during good behaviour, being removable only on an address from both Houses of Parliament[49]; and, subject to any statutory duties, he has complete discretion in the discharge of his functions, subject to the proviso that he takes into account proposals from the Committee of Public Accounts. The C. & A.G. is head of the National Audit Office (N.A.O.), and is responsible for the appointment and remuneration of such staff as he considers necessary.

The C. & A.G., as his title implies, has two main functions. First, as Comptroller, he controls the issue of money from the Consolidated Fund and the National Loans Fund. The Treasury sends an authority to the C. & A.G. requesting the payment of money to government departments. Before directing the Bank of England to pay, the C. & A.G. has to be satisfied that there is statutory authority for the payment and that all statutory requirements have been complied with.

Secondly, as Auditor General, through his staff at the N.A.O., he audits the appropriation accounts[50] of central government departments and various other public bodies, such as Regional Health Authorities and the universities. The extent and nature of this audit was reformed by the NAA. The C. & A.G. has statutory authority first to conduct a finance and regularity audit, that is to ensure that expenditure was made for the purposes authorised by Parliament, and report upon the accounts drawing attention to any irregularity that may have occurred. He is also able to conduct special investigations to examine "the economy, efficiency and effectiveness" of the use of resources to discharge the functions of any of the bodies to which the NAA applies, presenting the results as Value for

---

[44] The Committee of Public Accounts was established in 1861. The Exchequer and Audit Departments Act 1866 created the office of Comptroller and Auditor General.

[45] See Drewry [1983] P.L. 531.

[46] His full title is Comptroller General of the Exchequer and Auditor General of the Public Accounts.

[47] NAA s.1.

[48] Parliamentary and other Pensions and Salaries Act 1976, s.6.

[49] Exchequer and Audit Departments Act 1866.

[50] Until recently these accounts were based on cash sums, that is they recorded the cash to and from departments. A new system of accounting, resource accounting, has been phased in. This system requires account to be taken of all the economic cost of a service or activity, including the use of assets such as vehicles and properties. Department Resource Accounts should replace Appropriation Accounts from 2001–02. The Government Resources and Accounts Act 2000, s.6 gives the C. & A.G. powers to examine resource accounts.

Money (V.F.M.) reports.[51] In conducting V.F.M. inquiries the N.A.O. can not consider the merits of the policy objectives.[52] The question, over which bodies the C. & A.G. should have powers, has proved controversial, and the NAA did not greatly extend his jurisdiction.

12–019   To enable him to carry out his work the C. & A.G. has a statutory right of access to documents in the possession of any of the bodies concerned.[53] The reports from the C. & A.G. to the House of Commons forms the basis of the work of the Committee of Public Accounts.

The Committee of Public Accounts[54]

12–020   This Committee consists of not more than 16 members appointed at the beginning of each session to examine the accounts showing the appropriation of the money granted by Parliament to meet public expenditure and "such other accounts laid before Parliament as the Committee may think fit."[55] By tradition it is chaired by a member of the Opposition and the C. & A.G. attends all its meetings. It can propose to the C. & A.G. that he should conduct a V.F.M. audit into a body supervised by him.[56] In the light of reports by the C. & A.G. the Committee will examine whether Government policy has been carried out efficiently, effectively and economically. In carrying out these investigations it will examine the chief accounting and other senior officers of departments under investigation. It has identified fraud and corruption in the Property Services Agency[57] (the body responsible for building and maintaining government property); the extent of cost and time overruns in Ministry of Defence Major Projects[58] and the need for improvements in the working of the Further Education Funding Council for Wales.[59]

The Committee makes its reports to Parliament, and one day each session is devoted to debating its reports. The importance attached to these reports is shown by the Government undertaking to make a reply to the debate.

An additional function of the Committee is to look at "excess votes"—that is where a department has spent more upon a service in the financial year than the amount granted to it by Parliament. Before Parliament can approve an excess vote, a report will have been made to the Committee by the C. & A.G., which will have to report that it sees no objection to the sums being provided in this way.

---

[51] NAA s.6(1), s.7(1). See for *e.g.* the investigation into the administration of the Pergue Dam project, H.C. 908 (1992–93).

[52] NAA 1983 s.6(2).

[53] NAA s.8. The Pergau Dam affair revealed that the N.A.O. accepted limitations on its access to certain types of papers; see White, Harden and Donnelly, "Audit, accounting officers and accountability: the Pergue Dam affair", [1994] P.L. 526, for a discussion of the various issues raised by this affair.

[54] Flegmann, "The Public Accounts Committee; A Successful Select Committee?" XXXIII Parliamentary Affairs (1980), 166; Sheldon, "Public Sector Auditing and United Kingdom Committee of Public Accounts" LXV The Parliamentarian (1984), 91; *Holding Government to Account: Review of Audit and Accountability for Central Government*, Report by Lord Sharman, (2001).

[55] S.O. No. 148.

[56] The Public Accounts Committee is the only committee that has, in the shape of the N.A.O., a strong supporting bureaucracy.

[57] H.C. 295, (1983–84).

[58] H.C. 101 (1998–99). In this report it stated that the issues raised in the report had been identified by the Committee in many previous reports as far back as 1898.

[59] H.C. 641, (1998–99).

The P.A.C. and the NAO provide permanent oversight of Government expenditure, but the scope and extent of such spending means that it is not possible for them to track all such money. The 2001 Hansard Society Report suggested that each departmental select committees should establish a Finance and Audit subcommittee to consider departmental estimates, V.F.M. audits etc.

II. SCRUTINY OF THE ADMINISTRATION[60]

Party organisation usually ensures that government proposals will be adopted **12–021** by Parliament, and legislation passed to accord with the wishes of the Government. This increases the importance of Parliament's role in the scrutiny of the working of the administration. Parliament is assisted in this role by the law on parliamentary privilege,[61] which enables M.P.'s to criticise and comment freely on matters of public concern, and the rules whereby it is contempt for a witness to refuse to assist Parliament in carrying out this, and its various other functions.[62]

There are a several ways in which the Commons can participate in the scrutiny of the administration. A recent reform, Westminster Hall sittings,[63] is an example of how the House continues to try to reform its procedures so as to better perform this task. How effective Parliament is depends not only on the availability of suitable parliamentary proceedings, but also on the acceptance by Government of the authority and role of Parliament in the constitution.

Questions[64]

The device of parliamentary questions developed slowly in the eighteenth **12–022** century, and became increasingly important after the Reform Act of 1832. In addition to the more traditional purpose of questions, namely to check the activities of the executive, there are several other possible objectives for parliamentary questions:

(i) for backbenchers to raise grievances of constituents;

(ii) to illuminate the differences between the political parties on policy on major issues;

(iii) to enable the Government to disseminate information about particular policy decisions[65];

(iv) to obtain information from the Government. As the Procedure Committee reported, "The relative prominence assumed by the different purposes of parliamentary questions has varied from era to era".[66]

[60] See Adam Tomkins, "A right to mislead Parliament?", (1996) 16 L.S. 63.
[61] *post*, Chap. 13.
[62] *post*, para. 13–022.
[63] *ante* para. 11–017.
[64] See Select Committee on Procedure *Oral Questions* (1989–90) H.C. 379; *Parliamentary Questions* (1990–91) H.C. 178; *Parliamentary Questions* (1992–93) H.C. 687. D.N. Chester and N. Bowring, *Questions in Parliament* (1962); D.N. Chester in *The Commons Today* (S.A. Walkland and M. Ryle eds.), Chap. 8; *Parliamentary Questions* (Franklin and Norton eds., 1996). S.O. Nos. 21, 22.
[65] For example, the question which led to the naming of Anthony Blunt, H.C. Deb., Vol. 973, col. 679–681 (1979–80). The advantage of making announcements by written answer is that no further questions can be asked at that time on the subject matter on the answer.
[66] See H.C. 178 (1990–91) paras. 26–31.

Each year over 50,000 questions are tabled by M.P.'s. It is by asking questions that the private Member comes into his own, for he can put forward the grievances of individual citizens who have suffered at the hands of government departments, thereby reinforcing the convention of ministerial responsibility. It is also a useful tool for Members of the Opposition for, when used skilfully, the asking of questions may be made a source of considerable embarrassment to the Government.

12–023   Questions may be asked and answered orally or in writing. Oral answers are given at question time which lasts for about 55 minutes every sitting day except Friday. Three or four departments are allocated to each day, and the Ministers will answer questions according to a published rota, which means that each Minister will only have to answer oral questions about once every four weeks. The Prime Minister answers questions for thirty minutes on Wednesday. Unless the Speaker gives special leave, written notice of intention to ask a question must be delivered beforehand to the Clerk of the House at the Table.[67] Where an oral answer is required, an asterisk is affixed to the notice. A Member is limited to two oral questions a day but no more than one to any one Minister. Between 15 and 20 oral questions are answered each day, a ballot is used to determine the order in which questions will be asked.[68] There is no limit to the number of questions for written answer which a member may ask on the same day. If there is no asterisk, or the Member is not in the House, or the question is not reached by the time-limit, the Minister concerned has the answer printed in the Official Report. The Member may, however, postpone or withdraw his question. A Member who wishes to receive a written answer on a named day may indicate this by marking the question with the letter "N" and the specified date. Where a Member considers a Minister's reply to an oral question is unsatisfactory, supplementary questions may be asked. Unlike the original question, the Minister will not have advance notice of the supplementary question. "Originally, questions were asked in order to secure an answer," says Jennings[69]; "Today they often serve as pegs on which to hang a more insidious 'supplementary.'"

12–024   Questions addressed to a Minister[70] must relate to:

(i) public affairs with which he is officially connected,

(ii) proceedings pending in Parliament, or

(iii) matters of administration for which he is responsible, that is, which come within the work of his department or a Next Steps Agency,[71] or his official duties or powers.

[67] Private notice questions, which are not subject to the notice requirements for ordinary questions, may be allowed by the Speaker to enable urgent matters of public importance to be asked on the day on which they are raised.
[68] In 1990 the House agreed that only a specified number of oral questions put down would be drawn out of the ballot and printed.
[69] Jennings, op. cit. p. 106.
[70] Questions may be asked of non-official Members relating to Bills, motions or other matters concerned with the business of the House for which they are responsible, e.g. chairmen of certain Select Committees.
[71] See the House of Commons Resolution of March 19, 1997, H.C. Deb. vol. 292, cols. 1046–7. However when a question is on operational, as opposed to policy matters, Ministers will refer it to the Next Steps agency chief executive for reply, the question and letter in reply will be published in the Official Report, see Leopold [1994] P.L. 214.

An admissible question is one that asks for information or action, and not merely raises an interesting topic of the day. A question must relate to a matter within the Government's responsibility, or one that can be made so by legislation or administrative action.

The rules on the need for ministerial or government responsibility are amongst those that have been defined and redefined by the Speaker, and indeed by the House itself. An example is questions to Ministers relating to nationalised industries. For many years the tabling of questions to Ministers on the public corporations set up under various nationalisation Acts was limited on the grounds of constitutional propriety, rather than procedure. More recently because of the political interest in the remaining nationalised industries and the regulators of former nationalised industries, Ministers have been more inclined to exercise their discretion and answer a question rather than refer the Member to the public body concerned. In 1993 the House agreed that in this area, when applying the test of ministerial responsibility, the Table Office should give the benefit of doubt to Members especially when previous Ministerial answers revealed a lack of a regular pattern. A new area of uncertainty as to ministerial responsibility is with respect to the responsibilities of the Secretaries of State for Scotland, Wales and Northern Ireland. The Procedure Committee has recommended that rather than wait for a pattern to emerge from the territorial Secretaries of State, the House should adopt a resolution defining the extent to which questions could be put to these Ministers.[72]

A problem of responsibility also arises with regard to questions to the Prime **12–025** Minister who has few direct departmental responsibilities.[73] To circumvent this problem Members use "open" questions in which they ask for a list of the Prime Minister's official engagements for a certain day. The purpose of this type of question is to ask a topical or unexpected question as a supplementary. Despite criticisms of this procedure, the House has decided that it should continue.[74]

The Speaker is the final authority on the admissibility of questions, and in his decisions he implements the rules of the House on the form and content of questions.[75] For example, opinions must not be asked, and purely legal questions are not allowed, nor may a question refer to any debate that has occurred in either House in the current session. Questions may not be asked that bring the name of the Sovereign or the influence of the Crown directly before Parliament, or that cast reflections on the Sovereign or the Royal Family. The Prime Minister cannot be questioned on the date proposed for the dissolution of Parliament or on relations between himself and the Monarch. Imputations on private character are not permitted, but imputations on official character may be made with certain reservations. Questions may not be put on matters pending in a committee till the report of that committee is issued. A question must be a question: argument or statements of fact are not permitted. Following a recommendation from the

---

[72] Procedure Committee, *The Procedural consequences of Devolution*, H.C. 185 (1998–99). The committee recommended, and the House has agreed, a slight reduction in the time allocated for questions on Scotland, but not for Wales or Northern Ireland as the Ministers concerned had more extensive responsibilities.

[73] Select Committee on Procedure, *Questions to the Prime Minister* (H.C. 320; 1986–87).

[74] Report from the Procedure Committee: Prime Minister's Questions, H.C. 555 (1994–95) .

[75] See Erskine May, *Parliamentary Practice* (22nd ed., 1997) pp. 297–303. In February 2001, the apparent abuse of Question Time by Members of both the Government and Opposition, led the Speaker to remind the House of its purpose, see H.C. Deb. Vol. 341, col. 315, February 14, 2001.

Select Committee on Procedure[76] the House agreed that while the Speaker should have regard to the rules on the form and content of questions, he should not consider himself bound, when interpreting these rules, to disallow a question solely on the ground that it conflicted with any previous individual ruling. Nor is it any longer the case that questions will automatically be disallowed on the grounds that successive administrations have refused to answer questions on that matter.

12–026   No Minister is obliged to answer a question, but the House in 1997 resolved that Ministers should be, "as open as possible with Parliament, refusing to provide information only when disclosure would not be in the public interest, which should be decided in accordance with the relevant statute and the Government's Code of Practice on Access to Government Information."[77] This Code allows Ministers not to make information available where, for example, its disclosure would harm national security or the proper and efficient conduct of the operations of a Government department. The Government has agreed that if a Minister refuses to answer a question on grounds other than "disproportionate cost",[78] then reasons will be given and reference made to the relevant provision of the Code of Practice.[79]

The work required to answer questions is done by the civil servants in the department concerned. Guidance on answering parliamentary questions has been published.[80] This reminds officials of the obligations of Ministers to give as full information as possible about government policies and actions, and not to deceive Parliament or the public. Although the responsibilities of officials are to assist Ministers to fulfil those obligations, the Guidance also notes that Ministers are entitled to expect draft answers that will do full justice to the Government's position. However information should not be omitted merely because it could "lead to embarrassment or administrative inconvenience."

Debates[81]

12–027   There are a variety of occasions when private members in particular and the opposition in general, may use the technique of debate to scrutinise Government activities. The most frequent is the daily motion for adjournment of the House which provides a half-hour at the end of the day. In addition, from 1995 Wednesday morning adjournment debates of a total of five and a half hours were held on the floor of the House; these were transferred to Westminster Hall sittings in 1999,[82] and an extra three hours per week provided for such debates.[83] It is for

---

[76] H.C. 687 (1992–93), which was in fact endorsing a recommendation from the Select Committee on Parliamentary Questions H.C. 393 (1971–72).

[77] Resolution of March 19, 1997, H.C. Deb. Vol. 292, cols. 1046–7. The most recent Code of Practice is that of 1997. For discussion of the issues raised by the requirement of Ministers generally to account to Parliament see: Sir Richard Scott, "Ministerial Accountability," [1996] P.L. 416; Leigh and Lustgarten, "Five Volumes in Search of Accountability: The Scott Report", (1996) 59 M.L.R. 708; Oliver, "Freedom of information and Ministerial accountability," [1998] P.L. 172.

[78] The current figure of £550 for written answers was set in 2000, there is no advisory limit for oral answers. In a session the total annual cost of answering questions is about £4.5 m.

[79] See the Fourth Report from the Select Committee on Public Administration, *Ministerial Accountability and Parliamentary Questions*, H.C. 820 (1997–98). This includes a list of the questions blocked by government departments for the year 1996–97.

[80] See *Guidance to Officials on Drafting Answers to Parliamentary Questions*, H.C. 313, (1995–96).

[81] For the rules on debates see *ante*, para. 11–007.

[82] See *ante* para. 11–017.

[83] It was suggested that this will allow an additional 140 back-bench adjournments debates a year.

private members to choose the subject of and initiate adjournment debates and almost any matter not involving legislation may be discussed.[84] There is usually no division as adjournment is automatic when the time-limit is reached. A weekly ballot is held among those who wish to raise a matter on the daily or Westminster Hall adjournment debates. These debates are particularly valuable to private members who remain unsatisfied with answers to questions to Ministers. A Minister is obliged to attend an adjournment debate and to reply, but the member who has raised the issue cannot question or reply to the Minister's speech.

Each session there are 20 days *Opposition Days*, when the matters to be **12–028** debated can be decided by the Opposition. Seventeen of these are at the disposal of the Leader of the Opposition and three at the disposal of the leader of the second largest opposition party.[85] Examples of subjects debated include the implications of devolution for Westminster, pensions and industrial relations. The Opposition may also choose topics for debate during the five or six days of debate on the Annual Address in reply to the Queen's speech.

There are other occasions for general debates. These may be on a specific motion on for example the budget, foreign affairs or the European Union, or on a more general motion moved by a Minister for the adjournment of the House to enable a debate on foreign affairs or the environment where no decision by the House is required.[86] Debates may not be the best means of inquiring in depth into government administration, but they do enable topics to be aired in public and may result in further action elsewhere.

Select Committees

Parliament uses select committees[87] for a wide variety of purposes including **12–029** scrutinising the administration. We have already considered one such committee, the Committee of Public Accounts. The other committees which chiefly fulfil this function are the Departmental Select Committees established in 1979.[88] Each of these committees, as its name indicates, is concerned with a different government department. From 1997, until 2001 general election, there were the following committees: Agriculture; Culture, Media and Sport; Defence; Education and Employment; Environment Transport and Regional Affairs; Foreign Affairs; Health; Home Affairs; International Development; Northern Ireland Affairs; Science and Technology; Scottish Affairs; Social Security; Trade and Industry; Treasury; Welsh Affairs.[89] The existence of the committees is regulated by

---

[84] Matters for which the Government has no administrative responsibility may not be raised; this will restrict the ability of members to raise matters devolved to Scotland, Wales or Northern Ireland in these debates.

[85] S.O. No. 14.

[86] The Modernisation Committee indicated that one of the purposes of sittings in Westminster Hall was to enable more of this type of general debate, and it has been suggested that Westminster Hall sittings should enable an additional 17 or 18 extra general debates a year.

[87] *ante* para. 11–016.

[88] Following the First Report from the Select Committee on Procedure (1977–78; H.C. 588).

[89] After the 2001 election various departments were reorganised or renamed, and the following committees were established: Environment; Food and Rural Affairs; Culture, Media and Sport; Defence; Education and Skills; Environment, Food and Rural Affairs; Foreign Affairs; Health; Home Affairs; International Development; Northern Ireland Affairs; Science and Technology; Scottish Affairs; Trade and Industry; Transport, Local Government and the Regions; Treasury; Welsh Affairs; Work and Pensions.

standing order[90] and their continuation therefore is not dependent on the Government of the day. Although the selection of Members of the committees is by the Selection Committee (which is composed of private Members) and not by the party whips, it is clear that the composition is determined by the nominations made to the committee by the Whips.[91] This committee has refused to appoint to the select committees anyone with an official position in the political parties. Each committee elects its own chairmen,[92] has a permanent staff of three or four, and may recruit specialist advisers, such as professors and generals, who are paid on a *pro rata* daily basis. Most committees have 11 members and from the 2001 session all will be able to decide whether or not to appoint sub-committees, and decide whether to join with another committee for a particular enquiry.[93] There is also a *Liaison Committee* made up of most of the select committee chairmen, which considers general matters relating to the work of select committees, for example it can help to prevent more than one committee investigating the same subject. It also choices the select committee reports to be debated on three Wednesday mornings each session, and the estimates to be debated on Estimate Days. The Liaison Committee can express the joint views of the various select committees and from time to time makes reports to the House on the Select Committee system. It developed a higher profile in 2000–01, publishing three reports in which it indicated some of the concerns with the working of the select committee system.[94]

The powers of Select Committees

12–030   Each select committee is empowered "to examine the expenditure, administration and policy" of the department with which it is concerned, and also of "associated public bodies."[95] In common with all select committees, each committee has power delegated to it by the House to send for "persons, papers and records." Committees seldom need to rely on their formal powers, most witnesses attend or provide documents following an invitation to do so.[96] In the case of Members of either House, select committees do not have a power to summon, only to issue an invitation.[97] Governments have given repeated undertakings that Ministers will attend and answer questions from select committees. However this

---

[90] S.O. 152.
[91] See First Report, Liaison Committee, H.C. 323–I (1996–7). In July 2001 the House of Commons voted to refuse to accept some of the proposed nominations to select committees. A review of the procedure for nominations, to such committees was promised.
[92] By virtue of informal agreements between the parties a number of chairmen are members of the opposition; account is taken of the balance of the parties in the House in determining this.
[93] S.O. 152.
[94] See: H.C. 300 (1999–2000); H.C. 748 (1999–2000) H.C. 321 (2000–2001).
[95] Which is not defined. It is accepted that it applies to public bodies which exercise authority of their own, and over which Ministers do not have the same direct authority as they have over their own departments.
[96] In 1982 the Energy Select Committee made a formal order to summons Mr Arthur Scargill to attend, and in 1992 John and Kevin Maxwell were ordered to attend the Social Security Select Committee, but refused to answer most questions put to them, H.C. 353 (1991–92). See also: H.C. 421 (1996–97) where an order was made to require a lobbying company to produce papers to the Committee on Standards and Privileges; see H.C. 573 (1997–98) in respect of an order by the Home Affairs Select Committee for the production of a list of names of certain police officers and others who were freemasons.
[97] The House could order a Member to attend a select committee, but by convention one House does not compel the attendance of a member of the other House before its committees. This means that a Minister or former Minister who is elevated to the Lords could not be required to attend a Commons select committee, whereas if he left Parliament he could be so ordered.

does not necessarily mean that Ministers who appear before such committees are fully co-operative.[98] Where named civil servants have been invited or summoned by a select committee, Ministers have on occasion substituted other civil servants,[99] or appeared themselves in place of the named civil servant.[1] Select committees may only request, or order, the production of papers and records relevant to its work from private or public bodies or individuals. The means whereby select committees obtain papers and records from government departments are subject to "historical restrictions of little relevance today".[2] Where documents are in the possession of a government department, a select committee may order the production if they are of a public and official nature and not private or confidential. However if a department is headed by a Secretary of State then only the House by moving a Humble Address to the Queen, can take the formal step of ordering the production of the document.

Civil servants give their evidence or produce documents on behalf of Ministers, and successive Governments have issued published guidance for civil servants appearing before select committees.[3] These guidelines, while reminding officials that they appear before such committees on behalf of their Minister and under their directions, instruct them to be "as helpful as possible", and "as forthcoming as they can in providing information." Information should only be withheld where this is necessary in the public interest which should be decided in accordance with the law and the exemptions set out in the *Code of Practice on Access to Government Information* (1997). Information that may be withheld from select committees includes advice by officials to Ministers, information whose disclosure would harm national security or defence and information supplied to the Government in confidence. Governments have promised that if there was widespread concern in the House with respect to a Minister's refusal to allow the disclosure of information to a select committee, time would be provided for the House to express its view.[4]

Although wilful failure to attend a committee, to produce documents when formally summoned or to alter suppress or destroy a document requested or to refuse to answer questions, could amount to contempt of parliament, this is

12–031

---

[98] See for, *e.g.* the Westland affair in 1985–86, when Mr Leon Brittan refused to answer question from the Defence Select Committee on the leaking of a letter from the Solicitor General to another Minister, H.C. 519 (1985–86); the salmonella in eggs affair in 1988–89 where Mrs Currie initially refused to attend a meeting of the Agriculture Select Committee, when she reluctantly appeared, she refused to answer questions from the committee, H.C. 108 (1988–89).

[99] Or refused officials permission to attend as in the Supergun investigation in 1992, where it transpired that Ministers had prevented officials giving evidence to the Trade and Industry Select Committee, H.C. 86 (1991–92); see Phythian and Little, "Parliament and Arms Sales: Lessons of the Matrix Churchill Affair", (1993) 46 *Parliamentary Affairs* 293.

[1] Something that has been criticised by several select committees, Second Report of the Public Service Committee, H.C. (1995–96) 313, Liaison Committee *ante* note 94.

[2] D. Woodhouse, *Ministers and Parliament: Accountability in Theory and Practice* (1994), p. 189.

[3] These rules have which were know as the Osmotherly Rules have undergone several revisions and have progressively become less restrictive. The current edition, *Departmental Evidence and Response to Select Committees* (1999), is issued by the Cabinet Office.

[4] In 1998 the Foreign Affairs Select Committee successfully asked for the Government's repeated refusal to allow it to see copies of telegrams relating to breaches of the arms embargo to Sierra Leone to be debated, First and Second Special Report, Foreign Affairs Committee, H.C. 760, H.C. 852 (1997–98); H.C. Deb. vol. 315, col. 865–959, July 7, 1998. The motion to (debate on an Opposition Day, to criticise the Government for imposing conditions on the information sought by a Select Committee was defeated, the Government having agreed to provide the committee with a confidential summary of the telegrams.

unlikely to be enforced except in exceptional circumstances.[5] The Joint Committee on Parliamentary Privilege suggested that this type of contempt of Parliament should become a criminal offence, applicable to members and non-members alike.[6] Select committees have indicated that they are unhappy with their lack of formal powers with respect to Members, and the Liaison Committee has recommended that all select committees should have the power to order a Member to attend and give evidence[7]; something Governments continue to oppose.[8]

The work of Departmental Select Committees

12–032   The purpose of the departmental select committees is to assist the House of Commons to play an active role in the criticism and scrutiny of Government and to help enforce the accountability of Ministers to Parliament. In the early years of these committee there were some significant gaps in the fields of government activities covered: there was no committee for Northern Ireland affairs nor was there one for either the Lord Chancellor's or Law Officers' Departments. These gaps were eventually rectified.[9] In addition the Intelligence Services Act 1994, s.10 established a committee of members of both Houses to review the expenditure, administration and policy of the security and intelligence agencies,[10] and in 1997 a new select committee, the Environmental Audit Committee, was established to consider the extent to which the policies and programmes of governments and non-departmental bodies contribute to environmental protection and sustainable development.[11] This committee's work is cross-departmental and it can meet concurrently with other committees, in particular the departmental select committees.

The departmental select committees have a wide discretion as to how they do their work, but broadly speaking they are concerned with monitoring departments by taking evidence, questioning witnesses and making reports upon matters which they think should be investigated. They play an important role in helping to enforce the accountability of Ministers to Parliament. The committees normally meet to hear evidence in public, but meet in private to deliberate.[12] Witnesses before these committees can be questioned more thoroughly than would be possible on the floor of the House, and often by those with expertise in the matter under investigation. Evidence will be obtained not just from those in government, but also from those affected by government decision-making. Often

---

[5] *post* para. 13–020, see Patricia Leopold [1992] P.L. 541.

[6] H.L.Paper 43–I, H.C. 214–I (1998–99), para. 310–311. The legislation establishing the devolved Parliament and Assemblies provides that such actions are criminal offences triable in the courts.

[7] First Report, *The Work of Select Committees*, H.C. 323 (1996–97). At present only the Committee on Standards and Privileges has this power, S.O. No. 149(6), see *post* para. 13–023.

[8] The inability of a select committee to unearth all the available evidence in a matter can be see in a comparison between the report of the Foreign Affairs Select Committee into the Pergau Dam affair (H.C. 271 (1993–94)) and *R. v. Secretary of State for Foreign Affairs ex p. World Development Fund* [1995] 1 W.L.R. 386.

[9] The Northern Ireland Affairs Committee was established in 1994, and in 1991 the terms of reference for the Home Affairs Select Committee was extended to cover the work of the Law Officers, the Scottish Affairs Select Committee was given similar powers with respect to the Lord Advocate's functions.

[10] "A committee of Parliamentarians, but emphatically not a committee of Parliament." para. 90, H.C. 300 (1999–2000). The members are appointed by the Prime Minister in consultation with the Leader of the Opposition, so its independence from government is not as great as that of the departmental select committees.

[11] S.O. No. 152A. See Andrea Ross [1998] P.L. 190.

[12] Leaking of draft reports or the premature disclosure a report is a contempt of Parliament. See *post* para. 13–021.

a select committee report will be as important for the body of evidence it publishes, as its conclusions.[13] The committees attempt to achieve unanimous reports, which can make the report critical of government policy or administration more significant; alternatively there is a risk that a report will be bland. The desire for consensus may prevent committees considering politically controversial matters. Committee reports have been useful in giving the House background facts for particular debates, and so enable members to be better informed; this is assisted by the publication of White Papers by the Government in reply to committee reports. However fewer than ten per cent of the reports produced by select committees are debated[14] and less than a third are referred to in a motion as being relevant to a debate on something else. The proposal to hold debates on select committee reports at Westminster Hall sittings is expected to allow for an additional 36 such reports to be debated each session. Until now the vast majority of reports remained sources of information only.

There have been a variety of reports on the strengths and weakness of the **12–033** Departmental Select Committees.[15] The overall view is that they have made a contribution to strengthening parliamentary scrutiny of Government, but there remains room for further improvement.[16] The Liaison Committee reviewed the operation of the Select Committees in 1999 to explore ways in which they could be made more effective and more independent of Government. It made a series of proposals, which did not meet with an enthusiastic response from the Government.[17] The 2001 Hansard Society Report found that the quality of scrutiny provided by the select committees was variable and unsystematic. It suggested a variety of reforms including: defining their duties and functions more closely; the development of new methods of working; better monitoring of their recommendations; more opportunities for debates and questions on reports from committees and an increase in staffing and resources.[18]

---

[13] For example it was said of the report from the Home Affairs Committee, *Judicial Appointments Procedures*, H.C. 52 (1995–96), that its substantive value lay "almost entirely in the voluminous oral and written evidence from an impressive array of . . . witnesses, rather than in (its generally) bland and uncritical conclusions." Drewry and Oliver Chap. 3 in *The Law and Parliament* (ed. by Oliver and Drewry 1998).

[14] Originally these were debated were on the floor of the House on various Wednesday mornings, but for the 1999–2000 session they were transferred to sittings in Westminster Hall.

[15] *The New Select Committees: a Study of the 1979 Reforms* (Drewery, ed. 2nd. ed, 1989); Giddings, "Select Committees and Parliamentary Scrutiny", (1994) 47 *Parliamentary Affairs* 669; Woodhouse, *Ministers and Parliament* (1994) Chap. 10; Hennessey *The Hidden Wiring*, (1995).

[16] See note 27 *ante* for a proposal from the Procedure Committee.

[17] H.C. 300 (1999–2000), Government response Cm. 4737.

[18] *op. cit.*, see Chap. 3 and Appendix 5 of the Report.

CHAPTER 13

PARLIAMENTARY PRIVILEGE[1]

The nature of parliamentary privilege

13–001   Privilege, notably freedom from arrest, was originally part of the King's peace. It ensured the attendance of Members of the Council, judicial and other public officers, and Members of the royal household. From the reign of Henry VIII the Commons as well as the Lords have been left to enforce their own privileges.

Each House exercises certain powers and privileges which are regarded as essential to the dignity and proper functioning of Parliament. The Members also have certain privileges, although these exist for the benefit of the House and not for the personal benefit of the Members. "As every Court of justice hath laws and customs for its direction," says Coke, "so the High Court of Parliament *suis propriis legibus et consuetudinibus subsistit.* "[2] Erskine May defines parliamentary privilege as "the sum of the peculiar rights enjoyed by each House collectively as a constituent part of the High Court of Parliament,[3] and by Members of each House individually without which they could not discharge their functions, and which exceed those possessed by other bodies or individuals.[4] Thus privilege, though part of the law of the land, is to a certain extent an exemption from the general law."[5]

13–002   Privilege is part of "the law and custom of Parliament"—to be collected, says Coke, "out of the rolls of Parliament and other records, and by precedents and continued experience." Some of it has the authority of statute, notably the provision of the Bill of Rights 1688 relating to freedom of speech and debates or proceedings in Parliament. A Bill that concerns the privileges of either House should commence in the House to which it relates. Neither House can create new privileges except by statute.[6]

Parliamentary privilege consists of the rights and immunities which Parliament, its Members and officers possess to enable them to carry out their parliamentary functions. Over the years some privileges have modified to reflect wider political and social changes.[7] There is a need to keep privileges under review to ensure that they are effective and remain necessary for the proper functioning of Parliament. A general review of the privileges of the Commons was carried out

---

[1] See Erskine May, *Parliamentary Practice* (22nd ed., 1997). See also Anson, *Law and Custom of the Constitution*, Vol. I (5th ed., Gwyer), pp. 153–189, 242–247; Wittke, *Parliamentary Privilege* Holdsworth, *History of English Law* 1923–64, Vol. VI, pp. 92–100; Viscount Kilmuir, *The Law of Parliamentary Privilege* (Athlone Press, 1959).

[2] 4 Inst. 15.

[3] The House of Lords is a court of record, the House of Commons probably not.

[4] The power to commit for contempt, however, is not essential to the discharge of its functions; see *post*, para, 13–020.

[5] *op. cit.* p. 65.

[6] See, *e.g.* Parliamentary Commissioner Act 1967, s.10(5); Defamation Act 1996, s.13.

[7] *e.g.* the decision in 1971 by the Commons to waive its privilege in respect of the publication of its debates and proceedings, and the transfer in 1868 of election disputes from the Commons to the courts, *ante*, para. 10–061.

in 1967.[8] In 1997, a Joint Committee of both Houses was established to review privilege in both Houses; this committee reported in 1999.[9]

The relationship between the courts and Parliament

"After three and a half centuries, the boundary between the competence of the **13–003** law courts and the jurisdiction of either House in matters of privilege is still not entirely determined."[10] Although true, there is today a large measure of agreement between Parliament and the courts as to the areas where Parliament reigns supreme. By the nineteenth century Parliament accepted that the law of Parliament was part of the general law and its limits could be determined by the courts; the courts in turn accepted that there was a sphere in which the jurisdiction of the House of Commons was absolute and exclusive.[11] As Lord Simon of Glaisdale stated: " . . . for many years Parliament and the courts have each been astute to respect the sphere of action and the privileges of the other."[12] Cases to be discussed in this chapter illustrate how the boundary between the jurisdiction of the courts and Parliament has been drawn, and where the problem areas remain.

A consideration particularly to the fore in the light of the Human Rights Act 1998, is the right of citizens to have access to the courts. Two decisions, both by the Judicial Committee of the Privy Council, illustrate an interpretation of privilege which could result in a breach of the European Convention on Human Rights. In *Re Parliamentary Privilege Act* 1770[13] the Judicial Committee advised that the Commons would not be regarded as being in breach of this statute if it treated the issue of a writ of libel in respect of a proceeding in Parliament as a breach of privilege.[14] In the opinion of the Joint Committee the possibility of the exercise of Parliament's penal jurisdiction in these circumstances could be in breach of Article 6(1) of the E.C.H.R, and it recommended that this should be altered.[15] In *Prebble v. Television New Zealand*[16] the Judicial Committee advised that where an action could only be defended by citing proceedings in Parliament in such a way as to question those proceedings, then the case would have to be stayed. In this case the Judicial Committee decided that the need to ensure that the legislature could exercise its powers freely on behalf of its electors prevailed over the both the need to protect freedom of speech generally and the interests of

---

[8] Select Committee on Parliamentary Privilege (1967–68) H.C. 34. Very few of recommendations made by it, or in subsequent reports by the Committee of Privileges, have been implemented.

[9] Joint Committee on Parliamentary Privilege (1998–99) H.L. 43, H.C. 214, hereafter referred to as the Joint Committee. See P. M. Leopold [1999] P.L. p. 604–616.

[10] Erskine May, *op. cit.* p. 153, and see generally Chap. 11, which includes an account of the historical background to this conflict. Two pairs of cases are particularly important—*Ashby v. White*, (1703–1704) 2 Ld.Raym.938; 3 Ld.Raym.320; 14 St.Tr. 695, and *Paty's Case* (1704) 2 Ld.Raym. 1105, 1113; 14 St.Tr. 849, at the beginning of the eighteenth century; and *Stockdale v. Hansard*, (1839) 9 Ad. & E.1, and the *Case of the Sheriff of Middlesex*, (1840) 11 Ad. & E. 273, in the first half of the nineteenth century.

[11] Erskine May, *op. cit.* p. 160.

[12] *Pickin v. British Railways Board* [1974] A.C. 765, at p. 799.

[13] [1958] A.C. 331. The House of Commons consulted the Privy Council on the meaning of the 1770 Act, which had been passed at a time when court proceedings unconnected with proceedings in Parliament, were often delayed by members claiming immunity. The 1770 Act was intended to prevent this.

[14] For the dissenting opinion of Lord Denning, not published at the time, see the annex to G. F. Lock, "Parliamentary Privilege and the courts: the Avoidance of Conflict" [1985] P.L.67.

[15] It would be possible, in appropriate circumstances, for a court to decline jurisdiction to hear an action, *e.g.* if it concerned proceedings in Parliament, see *post* para. 13–006.

[16] [1995] 1 A.C. 321, see *post* para. 13–015.

justice in ensuring that all relevant evidence was available to the courts. This decision resulted in the enactment of section 13 of the Defamation Act 1996, which will not necessarily prevent a breach of Article 6.[17]

I. The Privileges of the Commons

13–004   The privileges of the Commons have been described as "the sum of the fundamental rights of the House and of its individual Memberse as against the prerogatives of the Crown, the authority of the ordinary courts of law and the special rights of the House of Lords."[18] Some are available against the Crown, some against the House of Lords, and others against the citizen. They are much more important at the present day than the privileges of the Lords owing to the predominant position attained by the Commons, and there have been few disputes relating to the Lords' privileges (except in relation to the Commons) in modern times.

At the opening of a new Parliament the Speaker claims in the name and on behalf of the Commons their "ancient and undoubted" privileges, in particular to:

(i) freedom of speech in debate;

(ii) freedom from arrest;

(iii) access of the Commons to the Crown through the Speaker[19]; and

(iv) that the Crown will place the best construction on the deliberations of the Commons. (This last is not now important.)

The Lord Chancellor, on behalf of the Sovereign, declares that they are "most readily granted and confirmed." Additional privileges not specifically claimed by the Speaker are:

(i) the right of the House to regulate its own composition;

(ii) the right to take exclusive cognisance of matters arising within the House;

(iii) the right to punish Members and strangers for breach of privilege and contempt; and

(iv) the right to control finance and initiate financial legislation.[20]

1. Freedom of speech and debate[21]
13–005   Freedom of speech and debate is the essential attribute of every free legislature, and may be regarded as inherent in the constitution of Parliament. By the

[17] See *post* para. 13–015.
[18] Redlich and Ilbert, *Procedure of the House of Commons*, Vol. I, p. 46.
[19] Privy Councillors have a customary right of individual access, but modern convention requires that the Sovereign should take political advice from Ministers only.
[20] See *ante*, para. 12–003.
[21] See David R. Mummery "The Privilege of Freedom of Speech in Parliament" [1978] 94 L.Q.R. 276; Patricia M. Leopold "Freedom of Speech in Parliament—its Misuse and Proposals for Reform," [1981] P.L. 30; "The Application of the Civil and Criminal Law to Members of Parliament and Parliamentary Proceedings", Chap. V in *The Law and Parliament* (Dawn Oliver and Gavin Drewery eds, 1998).

end of the fifteenth century the Commons had an (undefined) right to freedom of speech, but only as a matter of tradition and not as of right.[22] From the beginning of Elizabeth I's reign freedom of speech has been regularly claimed as a right,[23] although the monarch did not always respect it. In *R. v. Eliot, Hollis and Valentine*[24] three Members were imprisoned and fined by the Court of King's Bench for "seditious words" spoken in the House. The Houses in 1641 and 1667 passed resolutions against this judgment, and it was reversed by the Lords on a writ of error in 1668. After this case no legal proceedings were ever taken by the Crown for words spoken in the House. The Bill of Rights (1688) declares that "the freedom of speech and debates or proceedings in Parliament ought not to be impeached or questioned in any Court or place out of Parliament" (Article 9). The primary purpose of Article 9 was to allow the Commons to initiate business on its own and to protect its Members from legal action by the Crown. The effect of this today is that Members[25] enjoy complete civil and criminal immunity[26] in respect of things said by them in the course of proceedings in Parliament.[27] A citizen who regards himself as having been defamed will have no legal remedy, nor can someone who appears to say something which could be a contravention of the criminal law, be prosecuted.[28] However, Members are subject to the Houses' own internal rules of conduct and rules of order in debate,[29] breach of which can be punished by the House itself.[30]

Proceedings in Parliament

What is said or done by a Member is absolutely privileged provided it is part of a debate or "proceeding in Parliament." What this phrase means has not been comprehensively defined either by Parliament[31] or the courts. It is reasonably clear that certain activities are covered by this phrase including: speaking in a debate, voting, giving notice of a motion, presenting petitions or committee reports, taking part in committees nominated or appointed by either House, asking parliamentary questions.[32] It also includes actions taken by officers of the House in pursuance of its orders.[33] In *Rost v. Edwards*, Popplewell J. held that the Register of Members' Interests and related practice and procedure was not a

13–006

---

[22] Cases such as *Haxey's case* (397) Rot. Parl., iii, 434, and *Strode's Case* (1513) and the subsequent Strode's Act give some indication of the beginning of a privilege of freedom of speech in debate. See Erskine May, *op. cit* pp. 69–72; Taswell-Langmead, *Constitutional History* (11th ed. Plucknett), pp. 174–175, 195, 247–249, 377–378.

[23] J. E. Neale, "The Commons' Privilege of Free Speech in Parliament", in *Tudor Studies* (ed. Selton-Watson, 1924).

[24] (1629) 3 St. Tr. 294. The members were also charged with an assault on the Speaker.

[25] It also applies to anyone who takes part in proceedings in Parliament for, *e.g.* an officer of the House or a witness.

[26] The immunity is absolute, it is not destroyed by malice or fraudulent purpose.

[27] *Wason v. Walter* (1868) L.R. 4 Q.B. 73; *Dillon v. Balfour* (1887) 20 L.R.Ir. 600.

[28] The Duncan Sandys case concerning the Official Secrets Act (1938–39; H.C. 101).

[29] For *example*, the *sub judice* rule, see P. M. Leopold Chap. 5 in *Legal Structures, Boundary Issues Between Legal Categories*, (Richard Buckley ed., 1996). There is also a Code of Conduct established to assist Members in the discharge of their obligations to the House, see *post*, para. 13–032. A variety of types of misuse of free speech may be regarded as contempt of Parliament.

[30] *Post*, para. 13–020.

[31] s.13(4) of the Defamation Act 1996 contains a partial definition of proceedings in Parliament for the specific purposes of that section.

[32] See Erskine May, *op. cit.* pp. 95–98.

[33] *Bradlaugh v. Gossett* (1884) 12 Q.B.D. 271.

proceeding in Parliament.[34] However, Lord Woolfe M.R. in *Hamilton v. Al Fayed*, decided that the inauguration, and subsequent inquiries and reports by the Parliamentary Commissioner for Standards (PCS) and the Committee on Standards and Privileges as well as the resolutions of the House, amounted individually and collectively to proceedings in Parliament.[35] What is unclear is at what point a complaint to the PCS becomes a proceeding in Parliament: when it is made or when it is taken up for investigation by the PCS; the latter is clearly the better view.

The House of Commons resolved in the *Strauss* case in 1958 (contrary to the recommendation of the Committee of Privileges[36]) that a letter from a Member to a Minister was not a proceeding in Parliament. Although this could be regarded as anomalous, since a member's question to a Minister on the same matter would be a proceeding in Parliament, the Joint Committee did not recommend a change in the law partly because that there was little evidence that the decision had caused problems.[37] Letters to and from Members, Ministers and constituents will be protected by qualified privilege in respect of an action for defamation, provided there is a common interest between the parties and an absence of malice.[38]

Proceedings, precincts and criminal acts

13–007   Erskine May says that " . . . not everything that is said or done within the precincts forms part of proceedings in Parliament."[39] There are dicta in *Burdett v. Abbot*[40] and *Bradlaugh v. Gossett*[41] to the effect that privilege does not cover crimes or breaches of the peace committed within the House. The answer may depend on whether the act would be regarded as part of the proceedings of the House.[42] Erskine May suggests that it would be "hard to show how a criminal act committed by a Member . . . could form part of the proceedings of the House."[43] The Select Committee on the Official Secrets Act suggested that a member who disclosed secret information in the course of a casual conversation in the House was not doing so in the course of proceedings in Parliament.[44] In 1987 the Committee of Privileges was satisfied that private arrangements by a member to

---

[34] [1990] 2 Q.B. 460. The Joint Committee said it would not be appropriate for it to venture a view on the correctness of this decision, but suggested that if it was correct the law should be changed and legislation introduced to provide that the keeping of registers of the interests of members and others and the registers themselves were proceedings in Parliament.

[35] [1999] 3 All E.R. 317 at p. 330; [2001] A.C. 395.

[36] H.C. 305 (1956–57).

[37] Earlier reports, H.C. 34 (1966–67), H.C. 417 (1976–77), had suggested that legislation should be introduced to define proceedings in Parliament so as to cover such letters.

[38] *R. v. Rule* [1937] 2 K.B. 375 (letter from constituent to M.P. about conduct of police officer and magistrate); *Beach v. Freeson* [1972] 1 Q.B. 14 (letter from M.P. to Lord Chancellor and the Law Society); see Gatley, *Libel and Slander*, (9th ed, 1998) Chap. 14.

[39] *op. cit.* p. 98. Conversely parliamentary business conducted outside the precincts, such as select committee hearings, would amount to a proceeding in Parliament.

[40] (1811) 14 East 1.

[41] *op. cit.* note 33.

[42] Stephen J. suggested in *Bradlaugh v. Gossett op. cit.* that the accused in *R. v. Elliott, Hollis and Valentine* (1629) 3 St. Tr. 284, might have been properly charged in a separate indictment with assaulting the Speaker in the House.

[43] *op. cit.* p. 99.

[44] H.C. 101 (1938–39), and see *Coffin v. Coffin* (1808) 4 Mass. 1.

show a film about the Zircon defence project in a room within the precincts of the House would not be a proceeding in Parliament.[45]

A statutory definition

It may have been reasonably clear in 1688 what amounted to proceedings in Parliament, but developments in Parliament's methods of procedure and regulation have given rise to uncertainty. Several committees have proposed definitions, the latest is that from the Joint Committee, whose proposal is similar to that found in section 13(5) of the Defamation Act 1996, which is modeled on the Parliamentary Privileges Act 1987 (Australia). It also suggested that "court or place out of Parliament" should be defined, again in line with the Australian statute, to make it clear that the embargo on questioning proceedings in Parliament applied to courts and similar bodies and not elsewhere.

13–008

Bribery and Article 9 of the Bill of Rights 1688

It is a contempt of Parliament, punishable by Parliament to bribe a Member of either House and for a Member to accept such a bribe. However it is probably the case that the Prevention of Corruption Acts 1889–1916 do not apply to Members of Parliament in their capacity as such[46] and although it is possible that the common law offence of misuse of public office does apply to M.P.s this has yet to be determined by an appellate court.[47] The Salmon Report[48] and more recently the Nolan Report[49] recommended a clarification of the law. Any change in the law to bring the parliamentary activities of Members of either House within the law on bribery[50] would in certain circumstances have implications for parliamentary privilege. For example a court might have to decide whether a Member's action in respect of his parliamentary duties was corrupt, and either party in the case could seek to use parliamentary proceedings as evidence. Both these activities would require a court to question proceedings in Parliament contrary to Article 9. The Joint Committee has recommended that when the law on corruption is reformed it should apply to Members and that the legislation should include a provision permitting the admissibility of evidence notwithstanding Article 9.[51]

13–009

Right to exclude strangers[52]

The Commons has always exercised the right to exclude strangers, that is, persons who are not Members or officers of the House. This may be regarded

13–010

---

[45] H.C. 365 (1986–87), the Government had obtained an interim injunction to prevent a named individual from showing this film; an injunction preventing Members from showing the film in the precincts of the House was refused. The Speaker had ordered that the film should not be shown and the Committee of Privileges concluded that, on the basis of the information available to him, the Speaker had acted correctly. See A. W. Bradley [1987] P.L. 488.

[46] See the Royal Commission on Standards of Conduct in Public Life (1976) Cmnd 6524 (the Salmon Report); Graham Zellick, "Bribery of Members of Parliament and the Criminal Law" [1979] P.L. 31.

[47] See per Buckley, J. in R. v. Greenway reported in [1998] P.L. 357, contrary to the Salmon Report op. cit.

[48] op. cit.

[49] Cm. 2850 (1995).

[50] The Law Commission has issued a consultation paper and a final report on the general reform on the law on bribery and corruption, respectively Papers 145 (1997), and 248 (1998).

[51] op. cit. See Chap. 3 of the Report for a full discussion of the issues and proposals for additional protections for members.

[52] S.O. 163.

both as a corollary to the principle of freedom of speech, and as necessary for the orderly conduct of business where there is a danger of disorderly interruption. Since 1998 the procedure for this has been altered so that it is only the Speaker who has the power, whenever he think fit, to order the withdrawal of those other than Members or officers, from any part of the House.

It is possible for a member to move "That the House sit in private," this is put to the House, and if carried strangers (apart from Members of the House of Lords) must withdraw from proceedings for the rest of that day's sitting.[53] It would be a contempt of Parliament for a member to disclose anything said or done unless the House resolves otherwise.

Reporting Parliament and the publication of parliamentary papers

13–011   Another corollary of the privilege of freedom of speech and the right of Parliament to control its own affairs, was the right to restrain the publication of reports of proceedings. The publication of parliamentary debates was forbidden by the Commons in the sixteenth and seventeenth centuries.[54] Members initially desired secrecy of debate to protect themselves from the Crown; later they desired it to protect themselves from their constituents. However, from 1771 the Commons ceased to enforce their standing orders against the publication of reports of debates and, after the Reform Act 1832, reporters' galleries were provided.[55] However, it was not until 1971 that the House of Commons resolved to renounce their claim to treat such publication as a breach of privilege. Since 1980 the House has not regarded as a breach of privilege the publication of reports of evidence given at public sittings of Select Committees, before the evidence has been reported to the House.[56] The disclosure of the contents of a draft report is a contempt of Parliament.[57]

Parliamentary privilege does not provide any form of legal protection for the reports of parliamentary proceedings or the publication of papers or reports published on the authority of either House.[58] This was established in *Stockdale v. Hansard*[59] where it was held that an order of either House authorising the publication of papers outside Parliament did not render the publisher immune from liability for libel. The latter decision was correct but inconvenient, and it was nullified by the Parliamentary Papers Act 1840.[60] Section 1 provides that proceedings, criminal or civil, against persons for the publication of papers, reports, etc., printed *by order* of either House of Parliament are to be stayed. Section 2 provides that proceedings are to be stayed when commenced in respect of a correct *copy* of an authorised paper, report, etc. These provisions confer

---

[53] S.O. 163, which was amended in 1998 to alter the previous procedure in respect of strangers.

[54] In the Lords S.O. 13 (which dates from 1699) provides that the printing or publishing of anything relating to the proceedings of the House is subject to the privilege of the House.

[55] A series of unofficial reports of parliamentary debates began in 1803. It became known as *Hansard* after T. C. *Hansard* who was the printer and then the publisher of the first official series of debates. The present system, whereby official reports are prepared by staff employed by each House, was introduced in 1909.

[56] S.O. 136.

[57] See *post* para. 13–021.

[58] *cf. Lake v. King* (1668) 1 Wms. Saund. 131, which established that immunity from judicial proceedings attached to a petition containing defamatory matter and circulated only among Members of Parliament.

[59] (1839) 9 A. & E. 1.

[60] The Act declares and enacts that nothing therein affects the privileges of Parliament (s.4).

statutory absolute privilege, *i.e.* immunity from judicial proceedings, for Parliamentary reports such as Hansard, and for a variety of other types of papers and reports which Parliament has ordered to be printed.[61] Section 3 provides that in proceedings for printing any extract from or abstract of an authorised paper, report, etc., it is a defence to show that such extract or abstract was published *bona fide* and without malice.[62] This in effect confers "qualified privilege," *i.e.* immunity from judicial proceedings if the publisher can show that the publication was in good faith and without malice, such as spite or improper motive.

The Parliamentary Papers Act does not provide any assistance for those who publish unauthorised accounts of parliamentary papers or proceedings, such as newspaper reports which are not usually taken from *Hansard*. In these cases if an action for defamation were brought the publisher could rely on the common law defence of absolute privilege (when the whole of a debate or paper is reported) or qualified privilege (when less than the whole is published).[63] The report has to be fair and accurate and made without malice, and it is for the claimant to prove the contrary.[64] This defence does not apply to garbled or partial reports, but can apply to a parliamentary sketch[65] in which a reporter gives his impression of a debate. Section 15 of the Defamation Act 1996 provides a defence of qualified privilege in respect of fair and accurate reports of the proceedings of a legislature anywhere in the world.[66] It is doubtful whether there is a common law defence similar to that which was applied to defamation, in respect of the publication of criminal words, such as those that breach the Official Secrets Act, taken from a parliamentary paper or report.[67] An exception is the statutory defence in section 26 of the Public Order Act 1986 in respect of the publication of "fair and accurate reports of proceedings in Parliament", where those proceedings contain words that, if said elsewhere, could result in a prosecution.

13–012

Broadcasting of Proceedings; the Internet

Regular sound broadcasting from both Houses started in 1978, television broadcasting from the House of Lords in 1986, and the Commons in 1989.[68] It is possible that such broadcasts could fall within the protection of sections 1 and

13–013

---

[61] *e.g.* Act papers which are required by statute to be laid before Parliament and printed, many of which have little connection with the work of the House. If a Minister fears that a report of an inquiry into a matter of public concern could be the subject of a libel action, he can move a motion for an "unopposed return" which will ensure that the Commons will agree to print the report and it will fall within the protection of the 1840 Act, *e.g.* the Legg report on Sierra Leone H.C. 1016 (1997–98). See P. M. Leopold, "The Parliamentary Papers Act 1840 and its application today", [1990] P.L. 183; "The Publication of Controversial Parliamentary Papers", (1993) 56 M.L.R. 690.

[62] In *Dingle v. Associated Newspapers Ltd* [1960] 2 Q.B. 405, this defence was applied to an extract from the report of a Select Committee of the House of Commons. Section 3 has also been applied to broadcasting.

[63] *Wason v. Walter* (1868) L.R. 4 Q.B. 73.

[64] *cf.* s.3 of the 1840 Act where it is for the printer (or broadcaster) to prove that he was not actuated by an improper motive.

[65] A journalist's view or impression of a debate or other parliamentary proceeding started in the 1970s as an additional newspaper account of such proceedings; today it is likely to be the only account. *Cook v. Alexander* [1974] Q.B. 279.

[66] See also Sched. 1, paras 1 and 7. Fair and accurate copies of, or extracts from, material published by or on the authority of a government or legislature anywhere in the world will also be entitled to qualified privilege for defamation purposes.

[67] See H.C. 222 (1978–79), p. iv.

[68] For the arrangements and regulation of broadcasting, see Erskine May, *Parliamentary Practice* (22nd ed., 1997) p. 229–230.

2 of the 1840 Act.[69] Section 3 of the 1840 Act was extended in 1959[70] to include wireless telegraphy, and in 1990 to include any television or sound broadcasting service.[71] This means that the broadcasting of extracts, or abstracts of authorised papers, reports etc. has the protection of statutory qualified privilege. In addition in respect of defamation the common law defence of qualified privilege and section 15 of the Defamation Act 1996 would apply to the broadcasting of both live and recorded proceedings.[72] As with the publication of criminal words, the broadcaster is in an uncertain position. Since 1996 an increasing number of parliamentary reports and papers are available on the *Internet*, including the daily transcripts of the proceedings of each House. This type of publication is almost certainly covered by the 1840 Act.[73]

The uncertainty and variety of the law with respect to the publication and broadcasting of parliamentary papers and reports led the Joint Committee to recommend the replacement of the 1840 Act by a modern statute.

The use of Reports of proceedings in Parliament in Court proceedings: "ought not to be questioned"

13–014   In 1981 the House of Commons agreed that it was no longer necessary to seek its leave before referring to the official report of parliamentary proceedings in court. In consequence the use of *Hansard* in court proceedings increased. The use which can be made of reports is limited by Article 9 of the Bill of Rights in its requirement that proceedings in parliament "ought not to be questioned in any court or place out of parliament". In *Pepper v. Hart*[74] the House of Lords modified the rule whereby what was said in Parliament could not be cited in court as a direct evidence of the meaning of a statute. The Lords held that to use clear statements made concerning the purpose of legislation did not amount to a questioning of proceedings in Parliament. Nor in recent years have the courts regarded the use of parliamentary proceedings in judicial review proceedings as in breach of Article 9. In *R v. Home Secretary, ex p. Brind*[75] a ministerial statement was used as evidence that the Minister had properly used his power to impose broadcasting restrictions on terrorists; statements have also been used by applicants to support the argument that a government decision or policy statement was unlawful.[76] This use of parliamentary proceedings in the course of judicial review can be seen as complementary to ministerial accountability to Parliament. The Joint Committee accepted that both these developments should remain and that legislation should be introduced to make it clear that they were proper exceptions to Article 9.

---

[69] This interpretation would require the term "publication" in the 1840 Act to be interpreted as including radio and television broadcasting, even though these were unknown in 1840. See H.C. 146 (1965–66).

[70] Defamation Act 1959, s.9.

[71] Broadcasting Act 1990, s.203(1) and sched. 20, para. 1.

[72] s.1(3)(d) of the Defamation Act 1996 would appear to provide those who broadcast live proceedings in Parliament with an additional defence.

[73] But for a problem in respect to the uncorrected transcripts of witnesses before select committee see the Joint Committee Report paras 370–373.

[74] [1993] AC 593, see Geoffrey Marshall, "Hansard and the interpretation of statutes", Chap. IX in *The Law and Parliament op. cit.*

[75] [1991] 1 A.C. 696.

[76] *R. v. Secretary of State for Foreign Affairs, ex p. World Development Movement* [1995] 1 W.L.R. 386, *R. v. Home Secretary, ex p. Hindley* [1998] Q.B. 751.

A different situation arises with respect to the use of parliamentary proceedings in court even where to do so would not expose the speaker to legal liability. In *Church of Scientology of California v. Johnson-Smith*[77] it was held that reports of parliamentary debates could not be read in court to prove malice in an action against a member for libel uttered in the course of a television interview. In *Prebble v. Television New Zealand*,[78] a former government minister alleged that he had been defamed in a television broadcast. The television company sought to refer to statements made by the plaintiff, both outside and inside the New Zealand House of Representatives, to refute the allegations. The issue for the Judicial Committee of the Privy Council was whether it would be contrary to Article 9 to use things said in Parliament as part of a defence even if to do so would not expose the M.P. to any legal liability for those words. Lord Browne-Wilkinson expressly stated that there was no objection to a party in litigation referring to what has been said in parliamentary proceedings provided they did not allege impropriety.[79] The Judicial Committee was of the opinion that the correct statement of the effect of Article 9 was that found in section 16(3) of the Australian Federal Parliamentary Privileges Act 1987,[80] which in effect prohibits the use of parliamentary proceedings both to question the truth, motive, intention or good faith of anything that forms part of parliamentary proceedings and to draw inferences from those proceedings.[81] Consequently, a defamation action brought by the former M.P. Neil Hamilton against the *Guardian* was stayed, because the defence was precluded from using as evidence of justification things said or done by the Mr Hamilton in the course of proceedings in Parliament. In effect this prevented members and peers from using the courts to clear their names if they were alleged to have acted dishonestly in connection with their parliamentary duties.

Section 13 of the Defamation Act 1996[82]

This section was introduced to remedy the perceived injustices of the Hamilton type of case.[83] Section 13 provides that in a defamation action where "the conduct of a person in or in relation to proceedings in Parliament is in issue," that person[84] may waive the protection whereby proceedings in Parliament may not be questioned in any court. The immunity from legal liability for things said or done in the course of, or for purposes incidental to, proceedings in Parliament is

13–015

---

[77] [1972] 1 Q.B. 522; see also *Dingle v. Associated Newspapers Ltd* [1960] 2 Q.B. 405.

[78] [1995] 1 A.C. 321; see P. M. Leopold "Free Speech in Parliament and the Courts" (1995) 15 L.S. 204.

[79] *ibid.* at p. 321. It was also the opinion that the protection provided by Article 9 could not be waived by an individual or by the House.

[80] Passed to avoid the consequences of the interpretation of Article 9 in *R. v. Murphy* (1986) 5 N.S.W.L.R. 18.

[81] Since it was not possible for the defence to conduct its case without this evidence, the proceedings had to be stayed.

[82] Andrew Sharland and Ian Loveland, "The Defamation Act 1996 and Political Libels", [1997] P.L. 113; Enid Campbell, "Investigating the Truth of Statements made in Parliament. The Australian Experience", [1998] P.L. 125.

[83] The Commons' resolution of 1978 (*post* para. 13–020) was intended to encourage members to pursue defamation claims against the media through the courts rather than as contempt of Parliament.

[84] Which, in addition to members of either House, includes others such as witnesses before a House committee.

not affected (section 13(4)). Section 13 has been widely criticised[85]; it not only undermines the basis of privilege namely that it is the privilege of the House as a whole and not of individual members, it also creates uncertainty as to the position where more than one person is involved in the same action, and is anomalous as it is not possible to waive privilege in other civil actions or in criminal cases. The Joint Committee recommended the repeal of section 13 and its replacement by a statutory power for either House to waive Article 9 privilege in respect of any court action provided there was no question of the member, or the other person who made the statement, being exposed in consequence to a risk of legal liability.[86] This would enable either House to permit parliamentary proceedings to be examined in court when it is considered to be in the interests of justice to do so.

2. Freedom from arrest

13–016   Freedom from civil arrest[87] was in former times an important privilege necessary for the proper functioning of Parliament, because arrest was often part of the process for commencing civil proceedings by compelling the appearance of the defendant before the court, and also of distress, that is, enforcing a money judgment. Owing to reforms in civil procedure in the nineteenth century, and the abolition of imprisonment for debt by the Debtors Act 1869, this privilege has lost most of its importance and only applies to a few cases, *e.g.* attachment for disobeying a court order for the payment of money.[88] Those parts of the Insolvency Act 1986, which provides for bankruptcy and confers powers of arrest in connection with bankruptcy, also apply to those having privilege of Parliament.[89]

The privilege of freedom from arrest has never been allowed to interfere with the administration of criminal justice, emergency legislation or contempt of court where the sentence is of a quasi-criminal nature.[90] When a Member of Parliament commits a crime he may be arrested like anyone else,[91] and if he is convicted the court must notify the Speaker. The papers are then laid before the House at their request, and the member may be expelled. A member who is imprisoned by order of a court has no special privileges.

The abolition of this privilege was recommended in 1967, and again by the Joint Committee in 1999 on the ground that it is anomalous and of little value.[92]

---

[85] See generally the evidence to the Joint Committee, vols 2 and 3 and Report paras 67–90; see also, Lord Simon of Glaisdale, "A Question of Privilege: The crises of the Bill of Rights", *The Parliamentarian* April 1997, p. 121. In *Hamilton v. Al Fayed op. cit.* the House of Lords held that if Mr Hamilton waived his privilege, then in any subsequent court hearing it would be possible to question any proceeding in Parliament, including findings made about his conduct by the Standards and Privileges Committee. In consequence Mr Hamilton brought, and lost, an action for defamation against Mr Al Fayed in respect of remarks made by him in a television programme.

[86] *op. cit.* paras 72–90.

[87] Which applies in effect continuously, since it lasts during a session of Parliament and for 40 days before and after as well as where Parliament is dissolved or prorogued.

[88] See *Stourton v. Stourton* [1963] P. 302.

[89] With the exception of s.427.

[90] Erskine May, *op. cit.*, at p. 100. For a historical account of this privilege see Erskine May pp. 72–78; for the contemporary position see Erskine May, Chap. 7.

[91] But as to a crime committed in the House see *ante*, para. 13–007, *post*, para. 13–018.

[92] (1967–68) H.C. 34; (1998–99) H.L. 43, H.C. 214.

3. Right of the House to regulate its own composition

This privilege covers: (i) the filling of casual vacancies, (ii) the determination **13–017** of disputed election returns, (iii) the determination of legal disqualifications of persons returned to Parliament, and (iv) expulsion of members who are unfit to sit. These powers are exercised within the limits left by statute.

(i) *Filling casual vacancies.* The Speaker issues a warrant for the issue of a writ for an election to fill a casual vacancy.

(ii) *Determination of disputed elections.* The right of the Commons to decide questions of disputed election returns established in 1604 was exercised until the Parliamentary Elections Act 1868.[93] The Representation of the People Act 1983, s.144, which re-enacts with amendments the provisions of the Act of 1868 relating to election petitions, leaves nominally intact the privileges of the Commons, who in practice give effect to the findings of election courts.

(iii) *Determination of legal disqualifications.* The House retains the right to determine of its own motion whether a person, who has otherwise been properly elected, is legally disqualified from sitting. If the House holds that the person is disqualified it will declare the seat vacant, and may refuse to admit him or may expel him if he has already been admitted.[94]

(iv) *Expulsion of members who are unfit to serve.* The House may also expel a member who, although not subject to any legal disability, is in its opinion unfit to serve as a member. Until the Representation of the People Act 1981, which provides for the disqualification of any member who is detained for more than a year for any offence, this was commonly done when a court notified the Speaker that a member had been convicted of a serious criminal offence. The House cannot prevent an expelled member from being re-elected, as happened several times in the case of John Wilkes between 1769 and 1774, but it can refuse to allow him to take his seat.[95] Similar principles apply to expulsion for breach of privilege or contempt.

4. Exclusive right to regulate its own proceedings

Free speech in Parliament is one aspect of a wider principle that what happens **13–018** within Parliament is controlled by Parliament and is not reviewable by the courts. " ... the courts will not challenge or assault, by any order of their own, an assertion of authority issued by Parliament pursuant to Parliament's own procedures."[96] This includes the right of Parliament to determine its own procedures and to be the sole judge of the lawfulness of those procedures. In *Prebble v. Television New Zealand* Lord Browne-Wilkinson states that: "So far as the courts

---

[93] *ante* para. 10–061.

[94] The House may seek the opinion of the Privy Council: *e.g. Re MacManaway* [1951] A.C. 161. See *A.G. v. Jones* [1999] 3 W.L.R. 444, where the A.G. on behalf of the Speaker and the authorities of the House of Commons successfully sought a declaration that a M.P. whose conviction for a corrupt practice was overturned, was entitled to resume her seat in Parliament which had remained unfilled.

[95] But under the R.P.A. 1981 the nomination of a person who is disqualified by virtue of this Act, is void.

[96] *per* Lord Woolf M.R. in *Hamilton v. Al Fayed op. cit.* at p. 334.

are concerned, they will not allow any challenge to be made to what is said or done within the walls of Parliament in performance of its legislative functions and protection of its established privileges."[97] The case of *British Railways Board v. Pickin*[98] demonstrates that privilege is one of the main grounds on which the courts deny themselves jurisdiction to inquire into the legislative procedure in the House.

In *Bradlaugh v. Gossett*[99] the High Court declined to intervene when the Commons refused to allow Bradlaugh, an atheist who had been elected a member, to take the oath as required by the Parliamentary Oaths Act 1866. Stephen J. stated that the Commons was not "subject to the control of Her Majesty's Courts in the administration of that part of the statute law which has relation to its own internal proceedings."[1] In *R v. The Speaker ex p. McGuiness* the Northern Ireland High Court held that the decision of the Speaker that elected members who had refused to take the oath or affirm could not have access to the facilities available to members, was concerned with the internal arrangements of the House and was not amenable to judicial review.[2] Parliament's internal arrangements have also been held to include decisions of the Parliamentary Commissioner for Standards.[3] However the right to administer its own affairs does not give immunity from civil or criminal action within the precincts of Parliament (unless protected under Article 9 as proceedings in Parliament).[4]

13–019　　　As a consequence of *R. v. Graham-Campbell, ex p. Herbert*,[5] where the Divisional Court upheld the refusal of the Chief Metropolitan Magistrate for want of jurisdiction to try alleged breaches of a Licensing Act by the Kitchen Committee of the House, statutes on matters as diverse as the Prices and Incomes Act 1966, the Health and Safety at Work Act 1974, and the Food Safety Act 1990, have been regarded as not applying to the internal affairs of the House of Commons.[6] The activities covered by these statutes are not connected with the core activities of Parliament, and it is unsatisfactory that Parliament is not required to comply with its own laws on matters such as employment and the sale of alcohol. The Joint Committee has recommendation legislation to clarify those activities which fall within Parliament's exclusive jurisdiction, and a principle of statutory interpretation that in future, in the absence of a contrary intention, all legislation should bind both Houses of Parliament.

5. Parliament's disciplinary and penal powers

13–020　　　Each House has power to enforce its privileges and to punish those—whether members or strangers—who infringe them. Each House also has power (this is one of its privileges) to punish members or strangers for contempt. In 1978 the

---

[97] *op. cit.* at p. 332.
[98] [1974] A.C. 765 (H.L.); *ante*, para. 3–017.
[99] (1884) 12 Q.B.D. 271.
[1] *op. cit.* at p. 278.
[2] [1997] N.I. 359.
[3] *R. v. Parliamentary Commissioner for Standards ex p. Al Fayed* [1998] 1 All E.R. 93.
[4] Spencer Perceval, the Prime Minister, was shot dead in the lobby of the House of Commons in 1812 by John Bellingham, who had a grievance against the government. Bellingham was tried within four days of the assassination, convicted (although probably insane) and executed two days later. "The precincts of the House should not be treated as a sanctuary from the operation of the law." First Report from the Committee of Privileges H.C. 365 (1986–87) para. 30.
[5] [1935] 1 K.B. 594.
[6] From time to time legislation has been voluntarily applied to the activities of the House or the employment rights of its staff. See generally G.F. Lock, "Statute law and case law applicable to Parliament", Chap. IV in *The Law and Parliament op. cit.*

Commons resolved that it would exercise its penal jurisdiction as sparingly as possible, and in particular " . . . only when the House is satisfied that to exercise it is essential in order to provide reasonable protection for the House, its members or its officers, from such improper obstruction or attempt at or threat of obstruction as is causing or is likely to cause substantial interference with the performance of their respective functions."[7] This has resulted in a reduction in the number of complaints of breach of privilege or contempt.

Strictly speaking, "privileges"—and therefore breaches of them—are specific, whereas what constitutes "contempt," is not defined but is determinable by the House. A breach of privilege is also a contempt, but a contempt is not necessarily a breach of privilege. Something may be treated as a contempt even though there is no precedent for the offence, the categories of contempt are not closed. The general term contempt will be used here as it "focuses on the underlying mischief: interfering with Parliament in carrying out its functions."[8] The power to punish for contempt (as distinct from the ejection of persons who interrupt the proceedings), which has been exercised at least since the middle of the sixteenth century, is a judicial rather have a legislative power and not necessary to enable a legislature to function. The power is inherent in the Houses of the British Parliament for the historical reason that they are part of the High Court of Parliament and have been regarded as superior courts.[9]

Examples of contempt

Erskine May defines contempt as: "any act or omission which obstructs or impedes either House of Parliament in the performance of its functions, or which obstructs or impedes (or has a tendency to obstruct or impede) any member or officer of such House in the discharge of his duties."[10]   **13–021**

The following is a list of some types of contempt: **13–022**

(i) disorderly or disrespectful conduct by strangers, parties or witnesses in the presence of the House or one of its committees;

(ii) the refusal of a witness to answer questions from a committee,[11] to produce documents or to give false evidence[12];

(iii) disobedience to the rules or wishes of either House, for, *e.g.* to attend a committee when summoned to do so;

(iv) publication of false or perverted report of debates;

(v) molesting a member of the House while he is going to or from it;

(vi) bribery of a member (this would be contempt both by the member accepting and by the person giving the bribe);

---

[7] This had first been suggested in the 1967 Report, *op. cit.*, but no action was taken until after the proposal was made again in 1977 by the Committee of Privileges, H.C. 417 (1976–77).

[8] Joint Committee Report, *op. cit.* para. 263.

[9] *R. v. Richards, ex p. Fitzpatrick and Browne* (1955) 92 C.L.R. 157 (Australian House of Representatives has the same privileges by statute). *Cf. Kielley v. Carson* (1842) 4 Moo.P.C. 63 (although a colonial legislature can protect itself, *e.g.* by expelling those who disturb its proceedings, it cannot at common law punish for contempt).

[10] *op. cit.* p. 108, see generally Erskine May, Chap. 8.

[11] See H.C. 353 (1991–92) *The Conduct of Mr Ian Maxwell and Mr Kevin Maxwell*, and P. M. Leopold [1992] P.L. 541.

[12] The Perjury Act 1911 also applies to perjury before the House or its committees.

(vii) intimidation of members, or putting pressure on a member to execute his duties in a certain way;

(viii) molesting or taking judicial proceedings against officers of either House in connection with their official conduct;

(xi) obstructing or molesting witnesses summoned to either House or a committee thereof[13];

(x) the premature publication of committee papers either in breach of an embargo on publication or by the premature disclosure of a document not intended for publication, (a leaked document).[14]

The penal nature of contempt of Parliament makes it important that it should be clear and understandable by all: something the existing uncodified position is not. At present it could be a breach of Articles 6 and 7 of the E.C.H.R. to punish someone for a contempt where there was uncertainty prior to that case whether the particular conduct was contemptuous. The Joint Committee has proposed a statutory definition which would include as illustration a list of some of the types of contempt.[15]

Procedure on complaint of a matter of privilege

13–023 As soon as possible after the occurrence of the alleged breach of privilege or contempt a Member must give written notice to the Speaker, who will decide whether or not the matter should have precedence over other business of the House. The Speaker will inform the Member of his decision, and if it is in favour of giving the matter precedence, he will make an announcement in the House. This entitles the Member to table a motion the next day proposing that a reference should be made to the Committee on Standards and Privileges. The House will debate the motion and decide whether or not to approve it.

The Committee on Standards and Privileges is a Select Committee of 11 Members set up for the duration of Parliament with the power to send for persons, papers and records.[16] As with all committees with these powers, refusal to appear or to answer, or knowingly to give false answers, is itself a contempt. Unlike other such committees, this committee can order the attendance of any Member and require a Member to produce specified documents or records in his possession. Exceptionally, those who appear before this committee are allowed to be accompanied by an advisor. These additions powers and protections were introduced in consequence of the additional tasks assigned to the committee when it replaced the Committee of Privileges and the Select Committee on Standards in 1995.[17] Allegations of breach of privilege or contempt, are investigated by this committee.[18] The committee's recommendations are reported to the

---

[13] In addition, the Witnesses (Public Inquiries) Protection Act 1892 applies to witnesses before parliamentary committees.

[14] A special procedure for dealing with such publications was established in 1986 following a report from the Committee of Privileges (H.C. 555 (1984–85). See the 8th, 10th and 11th Reports from the Committee on Standards and Privileges, H.C. 607; H.C. 747 (1998–99).

[15] *op. cit.* para. 264.

[16] S.O. No. 149.

[17] *post* para. 13–031 for the other aspects of the work of this Committee.

[18] The Joint Committee considered that changes in the procedures of this committee in respect of this type of investigation were required to satisfy the requirements of fairness, *op. cit.* paras 280–285, 289, 292. The decision of the E.Ct.H.R. in *Demicoli v. Malta* (1992) 14 E.H.R.R., requires the deliberations of committees, such as that for Standards and Privileges, to comply with Art. 6 of the E.C.H.R. For the procedure of the committee in respect of its other functions see *post* para. 13–031.

House, which makes the ultimate decision, which may not necessarily be the same as that of the committee. At present the procedure is the same whether the complaint is against a Member or a non-Member, the Joint Committee has recommended that, with one exception, the House should continue to remain responsible for disciplining its own Members, but that it should transfer its jurisdiction for contempt of parliament over non-Members to the courts.[19] The exception would be to make it a criminal offence enforceable in the courts for Members and non-Members alike to willfully fail to attend before the House or a committee or to answer questions or produce documents.[20]

Penalties

(a) *Expulsion* of a Member is regarded rather as a declaration of unfitness **13–024** than a punishment.[21] It causes a vacancy; but as we have said the Commons cannot prevent his re-election, although they can refuse to let him take his seat if re-elected. The Commons admitted John Wilkes in 1774 after he had been expelled and re-elected several times.

(b) *Suspension* of a Member is available to assist the House of Commons to enforce discipline,[22] as well as to punish particular offences laid down in Standing Orders. The salary of a Member is withheld for the duration of the suspension.[23]

(c) *Imprisonment* of a Member or a non-Member. Neither House has used this power since 1880, and the Joint Committee suggested that such a power was no longer appropriate or needed.

(d) *Reprimand* and

(e) *Admonition*, the mildest form. In both these forms the Speaker addresses the offender, who is at the bar of the House either in the custody of or attended by the Serjeant-at-Arms; except that a Member (unless he is in the custody of the Serjeant) is reprimanded or admonished standing in his place.

Fine The House of Commons has not imposed a fine since 1666, and it is **13–025** doubtful whether it has the power to do so owing to the uncertainty whether it is a court of record. The power was denied by Lord Mansfield in *R. v. Pitt*.[24] The House of Lords has such a power, but it has not been exercised for nearly 200 years. The Joint Committee recommended that both Houses should have a statutory power to fine their Members and that this would be the penalty available to the courts in respect of contempt of parliament by non-Members.

---

[19] *op. cit.* paras 300–314; Parliament would retain a residual jurisdiction, for example to enable it to have summary powers to preserve security and good order.
[20] *op. cit.* paras 310–311. The penalty would be a fine not exceeding level 5 on the standard scale.
[21] The last time a Member was expelled, save following a criminal conviction and sentence of imprisonment of 12 months, was Garry Allingham in 1947.
[22] It is not clear whether the Lords have a power to suspend a peer within the life of a parliament, the Joint Committee recommended that it should have this power; it does not have the power to suspend a peer permanently. The Committee on Standards and Privileges recommended short suspensions for Members who either leaked or received copies of leaked Select Committee papers, see H.C. 607, 747 (1998–99).
[23] S.O. 45A.
[24] (1762) 3 Burr. 1335.

II. The Privileges of the Lords

Privileges of the House

13–026   The House of Lords has seldom come into conflict either with the Sovereign or with the courts in respect of its privileges. The juridical nature of the privileges of the House of Lords is similar to that of the privileges of the House of Commons, and strictly both are parts of the privileges of Parliament. The Lords passed a resolution in 1704 declaring that neither House has power to create for itself new privileges not warranted by the known laws and customs of Parliament, and the Commons assented.[25] Any matters as to privilege or contempt in the House of Lords, or as to a peerage claim is considered by its Committee for Privileges.[26]

(i) The power to declare the law with regard to its own composition, and to determine the validity of the creation of new peerages (*Wensleydale Peerage Case*),[27] and the succession to existing peerages.[28] This power will have limited application in the light of the House of Lords Act 1999.

(ii) The exclusive right to regulate its own internal proceedings, thought this probably does not include a power to suspend a peer within the life of a single Parliament.[29]

(iii) The power to commit for breach of privilege or contempt for a definite period and to fine.

(iv) The power to summon the judges for advice on points of law.

(v) The power to issue a warrant for the release of a peer who is improperly arrested.

Personal privileges of Peers

13–027   These include:

(i) Freedom from civil arrest, that is, except in cases of treason, felony (arrestable offence) or refusal to give security to keep the peace.[30] In addition the person of a peer (whether a Lord of Parliament or not) is by custom and statute[31] "for ever sacred and inviolable" during and for a period before and after a session. The privilege is not now of much importance since the abolition of arrest for debt.[32] It would appear to be uncertain whether or not the compulsory detention of a peer under the Mental Health Act 1983 would be a breach of the privileges of peerage

---

[25] 14, *Commons Journals* 555.

[26] A sub-committee of this committee has powers to investigate and advise on matters concerned with the registration of Lords' Interests, *post* paras 13–035 to 13–036.

[27] (1856) 5 H.L.C. 958.

[28] *Annandale and Hartfell Peerage Claim* [1986] A.C. 319.

[29] Unless available at common law (an underage peer) or by statute (bankruptcy). The Lords does not have a power to suspend a peer permanently.

[30] House of Lords S.O. No. 79.

[31] Parliamentary Privilege Acts 1700 and 1703.

[32] See *Stourton v. Stourton* [1963] P. 302; *cf. Peden International Transport v. Lord Mancroft* (1989), see P. M. Leopold [1989] P.L. 398.

or freedom from arrest or detention.[33] The Joint Committee recommended the abolition of the privilege of peerage as well as that of freedom from arrest and the introduction of legislation to enable Members of the House of Lords to be detained under the mental health legislation and disqualified for sitting and voting in Parliament.

(ii) Freedom of speech in Parliament. This privilege is similar to that of the Commons.

III Members' Conduct and Members' Interests[34]

As has been seen, an aspect of Parliament's claim to regulate its own proceedings is its right to regulate the conduct of its Members. To prevent Members from prejudicing the privileges of freedom of speech, the House of Commons resolved in 1947 that they were prohibited from entering into contracts or agreements which could limit their independence and freedom of action in Parliament.[35] The longstanding practice whereby M.P.s were expected to declare a pecuniary interest relevant to the proceedings when taking part in certain proceedings of the House or a committee, was formalised into a resolution in 1974.[36] A second resolution authorised the establishment of a compulsory (though unenforceable) register of members' interests. Until 1995 the Commons exercised its jurisdiction in respect of conduct and interests through the Committee of Privileges and the Committee on Members' interests. Allegations of impropriety by M.P.s and Ministers during the 1990s, as well as a more general disquiet in respect of standards of conduct in public life, led to the establishment in 1994 of a standing Committee on Standards in Public Life[37] whose task is: "To examine current concerns about standards of conduct of all holders of public office . . . and to make recommendations as to any changes in present arrangements which might be required to ensure the highest standards of propriety in public life."[38] Reports by this committee have resulted in significant changes to parliamentary procedures relating to the conduct of M.P.s and the registration of their pecuniary interests.[39] In its first report the committee stated its Seven Principles of Public Life which are now used as a touchstone to judge ethical behaviour in the public sector.[40]

13–028

---

[33] Report from the Committee of Privileges on Parliamentary Privilege and the Mental Health Legislation (1983–84; H.L. 254); see P. M. Leopold [1985] P.L. 9.

[34] Michael Rush, "The law relating to members' conduct," Chap. VII in *The Law and Parliament, op. cit.*

[35] See H.C. 118 (1946–47).

[36] The occasions when such a declaration is required were expanded in 1995 to include those circumstances when a member has to give written notice, *e.g.* questions, early day motions, presentation of a Bill. In 1996 it was further extended to applications for emergency debates and for adjournment debates.

[37] Initially chaired by Lord Nolan then by Lord Neill and since 2001 by Sir Nigel Wicks.

[38] In November 1997 additional terms of reference were announced, to enable the committee to review the funding of political parties, see *ante* para. 10–037.

[39] The committee has also dealt with Ministers and Civil Servants, appointments to Quangos, local government and local public spending bodies.

[40] *Standards in Public Life*, Cm. 2850 (1995). The seven principles are: selflessness, integrity, objectivity, accountability, openness, honesty and leadership. See also the Government response to this report, Cm. 2931 (1995).

13–029   In November 1995 the Commons agreed to the following proposals[41]:

(i) the appointment by the House of a Parliamentary Commissioner for Standards (PCS)[42];

(ii) the replacement of the former Committees on Privileges and Members' Interests by a new Committee on Standards and Privileges[43];

(iii) the drawing up of a Code of Conduct for M.P.s;

(iv) a restatement of the 1947 resolution to incorporate a prohibition on paid advocacy[44];

(v) a requirement that members should deposit with the PCS for public record, all agreements with outside bodies for the provisions of services in their capacity as M.P.s and the annual remuneration received from such employment.

The Parliamentary Commissioner for Standards

13–030   The PCS is appointed by the House of Commons and can only be removed by a resolution of the House. The tasks of the PCS are: to maintain the register of members' interests and any other register of interests established by the House[45]; to advise on registrable interests, the Code of Conduct and general matters of propriety; to make recommendations to the Committee on Standards and Privileges on the code and the registers; and, if he thinks fit, to investigate any complaints about a member's conduct and make a report to the Committee on Standards and Privileges.[46] Such a report will include the findings of fact and the opinion of the PCS on whether there were any breaches of the code.

The Role of the Committee on Standards and Privileges in Misconduct Cases

13–031   If the PCS finds that there was a *prima facie* case then its report will normally form the basis for the committee's inquiry. The committee will decide if there was a breach of the code, assess its gravity, and recommend what penalty, if any, should be imposed. The final decision is with the House. It is possible for the committee to hear oral evidence, in particular if the member complained about wishes to challenge the findings of the PCS. It did this in the case of the complaints by Mohamed Al-Fayed against Neil Hamilton, (hearing only Mr Hamilton) and in so doing revealed weaknesses in its procedures. It subsequently recommended that new procedure should be instituted for serious cases with the appointment of a legally qualified assessor to assist the PCS, and the introduction of an appeal procedure to be used in cases deemed appropriate by the committee,

---

[41] Which were based on the recommendations of the newly created Commons Select Committee on Standards in Public Life, appointed to advise on the implementation of relevant proposals from the Committee on Standards in Public Life; H.C. 637, 816 (1995–6).

[42] S.O. 150.

[43] S.O. 149, see *ante* para. 13–023.

[44] This went further than had been recommended in the First Report from the Committee on Standards in Public Life, Cm. 2850.

[45] In 1985 the House established registers on the relevant pecuniary interests of parliamentary journalists, members' staff and all-party and parliamentary groups; these registers have been open to public inspection since 1998.

[46] The investigation will normally be on the basis of written evidence, but the PCS may conduct oral hearings, see, *e.g.* H.C. 261 (1997–98). Details of the procedure are set out in H.C. 403 (1999–2000).

which would involve an *ad hoc* tribunal (whose composition would not include serving members of the House) to inquire into disputed questions of fact, and report to the committee.[47]

The Code of Conduct

The code is a system of self-regulation for M.P.s, and is designed to increase **13–032** members' awareness of their obligations as holders of public office. It was drawn up by the Committee on Standards and Privileges and consists of a short code of conduct setting out general principles, including the seven principles of public life, to guide members as well as more specific obligations, such as not to accept bribes, to register their interests, not to misuse confidential information, not to make improper use of their parliamentary allowances. There are then extensive guidelines on three areas: registration of interests; the declaration of interests; and paid advocacy. The code and the guidelines were adopted by resolution of the House in July 1996.[48] Any M.P. or member of the public may lay a complaint alleging breach of the code with the PCS.

The Advocacy Rule

The 1947 resolution was extended and reinforced to include a prohibition on **13–033** paid advocacy. Members are prohibited from accepting any remuneration, fee, payment or other reward or benefit in kind, in return for advocating or initiating any cause or matter on behalf of any outside body or individual, or urging any other member of either House to do so. The rule applies more strictly to *initiating* a parliamentary proceeding than it does to *participating* in a debate or other proceedings initiated by another Member.[49] One of the problems is what exactly is covered by "paid advocacy"? A consequence of the change in the rules has been a transfer of trade union sponsorship from individual candidates to local party organisations.[50]

The Register of Members' Interests

The number of M.P.s whose outside employment arises directly out of their **13–034** membership of the House of Commons has made the maintenance of such a register particularly important. Although there has been such a register since 1974 and its format was significantly improved in 1993, it was the view of the 1995 Nolan Report that the form of declaration failed to reflect the true nature of the interest being declared. Changes were made in 1996 to improve the position. The primary purpose of the register is: "to provide information of any pecuniary interest or other material benefit which a Member receives which might reasonably be thought to by others to influence his or her actions, speeches or votes in Parliament, or actions taken in his or her capacity as M.P.". Ten categories of registrable interest are specified on the registration form sent to all members at the beginning of each Parliament, and detailed guidance is issued to each member.[51] Members must also lodge copies of agreements with outside bodies,

---

[47] H.C. 1191 (1997–98). See also *Reinforcing Standards*, Cm. 4557 (2000); H.C. 267 (2000–01). None of the various proposals to reform investigations into the conduct of members had been debated by the House before the 2001 election.

[48] H.C. 688 (1995–96).

[49] See First Report from the Committee on Standards and Privileges H.C. 257 (1998–99).

[50] See Committee on Standards and Privileges, Fourth Report: Category 4, Sponsorship, H.C. 181 (1997–98). Members may still be paid to act as advisers to trade unions, companies, pressure groups etc.

[51] Register of Members' Interests, H.C. 291 (1997–98).

including remuneration, with the PCS. The collating of the returns is under the authority of the PCS and the register is published annually as a House of Commons paper. Complaints connected with the register have formed the bulk of complaints to the PCS and subsequently the Committee on Standards and Privileges.[52]

The Committee on Standards and Privileges and the Committee on Standards in Public Life keep the rules relating to conduct and registration under review, and it has proposed a variety of amendments to simplify and clarify the rules on the conduct of members and to reform the complaints procedure.[53]

The House of Lords

13–035   Lords speak on their personal honour, and it is a long-standing custom that members should declare any direct financial interest, or any non-financial interest, in a subject on which they speak. It was not until 1995 that the Lords accepted more formal rules.[54] The 1995 resolution restated both the principle that Lords speak on their personal honour and that Lords should never accept any financial inducement as an incentive or reward for exercising Parliamentary influence. The Lords also agreed to the establishment of a voluntary Register of Lords' interests covering three categories, registration is mandatory in the first two categories, and discretionary in the third. The categories were: (i) consultancies or similar arrangements, involving payment or other incentive or reward for providing Parliamentary advise or services; (ii) financial interests in business involved in Parliamentary lobbying on behalf of clients; (iii) other particulars relating to matters which Lords consider may affect the public perception of the way in which they discharge their Parliamentary duties. The operation of the register is overseen by the Committee on Lords' Interests, a sub-committee of its Committee for Privileges. In 2000, the Committee Standards in Public Life investigated and made recommendations in connection with standards of conduct in the House of Lords, which a House of Lords Working Group recommended should be accepted.[55]

13–036   In July 2001 the House agreed that it should have a Code of Conduct, *inter alia* to put in a more readily accessible form its existing standards. The Code of Conduct includes the seven general principles of public life,[56] and the principles stated in the 1995 resolution. The House has accepted that all *relevant interests*, both financial and non-financial, should be registered. The Code provides guidance as to what is covered, and a new *objective* test of relevance. The Register will continue to be overseen by the Committee on Lords' Interests, with an appeal to the Committee of Privileges. The Code requires the investigation and adjudication of complaints to be subject to safeguards "as rigorous as those applied in the courts and professional disciplinary bodies." It was agreed that there was no need for a PCS for the House of Lords. Members of the House have until 31, March 2001 to register their interests in accordance with the new Code.

---

[52] Between November 1995 when the new rules on conduct came into effect and July 2000 the Committee published 31 reports concerning complaints against 57 Members.
[53] H.C. 710 (1999–2000), and response by the Committee on Standards in Public Life, Cm. 4557 (2000); Fifth Report by the Committee on Standards and Privileges, H.C. 267 (2000–01).
[54] As a result of reports by the Procedure Committee, H.L. Papers 90, 98 (1994–95).
[55] *Standards of Conduct in the House of Lords* Cm. 4903–I; H.L. Paper 68 (2000–01).
[56] *op. cit.* note 40.

PART III

THE CENTRAL GOVERNMENT

CHAPTER 14

THE MONARCHY[1]

Constitutional law distinguishes between the roles of Head of State and Head of Government. In the United Kingdom the former office is hereditary and the current holder is described as monarch or sovereign. In legal theory (but not in political reality) the executive branch of the state, which in other constitutions has its own legal status and powers, exercises powers which belong to the royal head of state, usually referred to as the powers of the Crown, to distinguish the impersonal executive from the person of the monarch.[2]   **14–001**

Title to the Throne

The title to the Throne is both statutory and hereditary, while a trace of the   **14–002** Anglo-Saxon elective element is still found in the coronation ceremony. The Act of Settlement 1700[3] settled the Throne on Sophia, Electress of Hanover (granddaughter of James I), and the heirs of her body being Protestants. Sophia's son, George I (1714), succeeded Anne under this Act. Any person who is reconciled to or shall hold communion with the See or Church of Rome or shall profess the Popish Religion or shall marry a papist, is excluded from the succession. The successor to the Crown must take the Coronation Oath, in the manner and form prescribed by statute and must sign and repeat the declaration prescribed by the Bill of Rights. Any person who comes to the possession of the Crown must join in communion with the Church of England as by law established.

The desirability of amending the Act of Settlement to remove these discriminatory provisions, was raised in the course of 1999.[4] Any such reform would require the members of the Commonwealth to be consulted, at least the "Realms," if not also the Republics in accordance with the convention in the preamble to the Statute of Westminster 1931 that, since the Crown is the symbol of the free association of the members of the Commonwealth, any alteration in the law touching the succession to the Throne requires the assent of the Parliaments of all the "Dominions".[5]

Accession

When a Sovereign dies his successor accedes to the Throne immediately. The   **14–003** automatic succession of the new monarch is sometimes expressed in the maxim "the King never dies".[6] At common law a person is never too young to succeed to the Throne.

---

[1] V. Bogdanor, *The Monarchy and the Constitution* (1995).
[2] The various uses of the term "the Crown" are discussed later in Chapter 14 and Chapter 33.
[3] The Act of Settlement was amended by the Union with Scotland and Ireland Acts, and by His Majesty's Declaration of Abdication Act 1936. The legitimacy of the succession based on the Act of Settlement cannot be questioned in court: *Hall v. Hall* (1944) 88 S.J. 383 (Hereford C.C.).
[4] A motion to seek the permission of the Queen to debate a Succession to the Crown (Amendment) Bill was defeated in the House of Lords on December 2, 1999.
[5] Perhaps the assent is now required of all independent countries of the Commonwealth that recognise Her Majesty as Queen: *post*, para. 36–021.
[6] *Calvin's Case* (1608) 8 Co. Rep. 1a. 10b.

As soon as conveniently possible after the death or abdication of a Sovereign, an Accession Council meets to acclaim the new Sovereign. An Accession Council is composed of the Lords Spiritual and Temporal, assisted by Members of the Privy Council, with the Lord Mayor and Aldermen of the City of London and the high commissioners of the Commonwealth countries. The new Sovereign takes the oath for the security of the Presbyterian Church in Scotland prescribed by the Union with Scotland Act 1706. Before the first meeting of Parliament or at his coronation he must declare that he is a faithful Protestant, and promise to uphold the enactments securing the Protestant succession to the Throne.[7]

Coronation

14–004   Coronation customarily takes place in Westminster Abbey some months after accession, and is conducted by the Archbishop of Canterbury, assisted by the Archbishop of York.[8] Coronation is not legally necessary. Indeed Edward VIII reigned for nearly a year before abdicating, and was never crowned.[9]

The Coronation Oath is based on the Coronation Oath Act 1688, and is obligatory by the Act of Settlement as amended by the Acts of Union. The Oath taken by Elizabeth II was to govern the peoples of the United Kingdom of Great Britain and Northern Ireland, Canada, Australia, New Zealand, the Union of South Africa, Pakistan and Ceylon,[10] and her possessions and the other territories to any of them belonging or pertaining, according to the statutes in Parliament agreed on and their respective laws and customs; to maintain in the United Kingdom the Protestant reformed religion established by law; and to maintain and preserve inviolably the settlement of the Church of England, and the doctrine, worship, discipline and government thereof in England.

Abdication

14–005   There is no precedent for a voluntary abdication[11] before 1936, when Edward VIII was given the choice of abdicating or giving up his proposed marriage with Mrs. Simpson, whom the Prime Minister (Mr. Baldwin) and the Dominion Prime Ministers regarded as unsuitable for a King's consort. The King signed an Instrument of Abdication declaring his irrevocable determination to renounce the Throne for himself and his descendants. He then sent a message to Parliament asking that a Bill should be passed accordingly to alter the succession to the Throne, and issued a commission to signify his assent thereto. His Majesty's Declaration of Abdication Act 1936 accordingly provided that His Majesty should cease to be King and there should be a demise of the Crown, and the member of the Royal Family then next in succession to the Throne should succeed. It amended the Act of Settlement 1700 by excluding King Edward (thereafter Duke of Windsor) and his descendants from the succession to the

---

[7] Accession Declaration Act 1910.

[8] At the coronation of Elizabeth II in 1953 a minor part was played by the Moderator of the General Assembly of the Church of Scotland. It may well be that future coronations will follow a more ecumenical or multi-faith pattern.

[9] For a description of the coronation ceremony, see A. B. Keith, *The King and the Imperial Crown*, (1936) pp. 20–29.

[10] These were the independent kingdoms or realms in the Commonwealth at that time. India was already a republic.

[11] Following the defeat of James II in battle and his flight from the country, the Declaration of Rights 1688, embodied in the Bill of Rights, asserted that the late King James II had "abdicated the Government" and the Throne was "thereby vacant".

Throne, and exempted them from the provisions of the Royal Marriages Act 1772.

Royal Style and Titles

The Royal Style and Titles are altered from time to time by Act of Parliament, or by proclamation issued thereunder. Several changes have been made in the present century to take account of constitutional developments in the Commonwealth. The preamble to the Statute of Westminster 1931 recites the convention that any alteration of the Royal Style and Titles shall require the consent of the Parliaments of all the "Dominions".[12] Events since 1952, however, suggest that such consent is no longer required.[13] On the accession of Elizabeth II, the Sovereign was for the first time proclaimed by different titles in the various independent countries of the Commonwealth. The Royal Titles Act 1953 empowers the Queen to use, in relation to the United Kingdom and all other territories for whose foreign relations the Government of the United Kingdom is responsible, such style and titles as she may think fit having regard to the agreement made between representatives of the member governments of the Commonwealth. The style and titles proclaimed under this Act are: "Elizabeth II by the Grace of God of the United Kingdom of Great Britain and Northern Ireland and of her other Realms and Territories Queen, Head of the Commonwealth,[14] Defender of the Faith."[15]

14–006

The Royal family

The Sovereign.[16] The Queen Regnant has the same status and powers as a King. She is the Head of the State. The central government of the country is carried on in her name and on her behalf; she is an essential part of the legislature, and justice is administered in the royal courts in her name. But what were formerly the personal prerogatives of the Sovereign have now become largely the powers and privileges of the government.[17]

14–007

The official duties of the Queen in her capacity as Sovereign of the United Kingdom and of the other self-governing Commonwealth monarchies and the remaining colonial territories, Head of the Armed Services, and Supreme Governor of the Church of England and with her special responsibility to the Established Church of Scotland, include: (i) work arising out of the government such as approving and signing commissions, and reading ministerial, Cabinet, parliamentary and diplomatic papers for several hours a day; (ii) private audiences with ambassadors etc., receiving the Prime Minister and other Ministers, holding a Privy Council and investitures; (iii) attending at state occasions such as the opening of Parliament, Trooping the Colour and religious services; and (iv) exchanging state visits and visiting Commonwealth countries.[18]

The Sovereign's official expenditure is financed mainly out of the Civil List provided by Parliament.[19]

---

[12] *cf. ante*, para. 7–019.
[13] *post*, para. 36–021.
[14] *post*, para. 36–021.
[15] (1953) Cmd. 8748. See also S. A. de Smith, "The Royal Style and Titles" (1953) 2 I.C.L.Q. 263; and *post*, para. 36–021.
[16] See also *post*, para. 33–015.
[17] *post*, Chap. 15.
[18] *Report from the Select Committee on the Civil List* (1971) H.C. 29, para. 17 and Appendix 13.
[19] *post*, para. 15–013(d) And for the Crown private estates, see *post*, para. 15–009.

Husband of Queen Regnant. Prince Philip, Duke of Edinburgh, is granted precedence next to the Queen. He is a Privy Councillor. At common law he has the status of an ordinary subject, and is not protected by the law of treason.

The Prince of Wales. The life of the Sovereign's eldest son is protected by the Statute of Treason 1351. When the Sovereign's eldest son is born he immediately becomes by custom Duke of Cornwall.[20] When he succeeds to the Throne, the Duchy of Cornwall immediately vests in his eldest son. The Sovereign may create his of her eldest son Prince of Wales and Earl of Chester by letters patent. Prince Charles was created Prince of Wales and Earl of Chester in 1958, and his investiture as Prince of Wales took place at Caernarvon Castle in 1969.

For the avoidance of doubt, section 6 of the House of Lords Act 1999 provides that for the purposes of that Act "hereditary peerage" includes "the principality of Wales and the earldom of Chester".

Princes and princesses of the blood royal. The style of "Royal Highness" is conferred by letters patent[21] on the children of Sovereigns, and on the wives and children of the sons of Sovereigns.

Royal marriages. By the Royal Marriages Act 1772 no descendant of the body of George II (other than the issue of princesses married into royal families[22]) may marry without the royal consent signified under the Great Seal and declared in Council, and marriages by these persons without such consent are void (*Sussex Peerage Case*[23]). Further, all persons solemnising such marriages, or who are privy and consenting thereto, commit an offence. If the royal consent is refused, a descendant of George II aged 25 or more may give notice to the Privy Council and may contract a valid marriage at the expiration of 12 months unless Parliament has objected in the interim.[24]

Regency Acts 1937–1953

14–008   The common law made no provision for a regency or the delegation of royal functions when the Sovereign was ill or absent from the realm. These matters are now regulated by the Regency Acts 1937–1953.

14–009   (i) *Delegation of functions to Counsellors of State.* Before 1937 Counsellors of State were appointed under the Royal Prerogative and might include, in addition to members of the Royal Family, dignitaries such as the Archbishop of Canterbury, the Lord Chancellor and the Prime Minister. The Regency Act 1937 authorises the Sovereign to appoint Counsellors of State by letters patent, and to delegate to them such of the royal functions as may be specified in the letters

---

[20] Duchy of Cornwall Management Acts 1863 to 1982.

[21] *London Gazette*, February 5, 1864.

[22] It has been strongly argued that this exception largely nullifies the Act in modern circumstances: see C. d'O. Farran, "The Royal Marriages Act 1772" (1951) 14 M.L.R. 53), but it continues to be the practice to ask for the royal consent.

[23] (1844) 11 Cl. & F. 85.

[24] It is suggested that the Act should be amended so as to be confined to descendants of George V; and also that a marriage without the royal consent should not be void or punishable, but should merely exclude the parties and their descendants from the succession to the Throne.

patent, whenever he is absent or intends to be absent from the United Kingdom, or is suffering from infirmity of mind or body not amounting to incapacity such as would warrant a regency under the Act. The persons to be appointed to be Counsellors of State are the wife or husband of the Sovereign and the four persons next in succession to the Throne, excluding any person who would be disqualified from being Regent. The Regency Act 1953 includes Queen Elizabeth the Queen Mother among the persons who may be appointed Counsellors of State. This modern practice that only members of the Royal Family should be appointed to the exclusion of United Kingdom Ministers,[25] reflects the significance of the Monarchy to the Commonwealth. The Counsellors may not be given authority to dissolve Parliament otherwise than at the express instructions of the Sovereign—which may be given by telegraph—or to grant any rank, title or dignity of the peerage.

(ii) *Regency.* (a) The Regency Act 1937 provides that if *the Sovereign is under* **14–010**
18 years of age the royal functions are to be performed until he is 18 by a Regent, who shall act in the name and on behalf of the Sovereign. The Sovereign is deemed to accede to the Throne when he attains the age of 18 years for the purpose of taking statutory oaths and declarations. The Regent is to be the person of full age next in succession to the Throne who is a British subject resident in the United Kingdom and who is not disqualified on religious grounds. The Regency Act 1953, however, provides that the Duke of Edinburgh shall be Regent if a child of Queen Elizabeth and the Duke of Edinburgh succeeds to the Throne under the age of 18, or if a regency is necessary in the lifetime of the Queen. The Regent is to take oaths of allegiance, good government and maintenance of the Protestant religion in England and Scotland. He is empowered to exercise all royal functions, except that he may not assent to a Bill altering the succession to the Throne or repealing the Acts for securing the Scottish Protestant religion and Church.[26]

The Act of 1937 also provides for the *guardianship* of the person of a Sovereign under 18 years. Of an unmarried Sovereign his or her mother is to be the guardian; of a married Sovereign the Sovereign's spouse will be guardian. If in the first case the Sovereign has no mother or in the second case the Consort is under age, then the Regent will be guardian.

(b) The Regency Act 1937 further provides for the appointment of a Regent if a declaration is made by certain persons that they are "satisfied by evidence which shall include the evidence of physicians that *the Sovereign is by infirmity of mind or body incapable* for the time being of performing the royal functions", or that they are "satisfied by evidence that the Sovereign is for some definite cause *not available*" for the performance of those functions.[27] The regency will continue until a contrary declaration is made. The persons who may make such declaration are the wife or husband of the Sovereign, the Lord Chancellor, the Speaker, the Lord Chief Justice and the Master of the Rolls, or any three or more of them. It will be noticed that the person who would be Regent is not one of those who make this declaration. The declaration must be made in writing to the

[25] See J. W. Wheeler-Bennett, *King George VI*, (1958) App. A.
[26] *cf. ante*, para. 4–038.
[27] The Sovereign would not be available, *e.g.* if he were made a prisoner of war.

Privy Council, and is to be communicated to the governments of the "Dominions".

The Sovereign's Private Secretary[28]

14–011   The post of Private Secretary to the Monarch is comparatively modern. Before the reign of George III the theory was that the Home Secretary was the King's Private Secretary, and it was thought desirable that a person admitted to Cabinet secrets should be a Privy Councillor. George III for many years wrote his own letters, but in 1805, when he was almost blind, he appointed Sir Herbert Taylor his Private Secretary. William IV reappointed Taylor, who had by then become a Privy Councillor. Since the Prince Consort's death in 1861 the office has been regular and officially accepted, its prestige being built up by Sir Henry Ponsonby and Sir Arthur Bigge (Lord Stamfordham), who between them occupied that post from 1870 to 1931, except during Edward VII's reign.

The Sovereign's Private Secretary is always now sworn of the Privy Council. It appears that he informally seeks advice from various sources—governmental, opposition and official—and then briefs the Sovereign. His post is very important[29] as he is concerned with the relations not only between the Sovereign and the British Cabinet, but also between the Sovereign and Governors-General and Commonwealth Prime Ministers.

The publication of an article in *The Sunday Times* on July 20, 1986 which purported to describe the Queen's views on a wide range of political matters provoked, unusually, the Private Secretary to write a public letter denying the accuracy of the report.[30]

Treason

14–012   The law of treason is a reminder of the antiquity of much of the Constitution. It dates from a time when an attack on the monarch was likely to be the most effective way to undermine the government of the State.[31]

Treason is a betrayal (*trahison*) or breach of the faith and allegiance due to the Sovereign. Allegiance is correlative to protection. It is owed to the Crown by British citizens wherever they may be; by citizens of other Commonwealth countries and Irish citizens while they are in the United Kingdom[32]; and by aliens[33] while they are in British territory by the Sovereign's licence, express or tacit. It has been held that aliens resident in the Sovereign's dominions may

---

[28] Wheeler-Bennett, *King George VI* (1958) App. B; Arthur Ponsonby, *Henry Ponsonby, Queen Victoria's Private Secretary*, Chap. 3; Sir Ivor Jennings, *Cabinet Government* (3rd ed. 1959), pp. 343–351.
[29] "Crucial to the working of constitutional monarchy in Britain;" V. Bogdanor, *The Monarchy and the Constitution* (1995), p. 197.
[30] Letter to *The Times*, July 28, 1986; *post*, para. 36–023.
[31] It is worthy of note that even in the case of the most serious terrorist outrages of the last few years prosecutions have not been brought under the law of treason. No doubt that is explicable partly by the wish to avoid the uncertainties of an ancient part of the law but also, perhaps, because it was felt that the execution of persons convicted in peace time would cause undesirable controversy, and provoke further crimes of violence.
[32] Citizens of other Commonwealth countries which owe allegiance to the Queen as Queen also owe allegiance by the law of their respective countries.
[33] *Semble*, including civilian enemy aliens who remain at large within the realm by licence, and internees; *cf.* prisoners of war.

continue to owe allegiance even after protection is withdrawn.[34] Foreign diplomatic representatives and members of foreign invading or occupying forces, however, do not owe allegiance.

The earliest statute on the subject is the Treason Act 1351, which was supposed to be declaratory of the common law.[35] The statute is still in force, with amendments, and constitutes the following offences high treason[36]: (i) compassing or imagining the death of the King (or Queen Regnant) Queen Consort,[37] or the sovereign's eldest son and heir; or (ii) violating the King's consort or the King's eldest daughter unmarried or the wife of the king's eldest son and heir[38]; or (iii) levying war against the King in his realm; or (iv) adhering to the King's enemies in his realm, giving them aid or comfort in the realm or elsewhere; or (v) slaying the Chancellor, Treasurer[39] or the King's justices assigned to hear and determine, being in their places doing their offices.

Compassing or imagining the death of the Sovereign

The words "compass or imagine" import design, which must be manifested by an overt act.[40] The following are overt acts according to Blackstone[41]: providing weapons, conspiring to imprison the King though not intending his death, or assembling and consulting to kill the King.

14–013

Levying of war in the realm

This has been held to include not only levying of war to dethrone the King, but also levying war to reform religion, remove councillors or redress grievances. Resistance to the royal forces by defending a castle against them is levying War, and so is an insurrection with an avowed design to pull down all chapels and the like. In *Damaree's Case* (1709)[42] Damaree and Purchas were convicted of treason for burning Nonconformist meeting-houses, the court being of opinion that the design was a general one against the state, and therefore a levying of war. Blackstone says that merely conspiring to levy war is not a treasonable levying of war, but that it constitutes compassing the King's death where it is pointed at the royal person or government. To enlist men in the realm to go to the aid of the King's enemies abroad is not levying war in the realm, but it may be brought under compassing the King's death and adhering to the King's enemies.

14–014

Adhering to the King's enemies

It is an offence under (iv) above either to give the King's enemies in his realm aid and comfort in his realm, or to give aid and comfort elsewhere to the King's enemies elsewhere. "Enemies" here means public belligerents as understood in international law, and not mere pirates or British rebels; but to aid the latter in the

14–015

---

[34] *De Jager v. Att.-Gen. of Natal* [1907] A.C. 326.

[35] See J. G. Bellamy, *The Law of Treason in England in the Later Middle Ages* (1970); G. P. Bodet, "Sir Edward Coke's *Third Institute*: a primer for treason defendants" (1971) 20 U.T.L.J. 469.

[36] Petit treason under this statute consisted of: (a) the killing of a master by his servant, (b) the killing of a husband by his wife, and (c) the killing of a prelate by his ecclesiastical inferior. Since 1828 these offences have been regarded as ordinary murder.

[37] The consort of a Queen Regnant is not protected by the law of treason.

[38] Allegations of adultery by Diana, Princess of Wales, revived newspapers' interests in this provision of the Treason Act: P. Catley, "James Hewitt, the Princess of Wales and the Treason Acts", [1996] New L.J. 350.

[39] There has been no Treasurer since 1714; *post*, para. 18–007.

[40] *R. v. Thistlewood* (1820) 33 St.Tr. 681.

[41] Bl.Comm. IV, 74 *et seq.*

[42] *R. v. Damaree* (1709) 15 St.Tr. 521.

realm would constitute levying of war. Persons acting under duress as regards life or person cannot be convicted as traitors, provided that they leave the King's enemies at the first opportunity.

In *R. v. Lynch*,[43] where a British subject during the Boer War commanded an Irish brigade on the side of the Boers against the British forces, the court held that the words "adhering to the King's enemies in his realm" did not mean that the "accused person *being in the realm* has been adherent to the King's enemies *wherever they were*", to the exclusion of such a case as that before the court. So narrow a construction not only would enable an Englishman to engage with a foreign hostile power against his own country, so long as he took care to remain abroad, but also ignores the words "or elsewhere" in the same sentence of the section. *R. v. Lynch* also decided that section 6 of the Naturalisation Act 1870 did not enable a British subject to become naturalised in an enemy state in time of war, and, further, that the very act of purporting to become naturalised in those circumstances constituted an overt act of treason.[44]

In *R. v. Casement*[45] it was decided that a subject may "adhere to the King's enemies in his realm" and so be found guilty of treason under the statute of 1351, whether the act complained of was committed within or outside the realm. In that case Sir Roger Casement, a British subject,[46] was found guilty on the ground that he went to Germany when the United Kingdom was at war with that country, and while there endeavoured to persuade Irish prisoners of war (who were British subjects) to join the enemy's forces and thus to assist the liberation of Ireland. The Court of Criminal Appeal had to interpret the statute of Edward III, which was written without punctuation, according to its meaning when it was passed.

14–016   It was resolved by the judges in 1707[47] that a resident alien, who during a war with his native country returned there and adhered to the King's enemies, leaving his family and effects here, might be dealt with as a traitor: "For he came and settled here under the protection of the Crown; and though his person was removed for a time, his effects and family continued still under the same protection." The principle of this rule was extended by the House of Lords in *Joyce v. Director of Public Prosecutions*[48] to an alien who departed entirely from this country, but who was held in the particular circumstances to have remained under the protection of the Crown.

Mens rea is required for treason as for other crimes. In *R. v. Ahlers*[49] the accused was German Consul at Sunderland, and it was therefore part of his ordinary duty to give his compatriots assistance, monetary and otherwise. He took steps on the outbreak of war in 1914 to assist German subjects of military

---

[43] [1903] 1 K.B. 444; *post*, para. 23–011.

[44] *Quaere* extent of application of this rule to the British Nationality Act 1981 in the light of s.12(4); s.24; s.29; s.30.

[45] [1917] 1 K.B. 98. A. Wharam, "Casement and Joyce" (1978) 41 M.L.R. 681.

[46] An Irishman by birth: at that time the whole of Ireland was part of the United Kingdom.

[47] Foster's *Crown Cases* (3rd ed.), p. 185.

[48] [1946] A.C. 347. William Joyce (popularly known as "Lord Haw-Haw") was brought back from Germany at the end of the last war and charged with high treason in that he, while owing allegiance to the Crown, adhered to the King's enemies elsewhere than in the realm by broadcasting Nazi propaganda. He had obtained a British passport by falsely declaring himself to be a British subject, when he was in fact a citizen of the United States. For criticisms of the decision, see Cobbett's *Cases on International Law* (6th ed., W. L. Walker), i, p. 199; Glanville L. Williams, "The Correlation of Allegiance and Protection" (1948) 10 C.L.J. 54; S. C. Briggs, "Treason and the Trial of William Joyce" (1947) 7 U.T.L.J. 162. See also J. A. Cole, *Lord Haw-Haw, The Full Story of William Joyce*.

[49] [1915] 1 K.B. 616, CA.

age to return home to fight in the German army. A statutory Order in Council limited the time for the departure of alien enemies: of this the accused knew nothing, but he believed he was acting in accordance with international law. His conviction for treason by adhering to the King's enemies was quashed for lack of proof that he was aware that he was assisting the King's enemies.

Slaying the Chancellor, etc.

As the Lord Chancellor and judges represent the Sovereign in court, Black-stone considered them entitled to equal protection and justified this section of the statute accordingly. However, attempted murder of the Chancellor and judges in court is, according to the same authority, not treason.

14–017

Treason Acts subsequent to 1351

The Treason Act 1495 provided that a subject who obeyed a usurper while he was occupying the throne would not later be charged with treason after the lawful King had regained the throne, but no protection was given to any person who thereafter declined from his allegiance.[50]

14–018

Under the Treason Act 1702, endeavouring to deprive or hinder any person next in succession to the Throne under the Act of Settlement from succeeding thereto, and maliciously and directly attempting the same by any overt act, is treason. The Succession to the Crown Act 1707 made it treason maliciously and directly by writing or print to maintain and affirm that any other person has any right to the Crown other than in accordance with the Act of Settlement, or that Parliament has not power to make laws to bind the Crown and the descent thereof. The Treason Act 1708 applied the English law of treason to Scotland.[51]

Judicial interpretation of the statute of 1351 relating to compassing the King's death led to a number of "constructive treasons".[52] Some of these were enacted as treasons by the Treason Act 1795 which covered compassing, imagining, devising or intending the death, wounding or imprisonment of the King, whether within the realm or without, provided such compassing, etc. was expressed in writing or by any overt act. The temporary provisions of the 1795 Act were made permanent by the Treason Act 1817. Both statutes were replaced by the Crime and Disorder Act 1998.

Trial and punishment

The punishment prescribed for treason was, from 1814 until the coming into effect of section 36 of the Crime and Disorder Act 1998, death by hanging or, under royal warrant, by beheading.[53] Formerly a male traitor was hanged and quartered, after being drawn on a hurdle to the place of execution[54]; a female

14–019

---

[50] *Madzimbamuto v. Lardner-Burke* [1969] 1 A.C. 645, PC; A. M. Honoré, "Allegiance and the Usurper" (1967) C.L.J. 214; *cf.* Taswell-Langmead, *English Constitutional History* (11th ed. 1960), Plucknett), pp. 224–225, 446–447.

[51] 7 Anne c. 21. "Such crimes and offences which are high treason or misprision of high treason within England shall be construed adjudged and be taken to be high treason within Scotland."

[52] *e.g. R. v. Hardy* (1794) 24 St.Tr. 199; *R. v. Horne Took* (1794) 25 St.Tr. 1. See further, Stephen, *History of the Criminal Law*, Vol. II; Holdsworth, *History of English Law*, Vol. III, pp. 309–322. For criticism of the use of the term "constructive treason" see A. Wharam, "Treason in Rhodesia" [1967] C.L.J. 189.

[53] Treason Act 1814.

[54] These barbarous practices were gradually discarded and were finally abolished by the Forfeiture Act 1870.

traitor was burnt. Until the Forfeiture Act 1870 conviction was followed by forfeiture and corruption of blood.

Treason or misprision of treason committed abroad is triable in England.[55]

Treason committed within the realm must be prosecuted within three years after its commission, except in the case of designing or attempting the assassination of the Sovereign.[56] Bail cannot be granted by magistrates, but only by the Secretary of State or a judge of the Queen's Bench Division.

Misprision of treason

14–020   The Treason Act 1554 created a statutory offence of misprision of treason, punishable by imprisonment for life. Although that statute was repealed by the Criminal Law Act 1967, the common law offence of misprision of treason remains in existence[57] and is an offence punishable by fine or imprisonment at the discretion of the court. It is committed whenever a person knows that another has committed treason and fails to bring this information, or any material part of it, to the attention of the public authorities within a reasonable time.

Treason-felony

14–021   By the Treason Felony Act 1848 a person is guilty of felony if, by writing or overt act within or without the United Kingdom, he compasses, imagines, devises or intends to deprive or depose the Queen from the style, honour or royal name of the imperial crown of the United Kingdom, or of any other of Her Majesty's dominions and countries; or to levy war against Her Majesty within any part of the United Kingdom, in order to compel her to change her measures or counsels, or in order to intimidate or overcome both Houses or either House of Parliament; or to move any foreigner with force to invade the United Kingdom or any other of Her Majesty's dominions. Some of these offences had been enacted as treason by the Treason Act 1795 (*ante*). The Treason Felony Act does not affect the Act of 1795, but provides an alternative remedy in some cases. Its object was partly to cover Ireland, and partly to encourage juries to convict, which they had been loath to do in recent treason trials.

The maximum punishment under the Act of 1848 is imprisonment for life. If a person is indicted for treason-felony and the offence turns out to be treason, he may be convicted of treason-felony.

Attempt to alarm or injure the Sovereign

14–022   An attempt to alarm or injure the Sovereign by discharging or aiming or producing a gun, whether loaded or not, at or near the person of Her Majesty was made an offence punishable by imprisonment for seven years by the Treason Act 1842, after an incident involving Queen Victoria.

Proposals for reforming the law of treason

14–023   The present law of treason is clearly in need of reform. It is based on the concept of allegiance which has little connection with the modern concept of nationality. It covers a wide range of crimes, of varying degrees of gravity, some

---

[55] Treason Act 1543.
[56] Treason Act 1695.
[57] See the Law Commission Working Paper No. 72, para. 41 (1977).

of which can appropriately be dealt with by the ordinary criminal law. Proposals for reform were made by the Law Commission in 1977 but they were not acted upon.[58] The Crime and Disorder Act 1998 has, however, as seen above, abolished the death penalty for treason and effected minor changes in the scope of the offence.

---

[58] Working Paper No. 72, *supra* n. 57. See L. H. Leigh, "Law Reform and the Law of Treason and Sedition" [1977] P.L. 128.

CHAPTER 15

THE ROYAL PREROGATIVE[1]

I. GENERAL NATURE OF THE PREROGATIVE

15-001   The term "royal prerogative" is not a technical one. It is sometimes used to cover all the powers of the Sovereign, or at least those which the Sovereign does not share with his subjects. Sometimes it refers to the powers of the Sovereign in relation to his subjects, as distinct from "acts of state" done in relation to foreign affairs. More often, and preferably, it is limited to those powers which the Sovereign has by the common law as distinct from statute—in other words, the common law powers of the Crown.[2]

So far as the executive powers of the Crown are concerned (and for practical purposes these are the most important) it should be pointed out at the beginning that in the last 100 years the government of the country has been carried on largely under statutory powers. Further we must remember that, in so far as the Crown does exercise prerogative powers, the exercise is governed mainly by constitutional conventions, especially the doctrine of ministerial responsibility.[3] Nevertheless, emphasis on the prerogative does illuminate the historical basis of the Constitution, and it helps to explain much of the theory underlying the forms taken by governmental action.

The laws of England (and Northern Ireland) may differ from the laws of Scotland on the extent of the royal prerogative.[4] Nonetheless, "As the Constitution of Scotland has been the same as that of England since 1707 there is a presumption that the same constitutional principles apply in both countries."[5] (It remains to be seen whether this presumption survives the enactment of the Scotland Act.)

Historical introduction
15-002   The distinction between the natural and politic capacities of the King appears in the sixteenth century.[6] Further subtlety of reasoning led to a distinction in the early seventeenth century between the "absolute" and the "ordinary" powers of the King (*Bate's Case*[7]). By ordinary powers was meant such powers as those involved in the administration of justice, which had long been exercised without discretion in accordance with definite principles and procedure. The absolute powers we should now call discretionary, for example, the direction of foreign

---

[1] J. Chitty, *A Treatise on the Law of the Prerogatives of the Crown* (1820); *Hale's Prerogatives of the King* (ed. D. E. C. Yale, 1976); H. V. Evatt, *The Royal Prerogative* (1987).

[2] For "the Crown", see *post*, para. 15–007.

[3] *post*, para. 17–016 *et seq.*

[4] *Glasgow Corporation v. Central Land Board* 1956 S.C. (HL) 1; J. D. B. Mitchell, "The Royal Prerogative in Modern Scots Law", [1957] P.L. 304.

[5] *Macgregor v. Lord Advocate* 1921 S.C. 847, 848 *per* the Lord Ordinary (Lord Anderson). On appeal, Lord Salvesen said (at p. 853) "It would be anomalous if the liability of a Crown Department in Scotland differed from the liability of a Crown Department in England."

[6] *Case of the Duchy of Lancaster* (1562) Plowd. 212; *Calvin's Case* (1608) 7 Co.Rep. 1a.

[7] (1606) Lane 22; 2 St.Tr. 371; Broom, *Constitutional Law* (2nd ed.), pp. 245 *et seq.*

policy and the pardoning of criminals. There arose also a tendency to regard the absolute prerogatives as "inseparable," so that even Parliament could not detach them from the Crown (*Case of the King's Prerogative in Saltpetre*[8]). One certain principle was that the prerogative was limited by law: "the King hath no prerogative but that which the law of the land allows him" (*Case of Proclamations*[9]). Had not Bracton said in the thirteenth century that the King ought to be subject to God and the law, because the law makes him King?[10] Charles I might dispute the application of this principle in certain aspects of government, such as preventive detention (*Darnel's Case*[11]) and ship-money (*R. v. Hampden*[12]), but the Civil War and the Revolution of 1688 meant that henceforth the Sovereign would accept the limitation of the prerogative by law and its determination by the courts. It is now admitted, of course, that the Sovereign has no powers that are "inseparable"—none, that is, which cannot be taken away by Act of Parliament.[13]

Blackstone says: "By the word prerogative we usually understand that special **15–003** pre-eminence which the King hath, over and above all other persons, and out of the ordinary course of the common law, in right of his regal dignity. It signifies, in its etymology (from *prae* and *rogo*) something that is required or demanded before, or in preference to, all others."[14] The essential characteristic of the royal prerogative, then, is that it is unique and pre-eminent. It is not "out of the ordinary course of the common law" in the sense of being above the law: it is part of the Common law, but an exception to the principles that apply to citizens generally. Dicey's description of the royal prerogative as "the residue of discretionary or arbitrary authority, which at any given time is legally left in the hands of the Crown" has been more than once judicially approved.[15] Dicey emphasises the discretionary nature of the prerogative—the word "arbitrary" is misleading—and confines it according to the best usage to common law as distinct from statutory powers.

Dicey went on to say "Every act which the executive government can lawfully do without the authority of the Act of Parliament is done in virtue of this prerogative."[16] It has been pointed out that such a definition is much wider than

---

[8] (1607) 12 Co.Rep. 12. See Holdsworth, *op. cit.* Vol. IV, pp. 202–207.

[9] 12 Co.Rep. 74; 2 St.Tr. 723.

[10] (1610) *De Legibus et Consuetudinibus Angliae*, f. 5b.

[11] (1627) 3 St.Tr. 1; Broom, *op. cit.* pp. 158 *et seq.*

[12] (1637) 3 St.Tr. 825: And see Holdsworth, *op. cit.* Vol. VI, pp. 19–30; Broom, *op. cit.* pp. 303 *et seq.*

[13] *Att.-Gen. v. De Keyser's Royal Hotel Ltd* [1920] A.C. 508; *post*, para. 15–010.

[14] Bl.Comm. I, 239. Blackstone in defining the Prerogative referred to Locke who in the *True End of Civil Government*, Chap. 14, wrote: "This power to act according to discretion for the public good, without the prescription of the law and sometimes even against it, is that which is called prerogative; for since in some governments the law-making power is not always in being and is usually too numerous and so too slow for the dispatch requisite to execution, and because, also, it is impossible to foresee and so by laws to provide for all accidents and necessities that may concern the public . . . therefore there is a latitude left to the executive power to do many things of choice which the laws do not prescribe." See *Laker Airways Ltd v. Dept of Trade* [1977] Q.B. 643, 705, *per* Lord Denning M.R.

[15] Dicey, *Law of the Constitution* (10th ed. 1959), p. 424; approved, *e.g.* by Lord Dunedin in *Att.-Gen. v. De Keyser's Royal Hotel Ltd* [1920] A.C. 508, 526; *Burmah Oil Co Ltd v. Lord Advocate* [1965] A.C. 75, 99, *per* Lord Reid; *C.C.S.U. v. Minister for the Civil Service* [1985] A.C. 374, 416, *per* Lord Roskill.

[16] *op. cit.* p. 425.

that of Blackstone.[17] Whereas he confined the prerogative to "rights and capacities which the King enjoys alone, in contradistinction to others, and not to those which he enjoys in common with any of his subjects," Dicey's definition covers all the non-statutory power of the Crown, even those which it enjoys in common with its subjects, such as the power to enter into contracts. The correctness of Dicey's wide definition was assumed by the House of Lords in *Council of Civil Service Unions v. Minister for Civil Service*[18] where, however, there were also dicta that for the purposes of judicial review (which was the issue before the House), it was only of historical interest whether a power of the executive should be ascribed to the prerogative or not.[19]

15–004   The prerogative is a *residue* because Parliament can take away any prerogative and has frequently done so. It is seldom abolished expressly, however, but is impliedly abolished, curtailed or merely suspended (*Att.-Gen. v. De Keyser's Royal Hotel Ltd*[20]). Since the prerogative is part of the common law, the Queen cannot claim that a new prerogative has come into existence.[21] In *British Broadcasting Corporation v. Johns*,[22] where the BBC unsuccessfully claimed that the Crown had a monopoly of broadcasting exercised through the Corporation, and that the Corporation was entitled to Crown exemption from income tax, Diplock L.J. said: "It is 350 years and a civil war too late for the Queen's courts to broaden the prerogative." It can only be the residue at any given time of the rights and powers which the Sovereign had before the days of Parliament.

No new prerogative can be claimed, but to what extent can the prerogative be adapted to meet new situations? Being part of the common law, the prerogative is sufficiently adaptable, for example, to adjust itself to new dimensions and methods of warfare.[23] But the distinction between adapting a recognised prerogative and claiming a new power may be difficult to draw, as in *Malone v. Metropolitan Police Commissioner*[24] where Megarry V.-C. held that the Home Secretary had a limited power to authorise telephone tapping as an extension of the power to open articles sent through the post.[25]

There are dicta to the effect that a prerogative power in some circumstances may be lost by disuse.[26] The question may also arise whether a given prerogative

---

[17] H. W. R. Wade, *Constitutional Fundamentals* (1980) p. 46; "Procedure and Prerogative in Public Law" (1985) 101 L.Q.R. 180.

[18] [1985] A.C. 374 (The Cheltenham G.C.H.Q. Case).

[19] *post*, Chap. 17 and Chap. 31.

[20] [1920] A.C. 508.

[21] *Case of Monopolies* (1602) 11 Co. Rep. 84b.

[22] [1965] Ch. 32, CA.

[23] See *e.g. Re A Petition of Right* [1915] 3 K.B. 649, CA, (prerogative to requisition property in defence of the realm extended to aerodromes, although aeroplanes a modern invention) *Att.-Gen. v. De Keyser's Royal Hotel Ltd* [1920] A.C. 508, 565 *per* Lord Sumner.

[24] [1979] Ch. 344; *post*, para. 26–014. For the ability of the Crown to carry out lawful activities beyond the limits of the prerogative see B.V. Harris, "The Third Source of Authority for Government Action," (1992) 109 L.Q.R. 626.

[25] *cf.* now, Interception of Telecommunications Act 1985; *post* para. 20–014. In *Att.-Gen. of the Duchy of Lancaster v. G. E. Overton (Farms) Ltd* [1981] Ch. 333; [1982] Ch. 277 an attempt to extend the prerogative right to treasure trove so as to protect items of antiquarian value, whether or not gold or silver, failed: *post* p. 271. See generally, George Winterton, "The Prerogative in Novel Situations", (1983) 99 L.Q.R. 407.

[26] *e.g. per* Lord Lyndhurst and Lord Campbell, C.J. in *Wensleydale Peerage Case* (1856) 5 H.L.C. 958; and *per* Lord Simon of Glaisdale in *M'Kendrick v. Sinclair* 1972 S.C. 25 (H.L.), a Scots case concerning the old action of assythment; see J. M. Thomson, "Desuetude and the Common Law" (1973) 89 L.Q.R. 27.

survived the Bill of Rights 1688.[27] But generally we may say that a prerogative which has long fallen out of use, such as the sovereign's power to refuse the royal assent to Bills passed by both Houses of Parliament, is now bound by constitutional convention rather than by some legal doctrine of desuetude.

A prerogative power is *discretionary*, and, although its existence is determinable by the courts, the manner of the exercise was generally thought to be outside their jurisdiction. Dicta in the *G.C.H.Q.* Case,[28] however, suggest that prerogative powers, like discretionary powers of statutory origin, may be subject to judicial review.

The Prime Minister, as Minister for the Civil Service, gave instructions under an Order in Council made, as the House of Lords held, by virtue of the Royal Prerogative, forbidding staff at the Government Communications Headquarters from being members of trade unions. The House of Lords accepted the argument of the applicant unions and staff that past practice had created a legitimate expectation[29] that they would, in the normal course of events, be consulted before a decision affecting the terms of employment of civil servants at the headquarters was made. In so holding all the Law Lords agreed that the scope of judicial review of a Ministerial decision was the same whether it was made under statutory powers—whether Act of Parliament or delegated legislation made under an Act—or under an Order in Council deriving its authority from the prerogative. Lord Diplock, Lord Scarman and Lord Roskill were prepared to go further and were of the opinion that acts done directly under the royal prerogative were subject to judicial review, where the issues involved were *justiciable*.[30] Lord Fraser and Lord Brightman preferred to express no opinion on the point.[31] The House, however, accepted that the Minister had, on the facts, been entitled to issue the instruction without consultation because national security required such summary procedure.[32] (The issue of national security had not been raised at all before Glidewell J. who found for the unions, and only briefly before the Court of Appeal which reversed the first instance judgment).

The Law Lords in the *G.C.H.Q.* Case who asserted the existence of a jurisdiction to review acts done under the Royal prerogative confined that jurisdiction to justiciable acts. As examples of non-justiciable acts Lord Roskill listed, "the

15–005

---

[27] See, *e.g. per* Lord Parmoor in *Att.-Gen. v. De Keyser's Royal Hotel Ltd* [1920] A.C. 508, 570 and *per* Lord Reid in *Burmah Oil Co v. Lord Advocate* [1965] A.C. 75, 99.

[28] [1985] A.C. 374. See the earlier dicta of Lord Denning, M.R. in *Laker Airways v. Department of Trade* [1977] Q.B. 643.

[29] As to "legitimate expectations," see *post* para 31–018.

[30] at p. 407, *per* Lord Scarman; at p. 410, *per* Lord Diplock; at p. 417, *per* Lord Roskill.

[31] at p. 398 *per* Lord Fraser, who pointed out that to permit review would "run counter to the great weight of authority"; at p. 424 *per* Lord Brightman.

[32] The degree of control that the courts can exert over ministerial claims that a matter raises questions of national security is not clear. All the members of the House adverted to the need of evidence to justify such a claim by a minister. Lord Scarman envisaged, even in a case of national security, that the court might conclude that the opinion of a Minister that certain action was required was such that no reasonable minister could reasonably have held: [at p. 406]. Lord Diplock, on the other hand, having adverted to the need for evidence, went on to say that if a question of national security were established, the appropriate action was for the government: "It is par excellence a non-justiciable question. The judicial process is totally inept to deal with the sort of problems which it involves." (At p. 412) *cf. Chandler v. D.P.P.* [1964] A.C. 763. Judicial assertions of boldness in the areas of security and defence very often precede a refusal to upset the decision complained of on some other ground: *R. v. Home Secretary ex p. Ruddock* [1987] 1 W.L.R. 1482; *R. v. Ministry of Defence ex p. Smith* [1996] Q.B. 517, CA.

making of treaties[33] the defence of the realm,[34] the prerogative of mercy,[35] the grant of honours, the disolution of Parliament and the appointment of ministers as well as others ... ".[36] Thus there is no reason to doubt that the courts will continue to accept as conclusive Foreign Office certificates relating to the recognition of foreign states and governments,[37] the existence of a state of war[38] and whether individuals are entitled to claim sovereign[39] or diplomatic immunity[40] in the British courts.

15–006   Lastly, the prerogatives are *legally* vested in the Queen although this is now largely a matter of form. By custom and convention prerogative powers must be exercised through and on the advice of other persons. The necessity of knowing whether or not an executive act is an expression of the Sovereign's will and of making someone other than the Sovereign legally liable for its consequences has given rise to complex rules determining how the Sovereign's acts are to be authenticated. The forms in which the royal will is expressed are generally by: (i) proclamation, writ, letters patent, grant or other document under the Great Seal[41]; (ii) Order in Council; or (iii) warrant, commission, order or instructions[42] under the Sign Manual. The discretionary character of prerogative powers has also given rise to the doctrine of ministerial responsibility, the most important development in modern British constitutional history. There are very few occasions nowadays when the Queen can act without or against the advice of her Ministers; these exceptional cases may include the choice of Prime Minister[43] and the dissolution of Parliament or the dismissal of a ministry.[44]

For some years the Labour Party was committed to abolishing the prerogative so that all government decisions were subject to Parliamentary control. After the election in 1997 it was reported that the new government had abandoned plans to introduce legislation to give effect to this pledge.

Classification of the prerogative

15–007   (i) It is still possible to distinguish between *personal* and *political* prerogatives, that is, between those which the Queen has as a person and those which she has as Head of State. The personal, however, have tended to become absorbed by the political and in consequence they have lost most of their constitutional significance.

The political prerogatives are often spoken of as adhering to *"the Crown"*. Thomas Paine called the Crown "a metaphor shown at the Tower for sixpence or a shilling a piece",[45] and Maitland said the expression was often used as a cover

---

[33] *J.H. Rayner (Mincing Lane) Ltd v. Dept of Trade and Industry* [1990] 2 AC 418, HL.

[34] In *R. v. Ministry of Defence ex p. Smith* [1996] QB 517, the Court of Appeal refused to regard the Crown's policy with regard to the treatment of homosexual members of the Armed Forces as non-justiciable on this ground—but went on to refuse to find government policy irrational.

[35] *post* para. 20–004.

[36] At p. 418.

[37] *Duff Development Co v. Government of Kelantan* [1924] A.C. 797, HL; *Carl Zeiss Stiftung v. Rayner and Keeler Ltd.* (No. 2) [1967] A.C. 853, HL. See also *R. v. S. of State for Foreign and Commonwealth Affairs, ex p. Trawnik, The Times,* April 18, 1985.

[38] *R. v. Bottrill, ex p. Kuechenmeister* [1947] K.B. 41, CA.

[39] *Mighell v. Sultan of Johore* [1894] 1 Q.B. 149.

[40] *Engelke v. Musmann* [1928] A.C. 433. And *post* para. 15–032.

[41] *ante*, para 8–023.

[42] *e.g.* to colonial Governors, *post*, Chap. 35.

[43] *post*, para. 17–028.

[44] *ante*, para. 8–022.

[45] *Rights of Man* (1791).

for ignorance.[46] In effect "the Crown" is equivalent to the executive or the central government.[47] Each organ of the Government is in law, part of the one, indivisible Crown of the United Kingdom.[48] For specific purposes statutes may, however, distinguish between government departments, for example, the Crown Proceedings Act 1947, s.17 with regard to proceedings under that Act, or the Data Protection Act 1998, section 63(2) which provides that for the purposes of that Act each government department is to be treated as a person separate from any other government department. More precisely it means the Queen in her public capacity, either: (a) in rare cases acting at her own discretion, *e.g.* choice of Prime Minister in exceptional circumstances; (b) acting on the advice of Ministers, *e.g.* opening Parliament; (c) acting through or by means of Ministers, *e.g.* negotiating treaties and pardoning criminals; or (d) Ministers acting on behalf of the Queen.[49] With regard to the last, in modern times many powers are conferred by statute directly on Ministers, *e.g.* to approve town-planning schemes or to acquire land compulsorily; in theory the Ministers act on behalf of the Queen.

In the eyes of the law *the Crown* should probably be regarded as a corporation sole. The suggestion that the Crown has no legal personality[50] is untenable in the light of earlier authorities.[51] In *Re M*[52] Lord Woolf did not think it necessary to express a view on whether the Crown is better regarded as a corporation sole or a corporation aggregate.

Exceptionally individual ministers may be constituted corporations sole by statute in order to facilitate the acquisition and management of property: for example, the Secretary of State for Defence by section 2 of the Defence (Transfer of Functions) Act 1964.

(ii) So far we have spoken of the prerogatives as if they were composed **15–008** entirely of powers. Another classification shows that this is not so. They can be analysed into: (a) *rights, e.g.* the Crown Estate and *bona vacantia* (but these are regulated largely by statute); (b) *powers, e.g.* to summon Parliament and to make treaties; (c) *privileges, e.g.* to ask for and to receive supply from Parliament; and (d) *immunities, e.g.* exemption from statutes imposing taxes or rates unless expressly mentioned, and from being sued or have property taken in execution (*cf.* Crown Proceedings Act 1947). This method of classification is one of analytical jurisprudence rather than constitutional law, but it may sometimes help to a clearer understanding of the prerogative.

(iii) The most convenient classification for the present day is according to the branch of government to which the various prerogatives relate, *i.e. legislative, judicial* and *executive.* Those which relate to legislation and the administration of justice are mostly "ordinary" prerogatives in the sense used above, while those

---

[46] *Constitutional History*, p. 418.
[47] See further, Marshall, *Constitutional Theory* (1971), pp. 17–34. *The Nature of the Crown* (Sunkin and Payne eds, 1999).
[48] *Cmrs of Crown Lands v. Page* [1960] 2 Q.B. 274, CA. The Crown is, however, divisible with reference to its liabilities and obligations in respect of its various territories and realms: *R. v. Secretary of State for Foreign and Commonwealth Affairs ex p. Indian Association of Alberta* [1982] Q.B. 892, CA *post* para. 35–005.
[49] *Post*, Chap. 33.
[50] *Re Pan American's Application* [1992] Q.B. 854, 860 *per* Lord Donaldson M.R.
[51] Sir William Wade, [1992] New L.J. 1316.
[52] [1994] 1 A.C. 377, citing dicta of Lord Diplock and Lord Simon in *Town Investments Ltd v. Department of the Environment* [1978] A.C. 359.

which relate to the executive are mainly "absolute"[53] or discretionary and regulated by convention.

Personal prerogatives

15–009 These consist mainly of immunities and property rights.

(i) *"The King never dies."* The Common law knows no interregnum. But this theory was of limited effect, because the death of the Sovereign entailed the dissolution of Parliament and the determination of the tenure of offices under the Crown (including judicial offices), until these inconveniences were remedied by various statutes.[54]

(ii) *"The King is never an infant."* The common law made no provision for the Sovereign being a minor; but the contingency is now provided for by the Regency Acts.[55]

(iii) *"The King can do no wrong."* The Sovereign cannot be sued or prosecuted in the courts.[56] The significance of this immunity was greatly diminished by the Crown Proceedings Act 1947, which enables the citizen to sue government departments in contract or tort or for the recovery of property, while leaving unimpaired the Sovereign's personal immunity.[57]

(iv) *Crown private estates.*[58] At common law the general rule is that the same prerogatives attach to estates vested in the Sovereign in her natural capacity as apply to estates vested in the Sovereign in her political capacity in right of the Crown. The Crown Private Estates Acts 1800, 1862 and 1873 now regulate to some extent the disposition of such property. These Acts apply to property belonging to the Sovereign at the time of accession, property devised or bequeathed by any persons not being Kings or Queens of the realm, and property bought out of the privy purse. They render private estates subject to taxation in the same way as the property of any subject of the realm. Crown private estates may be disposed of by the Sovereign *inter vivos* or by will unless, like the Duchies of Lancaster and Cornwall (the incomes from which are not subject to income tax[59]), they are settled by charter having statutory effect. If undisposed of at the death of the Sovereign, they descend with the Crown and become lands held in right of the Crown.[60]

Effect of statute on the prerogative

15–010 A royal prerogative may be expressly abolished by Act of Parliament, as when the Crown Proceedings Act 1947 abolished the immunity of the Crown from being sued in contract and tort. An Act may be passed covering the same ground or part of the same ground as the prerogative, in which case the prerogative is to that extent by necessary implication abrogated, at least so long as the statute remains in force.

---

[53] *ante*, para. 15–001.

[54] For Parliament and the demise of the Crown, see *ante*, p. 139; and for judicial tenure, *post*, para. 20–029. And see Crown Proceedings Act 1947, s.32.

[55] *ante*, para. 14–008.

[56] The legend perpetuated by Bracton, that writs lay against the King down to Edward I's time, is refuted by other authorities; see Holdsworth, *History of English Law*, Vol. IX, p. 12.

[57] It would seem that proceedings against the Queen in her private capacity can now be brought (if at all) only by way of the common law (pre-1860) petition of right; *post*, para. 33–015.

[58] (1971) H.C. 29.

[59] *post*, para. 15–013.

[60] *cf.* Crown Estate, *post*, para. 15–013.

In *Attorney-General v. De Keyser's Royal Hotel Ltd*[61] the respondent's hotel was required by the War Office in the First World War. Negotiations broke down over the amount of the rent, and possession was taken compulsorily by the Army Council under the Defence of the Realm Regulations on terms that compensation would be paid *ex gratia*. The respondents gave possession but claimed the right to full compensation under the Defence Regulations. The House of Lords unanimously decided that the statutory Regulations specifying the manner in which compensation was to be assessed must be observed by the Crown. The Crown could not choose, said Lord Sumner, whether or not to act under the prerogative power (assuming that to exist) involving perhaps no compensation or only compensation *ex gratia*: it must act under the statutory power and in accordance with its terms for, as Lord Moulton said, that must be presumed to be the intention of Parliament in passing the statute. Their Lordships expressed various opinions on the question whether, where a statute impliedly covers the same ground as a prerogative power, the statute *pro tanto* abolishes the prerogative or merges it with the statute (Lord Parmoor); or whether, as Lord Atkinson preferred to say, the prerogative is merely in abeyance so long as the statute remains in force.

In *Laker Airways Ltd v. Department of Trade*[62] consideration was given to the effect of the Civil Aviation Act 1971 on the powers of the Crown under the Bermuda Agreement 1946, a treaty between the United Kingdom and the United States covering the grant and revocation of permits for transatlantic air services. The Act set up a Civil Aviation Authority for the licensing of air transport, subject to "guidance" given by the Secretary of State. In furtherance of changed government policy the Secretary of State gave "guidance" to the authority to revoke the licence granted to Laker Airways to operate their "Skytrain" service between London and New York. The Court of Appeal held that the Secretary of State's action was *ultra vires* the Act, which impliedly fettered the use of the prerogative to cancel the designation of the plaintiffs under the treaty.

In *R. v. Secretary of State for the Home Department ex p. Northumbria Police Authority*[63] the Court of Appeal accepted the existence of a prerogative power to maintain the Queen's Peace[64] and held that statutory provisions under the Police Act 1964 which gave local authorities responsibility for equipping police forces did not take away the prerogative power. Hence the Home Secretary could supply equipment which the local authority was unwilling to. This decision may be regarded as an instance where the statute was, as a matter of construction, not inconsistent with the continued exercise of the prerogative power but in reaching that conclusion the Court was influenced by the fact that, contrary to *De. Keyser's Royal Hotel*, there was no question of interference with private property rights. Indeed, the act here was for the public benefit.[65]

The relationship between prerogative and statute arose in unusual circum- **15–011** stances in *R. v. Secretary of State for the Home Department ex p. Fire Brigades*

---

[61] [1920] A.C. 508. See also *Egan v. Macready* [1921] 1 I.R. 265. *Walwin Ltd v. West Sussex C.C.* [1975] 3 All E.R. 604; *Herbert Berry v. I.R.C.* [1977] 1 W.L.R. 1437 (HL); *Manitoba Fisheries Ltd v. The Queen* (1978) 88 D.L.R. (3d) 462 (Can. Sup.Ct.).

[62] [1977] Q.B. 643, CA.

[63] [1989] Q.B. 26, CA.

[64] All three members of the court cited *O. Hood Phillips Constitutional and Administrative Law.* Croom-Johnson L.J. quoted a passage at p. 399 in the 6th ed., in this edition para. 21–001.

[65] In *Bethel v. Douglas* [1995] 1 W.L.R. 794 the Privy Council held that the Governor of the Bahamas retained his prerogative right to appoint a commission of inquiry despite having even more extensive statutory powers to do so.

Union.[66] The Criminal Justice Act 1988 had made provision for a statutory scheme for compensating the victims of crimes. The scheme would only come into effect on the making of a ministerial order under the Act. Some years later the statutory scheme never having come into effect, the Secretary of State purported to create a scheme offering less generous compensation in reliance on the royal prerogative.[67] The House of Lords held, by a majority, that the Home Secretary had a continuing duty under the Act to decide whether (or when) to bring the statutory scheme into operation. Parliament could not have intended that he might preclude himself from exercising the statutory powers by acting under the prerogative. The concern of the minority was that the question whether or when the provisions of the Act should be brought into effect was one of a political nature for Parliament not the courts. In the words of Lord Keith, any interference by the courts would be a most improper intrusion into a field lying peculiarly within the province of Parliament. Lord Mustill similarly was unhappy that the House was in danger of overstepping the boundaries of the distinction between court and Parliament established in, and recognised ever since, the Bill of Rights.

II. THE PREROGATIVE IN DOMESTIC AFFAIRS

These consist largely of powers, and in theory of some duties.

1. Executive prerogatives[68]

15–012   The prerogatives that may be classed as executive, administrative or governmental are a relic of the powers which the King had when he really governed the country. The government at the present day is largely carried on under statutory powers—a subject too vast for discussion in a general book on constitutional law. Prerogative powers nowadays are mainly of importance in relation to the Civil Service, the armed forces, colonial administration, Commonwealth relations and foreign affairs. Moreover, they have to be read subject to the principle of ministerial responsibility. The government does not have to consult, or even to inform, Parliament before exercising prerogative powers. This is convenient, for many matters falling within the prerogative are not suitable for public discussion before the decision is made or the action performed. On the other hand, the government must feel assured of parliamentary support afterwards, especially in a matter like war or where money will be required.

The Sovereign in theory also has duties, but these are not legally enforceable. "The principal duty of the King is, to govern his people according to law", says Blackstone, quoting Bracton and Fortescue to like effect. Blackstone cites the Coronation Oath, but adds that "doubtless the duty of protection is impliedly as much incumbent on the Sovereign before coronation as after".[69] The Sovereign is the general conservator of the peace of the Kingdom,[70] but although the

---

[66] [1995] 2 A.C. 513, HL.
[67] A scheme based on the prerogative had existed for many years before the 1988 Act: see *R. v. Criminal Injuries Compensation Board ex p. Lain* [1967] 2 Q.B. 864, CA.
[68] *Cf.* J. B. D. Mitchell, "The Royal Prerogative in Modern Scots Law" [1957] P.L. 304.
[69] Bl.Comm. I, Chap. 6.
[70] Bl.Comm. I, 266. *R. v. Secretary of State for the Home Department, ex p. Northumbria Police Authority*, [1989] Q.B. 26, CA.

preservation of the peace is a function of the Crown, police officers are not regarded as Crown servants.[71] In *China Navigation Co v. Attorney-General*,[72] it was held that there is no duty enforceable by the Courts on the Crown to afford such protection as was asked for in that case, *viz.* armed protection against pirates in foreign waters, and the subject is not obliged to pay for such protection; but if the Crown agrees to provide special protection for payment, such payment can be recovered from the subject. And in *Tito v. Waddell (No. 2)*[73] it was held that any obligation by the Crown to pay royalties for the extraction of phosphates from the colony of Ocean Island was governmental, and not a fiduciary duty enforceable in the courts. In *Mutasa v. Attorney-General*[74] Boreham J. held that he had no jurisdiction to enforce the sovereign's duty to protect her subjects at the instance of the plaintiff who claimed that the Crown had failed to prevent his unlawful detention by the illegal Smith regime in Southern Rhodesia.

For our immediate purpose the following is probably the most convenient classification of the prerogatives relating to executive government:

(a) **Appointment and dismissal** of Ministers, other government officials; offi- **15–013**
cers and men of the forces; the appointment and (subject to statute) dismissal of judicial officers and civil servants.

(b) **Control of the services.** The Queen is head of the Royal Navy, the Army and the Royal Air Force. The supreme command and government of all forces by sea, land and air, and of all forts and places of strength, is vested in the Crown both by common law and statute. The last Sovereign to exercise the command of the Army in person was George III in 1743 at the Battle of Dottingen. The raising of forces, their discipline and payment are now governed by statute,[75] but the movement and disposition of forces lawfully raised is entirely under the control of the Crown.[76] The control of the Civil Service is similarly vested in the Crown.[77]

(c) **Administration of dependencies.** It is still a function of the Crown to provide for the government of British colonies and other dependencies; and also to make laws for colonies acquired by conquest or cession until Parliament takes over or the colony is granted representative institutions.[78]

(d) **Revenue.** The Norman and early Plantagenet Kings had "ordinary" and "extraordinary" revenues, and this terminology was still used at the beginning of the nineteenth century.[79] The "ordinary" revenues consisted of customary hereditary revenues such as feudal dues,[80] *bona vacantia*, income from Crown lands and other miscellaneous sources of income that are now exchanged for the Civil

---

[71] *post* para. 21–009.
[72] [1932] 2 K.B. 197, CA.
[73] [1977] Ch. 106 (Megarry V.-C.).
[74] [1980] Q.B. 114. The learned judge quoted with approval the opening sentence of this paragraph from p. 272 of the 6th ed.
[75] *Post*, Chap. 19.
[76] *China Navigation Co v. Att.-Gen.* [1932] 2 K.B. 197, CA; *Chandler v. D.P.P.* [1964] A.C. 763, HL; see *per* Viscount Radcliffe.
[77] *Rodwell v. Thomas* [1944] K.B. 596. *Post*, Chap. 18.
[78] *post*, Chap. 35.
[79] Chitty, *Prerogatives of the Crown* (1820) p. 200.
[80] Most of these disappeared with the abolition of military tenure in 1660.

List (*infra*). "Extraordinary" revenues or "aids" were raised from time to time to meet the needs of war or other public emergency.

The Crown Estate consists of lands which have become vested in the Sovereign "in his body politic in right of the Crown," and include the ancient demesne lands of the Crown and lands subsequently acquired by prerogative right, *e.g.* by escheat or forfeiture, the foreshore and lands formed by alluvion. The Crown Estate is managed by the Crown Estate Commissioners, who are subject to the general directions of the Chancellor of the Exchequer and the Secretary of State for Scotland. Their annual reports are to be laid before Parliament.[81]

Bona vacantia include wreck,[82] treasure trove, waifs, estrays, royal mines and royal fish.[83] Land that formerly escheated[84] on failure of heirs goes to the Crown as *bona vacantia* under the Administration of Estates Act 1925. Treasure trove at common law consisted of gold or silver in coin, plate or bullion, hidden in the earth or other secret place, and subsequently found without trace of the owner.[85] It is hidden, and not abandoned, treasure. The finding of treasure trove was determined by a coroner[86] and a jury. Treasure trove went by law to the Crown, and it was an offence at common law to conceal the discovery.[87] The prerogative of treasure trove has been replaced by a statutory scheme designed to protect all ancient items of historic or archaeological interest when found.[88]

It is the privilege of the Crown to demand and receive supply from Parliament for the government of the country.[89] Since the Bill of Rights 1688 taxes can only be raised by authority of Parliament.

The Civil List. Since the accession of George III in 1760 it has been the custom for each Sovereign to surrender to the Exchequer for life the hereditary revenues held in right of the Crown, in exchange for an annual payment known as the Civil List. The revenues of the Duchies of Lancaster and Cornwall are excluded from the surrender. The surrendered revenues are paid into the Exchequer and form part of the Consolidated Fund. The main items of expenditure covered by the Civil List, which is charged on the Consolidated Fund, are the salaries and expenses of the official part of the royal household and royal bounty, and the Privy Purse (pensions for employees and the maintenance of Sandringham and Balmoral).[90] Provision is also made towards the expenses of performing public duties by certain other members of the Royal Family.[91] Various government departments meet other expenditure, *e.g.* the Queen's Flight and royal residences

---

[81] Crown Estate Act 1961.

[82] Regulated by the Merchant Shipping Act 1894. See *Pierce v. Bemis (The Lusitania)* [1986] 2 W.L.R. 501.

[83] For these, see Bl.Comm. I, 290–299; Keith, *The King and the Imperial Crown*, p. 390.

[84] See *Re Lowe's Will Trusts* [1973] 1 W.L.R. 882 (Claim by Crown to the Phoenix Inn, Stratford-on-Avon, arising from death in 1851 of tenant in fee simple without heirs).

[85] *Att.-Gen. of the Duchy of Lancaster v. G. E. Overton (Farms) Ltd* [1981] Ch. 333; [1982] Ch. 277. See generally, Sir George Hill, *Treasure Trove in Law and Practice: from the earliest time to the present day* (1936).

[86] The chief duty of the coroner, whose court dates back to 1194, is to hold an inquest where a person has died in his district and there is reasonable cause to suspect that he died a violent or unnatural death, or where death was sudden and the cause unknown, or where the person died in prison: Coroners Courts Act 1887–1954; Criminal Law Act 1977.

[87] *R. v. Toole* (1867) 11 Cox C.C. 75.

[88] Treasure Act 1996.

[89] *ante*, Chap. 12.

[90] The Queen does not, in fact, draw the money allocated to her Privy Purse and her personal expenditure is paid from her own resources.

[91] *Report from the Select Committee on the Civil List* (1971) H.C. 29.

occupied by members of the Royal Family. The amounts fixed by Parliament on the accession of Queen Elizabeth II in 1952 were increased by the Civil List Act 1972 to offset inflation. Section 6 provides that the Treasury may increase from time to time the financial provision allocated for certain purposes by statutory instrument subject to annulment by resolution of the House of Commons; and the Civil List Act 1975 allows the Treasury to supplement such sums out of moneys provided by Parliament. It is unclear whether the amounts paid by the Treasury and other Departments for the Monarchy exceed the hereditary revenues and income made over by the Queen to the Treasury.[92]

(e) Ecclesiastical prerogatives. Elizabeth I was described as the supreme eccle-   **15–014**
siastical and temporal "Governor" of the realm by the Act of Supremacy 1558,[93] and the Book of Common Prayer refers to the Sovereign as "our Queen and Governor". The title suggests administrative rather than lawmaking powers; ecclesiastical but not spiritual. "Conceive it thus", says Selden, "there is in the Kingdom of England a college of physicians; the King is supreme governor of those, but not the head of them, nor president of the college, nor the best physician." The Queen nominates bishops diocesan[94] of the Church of England on the advice of the Prime Minister. The Church has not been given the decisive voice in appointing its bishops,[95] mainly because its senior bishops sit in the House of Lords. The current practice is that the Church Commission on Crown Appointments[96] puts forward to the Prime Minister two names for a vacant bishopric, expressing a preference for one of them.[97] In 1998 Mr Blair is believed to have rejected both names put forward for the bishopric of Liverpool.

Otherwise, the functions and powers of the Queen in relation to the Church of England are mainly regulated by statute, for example, the calling together and dissolving of the General Synod and the Convocations of Canterbury and York.[98] The Queen in person opened the Second General Synod in 1975. The Clergy Act 1533 requires the Queen's assent and licence for the making of Canon laws and also provides that no Canons may be made which are contrary or repugnant to the royal prerogative or the customs, laws or statutes of the realm. Since the

[92] See further, Bogdanor, *op. cit.*, Chap. 7; A. Tomkins, "Crown Privileges", in *The Nature of the Crown* (eds, Sunkin and Payne).

[93] Repealed, except section 8 by various Acts. The sidenote to that section reads "All Spiritual Jurisdiction United to the Crown." The Act of Supremacy 1534 (repealed in 1554) called Henry VIII the supreme "Head" on earth of the Church of England.

[94] Suffragan bishops are appointed on the nomination of diocesan bishops. The appointment of Deans is on the advice of the Prime Minister.

[95] The prerogative and procedure for confirming the election of bishops were preserved by the Ecclesiastical Jurisdiction Measure 1963, as amended.

[96] Consisting of the two Archbishops, six members elected by the General Synod, and two non-voting members (the Prime Minister's appointments secretary and the Archbishop's appointments secretary). Proposals for reform of the present system, involving less secrecy and the opportunity for clergy to apply for consideration as possible bishops were published in May, 2001. (*Working with the Spirit: Choosing Diocesan Bishops*). The Commission would be renamed the Episcopal Nominations Commission and given an enlarged membership.

[97] A *congé d'elire* (permission to elect) is sent to the dean and chapter of the cathedral of the vacant bishopric (or to the cathedral chapter in the case of "a parish church cathedral" which does not have a dean), accompanied by a "letter missive" containing the name of the nominee. (In the case of the Bishopric of Sodor and Man where there is no chapter at all, nomination is effected by letters patent).

[98] Synodical Government Measure 1969, modifying the Church of England Assembly (Powers) Act 1919 and the Church of England Convocations Act 1966.

Reformation new Canons, or changes in customary or Canon Law, can only bind the laity by authority of Act of Parliament (*Middleton v. Croft*[99]). Forms of service alternative to those prescribed by the Book of Common Prayer may now be authorised by the General Synod, without the need for an Act of Parliament.[1]

15–015   **(f) The "fountain of honour".** The Queen is the "fountain of honour."[2] The creation of peers is done on the advice of the Prime Minister.[3] Most honours in the United Kingdom are also conferred on the advice of the Prime Minister.[4]

Recommendations for *all* honours have, since 1979, been submitted for scrutiny to the Political Honours Scrutiny Committee, a body which was established in the 1920s in the wake of disquiet about the sale of titles by Lloyd George. The Committee consists of three Privy Councillors. If the Prime Minister persists with a recommendation against the advice of the Committee, its adverse view is made known to the Queen which, it has been suggested, must imply that the monarch, in such circumstances, has a discretion to reject the recommendation.[5]

(g) Miscellaneous prerogatives. Other prerogatives or former prerogatives relating to coinage, mining of precious metals, administration of charities, guardianship of infants and mental patients,[6] the use of patents and the creation of boroughs, are now largely regulated by statute.[7] The prerogative to issue the writ *ne exeat regno*[8] (to forbid a person to leave the realm) at the instance of a Secretary of State is obsolescent.[9] The right to publish the Bible and the New Testament does not extend to breach of copyright in modern translations.[10] It has

---

[99] (1743) Cas. T. Hard. 326 (Eccles. Ct.).

[1] Church of England (Worship and Doctrine) Measure 1974 (No. 3).

[2] *The Prince's Case* (1606) 8 Co.Rep. 1a, 18b; Bl.Com. I, 271.

[3] George V in 1924 personally offered Asquith, an ex-Prime Minister, a peerage on the day on which he lost his seat at a general election, when Baldwin was about to succeed MacDonald and the premiership was momentarily vacant; Roy Jenkins, *Asquith*, pp. 505–506.

[4] Some Orders are a matter for the Queen's personal choice; *viz*: awards to the Order of Merit, Orders of the Garter and the Thistle and the Royal Victorian Order. Thus the Queen made the Governor of Southern Rhodesia a K.C.V.O. at the time of U.D.I. in November 1965.

[5] G. Marshall, *Constitutional Conventions* (1984), p. 23. Questions may not be asked of the Prime Minister relating to the grant of honours: Erskine May, *Parliamentary Practice* (22nd ed.), p. 298. The role of the Committee will be affected by the establishment of an Appointments Committee to advise on the conferment of life peerages; *ante*, para. 9–011.

[6] See *R.F. (Mental Patient: Sterilisation)* [1990] 2 AC 1, HL for resort by the courts to their inherent jurisdiction.

[7] The Wild Creatures and Forest Laws Act 1971 abolished the prerogative right to wild creatures (except royal fish and swans), and any franchises of forest, free chase, park or free warren; abrogated the forest laws and repealed the statutes dating back to Edward I. On the coinage see now, Coinage Act 1971; Currency Act 1983. The determining of weights and measures was formerly done by the prerogative: A. Wharam, "The History of the Mile" [1979] N.L.J. 51.

[8] *Ne exeat regnum*: Bl.Comm. I. 265–266.

[9] *Felton v. Callis* [1969] 1 Q.B. 200 (Megarry J.), *Lipkin Gorman v. Cass The Times* May 29, 1985; *Al Nahkel for Contracting and Trading Ltd v. Lowe* [1986] 2 W.L.R. 317. And see J. W. Bridge, "The Case of the Rugby Football Team and the High Prerogative Writ" (1972) 88 L.Q.R. 83; F. M. Auburn, *"Ne Exeat Regno"* [1970] C.L.J. 183. L.J. Anderson, " 'Antiquity in Action,'—*Ne Exeat Regno* Revived," (1987) 104 L.Q.R. 246. A similar effect can be achieved by resort to the equitable jurisdiction of the High Court: *Bayer A.G. v. Winter (No. 2)* [1986] 1 W.L.R. 497, CA.

[10] *Universities of Oxford and Cambridge v. Eyre and Spottiswoode* [1964] Ch. 736.

been held that there is a prerogative to issue free information, *e.g.* a government pamphlet about the Common Market.[11]

(h) Emergency and Defence. The Crown may use such force as is reasonably necessary to put down riot or insurrection.[12]   **15–016**

The Crown is responsible for the defence of the realm by sea and land, and is the only judge of the existence of danger to the realm from external enemies (*R. v. Hampden*[13]), although it is not the sole judge of the means by which such danger is to be averted, *e.g.* the imposition of taxation or conscription (Bill of Rights 1688). In time of war the Crown may requisition ships, at least British ships in territorial waters, on payment of compensation (*The Broadmayne*[14]), and may enter upon and use the lands of the citizen near the coast in order to repel invasion (*Case of the King's Prerogative in Saltpetre*[15]). After the danger is over the bulwarks ought to be removed: nothing otherwise was said about compensation in that case. But in modern times the Crown relies in time of war and other grave emergency on statutory powers, such as the Emergency Powers (Defence) Acts of the late war.[16]

Dicey goes so far as to say: "There are times of tumult or invasion when for the sake of legality itself the rules of law must be broken. The course which the Government must then take is clear. The Ministry must break the law and trust for protection to an Act of Indemnity."[17] If this is so, the duty of the Crown to protect the realm is paramount. Darling J. in *Re Shipton*[18] construing a Defence of the Realm Act approved *obiter* the old maxim, *salus populi suprema lex* (the safety of the people is the highest law).[19]

The question whether compensation is payable for loss or damage caused by (lawful) exercise of the prerogative was argued for the first time in the House of Lords as a preliminary question of law in *Burmah Oil Co v. Lord Advocate*.[20] The company's oil installations had been destroyed by order of the British commander of the forces in Burmah (then a colony) in 1942, to prevent them from falling into the hands of the invading Japanese forces who would have found them of great strategic value. Their Lordships held by a majority of three to two that, although compensation had never been payable at common law for "battle" damage, whether accidental or deliberate, this was "denial" damage—really economic warfare—and there was no general rule that the royal prerogative can be exercised without compensation. Lord Reid in his majority speech said that there was no precedent of a claim for compensation in such cases not being paid,   **15–017**

---

[11] *Jenkins v. Att.-Gen.* (1971) 115 S.J. 674. "Since all the Crown's subjects are at liberty to issue as much free information as they like … I offer you this as a choice example of a non-prerogative"; H. W. R. Wade, *Constitutional Fundamentals* (1980), p. 49. The Crown's subjects, however, would be using their own money. "Free" information from the government must be paid for by the taxpayer. See further, C. Munro, "Government Advertising and Publicity", [1990] P.L. 1.

[12] See further, *post*, Chap. 19.

[13] (1637) 3 St.Tr. 825.

[14] [1916] P. 64; and see *The Sarpon* [1916] p. 306.

[15] (1606) 12 Co.Rep. 12.

[16] *post*, Chap. 19.

[17] Dicey, *Law of the Constitution* (10th ed. 1959), pp. 412–413.

[18] *Re Shipton, Anderson & Co and Harrison Brothers & Co* [1915] 3 K.B. 676, 684.

[19] The maxim was addressed by Cicero to a military commander. It is found in Bracton, Hobbes, Bacon, Coke, Hale and Hawkins. Sometimes, as in Selden's *Table Talk*, the verb is imperative (*esto*).

[20] [1965] A.C. 75. See A. L. Goodhart, "The Burmah Oil Case and the War Damage Act 1965" (1966) 82 L.Q.R. 97; and note by Paul Jackson in (1964) 27 M.L.R. 709.

and it was therefore payable.[21] Lord Radcliffe in his dissenting speech said the prerogative was so vague and uncertain that he preferred to base his opinion on the idea of necessity: the Crown had as much a duty as a right to do what it did, and it was not a source of profit to the Crown. With logic equal to Lord Reid's he said there was no precedent of such a claim being paid, and therefore it was not payable.[22]

The War Damage Act 1965 abolished retrospectively[23] any right which the subject may have had at common law to compensation from the Crown in respect of lawful acts of damage to, or destruction of property done by, or under the authority of, the Crown during, or in contemplation of, a war in which he Sovereign was or is engaged. The Act thus nullified the decision of the House of Lords in the *Burmah Oil Company* case so far as war damage is concerned. It does not deal with unlawful acts by officers or servants of the Crown,[24] nor the mere taking possession of property (requisition or angary).[25] Any payment of compensation by the government for war damage, whether caused by the Crown in prosecution of a war or by enemy action, must therefore be authorised by Act of Parliament.

2. Judicial prerogatives

15–018   These are discussed later in Chapter 20 under "The Administration of Justice."

3. Legislative prerogatives

15–019   The prerogatives in relation to the legislature include the power to summon, prorogue and dissolve Parliament, and the giving of the Royal Assent to Bills. These have already been discussed in Chapter 7. It has also been seen that the Sovereign has no prerogative power to legislate within the realm (*Case of Proclamations*[26]). The Crown has a prerogative right to print and publish statutes.[27]

---

[21] Cited as authority for this proposition in the Privy Council: *Société United Docks v. Government of Mauritius* [1985] A.C. 585, 600 *per* Lord Templeman.

[22] In *United States v. Caltex* (1952) 344 U.S. 149, a similar case relating to property in the Philippines, the majority of the United States Supreme Court held that no compensation was payable at common law, while the minority thought compensation was payable under the Fifth Amendment to the Constitution (private property not to be taken for public use without just compensation).

[23] Lawyers in both Houses objected strongly to the retroactive effect of the Bill, but: (i) the company had been offered reasonable compensation by successive Chancellors of the Exchequer, and had been warned that if their claim were successful in the courts, legislation would be introduced to indemnify the Crown, *i.e.* the taxpayer; (ii) it is unlikely that the company destroyed the property acting in the belief that there was a common law right to compensation; *cf. Phillips v. Eyre* (1870) L.R. 6 Q.B. 1; (iii) the provision in the American Constitution against *ex post facto* laws is interpreted to refer to penal laws: *Calder v. Bull* (1798) 3 Dall. 386; (iv) by what method, and on what basis, would compensation be assessed? The Japanese captured the site on the day after the installations were destroyed, and the loss was estimated at anything from nil to £100,000,000; (v) by what common law procedure (*e.g.* petition of right) could compensation have been claimed before the Crown Proceedings Act 1947?

[24] *cf.* Crown Proceedings Act 1947, s.2.

[25] Angary is the power of the Crown in time of war to requisition neutral chattels found within the realm on payment of compensation: *Commercial and Estates Co of Egypt v. Board of Trade* [1925] 1 K.B. 271.

[26] (1610) 2 St.Tr. 723; *ante*, para. 3–003. For prerogative legislation by Order in Council for British dependencies, see *post*, Chap. 35.

[27] Paul Von Nessen, "Law Reporting: Another Case for Deregulation", (1985) 48 M.L.R. 412.

It is a parliamentary custom that legislation affecting the prerogatives or property of the Crown should be preceded by a message from the Crown; and the Speaker must not allow a Bill that affects the prerogative to be read a third time unless the royal consent has been signified by a Privy Councillor.[28]

The Crown is not bound by an Act of Parliament—at any rate, to its detriment—except by express words or necessary implication. It was said in some earlier cases that the Sovereign is bound, even though not named therein, by statutes for the public good, for the preservation of public rights, suppression of public wrong, relief and maintenance of the poor, advancement of learning, religion and justice, the prevention of fraud, and by statutes tending to perform the will of a grantor, donor or founder.[29] In *Bombay Province v. Bombay Municipal Corporation*,[30] however, the Judicial Committee held that the inference that the Crown agreed to be bound by a statute could only be drawn if it was apparent from its terms at the time of its enactment that its beneficial purpose would be wholly frustrated if the Crown were not bound.

For the court to hold that Parliament intended an Act to bind the Crown there must be either express words to that effect, *e.g.* Crown Private Estates Acts; Crown Proceedings Act 1947; Law Reform (Limitation of Actions, etc.) Act 1954, s.5, Health and Safety At Work etc. Act 1974, s.48 and s.72, or words giving rise to such a strong implication that the court cannot reasonably help drawing it (*Attorney-General v. Donaldson*[31]). Thus it has been held that houses let by the Crown were not protected by Rent Restriction Acts,[32] royal palaces are not bound by the Licensing Acts,[33] vehicles driven by Crown servants were not subject to a statutory speed limit,[34] the Administrator of Austrian Property was not subject to statutes of limitation,[35] and land occupied by government departments does not require planning permission under Planning Acts.[36]

A corollary of that principle is the immunity of the Crown from income tax and rates, which can only be imposed by authority of Act of Parliament. The basis of the *prima facie* exclusion of the Crown from a taxing Act was discussed by the House of Lords in *Madras Electric Supply Corporation v. Boarland*.[37] While Lords Oaksey and Tucker thought it was not necessary to decide whether the Crown's immunity depended on the construction of the Act or arose from the

15–020

---

[28] Erskine May, *Parliamentary Practice* (22nd ed. 1997) 603.

[29] *Case of Ecclesiastical Persons* (1601) 4 Co.Rep. 14b; *Magdalen College Case (Warren v. Smith)* (1615) 11 Co.Rep. 66b. In *Willion v. Berkley* ((1561) Plowd. 223) counsel argued that the presumption is that the Sovereign "does not mean to prejudice himself or to bar himself of his liberty and privilege."

[30] [1947] A.C. 58. See too *Department of Transport v. Egoroff, The Times* May 6, 1986.

[31] (1842) 10 M. & W. 117; *Gorton Local Board v. Prison Commissioners* (1887) reported in *Cooper v. Hawkins* [1904] 2 K.B. 165 (local byelaws); *Re Wi Matua's Will* [1908] A.C. 448.

[32] *Tamlin v. Hannaford* [1950] 1 K.B. 18; *cf.* Crown Lessees (Protection of Sub-Tenants) Act 1952. But tenants of the Crown Estates Commissioners, of the Duchy of Cornwall and the Duchy of Lancaster do enjoy statutory protection: Housing Act 1980, s.73; *Crown Estates Commissioners v. Wordsworth* (1982) 44 P. & C.R. 302, CA.

[33] *R. v. Graham Campbell, ex p. Herbert* [1935] 1 K.B. 594.

[34] *Cooper v. Hawkins* [1904] 2 K.B. 164; for subsequent developments see (1983) 99 L.Q.R. 341 and *post*, para. 33–002.

[35] *Administrator of Austrian Property v. Russian Bank for Foreign Trade* (1931) 48 T.L.R. 37, CA. But see now, Limitation Act 1980, s.37.

[36] *Ministry of Agriculture, Fisheries and Food v. Jenkins* [1963] 2 Q.B. 317, CA; *Campbell (A.G.) (Arcam) v. Worcestershire County Council* (1963) 61 L.G.R. 321. See now Town and Country Planning Act 1984.

[37] [1955] A.C. 667. The Crown is not bound by an admission made on its behalf that a statute applies to the Crown: *Att-Gen. for Ceylon v. A. D. Silva* [1953] A.C. 461, PC.

prerogative, Lord Mac-Dermott regarded it as a rule of construction, Lord Keith of Avonholm offered the questionable explanation that words in a statute capable of applying to the Crown might be overridden by the exercise of the prerogative, and Lord Reid expressed the preferable opinion that the presumption is a rule of construction taking account of the prerogative.

The question who represents the Crown for this purpose was reviewed in *Bank voor Handel en Scheepvaart N.V. v. Administrator of Hungarian Property*,[38] where the House of Lords by a majority held that the Custodian of Enemy Property was a servant of the Crown, and that the Crown had a sufficient interest in the disposal of property held by him in that capacity to entitle him to claim exemption from tax on the income. The majority of their Lordships approved of the classification made by Blackburn J. in *Mersey Docks and Harbour Board v. Cameron* (1864)[39] that the immunity extends to: (i) the Sovereign personally; (ii) Crown servants, *e.g.* government departments[40]; and land occupied or funds held for Crown purposes by persons in *consimili casu, e.g.* assize courts and judges' lodgings,[41] county courts,[42] police stations[43] and prisons.[44] The difficulty was to decide, first, whether the Custodian of Hungarian Property fell into any of the categories enumerated above, and (if so) whether the property held by him was entitled to Crown immunity. Their Lordships (except Lord Keith) were agreed that the Crown, through the Board of Trade and the Treasury, had sufficient control of him to make him a Crown servant, so that he fell into category (ii).

The general rule is subject to criticism. It has been suggested that the presumption ought to be reversed by legislation, so that the Crown would be bound by statute unless it was expressly declared not to be bound, or public policy required the exemption of the Crown in a particular case.[45]

III. THE PREROGATIVE IN FOREIGN AFFAIRS

Acts of state

15–021   There is no technical definition of "act of state" in British constitutional law,[46] but the expression, as considered here, is generally used for an act done by the

---

[38] [1954] A.C. 584.

[39] 11 H.L.C. 443, 465. See also *Mersey Docks and Harbour Board v. Gibbs* (1866) L.R. 1 H.L. 93; And see Holdsworth, *History of English Law*, Vol. X, pp. 295–299.

[40] *R. v. Stewart* (1857) 8 E. & B. 360. And see *Smith v. Birmingham Guardians* (1857) 7 E. & B. 483; *R. v. Kent Justices* (1890) 24 Q.B.D. 181; *Wirral Estates v. Shaw* [1932] 2 K.B. 247.

[41] *Hodgson v. Carlisle Board of Health* (1857) 8 E. & B. 116; and see *Coomber v. Berkshire Justices* (1883) 9 App.Cas. 61, HL.

[42] *R. v. Manchester Overseers* (1854) 3 E. & B. 336.

[43] *Justices of Lancashire v. Stretford Overseers* (1858) E.B. & E. 225.

[44] *R. v. Shepherd* (1841) 1 Q.B. 170. And see *Territorial, etc. Forces Association v. Nichols* [1949] 1 K.B. 35.

[45] Glanville Williams, *Criminal Law*, I (1961). And see H. Street, *Governmental Liability* (1953) pp. 143–152; Peter W. Hogg, *Liability of the Crown* (2nd ed., 1989), Chap. 10. In *Cain v. Doyle* (1946) 72 C.L.R. 409, the majority in the High Court of Australia speaking *obiter* did not reject the possibility of the Crown being convicted of a criminal offence, *e.g.* the State as employer. See W. Friedmann, "Public Welfare Offences, Statutory Duties, and the Legal Status of the Crown" (1950) 13 M.L.R. 24.

[46] See Harrison Moore, *Act of State in English Law* (1906); Holdsworth, "The History of Acts of State in English Law" (1941) 41 *Columbia Law Rev.* 1313; E. C. S. Wade, "Act of State in English Law" (1934) 15 B.Y.I.L. 98. P. Cane, "Prerogative Acts, Acts of State and Justiciability", (1980) 29 I.C.L.Q. 680.

Crown as a matter of policy in relation to another state, or in relation to an individual who is not within the allegiance to the Crown.[47] The two parts of this definition are best considered separately. Cases on acts in relation to foreign states usually arise out of attempts by private individuals to enforce contract or property rights *indirectly* accruing, while cases on acts in relation to individuals normally arise out of an attempt to obtain a remedy for a supposed wrong *directly* resulting; and, as will be seen, the class of individuals against whom acts of state may be done is not free from doubt.

A distinct use of the term which Lord Wilberforce identified in *Buttes Gas and Oil Co v. Hammer*[48] relates to cases which are concerned with the applicability of foreign municipal legislation within its own territory and with the recognition of such legislation in the British courts. It is in this context that Lord Millett said, "the Act of state doctrine is a rule of domestic law which holds the national court incompetent to adjudicate upon the lawfulness of the sovereign acts of a foreign state".[49]

1. Acts of state in relation to foreign states

Acts of state in this class include the declaration of war and peace; the making **15–022** of treaties[50]; the annexation and cession of territory; the sending and receiving of diplomatic representatives; and the recognition of foreign states and governments. A claimant whose property or contracts are indirectly affected will be unsuccessful in his attempt to use an act of state as a foundation of an action. Such acts are outside the jurisdiction of British courts in the sense that they cannot be questioned. They are non-justiciable. Nor can a citizen claim to enforce directly any rights to which he may be entitled under them.[51] One view is that they are not properly described as an exercise of the "prerogative" as they are not done in relation to British subjects.[52] (This was the term traditionally used. Its ambit in this context was never precisely defined as is shown by the discussion below of *Nissan v. Attorney-General*[53] In terms of the British Nationality Act 1981 it no doubt includes British citizens[54] and some, or all, categories of Commonwealth citizens[55] and, perhaps, those who under the Act are British subjects[56]). There seems to be no good reason why the term "prerogative" should be limited in this way; indeed, Lord Coleridge C.J. described the making of peace and war as "perhaps the highest acts of the prerogative of the Crown".[57]

---

[47] "An act of the executive as a matter of policy performed in the course of its relations with another State, including its relations with the subjects of that State, unless they are temporarily within the allegiance of the Crown": Wade, *op. cit.* p. 103. *Cf. per* Lord Wilberforce in *Nissan v. Att.-Gen.* [1970] A.C. 179, *post*, para. 15–025.

[48] [1982] A.C. 888 (As a general rule such matters are "non-justiciable": in exceptional cases the British courts may consider the effects of foreign legislation which is confiscatory or contrary to public policy).

[49] *R. v. Bow Street Magistrate ex p. Pinochet Ugarte* [2000] 1 A.C. 147, 269, HL. See further *Fayed v. Al-Tajir* [1998] Q.B. 712, 714 *per* Mustill L.J.

[50] *post*, para. 15–028 *et seq.*

[51] Unless there is a special statutory provision to this effect, *e.g.* Foreign Compensation Act 1950.

[52] *Per* Warrington L.J. in *Re Ferdinand, Ex-Tsar of Bulgaria* [1921] 1 Ch. 107, 139.

[53] [1970] A.C. 179.

[54] s.1.

[55] s.37.

[56] s.30 and s.31.

[57] *Rustomjee v. R.* (1876) 2 Q.B.D. 69, 73.

In *Salaman v. Secretary of State for India*,[58] where a claim was brought to enforce an agreement between the Secretary of State for India and the Maharajah of the Punjab, Fletcher Moulton L.J. said: "An act of state is essentially an act of sovereign power, and hence cannot be challenged, controlled, or interfered with by municipal courts." He went on to say that the court must accept an act of state as it is without question; but the court may be called upon to decide whether or not there has been an act of state, and (if so) its nature and extent.[59] Further, the court may have to consider the effect of an act of state on the rights of the government or of individuals. Thus, while the court will not enforce private rights arising under a treaty,[60] it may be concerned if the treaty creates or modifies rights between the Crown and individuals who are, or who thereby become, subjects. For example, the Crown may recover in the courts debts due to it as a result of annexation, and presumably debts can similarly be recovered from it. The Crown decides what rights and obligations it takes over from the government of a state which it has extinguished by conquest and annexation (*West Rand Central Gold Mining Co v. The King*[61]); and so there was no redress where a colonial government declined to recognise concessions made to people who under the law then in force were British subjects[62] by the former ruler of territory that has been annexed (*Cook v. Sprigg*[63]). It will be noticed that in these cases the act of state was not done in relation to "British subjects," although it affected their interests.

15–023   A declaration of war affects the citizen's trading and contract rights with persons of enemy character, formerly prevented a British subject from becoming naturalised in the enemy state (*R. v. Lynch*[64]), and alters the status in this country of nationals of the enemy state. The court must accept the certificate of the Foreign Secretary as to whether the Crown is at war, or has ceased to be at war, with a foreign country (*R. v. Bottrill, ex p. Kuechenmeister*[65]). The recognition by the Crown of foreign states, Sovereigns and governments may affect the rights of private individuals because of the immunity,[66] from the jurisdiction of the courts which such recognition confers (*Duff Development Co v. Government of Kelantan*[67]). The court must accept the certificate of the Crown as to recognition, although it will examine the declaration in order to see that the proper facts have

---

[58] [1906] 1 K.B. 613, CA. And see *Secretary of State for India v. Kamachee Boye Sahaba* (1859) 13 Moo.P.C. 22.

[59] *Forester v. Secretary of State for India* (1872) L.R.Ind.App., supp. Vol., p. 10; *Musgrave v. Pulido* (1879) 5 App.Cas. 102, PC.

[60] *Nabob of the Carnatic v. East India Co* (1793) 2 Ves. 56; *Civilian War Claimants' Association v. The King* [1932] A.C. 14.

[61] [1905] 2 K.B. 391 (South African Republic).

[62] At that time "British subject" meant anyone born within the King's dominions who thereby owed allegiance to the King. Not until the British Nationality Act 1948 was the distinct category of citizen of the United Kingdom and Colonies recognised: *post* Chap. 23.

[63] [1899] A.C. 572 (annexation of Pondoland to Cape Colony).

[64] [1903] 1 K.B. 444. *Quaere* how far this prohibition extends.

[65] [1947] K.B. 41 (CA).

[66] Now limited by the State Immunity Act 1978; *post* para. 15–032.

[67] [1924] A.C. 797, HL. And as to the Commonwealth, see *Mighell v. Sultan of Johore* [1894] 1 Q.B. 149; *Kahan v. Pakistan Federation* [1951] 2 K.B. 1003; *Mellenger v. New Brunswick Development Corporation* [1971] 1 W.L.R. 604, CA. cf. *Sultan of Johore v. Abubakar Tunku Aris Bendahar* [1952] A.C. 218, PC. The practice of recognising *governments* which have come to power by unconstitutional means was abandoned by the British government in 1980. Future certificates will merely indicate what links exist between the regime in question and HM Government so, presumably, leaving the question of recognition to the courts: C. R. Symmons, "United Kingdom Abolition of the Doctrine of Recognition of Governments: A Rose by Another Name?" [1981] I.L. 249.

been considered by the appropriate Ministers.[68] Similar considerations apply to the recognition of diplomatic representatives, which confers diplomatic immunity (*Engelke v. Musmann*[69]).

The decisions of the British courts in such cases illustrate according to Lord Wilberforce, the undoubted judicial acceptance of the principle that, "In a matter affecting the sovereignty of the United Kingdom the courts are entitled to take account of the declared policy of Her Majesty's Government. . . . The courts should in such matters speak with the same voice as the executive."[70]

An act of state cannot alter the law administered by British courts. Thus in *The Zamora*[71] the Privy Council held that a prerogative Order in Council authorising reprisals could not increase the right of the Crown to requisition neutral ships and cargo. Although prize courts are said to administer "international law", it is such law—having its source in international law—as is recognised by English law. It may be modified by statute, but not by the prerogative.

2. *Acts of state in relation to individuals*

Acts done under the authority of the Crown in relation to individuals have been **15–024** held to be acts of state, so as to prevent an aggrieved person from obtaining redress for damage done,[72] in the following classes of case. Where the plea "act of state" is successful, this means that the court declines jurisdiction. In such cases the Crown uses "act of state" as a shield in an action brought by a private individual.

(a) *An alien outside British territory.* In *Buron v. Denman*[73]) the captain of a British warship was held not liable for trespass for setting fire to the barracoon of a Spaniard on the west coast of Africa (not British territory) and releasing his slaves: the captain had general instructions to suppress the slave trade, and his conduct in this case was afterwards approved by the Admiralty and the Foreign and Colonial Secretaries. An act of state in relation to individuals, it was held, may be either previously authorised or subsequently ratified by the Crown. There is probably a prerogative power to exclude aliens from entering British territory, and at any rate aliens have no enforceable right at common law to enter (*Musgrove v. Chun Teeong Toy*[74]).

(b) *An enemy alien within that country.* In *R. v. Bottrill, ex p. Kuechenmeister*[75] a German national, who had lived in England since 1928 without being naturalised and was interned by the Home Secretary during the war, was unsuccessful in his application for a writ of habeas corpus, detention by the Crown of

---

[68] *Sayce v. Ameer Ruler Sadig Mohammed Abbasi Bahawalpur State* [1952] 2 Q.B. 390, CA.

[69] [1928] A.C. 433.

[70] *Re Westinghouse Electric Corporation Uranium Contract Litigation M.D.L. Docket No. 235* [1978] A.C. 547, *per* Lord Wilberforce. See too, *British Airways v. Laker Airways* [1985] A.C. 58, *per* Lord Diplock.

[71] [1916] 2 A.C. 77; "One of the most courageous of judicial decisions even in our long history"; *per* Lord Scarman, *C.C.S.U. v. Minister for Civil Service* [1985] A.C. 374, 404.

[72] Act of state may also be a defence to a criminal charge; see Stephen, *History of the Criminal Law*, II, pp. 61–65. And see *Carr v. Fracis Times & Co* [1902] A.C. 176 (act of state by foreign ruler authorising British subjects to seize British-owned goods in British ships in foreign territorial waters).

[73] (1848) 2 Ex. 167. The case was settled on terms. Captain Denman, the successful defendant, was a son of Denman C.J.

[74] [1891] A.C. 491, PC. The entry of aliens into this country is now regulated by the Immigration Act 1971 and Community Law.

[75] [1947] K.B. 41, CA.

an enemy alien being an act of state. A similar principle applies to the deportation of an enemy alien (*Netz v. Chuter Ede*[76]).

(c) Formerly acts done by the Crown in British protectorates in relation to the local inhabitants were regarded as acts of state, protectorates being technically foreign countries.[77] This principle probably became untenable after the creation of the new status of British protected persons by the British Nationality Act 1948, but the question is no longer of practical importance.[78]

With regard to the defence of "act of state" against British citizens, Commonwealth citizens and British subjects outside British territory, there is no direct judicial authority.[79]

15–025   The Crown must claim "act of state" specifically.[80] But the mere plea "act of state" is not enough: the court can examine the facts in order to decide whether what has been done is an act of state. Thus in an action of trespass against the Governor of Jamaica for seizing and detaining the plaintiff's schooner, it was not enough for the defendant to plead that the acts were done by him in the exercise of his discretion as Governor and as acts of state; he had to show that the acts were done under and within the limits of his commission, or that they were really acts of state policy done under the authority of the Crown (*Musgrave v. Pulido*).[81]

On the other hand, if a wrong is committed by a servant of the Crown against a British citizen and, possibly Commonwealth citizens and British subjects or friendly aliens in British territory, it is no defence to plead "act of state." In *Walker v. Baird*,[82] where the commander of a British warship had taken possession of a lobster factory belonging to a British subject (under the law then in force) in Newfoundland, it was held no defence that the commander was acting under the orders of the Crown to implement a treaty with France. And in *Johnstone v. Pedlar*[83] the House of Lords held that a United States citizen in Dublin (at that time within the United Kingdom) was entitled to claim from the police commissioner money found on him at the time of his arrest for illegal drilling, "act of state" not being available as a defence to an action brought by the citizen of a friendly state for wrongful detention of property in this country.

In *Nissan v. Attorney-General*.[84] Nissan, a citizen of the United Kingdom and Colonies, was lessee of an hotel in Cyprus, an independent republic in the Commonwealth.[85] The hotel was occupied by British troops for several months as part of a truce force under an agreement between the Governments of the

---

[76] [1946] Ch. 224.
[77] *R. v. Earl of Crewe, ex p. Sekgome* [1910] 2 K.B. 576, CA; *Sobhuza II v. Miller* [1926] A.C. 518 PC; *Eshugbayi (Eleko) v. Government of Nigeria (Officer Administering)* [1931] A.C. 662, PC; *R. v. Ketter* [1940] 1 K.B. 787. *cf. Ex p. Mwenya* ([1960] 1 Q.B. 241, CA, where the petitioner was assumed to be a British subject by virtue of local citizenship laws (Federation of Rhodesia and Nyasaland). *cf.* K. Polack, "The Defence of Act of State in Relation to Protectorates" (1963) 26 M.L.R. 138; L. L. Kato, "Act of State in a Protectorate—in Retrospect" [1969] P.L. 219.
[78] The status of British protected persons is preserved by the British Nationality Act 1981; s.38.
[79] See *Nissan v. Att.-Gen.* [1970] A.C. 179, HL, *post*.
[80] *Nissan v. Att.-Gen.* [1970] A.C. 179, *post*.
[81] (1879) 5 App.Cas 102, PC.
[82] [1892] A.C. 491, PC. And see the *General Warrant Cases, post,* Chap. 24.
[83] [1921] 2 A.C. 262.
[84] [1970] A.C. 179. See J. G. Collier, "Act of State as a Defence against a British Subject" (1968) C.L.J. 102, and note in (1969) C.L.J. 166; S. S. de Smith in (1969) 32 M.L.R. 427; *cf.* D. R. Gilmour, "British Forces Abroad and the Responsibility for their Actions" [1970] P.L. 120.
[85] But not one of Her Majesty's dominions.

United Kingdom and Cyprus for the purpose of restoring peace in the civil strife between the Greek and Turkish communities. The British forces then continued to occupy the hotel for a period as part of a United Nations peace-keeping force, on the recommendation of the Security Council of the United Nations and with the consent of the Cyprus Government. Nissan brought an action against the Crown in England, claiming declarations that he was entitled to compensation for damage to the contents of the hotel and the destruction of stores, on the ground that this was a lawful exercise of the prerogative[86]; and that the Crown was liable in damages for trespass to chattels by the British troops.[87] This case was fought on preliminary issues, in particular, whether the acts of the British forces were acts of state.[88] The House of Lords upheld the Court of Appeal in deciding that the acts of the British forces were not non-justiciable as acts of state. Although the agreement of the British Government with the Cyprus Government to send peace-keeping forces to Cyprus was no doubt an act of state, not all acts done incidentally in relation to individual persons or their property (such as occupying a particular hotel or damaging its contents) in the course of executing an act of state are themselves acts of state. All the Law Lords said it was unnecessary to discuss whether the acts of the Crown were an exercise of the prerogative, although Lord Denning M.R. in the Court of Appeal based the liability of the Crown to pay compensation on the exercise of the prerogative, referring to the *Burmah Oil Company* case.[89]

There are a number of dicta, which are not easily reconcilable, in the various **15–026** judgments concerning "act of State" and its availability as a defence against British subjects. Their Lordships recognised that the latter term itself was open to various interpretations. Lord Morris wondered, without expressing a final opinion, whether the phrase was equivalent to "those owing allegiance to the Crown?" Lord Pearson was uncertain whether "British subject" extended only to a citizen of the United Kingdom and Colonies or to anyone within the wide definition of section 1 of the British Nationality Act 1948 or even whether, in the context, it had some other meaning. In the light of the British Nationality Act 1981 these doubts may be rephrased to ask: does "British Subject" for this purpose mean "British citizen" or does it include some or all of the following classes, Commonwealth citizens, British protected persons and British subjects (within the meaning of sections 30 and 31 of the 1981 Act)? If Commonwealth citizens *are* included, should a distinction be drawn between citizens of Commonwealth countries which are still realms and those which recognise the Queen merely as Head of the Commonwealth. (In view of the disintegration of the common law throughout the Commonwealth, also, the earlier cases may have to be reviewed on the questions: what is meant by "British territory", "abroad" and "foreign country"?)

With regard to the question whether act of state might be pleaded against a British subject, in whatever sense that phrase is used in this context, Lord Reid stated the traditional doctrine that "act of state" is not available as a defence to

---

[86] See *Burmah Oil Co v. Lord Advocate* [1965] A.C. 75; *ante*, para. 15–017.

[87] Nissan also claimed that there was a contract by the High Commissioner on behalf of the Crown, with the consent of the Secretary of State, that he would receive compensation for occupation of the hotel.

[88] Also on the questions whether there was a contract, express or implied, that he would be compensated (a question of fact left to the trial court); and whether the British troops in the first period were agents of the Cyprus government, and whether in the second period they were agents of the United Nations, the decision as to both periods being "no".

[89] *ante*, para. 15–017.

interference with the rights of British subjects abroad, but Lord Morris, Lord Pearce and Lord Pearson were doubtful.[90] Lord Wilberforce thought that act of state *could* be pleaded; but in his speech he was concerned mainly not with acts *directly* causing harm which if done by a private individual would constitute a tort but non-justiciable acts of the Crown which *indirectly* cause harm. Lord Pearce thought there was an exercise of the prerogative, involving the obligation to pay, as the case was not covered by the War Damage Act 1965[91]; while Lords Reid and Wilberforce doubted whether the principle of the *Burmah Oil Company*[92] case applied to acts done on foreign soil.

Passports[93]

15–027   The Secretary of State has a discretion to grant, refuse, impound or revoke passports, which remain Crown property.[94] A passport was defined by Lord Alverstone C.J. in *R. v. Brailsford*[95] as "a document issued in the name of the Sovereign on the responsibility of a Minister of the Crown to a named individual, intended to be presented to the governments of foreign nations and to be used for that individual's protection as a British subject in foreign countries". It contains a request in the name of Her Majesty to allow the bearer pass freely, and to afford him such assistance and protection as may be necessary. The Crown has a duty to protect its citizens abroad, although this is not legally enforceable.[96] A passport is not legally necessary at common law in order to go abroad, but it is universally used as a certificate of identity and nationality. Other countries may refuse entry without possession of one, and therefore transport companies may be expected to refuse to carry passengers abroad without passports.

The alleged prerogative power of the Crown to refuse or impound passports has been described as arbitrary, objectionable and of doubtful legality. Further, the right of establishment in Community Law means that nationals are entitled to identity cards or passports enabling them to leave and re-enter the country freely, subject to public policy, security and health.

Treaties

15–028   The treaty-making power is an executive power which in British constitutional law is vested in the Crown.[97] A treaty is analogous to a contract between states. Its binding force is a matter of international law. The negotiations are conducted

---

[90] H. W. R. Wade suggests that the test whether "act of state" is a defence to an action for a tort against a British subject should be a matter of geography rather than nationality, *e.g.* British troops seizing Suez Canal damage house of British subject living in Egypt: *Administrative Law* (5th ed., 1982) pp. 718–719 citing *Cook v. Sprigg* [1899] A.C. 572.

[91] *ante*, para. 15–017.

[92] [1965] A.C. 75.

[93] H. Street, *Freedom, the Individual and the Law* (5th ed., 1982), pp. 291–296; D. W. Williams, "British Passports and the Right to Travel" (1974) I, C.L.Q. 642; Justice, *Going Abroad: A Report on Passports* (1974); J. Jaconelli, (1975) 38 M.L.R. 314; D. C. Turack, "Selected Aspects of International and Municipal Law Concerning Passports" (1971) 12 *William & Mary Law Review*, 805.

[94] *cf. Ghani v. Jones* [1970] 1 Q.B. 693, CA, where the Pakistani passports taken by the police were not the property of the Crown.

[95] [1905] 2 K.B. 730, 745; approved *Joyce v. D.P.P.* [1946] A.C. 347, *per* Lord Jowitt, L.C.

[96] But the obtaining of a British passport, even by an alien, involves allegiance to the Crown: *Joyce v. D.P.P.* [1946] A.C. 347, HL.

[97] *Att.-Gen. for Canada v. Att.-Gen. for Ontario* [1937] A.C. 326, PC, *per* Lord Atkin. The relevant rules of English law are conveniently set out by Lightman J. in *Lonrho Exports v. Export Credits Guarantee Department* [1999] Ch. 158, at p. 178.

by agents of the Crown, *e.g.* the Foreign Secretary or a diplomatic representative, and are usually made subject to ratification by the Crown under the Great Seal. Treaties are acts of state, and do not in general require parliamentary sanction.[98] Where treaties require ratification by the Crown (*i.e.* treaties between Heads of State, but not commercial or technical agreements at official level), it has been the practice since 1924 to lay them when signed before both Houses of Parliament for 21 days before they are ratified ("the Ponsonby Rule").[99] It is open to argument whether this practice may be regarded as a constitutional convention. It has also been described as a "so-called rule ... no more than a self denying ordinance on the part of the government; on occasions it has been waived or modified if expediency requires a treaty to be ratified more hurriedly".[1] On important treaties the government initiates a discussion; otherwise the Opposition may ask for a discussion.

There are, however, three classes of treaty which do require confirmation by Parliament[2]:

(i) *Treaties expressly made subject to confirmation by Parliament.* A treaty **15–029** expressly made subject to confirmation by Parliament will not come into force, either by international law or by English law, unless an Act of Parliament is passed confirming it; for that is a condition in the treaty itself. Such parliamentary sanctions is sometimes spoken of as "ratification", but that word is properly used of the final authentication by the Crown.

(ii) *Treaties involving an alteration of English law or taxation.* Any alteration of English law involved in implementing a treaty, including the imposition of taxes or the expenditure of public money, needs to be authorised by Act of Parliament.[3] The most striking example is the European Communities Act 1972. The courts cannot have regard to the provisions of treaties until enacted by Parliament,[4] except to the extent that they relate to international relations within the "narrow field" where the courts are prepared to defer to the declared policy of Her Majesty's Government.[5] In other cases courts cannot take into account the terms of international agreements, as Lord Fraser emphasised in the *G.C.H.Q.* Case when criticising the Court of Appeal for taking into account I.L.O. Conventions which had not been enacted as part of United Kingdom law.[6] Dicta in some cases suggests that there is one exception to the general principle; the European Convention on Human Rights. In *Attorney-General v. BBC*,[7] for example, Lord

---

[98] *Att.-Gen. for Canada v. Att.-Gen. for Ontario* [1937] A.C. 326, PC.

[99] H.C.Deb., Vol. 171, ser. 53, col. 2001 (1924). An unsuccessful attempt to subject the treaty-making power to Parliamentary approval occurred in 1996 when Lord Lester introduced in the House of Lords the Treaties (Parliamentary Approval) Bill.

[1] K. Bradshaw and D. Pring, *Parliament and Congress* (1972), p. 401.

[2] Lord McNair, *The Law of Treaties*, Chap. 2; "When do British Treaties involve Legislation?" (1928) B.Y.I.L. 59.

[3] [1937] A.C. 326, 347 *per* Lord Atkin. This is the effect of the *Case of Proclamations* ((1610) 12 Co.Rep. 74) and the Bill of Rights.

[4] *Rustomjee v. The Queen* (1876) 2 Q.B.D. 69 *per* Lord Coleridge C.J. (treaty with China; subject could not claim against Crown share of compensation for loss of trading rights); *Blackburn v. Att.-Gen.* [1971] 1 W.L.R. 1037, CA *per* Lord Denning M.R.; *Littrell v. United States of America (No. 2)* [1995] 1 W.L.R. 82, CA. See D. C. T. Williams, "Prerogative and Parliamentary Control" [1971] C.L.J. 178.

[5] *British Airways v. Laker Airways* [1985] A.C. 58, 85–86, *per* Lord Diplock; *post* para. 20–007.

[6] *C.C.S.U. v. Minister for Civil Service* [1985] A.C. 374.

[7] [1981] A.C. 303. See *post* para. 20–007 for further discussion.

Fraser said that the courts should have regard to the provisions of the Convention "where our domestic law is not firmly settled. But the Convention does not form part of our law and the decision on what that law is for our domestic courts and for this House".

The courts must apply a statute whose terms are clear, irrespective of whether it is alleged to conflict with the terms of a treaty.[8] Where a statute incorporating a treaty into United Kingdom law is ambiguous the courts will interpret its provisions in the light of the treaty.[9]

15–030   (iii) *Treaties affecting private rights.* In *The Parliament Belge*[10] Sir Robert Phillimore said that treaties affecting the private rights of British subjects were inoperative without the confirmation of the legislature. The Crown, therefore, could not by a treaty with Belgium confer on a private ship engaged in trade the immunities of a public ship so as to deprive a British subject of the right to bring proceedings against the ship for damage sustained in a collision. This is really a particular aspect of (ii) above (treaties involving an alteration of English law). It is the reason why the European Communities Act 1972 was needed to cover enforceable Community rights and obligations, and also why Extradition Acts are required to give legal effect to treaties made for surrendering persons accused of crimes committed abroad.[11]

In the exceptional case of treaties providing for any increase in the powers of the European Parliament the Crown cannot even *ratify* a treaty without Parliamentary approval: European Assembly Election Act 1978, s.6(1).[12] (Such approval was given, by section 2 of the European Communities (Amendment) Act 1998, to an increase in powers under the Treaty of Amsterdam.)

By the making of a treaty the Crown may morally bind Parliament to pass any legislation needed to give full effect to it. The negotiation of treaties, which must often be done in secret,[13] is less under parliamentary control than almost any other branch of the prerogative, and Parliament may be met with a *fait accompli*. But there is an increasing tendency to keep Parliament informed and to invite expressions of opinion before the Crown finally commits itself, as was done during the Common Market negotiations in 1962–1971. This is only expedient, as the government relies on the support of Parliament, and especially of the Commons. Where legislation will be required to supplement a treaty, there is probably a convention that Parliament should be consulted in principle before the treaty is concluded. Parliament will also be consulted in very important matters, such as the declaration of war or the conclusion of a peace treaty.

---

[8] *Cheney v. Conn* [1968] 1 W.L.R. 292.

[9] *Buchanan (James) & Co Ltd v. Babco Forwarding & Shipping (UK) Ltd* [1978] A.C. 141; *Fothergill v. Monarch Airlines Ltd* [1981] A.C. 251.

[10] (1879) 4 P.D. 129, 154. The Court of Appeal ((1880) 5 P.D. 197) reversed Sir Robert Phillimore's decision on the ground that the ship in that case was a public ship, but they carefully refrained from expressing disapproval of the principle stated by him, which is regarded as good law; applied by MacKenna J. in *Swiss-Israel Trade Bank v. Government of Malta* [1972] 1 Lloyd's Rep. 497. See also *British Airways v. Laker Airways* [1983] 3 W.L.R. 544, 580 *per* Sir John Donaldson, M.R.

[11] Maitland, *Constitutional History*, (1908) pp. 424–425.

[12] The European Communities (Amendment) Act 1993, s.2 provides expressly that the United Kingdom cannot move to the third stage of economic and monetary union under the Maastricht Treaty without prior Parliamentary approval.

[13] For example, negotiations with China *re* Hong Kong in 1984.

Treaties of cession and delimitation of maritime boundaries

Doubt has been expressed whether the Crown can by virtue of the prerogative cede territory, so as to deprive British subjects of their nationality and perhaps property and contract rights.[14] It may be that a distinction should be drawn between the United Kingdom, where the prerogative does not apply, and territories of the Crown overseas. The Crown was persuaded to seek parliamentary approval for the cession of Heligoland to Germany in 1890,[15] and since then it has been the practice to ask Parliament to confirm cessions.[16] Whatever the law may be, this seems to be now the convention. Indeed, convention probably demands that Parliament should be consulted beforehand, as in the case of the cession of Jubaland to Italy in 1927. **15–031**

It has been asserted that the Crown possesses a prerogative to delimit the maritime boundaries of the United Kingdom and, in cases of doubt to provide conclusive certificates for the guidance of the courts.[17] The existence of such a prerogative is, however, open to doubt.[18]

Sovereign Immunity and Diplomatic representation

It is part of the royal prerogative in relation to foreign affairs to recognise, or to withhold recognition from, foreign states, their heads and, before 1980, governments.[19] Foreign states, their head, governments and diplomatic envoys recognised by the Crown enjoy certain immunities from the jurisdiction of English courts. **15–032**

The main purpose of the State Immunity Act 1978 is to restrict the immunities of foreign governments and States by bringing the British rules on state immunity into line with the more restrictive rules adopted in other States. The Act lists various circumstances in which civil actions may be brought against foreign states in the British courts. Section 3, for example, gives jurisdiction over commercial transactions as opposed to those entered into by a State in the exercise of its sovereign authority. Section 4 deals with contracts of employment made in the United Kingdom or under which the work is to be performed in the United Kingdom. Other sections relate to personal injuries and damage to property arising from acts or omissions in the United Kingdom (section 5); the ownership and use of immovable property (section 6); patents (section 7) and ships used for commercial purposes (section 10). Entities separate from the government of a foreign state enjoy immunity with regard to acts done by them in the exercise of sovereign authority (within the limits of immunity recognised by the Act (s.14)[20] Important provisions in section 16 ensure that nothing in the Act curtails any privileges conferred by the Diplomatic Privileges Act 1964 or

---

[14] See Anson, *Law and Custom of the Constitution*, II, ii (4th ed, 1935), Keith), pp. 137–142; Holdsworth, "The Treaty-making power of the Crown" (1942) 58 L.Q.R. 177, 183; Roberts-Wran, *Commonwealth and Colonial Law*, p. 118. *Cf. Damodhar Gordhan v. Deoram Kanji* (1876) 1 App.Cas. 352, PC. And *cf.* Treaty of Paris 1783, recognising the independence of the former American colonies.

[15] Anglo-German Agreement Act 1890.

[16] *e.g.* Anglo-Italian (East African Territories) Act 1925; Dindings Agreement Approval Act 1934; Anglo-Venezuelan Treaty (Island of Patos) Act 1942.

[17] *The Fagernes* [1927] P.L. 311, CA; *R. v. Kent Justices, ex p. Lye* [1967] 2 Q.B. 153; *Post Office v. Estuary Radio* [1968] 2 Q.B. 740.

[18] W. R. Edeson, "The Prerogative of the Crown to Delimit Britain's Maritime Boundary" (1973) 89 L.Q.R. 364.

[19] *Carl Zeiss Stiftung v. Rayner and Keeler Ltd (No. 2)* [1967] 1 A.C. 853, HL. see *per* Lord Reid (German Democratic Republic).

[20] *Kuwait Airways Corporation v. Iraqi Airways Co* [1995] 1 W.L.R. 1147.

the Consular Relations Act 1968. The Act was successfully relied on by a landlord in an action against the French government to which property had been let to be used as a private dwelling.[21] In *Alconi Ltd v. Republic of Colombia*[22] the House of Lords, reversing the Court of Appeal, interpreted complicated provisions relating to the enforcement of judgments (section 13) as generously as possible in favour of the respondent state to deny jurisdiction in the circumstances to the English courts.

15–033   The privilege and immunities of the heads of foreign states were placed on a statutory basis by section 20 of the State Immunity Act which was the subject of detailed consideration in the prolonged *Pinochet* litigation.[23] Senator Pinochet, the former Head of State of Chile, had been arrested while in the United Kingdom in response to a request for his extradition[24] by the Spanish authorities to face charges of torture. Section 20 equates the position of a head of state to that of diplomats for the purpose of determining the extent of immunity from municipal courts.[25] The latter, while in post as diplomatic representatives, enjoy full immunity from the courts of the receiving State—immunity *ratione personae*—but after the termination of their diplomatic status immunity applies only to acts carried out in the exercise of their official functions—immunity *ratione materiae*. The House of Lords, by a majority, held that a similar distinction applied to former heads of states and that authorising acts of torture could not be part of a head of state's official functions so as to entitle a former head to immunity from prosecution—even although the definition of torture under the Convention on Torture, which became part of United Kingdom law by the Criminal Justice Act 1988, section 134, refers to the infliction of pain or suffering by a public official or other person acting in an official capacity. Lord Goff, dissenting, found the view of the majority contrary to "principle, authority and commonsense".[26]

Statutory recognition of the customary rules of international law regulating diplomatic immunity dates back to the Diplomatic Privileges Act 1708 which arose out of *Mattueof's Case*,[27] in which the Russian Ambassador had been arrested for debt and taken out of his coach in London. The Court of Queen's Bench was uncertain whether the Sheriff of Middlesex and his assistants were guilty of a criminal offence. Peter the Great demanded that they should be punished with instant death. Queen Anne replied that she could not punish any of her subjects except in accordance with law. The Act of 1708, which was largely declaratory, was therefore passed, providing that judicial proceedings brought against diplomatic envoys or their servants should be null and void, and that it should be a misdemeanour to commence such proceedings.[28]

---

[21] *Intro Properties (UK) Ltd v. Sauvel* [1983] Q.B. 1019, CA.

[22] [1984] A.C. 580; noted, S. Ghandhi (1984) 37 M.L.R. 597.

[23] *R. v. Bow Street Magistrate, ex p. Pinochet (No. 1)* [2000] 1 A.C. 61 (No. 2) [2000] 1 A.C. 119; (No. 3) [1999] 2 W.L.R. 827; J.C. Barker, (1999) 48 I.C.L.Q. 937.

[24] *post* Chap. 23.

[25] The inadequacies of the drafting of the section are considered by Lord Browne-Wilkinson at [2000] 1 A.C. 147, 202–203 845; E. Denza, (1999) 48 I.C.L.Q. 949.

[26] [2000] 1 A.C. 147, 223.

[27] (1709) 10 Mod.Rep. 4; Bl.Comm. I, 255–356; Martens, *Causes Célèbres du Droit des Gens* (1827), Vol. I, p. 47.

[28] The Queen sent an illuminated copy of the Act to Moscow, which appeased the Czar, and the offenders were discharged at his request. It is uncertain how far the 1708 Act covered the bringing of criminal proceedings. There is no record of a prosecution for contravening the Act.

The Diplomatic Privileges Act 1964, giving effect to most of the provisions of the Vienna Convention on Diplomatic Relations 1961, replaces the previous law on the privileges and immunities of diplomatic representatives in the United Kingdom. The Act distinguishes between members of the diplomatic staff, who have full personal immunity, civil and criminal, with certain exceptions; members of the administrative and technical staff, who enjoy full immunity for official acts, but are liable civilly (though not criminally) for acts performed outside the course of their duties[29]; and members of the service staff, who enjoy immunity only for official acts.

Privileges and immunities may be withdrawn by Order in Council from any state that grants less to British missions.

The certificate of the Foreign Secretary is conclusive as to whether a person falls into any (and, if so, which) of the above three classes. No question of diplomatic immunity can arise until a person has been notified to the Foreign and Commonwealth Office as a diplomat.[30]

Members of the diplomatic mission of a Commonwealth country or of Ireland and their private servants are entitled, if they are both citizens of that Commonwealth country or Ireland and also citizens of the United Kingdom and Colonies, to the privileges and immunities to which they would have been entitled if they had not been citizens of the United Kingdom and Colonies.

Diplomatic privilege may be waived in any particular case. Where an ambassador or other head of mission is concerned, waiver must be with the consent of his Sovereign (*Re Suarez*[31]); where a subordinate is concerned, waiver must be by head of the mission.[32] Unless the waiver extends to execution, which is unlikely, judgment in such a case cannot be enforced until a reasonable time after the envoy has been recalled.[33]

15–034

If a diplomatic envoy commits a breach of the law, the Foreign Secretary may request his government to recall him as *persona non grata*, as was done in the case of the Swedish Ambassador, Count Cyllenburg, in 1717.

Various incidents in the last few years, particularly the killing of a policewoman in April 1984 outside the Libyan People's Bureau in London, have led to calls for the revision of the Vienna Convention on Diplomatic Relations. It is believed that diplomatic premises may be used to harbour terrorists and that guns and explosives are smuggled into countries in diplomatic "bags", *i.e.* officially sealed packages which under the Convention are exempt from examination. Revision of such an international agreement is likely to prove difficult. In the meantime states could act more promptly to expel "diplomats" whose status is open to doubt.[34]

Under the International Organisations Acts 1968 and 1981 immunities and privileges may be accorded to international and Commonwealth organisations of which the United Kingdom is a member, and to persons connected with such organisations. Provision is also made for granting immunities and privileges to

---

[29] For applications of the Act see *Empson v. Smith* [1966] 1 Q.B. 426, CA noted (1965) 28 M.L.R. 710; *Shaw v. Shaw* [1979] Fam. 62. Whether an act is performed inside or outside the scope of a diplomat's duties is to be determined by the Courts.

[30] *R. v. Lambeth Justices ex p. Yusufu, The Times* February 20, 1985, CA.

[31] *Re Suarez, Suarez v. Suarez* [1918] 1 Ch. 187.

[32] *Dickinson v. Del Solar* [1930] 1 K.B. 376; *Re Republic of Bolivia Exploration Syndicate Ltd.* [1914] 1 Ch. 139.

[33] *Re Suarez, ante.*

[34] J. C. Barker, *The Abuse of Diplomatic Privileges and Immunities* (1996).

judges and suitors of the International Court of Justice, and to representatives of other states attending international conferences in the United Kingdom.

Diplomatic privileges and immunities have been extended to the high commissioners or ambassadors of the independent members of the Commonwealth, Associated States and the Republic of Ireland, their staff, families and servants; and to certain representatives of Commonwealth governments and of the Government of the Republic of Ireland attending conferences with the British Government.[35] Diplomatic immunity and privileges may also be extended by Order in Council to any international headquarters or defence organisations set up under an arrangement for common defence, *e.g.* NATO, and the Visiting Forces Act 1952 may be applied to them.[36]

The privileges and immunities of consuls are governed by the Consular Relations Act 1968, which gives effect to the Vienna Convention on Consular Relations; and (as to Commonwealth and Irish consuls) by section 4 of the Diplomatic and other Privileges Act 1971.

---

[35] Diplomatic Immunities (Conferences with Commonwealth Countries and Republic of Ireland) Act 1961.
[36] International Headquarters and Defence Organisations Act 1964.

CHAPTER 16

THE PRIVY COUNCIL

I. The Council as an Instrument of Government

Historical introduction[1]

The *Curia Regis* exercised supreme legislative, executive and judicial powers, subject to general feudal customs. From the *Curia Regis* there developed in course of time the most important institutions of English central government, namely, the Exchequer and the Treasury (12th century), the courts of common law (13th–14th centuries) and Chancery (14th–15th centuries), and the House of Lords, *i.e.* the King's Council in Parliament[2] (14th century). **16–001**

The Privy Council has been generally regarded as a continuation of the *Curia Regis* after these other bodies had separated, but it may be more precise to say that the *Curia Regis* ceased to exist, and that the Council which emerged as a distinct body in the thirteenth and fourteenth centuries was something new. The Council was used as a powerful instrument of government by the Tudors. In Henry VIII's reign the distinction was first drawn between "Ordinary Councillors," a fairly large number of lawyers and administrators, and "Privy Councillors," a select body of nobles who acted as the King's advisers. As the Tudor period progressed the tendency was for Privy Councillors to be drawn from humbler ranks of society.

Coke, in his treatment of the courts, deals after the High Court of Parliament with "the Councell Board or Table," and says: "This is a most noble, honourable, and reverend assembly of the King and his privy councell in the King's court or palace; with this councell the King himself doth sit at pleasure. These councellors like good centinels and watchmen, consult of and for the publique good, and the honour, defence, safety and profit of the realm."[3] **16–002**

Committees composed of some only of the members of the Council were sometimes used by the Tudors for particular purposes or occasions, and temporary or permanent committees were used frequently in the seventeenth century. For various reasons Committees of the whole Council came to be employed in the eighteenth century, and, indeed, most of the Council's work was then carried on in Committee. Some of these committees in their turn became, or transferred their administrative functions to, separate government departments such as the Board of Trade and the former Boards of Agriculture and Education.

The eclipse of the Privy Council as a practical instrument of government came with the development in the eighteenth century of the Cabinet as the policy-making organ and advisory body of the Crown, which is discussed in the next chapter.

[1] Holdsworth, *History of English Law*, Vol. I, Chap. 6; (1860) Baldwin, *The King's Council during the Middle Ages*; Turner, *The Privy Council, 1603–1784*; Dicey, *The Privy Council*; Williamson, *Studies in the Constitutional History of the Thirteenth and Fourteenth Centuries*.
[2] The House of Lords was not so called until Henry VII's reign.
[3] 4 Inst. 53. The official spelling now used is "Counsellor" although, according to the Clerk of the Council "Councillor" cannot be "called wrong." (*Observer*, August 1, 1982).

The Privy Council at the present day: the composition of the Privy Council[4]

16–003   "The Lords, and others of Her Majesty's most Honourable Privy Council," now about three hundred in number, consist of persons who hold or have held high political or legal office, peers, Church dignitaries and persons distinguished in the services and professions. They are appointed by letters patent, and include the Lord President of the Council, all Cabinet Ministers by convention, the two Archbishops by prescription, and customarily some of the leading Commonwealth statesmen, British Ambassadors, the Speaker of the House of Commons, the Lords of Appeal in Ordinary, the Lord Chief Justice, the Master of the Rolls, the President of the Family Division, and the Lords Justices of Appeal.

A new member of the Privy Council must take the oath of allegiance and the special Privy Councillor's oath, which binds him to keep secret all matters committed or revealed to him or that are treated of secretly in council.[5] An affirmation may be made in lieu of oath.[6] The oath or affirmation probably does not add anything to the obligation later imposed by the Official Secrets Acts. The disclosure of such confidential information requires the consent of the Sovereign, which in practice means the Prime Minister of the day. Privy Councillors must be British subjects. They are addressed as "Right Honourable." Since the Demise of the Crown Act 1901 membership of the Privy Council is apparently not affected by a demise of the Crown.

Functions of the Privy Council[7]

16–004   The Privy Council became too unwieldy as an instrument of government. Owing to the development of the Cabinet and government departments, the Council lost most of its advisory and administrative functions and is today little more than an organ for giving formal effect to certain acts done under prerogative or statutory powers.

Proclamations and Orders in Council

16–005   The most important acts done by Her Majesty "by and with the advice of her Privy Council" take the form of proclamations or Orders in Council, the former normally being authorised by the latter. Proclamations are employed for such matters as proroguing, dissolving and summoning Parliament[8] and declaring war or peace—solemn occasions requiring the widest publicity. Orders in Council may be made under the Royal Prerogative or, more commonly, under statutory powers.[9] The nature of an Order in Council may be legislative, *e.g.* making laws for certain overseas territories and Statutory Instruments under a wide range of modern statutes; executive, *e.g.* setting up a new government department, issuing regulations for the armed forces, determining the conditions of employment of

---

[4] The Union with Scotland (Amendment) Act 1707 provided that there should be one Privy Council for Great Britain. The Union with Ireland Act 1800 provided for the continuance of a separate Privy Council for Ireland. A Council for Northern Ireland was established by the Irish Free State (Consequential Provisions) Act 1922. The Northern Ireland Constitution Act 1973, s.32(3) provided that no further appointments would be made to the Council.

[5] The oath dates back to the time of Edward I. For the modern form of Privy Councillor's oath, see Anson, *Law and Custom of the Constitution* (4th ed.) Vol. II, Pt. I, p. 153.

[6] Oaths Act 1978.

[7] For a descriptive account, see Sir Almeric Fitzroy, *The History of the Privy Council* (1928) pp. 294 *et seq.*

[8] For a specimen, see Anson, *op. cit.* (5th ed. Gwyer), Vol. I, pp. 55–56.

[9] For the form, see Anson, *op. cit.* (4th ed. Keith), Vol. II, Pt. I, p. 62.

civil servants[10] or declaring a state of emergency to exist or to be at an end; or judicial, *e.g.* giving effect to a judgment (technically advice) of the Judicial Committee of the Privy Council.

Miscellaneous functions

A Privy Council is also summoned for certain special occasions, such as the acceptance of office by newly appointed Ministers, and the annual "pricking" of sheriffs on Maundy Thursday.   **16–006**

Meetings of the Privy Council

Privy Councillors are summoned to attend at Buckingham Palace, or wherever else the Sovereign may be.[11] The quorum is three. Usually four are summoned, being Ministers concerned with the business in hand. The whole Council has not met (except at an Accession) since 1839, when Queen Victoria's forthcoming marriage was announced.[12] The marriage of the Prince of Wales to Lady Diana Spencer was approved at a special meeting of the Privy Council in March 1981 where those present, in addition to The Queen, the Prime Minister, the Lord Chancellor, the Lord President and other senior ministers, included the Prince of Wales, the Archbishop of Canterbury, the Speaker of the House of Commons, Leaders of the Opposition Parties and Privy Councillors from Australia, New Zealand and other Commonwealth Countries.[13]   **16–007**

Committees of the Council

Any meeting of Privy Councillors at which the Sovereign or Counsellors of State are not present can only be a committee.[14] Apart from the Judicial Committee, which is discussed below, there are advisory or *ad hoc* committees concerned with such matters as scientific research and the grant of charters.[15]   **16–008**

An *ad hoc* committee was set up to hear and advise on an appeal to the Visitor of the University of London, the Queen in Council, which led to proceedings reported in *R. v. Her Majesty The Queen in Council ex p. Vijayatunga.*[16]

---

[10] See, for example, *C.C.S.U. v. Minister for the Civil Service* [1985] A.C. 374.

[11] *e.g.* Balmoral or aboard the Royal Yacht.

[12] *ante* para. 14–003 (Accession Council).

[13] For a description of a meeting of the Council, see Herbert Morrison, "The Privy Council today" (1948) 2 *Parliamentary Affairs* (Hansard Society), pp. 10, 12–13. See also Dermot Morrah, *The Queen at Work* (1958), pp. 142–144. R.H.S. Crossman, who resented having to travel to Balmoral for meetings of the Privy Council in his capacity as Lord President of the Council (particularly when there was no restaurant car on his train), described meetings as "the best example of pure mumbo jumbo you can find." (*Diaries of a Cabinet Minister*, Vol. 2, p. 44).

[14] This idea dates from the middle of the eighteenth century.

[15] In addition to the *ad hoc* exercise of its power to grant royal charters (and amend their terms) to particular bodies, the Education Reform Act 1988, s.205 required a general revision of university charters, pursuant to the recommendations of statutory university commissioners.

[16] [1990] 2 Q.B. 444, CA. The Committee consisted of Lord Brightman, Mr Fred Mulley and Mr Mark Carlisle Q.C., M.P.. Normally, in the case of universities created by royal charter, the visitor is simply the Queen and her visitatorial duties are discharged by the Lord Chancellor who, typically, appoints a senior judge or law lord to hear any appeal: *Thomas v. University of Bradford* [1987] A.C. 795. On the law relating to Visitors, see H. Picarda, *The Law and Practice Relating to Charities* (3rd ed. 1999) Chap. 42. The role of Visitors in universities was considerably restricted by the Education Reform Act 1988, in relation to disputes about employment of academic staff, and the abolition of their jurisdiction has been proposed.

II. The Judicial Functions of the Privy Council[17]

Historical introduction

16–009   Even after the separation of the courts of common law and the Court of Chancery, the King's Council retained some jurisdiction (i) in cases which in some way concerned the state, and (ii) in private cases where the ordinary courts could not provide a remedy. This jurisdiction, especially in the latter element, represented the residue of justice that always lay with the King. In the early Middle Ages the Council was not a court of record; it had no seal, and indeed it was not called a "court" at all.[18]

In the Tudor period most of the Council's jurisdiction relating to state offences and cases in which great men were involved was exercised by the Court of Star Chamber. In this period the Court of High Commission was set up to deal with important ecclesiastical causes, and the Court of Requests as a "minor Court of Equity" to hear the suits of poor persons. It was part of the struggle between Parliament and the King in the early seventeenth century that these courts of an "arbitrary" jurisdiction should be attacked as being closely associated with the royal prerogative. The Long Parliament, in the same year in which it abolished the Court of High Commission, also passed a statute commonly known as the Act for the Abolition of the Star Chamber 1640. Certain other prerogative jurisdictions, such as those of the Councils of Wales and the Marches and of the North, were also expressly abolished. The Act further declared and enacted that neither His Majesty nor his Privy Council have or ought to have any jurisdiction over the land or chattels of English subjects. Although the Court of Requests was not mentioned, it ceased to function almost immediately afterwards.

The ancient judicial powers of the Privy Council survived only in the form of an appellate jurisdiction from the King's overseas dominions, namely, the Channel Islands, the Isle of Man, the colonies (or "foreign plantations," as they were at first called)[19] and, later, India. In the eighteenth century the Judicial Committees formed for this purpose acquired many of the characteristics of courts; they usually sat in public, and reports began to be published in 1829.

Appeals from the ecclesiastical courts, the Court of Admiralty and the vice-admiralty courts of the colonies were given to the Privy Council by statute in 1832. This statutory extension of the Privy Council's jurisdiction necessitated a reorganisation of its constitution.

The Judicial Committee—composition

16–010   The Judicial Committee Act 1833, passed "for the better administration of justice in His Majesty's Privy Council," constituted a Judicial Committee. The Judicial Committee Act 1844 authorised the Queen by Order in Council to admit

[17] Holdsworth, *History of English Law*, Vol. I; N. Bentwich, *Privy Council Practice* (3rd ed. 1937), Chap. I; P. A. Howell, *The Judicial Committee of the Privy Council, 1833–1876*; J. H. Smith, *Appeals to the Privy Council from the American Plantations*. Viscount Haldane, "The Judicial Committee of the Privy Council" (1922) 1 C.L.J. 143; Sir George Rankin, "The Judicial Committee of the Privy Council" (1939) 7 C.L.J. 2; Lord Normand, "The Judicial Committee of the Privy Council—retrospect and prospect" (1950) C.L.P. 1; Robert Stevens, "The Final Appeal: Reform of the House of Lords and Privy Council 1867–1876" (1964) 80 L.Q.R. 343. Loren P. Beth, "The Judicial Committee: Its Development, Organisation and Procedure," [1975] P.L. 219.
[18] Leadam and Baldwin, Introduction to *Select Cases before the King's Council* (Selden Society Publications).
[19] *Fryer v. Bernard* (1724) 2 P.W. 262.

any appeals to the Privy Council from any court within any British colony or possession abroad, even though such court might not be a court of error or of appeal. Hence appeals lay from the Australian states after federation. It has been questioned whether this Act put the prerogative power on a statutory basis, or merely regulated the manner of its exercise.

As a result of the Act of 1833 and various later statutes,[20] the Judicial Committee is composed of:

(a)   the Lord Chancellor; the Lord President and ex-Lord Presidents of the Council (who do not sit)[21]; the Lords of Appeal in Ordinary; and the Lords Justices of Appeal (who seldom sit);

(b)   ex-Lord Chancellors and retired Lords of Appeal;

(c)   selected senior judges or ex-judges of Australia, New Zealand and other Commonwealth countries from which appeal lies.

The quorum is three.

It will be seen that the composition of the Judicial Committee is wider than that of the House of Lords sitting as a final court of appeal.

Jurisdiction

The Judicial Committee was given the jurisdiction of the Privy Council set out above, namely, appeals from the courts of the Channel Islands, the Isle of Man, the colonies and British India, and from the ecclesiastical courts and Admiralty Court, to which were later added appeals from prize courts.   **16–011**

Appeals in probate, divorce and admiralty causes (other than prize) were later transferred to the House of Lords. The Judicial Committee also has a limited appellate jurisdiction over the ecclesiastical courts of the Church of England.[22] A number of former colonies and protectorates, as well as India, have become independent members of the Commonwealth, and in most instances appeals from their courts to the Judicial Committee of the Privy Council have been abolished by local legislation.[23]

Modern statutes have given a right of appeal to the Judicial Committee from the tribunals of various professional organisations having power to strike a member off the register.[24]

A new role

Until recently the most controversial aspect of the Judicial Committee's work has been the hearing of appeals from overseas against the infliction of the death penalty.   **16–012**

The devolution legislation contains provisions likely to provoke controversy of a different kind. The Scotland Act, the Northern Ireland Act and the Government of Wales Act confer wide powers on the Judicial Committee, to advise on the

[20] Appellate Jurisdiction Acts 1876, 1887, 1908; Judicial Committee Amendment Act 1895.

[21] The Lord President, Secretaries of State and other laymen often sat until the middle of the nineteenth century; for example, the Duke of Buccleuch, of whom the future Lord Kingsdown said: "Depend upon it, the natives of India would much rather have this case decided by a great Scottish Duke than by lawyers alone": Stevens, *op. cit.* p. 349.

[22] Ecclesiastical Jurisdiction Measure 1963, s.8.

[23] For appeals to the Privy Council from courts overseas, see *post*, Chap. 37.

[24] *e.g.* Medical Act 1983, Dentists Act 1984; Osteopaths Act 1993; Chiropractors Act 1994.

constitutionality of legislation before enactment, to hear devolution issues referred to it in the course of litigation and to determine appeals on devolution issues arising in courts in the devolved jurisdictions.[25]

It was thought that it would be inappropriate to refer such issues to the House of Lords (although the House has power to decide devolution matters in litigation arising before it.) But in terms of personnel, there is considerable overlap between the House of Lords in its judicial capacity and the Judicial Committee. The role of the Lord Chancellor as a member of the United Kingdom cabinet becomes even more anomalous. Were he to sit in a case involving devolution issues litigants would surely consider challenging his participation under the Human Rights Act 1998 and Article 6 of the European Convention.[26]

Judges from Commonwealth jurisdictions outside the United Kingdom are excluded by the legislation from sitting in devolution cases—thus excluding those judges with experience of constitutional cases which, at least, have a degree of similarity to those likely to arise in devolution litigation.

Questions may arise—will arise—about the composition of the Judicial Committee on these occasions. No doubt every judge is impartial *virtute officii* but the impartiality of an English judge may not be so obvious to citizens of Belfast or Edinburgh. At present the responsibility for determining the composition of the Committee rests with the Lord Chancellor but is delegated to the senior Law Lord. (The gravity of that responsibility is in no doubt after the *Pinochet* litigation.)

In the nineteenth century there had been proposals to merge the Judicial Committee and the Appellate Committee of the House of Lords. Reform of the House of Lords in this century and the introduction of devolution should have provided the opportunity to consider seriously a fundamental reform of the highest courts in the United Kingdom.[27]

It has been suggested that the judicial functions of the Privy Council should be merged with those of the House of Lords, and that the Judicial Committee should become a peripatetic Commonwealth Court.[28] The former idea was often discussed in the nineteenth century. The latter idea is not new, but seems to be no longer practicable in the present stage of Commonwealth development or disintegration.

Procedure

16–013   Rules of practice are made under the Act of 1833. Appeals, or requests for leave to appeal, are commenced by petition to the Crown. Usually only one "judgment" is given by the Board. This is in theory a report made to Her Majesty of the reasons why judgment should be given in favour of a particular party; but the Committee is regarded for practical purposes as a court, and the Queen is bound by convention to give effect to its advice, which is done by Order in Council.[29] Indeed, the report is made public before it is sent up to the Sovereign in Council.[30]

---

[25] For details, *ante* Chapter 5. In the case of Northern Ireland the Government of Ireland Act had provided for seeking the opinion of the Judicial Committee on the validity of legislation. Only one reference was made: *Re a Reference under the Government of Ireland Act 1920* [1936] A.C. 352.
[26] *post*, para. 22–036. See also para. 31–014 for the *Pinochet* litigation.
[27] D. Olivier, "The Lord Chancellor, the Judicial Committee of the Privy Council and devolution," [1999] P.L.I.
[28] Gerald Gardiner and Andrew Martin, *Law Reform Now* (1963), p. 16; *post*, Chap. 3.
[29] *British Coal Corp. v. The King* [1935] A.C. 500; *Ibralebbe v. R.* [1964] A.C. 900.
[30] *Hull v. M'Kenna* [1926] I.R. 402, *per* Viscount Haldane.

The advice was formerly required to be unanimous,[31] but an Order in Council in 1966[32] allowed dissenting opinions to be delivered.

Special reference

Section 4 of the Judicial Committee Act 1833[33] provides that the Crown may **16–014** refer to the Committee for an advisory opinion any matter it may think fit. In practice, references under this section are confined to justiciable matters.[34] Thus in 1927 the Committee was asked to give an opinion on the Labrador boundary dispute between Canada and Newfoundland,[35] and in 1924 on the interpretation of the provisions of the Anglo-Irish Treaty of 1921 relating to the settlement of the boundary between Northern Ireland and the Irish Free State.[36] It was called on to advise on the elements of the international crime of piracy in *Re Piracy Iure Gentium*.[37] Its advice has also been sought by the Commons, through the Attorney-General, on whether a member was disqualified from sitting in the House[38] the law relating to Parliamentary privilege.[39]

---

[31] *cf. Cowie v. Remfrey* (1846) 5 Moo.P.C. 232.
[32] Judicial Committee (Dissenting Opinions) Order in Council, 1966.
[33] 3 & 4 W.4. c. 41.
[34] See Sir Kenneth Roberts Wray, *Commonwealth and Colonial Law* (1966), p. 448 *et. seq.*
[35] (1927) 43 T.R. 289.
[36] (1924) Cmd. 2214.
[37] [1934] A.C. 584.
[38] *Re Sir Stuart Samuel* [1913] A.C. 514; *Re MacManaway, Re House of Commons (Clergy Disqualification) Act 1801* [1951] A.C. 161.
[39] *Re Parliamentary Privilege Act 1770* [1958] A.C. 352.

CHAPTER 17

THE CABINET AND THE PRIME MINISTER

I. DEVELOPMENT OF THE CABINET[1]

Origins in the Privy Council

17–001   The seventeenth and eighteenth centuries saw the growth of the practice of withdrawing the discussion and direction of government policy, as distinct from administration, into the hands of a few of the King's *confidential* advisers. The history of this subject is very obscure, owing to the secrecy of the proceedings and the lack of official and connected records, and the fact that during most of this period the practice was unpopular with Parliament and in the country, and was not openly avowed. The historian's difficulty is further increased by the confusing terminology employed by the writers of that time. The better opinion probably is that the body which we now know as the Cabinet should never at any stage in its history be identified with any particular committee of the Privy Council, such as the Committee for Foreign Affairs. No doubt the use of committees helped to crystallise the form that the Cabinet was to take. The process was further assisted by the appointment of regency councils, known as "the Lords Justices," during the frequent absence abroad of William III, George I and George II. In this case the absence of the King made it necessary to commit resolutions to writing, and even to frame rules of procedure.

In the eighteenth century the members of the Cabinet came to call themselves "His Majesty's servants" or "His Majesty's *confidential* servants." The names given to Charles II's group of confidential advisers were intended as terms of reproach. *Cabinet* was a French word then in vogue for a private room set apart for interviews, and the "Cabinet Council" or "Cabinet" was so called because it met literally or metaphorically in the King's cabinet or closet. Similarly *cabal* was a French term for a secret group of advisers.[2]

George I attended Cabinet meetings at the beginning of his reign, but is traditionally said to have ceased attending regularly after 1717, because he was little interested in English affairs, ignorant of the English language and institutions, and unable to influence policy owing to his dependence for support on the Whig leaders.[3] Both George II and George III seem occasionally to have been present at Cabinet meetings for some special reason. The absence of the Sovereign marks a definite epoch in the development of the power of the principal Ministers, although the decline of the royal power was gradual. Kings in the

---

[1] Turner, *The Cabinet Council, 1622–1784*; A. B. Keith, *The British Cabinet System, 1830–1938* (2nd ed. Gibbs); D. L. Keir, *A Constitutional History of Modern Britain*; M. A. Thomson, *A Constitutional History of England, 1642–1801*; C. S. Emden, *The People and the Constitution*; Richard Pares, *King George III and the Politicians* (1953); Sir Lewis Namier, *Crossroads of Power* (1962), Chaps. 7 and 8.

[2] Fortuitously appropriate because of the names of the ministers, Clifford, Arlington, Buckingham, Ashley and Lauderdale.

[3] See, however, R. Hatton, *George I, Elector and King* (1979).

eighteenth century still exercised influence from their closet, and were "sometimes near, if not present."[4]

A further process of division took place in the reign of George II, when a distinction was drawn between the "inner," "efficient," or "effective" Cabinet and the "outer" or "nominal" Cabinet. The former, also known as the "conciliabulum," had special access to important state papers, while the latter disclaimed responsibility for acts of the Ministry on which they had not been consulted. The inner Cabinet, which may be regarded as the direct ancestor of the modern Cabinet, was in existence at least as early as 1740.[5] The size of the Cabinet had increased from five to about twenty in George III's reign. Indeed, the Cabinet had become considerably larger than Elizabeth I's Privy Council, which numbered only twelve.

Opposition of Parliament

The practice of consulting confidentially a small group of Ministers, which had **17–002** been intermittent in the reign of Charles I, was habitual in the reign of Charles II, and Parliament objected strongly to the secrecy of the deliberations, for it was difficult to know who were the responsible Ministers and how to enforce that responsibility. In order to put a stop to the practice, and to keep the House of Commons from being contaminated by the Sovereign's influence, Parliament inserted two clauses in the Act of Settlement 1700 to the effect that: (1) matters theretofore discussed in the Privy Council must be dealt with there and not elsewhere, and all resolutions must be signed by the members present, and (2) no person holding a place of profit under the Crown was to sit in the House of Commons. The operation of these provisions was postponed until the death of Queen Anne, by which time they had been repealed, although the second emerged in a modified form in the Succession to the Crown Act 1707.[6]

Growth of political ideas relating to the Cabinet

Political ideas grow gradually. The party system and the principle of the **17–003** dependence of the government on the confidence of Parliament, and especially of the House of Commons, were developing in the eighteenth century.[7] The Cabinet often had political unity. Walpole, during his long period of office between 1721 and 1742, was skilful both in holding the favour of the King, partly through his friendship with Queen Caroline, and also in controlling the Commons, largely through bribery. At first the King chose as members of his Cabinet persons whom he liked and could trust. Eventually he had imposed upon him such advisers as Parliament, or the chief Ministers or the Prime Minister, wanted. There was an intermediate stage when the King no longer chose but could obstruct: when he was cajoled into accepting Ministers whom he did not like but to whom he did not profoundly object. This stage is illustrated by the long opposition of George II to the elder Pitt.

It was still possible for George III to hold a personal ascendancy during the earlier part of his reign by trading on the lack of political unity among his

---

[4] Turner, *op. cit.* Vol. II, pp. 92–100.
[5] R. R. Sedgwick, "The Inner Cabinet from 1732 to 1741" 34 *English Historical Review* 290–302.
[6] *ante*, para. 10–003.
[7] See Sir Ivor Jennings, *Party Politics*, Vol. II, "The Growth of Parties" (1961), for an account of the development of political parties since 1783.

Ministers, manipulating the two Houses, and making use of "honorary" members of the Cabinet. Some time during his reign, however, the Cabinet established the right to consider matters without reference from the King. The normal course had been for departmental matters to go from the Minister concerned to the King, and thence to the Cabinet if the King so willed. It now came to be recognised that, if the King had not actually a duty to consult the Cabinet, he was generally expected to do so. The King consulted Ministers individually in the closet, but they could agree beforehand in the ante-room what they would say. When the Cabinet were all of one party (which was not always so) they sometimes met, not as the King's advisers but as party leaders; and this paved the way for the Cabinet to become the general initiator of policy. The decline of the King's influence after the fall of the North Ministry in 1782 was accentuated by "the mental derangement which afflicted George III, the contemptible personal character of George IV, and the negligible qualities of William IV."[8] The younger Pitt asserted the necessity of having the King's confidence. In 1803 he insisted that it was essential that there should be "an avowed and real minister, possessing the chief weight in the Council and the principal place in the confidence of the King."[9]

17–004 The turning point came with the Reform Act 1832, which soon showed that henceforth a Ministry would depend on the support of a majority in the House of Commons, and ultimately on the electorate. Peel accepted responsibility for the King's action in forcing Melbourne to resign in 1834. The King granted Peel a dissolution, but he was returned with a minority and Melbourne displaced him in office until 1841. In the latter year the Whig Ministry was defeated in the Commons on the budget, but preferred to retain office. Peel moved a resolution that their continuance in office in such circumstances was at variance with the spirit of the Constitution; this was carried by one vote, and a dissolution followed. Nonetheless in 1851, when a Committee of the House of Commons proposed that some precedence be given to Cabinet Ministers at the opening and prorogation of Parliament the House rejected the proposal on the ground that the Cabinet was unknown to the Constitution.[10]

II. THE CABINET[11]

Functions of the Cabinet

17–005 The Cabinet system, or system of Cabinet government, was generally agreed to prevail between the wars. The main functions of the Cabinet at the end of the first war were summarised in the following way: "(a) the final determination of the policy to be submitted to Parliament; (b) the supreme control of the national executive in accordance with the policy prescribed by Parliament; and (c) the

---

[8] Keir, *op. cit.* pp. 381–382.
[9] Quoted, Keith, *op. cit.* pp. 16–17.
[10] G. H. Le May *The Victorian Constitution* (1979), p. 96. The word "Cabinet" first appeared on the order paper of the House of Commons in 1900: Le May, *loc. cit.*
[11] J. P. Mackintosh, *The British Cabinet* (3rd ed., 1977); Sir Ivor Jennings, *Cabinet Government* (3rd ed., 1959); P. Gordon Walker, *The Cabinet* (revised ed., 1972); Harold Wilson, *The Governance of Britain* (1976); Herbert Morrison, *Government and Parliament* (1954); L. S. Amery, *Thoughts on the Constitution* (2nd ed., 1953); R. H. S. Crossman, *Inside View* (1972); *Memoirs of a Cabinet Minister* (3 Vols.); Ronald Butt, *The Power of Parliament* (2nd ed., 1969); Ian Colvin, *The Chamberlain Cabinet* (1971).

continuous co-ordination and delimitation in the interests of the several Departments of State."[12] The Cabinet, giving collective "advice" to the Sovereign through the Prime Minister, was said to exercise under Parliament supreme control over all departments of state, and to be the body which co-ordinated the work on the one hand of the executive and the legislature, and on the other hand of the organs of the executive among themselves. The concept of the "Cabinet system" or "system of Cabinet government" may now need to be revised in the light of more recent developments, such as the predominance of the Prime Minister, the greater use of Cabinet committees and the growing influence of senior civil servants.[13] And the expression "policy prescribed by Parliament" must be read subject to the government's control of its party in the Commons, so that Parliament prescribes what the government wants.

Most important matters of policy are discussed at Cabinet meetings. For security reasons, however, specific Budget proposals (as distinct from the general Budget strategy) are disclosed orally to the Cabinet only a few days before the Chancellor of the Exchequer is to introduce them in the Commons, and for diplomatic reasons it is not always possible to consult the Cabinet before taking action in foreign affairs. Among matters not usually discussed by the Cabinet are the exercise by the Home Secretary of the prerogative of mercy (not of great importance since the abolition of the death penalty),[14] the personnel of the Cabinet itself, the making of appointments and the conferment of honours, which are matters within the patronage of the Prime Minister.

The dissolution of Parliament after 1841 was formerly a matter for Cabinet decision; but in 1918 Lloyd George and Bonar Law, the party leaders in a Coalition Government, alone made the decision, the lapse of time since the last general election in 1910 having caused Ministers to forget what the practice was.[15] Lloyd George consulted a number of Cabinet colleagues about dissolution in 1922 because he had difficulty making up his mind.[16] Mr Heath consulted his Cabinet before the ill-fated dissolution in February 1974, and they unanimously supported him.[17] A Prime Minister consults at least a few colleagues, of course, including the Chief Whip and the Chairman of the party. The principle may be discussed by members of the Cabinet, but the details are left to the Prime Minister.[18] It seems to have been generally assumed that in regard to the timing of the 2001 Election the Cabinet was left in the dark while the Prime Minister relied on advice from a circle of close aides.

17–006

It has been argued that this supposed convention lacks the essential quality that should mark a constitutional convention, namely the combination of consistent historical precedents and a convincing *raison d'être*.[19] It has been suggested that it is desirable to restore the balance of ministerial power by reverting to the

---

[12] Report of the Machinery of Government Committee Cd. 9230 (1918), p. 5.

[13] *post*, para. 17–034.

[14] But the decision not to exercise the prerogative of mercy in the case of Sir Roger Casement (1916) was made by the Cabinet for political reasons: Roy Jenkins, *Asquith*, pp. 403–404.

[15] Ivor Jennings, *Parliament must be Reformed* (1941); L. S. Amery, *op. cit.*, p. 23.

[16] Lord Beaverbrook, *The Decline and Fall of Lloyd George* (1963), Chaps. 7, 8, 11.

[17] Lord Hailsham, *The Door Wherein I Went* (1975), p. 298.

[18] B. E. Carter, *The Office of Prime Minister* (1956), pp. 289–291. Harold Wilson, "Why I chose June," *Observer* March 21, 1971. For a discussion of the request for, timing of, and reasons for dissolutions in the present century, see B. S. Markesinis, *The theory and practice of Dissolution of Parliament* (1972) Pt. II and App. I.

[19] G. Marshall, *Constitutional Conventions* (1984), Chap. 3.

convention that dissolution should be advised by, and granted to, the Cabinet.[20]

The Cabinet may meet anywhere, for example, in the Prime Minister's room in the House of Commons or at Chequers. Most often it meets at No. 10 Downing Street, usually once or twice a week. A summons to a Privy Council takes precedence. There is no quorum for a Cabinet. The agenda is determined by the Prime Minister. The regular items begin with parliamentary business and then foreign and Commonwealth affairs. These are followed by White Papers, which have been processed by committees; statistical reports on such subjects as unemployment and balance of payments. Finally there are current matters from committees, emergencies, etc. Elaborate precautions are taken to ensure secrecy: the Cabinet room has double doors, and a person waiting in attendance outside is brought in by a Cabinet Minister.[21] Every attempt is made to promote unanimity by refraining where possible from formal voting. The Prime Minister "collects the voices" and announces the decision.[22]

Composition of the Cabinet

17–007   The Cabinet consists of a group of Ministers, normally something over 20 in number, who are agreed to pursue a common policy and who are invited by the Prime Minister to attend Cabinet meetings. Most of them are heads of the chief government departments, for example, the Chancellor of the Exchequer, the Foreign Secretary and the Home Secretary, but a number of heads of departments will be outside the Cabinet, and the Cabinet will include some Ministers whose offices involve few or no departmental responsibilities. These last are free to carry out miscellaneous tasks, such as the co-ordination of policy and administration, responsibility for research, acting as chairmen of Cabinet committees and giving advice as elder statesmen. The "Ministry," "Government" or "Administration" is the name given to the whole body of about a hundred holders of ministerial office, all of whose offices are known to the law,[23] and who are appointed by the Sovereign on the advice of the Prime Minister. Under the standing orders adopted by the Parliamentary Labour Party in 1981 a Labour Prime Minister is required on election to appoint as Cabinet Ministers the individuals who had formerly been elected as members of the Shadow Cabinet.

The Cabinet itself has been mentioned a few times in statutes. The Ministers of the Crown Act 1937 provided additional salaries to "Cabinet Ministers" who held offices at salaries less than a certain amount. The additional salary was made payable "if and so long as any Minister of the Crown to whom this section applies is a member of the Cabinet." The date on which any such Minister ceased to be a member of the Cabinet was to be published in the *London Gazette*, and such notification was to be "conclusive evidence" for the purposes of the Act.[24]

---

[20] O. Hood Phillips, *Reform of the Constitution* (1970), pp. 44–45, 51–52.

[21] Despite the formal position, inspired "leaks" and the activities of "spin doctors" ensure that the media are not short of accounts of what passed if the parties involved so wish.

[22] For descriptions of a Cabinet meeting, see Morrison, *op. cit.* pp. 4–6; Gordon Walker, *op. cit.* Chap. 6.

[23] They (except the Lord Chancellor) are listed in the Second Schedule to the House of Commons Disqualification Act 1975, as amended.

[24] See now, Ministerial and other Salaries Act 1975, under which additional salaries are payable to the Lord President of the Council, the Lord Privy Seal, the Chancellor of the Duchy of Lancaster, the Paymaster General, the Chief Secretary to the Treasury, the Parliamentary Secretary to the Treasury, and Ministers of State so long as they are members of the Cabinet.

The Parliamentary Commissioner Act 1967, s.8(4) provides that no person shall be required or authorised "by virtue of this Act" to furnish any information or documents or answer any question relating to proceedings of the Cabinet or any Cabinet Committee. For the purposes of the subsection any certificate issued by the Secretary of the Cabinet with the approval of the Prime Minister is conclusive.[25] The Data Protection Act 1998, s.28 entitles a Minister of the Crown to exempt certain information from the provisions of the Act if the Minister is a member of the Cabinet or the Attorney-General or the Lord Advocate. Cabinet meetings and the question of joint responsibility of the Cabinet were referred to by Lord Widgery C.J. in *Attorney-General v. Jonathan Cape Ltd.*[26]

The Cabinet is, then, the nucleus of the Ministry. In choosing the Cabinet the Prime Minister has a number of factors to consider, such as the importance of the various offices, the influence of members in the country, the authority of members in the Commons and their value in debate, the value of members as advisers in Committee, and the representation of the government in the House of Lords.[27] They are not generally experts in the subject-matter of their departments. By custom Cabinet Ministers are made Privy Councillors if they are not so already. Since 1951 the Chief Whip has been invited to attend, so that he may be asked what would be the probable attitude of the party.[28]

Cabinet Ministers in the House of Lords

Convention requires that all Ministers must sit in one or other of the Houses   **17–008**
of Parliament, in order that their activities may be subject to parliamentary supervision.[29] The House of Commons Disqualification Act 1975 limits the number of Ministers who may sit in the House of Commons: the rest must therefore be peers. The Government in any case will want to be adequately represented in the House of Lords. As regards the House of Lords, the Lord Chancellor will be automatically included,[30] and in a Labour Government he may be the only Cabinet Minister there. It is inconceivable that the Chancellor of the Exchequer should be in the House of Lords, since the Commons have a monopoly of financial affairs. Another office that has raised controversy (apart from Prime Minister[31]) is that of Foreign Secretary. The appointment of Lord Halifax as Foreign Secretary in 1938 provoked some comment.[32] Considerable controversy arose in 1960 when the Earl of Home (now Lord Home of the Hirsel) was appointed Foreign Secretary. In 1979, however, Mrs Thatcher appointed

[25] It has been suggested, (G. Marshall, *Constitutional Conventions* (1984), p. 89) that a Minister may, if he wishes produce such documents or give such information.

[26] [1976] Q.B. 752; *post*, p. 313.

[27] See *The British Prime Minister* (Anthony King ed. 1969), pp. 60–79 (Attlee, "The Making of a Cabinet").

[28] The Chief Whip (Parliamentary Secretary to the Treasury) has recently been included as a member of the Cabinet. It appears that the Principal Private Secretary to the Prime Minister since Mr Macmillan's time sits in at meetings of the full Cabinet and at most Cabinet committees.

[29] A temporary exception to this convention was the appointment of Mr R. G. Casey, an Australian, as Minister of State in 1942, which was presumably made under the Re-election of Ministers Act 1919, s.2. And see as regards Asquith, para. 17–025n; Mr Gordon Walker and Mr Frank Cousins (1964–65) *ante*, para. 7–015.

[30] It was wholly exceptional that in the "caretaker government" formed after the with-drawal of the Labour Party from the National Coalition in 1945, the Lord Chancellor—Viscount Simon, a National Liberal—was not a member of the Cabinet.

[31] *post*, para. 17–033.

[32] He even remained a member of the Cabinet after being appointed Ambassador to the United States.

Lord Carrington to be Foreign Secretary, a post which he held until his resignation in 1982.[33] The Prime Minister in modern times is the overseer of foreign policy, and communicates personally with the heads of foreign governments or states and can answer for foreign affairs in the house of Commons if the Foreign Secretary is in the other House.[34]

There was criticism of Mrs Thatcher's decision in 1985 to appoint Lord Young of Graffham as Secretary of State for Employment. Lord Young had been created a life peer in the previous year and appointed a Minister without Portfolio. To meet the argument that employment was a matter of particular concern to the Commons, the Paymaster General was designated as chief Commons spokesman on employment.

Mr Blair has not hesitated to use the device of life peerages to secure the appointment of individuals to ministerial office, for example, Lord Falconer, formerly Minister of State in the Cabinet Office, currently Minister of State for Housing and Planning, Lord Macdonald, formerly Minister of Transport, currently Chancellor of the Duchy of Lancaster[35] and Lady Morgan of Huyton, Minister of State in the Cabinet Office.

Size of the Cabinet

17–009 The size of the Cabinet varies from time to time. Prime Ministers usually begin by hoping to cut the size of the Cabinet but find it impracticable. Between the wars there "full" Cabinets of over twenty members. After the last war there were "medium" Cabinets of sixteen to eighteen, but Sir Alex Douglas-Home and Mr Wilson had Cabinets of 23. Mrs Thatcher reduced the Cabinet to 22 and in June 1987 to 21. The current figure is 23, which includes the Labour Party Chairman who is Minister without portfolio. During the two world wars there were "small" Cabinets of from six to ten members, although other Ministers were often present, and Chiefs of Staff, Dominion Prime Ministers and others were in attendance. It has been persuasively argued that the large volume of work assumed by the Cabinet is too great to be efficiently performed by a group of Ministers most of whom have heavy departmental responsibilities as well as the duty of constant attendance at the House. One suggestion is that there should be a small policy-making Cabinet of about six, whose members would not be departmental heads.[36] Another is that more use should be made of Standing Committees of the Cabinet to co-ordinate the work of groups of departments

---

[33] *post*, para. 17–017.

[34] In 1923 Curzon inquired of King George V why, if in the circumstances of the times His Majesty thought that a peer ought not to be Prime Minister he had no objection to a peer being Foreign Secretary: "Because the Prime Minister is responsible for everything you do"; Kenneth Rose, *King George V* (1983), pp. 272–273.

[35] In the case of Lord Macdonald there was a period of four months between his appointment as a minister (in August 1998) and becoming a peer at the beginning of the next session of Parliament.

[36] Amery, *op. cit.* pp. 87, 90–93. This would be something like the small war Cabinets in the two world wars, although these were reinforced from time to time by Commonwealth statesmen: Lord Hankey, *Government Control in War* (1945); Winston S. Churchill, *The Second World War*, Vol. II, Chap. 3; Vol. III, pp. 784–786; Vol. IV, Chap. 5 and App. G; Vol. V, App. G; Vol. VI, App. H; Jennings, *op. cit.* pp. 287–291; Keith, *op. cit.* pp. 136–141; *Memoirs of Lord Chandos* (1962), Chaps. 12–14. Several meetings were also held in the first war with Dominion Prime Ministers, and called the "Imperial War Cabinet"; D. Lloyd George, *War Memoirs*, Chaps. 38 and 55; Report of the Machinery of Government Committee Cd. 9230 (1918), pp. 4–6; The War Cabinet, Report for the Year 1917 Cd. 9005 (1918), pp. 1–10.

whose interests overlap.[37] Attlee thought 16 the best number. There is difference of opinion on how many members of this supreme policy-making body should be free from departmental duties, the manner in which the work of the departmental (non-Cabinet) Ministers should be co-ordinated, and the way in which Parliament can call Ministers to account.

Churchill's experiment from 1951–1953 of having several Ministers as "Overlords," who without statutory authority supervised groups of other Ministers, was not successful as it degraded the Ministers who were supervised and confused ministerial responsibility. Since 1970, however, Cabinets have included several "super-Ministers" directly responsible for multiple departments formed by the merger of a number of previous departments—for example, the Secretary of State for the Environment embraced for a time the former Ministries of Housing and Local Government, Public Building and Works, and Transport, until a separate Department of Transport was established. In the previous Cabinet Transport was absorbed again by Environment, the Minister, however, attending Cabinet meetings, and the Department's name expanded to Environment, Transport and the Regions.[37a]

Ministers who are not members of the Cabinet may be called in if matters specially affecting their department are under discussion. Civil servants are rarely present, although the Permanent Secretary to the Treasury or the Permanent Under-Secretary of State of the Foreign Office may be summoned. Law Officers may be summoned when legal issues are being discussed and Chiefs of Staff, may be present when military questions are being discussed.

Shadow Cabinet[38]

It has come to be an accepted part of the working of our Constitution that the **17–010** Opposition should organise itself on parallel lines to the government. The idea emerged gradually, and the Shadow Cabinet in an inchoate form came into existence by the 1860s. It may be said to have become a convention that there should be a Shadow Cabinet. Statutory salaries are now provided for the Leader of the Opposition and the Chief Opposition Whip in each House. The Shadow Cabinet constitutes an alternative team from which the prospective Prime Minister can choose his senior colleagues, and which provides the electorate with an alternative choice of government.

The Conservative Party's Shadow Cabinet is technically its Consultative Committee, and the Labour Party's is its Parliamentary Committee. The Labour Shadow Cabinet since 1923 has been elected annually by the parliamentary Labour Party in the Commons. The Conservative Shadow Cabinet is chosen by the Leader of the Opposition.[39]

Like the Cabinet itself, the Shadow Cabinet observes the convention of collective responsibility—described by Mr Foot, when Leader of the Opposition, in 1981 as a rule accepted by the Labour Party for generations.[40]

---

[37] Sir John Anderson, *The Machinery of Government* (Romanes Lecture, 1946). See also (1918) Cd. 9230 (*ante*): Lord Samuel, "A Cabinet of Ten." *The Times*, September 9, 1947.

[37a] *post*, para. 18–020.

[38] D. R. Turner, *The Shadow Cabinet in British Politics* (1969); Mackintosh, *op. cit.* pp. 259–261, 536–541, Jennings, *Parliament* (2nd ed.), pp. 81–83.

[39] *Quaere*, if a third party were the largest opposition party?

[40] *The Times*, November 14, 1981. For recognition of the principle by Mrs Thatcher when in opposition see D. Ellis, "Collective Ministerial Responsibility and Solidarity" [1980] P.L. 367, 392.

Cabinet Committees[41]

17–011   Committees of the Cabinet were set up ad hoc in the nineteenth century to expedite government business. An example was the War Committee (1855) at the time of the Crimean War. The first Standing Committee was the Committee of Imperial Defence set up by Balfour in 1903. This was not confined to Ministers, and it used the Privy Council secretariat. During the First World War a large number of committees were set up unsystematically by Asquith and Lloyd George. Between the wars committees came and went, there being on an average twenty ad hoc Committees at any one time. A system of Cabinet committees was developed in the last war. Attlee (Deputy Prime Minister) gave an account of these to the House of Commons in 1940, as did Churchill (Prime Minister) in 1941. Herbert Morrison has also given a full written account of the committees during the last war.[42] The most important of these was the Home Affairs Committee, which was responsible for a major part of domestic policy, such as the Education Bill. A new principle developed that a Cabinet committee had equal authority to the Cabinet, subject to possible reference to the Cabinet.

Attlee was the first Prime Minister to have a permanent committee structure in peace time. The pattern continued during the 1950s and 1960s, ad hoc committees continuing alongside Standing Committees. "The Prime Minister sets up and disbands committees, appoints the chairman and members and sets the terms of reference."[43] Some committees are chaired by the Prime Minister at No. 10; some by other Ministers in the Cabinet Office or at the House of Commons. Mr Wilson raised the authority of Cabinet committees by ruling that a member could only appeal from a committee to the Cabinet with the agreement of the chairman. The recommendations of a committee can be turned down by the Cabinet.

17–012   The existence of a Cabinet committee, the name of its chairman and the terms of reference formerly were not disclosed during the lifetime of a government, because of the principle of the unity and collective responsibility of the Cabinet. Despite the fact that their existence has been well known for many years Prime Ministers as recently as Mr Callaghan in 1978 urged the need for secrecy.[44] In May 1979 Mrs Thatcher announced in the House of Commons the existence of four standing committees of the Cabinet: Defence and Overseas Policy, Economic Strategy, Home and Social Affairs, and Legislation. Paradoxically, we were told most about the Defence Committee from White Papers on Defence.[45] The existence of Cabinet Committees was further recognised by Mr Major and lists of Committees with details of membership are now made public.

The committee system has increased the efficiency of the Cabinet, and enables a great deal more work to be done by Ministers. The Cabinet itself is left free to discuss controversial matters and to make more important decisions,[46] and its business is better prepared. The system also enables non-Cabinet Ministers to be brought into discussions.

---

[41] Walker, *op. cit.* pp. 38–47; App. (List of Standing Committees, 1914–64); Mackintosh, *op. cit.* pp. 521–529; Jennings, *Cabinet Government*, pp. 255–261; Wilson, *The Governance of Britain*; P. Hennessy and A. Arends, *Mr Attlee's Engine Room: Cabinet Committee Structure and the Labour Government 1945–51* (1983) (Strathclyde Papers on Govt. & Politics, No. 26); M. Cockerell, P. Hennessy and D. Walker, *Sources Close to the Prime Minister* (1984).
[42] Herbert Morrison, *op. cit.* pp. 19–26.
[43] Walker, *op. cit.* p. 45.
[44] *New Statesman*, November 10, 1978.
[45] *Central Organisation for Defence Cmd.* 6923 (1946); Cmnd. 576 (1958); Cmnd. 2097 (1963).
[46] Mr Wilson thought EEC affairs too important for a committee.

Cabinet committees come and go, change their names and are impossible to enumerate. Modern Standing Committees include (or have included) Home Affairs (currently, Home and Social Affairs)[47]; Future Legislation (principles and provisional priority of government Bills); Legislation (drafting and settling priority of government Bills and important Statutory Instruments[48]); Defence[49]; Economic Policy; Incomes Policy; Public Expenditure Scrutiny (PESC); and Social Services. The first list of Cabinet Committees issued after the 1997 election included new bodies to deal with Constitutional reform policy and Devolution. There is also a long list of miscellaneous committees ("Miscs"). Mr Wilson in 1968 announced the formation of a Parliamentary Committee to co-ordinate the work in Parliament, and to consider the broader aspects of the government's business. In his memoirs he speaks of a Management Committee to hold preliminary discussions on matters of policy, such as the Industrial Relations Bill, before putting the matter to the full Cabinet.[50] Commentators regarded both these as an Inner Cabinet.

The Committee on the South Atlantic which was established at the time of the Falklands crisis in 1982 has been described as a "War Cabinet" although, on the other hand, it has been argued that the need to secure Cabinet approval for major decisions throughout that undertaking helped to re-establish the importance of the Cabinet as a whole.[51]

"Inner Cabinet"

Prime Ministers in recent years are said to be in the habit of summoning an "Inner Cabinet."[52] The practice has been ascribed to Neville Chamberlain, Churchill, Attlee and Eden. Mr Wilson's Parliamentary Committee and Management Committee (*supra*) were described as an Inner Cabinet. An Inner Cabinet is supposed to be the efficient part that directs the Cabinet's activities. Lord Gordon Walker, however, calls it a misnomer. According to him it is not a Cabinet or a Cabinet committee. It has no organic or set place in the Cabinet structure. It is merely an informal, small group of friends or confidants of the Prime Minister drawn from members of the Cabinet.[53] It is not formally set up; it has no papers or records; it is not served by the Cabinet secretariat. An Inner Cabinet has as such no power. It does not predigest Cabinet business, although it may among other things discuss questions that are to come before the Cabinet. The practice of different Prime Ministers in this respect varies. The Inner Cabinet, says Lord Walker, is "a loose and informal thing."[54] Similarly, Mackintosh describes an Inner Cabinet as a number of Cabinet Ministers who are

17–013

---

[47] The Attorney-General often attends: see Sir Jocelyn Simon in (1965) 81 L.Q.R. 292–293.

[48] The Attorney-General is a member. Civil servants may be present by permission of the Prime Minister or chairman of the committee.

[49] Chiefs of Staff are in attendance: Cmnd. 2097 (1963).

[50] Harold Wilson, *The Labour Government, 1964–70: A Personal Record* (1971).

[51] P. Hennessy, "The Quality of Cabinet Government in Britain," (1985) 6 Pol. Stud. (Part 2), 15. See further P. Hennessy, *The Prime Minister* (Allen Lane, 2000) pp. 416–421.

[52] Walker, *op. cit.* pp. 37–38; Anthony King, *op. cit.* pp. 64, 91, 174, 185–186. Attendance at an Inner Cabinet was referred to in evidence in *Churchill (Randolph) v. Nabarro, The Times*, October 25–29, 1960. P. Hennessy, *op. cit.* p. 306.

[53] *cf.* Churchill's "cronies" with whom he liked to talk late into the night: they were personal friends, not men of influence. The Prime Minister probably did most of the talking; *cf.* "Kitchen Cabinet," *post*, note 55.

[54] Mr Gordon Walker, together with Mr George Brown and Mr Callaghan, was a member of Mr Wilson's Inner Cabinet that discussed such questions as devaluation and the Bank Rate.

regularly consulted by the Prime Minister, often singly; there is "no clearcut line which separates an inner from an outer ring."[55]

In contrast, Lord Walker talks of a *Partial Cabinet*, which can act for the Cabinet. This is a standing or ad hoc committee, presided over by the Prime Minister, but acting for a time as if they were the Cabinet. Examples are Attlee's group of Ministers who decided to make the atom bomb, and Eden's group who determined the Suez policy.[56]

The Cabinet Office[57]

17–014   Cabinet minutes were sometimes kept in the reigns of George II, III and IV, but the practice lapsed until the First World War. Ministers were expected to remember what was decided and to carry out those decisions in their departments. The Sovereign was kept informed by a letter from the Prime Minister after each meeting, retailing the topics considered and the decisions taken. It was a confidential letter written in the Prime Minister's own hand, and not shown to other members of the Cabinet.[58] Lloyd George, when Prime Minister, introduced a secretariat in 1916 by borrowing as Secretary of the War Cabinet Sir Maurice Hankey (later, Lord Hankey), at that time Secretary to the Committee of Imperial Defence.[59] Since then minutes of Cabinet meetings have been sent to the Sovereign and circulated to members of the Cabinet.

The Secretariat, which has steadily grown in numbers and influence, serves all Cabinet committees as well as the full Cabinet. It organises the agenda, circulates reports, and records the Cabinet "Conclusions." This record contains not only the actual "Conclusions" or decisions, but also the subjects discussed and the relevant Papers, and a summary of the discussion. The arguments of individual Ministers are not usually recorded, in the interest of both of anonymity and secrecy. The Conclusions are circulated to the Cabinet, unless the matter is one of exceptional secrecy.

17–015   The Cabinet secretariat has always been on the Treasury vote: there is no Cabinet vote. The Secretary to the Cabinet also serves as Principal Private Secretary to the Prime Minister.

Mr Heath in 1970 appointed a *Central Policy Review Staff* (CPRS or "Think-tank"), staffed partly by non-civil servants, to consider long-term and trans-departmental problems and to make recommendations for action.[60] It was located in the Cabinet Office, and a few years later became part of the civil service. The C.P.R.S. was abolished by Mrs Thatcher in 1983. In 1974 Mr Wilson introduced a *Policy Unit* of non-civil servants to help him in his political and administrative

[55] Mackintosh, *op. cit.* p. 542. *Cf.* "Kitchen Cabinet," a body of non-ministerial confidants "giving advice in a sympathetic manner"; *ibid.* p. 520. "Kitchen Cabinet" is a pejorative term, most frequently used in recent years in relation to Harold Wilson's circle of intimates: P. Hennessy, *op. cit.* p. 294 *et seq.*

[56] Walker, *op. cit.* pp. 87–91.

[57] R. K. Mosley, *The Story of Cabinet Office* (1969); Walker, *op. cit.* pp. 48–57; Jennings, *op. cit.* pp. 242–245; Mackintosh, *op. cit.* pp. 517 *et seq.* Stephen Roskill, *Hankey, Man of Secrets* (1972).

[58] The Public Record Office contains photographic copies of the 1,700 "Cabinet letters" written by Prime Ministers to the Sovereign from 1868 to 1916. The originals are at Windsor Castle. The letters constitute the only official record of decisions by the Cabinet in that period. There are also in the Public Record Office photographic copies of Cabinet memoranda from 1880 to 1914, and the Committee of Imperial Defence from 1902 to 1914.

[59] Lord Hankey, *Diplomacy by Conference*, Chaps. 2 and 3. See also John F. Naylor, A Man and an Institution: Sir Maurice Hankey, the Cabinet Secretariat and the custody of Cabinet secrecy, (1984).

[60] Cmnd. 4506.

work. The Policy Unit has survived and, under Mr Blair, has been increased from eight to twelve in number. He has also added two further bodies, the Social Exclusion Unit and the Performance and Innovation Unit.

A British Prime Minister has not been thought to need a department, as not only is he briefed by the Cabinet Secretary but also he can call on the Permanent Secretaries of any of the various departments. Since the last War, however, the Prime Minister has had a small *"No. 10 Office"* working as his and serving his personal needs. Under Mr Blair this Office has expanded and, controversially, two members of his staff, although not themselves civil servants, were given authority over civil servants. The newly appointed Secretary to the Cabinet, Sir Richard Wilson carried out a review of the working of the Cabinet Office and the Prime Minister's Office (which has not been published). Unease at the growth in numbers and influence of special advisers at No. 10 has been expressed by the House of Commons Select Committee on Public Administration.[61]

Ministerial responsibility and accountability

The responsibility of Ministers, as was indicated in Chapter 6, is both individ-   **17–016** ual and collective. The individual responsibility of a Minister for the performance of his official duties is both legal and conventional: it is owed legally to the Sovereign, and also by convention to Parliament. "Responsible" here does not mean morally responsible or culpable, but accountable or answerable.[62] The responsible Minister is the one under whose authority an act was done, or who must take the constitutional consequences of what has been done either by himself or in his department.[63] The traditional method of expressing no confidence in an individual Minister has been to move that his salary be reduced by a nominal sum, though it was pointed out in February 1976 that as ministerial salaries are fixed by statute, legislation would be required to reduce it.[64] A Minister must accept responsibility for the actions of the civil servants in his department, and he is expected to defend them from public criticism, unless they have done something reprehensible which he forbade, or of which he disapproved and of which he did not have and could not reasonably be expected to have had previous knowledge. In the latter case, which is unusual, he may dismiss them.[65] In normal circumstances, then, a Minister acts as a shield for his civil servants who are expected to be impartial and not able to answer public criticism for themselves; though this position is being eroded to some extent by the existence of the Parliamentary Commissioner[66] and Specialist Select Committees of the House.

It has been argued that an examination of ministerial resignations in the past   **17–017** century shows that the doctrine of individual responsibility in practice has no punitive effect, because either: (i) the erring Minister who resigns is appointed to another post; (ii) a timely reshuffle of ministerial posts renders resignation unnecessary; or (iii) a Minister who is unpopular with the Opposition is protected

---

[61] H.C. 293 (2000–2001).

[62] It also connotes a state of mind that acts as may be thought right after weighing the consequences: Amery, *op. cit.* p. 30.

[63] See G. K. Fry, "Thoughts on the Present State of the Convention of Ministerial Responsibility" (1969–70) XXIII *Parliamentary Affairs* 10.

[64] A motion to reduce the salary of the Secretary of State for Industry by £1,000 was carried as the result of a muddled vote, but the cut was restored after another motion a few days later.

[65] 520 H.C. Deb. cols. 1287 *et seq.*: following the Report of the Crichel Down Enquiry Cmd. 9176 (1954).

[66] *post*, para. 34–005.

by the solidarity of his colleagues.[67] Often too the unearthing of incompetence and inefficiency is such a slow process that the minister responsible has long ceased to hold the position in question.[68] The number of resignations in the last 50 years is small. Those that involve personal misbehaviour or alleged immorality do not help establish a principle of accountability for the proper working of a minister's department. Mr Ian Harvey in 1958, Mr Galbraith in 1962, Lord Jellicoe in 1973 and Mr Cecil Parkinson in 1983 resigned as a result of publicity about their private lives.[69] Mr Profumo resigned in 1963 but in his case, in addition to private immorality which was said to involve risks to the national security, there was the added factor of misleading Parliament.[70] Similarly in 1992, David Mellor's resignation was linked to allegations of improperly accepting hospitality without declaring it under the Ministerial Code, although newspapers had amused themselves by recounting stories of his extra-marital sexual activities. Other ministers had been guilty of disclosing Budget proposals prematurely—J. H. Thomas in 1936 and Hugh Dalton in 1947. More remarkable is the list of ministers who have not resigned despite serious errors in areas within their responsibility: Mr Lennox Boyd, the Colonial Secretary, despite the atrocities at Hola Prison Camp in Kenya[71]; Mr Whitelaw, when Home Secretary, despite the defects in police security which allowed an intruder to make his way into the Queen's bedroom[71a]; Mr Prior, when Secretary of State for Northern Ireland, despite the escape of terrorists from the Maze Prison.[72] Mr Howard's two escapes from resignation in 1995 and 1996 are significant because they illustrate the difficulties arising from the semi-independent status of Next Step Agencies.[73] Two examples may seem to support the convention that ministers are ultimately responsible for misjudgment in the performance of their duties or errors of policy in their departments. First, the resignation of Sir Thomas Dugdale in 1954 over the Crichel Down affair where he admitted maladministration in his department although he defended its policy.[74] Secondly, the resignation in 1982 of Lord Carrington the Foreign Secretary, Mr Luce and Mr Atkins who accepted personal responsibility for what in retrospect was found to be the miscalculation by the Foreign Office of the threat posed to the Falkland Islands by Argentina. A possible third example is the resignation of Mr Brittan, Secretary

---

[67] S. E. Finer, "The Individual Responsibility of Ministers" (1956) *Public Administration* 377. *Cf.* R. K. Alderman and J. A. Cross, *The Tactics of Resignation* (1967); K. C. Wheare, *Maladministration and its remedies* (1973), Chap. 3; G. Marshall, *Constitutional Conventions* (1984), pp. 61 *et seq.*; A. Barker, "Spreading the Blame", *The Listener* September 13, 1984.

[68] See G. Ganz "Parliamentary Accountability of the Crown Agents" [1980] P.L. 454.

[69] It is possible to add more recent examples to this list—proof, if of anything—that this generation should be more cautious about accusing the Victorians of hypocrisy.

[70] Cmnd. 2152 (1963) (Lord Denning's Report); P. J. Madgwick, "Resignations" (1966–67) *Parliamentary Affairs* 59.

[71] 607 H.C. Deb. col 248 and 610 H.C. Deb. col. 182.

[71a] Mr Michael Fagan, on July 9, 1982.

[72] H.C. Deb., cols. 1041–1047 (February 9, 1984).

[73] *post*, para. 18–023.

[74] Farmland had been compulsorily purchased during the Second World War. The owners from whom it was acquired were given an assurance that they would be given an opportunity to buy it back if the Crown subsequently had no use for the land. In due course the previous owners sought, unsuccessfully, to re-acquire the land. Various allegations were made of inefficiency and shortcomings of various kinds on the part of the civil servants concerned. Sir Andrew Clark Q.C. was appointed to hold an inquiry: he found evidence of muddle, bias and bad faith; Cmd. 9176 (1954). See J. A. G. Griffith, "The Crichel Down Affair" (1955) 18 M.L.R. 557.

of State for Trade and Industry in January, 1986, following the "leaking" of parts of a confidential letter from the Solicitor General by a civil servant in Mr Brittan's Department. That resignation formed part of the remarkable Westland Affair.[75] Apparently Mr Brittan resigned because he accepted responsibility for having authorised an action by a member of his Department which was improper and, as it turned out, inexpedient. At the other extreme the resignation of Ministers as in the case of Sir Samuel Hoare, over the Hoare-Laval Pact concerning Abyssinia in 1935, may be cases of ministers being "thrown to the wolves."

Such too may be the explanation of the second resignation of Mr Mandelson **17–018** on January 24, 2001. An earlier resignation related to the failure to disclose a loan by a fellow minister in circumstances where it should have been revealed. The second resignation arose from differing and ultimately unresolved accounts of the role he had played in an application for naturalisation by a wealthy Indian businessman. Mr Mandelson "resigned" first and then the Prime Minister appointed Sir Anthony Hammond to hold an inquiry to establish the facts. The inquiry concluded there was no evidence of any improper conduct and it was impossible to establish the facts in relation to telephone calls which had allegedly been made.

The Scott Inquiry[75a] into the export of defence equipment to Iraq, following the collapse of prosecutions relating to such exports, considered ministerial responsibility and drew a distinction between responsibility and accountability. The former relates to ministerial culpability, for example for an error in policy. The latter relates to the minister's duty to give an account to Parliament of everything that happens in his department or its associated Next Step Agencies, without implying any personal blameworthiness. Thus Mr Howard could successfully argue that he was not *responsible* for operational shortcomings in the Prison Service and had discharged his accountability to Parliament by, in 1995, sacking the Director General of the Prison Service. In the case of the Scott Inquiry, Sir Richard Scott concluded that two ministers had misled Parliament but "without duplicitous intention." Defendants had been prosecuted and only the production of departmental files, for which public interest immunity had been unsuccessfully sought, led to their trials being abandoned. Nonetheless no ministerial resignations were deemed appropriate.

Both Houses subsequently adopted resolutions, now enshrined in the Ministerial Code, which recognise that ministers have a duty to account and be held to account for the policies, decisions and actions of their Departments and Next Step Agencies. They must give accurate and truthful information to Parliament. Ministers who knowingly mislead Parliament will be expected to offer their resignation to the Prime Minister.

The conclusion must be that while there is no doubt that a minister is **17–019** responsible in the sense that he is answerable for his department it is not clear in what circumstances convention requires that he resign when his department errs. So long as he retains the support of the Prime Minister he is safe in effect unless his own party is willing to risk bringing down the Government.

---

[75] For a chronology and comment see G. Marshall, "Cabinet Government and the Westland Affair," [1986] P.L. 184. See further *The Defence Implications of the Future of Westland plc.*, Third Report from the Defence Committee, July 1986.
[75a] 1995–96, H.C. 115. For a collection of reactions to the Report, see [1996] P.L.

The doctrine of the individual responsibility of ministers is frequently cited as an important feature of the British Constitution. "The enduring effect of the doctrine of ministerial responsibility has been over the past century or so that powers have been vested in ministers and on a relentlessly increasing scale."[76] The Courts have referred to the doctrine in seeking the intention of Parliament when interpreting statutes.[77] The existence of the doctrine has been invoked to disprove the need for proposed new remedies against abuse of power or malad-ministration.[78] On the other hand it was derided as "the mere shadow of a name" in 1911 by Farwell L.J. in *Dyson v. Attorney-General*.[79] There is, it may be thought, something unsatisfactory in putting so much weight on such an uncertain foundation.

It should be borne in mind that the Prime Minister may always advise the Sovereign to dismiss a Minister, as in the case of Mr Heffer, a Minister of State who spoke in the House in April, 1975, against continued membership of the EEC, but it is seldom necessary to resort to this expedient, for it is usually sufficient if the Prime Minister invites a Minister to resign.

17–020 The collective responsibility is owed by convention both to the Sovereign and to Parliament. As we have seen in connection with the dissolution of Parliament the Ministry as a whole (including the Cabinet) must retain the confidence of the House of Commons. To the Sovereign Ministers must tender unanimous advice: to Parliament and the nation they should show a united front by vote and speech. Cabinets in the late nineteenth and early twentieth centuries sometimes agreed that certain topics should be treated as "Open Questions" where collective responsibility did not apply and each minister might speak and voted as he pleased.[80] The convention is illustrated by the resignations of dissenting Ministers—Eden in 1938 over the policy of appeasement, Aneurin Bevan in 1951 over National Health Service charges, and Lord Salisbury in 1957 over the release of Archbishop Makarios. Mr Frank Cousins resigned from his post of Minister of Science and Technology in 1966 because he disagreed with the Government's Prices and Incomes Bill: being a trade union leader he could not keep quiet about it. Mr Heseltine resigned as Secretary of State for Defence in January 1986, the first of the two ministers to do so in the course of the Westland affair. To the extent that he resigned because he felt unable to accept the view of the rest of the Cabinet on the matters in issue his resignation illustrates the continued working of the traditional convention. Mr Heseltine himself, however, gave different reasons at different times for his resignation and on one occasion denied that it was required by the doctrine of collective responsibility.[81] Custom allows a dissenting Minister who resigns to make a personal statement in the House.

The principle of collective responsibility is not applied in its full rigour to non-Cabinet Ministers, for they are often not consulted in matters that do not affect their department. In their case the responsibility is passive rather than active. Sir

---

[76] N. Johnson, *In Search of the Constitution* (1977), p. 84.

[77] *e.g. Liversidge v. Anderson* [1942] A.C. 206; *Raymond v. Att.-Gen.* [1982] 2 W.L.R. 849.

[78] *e.g.* the need for, and appropriateness of, the Parliamentary Commissioner for Administration: *post*, para. 34–005.

[79] [1911] 1 K.B. 410, 424.

[80] *e.g.* Catholic emancipation 1812–1829; Women's Suffrage 1884 and 1906–1914; tariff reform 1903–1905.

[81] See Marshall, *op. cit. supra* n. 75.

Edward Boyle, one of the two junior Ministers who resigned from Sir Anthony Eden's Government in 1956 because they disagreed with the Government's intervention in the Suez Canal Crisis, joined the Government formed by Mr Harold Macmillan early in 1957 although the new Ministry confirmed its support for Eden's Suez policy. Technically they were different Ministries, but the policy disapproved of was the same, although it was no longer possible to pursue it.

The convention of the collective responsibility of Ministers, as we have seen,[82] **17–021** has been weakening in recent years.[83] Mr Wilson in the period 1974–76 had to remind his colleagues several times of this principle, and Mr Callaghan in April, 1976 rebuked the Secretary of State for Energy (Mr Benn) in the House of Commons for abstaining at a meeting of the Labour Party National Executive in a vote concerning proposed cuts in public expenditure. In March–April, 1975 Mr Wilson allowed Ministers as well as Labour back-benchers "in the unique circumstances of a referendum" to advocate, outside Parliament, opposition to continued membership of the EEC, although continued membership was Government policy. Later in a broadcast he said "after June 6 there will be one Cabinet and one Cabinet view."[84] Another episode was that of the European Assembly Elections Bill 1977 to provide for direct elections to the European Assembly, an item of Government policy contained in the Queen's Speech and implementing a Treaty obligation. Mr Callaghan, the Prime Minister, stated that Ministers as well as Labour back-benchers would be free to vote against the Bill on second reading. When questioned by Mrs Thatcher, Leader of the Opposition, Mr Callaghan replied: "I certainly think that doctrine [collective responsibility] should apply except in cases where I announce that it does not."[85] In the event 31 Ministers, including six Cabinet Ministers, voted against the Bill, but it was easily carried with the help of Opposition parties.[86] So long as a Government can keep its majority in the House of Commons, its main concern nowadays appears to be its image amongst the electorate. Dissent in public is allowed if it is thought it will do the party less harm than resignations and press reports of "splits."[87]

Confidentiality

Access to, and use of Cabinet papers is governed by convention.[88] Cabinet and **17–022** other government papers are, in law, Crown property. In deciding who may have access to such papers the Crown by convention acts on the advice of the Government. It is accepted that, as a general rule, Cabinet ministers may not see Cabinet papers of former ministers of a different party. Nor may they see other papers (with certain exceptions) which contain unpublished views or comments of those predecessors on advice submitted to them. Ministers may normally see

[82] *ante*, para. 7–017.
[83] Unless Mr Heseltine's resignation can be seen as a strengthening of the convention.
[84] *The Times*, May 12, 1975. *Cf.* the "agreement to differ" in 1932, when there was a coalition Government, no referendum or general election was involved, and the dissentients in fact soon resigned office: *ante*, para. 7–017.
[85] *The Times*, June 15, 16 and 17, 1977.
[86] Not so basic was the defeat at the Committee stage of the Prime Minister's recommendation of the regional list system of proportional representation for the first direct elections to the European Assembly, in favour of the first-past-the-post system.
[87] Mackintosh, *op. cit.* p. 533. And see R. Brazier, "The Constitution in the New Politics" [1978] P.L. 117.
[88] Lord Hunt of Tanworth, "Disclosure of Government Papers" [1982] P.L. 514; *ante* para. 7–005.

papers of their predecessors of their own party in the course of their duties, with the agreement, where appropriate, of any former Prime Minister. Former ministers may have access to but not retain, any documents which they saw when in office.[89]

A highly unusual exception to the general principle was supplied when a Committee of Privy Councillors was established in 1982 under the Chairmanship of Lord Franks to review the way in which government departments had discharged their responsibilities to the Falkland Islands in the period before the Argentinian invasion.[90] The Committee was given access to departmental papers, Cabinet and Cabinet committee memoranda and minutes, and intelligence assessments which had been prepared for previous governments of both major parties. On a matter of less grave political controversy, in 1986 Mr Callaghan agreed to allow Conservative ministers to examine papers prepared when he was Prime Minister relating to the controversy whether to equip the Royal Air Force with the Nimrod early warning system or the American Awacs system.[91] The decision to adopt the Nimrod system had been taken in 1977, with the support of both the Labour and Conservative parties but the subsequent delay in producing the equipment and the increase in cost had called in question the wisdom of the original decision.

17–023 Cabinet or ex-Cabinet ministers who wished to refer in their memoirs to Cabinet discussions or papers during the period when official documents are protected by statute,[92] were formerly required by convention to obtain the consent of the Sovereign expressed through the Prime Minister, who delegated the vetting to the Secretary of the Cabinet.[93] Convention also required the disclosure of confidential State or official papers or information by Ministers or ex-Ministers to have the approval of the Government of the day, application being made to the Secretary of the Cabinet. Ex-civil servants were expected to apply for such permission to their Department. The legal effect of these requirements was tested in *Attorney-General v. Jonathan Cape Ltd*[94] where the Attorney-General sought to restrain the posthumous publication of volume I of Richard Crossman's *Diaries of a Cabinet Minister*, covering events of about 10 years before. Lord Widgery C.J., declined to grant the injunction. It was conceded by the Attorney-General that there was no breach of the Official Secrets Acts.[95] Lord Widgery held that the court has power on the ground of public policy to restrain publication of information in breach of confidence,[96] but this volume disclosed no details that should still remain confidential.

---

[89] In 1980 Mrs Thatcher, while recognising the convention that Mr Alfred Morris, former Minister for the Disabled, could consult papers prepared by officials while he was minister, refused to agree to allow the photocopying of the papers: *The Times*, February 7, 1980.

[90] *Falkland Islands Review* Cmnd. 8787 (1983).

[91] *ante*. para. 7–005n.

[92] The Public Records Acts 1958 and 1967 provide that public records in the Public Record Office (including Cabinet minutes) shall not be available for public inspection until they are 30 years old. The period may be extended by the Lord Chancellor if they include information received in confidence or liable to prejudice national security or trade.

[93] Because it is difficult for the Prime Minister to deal with comments about his colleagues or predecessors, and he does not know about the activities of members of opposite parties when they were in office.

[94] [1976] Q.B. 752.

[95] Nor does the Privy Councillor's oath add to the Cabinet Minister's legal obligation.

[96] In its equitable jurisdiction: see, *e.g. Argyll (Duchess) v. Argyll (Duke)* [1967] Ch. 302.

A Committee of Privy Councillors on Ministerial Memoirs under the chairmanship of Lord Radcliffe, whose report[97] came out after the decision in *Attorney-General v. Jonathan Cape*, recommended that ministerial authors should be precluded for fifteen years from publishing information falling within three categories: (i) the requirements of national security operative at the time of publication; (ii) injury to foreign relations; and (iii) destructive of the confidential relationships on which the system of government is based, *i.e.* relations between Ministers and colleagues or their advisers in the civil service or outside. "Government is not to be conducted," said the report, "in the interests of history." The report was accepted by the Prime Minister, Mr Wilson, who said manuscripts should still be submitted for inspection and these working rules of reticence should be accepted as an obligation of honour.[98]

Influence of the Sovereign

Since the Sovereign acts on the advice of the Cabinet, tendered through the **17–024** Prime Minister, and the government is carried on in the name of the Sovereign, the Cabinet is expected to keep the Sovereign informed of any departure in policy, of the general march of political events, and in particular of the deliberations of the Cabinet. The *power* of the Monarch in modern times is confined—in Bagehot's well-known words[99]—to "the right to be consulted, the right to encourage, the right to warn." The *influence* of a Sovereign who has been on the Throne for some years, however, is far from negligible, for his experience will be wider and more continuous than that of most or all of his Ministers.

Queen Victoria cannot perhaps be taken as a model for the twentieth century, but George V's reign of a quarter of a century shows a number of examples of the influence exerted by the Throne. By his advice, warnings and encouragement the King helped to bring the parties together in negotiating the Anglo-Irish Treaty of 1921; but he left the conduct of the negotiations entirely to the Prime Minister, Lloyd George, and refrained from any comment or intervention while the conference lasted.[1] In 1923 the King tried unsuccessfully to dissuade Baldwin from a dissolution,[2] and later in the same year he persuaded Baldwin not to resign before meeting Parliament when the Conservatives at a general election had lost their absolute majority but were still the largest party in the Commons.[3] George V took the initiative in the formation of the National (coalition) Government under Ramsay MacDonald in 1931 when the "economic crisis" caused the latter's minority Labour Government to break up. The King consulted the Conservative and Liberal leaders, each of whom had a considerable following in the House, and then entrusted MacDonald with the task of resuming office as the head of a coalition and in spite of the defection of his own Labour Party.[4]

As the Sovereign's influence may be underestimated, so on the other hand it may be exaggerated. Thus Lord Attlee discounts certain incidents given in the

---

[97] Cmnd. 6386 (1976).

[98] On the security of Cabinet documents, see Report of Houghton Committee Cmnd. 6677 (1976).

[99] Bagehot, *The English Constitution* (World's Classics ed.), p. 67.

[1] Harold Nicolson, *King George the Fifth*, p. 360.

[2] *ibid.* pp. 379–380.

[3] *ibid.* pp. 382–384.

[4] *ibid.* pp. 460–469; G. M. Young, *Stanley Baldwin*, Chap. 16; K. Middlemas and J. Barnes, *Baldwin* (1969), Chap. 23; D. Macquand, *Ramsay MacDonald* (1977), Chaps. 25 and 26. The importance of the King's role is described in Kenneth Rose, *King George V* (1983), pp. 371–379.

official biography of George VI[5] as examples of interference by that King, notably the choice of Ernest Bevin as Foreign Secretary and the holding of a general election in 1951. Attlee later said that the reason for the first was that he, as Prime Minister, wanted to keep Ernest Bevin away from Herbert Morrison; and the reason for the second was that he did not want the King to worry about the precarious position of the Government (majority 6) while he was abroad.[6] It is too early to say what influence, if any, the present monarch has exercised.[7]

The exchange of views between Sovereign and Prime Minister on any matter is strictly confidential between them. It would be improper for the Sovereign herself or for any member of the Royal Household to give public expression to her opinions on political matters.[8] (Conversely the Prime Minister does not answer questions in the House of Commons relating to her relations with the monarch[9]).

III. THE PRIME MINISTER[10]

Formal position

17–025   The emergence of the position of Prime Minister in the modern sense begins with the Ministries of Sir Robert Walpole (1721–42) and the younger Pitt (1783–1801; 1804–1806), although the former disclaimed the title. It was brought about by a combination of a number of factors, including royal confidence, pre-eminence among Ministers, patronage as First Lord of the Treasury, and especially control of the Commons (not necessarily as leader of the largest party). The authority of the Prime Minister was firmly established during the latter part of the nineteenth century by the outstanding personalities of Disraeli and Gladstone, making use of the effects brought about by the Representation of the People Acts and the development of the party system. As we have seen, the Prime Minister was until recently hardly known to the law: like the Cabinet, he was the creature of convention. He is mentioned in the Treaty of Berlin 1878; a royal warrant of 1905 which gives him precedence next after the Archbishop of York; the Schedule to the Chequers Estate Act 1917, in which Parliament gave effect to the gift of the Chequers estate as a country residence for the Prime Minister of the day[11]; the Physical Training and Recreation Act 1937; the

---

[5] Wheeler-Bennett, *King George VI.*

[6] "The Role of the Monarchy" *The Observer*, August 23, 1959.

[7] Newspapers discussed the possibility (and propriety) of the Queen raising with the Prime Minister the desirability of postponing the date of the local elections and, if appropriate, of the general election, in the days following the outbreak of foot and mouth disease in March 2001.

[8] Letter from the Private Secretary to The Queen (Sir William Heseltine) *The Times* July 28, 1986. *post* para. 36–022.

[9] *ante* para. 12–025.

[10] B. E. Carter, *The Office of Prime Minister* (1956); Anthony King (ed.), *The British Prime Minister* (1969); Lord Blake. "The Office of Prime Minister" (British Academy Lecture), (1975); Mackintosh, *op. cit.*; Humphry Berkeley, *The Power of the Prime Minister* (1968); P. Hennessy, *The Prime Minister* (Allen Lane, 2000); P. Gordon Walker, *op. cit.* Chap. 5; Jennings, *op. cit.*; Thomson, *Constitutional History of England*, 1642–1801.

[11] *Robertson v. Secretary of State for Environment* [1976] 1 W.L.R. 371 (QBD).

Parliamentary and other Pensions Act 1972; the House of Commons Disqualification Act 1975 ("Prime Minister and First Lord of the Treasury") and the
Chevening Estate Act 1959, under which this Kent estate was given on certain
trusts as regards occupation, including "any Minister of the Crown nominated by
the Prime Minister."[12]

The Prime Minister now invariably takes the office of First Lord of the
Treasury,[13] and occasionally some other office as well, such as that of Chancellor
of the Exchequer (Gladstone), War Office (Asquith),[14] Foreign Secretary (Ramsay MacDonald) or Minister of Defence (Winston Churchill). The Prime Minister
has no legal powers except as First Lord of the Treasury and (since 1968)
Minister for the Civil Service (apart from the miscellaneous examples in Acts
such as those cited earlier). The office of First Lord of the Treasury down to 1937
provided him with his salary. It places him technically at the head of the most
important government department (the Treasury), yet with departmental duties
which (apart from patronage) are only nominal, as the working head of that
department is the Chancellor of the Exchequer. In the eighteenth and early
nineteenth centuries, before the reform of the Civil Service and the parliamentary
franchise, the fact that the First Lord of the Treasury exercised a very extensive
patronage over many kinds of official appointments meant that the Prime Minister could control departmental appointments, and this helped him to obtain a
parliamentary majority for his party. The Ministers of the Crown Act 1937 first
provided for a salary to be paid to "the person who is Prime Minister and First
Lord of the Treasury." The Ministerial and other Salaries Act 1975 now provides
a salary to the "Prime Minister and First Lord of the Treasury," so it is unlikely
that these positions will be held separately in future, although the Act does not
require them to be held together. The Act of 1937 also provided former Prime
Ministers with a pension. The Parliamentary and other Pensions Act 1972, s.26,
now provides that any person who has been Prime Minister and First Lord of the
Treasury shall be entitled to a pension charged on the Consolidated Fund.

Functions of the Prime Minister

The primary functions of the Prime Minister are to form a government, and to   **17–026**
choose and preside over the Cabinet. He gives advice to his ministerial colleagues on matters before they come to the Cabinet, and he is the main channel
of communication between the Cabinet and the Sovereign, with whom he has a
weekly audience.[15] He advises the Sovereign on a dissolution.[16]

The Prime Minister is normally the leader of his party, having either been
chosen as Prime Minister because he is the leader of the largest party or elected
leader because he is Prime Minister.[17] He is primarily responsible for the
organisation of the business of the House, even if (as is now usual) this work is

[12] See further the National Audit Act 1983, s.1 and the Museums and Galleries Act 1992.
[13] They were last separated when Balfour was First Lord of the Treasury in Lord Salisbury's
administrations (1891–92, 1895–1902).
[14] At that time (1914) a member accepting this office had to seek re-election, so that for a time
Asquith was Prime Minister without a seat in the House.
[15] Other Ministers may communicate with the Sovereign on matters concerning their department.
[16] Lord Beaverbrook recounts that the decision of Lloyd George and his colleagues in January, 1922
not to hold a general election was induced by the intervention of a parrot: *Men and Power* (1956),
pp. 340–341. And see *ante*, para. 17–006.
[17] Lloyd George (1916), MacDonald (1931) and Churchill (1940) were not leaders of their party
when appointed Prime Minister, though Churchill soon accepted the leadership.

delegated to the Leader of the House.[18] In the House he is expected to speak in debates, and to answer questions on general government policy, the future business of the House and any residual matters. A Prime Minister is willing to give confidential information to the Leader of the Opposition on such matters as defence, security, the EEC and Northern Ireland.

The Prime Minister has special responsibilities in the areas of Security and Intelligence. A Cabinet Committee of Ministers, chaired by the Prime Minister, supervises MI5, MI6 and G.C.H.Q. A Joint Intelligence Committee (J.I.C.) chaired by a Cabinet Office official, collates intelligence reports and prepares assessments for ministers. Since 1952 the Director General of the Security Service has been responsible to the Home Secretary and not, as formerly, to the Prime Minister. The Director General has, however, the right of direct access to the Prime Minister, as has the Chairman of J.I.C.[19] The decision to refer any matter relating to security to the Security Commission[20] for investigation is taken by the Prime Minister. The Prime Minister alone can authorise the launching of a nuclear attack by United Kingdom forces.[21]

17–027   The Prime Minister sees that Cabinet decisions are carried out by the departments, although, as we have said, the extent to which he supervises the administration varies with different holders of the office. His contact with the affairs of the Foreign Office is often especially close. The Cabinet secretariat is under his control, and consults him in preparing the agenda. He communicates directly with the other Commonwealth Prime Ministers, and presides when they meet in this country.

Many Crown appointments, in addition to ministerial offices, are made on his advice. These include the Lords of Appeal in Ordinary, the Lords Justices of Appeal, bishops and deans of the Church of England, peerages, Privy Councillors and most honours.[22] As First Lord of the Treasury and Minister for the Civil Service,[23] the Prime Minister approves the senior appointments in the Civil Service.

Choice of Prime Minister[24]

17–028   The Sovereign chooses the Prime Minister. Conventions ensure that in most cases the "choice" is formal, for the Sovereign is expected to send for the leader of the party or group of parties that has, or can control, a majority in the House of Commons. The choice became formal owing to the development of the party system. Thus in 1855 Queen Victoria, who preferred Derby, was constrained to appoint Palmerston; and in 1880 she reluctantly appointed Gladstone when she would have preferred Hartington, though Rosebery was Victoria's choice after

---

[18] The Leader of the House is responsible for steering the Government's legislative programme through the House of Commons and must also pay regard to the interests of the House as a whole.

[19] See G. Marshall, *Constitutional Conventions* (1984) pp. 122 *et seq.*; G. Drewry, "The House of Commons and the Security Services" [1984] P.L. 370; G. Zellick, "Government Beyond the Law" [1985] P.L. 283, 299.

[20] A non-statutory body, established in 1964, consisting of distinguished public figures, chaired by a senior judge.

[21] Hennessy, *op. cit.* p. 90 for details of the appropriate procedure.

[22] Recommendations for some honours and decorations are also made by the Foreign Secretary, the Defence Minister, Commonwealth Prime Ministers, and on the Queen's personal initiative.

[23] *post*, para. 18–022.

[24] V. Bogdanor, *The Monarchy and the Constitution* (Oxford, 1997), Chap. 4.

Gladstone's resignation. If the government is defeated at a general election the Prime Minister resigns[25] (and with him the other Ministers), and the Sovereign on the advice of the resigning Prime Minister sends for the Leader of the Opposition. The Leader of the Opposition is known, because both the Labour Party and (since 1964) the Conservative Party in opposition select a leader by ballot, and he has a statutory salary. The Leader of the Opposition will accept office if his party commands a majority in the Commons, which it usually will if the Government was defeated at a general election.[26]

If the Prime Minister dies in office or retires on *personal* grounds, such as ill health or old age, the Sovereign has really no discretion in the common case where the government has an absolute majority and one other Cabinet Minister in the Commons is obviously regarded as ranking next to the Prime Minister. In this way Neville Chamberlain succeeded Baldwin in 1937 and Mr Eden succeeded Sir Winston Churchill in 1955,[27] A *retiring* Prime Minister is probably not entitled to proffer advice as to his successor,[28] but he can make his views known before-hand, and anyway the Sovereign is free to consult him and other members of the government party.

There are exceptional circumstances when the Sovereign really has to exercise a personal discretion within limits; and this is perhaps the most important function of the Sovereign at the present day. There may be more than two parties in the House of Commons with no one party having an absolute majority, either as a result of a general election or on a defeat in the Commons of a government that has already been granted one dissolution; and the question arises whether one of the minority parties, and if so which, will be able to carry on the government with the support of one of the other parties, or whether a coalition shall be formed; or the government may break up owing to internal dissension. **17–029**

---

[25] See G. H. Le May, *The Victorian Constitution* (1979), pp. 57–58; "Disraeli created a constitutional precedent after the general election of 1868, when he chose to accept defeat at the hands of the constituencies instead of those of the new House of Commons, and resigned without meeting Parliament. This was a clear example of precedent crystallising about accident. Disraeli had no wish to consolidate the Liberal Party by presenting himself as a common target for its various elements. The party had disintegrated in the previous Parliament, it might do so again, and the chances of that happening would be better if it was not allowed to bind itself together in a vote of censure. In spite of its peculiar origin, the precedent was found to be convenient; it was followed by Gladstone in 1874 and by Disraeli (then Earl of Beaconsfield) in 1880. [Queen Victoria] did not think that immediate resignation ought to become a general rule, 'because it might be a means for a Government, who had committed some grievous fault, to escape condemnation by Parliament, as the adverse party was seldom inclined to attack a fallen Government.' But become a general rule it did, whenever the result of a general election was sufficiently clear to make the carrying of a vote of no confidence a certainty; its adoption may be taken as a measure of the development of party cohesion and solidarity. Gladstone resigned at once after the election of 1886. Salisbury chose to meet Parliament after the election of 1885, as Baldwin did after that of 1923; both were turned out almost at once. In 1929, in conditions roughly similar to those of 1923, Baldwin resigned at once: however obscure the result might be, he said, it showed that the electorate did not want him."
[26] The Leader of the Opposition is not bound to accept office. Disraeli in 1873, when the parties were very even, thought it would be more advantageous if Gladstone carried on for a while.
[27] Partly at least through the influential advice of Lord Kemsley, proprietor of the *Sunday Times* and Lord Woolton, Chairman of the Conservative Party: J. Margach, *The Abuse of Power* (1978), pp. 104–105.
[28] In March, 1955 Churchill said to Mr Eden and Mr Butler: "I am going and Anthony will succeed me. We can discuss details later": Lord Butler, *The Art of the Possible* (1971), p. 176; but he refrained from mentioning to the Queen the question of his successor: J. Wheeler-Bennett (ed.) *Action This Day* (1968), p. 234.

The Sovereign then may consult all interested parties with a view to the formation of a Ministry that can hold a majority in the House. When Baldwin's minority Conservative Government was defeated in the House in 1924 not long after a general election, the King did not seek any advice before sending for Ramsay MacDonald, the leader of the second largest party.[29]

Neville Chamberlain, the Conservative Prime Minister, resigned in 1940 because, although he had not been defeated in the House (his normal majority of about 200 was reduced to 81, a number of Conservatives voting against him or abstaining) he realised that he had lost the confidence of his own party as well as of the Labour Party, which was supporting the Government in the conduct of the war. A coalition government was needed, and Labour members intimated that they would not serve under Chamberlain. The possible choice of a successor lay between Winston Churchill, First Lord of the Admiralty, and Lord Halifax, Foreign Secretary. The Labour Party were willing to serve under Churchill. Lord Halifax expressed the view, in a conference between the three statesmen, that it would be impracticable to try to lead the government from the Lords in wartime.[30] Chamberlain then tendered his resignation to George VI, who accepted it. In an informal discussion as to his successor the King suggested Lord Halifax, but Chamberlain told the King what Lord Halifax had said. "I asked Chamberlain his advice," the King recorded, "and he told me Winston was the man to send for . . . . I sent for Winston and asked him to form a Government."[31]

17–030   The most difficult case is where a Prime Minister dies in office or resigns on personal grounds, such as health or age, leaving no obvious successor. It was wholly exceptional that twice during the last war George VI asked Churchill to advise him on his successor if the Prime Minister should die as a result of enemy action while abroad. George VI objected to Mr Eden being described as Deputy Prime Minister in 1951, as it would imply a line of succession and so restrict the royal prerogative.[32] There have been appointments by both the main parties of Deputy Prime Minister, notably Attlee (Leader of the Labour Party) in the coalition Government during the last war.[33] The title does not imply any right of succession to the Prime Minister,[34] but it is increasingly used, whether to indicate the trust a Prime Minister puts in a valued senior colleague (Mrs Thatcher and Lord Whitelaw) or as a consolation prize designed to mollify the vanity of a colleague perhaps not entirely trusted.

In 1923 Bonar Law, the Conservative Prime Minister, was so ill that he sent his resignation to George V. The choice of successor lay between Lord Curzon, Foreign Secretary and former Viceroy of India, a statesman of brilliant gifts and vast experience; and Mr Baldwin who, although recently appointed Chancellor of the Exchequer, had little political experience and was not well known either inside or outside the House. After the King or his Private Secretary had consulted Lord Balfour (former Prime Minister) and Lord Salisbury (Lord President of the Council) and members of the government party, the King chose Baldwin both on

---

[29] Nicolson, *op. cit.* pp. 382–386; *cf.* Sidney Webb, "The First Labour Government" (1961) 32 *Political Quarterly* 6.

[30] Winston S. Churchill, *Second World War*, Vol. I, pp. 523–526; K. Feiling, *The Life of Neville Chamberlain*, pp. 439–441; Earl of Halifax, *Fulness of Days*, pp. 218–220; Earl of Birkenhead, *Halifax* (1965), pp. 453–455.

[31] Wheeler-Bennett, *King George VI*, pp. 438–445.

[32] Wheeler-Bennett, *op. cit.* p. 797.

[33] See K. Harris, *Attlee* (1982), pp. 192–254.

[34] Butler, *op. cit.* p. 234; R. Brazier, "The Deputy Prime Minister," [1988] P.L. 176.

personal grounds and because he was in the Commons, although the latter reason was emphasised in breaking the news to Curzon.[35]

When Sir Anthony Eden, Conservative Prime Minister, resigned in 1957 because of serious ill-health, the succession lay by common consent between Mr R. A. Butler (Lord Privy Seal and Leader of the House of Commons) and Mr Harold Macmillan (Chancellor of the Exchequer). All that was publicly known was that the Queen consulted two elder statesmen of the Conservative Party—Lord Salisbury (Lord President of the Council and son of the adviser of 1923) and Sir Winston Churchill, the former Prime Minister—and selected Mr Macmillan. We now know that they both recommended Mr Macmillan, and that only one member of the Cabinet supported Mr Butler.[36] Eden was neither asked for his advice nor did he volunteer it.[37]

In 1963 (after the Peerage Act had been passed) Mr Macmillan became ill, **17–031** entered hospital for an operation and announced his intention to resign. In accordance with the practice of the Conservatives at that time "soundings" were taken in the party. The result of these soundings was communicated by the Lord Chancellor to the Prime Minister, who then sent a letter of resignation to the Queen, presumably intimating that he had advice to give if requested. The Queen (who is not known to have sought any other advice) visited Mr Macmillan in hospital, and immediately afterwards sent for the Earl of Home and invited him to form an Administration.[38] A day or two later Lord Home informed the Queen that he was able to form an Administration.[39]

In 1964 the Conservatives adopted a new method of selecting their party leader. A ballot was taken of the party in the Commons, and the candidate so selected was then presented for election at a party meeting.[40] On Sir Alec Douglas-Home's resignation (after the defeat of his party general election) this led to the election of Mr Heath. A more elaborate procedure was introduced after defeat in a general election in 1974 for filling a vacancy in the leadership, involving consultation with Conservative peers and constituency associations and holding (if necessary) three secret ballots among the party's M.P.s. The candidate elected by the latter is presented for confirmation as leader to a party meeting consisting of M.P.s, peers and parliamentary candidates. The first election by ballot resulted in the defeat of Mr Heath by Mrs Thatcher. Under the

---

[35] Robert Blake, *The Unknown Prime Minister* (1955), pp. 514–527; Winston S. Churchill, *Great Contemporaries*, pp. 215–220; L. S. Amery, *op. cit.* pp. 21–22; Harold Nicolson, *King George the Fifth*, pp. 375–379; *Curzon. The Last Phase*, pp. 353–355; G. M. Young, *Stanley Baldwin*, pp. 48–49; Keith Middlemas and John Barnes, *Baldwin*, Chap. 8. K. Rose, *King George V* (1983), pp. 266–273.

[36] Mackintosh, *op. cit.* pp. 522–523. Lord Salisbury and Lord Kilmuir (Lord Chancellor) sounded the Cabinet Ministers. "What they wanted was a straight answer to the question: 'Who's best—Rab or Harold?' They got it": Lord Egremont, *Wyndham and Children First* (1968), pp. 158–159.

[37] Harold Macmillan, *Riding the Storm* 1956–1959 (1971), Vol. 4, Chap. 5.

[38] "What is certain is that Macmillan ... acted ... with utter determination and dispatch, making a definite recommendation of Home": Lord Butler, *The Art of the Possible* (1971) pp. 247–248. Lord Hailsham says that Macmillan in 1963 favoured him as a leader of the Conservative Party and Prime Minister. Viscount Hailsham (as he then was) did not disclaim his hereditary title until after Home had been appointed Prime Minister: *The Door Wherein I Went* (1975), Chap. 32. Controversy continues over the circumstances surrounding the invitation to Lord Home: see letter from V. Bogdanor, *Daily Telegraph*, March 10, 2001 and riposte from Lady Butler, March 2001.

[39] He forthwith renounced his peerage under the new Act, and (being a Knight of the Thistle) became known as Sir Alec Douglas-Home. He had then, of course, to fight a by-election to get into the House of Commons. See A. Howard and R. West, *op. cit.* Chap. 4.

[40] See Humphry Berkeley, *Across the Floor* (1972).

current rules, two candidates are elected by the party's M.P.s and the final choice is made by the members of the party through a postal ballot.

17–032   The leadership of the Labour Party until 1976 had never changed while the party was in office.[41] The party expressed the view in 1957 that they would not expect anyone to accept office as Prime Minister until he had been elected leader of the parliamentary party. There is much to be said for this practice, which is adopted in Australia and New Zealand.[42] In March, 1976 Mr Wilson, Labour Prime Minister, announced his intention to retire from office and to return to the back-benches when the parliamentary Labour Party had had the opportunity to elect a new leader. A ballot led to the election of Mr Callaghan, and the Queen appointed him Prime Minister. Mr Wilson in the previous December had informed the Queen of his intention, and presumably Her Majesty approved of this course.

It is probable that in future the Conservatives in office would follow the Labour practice of filling a vacancy by electing a new leader, who would then be appointed Prime Minister. In view of the Conservative Party's new system of electing a leader, it would appear that the Sovereign in practice no longer has a discretion in the choice of Prime Minister, at least when the normal two-party system is operating.[43]

Should a Prime Minister be a peer?

17–033   The question whether it is constitutionally proper for a Prime Minister to be in the House of Lords in modern times was formerly discussed, especially in connection with the resignation of Bonar Law in 1923. No peer has been Prime Minister[44] since Lord Salisbury (1895–1902). Even in the nineteenth century Prime Ministers who were peers found it difficult to control the Commons; but as late as 1921 Cabinet colleagues seriously considered Lord Birkenhead (Lord Chancellor) as Prime Minister to succeed Lloyd George, and in 1922 they offered the position to Lord Derby.[45] Lord Halifax saw the difficulty in 1940, but neither he nor Neville Chamberlain acknowledged a convention. George VI suggested to Chamberlain that Lord Halifax's peerage could be "placed in abeyance for the time being," apparently meaning that legislation should be passed allowing Lord Halifax to speak in the House of Commons.[46] In 1957 Lords Salisbury and Kilmuir considered themselves excluded by virtue of their peerage.[47]

The weight of opinion is in favour of the view that it is undesirable and impracticable for the Prime Minister to have a seat in the Lords. The House of Commons is the centre of interest and influence; it has exclusive control over national finance and, although the office of First Lord of the Treasury is only nominally concerned with financial matters, it would be absurd for the holder of

---

[41] Since 1981 the Leader is elected by a process in which the members of the Parliamentary Labour Party have 30 per cent of the votes, the constituencies 30 per cent and the Trades Unions 40 per cent.

[42] E. M. McWhinney, "Constitutional Conventions" (1957) 35 Can. Bar Rev. 92, 242, 368, 369.

[43] See also R. Brazier, "Choosing a Prime Minister," [1982] P.L. 395.

[44] Apart from the Earl of Home in 1963 for a period of four days before the renunciation of his hereditary title took effect.

[45] Lord Beaverbrook, *The Decline and Fall of Lloyd George* (1963), pp. 68 *et seq.*; pp. 181.

[46] Wheeler-Bennett, *op. cit.* p. 444.

[47] Mackintosh, *op. cit.* p. 425. *Cf.* Lord Moran, *Churchill: The Struggle for Survival 1940–65*, where Lord Salisbury is said to have suggested in 1953 that Churchill, who had had a stroke, ought to go the Lords while remaining Prime Minister—an idea that commended itself to the Queen's Private Secretary but not to Churchill, who was 77.

that office to sit in the upper House; it is in the elected Second Chamber that governments are made and defeated; and the Labour Party is under-represented in the Lords, so that the real opposition to a Conservative Government is in the lower House. The question lost much of its importance after the Peerage Act 1963 allowed existing hereditary peers, and persons who later succeed to hereditary peerages, to renounce their peerages within a time limit. It might be said to have become an increasingly unrealistic issue with current attitudes to the role of hereditary peers as expressed in the House of Lords Act 1999.

Prime Ministerial government?[48]

Some writers say we no longer have Cabinet government as we used to know **17–034** it, but that since the last war—if not before—we have had "Prime Ministerial government." Policy is not usually initiated by the Cabinet. Decisions tend to be taken either by the Prime Minister alone or by him after consulting one or two Ministers, or else by Cabinet committees or informal meetings of the Ministers concerned. To these factors may be added the unification and centralisation of an expanding Civil Service under the Prime Minister, who is the only political master of the powerful trinity consisting of the Permanent Secretary of the Treasury, the head of the Civil Service, and the Secretary to the Cabinet.

Crossman attached great importance to committees of officials or inter-departmental meetings of civil servants, which he described as "the key to the control of the civil service over the politicians."[49] Mr George Brown (later Lord George Brown), Deputy Prime Minister and Foreign Secretary, resigned over an emergency decision for a bank holiday because it seemed to him that the Prime Minister (Mr Wilson) was introducing a presidential system.[50]

In considering the relative positions of the Prime Minister and the Cabinet we have to take note of such factors as the moral authority of his office as Leader in the eyes of the public and his standing in his party; the power of the Prime Minister to appoint and reshuffle Ministers, to determine the scope of the various offices, to control the Cabinet agenda and to advise a dissolution. The Prime Minister has the advantage of knowing more than his colleagues what is going on. It is difficult to overthrow a Prime Minister, because the Cabinet must not only be united against him but agreed on his successor, and backbenchers are not likely to want to precipitate a general election in which many of them may lose their seats. On the other hand, if the Cabinet does not often initiate policy, it co-ordinates. The Cabinet "reconciles, records and authorises."[51] The Cabinet is not the only decision-making body in the central government, but all important matters must go before the Cabinet at some stage. Also, the Cabinet have greater *legal* powers than the Prime Minister.

The relative positions of the Prime Minister and the Cabinet are variable, **17–035** depending on personalities, not only that of the Prime Minister but also those of

---

[48] Richard Crossman, *The Diaries of a Cabinet Minister*; G. W. Jones, "Prime Ministers and Cabinets" (1972) 20 Pol. Stud. 213; A. H. Brown, "Prime Ministerial Power" [1968] P.L. 28, 96; Harold Wilson, "Where the Power Lies," *Listener*, February 9, 1967. And see: Mackintosh, *op. cit.*; Gordon Walker, *op. cit.*; King, *op. cit.*; Hood Phillips, *Reform of the Constitution*, (1970) pp. 42–47, 51–54. G. Marshall, "The End of Prime Ministerial Government?" [1991] P.L.I.

[49] *The Diaries of a Cabinet Minister*, Vol. I, p. 616.

[50] George Brown, *In My Way* (1971), p. 169.

[51] Mackintosh, *op. cit.* p. 630. Mackintosh pictures the form of government as a cone with the Prime Minister at the apex. Beneath him is a widening series of rings of senior Ministers, the Cabinet, its committees, non-Cabinet Ministers and departments. The only one above the level of the civil service that has formal existence is the Cabinet, *op. cit.* p. 543.

his colleagues. A Prime Minister cannot ride roughshod over his Cabinet—even Churchill gave way on occasion, and Mrs Thatcher was finally brought down by her own Cabinet and party. Their positions may also vary in different aspects of policy and administration. The main influence of the Prime Minister tends to lie in foreign policy, defence and national security, and in emergencies, like a general strike, abdication, the Rhodesian U.D.I. and the Falkland Islands crisis. His influence fluctuates in economic policy, and he does not usually intervene in person in such matters as education and housing. Thus the Prime Minister is more powerful than any other Minister, and than most combinations of Ministers, but less powerful than the Cabinet collectively.

Mr Harold Wilson saw the role of the Prime Minister as "if not that of a managing director, as that of an executive chairman." According to Mr Wilson power still lies in the Cabinet, but as the Cabinet must keep the confidence of the House, it is the Cabinet in Parliament. The power-base lies in his party in Parliament. A similar conclusion was reached by Lord Gordon-Walker, who found "the Cabinet in Parliament" to be the central feature of the British Constitution.

Nonetheless under Mrs Thatcher and even more under Mr Blair the importance of the *full* Cabinet has declined, as is evident from a decrease in the number of meetings and their brevity.[52] More significance belongs to the deliberations of Cabinet Committees and ad hoc groups of advisers and others who have the Prime Minister's ear. Nonetheless we cannot say we have "Presidential government."[53] The American Presidential or Congress system is so different from ours that comparison is difficult. The American party system is looser, the President has a fixed term of office and he is not immediately dependent on Congress.[54]

---

[52] See Hennessy, *op. cit.* pp. 427 and 481.

[53] See Berkeley, *The Power of the Prime Minister; cf.* Max Beloff, "Prime Minister and President" (Hugh Gaitskell Memorial Lecture, University of Nottingham, 1966), who admits, however, that the pull of the American pattern is very strong.

[54] It is only necessary to think of the impeachment proceedings against President Clinton to realise the vast differences between American and the British systems of government.

CHAPTER 18

CENTRAL GOVERNMENT DEPARTMENTS AND CIVIL SERVICE

I. CENTRAL GOVERNMENT DEPARTMENTS

Offices of state

The origin of the great offices of state is to be found in the royal household of **18–001** the Saxon and Norman Kings. The Saxon King had his chamberlain, steward, marshal and cupbearer, and the Norman King his Lord High Steward, Lord Great Chamberlain, Constable and Marshal. In the process of time these offices became hereditary and honorary. Their public, as distinct from purely personal, services came to be performed by others who duplicated the offices and were appointed from time to time on merit and received a salary.[1] Two of the original offices survive as non-political appointments, namely, the hereditary Earl Marshal (Duke of Norfolk) in charge of styles and precedence, and the Lord Great Chamberlain.[2] Their "doubles," Master of the Horse and Lord Chamberlain (former censor of plays), and the Lord Steward of the Household (who was the "double" of the Lord High Steward who presided over the trial of peers and the Court of Claims which determined the validity of claims to perform honorary services at coronations)[3] used to be political officers. The offices of Treasurer, Comptroller and Vice-Chamberlain of the Household are still often given to members of the House of Commons who, together with the Joint Parliamentary Secretaries and the Junior Lords of the Treasury, act as Government Whips.

As the work of government grew, it became necessary for the King to employ secretaries and other officers to transact state business as distinct from the administration of the affairs of the royal household. The earliest and most important of these was the Lord Chancellor, who, as the King's chaplain, was both an educated "clerk" and the Keeper of the King's Conscience. His name is derived, says Holdsworth,[4] from "the *cancelli* or screen behind which the secretarial work of the royal household was carried on." To him was entrusted the custody of the Great Seal, under which the most important state documents were issued. For more than 400 years the use of the Privy Seal, held by the Lord Privy Seal, was a necessary prerequisite before letters patent under the Great Seal could be passed. Other secretaries were appointed in Plantagenet times, and they also held royal seals for affixing to appropriate documents. There is strictly only one office of Secretary of State, although it may be held by several persons whose

---

[1] Maitland, *Constitutional History*, pp. 390–394; S. B. Chrimes, *Introduction to the Administrative History of Medieval England* (1952), describes the origins and early history of the royal household; Randolph S. Churchill, *They Serve the Queen* (1953) is a popular account.

[2] This office descends in tail general, daughters, in the absence of a male heir, taking as co-heirs. Since 1779, the office has been vested in co-heirs who nominate a deputy to perform the duties of the office.

[3] Such claims are now dealt with by a Committee of Claims, the office of Lord High Steward having become merged in the Crown in the reign of Henry IV. Trials in the House of Lords were, thereafter, presided over by a peer appointed Lord High Steward, *pro hac vice*; L.W. Vernon Harcourt, *His Grace the Steward and Trial of Peers* (1907).

[4] Holdsworth, *History of English Law* (5th ed.), Vol. I, p. 37.

powers are, with certain statutory exceptions,[5] equal and interchangeable. For the purposes of holding property Secretaries of State may be constituted as separate corporations sole for example the Secretary of State for Defence under the Defence (Transfer of Functions) Act 1964 or under the general provision contained in the Ministers of the Crown Act 1975. They are appointed by the delivery of three seals, namely, the signet, a lesser seal and a small seal called the *cachet*.[6] Since 1964, when the title was conferred on George Brown, from time to time a minister may be designated "First Secretary" to indicate the political importance attached to his role in the government. Since the June 2001 election Mr Prescott has been both Deputy Prime Minister and First Secretary of State, with his own Office as one of the ministers in the Cabinet Office.

18–002   For the functions of finance and defence the great officers of state were the Lord High Treasurer, the Lord High Admiral, the Lord High Constable and the Earl Marshal. The first office has been in commission since the early eighteenth century, the work being carried on by the First Lord of the Treasury and the Chancellor of the Exchequer, the two most important members of the Treasury Board. Queen Elizabeth II assumed the title of Lord High Admiral in 1964 in order to perpetuate the name of an office dating back 600 years, which would otherwise have been lost on the abolition of the Lords Commissioners of the Admiralty. The Constable and the Earl Marshal issued regulations for the army. A Lord High Constable is still appointed for the coronation ceremony. The courts in which the Constable and Earl Marshal enforced military discipline disappeared soon after the Bill of Rights, giving way to the courts martial which now function under statutory authority. The only vestige is the High Court of Chivalry presided over by the Earl Marshal to try complaints of usurpation of arms. The English law of arms is a civilian jurisdiction.[7] This court was revived in 1954 after a lapse of 223 years.[8]

The Lord President of the Council is in charge of the Privy Council Office, but his departmental duties are light. He is usually a member of the Cabinet entrusted by the Prime Minister with special duties. Since the advent of the Blair Government in 1997 the office has been referred to simply as President of the Council and held with the position of Leader of the House of Commons.

18–003   The office of Lord Privy Seal was considered important in the Middle Ages, but since the Great Seal Act 1884 the use of the Privy Seal is no longer necessary. The Lord Privy Seal has now no departmental duties. He is generally used by the Prime Minister for special duties, although he is not always in the Cabinet. The same applies to the Chancellor of the Duchy of Lancaster, whose department administers the estates of the Duchy of Lancaster, and who appoints and removes justices of the peace within the Duchy.[9] Both office holders were included in the

---

[5] An example is provided by the Somerset House Act 1984 which confers powers of leasing part of Somerset House on the Secretary of the State for the Environment.

[6] For an account of these seals and their use, see Anson, *Law and Custom of the Constitution*, (4th ed. Keith) Vol. II, Pt. I, pp. 182–184. See also, F. M. G. Evans, *The Principal Secretary of State* (1923); A. J. C. Simcock, "One and Many—The Office of Secretary of State," (1992) 70 Publ. Admin. 535.

[7] See G. D. Squibb Q.C., *The High Court of Chivalry*.

[8] *Manchester Corporation v. Manchester Palace of Varieties* [1955] P. 133; verbatim report, The Heraldry Society, 1955. The Earl Marshal (Duke of Norfolk) was assisted by his surrogate (Lord Goddard D.C.L.), who delivered judgment, and the officers of arms. Lord Goddard was Lord Chief Justice, but he sat as a Doctor of Civil Law, his robes including a scarlet D.C.L. (Oxon.) gown, white bow tie and bob wig. The comparable Scottish Court of the Lord Lyon has always retained—and retains—an active jurisdiction.

[9] Justices of the Peace Act 1979, s.68.

Cabinet after the re-shuffle of July 1999, the Lord Privy Seal being also Leader of the House of Lords and Minister for Women (Baroness Jay) while the Chancellor of the Duchy of Lancaster was also Minister for the Cabinet Office.

Until recent times some government departments were boards that were once committees of the Privy Council.[10] The last survival was the Board of Trade, dating from the seventeenth century. The post of President of the Board of Trade is now held by the Secretary of State for Trade and Industry. It amused Mr Heseltine to be known by his title of President of the Board of Trade, presumably to distinguish him from the increasing number of ministers known as Secretaries of State.

The Sovereign can create Ministers by virtue of the prerogative; but statutory authority is requisite in most cases, first, because it will usually be necessary for the Minister and his staff to be paid out of money voted by Parliament, and, secondly, because of the statutory restrictions on the number of Ministers who may sit in the House of Commons.

Examples of statutory creation which reflect the increasing range of governmental activities may be found in the Ministry of Agriculture and Fisheries Act 1919, the Minister of Works and Planning Act 1942, the Ministry of National Insurance Act 1944 and the two Acts establishing what is now the Department of Defence: the Ministry of Defence Act 1946 and the Defence (Transfer of Functions) Act 1964.

Statutory provisions which allow for the transfer of functions from one department to another, the dissolution of departments and the change of titles of ministers by Order in Council, without the need for specific legislation, are now to be found in the Ministers of the Crown Act 1975, which re-enacts earlier legislation. Thus, in 1955, the functions of the Ministry of Food were transferred to the newly named Ministry of Agriculture, Fisheries and Food under the predecessor of the 1975 Act. In 1983 the Departments of Trade and Industry were amalgamated. The Department of Education became the Department for Education and Employment in 1995. The Department of the Environment, itself created from Housing and Local Government, Transport, and Public Buildings and Works, became, in 1997, the Department of the Environment, Transport and the Regions. Section 5(5) of the 1975 Act expressly preserves the royal prerogative in respect to the functions of Ministers of the Crown.

The Ministry

As has been seen in connection with a discussion of the disqualification for membership of the House of Commons,[11] the number of holders of ministerial posts is now about 100, including Cabinet Ministers, Ministers not in the Cabinet and Junior Ministers. The Ministerial and other Salaries Act 1975 provides a salary to the Chancellor of the Exchequer, the Secretaries of State and the holders of the senior ministerial posts mentioned in Schedule 1. Ministers of State are to be paid such an amount (within the statutory limits) "as the First Lord of the Treasury may determine." The same applies to the Lord President of the Council, the Lord Privy Seal, the Chancellor of the Duchy of Lancaster or the Paymaster-General "when not a member of the Cabinet." Parliamentary Secretaries are also provided with a salary.

18–004

[10] Anson, *op. cit.* p. 160.
[11] *ante*, Chap. 9.

Part V of Schedule 1 to the Act fixes a maximum number of paid Ministers in various classes, namely: holders of the office of Secretary of State; Ministers of State; Treasury Secretaries; Junior Lords of the Treasury; Assistant Government Whips in the House of Commons; Lords in Waiting; and Parliamentary Secretaries.

Organisation of Government Departments[12]

Ministers

18–005   At the head of each political department or Ministry is the Secretary of State or Minister. The most notable exception until June 2001 was the Minister of Agriculture, Fisheries and Food. In practice, nowadays, the head of a department is a Secretary of State. Every minister is, of course, a member of the government and changes with the Ministry of the day; he may also be a member of the Cabinet.

Parliamentary Secretaries[13]

18–006   Under the Secretary of State or Minister will be one or more Parliamentary Under-Secretaries of State or Parliamentary Secretaries. As their name implies, they are members of one or other of the Houses of Parliament; they are Junior Ministers[14] who change with the government of the day. They assist their chief in the parliamentary or political side of his work, as well as the administration of his department. In the past they were usually chosen from the House in which the Minister did not sit,[15] but since 1945 Junior Ministers, as well as the heads of departments, have been recruited mainly from the lower House.

The Treasury[16]

18–007   The Treasury is the department entrusted by the Crown and by Parliament with the supervision and control of national finance. It is regarded as the senior government department. The Treasury was an offshoot of the Exchequer, which in the twelfth century was the *Curia Regis* sitting for revenue purposes. The Upper Exchequer, which audited and managed the King's accounts, developed into the Court of Exchequer; while the Lower Exchequer, from which the Treasury emerged, was concerned with the receipt of the royal revenue. The office of Treasurer, which is described in the *Dialogus de Scaccario* (1177), has been in commission since 1714.[17]

The Treasury Board consists of the First Lord of the Treasury (nowadays invariably the Prime Minister), the Chancellor of the Exchequer (whose office dates from Henry III) and five Junior Lords. Meetings of the full Board became less frequent by the beginning of the nineteenth century, and were discontinued altogether in 1856. The Junior Lords (who act mainly as Government Whips) still

---

[12] T. Daintith and A. Page, *The Executive in the Constitution* (1999).

[13] These are to be distinguished from Parliamentary Private Secretaries, whose office is unofficial and unpaid: See N. Henderson, *The Private Office* (1984).

[14] Junior Ministers include the Parliamentary Secretaries, Treasury Commissioners (Government Whips) and H.M. Household.

[15] A Minister has not the right—as he has in some constitutions—to address both Houses of the legislature.

[16] Lord Bridges, *The Treasury* (2nd ed., 1966) H. Roseveare, *The Treasury* (1969); H. Heclo and A. Wildavskyu, *The Private Government of Public Money* (1973); J. Barnett, *Inside the Treasury* (1982). C. Thain and M. Wright, *The Treasury and Whitehall* (1995).

[17] Holdsworth *History of English Law* (5th ed.), Vol. I, pp. 42–44.

have certain formal functions, such as signing Treasury warrants.[18] The management of the department is in the hands of the Chancellor of the Exchequer, who is also Under-Treasurer. In addition to his traditional duties with regard to national finance, the Chancellor in recent times has acquired responsibilities relating to economic policy.[19] Under him are a number of ministers. The fact that one of these, the Chief Secretary, has a seat in the Cabinet is evidence of the pre-eminent position of the Treasury.

The Treasury is ultimately responsible for the two tax collecting departments, the Inland Revenue and Customs and Excise. Both bodies are of statutory origin and run not by ministers but Commissioners appointed by the Queen.[20] **18–008**

Until 1968 the Treasury was also responsible for the management of the Home Civil Service. In that year, however, responsibility was transferred to the newly established Civil Service Department. Since 1995 all responsibility belongs to the Minister for the Civil Service, a post held by the Prime Minister, and is exercised through the Cabinet Office.[21]

Lord Chancellor's Department

The Lord Chancellor's Department in its modern form owes its origin to Lord Halsbury who in 1885 appointed a Permanent Secretary to the Lord Chancellor.[22] Before then the Lord Chancellor had been assisted by three Secretaries, regarded as his personal servants, to the extent that when a Chancellor resigned the Great Seal they destroyed all the files relating to his term of office! The office of Permanent Secretary has, since Lord Halsbury's reforms, been combined with the ancient office of Clerk of the Crown in Chancery.[23] **18–009**

The Department remained small and somewhat out of the mainstream of government activity, concerned largely with judicial and ecclesiastical appointments, until after the Second World War. Two developments since then have turned it into one of the larger spending departments of state: the introduction and growth of legal aid, beginning with the Legal Aid Act 1949, and the coming into effect of the Courts Act 1971 which made the department responsible for the administration of the court system,[24] other than magistrates' courts which are run by local Magistrates' Courts Committees.[25]

In addition to these new responsibilities, the role of the Lord Chancellor himself has increasingly come under scrutiny for various reasons. The procedure for judicial appointments has become the subject of criticism and the coming into effect of the Human Rights Act 1998[26] has strengthened calls for reform and

---

[18] Treasury Instruments (Signature) Act 1849.
[19] *Control of Public Expenditure* Cmnd. 1432, (1961). And see *Report of the Machinery of Government Committee* Cmd. 9230 (1918), pp. 18–19; S. H. Beer, *Treasury Control: The Co-Ordination of Financial and Economic Policy in Great Britain* (1956); Sir Ivor Jennings, *Cabinet Government* (3rd ed.), Chap. 7.
[20] Inland Revenue Regulation Act 1890; Customs and Excise Management Act 1979.
[21] *post*, para. 18–022.
[22] R. F. V. Heston, *Lives of the Lord Chancellors 1885–1940* (1964, Oxford); *Lives of the Lord Chancellors 1940–1970* (1987, Oxford), 31.
[23] The Clerk of the Crown in Chancery is an officer of the Supreme Court (Supreme Court Act 1981; Supreme Court (Offices) Act 1997) and has an important role in the conduct of general elections under the Representation of the People Acts.
[24] This responsibility is discharged through the Court Service, an executive agency (see *post*, para. 18–023). For judicial unease, see Nicolas Browne-Wilkinson, "The Independence of the Judiciary", [1988] P.L. 44.
[25] See, Police and Magistrates' Courts Act 1994, Part IV.
[26] *ante*, para. 2–020 and *post*, para, 22–036.

highlighted the anomalous position of a judge without security of tenure who is at the same time a Cabinet Minister and the Speaker of one of the Houses of Parliament.[27]

In 1994 a Parliamentary Secretary was appointed to represent the Department in the House of Commons. There are currently two Parliamentary Secretaries in the House of Commons and one in the House of Lords.

Law Officers' Departments[28]

18–010   The Law Officers are legal advisers to the Crown and the Houses of Parliament. They hold ministerial posts and therefore change with the government. The Law Officers consist of the Attorney-General[29] and Solicitor-General for England and Wales, and the Lord Advocate and Solicitor-General for Scotland.[30] Advice to the United Kingdom government on Scottish legal matters is given, following devolution, by the newly created law officer, the Advocate-General for Scotland.

The Attorney-General was so called in 1461. The Solicitor-General dates from 1515. Formerly the Law Officers were summoned to advise the House of Lords,[31] and there was some doubt whether the Attorney-General was entitled to sit in the Commons; but his attendance in the Lords is dispensed with except in peerage cases, and his right to sit in the Commons has not been seriously questioned since Bacon's time.[32] The current Attorney-General like his predecessor, is a member of the House of Lords. Neither appointment caused a stir and both cases are presumably a reflection on the calibre of lawyers in the House of Commons, at least on the government benches. The Solicitor-General also became entitled to sit in the Commons during the seventeenth century, although strictly he need not be a member.

18–011   The Attorney-General represents the Crown in civil proceedings in which it is specially concerned. His consent is necessary for the prosecution of certain offences, *e.g.* under the Official Secrets Acts. In criminal proceedings he or the Solicitor-General, or their deputies, prosecute in important cases.[33] It is the practice for the Attorney-General to lead in treason and important constitutional cases. He may intervene in a private law suit whenever it may affect the prerogatives of the Crown. He may at the invitation or with the permission of the court intervene whenever a suit raises any question of public policy on which the executive has a view which it wishes to bring to the notice of the court.[34] The Attorney-General can sue on behalf of the public to enforce public rights. He

---

[27] The Labour Party's enthusiasm for reform waned after its electoral victory in 1997: R. Brazier, "The Judiciary", in *Constitutional Reform* (R. Blackburn and R. Plant eds., Longman, 1999). See further, G. Dewry and D. Oliver, "Parliamentary accountability for the administration of justice," Chap. 3 in *The Law and Parliament* (D. Oliver and G. Drewry eds., Butterworths, 1998). See also D. Woodhouse, *The Office of Lord Chancellor* (Hart, 2001).

[28] J. Ll. J. Edwards, *The Law Officers of the Crown* (1964); and review by Sir Jocelyn Simon in (1965) 81 L.Q.R. 289; Sir Elwyn Jones, "Office of Attorney-General" (1969) 27 C.L.J. 43. J. Ll. J. Edwards, *The Attorney-General, Politics and the Public Interest* (1984).

[29] Under the Northern Ireland Constitution Act 1973, s.10 the Attorney-General for England and Wales is also Attorney-General for Northern Ireland.

[30] Other Officers are the Attorney-General of the Duchy of Lancaster, the Attorney-General and Solicitor-General of the County Palatine of Durham, and the Attorney-General to the Prince of Wales in respect of the Duchy of Cornwall.

[31] They still are, but they attend for ceremonial purposes only.

[32] Lord Campbell, *Lives of the Chancellors*, III, Chap. 54.

[33] *R. v. Wilkes* (1768) Wilson 322; (1678) 4 Burr. 2829.

[34] *Adams v. Adams* [1971] P. 188, 197, *per* Sir Jocelyn Simon P.

may lend his name to such an action at the instance of a private citizen—a proceedings known as a relator action. If he refuses to consent to the bringing of a relator action, his refusal cannot be questioned in the courts.[35] Owing to the increase in their ministerial work, the Law Officers appear less frequently in criminal cases nowadays. Actions may be brought against the Attorney-General under the Crown Proceedings Act 1947 if there is no appropriate department in respect of matters relating to the Crown in England, Wales and Northern Ireland only; he cannot be sued in relation to matters concerning acts of the Crown in its other dominions.[36] The Law Officers are forbidden by Treasury Minute to engage in private practice, but they receive a salary which takes some account of the loss entailed by being unable to practice. Fees which are paid when they appear in contentious business on behalf of the Crown are set-off against their salaries.

The better opinion is that the Attorney-General should not be in the Cabinet **18–012** because of his quasi-judicial functions with regard to prosecutions, and also because it is desirable to separate the giving of advice from those who decide whether to act on the advice.[37] Indeed it must be open to question in view of his unfettered discretion to refuse to initiate proceedings[38] and his power to terminate criminal proceedings[39] whether the appointment should not be non-political. The Attorney-General (and sometimes the Solicitor-General) is a member of the Legislative Committee of the Cabinet, and he is sometimes a member of (and in any case frequently attends) the Home Affairs Committee.[40] As regards the decision whether or not to institute public prosecutions, the Attorney-General acts in a quasi-judicial capacity, and does not take orders from the government that he should or should not prosecute in particular cases.[41] In political cases, such as sedition, he may seek the views of the appropriate Ministers, but he should not receive instructions. He may consider broad questions of public policy, but he should not be influenced by party political factors. Ministers may not be questioned in the House as to what advice the Law Officers have given, although they may be asked whether they have sought such advice. The fact that the Attorney-General consults informally and selectively, emphasises that both the decision whether or not to prosecute and the responsibility are his alone.[42] This makes his position anomalous in relation to the doctrine of collective ministerial responsibility.

The Solicitor-General is a subordinate of the Attorney-General, and often gives a joint opinion with him on legal matters. His duties are in general similar to those of the Attorney-General, and he usually succeeds to that post if it

[35] *Gouriet v. U.P.W.* [1978] A.C. 435 *post* para. 32–022. On the Attorney-General's right to stop a trial by entering a *nolle prosequi* see *post*, para. 20–003.
[36] *Trawnik v. Gordon Lennox* [1985] 2 All E.R. 368, CA.
[37] Lord Silkin, a former Attorney-General, has expressed the view that it is desirable that the Attorney-General should normally be in attendance at Cabinet meetings: [1984] P.L. 179, 183. Sir Michael Havers thinks it is better that the Attorney-General attend only on the occasions when his advice is specifically required so that he will be listened to as an impartial adviser: *The Times*, December 6, 1984.
[38] *ante*, para. 18–011.
[39] *post*, para. 20–003.
[40] The Attorney-General is in the Cabinet in some Commonwealth countries, *e.g.* Australia. In other Commonwealth countries the corresponding office is not regarded as a political one.
[41] H.C. Deb., Vol. 600, col. 58 (1959). And see Lord MacDermott, *Protection from Power under English Law*, pp. 25–40; Sir Patrick Devlin, *The Criminal Prosecution in England*, p. 18; Marshall and Moodie, *Some Problems of the Constitution*, pp. 172–180; Jennings, *op. cit.* pp. 236–257. J. Ll. J. Edwards, *The Attorney-General, Politics and the Public Interest*, (1984) Chap. 11.
[42] Sir Jocelyn Simon, *loc. cit.*

becomes vacant. He may deputise for the Attorney-General if the office becomes vacant, or if the latter is absent or ill or authorises him to do so.[43]

18–013   Until recently the Attorney-General and Solicitor-General were, in effect ministers without departments. However, following the report in 1989 by Sir Robert Andrew on government legal services, the Attorney-General acquired responsibility for a number of bodies henceforth known as the Law Officers Departments.

The Legal Secretariat is composed of a small group of lawyers and non-legal staff who provide the law officers with essential support and back-up services in their duty of providing legal advice and exercising the discretions vested in them.

The Treasury Solicitor's Office,[44] which is staffed by barristers and solicitors, is available to the departments for legal advice and conveyancing. The senior official of this department is H.M. Procurator-General and Treasury Solicitor, who in the latter capacity acts as a solicitor to government departments in litigation. He is also appointed *Queen's Proctor* in connection with proceedings for Admiralty droits and matrimonial causes. The general practice is that departments whose work is primarily the administration of detailed legal rules have their own solicitor's department, while departments whose legal problems are likely to be involved with policy rely on the Treasury Solicitor, whose position is independent of department policy. Since 1996 the Treasury Solicitor's Office has been itself an executive agency[45] while its conveyancing work is undertaken by a second executive agency, the Government Property Lawyers.

The Crown Prosecution Service was established by the Prosecution of Offences Act 1985. The head of the service, which has a general responsibility for initiating criminal proceedings, is the Director of Public Prosecutions.[46]

The Serious Fraud Office was established under the provisions of the Criminal Justice Act 1987 and is headed by a Director.[47]

Home Office[48]

18–014   The work of the two Secretaries of State then existing was divided in 1782 into home affairs and foreign affairs. The Home Secretary collaborates with the Secretary of State for Scotland in certain matters affecting that country. He was traditionally the medium of communication between the British Government, the Channel Islands and the Isle of Man but under the reorganisation of departmental responsibilities following the election in June 2001 the relevant minister is now the Lord Chancellor.[49] Formerly, this arrangement extended to Northern Ireland.

The Home Secretary exercises the prerogative of the Queen's pleasure in many ways. He is the channel of communication between the subject and the Queen for addresses and petitions, and he authorises many of the royal commissions set up

---

[43] Law Officers Act 1944.
[44] G. Drewry, "The Office of Treasury Solicitor," (1980) 130 N.L.J. 753; Daintith and Page, *op. cit.*, 217, *et seq.*
[45] *post*, para. 18–023.
[46] *post*, para. 20–014.
[47] The Parliamentary Counsel Office is not one of the Law Officers Departments but forms part of the Cabinet Office: see *ante*, para. 17–014.
[48] Sir Frank Newsam, *The Home Office* (1954); Report of the Committee on the Machinery of Government Cd. 9230 (1918), pp. 63–78.
[49] See, now, *post*, Chap. 35.

from time to time to examine various matters. He is also the medium of communication between the Church of England and the Queen, its Governor.

Matters connected with the administration of justice which are not dealt with by the Lord Chancellor or the Attorney-General come within the sphere of the Home Secretary. He is ultimately responsible for the maintenance of the Queen's peace, and in this capacity he is in direct control of the Metropolitan Police and indirectly supervises the local police forces, and provides for co-operation between magistrates, the police, special constables and the armed forces. He exercises the prerogative of mercy.[50] He is also responsible for prisons[51] and other penal institutions; the treatment of offenders; the probation and aftercare services and legislation on criminal justice.

The Home Secretary administers the law relating to naturalisation, supervision of aliens, immigration, deportation and extradition.[52]

The Home Office, being the residuary department of state, is concerned with many other miscellaneous matters under various statutes, including the supervision of the fire service; civil defence; community relations; the law relating to parliamentary and local government elections; explosives; fire-arms; dangerous drugs; liquor licensing; betting and gaming; and such other internal affairs of England and Wales as are not assigned to other departments.

Foreign and Commonwealth Office[53]

The Foreign Office is concerned with the formulation and conduct of foreign **18–015** policy, and controls the Foreign Service. The Foreign Office combined in 1968 with the Commonwealth Office which (as the Commonwealth Relations Office) had merged with the Colonial Office in 1966. The Secretary of State maintains direct contact with the diplomatic representatives of foreign and Commonwealth states, with foreign and Commonwealth governments, and with the British diplomatic representatives overseas. He is in constant communication with the Queen, the Prime Minister and the Cabinet on all important matters relating to foreign and Commonwealth affairs. The Passport Office is a subordinate directorate. The Permanent Under-Secretary is head of the Diplomatic Service.

The Secretary of State is ultimately responsible for the government of British dependent territories.

Privy Council Office

As we saw earlier, the (Lord) President of the Council is also, at present, the **18–016** Leader of the House of Commons. The Lord Privy Seal is also Leader of the House of Lords.

Scottish Office[54]

Scottish affairs were formerly conducted by the Home Secretary and various **18–017** other departments. In 1885 a Secretary for Scotland, with a Scottish Office, was

---

[50] See *post*, para. 20–044.
[51] See *R. v. Home Secretary, ex p. McAvoy* [1984] 1 W.L.R. 1408.
[52] *post*, Chap. 23.
[53] Lord Strang, *The Foreign Office* (1955); Sir Charles Jeffries, *The Colonial Office* (1956); Sir George Fiddes, *The Dominions and Colonial Offices* (1926); J. A. Cross, *Whitehall and the Commonwealth* (1967).
[54] *The Thistle and the Crown: A History of the Scottish Office* (H.M.S.O. 1985). See *ante*, Chap. 5.

created by statute, and in 1926 he was made a Secretary of State. The continued existence of a Secretary of State after the implementation of the Government of Scotland Act 1998 may owe more to political expediency than to constitutional appropriateness.

Welsh Office[55]

18–018   A Minister for Welsh Affairs was appointed in 1951, but for some years this office was held by the Minister of another department, usually of Cabinet rank. Since 1964 there has been a Secretary of State for Wales. The continued existence of this office, too, may be questionable, although perhaps explicable in the light of the limited degree of devolution in the case of Wales.

Northern Ireland Office[56]

18–019   A Secretary of State for Northern Ireland was appointed in 1972 on the suspension of the then existing system of devolved government. In the ensuing years the position has been one of great responsibility both in terms of attempting to establish a constitutional settlement acceptable to all parties and, in effect, governing the Province through Statutory Instruments passed at Westminster.

Other government departments

18–020   The creation and transfer of functions between departments is effected by reliance on both statutory and prerogative powers.[57] The wish to keep the size of the Cabinet within bounds has encouraged the merger of ministries into large departments under the supervision of a Secretary of State.[58] The distribution of functions between departments and their titles also reflect changes in the importance of their activities, changes in the emphasis governments wish to give—or be seen to give—to particular elements in their overall programmes and, even, the need to find an appropriate role for a particular member of the governing party. The evolution of the Department of Defence was mentioned earlier.[59] The Department of the Environment was created from the former Ministries of Housing and Local Government, Public Building and Works, and Transport. In the previous government it became the Department of Environment, Transport and Regions, to reflect the importance of these issues and, no doubt, of the Deputy Prime Minister, Mr Prescott. The Department for Education and Employment was created in 1995 from two separate departments to reflect what are now seen as the obvious links between these two areas. On the other hand, the importance of Health and Social Security is reflected by their currently being entrusted to two separate departments, having formerly been the responsibility of one Secretary of State. The appointment, by Mrs Thatcher, of a Minister for the Arts, located in the Privy Council Office, led to the growth of a department for the National Heritage, under a Secretary of State who is currently styled the Secretary of State for Culture, Media and Sport. The establishment of a Department of International Development in 1997 reflected the importance attached by

[55] See *ante*, Chap. 5.
[56] *ante*, Chap. 5.
[57] *ante*, para. 18–003.
[58] *ante*, para. 18–003.
[59] *ante*, para. 18–003.

the Labour Government to what, as Overseas Development, had been the responsibility of a minister in the Foreign Office.

Post Election Changes

Following the election of June 2001 a number of changes were made to the departmental structure described in the preceding sections of chapters 17 and 18. The Department of Environment, Transport and Regions became the Department for Environment, Food and Rural Affairs. The Ministry of Agriculture, Fisheries and Food came to an end, after a period of sustained criticism relating to its handling of such issues as BSE and the Foot and Mouth epidemic in the months leading up to the election. A new Department was established for Transport, Local Government and the Regions. As before, the Minister for Transport, although not a member of the Cabinet, attends Cabinet meetings. The Department for Education and Employment has been renamed Education and Skills, while the Department of Social Security has become the Department for Work and Pensions. The Deputy Prime Minister and First Secretary of State now heads his own office which is located in the Cabinet Office where also are to be found the Chancellor of the Duchy of Lancaster (and Minister for the Cabinet Office) and two Ministers of State.

II. THE CIVIL SERVICE[60]

The detailed administration of the work of a government department is carried out by civil servants. Although, like Ministers, they are servants of the Crown, civil servants are called "permanent" since their appointment is non-political and in practice lasts during good behaviour, as opposed to Ministers and Parliamentary Secretaries who are responsible to Parliament and change office with the government. **18–021**

The backbone of the department or Ministry is the secretariat under the Permanent Under-Secretary of State or Permanent Secretary. There used to be a hierarchy of administrative, executive and clerical classes; but following the recommendation of the Fulton Report,[61] these classes (up to and including the level of assistant secretary) were merged in one administrative group. Departments with technical functions will also require a number of inspectors, accountants, contract officers, production officers, scientific officers and others with professional or technical qualifications.

Organisation and Management of the Civil Service

The modern civil service owes its origins to the Northcote-Trevelyan Report of 1854 which led to the establishment of a centralised service to which entry was by competitive examination, controlled and operated by the Civil Service Commissioners. The management of the service was in the hands of the Treasury, the Permanent Secretary to the Treasury being also the Permanent Head of the Civil Service. In 1968 control was given to the newly established Civil Service Department and a Minister for the Civil Service, a position, in fact, held by the Prime Minister. The Department was abolished in 1981 and responsibility for the **18–022**

---

[60] T. Daintith and A. Page, *The Executive in the Constitution*, Chap. 3.
[61] Cmnd. 3638, (1971).

management of the service was transferred to a Management and Personnel Office in the Cabinet Office. In 1998 the Office was merged into the Cabinet Office. The Prime Minister remains Minister for the Civil Service.

The role and structure of the present day Civil Service have been profoundly affected by two recent developments, the creation of Next Step Agencies which are discussed in the following section and, secondly, reforms to recruitment and management introduced by the Civil Service Order in Council 1995 which find detailed expression in the Civil Service Management Code. Inevitably the coming into effect of devolution will see further fundamental changes.[62]

The legal basis for the operation and control of the Civil Service is the exercise by the executive of the royal prerogative. Almost the only example of statute is to be found in the Civil Service (Management Functions) Act 1992 which provides authorisation for delegation by ministers of powers in relation to the management of the civil service to particular departments or agencies.

Next Steps Agencies

18–023   Next Steps Agencies[63] have been described as the most significant development in the machinery of government in the last hundred years.[64] They reflect a belief that the provision of services to the public can best be carried out by agencies under the control of chief executives, leaving a greatly reduced central core of civil servants to be responsible for general issues of policy and advice to ministers. Almost three quarters of the civil service now work in agencies which deal with a range of activities whose width can be gathered from a sample of their names: from the Land Registry, the Driver and Vehicle Licensing Agency, the Passport Agency and the Patent Office to the Social Security Benefits Agency. Some, such as the Treasury Solicitor's Department are departments in their own right but the majority remain linked to the department from which they emerged.

In terms of the civil service as a unified service the development of Next Steps Agencies raises questions about the relationship between the central core of the service and the members working in agencies. How unified will the service remain? Will there be a genuine interchange between the staff of the agencies and the central core of civil servants leading to an exchange of their differing skills and experience?

The financial arrangements for next step agencies vary from one to another.[65] The proliferation of such bodies has given significance to the use of trading funds, a device introduced by the Government Trading Funds Act 1973, but initially little used. Since, however, the Government Trading Act 1990 a wide range of agencies has been financed by this method which is used where revenue is generated by the receipt of monies in respect of goods and services provided

---

[62] The Scotland Act 1998, s.51(2) and the Government of Wales Act 1998, s.34(2) provide that civil servants working in Scotland and Wales remain members of the Home Civil Service but difficulties will arise as questions of conflicting loyalties emerge: *ante*, Chap. 5.

[63] So called from the title of the report, *Improving Management in Government: The Next Steps*, by the Cabinet Office Efficiency Unit under Sir Robin Ibbs, published in 1988. G. Drewry, "Forwards from F.M.I.," [1988] P.L. 505; "Next Steps, The Pace Falters," [1990] P.L. 322; *Parliamentary Accountability, A Study of Parliament and Executive Agencies* (P. Giddings ed., Macmillan, 1995); D. Oliver and G. Drewry, *Public Service Reforms* (Pinter, 1996).

[64] Daintith and Page, *op. cit.* p. 37. M. Freedland, "The Crown and the Changing Nature of Government" in *The Nature of the Crown* (M. Sunkin and S. Payne eds.) Chap. 5.

[65] Daintith and Page, *op. cit.* p. 134.

by an agency. The object of the system is to encourage agencies to operate as far as possible like normal commercial undertakings.

In terms of constitutional law the development of Next Steps Agencies raises two issues, the extent to which the *Carltona* principle applies to them and their impact on the convention of ministerial responsibility.[66] **18–024**

In *Carltona v. Commissioners of Works*[67] the Court of Appeal recognised that ministerial powers could, in appropriate cases, be exercised on their behalf by civil servants in their department without infringing the legal principle that delegated powers cannot normally be further delegated: *delegatus non potest delegare*. Thus a decision relating to deportation may validly be taken by a senior civil servant in the Home Office, acting as the Home Secretary's *alter ego*: *R. v. Secretary of State for the Home Office, ex p. Oladehinde*.[68] The same principle was applied to the Social Services Benefits Agency in *R. v. Secretary of State for Social Services, ex p. Sherwin*[69] although Latham J. was prepared to consider that ministerial accountability to Parliament for a particular agency might be so attenuated that the *Carltona* principle could no longer apply.[70]

The impact of Next Steps Agencies on the convention of ministerial responsibility to Parliament remains to be fully worked out although it is already clear that it represents a further weakening of a fragile constitutional control. Reference was made earlier to the increasing emphasis on a distinction between ministerial responsibility and ministerial accountability.[71] The development of next step agencies has had a significant role in the growth of this terminology. Ministers are accountable to Parliament for Next Steps Agencies but not responsible for agencies "operational decisions". Where an error occurs at the level of operations as opposed to policy the minister may, for example, discharge his accountability by reporting to Parliament that he has dismissed or disciplined the head of the agency.[72] Whatever it means in practice the principle of accountability for agencies as for departments is explicitly recognised in the Ministerial Code, repeating the language of resolutions passed by the House of Commons and the House of Lords on March 19 and 20, 1997.[73]

Who is a civil servant?

A civil servant is one kind of Crown servant, and whether or not a person is a Crown servant depends on the facts of the case.[74] There is no formal definition of "Crown servant," although we may say that generally he is appointed by or on behalf of the Crown to perform public duties which are ascribable to the **18–025**

---

[66] *ante*, para. 17–018; M. Freedland, "The rule against delegation and the Carltona doctrine in an agency context," [1996] P.L. 19.

[67] [1943] 2 All E.R. 560.

[68] [1991] A.C. 254.

[69] (1996) 32 B.M.L.R.I.

[70] The Civil Service (Management Functions) Act 1992 provides for delegation by ministers of powers delegated to them in respect of the management of the civil service—for example, pay and conditions of service. Hence the Act is inapplicable to the typical *Carltona* situation.

[71] *ante*, para. 17–018.

[72] Thus in 1995 Mr Howard, the Home Secretary, dismissed the Director-General of the Prison Service. In 1996 he felt able to discharge his accountability to Parliament by calling for an apology from the Director-General of the Prison Service and an assurance that similar errors would in future be avoided.

[73] 291 H.C. Debs, cols 273–293; 579 H.L. Debs, cols 1055–1062.

[74] *post*, Chap. 33.

Crown; usually, but not necessarily, he is paid by the Crown out of the Consolidated Fund or out of moneys voted by Parliament. Modifications must be made for servants of the Crown in overseas territories.[75]

All civil servants are Crown servants, but not all Crown servants are civil servants, for the term is not applied to Ministers, their Parliamentary Secretaries and Parliamentary Private Secretaries, or other holders of political offices, nor to members of the armed forces. Local government officers and the employees of public corporations are not civil servants, although the nature of their work and their conditions of employment bear many similarities. A subordinate engaged by, or working under, a civil servant is himself a servant of the Crown and not of his superior.[76]

Civil servants may be established (*i.e.* entitled to statutory superannuation), non-established or temporary. Civil servants who may render the Crown liable in actions of tort by third parties are those appointed directly or indirectly by the Crown and paid wholly out of the Consolidated Fund or moneys provided by Parliament, or holding an office which would normally be so paid: Crown Proceedings Act 1947, s.2(6).[77]

The legal status of civil servants

18–026   Although there has been controversy about the status of the civil servant and the nature of the relationship between the Crown and civil servants,[78] the House of Lords has recently indicated very clearly its view that the employment of civil servants is governed by the royal prerogative; *Council of Civil Service Unions v. Minister for the Civil Service*[79]; *Hughes v. D.H.S.S.*[80]

At common law a civil servant was dismissible at pleasure,[81] even if he was engaged for a definite period that had not yet expired.[82] There was an implied term to this effect, resting on public policy and not on the incapacity of the Crown to bind itself.[83] In such cases no action for damages lay against a superior

---

[75] H. H. Marshall, "The Legal Relationship between the State and its Servants in the Commonwealth" (1966) 15 I.C.L.Q. 150.

[76] *Lane v. Cotton* (1701) 1 Ld.Raym. 646; *Bainbridge v. Postmaster-General* [1906] 1 K.B. 178; *Town Investments v. Department of the Environment* [1978] A.C. 359.

[77] *post*, Chap. 33.

[78] It has been argued that the civil servant, like the soldier, has a status and is subject to a special kind of law contained in Royal Warrants, Treasury Minutes, etc.; and on the other hand that civil servants (unlike the armed forces) are not governed by prerogative; *cf.* L. Blair, "The Civil Servant—A Status Relationship?" (1958) 21 M.L.R. 265; "The Civil Servant—Political Reality and Legal Myth" [1958] P.L. 32; J. D. B. Mitchell, *The Contracts of Public Authorities*, pp. 32 *et seq.*; H. Street, *Governmental Liability*, pp. 111 *et seq.*; R. Watt, "The Crown and its Employees," in *The Nature of the Crown* (M. Sunkin and S. Payne, eds, 1999), Chap. 11.

[79] [1985] A.C. 374.

[80] [1985] A.C. 716, 782 *per* Lord Diplock.

[81] *Shenton v. Smith* [1895] A.C. 229, PC; *Gould v. Stuart* [1896] A.C. 575; *Nobrega v. Att.-Gen.* (1966) 10 W.I.R. 187; *Kodeeswaran Chelliah v. Att.-Gen. of Ceylon* [1970] A.C. 1111, PC.

[82] *De Dohsè v. R.* (1886) 3 T.L.R. 114, HL; *Dunn v. The Queen* [1896] 1 Q.B. 116, CA; *Hales v. R.* (1918) 34 T.L.R. 589, CA; *Denning v. Secretary of State for India* (1920) 37 T.L.R. 138 (Bailhache J.); *Terrell v. Secretary of State for the Colonies* [1953] 2 Q.B. 482; Nettheim, "*Dunn v. The Queen* Revisited" (1975) 35 C.L.J. 253.

[83] *Inland Revenue Commission v. Hambrook* [1956] 2 Q.B. 640; *Att.-Gen. for New South Wales v. Perpetual Trustee Co. Ltd* [1955] A.C. 457, PC; *Riordan v. War Office* [1961] 1 W.L.R. 210, CA; *Denning v. Secretary of State for India* (1920) 37 T.L.R. 138; *Rodwell v. Thomas* [1944] K.B. 596; *Thomas v. Att.-Gen. of Trinidad and Tobago* [1982] A.C. 113.

Crown servant[84]; nor, apparently, did an action lie for breach of warranty of authority.[85]

Further evidence of the anomalous legal status of the civil service may be **18–027** found in cases that doubt, or deny, a right to recover arrears of pay for services rendered, either during the subsistence of his employment or after his employment has been terminated. It was held in an early case that no action lay against the East India Company to recover a non-statutory pension.[86] In *Mulvenna v. Admiralty*[87] it was held that the rule that members of the forces may only claim on the bounty of the Crown and not for a contractual debt applies also to civilians as an implied condition in the terms of their contract. The latter case was followed in *Lucas v. Lucas and High Commissioner for India*,[88] where Pilcher J. held that the salary due to a civil servant was not a debt for the purpose of garnishee proceedings. The decision was much criticised, and in any case it could have been based on another ground.[89] In *Sutton v. Att.-Gen.*,[90] on the other hand, the House of Lords assumed that a civil servant's pay was recoverable, and the only question in that case was, how much was due. The question was regarded as one of the interpretation of an enlistment circular for Post Office[91] telegraphists in the first war. None of the judgments raised the question whether the pay was legally recoverable at all, and counsel for the Crown do not seem to have argued the point. Lord Goddard C.J. expressed the opinion *obiter* in *Terrell v. Secretary of State for the Colonies*[92] that a civil servant who had been dismissed could recover arrears of salary up to the time of dismissal, and in *Inland Revenue Commissioners v. Hambrook*[93] that civil servant (although perhaps not a soldier) could recover for services rendered on a *quantum meruit*.

On the question whether at common law there subsists between the Crown and a civil servant a contractual relationship, a contract of service the terms of which are enforceable, the decisions and dicta are conflicting. In *Sutton v. Att.-Gen. (ante)* all the judgments in the Court of Appeal and the House of Lords assumed that there was a contract of employment and that the terms as regards pay were enforceable. On the other hand, Pilcher J. in *Lucas v. Lucas (ante)* based his judgment on the ground that there was no contract the terms of which could be enforced by the civil servant. Further support for the latter view is to be found in

---

[84] *Gidley v. Lord Palmerston* (1822) 3 Brod. & B. 275; *Worthington v. Robinson* (1897) 75 L.T. 446.

[85] *Dunn v. MacDonald* [1896] 1 Q.B. 555; see also *Kenny v. Cosgrave* [1926] I.R. 517; *Riach v. Lord Advocate*, 1932 S.C. 138; *The Prometheus* (1949) 182 Ll.L.Rep. 859, CA.

[86] *Gibson v. East India Co* (1839) 5 Bing.N.C. 262.

[87] 1926 S.C. 842.

[88] [1943] P. 68.

[89] D. W. Logan, "A Civil Servant and his Pay" (1945) 61 L.Q.R. 240. *Cf.* Crown Proceedings Act 1947, s.27(1). *cf. Considine v. McInerney* [1916] 2 A.C. 162, HL; *ex gratia* pension paid to civil servant should be taken into account in fixing the amount of compensation under Workmen's Compensation Acts.

[90] (1923) 39 T.L.R. 294. Considered by the Privy Council in *Kodeeswaran Chelliah v. Att.-Gen. of Ceylon* [1970] A.C. 1111, where dicta of Lord Blackburn in *Mulvenna v. The Admiralty, ante* were strongly criticised as being a *non sequitur* from the Crown's right to terminate a contract of service at will. It was not necessary in *Dudfield v. Ministry of Works and Faithful v. Admiralty* (1964) 108 S.J. 118, to decide whether industrial civil servants could have sued their departments for arrears of pay, because there was no contractual right to receive the negotiated increases that were postponed by a "pay pause."

[91] The Post Office was at that time a government department.

[92] [1953] 2 Q.B. 482, 499.

[93] [1956] 2 Q.B. 641, 654. See further *Nobrega v. Att.-Gen.* (1966) 10 W.I.R. 187; *Kodeeswaran Chelliah v. Att.-Gen. of Ceylon ante*.

the G.C.H.Q. Case where "It was common ground before your Lordships, although it was not common ground below, that there was no contractual relationship between the Crown and the staff at the G.C.H.Q."[94]

18–028   As far as third parties are concerned, a contractual relationship may be said to exist between the Crown and a civil servant. The House of Lords in *Owners of S.S. Raphael v. Brandy*,[95] where a stoker on board a merchant ship was injured in an accident, held that the retainer he was paid as a member of the Royal Naval Reserve must be taken into account as earnings under a concurrent contract of service in assessing compensation under the Workmen's Compensation Act 1906. In *Picton v. Cullen*[96] the Irish Court of Appeal held that, where a judgment debt had been entered against a school teacher employed by the Board of National Education, the court could appoint a receiver over an instalment of salary that had actually become due, although there could be no attachment of such future income.

In *Reilly v. The King*[97] the appellant had been appointed a member of a statutory board in Canada for a term of five years, but after two years the board was abolished by a Canadian statute. His office was therefore terminated, and he brought a petition of right for breach of contract. It was held that further performance of the contract had become impossible by legislation, and the contract was therefore discharged. The case is notable for Lord Atkin's dicta[98] because, although they were *obiter*, he was delivering the opinion of a strong Judicial Committee. He said that "in some offices at least it is difficult to negative some contractual relations, whether it be as to salary or terms of employment on the one hand, and duty to serve faithfully and with reasonable care and skill on the other." Lord Atkin also said: "If the terms of the appointment definitely prescribe a term and expressly provide for a power to determine 'for cause' it appears necessarily to follow that any implication of a power to dismiss at pleasure is excluded." This statement is difficult to reconcile with Lord Goddard's statement in *Terrell's* case[99] that, where the Crown has the right to dismiss at pleasure, it cannot be taken away by any contractual arrangement made by a Secretary of State or an executive officer or department of state.

The answer seems to be that statute or letters patent creating an office may prescribe a definite term with power to determine "for cause" within that period, excluding the implication of a power to dismiss at will, but no such binding arrangement can be made *ad hoc* between an officer on behalf of the Crown and a prospective Crown servant. In *Riordan v. War Office*[1] Diplock J. gave reason for saying that the Crown might be held bound by other terms in the regulations than length of service or dismissal, and that the civil servant for his part would be bound by the express terms; but this also was *obiter*.

In practice nowadays disputes relating to the employment of civil services will be dealt with by reference to the Codes referred to in the following section and to the statutory rights which, to a large extent, apply to civil servants as to other

---

[94] *C.C.S.U. v. Minister for the Civil Service* [1985] A.C. 374, 419, *per* Lord Roskill.
[95] [1911] A.C. 413. The Crown itself would have been expressly not liable under the Workmen's Compensation Act.
[96] [1900] 2 I.R. 612.
[97] [1934] A.C. 176, PC.
[98] *ibid.* at pp. 179–180. And see *per* Denning J. in *Robertson v. Minister of Pensions* [1949] 1 K.B. 227, 231.
[99] *Terrell v. Secretary of State for the Colonies* [1953] 2 Q.B. 482, 497–500.
[1] [1959] 1 W.L.R. 1046; [1959] 3 All E.R. 552. And see note by C. Grunfeld in (1960) 23 M.L.R. 194.

employees under the Employment Rights Act 1996 and the Public Interest Disclosure Act 1998.

Conduct and Discipline

The terms and conditions of employment of civil servants continue to be governed by Orders in Council made under the royal prerogative.[2] **18–029**

Disputes relating to employment matters may be taken to the Civil Service Appeal Board whose decisions were held to be subject to judicial review by the Divisional Court in *R. v. Civil Service Appeal Board ex p. Bruce*.[3] That decision, however, was distinguished in *R. v. Lord Chancellor's Department ex p. Nangle*[4] where the Divisional Court held that disputes relating to the employment of civil servants, whether they should be regarded as employed under contracts of employment or not, did not raise questions of public law.

The constitutional role and importance of the civil service give rise to questions which do not normally arise in the case of other types of employees, or not to the same degree. Issues peculiar to public employment are addressed in the Civil Service Management Code and the Civil Service Code which, *inter alia*, set out the standards expected of civil servants in terms of impartiality, loyalty to the government of the day and confidentiality.

The importance of the impartiality of the civil service—so that a change of government does not, as in some countries, involve a wholesale dismissal of officials and the appointment of replacements—is emphasised in the Ministerial Code which provides for the appointment by ministers of Special Advisers to add a political dimension to the advice available to Ministers while reinforcing the politicians impartiality of the Civil Service.

The extent of the civil servant's obligation to preserve the confidentiality of information which has come to his notice in an official capacity became a controversial issue as a result of the unsuccessful prosecution of Clive Ponting in 1985 for sending departmental papers relating to the sinking of the Argentinean warship, *General Belgrano* to a member of Parliament.[5] Subsequently a memorandum was circulated by Sir Robert Armstrong, Secretary to the Cabinet and Head of the Home Civil Service. The position is currently dealt with in the Civil Service Code which provides that where a civil servant is unhappy with the propriety or legality of something which has come to his knowledge he should rely on departmental procedures for drawing the matter to the attention of superior officials and, if dissatisfied with their reaction, may refer the issue to the Civil Service Commissioners. The civil servant who does engage in what is now known as "whistleblowing" can claim the protection of the provisions of the Public Disclosure Act 1998. **18–030**

That there may be circumstances in which a citizen finds himself faced with a moral imperative which is inconsistent with the law of the land was recognised judicially by Sir John Donaldson M.R. in *Francome v. Mirror Group Newspapers Ltd*.[6] But, the Master of the Rolls added, such circumstances must be "very rare." He might have added that they also require the courage to defy the law openly

---

[2] *e.g.* Civil Service Order in Council 1995. Statutory authority for delegation of powers of management is contained in the Civil Service (Management Functions) Act 1992.

[3] [1988] I.C.R. 649, [1988] 3 All E.R. 686. On the facts the Div. Ct. refused relief and was upheld on that refusal by CA; [1989] I.C.R. 171, [1989] 2 All E.R. 907.

[4] [1991] I.C.R. 743; [1992] 1 All E.R. 897, DC.

[5] *R. v. Ponting* [1985] Crim. L.R. 318.

[6] [1984] 1 W.L.R. 892, 897.

and accept the consequences. The anonymous informer hardly shows the courage of his moral conviction and by his conduct may well involve others in suspicion.

In a rather different position is the unfortunate civil servant who "leaks" information with the authorisation and approval of his or her minister, as happened during the Westland affair when the Director of Information at the Department of Trade and Industry "leaked" parts of a confidential letter from the Solicitor General with the approval of Mr Brittan, then Secretary of State for Trade and Industry. In theory—and in this case, in practice—the minister is responsible for such wrong-doing and should accept responsibility by resigning. Normally the circumstances of such a leak would not come to light since the minister most closely concerned would have no interest in pursuing the matter. In this instance, however, a full inquiry was undertaken by Sir Robert Armstrong, Secretary to the Cabinet and Head of the Home Civil Service at the request of the Prime Minister. The extent to which pressure from the Attorney-General resulted in the setting-up of the inquiry is unlikely ever to be known fully.[7] Newspaper reports spoke of threats to "have the police into No. 10," if an inquiry were not established.

Political activities of civil servants

18–031   In determining the extent to which civil servants shall be free to take part in political activities, the government has to effect a compromise between two conflicting principles. On the one hand it is desirable in a democratic society "for all citizens to have a voice in the affairs of the state and for as many as possible to play an active part in public life"; on the other hand "the public interest demands the maintenance of political impartiality in the Civil Service and confidence in that impartiality as an essential part of the structure of government in this country."[8]

   (i) As we have seen, civil servants are disqualified by statute from sitting in the House of Commons, and by the Servants of the Crown (Parliamentary Candidature) Order 1960 a civil servant must resign his office before standing as a candidate for a parliamentary election.

   (ii) With regard to other political activities, civil service regulations issued in 1953 distinguished, first, between three classes of civil servants and, secondly, between national and local politics.[9]

   (a) The administrative and professional grades, and those members of the executive and clerical grades who work with them and come into contact with the public, are restricted from taking an active part in national politics. They may be permitted where possible to take part in local government, but most would probably not have time to do so.

---

[7] For references to the Westland affair, see, *ante*, para. 17–017. To ensure her full co-operation with the inquiry the Director of Information was offered immunity from prosecution by the Attorney-General for any criminal offences which her evidence might show her to have committed: *post*, para. 20–003.

[8] *Report of the Committee on the Political Activities of Civil Servants* (Masterman), Cmd. 7718 (1949).

[9] *Political Activities of Civil Servants* Cmd. 8783 (1953). The merger of the administrative and executive classes following the Fulton report (cnd. 3638, 1971) has not affected these regulations.

(b) The remaining members of the executive and clerical grades may be permitted to take part in national as well as local politics (except parliamentary candidature), subject to a code of "discretion" with regard to the expression of views on governmental policy and national political issues.

(c) The minor, manipulative and industrial grades are free to engage in both national and local politics (other than parliamentary candidature), except when on duty or on official premises or while wearing uniform. They remain subject, of course, to the Official Secrets Acts.

A Committee to review the rules governing the participation in political activities of Civil Servants was set up in May 1976, under the Chairmanship of Sir Arthur Armitage and reported in 1978,[10] recommending the relaxation of the rules then in force. In 1984 the Government agreed that the numbers in the most severely restricted class should be substantially reduced. All but a small part of the restricted class are now subject to the rules governing class (b).

The continued validity of these restrictions is now open to question under the Human Rights Act 1998. Restrictions on the right of freedom of expression under Article 10 may be justified in the case of public servants but the need for such restrictions must be clearly demonstrated and they must be limited to what is necessary: *Ahmed v. United Kingdom.*[11]

---

[10] (1978) Cmnd. 7057.
[11] (1998) 5 B.H.R.C. III; H.R.C.D. 823.

CHAPTER 19

THE ARMED FORCES: EMERGENCIES: THE SECURITY SERVICES AND TERRORISM

19–001   The first duty of any state or ruler is to protect citizens from violence and threats of violence, whether in the form of external aggression or internal disorder and crime. This may lead to the executive claiming wide powers to use force and other techniques—such as espionage and surveillance—to protect itself and citizens generally. On the other hand, unless the activities of the executive are subject to effective legal and Parliamentary scrutiny they can themselves constitute a threat to individuals' basic freedoms. This dilemma unites the different sections of this chapter and, as will be seen, it exemplifies strikingly the relationship between prerogative and statute, as well as the role of the judiciary.

I. THE ARMED FORCES[1]

Introduction

19–002   In 2001 the legal situation of the armed forces reflects a mixture of prerogative and statutory powers. Before the revolution of 1688 the legal authority for raising and maintaining an army and navy was the royal prerogative. To ensure Parliamentary control over the arm the Bill of Rights 1688 provided that "the raising or keeping of a standing arm within the Kingdom in time of peace, unless it be with the consent of Parliament, is against law."

It was soon realised, however, that a standing army was necessary for the national safety. The solution was found in the Mutiny Act 1688, which authorised the keeping of an army for one year, and provided that the Act should not exempt any officer or soldier from the ordinary process of law. This force was maintained (except for short intervals) by annual Mutiny Acts down to 1879 and continued by the Army Act 1881, which formed to a large extent a military code. The Act of 1881 was annually renewed with amendments by short Army (Annual) Acts down to 1956. Meanwhile the Royal Air Force was established as a separate force by Parliament in 1917. Authority for this was renewed by Army and Air Force (Annual) Acts down to 1956.

19–003   From 1955 Parliament, instead of passing annual Acts, gave the Army and Air Force Acts a maximum life of five years, subject to annual renewal by Order in Council. Such Orders in Council must be laid in draft before Parliament and are subject to an affirmative resolution by each House. The current legislation is to be found in the Armed Forces Act 2001.

---

[1] Clode, *Military Forces of the Crown* (1869); Bl.Comm. I, Chap. 13; Anson, *Law and Custom of the Constitution*, II, ii (4th ed. Keith), pp. 199–222; *Manual of Military Law, Part II, Section 1; Maitland, Constitutional History*, pp. 275–280.

The consideration of such legislation by an *ad hoc* Select Committee affords an opportunity for detailed discussion of matters relating to the organisation and discipline of the armed forces.

Legislation was necessary to legalise not only the raising of a standing army but also the enforcement of military discipline, which would infringe the common law, as well to provide the money for its upkeep. The practice of authorising the keeping of an army for one year at a time was devised to ensure the observance of the convention that Parliament should be summoned at least once a year. The money is now provided by annual Appropriation Acts, which might be taken to imply the lawfulness of maintaining the forces for which funds are appropriated.

Public opinion has never feared the existence of a standing navy, so that the history of the Royal Navy has been free from constitutional problems.[2] It was the customary duty of the coastal towns, and especially the Cinque Ports, to provide ships and men in an emergency. The maintenance of the Navy has always been, and still is, within the royal prerogative; but terms of enlistment and naval discipline are now regulated by the Naval Discipline Act, and of course in modern times the money has come from Parliament. The Naval Discipline Act is now subject to continuance in the same manner as the Army and Air Force Acts.

Conscription, or compulsory military service, was introduced by statute in both world wars.[3]

The law relating to the various Reserve forces is now to be found in the Reserve Forces Act 1980 and the Reserve Forces Act 1996.

Legal position of members of the armed forces[4]

The control of the armed forces is part of the royal prerogative: *Chandler v. D.P.P.*[5] Despite the power of judicial review claimed in the *G.C.H.Q.*[6] case over acts done by virtue of the royal prerogative it is probable that the direction and disposition of the forces of the Crown will continue to be regarded as non-justiciable. The prerogative powers in relation to such matters as the training of the forces are preserved by section 11 of the Crown Proceedings Act 1947. The provisions of the Employment Rights Protection Act 1996 apply for the most part to members of the armed forces.[7]

19–004

Contract of service

Officers are commissioned by the Crown. They may be dismissed at the pleasure of the Crown, but may not resign their commission without leave.[8]

Other ranks are recruited—apart from statutory conscription or compulsory national service—by voluntary enlistment by attestation before a recruiting

19–005

---

[2] But *cf. The Case of Ship Money (R. v. Hampden)* (1637) 3 St.Tr. 825.

[3] The prerogative of "impressment" or "pressing" mariners into the Navy whenever the public safety requires, has never been abolished by statute although in practice it is obsolete: *R. v. Broadfoot* (1743) 18 St.Tr. 1323; Foster, *Crown Law*, p. 154; *R. v. Tubbs* (1776) Cowp. 512, *per* Lord Mansfield; *Ex p. Fox* (1793) 5 St.Tr. 276, *per* Lord Kenyon; *Barrow's Case* (1811) 14 East 346; Foster, 158.

[4] Peter Rowe, "The Crown and Accountability for the Armed Forces", in *The Nature of the Crown* (Sunkin and Payne ed. 1999).

[5] [1964] A.C. 763 (HL). *ante* para. 15–013; *post*, para. 26–003.

[6] *C.C.S.U. v. Minister for Civil Service* [1985] A.C. 374; *ante*, para. 15–004.

[7] s.192.

[8] *Vertue v. Lord Clive* (1769) 6 Burr. 2472; *R. v. Cuming, ex p. Hall* (1887) 19 Q.B.D. 13; *Hearson v. Churchill* [1892] 2 Q.B. 144; *Marks v. Commonwealth of Australia* (1964) 111 C.L.R. 548.

officer. Enlistment being a civil contract, its terms cannot be varied without the consent of the soldier, but he can be discharged at the pleasure of the Crown.

No action lies against the Crown to enforce the terms of service for damages for wrongful dismissal or to recover arrears of pay.[9]

Subject to ordinary law

19–006   A soldier becomes subject to military law, but he also remains bound by the ordinary civil and criminal law.[10] It is hardly correct to say that he is governed by two systems of law, for military law is part of the law of the land.[11] Statutory exceptions include the right to make an informal will on actual military service[12] or at sea, exemption from jury service, and the right to a "service qualification" under the Representation of the People Act 1983, ss.14–17.[13]

Superior orders as a defence

19–007   A member of the armed forces is primarily bound to obey the civil (*i.e.* non-military) law, even though such obedience may render him liable to be tried by court-martial. "A soldier for the purpose of establishing civil order," it has been said,[14] "is only a citizen armed in a particular manner." Although military regulations forbid the firing on rioters except under an order from a magistrate who is present, the existence or absence of a magistrate's order neither justifies what is done nor excuses what is not done in the eyes of the civil law. The soldier may therefore sometimes find himself in a dilemma if he is ordered by a superior officer to do something which is unlawful; and the question has arisen how far, if at all, he can plead obedience to superior orders—one of the first duties of a soldier—as a defence. In *R. v. Smith*,[15] a case heard by a special tribunal of three civilian judges set up in the Cape of Good Hope during the Boer War, Solomon J. said: "I think it is a safe rule to lay down that if a soldier honestly believes he is doing his duty in obeying the commands of his superior, and if the orders are not so manifestly illegal that he must or ought to have known that they were unlawful, the private soldier would be protected by the orders of his superior officer." In that case it was held that the order to shoot an African if he did not fetch a bridle was not so plainly illegal that the accused would have been justified in the circumstances in refusing to obey it, and it was therefore not necessary to decide whether in the circumstances the order was unreasonable or unnecessary. The accused was therefore not guilty of murder.

In *Keighley v. Bell*,[16] Willes J., a great authority on the common law, said *obiter*: "I hope I may never have to determine that difficult question, how far the orders of a superior officer are a justification. Were I compelled to determine that

---

[9] *Grant v. Secretary of State for India* (1877) 2 C.P.D. 445; *Mitchell v. R.* [1896] 1 Q.B. 121; *Leaman v. R.* [1920] 3 K.B. 663. See Z. Cowen, "The Armed Forces of the Crown (1950) 66 L.Q.R. 478.
[10] The subjection of the soldier to English law is indeed wider than that of a civilian in that the soldier takes English law with him wherever he goes; *post*, para. 19–008.
[11] *Burdett v. Abbot* (1812) 4 Taunt. 401, *per* Mansfield C.J.; *Grant v. Gould* (1792) 2 H.Bl. 98, *per* Lord Loughborough.
[12] *Re Wingham* [1949] P. 187. *Re Jones decd.* [1981] Fam. 7. (Privilege extends to service in N. Ireland: actual military service not confined to war between sovereign states).
[13] *ante* para. 10–029.
[14] *Report of the Commission on the Featherstone Riots* (1893) C. 7234. See also *Att.-Gen. of Northern Ireland's Reference (No. 1 of 1975)* [1977] A.C. 105; *post*, para. 19–021, where Lord Diplock pointed out the unreality of the comparison in many cases, such as that of the continuing emergency in Northern Ireland.
[15] [1900] Cape of Good Hope S.C. 561.
[16] (1866) 4. F. & F. 763, 790.

question, I should probably hold that the orders are an absolute justification in time of actual war—at all events, as regards enemies or foreigners—and I should think, even with regard to English-born subjects of the Crown, unless the orders were such as could not legally be given. I believe that the better opinion is, that an officer or soldier acting under the orders of his superior—not being necessarily or manifestly illegal—would be justified by his orders." If modified to the extent that the soldier's belief in the lawfulness of the order must be reasonable. Willes J.'s opinion would probably be accepted by the legal profession.

The soldier's obligation is to obey any *lawful* command. "Lawful command"   **19–008**
is described in the *Manual of Military Law*[17] as a command which is not contrary to English or international law and is justified by military law. "A superior has the right," says the *Manual* "to give a command for the purpose of maintaining good order or suppressing a disturbance or for the execution of a military duty or regulation or for a purpose connected with the welfare of troops. . . .   If a command is manifestly illegal the person to whom it is given would be justified in questioning and even refusing to execute it." With regard to a soldier's responsibility for carrying out an order which is not manifestly illegal, on the other hand, the *Manual* disagrees with the dictum in *Keighley v. Bell* (*ante*), but says that "It may give rise to a defence on other grounds, *e.g.* by establishing a claim of right made in good faith in answer to a charge of larceny, or by negativing a particular intent which may be a complete defence or reduce the crime to one of a less serious nature, or by excusing what appears to be culpable negligence.[18]

Whichever view is accepted it is obvious that a soldier may be placed in a serious dilemma, with the prospect of being proceeded against in the ordinary courts if he commits a crime or tort and of being court-martialled if he refuses to obey the command. So far as criminal liability is concerned, the soldier's position is somewhat mitigated by the power of the Crown to enter a *nolle prosequi* or to pardon after conviction, and the jurisdiction of the Courts-Martial Appeal Court to hear appeals from courts-martial which provides a forum for resolving any conflict of jurisdictions. Ultimately, the House of Lords could dispose of the problems as regards liability in tort as well.

With regard to liability for war crimes, *i.e.* violations of the principles of international law relating to warfare, the edition of the *Manual of Military Law* still issued at the beginning of the Second World War allowed superior orders as a valid defence. An amendment drafted by the Law Officers of the Crown was made in 1944 so as to read: "Obedience to the orders of a government or of a superior, whether military or civil, or to a national law or regulation, affords no defence to a charge of committing a war crime but may be considered in mitigation of punishment."[19] The Nuremberg Charter similarly provided that: "The fact that the defendant acted pursuant to orders of his government or of a superior shall not free him from responsibility, but may be considered in mitigation of punishment" (Art. 8). The true test, said the International Military Tribunal, is not the existence of the order, but whether moral choice is in fact possible.[20]

[17] Part I (12th ed., 1972). *The Manual* is not authoritative: *R. v. Tucker* [1952] 2 All E.R. 1074; 36 Cr.App.R. 192.
[18] Citing *R. v. James* (1839) 8 C. & P. 131; *R. v. Trainer* (1864) 4 F. & F. 105.
[19] Part III, p. 176. *cf.* Shakespeare, *Henry V,* Act IV, sc. 1, 11. 138–140.
[20] See Viscount Kilmuir, *Nuremberg in Retrospect* (Holdsworth Club, University of Birmingham, 1956), pp. 14–17.

Military law[21]

19–009   When a person joins the armed forces he becomes subject to the special code of military law in addition to the ordinary law. The objects of military law are disciplinary and administrative. It provides in the first place for the maintenance of discipline and good order among the troops, and secondly, for administrative matters such as terms of service, enlistment, discharge and billeting.

The sources of military law are statutes supplemented by the Queen's Regulations and royal warrants. The laws and customs of war established by international conventions (*i.e.* multilateral treaties) are also required to be observed by members of the forces. It was argued in *R. v. Durkin*[22] that there is also a "common law of the army," and the Courts-Martial Appeal Court did not reject it, but the existence of such a common law is doubtful. In addition to legally binding rules, there is "the custom of the service and military usage."

Employed civilians and followers with the Regular forces anywhere whether or not on active service are subject (with modifications) to Part II of the Army Act, which deals with discipline and the trial and punishment of military offences. All civilians listed in Schedule 5 to the Army Act are subject to the "civil offences" and certain specific offences within the jurisdiction of the Act, when in the command area of any part of the Regular forces abroad at any time. These include employed persons, persons attached to the forces for the purposes of their profession, and resident families.[23] The Armed Forces Act 1976 provides for the creation of Standing Civilian Courts to deal, in the case of minor offences, with civilians who would otherwise be liable to be tried by courts-martial.[24]

The civil courts have jurisdiction to determine in proceedings brought before them, *i.e.* in the exercise of their supervisory jurisdiction by way of judicial review and in actions for damages in tort, whether a person is subject to military law.

Courts-martial

19–010   The King's troops in medieval times were governed by regulations or articles of war issued by the King and administered in the Court of the Constable and the Marshal, two hereditary officers of state.[25] The office of Constable became extinct in the reign of Henry VIII, but the Court of the Constable and the Marshal continued to exist. During the early eighteenth century the Court ceased to function although it was never formally abolished.[26] From that time articles of war governing Army discipline were issued under parliamentary authority. The modern system of courts-martial for the trial of persons subject to *military law*

---

[21] It is convenient here to speak of "military law," which is the law of the Army; but similar considerations apply to Air Force law and Naval discipline. Stuart Smith J., "Military Law: Its History, Administration and Practice," (1969) 85 L.Q.R. 478.

[22] [1953] 2 Q.B. 364 (C.-M.A.C.).

[23] See G.J. Borrie, "Courts-martial, civilians, and civil liberties" (1969) 32 M.L.R. 35. In *R. v. Martin* [1998] A.C. 917, the House of Lords upheld the trial by court martial in Germany of the 19 year old civilian son of a soldier who had, with his son, returned to England more than a year before the trial.

[24] ss.6–8.

[25] For the history of this Court, see Holdsworth, *History of English Law* (5th ed.), Vol. I, pp. 573–580. See also Clode, *Military Forces of the Crown*, Vol. I, pp. 76–77; Richard O'Sullivan, *Military Law and the Supremacy of the Civil Courts* (1921), pp. 1–12.

[26] The last case tried by the Court of the Marshal appears to be *Sir H. Blount's Case* (1737) 1 Atk. 296. *Cf.* Court of Chivalry, *ante*, para. 18–002.

was established by the Mutiny Act 1688, and the Army Act 1881 combined it with the statutory articles of war.

The courts-martial that exist today enforce military law, Air Force law and Naval discipline, but do not administer martial law, although there has inevitably been some confusion on the point. "As a matter of etymology," says Maitland,[27] "*marshall* has nothing whatever to do with *martial*—the marshall is the master of the horse—he is marescallus, mareschalk, a stable servant—while of course Martial has to do with Mars, the God of war. Still, when first we hear of martial law in England, it is spelt indifferently *marshall* and *martial*, and it is quite clear that the two words were confused in the popular mind. . . . " Courts-martial have jurisdiction to try and to punish persons subject to military law for two classes of offences: first, military offences created by Part II of the Army Act, as to which their jurisdiction is exclusive; and secondly, under certain conditions, civil offences (*i.e.* criminal offences under non-military law), as to which their jurisdiction in this country is concurrent with the civil (*i.e.* non-military) courts.[28] Civil offences are acts or omissions punishable by the law of *England*, even where the accused is a Scottish soldier in a Scottish regiment stationed in Scotland.[29] Courts-martial have no jurisdiction, however, to try cases of treason, murder, manslaughter, treason-felony or rape committed in the United Kingdom.

The Army Act does not restrict the offences for which persons may be tried in the civil courts, or the jurisdiction of the civil courts to try a person subject to military law for any offence; but where a person is tried by a civil court the fact that he has been punished by a court-martial must be taken into consideration in awarding punishment. On the other hand, a person subject to military law who has been tried by a civil court may not subsequently be tried by court-martial for the same offence. **19–011**

The functioning of the Courts Martial system was reformed by the Army Act 1996, following the decision of the European Court of Human Rights in *Findlay v. United Kingdom*[30] that the system as it existed before that Act did not comply with the terms of Article 6 of the European Convention on Human Rights which guarantees a right to a hearing before an independent and impartial tribunal in the determination of any criminal charge. The Commission was concerned at the role of the Convening Officer who carried out the role of prosecutor, chose the members of the Court (who were fellow officers and often junior to him) and had the power to confirm the decision and confirm or vary the sentence. Advice on questions of law is given to a court martial by a Judge Advocate but formerly he was not a member of the court, another matter of concern for the Commission. **19–012**

---

[27] *Constitutional History*, p. 266. For martial law, see *post*, para. 19–023.
[28] See, *e.g. R. v. Gordon-Finlayson* [1941] 1 K.B. 171; *Cox v. Army Council* [1963] A.C. 48 (HL, on appeal from C.-M.A.C.). With regard to murder committed abroad, see *R. v. Page* [1954] 1 Q.B. 170 (C.-M.A.C.); *cf.* M. J. Prichard, "The Army Act and Murder Abroad" (1954) C.L.J. 232.
[29] Army Act 1955, s.70(2); Air Force Act 1955, s.70(2); Naval Discipline Act 1957, s.42(1). For comments on this anomalous position see Sir T. B. Smith, *British Justice: The Scottish Contribution* (1961), pp. 30–33; *Studies Critical and Comparative* (1962), p. 20.
[30] (1997) 24 E.H.R.R. 221. The decision of the Court was based on the law in effect before the 1996 Act. The Court refrained from expressing any view on whether the reforms, introduced following the decision of the Commission on Human Rights, were sufficient to satisfy Article 6. Nine other signatory states had the foresight to sign the Convention subject to a reservation relating to military discipline.

Following *Findlay,* the role of Convening Officer has been split between a Prosecuting Authority, an officer with legal qualifications, independent of the military chain of command, and a Court Administration Officer. The Judge Advocate is now a member of the court and the power of the Convening Officer to confirm the court's decision has been transferred to a Reviewing Authority, an officer entirely independent of the prosecution.[31] The presidents of courts martial are now appointed on a four year term of office: the appointment constitutes an officer's last posting and offers no prospect of further promotion.

In the light of these changes the Court Martial Appeal Court concluded in *R. v. Spear*[32] that the new system satisfied the requirements of Article 6 of the Convention: to hold otherwise would involve the court according to Laws L.J., in adopting an unduly formalistic approach, one approaching a neurotic distrust.[33]

The system of detention of members of the Armed Forces pending trial by court martial and the exercise by commanding officers of powers of summary jurisdiction in cases not regarded as sufficiently serious to merit trial by court martial have been reformed by the Armed Forces Discipline Act 2000 in an attempt to make them compatible with the terms of the European Convention.[34] The procedures for investigating offences including powers of entry and seizure have been placed on a statutory footing by the Armed Forces Act 2001.

19–013   Since 1951[35] it has been possible to appeal against conviction by a court-martial to a Courts-Martial Appeal Court, composed of judges of the Court of Appeal and Queen's Bench Division, nominated by the Lord Chief Justice; Lords Commissioners of Justiciary nominated by the Lord Justice General; judges of the Supreme Court of Northern Ireland, nominated by the Lord Chief Justice of Northern Ireland, and other persons of legal experience, nominated by the Lord Chancellor. Appeal lies to the House of Lords with leave of the Appeal Court or the House where the Appeal Court has certified that a point of law of general public importance is involved in the decision and the Court or the House of Lords thinks that the point is one which ought to be considered by the House.[36]

Jurisdiction of the High Court

19–014   Formerly courts martial were regarded as inferior courts, subject to the supervisory jurisdiction of the High Court exercised through an application for judicial review.[37] The Armed Forces Act 2001, section 23, however, puts courts martial on the same footing as the Crown Court and excludes the High Court's supervisory jurisdiction. A sufficient remedy is provided by the right of appeal to the Courts-Martial Appeal Court.

---

[31] P. Camp, "Court Martial—an independent impartial trial?", (1998) New L.Jo. 1156 and 1209.

[32] *The Times,* January 30, 2001.

[33] Nor, clearly, was Laws L.J. favourably disposed to the suggestion, made after the hearing of the case, that his own earlier appointment as junior counsel to the Treasury had involved him acting on behalf of the Ministry of Defence and he could therefore be suspected of partiality.

[34] *Hood v. United Kingdom* (2000) 29 E.H.H.R. 365.

[35] Courts-Martial (Appeals) Act 1951. See now the Courts-Martial (Appeals) Act 1968. See, *e.g. R. v. Tucker* [1952] 2 All E.R. 1074; 36 Cr.App.R. 192; *R. v. Bisset* [1980] 1 W.L.R. 335 (unsuccessful attempt to rely on defence of "condonation" by superior officer under Army Act 1955, s.134; for comment on this "most unusual" provision see *per* Lawton L.J. at p. 339.

[36] *e.g. R. v. Garth* [1986] A.C. 268, HL.

[37] *post* para. 32–011.

Civil actions may be brought against individual officers for damages for false imprisonment, assault, malicious prosecution, defamation, etc. Criminal proceedings against officers may take the form of a prosecution for *e.g.* murder, manslaughter or assault.

Actions for damages

As regards actions in tort the true principles are probably those stated by **19–015** McCardie J. in *Heddon v. Evans*,[38] an action brought by a private soldier against his commanding officer for false imprisonment and malicious prosecution in confining him to barracks on charges of making a frivolous complaint and conduct to the prejudice of good order and military discipline. His Lordship stated that: (1) an action lies if the court-martial or officer commits what would be a wrong at common law while acting without or in excess of jurisdiction[39]; but (2) no action lies if the court-martial or officer commits what would be a common law wrong while acting within its or his jurisdiction, even if the act was done maliciously[40] or without reasonable and probable cause.[41] The first proposition His Lordship thought was clear from the authorities as well as on principle. The second proposition he based on five cases, two of them in the Court of Appeal.[42] Only the House of Lords is free to hold that an action will lie for malicious abuse of military authority (within jurisdiction) without reasonable and probable cause.

In *Dawkins v. Lord F. Paulet*[43] an officer sued a superior officer for libels contained in letters written by the superior to the Adjutant-General in the course of his duty. The majority of the Court of Queen's Bench (Cockburn C.J. dissenting) held that the civil courts would not interfere in such cases even if the superior officer acted maliciously,[44] first, because the alleged wrong was done in the course of duty, and motive is therefore irrelevant; secondly, on grounds of convenience and public policy, as otherwise a superior officer would be unduly hampered in the performance of his duty; and, thirdly, because the party complaining of injustice has his remedy under military law.

In *Johnstone v. Sutton*[45] Lord Mansfield and Lord Loughborough in the Court **19–016** of Exchequer Chambers gave it as their opinion that even if malice were proved, an action would not lie by a person subject to naval or military law against someone who had used his authority under that law to injure him; but the question was admittedly left undecided. Johnstone, an admiral, had Sutton, a naval captain, put under arrest for disobedience to orders and sent to England to be tried by a court martial. He was honourably acquitted and then brought an action for malicious prosecution against Johnstone. The jury found for Sutton. Johnstone moved for arrest of judgment and was successful in the Court of

---

[38] (1919) 35 T.L.R. 642. McCardie J. went on to hold (although he did not consider it necessary for the decision) that the plaintiff had not established that the defendant did act maliciously or without reasonable and probable cause. A verbatim report is given in R. O'Sullivan, *Military Law and the Supremacy of the Civil Courts* (1921), pp. 43 *et seq.*

[39] *Grant v. Gould* (1792) 2 H.Bl. 100.

[40] *Dawkins v. Lord F. Paulet* (1869) L.R. 5 Q.B. 94.

[41] *Johnstone v. Sutton* (1786) 1 T.R. 493, 510, 784.

[42] *Dawkins v. Lord F. Paulet (ante)*; *Dawkins v. Lord Rokeby* (1866) 4 F. & F. 806; *Marks v. Frogley* [1898] 1 Q.B. 888; *Fraser v. Hamilton* (1917) 33 T.L.R. 431; *Fraser v. Balfour* (1918) 34 T.L.R. 502.

[43] (1869) L.R. 5 Q.B. 94.

[44] The occasion was privileged; see *Dawkins v. Lord Rokeby* (1875) L.R. 7 H.L. 744.

[45] (1786) 1 T.L.R. 493, 510, 784.

Exchequer Chamber and the House of Lords, not, however, on the broad ground that an action did not lie against a superior officer but because there had been reasonable and probable cause for the prosecution.

A court-martial would act without jurisdiction if it proceeded against a person who was not subject to military law,[46] or if it was not properly convened or properly constituted in accordance with the relevant Act, or if it convicted a man of an offence which is not an offence under the Act. It would exceed its jurisdiction if it awarded a heavier punishment than it had authority to award.

Visiting Forces

19–017   The Visiting Forces Act 1952 provides that visiting forces belonging to the member states of the Commonwealth and other countries specified by Order in Council under arrangements for common defence (*e.g.* NATO),[47] may be tried in the United Kingdom by the service courts of their own country according to their own service flaw; but a death sentence may not be carried out in the United Kingdom unless the law of the United Kingdom provides for the death sentence in such a case. In *R. v. Thames Justices, ex p. Brindle*,[48] the Court of Appeal held that although the jurisdiction of the relevant military courts under Part I of the Act extended only to members of visiting forces stationed in the United Kingdom, the provisions in Part II of the Act dealing with deserters were not so limited. Hence a deserter from an American army unit stationed in Germany who was arrested in England could properly be handed over to the American army authorities under the Act.

This jurisdiction does not oust the jurisdiction of British criminal courts over such visiting forces except in relation to offences arising in the course of service duty, offences against the person of a member of the same or another visiting force, and offences against the property of the visiting force or of a member of such force; and in these cases the appropriate authority may waive its jurisdiction. British courts may not try a member of a visiting force for an offence for which he has already been tried by his service court.

19–018   Civil actions may be brought in the ordinary courts against members of visiting forces; but the Secretary of State for Defence may arrange, under regulations issued by the Lord Chancellor's department, for the settlement of claims in tort. (Section 9).

Although the Act gave effect to certain provisions of the Agreement regarding the status of Forces of Parties to the North Atlantic Treaty 1951 it did not enact the Agreement as a whole into the law of the United Kingdom. Thus in *Luttrell v. U.S.A. (No. 2)*[49] a claim in tort by an American serviceman who alleged that he had been negligently injured in a British military hospital failed because his right of action depended on a provision in the Agreement. In the absence of legislation, however, a treaty cannot create rights enforceable at the instance of individual litigants.[50]

---

[46] *R. v. Wormwood Scrubs Prison (Governor), ex p. Boydell* [1948] 2 K.B. 193.
[47] See G.I.A.D. Draper, *Civilians and the Nato Status of Forces Agreement* (1966).
[48] [1975] 1 W.L.R. 1400. See also *R. v. Tottenham Magistrates' Court ex p. Williams* [1982] 2 All E.R. 705, DC. (Magistrate must be satisfied beyond reasonable doubt that prisoner is subject to foreign military law and that there is evidence to justify the bringing of proceedings against him).
[49] [1995] 1 W.L.R. 82, CA.
[50] *ante*, para. 15–030.

II. Emergency Powers of the Executive

Common Law Powers to Deal with an Emergency

Use of force to maintain public order[51]

Before the development of statutory professional police forces during the   **19–019**
nineteenth century, the duty of maintaining internal order rested mainly on
the sheriffs, mayors of boroughs and county magistrates, who were charged with
the duty of suppressing riots and dispersing unlawful assemblies. This duty has
never been expressly abrogated, but in practice the function of maintaining order
is now the responsibility of the local chief constable.[52] Force must not be used
unless necessary, and then only in a degree proportionate to the necessity. Those
who adopt excessive or cruel measures will be criminally liable (*Wright v.
Fitzgerald*[53]), but if the right amount of force is applied, incidental assaults or
trespasses will be justified. It is only as a last expedient that the civil authority
should invoke the assistance of the military.

At the time of the Gordon Riots in 1780 Wedderburn, the Attorney-General,
advised that as soldiers are also citizens they may lawfully be used to prevent
felony, even without the Riot Act proclamation being read. The military, if
invoked, should act under the direction of the civil authority (usually a magistrate): they should not, in ordinary cases, fire without his orders, nor fail to fire
when ordered by him. Exceptional circumstances may exist which make it the
duty of the troops to ignore or act in independence of the orders of the magistrate.
In *R. v. Kennett*[54] Lord Mansfield laid it down that magistrates who neglected
their duty of "reading the Riot Act" were guilty of misdemeanour. Alderman
Kennett, Lord Mayor of London, was convicted of neglect of duty in failing to
act during the Riots and releasing some prisoners, but he died before sentence
was passed.

In *R. v. Pinney*[55] the Mayor of Bristol was charged with neglect of duty in
failing to suppress a serious riot, directed in the first instance against the
Recorder who had expressed unpopular views in Parliament about parliamentary
reform. "A person, whether a magistrate or peace officer, who has the duty of
suppressing a riot," Littledale J. told the jury, "is placed in a very difficult
situation; for if, by his acts, he causes death, he is liable to be indicted for murder,
or manslaughter, and if he does not act he is liable to an indictment on an

---

[51] G. Marshall, *Constitutional Conventions* (1984) Ch. 9; D. Bonner, *Emergency Powers in Peacetime*
(1985); C.J. Whelan, "Military Intervention in Industrial Disputes," (1979) 8 Ind. L.J. 222; S. L.
Greer, "Military Intervention in Civil Disturbances: The Legal Basis Reconsidered," [1983] P.L. 573;
K. Jeffery and P. Hennessy, *States of Emergency: British Governments and Strikebreaking since 1919*
(1983).
[52] *post* Chap. 21.
[53] (1799) 27 St.Tr. 759; Forsyth, *Cases and Opinions on Constitutional Law*, p. 557; and *cf. Wolfe
Tone's Case* (1798) 27 St.Tr. 613, 624–625.
[54] (1781) 5 C. & P. 282. The Riot Act 1714 was repealed by the Criminal Law Act 1967; *post*
para. 27–019.
[55] (1832) B. & Ad. 947. See also *Case of Armes* (1597) Pop. 121. Mayors were formerly *ex officio*
magistrates. And see the charge of Tindal C.J. to the Bristol Grand Jury, as reported in 3 St.Tr.(N.S.)
11, approved by Willes J. in *Phillips v. Eyre* (1870) L.R. 6 Q.B. 1, 15. (Ct.Exch.Ch.). The plaintiff,
in the latter case brought a civil action for damages against the defendant, the former Governor of
Jamaica, for assault and false imprisonment in the course of suppressing rebellion. The defendant
successfully pleaded an Act of Indemnity passed by the legislature of Jamaica; *post*, para.
35–023n.

information for neglect. He is, therefore, bound to hit the exact line between excess and failure of duty." The jury found that the Mayor had acted "according to the best of his judgment, with zeal and personal courage," and acquitted him. A prosecution for such neglect of duty is in fact extremely rare.

19–020   The common law principles, particularly in relation to the use of military force, were explained in the report of the commission appointed to report on the disturbances at Featherstone Colliery, near Wakefield, during a coal strike in 1893. All the available Yorkshire constables were concentrated at Doncaster, and the Home Secretary (Asquith) at the request of the local magistrates approved the sending of an infantry platoon. A magistrate, who was present with the troops, appealed repeatedly to the crowd to cease destroying property; the proclamation in the Riot Act was read; a bayonet charge proved unavailing; and as the defensive position held by the soldiers was becoming untenable and the complete destruction of the colliery was imminent, the magistrate gave orders to the commander to fire. Two men on the fringe of the crowd were killed. The coroners' juries disagreed on whether there had been sufficient reason for the troops to fire. Asquith appointed a Special Commission consisting of Lord Justice Bowen (afterwards Lord Bowen), Haldane (later Lord Chancellor), and Sir Albert Rollitt, M.P., a solicitor.[56] "Officers and soldiers," said the Commissioners in their Report,[57] "are under no special privileges and subject to no special responsibilities as regards this principle of the law. A soldier for the purpose of establishing civil order is only a citizen armed in a particular manner. . . .   One salutary practice is that a magistrate should accompany the troops. The presence of a magistrate on such occasions, although not a legal obligation, is a matter of the highest importance. . . .   The question whether, on any occasion, the moment has come for firing on a mob of rioters, depends, as we have said, on the necessities of the case. . . .   An order from the magistrate who is present is required by military regulations . . . but the order of the magistrate has at law no legal effect. Its presence does not justify the firing of the magistrate is wrong. Its absence does not excuse the officer to fire when the necessity exists. . . .   The justification of Captain Barber and his men must stand or fall entirely by the common law [*i.e.* it was not affected by the Riot Act]. Was what they did necessary, and no more than was necessary, to put a stop or to prevent felonious crime? In doing so, did they exercise all ordinary skill and caution, so as to do no more harm than could reasonably be avoided?" The Commission exonerated the magistrates, officers and troops from blame.

19–021   In *Attorney-General for Northern Ireland's Reference (No. 1 of 1975)*,[58] which concerned the use of force by soldiers to effect an arrest under the Northern Ireland (Emergency Provisions) Act 1973, Lord Diplock, speaking of the position at common law, said[59] that the little authority in English law concerning the rights and duties of a member of the armed forces of the Crown when acting in aid of the civil power relates almost entirely to the duties of soldiers when troops are called on to assist in controlling a riotous assembly. Where used for such temporary purposes it may not be inaccurate to describe the legal rights and duties of a soldier as being no more than those of an ordinary citizen in uniform. But such a description was misleading in the circumstances in which the army

---

[56] H. H. Asquith, *Memories and Reflections*, Vol. I, p. 130.
[57] (1893) C. 7234. See also *Lynch v. Fitzgerald* [1938] I.R. 382, *per* Hanna J.
[58] [1977] A.C. 105. The common law rule had been replaced by the Criminal Law (Northern Ireland) Act 1967, s.3 which, like the English Act, refers to force "reasonable in the circumstances."
[59] At p. 136.

was employed in aid of the civil power in Northern Ireland where in some parts of the province there has existed for some years a state of armed and clandestinely organised insurrection against the lawful government.

Although the duty on a private citizen may be described as one of imperfect obligation, it was held in *R. v. Brown*[60] to be an indictable misdemeanour for a bystander to refuse to aid a police officer in suppressing a riot, if reasonably called upon by him to do so. Alderson B. said that liability for this offence requires three conditions: (i) the constable must actually see a breach of the peace committed by two or more persons; (ii) there must be a reasonable necessity for the constable to call on other persons for assistance; and (iii) the defendant must have refused to render assistance without any physical impossibility or lawful excuse. It is immaterial whether the help the defendant could have given would have proved sufficient or useful. Prosecutions for failing to assist the police are very rare.

The degree of force that may properly be exercised in the preservation of the Queen's peace is unclear. Section 3 of the Criminal Law Act 1967, which replaces the common law rule, refers to "such force as is reasonable in the circumstances." It is thought that the destruction of life or property might well be reasonable in circumstances of grave disorder.[61] The question, what degree of force is reasonable, is one of fact for the jury.[62]   **19–022**

In circumstances where a chief constable felt unable to cope with serious civil disturbance, even with the help of men from other police forces,[63] the decision to use troops would be taken by the Home Secretary and not, as in earlier times, by the local magistrates.[64] In such circumstances he would, no doubt, consult colleagues including the Prime Minister and the Secretary of State for Defence, if, indeed, the decision were not regarded as one to be taken by the Cabinet.

Martial Law[65]

Uses of the term "martial law"

The question is often raised, whether the Crown has a prerogative power to declare martial law. The term "martial law" is sometimes incorrectly used to cover any one or more of the following: **19–023**

(i) Military law, *i.e.* the codes governing the armed forces at home and abroad, in war and in peace. In former times, what we now call military law was sometimes referred to as martial law.

---

[60] (1841) C. & Mar. 314. See also *R. v. Pinney*, 1832 3 S.T. (N.S.) 4; H.E.L., viii, 350. *cf. Miller v. Knox* (1838) 4 Bing N.C. 574.

[61] Lord Diplock in *Att.-Gen. for Northern Ireland's Reference (No. 1 of 1975)* [1977] A.C. 105, quoted *ante*, seems so to have assumed. See also Report of the Widgery Tribunal of Inquiry (H.C. 200 1971–72)). *Farrell v. Secretary of State for Defence* [1980] 1 W.L.R. 172. Possibly a private citizen acting on his own initiative may not be justified in using as much force as the Crown itself may be entitled to use; *cf. Burmah Oil v. Lord Advocate* [1965] A.C. 75.

[62] *Att.-Gen. for Northern Ireland's Reference (No. 1 of 1975)*.

[63] Police Act 1966, s.24. Mutual help is now co-ordinated through the Mutual Aid Co-ordination Centre. The effectiveness of the Centre was demonstrated during the Miners' Strike of 1984–1985; *post* p. 415.

[64] Mr Jenkins, replying as Home Secretary, to a question in the House of Commons on April 8, 1976; H.C.Deb., Vol. 909, col. 617. See further Wilcox, "Military aid to the civil power" (1976) 126 New L.J. 404.

[65] "Martial Law" in D. Clark and G. McCoy, *The Most Fundamental Legal Right* (2000), pp. 61–82.

(ii) The law administered by a military commander in occupied enemy territory in time of war. This is sometimes called martial law by international lawyers. It is unnecessary to say more than that the law so administered amounts to arbitrary government by the military, tempered by international custom (*e.g.* the Hague Convention), and such disciplinary control as the British Government think fit to exercise.

(iii) The common law right and duty to maintain public order by the exercise of any degree of necessary force in time of invasion, rebellion, insurrection or riot (*ante.*)

Martial law in the strict sense means the suspension of the ordinary law, and the substitution therefor of discretionary government by the executive exercised through the military.[66]

Is martial law known to English law?[67]

19–024   Dicey asserted that martial law in this last sense is unknown to our Constitution.[68] Other writers have drawn a distinction between martial law in time of peace and in time of war, and contend that while the Petition of Right (1628) declared it illegal in the former case, it may still validly be proclaimed in the latter. The Petition of Right complained that commissions had been issued to certain persons giving them power to proceed "within the land" against such soldiers or mariners or other dissolute persons joining with them as should commit crimes, and to try them by such summary course "as is agreeable to martial law and as is used in armies in time of war"; and it prayed that no such commissions should thereafter issue. Cockburn C.J. in his charge to the grand jury in *R. v. Nelson and Brand*[69] pointed out that no distinction was made until after the time of Blackstone between "martial law" in the modern sense and what is now called "military law." In Great Britain, at any rate, the Crown cannot proclaim martial law by prerogative in time of peace. Nor has the Crown purported to proclaim it in time of war since the reign of Charles I, and it makes no difference whether or not a state of war has been proclaimed.

What on rare occasions has been called "martial law" since 1628 by British constitutional writers has been a state of affairs outside Great Britain in which, owing to civil commotion, the ordinary courts were unable to function, and it was therefore necessary to establish military tribunals. It is merely an extended application of the principle, discussed above, that the executive has such powers as are necessary for the preservation of public order. Even then specific powers have usually been obtained from Parliament, as in Ireland in 1799 and Jamaica in 1865.

Some authorities hold, nevertheless, that martial law may validly be called into operation in time of war both in Great Britain and outside, and that when this has been done the civil courts have no authority to call in question the actions of the

---

[66] The principles generally recognised for the imposition of martial law are: (i) necessity, *i.e.* the ordinary courts are unable to function; (ii) proportionality *i.e.* acts done should be proportional to the need; (iii) limitations of area *i.e.* only in areas (which might include the whole country) where the ordinary courts are unable to function; (iv) limitation of time, *i.e.* martial law should continue only so long as the necessity lasts.

[67] On the position before the Petition of Right see J. V. Capua, "The early history of Martial Law in England from the fourteenth century to the Petition of Right" (1977) 36 C.L.J. 152.

[68] Dicey, *Law of the Constitution* (10th ed.), p. 293.

[69] (1867) *Special Report*, pp. 99–100.

military authorities. They rely on the preamble to certain Irish Acts of Parliament, *e.g.* (1799) 39 Geo. 3, c.11, which referred to "the wise and salutary exercise of His Majesty's undoubted prerogative in executing martial law." They also pray in aid language used by Lord Halsbury in *Ex p. D. F. Marais*[70]: "The framers of the Petition of the Right well knew what they meant when they made a condition of peace the ground of the illegality of unconstitutional procedure." One answer to this line of reasoning was anticipated by Lord Blackburn when he said in his charge in *R. v. Eyre*[71]: "It would be an exceedingly wrong presumption to say that the Petition of Right, in not condemning martial law in time of war, sanctioned it." Another answer is afforded by the fact that when martial law has been proclaimed, the Crown has almost invariably protected its servants after the event by obtaining the passing of Acts of Indemnity.[72]

It is sometimes difficult to determine when a state of war exists in a particular **19–025** district. Coke, Rolle and Hale were of the opinion that time of peace is when the civil courts are open, and that when they are closed it is time of war. The decision of the Privy Council in *Ex p. D. F. Marais*,[73] however, shows that this test is not conclusive and that the existence of a state of war in a given district is compatible with the continued functioning for some purposes of the civil courts within that district. To exclude the legality of martial law, says Holdsworth,[74] "the courts must be sitting in their own right and not merely as licensees of the military authorities."

The judicial decisions are few and inconclusive and mostly Irish, but the following seem to be the general principles:

(i) The ordinary courts have jurisdiction to determine as a question of fact whether a state of war exists, or did exist at the relevant time, in a given area so as to justify the setting up of a military tribunal (*R. v. Allen*[75]; *R. (Garde) v. Strickland*[76]).

(ii) If it is held that a state of war does or does not exist, then the military tribunal—not being a court but merely a body of military officers to advise the military commander—would not be bound by the ordinary law or procedure. In *Re Clifford and O'Sullivan*[77] the appellants had been sentenced to death for being in possession of firearms by a military tribunal constituted under the authority of the Commander-in-Chief in Ireland, and they applied for a writ of prohibition. The House of Lords held that if in fact a state of war exists or existed at the time of question, a military tribunal is not a court in the ordinary sense, but merely a body of military officers advising their commander; such a tribunal is not bound by the ordinary law of procedure, and therefore prohibition would not lie. Further, in this case the military "court" had concluded its business, so that prohibition was too late anyway: relief might be sought by habeas corpus when order was restored if the appellants were still alive. There is no remedy during the

---

[70] [1902] A.C. 109. This decision gave rise to four articles on martial law in (1902) 18 L.Q.R. 117, 133, 143 and 152.

[71] (1868) Finlayson, 73.

[72] See *R. v. Nelson and Brand* (1867) F. Cockburn's Reports, 59, 79; Forsyth, *Cases and Opinions on Constitutional Law*, pp. 198, 199, 553, 556–557; Holdsworth, *History of English Law*, Vol. X, pp. 705–713.

[73] [1902] A.C. 109, and see *Elphinstone v. Bedreechund* (1830) 1 Knapp 316.

[74] Holdsworth, *History of English Law*, Vol. I, p. 576.

[75] [1921] 2 I.R. 241.

[76] [1921] 2 I.R. 313. And see *R. (O'Brien) v. Military Governor, N.D.U. Interment Camp* [1924] 1 I.R. 32.

[77] [1921] 2 A.C. 570.

state of war (*Ex p. D. F. Marais, ante*). During the disturbances in Ireland that followed the passing of the Irish Free State Constitution Act 1922, many persons were sentenced to death by courts-martial, among them Erskine Childers. He applied for a writ of habeas corpus, which was refused on the ground that a state of war existed in Ireland at the time, and that the civil courts were unable to discharge their duties (*R. v. Portobello Barracks Commanding Officer, ex p. Erskine Childers*[78]). Nor is there any remedy after the war is over, if what was done was done in good faith or at least was dictated by necessity (*Wright v. Fitzgerald*[79]).

(iii) If on the other hand it is held that a state of war does not or did not exist at the relevant time, the person injured has his remedy by habeas corpus (*Wolfe Tone's Case*[80]) or otherwise for injury done to him, subject to the terms of an Act of Indemnity which will probably have been passed in the meanwhile (*Tilonko v. Att.-Gen. for Natal*[81]).

Statutory Powers to Deal with an Emergency: In Time of Peace[82]

The Emergency Powers Act 1920

19–026   This is a *permanent* statute, and was designed to meet emergencies such as the coal strike of 1921 or the General Strike of 1926. The Act, as amended in 1964,[83] provides that Her Majesty may by proclamation declare a state of emergency if at any time it appears that there have occurred, or are about to occur, events of such a nature as to be calculated, by interfering with the supply and distribution of food, water, fuel or light, or with the means of locomotion, to deprive the community, or any substantial portion of the community, of the essentials of life. No such proclamation remains in force for more than a month, without prejudice to the issue of a fresh proclamation during that period (section 1(1)). Where a proclamation of emergency has been made Parliament is to be informed thereof forthwith, and if the Houses be then adjourned or prorogued they are to be summoned to meet within five days (section 1(2)).

Where a proclamation of emergency has been made, and so long as it is in force, Her Majesty in Council may make regulations for securing the essentials of life of the community; and those regulations may confer on a Secretary of State or other government department, or any other person in Her Majesty's service or acting on Her Majesty's behalf, such powers and duties as Her Majesty may deem necessary for preserving the peace, securing to the public the necessaries of life, the means of locomotion and the general safety. Nothing in the Act authorises the making of regulations imposing military or industrial conscription, the alteration of the rules of criminal procedure, or making it an offence to take part in a strike or peacefully to persuade other persons to take part in a strike (section 2(1)).

All regulations so made must be laid before Parliament as soon as may be after they are made, and cease to remain in force after the expiration of seven days

---

[78] [1923] I.R. 5.

[79] (1799) 27 St.Tr. 759; P. O'Higgins, "*Wright v. Fitzgerald Revisited*" (1962) 25 M.L.R. 413.

[80] (1798) 27 St.Tr. 613. "No more splendid assertion of the supremacy of the law can be found than the protection of Wolfe Tone by the Irish Bench"; Dicey, *Law of the Constitution* (10th ed.), p. 294. See further, R. F. V. Heuston, *Essays in Constitutional Law* (2nd ed., 1969) pp. 36 *et seq.* Before the dispute between the Courts and the military could be settled, Wolfe Tone had cut his throat.

[81] [1907] A.C. 93.

[82] K. Jeffery and P. Hennessy, *States of Emergency* (Routledge & Kegan Paul, 1983).

[83] Emergency Powers Act 1964.

from the time they were laid before Parliament unless a resolution is passed by both Houses providing for their continuance (section 2(2)). Regulations may provide for the trial by courts of summary jurisdiction of persons offending against the regulations. The maximum penalty for breach of the regulations is imprisonment for three months or a fine of £100 or both, together with the forfeiture of any goods or money in respect of which the offence has been committed. Regulations may not alter criminal procedure or confer any right to punish without trial (section 2(3)).

The Act was fully invoked during the General Strike of 1926. Proclamations of a state of emergency have been issued during strikes a number of times since. On some occasions regulations have been laid before Parliament, but they are usually dormant until put into force by orders, and they have not often needed to come into operation as most strikes are not sufficiently serious or are settled before the need arises. A proclamation of emergency was issued at the time of the seamen's strike in 1966. Regulations were then laid before Parliament making provision for control over maximum prices for such foods as might be specified; control of ports and dock labour; direction of the supply of fuel, food and animal foodstuffs, restriction of postal services, and control of home trade, shipping and cargoes; and the requisitioning of land, including houses and buildings. At the time of a miners' strike in February 1972, which cut off supplies of coal to power stations, emergency regulations come into force authorising electric power cuts and restricting the use of electricity in advertising and display-lighting. In 1973, emergency regulations were made to deal with the consequences of industrial action taken by miners and electricity workers.

The Emergency Powers Act 1964

19–027   Section 1 of the 1964 Act amended and expanded section 1 of the Emergency Powers Act 1920. Section 2 gives permanent effect to a regulation made under wartime legislation which permits the Defence Council to authorise the temporary employment of members of the Armed Forces in agricultural work or other urgent work of national importance. Under this section troops may be employed without any need for Parliamentary approval or the proclamation of a state of emergency. The section has been relied on in a number of cases; troops, for example, in 1975 went into action to remove refuse when Glasgow dustmen went on strike and in 1977–1978 when there was a national strike of firemen. In 2001 the Army was called on to help deal with the crisis following an outbreak of foot and mouth disease among farm animals.

Energy Act 1976

19–028   The sudden crisis in the distribution of petrol in the Autumn of 2000 required the government to exercise its powers under the Energy Act 1976, section 1 to regulate the production, supply, acquisition or use of liquid petroleum, allied products, and electricity.

Civil Contingencies Unit The co-ordination of measures to deal with emergencies   **19–029** is the responsibility of the Civil Contingencies Unit, a standing Cabinet Committee of ministers and civil servants which was set up in 1972 to replace the Emergencies Committee.

It is understood that in the light of experience gained in the recent emergencies the Home Office is reviewing government procedures for dealing with such occurrences.

Emergency Legislation in Northern Ireland

19–030   Members of the Armed Forces have not, since the General Strike, been employed in England, Scotland or Wales for the purposes of maintaining law and order. In Northern Ireland, however, the Army has been involved in preventing civil disorder since 1969. To rely on vague common law powers would have been impossible. At first legislation was passed by the Northern Ireland Parliament. When that was successfully challenged in the Courts,[83a] legislation was passed by the Westminster Parliament. The Northern Ireland Act 1972, in one short section provided that

> "The limitations imposed on the powers of the Parliament of Northern Ireland to make laws shall not have effect, and shall be deemed never to have had effect, to preclude the inclusion in laws made by that Parliament for the peace, order or good government of Northern Ireland of all provisions relating to members of Her Majesty's forces as such or to things done by them when on duty, and in particular shall not preclude, and shall be deemed never to have precluded, the conferment on them by, under or in pursuance of any such law of powers, authorities, privileges or immunities in relation to the preservation of the peace or maintenance of order in Northern Ireland."

In 1972 direct rule was introduced[84] and subsequently various statutes have been passed by the United Kingdom Parliament conferring emergency powers on the civil authorities and armed forces in Northern Ireland.[85] The legislation gave wide powers of arrest, search and entry to troops, as well as police constables. It created new offences and provided for the proscribing of organisations. It provided for detention without trial and for trial without jury. Without considering the details of such provisions it is necessary to emphasise the width of the powers conferred. Apart, for example, from specific provisions relating to entering and searching premises, section 19(1) of the 1978 Act allowed any member of the forces or any constable to enter any premises if he considers it necessary to do so in the course of operations for the preservation of peace or the maintenance of order; or if authorised to do so by or on behalf of the Secretary of State. Powers of detention—which have not been used since 1975—allowed persons to be detained

> "where it appears to the Secretary of State that there are grounds for suspecting that a person has been concerned in the commission or attempted commission of any act of terrorism or in directing, organising or training persons for the purpose of terrorism,"

(defined as the use of violence for political ends and includes any use of violence for the purpose of putting the public or any section of the public in fear).

Fears of widespread intimidation of juries led to the introduction of trials of "Scheduled Offences" by a judge sitting alone. These courts were known as Diplock Courts, after the author of the report which led to their adoption.[86]

[83a] *R. (Hume) v. Londonderry Justices* [1972] N.I. 91.

[84] *ante*, para. 5–003 *et seq.*

[85] Northern Ireland (Emergency Provisions) Act 1973; Northern Ireland (Emergency Provisions) Act 1978; Northern Ireland (Emergency Provisions) Act 1991; Northern Ireland (Emergency Provisions) Act 1996.

[86] *Report of the Commission to consider legal procedures to deal with terrorist activities in Northern Ireland, Cmnd* 5185 (1972).

The present constitutional situation in Northern Ireland, following the Good Friday Agreement of 1998 has been discussed earlier in Chapter 5. The emergency, anti-terrorist legislation will be discussed in Part IV of this chapter where it will be seen that the law relating to scheduled offences and trial by Diplock Courts will be continued for a fixed period as part of a permanent Terrorist Act which will apply throughout the United Kingdom.

Statutory Powers to Deal with an Emergency: In Time of War

Defence of the Realm Act 1914–15

The experience of the two great wars of the last century shows that the **19–031** executive rely in time of war almost exclusively on statutory powers. Shortly after the outbreak of war in 1914, the United Kingdom was in effect placed under military law by the Defence of the Realm Act 1914, and British subjects and aliens were triable by court-martial in connection with certain offences for some months. Subsequent Defence of the Realm Acts allowed British subjects to claim a civil trial on taking the prescribed steps, and gave to the King in Council such powers as were necessary for the efficient prosecution of the war. The doctrine of *ultra vires*, of course, still applied (*Chester v. Bateson*[87]; *Att.-Gen. v. Wilts. United Dairies*.[88] But as Scrutton L.J. is reported to have said in *Ronnfeldt v. Phillips*[89]; "It has been said that a war could not be conducted on the principles of the Sermon on the Mount. It might also be said that a war could not be carried on according to the principles of Magna Carta. Very wide powers had been given to the Executive to act on suspicion on matters affecting the interests of the State."

The Indemnity Act 1920 The liability of the executive for action taken to put down grave civil disturbances, and acts done in the prosecution of a war, may be greatly limited by Acts of Indemnity. These may be quite narrow in scope, or they may be framed in general terms as in the Indemnity Act 1920. This provided that no civil or criminal proceedings should be instituted for anything done in or outside British territory during the war before the passing of the Act, if done in good faith, and done or purported to be done in the execution of duty or for the defence of the realm or the public safety, or for the enforcement of discipline or otherwise in the public interest, by any servant of the Crown, military or civil, or any person acting under his authority.

The Emergency Powers (Defence) Acts 1939 and 1940

The main provisions of the Emergency Powers (Defence) Act 1939, which was **19–032** passed a week before the outbreak of war with Germany, were as follows: section 1 gave a special power to His Majesty by Order in Council to make such Regulations "as appear to him to be necessary or expedient for securing the public safety, the defence of the realm, the maintenance of public order and the efficient prosecution of any war in which His Majesty may be engaged, and for maintaining supplies and services essential to the life of the community." Without prejudice to the generality of the preceding powers, it specified certain particular matters which might be the subject of Defence Regulations, *viz*.: the

---

[87] [1920] 1 K.B. 829.
[88] (1922) 91 L.J.K.B. 897. *cf. Yoxford and Darsham Farmers' Association Ltd. v. Llewellin* (1946) 62 T.L.R. 347.
[89] (1918) 35 T.L.R. 46, 47 (confirming Darling J. at (1917) 34 T.L.R. 556).

apprehension, trial and punishment of persons offending against the Regulations; the detention of persons whose detention appeared to the Secretary of State to be expedient in the interests of public safety or the defence of the realm; the taking of possession or control of any property or undertaking; the acquisition of any property other than land; the entering and searching of any premises; and the amendment, suspension or modification of any enactment.[90]

Section 2 of the Act of 1939 authorised the Treasury to impose charges in connection with any scheme of control authorised by Defence Regulations, *e.g.* the grant of licences or permits (*cf. Att.-Gen. v. Wilts. United Dairies, ante*); but any such order had to be laid before the Commons and would cease to have effect unless approval within 28 days by a resolution of the House.

19–033   Every Order in Council containing Defence Regulations had to be laid before Parliament, subject to annulment by either House within 28 days.

The Emergency Powers (Defence) Act 1940, passed at a time when invasion seemed to be imminent, allowed Defence Regulations, issued for the purposes prescribed by the Act of 1939, to make provision *"for requiring persons to place themselves, their services, and their property at the disposal of His Majesty."* This very remarkable piece of legislation, which was passed through all its stages in both Houses and received the Royal Assent in one day, described itself as an extension of powers, but it is doubtful whether it did extend the powers already contained in the earlier Act.[91] The Emergency Powers (Defence) (No. 2) Act 1940, which was passed a few months later in order to remove doubts, declared that provision might be made by Defence Regulations "for securing that, where by reason of recent or immediately apprehended enemy action the military situation is such as to require that criminal justice should be administered more speedily than would be practicable by the ordinary Courts, persons, whether or not subject to the Naval Discipline Act, to military law, or to the Air Force Act, may . . . be tried by such special courts, not being courts-martial, as may be so provided."

The Emergency Powers Act 1964, s.2, as we have seen, made permanent the Defence (Armed Forces) Regulations 1939, which authorise the temporary employment of members of the armed forces in agricultural work or other urgent work of national importance. Otherwise the Emergency Laws (Re-enactments and Repeals) Act 1964 repealed the remaining Defence Regulations, re-enacting some of them with modifications.

Emergency powers and personal freedom

19–034   Judicial review of the legality of ministers' acts under legislation conferring emergency powers and of the validity of delegated legislation made under such legislation is subject to the same principles as apply to other cases involving statutory interpretation, which must, of course, now take account of the Human Rights Act 1998.[92] Nonetheless cases dealing with this particular type of legislation cannot safely be taken as authorities in other spheres because of the courts' reluctance to interfere with ministerial decisions when the safety of the state may be at risk.

---

[90] This meant any enactment passed before the Emergency Powers (Defence) Act 1940.
[91] Sir Ivor Jennings suggested that it was rather an act of defiance to the all-conquering Germans which "put into a legal formula the 'blood and tears and sweat' that Mr Churchill had promised as the British contribution to the war effort": *Law and the Constitution* (3rd ed.) pp. xxv–xxvi.
[92] *post* para. 31–005.

In *Liversidge v. Anderson*[93] Regulation 18B(1) of the Defence (General) Regulations issued under the Emergency Powers (Defence) Act 1939 provided that: "If the Secretary of State *has reasonable cause to believe* any person to be of hostile origin or associations . . . and that by reason thereof it is necessary to exercise control over him, he may make an order against that person directing that he be detained." Persons aggrieved by a detention order might make objections to an advisory committee, and it was the duty of the chairman to inform the objector of the grounds on which the order had been made against him. A detention order was made by the Home Secretary against Liversidge (alias Perlzweig) on the ground that he had reasonable cause to believe that Liversidge was a person of hostile associations, and that by reason thereof it was necessary to exercise control over him. Liversidge was accordingly detained in Brixton Prison, and next year he issued a writ against the Home Secretary claiming a declaration that his detention was unlawful and damages for false imprisonment. The Home Secretary did not make any affidavit showing why, or on what information, he had reached his decision, but merely produced the order purporting to be made under Regulation 18B(1).[94] The action proceeded on a claim for particulars of defence: there was no suggestion that the Home Secretary had not acted in good faith; and the House of Lords (Lord Maugham L.C. and Lords Macmillan, Wright and Romer, with Lord Atkin dissenting) held that the order was valid and the Home Secretary's answer sufficient.

Lord Maugham L.C. emphasised the points that this was a matter for executive discretion; the Home Secretary was not acting judicially, his decision must necessarily be based on confidential information, and he was responsible to Parliament. It may be noticed that this last point was not merely a constitutional convention, for the Regulation required the Home Secretary to make a monthly report to Parliament of his exercise of this power. His Lordship further said that the words "if he has reasonable cause to believe" drew the attention of the Home Secretary to the fact that he should personally consider the matter himself: the only requirement was that he must have acted in good faith. The other majority opinions emphasised the facts that these were emergency executive powers, conferred at a time of great national danger on a responsible Minister who was answerable to Parliament, and whose sources of information were confidential on security grounds.

Lord Atkin, in his spirited dissenting judgment,[95] contended that the words "if **19–035** he has reasonable cause" to believe did not mean "if he *thinks* he has reasonable cause": they have an objective meaning and give rise to justiciable issue. He supported his argument by references to the common law and statutory power of arrest, statutes dealing with other criminal matters, and actions at common law for malicious prosecution. His Lordship did not consider that the case of *R. v. Halliday (ante)* was relevant, as in that case (on which he had sat as a member of the Divisional Court) the appellant's contention was that the Regulation was *ultra vires*. Nor was he suggesting that the courts should substitute their opinion

---

[93] [1942] A.C. 206. See R. F. V. Heuston, "*Liversidge v. Anderson* in retrospect" (1970) 86 L.Q.R. 331, and note in (1971) 87 L.Q.R. 161.
[94] *cf. R. v. Home Secretary, ex p. Lees* [1941] 1 K.B. 72 (application for habeas corpus; Court of Appeal held Home Secretary's affidavit sufficient answer).
[95] *ibid.* at pp. 225–247. See further, G. Lewis, *Lord Atkin*, (Butterworths, 1983) pp. 132–57; D.N. Pritt, *Autobiography: From Right to Left* (Lawrence and Wishart 1967). Pritt was counsel for Liversidge. A similar stand had been taken in his dissenting speech by Lord Shaw in *R. v. Halliday, Ex p. Zadig* [1917] A.C. 260.

for that of the Home Secretary as to whether, for example, a person is of hostile origin; the question was, whether the Home Secretary had reasonable cause to believe that he was of hostile origin.

In *Greene v. Home Secretary*[96] the House of Lords dismissed an appeal on an application for habeas corpus arising out of the same regulation. Lord Atkin in this case agreed with his colleagues, as the Home Secretary had filed an affidavit setting out a number of particulars and stating that he had acted on information from responsible and experienced persons.

Both Liversidge and Greene were, in fact, released shortly after these decisions.

Liversidge v. Anderson and *Greene v. Home Secretary* were applied by Asquith J. in *Budd v. Anderson*[97] a case arising out of Regulation 18B(1A). The decision in *Liversidge v. Anderson*, however, met with a mixed reception outside the courts,[98] and we cannot do better than adopt the conclusion of the late Professor Berriedale Keith: "The question is one of great difficulty, but the concurrent view of so many judges leaves little doubt that the decision has been rightly taken on the wording of the regulation."[99]

19–036   In *Nakkuda Ali v. Jayaratne*[1] a strong Privy Council held that *Liversidge v. Anderson* must not be taken to lay down any general rule on the construction of the expression "has reasonable cause to believe." Subsequently *Liversidge v. Anderson* was described by Lord Reid in *Ridge v. Baldwin*[2] as a "very peculiar decision." Lord Diplock in *I.R.C. v. Rossminster Ltd*[3] thought that "the time has come to acknowledge openly that the majority of this House in *Liversidge v. Anderson* were expediently and, at that time, perhaps, excusably, wrong and the dissenting speech of Lord Atkin was right." Lord Scarman, in the same case, said that the ghost of *Liversidge v. Anderson* had been laid to rest by Lord Radcliffe in *Nakkuda Ali v. Jayaratne*.[4] It should not, however, be forgotten that the House of Lords, as evidenced by *McEldowney v. Forde*[5] in construing powers for dealing with emergencies may still give greater scope to ministerial discretion than subsequent judicial criticisms of *Liversidge v. Anderson* might suggest.

---

[96] [1962] A.C. 284. See R. F. V. Heuston in (1971) 87 L.Q.R. 163. The Court of Appeal refused habeas corpus in *R. v. Home Secretary, ex p. Lees* [1941] 1 K.B. 72, in a case arising under Regulation 18B(1A).

[97] [1943] K.B. 642. *cf. R. v. Home Secretary, ex p. Budd* [1942] 2 K.B. 14, where the Court of Appeal held that the Home Secretary must apply himself to each case under the Regulation, and sign the detention order, otherwise the person detained was entitled to release under habeas corpus; but if the procedure is regularised after release, the person may be detained again for the same cause. For a survey of other jurisdictions, see Clark and McCoy, *op. cit.*, Chapter 4.

[98] For: Keith, *Journal of Comparative Legislation* (1942) 3rd Ser., Vol. XXIV, Pt. I, pp. 63–64; Holdsworth (1942) 58 L.Q.R. 1–3; Goodhart, *ibid.* pp. 3–8 and 243–246. Against: Allen, *ibid.* pp. 232–242; Keeton (1942) 5 M.L.R. 162–173; Allen, *Law and Orders* (2nd ed.), App. 1. Neutral: Jennings, *The Law and the Constitution* (3rd ed.), pp. xxx–xxxi. For an account generally of detention and the role of the Security Services, A.W.B. Simpson, *In the Highest Degree Odious: Detention Without Trial in Wartime Britain.*

[99] *The Constitution under Strain* (1942), p. 51.

[1] [1951] A.C. 66. The application for certiorari failed on the ground that the Controller's function was executive and not judicial.

[2] [1964] A.C. 40.

[3] [1981] A.C. 952, 1011.

[4] At p. 1025. See also *Att.-Gen of St. Christopher v. Reynolds* [1980] A.C. 637, PC.

[5] [1971] A.C. 632, Lord Diplock and Lord Pearce dissenting; *post* para. 31–005. Further evidence is to be found in *McKee v. Chief Constable for Northern Ireland* [1984] 1 W.L.R. 1358. (H.L.) (Power of arrest under anti-terrorist legislation: question is state of mind of constable, not reasonableness of his belief).

Other war legislation

Legislation for the purposes of the last war was mostly carried out by means   **19–037**
of Defence Regulations, but Acts of Parliament were necessary where: (i) what
was wanted to be done was outside the scope of the Emergency Powers
(Defence) Acts 1939 and 1940, or (ii) the provisions were not to be limited to the
war period, or (iii) it was necessary to raise money. The practice with regard to
the last was for the Government to ask Parliament periodically for votes of
£1,000,000,000, while for security reasons the estimates for each of the service
and supply departments were put at the nominal figure of £100.

Many of the Emergency Acts[6] passed on account of the war contained a
provision to the effect that they were to continue in force until such date as His
Majesty might by Order in Council declare to be the date on which the emergency which was the occasion of the passing of the Act should have ended. In
Willcock v. Muckle[7] it was held that there must be an order in Council declaring
the end of the emergency in relation to the particular Act.

The reluctance of the executive to abandon the powers contained in such
legislation was revealed in the Scott Inquiry Report[8] which drew attention to
continued reliance on the Import, Export and Customs Powers (Defence) Act
1939 until, finally, the Import and Export Control Act 1990 removed the reference in the 1939 Act to "the emergency which was the occasion for its passing"
and so made permanent an Act which should long before have been terminated
by Order in Council.

The dearth of judicial decisions after 1939 on the nature and extent of the
prerogative in time of war is due to the fact that the Emergency Powers (Defence)
Acts and the other emergency statutes mentioned covered practically everything
that the Government would want to do, except for taxation and the acquisition (as
distinct from the taking possession) of land.[9]

III. The Security Services

Although it has been suggested that the covert gathering of intelligence can be   **19–038**
traced back for over three thousand years to the sending of secret agents by
Moses to spy out the land of Canaan,[10] the origins of the modern British
intelligence services date to the last quarter of the nineteenth century when the
War Office, in 1873, and the Admiralty, in 1886, established departments to
obtain information on military and naval developments in Germany. In 1883 the
Special Irish Branch was established as part of the Metropolitan Police; in 1887
it became the Special Branch of the Metropolitan Police. In the twentieth century
there evolved MI5 (the Security Service) which dealt with internal issues of
espionage and state security and MI6 (Secret Intelligence Service) which dealt
with intelligence gathering outside the United Kingdom. Following the lead of
the Metropolitan Police, each police force established its own Special Branch.

[6] See Carr, *Concerning English Administrative Law*, Chap. 3, for the spate of legislative activity in
the first week of the war.
[7] [1951] 2 K.B. 844.
[8] *Inquiry into the Export of Defence Equipment to Iraq*, 1995–1996, H.C. 115.
[9] *cf.* Requisitioned Land and War Works Acts 1945 and 1948; Land Powers (Defence) Act 1958. And
cf. Burmah Oil Co case, *ante*, para. 15–017.
[10] Numbers, Chap. 13, cited by C. Andrew, *Secret Service* (1985).

Until the last quarter of the twentieth century MI5 and MI6 operated on a non-statutory basis, their very existence hardly officially acknowledged. A central part of the government's intelligence gathering activities was, of course, given considerable publicity by the litigation following the banning of trades union activities at the Government Communications Headquarters: *Council of Civil Service Unions v. Minister of Civil Service.*[11] Legislation to put these services on a statutory footing was passed as a result of the decision of the European Court of Human Rights in *Harman and Hewitt v. United Kingdom.*[12] The Security Service Act 1989 provided that "there shall continue to be a Security Service" whose function is to be the protection of national security, in particular its protection against threats from espionage, terrorism and sabotage, from the activities of agents of foreign powers and from actions intended to overthrow or undermine parliamentary democracy by political, industrial or violent means. The Security Service was also given the responsibility of safeguarding the economic well-being of the United Kingdom against threats posed by the actions or intentions of persons outside the British Islands. These functions have been extended by the Security Services Act 1996, the Police Act 1997 and the Regulation of Investigatory Powers Act 2000 to enable the Security Service to act in support of the police in the prevention and detection of serious crime. The Intelligence Services Act 1994 similarly "recognised" the continued existence of a Secret Intelligence Service whose role related to obtaining information relating to persons outside the British Islands in the interests of national security with particular reference to defence and foreign policies or in the interests of the economic well-being of the United Kingdom or in support of the prevention or detection of serious crime. The 1994 Act also recognised the existence of the Government Communications Headquarters and made explicit its role in monitoring electromagnetic, acoustic and other emissions and in the field of cryptography.

19–039 As further evidence of the changing climate the names of the Directors of the services became public and, indeed, the former Director of MI5, Dame Stella Rimington, has announced plans to publish her memoirs. The locations of the headquarters of the services similarly were formally acknowledged—new and very visible buildings in London for MI5 and MI6 and a new home for GCHQ at Benhall, near Cheltenham.[13] Less desirable publicity has, of course, been attracted to their activities by the publication of the memoirs of Peter Wright, leading to the *Spycatcher* litigation,[14] the further memoirs of Richard Tomlinson and, most recently, criminal proceedings against David Shayler, a former member of MI5 on charges of breaches of the Official Secrets Act.

The Acts of 1989 and 1994 provided a statutory basis for the surveillance activities of both security services[15] and a system of control via a need for authorisation before exercising these powers, a tribunal to which complaints of misuse of powers could be made and annual reports by a Commissioner to the Prime Minister which would be laid before Parliament after the deletion of any

---

[11] [1985] A.C. 374.

[12] [1989] 14 E.H.R.R. 657.

[13] MI5 at Thames House and MI6 at Vauxhall Cross. The costs of fitting out both buildings exceeded estimates by £300m. GCHQ's new home has so far cost £400m, against an original estimate of £20m.

[14] *post* para. 25–020.

[15] And so made glaringly anomalous the exercise of similar powers by the police without statutory authority which was exposed by *R. v. Khan* [1996] 2 Cr.App.R. 440, HL. Legislation followed: the Police Act 1997.

material required by considerations of national security.[16] The efficacy of this régime as a guarantee against abuse of an individual's rights was open to question.[17] A new basis for the exercise and regulation of powers of surveillance and investigation has been introduced by the Regulation of Investigatory Powers Act 2000, the provisions of which are discussed in Chapter 26.[18]

A degree of Parliamentary accountability was introduced by section 10 of the **19–040** Intelligence Services Act 1994 which established the Intelligence and Security Committee, composed of nine members drawn from both Houses of Parliament with the responsibility of examining the expenditure, administration and policy of the security services and G.C.H.Q. The Committee lacks the powers of a Select Committee. It reports to the Prime Minister who must lay its report before Parliament but with the deletion of any material prejudicial to the functioning of the services.

The Committee's lack of effectiveness is clear from its Interim Report for 2000–2001[19] in which it points out that the Cabinet Committee on the Intelligence Services has not met despite an assurance from the Prime Minister that it would do so while the Chief Secretary to the Treasury continues to refuse to talk to the Committee and the government continues to refuse to give any breakdown of the allocation of funds to specific agencies within the overall role for the Intelligence Services. Not merely were the Tribunals established under the 1989 and 1994 Acts of limited efficacy in terms of jurisdiction: the Committee reveals that they were so deprived of resources that they lacked the staff to open the mail which they received, let alone deal with complaints. Meanwhile the Committee continues to look at the systems of oversight of intelligence services in countries such as America, Australia, Canada and New Zealand which operate through an Inspector General.

IV. TERRORISM

In earlier[20] and later[21] chapters we discuss threats posed to the state by treason **19–041** and sedition, both topics which reflect the realities of earlier centuries of constitutional law. Terrorism is a phenomenon of more recent years[22] which poses the dilemma of how to take effective steps to curtail its evils without, at the same time, destroying the very liberties which the law is seeking to protect.[23] Article 17 of the European Convention on Human Rights provides that nothing in the Convention creates any right to engage in any activity or perform any act aimed at the destruction of any of the rights and freedoms contained in the Convention.

---

[16] The two Acts followed the model of the Interception of Communications Act 1985.

[17] H. Fenwick, *Civil Rights* (Longman, 2000) Chap. 8. The author concludes that the systems for dealing with complaints share characteristics which "render them almost irrelevant as a means of providing oversight" (p. 313).

[18] Fenwick, *op. cit.*, Chaps 9 and 10.

[19] Cm 3126. Its effectiveness is unlikely to be increased by the appointment, following the election in June 2001, of the former Government Chief Whip to the position of Chair of the Committee.

[20] Chap. 14.

[21] Chap. 25.

[22] But not unknown in earlier times, as shown by cases such as *Re Meunier* [1894] 2 Q.B. 415 or novels such as Joseph Conrad's *The Secret Agent*. See George Woodcock, *Anarchism* (2nd ed., 1986).

[23] H. Fenwick, *Civil Rights* (Longman, 2000) Chap. 3.

Nonetheless it recognises certain rights are not subject to any restriction: no-one shall be subjected to torture or to inhuman or degrading treatment or punishment (Article 3). But other rights, as will be seen in Chapter 22, may be restricted on grounds such as the protection of public order and states may, by Article 15, derogate from their obligations under the Convention "in time of war or other public emergency threatening the life of the nation ... to the extent strictly required by the exigencies of the situation, provided that such measures are not inconsistent with its other obligations under international law."

Terrorism often raises issues of extra-territorial jurisdiction, and international agreements to suppress a particular type of activity, for example, the hi-jacking of aircraft or to simplify extradition proceedings between the requesting state and the state where the alleged terrorist has taken refuge.[24] All these matters are reflected in a wide range of United Kingdom statutes—for example the Aviation Security Act 1982, the Taking of Hostages Act 1982 and the Aviation and Maritime Security Act 1990. The Suppression of Terrorism Act 1978 amended the law of extradition in the light of the European Convention on the Suppression of Terrorism. The Terrorism Act 2000 contains provisions amending the Extradition Act 1989 and enabling the United Kingdom to ratify United Nations Conventions for the Suppression of Terrorist Bombings and the Suppression of the Financing of Terrorism (Sections 62–64).

19–042   The original impetus for anti-terrorist legislation at the end of the last century was provided by the situation prevailing in Northern Ireland which led, *inter alia* to the enactment of the Prevention of Terrorism (Temporary Provisions) Act 1974.[25] Later, similarly named, Acts in 1976, 1984 and 1989 extended anti-terrorist provisions to the whole of the United Kingdom while further powers were included in other statutes of which the last, rushed through Parliament in two days, was the Criminal Justice (Terrorism and Conspiracy) Act 1998.

The current legislation is to be found in the Terrorism Act 2000,[26] which contains complicated transitional provisions in relation to the earlier statutes.[27] In accordance with the requirements of the Human Rights Act 1998, section 19, ministers in both Houses certified that the Act is compatible with the terms of the European Convention on Human Rights.[28] As will be seen, however, a number of provisions in the legislation may be open to question on the ground of incompatibility with the Convention.

Whereas earlier legislation required periodic renewal by Parliament, the 2000 Act represents a belief in the need for permanent anti-terrorist legislation. Section 126, however, requires the laying before Parliament of an annual report on the working of the Act.

Terrorism is defined in section 1 as the use or threat of action for the *purposes* set out in subsection (1) when the action is of the *kind* set out in subsection (2). To fall within subsection (1) the use or threat of action must satisfy a twofold test: it must (i) be designed to influence the government or to intimidate the public or a section of the public, and (ii) be made for the purpose of advancing a political, religious or ideological cause.

---

[24] Chap. 23.
[25] Chap. 5.
[26] On the background to the legislation, see the report of Lord Lloyd of Berwick, *Inquiry into legislation against terrorism*, Cm 3420 (1996) and the White Paper, *Legislation Against Terrorism*, Cm 4178.
[27] s.2 and Sched. 1; Pt VII.
[28] *post*, para. 22–016, for the need for and the effect of such ministerial statements.

The *kind* of action defined in subsection (2) is any that (a) involves serious **19–043** violence against a person, or (b) serious damage to property, or (c) endangers a person's life other than that of the person committing the action, or (d) creates a serious risk to the health or safety of the public or a section of the public, or (e) is designed seriously to interfere with or seriously to disrupt an electronic system. The use of firearms or explosives in circumstances falling with in subsection (2) is terrorism if it satisfies subsection (1)(c)—the advancement of a political, religious or ideological cause—whether or not it also satisfies subsection 1(b)— influencing the government or intimidating the public or a section of a public: subsection (3). Subsection 4 explicitly provides that all the elements of the definition of terrorism are to be given extraterritorial effect.[29] In relation to later provisions of the Act, subsection (5) provides that any reference to action taken for the purposes of terrorism includes a reference to action taken for the benefit of a proscribed organisation (that is an organisation falling within section 3). A terrorist is defined for the purposes of Part V of the Act (which confers on the police counter-terrorist powers) as a person who has committed any of a number of offences under the Act or is or has been concerned in the commission, preparation or instigation of acts of terrorism (section 40).[30]

Part II of the Act deals with the proscribing of organisations and offences connected with membership of proscribed organisations. Under section 3, an organisation is proscribed if it is listed in Schedule 2 of the Act or if it is added to the list by the Secretary of State if it believes it is concerned in terrorism, as defined in the wide terms of subsection 5 which after listing such specific forms of being concerned in terrorism as committing or participating in acts of terrorism or prepares for terrorism goes on to conclude "or is otherwise concerned in terrorism". The proscription of organisations has a long history in Northern Ireland.[31] Modern anti-terrorist legislation contained distinct provisions for Northern Ireland and Great Britain. The Terrorism Act provides a system for the whole of the United Kingdom and extends it to all terrorist organisations, not merely those concerned with terrorism in Northern Ireland—although only such bodies appear in the original list forming Schedule 2. Any organisation which has been proscribed, or any person affected by the organisation's proscription may apply to the Secretary of State to remove the organisation from the list: section 4. Where an application is unsuccessful, the applicant may appeal to the Pro-scribed Organisations Appeal Commission, established by section 5, from which there is a further right of appeal to the Court of Appeal under section 6.[32] The constitution and procedure of the Commission are set out in Schedule 3. These provisions are intended to ensure that the proscription and (in the language of the sidenote to section 5) deproscription procedures are compatible with the Human Rights Act 1998.[33] Whether they are held to be so, or not, Schedule 3 makes it clear that the Commission does not function like a conventional court. Full particulars of the reason for proscription or refusal to deproscribe may be

---

[29] Thus eliminating any doubt arising from the normal presumption of non-extraterroriality: *ante* para. 3–020.

[30] s.11 (membership of a proscribed organisation); s.12 (inviting support for a proscribed organisa-tion); ss.15–18 (fund-raising offences); s.54 (weapons training); ss.56–63 (directing, possessing, inciting offences).

[31] See, for example, *McEldowney v. Forde* [1971] A.C. 632, HL.

[32] Or, as appropriate, the Court of Session or the Court of Appeal in Northern Ireland.

[33] See further the detailed, consequential provisions of s.9. Evidence given in the course of depro-scription proceedings is not admissible in proceedings relating to certain statutory offences connected with membership of terrorist organisations: s.10.

withheld from the organisation or applicant and from any person representing such parties; parties and their representatives may be excluded from all or part of proceedings (paragraph 4(4)). It is open to question whether these provisions satisfy Article 6 of the Convention.[34]

19–044   Part II creates three criminal offences relating to proscribed organisations; membership (section 11): inviting support (beyond the provision of money or property) (section 12) and the wearing in a public place of an item of clothing or the wearing or carrying of an article so as to arouse reasonable suspicion of membership of a proscribed organisation (section 13).[35] These sections are similar to those familiar in earlier legislation such as the various Prevention of Terrorism (Temporary Provisions) Acts and the Northern Ireland (Emergency Provisions) Acts.

The later Parts of the Act deal with offences relating to terrorism generally, as defined in section 1, and grant wide powers to the police in conducting terrorist investigations and engaging in counter-terrorist activities. Part III deals with terrorist property, that is property likely to be used for the purposes of terrorism (including any resources of a proscribed organisation) and the proceeds of the commission of acts of terrorism (section 14). Subsequent sections render criminal the raising of funds for the purposes of terrorism (section 14), the use or possession of property for such purposes (section 16), and money laundering (section 18). Courts may, after convictions under sections 15–18 make forfeiture orders (section 23). Cash which is being taken from or brought into the United Kingdom may be seized by an authorised officer if he has reasonable grounds that it is intended to be used for the purposes of terrorism, forms part of the resources of a proscribed organisation or is terrorist property within the meaning of section 14 (section 25). Provision is made for detention of the property and ultimately forfeiture by court order (sections 26–31). Part IV empowers the police to designate "cordoned areas" for the purpose of carrying out terrorist investigations as defined in section 32. Extensive powers of search in such areas are conferred by section 37 and Schedule 5. Part V deals with counter-terrorist powers. Section 41, for example, provides for arrest without warrant of a person reasonably suspected of being a terrorist. Section 42 authorises searching premises for the purpose of arresting a person reasonably suspected of being a terrorist. Section 43 authorises the stopping and searching of anyone whom a police constable suspects to be a terrorist to discover whether he has in his possession anything which may constitute evidence that he is a terrorist. Powers of stopping and searching vehicles or persons in designated areas are conferred by section 44.

19–045   Those provisions may raise questions in relation to the European Convention. Article 5, for example, refers to arrest on reasonable suspicion of having committed an offence. But the 2000 Act does not make "being a terrorist" an offence in itself.[36] Similarly rights of search may infringe Article 8 which protects the right to respect for one's home and private life.[37] The powers of detention conferred by section 41(3) have been drafted to require judicial approval for any

---

[34] *post* para. 22–036.

[35] *cf.* Public Order Act 1936, s.1; *O'Moran v. D.P.P.* [1975] Q.B. 864; *post* para. 27–040. The Public Order Act uses the word uniform in the body of the section. In the Terrorism Act uniform is used only as a sidenote.

[36] A point made by Lord Lloyd of Berwick during debates on the Bill in the House of Lords. H.L.Debs. vol. 613, col. 676. On Article 5, see later, para. 22–033.

[37] *post*, para. 22–039.

extension after the initial period of 48 hours, up to the maximum period of 7 and as a response to the decision in *Brogan v. UK* which held a system of detention dependent on authorisation by the executive to be in breach of Article 5(3).[38]

Part VI creates a number of specific offences. Section 54 relates to training or providing instruction in the making of firearms, explosives or chemicals, biological or nuclear weapons, or receiving training or instruction in using such weapons. It is for the defence to prove that such training or instruction was wholly for a purpose other than assisting or participating in an act of terrorism. The compatibility of this shifting of the burden of proof from the prosecution to the defence will be considered later in connection with section 118 of the Act. A similar shift is to be found in section 57 (possession of article for the commission of an act of terrorism) and section 58 (collecting or recording information of a kind likely to be useful in the commission of an act of terrorism). Sections 59–61 relate to inciting terrorism outside the United Kingdom.[39] Sections 62 and 63 give jurisdiction to the courts of the legal systems in the United Kingdom over acts committed abroad which fall within the terms of the United Nations Conventions for the Suppression of Terrorist Bombings and the Suppression of the Financing of Terrorism.

A number of sections of the Act require the defendant to prove a defence to an **19–046** offence arising, for example, from possession of articles for the commission of terrorism (section 57). Article 6(2) of the European Convention on Human Rights recognises the right to be presumed innocent until proved guilty. The shifting of the burden of proof to the defence in criminal proceedings raises questions about the meaning and scope of the Convention guarantee. Section 112 of the Act is intended to strike an acceptable balance between the presumption of innocence and placing on the defence the burden of disproving a criminal inference from facts proved by the prosecution. Where it is a defence for a person charged with an offence to prove a particular matter it is only necessary to adduce evidence which is sufficient to raise an issue with respect to that matter. The court shall then assume that the defence is satisfied unless the prosecution proves beyond reasonable doubt that it is not: subsections 1 and 2.[40] In those provisions where the court makes an assumption unless a particular matter is proved or may accept a fact as sufficient evidence unless a particular matter is proved, the defence again is only required to adduce evidence sufficient to raise an issue— unless the prosecution can disprove the issue beyond reasonable doubt: subsections 3 and 4.[41]

Section 118 had no counterpart in earlier legislation and is a response to dicta *R. v. D.P.P. ex p. Kebilene*[42] where the House of Lords refused to interfere with a decision of the Director of Public Prosecutions to consent to the prosecution of the applicants under section 16A of the Prevention of Terrorism (Temporary

---

[38] (1989) 11 E.H.R.R. 177. As a result the United Kingdom entered a derogation (which was upheld in *Brannigan and McBride v. UK* (1999) 17 E.H.R.R. 539, *post* para. 22–026). As a result of the new procedure the Government has felt able to withdraw the derogation.

[39] In s.59 (inciting terrorism overseas) subs. 5 deserves special mention: "Nothing in this section imposes criminal liability on any person acting on behalf of, or holding office under, the Crown."

[40] s.12(4), defence to prove no reasonable cause to believe address supporting proscribed organisation would be made; s.39(5)(a), disclosure of information; s.54(5) instruction or training in weapons; s.57(2), possession of articles; s.58(3) collection of information.

[41] This refers to two sections in Pt VII, which relates to Northern Ireland: s.77, possession of article in circumstances such as to constitute an offence under certain statutes; s.103, terrorist information.

[42] [2000] 2 A.C. 326, HL.

Provisions) Act 1989 (the terms of which are re-enacted in the Terrorism Act 2000, section 57). The House expressed views, in the event the trial took place, of the possibility of interpreting section 16A in a way which was consistent wit the European Convention's recognition of the presumption of innocence. Contrary to the Divisional Court their Lordships thought section 16A could be interpreted as being consistent wit the Convention if it were read, not as requiring he defendant to *prove* his innocent possession but to put on the defendant the obligation to produce evidence which raised a reasonable doubt on the issue. Section 118 clearly attempts to enact the substance of the dicta in *Kebilene*.

PART IV

JUSTICE AND POLICE

CHAPTER 20

THE ADMINISTRATION OF JUSTICE

In much of the earlier part of this book it has been convenient, and often **20–001** correct, to refer to the British Constitution or to the United Kingdom without adverting to the existence of separate legal systems in England, Scotland and Northern Ireland. In this chapter, however, it is impossible to ignore the fact that the legal systems of England and Scotland developed separately in the centuries before 1707 and have remained largely distinct since then.[1] Although the Scotland Act 1998 will ensure that the systems remain distinct, the single system of courts in Scotland: "has to be made serve both the devolved Scottish and reserved UK interests".[2] The differences between the legal systems of England and Northern Ireland are less marked. Ireland it has been said, was the scene of "The First Adventure of the Common Law"[3] and over 800 years the law developed along similar lines in both countries.

The main emphasis of this chapter will be on the English legal system and while important distinctions between the systems will be referred to, it must not be assumed that any statement is equally true of the three parts of the United Kingdom unless such is said to be the case.

I. PREROGATIVE AND ADMINISTRATION OF JUSTICE

The administration of justice is one of the prerogatives of the Crown, but it is **20–002** a prerogative that has long been exercisable only through duly appointed courts and judges.[4] The various courts and their jurisdictions are now almost entirely on a statutory basis. The Sovereign is "the fountain of justice" and general conservator of the peace. "By the fountain of justice," Blackstone explains,[5] "the law does not mean the *author or original*, but only the *distributor. . . .* He is not the spring, but the reservoir; from whence right and equity are conducted, by a thousand channels, to every individual." In the contemplation of the law the Sovereign is always present in court and therefore cannot be non-suited. Instances are recorded of Plantagenet Kings personally dealing with criminal cases, and Edward IV sat with his judges for three days to see how they did their work; but the personal interference of the Sovereign with the judges was infrequent, and Coke told James I that although he might be present in court he could not give an opinion (*Prohibitions del Roy*[6]). Criminal proceedings, whether

---

[1] See in particular Articles XIX and XVIII of the Union with Scotland Act 1807 *ante*, para. 4–006.

[2] C.M.G. Himsworth, "Securing the tenure of Scottish judges: a somewhat academic exercise", [1999] P.L. 14, at p. 14.

[3] W.J. Johnston, "The First Adventure of the Common Law", (1920) 36 L.Q.R. 9; A.G. Donaldson, *Some Comparative Aspects of Irish Law* (1957) Chap. 1 and *passim*; F. E. Moran, "The Migration of the Common Law: The Republic of Ireland", (1960) 76 L.Q.R. 69.

[4] *Prohibitions del Roy* (1607) 12 Co.Rep. 63.

[5] Bl.Comm.I, 266.

[6] (1607) 12 Co.Rep. 63, 64. And see Holdsworth, *History of English Law* (5th ed.), Vol. 1, pp. 194, 207.

initiated by the Crown or a private individual, are conducted on behalf of the Crown and indictments are in the Queen's name. Claim forms commencing civil actions are not issued in the Queen's name,[7] and although judgment is executed in her name, the Crown has no control over the conduct of civil cases. The prerogative power to create courts is now virtually useless, because, first (if Coke was right), such courts could not administer equity or any other system except the common law; and secondly, the expense of maintaining such courts would require parliamentary authority. For practical purposes, then, the following may be regarded as the most significant of the existing prerogatives relating to the administration of justice.

The maxim "the King can do no wrong" extended to the Sovereign in his public capacity and in effect to the government generally. The common law rule that no civil action might be brought against the Crown must now be read subject to the important exceptions contained in the Crown Proceedings Act 1947; although even then there are savings with regard to prerogative powers, such as defence and the training of the forces. The Crown still has procedural privileges with regard to disclosure and interrogatories, and no execution may be levied against the Crown.[8]

20–003 Time does not run against the Crown at common law. *Nullum tempus occurrit regi.*[9] But there are numerous statutes providing that specified criminal proceedings must be taken within a limited period; and the Crown Proceedings Act 1947 expressly makes the Crown bound by statutes limiting the time within which civil proceedings must be commenced, *e.g.* Limitation Acts.

The Attorney-General has a discretion by his fiat (*nolle prosequi*) to discontinue any criminal proceedings on indictment, whether the proceedings were initiated by the Crown or a private prosecutor.[10] He is answerable *ex post facto* to Parliament for the exercise of this power, although it is seldom questioned. The wide statutory powers given to the Director of Public Prosecutions by the Prosecution of Offences Act 1985 to discontinue criminal proceedings[11] means that this power is seldom used.[12] A *nolle prosequi* does not have the effect of an acquittal, although if further proceedings were brought the Attorney-General could enter a *nolle prosequi* again.

The prerogative of mercy[13]

20–004 The Sovereign, acting in England and Wales by the Home Secretary,[14] may pardon offences of a public nature, which are prosecuted by the Crown.[15] Although it is a personal power of the Sovereign, it was described by Lord Slynn

---

[7] In 1999, claim forms replaced writs, which had ceased to be issued in the name of the Crown in 1980.

[8] *post*, Chap. 33.

[9] *Magdalen College Case* (1615) 11 Co.Rep. 66b.

[10] *R. v. Allen* (1862) 1 B. & S. 850. See J. Ll.J. Edwards, *The Law Officers of the Crown* (1964), pp. 227–237.

[11] *post*, para. 20–015.

[12] It was used in 1998 to stop the trial of Richard Gee J. who had been accused of a £1m fraud.

[13] C.H. Rolph, *The Queen's Pardon* (1979). A.T.H. Smith, "The Prerogative of Mercy, The Power of Pardon and Criminal Justice", [1983] P.L. 398; C.H.W. Gane, "The Effect of a Pardon in Scots Law", [1980] J.R. 18.

[14] In Scotland and Northern Ireland, pardons are granted on the advice of the respective Secretaries of State.

[15] Although this is the traditional formulation of the extent of the prerogative it has been suggested that there are no legal obstacles to the pardoning power being exercised after a private prosecution. A.T.H. Smith, *op. cit., supra*, p. 409.

as, "part of the whole constitutional process of conviction, sentence and the carrying out of the sentence."[16] Since 1997 the Home Secretary may seek the assistance of the Criminal Cases Review Commission in connection with the exercise of this power; in addition the Commission can suggest to the Home Secretary that he should exercise the prerogative of mercy.[17] A full or free pardon removes all "pains penalties and punishments whatsoever" ensuing from a conviction but does not eliminate the conviction itself which can only be quashed by a court.[18] In addition to a full pardon it is possible to grant a posthumous pardon, to partially remit the penalty imposed, or to grant a conditional pardon whereby a lesser penalty is imposed.[19]

For many years the view was that the exercise of the prerogative was not subject to judicial review: "Mercy is not the subject of legal rights. It begins where legal rights end."[20] In *R. v. Secretary of State for the Home Department, ex p. Bentley*[21] the Divisional Court suggested that review of the prerogative of mercy was possible for error of law. The Home Secretary in refusing a posthumous exercise of the prerogative of mercy had applied the practice of previous Home Secretaries that a free pardon should only be granted in cases where the convicted individual was both technically and morally innocent. The court concluded that he had made an error of law in not considering the alternative forms of pardon available, and invited him to reconsider his decision in the light of the court's conclusion that a posthumous conditional pardon, retrospectively annulling the sentence of death, would be possible.[22] In *Reckley v. Minister of Public Safety (No. 2)*,[23] *Bentley* was distinguished and it was held that the exercise of the prerogative of mercy by the Governor-General of the Bahamas in a death sentence case was not amenable to judicial review. However in *Lewis v. Attorney General*[24] *Reckley* was not followed, and the majority of the Privy Council accepted that the prerogative of mercy was capable of judicial review, and that the rules of natural justice applied to the exercise of this prerogative power. The Privy Council accepted that the exercise of the prerogative of mercy involved an exceptional breadth of discretion, but did not consider that it was inconsistent with that discretion to require proper procedures to be followed.[25]

[16] *Lewis. v. Attorney-General of Jamaica* [2001] 2 A.C. 50; [2000] 3 W.L.R. 1785 at p. 1804.

[17] Criminal Appeal Act 1995, s.16.

[18] *R. v. Foster* [1985] Q.B. 115, CA. The quashing of a conviction does not operate as a declaration of a defendant's innocence: *R. v. McIlkenny and others* 93 Cr.App.R. 287, CA.

[19] There are certain restrictions to granting a pardon: it may not be pleaded as a bar to impeachment (Act of Settlement 1700) *cf. Danby's Case* (1679) 11 St.Tr. 599; the penalties prescribed by the Habeas Corpus Act 1679 for sending a prisoner out of the realm cannot be remitted; a third party cannot be deprived of his rights, *Thomas v. Sorrell* (1674) Vaughan 330.

[20] *De Freitas v. Benny* [1976] A.C. 239, 247, *per* Lord Diplock; *dicta* in *Council of Civil Service Unions v. Minister for the Civil Service* [1985] A.C. 374.

[21] [1994] Q.B. 349, and see Hare, (1994) 53 C.L.J. 4.

[22] The court had declined to make a formal order against the Home Secretary; the Home Secretary accepted its invitation to grant Bentley a partial posthumous pardon, recognising in effect that he should not have been executed. The conviction was eventually quashed by the Court of Appeal, *Derek William Bentley (Deceased)* [2001] 1 Cr.App.R. 307.

[23] [1996] A.C. 239, PC.

[24] [2000] 3 W.L.R. 1785; [2001] 2 A.C. 50.

[25] See also *Burt v. Governor-General* [1992] 3 N.Z.L.R. 672. The Privy Council declined to follow *de Freitas v. Benny* [1976] A.C. 239, PC.

20–005   Pardons also used to be granted before conviction in order to guarantee immunity from prosecution to Crown witnesses. There is no reason to believe that such a prerogative no longer exists.[26]

The prerogative power of pardon exists to remedy the miscarriages of justice which must occur from time to time in any legal system. Such occasions should be exceptional. The first safeguards against the conviction of the innocent are to be found in the rules of evidence and procedure to be applied in criminal trials. Further protection is given by statutory rights of appeal to higher courts. Dissatisfaction with the system dealing with alleged cases of wrongful conviction[27] and a spate of miscarriage of justice cases[28] lead to the establishment of a Royal Commission on Criminal Justice which reported in 1993.[29] Among the recommendations made by the Royal Commission and accepted by the Government was the establishment of a Criminal Cases Review Commission (CCRC) independent of the court structure which could consider and investigate allegations of miscarriages of justice. The CCRC was established by the Criminal Appeal Act 1995, and came into existence in 1997. It took over the power previously exercised by the Home Secretary to refer possible miscarriages of justice cases back to the Court of Appeal.[30] In addition it has power in certain circumstances to refer cases to the Crown Court (section 13). The CCRC can act on its own initiative or after an application by or on behalf of the convicted person. However there is evidence that the CCRC is under-resourced and under-funded, casting doubt on its effectiveness.[31] The 1995 Act also amended the Court of Appeal's powers when dealing with appeals against convictions.

Appointment of judges

20–006   The appointment of judges by the sovereign will be considered below[32] in the context of the discussion of judicial independence.

II. The Courts

20–007   In states with written constitutions it may be a matter of great moment whether a particular body which has power to deal with certain matters or disputes is a "court" exercising "judicial powers". It is common for written constitutions to provide that only courts established under the constitution or by a special

---

[26] Prerogative powers are not lost by disuse: *ante*, para. 15–04. Immunity from the risk of prosecution for treason was granted to Bishop Muzurewa and Mr Ian Smith when they attended the constitutional conference on Rhodesia in London in 1979 by the making of the Southern Rhodesia (Immunity for Persons attending Meetings and Consultations) Order 1979 (S.I. No. 820), p. 2, under powers conferred by the Southern Rhodesia Act 1965: see J.Ll.J. Edwards, *The Attorney General, Politics and the Public Interest* (1984), p. 475. The Attorney-General has said of the undertaking given with respect to statements of evidence given at the Saville Inquiry into the events of "Bloody Sunday" that it is not an immunity, see www.bloody-sunday-inquiry-org.uk.

[27] Sixth Report, Home Affairs Committee of the House of Commons, *Miscarriages of Justice* (1981–82; H.C. 421); Government Reply Cmnd. 8856 (1983).

[28] See Joshua Rozenberg, "Miscarriages of Justice", in *Criminal Justice under Stress* (Stockdale and Casale eds, 1993).

[29] Cmnd. 2263.

[30] *e.g.* the case of *Bentley op.cit.*, note 24.

[31] See remarks in *R. v. Secretary of State for the Home Dept, ex p. Simms* [2000] A.C. 115 at p. 128 and in *Arthur J.S. Hall v. Simons* [2000] 3 All E.R. 673, HL at 681.

[32] *ante* para. 12–026.

legislative procedure can exercise judicial power. In the United Kingdom the question whether a body is a court or not is most likely to arise when there is a doubt about whether its activities are protected by the law of contempt, whether its members are entitled to absolute privilege under the law of defamation and whether they are immune from liabilities for errors they have committed in performing their duties.[33] The difficulties in answering such questions are illustrated by *Attorney-General v. BBC*[34] where the House of Lords considered whether a local valuation court, which determined appeals from the rating assessments of valuation officers, was a court to which the law of contempt applied. The House of Lords held that it was not such a body but their Lordships gave various reasons for their conclusions. Viscount Dilhorne, Lord Fraser and Lord Scarman thought that it was a court, but one discharging administrative functions, not a court of law and only the latter type of court was within the law of contempt. Lord Salmon was prepared to hold that it was an "inferior court" but the law of contempt did not extend to "the host of modern inferior courts and tribunals". Lord Edmund-Davies concluded that the valuation court was not, despite its name, a court at all. There is, as Lord Edmund-Davies said, no sure guide, no unmistakable hall-mark by which a court may unerringly be identified. (The problem will be discussed later in Chapter 30). Various features have been suggested as the means of distinguishing courts from other bodies. While, as we have seen, there is no unmistakable hall-mark, the more of these features possessed by a particular institution the less likelihood there is of its not being regarded a court. For our present purposes some of the more important features, all of which are possessed by the courts considered in the following pages, are that:

(1) The tribunal is established by the State, as opposed, for example, to an arbitral tribunal established by the parties.

(2) It usually decides a dispute between two parties.

(3) Its decision is on the basis of evidence given to it by the parties.

(4) The hearing of a dispute takes place in public unless of national security or public decency.

(5) Its decision is on the basis of law and legal rights.

(6) Its decision is final, subject only to an appeal to a higher court.

The name of a tribunal does not necessarily settle whether it is a court: the Employment Appeal Tribunal, for instance, is a superior court of record.[35] Nor must the members of a court be legally qualified, as evidenced in England by the magistrates' courts. The fact that a body is exercising a judicial function and does so in the public interest, does not mean that it is part of the judicial system of the state.[36]

[33] See *post*, para. 20–041.
[34] [1981] A.C. 303. See also *R. v. Cripps, ex p. Muldoon* [1984] Q.B. 68, CA. (Is local election court an "inferior court"?)
[35] Employment Tribunals Act 1996, s.20; *Pickering v. Liverpool Daily Post and Echo Newspapers plc and others* [1991] 2 A.C. 370, where it was held that a mental health tribunal was a court for the purpose of the law on contempt of court.
[36] *General Medical Council v. British Broadcasting Corporation* [1998] 1 W.L.R. 1573, CA, where it was held that the Professional Conduct Committee of the General Medical Council was not a court.

The United Kingdom

20–008   Although within the United Kingdom there are three separate systems of courts, two courts are shared by all three systems.

The House of Lords has appellate jurisdiction over the three systems although in the case of Scotland, appeal lies only on civil matters.

The Judicial Committee of the Privy Council[37] has jurisdiction under the Government of Wales Act 1998, the Scotland Act 1998 and the Northern Ireland Act 1998 to determine "devolution questions".[38]

In many matters the Courts, in whatever part of the United Kingdom they sit, administer the same statutory provisions and the English Court of Appeal may, for example, follow a decision of the Court of Session on the interpretation of an Act which both Courts have to apply.[39]

England

20–009   Since the Judicature Act of 1873 the superior English courts have formed part of one Supreme Court of Judicature which is divided into a Court of Appeal and a High Court.[40] The latter, for convenience of business, is divided into three divisions but each judge of each division possesses unlimited jurisdiction. Two judges of a particular division may sit together in a Divisional Court which has powers not possessed by a single High Court Judge.[41] The Divisional Court through its supervisory jurisdiction[42] plays a particularly important role in the field of constitutional and administrative law.

The Courts Act 1971 which reformed the administration of criminal justice created the Crown Court which also forms part of the Supreme Court. County Courts were created by statute in the mid-nineteenth century to provide a cheaper and more expeditious trial of civil matters, falling within certain limits, than could the superior courts of law sitting at Westminster.[43]

One of the most remarkable features of the English system of the administration of justice is the large part played by laymen, either as lay magistrates or as jurymen.[44] The appointment of lay justices dates from the earliest days of English law. Statutes of Edward I (Statutes of Winchester 1285) and Edward III confirmed and extended the practice of commissioning conservators, custodians or guardians of the peace. They have been known as Justices of the Peace since the justices of the peace Act 1361 which remains in force, despite later consolidating

---

[37] *ante*, para. 16–009.
[38] *ante*, para. 5–015.
[39] *Prasad v. Wolverhampton B.C.* [1983] Ch. 333.
[40] See now Supreme Court Act 1981. On the long history of the many ancient courts swept away by the Judicature Act 1873, see *Radcliffe and Cross The English Legal System* (G.J. Hand and D.J. Bentley eds, 6th ed 1997). The Civil Procedure Act 1997 facilitated reform of the civil justice system, including the establishment of an advisory body, the Civil Justice Council.
[41] Paul Jackson, "The Divisional Court, Precedent and Jurisdiction" (1985) 101 L.Q.R. 157. The Access to Justice Act 1999 provides for cases to be heard by a single judge, apart from substantive applications for judicial review.
[42] *post*, Chap. 31
[43] See now County Court Act 1984, the jurisdiction of the County Courts can be extended by the Lord Chancellor under powers given to him by the Courts and Legal Services Act 1990.
[44] Sir Carleton Allen, *The Queen's Peace* (1953) Chap. 5; Glanville Williams, *The Proof of Guilt*, Chap. 11; Maitland, *Justice and Police* (1885), Chaps. 8 and 9; Leo Page, *Justice of the Peace* (3rd ed.); B. Osborne, *Justices of the Peace, 1361–1848* (1960).

legislation,[45] and is the source of the useful and sometimes controversial power of justices to "bind over".[46] Lay magistrates are supplemented by district judges (magistrates' courts) who are legally qualified[47]; but the system they represent— involving the trial of 97 per cent of all criminal cases, and the preliminary examination of the rest—is perhaps an even more remarkable feature of our judicial system than the jury system as it now survives. In addition to their criminal jurisdiction magistrates also have an important civil jurisdiction in the field of family proceedings.

Northern Ireland

The structure of the superior courts in Northern Ireland is similar to that in England.[48] Justices in the Magistrates' Courts is administered by legally qualified Resident Magistrates. Lay justices of the peace perform such tasks as signing warrants and issuing summonses.

20–010

Scotland[49]

The Court of Session, which dates from 1532, is the superior court of civil jurisdiction in Scotland. The Outer House corresponds to the High Court in that its jurisdiction is first instance and an appeal from a judge of the Outer House (Lord Ordinary) lies to the Inner House which sits in two Divisions. Criminal jurisdiction is exercised by the High Court of Justiciary which consists of the same judges as the Court of Session. The senior judge of the Court of Session is the Lord President who, as Lord Justice—General, presides in the High Court of Justice.

20–011

Limited but important civil and criminal jurisdiction is exercised by Sheriffs, legally qualified judges. The role of stipendiary magistrates and lay justices of the peace who, since 1975, sit in District Courts, is far less significant in England.[50]

Initiation of proceedings

Article 6 of the E.C.H.R. provides for a right to a fair trial. This article has been interpreted widely and applies to the pre-trial processes as well as the trial itself. It has also been interpreted so that, for example, rights specifically granted with respect to criminal offences, such as the right to legal assistance (Article 6(3)(c)), have been implied as applying to civil proceedings as a necessary aspect of the general right to a fair hearing.[51] Aspects of Article 6 which could cause future reconsideration of civil and criminal proceedings include: the requirement that a trial is held within a reasonable time; that a case is heard in the open and by an independent and impartial tribunal; and rules of evidence.

20–012

---

[45] Magistrates' Courts Act 1980, Justices of the Peace Act 1997.

[46] *post*, Chap. 27.

[47] Justices of the Peace Act 1997, s.10A–D, as inserted by the Access to Justice Act 1999. Unlike lay justices, district judges, (formerly known as stipendiary magistrates) may sit alone. The 1999 Act expanded their jurisdiction.

[48] See the Judicature (Northern Ireland) Act 1978, as amended by the Administration of Justice Act 1982, s.70 and Sched. 8.

[49] D.M. Walker, *The Scottish Legal System* (8th ed., 2001).

[50] District Courts (Scotland) Act 1975.

[51] *Airey v. Ireland* (1979) 2 E.H.R.R. 305.

Civil litigation

20–013　　The right of access to the courts is in itself an important constitutional right, and for that reason, the courts have been unwilling, for example, to accept that Parliament meant to authorise a Minister to remove the right of access by delegated legislation.[52] Anyone may commence a civil action, subject to the risk of losing money if he is unsuccessful. The courts also possess jurisdiction to strike out actions which are frivolous, vexatious or an abuse of process[53] and under section 42 of the Supreme Court Act 1981 any person who has habitually instituted vexatious legal proceedings may, on the application of the Attorney-General, be restrained from instituting further proceedings without the leave of the High Court. A review of the civil justice system was carried out by Lord Woolf, and his 1996 report[54] recommended far reaching reforms many of which were implemented by the Civil Procedure Act 1997, and new Civil Procedure Rules (1998).[55]

For many people, a right of access to the courts is meaningless unless they can claim assistance from the State with the costs of litigation. Legal aid in civil proceedings was first introduced on a statutory basis by the Legal Aid 1949, and before the 1999 reforms there were several different schemes making up the legal aid scheme. Although legal aid is extremely costly, there were allegations that it was underfunded and that too many people were ineligible by virtue of a lowering of the means test level in 1992. There were also allegations of fraud and misuse and criticisms of the gaps in its availability. The Access to Justice Act 1999 provides for a complete overhaul of legal aid and advice. A Community Legal Service Fund to be run by a *Legal Services Commission* is established. Each year, as part of government spending plans, a fixed amount of money will be allocated to this fund. The Commission, with the approval of the Lord Chancellor, has established a Funding Code containing the criteria and procedures for how this fund is to be spent. The 1999 Act removes certain types of case from the legal aid scheme completely. These include: personal injury[56] (except clinical negligence); defamation and malicious falsehood[57]; disputes arising in the course of business; the law relating to companies, trusts or partnership disputes; boundary disputes. It was estimated that the above list accounted for 60 per cent of the civil cases previously funded by the State. Eligibility is based on both merit[58] and need, and the Lord Chancellor can set different limits for eligibility for different types of case. Clients who want to take advantage of the new scheme may only do so with those law firms to which a contract to provide such services has been awarded. The Commission has additional functions to liaise with other funders of legal services and to help and encourage the voluntary sector to reach more people.

---

[52] *Chester v. Bateson* [1920] K.B. 829, DC; *R. v. Secretary of State for the Home Dept, ex p. Anderson* [1984] Q.B. 778, DC; *R. v. Lord Chancellor ex p. Whitham* [1997] 2 All E.R. 779, (changes to court fees which also removed the right to exemptions to those suffering various types of financial hardship were declared illegal; the exemptions were reinstated).
[53] R.S.C. Ord. 94, r.15
[54] *Access to Justice: Final Report* (1996).
[55] See Ian Grainger, *The Civil Procedure Rules in Action* (2000).
[56] The Courts and Legal Services Act 1991 made provision for the introduction of contingency fee schemes, which the Government thought provided sufficient access to justice for these cases.
[57] The former was not covered by the previous scheme.
[58] As provided in the Funding Code.

Criminal proceedings

In general, anyone may commence criminal proceedings subject to the risk of **20–014** paying the costs of an unsuccessful action and, in some cases, of being sued for malicious prosecution. Certain statutes, however, require the consent of the Attorney-General[59] or the Director of Public Prosecutions[60] to the bringing of prosecutions. The Law Commission has recommended a rationalisation of the consent regime.[61]

The prosecution system was reformed by the Prosecution of Offences Act 1985.[62] Until 1986 in England and Wales,[63] most criminal offences were both investigated and brought by the police; in theory they were private prosecutions. The 1985 Act does not take away the right of private prosecution,[64] nor does it deprive the police of their investigatory role or their power to decide whether or not to initiate proceedings. It entrusts the final decision whether or not to prosecute and the conduct of prosecutions begun at the instance of the police, to a national Crown Prosecution Service (CPS), and gives to that Service the power to discontinue proceedings. Thus indirectly, there is a control over the police discretion to prosecute in individual cases.

The Director of Public Prosecutions is the head of the Crown Prosecution Service. The office of Director of Public Prosecutions was established in 1879.[65] He is appointed by and acts under the general "superintendence" of the Attorney-General (section 2 of the 1985 Act), and his powers and duties are to be found largely in that section. He is under a duty to take over the conduct of all criminal proceedings (other than those excluded from the section by the Attorney-General) which have been instituted by a police force; to institute and conduct proceedings where the importance or the difficulty of a case makes it appropriate that he should do so, or where it is otherwise appropriate; to appear for the prosecution when directed by the Court to do so in certain categories of criminal appeals. He may give advice to police forces on all matters relating to criminal offences and must discharge such other functions as may be assigned to him by the Attorney-General.

The conduct of proceedings is the responsibility of members of the Service **20–015** designated Crown Prosecutors. Since 1999 the CPS is divided into 42 prosecution areas each headed by a Chief Crown Prosecutor; within each area there are one or more local branches headed by a Branch Crown Prosecutor who is responsible for a teams of lawyers and caseworkers.[66] Section 10 of the Act requires the Director to issue a code to Crown Prosecutors giving guidance on the

---

[59] *e.g.* Explosive Substances Act 1883; Official Secrets Act 1911; Public Order Act 1986.

[60] *e.g.* Theft Act 1968, s.30(4); the power to consent can be exercised by any member of the CPS see below.

[61] Law Commission Report No. 255, H.C. 1085 (1997–98).

[62] See the Royal Commission on Criminal Procedure, Cmnd. 8092 (1981) and *An Independent Prosecution Service for England and Wales*, Cmnd. 9074 (1983).

[63] *cf.* Scotland where the decision to prosecute was, and still is taken by procurators fiscal who, under the Lord Advocate, are entirely independent of the police.

[64] It is expressly preserved by s. 6 which is of importance not merely to the individual but to government departments, local authorities and other public bodies such as the RSPCA and the NSPCC. In magistrates' courts 25 per cent of prosecutions are private prosecutions.

[65] Prosecution of Offences Act 1879. See J.Ll.J. Edwards, *Law Officers of the Crown* (1964), Chaps 16 and 17; *The Attorney General, Politics and the Public Interest* (1984), Chap. 2; Sir Theobald Mathew, *The Office and Duties of the Director of Public Prosecutions* (1950); Sir Norman Skelhorn, *Public Prosecutor* (1981).

[66] These reforms were introduced in 1999 following recommendations made in the Glidewell Report: *The Review of the Crown Prosecution Service* (1998) Cm. 3960.

general principles to be followed by them in deciding whether to institute proceedings, and what charges should be preferred. The terms of the code, which has been revised from time to time, is contained in the report which the Director must make each year to the Attorney-General who then lays it before Parliament (section 9).[67] Crown Prosecutors have all the powers of the Director as to the institution and conduct of proceedings but they must exercise their powers under his direction. The most important power is that contained in section 23[68] which authorises the Director to discontinue proceedings. This helps to provide an independent check on whether or not police prosecutions are justified.[69] The accused may, however, give notice that he requires the proceedings to continue. (He may wish to establish his innocence clearly in open court.) If the Director does not discontinue, or the accused wishes the proceedings to proceed, there is nothing to stop the Director (or Crown Prosecutor) from deciding to offer no evidence, with the inevitable result of an acquittal: *Raymond v. Attorney-General.*[70] The Attorney-General may also end any criminal proceedings brought on indictment by entering the *nolle prosequi.*[71] Section 24 extends the law relating to vexatious litigation[72] to criminal proceedings.

20–016 Legal aid in criminal proceedings was introduced in 1903.[73] In addition to assistance with the cost of legal representation the Legal Aid Act 1982 introduced a Duty Solicitor Scheme under which solicitors were available at magistrates' courts to advise accused persons. Following the provision in section 59 of the Police and Criminal Evidence Act 1984 for legal advice and assistance to be available to persons detained at police stations, a scheme was established for police stations.[74] Problems with criminal legal aid identified by the Royal Commission on Criminal Justice 1993,[75] included poor standards in legally aided criminal defence work in general and in particular at the police station. There were also concerns about underfunding and with the application of the means test. The Access to Justice Act 1999 also reforms criminal legal aid, which is to be covered by the newly created Criminal Defence Service. Like its civil equivalent it is run by the Legal Services Commission, and consists of a mix of private practitioners and salaried defenders employed by the Commission. Unlike civil legal aid there is not a set budget for criminal legal aid; all cases which fit the merits test—which is unaltered from the previous legislation—will be funded. However there are new powers to enable the recovery of some or all of the costs incurred in defending an individual. As in civil cases, solicitors who

[67] The most recent version was issued in November 2000; it takes account of the Human Rights Act 1998, and other developments in the criminal justice system.
[68] As amended by s.119 and sched. 8 of the Crime and Disorder Act 1998, to enable the discontinuance of proceedings after the accused has been sent for trial at Crown Court.
[69] The courts in certain circumstances have been willing to consider applications for judicial review of prosecution decisions: *R. v. Chief Constable of Kent ex p. L* [1993] 1 All E.R. 756; *R. v. Secretary of State for the Home Department ex p. Manning* [2000] W.L.R. 463. Dotan, "Should Prosecution Discretion Enjoy Special Treatment in Judicial Review? A Comparative Analysis of the Law in England and Israel", [1997] P.L. 513. The Crown Prosecution Service Inspectorate Act 2000, established a new independent inspectorate to scrutinise the CPS.
[70] [1982] Q.B. 839, CA.
[71] *ante*, para. 20–003.
[72] *ante*, para. 20–013.
[73] Poor Prisoners' Defence Act 1903.
[74] *post*, Chap. 24, para. 24–016.
[75] Cmnd. 2263.

wish to provide services to defendants will have to secure a contract with the Commission and meet certain standards.

Trial by Jury[76]

Despite the exalted terms in which the right to trial by jury has been described **20–017** in earlier centuries,[77] the use of the jury has declined in both civil and criminal cases over the last fifty years. The Royal Commission on Criminal Justice challenged the "so-called right to jury trial",[78] and it is not a right mentioned in, or required by, the E.C.H.R.

A prisoner who is indicted is tried by a petty jury, except that some indictable offences may be dealt with summarily by the magistrates with the consent of the accused.[79] Summary offences are triable on information by magistrates' courts without formal indictment or jury. At the present day about 90 per cent of *indictable* offences are in fact tried summarily. Of those sent for trial by jury, about 60 per cent plead "guilty".[80] Only about 2 to 3 per cent even of indictable offences are actually tried by jury. A majority verdict may be accepted in criminal proceedings where not fewer than ten out of 12 (or nine out of 11) jurors agree, provided that the jury have had at least two hours for deliberation.[81]

A coroner must summon a jury (or seven to 11 jurors) in certain cases, and **20–018** may accept a majority verdict if the dissentients are not more than two.[82]

The use of the jury in civil cases has declined greatly since World War I. The Supreme Court Act 1981, s.69 provides that where a party to an action in the Queen's Bench Division so requests the action will be tried by a jury if the Court is satisfied (i) that there is in issue a charge of fraud; a claim in respect of libel, slander,[83] malicious prosecution or false imprisonment or any other issue added to the list by a Rule of Court; and (ii) that the trial will not involve any prolonged examination of documents or accounts or any scientific or local investigation which cannot conveniently be made with a jury. In other cases the court may in its discretion order a trial with a jury. Less than 1 per cent of all civil cases are tried by a jury. The power to summon jurors in the Chancery Division introduced by the Chancery Amendment Act 1858, and the right to apply for a jury (of eight) in the county courts are practically obsolete.[84] Majority verdicts may now be accepted in civil proceedings in the High Court if ten out of 12 (or nine out of 11) jurors agree, and in a country court if seven (out of eight) jurors agree;

---

[76] See W.R. Cornish, *The Jury* (1968); J. Baldwin and M. McConville, *Jury Trials* (1979), James Gobert, *Justice Democracy and the Jury* (1997).

[77] See Blackstone, Bl.Comm.III, 379, and more recently Lord Devlin, *Trial by Jury* (1971).

[78] Cmnd. 2263 (1993).

[79] Magistrates' Courts Act 1980, ss.17A–17C, as inserted by the Criminal Procedure and Investigations Act 1996.

[80] The figure has dropped since October 1997 as a system of "plea before venue" under the Crime Sentence Act 1997 allows the magistrates' courts in triable-either-way cases to deal with defendants who indicate that they will plead guilty.

[81] Juries Act 1974, s.17; *R. v. Pigg* [1983] 1 W.L.R. 6 (HL). A verdict of "not guilty" similarly requires unanimity or not more than two dissentients. For a criticism of this rule see G. Maher, "Jury Verdicts and the Presumption of Innocence", (1983) 3 Leg.Stud. 146.

[82] Coroners Acts 1988, which consolidated and amended the previous legislation.

[83] The right to jury trial in civil cases is exercised most frequently in defamation cases; the Defamation Act 1996 introduced a summary procedure before a judge for claims of less than £10,000, which may reduce the number of jury trials.

[84] The current statutory provision is the County Courts Act 1984, s.66(3).

provided that it appears to the court that the jury have had a reasonable time for their deliberations having regard to the nature and complexity of the case.[85]

Jury service

20–019   Persons between the ages of 18 and 70 are liable to jury service if they have been resident for five years in the United Kingdom.[86] Jurors are entitled to travelling and subsistence allowances, and compensation for loss of earnings. The jury list is based on the Electoral Register. Various classes of person are ineligible for jury service, including councillors, clergymen, practising barristers, solicitors, police and prison officers, medical practitioners, members of the armed forces, justices of the peace and persons who are mentally ill.[87]

The Juries Act 1974 and the Juries (Disqualification) Act 1984[88] disqualify from jury service anyone who at any time has been sentenced within the United Kingdom, the Channel Islands or the Isle of Man to imprisonment for life, for a term of five years or more or to be detained during Her Majesty's pleasure. No one may serve on a jury who, within the preceding ten years, has served any sentence of imprisonment, youth custody or detention; been detained in a Borstal or been the subject of a suspended prison sentence of imprisonment or detention or of a community service order. An order of probation disqualifies a person from serving on a jury for the following five years. A person who is on bail in criminal proceedings is disqualified from jury service in the Crown Court. Any prospective juror may be questioned by the appropriate officer to establish whether he is disqualified from jury service.[89]

Certain persons are entitled if they so wish to be excused as of right from jury service. These include: members of either House of Parliament, of the devolved legislative bodies and the European Parliament; doctors, nurses, vets; those who can show that they have served on a jury within the previous two years; members of certain religious bodies; those over the age of 65. Failure to attend jury service without excuse, or serving on a jury while disqualified, is punishable by fine.

The impartiality of the jury: challenge and vetting

20–020   The Lord Chancellor undertakes the responsibility for summoning and preparing panels of jurors, and making arrangements for payment in respect of jury service. The right to a jury chosen at random from among those qualified to serve is recognised by "the right of challenge to the array" that is the right of challenge on the ground that the official responsible for summoning the jurors was biased or acted improperly.[90] Although a trial judge has a residual power to stand a juror down, he has no jurisdiction to order a multiracial jury[91] or order that a jury should be brought in from outside the normal catchment area.[92] Both prosecution and defence can challenge as many individual jurors as they wish for cause, on the basis that a juror is ineligible or disqualified from jury service, or on the basis that he is, or is reasonable suspected of being, biased.

[85] Juries Act 1974, s.17.
[86] Juries Act 1974, s.1, as amended by the Criminal Justice Act 1988.
[87] Juries Act 1974, Sched. 1.
[88] As amended or added to by the Criminal Justice and Public Order Act 1994. Similar provisions apply to Coroners' Juries by virtue of the Coroners' Juries Act 1983.
[89] Juries Act 1974, s.2(5); Administration of Justice Act 1982, s.61.
[90] Juries Act 1974, s.12(6); such challenges are virtually unknown today.
[91] *R. v. Ford* [1989] 3 All E.R. 445, CA; but see the recommendations from the R.C.C.J. Cmnd. 2263 (1993), p. 133.
[92] *R. v. Tarrant* [1998] Crim.L.R. 342.

The alleged bias may be thought to arise from some particular circumstances such as the relationship of a juror to someone involved in the proceedings.[93] In the absence of *prima facie* evidence a juror cannot be questioned in an attempt to discover a disqualifying bias.[94] A juror is not disqualified from serving by reason of some possible general prejudice based on racial or religious or sexual grounds and a judge should not excuse a juror on such general ground.[95] In *R. v. Pennington*[96] the Court of Appeal held that a miner who had not been on strike was not thereby disqualified from serving on a jury which was trying miners on various charges arising out of the strike in which the accused had been involved.

The trial judge may discharge individual jurors in certain circumstances, which include where there was a real danger of bias affecting the mind of an individual juror.[97] He may also discharge a whole jury in these circumstances if the matter cannot be satisfactorily dealt with by the discharge of individual jurors. A failure to dismiss a jury where there were doubts as to its impartiality could mean that the defendant had not been tried by an impartial tribunal as required by Art. 6 E.C.H.R.[98] **20–021**

The right of a defendant to challenge up to three jurors without cause was abolished by section 118(1) of the Criminal Justice Act 1988. However the Crown retains its power to "stand-by" without cause, potential jurors. Although there is no limit to the exercise of this right,[99] a *Practice Note*[1] published after the 1988 Act stated that this power should be exercised sparingly and only in exceptional circumstances, and that it should not be used to influence the overall composition of a jury. One circumstance when it can be used is where a jury check or vet has revealed information which strongly suggests that in the circumstances of the case a particular juror might be a security risk, be susceptible to improper approaches or influenced by improper motives. This practice of jury vetting became public knowledge in the late 1970s, and in 1978 after pressure from M.P.s the Attorney-General published his *Guidelines on Jury Checks*.[2] There is no statutory authority for jury vetting and the permission of a judge is not required before it can take place. The legality of vetting a jury panel for criminal convictions was upheld in *R. v. Mason*,[3] and in *R. v. McCann and others*[4] the Court of Appeal accepted that the jury vetting in accordance the Attorney-General's Guidelines was constitutional.

The Guidelines on jury vetting state as a basic principle that a jury should be chosen by random selection and only those who fall within the provisions of the **20–022**

---

[93] *R. v. Spencer* [1987] A.C. 128. Trial of nurses at Rampton Hospital accused of ill-treating patients: juror discharged when it became known that his wife worked at another mental hospital which had been mentioned in evidence; risk of bias arising from remaining jurors having discussed case with him. See *Practice Note (jury; juror; excuse)* [1988] 3 All E.R. 177.

[94] *R. v. Chandler (No. 2)* [1964] 2 Q.B. 322; *R. v. Andrews The Times* October 15, 1998, trial judge right to refuse defence request to issue a questionnaire to the jury panel to discover if any of them was biased against her; questioning of the panel should be avoided in all but the most exceptional cases.

[95] *Practice Note (Jurors: Excusal from Service)* [1988] 3 All E.R. 177.

[96] (1985) 81 Cr.App.R. 217.

[97] *R. v. Gough* [1993] A.C. 646.

[98] *Sander v. United Kingdom* [2000] Crim.L.R. 767.

[99] *R. v. Burns* [1982] Crim.L.R. 522.

[1] [1988] 3 All E.R. 1086.

[2] For the latest version see (1989) 88 Cr.App.R. 123.

[3] [1981] Q.B. 881; *c.f. R. v. Crown Court at Sheffield, ex p. Brownlow* [1980] Q.B. 530.

[4] (1990) 92 Cr.App.R. 239.

Juries Act 1974 should be excluded. Jury vetting is envisaged in two types of case, (a) cases involving national security and part of the evidence is likely to be heard *in camera* and (b) terrorist cases. In security cases there is a danger that a juror, either voluntarily or under pressure, may make an improper use of evidence which has been given *in camera*. In both security and terrorist cases there is a danger that a juror's political beliefs may be biased as to go beyond normally reflecting the broad spectrum of views and interest in the community to reflect the extreme views of sectarian interest or pressure group to a degree which might interfere with his fair assessment of the facts of the case or lead him to exert improper pressure on his fellow jurors. In order to ascertain whether in such cases either of these factors might seriously influence a potential juror's impartial performance of his duties, further investigation beyond one on criminal records made for disqualifications may only be made on the records of police Special Branches. No investigation of the records of police Special Branches should be made save with the personal authority of the Attorney-General on the application of the Director of Public Prosecutions, to whom the matter has been referred by a chief officer of police.

The result of any authorised check is sent to the Director of Public Prosecutions who decides what information ought to be brought to the attention of prosecuting counsel.

20–023   No right of stand-by should be exercised by counsel for the Crown on the basis of information obtained as a result of an authorised check unless the information is such as, having regard to the facts of the case and the offences charged, to afford strong reason for believing that a particular juror might be a security risk, be susceptible to improper approaches or be influenced in arriving at a verdict. Where a potential juror is asked to stand by for the Crown, there is no duty to disclose to the defence the information on which it was founded; but counsel may use his discretion to disclose it if its nature and source permit it.

When information revealed in the course of an authorised check is not such as to cause counsel for the Crown to ask for a juror to stand by, but does give reason to believe that he may be biased against the accused, the defence should be given, at least, an indication of why that potential juror may be inimical to their interests.

Reform[5]

20–024   The jury system has been under attack for some years. Since 1977 the right to jury trial has been significantly reduced, with more and more offences being made summary only. The RCCP in 1993 recommended that in either way offences defendants should no longer have the right to insist on a trial by jury, and the Narey Report (1997) recommended that the choice of venue in either way offences should be for the magistrates.[6] Despite being against further reforms to the availability of trial by jury when in opposition, the Labour Government changed tack, and legislation was introduced to give effect to the Narey proposals.[7] However the Criminal Justice (Mode of Trial) Bill 2000 was defeated by the House of Lords, as was a No. 2 Bill, and the Government abandoned the

---

[5] See Derbyshire, "The Lamp that Shows that Freedom Lives: is it worth the candle?" [1991] Crim.L.R. 740.

[6] *Review of Delay in the Criminal Justice System*, Home Office (1997).

[7] A consultative paper, *Determining Mode of Trial in Either Way Offences* Home Office (1998), put forward a variety of alternatives.

measure.[8] A possible alternative reform would be to establish a unified criminal court to replace the separate system of Crown and Magistrates' courts, with most offences being tried by a district judge and two lay magistrates, jury trial would be available only for the most serious cases.[9] The Government has also proposed restricting the use of juries in trials for fraud.

III. THE JUDICIARY[10]

Judicial independence[11]

The independence of the judiciary from interference by the executive has been mentioned in Chapter 2 as one of the most important principles of British constitutional law. Here we will say something more about the means by which this independence is secured. The main topics under this heading are the appointment of the judiciary, tenure of the judicial office and the manner in which judges may be disciplined and removed. Aspects of these procedures must now be considered in the light of, in particular, Article 6, E.C.H.R.

20–025

Judicial appointments

The appointment of judges by the sovereign is now largely governed by statute[12] supplemented by convention.[13] The fact that members of a court are appointed by the executive is not in itself incompatible with the E.C.H.R.[14] The sovereign appoints the Lords of Appeal in Ordinary,[15] the Lord Chief Justice, the Master of the Rolls, the President of the Family Division, the Vice-Chancellor and the Lords Justices of Appeal,[16] by convention on the advice of the Prime Minister, who consults the Lord Chancellor. The Queen appoints the puisne judges of the High Court by convention on the advice of the Lord Chancellor, who no doubt consults the Prime Minister.

The Queen on the recommendation of the Lord Chancellor also appoints Circuit judges to serve in the Crown Court and country courts, and Recorders to act as part-time judges of the Crown Court.[17] District judges (magistrates'

20–026

---

[8] See *ante*, para. 7–023.

[9] Auld Report (2001); *Criminal Justice: The Way Ahead* Cm. 5074 (2001). Legislation to reform the criminal courts system in the light of this report was promised in the 2001 Queen's Speech.

[10] Lord Devlin *The Judge* (1979), David Pannick, *Judges* (1987).

[11] See generally, S. Shetreet, *Judges on Trial* (1976); Aiden O'Neill, "The E.C.H.R. and the Independence of the Judiciary—The Scottish Experience", (2000) 63 M.L.R. 429.

[12] Which provides the qualifications required to fill each post. By changing the necessary qualifications it is possible to make certain judicial appointments open to a wider pool *e.g.* the Courts and Legal Services Act 1990 opened the way for solicitors to be judges in the higher courts.

[13] For the appointment of judges to the Court of Session and the High Court of Justiciary in Scotland see Scotland Act s.95, which puts in legislative form requirements as to appointment that are constitutional conventions for non-Scottish judicial appointments. The practice of appointing temporary sheriffs (s.11(4) Sheriff Courts (Scotland) Act 1971) was held *Starrs v. Ruxton* 2000 S.L.T. 42 to infringe Art. 6 E.C.H.R.; in consequence the office of temporary sheriff was abolished and replaced by part-time sheriffs, see Bail, Judicial Appointments etc. (Scotland) Act 2000.

[14] *Campell and Fell v. United Kingdom* (1984) 7 E.H.R.R. 165.

[15] Appellate Jurisdiction Act 1876, s.2.

[16] Supreme Court Act 1981, s.10. See too Judicature (Northern Ireland) Act 1978, s.12.

[17] Courts Act 1971, ss.16, 21. The possibility that such appointments could be in breach of the E.C.H.R. (see *Starrs v. Ruxton* S.L.T. 42, H.C.J.) caused a review of the of arrangements for part-time judicial appointments for which the Lord Chancellor is responsible, see H.C.Deb. Vol. 348, *col. 222W*, April 12, 2000.

courts)[18] are appointed by the Crown on the advice of the Lord Chancellor.[19] Lay justices are appointed to the Commission of the Peace in the name of the Queen, but on the nomination of the Lord Chancellor in consultation with local advisory committees by or the Chancellor of the Duchy of Lancaster.[20] The Lord Mayor and aldermen of the City of London are *ex officio* justices of the peace.[21] The method of appointing lay members to the Employment Appeals Tribunal by the Secretary of State for Trade and Industry was revised to take account of E.C.H.R. requirements.[22]

Judges and magistrates on appointment take the judicial oath, by which they promise "to do right to all manner of people after the laws and usages of this realm, without fear or favour, affection or ill-will."[23]

Reform of the judicial appointment system[24]

20–027
The selection process followed by the Lord Chancellor in advising on and making judicial appointments is described in a booklet issued by the Lord Chancellor's Department.[25] The system of judicial selection and appointment has been subject to a variety of criticisms: the extensive involvement of the Lord Chancellor, a government minister, means it is a political process, and until after World War II it was perceived as having been used in a partisan way; the reliance on "secret soundings" taken by civil servants in the Lord Chancellor's Department from leading barristers and judges, is one that favours the appointment of similar types of people and is potentially discriminatory to women and ethnic minorities[26]; the emphasis in advocacy skills excludes most solicitors; the higher judiciary does not reflect the composition of the community.[27]

20–028
Changes have been made in recent years: since 1994 appointments to circuit judge and below are filled by open competition following advertisements; since 1998 High Court judges may be appointed on application following advertisement or by invitation[28]; since 1998–99 the Lord Chancellor has made an annual report to Parliament on the judicial appointments system[29]; new directions were issued in 1998 which set out a job description for magistrates and the qualities

[18] Formerly known as stipendiary magistrates.
[19] Justices of the Peace Act 1997, s.10 A–E as inserted by the Access to Justice Act 1999.
[20] Justices of the Peace Act 1997, s.5.
[21] Justices of the Peace Act 1997, s.21 retains this anomaly.
[22] See *Scanfuture UK Ltd. v. Secretary of State for Trade and Industry, The Times*, April 26, 2001 [2001] I.R.L.R. 416.
[23] Promissory Oaths Act 1868.
[24] "*JUSTICE*" *The Judiciary in England and Wales* (1992); Third Report from the Home Affairs Committee, *Judicial Appointments Procedures*, H.C. 52 (1995–96); Sir Thomas Legg, "Judges for the New Century", [2001] P.L. 62; Report to the Lord Chancellor by Sir Leonard Peach, *An Independent Scrutiny of the Appointment Processes of Judges and Queen's Counsel in England and Wales* (1999; *Broadening the Bench: Law Society proposals for reforming the way judges are appointed* (2000); Malleson and Banda, *Factors Affecting the Decision to Apply for Silk and Judicial Office*, Lord Chancellor's Department Research Series No. 2/2000.
[25] *Judicial Appointments* (1999) it was first published only in 1985.
[26] See H.C. Deb. Vol. 336, *col. 565W*, October 19, 1999, for details of the procedures used and the persons and organisations consulted. In 1999 the Law Society announced that it would no longer participate in the process.
[27] The argument does not apply with such force to the magistracy, where women and ethnic minorities are better represented. For a defence of the system see Gladwell, "Judicial appointments", (2001) 152 N.L.J. 737.
[28] Of the 19 High Court judges appointed between February 1998 and May 2000, eight had applied for appointment and 11 were invited to accept appointment, H.C.Deb. Vol. 350, *col. 458W*, May 23, 2000.
[29] See Cm. 4783 (2000).

required for the position, as well as new application forms; an independent Judicial Appointments Commissioner, to oversee and monitor the appointment process was appointed in 2000.[30] The most senior appointments are not advertised, and appointment is not subject to any formal interview or selection panel; the Lord Chancellor makes such appointments from eligible judges having taken "soundings". Lower level judges are interviewed, but the final decision is for the Lord Chancellor. Before coming into office the Labour Party had favoured a Judicial Appointments Commission composed of lay members and lawyers to advise the Lord Chancellor on judicial appointments, but Lord Irving indicated in 1998 that such a change was not a priority. A further possibility, which could be used in conjunction with an Appointments Commission, would be to introduce a hearings system whereby a candidate for judicial office could be questioned by a parliamentary committee as to his views or opinions.[31] The role of the higher judiciary in the application of the Human Right Act 1998, has given impetus to this suggestion.

Judicial tenure[32]

Judges of superior courts[33] Before the Act of Settlement 1700, judges in England **20–029**
(other than the Barons of the Exchequer) usually held office *durante bene placito nostro* (during the King's pleasure).[34] The Act of Settlement, which was to come into force when the Hanoverians ascended the throne, provided "that . . . judges' commissions be made *quamdiu se bene gesserint*, and their salaries ascertained and established, but upon the address of both Houses of Parliament it may be lawful to remove them." The statutory provisions now in force are the Supreme Court Act 1981, s.11 under which all the Judges of the High Court and the Court of Appeal, with the exception of the Lord Chancellor, hold their offices during good behaviour subject to a power of removal by Her Majesty on an address presented to Her Majesty by both Houses of Parliament,[35] and the Appellate Jurisdiction Act 1876, s.6: "Every Lord of Appeal in Ordinary shall hold his office during good behaviour . . . but he may be removed from such office on the address of both Houses of Parliament." Such an address must be introduced in the House of Commons. Most Commonwealth countries prescribe a more judicial procedure for the removal of judges, in some cases involving a reference to the Judicial Committee of the Privy Council.

It is commonly but erroneously stated that since the Act of Settlement judges can be dismissed by the Crown *only* on an address from both Houses of Parliament.[36] The true position, however, is stated by Anson: "the words mean simply that if, in consequence of misbehaviour in respect of his office or from any other cause, an officer of state holding on this tenure has forfeited the

---

[30] Following a recommendation in the Peach Report *op. cit.* note 24, p. 432.

[31] Following a report by the Home Affairs Select Committee, *Freemasonary in the Police and Judiciary*, H.C. 192 (1996–97); in July 1998 the Lord Chancellor's Department sent a questionnaire to all judges and magistrates in connection with membership of the freemasons, see H.C. 467 (1998–99). There was judicial disquiet at the subsequent decision of the Lord Chancellor to publish a register of all judges indicating whether or not they were masons, or had refused to answer a question on membership.

[32] See Rodney Brazier, *Constitutional Practice* (3rd. ed., 1999), Chap. 12.

[33] For the position of judges in Scotland see Scotland Act s.95; C.M.G. Himsworth, "Securing the tenure of Scottish judges: a somewhat academic exercise?" [1999] P.L. 14.

[34] See *ante*, para. 2–018.

[35] Re-enacting Judicature Act 1875, s.5; Supreme Court of Judicature (Consolidation) Act 1925, s.12(1). For Northern Ireland, see Judicature (Northern Ireland) Act 1978, s.13(1).

[36] This is the position in some Commonwealth countries.

confidence of the two Houses, he may be removed, although the Crown would not otherwise have been disposed or entitled to remove him."[37] The Crown could remove without an address for official misconduct, neglect of official duties, or (probably) conviction for a serious offence (*Earl of Shrewsbury's Case*[38]). The Queen would be bound by convention to act on an address from both Houses.[39] The first case in which Parliament initiated proceedings for the removal of a judge under the Act of Settlement was that of Mr Justice Fox, of the Irish Bench, in 1805; but it was abandoned on the ground that the proceedings should have commenced in the Commons instead of in the Lords. The only case which has resulted in removal under the Act of Settlement procedure was that of Sir Jonah Barrington, another Irish judge, in 1830. Most of the cases—and they are few—have concerned colonial judges, or judges accused of partiality in hearing election petitions.[40]

There is a compulsory retiring age of 70 for Lords of Appeal in Ordinary and judges of the Supreme Court.[41] However, beyond that age retired judges may be asked to sit from time to time under the Supreme Court Act 1981, s.9. It is hardly necessary to add that judges could be removed by Act of Parliament.

Judges' salaries are charged by statute on the Consolidated Fund, so that they do not come up for review by the Commons every year as do most estimates of national expenditure. They may be increased, though not reduced, by Order in Council.[42]

20–030   *Circuit judges*[43] Circuit judges are judges of the superior courts in so far as they sit in the crown court which is a superior court of record.[44] They also sit in the county court which is not a superior court. They may be removed by the Lord Chancellor "on the ground of incapacity of misbehaviour".[45] They are subject to a retiring age of 70, except that the Lord Chancellor may in the public interest continue them in office up to the age of 75.[46] The Lord Chancellor may terminate

---

[37] Anson, *Law and Custom of the Constitution* (4th ed., Keith 1922). Vol. II, Part I, pp. 234–235.

[38] (1611) 9 Co.Rep. 42a, 50.

[39] As to what amounts to misbehaviour in a public office, and the methods by which an office in which a person has a life interest may be forfeited, see Todd, *Parliamentary Government in England* (2nd ed.), Vol. II, pp. 857–859; Anson, *ibid.*, at pp. 235–236. But all judges (except the Lord Chancellor) are now subject to a statutory age of retirement.

[40] For an account of a number of cases, and the principles and proceedings established, see Keith, *Responsible Government in the Dominions*, II, pp. 1073–1074. In 1991 a motion supported by more than 100 M.P.s called for the removal of the Lord Lane L.C.J. after revelations of a miscarriage of justice in the case of *R. v. McIlkenny* 93 Cr.App. R. 287, CA.

[41] Judicial Pensions Act 1959; Supreme Court Act 1981, s.11(2), as amended by the Judicial Pensions and Retirement Act 1993. See Supreme Court Act 1981, s.11(8) for the compulsory retirement of judges incapacitated by ill health from resigning.

[42] Administration of Justice Act 1973; Supreme Court Act 1981, s.12. On judicial pensions see Judicial Pensions and Retirement Act 1993; Supreme Court Act 1981, s.12(7).

[43] For the position of Scottish Sheriffs see, Sheriffs Courts (Scotland) Act 1971, s.12; *Stewart v. Secretary of State for Scotland* 1998 S.L.T. 385.

[44] Courts Act 1971, s.4.

[45] Courts Act 1971, s.17(4). A circuit judge who was convicted on a charge of smuggling was removed from office by the Lord Chancellor in 1983: *The Times*, December 6, 1983. In July 1994 the Lord Chancellor stated that "misbehaviour" could include: a conviction for drink-driving; any offence involving violence, dishonesty, or moral turpitude; behaviour likely to cause offence on religious or racial grounds or which amounted to sexual harassment. The resignation of Richard Gee J., *ante*, note 12, p. 418, pre-empted any decision by the Lord Chancellor to remove him from office.

[46] Courts Act 1971, s.17 as amended by the Judicial Pensions and Retirement Act 1993.

the appointment of a Recorder on the ground of incapacity or misbehaviour or of failure to comply with the terms of his appointment.[47]

Other judicial officers Justices of the peace may be removed from the Commission of the Peace by the Lord Chancellor[48] if he thinks fit, although by convention he does not remove them except for good cause, such as refusal to administer the law because the justice does not agree with it. The Justices of the Peace Act 1997 also requires the Lord Chancellor to keep a Supplemental List of justices who are no longer entitled to exercise judicial functions. The Lord Chancellor may direct that the name of a justice be put on the Supplemental List on the ground of "age or infirmity or other like cause," or if he "declines or neglects" his judicial functions, and his name must be put on this List when he reaches the age of 70.[49] A district judge (magistrates' court) is only dismissable by the Lord Chancellor on grounds of incapacity or misbehaviour.[50]

Discipline, resignation and training

There is no formal machinery for complaints against judges. It is very difficult   **20–031** to remove members of the senior judiciary from office,[51] although on occasion criticism from colleagues may induce resignation.[52] Criticism by the appellate courts may be viewed as part of the disciplinary machinery.[53] It has been suggested that the importance attached to the separation of powers and the independence of the judiciary has resulted in pressure being put on judges to resign on the grounds of ill-health rather than invoke more formal measures.[54] Occasionally the Lord Chancellor may make it known that he has rebuked a judge.

Judicial training by the Judicial Studies Board was established in 1979 and reconstituted in 1985 when it was given additional responsibilities. It responsibilities now include training on sentencing, criminal law, family law, civil matters and the Human Rights Act 1998. It has been questioned whether it was proper for the Home Secretary to describe the purpose of training the judiciary to deal with the Human Rights Act as including explaining how to deal with "sharp lawyers" who would make "disruptive points".[55]

No general duty to advise the executive[56]

It is often said that one of the hallmarks of the independence of the English   **20–032** judiciary is that they have no duty to advise the executive on cases that do not come before the courts in the ordinary course of litigation. In 1925 a great outcry was raised in the House of Lords when it was proposed in the Rating and

---

[47] Courts Act 1971, s.21(6). Section 21(3) provides that a Recorder's appointment shall specify the frequency and duration of the occasions on which he must be available to perform his duties.
[48] Or the Chancellor of the Duchy of Lancaster; Justices of the Peace Act 1997, s.26.
[49] Justices of the Peace Act 1979, s.7(2).
[50] Justice of the Peace Act 1997, s.10A as substituted by the Access to Justice Act 1999.
[51] See Brazier *Constitutional Practice* (1999), pp 294–6.
[52] Harman J. resigned in 1998 following criticism of his conduct by the Court of Appeal in *Goose v. Wilson Sandford, The Times,* February 13 and 19, 1998.
[53] See Brazier *op. cit.,* pp. 289–92 for examples.
[54] A. Patterson and St. J. Bates, *The Legal System of Scotland* (4th ed., 1999).
[55] J.A.G. Griffith, *Daily Telegraph,* April 23, 2001.
[56] See J.A.G. Griffith, *Politics of the Judiciary,* (5th ed., 1997), Chap. 2.

Valuation Bill that advisory judgments should be allowed on rating questions.[57] That such a duty does not necessarily impair the independence of the courts is shown by the fact that it exists in many constitutions, including some in the Commonwealth, and also in our judicial system in the case of the Judicial Committee[58] and the Courts-Martial Appeal Court. In addition, following an acquittal, the Attorney-General may refer a case to the Court of Appeal for its opinion a point of law which has arisen in the case.[59]

Such advisory functions should be distinguished from the ancient duty of the judges to advise the House of Lords in its judicial capacity, and from the binding declaratory judgments that may be given in certain cases.[60]

The role of the Law Lords in the legislative function of the House of Lords is governed by convention.[61] Their position is arguably more problematic since the enactment of the Human Rights Act 1998. Lord Phillips M.R. has indicated that he will not get involved in the legislative function of the House of Lords.[62]

20–033 Apart from their strictly judicial duties, judges of the superior courts are, from time to time, called upon to conduct inquiries of one kind and another[63]: "a role which the judiciary do not seek, but which is thrust upon them."[64] The inquiries have been formally established under the Tribunals of Inquiry (Evidence) Act 1921,[65] under a specific statutory provision, or on an *ad hoc* basis.[66] The matters inquired into have included events in Northern Ireland,[67] rail crashes, public health matters, standards in public life,[68] murder.[69] Whether such a practice is desirable is a question on which different views have been expressed. "The employment of judges in extra-judicial inquiries may be entirely acceptable, as a means of reassuring the public, where there has been a tragic event such as Aberfan or Dunblane or Paddington. There are more serious issues of the separation of powers where the inquiry raises overtly political and contentious matters . . . ".[70] A further danger of relying on judges to examine contentious issues is that they become themselves controversial figures. The new and important roles of the House of Lords and the Judicial Committee of the Privy Council in constitutional matters such as the interpretation of the Human Rights Act 1998 and the devolution legislation could result in a reduction in this type of extra-judicial activity in order to avoid compromising judicial impartiality. There is

---

[57] See E.C.S. Wade, "Consultation of the Judiciary by the Executive" (1930) 46 L.Q.R. 169.

[58] *ante*, para. 16–009.

[59] Criminal Justice Act 1972, s.36. This section has not, however, "created a system for referring mere 'moots' to appellate courts"; *Att.-Gen. for Northern Ireland's Reference No. 1 of 1975* [1977] A.C. 105, 156 *per* Lord Edmund Davies.

[60] *Dyson v. Att.-Gen.* [1911] 1 K.B. 410.

[61] See *ante*, para. 9–012

[62] *The Times*, May 22, 2001.

[63] See S. Shetreet, *Judges on Trial* (1976), pp. 354–363; Zellick [1972] P.L. 1.

[64] Lord Woolf in the course of a debate in the House of Lords. H.L. Deb., Vol. 572, col. 1272, June 5, 1996.

[65] The Crown Agents inquiry, H.C. 364 (1981–82); the inquiry by Lord Cullen into the Dunblane massacre 1996.

[66] The Scott inquiry into the "Arms for Iraq" affair, H.C. 115 (1995–96).

[67] *e.g.* by Lord Widgery C.J., into the events of "Bloody Sunday" H.L. 101, H.C. 220 (1971–72), being re-investigated by Lord Saville (1998); Bennett J. into interrogation methods, Cmnd. 7497.

[68] Lord Nolan Cm. 2850 (1995).

[69] The Macpherson inquiry into the death of Stephen Lawrence, Cm. 4262 (1999).

[70] Sir David Williams, "Bias; the Judges and the Separation of Powers", [2000] P.L. 45 at p. 54; see also Drewry, "Judicial Inquiries and Public Reassurance", [1996] P.L. 368.

also the practical matter of availability: if judges are busy with a lengthy inquiry they will not be available in court.

Terms, conditions and administration

The independence of the judiciary can be threatened by changes to the administration of the courts,[71] by increasing the powers of the Lord Chancellor to control the education, training and conduct of advocates, or by changes in the rules relating to judicial pensions. The relaxation of the doctrine or convention that judges—except the Lord Chancellor—should not take part in political and party controversy,[72] has ensured that these matters are not ignored.[73] The jurisdiction of the Parliamentary Commissioner for Administration was extended in 1990 to include alleged maladministration in the courts.[74] **20–034**

Sentencing[75]

An aspect of judicial independence is the discretion that judges have in determining the sentences of those convicted. Attempts have been made from time to time to restrict this discretion by the use of legislation to enable government policy on sentencing to be reflected by the judiciary. A White Paper published in 1996 proposed to increase the availability of mandatory sentences for certain offences, and to impose heavy mandatory minimum sentences. Despite criticisms of the proposals, many of the proposals made in the White Paper were enacted in the Crime (Sentence) Act 1997. One of the provisions in this Act is the requirement that where an offender is convicted of a second serious offence (as defined in section 2) no matter how long between the two offences, the court is obliged to impose a sentence of life imprisonment unless there are "exceptional circumstances". This section requires careful interpretation to avoid being incompatible with Articles 3 and 5 of the E.C.H.R.[76] **20–035**

Judicial impartiality

The impartiality of the judiciary is recognised as an important, if not the most important element, in the administration of justice. It is recognised in British law and by Article 6(1) E.C.H.R. which establishes a right to a fair and public hearing by an independent and impartial tribunal established by law. The E.C.t.H.R. has held that impartiality requires a judge not only to be impartial, but also to appear to be impartial.[77] Certain legal rules and constitutional conventions are clearly intended to facilitate the impartial administration of justice so far as that is possible.[78] **20–036**

---

[71] See Sir Nicolas Brown-Wilkinson, "The Independence of the Judiciary in the 1980s", [1988] P.L. 44.

[72] The relevant rules were referred to as the Kilmuir Rules, although in one form or another restrictions on judicial utterances ante-dated that Lord Chancellor. See also [1986] P.L. 383. They were relaxed by Lord Mackay in 1987, who reminded judges that they should not say anything that might damage their authority or prejudice the performance of their judicial work.

[73] Sir Francis Purchas, "Lord Mackay and the judiciary", (1994) 144 N.L.J. 527, "What is happening to judicial independence?", (1994) 144 N.L.J. 1306; Lord Ackner, "The erosion of judicial independence" (1996) 146 N.L.J. 1789, "More power to the Executive?" (1998) 148 N.L.J. 1512.

[74] s. 110 Courts and Legal Services Act 1990.

[75] See Ashworth, *Sentencing and Criminal Justice* (3rd ed., 2000), Chap. 2.

[76] See *R. v. Offen* [2001] Cr.App.R. 24.

[77] *McGonnell v. United Kingdom* (2000) 30 E.H.R.R. 241.

[78] *e.g.* both Houses of Parliament have *sub judice* rules, see P. M. Leopold "The Changing Boundary between the Courts and Parliament," in *Legal Structures* (Buckley ed., 1998).

Exclusion from the House of Commons

20–037   The exclusion by law of the holders of judicial office (other than lay magistrates) from sitting in the House of Commons[79] is now based on the doctrine that judges should not take part in political controversy. Formerly, the exclusion of judges from the House of Commons was based on different principles. When the Commons asserted their right to exclude James I's judges they did so on the ground of parliamentary privilege, because the judges of the common law courts were advisers of the House of Lords. For the same reason the Law Officers of the Crown should have been disqualified, but in this case the disqualification was eventually waived.[80]

Natural justice

20–038   The principles of natural justice which are discussed in Chapter 32 in relation to the judicial control of public authorities, apply *a fortiori* to the conduct of the courts. The right of each side to a dispute to be heard (*audi alteram partem*) and the requirement that a judge should not be a party to a case and should be free from personal interest or bias in the case before him (*nemo iudex in re sua*)[81] help to insure the impartial discharge of judicial duties. Where a judge has a pecuniary interest or has a direct personal interest in the outcome of a case, he is automatically disqualified from hearing the action, and any judgment he gives will be automatically set aside. The case of *R. v. Bow Street Magistrates, ex p. Pinochet (No. 2)*[82] established that the automatic disqualification rule goes further, and covers the situation where a judge does not have an interest in the outcome of the case, but where some affiliation or personal interest of the judge gives rise to a suspicion that he might not be impartial. This case arose out of the decision of the House of Lords, by a majority of three to two, that Senator Pinochet, a former Head of State, did not have immunity from the criminal process for international crimes which he allegedly committed when he was in office. The House of Lords before reaching this decision, had given a variety of human rights bodies, including Amnesty International, leave to intervene in the appeal process. It became known after the decision that Lord Hoffmann, one of the majority, was Chairperson of a trust set up by Amnesty to research into human rights issues. In *ex p. Pinochet (No. 2)* the House of Lords held that since the trust in question was owned and controlled by Amnesty, the two bodies were effectively one, and although the link was not sufficiently close to say that Lord Hoffmann was a party to the appeal, it was sufficiently close to establish that he had an interest in the proceedings. Their Lordships held that Lord Hoffmann should have been automatically disqualified from hearing the case and in consequence the earlier decision of the House should be set aside. This decision left the law in some confusion as it expanded the notion of automatic disqualification and, in remarks by members of the House of Lords, cast doubts on *R. v. Gough*.[83] *Gough* had established that where there was evidence of bias, and it was not a case of

---

[79] House of Commons Disqualification Act 1975.

[80] *Report and Minutes of Evidence on the Select Committee on Offices or Places of Profit under the Crown* (1941; H.C. 120, 147).

[81] *Dimes v. Grand Junction Canal* (1852) H.L.C. 759. In the light of the requirements of the E.C.H.R. the convention that the Lord Chancellor and ex-Lord Chancellors do not participate in appeals involving controversial political issues with which they have been concerned, *e.g. Heaton's Transport Co v. T.G.W.U.* [1973] A.C. 15, is of even greater importance.

[82] [2000] 1 A.C. 119; see Timothy H. Jones, "Judicial bias and disqualification in the *Pinochet* case," [1999] P.L. 391.

[83] [1993] A.C. 646.

automatic disqualification, the test to be applied in determining whether a decision should be set aside was whether there was a "real danger" of bias. However, in *Locabail (UK) Ltd v. Bayfield Properties Ltd*[84] the Court of Appeal, in a single judgment of the court, applied *Gough* and dismissed four of the five appeals[85] before them on the ground that although there was evidence of apparent bias, there was no real danger of bias. The Court of Appeal refused to attempt to define the factors which could give rise to a real danger of bias, stating that it would depend on the facts and the nature of the issue to be decided in the case. However it went on to suggest that objection could not be based on the religious, ethnic or national origin, age, class, education, means or sexual orientation of a judge. It also suggested that objection could not ordinarily be based on a variety of other interests or experiences including a judge's membership of social, sporting or charitable bodies; masonic associations; previous judicial decisions; extra-curricular utterances in lectures, books, etc.[86]

A judge who has a possible conflict of interest in a case may continue to hear **20–039** the case if he discloses this interest and the parties do not object. It may be questioned if this satisfies the requirement that justice should be seen to be done. It is clear that judges must take care to disclose to the parties anything which could give rise to a suspicion of a conflict of interest. The relaxation of the convention whereby judges should not take part in political controversy[87] can give rise to concerns as to judicial impartiality. In *Hoekstra and others v. H.M. Advocate*[88] it was held that extra judicial comments by Lord McClusky, in which he indicated misgivings with respect to the enactment of the Human Rights Act 1998, cast doubt on his impartiality in any case where arguments were based on the Act or the E.C.H.R.

Publicity of proceedings[89]

One of the chief safeguards of the impartial administration of justice lies in the **20–040** common law right of the public, including the press, to be present and to publish accurate reports and fair comments on the proceedings. This is embodied, too, in the maxim that it is not sufficient that justice be done, but it must be seen to be done: *Scott v. Scott*.[90] "Proceedings in open court ensure that justice is done and is seen to be done and that the public may be able to ponder whether justice has been done": *Home Office v. Harman*.[91] It is also a requirement of Article 6(1) E.C.H.R., and a pre-condition of the right to freedom of expression (Article 10).

The courts have a discretion, which must be carefully exercised, to hear proceedings *in camera* on grounds of public policy, *e.g.* where secret information that might endanger the safety of the state is to be divulged, or to clear the court for the suppression of disorder.[92] In *R. v. Chief Registrar of Friendly Societies, ex*

---

[84] [2000] 2 W.L.R. 870, CA.
[85] It allowed the appeal in a personal injury case where the trial judge had previously written articles critical of insurance companies in such cases.
[86] At p. 888.
[87] *ante*, para. 20–034, and note 71 on p. 437
[88] [2001] 1 A.C. 216, 2001 S.L.T. 28
[89] Miller, *Contempt of Court* (3rd ed. 2000), Chap. 10.
[90] [1913] A.C. 417.
[91] [1981] Q.B. 534, *per* Templeman L.J.; see *Storer v. British Gas plc, The Times*, March 1, 2000, where the Court of Appeal held that an industrial tribunal had no jurisdiction to sit in private.
[92] See *R. v. Denbigh J.J., ex p. Williams* [1974] Q.B. 759.

p. New Cross Buildings Society,[93] the Court of Appeal pointed out that in exceptional circumstances the paramount object of the courts—to do justice in accordance with the law—could only be achieved by proceedings *in camera.* Here a public hearing—irrespective of the decision—would have caused financial loss. Statutory limitations on grounds of public morality are imposed in certain cases on the details that may be published, *e.g.* under the Judicial Proceedings (Regulation of Reports) Act 1926 and various statutes relating to children and young persons, divorce, nullity, and domestic proceedings.[94]

Fair reports of contemporary judicial proceedings are privileged.[95] Restrictions on reporting may be imposed to prevent the risk of prejudicing proceedings under the Contempt of Court Act 1981.[96]

Judicial immunity[97]

20–041   Immunity from suit is a derogation from a person's fundamental right of access to the court, and both common law and the E.C.H.R. require such derogations to be justified.[98] The law of defamation accords absolute privilege to judges[99] taking part in judicial proceedings. With regard to torts other than defamation the law is not altogether clear. The distinction usually taken is that between superior courts and inferior courts.

Judges are exempt from civil or criminal liability for things done or said while acting within their jurisdiction, even if done maliciously and without reasonable or probably cause.[1] Judges of *superior* courts are apparently not liable for judicial acts done outside their jurisdiction,[2] (*Anderson v. Gorries, ante*), and the acts of a superior court are presumed to be within their jurisdiction[3]). Anyway, there is no tribunal to enforce such liability.

Judges of *inferior* courts, including county courts,[4] courts—martial[5] and consular courts,[6] had been traditionally regarded as liable for judicial acts done without, or in excess of, their jurisdiction (*Peacock v. Bell, ante*). The judge of an inferior court will not be deemed to have acted without jurisdiction if he was induced to act by some false allegation of fact which, if true, would have given

---

[93] [1984] 2 Q.B. 227.
[94] *e.g.* Domestic and Appellate Proceedings (Restriction of Publicity) Act 1968; *Barritt v. Att.-Gen.* [1971] 1 W.L.R. 1713; Magistrates' Courts Act 1980, s.71; Youth Justice and Criminal Evidence Act 1999, s.44.
[95] *Kimber v. The Press Association* (1893) 62 L.J.Q.B. 152, and see s.14 Defamation Act 1996.
[96] *post*, para. 25–012.
[97] Winfield, *The Present Law of Abuse of Legal Procedure* (1921), Chap. 7; *cf.* D. Thompson, "Judicial Immunity and the Protection of Justices", (1958) 21 M.L.R. 517; L.A. Sheridan, "The Protection of Justices" (1951) 14 M.L.R. 267; Abimbola Olowofoyeku, "State Liability for the Exercise of Judicial Power", [1998] P.L. 444.
[98] See *Fayed v. United Kingdom* (1994) 18 E.H.R.R. 393 at para. 65; *Tinnelly and Sons Ltd v. United Kingdom* (1998) 27 E.H.R.R. 249 at para. 74.
[99] Including magistrates: *Law v. Llewellyn* [1906] 1 K.B. 487.
[1] *Anderson v. Gorrie* [1895] 1 Q.B. 668 (colonial court); see also *Scott v. Stansfield* (1868) L.R. 3 Ex. 220 (county court).
[2] *Hammond v. Howell* (1677) 2 Mod. 219, *cf.* ministerial acts; *Ferguson v. Earl of Kinnoull* (1842) 9 Cl. & F. 251, 311 (HL).
[3] *Peacock v. Bell* (1666) 1 Wms.Saund. 74. See also *Taffe v. Downes* (1813) 3 Moo. P.C.
[4] *Houlden v. Smith* (1850) 14 Q.B. 841.
[5] *Dawkins v. Lord F. Paulet* (1869) 5 Q.B. 94; *Dawkins v. Lord Rokeby* (1873) L.R. 8 Q.B. 255; *Heddon v. Evans* (1919) 35 T.L.R. 642.
[6] *Haggard v. Pelisier Frères* [1892] A.C. 61.

him jurisdiction.[7] The distinction between superior and inferior courts began to develop in the seventeenth century, and was the product of two principles: first, the jurisdiction of inferior courts is limited by subject-matter, persons or place, while superior courts are not so limited; and, secondly, inferior courts are answerable to the superior courts if they exceed their jurisdiction, while superior courts are answerable only to God and the King.[8]

In *Sirros v. Moore*,[9] the Court of Appeal, in refusing to hold a judge of the **20–042** Crown Court liable for a wrongful order of imprisonment, expressed the view that the immunity of judges of inferior courts should be assimilated to that of judges of superior courts. Magistrates have statutory protection from acts within their jurisdiction, but did not have immunity for acts beyond jurisdiction until 1991.[10]

In order to protect the administration of justice, immunity from suit also attaches to words spoken in the course of judicial proceedings by the parties,[11] witnesses[12] and counsel[13] and to the verdics of juries.[14] However, in 2000, in *Arthur J.S. Hall and Co (a firm) v. Simmons*[15] the House of Lords, in a change of policy which was based on the changes in society and law in the previous thirty years,[16] held that the immunity of advocates from suits for negligence no longer applied. All of their Lordships held this to be the case in respect of the conduct of civil cases, and a majority of the House held it to apply to criminal proceedings also. Although the decision was not based on the requirements of the E.C.H.R., it is likely that had it been maintained a challenge could have been made on the basis that the restriction that the immunity imposed on the rights of individuals was disproportionate to its public policy aim.

Immunity for words spoken is absolute in the case of the courts in the strict sense and tribunals which have similar attributes to a court. The extent of absolute immunity was considered by the House of Lords in *Trapp v. Mackie*.[17] Lord Diplock emphasised that the first requirement was that the tribunal had been established by law, although not necessarily by statute[18] so that absolute immunity does not extend to domestic tribunals. A tribunal may be entitled to absolute immunity even although its decision may be subject to confirmation by another body as in the case of a military court of inquiry; *Dawkins v. Lord Rokeby*.[19] It

---

[7] *Houlden v. Smith, ante.*; *Calder v. Halket* (1839) Moo. P.C. 28.

[8] Holdsworth, *op. cit.* Vol. VI, pp. 234–240.

[9] [1975] Q.B. 118.

[10] For the situation prior to 1991, see *R. v. Manchester City Justices, ex p. Davies* [1989] Q.B. 631, CA and *Re McC.* [1985] A.C. 528, HL, a case from Northern Ireland. See now Justice of the Peace Act 1997, ss.51, 52.

[11] *Astley v. Younge* (1759) 2 Burr. 807. See also *Re Hunt* [1959] 2 Q.B. 69, CA.

[12] *Seaman v. Netherclift* (1876) 2 C.P.D. 53. See *Taylor v. Director of Serious Fraud Office* [1999] 2 A.C. 177, where it was explained that the immunity was limited to cases where "the alleged statements constitute the cause of the action." *per* Lord Hoffmann.

[13] *Munster v. Lamb* (1883) 11 Q.B.D. 588.

[14] *Bushell's Case* (1670) 6 St.Tr. 999; (1677) Vaughan 135. The practice of punishing jurors for finding against the evidence of direction of the judge was finally stopped by this case.

[15] [2000] 3 All E.R. 673.

[16] When in *Rondel v. Worsley* [1969] 1 A.C. 191, it was held on the grounds of public policy that barristers had immunity from actions in negligence.

[17] [1979] 1 W.L.R. 177. (A Scottish appeal, the House declaring that on this point English and Scottish law are the same.)

[18] *e.g. Lincoln v. Daniels* [1962] 1 Q.B. 237, CA: (disciplinary proceedings in Inns of Court); *Marrinan v. Vibart* [1963] 1 Q.B. 528.

[19] (1873) L.R. 8 Q.B. 255; (1875) L.R. 7 H.L. 744.

is important, although not an essential requirement,[20] that the tribunal's proceedings are held in public. Other characteristics listed by Lord Diplock included the right to legal representation, the calling of witnesses by each party; the compellability of the witnesses and the right to cross-examine witnesses.

IV. CONTEMPT OF COURT[21]

20–043   Courts, if they are to serve their purpose of administering justice, must have the power to secure obedience to their judgments, to prevent interference with their proceedings and to ensure a fair trial to parties who resort to them to vindicate their rights. It is the public interest in seeing these ends achieved that is served by the law relating to contempt of court.[22] The latter phrase has been described as "inaccurate and misleading",[23] particularly because it suggests that the purpose of the law is to protect the dignity of the court. "It is justice itself that is flouted by contempt of court, not the individual court or judge who is attempting to administer it."[24] Lord Scarman has expressed the view that "It is high time . . . that we re-arranged our law so that the ancient but misleading term 'contempt of court' disappeared from the law's vocabulary."[25] However an acceptable alternative has not yet been suggested.

The law relating to contempt covers a variety of very different situations, from the disgruntled litigant who throws a tomato at a judge to the publication of an article on a matter of public interest by a newspaper before litigation on some aspect of that matter has even begun. Thus, in varying degrees the law of contempt will be in conflict with the right of free speech. In all cases judges will be judging in matters in which they may be thought to have a personal interest.[26] It is not, then, surprising that the law of contempt is an area of controversy. It is an area of law that has to be considered in the light of the E.C.H.R. and in particular Articles 6 and 10; even before the enactment of the Human Rights Act, the E.C.H.R. caused aspects of the law on contempt to be changed.[27] The Contempt of Court Act 1981 was enacted because of the decision of the European Court of Human Rights in *Sunday Times v. UK*[28] The 1981 Act reforms but does not entirely replace the common law of contempt.[29] Although the law of contempt in Scotland differs from the common law, the Act applies to both jurisdictions.[30]

---

[20] *Addis v. Crocker* [1961] 1 Q.B. 11 (CA) (Disciplinary Committee constituted under Solicitors Act 1957).

[21] Miller, *Contempt of Court* (3rd ed., 2000), Arlidge, Eady and Smith, *Contempt of Court* (2nd ed., 1999).

[22] The difficulty of determining what constitutes a court is discussed *ante*, para. 20–007.

[23] *Att.-Gen. v. Times Newspapers Ltd* [1992] 1 A.C. 191.

[24] *Att.-Gen. v. Leveller Magazine* [1979] A.C. 440, 449, *per* Lord Diplock.

[25] *Att.-Gen. v. BBC* [1981] A.C. 303, 362.

[26] See Willes J.'s answer to such a charge in *ex p. Fernandez* (1862) 19 C.B. (N.S.) 3, 56.

[27] See *Saunders v. United Kingdom* (1997) 23 E.H.R.R. 313. The Companies Act 1985 allowed information obtained by inspectors from a company official to be used in evidence against that person, failure to answer such questions could be punished as contempt of court. This was held to be in breach of Art. 6 E.C.H.R. Other legislation had similar provisions; s.59 and Sch. 3 of the Youth Justice and Criminal Evidence Act altered the law to conform with the E.C.H.R.

[28] [1979] 2 E.H.R.R. 245. The Phillimore Report (Cmnd. 5794 (1974)), had recommended reform.

[29] See para. 25–014.

[30] Rosalin McInnes and Douglas Fairley, *Contempt of Court in Scotland* (2001).

The common law distinguishes between civil and criminal contempt. Scots **20–044** law draws no such distinction but recognises all forms of contempt as *sui generis*. That is more logical because, on the one hand civil contempt at common law is, like a criminal offence, punishable with imprisonment and the standard of proof required is the standard in criminal law, proof beyond reasonable doubt.[31] On the other hand criminal contempt is usually tried summarily,[32] that is without a jury, a form of procedure otherwise confined to minor offences dealt with by magistrates. The importance of the distinction in English law formerly lay in the fact that no appeal was possible in the case of criminal contempt,[33] however the Administration of Justice Act 1960, s.13 provided a right of appeal in all cases of contempt. Legal aid is available in the case of some criminal contempts only.[34] Magistrates' courts, the county court and all superior courts have a discretion to grant emergency legal aid for criminal contempts committed in the face of the court or in its immediate vicinity.[35] One remaining difference is that in cases of criminal contempt enforcement of the law is a matter for the Attorney-General[36] or the court itself; in civil contempt the choice of whether to pursue the matter of disobedience to the order of the court is usually a matter for the private litigant in whose favour the order has been made.[37]

In many instances conduct which is punishable as a contempt may equally constitute a distinct common law or statutory crime. In addition to a variety of specific (and, in some instances, largely obsolescent) offences,[38] there exists the extremely wide offences of perverting (or attempting or conspiring to pervert) the course of justice.[39] The Criminal Justice and Public Order Act 1994, s.51 provides several offences in connection with the intimidation of witnesses, jurors, etc.

Civil contempt

Civil contempt of court consists of disobedience to an order of the court made **20–045** in civil proceedings. In *M. v. Home Office*[40] it was established that although a finding of contempt could not be made against the Crown, it could be made against a Minister of the Crown acting in his official capacity and against a

---

[31] *Dean v. Dean*, (1987) 17 Fam. Law 200, CA.

[32] Trial on indictment, where the facts permit, was recommended by the Court of Appeal in *Balogh v. Crown Court of St Albans* [1975] Q.B. 73. Stephenson L.J. said that the jurisdiction to deal summarily with a case in which the judge himself was interested should "never be invoked unless the ends of justice really require such drastic means: it appears to be rough justice, it is contrary to natural justice, and it can only be justified if nothing else will do." (*ibid.*, p. 90). See also *D.P.P. v. Channel Four Television Co Ltd* [1993] 2 All E.R. 517, *per* Woolfe L.J., but *cf. R. v. Griffin* (1989) 88 Cr. App. Rep. 63.

[33] *Scott v. Scott* [1913] A.C. 417.

[34] Which may not be sufficient for Art. 6.3(c) of the ECHR.

[35] s.29, Legal Aid Act 1988; the provision for legal aid in these circumstances is now included within the scope of the Criminal Defence Service created by the Access to Justice Act 1999.

[36] s.7, Contempt of Court Act 1981. The Law Commission's view is it is justifiable to give the Attorney-General an exclusive role to protect freedom of expression: Consultation Paper 149 (1997) and Report, No. 255, H.C. 1085, (1998–99).

[37] *Home Office v. Harman* [1983] 1 A.C. 280, 310 *per* Lord Scarman; but in exceptional circumstances the court itself may act: *Re M. and others (minors) (breach of contract order: committal)* [1999] 2 All E.R. 56, CA.

[38] See *Offences Relating to Interference With the Course of Justice* (Law Comm. Report No. 96, 1979).

[39] *R. v. Machin* [1980] 1 W.L.R. 763, CA; *R. v. Selvage* [1982] Q.B. 372, CA.

[40] [1994] 1 A.C. 377; see H.W.R. Wade, "Injunctive Relief Against the Crown and Ministers", (1991) 107 L.Q.R. 4; T.R.S.Allan, "Courts, Crown, Contempt and Coercion", [1994] C.L.J. 1.

government department. Here the Home Secretary, on legal advice, had ignored an order of a High Court judge requiring him to procure the return of M to this country to enable a further hearing on M's application for judicial review of the Home Secretary's decision not to grant him asylum. Lord Templeman referred to the dangers of exempting Ministers of the Crown from the coercive jurisdiction of the courts, and said of the argument that there was no power to enforce the law by injunction or contempt proceedings against a Minister in his official capacity that it would, if upheld: "establish the proposition that the executive obey the law as a matter of grace and not as a matter of necessity, a proposition that would reverse the result of the Civil War."[41]

Formerly a contemnor was liable to punishment for an indefinite period until he was prepared to "purge" his contempt by apologising and complying with the order of the court. Section 14 of the Contempt of Court Act 1981 provides a maximum sentence "on any occasion" of two years for any contempt in the case of a superior court and one month in the case of an inferior court.[42] In *Lee v. Walker*[43] the Court of Appeal held that the High Court retained an inherent jurisdiction to impose consecutive sentences of imprisonment where there are a number of separate acts of contempt. Where it is possible to ensure obedience to a court order in some way other than imprisonment, such as a warrant for possession, that is preferable.

Because of the gravity of the consequences of breach of an order made in contempt proceedings the Court of Appeal has emphasised in several decisions the need for certainty and clarity in the order with which the alleged contemnor must comply if he is to avoid imprisonment[44], and "meticulous adherence to the required formalities".[45] Although there is authority for the view that a person in contempt cannot subsequently bring proceedings in the same cause until he has purged his contempt, "It is a strong thing for a court to refuse to hear a party . . . and it is only to be justified by grave considerations of public policy."[46] In all cases the court, probably, has a discretion whether or not to hear the party, and in so deciding it should take account of the requirements of the ECHR and the need for any restriction on the right of access to the courts to be in proportionate to the aim sought.[47]

20–046   The Official Solicitor has a responsibility to keep under review the cases of all persons imprisoned for contempt and to bring to the notice of the court any circumstances which might lead to a prisoner's release. He may act irrespective of the prisoner's own wishes.[48]

Disobedience to a court order may take many forms, from the obvious case of defiance of an injunction[49] to the breach of an undertaking given to a court. The

---

[41] At p. 395 Since the normal penalties for contempt were inappropriate, an order for cost was made against the Minister.

[42] For penalties in Scotland, see s.15. In the case of a corporate body there is a power to fine or to sequestrate assets, see *D.P.P. v. Channel Four Television Co Ltd* [1993] 2 All E.R. 517.

[43] [1985] 1 All E.R. 781. A similar power is possessed by the County Court by virtue of the Supreme Court Act 1981, s.14(4A), see the County Courts (Penalties for Contempt) Act 1983.

[44] *Chiltern D.C. v. Keane* [1981] 1 W.L.R. 619. See also *Lee v. Walker* [1985] Q.B. 1191.

[45] *Re C. (a Minor)*, (1986) 16 Fam. Law 187, CA.

[46] *Hadkinson v. Hadkinson* [1952] p. 285, 298.

[47] See *X Ltd v. Morgan-Grampian Ltd* [1991] A.C. 1, where a flexible approach was favoured.

[48] See *Churchman v. Joint Shop Stewards' Committee* [1974] 1 W.L.R. 1094 (CA). (Release of three dockers imprisoned for contempt by N.I.R.C.): *Midland Cold Storage Ltd v. Turner* [1972] I.C.R. 230; *Enfield L.B.C. v. Mahoney* [1983] 1 W.L.R. 749, CA. (Refusal to deliver up the "Glastonbury Cross": inherent power of Court to release before termination of fixed period of imprisonment).

[49] *e.g. Clarke v. Chadburn* [1985] 1 W.L.R. 78. (Contempt by N.U.M.).

place of contempt in the law on discovery (now disclosure) arose in *Home Office v. Harman*,[50] and resulted in a change in the Civil Procedure Rules.[51] The problem was the need to balance open justice and the need to have a mechanism for making available to the parties confidential or embarrassing documents.

Criminal contempt

Criminal contempt of court takes various forms.   **20–047**

(i) *Scandalising the court*[52]

This form of contempt, picturesquely also known in Scotland as "murmuring judges"[53] is intended to preserve public confidence in the administration of justice by punishing words and conduct which are scurrilously abusive or impugn the impartiality of the courts. O'Higgins C.J. in *The State (D.P.P.) v. Walsh*[54] said "Such contempt occurs where wild and baseless allegations of corruption or malpractice are made against a court." In *R. v. Gray*[55] it was held to be contempt to say, in a newspaper, of Darling J., that he was an "impudent little man in horsehair ... a microcosm of conceit and empty headedness." The article went on to say, "No newspaper can exist except upon its merits, a condition from which the Bench, happily for Mr Justice Darling, is exempt." In *R. v. Editor of New Statesman, ex p. D.P.P.*[56] it was held to be contempt to say that it was impossible for certain people to hope for a fair trial from Avery J.. To commit this type of contempt, the words have to be directed at a judge in his judicial capacity: *Badry v. D.P.P.*[57]

The risk of judges confusing their own self esteem with the interests of justice is more serious here than in other areas of the law of contempt. It is necessary to bear in mind Lord Atkin's words, "Justice is not a cloistered virtue, she must be allowed to suffer the scrutiny and respectful, though outspoken comments of ordinary men."[58] In *R. v. Commissioner of Police of the Metropolis, ex p. Blackburn (No. 2)*,[59] for example, where Mr Quintin Hogg Q.C., M.P., as he then was, had published an article in *Punch* criticising the decisions of Court of Appeal on the Gaming Acts, the court held that criticisms of a court's decisions do not amount to contempt of court, even though they are in bad taste and contain inaccuracies of fact, provided they are in good faith and do not impute improper motives to those taking part in the administration of justice.

This type of contempt is virtually obsolete in English law; it would be difficult to justify it as a legitimate restriction to freedom of expression under the E.C.H.R.

---

[50] [1983] 1 A.C. 280; a friendly settlement was reached after the decision of the European Commission on Human Rights, *Harman v. United Kingdom* (1985) 7 E.H.R.R. 146.

[51] See Civil Procedure Rules 1998, r. 31.22.

[52] C. Walker, "Scandalising in the Eighties" (1985) 101 L.Q.R. 359.

[53] The Judges Act 1540 (no longer in force) provided that if "any maner of persoun murmuris any Juge temporale or spirituale als weill lordis of the sessioune as vtheris and previs nocht the samin sufficientlie ".

[54] [1981] I.R. 412, 421; see also *Attorney-General v. Connolly* [1947] I.R. 213.

[55] [1900] 2 Q.B. 36.

[56] (1928) 44 T.L.R. 301.

[57] [1983] 2 A.C. 297, PC.

[58] *Ambard v. Att.-Gen. for Trinidad and Tobago* [1936] A.C. 323, 335.

[59] [1968] 2 Q.B. 150, CA.

(ii) *Interference with justice as a continuing process*

20–048   Here again, the concern of the law is not to protect the conduct of particular proceedings but the administration of justice in general and public confidence in the courts. The Contempt of Court Act 1981, s.8 provides that it is contempt of court to obtain, disclose[60] or solicit any information about the details of the deliberations of a jury in any legal proceedings. In *R. v. Young*[61] the Court of Appeal held that it could take account of what had happened in the hotel where the jury had spent the night, as that was not part of their deliberations.[62] Proceedings under the section may only be instituted by or with the consent of the Attorney-General or on the motion of a court having jurisdiction to deal with the alleged contempt.[63] Section 8 is a restriction on freed expression, but in *Attorney-General v. Associated Newspapers Ltd*[64] the view was expressed that it did not breach the E.C.H.R.

The publication of the names of blackmail victims has been held to be a contempt because it interferes with the administration of justice by deterring future victims of such crimes from resorting to the courts: *R. v. Socialist Worker Printers and Publishers Ltd, ex p. Attorney-General.*[65] The House of Lords, however, in *Attorney-General v. Leveller Magazine Ltd*[66] emphasised that at common law there is no general right to anonymity on the part of witnesses and parties. Differing views were expressed on whether courts possessed a power specifically to order the press to refrain from revealing the identity of a witness and whether, if such a power existed, the magistrates had purported to make such a ruling. Section 11 of the Contempt of Court Act 1981 provides that where a court (having power to do so) allows a name or other matter to be withheld from the public in judicial proceedings the court may give such directions prohibiting the publication of that name or matter as appear to the court to be necessary for the purpose for which it was ordered to be withheld.[67] The section does little to clarify the common law position. It refers to courts which have the power to make directions without conferring those powers or making clear which courts possessed them under the common law. It does not make clear the effect of a breach of a direction and it does not deal with the publication of information in the absence of an express direction. Clearly the power provided by section 11 must be exercised with caution, as it creates an exception to the idea of open justice,[68] and must be interpreted in the light of Articles 6 and 8 of the E.C.H.R.[69]

20–049   "Victimising" witnesses after the conclusion of legal proceedings provides another example of conduct which generally undermines public willingness to participate in legal proceedings and confidence in the ability of courts to protect

---

[60] See *Attorney-General v. Associated Newspapers Ltd* [1994] 2 A.C. 238.

[61] [1995] Q.B. 344, CA.

[62] Four of the jurors has taken part in a seance where it was claimed the deceased told them to vote guilty; the appeal was allowed.

[63] The R.C.C.J. Cm. 2263 (1993) recommended that s.8 should be amended to allow for research into how juries reach their verdicts.

[64] [1994] 2 A.C. 238, HL.

[65] [1975] Q.B. 637.

[66] [1979] A.C. 440.

[67] A court which has not allowed a name to be withheld during proceedings cannot later attempt to prohibit publication of the name under s.11: *R. v. Arundel Justices ex p. Westminster Press Ltd* [1985] 1 W.L.R. 708.

[68] *R. v. Legal Aid Board, ex p. Kaim Todner* [1998] 3 All E.R. 541, CA.

[69] Specific statutory powers exist to shield, *e.g.* young people and vulnerable witnesses from publicity, see Youth Justice and Criminal Evidence Act 1999.

those who appear before them. "The administration of justice is, after all, a continuing thing. It is not bounded by the day's cases. It has a future as well as a present. And, if somebody pollutes the stream today so that tomorrow's litigant will find it poisoned, will he appeal to the court in vain?"[70]

In *Attorney-General v. Royal Society for the Prevention of Cruelty to Animals*[71] the society had brought disciplinary proceedings against one of its officers for giving evidence for the defence at the hearing of a private prosecution brought by the society. The Divisional Court described such conduct as, "a serious and unmitigated contempt", and imposed a heavy fine on the society.

(iii) *Contempt in the face of the court*

Conduct in a court designed to interrupt the administration of justice or expose the court to ridicule falls within this category. It covers assaults, threats, insults[72] or disturbing proceedings, for example by shouting slogans and singing songs: *Morris v. Crown Office*.[73] Witnesses who fail to attend court, produce documents or answer relevant questions, may be guilty of contempt.[74] The particular position of journalists, and others, who refuse to reveal the source of information is dealt with in section 10.[75] The alleged contempt does not have to be committed in the court room itself so long as it is closely connected with the case in progress, for example, threatening a witness outside the court room or putting a cylinder of laughing gas on the roof of the court building with the object of introducing gas into a particular court: *Balogh v. St Albans Crown Court*.[76]

Whatever the position at common law the taking of photographs and the making of sketches in court is forbidden by the Criminal Justice Act 1925, s.41.[77] The use of tape recorders or other instruments for recording sound, without the consent of the court, is made contempt by section 9 of the Contempt of Court Act 1981.[78]

20–050

(iv) *Deliberate interference with particular proceedings*

Any act interfering with the outcome of particular proceedings, such as an attempt to bribe or intimidate judges, jurors or witnesses may constitute common law contempt which was preserved by section 6(c) of the 1981 Act.[79]

20–051

(v) *Unintentional interference by prejudicial publications*

This type of contempt, which is concerned with publications which create a substantial risk of impeding or prejudicing the course of justice, is covered by the 1981 Act.[80]

20–052

[70] *Re Att.-Gen.'s Reference, Att.-Gen. v. Butterworth* [1963] 1 Q.B. 696, 725, *per* Donovan L.J.

[71] *The Times*, June 22, 1985.

[72] See *R. v. Powell* (1994) 98 Cr.App.R. 224: wolf whistling at a juror was contempt, but a sentence of 14 days' imprisonment was inappropriate.

[73] [1970] 2 Q.B. 114, CA.

[74] *R. v. Montgomery* [1995] 2 All E.R. 28, CA.

[75] See *post*, para. 25–016 for a discussion of this section.

[76] [1975] Q.B. 73, CA.

[77] It is this section which prevents the televising of court proceedings in England and Wales.

[78] See the Practice Direction [1981] 3 All E.R. 848.

[79] See *post*, para. 25– 014.

[80] See *post*, para. 25–013.

Jurisdiction to punish contempts

20–053   Although the law of contempt applies to protect proceedings in all courts, inferior courts have limited jurisdiction to enforce the law of criminal contempt. At common law an inferior court of record such as a coroner's court has jurisdiction to punish contempts in the face of the court: *R. v. West Yorkshire Coroner, ex p. Smith.*[81] Inferior courts, not of record, have no jurisdiction except where there is statutory authority; for example, magistrates' courts under the Contempt of Court Act, 1981, s.12[82] and county courts under the County Courts Act 1984, s.118.[83] In other cases provision is made for enforcement of the law by the Divisional Court.[84]

---

[81] [1985] 1 All E.R. 100.
[82] See *R. v. Newbury Justices, ex p. du Pont* (1983) 78 Cr.App.R. 255, DC. For the purposes of civil contempt county courts are superior courts: County Courts (Penalties for Contempt) Act 1983.
[83] *Bush v. Green* [1985] 1 W.L.R. 1143, CA.
[84] R.S.C., Ord. 52.

Chapter 21

THE POLICE[1]

Although the preservation of the peace, which is a royal prerogative,[2] is one of the primary functions of any state, the administration of the police has always been on a local basis in this country. That there is still no national police force today is partly a historical accident. In the sixteenth and seventeenth centuries constables were controlled both administratively and judicially by the justices of the peace, and they in their turn were controlled by the Council. The Long Parliament put an end to conciliar government by abolishing in 1642 the Star Chamber, through which this control was exercised. The Revolution Parliament had an equally strong fear of government by means of a standing army, as is witnessed by the famous declaration in the Bill of Rights 1688, and this traditional fear has since then been sufficient to prevent the formation of a national police force.

21–001

History of the police[3]

In early English law the duty of seeing that the peace was preserved and of apprehending malefactors lay on the local communities of township and hundred. These duties—represented by such terms as frank-pledge, hue and cry and sheriff's tourn—were reinforced by the Assize of Arms 1181, an ordinance of 1252 which first mentions constables, and the Statute of Westminster 1285. Under this legislation a high constable was appointed for each hundred,[4] and one or more petty constables in each township. The office of constable was an annual duty and unpaid. The constables gradually came under the control of the justices of the peace, who were introduced in the fourteenth century. In the latter part of the seventeenth century the petty constables, appointed and dismissed by the local justices, came to be identified with the parish.[5] Towns had also an inefficient system of watch by night and ward by day.

21–002

No one did more to rouse public opinion in the eighteenth century on the necessity for efficient organisation for the prevention of crime than Henry Fielding, both as author and magistrate. Sir Robert Peel, when Home Secretary, laid the foundation of a permanent professional police force for the metropolis. Nineteenth-century legislation made away with the ancient arrangements for trying to preserve the peace. Following on Peel's Metropolitan Police Act 1829,[6]

[1] T. Jefferson and R. Grimshaw, *Controlling the Constable* (1984); L. Lustgarten, *The Governance of Police* (1986). S. Uglow *Policing Liberal Society* (1988); Ian Oliver, *Police and Accountability* (2nd. ed., 1997); Neil Walker, *Policing in a Changing Constitutional Order* (2000); Robert Reiner, *The Politics of the Police* (3rd ed. 2000).
[2] Cited with approval in *R. v. Secretary of State for the Home Department, ex p. Northumbria Police Authority* [1989] Q.B. 26.
[3] L. Radzinowicz, *History of English Criminal Law and its Administration* (1956), Vol. III (1968), Vol. IV, Chap. 7; Sir Carleton Allen, *The Queen's Peace* (1953) Chap. 4; T. A. Critchley, *A History of the Police in England and Wales* (1967).
[4] High constables were abolished by the High Constables Act 1869.
[5] Parish constables were abolished by the Police Act 1964.
[6] See D. Ascoli, *The Queen's Peace: the Origins and Development of the Metropolitan Police 1829–1979* (1979). Modern statutory police forces may be traced back to the Dublin Police Act passed by the Irish Parliament in 1786, which established the Royal Irish Constabulary.

the Municipal Corporations Act 1835 required boroughs to maintain a paid police force. Every borough at one time maintained its own police force, but many of these were too small for efficiency and a series of statutes pursued a general policy of reducing their number. The borough police were administered by a Watch Committee of the Council, consisting of not more than one-third of the councillors. Meanwhile the City of London had obtained similar powers under a local Act, the City of London Police Act 1829. Optional powers were conferred on county Quarter Sessions by the Rural Police Act 1839. Not all counties availed themselves of these powers, and eventually the County and Borough Police Act 1856 extended the metropolitan scheme with modifications to all counties in England and Wales. When county councils were created by the Local Government Act 1888, the control of county police was transferred by way of compromise to a Joint Standing Committee of county councillors and justices.

21–003   As can be seen, the organisation of police administration and the legal status of the police officer grew up piecemeal. A Royal Commission was set up in 1960 to consider the constitutions and functions of local police authorities; the status and accountability of members of police forces, including chief officers of police; the relationship of the police with the public, and the means of ensuring that complaints by the public against the police are effectively dealt with. The Police Act 1964[7] accepted in general the majority of the recommendations of the Royal Commission.[8] In particular it established the tripartite structure of: police authorities, Chief constables and central government, which remains the basis of police governance in England and Wales,[9] but the powers of each part of this structure and their relationship to each other altered in 1994.

An important exception was London: the range of national functions and other tasks which arose from London's role as a capital city was seen as justification for a different control system for the Metropolitan Police, which since 1829 was under the direct control of the Home Secretary acting as its police authority.[10]

During the 1980s the government's general concern about efficiency, effectiveness and value for money in all aspects of public service included the police service.[11] The police service responded by undertaking a variety of internal reviews and initiatives aimed at addressing these demands, and unsuccessfully requested the establishment of Royal Commission on Policing. Instead the Sheehy Inquiry was established in 1992 to assess the modern needs of the police service. In 1993 a White Paper with new proposals for the structure of policing,[12] and the Sheehy Report were published. The Police and Magistrates' Court Act 1994 was broadly based on these two reports.[13] The Police Act 1996 consolidated the 1964 Act, aspects of the Police and Criminal Evidence Act 1984 and the 1994

[7] It also re-enacted certain previous statutes.
[8] Final Report (1962) Cmnd. 1728. *cf.* Dr A. L. Goodhart's Memorandum of Dissent, pp. 157, *et seq.*
[9] The position of the police in Scotland and Northern Ireland is not dealt with in this Chapter, but see Neil Walker, *op. cit.* Chaps 5 and 6; the Police (Northern Ireland) Act 2000 will make extensive alterations to policing in Northern Ireland.
[10] The other London police force is the City of London Police which had as its police authority the Common Council of the Corporation of London, which in 1985 delegated its functions to a Police Committee; the Home Secretary has particular powers in connection with this force.
[11] In the 1980s there were also conflicts between several Chief Constables and their respective police authorities; and see *R. v. Secretary of State for the Home Department, ex p. Northumbria Police Authority* [1989] 1 Q.B. 26.
[12] *Policing Reform: The Government's Proposals for the Police Service for England and Wales*, Cm. 2281.
[13] The Bill was extensively amended in the House of Lords.

Act, and provides the framework for police governance in England and Wales. The 1994 reforms sought to clarify accountability for policing and to strengthen the bonds between local communities and their police services; some commentators have suggested that they achieved the opposite.[14]

The 1962 Royal Commission had accepted that in policing the capital city the **21–004** Metropolitan Police dealt with matters of national and international importance with responsibilities which transcended local and disparate interests; in consequence there remained good reasons why it should have a different constitutional arrangement from the rest of England and Wales. However there was some dissatisfaction with the lack of accountability of the Metropolitan Police to the people of London. In 1995 a non-statutory advisory body, the Metropolitan Police Committee, was established to assist the Home Secretary oversee the performance of the Metropolitan Police.[15] The election of a Labour government committed to reforming government in London[16] resulted in the enactment of the Greater London Authority Act 1999 which, in Part VI, makes extensive alterations to the constitutional position of the Metropolitan Police. In particular it provides for the establishment of a Metropolitan Police Authority as the police authority for the Metropolitan Police.[17]

Centralising and nationalising trends in policing

The 1964 Royal Commission report rejected the case for creating a national **21–005** police system,[18] although many of the members thought a national police service would be more effective in fighting crime and handling road traffic, and the Commission did not think it would be constitutionally objectionable or politically dangerous. As a consequence of the report greater responsibilities were conferred on the Home Secretary, and provision was made for collaboration and mutual aid between forces. One of the recommendations of the Royal Commission was the further amalgamation of small police forces, and in consequence there are now 43 police forces compared to 122 in 1962.

There have been significant developments in policing since 1964 which, while not *de facto* creating a national police force, indicate a centralising trend. One of the main influences is the Home Office which, in addition to its policy-making and co-ordination role within the system of police governance,[19] provides specialised areas of support to the police forces such as the police national computer, the national automated fingerprint system and a D.N.A. database. The existence of a national Inspectorate of Police, the role of the Audit Commission and the powerful Association of Chief Officers of Police (ACPO) have contributed to this trend. Intelligence-led policing to tackle serious and organised crime on a national basis has been a further influence. The National Criminal Intelligence Service, whose role is to provide criminal intelligence to police forces, was established in 1992, but did not come under statutory authority until the Police

---

[14] Marshall and Loveday, "The Police: Independence and Accountability", in *The Changing Constitution*, (Jowell and Oliver eds., 3rd. ed., 1994). See *post*, para. 21–012 for a discussion of police accountability.

[15] For details of this Committee see Ian Oliver, *op. cit.* Chap. 7.

[16] Cm. 3727 (1997), Cm. 4014 (1998).

[17] The Police Act 1996 is amended to give the Metropolitan Police Authority similar powers to other police authorities and to give the Commissioner a similar role to Chief Constables.

[18] There are a variety of specialist national forces: the British Transport Police, the Ministry of Defence Police and the Atomic Energy Authority Constabulary, each regulated by statute.

[19] See *post*, para. 21–016 for further discussion of these and other the powers of the Home Secretary.

Act 1997. This Act also created the National Crime Squad, which developed from the existing six regional crime squads set up to deal with serious crime.[20] The remit of the Security Services[21] was extended in 1994 to include the prevention or detection of serious crime[22] and was further extended in 1996 to enable them to act in support of police forces in the prevention and detection of crime.[23] The changes in police accountability introduced in 1994 have been criticised as shifting the balance of power away from local government to central government.[24] In contrast, the relinquishment of the Home Secretary of his position as police authority for the Metropolitan Police is contrary to the centralising trends.

Main functions of the police

21–006 The Royal Commission on the Police (1962) outlined the main functions of the police as follows[25]:

(i) The duty to maintain law and order, and to protect persons and property.

(ii) The duty to prevent crime.[26]

(iii) Responsibility for the detection of criminals. Particularly in the case of terrorists and other politically motivated criminals this may involve infiltration by the police of suspect groups. The gathering of intelligence is the particular responsibility of Special Branch officers who are in close contact with the Security Services. They should not, however, procure the commission of crimes through agents provocateurs in order to secure the evidence required for conviction. Nonetheless, English law does not have a defence of "entrapment", although evidence obtained by entrapment may be excluded if its admission would have such an adverse effect on the fairness of the proceedings that the court should not admit it.[27]

(iv) Responsibility in England and Wales for making the initial decision whether to prosecute suspected criminals; the final decision is for the Crown Prosecution Service.

(v) The duty of controlling road traffic, and advising local authorities on traffic questions.[28]

---

[20] This Act established a Service Authority for each of these bodies and a framework for their control, direction and funding.

[21] *ante*, paras 19–047 to 19–050.

[22] Intelligence Services Act 1994, ss.1 and 3.

[23] Security Service Act 1996, s.1(1).

[24] See Leishman, Cope and Starie, "Reinventing and Restructuring: Towards a New Policing Order" Chap. 1 in *Core Issues in Policing* (1996).

[25] Cmnd. 1728, pp. 157, *et seq.*

[26] This duty extends to the suppression of crime in other parts of the world through cooperation with Europol and Interpol: *X. v. Metropolitan Police Commissioner* [1985] 1 W.L.R. 420.

[27] *R. v. Smurthwaite* [1994] 1 All E.R. 898, CA, applying s.78 of the Police and Criminal Evidence Act 1984. Allegations of police encouragement in the committing of a crime may result in proceedings being stayed: *R. v. Latif* [1996] 1 All E.R. 353, HL, or go to the question of sentence. See *Attorney-General's Reference No. 3 of 2000* [2001] Crim. L.R. 645, (relationship between English law and Art. 6 E.C.H.R.).

[28] The police have been assisted in this role since 1960 by traffic wardens.

Duty and discretion

Detailed consideration of what is implied in these duties and of the powers and **21–007** privileges that the police also possess in connection with them will be found in later chapters.[29] Some general points may be made here. First, the police have no privilege in carrying out their work to break the law: *Morris v. Beardmore*.[30] Secondly, they may (and must), as will be seen later, possess powers not possessed by ordinary citizens, for example, to question, search, detain and arrest. Thirdly, although the police are described as being under a duty to maintain law and order and to prevent crime, in most cases that duty involves a large element of discretion and judgment. In some, unusual cases, the duty may allow of little or no discretion; the police constable who takes no action when an assault occurs before his eyes may be guilty of the common law offence of misconduct in a public office.[31] But usually even the ordinary constable is possessed of a wide discretion; should he arrest wrongdoers or merely warn them; arrest all or some of the participants in a brawl? Superior officers, too, must exercise a discretion whether to charge offenders and, if so, with what offence or offences. In the case of a Chief Constable the element of discretion extends to general questions of policy: should he concentrate his resources on suppressing illegal trafficking in drugs, on catching burglars or enforcing the laws against pornography. During a strike should he take steps to enable non-strikers to work if they wish, and, if so, what steps?[32]

In exercising their discretionary powers the police, like other public authorities, are ultimately subject to judicial review. A constable's decision to arrest, for example, is open to challenge on the ground that it was unreasonable (in the sense given to that term in the law of judicial review[33]): *Mohammed-Holgate v. Duke*.[34] The exercise by a Chief Constable of his wider discretionary powers has been considered by the Court of Appeal, and the House of Lords. The earliest cases concerned the Metropolitan Police Force whose Commissioner is not in law a constable,[35] although the Court of Appeal equated his position with what they asserted to be that of a constable. A private citizen challenged the legality of directions issued by the Commissioner which, he alleged, meant in effect that the Metropolitan Police were not enforcing the laws against gaming[36] and pornography.[37] In all the cases the citizen failed in his applications; in the gaming case the Commissioner withdrew the offending instructions in the course of the litigation in the light of a decision of the House of Lords relating to the legality of certain forms of gambling. In the cases relating to pornography, however, he lost because the Court of Appeal emphasised that it could not tell the Commissioner how to exercise his discretion; it could only interfere if he did not exercise his discretion at all.

---

[29] *e.g.*, Chaps. 24 and 27.

[30] [1981] A.C. 446.

[31] *R. v. Dytham* [1979] Q.B. 722, CA.

[32] The discretion given to the police in connection with public assemblies and demonstrations has now to be exercised in such a way that it complies with the Human Rights Act 1998, see *post*, Chaps 22 and 27.

[33] *post*, para. 33–011.

[34] [1984] A.C. 437.

[35] Metropolitan Police Act 1829.

[36] *R. v. Commissioner of Police of the Metropolis, ex p. Blackburn* [1968] 2 Q.B. 118.

[37] *R. v. Commissioner of Police of the Metropolis (No. 3)* [1973] Q.B. 241; *R. v. Commissioner of Police of the Metropolis, The Times*, March 7, 1980, CA.

21–008   In *R. v. Chief Constable of Devon and Cornwall*[38] the Central Electricity Generating Board sought the assistance of the police to remove demonstrators who for some months had been occupying land in order to prevent the Board beginning the construction of a nuclear power station. The Court of Appeal held that the Board was entitled to the help of the police but refused to issue an order of mandamus. Templeman L.J. said that the police are not bound in all circumstances to act every time there is a breach of the law. On the other hand there came a time when they should act; but even then it was not for the court to tell the police how and when their powers should be exercised.[39] *R. v. Chief Constable of Sussex, ex p. International Trader's Ferry Ltd*[40] raised for the first time a European element to this discretion. Violent protests by those opposed to the export of veal calves required an extensive police presence to enable International Trader's Ferry Ltd (ITF) to carry on this trade. After several months the Chief Constable indicated that he was unable to continue the existing level of cover and provide an efficient and effective general police service. ITF sought judicial review on two grounds: first, unreasonable exercise of his discretion over the deployment of his resources, and secondly that his failure to guarantee safe transit of the livestock was a quantitative restriction on exports and in breach of Article 34 of the E.C. Treaty. The first argument was dismissed by all three courts, the House of Lords confirming that the police had a discretion as to how they allot the funds available to them, which would only be interfered with if it was *Wednesbury* unreasonable.[41] On the second ground, the House of Lords held that, on the assumption that the Chief Constable's decision was a "measure" for the purpose of Article 34, the decisions he took fell within the public policy exception in Article 36. The actions of the Chief Constable to maintain public order and adequate policing in his region were not disproportionate to the restrictions involved on ITF's trade.[42]

A final point to be made at this stage is that the execution by the police of their powers and the carrying out of their duties may interfere with the rights and powers of law abiding citizens. A citizen who obstructs a constable in the execution of his duty is guilty of an offence under the Police Act 1996, s.89. It may, however, be a matter of controversy whether a constable has a particular power or is acting within the scope of his duty. To what extent must the citizen in a particular instance accept the constable's view of his powers or his judgment on what is necessary in certain circumstances to prevent a breach of law? This problem will be discussed later.[43]

Legal status of police officers

21–009   The Queen's peace is part of the prerogative.[44] Police officers are not, however, Crown servants. A constable, including a Chief Constable, is an officer of

---

[38] [1982] 2 Q.B. 458, CA.

[39] See also *R. v. Oxford, ex p. Levey*, (1987) 151 L.G. Rev. 371; *Harris v. Sheffield United Football Club* [1988] 1 Q.B. 77.

[40] [1999] 1 All E.R. 129, HL; [1999] 2 A.C. 418, HL.

[41] For a discussion of the implications for accountability of where the funds come from see Barnard and Hare "The Right to Protest and the Right to Export: Police Discretion and Free Movement of Goods", (1997) 60 M.L.R. 394.

[42] Estell Baker, "Policing, Protest and Free Trade: Challenging Police Discretion under Community Law," [2000] Crim. L. Rev. 95.

[43] *post* paras 24–019 to 24–022.

[44] *Coomber v. Berks. Justices* (1883) 9 App.Cas. 61, 67, *et seq.*, *per* Lord Blackburn.

the peace, and as such has common law powers and duties.[45] These powers are exercised by a constable by virtue of his office, and not on the responsibility of anyone else, nor as a delegate or agent.[46] The legal position whereby a police officer exercises his authority by virtue of the common law as supplemented and amended by statute,[47] has to be seen in the context of his being a member of a disciplined body subject to the lawful orders of his superior officers.[48] The conflict between a police officer's individual responsibility for his actions and his duty to obey orders was referred to in *O'Hara v. Chief Constable of the Royal Ulster Constabulary*.[49] Lord Styne stated that where a statute vested an independent discretion to arrest on an individual constable, the fact that a superior officer had ordered that a particular arrest should be made, would not in itself be sufficient grounds to afford the constable reasonable grounds for the necessary suspicion. To decide otherwise would "be contrary to the principle . . . which makes a constable individually responsible for the arrest and accountable in law."[50]

21–010   The Police and Criminal Evidence Act 1984 (PACE Act) and the Public Order Act 1986 in conferring certain powers, distinguishes between different ranks of police officers. Under the PACE Act, section 55, for example, what are euphemistically described as "intimate searches" can only be authorised by an officer holding at least the rank of inspector.[51] The Public Order Act 1986 provides that "the senior police officer" may impose conditions on public processions (section 12) or public assemblies (section 14). In both sections this refers to the "most senior in rank of the police officers present at the scene".

A police officer who exceeds or abuses his powers to the injury of another may make himself personally liable in tort.[52] These cases seldom reach the courts; in the vast majority of cases the police negotiate a cash settlement. It is also possible to prosecute a police officer, but such action is rare.[53]

Vicarious liability

21–011   Since there is no master-servant relationship between a police constable and the police authority, vicarious liability for the wrongful actions can not apply.[54] This lacuna was rectified by statute, and section 88 of the 1996 Act[55] provides for

---

[45] *Lewis v. Cattle* [1938] 2 K.B. 454, DC. The office of constable is very ancient, older than that of justice of the peace.

[46] *Enever v. The King* (1906) 3 C.L.R. 969, *per* Griffiths C.J. at p. 977; approved in *Fisher v. Oldham Corporation* [1930] 2 K.B. 364, and *Att.-Gen for New South Wales v. Perpetual Trustee Co* [1955] A.C. 457, PC. *Sheilch v. Chief Constable of Greater Manchester Police* [1989] 2 W.L.R. 1102: a special constable also hold the office of constable.

[47] Today many of the powers of the police are found in the Police and Criminal Evidence Act 1984, see *post* Chap. 24.

[48] The 1962 Royal Commission acknowledged that it was not easy to reconcile these two positions, Cmnd. 1738 para. 66–67. See s.10 of the 1996 Act, which provides that the Chief Constable has "direction and control" of the force.

[49] [1997] 1 All E.R. 129, HL. The case was concerned with the meaning of reasonable suspicion in connection with a power to arrest; see *post* para. 24–009.

[50] At p. 135.

[51] As amended by the Criminal Justice and Police Act 2001 s.79. The substitution of inspector for superintendent was said by the Government to be necessary as part of the, "flexible reconstructing of the police."

[52] See Clayton and Tomlinson, *Civil Actions Against the Police* (1992); F. Belloni and J. Hodgson, Chap. 4 "Remedies for Police Misconduct" in *Criminal Injustice* (2000).

[53] See *post* para. 21–021 on police complaints.

[54] *Fisher v. Oldham Corporation* [1930] 2 K.B. 364.

[55] Re-enacting s.48 of the 1964 Act.

the vicarious liability of a Chief Constable for torts committed by constables under his direction and control in the performance or purported performance of their functions[56] in the same way as a master is liable for the torts of his servants. This is straightforward when the claimant has suffered an injury or damage as a result of the acts or omissions of a police officer,[57] it is more difficult and controversial when the damage has been caused by a third party.[58] The Race Relations (Amendment) Act 2000 makes Chief Constables vicariously liable for acts of racial discrimination by police officers.[59]

Police Accountability[60]

21–012   The following account is concerned with police forces in England and Wales; following amendments to the Police Act 1996 by the Greater London Authority Act 1999, much of it also applies to the Metropolitan Police.[61]

Police authorities

21–013   The establishment of a police authority[62] for every police area is provided for in section 3 of the 1996 Act. A police authority has the status of a body corporate (section 3(2) and section 5B), which reinforces its post 1994 independence from the local council. Prior to 1994 outside London, the police authority was a committee of the main council, with two thirds of its membership being drawn from the elected members of the council, and one third being drawn from the justices of the peace for the area. The 1994 Act reduced the size of the police authority (normally to be 17 members) and altered its composition. The membership now consists of nine members drawn from the relevant council, three magistrates and five independent members. The latter are appointed under a complex procedure, in which the Home Secretary plays a significant part (section 4 and Schedules 2 and 3 of the 1996 Act).[63]

In England and Wales every police authority is required to secure the maintenance of an efficient and effective police force for its area (Police Act 1996, s.6(1)).[64] The 1994 Act also introduced more concrete functions for the police authorities which have been repeated and expanded in the 1996 Act: to determine

---

[56] There will be no liability if the police officer was acting on "a frolic of his own": *Makanjuola v. Metropolitan Police Commissioner* [1990] 2 Admin. L.R. 214.

[57] See for example *Rigby v. Chief Constable of Northamptonshire* [1985] 1 W.L.R. 1242.

[58] See *Hill v. Chief Constable of West Yorkshire* [1989] 1 A.C. 53, and *Osman v. Ferguson* [1993] 4 All E.R. 344; *post* para. 31–024.

[59] This was proposed by the Commission for Racial Equality in its Third Review of the Race Relations Act, and by the Macpherson Inquiry into the death of Stephen Lawrence, Cm. 4262, recommendation 11.

[60] Ian Oliver, "Police Accountability in 1996", [1996] Crim. L. Rev. 611.

[61] The City of London Police was exempted from the 1994 Act following an undertaking from the Common Council of the Corporation of London to limit the size of its police committee, and to have regard to Home Office guidance issued to other forces by virtue of the 1994 Act.

[62] Unless otherwise indicated, the Metropolitan Police Authority is included in the term police authority.

[63] The police authority for London consists of 23 members: 12 London Assembly members appointed by the Mayor, one of whom must be the Deputy Mayor; seven independent members, six of whom are appointed by the police authority in accordance with a similar complex procedure as for other police authorities, and one appointed by the Home Secretary; the reminder are magistrates (Sched. 2A).

[64] A number of public bodies have statutory powers to maintain bodies of constables not subject to the Police Act 1996; see note 18 *ante*.

local policing objectives (section 7 1996 Act), which may simply reflect the national objectives laid down by the Home Secretary, if they identify local priorities these must be consistent with the national objectives[65]; and to publish a local policing plan for the force area (section 8 1996 Act[66]). In discharging its functions the police authority has to have regard to all such objectives, performance indicators and plans (section 6). The 1994 Act gave the Home Secretary the power to instruct the inspectors of constabulary to inspect any force at any time. If the force is found to be not efficient or not effective, then he can instruct the police authority to take such measures as necessary (section 40 1996 Act) and the police authority must comply with those directions (section 6(4), 1996 Act).

The police authority, subject to the approval of the Home Secretary, appoints the Chief Constable (section 11); after consulting the Chief Constable and with the approval of the Home Secretary, it also appoints the Assistant Chief Constable (section 12).[67] It may also, with the approval of the Home Secretary, call on the Chief Constable, or Assistant Chief Constable to retire in the interests of "efficiency or effectiveness" (section 11 of the 1996 Act). Before seeking the approval of the Home Secretary, the police authority is required to give the Chief Constable or other officer an opportunity to make representations, and to consider any representations so made (section 11(3) of the 1996 Act).

By contrast the Commissioner of the Metropolitan Police is appointed by the **21–014** sovereign under the sign manual and holds office during Her Majesty's pleasure. Before recommending an appointment to Her Majesty, the Home Secretary has to have regard to recommendations made to him by the Metropolitan Police Authority and representations made to him by the Mayor (section 9B 1996 Act).[68] The Metropolitan Police Authority has similar powers to other police authorities to remove the Commissioner or Deputy Commissioner (section 9E 1996 Act).

The police authority has a statutory obligation to set a budget for the year. Its sources of income are: the central police grant (51 per cent of income), a revenue support grant (administered by the Department of the Environment), nationally pooled council tax. In addition both central and local government may make grants. The police authority may accept gifts of money and loans of other property "on such terms as appear to the authority to be appropriate", which may include commercial sponsorship (section 93(1)). Day to day financial management is in effect the responsibility of the Chief Constable who must "have regard to the local policing plan".

The police authority is required to make an annual report to the Home Secretary with respect to the policing of the area (section 9 of the 1996 Act); since 1994 the Home Secretary has also been able to require a police authority to submit a report to him on any matter connected with the discharge of the authority's functions (section 43 of the 1996 Act).

---

[65] s.37 1996 Act.

[66] s.24(1) of the Local Government Act 1999 inserted s.8(2)(d) which requires police authorities to prepare "Best Value" performance plans as part of the local policing plan. Best Value is concerned with securing continuous improvements to local services.

[67] These appointments have become "fixed term" appointments.

[68] There is a similar provision for the appointment of the Deputy Commissioner, the only difference is that the Home Secretary has to have regard to representations made to him by the Commissioner.

Functions of Chief Constables[69]

21–015   The Chief Constable has direction and control of his force (sections 9A and 10 of the 1996 Act). In exercising this operational control the Chief Constable is autonomous, subject only to the powers of the police authority and the Home Secretary. In discharging his functions he is required to "have regard to the local policing plan issued by the police authority" (sections 9A and 10(2)).[70] Appointments and promotions below the rank of Assistant Chief Constable are made by the Chief Constable, subject to regulations made by the Home Secretary (section 13 of the 1996 Act). These regulations give the Chief Constable the main role in monitoring conduct and exercising discipline within the force. Since 1994 Chief Officers have had similar powers to direct and control and to hire and fire civilian employees (section 15 1996 Act). Detailed powers of financial management in respect of manpower, buildings and other equipment were also transferred from police authorities to Chief Officers. The Chief Officer of Police must submit an annual report to the police authority, and the latter may require him to report on specific matters from time to time (section 22 of the 1996 Act).

Provision is made for collaboration and mutual aid between police forces, to be arranged by Chief Officers of Police with the approval of their police authorities (sections 23 and 24 of the 1996 Act). Collaboration enables two or more Chief Officers to agree to make joint use of premises, equipment or other facilities where they believe this would be advantageous. This enabled the foundation of the regional crime squads in 1965 and the National Criminal Intelligence Service in 1992.[71] Mutual aid[72] enables Chief Officers to ask one another for manpower or other assistance to enable then to meet special demands on their resources. The Mutual Aid Co-ordination Centre (formerly the National Reporting Centre) co-ordinates the requirements and needs of police forces during, for example, strikes such as the miners' in 1984–1985 and large scale disorders. The Home Secretary has power, in certain circumstances, to direct that mutual aid arrangements should be made (section 24(2)).

The Chief Officer may agree to provide special police services at any premises in his area, *e.g.* at demonstrations on private premises, sporting events; charges are payable to the police authority on such a scale as may be determined by that authority (section 25 of the 1996 Act).[73]

Functions of the Secretary of State

21–016   Although the tripartite system of police governance gives the Home Secretary the dominant role, on the ground that the basic function of government is to preserve law and order, he does not have a general responsibility for the efficiency of policing. He has specific powers under the Act which he is required to exercise "in such manner and to such extent as appears to him to be best

---

[69] Unless otherwise indicated this account also applies to the Commissioner of Police for the Metropolis. Where appropriate, the 1996 Act has been amended by the substitution of "chief officer" for "chief constable" to reflect the changes made by the Greater London Authority Act 1999; the 1996 Act already used that term when a provision applied to both Chief Constables and Commissioners.

[70] Although it is the police authority which takes the final decision on the local policing plan, it is the Chief Constable who takes the initiative in its drafting (section 8(3) 1996 Act).

[71] These bodies are now subject to the Police Act 1997.

[72] See Lustgarten, *Governance of the Police* (1986) Chap. 8.

[73] In *Harris v. Sheffield United Football Club* [1987] 2 All E.R. 838, it was held that police presence inside the ground went beyond the Chief Constable's duty to enforce the law, and should be paid for as a special service.

calculated to promote the efficiency and effectiveness of the police" (section 36 of the 1996 Act).[74] The Home Secretary is accountable to Parliament in a general way for the provision of an efficient and effective police service. His powers include: alteration of force areas; strategic policy-making; influence and oversight of the police authorities and chief officers of police; budgetary powers; powers to provide central services and power to make general regulations on discipline and conditions of service of police officers; powers in connection with the Inspectorate of Constabulary. The 1994 reforms gave the Home Secretary greater powers in respect of the broad strategy of policing, but less involvement in the details of force management. The Greater London Authority Act 1999 transferred responsibility for the Metropolitan Police Service from the Home Secretary to the newly established Metropolitan Police Authority.

The Home Secretary may by order make alterations in police areas, other than the City of London police area, if he considers it expedient in the interests of efficiency or effectiveness (section 32 of the 1996 Act). Police authorities may propose amalgamation, in which case the proposals must be submitted to the Home Secretary for his approval. This provision, which originated in the 1964 Act, is a means by which central government can reduce the number of police forces and thereby reduce the local connection with a police force. The Home Secretary must give notice of his intention to use this section, and consider any objections (section 33 of the 1996 Act); the relevant order has to be laid in draft before Parliament and approved by each House.

The Home Secretary gained new powers in 1994 over police authorities. Section 37 of the 1996 Act allows the Home Secretary, after consultation, to lay down national policy objectives.[75] Where an objective has been laid down then he may direct police authorities to establish performance targets aimed at achieving those objectives (section 38). This power enables the Home Secretary to determine national strategies for the police. He may also issues codes of practice to police authorities, for example on Financial Management and Race Relations.

21–017

The Home Secretary shares power with the police authorities in the appointment and dismissal of Chief Constables,[76] and may require a police authority to exercise its power to call on a Chief Constable to retire in the interests of efficiency or effectiveness, after hearing his representations and holding an inquiry (section 42 of the 1996 Act).

The powers of the Home Secretary over Chief Constables did not undergo such extensive reforms in 1994, and are based on the 1964 Act. In addition to his powers of appointment and dismissal, and general powers to make disciplinary regulations (section 50 of the 1996 Act), he has a variety of powers to require reports from the police authorities.[77] As well as receiving reports on forces from the Inspectors of Constabulary, he can cause a local inquiry to be held into any matter connected with the policing of any area (section 49).[78] He may require a Chief Officer to submit a report on specific matters concerned with the policing

21–018

---

[74] This formulation of the general duty of the Home Secretary is the basis for questioning him in Parliament about the police, but it does not enable questions on operational matters, which are the responsibility of the Chief Constable.

[75] S.I. 1999 No. 543, this is the third such plan to be issued.

[76] *ante* para. 21–013.

[77] *ante* para. 21–013.

[78] *e.g.*, the Scarman inquiry into the Brixton disturbances Cmnd. 8427 (1982), the Macpherson inquiry into the death of Stephen Lawrence Cm. 4262 (1999).

of an area and a copy of the Chief Officer's annual report to the police authority must be sent to him (section 44 of the 1996 Act). He may also require Chief Officers to provide him with a variety of criminal statistics (section 45 of the 1996 Act).

The Home Secretary may make grants to police authorities of such amounts as he may with the approval of the Treasury determine (section 46 of the 1996 Act). The 1994 Act introduced a new scheme of funding. Previously central government provided 51 per cent of whatever was spent by the police authority, under section 46 the amount of police grant is cash limited, and the figure is based on 51 per cent of assessed police costs. The procedure for calculating this figure has to be published. Grants for capital expenditure may be made to police authorities, either unconditionally or subject to conditions (section 47 of the 1996 Act), as can grants for expenditure on safeguarding national security (section 48 of the 1996 Act). The Home Secretary has fewer constraints on his funding decisions than the local authority; his ability to make grants to police authorities to enable a local police force to cope with a particular occurrance with little need to account for such decisions could be significant.[79]

21–019   The power of the Home Secretary to provide specific common services found in section 41 of the 1964 Act[80] was made more general in the 1994 Act, permitting him to provide such facilities and services "as he considers necessary or expedient for promoting the efficiency or effectiveness of the police" (section 57 of the 1996 Act). His statutory powers to encourage collaboration or mutual aid contribute to his powers to provide common services.

The Home Secretary determines the number of Inspectors of Constabulary who are appointed by the Crown, on the advise of the Home Secretary[81] (sections 54 and 55 of the 1996 Act). The *Inspectorate of Constabulary* is required to report to the Home Secretary on the efficiency and effectiveness of every police force in England and Wales, and to carry out other duties as directed by the Secretary of State. The latter requirement has enabled the reviews to become thematic, for example to consider the policing of ethnic minorities. New powers were given to the Inspectorate in 1999 to allow it to report on whether a police authority has improved the ways in which its functions are exercised.[82] Reports from the Inspectorate have to be published by the Home Secretary, and copies sent to the Chief Officers and the police authority, who must respond. The Chief Inspector of Constabulary must report annually to the Home Secretary, and his report is laid before Parliament. The work of the Inspectorate takes place in the context of a national policy framework laid down by the Home Secretary; it provides an important link between the centre and the police forces.

Public Accountability

21–020   Section 20 of the 1996 Act provides that every relevant council had to make arrangements to enable questions on the discharge of the police authority's functions to be asked, and answered, at council meetings. The 1999 Act provides for the first time for a similar provision in respect of the London Assembly (section 20A of the 1996 Act). Since 1984 each police authority, in consultation

---

[79] For examples to support the policing of an industrial dispute.

[80] This was interpreted widely in *R. v. Secretary of State for the Home Department, ex p. Northumbria Police Authority* [1989] 1 Q.B. 26.

[81] Formerly the Inspectors were all ex-chief officers, but increasingly serving chief officers have become Inspectors, and since 1991 part-time non-police officers have been appointed.

[82] "The Best Value framework" as established in the Local Government Act 1999 Part I.

with the Chief Constable,[83] has been required to obtain the views of the people of the area about matters concerning the policing of the area, and their co-operation with the police in crime prevention.[84] This has been implemented by non-elected consultative committees, which have been assessed as "talking shops" which have little influence on policing.[85] The requirement that police authorities establish a local policing plan, should provide a more effective forum for such groups.

The Home Secretary has a limited requirement to account to Parliament for policing since his responsibilities are to set national policing objectives and performance indicators; he cannot be questioned in Parliament about how a Chief Constable or an individual police officer has exercised his discretion, although these decisions may be influenced by objectives established by the Home Secretary. Since the 1999 reform, this is also the position with respect to the Metropolitan Police.

Complaints against police officers

An important aspect of genuine accountability of the police to the public, as opposed to the members of a police authority, is the existence of a satisfactory system to deal with complaints against the police. To say that the citizen has the right of recourse to the courts is unrealistic on various accounts. He may not be able to obtain the necessary evidence by his own efforts[86]: the conduct he complains of may not constitute a crime or tort but still fall below the standard properly expected of a public servant. The Police Act 1964, left the investigation and adjudication of complaints against the police to other police officers, a system reformed by the Police Act 1976 which established a Police Complaints Board, which looked at all reports of investigations into complaints except those involving possible criminal charges which went to the D.P.P. This system was criticised for its limited independent element and its failure to distinguish between minor and serious complaints. The Police and Criminal Evidence Act 1984 introduced a new scheme for dealing with complaints which was subject to further reform in 1994. The present law, based on the 1984 Act, is found in Part IV of the 1996 Act. There has also been dissatisfaction with this system,[87] and legislation to establish a new complaints system was promised in the 2001 Queen's Speech.

21–021

The 1984 Act established the Police Complaints Authority whose independence was emphasised by the provision that its chairman shall be appointed by the Queen. The other members, none of whom may be, or have been, police constables, are appointed by the Secretary of State (section 66 and Schedule 5 of the 1996 Act). Complaints may be made by a member of the public or by anyone on behalf of a member of the public—for example, the M.P. of a person aggrieved. The chief officer in whose area a complaint is made must take steps to obtain or preserve evidence relating to the complaint although he may subsequently refer the complaint to the Chief Officer of another force if it appears that

[83] Since the 1999 Act, s.96 applies in the same way to the Metropolitan Police.
[84] This was one of the proposals made in the Scarman Report, Cmnd. 8427 (1982).
[85] R. Morgan, "Talking about Policing", in *Unravelling Criminal Justice* (Downes, ed., 1992).
[86] Despite these problems the number of civil actions against the police, settled either in or out of court has risen in recent years, see H.C. 258 (1997–98) paras. 31–34.
[87] See Royal Commission on Criminal Justice, Cm. 2263 (1993), Chap. 3; the Home Affairs Select Committee First Report H.C. 258 (1997–98); Second Special Report H.C. 683 (1998–99); Macpherson inquiry, *op cit.*; Home Office Consultation Paper *Complaints Against the Police*, 2000.

it is appropriate to do so (section 67 of the 1996 Act). Complaints relating to officers above the rank of chief superintendent (senior officers) cannot be dealt with by a chief officer of a force but must be referred to the relevant police authority (section 68 of the 1996 Act). In the case of other ranks the procedure subsequent to the making of a complaint is the responsibility of a chief officer. Provision is made in section 69 of the 1996 Act for the informal resolution of complaints where that is appropriate. Chief Constables or police authorities must refer to the Police Complaints Authority any complaint alleging that conduct complained of resulted in death or serious injury (section 70 of the 1996 Act). Any matter *may* be referred to the Complaints Authority where it appears that a police officer has committed a criminal offence or an offence against discipline and the matter has not been made the subject of a complaint and it is the view of the police authority or the Chief Constable, as appropriate, that the matter ought to be referred by reason of its gravity or exceptional circumstances (section 71 of the 1996 Act). In the light of the discussion earlier of the accountability of chief officers it should be noted that it is expressly provided by section 67(4) of the 1996 Act that the complaints procedure does not apply to any complaint "in so far as it relates to the direction or control of a police force by the chief officer or the person performing the functions of the chief officer."

21–022   A feature of the procedure is that the investigation stage of complaints is to be subject to the supervision of the Complaints Authority in all cases involving death or serious injury and in other cases if it considers it desirable in the public interest (section 72 of the 1996 Act). Supervision may take the form of approving a particular officer to carry out the investigation and imposing specific requirements as to the carrying out of the investigation.

Once the investigation is complete the procedure depends on whether the complaint relates to senior officers or not. In the case of senior officers the report must be sent to the Director of Public Prosecutions unless the police authority (of the relevant force) is satisfied that no criminal offence has been committed (section 74 of the 1996 Act). In the case of other officers the chief officer of the force must decide whether the report indicates that a criminal offence has been committed: if he does so decide he must forward the report to the Director of Public Prosecutions.[88] He must, after the Director has dealt with the question of criminal proceedings, inform the Complaints Authority whether he intends to prefer disciplinary charges. If the chief officer decides that the officer ought not to be charged with a criminal offence he must inform the Complaints Authority and again indicate whether he intends to prefer disciplinary proceedings. Finally if the chief officer concludes that the report does not indicate the commission of a criminal offence he must relay his conclusion to the Complaints Authority and indicate whether he intends to prefer disciplinary proceedings (section 75 of the 1996 Act); the Complaints Authority may recommend that disciplinary charges should be laid (section 76 of the 1996 Act). Charges laid under section 76, or in other cases where the Complaints Authority direct, are to be heard by a disciplinary tribunal, consisting of the chief officer and two members of the Authority.[89]

---

[88] Prosecutions are rare; in the light of several cases where the DPP had been asked to look again at decisions not to prosecute police officers, an independent inquiry was established: Butler Report, *Inquiry into C.P.S. Decision Making in Relation to Deaths in Custody and Related Matters* (1999). G. Smith, "Police Complaints and Criminal Prosecutions", (2001) 64 M.L.R. 372.

[89] s.78 provides for the application of the complaints procedure to constables maintained by bodies other than local government police authorities, *e.g.* British Transport Police.

Police authorities and Inspectors of Constabulary are required to keep them- **21–023** selves informed about the way in which complaints are dealt with (section 77 of the 1996 Act). The Complaints Authority is required to make an annual report to the Secretary of State and may make other reports on any matter coming to their notice in connection with their responsibility (section 79 of the 1996 Act).

Discipline

Connected with police complaints is police discipline. In 1999 new regula- **21–024** tions, which extensively reformed the previous scheme, were introduced.[90] In particular the double jeopardy rule, whereby an officer acquitted of a criminal offence could not be charged with an equivalent disciplinary, was abolished[91] and the standard of proof in disciplinary proceedings was changed to the civil standard of the balance of probabilities.

---

[90] S.I. 1999 No. 730, made under ss.50 and 84 of the 1996 Act.
[91] This was provided for by s.37(f) of the 1994 Act, but only took effect in April 1999.

PART V

RIGHTS AND DUTIES OF THE INDIVIDUAL

CHAPTER 22

RIGHTS AND DUTIES GENERALLY

I. INTRODUCTION

In this Part we discuss the civil rights which have been traditionally recognised   **22–001**
as the hall marks of a free society. We discuss also some areas of the criminal law
which are designed to preserve a society in which these rights can be exercised
and to protect individuals against undue invasion of their rights by the actions of
others. Dicey was concerned in his discussion of basic civil rights to demonstrate
that they had been deduced as principles from judicial decisions determining the
rights of private persons in particular cases brought before the Courts "whereas
under many foreign constitutions the security (such as it is) given to the rights of
individuals results, or appears to result, from the general principles of the constitution." [1]

Rights of the individual under the United Kingdom Constitution[2]

As has been seen in Chapter 2, there are under the constitution of the United   **22–002**
Kingdom no rights strictly fundamental, in the sense of entrenched (basic,
inalienable), because of the supremacy of Parliament and the absence of a written
constitution with entrenched provisions and judicial review of Acts of Parliament.[3] However, as was also mentioned, the Courts have increasingly in recent
years adverted to the importance of generally recognised rights and suggested
that they are so fundamental to the common law that statutes must be read in the
light of their existence and they will be restricted only by the clearest words. The
right of unimpeded access to a court, for example, must "even in our unwritten
constitution . . . rank as a constitutional right".[4] Freedom of expression is "the
primary right" in a democracy.[5]

At the same time, however, support was increasingly being expressed for the
adoption by the United Kingdom of some form of written constitutional statement of basic rights not only by academic writers but also by senior members of
the judiciary.[6] Various proposals were made. Some writers preferred the drafting

[1] *The Law of the Constitution* (10th ed.), p. 195.
[2] D. Feldman, *Civil Liberties and Human Rights in England and Wales* (2nd ed., 2001); G. Robertson, *Freedom, The Individual and the Law* (6th ed., 1989); S. H. Bailey, D. J. Harris and B. L. Jones, *Civil Liberties, Cases and Materials* (3rd ed., 1991); C. Palley, *The United Kingdom and Human Rights* (1991).
[3] *ante*, para. 2–034.
[4] *R. v. Secretary of State for the Home Department ex p. Leech* [1994] Q.B. 198, 210, *per* Steyn L.J. (Prison Act 1952 not sufficiently unambiguous to justify making Prison Rule which interfered with right of access to legal advisers). *R. v. Secretary of State for the Home Department ex p. Ruddock* [1987] 1 W.L.R. 1482; *cf. R. v. Lord Chancellor ex p. Witham* [1998] Q.B. 575, DC; distinguished, *R. v. Lord Chancellor ex p. Lightfoot* [2000], 2 Q.B. 597, CA.
[5] *R. v. Secretary of State for the Home Department ex p. Simms* [2000] 2 A.C. 115, HL. See too *Derbyshire C.C. v. Times Newspapers Ltd* [1993] A.C. 534, HL.
[6] Lord Lloyd of Hampstead, "Do we Need a Bill of Rights?" (1976) 39 M.L.R. 121; C. Campbell, ed., "*Do We Need a Bill of Rights?*" (1980); J. Jaconelli, *Enacting a Bill of Rights: The Legal Problems* (1980, Oxford); M. Zander, *A Bill of Rights* (4th ed., 1997, Sweet & Maxwell); J. Wadham, "A British Bill of Rights" in *Constitutional Reform* (R. Blackburn and R. Plants, eds, 1999,

of a Bill of Rights, adapted to the needs of the nation at the time of drafting.[7] Others supported incorporation into domestic law of the European Convention on Human Rights on the grounds that, whatever its shortcomings, the United Kingdom had been a signatory to the Convention for many years and its adoption would not involve the same degree of controversy that would inevitably flow from attempting to draft a Bill of Rights from scratch.[8] Scepticism about the wisdom of conferring new and potentially controversial powers on the judiciary was voiced, however, forcefully by Professor J. A. G. Griffith.[9]

22–003   In its Manifesto at the 1997 Election the Labour Party included a pledge to introduce legislation incorporating the European Convention into United Kingdom law. Its election victory resulted in that pledge leading to the enactment of the Human Rights Act 1998 with which much of the rest of this chapter will be concerned.

In addition to the question, what rights should be protected, in the period before 1998 the issue of the possibility of entrenching any legislation on rights was discussed. Dicey's view of Parliamentary supremacy is inconsistent with the possibility of entrenching a statute of the United Kingdom Parliament. The government in introducing the proposed legislation simply—and probably wisely—ignored the issue.[10]

International Covenants[11]

22–004   Popularisation of the concept of human rights in the western world began in 1941[12] during the Second World War with the Atlantic Charter, a joint declaration by the United State President (Franklin Roosevelt) and the United Kingdom Prime Minister (Churchill), and Roosevelt's message to Congress proclaiming the Four Freedoms—freedom of speech and expression, freedom of religion, freedom from fear and freedom from want; followed by a declaration of United Nations war aims in 1942 that victory was essential to defend life, liberty, independence and religious freedom, and to preserve human rights and justice. These rights were elaborated in the Universal Declaration of Human Rights adopted and proclaimed in 1949 by the General Assembly of the United Nations, including the United Kingdom.[13] No attempt was made at the time to specify limitations on those rights; to distinguish political, economic and social rights; or

Longman). Judicial contributions include, Sir Leslie Scarman, *English Law—The New Dimension* (Hamlyn Lectures, 1974); Lord Browne-Wilkinson, "The Infiltration of a Bill of Rights" [1992] P.L. 397; Lord Bingham, "The European Convention on Human Rights: Time to Incorporate" (1993) 109 L.Q.R. 390; Laws L.J., "Is the High Court the Guardian of Fundamental Rights?" (1993) P.L. 59; "Law and Democracy" [1995] P.L. 72; Lord Woolf, "Droit Public—English Style" [1995] P.L. 57. Laws L.J., "The Constitution: Morals and Rights" [1996] P.L. 623; Lord Irvine, "Response to Lord Justice Laws" [1996] P.L. 636.

[7] Although it might be thought that the concept of fundamental rights is undermined by the admission that they can arise or fade away within a period of 50 years.

[8] Bills were introduced in both Houses of Parliament from 1975 onwards by the Liberal Party. Lord Scarman introduced a Bill for incorporating the Convention in 1985. Sir Edward Garner, Q.C., a Conservative M.P. introduced a Bill in 1987 and Lord Lester of Herne Hill, Q.C., a Liberal Democrat peer, introduced bills in 1994 and 1996.

[9] *The Politics of the Judiciary* (5th ed., 1997).

[10] "It would not be necessary or desirable to attempt entrenchment": White Paper, (1997) Cm 3782, para. 2.16.

[11] Ian Brownlie (ed.), *Basic Documents on Human Rights* (3rd ed., 1992). P. R. Ghandhi, *International Human Rights Documents* (2nd ed., 1995).

[12] But *cf.* the work of the International Labour Organisation which was established after the First World War.

[13] *ante,* para. 1–020.

to provide machinery for enforcement. The United Nations drew up more elaborate formulations in 1966—in some respects improving on the European Convention—in the International Covenant on Economic, Social and Cultural Rights[14] and the International Covenant on Civil and Political Rights, which were ratified by the United Kingdom in 1976 with certain reservations in relation to education and dependent territories.[15] Subsequent developments have included the adoption of Conventions on the Elimination of All Forms of Discrimination against Women (1979), against Torture and other Cruel, Inhuman or Degrading Treatment or Punishment (1984), which was incorporated into the law of the United Kingdom by the Criminal Justice Act 1988, section 134,[16] and the Convention on the Rights of the Child, (1989).

The increasing international emphasis on the recognition of human rights had led to attempts to draft conventions on a regional basis, with emphasis on effective machinery for enforcement and the provision of remedies for infringement of guaranteed rights. In the United Kingdom the European Convention on Human Rights is the most important example of this development. Other significant important examples include the inter-American system of Human Rights.[17]

The European Convention[18]

The Member States of the Council of Europe,[19] being a number of democratic **22–005** European countries including the United Kingdom, drew up the European Convention for the Protection of Human Rights and Fundamental Freedoms in 1950 as a first step in the collective enforcement of certain of the rights stated in the Universal Declaration. The United Kingdom ratified the Convention in 1951.[20] Although it was not part of English or Scots law the Convention began to exert a strong influence on the way civil rights were regarded in this country.

An important feature of the European Convention from its inception was the provision of effective machinery to enforce the rights which it proclaimed. Provision was made for complaints to be laid by a State alleging breach of the provisions by another State[21] and, more remarkably, for a right of individual petition by a citizen of a signatory state.[22]

Until the reforms to the Convention which took effect in 1998, all applications **22–006** alleging breaches of the Convention were made to the Commission on Human

---

[14] M. Craven, *The International covenant on Economic, Social and Cultural Rights* (1998).

[15] D. Harris and S. Joseph, *The International covenant on Civil and Political Rights and the United Kingdom* (1995).

[16] See *R. v. Bow Street Magistrate ex p. Pinochet (No. 3)* [2000] 1 A.C. 147, HL.

[17] D. J. Harris and S. Livingstone, *The Inter-American System of Human Rights* (1998).

[18] D. J. Harris, M. O'Boyle and C. Warbrick, *Law of the European Convention on Human Rights* (1995); F. G. Jacobs and R. C. A. White, *The European Convention on Human Rights* (2nd ed., 1996); A. H. Robertson and J. G. Merrills *Human Rights in Europe* (3rd ed., 1993); R. Beddard, *Human Rights and Europe* (3rd ed., 1993); A. Drzemczewski, *European Human Rights Convention in Domestic Law* (1983).

[19] The Council of Europe was established in 1949: the aim of the Council was declared by its founding Statute to be "to achieve a greater unity between its Members for the purpose of safeguarding and realising the ideals and principles which are their common heritage and facilitating their economic and social progress."

[20] Lord Jowett, then Lord Chancellor, thought that accepting the Convention would "jeopardise our whole system of law, which we have laboriously built up over centuries, in favour of some half baked scheme to be administered by some unknown court": see Anthony Lester, "Fundamental Rights, The United Kingdom Isolated" [1984] P.L. 46, 51.

[21] *e.g. Ireland v. United Kingdom* (1978) 2 E.H.R.R. 25.

[22] *e.g. Lawless v. Ireland* (1961) 1 E.H.R.R. 15.

Rights. The Commission decided whether a complaint was admissible, the Commission then established the facts and gave a legal opinion which was transmitted to the Committee of Ministers. The Commission was empowered to refer a case to the Court by Article 48, the normal way by which the Court became seized of a dispute.[23]

Under the revised Convention, following the coming into effect of the Eleventh Protocol, the Commission and the Court have been merged.[24] A new procedure had been required to cope with the continual increase in the number of applications each year arising from a greater awareness of the roles of the Commission and the Court and the expansion in the number of signatory states since the foundation of the Council of Europe in 1949.

The newly constituted Court consists of full-time judges, equal in number to the states which are parties to the Convention.[25] The work of the Court will be carried out by Committees, consisting of three judges, Chambers, consisting of seven judges, and a Grand Chamber of 17 judges. Although each judge sits in his individual capacity and not as a representative of the State which nominated him,[26] each State involved in litigation is entitled to have its national judge (or another of its choice) included as an *ex officio* member of the relevant Chamber or Grand Chamber (Article 27(2)).

A second important change to the previous law relates to the right of individual petition. Formerly, under Article 25 the right was subject to the lodging of a declaration by the relevant State which might be for a fixed period, subject to renewal, or indefinitely.[27] Under Article 34, however, the right is now independent of State agreement.

The European Convention before the Human Rights Act 1998

22–007   Increasingly as litigants obtained judgments at Strasbourg against the United Kingdom the Convention began to be cited in our domestic courts. This was despite the fundamental constitutional principle that treaties cannot affect rights and duties of persons in the United Kingdom unless their provisions have been incorporated into domestic law by legislation. That fundamental principle, was illustrated in the *G.C.H.Q.* Case[28] when Lord Fraser in the part of his speech headed "Minor matters" declined to consider the interpretation of certain international labour conventions because they were "not part of the law in this country". In *British Airways Board v. Laker Airways Ltd*[29] Lord Diplock said, "The interpretation of treaties to which the United Kingdom is a party but the terms of which have not either expressly or by reference been incorporated in English domestic law by legislation is not a matter that falls within the interpretative jurisdiction of an English court of law". Nonetheless the Convention was frequently cited in the courts and judges on various occasions referred to its

---

[23] For details of the earlier procedure, see Harris, O'Boyle and Warbrick, *op. cit.*

[24] Decisions and Opinions of the Commission remain of importance in interpreting the terms of the Convention and are expressly mentioned in s.2(1)(b) and (c) of the Human Rights Act.

[25] A. R. Mowbray, "A new European Court of Human Rights" [1994] P.L. 540; "The composition and operation of the new European Court of Human Rights" [1999] P.L. 219.

[26] Each State nominates three names from which the final selection is made by the Parliamentary Assembly: Art. 22.

[27] Thus under Article 25 the United Kingdom withdrew the right of individual petition in relation to the Isle of Man after *Tyrer* (1978) 2 E.H.R.R. 1; *post* para. 22–032 and para. 35–001.

[28] *Council of Civil Service Unions v. Minister for the Civil Service* [1985] A.C. 374.

[29] [1985] A.C. 58.

provisions although no decision can be said to have been based on the Convention. In *Kynaston v. Secretary of State for the Home Department*[30] the Court of Appeal held that the clear words of the United Kingdom mental health legislation prevailed over the provisions of Article 5 (right to liberty of the person). Article 6 (right to a hearing) was involved in *Trawnik v. Lennox*.[31] Sir Robert Megarry V.-C., said "The [European] Convention [of Human Rights] is not, of course, law though it is legitimate to consider its provisions in interpreting the law; and naturally I give it full weight for this purpose."[32] Nonetheless, he (and subsequently the Court of Appeal) applied the letter of the Crown Proceedings Act 1947. Article 8 (respect for private and family life) was similarly invoked in vain in an attempt to challenge the legality of telephone tapping in *Malone v. Commissioner of Police of the Metropolis*.[33] Article 8 and Article 14 (enjoyment of rights without discrimination) have failed to aid immigrants in the light of the provisions of the Immigration Act 1971 and the Immigration Rules: "The Convention is not part of the law of this country. If it happens to be in accord with the law so much the better. But on the other hand if it does not accord with the law ... then it is a matter of which we cannot take any account: *R. v. Immigration Appeal Tribunal ex p. Ali Ajmal*,[34] per Lord Lane C.J. In *R. v. Ministry of Defence ex p. Smith*[35] the Divisional Court and Court of Appeal felt bound to disregard Article 8 when considering the dismissal from the armed forces of the applicants because of their sexual orientation—although they had little doubt of the applicants' ultimate success at Strasbourg.

Article 9 (freedom of religious expression) was unsuccessfully relied on in **22–008** *Ahmed v. Inner London Education Authority*.[36] The same Article was invoked by Lord Scarman in *R. v. Lemon*[37] to justify limitations on free speech. Article 10 (freedom of speech) was cited by Lord Simon and Lord Scarman in their dissenting speech in *Home Office v. Harman*[38] (as well as Milton and the Constitution of the United States). In *R. v. Wells Street Stipendiary Magistrate ex p. Deakin*[39] the House of Lords indicated the need for a reform of the law of criminal libel and Lord Diplock described the present English law as being contrary to Article 10. In *Schering Chemicals v. Falkman*[40] a majority in the Court of Appeal upheld the granting of injunction to prevent the showing of a television programme which had been sought on various grounds. Lord Denning M.R. (dissenting) referred to the importance of freedom of expression and quoted both Blackstone and Article 10. He said, "I take it that our law should conform as far as possible with the provisions of the European Convention of Human Rights". In *Derbyshire C.C. v. Times Newspapers Ltd*[41] the House of Lords in refusing a claim to sue in libel by the county council, considered that the common law on freedom of speech was in accordance with Article 10. In a

---

[30] (1981) 73 Cr.App.R. 281.
[31] [1985] 1 W.L.R. 532.
[32] At p. 541.
[33] [1979] Ch. 344; *post*, para. 22–012 and para. 26–014.
[34] [1982] Imm.A.R. 102, CA.
[35] [1996] Q.B. 517.
[36] [1978] Q.B. 36, CA; Scarman L.J. dissenting. See also *Panesar v. Nestlé Co.* [1980] I.C.R. 144, CA.
[37] [1979] A.C. 617.
[38] [1983] 1 A.C. 280.
[39] [1980] A.C. 477.
[40] [1982] Q.B. 1.
[41] [1993] A.C. 534.

number of cases relating to trades unions references have been made to Article 11 (right to join and form unions)[42] but judges have differed sharply about the correct significance to draw from the Article when applied to particular facts. In *Cheall v. APEX*,[43] for example, Donaldson L.J. agreed with Lord Denning M.R. that "in matters of legal policy regard should be had to this country's international obligations to observe the treaty as interpreted by the European Court of Human Rights." Nonetheless, he found the conclusion drawn by the Master of the Rolls from Article 11 a "somewhat surprising proposition".

At most, therefore, it could be said that the courts were entitled to look at the Convention, when faced, as Donaldson L.J. suggested in *Cheall v. APEX (supra)*,[44] with a question of legal policy (or public policy), or where the substantive law was unclear as Lord Fraser suggested in *Attorney-General v. BBC*,[45] "The House, and other courts in the United Kingdom should have regard to the provisions of the Convention [on Human Rights] and to the decisions of the Court of Human Rights in cases . . . where our domestic law is not firmly settled. But the Convention does not form part of our law and the decision on what that law is for our domestic courts and for this House."

The Construction of Statutes

22–009   A particular example of the use of the Convention to aid in resolving uncertainty in the law may be said to be found in having recourse to its provisions as an aid to statutory interpretation.

The justification for doing so was that Parliament must know that the United Kingdom has ratified the Convention and so must be taken to intend not to legislate contrary to it. Thus in *Waddington v. Miah*,[46] where the question was whether penal provisions of the Immigration Act 1971 were retrospective, Lord Reid referred to Article 11 of the Universal Declaration and Article 7 of the European Convention (no *ex post facto* criminal laws) and said: "It is hardly credible that any government department would promote or that any Parliament would pass retrospective criminal legislation." In *Birdi v. Secretary of State for Home Affairs*,[47] where a detained illegal immigrant applied unsuccessfully for habeas corpus alleging violations of Article 5 (liberty of person), Article 6 (fair trial) and Article 13 (effective remedies), Lord Denning M.R. stated *obiter* that the courts could and should take the Convention into account when construing statutes, since all concerned with framing legislation after the Convention came into force must be assumed to have borne the Convention in mind. His Lordship even went so far as to suggest that an Act which did not conform might be held invalid. Lord Denning in *ex p. Bhajan Singh*,[48] where an illegal immigrant applied unsuccessfully for mandamus against the Home Office to permit him to

---

[42] e.g. *R. v. G.L.C., ex p. Burgess* [1978] I.C.R. 991, DC; *U.K.A.P.E. v. A.C.A.S.* [1979] 1 W.L.R. 570; [1981] A.C. 424; *Taylor v. Co-operative Retail Services Ltd* [1982] I.C.R. 600, CA.

[43] [1982] I.C.R. 231. Article 11 was also referred to in the House of Lords which reversed the decision of the Court of Appeal: [1983] 2 A.C. 180.

[44] See similarly F. A. Mann, "Britain's Bill of Rights" (1978) 94 L.Q.R. 512. *cf. R. v. Secretary of State for the Home Dept. ex p. Fernandes, The Times*, November 21, 1980; [1981] Imm.A.R. 1; *R. v. Secretary of State for the Home Dept ex p. Kirkwood* [1984] 1 W.L.R. 913 (Secretary of State under no duty to consider Convention before deporting).

[45] [1981] A.C. 303.

[46] [1974] 1 W.L.R. 683, HL. On the first reference to the Convention in an English court, see note by Stephenson L.J., (1979) 85 L.Q.R. 35.

[47] February 11, 1975, CA, unreported. *cf. Minister of Home Affairs v. Fisher* [1980] A.C. 319, PC. (Interpretation of Constitution of Bermuda in light of United Nations Conventions).

[48] *R. v. Secretary of State for Home Department, ex p. Bhajan Singh* [1976] Q.B. 198, CA.

marry while in custody and relied on Article 12 (marriage and family), stated *obiter* that the courts should take account of the Convention when interpreting statutes affecting the rights and liberties of the citizen; and that it was hardly credible that Parliament or any government department would act contrary to the provisions of the Convention, and regard must be had to them by Ministers and government officials. But His Lordship admitted he went too far in *Birdi (supra)*: if an Act did not conform to the Convention the Act would prevail. And Scarman L.J. in *ex p. Phansopkar*,[49] where a Commonwealth immigrant wife of a patrial was refused entry under the Immigration Act 1971 on the ground that she had not obtained a certificate of patriality, referring to Article 8 (respect for family life) said it was the duty of the courts to have regard to the Convention and to construe statutes so as to promote those rights, so long as they do not disregard clear and unequivocal provisions of the statute.

In *ex p. Salamat Bibi*[50] where the wife and children of a Pakistani resident who   **22–010** sought to join him here after Pakistan had left the Commonwealth, were treated as foreign nationals and the wife cited Article 8 of the Convention (family life), Lord Denning, after stating that the courts can look to the Convention as an aid to clear up ambiguity in our statutes or uncertainty in our law,[51] added: "But I would dispute altogether that the Convention is part of our law. Treaties and declarations do not become part of our law until they are made law by Parliament. I desire, however, to amend one of the statements I made in the *Bhajan Singh* case [*ante*] . . . that the immigration officers ought to bear in mind the principles stated in the Convention . . . They must go simply by the immigration rules laid down by the Secretary of State, and not by the Convention." A Muslim teacher was held in *Ahmad v. I.L.E.A.*[52] not to be entitled, either by the Education Act 1944 or by the European Convention, to preferential treatment to enable him to attend a Mosque in school hours; Lord Denning saying that, although the Convention is not part of our law the courts do their best to see that their decisions are in conformity with it, but Article 9 (freedom of religion) was too vague to be relied on here. Scarman L.J. in his dissenting judgment, however, thought the Education Act 1944 had to be construed today in accordance with that Article.[53]

Even this moderate approach was criticised in Scotland. Lord Ross in *Kaur v. Lord Advocate*[54] said "With all respect to the distinguished judges in England who have said that the courts should look to an international convention such as the European Convention of Human Rights for the purposes of interpreting a United Kingdom statute, I find such a concept extremely difficult to comprehend. If the Convention does not form part of the municipal law, I do not see why the court should have regard to it at all. It was His Majesty's government in 1950 which was High Contracting Party to the Convention. The Convention has been ratified by the United Kingdom but . . . its provisions cannot be regarded as

---

[49] *R. v. Secretary of State for Home Department, ex p. Phansopkar* [1976] Q.B. 606, CA.
[50] *R. v. Chief Immigration Officer, Heathrow Airport, ex p. Salamat Bibi* [1976] 1 W.L.R. 979, CA.
[51] If this means common law, the statement is questionable.
[52] *Ahmad v. Inner London Education Authority* [1978] Q.B. 36, CA. A subsequent application to the Commission was ruled inadmissible: (1982) 4 E.H.R.R. 126.
[53] See also *Broome v. Cassell & Co* [1972] A.C. 1927, 1133, HL, *per* Lord Kilbrandon (free speech); *Blathwayte v. Baron Cawley* (1976) A.C. 397, 426, *per* Lord Wilberforce (public policy); *R. v. Deevey* [1977] Crim.L.R. 550, *per* Sir Robert Lowry C.J.N.I. (Firearms Act); *R. v. Secretary of State for Home Department, ex p. Hosenball* [1977] 1 W.L.R. 766, CA (deportation on security grounds).
[54] [1980] 3 C.M.L.R. 79; 1981 S.L.T. 322.

having the force of law . . . Under our constitution it is the Queen in Parliament who legislates and not Her Majesty's government, and the court does not require to have regard to acts of Her Majesty's government when interpreting the law."

22–011   The House of Lords in *R. v. Home Secretary ex p. Brind*[55] while recognising that the courts could have recourse to the Convention when faced with an ambiguous statute refused to go a step further and hold that where wide powers of decision making were given to a minister by an unambiguous statutory provision, the minister in exercising those powers should conform to the provisions of the Convention. To do so, in the words of Lord Ackner, would be to incorporate the Convention into English law by the back door.[56]

No decision of the British courts before the coming into effect of the Human Rights Act was actually based on the European Convention. The dicta on the construction of statutes not purporting to implement a treaty do not follow from precedents concerned with construing statutes consistently with the general principles of international law[57] or statutes designed to implement particular treaties on such matters as diplomatic privilege. It is submitted, further, that their approach is potentially dangerous.[58] The judges wish to keep government officers to their international obligations, but in fact they are challenging the cardinal principle laid down in the *Case of Proclamations*[59] and our own Bill of Rights of 1688, that the Executive by itself cannot make law for this realm. Indeed, one might argue that the fact that Parliament had refrained from incorporating the European Convention into our law indicated an intention that its provisions should not be taken into account by the courts, so that the Convention ought not to be cited by counsel or looked at by judges.[60]

Cases against the United Kingdom in the European Court of Human Rights

22–012   Although unable to rely on the Convention in the domestic courts before the coming into effect of the Human Rights Act 1998, litigants were able, in reliance on the right of individual petition to argue before the European Court of Human Rights that United Kingdom law was in breach of the terms of the Convention. Cases in which they did so successfully will be cited in Part II in discussing the scope of Convention Rights. Here the emphasis is on the way the United Kingdom government reacted to these decisions, usually changing domestic law by legislation, or administrative action. After the decision in *Sunday Times v. United Kingdom*[61] that the English law of contempt of court was in breach of Article 10, Parliament enacted the Contempt of Court Act 1981. The law relating to corporal punishment in schools was changed by legislation following the decision in *Campbell and Cosans v. United Kingdom*[62] that the infliction of such

---

[55] [1991] 1 A.C. 696.

[56] At p. 762.

[57] *ante*, para. 3–026. The dicta may claim support of a dictum of Diplock L.J. in *Salamon v. Commissioners of Customs and Excise* [1967] 2 Q.B. 116, for which, however, he cited no authority.

[58] This sentence was quoted with approval from the 6th ed. (p. 446) by Lord Ross in *Kaur v. Lord Advocate (supra)*.

[59] (1610) 12 Co.Rep. 74.

[60] The fact that the treaty was presumably laid before both Houses of Parliament before being ratified by the Crown (*ante*, para. 15–028) does not affect the argument.

[61] (1979) 2 E.H.R.R. 245.

[62] (1982) 4 E.H.R.R. 293; Education (No. 2) Act 1986; see now School Standards and Framework Act 1998.

punishment, contrary to parental wishes, was in breach of Protocol 1, Article 2 (right to respect for religious and philosophical principles in education). Telephone tapping was regulated by the Interception of Telecommunications Act 1985 following the decision in *Malone v. United Kingdom*.[63] In *Chahal v. United Kingdom*[64] the Court held that the decision to deport the applicant despite the risk of him being subjected to torture on return to India was in breach of Article 3 (torture, inhuman or degrading treatment) and of Articles 5 and 13 because the procedures for challenging the Home Secretary's decision did not constitute an effective remedy. The result was the passing of the Special Immigration Appeal Commission Act 1997. The law relating to courts martial and military discipline has been amended by the Armed Forces Act 1996 and the Armed Forces Discipline Act 2000 as a result of cases such as *Findlay v. United Kingdom*.[65]

In other cases it has been sufficient to amend delegated legislation, for example following *Golder v. United Kingdom*[66] where the Court held that prison rules relating to the rights of prisoners were in breach of the Convention or in *Dudgeon v. United Kingdom*[67] where the law in Northern Ireland prohibiting homosexual acts between consenting adults was held to be in breach of Article 8 (right to privacy). **22–013**

Some victories at Strasbourg turned out, on the other hand, to be pyrrhic. The decision in *Tyrer v. United Kingdom*[68] that birching as a judicial punishment was a degrading punishment contrary to Article 3 led to the withdrawal of the right of individual petition from the Isle of Man, in which jurisdiction the case had originated. In *Abdulaziz v. United Kingdom*[69] a finding that immigration rules restricting the rights of women settled in the United Kingdom was met by extending the restriction to men. In *Brogan v. United Kingdom*[70] a decision that powers of detention in terrorist legislation violated Article 5 led to the United Kingdom entering a derogation on the grounds of a public emergency threatening the life of the nation under Article 15.

Community Law

We saw in Chapter 6 that the law of the European Communities does have legal effect inside the United Kingdom. Unlike the European Convention, the Treaties establishing the Communities were adopted by legislation of the United Kingdom Parliament. In some areas, particularly that of discrimination on the grounds of sex, British citizens have successfully claimed rights under EEC law and aliens, if citizens of Community states, have established rights in the field of immigration and deportation. **22–014**

The European Court has recognised respect for fundamental human rights as one of the general principles of law which form part of Community law[71] and the Commission has accepted the desirability of the EEC becoming a signatory to the

---

[63] (1985) 7 E.H.R.R. 14. See now also the Regulation of Investigatory Powers Act, 2000, *post* para. 26–014 *et seq.*

[64] (1997) 23 E.H.R.R. 413.

[65] (1997) 24 E.H.R.R. 221; *Hood v. United Kingdom, The Times* March 11, 1999; *Moore and Gordon v. United Kingdom* (2000) 29 E.H.R.R. 728.

[66] (1975) 1 E.H.R.R. 524; a decision described as "almost grotesque": F. A. Mann, "Britain's Bill of Rights" (1978) 94 L.Q.R. 512, 524.

[67] (1981) 4 E.H.R.R. 149; Homosexual Offences (N.I.) Order 1982.

[68] (1978) 2 E.H.R.R. 1.

[69] (1985) 7 E.H.R.R. 471.

[70] (1988) 11 E.H.R.R. 117; *ante*, para. 14–054.

[71] For references, see *ante*, para. 6–011 and para. 6–038.

Convention on Human Rights.[72] The possible impact on domestic law of this approach is shown in *Johnston v. Chief Constable of the R.U.C.*[73] where the applicant was held entitled under Community law to challenge, on the ground of discrimination, the prohibition on women members of the R.U.C. carrying weapons.

An E.U. Charter of Human Rights was adopted at the Nice Summit but its impact on the work of the European Court and its legal status remain matters of conjecture.[74]

II. THE HUMAN RIGHTS ACT 1998[75]

The Scheme of the Act

22–015   A commitment to introduce legislation to incorporate the European Convention on Human Rights into United Kingdom Law had been included in the manifesto of the Labour Party before the election of 1997. The introduction of the necessary legislation was preceded by a White Paper (Rights Brought Home: The Human Rights Bill)[76] in which the Prime Minister referred to the Government's desire to modernise British politics and, as part of a comprehensive programme of constitutional reform, to enable people to enforce rights under the European Convention in British courts and to enhance the awareness of human rights.

The Human Rights Act 1998 does not directly incorporate the European Convention into the various legal systems in the United Kingdom. As the long title states, it is an Act to give further effect to rights and freedoms guaranteed under the Convention. Section 3 of the Act creates a rule of interpretation of legislation for the courts. Section 6 creates an obligation on public authorities not to act in a way incompatible with a Convention right. Whether the Act has any relevance to litigation between private litigants is, as will be seen, a controversial issue.

Section 1 of the Act defines Convention rights as the rights and fundamental freedoms contained in the Articles of the Convention and two Protocols to the Convention set out in Schedule 1 to the Act. Provision is made for subsequent amendments to the Act whenever the United Kingdom ratifies further protocols. Section 2 of the Act directs courts in determining any question which arises in connection with a Convention right *to take into account* judgments, decisions or advisory opinions of the European Court of Human Rights, opinions or decisions of the Commission and decisions of the Committee of Ministers.

22–016   Section 3 constitutes a general direction that *so far as it is possible to do so* primary and secondary legislation—whether enacted before or after the 1998 Act—must be read and given effect in a way which is compatible with Convention rights. The Act itself recognises that it will not always be possible to achieve

---

[72] See too the reference to the European Convention in the Preamble to the Single European Act (1986).

[73] [1986] E.C.R. 1651.

[74] *ante*, para. 6–039.

[75] S. Grosz, J. Beatson and P. Duffy, *Human Rights, The 1998 Act and the European Convention* (2000 Sweet & Maxwell); *Human Rights Act 1998: A Practitioner's Guide* (C. Baker ed.,) (Sweet & Maxwell, 1998); J. Wadham and H. Mountfield, *Human Rights Act 1998* (Blackstone, 1999); R. Clayton and H. Tomlinson, *The Law of Human Rights* (Oxford, 2000).

[76] Cm 3782.

the desired compatibility because it goes on to provide in section 4 that the superior courts listed in section 4(2)[77] can make a declaration of incompatibility where satisfied that primary legislation or secondary legislation which is validly made within the terms of the empowering statute, is incompatible with a Convention right. This is in deliberate contrast to the position under the European Communities Act 1972,[78] a contrast specifically adverted to and defended in the White Paper. Section 5 makes provision for the right of the Crown to intervene in any proceedings where a court is considering whether to make a declaration of incompatibility.[79]

Since the Courts cannot strike down legislation for incompatibility, section 10 provides power for ministers to amend offending legislation by *remedial order* (see later at paragraph 29–034). This special procedure applies only where the minister considers there are compelling reasons for proceeding under section 10. In other cases amendment will require legislation in the normal way.

In an attempt to ensure that legislation enacted in the future does not inadvertently infringe Convention rights, section 19 requires the minister in charge of a Bill to make a statement of compatibility before the Second Reading or to draw the House's attention to the Government's wish to proceed with the Bill although a statement of compatibility with Convention rights cannot be made.

Section 6 makes it unlawful for a public authority to act in a way which is incompatible with a Convention right except where the public body could not have acted differently. Public authority is defined as including a court or tribunal and any person certain of whose functions are functions of a public nature.

Section 7 allows any person who claims that a public authority, other than a   **22–017** court, has acted or proposes to act in a way which is unlawful under section 6, to bring proceedings in the appropriate court or tribunal or rely on the relevant Convention right in any proceedings, but only if he is (or would be) a victim of the unlawful act. Section 7(7) specifically states that a person is a victim for the purpose of such proceedings if he would be a victim for the purposes of Article 34 of the Convention in relation to proceedings in the Court of Human Rights.

In the case of a claim that a judicial act infringes a Convention right, section 9 requires that proceedings must be brought by way of appeal or judicial review or in such forum as may be prescribed by rules.[80]

Section 8 provides that a court which finds that a public body is acting unlawfully under the Act may grant such remedy within its power as it considers just and appropriate. This may, in the case of a court with power to order damages or the payment of compensation, include an order for damages. In awarding damages the court is specifically directed by section 8(4) to take into account the principles applied by the European Court of Human Rights in exercising its jurisdiction under Article 41 of the Convention.[81]

Article 13 of the Convention, which guarantees an effective remedy to any one whose rights have been infringed, is not included among the Convention rights

---

[77] The House of Lords, the Judicial Committee, the Courts-Martial Appeal Court, the High Court of Justiciary sitting otherwise than as a trial court of the Court of Session, the High Court or the Court of Appeal in England, Wales or Northern Ireland.

[78] *R. v. Secretary of State for Trade and Industry ex p. Factortame Ltd* [1990] 2 A.C. 85; *R. v. Secretary of State for Employment ex p. Equal Opportunities Commission* [1995] 1 A.C. 1, HL.

[79] *R. v. A. (Joinder of Appropriate Minister) The Times*, March 21, 2001.

[80] Grosz, Beatson and Duffy, *op. cit.* p. 142.

[81] L. Leigh and L. Lustgarten, "Making Human Rights Real. The Courts, Remedies and the Human Rights Act" (1999) 58 Camb. L.J. 509.

set out in Schedule 1 to the 1998 Act. While this omission may seem curious,[82] it is doubtful if it has any significance since section 8 is sufficiently widely worded to allow the courts to grant effective remedies and, in the case of damages, specific reference is, as has been seen above, made to the jurisprudence of the European Court. If, of course, a litigant feels that he has been deprived of an effective remedy he will be able, as before the Act, to appeal to Strasbourg.

22–018   Sections 12 and 13 of the Act are responses to misgivings expressed by the media and religious organisations during the passing of the Act. To the extent that they are consistent with the Convention they are otiose; to the extent that they are inconsistent they are storing up trouble for the future. Section 12(2) prevents the making of interim injunctions without the party affected being warned, unless there are compelling reasons why he should not be. Section 12(3) restricts the discretion of courts to make such orders unless the court is satisfied that the applicant is likely to establish at trial that publication should not be allowed. This provision applies to all cases involving freedom of expression.[83] Section 12(4) directs the court to have particular regard to the importance of the Convention right to freedom of expression and, in cases involving "journalistic, literary or artistic material", to have regard to the extent to which the material has, or is about to, become available to the public or it is or would be in the public interest for the material to be published; and any relevant privacy code. The latter remarkably vague phrase presumably includes, for example, the Press Complaints Commission Code to which newspapers are expected to adhere and similar voluntary codes which may be adopted by self regulatory bodies such as the Broadcasting Standards Commission.

Section 13 provides that a court, in determining any question arising under the Act which may affect the exercise by a religious organisation (itself or its members collectively) of the Convention right to freedom of thought, conscience and religion, must have particular regard to the importance of that right.[84] As will be seen below, only the Church of England (or Church of Scotland) can be regarded as a public authority for the purposes of the Act. Thus this section can only have any significance in cases involving other religious organisations to the extent that the Act may be invoked against parties under section 6(3) or as discussed later, against private individuals.

22–019   Finally it should be noted that section 11 provides that nothing in the Act restricts any rights under the existing laws of any part of the United Kingdom or prevents the bringing of proceedings which can be brought apart from those provided for in section 7 to 9.

The wording of the Human Rights Act raises a number of problems, in the solving of which commentators have been quick to refer to the debates in both Houses, as reported in Hansard, in reliance on *Pepper v. Hart*.[85] Ministers, too, were well aware of that case which leads to one reason for doubting the wisdom of the rule laid down there: it may result in ministers deliberately tailoring

---

[82] Inspired, according to ministerial comments during debates on the Bill, by a fear that its inclusion might encourage the courts to be too adventurous in devising remedies and awarding damages.

[83] Equity had confined its extreme reluctance to grant interim injunctions to cases of libel: *Bonnard v. Perryman* [1891] 2 Ch. 269.

[84] P. Cumper, "The Protection of Religious Rights Under Section 13 of the Human Rights Act" [2000] P.L. 254.

[85] [1993] A.C. 593, HL. See *ante* for critical comment para. 4–037.

remarks in both Houses with a view to affecting the interpretation of legislation.[86]

The fundamental conundrum with which the courts will have to grapple is the meaning of the rule about the interpretation of legislation contained in section 3. In solving that, as in dealing with other issues, there will be invocations of the need for the courts to approach the legislation broadly and purposively, not in a narrow and legalistic way.[87] Whether this approach can or should be described as a generous approach is itself a matter of dispute.[88]

Where a statutory provision is genuinely ambiguous a court, following section 3, will have no difficulty in finding a meaning that is consistent with the Convention—which may mean a claim fails, of course. For example, a section which in ambiguous terms restricts the right of free speech may be consistent with the Convention because the ambiguous restrictions can be read as justifiable within the meaning of Article 10. Interpreting ambiguous provisions in a way which is consistent with the Convention[89] or principles of International law[90] or principles of the common law[91] is nothing new. But if a statute unambiguously, for example, requires an accused person, contrary to Article 6(2), to prove his innocence, what is the court to do? Mr Straw and Lord Irvine may believe that the courts can "read words" into the section,[92] but what words? It is assumed in the Act that in some cases the courts will not be able to twist a statute into consistency with the Convention: hence the need for the declaration of incompatibility provided by section 4. Examples taken from cases relating to Community law are not authoritative, precisely because the Human Rights Act is not based on the supremacy of Convention law. Moreover, in cases such as *Litster v. Forth Dry Dock and Forth Estuary Engineering*,[93] the House of Lords knew what Community law required and so could fairly precisely identify the words necessary to make the United Kingdom regulations consistent with that law. In a case involving alleged incompatibility with the Convention the issues may be far less clear. Should the Court imply words to deal with the facts of the case before them? Or try to redraft the relevant legislation to ensure compatibility in all future potential litigation involving that provision.[94]

The government has indicated that where a court does conclude that a statute is incompatible with the Convention and makes a declaration to that effect, amending legislation may not necessarily be introduced. In such cases litigants could, of course, pursue their claims at Strasbourg.[95]

22–020

---

[86] Anthologies of extracts from Hansard are available in Wadham and Mountfield, *op. cit.* Appendix 4; F. Klug, "The Human Rights Act 1998, *Pepper v. Hart* and All That" [1999] P.L. 246.

[87] *Att.-Gen. of Trinidad and Tobago v. Whiteman* [1991] 2 A.C. 240, 247, *per* Lord Keith who said this approach to interpreting written constitutions is particularly true of those provisions which are concerned with the protection of human rights.

[88] R. A. Edwards, "Generosity and the Human Rights Act: the right interpretation" [1999] P.L. 400. "It [s.3] drastically alters existing methods", F. Bennion, "What interpretation is possible under section 3(1) of the Human Rights Act 1998?" [2000] P.L. 77, 91.

[89] *e.g. Attorney-General v. BBC* [1981] A.C. 303, HL.

[90] *The Zamora* [1916] A.C. 77, PC.

[91] *Waddington v. Miah* [1974] 1 W.L.R. 683, HL; *R. v. West Yorkshire Coroner ex p. Smith* [1983] Q.B. 335.

[92] Klug, *op. cit.* 252–255. Are Acts of Parliament really to be interpreted by the words of Lord Chancellors taken from lectures, however "robust"?

[93] [1990] 1 A.C. 546, HL.

[94] See further, G. Marshall, "Two kinds of compatibility: more about section 3 of the Human Rights Act 1998" [1999] P.L. 377.

[95] Statement by the Lord Chancellor, September 20, 2000.

22–021   The next issue which arises has been described as that of the horizontal effect of the Act[96]—although it is suggested that that term is best avoided because of the risk of confusion with the position in Community law.[97] The object of the Act, effected in section 6, is to make it unlawful for public authorities to act in a way which is incompatible with a Convention right unless required to do so by primary legislation. Is it, however, possible that the Act may also impose duties on private parties relating to Convention rights? The argument for such effect mainly centres on section 6(3), a seemingly innocuous definition provision to the effect that for the purposes of the section "public authority" includes "a court or tribunal". But since section 6(1) forbids public authorities to act in ways which are incompatible with Convention rights, courts, it is argued, are similarly so forbidden—a prohibition which applies to all their activities including deciding the law in disputes between private parties. Thus, if the right to privacy guaranteed by Article 8 can be invoked in an action against public authorities it follows that since the Courts are public authorities they too must recognise and abide by the Convention rules on privacy if X sues a newspaper or his neighbour. Put in such terms the argument destroys what is clearly the basic concept of the Act and it is difficult to believe the Courts would accept it.

Full effect is given to section 6(3) in a way which is consistent with the concept underlying the Act if it is interpreted to mean that the courts as public authorities are bound by those Convention rights which affect them as *courts*. Thus courts are bound, in hearing cases, by Article 6 of the Convention to ensure a fair hearing and to respect the other procedural rights guaranteed by that Article.

The acts of private individuals may be relevant in actions under the Act because of the possibility recognised by the Strasbourg case law, that public authorities may be under positive duties to take steps to prevent breaches of the Convention[98]: that, however, is not giving the Act "horizontal effect".

22–022   The increased emphasis on human rights which is expected as a consequence of the Act may, independently of the legal effects of the statute, lead to a greater willingness on the part of the courts to develop common law rules in this area, as other factors had, as seen above,[99] encouraged judicial recognition of fundamental rights in the years before the Act's enactment. Conversely, the argument might prevail that implicitly at least the Act makes out the proper sphere for the protection of human rights and in implementing its possibly far-reaching effects the courts should not be over anxious to inaugurate controversial developments in other areas of the legal system.

22–023   In describing the scope of the Convention rights and their interpretation by the Strasbourg Court reference will be made to "the margin of appreciation"[1] allowed to national authorities in determining what limitations on rights are required by the realities of their own societies: thus in *Lawless* it was for the Irish Government to determine whether there existed a public emergency threatening

---

[96] M. Hunt, "The Horizontal Effect of the Human Rights Act", [1998] P.L. 423; Sir William Wade, Q.C., "Horizons of Horizontality" (2000) 116 L.Q.R. 217. See for a survey of various views, Clayton and Tomlinson, *op. cit.*, paras 5.74–5.99. See also J. Howell, "Horizontal Application: Its Possible Impact on Land Law", Chap. 9 in *Modern Studies in Property Law* (E. Cooke ed., Hart, 2001).
[97] Buxton L.J., "The Human Rights Act and Private Law" (2000) 116 L.Q.R. 48.
[98] *post*, para. 22–030.
[99] *post*, para. 22–002.
[1] *post*, para. 22–030.

the life of the nation, unless the Strasbourg Court concluded such determination could not be justified.[2] As a doctrine developed by Strasbourg to reflect "the subsidiary role of the Convention in protecting human rights" [as opposed to] the initial and primary responsibility for the protection of human rights [which] lies with the contracting parties"[3] the margin of appreciation logically cannot be applied as such by domestic courts.[4] That does not, however, mean that a court can substitute its decision on the need for legislation restricting freedom of expression for that of Parliament or substitute its decision for that of a minister refusing access to the media to prisoners. The roles of judge, administrator and legislature remain distinct.[5] The approach of the courts will be analogous to that with which they are familiar from judicial review. The role of the court is not to approve legislation or ministerial decisions but to decide that they are lawful because they fall within the limits of their powers. Traditionally this has often involved using the terminology of *Wednesbury* unreasonableness[6]: was this a decision no reasonable minister could reach. (Review of primary legislation could not, before the Human Rights Act, take place. Delegated legislation was examined for its legality by reference to *ultra vires*). In its new duties under the 1998 Act the Courts, taking account of the Strasbourg jurisdiction, will have to develop a more clearly articulated set of principles for setting acceptable legal limits to legislation and executive actions. These will largely be found in the terminology of the European Court as it developed its case law on justifiable grounds for restricting Convention rights, for example, is the restriction proportionate to the aim in view? Is the restriction necessary in a democratic society? Domestic courts, too, will presumably be justified in deferring more willingly to the views of the legislature and executive in such fields as national security than in an issue such as restriction of land use in peace time.[7]

The existence of an English (or Scottish) decision on a dispute relating to a Convention right may affect the application of the margin of appreciation doctrine by the Strasbourg Court if that dispute finally goes to that Court. For example, if an English court found a new statute extending the law of blasphemy to be incompatible with the freedom of religion guaranteed by Article 9 and freedom of speech guaranteed by Article 10, the Strasbourg Court in such circumstances might well feel less need to defer the views of the State authorities that such restrictions were needed by the "vital forces of their countries" when the courts of that country had reached a different conclusion.

Whatever the outcome of the debate on the misleadingly named "horizontal effect" of the Act, the meaning of public authority will be of central importance in future litigation. Section 6 offers no definition of a concept central to the legislation. It includes, by subsection 3, (a) a court or tribunal and (b) any person certain of whose functions are functions of a public nature. It excludes Parliament, except the House of Lords in its judicial capacity (subsections 3 and 4). It

---

[2] *post*, para. 22–026.
[3] Harris, O'Boyle, Warbrick, *op. cit.* p. 14.
[4] Clayton and Tomlinson, paras 6.82–6.85. Hence the importance of s.2 of the Human Rights Act: the domestic courts are not bound by decisions of the European Court; they are to "take into account" any such decisions, so enabling them to disregard the margin of appreciation.
[5] See *R. v. D.P.P. ex p. Kebilene* [2000] 2 A.C. 326, 380 *per* Lord Hope.
[6] *Associated Provincial Pictures Houses Ltd v. Wednesbury Corporation* [1948] 1 K.B. 223, CA; *post* Chap. 31.
[7] *post*, Chap. 31.

also provides that any person within subsection 3(b) is not a public authority if the nature of the act is private. Public authority is not a term of art in English law and the courts will have to determine the applicability of section 6 on a case by case basis. No doubt, in so doing, they will be guided by case law on the availability of Judicial Review and the developing distinction between public and private law.[8] Bodies exercising legislative or common law powers, as opposed to those resting on a contractual basis, are *prima facie* public authorities and for the purposes of section 6, *all* their activities are subject to the Act.[9] Within this category will fall government departments, local authorities, the police, the armed forces.

22–024   The Church of England, it is arguable, unlike other religious bodies, is a public authority. It has law-making powers, exercised through the making of Measures, which, with Parliamentary sanction, become law and are for the purposes of the Human Rights Act, primary legislation[10] and are exempt from the ministerial amending provisions of section 10(6). The structure of its ecclesiastical courts has Parliamentary authority and appeal from them lies to the Privy Council.[11] Its episcopacy is appointed by the monarch, on the advice of the Prime Minister and the two Archbishops and twenty four other bishops sit in the House of Lords as Lords Spiritual. Against this legal background Mr Straw's belief that the Church of England is not a public authority is hardly conclusive of the question.[12] The basis of the authority of other churches in England, according to English law, is contractual and the reluctance of the courts to become involved in religious matters is illustrated in *R. v. Chief Rabbi of United Hebrew Congregations ex p. Wachmann*.[13] Nonetheless, arguably, religious organisations and authorities, other than those of the Church of England may fall within section 6(3)(b) in relation to any of their functions which are of a public nature, for example, running schools. Section 13, as mentioned above, directs courts to pay particular regard to the right to freedom of thought, conscience and religion in any litigation which might affect the exercise by a religious organisation of that right. Either that provision is superfluous or it is directing the Courts to give undue weight to the right in breach of the general principle that they decide cases under the Act by taking account of the decisions of the Court of Human Rights.

In judicial review proceedings the courts have identified as public bodies, in addition to those exercising statutory or common law powers, bodies created under the Royal Prerogative[14] and even bodies exercising *de facto* powers in areas where in the absence of such a body the State would have had to provide

---

[8] See further, Grosz, Beatson and Duffy, *op. cit.* 17–21 and 114–118.

[9] For the purposes of Judicial Review, the activities of a public body may be public (subject to review) or private (subject to the private law of tort and contract).

[10] s.21(1).

[11] Ecclesiastical Jurisdiction Measure 1963. Reports of cases decided on ecclesiastical law appear regularly in the Law Reports. Ecclesiastical courts, although not subject to certiorari, are subject to control by judicial review, for example by prohibition: *R. v. Chancellor of St Edmundsbury and Ipswich Diocese ex p. White* [1948] 1 K.B. 195, CA.

[12] 12 H.C. 1015 (May 20, 1998). On the legal status of the Church of Scotland, see *Stair Memorial Encyclopedia*, vol. 5 paras 679 *et seq.*

[13] [1992] 1 W.L.R. 1036. The courts may have to be drawn into religious controversies when warring groups lay claim to property: *Free Church of Scotland v. Lord Overtown* [1904] A.C. 515, HL. The property of the non-established Churches is held by trustees, subject to the normal laws of property. Exceptionally there are statutory provisions, *e.g.* Methodist Church Union Act 1929.

[14] *R. v. Criminal Injuries Compensation Board ex p. Lain* [1967] 2 Q.B. 864, CA.

a legal framework for regulation.[15] Thus there seems no difficulty in regarding the Press Complaints Commission as subject to judicial review and a public authority within section 6(1) or 6(3) as a body certain of whose functions are of a public nature.[16]

Section 7(1) provides that a claim that an act is unlawful under section 6 may **22–025** only be brought by a victim of that act and section 7(7) provides that a person is a victim of an unlawful act only if he would be for the purposes of the Convention in the case of proceedings before the European Court of Human Rights. In judicial review proceedings the relevant requirement is that of "sufficient interest"[17] which encompasses almost any litigant other than the mere busybody.[18] Thus recent cases have allowed the lawfulness of government and to foreign governments to be challenged by environmental groups and organisations such as the Equal Opportunities Commission to challenge legislation on behalf of litigants unlikely to be in a position to do so themselves.[19] The Court of Human Rights interprets "victim" more narrowly, perhaps inevitably given its role in relation to municipal legal systems. It is not necessary that an individual *has* suffered interference with his rights; it suffices if he may be directly affected, for example, a complaint that the absence of a clear legal regime puts the complainant at risk of having his telephone tapped.[20] The Strasbourg jurisprudence also allows proceedings by the family or relatives of the person directly affected, for example to challenge an immigration decision,[21] or where the alleged wrong is a breach of Article 2.[22] Governmental organisations are excluded from bringing actions by the explicit wording of Article 34 of the Convention. Non-governmental organisations may bring proceedings if they are affected in their own right, for example, churches or trades unions.

The existence of the two tests, victim and sufficient interest, is almost certain to lead to confusion and difficulties. Organisations and individuals will be entitled to sue if they can bring their challenges within the limits of judicial review under Order 53 when they would be ineligible to litigate under the Human Rights Act.[23]

Section 1 of the Act subjected the effect of the Convention Rights to "any **22–026** designated derogation or reservation". The reservation to Article 2 of the First Protocol (the right to education) has been considered earlier. The possibility of

---

[15] R. v. Take-Over Panel ex p. Datafin [1987] Q.B. 815. Contrast R. v. Disciplinary Committee of the Jockey Club ex p. Aga Khan [1993] 1 W.L.R. 909.

[16] A fortiori in the case of regulatory authorities established by statute such as the Broadcasting Standards Commission and the Independent Television Commission.

[17] post, para. 32–010.

[18] R. v. Inland Revenue Commissioners ex p. National Federation of Self Employed and Small Businesses Ltd [1982] A.C. 617.

[19] R. v. Secretary of State for Foreign and Commonwealth Affairs, ex p. World Development Movement [1995] 1 W.L.R. 386. R. v. Secretary of State for Employment, ex p. Equal Opportunities Commission [1995] 1 A.C. 1, HL. See similarly, R. v. Secretary of State for Social Services ex p. Child Poverty Action Group [1990] 2 Q.B. 540, CA; R. v. Secretary of State for Social Security ex p. Joint Council for the Welfare of Immigrants [1997] 1 W.L.R. 275, CA.

[20] Klass v. Germany (1978) 2 E.H.R.R. 214; Open Door Counselling and Dublin Well Woman v. Ireland (1993) 15 E.H.R.R. 244 (Women of child-bearing age, although not pregnant, entitled to challenge laws relating to abortion).

[21] Abdulaziz, Cabales and Balkandali v. UK (1985) 7 E.H.R.R. 471.

[22] Wolfgram v. Germany (1986) 46 D.R. 213.

[23] The requirement imposed by section 7 that a claimant under the Act must be a victim is identified as one of the weaknesses of the Act by Clayton and Tomlinson, paras 3.84–3.87.

derogations from the Convention raises wider and potentially more controversial issues.

The Convention on Human Rights, in addition to the specific restrictions in particular Articles referred to earlier, recognises in Article 15 the right of States "in time of war or other public emergency threatening the life of the nation" to derogate from its obligations under the Convention to the extent strictly required by the exigencies of the situation.[24] In 1988 the United Kingdom Government notified the Council of Europe of its decision to exercise this right in relation to Article 5(3) following the decision of the Court that the powers of detention granted by the Prevention of Terrorism (Temporary Provisions) Act 1984 were in breach of that provision.[25] The government referred to "campaigns of organised terrorism . . . repeated murder, maiming, intimidation and violent civil disturbance . . . bombing and fire-raising which have resulted in death, injury and widespread destruction of property". In the view of the government a public emergency existed within the meaning of Article 15(1). In the light of the provisions of the Terrorism Act 2000 which replaces earlier legislation the government has concluded that it no longer needs to maintain this derogation.[26] Section 14 of the Act defines as a *designated derogation*, the derogation at present in effect relating to Article 5(3) and any later derogation which is designated by the Secretary of State as a designated derogation. Section 16 provides for a system of five yearly reviews by Parliament of derogations; in the case of the existing derogation the five year period runs from the coming into effect of section 1(2), that is October 2, 2000, and in the case of later derogations from the date on which the designating order was made.

22–027   In litigation before the Strasbourg Court the question whether there is a public emergency and whether the measures derogating from the Convention are strictly required are issues for the Court which, not surprisingly, in this area leaves to State authorities a wide margin of appreciation.[27] Is it, however, open to domestic courts to consider the validity of the current or later derogations? At first sight it might seem that they can not. Section 1(2) provides that the Act takes effect subject to designated derogations; the only question for the domestic courts is whether a derogation is duly designated within section 14.[28] On the other hand, the courts are directed, in determining questions arising in connection with Convention rights, to take into account judgments of the European Court (S.2(1)). Can it be argued that this requires them to examine for themselves the validity of a derogation? The assertion of a government cannot, under the Convention, be conclusive. Section 3 also directs them to interpret legislation where is can be done in a way which is compatible with Convention rights. That can very easily be done with reference to sections 1(2) and 14 by interpreting them as referring to derogations which are *prima facie* effective but open to examination in the light of the prevailing facts. Once it is admitted that there is an ambiguity in the Act it can hardly be argued that it cannot be resolved in favour of the meaning which is compatible with the Convention.

---

[24] Derogations are not permitted in the cases of Article 2 (except in respect of deaths resulting from lawful acts of war), Articles 3, 4(1) and 7.

[25] *Brogan v. United Kingdom* (1989) 11 E.H.R.R. 11. An earlier derogation had been withdrawn in the belief that the Prevention of Terrorism (Temporary Provisions) Act 1984 complied with the Convention.

[26] *ante*, para. 19–054.

[27] *Ireland v. United Kingdom* (1978) 2 E.H.R.R. 35.

[28] Grosz, Beatson and Duffy, *op. cit.* para. C15–03.

The Convention Rights 22–028

It is impossible here to examine in detail the rights guaranteed by the Convention as these have been developed by the European Court of Human Rights.[29] Some important general issues and possible areas likely to be of particular concern in domestic litigation can, however, be identified.

The case law of the Court of which the United Kingdom courts must take account (Section 2)—has established a number of general principles. The Court has emphasised that the Convention must be interpreted in accordance with the general principles governing the interpretation of treaties. It must be interpreted in good faith, in the light of its object and purpose[30]—the purposive or teleological approach to interpretation. The protection given to Convention rights must be real and effective, for example the right to a fair trial (Article 6) may be illusory in the absence of a right to legal aid.[31] The Convention is a "living instrument" which is to be interpreted in the light of changing conditions.[32] This approach is particularly important in areas where the views of society are subject to variation from generation to generation for example in the field of sexual mores.[33]

The Court has also developed general guidelines in determining the extent to which rights guaranteed by the Convention may be restricted. Apart from Article 3, which prohibits absolutely torture or human or degrading treatment or punishment, Articles normally state a right in general terms and then go on to recognise the possibility of restrictions such as are prescribed by law and necessary in a democratic society for example in the interests of public security, for the prevention of disorder or crime, for the protection of health or morals, or for the protection of the rights and freedoms of others.[34]

The court has held that where a State seeks to justify a restriction on a 22–029 Convention right it must be able to point to a specific legal rule, whether of domestic, international or Community law. To justify a restriction a "law" must be accessible to citizens affected by it and it must be formulated with sufficient precision to enable citizens to regulate their conduct. Thus restrictions on prisoners' correspondence which were imposed on the basis of unpublished Prison Orders could not be said to be imposed by law.[35] A binding over order for conduct "*contra bonos mores*" imposed on hunt sabateurs was too imprecise to

---

[29] For comprehensive accounts see D. J. Harris, M. O'Boyle and C. Warbrick, *Law of the European Convention on Human Rights* (1995), F. G. Jacobs and R. C. A. White, *The European Convention on Human Rights* (2nd ed., 1996); R. Clayton and H. Tomlinson, *The Law of Human Rights* (Oxford, 2000).

[30] *Golder v. United Kingdom* (1975) 1 E.H.R.R. 524.

[31] *Airey v. Ireland* (1979) 2 E.H.R.R. 305. In *Artico v. Italy* (1981) 3 E.H.R.R. 1 the Court said the Convention was intended to protect "not rights that are theoretical or illusory but rights that are practical and effective."

[32] *Tyrer v. UK* (1978) Series A, No. 26; 2 E.H.R.R. 1.

[33] "A belief which represented unquestioned orthodoxy in year X may become questionable by year Y and unsustainable by year Z"; *per* Lord Bingham M.R. in *R. v. Ministry of Defence ex p. Smith* [1996] Q.B. 517, 554.

[34] The prevention of disorder or crime occurs in Art. 8 (right to respect for private and family life), Art. 10 (freedom of expression), Art. 11 (freedom of assembly and association). Other factors listed above are referred to, *e.g.* in Art. 6 (right to a fair trial), Art. 8, Art. 9 (freedom of thought, conscience and religion), Art. 10, Art. 11. Reference to restrictions prescribed by law are found in the Articles cited here and others, *e.g.* Art. 5 (right to liberty and security), Art. 1 of the First Protocol (protection of property). Other Articles require the establishment or protection of rights by law—*e.g.* Art. 6 (right to a fair trial before an independent and impartial tribunal established by law), Art. 12 (right to marry according to the national laws governing the exercise of this right).

[35] *Silver v. United Kingdom* (1983) 5 E.H.R.R. 347.

be justifiable within the limits on free speech in Article 10.[36] French law which authorised the tapping of telephones was held to be insufficiently precise in the light of the gravity of the interference with the right to privacy posed by telephone tapping.[37]

The burden of showing that a restriction is necessary in a democratic society is on the State. "Necessary" does not mean indispensable, at one extreme, but neither does it equate with useful or desirable.[38] The Court requires, before a restriction can be justified as necessary, to be satisfied that there is a pressing social need for interference with the right and that the interference is no more than is required—that it is proportionate to the legitimate aim being pursued. Exceptions to rights are to be narrowly construed.[39]

22–030 On the other hand the Court is conscious of the fact that state authorities are better placed to evaluate the necessity of a particular restriction in a particular situation and hence allows to national authorities "a margin of appreciation".[40] This is likely to be particularly significant in areas of subjective judgment where cultural and religious traditions vary among the signatory states.

Although much of the Convention, and the case law of the Court, deals with interference with rights, the Court has recognised that positive obligations may have to be imposed on States if the protection given to Convention rights is to be real and effective.[41] The right to peaceful assembly may require, for example, positive steps on the part of State authority to protect citizens who wish to assemble against threats from others.[42] Again a group of citizens may be entitled to expect the authorities to take positive steps to protect their religious feelings from being offended by the publication of material which, to them, is blasphemous or, in similar ways, upsetting.[43]

Article 1 of the Convention, which is not reproduced in the Schedule to the Human Rights Act, imposes an obligation on the signatory states to secure to everyone within their jurisdiction the rights and freedoms defined in the Convention. In the case of the United Kingdom the enactment of the Human Rights Act is itself a significant event in discharging that obligation.

22–031 Article 2 guarantees the right to life. It did not outlaw capital punishment following conviction by a court for a crime for which that penalty was provided by law. The Sixth Protocol, however, now forbids the death penalty except in time of war or imminent threat of war.[44] The Article refers to the right to life being protected by the law. The meaning of that provision was considered in *Osman v. United Kingdom*[45] where the Court held that the failure of the police to prevent injury to a young boy and the death of his father at the hands of a teacher who had developed an obsessive attachment to the boy was not a breach of Article 2. What is required in each case depends on all the circumstances and involves, in a case such as *Osman* the balancing of the rights of the alleged

---

[36] *Hashman and Harrup v. United Kingdom* (2000) 30 E.H.R.R. 241.
[37] *Kruslin v. France* (1990) 12 E.H.R.R. 547. *A fortiori, Malone v. United Kingdom* (1985) 7 E.H.R.R. 14 (telephone tapping regulated by unpublished ministerial guidelines).
[38] *Handyside v. United Kingdom* (1976) 1 E.H.R.R. 737.
[39] *Silver v. United Kingdom* (1983) 5 E.H.R.R. 347.
[40] *Handyside v. United Kingdom supra.* For the position of domestic courts, see *ante* para. 22–023.
[41] See above, n. 12 on para. 22–038: *Airey v. Ireland* (legal aid).
[42] *Plattform Ärtzte für das Leben v. Austria* (1991) 13 E.H.R.R. 204.
[43] *Otto-Preminger-Institut v. Austria* (1994) 19 E.H.R.R. 34.
[44] See *post*, para. 22–045, n. 19.
[45] [1999] Fam.L.R. 86. See too *Re A (Children)* [2000] 4 All E.R. 961, CA.

wrongdoer against the feared risks to the potential victim. In *Jordan v UK*[45a] the European Court held that a failure by the State to conduct appropriate investigations into deaths of persons caused by agents of the State was in itself a violation of the right to life guaranteed by Article 2. The second paragraph provides that the deprivation of life is not in contravention of the Article when it results from the use of force which is no more than absolutely necessary in the defence of persons against unlawful violence, to effect a lawful arrest or to prevent an escape by a person lawfully detained or to quell a riot or insurrection.[46] Obviously Article 2 will be relevant in any situation where, for example, a householder has killed an intruder or police have caused death in the circumstances envisaged in the Article: in such cases the question for the court will be the extent to which the Convention imposes a stricter test than that of the common law or the Criminal Law Act 1967, section 3, namely such force as is reasonable in the circumstances.

Article 2 may, however, turn out to be relevant in other areas. It might be argued, for example, that public health authorities have failed to protect life by failing to provide adequate resources in terms of intensive care units, facilities for surgical procedures of various kinds such as organ transplantation or the provision of expensive drugs. The question of withholding treatment from a patient in a permanent vegetative state may be open to reconsideration.[47] Legislation on highly charged issues such as abortion and euthanasia will also now be subject to judicial consideration in the light of their compliance with the Convention.[48]

Article 3 (the prohibition of torture and inhuman or degrading treatment or **22–032** punishment) is interesting in not allowing any derogation from its terms. Torture is never permitted even to extract information in times of war or terrorist violence. Torture involves suffering of particular intensity and cruelty. Sophisticated techniques of interrogation may be inhuman or degrading without amounting to torture.[49] Notions of what is degrading change with the times, as evidenced by the decisions of the Court finding corporal punishment as a judicial sanction degrading[50] and, at least in some circumstances, domestically administered punishment.[51] In *Costello-Roberts v. United Kingdom*[52] the Court did not find, on the facts, that corporal punishment of a young boy in school was degrading. In

---

[45a] *The Times*, May 18, 2001.

[46] *McCann, Farrell and Savage v. United Kingdom* (1996) 21 E.H.R.R. 97; *Kaya v. Turkey* (1999) 28 E.H.R.R. 1.

[47] For the present law, see *Airdale NHS Trust v. Bland* [1993] A.C. 789, HL and *Re A (Children). supra.*

[48] For an unsuccessful attempt to invoke the Convention, see *Paton v. United Kingdom* (1980) 3 E.H.R.R. 409: application by father complaining wife had had abortion against his wishes rejected by Commission.

[49] *Ireland v. United Kingdom* (1978) 2 E.H.R.R. 25 (Prisoners made to stand against walls; deprived of sleep, food and drink; made to wear hoods, subjected to continuing noise). *Tomasi v. France* (1993) 15 E.H.R.R. 1 (Slapping, kicking, threatening with a firearm, handcuffed, deprived of food "and so on"). A number of cases have concerned Turkey, *Askoy* (1996) 23 E.H.R.R. 553; *Aydin* (1997) 25 E.H.R.R. 251; *Selçuk and Asker* (1998) 26 E.H.R.R. 477. See too *Ribitsch v. Austria* (1995) 21 E.H.R.R. 573.

[50] *Tyrer v. United Kingdom* (1978) 2 E.H.R.R. 1. (Isle of Man: see *post* para. 35–002).

[51] *A. v. United Kingdom* (1999) 27 E.H.R.R. 611.

[52] (1995) 19 E.H.R.R. 112. *Campbell and Cosans v. United Kingdom* (1982) 4 E.H.R.R. 293 involved a breach of Art. 2 of Protocol 1; parents' objection to threat of corporal punishment based on philosophical convictions which were entitled to be respected. Corporal punishment in all schools is now forbidden by section 31, School Standards and Framework Act 1998.

Price v. United Kingdom[52a] the Court held that the detention of a severely disabled person in a police cell and later in prison amounted in the circumstances to degrading treatment contrary to Article 3. Although there was no intention to humiliate or degrade the prisoner her ill treatment reached the minimum level required to constitute a breach of the Article.

Although the English courts have been reluctant to allow litigation about the conditions in which prisoners are held,[53] they will now have to be prepared to consider whether the treatment of prisoners is degrading within the meaning of the Convention, for example the use of handcuffs, intimate body searches, the use of solitary confinement or other punitive regimes. Similar consideration may apply to claims by patients detained in mental hospitals.[54]

22–033   Another area of law where reliance may well be placed on Article 3 is that of extradition and deportation. In *Soering v. United Kingdom*[55] the Court held that the extradition of a German national to the United States to face a charge of murder and the likelihood of a sentence of death was contrary to Article 3. Although the death penalty itself could not (before the adoption of the Sixth Protocol) amount to inhuman or degrading punishment, the Court took account of the likely conditions of detention after conviction, the lengthy period spent in "death row" subject to a harsh regime and exposed to mental stress.[56] A similar approach was taken with regard to deportation in *Cruz Varas v. Sweden*[57] where, however, the claim, of a real risk of ill-treatment by the Chilean authorities, if returned to that country, failed on the facts.

Article 4 prohibits slavery and forced or compulsory labour. It has given rise to little case law and seems to offer little hope to even the most imaginative litigant.

Article 5 (the right to liberty and security of the person) on the other hand has been the basis for considerable case law and may provide opportunities for challenges to domestic law over a wide area. Many of the provisions of Article 5 are relevant to issues discussed later in Chapter 23, Immigration and Deportation, in Chapter 24, Freedom of Person and Property and in some specific instances to Terrorism, discussed earlier in Chapter 19. An important aspect of Article 5, which has already had an impact on our domestic law through decisions of the Court is the requirement in paragraph 4 that anyone deprived of liberty by arrest or detention can take proceedings by which the lawfulness of his detention can be speedily determined by a court and his release ordered if the detention is not lawful.

22–034   The person or body determining the lawfulness of detention need not be part of the normal judicial structure of the state but must be independent of the executive and the parties, and impartial. The judicial character of the body also involves the ability to make a legally binding decision. Thus a mental health review tribunal was held not to satisfy paragraph 4 because it could only make

---

[52a] *The Times*, August 13, 2001. (Difficulties in using lavatory; humiliating treatment at hands of male prison officers; initial period in prison cell when she suffered from extemely cold conditions; lavatory inaccessible; emergency buttons and light switches out of her reach.)

[53] *R. v. S. of S. for Home Dept ex p. McAvoy* [1984] 1 W.L.R. 1408; *R. v. Deputy Governor of Parkhurst ex p. Hague* [1992] 1 A.C. 58, HL and see *post* Chap. 24.

[54] For details of case law involving a variety of unpleasant situations see Harris, O'Boyle and Warbrick, *op. cit.* pp. 61–73.

[55] (1989) 11 E.H.R.R. 439. See too *Chahal v. United Kingdom* (1996) 23 E.H.R.R. 413.

[56] See *post* Chap. 37 for Privy Council decisions on inhuman and degrading treatment in relation to the death penalty.

[57] (1991) 14 E.H.R.R. 1.

a recommendation.[58] Similarly, although the Parole Board had the necessary independence and impartiality it lacked judicial character in cases where it lacked power to make binding decisions.[59] Difficulties have arisen under the English legal system where convicted prisoners are sentenced to indeterminate periods of imprisonment, for example, a discretionary life sentence or, in the case of juveniles, to be detained during Her Majesty's pleasure. In such cases, in the view of the Court, there is a right to a regular judicial review of the detention to take account of possible changes in such factors as likely risk to the public and, particularly in the case of juveniles, intellectual and emotional development.[60]

Even where there is a right of challenge to a judicial tribunal it may fail to satisfy the requirements of Article 5 if the grounds which the tribunal may investigate are too narrowly restricted—an issue which may arise in English law in connection with the distinction between "appeal" and "review".[61] Thus in *Weeks v. United Kingdom*[62] a right to challenge the continued detention of a discretionary life prisoner did not satisfy the Article since the ground of the decision by the Home Secretary—that the prisoner remained a danger to the public—was not open to question by the court. But the Court, even in a case where it found English law defective in its remedies, has emphasised that Article 5(4) does not mean that in examining the legality of detention a court must be entitled to substitute its won decision for that of the decision-making authority "on all aspects of the case including questions of pure expediency."[63]

22–035 A right to compensation for wrongful arrest or detention is given by Article 5(5). Compatibility with the Convention is achieved under the Human Rights Act by two provisions; section 8(2) provides generally for the awarding of damages by courts for the wrongful acts of public bodies. In the case of "judicial acts done in good faith" damages are not available in proceedings brought under the Act, otherwise than to compensate a person to the extent required by Article 5(5)(section 9(3)).

Article 6 (the right to a fair trial) has been described as having a position of pre-eminence in the Convention, both because of the importance of the right involved and the volume of applications it has attracted.[64] There is no reason to believe it will be less significant in a domestic setting, extending as it does over the entire field of civil and criminal litigation and, to a certain extent, to proceedings before disciplinary and administrative tribunals and beyond.

22–036 Paragraph (1) applies to the determination of "civil rights and obligations" and criminal charges, the subsequent paragraphs to criminal proceedings alone. Civil rights and obligations are not confined to what continental systems would regard as private law rights, in common law systems typically claims in tort and contract

---

[58] *X v. United Kingdom* (1981) 4 E.H.R.R. 188. This necessitated a change in the law: Mental Health Act 1983, ss.72–74. A number of outstanding difficulties in English law in the light of the Court's decision in *Winterwerp v. The Netherlands* (1979) 2 E.H.R.R. 387 are discussed in *Human Rights Act 1998: A Practitioner's Guide* (ed. Baker 1998), Chap. 10,

[59] *Weeks v. United Kingdom* (1988) 10 E.H.R.R. 293. Again, the law was changed: Criminal Justice Act 1991, s.34.

[60] *Thynne, Wilson and Gunnell v. United Kingdom* (1991) 13 E.H.R.R. 666 (discretionary life sentences); *Hussain v. United Kingdom* (1996) 22 E.H.R.R. 1 (detention during Her Majesty's pleasure); *T. and V. v. United Kingdom* [2000] 30 E.H.R.R. 121.

[61] See *post* Chap. 32.

[62] (1988) 10 E.H.R.R. 293.

[63] *Chahal v. United Kingdom* (1996) 23 E.H.R.R. 413. The scope of review appropriate may vary with the various categories of cases listed in Article 5(1) which, in turn, may lead to differing views on the adequacy of *habeas corpus* as a remedy under the Convention); *post* para. 24–034 *et seq.*

[64] Harris, O'Boyle, Warbrick, *op. cit.*, p. 164.

or the law of trusts. The Court has extended the protection of Article 6 to such issues as disputes between citizens and public authorities relating to land use, planning, water rights and other property matters. The granting of licences to run businesses or to practice a profession have similarly been brought within the Article. Social security benefits may be regarded as giving rise to civil rights for the purposes of Article 6.[65] Criminal charges are those which the relevant state so characterises but also other proceedings which share the qualities normally regarded as typical of criminal proceedings, in particular the nature of the offence and the severity of the sanction.[66] This leaves open the question whether, in particular cases, proceedings are criminal and entitled to the full protection of the provisions of Article 6 or merely disciplinary, when they might well still fall within Article 6(1).[67] The right guaranteed by Article 6(1) is to a fair and public hearing within a reasonable time by an independent and impartial tribunal established by law. In *Golder v. United Kingdom*[68] the Court held that Article 6(1) was meaningless unless it impliedly guaranteed the right of access to a court. Hence the refusal by the Home Secretary of permission to a prisoner to write to a lawyer with a view to initiating legal proceedings was in breach of the Convention. A court or tribunal cannot be independent unless its members have security of tenure and are free from pressure from particularly, the executive. The Court has held, for example, that a planning inspector lacks the necessary independence because he is appointed by a Secretary of State and his appointment can be revoked at any time.[69] In *McGonnell v. United Kingdom*[70] the Court found a breach of Article 6 where the same person was President of the States of Deliberation (the legislature of Guernsey) and the sole professional judge in the Royal Court where he sat with lay jurats.

Reference has already been made to the impact of the Convention on the system of courts-martial,[71] following the finding of the Commission, upheld in *Findlay v. United Kingdom*,[72] that the extensive powers of the convening officer in relation to the decision to prosecute, the composition of the court, the confirmation of the decision and confirmation or variation of sentence meant that such courts could not be regarded as sufficiently independent and impartial.

22–037   The right to a fair and public hearing is already well recognised in English law,[73] even if in particular cases it will always be open to argument whether, for

[65] Harris, O'Boyle, Warbrick, *op. cit.* pp. 174–186.

[66] *Engel v. The Netherlands* (1976) 1 E.H.R.R. 647; *Campbell and Fell v. United Kingdom* (1984) 7 E.H.R.R. 165.

[67] Consider proceedings to remove a doctor's name from the medical register, for medical incompetence? For conviction of a criminal offence? Is it relevant that dismissal from an appointment following such proceedings results in loss of pension rights? What is the nature of University proceedings to expel student on a charge of cheating in examinations? Or to expel for failing an examination? Or for behaviour, *e.g.* relating to illegal dealing in drugs, which has not been the subject matter of proceedings in the courts?

[68] (1975) 1 E.H.R.R. 524. In *Osman v. United Kingdom* (2000) 29 E.H.R.R. 245 the Court treated as a question of access under Art. 6, what in reality was a substantive question of liability under English tort law and not, therefore, a matter for the Strasbourg Court. See Lord Hoffman, "Human Rights and the House of Lords" (1999) 62 M.L.R. 159.

[69] *Bryan v. United Kingdom* (1996) 21 E.H.R.R. 342.

[70] [2000] 30 E.H.R.R. 289. R. Cornes, "*McGonnell v. United Kingdom*, The Lord Chancellor and the Law Lords" [2000] P.L. 166.

[71] *ante*, para. 19–021.

[72] (1997) 24 E.H.R.R. 221. The Armed Forces Act 1996 introduced changes to the system to take account of the earlier Commission's findings.

[73] *ante*, para. 20–038 *et seq.*

example, in particular circumstances a private hearing is justified.[74] The Court has emphasised that the right to a fair hearing is not to be confined to the specific factors mentioned in Article 6 and, for instance, has developed the principle of "equality of arms" (*égalité des armes*) under which, quite generally, each party must have a reasonable opportunity to present his case under conditions that do not place him at a substantial disadvantage against his opponent.[75]

Of the specific requirements mentioned in Article 6, one that has already provoked discussion in the English courts is the presumption of innocence, Article 6(2) which will be discussed below.[76]

Article 7 enshrines a fundamental principle of legality, *nullum crimen, nulla poena sine lege*. If its prohibition of retroactive criminal liability is unlikely to generate the litigation arising under Article 6 (or the succeeding Article 8) it is, nonetheless, important, particularly in its historic context, for recognising and outlawing what is almost a defining characteristic of tyrannies. It is a principle of the common law that statutes should be construed not to have a retrospective operation in the absence of language that plainly requires such operation.[77] Here the Convention merely strengthens the existing position. A difficulty might, however, have been thought to arise from the inherently retrospective nature of judge made law. The Court, however, has accepted that "clarification" of the law by judicial decision is not forbidden by Article 7: *Gay News and Lemon v. United Kingdom*[78]; *S.W. v. United Kingdom.*[79]

The prohibition on retrospective penalties has been widely construed[80] and may well lead to challenges to attempts by legislation to extend, for example, the making of orders confiscating the assets of convicted persons.

Article 7(2), which ensures that nothing in the Article prevents the trial and punishment of any person for acts which at the time they were committed were criminal according to the general principles of law recognised by civilised nations, again reflects very clearly its historic context when memories of the Nuremburg trials were still very fresh. It effectively undermines any argument that the War Crimes Act 1991 is contrary to the Convention.   **22–038**

Articles 8 to 11 follow a common structure; they affirm a right and then   **22–039**
describe justifications for restrictions on the right.[81] Article 8 recognises the right to respect for everyone's private and family life, home and correspondence. It is likely to have a profound impact because of the width of the rights it protects, their inherent vagueness, the undeveloped state of the domestic law in many areas covered by the Article and because, more than in the case of any other Article, the content of these rights is likely to change with changing social

---

[74] *Campbell and Fell v. United Kingdom* (1984) 7 E.H.R.R. 165. (Prison disciplinary proceedings can justifiably be held in private on grounds of public order and security.)

[75] *Dombo Beheer BV v. The Netherlands* (1994) 18 E.H.R.R. 213.

[76] [1999] 3 W.L.R. 175. The question did not arise on the view taken of the law by the House of Lords: [1999] 3 W.L.R. 972.

[77] *Midland Ry Co v. Pye* (1861) 10 CBNS 179, 191 *per* Erle C.J. (Retrospective legislation a manifest shock to our sense of justice). *Waddington v. Miah* [1974] 1 W.L.R. 683; *Tracomin S.A. v. Sudan Oil Seeds Co. Ltd* [1983] 1 W.L.R. 1026.

[78] (1983) 5 E.H.R.R. 123. (*Mens rea* of blasphemy).

[79] (1995) 21 E.H.R.R. 363 (marital rape). Both decisions of the House of Lords are open to the same criticisms as were levelled, forcefully and tellingly, against *Shaw v. D.P.P.* [1962] A.C. 220 (Common law conspiracy: "Ladies Directory" Case).

[80] *Welch v. United Kingdom* (1995) 20 E.H.R.R. 247.

[81] See *ante* para. 22–028; Harris, O'Boyle, Warbrick, *op. cit.* Chap. 8.

standards, cultural beliefs and values.[82] Cases before the Court from the United Kingdom which illustrate the importance of Article 8 include *Smith and Grady v. United Kingdom*[83] (policy of exclusion of homosexuals from the Armed Forces; investigations into applicants' sexual orientations and subsequent discharge from the armed forces constituted grave interferences with the private lives); *Dudgeon v. United Kingdom*[84] (criminalisation of homosexual activity in Northern Ireland); *Halford v. United Kingdom*[85] (bugging of office telephone); *Gaskin v. United Kingdom*[86] (right of access of applicant to local authority's records of his upbringing by foster parents); *X, Y and Z v. United Kingdom*[87] (relationship between post-operative male transsexual, natural born woman and her child constituted a family); *Powell and Rayner v. United Kingdom*[88] (aircraft noise wrongful interference with right of enjoyment of home); *Malone v. United Kingdom*[89] (telephone tapping unregulated by precise and ascertainable rules of law); *Khan v. United Kingdom*[90] (installation of bugging devices on private property unregulated by law).

Applications which have been successful under other Articles show the potential for further reliance on Article 8. For example, in *Abdulalaziz, Cabalas and Balkandali v. United Kingdom*[91] the applicants established that United Kingdom immigration law was in breach of Article 14 which forbids discrimination in the enjoyment of Convention rights. The court went on to point out that immigration rules may affect the right to respect for family life under Article 8—for example if X is lawfully settled in the United Kingdom and his or her family is refused admission and there is no other state in which they could establish a home together.

22–040   The importance of the opening phrase of Article 8—"the right to respect for . . . "—lies in its use by the court to justify its view that the Article goes beyond a prohibition on interference with the relevant rights. It guarantees positive protection by State authorities, which may require the State to take steps against third parties. In *Marck v. Belgium*[92] the Court held that the failure to provide by legislation for the rights of illegitimate children was a breach of the duty to respect family life.

The impact of Article 8 on English law with regard to a right to privacy is likely to be considerable, precisely because the English courts have affirmed on many occasions that no such general right is known to English law. Other areas of the law which may call for re-examination under Article 8 include the right to

---

[82] *cf. R. v. Ministry of Defence ex p. Smith* [1996] Q.B. 17, 554, *ante*, para. 22–028, n. 33; *Fitzpatrick v. Sterling Housing Association Ltd* [1998] Ch. 304 (CA); [1999] 3 W.L.R. (HL) (Rent Act 1977, Sched. 1, Part 1, para. 2(1): can "living with the original tenant as his wife or her husband" extend to the survivor of a homosexual relationship?)

[83] (2000) 29 E.H.R.R. 493.

[84] (1981) 4 E.H.R.R. 149. The State has a margin of appreciation in taking account of issues of public health and morality when restricting sexual activities even in private: *Lasky, Jaggard and Brown v. United Kingdom* [1997] 24 E.H.R.R. 39. But the limits to that right were emphasised in *ADT v. United Kingdom, The Times* August 1, 2000.

[85] (1997) 24 E.H.R.R. 523.

[86] (1990) 12 E.H.R.R. 36; *post* Chap. 33.

[87] (1997) 24 E.H.R.R. 143.

[88] (1990) 12 E.H.R.R. 355.

[89] (1985) 7 E.H.R.R. 14.

[90] [2000] Crim.L.R. 684.

[91] (1985) 7 E.H.R.R. 471.

[92] (1979) 2 E.H.R.R. 330.

search premises, the law relating to sexual offences and restrictions on prisoners.

Article 9 (freedom of thought, conscience and religion) by contrast has played a less significant part in the jurisprudence of the Court and there is little reason to see it provoking litigation in the United Kingdom. Where questions of freedom of thought, conscience and religion do arise they are likely to involve also Article 10 (freedom of expression) and Article 14 (freedom from discrimination in the exercise of Convention rights).[93] The scope of the protection given by Article 9 is not clear. A different phrase is used in the First Protocol, Article 2 which refers to parents' "religious and philosophical convictions". It is not clear whether the two provisions should be interpreted separately or, together to indicate that the Court should give the widest possible protection to ideas, philosophies and beliefs of all kinds. In *Arrowsmith v. United Kingdom*[94] the Commission concluded that pacifism was a "philosophy" which fell "within the ambit" of the Article. Otherwise, at present, the case law offers little help.

In *Otto-Preminger-Institut v. Austria*[95] the Court upheld blasphemy laws on **22–041** the grounds that Article 9 requires the State to protect religious believers from expressions of views and opinions which are gratuitously offensive to them. But in *Kokkinakis v. Greece*[96] the Court refused to hold that attempting to convert citizens from one religious belief to another could be prohibited consistently with Article 9—unless it could be shown that the law was proportionate to the aim of protecting the rights of others.

In domestic law Article 9, again, is unlikely to have a large impact. It may, directly or indirectly, lead to a recommendation of the present position under which the law of blasphemy protects only believers in Christianity.[97]

Article 10 (freedom of expression) deals with a right of fundamental importance in a free society, which is dealt with at length in Chapters 25 and 26. The House of Lords in *Derbyshire County Council v. Times Newspapers Ltd*[98] felt able to assert the essential compatibility of the common law and Convention rules on freedom of speech. That case involved an unsuccessful action of libel brought by an elected public body against a newspaper for criticisms of the local authority's management of its employees' pension fund.

Nonetheless, the adoption of the Convention into domestic law will require the courts in other, more difficult cases to examine in a principled manner what is meant by "expression".[99] Do differing forms of expression deserve differing degrees of protection.[1] It will no longer be possible, or sufficient, for courts to

---

[93] *e.g. Ahmed v. Inner London Education Authority* [1978] Q.B. 36, CA. (Lord Denning M.R. described the Convention as "drawn in such vague terms that it can be used for all sorts of unreasonable claims and provoke all sorts of litigation"). An application to the European Commission on Human Rights was unsuccessful (1981) 22 DR 27.

[94] (1980) 3 E.H.R.R. 218.

[95] (1994) 19 E.H.R.R. 34; *ante*, para. 22–030. See also *Wingrove v. United Kingdom* (1997) 24 E.H.R.R. 1.

[96] (1994) 17 E.H.R.R. 397.

[97] *ex p. Choudhury* [1991] 1 Q.B. 429, DC; S. Ghandhi and J. James, "The English Law of Blasphemy and the European Convention on Human Rights" [1998] E.H.R.L.R. 430.

[98] [1993] A.C. 534.

[99] For example, the wearing of particular clothes to symbolise support for a political group? Burning a flag to indicate disapproval of government policy? See E. Barendt, *Freedom of Speech* (1985).

[1] Forms of expression may range from criticism of a political system to advocacy of the merits of soap powder or ridicule of generally accepted religious or social beliefs; *Barendt, op. cit.*

reject challenges to legislation restricting freedom of expression by reference to the supremacy of Parliament, as was appropriately done in *R. v. Jordan*.[2]

22–042   Article 11 (freedom of assembly and association) similarly deals with an area of the law which has been the subject of considerable domestic legislation and case law which is considered in Chapter 27. In preparation, perhaps, for the coming into effect of the Human Rights Act, Lord Irvine had already recognised the importance of a public right of assembly.[3] Article 10 will require the scrutiny of all legislation in the light of that basic right. The case law of the Court has emphasised that the right of association entails the right of non-association an important principle which domestic legislatures may prefer for political or practical reasons to overlook. Here again British legislation will now be open to judicial scrutiny.[4] The Commission has also held that the State, in appropriate cases, must protect the rights of individual members against associations to which they belong.[5]

Article 12 recognises the right to marry and found a family, according to the national laws governing the exercise of this right. The case law of the Court does not suggest the likelihood of any great impact on domestic law. The right guaranteed "refers to the traditional marriage between persons of opposite biological sex . . . Article 12 is mainly concerned to protect marriage as the basis of the family."[6]

The limits on the right of the State to lay down rules governing the exercise of the right to marry were considered by the Commission in *Hamer v. United Kingdom*[7] which concluded that while the State was entitled to lay down rules concerning formalities or relating to matters recognised as involving a genuine public interest, for example, degrees of consanguinity, prohibitions on prisoners marrying could not be justified.[8]

22–043   Article 13 guarantees a right to an effective remedy for a violation of any right protected by the Convention. Although this Article was deliberately omitted from the Act,[9] section 8 gives the Courts wide powers to grant remedies and section 2 directs them to take account of the jurisprudence of the Court which, of course, includes the role of Article 13. If the exclusion of Article 13 from Schedule 1 of the Act does, in the view of the courts, restrict their ability to award an effective remedy, litigants will, of course, be free to resort to Strasbourg.

Article 13 has been interpreted by the Court to mean that everyone has a right to a remedy in relation to an arguable *claim* that a Convention right has been breached, as well as an effective remedy if such breach is established.[10]

The remedy, to be effective, need not be to a judicial authority, for example a right of petition to the Home Secretary by a prisoner could be an effective

---

[2] [1967] Crim. L.R. 483.

[3] *D.P.P. v. Jones* [1999] 2 A.C. 240.

[4] *Young, James and Webster v. United Kingdom* (1982) 4 E.H.R.R. 38 (right not to join a trades union); *Sigurjonsson v. Iceland* (1993) 16 E.H.R.R. 462 (right not to join automobile association before applying for taxi-driver's licence); *Chassagnou v. France* (2000) 29 E.H.R.R. 615 (right of landowner not to join hunting association).

[5] *Cheall v. United Kingdom* (1985) 42 D.R. 178.

[6] *Rees v. United Kingdom* (1986) 9 E.H.R.R. 56. See also *Cossey v. United Kingdom* (1990) 13 E.H.R.R. 622; *Sheffield and Horsham v. United Kingdom* (1998) 27 E.H.R.R. 163.

[7] (1979) 4 E.H.R.R. 139.

[8] See now Marriage Act 1983, s.1.

[9] *ante*, para. 22–017.

[10] *Klass v. Germany* (1978) 2 E.H.R.R. 214; *Silver v. United Kingdom* (1983) 5 E.H.R.R. 347.

remedy: *Silver v. United Kingdom.*[11] On the other hand in *Chahal v. United Kingdom*[12] a right of appeal against a decision to deport on the ground of national security to a panel which could not reach a decision but only advise the Secretary of State was not an effective remedy.

Of particular importance is the possibility that judicial review may not constitute an effective remedy because of the limitations on the ability of the courts to examine the legality of a minister's decision. Thus in *Smith* and *Grady v. United Kingdom*[13] the Court held that the difficulty of establishing the required degree of irrationality before a ministerial decision could be impugned meant that the court was prevented from considering whether the decision (to ban all homosexuals from serving in the armed forces) could be justified by a pressing social need or proportionality to legitimate concerns such as national security.

Article 14 prohibits discrimination in the enjoyment of other rights and freedoms set out in the Convention on any ground. The list given in the Article is regarded as merely illustrative, not exhaustive. In the fields covered by United Kingdom statute law such as employment and discrimination on the grounds of race and sex, Article 14 has little, if anything, to add to domestic law. In areas where it might be invoked its usefulness may be limited by the fact that it is not clear if it extends to indirect discrimination, unlike British legislation in the areas where that applies.[14]   **22–044**

It is not necessary to establish a breach of a substantive right before Article 14 can be invoked; that would render the Article useless. It is sufficient to show that a measure which in itself is in conformity with the requirements of the Convention infringes the relevant Article when read in conjunction with Article 14.[15] Thus, as the Court pointed out, the establishment of a system of appellate courts, although not required by Article 6 is entirely consistent with it. But if those courts were only available to an arbitrarily defined group of litigants there would be a breach of Article 6, read with Article 14.

Discrimination does not mean "any distinction".[16] A distinction is not discriminatory where it has objective and reasonable justification. The existence of such a justification is to be assessed in relation to the aims and objects of the measure under consideration, regard being had to the principles which normally prevail in democratic societies.

Article 16 which entitles States to impose restrictions on the political activities of aliens is unlikely to be of any significance and has been recognised as outdated by the Court in the only case before it involving this Article.[17]   **22–045**

Article 17 prevents any person or State relying on rights guaranteed under the Convention to destroy those rights, for example a totalitarian party seeking to rely on the freedom of speech, guaranteed by Article 10, to advocate the overthrow of democracy. Nonetheless, restrictions imposed under Article 17 must be strictly proportionate to any threat posed to the rights of others and, for

[11] *ante*, n. 10. *N.b.* The question of an effective remedy for a breach of a Convention right under Art. 13 is distinct from the right to a trial before an independent and impartial tribunal under Art. 6.
[12] (1998) 23 E.H.R.R. 413. In addition the applicant had no legal representation, was given only an outline of the case against him and was unable to see the panel's advice. The decision led to a change in the law; see *post*, para. 23–034.
[13] (2000) 29 E.H.R.R. 493.
[14] Harris, O'Boyle and Warbrick, *op. cit.* p. 477.
[15] *Belgian Linguistic case* (1968) 1 E.H.R.R. 252.
[16] Despite the French text, *sans distinction aucune*.
[17] *Piermont v. France* (1995) 20 E.H.R.R. 301. (German M.E.P. taking part in anti-nuclear demonstrations in French Polynesia: not an alien for the purposes of Art. 16).

example, while it may be justifiable to restrict the rights of members of terrorist organisations the State is not therefore entitled to take away the rights guaranteed by Article 5 and Article 6.[18]

Article 18 provides that permitted restrictions on Convention rights may not be resorted to for any purpose other than those which justified their imposition. No litigant has yet persuaded the court that a restriction, *prima facie* justifiable, has been wrongfully relied on.

In addition to the rights and freedoms guaranteed by the original Convention the Human Rights Act incorporates the First Protocol to the Convention (which deals with the Protection of Property, the Right to Education and the Right to Free Elections) and the Sixth Protocol which outlaws the death penalty except in time of war or imminent threat of war. The latter calls for no comment since United Kingdom law now accords with its provisions.[19]

22–046   Article 1 of the First Protocol recognises the right of every natural or legal person to the peaceful enjoyment of his possessions. No one shall be deprived of his possessions except in the public interest and subject to conditions provided for by law and by the general principles of international law. The Article in its second paragraph expressly recognises the right of the State to control the use of property in accordance with the general interest or to secure the payment of taxes or other contributions or penalties. The Court has given a wide meaning to the term "possessions", including tangible and intangible property such as the right to a sum of money under an arbitral award,[20] hunting rights[21] and the goodwill of a business.[22]

In practice, the Court while requiring "a fair balance" to be struck between the individual's right to property and the demands of the general interest of the community[23] has allowed states a wide power to interfere with private rights in the public interest. The availability of compensation is an important element in striking the balance although Article 1 does not guarantee a right to full compensation in all circumstances.[24]

22–047   The retrospective nature of legislation depriving an applicant of his property is not in itself sufficient to render the taking unlawful but the Court is particularly mindful in such cases of the dangers of retrospective legislation.[25]

Article 1 may, in the domestic courts, be invoked to challenge legislation to ban or control hunting and, more generally, to challenge various aspects of tax law.[26]

Article 2 of the First Protocol, despite its negative phraseology—No person shall be denied the right to education—recognises a right to education. Where the State assumes the function of providing education (as opposed to provision by

---

[18] *Lawless v. Ireland* (1961) 1 E.H.R.R. 15.
[19] Murder (Abolition of Death Penalty) Act 1965; Crime and Disorder Act 1998, s.36; Human Rights Act 1998, s.21(5).
[20] *Stran Greek Refineries & Stratus Andreadis v. Greece* (1995) 19 E.H.R.R. 293 (Greek law retrospectively cancelling award in favour of applicants).
[21] *Chassagnou and Others v. France* [2000] 29 E.H.R.R. 615.
[22] *Van Marle and Others v. The Netherlands* (1986) 8 E.H.R.R. 491.
[23] *Sporrong and Lönnroth v. Sweden* (1983) 5 E.H.R.R. 35.
[24] *James v. United Kingdom* (1986) 8 E.H.R.R. 123. (Leasehold reform legislation: compensation to landlord justifiably limited to value of site, excluding value of buildings). See also *Lithgow v. United Kingdom* (1986) 8 E.H.R.R. 329.
[25] *The National and Provincial Building Society, The Leeds Permanent Building Society and the Yorkshire Building Society v. United Kingdom* (1997) 25 E.H.R.R. 127. (Retrospective validation of tax regulations to prevent windfall from defects in earlier tax legislation.)
[26] See further *Human Rights Act 1998* (ed. C. Baker 1998), Chap. 14.

religious or other organisations) it must respect the religious and philosophical convictions of parents.[27] The United Kingdom ratified Article 2 subject to the reservation that this principle is accepted only so far as it is compatible with the provision of efficient instruction and training and the avoidance of unreasonable public expenditure.[28] Article 2 does not require States to establish particular forms of educational systems at their own expense but it does require, in conjunction with Article 14, that access to state funded institutions is on a non-discriminatory basis.[29]

The meaning of religious and philosophical convictions has been considered in a number of cases.[30] To be protected the convictions must be worthy of respect in a democratic society and not inconsistent with the fundamental right of a child to education. In determining the meaning of religious or philosophical convictions for the purpose of Article 2 of the Protocol the Court takes account of its jurisprudence on Articles 8, 9 and 10 of the Convention. Parental view on sex education[31] and corporal punishment[32] have been held to fall within the limits of convictions to which respect must be paid.

The emphasis of the Article is on primary and secondary education, as might **22–048** seem to be obvious from the reference to parental convictions. Where the State provides tertiary education it is entitled to limit it to those likely to benefit from it.[33]

Despite the United Kingdom's reservation, Article 2 in conjunction with Article 14 of the Convention, may well encourage litigation involving allegations that particular ethnic or religious groups have been less generously provided for by the State-funded educational system than others. In an area of increasing litigation and parental choice, litigation may equally focus on the adequacy of the provision of facilities to meet special educational needs, despite the United Kingdom reservation. Questions may also arise about the independence of tribunals in the education field where there is a close link with the education authorities against whose decisions parents may be appealing.[34]

Article 3 of the First Protocol imposes an obligation on the Contracting Parties **22–049** to hold free elections at reasonable intervals by secret ballot under conditions which ensure the free expression of the opinion of the people. The traditional British system of voting—"first past the post"—has been held by the Commission to be compatible with Article 3 despite the fact that a small party with support spread throughout the United Kingdom will inevitably obtain fewer seats in Parliament than its percentage of the votes would indicate.[35] The same principle would presumably apply *mutatis mutandis* to elections to the new devolved legislatures although, as discussed earlier, in all these cases varying systems of voting designed to produce, in some cases at least, "fairer" results have been introduced[36] and reform of voting methods for the Westminster

---

[27] *post* n. 52.
[28] See the Human Rights Act 1998, ss.1(2) and 15; Sched. 3, Pt II.
[29] *Belgian Linguistics Case* (1968) 1 E.H.R.R. 252.
[30] See *e.g. Campbell and Cosans v. United Kingdom* (1982) 4 E.H.R.R. 293; *Valsamis v. Greece* (1996) 24 E.H.R.R. 294.
[31] *Kjeldsen, Busk Madsen and Pedersen v. Denmark* (1976) 1 E.H.R.R. 711.
[32] *Campbell and Cosans, ante* n. 30.
[33] *X v. United Kingdom* (1981) 23 D.R. 228; *Glasewska v. Sweden* (1986) 45 D.R. 300.
[34] *Human Rights Act 1998* (ed. Baker), p. 349.
[35] *Liberal Party, R. and P. v. United Kingdom* (1980) 21 D.R. 211.
[36] *ante*, para. 5–013.

Parliament is allegedly under consideration.[37] The Court has emphasised that electoral systems must be assessed in the light of the political evolution of the country concerned; features that would be unacceptable in the context of one system may be justified in another.[38]

Domestic law relating to expenditure by political parties and other organisations may fall for consideration in the light of this Article and the right to freedom of expression under Article 10.[39]

Arguably the system of voting at present in use in the United Kingdom which allows for identification of a voter from the electoral roll number which is recorded on the counterfoil of each ballot paper is not "secret" for the purposes of the Protocol.[40]

Applying the Act[41]

22–050 The Human Rights Act 1998 took effect in England on October 2, 2000 but as explained in Chapter 5 it became effective in Scotland and Wales and Northern Ireland earlier under the terms of the devolution legislation. As a result of this timetable, and the accidents of litigation, the first decisions to demonstrate the potential of the Act were from Scotland. Article 6 (the right to a fair hearing) has, as had been expected, been the most commonly invoked provision of the Convention.

In *R. v. Lambert*[41a] the House of Lords held that the Human Rights Act 1998 does not have retrospective effect and can not be invoked to challenge the legality of a trial held before the Act took effect.

Article 2, the right to life, has been referred to, without English law being found incompatible, in cases involving the separation of conjoined twins[42] and the withdrawal of treatment from a patient in a persistent vegetative state, with no hope of recovery: *NHS Trust A v. M.*[43]

Article 3 (inhuman or degrading treatment) was also unsuccessfully relied on in the *NHS Trust* case and in *R. v. Offen*[44] where it was argued that the Crime (Sentences) Act 1997, s.2, which required the imposition of a life sentence on certain offenders except where there were "exceptional circumstances" was contrary to the terms of the Article. The Court of Appeal (Criminal Division) held that while the automatic imposition of a life sentence might amount to inhuman or degrading punishment the discretion given to the Court by the words "exceptional circumstances" avoided that risk, enabling the Court, for example, not to impose a life sentence where an offender did not pose a considerable risk to the public. In *Offen* the Court of Appeal for similar reasons rejected the argument that section 2 might amount to the imposition of an arbitrary punishment contrary to Article 5.

---

[37] Jenkins Commission Report, Cm. 4090 (1998), *ante* para. 10–060.

[38] *Mathieu-Mohin and Clerfayt v. Belgium* (1998) 10 E.H.R.R. 1.

[39] *e.g. Bowman v. United Kingdom* (1998) 26 E.H.R.R.1, but see now Political Parties Elections and Referendums Act 2000, s.131.

[40] See Representation of the People Act 1983, s.23 and Sched. 1, Part III; *ante* para. 10–057.

[41] J. Croft, *Whitehall and the Human Rights Act 1998* (The Constitution Unit, 2000).

[41a] *The Times*, July 6, 2001, HL Lord Slynn recanted his comments to the contrary in *R. v. D.P.P. ex p. Kebilene* [2000] 2 A.C. 326, HL; *post*, para. 22–052.

[42] *Re A (Children) (conjoined twins: surgical separation)* [2000] 4 All E.R. 961, CA.

[43] [2001] 1 All E.R. 801. Butler-Sloss P. followed and applied *Airedale NHS Trust v. Bland* [1993] A.C. 789, HL.

[44] [2001] 1 W.L.R. 253, CA.

Article 5 has, however, been successfully invoked in two relating to mental health legislation and practice. In *R(H) v. Mental Health Tribunal, North and East London Region*[44a] the Court of Appeal held that section 73 of the Mental Health Act 1983 placed the burden of proving that he was no longer suffering from a mental illness on the patient seeking an order for his discharge and that this was incompatible with the right to liberty guaranteed by Article 5. In *R(C) v. Mental Health Review Tribunal*[44b] the Court of Appeal held that the practice of listing hearings before the Tribunal eight weeks after the date of the application was incompatible with Article 5(4) which required that such hearings should take place as soon as practicable.

The potential of Article 6 (right to a hearing) to cause serious upheavals in the domestic legal systems of the United Kingdom was strikingly demonstrated when, within months of the Scotland Act 1998 taking effect the High Court of Justiciary held, on appeal, that a temporary Sheriff whose appointment and continuance in office was, in practice, dependent on the Lord Advocate, a member of the Scottish Executive, in whose name prosecutions were undertaken, could not constitute an independent tribunal within Article 6(1): *Starrs v. Procurator Fiscal (Linlithgow)*.[45] With these consideration in mind, the appointments of deputy High Court judges and Assistant Recorders in England and Wales have been amended to give them a fixed term of office likely to be sufficient to ensure their independence for the purposes of Article 6.[46] The judicial role of the Lord Chancellor is unique and will inevitably come under scrutiny. It can hardly be argued that he has the guarantee of tenure which entitles him to be regarded as independent.[47] His multiplicity of roles, as judge, minister and Speaker of the Upper House of the legislature call to mind the decision of the Strasbourg Court in *McGonnell v. United Kingdom*.[48]

22–051

Apart from the Convention, the Law Lords have had to address the question of bias in relation to their own proceedings[49] and inevitably increasing attention will be paid to this issue. The increasing willingness of the law lords to participate in controversial issues before the House of Lords in its legislative role for example may lead to challenges to their judicial impartiality—which, as the Court of Human Rights emphasised in *McGonnell*[50] is a question, not of actual bias, but of impartiality from an objective viewpoint. The risk of judicial figures imperilling their own impartiality is starkly demonstrated by the Scottish decision, *Hoekstra v. H.M. Advocate*[51] where the appearance of bias, arising from the judge's journalistic writings, related to his views on the wisdom of adopting conventions of human rights.[52]

[44a] [2001] H.R.L.R 752, CA. For remedial action under s.10, see *post*, para. 29–034.

[44b] *The Times*, July 11, 2001, CA.

[45] 2000 J.C. 208.

[46] H.C. Deb. Vol. 348, *col. 222w* April 12, 2000.

[47] See R. F. V. Heuston, *Lives of the Lord Chancellors 1940–1970*, p. 176 for an account of the abrupt nature of Lord Kilmuir's dismissal. He was called from a Cabinet committee meeting at 11.15 a.m. to see the Prime Minister, Mr Macmillan. At 11.30 the Lord Chancellor's Office was telephoned to be told, "you have a new Lord Chancellor".

[48] (2000) 30 E.H.R.R. 289; *ante*, para. 22–036.

[49] *R. v. Bow Street Magistrate ex p. Pinochet (No. 2)* [2000] 1 A.C. 119, HL, *post*, para. 31–014.

[50] (2000) 30 E.H.R.R. 289.

[51] [2001] A.C. 216, 2001 S.L.T. 28, PC.

[52] "A field day for crackpots, a pain in the neck for judges and legislators, and a goldmine for lawyers"; Lord McCluskey's view of the Canadian Charter of Rights and Freedoms, as reported in Scotland on Sunday.

22–052   Challenges in the English courts to the status of courts martial in relation to Article 6 failed in *R. v. Spear*[53] and in *Scanfuture UK v. Secretary of State for Trade and Industry*[54] the Employment Appeal Tribunal held that new procedures for appointing lay members of employment tribunals were in compliance with the European Convention.

Article 6(2) expressly recognises the presumption of innocence in criminal trials. Is it compatible with this provision for a statute to, for example, enact that the possession of drugs, or housebreaking equipment, or other items constitutes an offence unless the accused can provide an explanation for the possession? In legislation suppressing terrorism or bribery it is often said to be necessary to shift the burden of proving innocence to the accused once the prosecution has established the existence of certain defined *prima facie* incriminating facts. In *R. v. D.P.P. ex p. Kebilene*,[55] decided before the Human Rights Act had come into effect, the Divisional Court and House of Lords considered the compatibility with Article 6(2) of sections 16A and 16B of the Prevention of Terrorism Act 1989. Section 16A provided that a person was guilty of an offence if he had any article in his possession in circumstances giving rise to a reasonable suspicion that the article was in his possession for a purpose connected with the commission of acts of terrorism. Subsection 3 provided that it was a defence for a person charged to prove that the item in question was not in his possession for such a purpose. Section 16B related to the collecting of information useful for terrorist purposes. The person charged could avoid liability by proving "lawful authority or reasonable excuse" for the collecting. Both provisions, in the view of the Divisional Court undermined, in a blatant and obvious way the presumption of innocence and were incompatible with Article 6(2). The Court did not, however, consider whether, had the Human Rights Act 1998 been in force, the sections could, under section 3 of the Act, have been read in a way which was consistent with the Convention. The House of Lords, however, did venture to express a view on the hypothetical possibility of reconciling the sections with the 1998 Act and concluded such reconciliation was possible.

22–053   Their Lordships thought the provisions were compatible if they merely imposed an evidential burden on the defendant. If evidence was adduced which raised a real issue as to the innocence of their possession, the burden of proving guilt would have to be undertaken by the prosecution.[56] In *R. v. Benjafield*[57] a challenge to a confiscation order under the Drug Trafficking Act 1994 on the ground that it deprived the applicant of the presumption of innocence failed. Lord Woolf C.J. said that Article 6(2) was only an application of the broad principle of a fair trial contained in Article 6(1) and the question was one of the fairness of the trial overall.

Two cases before the Judicial Committee of the Privy Council involving Article 6 also illustrate the application of the Convention in the context of devolution. In *Brown v. Stott*[58] the Judicial Committee held that a devolution issue had arisen within the Scotland Act 1998, Schedule 6 which the Committee

---

[53] *The Times*, January 30, 2001; *ante* para. 19–021.
[54] *The Times*, April 26, 2001.
[55] [1999] 3 W.L.R. 175; [2000] 2 A.C. 326; *ante* para. 19–055. See, too, *Att.-Gen. of Hong Kong v. Lee Kwong Kut* [1993] A.C. 951, PC.
[56] Their Lordships' explication of ss.16A and 16B have found statutory expression in the Terrorism Act 2000, s.118; *ante* para. 15–055.
[57] [2001] 2 W.L.R. 75, [2001] 2 Cr.App.R. 87, CA.
[58] [2001] 2 W.L.R. 817, PC.

was entitled to determine and went on to hold that it was not a breach of Article 6 for a prosecutor at her trial to rely on an admission by a defendant that she had been driving a car at the time of an alleged offence, made compulsorily under section 172 of the Road Traffic Act 1988. In *Montgomery v. H.M. Advocate*[59] the Judicial Committee refused to interfere with the findings of the High Court of Justiciary that pre-trial publicity had deprived the appellants of a fair trial on a charge of murder.

The compatibility of the power of the Secretary of State to decide planning appeals under the Town and Country Planning Act 1990, and appeals against orders under the Transport and Works Act 1992, the Highways Act 1980 and the Acquisition of Land Act 1981 with Article 6 was upheld by the House of Lords in the important case of *R. (Alconbury Developments Ltd) v. Secretary of State for the Environment, Transport and Regions*[60] Lord Slynn held that the European Court had consistently accepted the propriety of administrative law decisions being taken by ministers, answerable to elected bodies, provided that those decisions are subject to judicial control.

The prohibition on retrospective criminal legislation contained in Article 7 was unsuccessfully relied on in *Gough v. Chief Constable of Derbyshire*[60a] where the Court of Appeal held that banning orders under the Football Spectators Act 1989 were not penalties within the Article and hence legislation could retrospectively lengthen the terms of such orders.

Article 8 (right to privacy and family life) is potentially of significance because **22–054** of the undeveloped state of English law in this field[61] and the controversial nature of many of the issues involved at a time when society's views are changing and technological developments are raising new questions.[62] The Article was invoked successfully in *R. (Daly) v. Secretary of State for the Home Department*[62a] where the House of Lords held that a rule that prisoners cannot be present during searches of their cells was contrary both to the common law and Article 8 as an infringement of their right to confidentiality of privileged legal correspondence. In *Secretary of State for the Home Department ex p. Montana*[63] the father of an illegitimate child challenged the refusal of the Secretary of State to register that child as a British citizen. The relevant provisions of the British Nationality Act 1981 which dealt with the citizenship of children born outside the United Kingdom to British citizens distinguished between the position of illegitimate children claiming citizenship by reference to their mothers and those seeking citizenship by reference to the status of their fathers. The Court of Appeal held that the distinction did not violate Article 8. The right to respect for family life did not entail a right to have the same nationality as one's parent.

---

[59] [2001] 2 W.L.R. 779, PC.

[60] [2000] 2 W.L.R. 1389, HL. See also *R Carroll and Another) v. Secretary of State for the Home Department, The Times* August 16, 2001, CA (Prison discipline proceedings not criminal proceedings within Article 6); *Preiss v. General Dental Council, The Times* August 14, 2001, PC (GDC disciplinary procedure lacked necessary independence and impartiality required by Art. 6.1 but no breach of Convention because of availability of unrestricted right of appeal to PC).

[60a] *The Times* July 19, 2001, CA. Nor were such orders in breach of right of freedom of movement under Community law: see para. 6–021, n. 54.

[61] *e.g. Malone v. Metropolitan Police Commissioner* [1979] Ch. 344; For later judicial thoughts see *Hellewell v. Chief Constable of Derbyshire* [1995] 1 W.L.R. 804, 807, *per* Laws J; *Douglas v. Hello! Ltd, The Times*, January 16, 2001, CA.

[62] *post*, Chap. 26.

[62a] [2001] 2 W.L.R. 1622, HL.

[63] *The Times*, December 5, 2000, CA. See *post*, para. 23–009. The Family Law Reform Act 1987 and the Children Act 1989 do not apply to the British Nationality Act.

In *Payne v. Payne*[64] the Court of Appeal held that the principles of English law governing the awarding of custody of children, with the welfare of the child as the paramount consideration were not inconsistent with Article 8. In *R. v. Bracknell Forrest D.C.*[65] the right of a local authority to terminate a tenancy under the Housing Act 1996 was held not to be in breach of Article 8.

The prohibition on discrimination in Article 14 was raised in *R. v. Secretary of State for the Home Department ex p. Montana*[66] as a second ground of challenge to the impugned provisions of the British Nationality Act 1981. The Court of Appeal, however, held that there was no discrimination within the Article because there were objective and reasonable grounds for distinguishing between the rights of illegitimate children in relation to their mothers as opposed to fathers.

22–055   Article 1 of the First Protocol (peaceful enjoyment of possessions) was invoked in *Regina (Professional Contractors Group Ltd and Others) v. Inland Revenue Commissioners*[67] in which the applicants challenged legislation known as IR35, which was aimed at eliminating a particular form of tax avoidance. Burton J. held that the legislation—a mixture of statutory provisions and delegated legislation—did not, in its effects on the taxpayers it was aimed at, come anywhere near to a de facto confiscation of property or an abuse of the government's right to levy tax.

The feudal liability of some landowners to contribute to the cost of repairing the chancel of their parish church[68] was held by the Court of Appeal in *Parochial Church Council of Aston Cantlow and Wilmcote with Billesley Warwickshire v. Wallbank*[69] to be contrary to Article 1 of the Protocol because of the arbitrariness of the way the liability fell, both in terms of its incidence and the scope of liability.

Parliamentary supervision of the working of the Act will be exercised through the Joint Committee on Human Rights, a Select Committee of both Houses of Parliament which was established in February 2001.

Despite suggestions that Human Rights Commission be established to promote the rights guaranteed under the 1998 Act the government finally decided against including provision for such a body in the Human Rights Act. The creation of such a body and its possible role and structure was envisaged as a suitable topic for consideration by what is now the Joint Committee.[70]

---

[64] *The Times*, March 9, 2001, CA.
[65] *Daily Telegraph*, February 13, 2001. See also *Poplar Housing and Regeneration Community Association Ltd. v. Donoghue, The Times* June 21, 2001, CA.
[66] *The Times*, December 5, 2000, CA.
[67] *The Times* April 5, 2001.
[68] *Wickhambrook Parochial Church Council v. Coxford* [1935] 2 K.B. 417, CA; *Chivers & Sons Ltd v. Air Ministry* [1955] 1 Ch. 585.
[69] *The Times* June 15, 2001, CA. The CA rejected an argument that the parochial council was not a public body within s.6 of the Human Rights Act: the relationship was based on law, not contract.
[70] S. Spencer, "A Human Rights Commission", Chap. 5 in R. Blackburn and R. Plant (eds), *Constitutional Reform* (Longman, 1999).

CHAPTER 23

NATIONALITY, CITIZENSHIP, IMMIGRATION AND EXTRADITION

I. INTRODUCTION

"British nationality law is probably more complex than that of any other country and, on its own, certainly more complex today than at any time in the past."[1]

Nationality and allegiance[2]

Nationality is a nineteenth-century concept. It is important in international law **23–001** as well as constitutional law in connection with such matters as diplomatic protection abroad, immigration, deportation and the negotiations of treaties. In constitutional law the distinction between nationals and aliens is also important because the latter are subject to certain disabilities, especially as regards public or political rights.

Until 1948, British nationality law, which had been put on a statutory basis in 1914, was founded on the common law doctrine of allegiance. Allegiance was defined by Blackstone as "the tie, or *ligamen*, which binds the subject to the King, in return for that protection which the King affords the subject."[3] A natural or permanent allegiance was owed by subjects, who at common law were persons born within the King's dominions: while aliens within the King's dominions owed the Sovereign a local or temporary allegiance. No one could relinquish his nationality (*"nemo potest exuere patriam"*). Conversely, a special Act of Parliament was necessary to give an alien English or British nationality.

The distinction between natural-born subjects and others (including naturalised aliens) was in earlier times more important than that between subjects and aliens.[4] General provision was made by the Naturalisation Act 1870 to enable aliens to acquire British nationality by executive grant of the Home Secretary instead of by private Act of Parliament.

The common law doctrine of allegiance plays no part in the new concept of nationality. Allegiance is no longer a source of British nationality, although it

---

[1] *Fransman's British Nationality Law* (3rd ed, 1989) p. viii.

[2] A Dummett and A. Nicol, *Subjects, Citizens, Aliens and Others* (Weidenfeld and Nicolson, 1990)

[3] Bl.Comm. I, 366. See also *Calvin's Case* (1608) Co.Rep. 1a, where it was decided that *"postnati,"* i.e. persons born in Scotland after the accession of James VI of Scotland to the English throne as James I, were not aliens in England. *cf. Isaacson v. Durant* (1886) 17 Q.B.D. 54 (Hanoverian born before accession of Queen Victoria).

[4] An Act of 1705 provided that the lineal descendants of Princess Sophia should be deemed to be natural-born British subjects: see *Att.-Gen. v. Prince Ernest Augustus of Hanover* [1957] A.C. 436; Clive Parry, "Further Considerations upon the Prince of Hanover's Case" (1956) 5 I.C.L.Q. 61; note by C. d'O. Farran in (1956) 19 M.L.R. 289. And see *Duke of Brunswick v. King of Hanover* (1844) 6 Beav. 1, 19, 34.

may be a consequence of it. It must be regarded henceforth as relevant to the law of treason rather than nationality, and perhaps also to "acts of state."[5]

The Act of 1914

23–002   The British Nationality and Status of Aliens Act 1914 repealed the Naturalisation Act 1870 (except as regards persons born before 1915) and provided a comprehensive code for the acquisition and loss of British nationality. Part I, relating to natural-born British subjects, applied throughout the British Empire. The general principles governing the status of natural-born British subjects were: (a) birth in British territory; or (b) birth abroad of a father who was a British subject; and (c) a married woman acquired British nationality if she married a British subject, and she lost British nationality if she married an alien. Part II related to naturalisation.[6]

British Nationality Act 1948[7]

23–003   Before 1948 British nationality was based on the common law doctrine that (with certain exceptions) every person born in British territory was a natural-born British subject. The pre-1948 statutes embodied this doctrine, but also laid down conditions on which persons born outside British territory might become natural-born British subjects, and made rules regarding naturalisation, the status of married women and children, and loss of British nationality. The combination of United Kingdom legislation and Dominion legislation along similar lines would constitute, it was hoped, a common code of British nationality for the British Commonwealth.

In the course of time divergencies began to appear between the laws of various members of the Commonwealth, in particular in relation to married women. In 1946 Canada enacted a Citizenship Act which defined Canadian *citizens*, provided that all Canadian citizens were British subjects, and further provided that all persons who were British subjects under the law of any other Commonwealth country would be recognised by Canada as British subjects. The Act thus retained the common status of British subjects, but abandoned the common code of nationality. A Commonwealth legal conference was held in London in 1947, and it was decided to accept the principles of the Canadian Citizenship Act 1946 for general application throughout the Commonwealth. The British Nationality Act 1948, as amended from time to time, gave effect to these principles so far as the United Kingdom and British colonies are concerned. It provided a new method of giving effect to the principle that people of each of the self-governing countries within the Commonwealth have both a particular status as citizens of their own country and a common status as members of the wider association of peoples comprising the Commonwealth. The Act was divided into two main parts: Part I dealt with British nationality, Part II with citizenship of the United Kingdom and colonies.

---

[5] *ante*, Chap. 15.

[6] Further Acts were passed dealing notably with the status of married women, and this legislation was known as the British Nationality and Status of Aliens Act 1914–1943. These Acts were almost entirely repealed by the British Nationality Act 1948, but they are still of practical importance for they determine whether any person born before 1949 was a British subject, so as to retain British nationality under the transitional provisions of the Act of 1948.

[7] See E. C. S. Wade, "British Nationality Act, 1948" (1948) xxx *Journ. Comp. Leg.* 67; Clive Parry, *Nationality and Citizenship Laws of the Commonwealth* (2 vols. 1957–60).

Section I of the British Nationality Act 1948 provided that:

"(1) Every person who under this Act is a citizen of the United Kingdom and Colonies,[8] or who under any enactment for the time being in force in any country mentioned in subsection (3) of this section is a citizen of that country, shall by virtue of that citizenship have the status of a British subject.

(2) Any person having the status aforesaid may be known either as a British subject or as a Commonwealth citizen: and accordingly in this Act and in any other enactment or instrument whatever, whether passed or made before or after the commencement of this Act, the expression 'British subject' and the expression 'Commonwealth citizen' shall have the same meaning."

Subsection (3), specifying the Commonwealth countries concerned, was amended from time to time so as to include all independent members of the Commonwealth, Southern Rhodesia, as it then was, and any other Commonwealth country that had been granted power to enact its own citizenship laws. Each of the countries mentioned in subsection (3), as amended, was a legislative unit for nationality or citizenship purposes. It was intended that each of them should enact a citizenship law containing the principle of section 1(1), *ante*, by which mutual recognition as British subjects would be given to the citizens of other Commonwealth countries. The result would be that "British subjects," instead of being ascertained by a common code, would simply comprise the citizens of all Commonwealth countries, as is shown by the alternative title "Commonwealth citizens."

The 1948 Act provided for the acquisition of citizenship by *birth* in the United **23–004** Kingdom and Colonies on or after January 1, 1948 (s.4)[9]; and by *descent* if a child's father was a citizen of the United Kingdom and Colonies at the time of the birth (s.5).[10]

Any person who was a British subject immediately before January 1, 1949[11] became a citizen of the United Kingdom and Colonies if: (a) he was born in the United Kingdom and Colonies; or (b) he was naturalised in the United Kingdom and Colonies; or (c) he became a British subject by annexation of territory to the United Kingdom and Colonies; or (d) his father was a British subject and fulfilled any of the above conditions: or (e) he was born in a British protectorate, protected state or trust territory (s.12).[12]

Provision was also made for the acquisition of citizenship by *naturalisation* (in the case of aliens and British protected persons) and by *registration* in the case

---

[8] *post*, para. 23–007.

[9] Unless (a) the father of the child enjoyed diplomatic immunity and was not a citizen of the United Kingdom and Colonies, or (b) the father was an enemy alien and the birth occurred in a place then under enemy occupation.

[10] Subject to the proviso that if the father were a citizen by descent one of a number of other conditions had to be satisfied.

[11] Under the British Nationality and Status of Aliens Act 1914–1943 the following persons born after 1914 were natural-born British subjects:

(a) Any person born within His Majesty's dominions and allegiance; and

(b) Any person born out of His Majesty's dominions whose father was, at the time of that person's birth, a British subject and fulfilled one of a number of conditions; and

(c) Any person born on board a British ship.

[12] See *post*, para. 35–008 *et seq.* for protectorates, protected states and trust territories.

of Commonwealth citizens and the wives of citizens of the United Kingdom and colonies.

II. THE BRITISH NATIONALITY ACT 1981[13]

Introduction

23–005   British subjects were free at common law to come into or leave the "mother country." The British Nationality Act 1948, which created citizenship of the United Kingdom and Colonies, retained the old term "British subject" as an alternative to the new term "Commonwealth citizen" for the citizens of other independent Commonwealth countries. In 1962 Parliament passed the Commonwealth Immigrants Act 1962 to give some power to control immigration into the United Kingdom by citizens of Commonwealth countries. All other Commonwealth countries had power to control such immigration.[14] The power of control conferred in 1962 applied to all Commonwealth citizens except those born in the United Kingdom and those holding United Kingdom passports, and also to British protected persons and Irish citizens.

The Home Secretary was also given for the first time a limited power to deport from the United Kingdom Commonwealth citizens,[15] British protected persons and Irish citizens on the recommendation of a court that had sentenced them to imprisonment. The power to deport in such cases was possessed by practically every other territory in the Commonwealth.

The Commonwealth Immigrants Act 1968 amended the Act of 1962 with regard to (*inter alia*) exemption from control enjoyed by citizens of the United Kingdom and Colonies holding United Kingdom passports, and made it an offence to land otherwise than in accordance with immigration regulations. The Acts of 1962 and 1968 were repealed and replaced by the Immigration Act 1971.

The result of the introduction of immigration controls was that there were two categories of citizens in the United Kingdom and Colonies: those entitled to enter and reside in the United Kingdom (called by the Immigration Act "patrials") and those not entitled ("non-patrials"). The object of the British Nationality Act 1981[16] is to distinguish clearly a category of citizenship which carries with it the right of entry and residence from other categories. The old law which was outlined in the previous section remains of importance because (i) it defines the nationality or citizenship of people born before the 1981 Act came into effect (January 1, 1983); (ii) claims under the 1981 Act may turn on the status of parents and grandparents born under the old law[17] and (iii) the terminology of the old law is to be found in the case law and confusion can be caused unless it is realised that, for example, British subject is used in the new law in an entirely different sense from that in which it was formerly used.

---

[13] *Fransman's British Nationality Law* (3rd ed, 1989).
[14] Colonies can also restrict immigration: see *Thornton v. The Police* [1962] A.C. 339, PC.
[15] *cf. R. v. Sabri, The Times*, November 10, 1964, CCA. Before 1962 a deportation order against a British subject would be quashed: *R. v. Home Secretary, ex p. Château Thierry (Duke)* [1917] 1 K.B. 922, 930 *per* Swinfen Eady L.J.
[16] See commentaries by C. Blake, "Citizenship, Law and the State" (1982) 45 M.L.R. 179 and R. White and F. J. Hampson, "The British Nationality Act 1981" [1982] P.L. 6.
[17] In *R. v. Secretary of State for Foreign and Commonwealth Affairs, ex p. Ross-Clunis* [1991] 2 A.C. 493, HL a claim to citizenship under the 1981 Act hinged on events dating back to 1905.

Categories of citizenship

The 1981 Act recognises three categories of citizenship: **23–006**

(i) British;

(ii) British Dependent Territories;

(iii) British Overseas.

It also recognises the special status of

(i) British protected persons; and

(ii) British subjects without citizenship (British subjects).

A further category of British National (Overseas) was created by the Hong Kong Act 1985.

The term Commonwealth citizen embraces all categories (apart from that of British Protected Persons) and citizens of independent Commonwealth countries.[18]

Citizens of Eire continue to enjoy their own unique status; they are not aliens and possess the right to vote when resident in the United Kingdom.[19]

British citizenship

British citizenship is the only type of citizenship under the 1981 Act which   **23–007**
confers a legal right to live in, and to come and go into and from, the United Kingdom by right.

British citizenship is acquired, as a general rule, in the case of persons born before January 1, 1983 if they were patrials, that is citizens of the United Kingdom and Colonies who under the Immigration Act 1971, were entitled to enter the United Kingdom by right.[20]

Patrials were (a) citizens of the United Kingdom and Colonies and (b) Commonwealth citizens who possessed one of the special links with the United Kingdom defined in the Immigration Act. That status largely corresponds to British citizenship as defined in the 1981 Act in the case of persons born after January 1, 1983.[21]

In the case of persons born after the commencement of the Act, British citizenship may be acquired by

(i) *Birth* in the United Kingdom provided that one parent was at the time of birth a British citizen or was settled in the United Kingdom.[22] This provision marks the abandonment of the former principle that, subject to minor exceptions, birth in the United Kingdom conferred British nationality.[23] A person who does not acquire citizenship by birth in the United

---

[18] s.37.

[19] s.50(1); Representation of the People Act 1983, s.1. Citizens of Eire can continue to claim to be British subjects under s.31.

[20] The term patrial was given legal significance and currency but not invented by the Immigration Act 1971. It has been removed from the 1971 Act by s.39 of the 1981 Act and replaced by British citizen.

[21] Some patrials do not become British citizens; and lose their right of abode: s.11(2). Some patrials do not become British citizens but retain a right of abode: s.39(2).

[22] s.1. "Settled" has a technical meaning: s.50(1)–(4); *post*, para. 23–028.

[23] *ante*, para. 23–003.

Kingdom may, however, be subsequently entitled to citizenship, for example, if one of his parents later acquires citizenship or he spends the first 10 years of his life in the United Kingdom.[24]

(ii) *Descent*: when birth occurs abroad but one parent is a British citizen other than by descent.[25] This represents an extension of the rule in the 1948 Act which allowed the acquisition of citizenship by descent only through the father. The new rule, however, is more restrictive than the old in that, subject to exceptions, it allows acquisition by descent for one generation only. Formerly United Kingdom citizenship could be transmitted indefinitely by registration at a British consulate in a foreign country. Persons born abroad whilst a parent possessing British citizenship is in the service of the Crown are treated as acquiring citizenship by birth and can transmit that citizenship even if the relevant parent was a citizen by descent.[26] In some cases British citizenship may be claimed following birth abroad where one of the parents was a British citizen by descent but had resided in the United Kingdom for the three years preceding the birth.[27]

Citizenship by naturalisation

23–008   Naturalisation is now governed by section 6 of and Schedule 1 to the British Nationality Act 1981. Naturalisation is a matter within the discretion of the Secretary of State. Section 44 provides that in exercising any discretion under the Act the Secretary of State must pay no regard to "race, colour or religion."[28] Section 6 distinguishes between applications by persons of full age and capacity (subsection 1) and applications by persons of full age and capacity who at the date of the application are married to a British citizen (subsection 2). In the case of naturalisation under subsection 1 the applicant must first satisfy a residence requirement which involves within the five years before the application presence in the United Kingdom, subject to absences not exceeding 450 days, and in the 12 months before application presence except for a maximum absence of 90 days.[29] In the alternative an application can show that at the date of application he is serving outside the United Kingdom in Crown service under the United Kingdom government. Secondly he must establish that he is of good character; thirdly that he has sufficient knowledge of the English, Welsh or Scottish Gaelic language, and fourthly that he intends (i) to reside in the United Kingdom, or (ii) to enter into or continue in Crown service under the United Kingdom Government, or service under an international organisation of which the United Kingdom Government is a member, or service in the employment of a society or company established in the United Kingdom. The Home Secretary is expressly given a wide discretion to waive the requirements relating to residence and language proficiency.

---

[24] s.1(3); s.1(4).

[25] s.2.

[26] s.2.

[27] s.3(3).

[28] Although subs. 2 provides that the Secretary of State is not required to give any reason for his decision, the Court of Appeal has held that fairness requires him to give such explanation as to enable the applicant to challenge the exercise of his discretion in the courts: *R. v. Secretary of State for the Home Department, ex p. Fayed* [1998] 1 W.L.R. 763; *post* para. 31–016.

[29] Furthermore the applicant must not at any time in the five year period have been in breach of the immigration laws and in the final twelve months must not at any time have been subject to any restriction on the period for which he might remain in the United Kingdom.

The requirements to be satisfied by the spouse of a British citizen who seeks naturalisation under subsection 2 are less onerous. The period of five years is reduced to three (subject to absences not exceeding 270 days) and there is no need to show "sufficient knowledge" of the three listed languages.

Naturalisation is only available to allow aliens to acquire British citizenship. A British citizen by descent, for example, cannot apply for naturalisation.[29a]

Citizenship by registration

The Home Secretary is given a discretion to register minors as British citizens by Section 3 which spells out particular requirements to be satisfied in specific types of application.[30]   **23–009**

Registration by right is available to British Dependent Territories citizens, British Overseas citizens, British subjects and British protected persons who satisfy the residence requirements of section 4.

An applicant whose right to be registered depends on her own antecedent fraud is not entitled to challenge the Secretary of State's refusal to register her as a British citizen: *R. v. Secretary of State for the Home Department, ex p. Puttick*.[31]

Registration is available by right to British Dependent Territories citizens who are nationals of the United Kingdom for the purpose of the Community Treaties, that is people having a link with Gibraltar (section 5).[32]

Transitional provisions preserve for five years after the commencement of the 1981 Act the rights of individuals to register as British citizens who could formerly have registered as citizens of the United Kingdom (i) by virtue of residence (section 7); (ii) in the case of women, by marriage to a citizen of the United Kingdom (section 8) and (iii) by registration at a United Kingdom consulate (section 9).

British Nationality (Falkland Islands) Act 1983

This Act which is deemed to have come into effect on the same day as the British Nationality Act confers British citizenship on inhabitants of the Falkland Islands born before January 1, 1983 who would otherwise be British Dependent Territories citizens by virtue of a link with the Falkland Islands—for example, birth, naturalisation or registration there. In the case of persons born after January 1, 1983 British citizenship is conferred on persons born in the Islands who satisfy *mutatis mutandis* the requirements of the 1981 Act. Provision is also made for acquisition of British citizenship by registration and descent.   **23–010**

Loss of citizenship

In the case of naturalised citizens and citizens by registration, citizenship may be lost by *deprivation* under section 40 of the British Nationality Act 1981. The   **23–011**

[29a] *R. v. Secretary of State for the Home Department ex p. Ullah, The Times* June 27, 2001, CA. (Application presumably inspired by limitation on transmission of citizenship by citizens by descent).

[30] Statutory distinction between illegitimate male/female children for purposes of registration not contrary to European Convention on Human Rights: *R. v. Secretary of State for the Home Department, ex p. Montana, The Times*, December 5, 2000, CA; *ante* para. 22–054.

[31] [1981] 1 Q.B. 767, CA (Marriage to British subject procured only by deceiving registrar as to identity of P, a German national wanted in Germany on charges of terrorism). See too *Puttick v. Attorney-General* [1980] Fam. 1 where Sir George Baker P. refused to grant a declaration of the validity of the marriage.

[32] K. Simmonds, "The British Nationality Act 1981 and the definition of the term 'national' for Community purposes" (1984) C.M.L. Rev. 675.

Home Secretary may deprive any person to whom the section applies of citizenship if satisfied that the registration or certificate of naturalisation was obtained by fraud, false representation or concealment of any material fact; or if he is satisfied that the person has shown himself disloyal to Her Majesty, or has traded with the enemy during any war, or (unless the effect of deprivation would be to render that person stateless) has been sentenced to not less than twelve months' imprisonment within five years of naturalisation. A person is not to be deprived of citizenship under the section unless the Home Secretary is satisfied that it is not conducive to the public good that that person should continue to be a British citizen; and except in the case of continuous residence abroad, a person against whom an order is proposed to be made may require that the case be referred to a committee of inquiry called the Deprivation of Citizenship Committee.[33]

A British citizen of full age and capacity may under section 12 of the 1981 Act *renounce* his British nationality.[34] A declaration must be made in a prescribed form and registered by the Home Secretary if he is satisfied that after registration the person concerned will acquire some citizenship or nationality other than British citizenship. If another citizenship or nationality is not acquired within six months of registration the person shall be deemed to be and have remained a British citizen. It is provided, however, that the Home Secretary may withhold registration of any such declaration if made during any war in which Her Majesty may be engaged in right of Her Majesty's government in the United Kingdom.[35]

Resumption of citizenship

23–012   Provision is made for resumption of citizenship by persons who have earlier renounced citizenship, for example a wife might have to renounce British citizenship under the law of her husband's state and wish to return to the United Kingdom on divorce or following his death.[36]

British Dependent Territories Citizenship

23–013   This, in effect, is a colonial citizenship, acquired by a connection with a colony analogous to that needed with the United Kingdom to establish the status of British citizenship.[37] The status does not confer a right of entry to the United Kingdom or to any particular colony, immigration being a matter left to each colony to determine for itself. As we have seen, Gibraltarians and Falkland Islanders have, within this category, special rights to British citizenship; on the other hand the Hong Kong Act 1985 makes provision for converting this type of citizenship arising from a connection with Hong Kong into "a new form of

---

[33] There is no right to an inquiry where the registration or naturalisation has been procured by fraud as to identity: *R. v. Secretary of State for the Home Department, ex p. Akhtar* [1981] Q.B. 46.

[34] For the purposes of s.40 any person who has been married is deemed to be of full age.

[35] At common law a British subject could not become naturalised in a foreign country (*ante*, para. 23–001). The Naturalisation Act 1870 provided that if he did so he should be deemed to have ceased to be a British subject and be regarded as an alien. The 1948 Act in order to prevent statelessness provided that the acquisition of a foreign nationality or of another Commonwealth citizenship, instead of involving automatic forfeiture, should entitle a person to renounce his citizenship of the United Kingdom and Colonies if he so desired. In *R. v. Lynch* [1903] 1 K.B. 444, it was held that naturalisation in a country with which Britain was at war not only amounted to treason, but was probably null and void: *ante*, para. 23–001.

[36] s.13. See also s.10.

[37] British Nationality Act 1981, Part II. For dependent territories, see *post*, Chap. 35.

British nationality the holders of which shall be known as British Nationals (Overseas)".[38]

British Overseas Citizenship[39]

This status was conferred on citizens of the United Kingdom and Colonies **23–014** who did not, when the 1981 Act came into effect, acquire British citizenship or British Dependent Territories Citizenship. It is a transitional and residual status. They may at the same time hold another citizenship.

British subjects[40]

Unlike British Overseas Citizens, British subjects cannot possess any other **23–015** citizenship. They are persons who were British subjects under the 1948 Act who failed to acquire citizenship when the country in which they lived adopted its own nationality laws. This, too, is a transitional status, destined to disappear.

British Overseas Citizens and British subjects are entitled to British passports but, as will be seen, have no right of entry to the United Kingdom. If admitted to the United Kingdom they may under section 4 acquire British citizenship by registration.

British Protected Persons

British Protected Persons are defined by Order in Council made under section **23–016** 38 of the 1981 Act and the Solomon Islands Act 1978.[41] They are connected with territories which were protectorates, protected states of United Kingdom trust territories.[42] They may hold citizenship of a non-Commonwealth country. Like the two preceding categories, the significance of this one is the right to a British passport and, if admitted to the United Kingdom, the chance of registration as a British citizen.

British National (Overseas)

This new form of British nationality was created by the Hong Kong Act 1985 **23–017** and was intended to replace the British Dependent Territories citizenship which would come to an end for inhabitants of the Colony formerly entitled to it on the handing-over of Hong Kong to China. The new form of nationality was in effect no more than a right to a British passport. The value of this new status was a matter of controversy between the United Kingdom government and residents of Hong Kong and their supporters in Parliament. As a result three further statutes were enacted.

The British Nationality (Hong Kong) Act 1990 authorised the conferment by registration of British citizenship on up to 50,000 persons and their dependents, recommended by the Governor of Hong Kong. It was hoped that this would encourage those registered to feel able to stay in Hong Kong under the new administration.

---

[38] See further, *post*, Chap. 35.
[39] Pt III. This category includes East African Asians in India and East Africa and certain classes of inhabitants of Malaysia.
[40] Pt IV. British subjects are believed to number about 50,000 and reside mainly in Sri Lanka, India and Pakistan.
[41] The Solomon Islands Act 1978 was unusual in the provision it made for citizenship on the coming into effect of independence. Only "indigenous Solomon Islanders" became citizens of the new state. Other residents who lacked a nationality as a consequence of the new legislation became British Protected Persons.
[42] *post*, Chap. 35.

The Hong Kong (War Wives and Widows) Act 1996 authorised the conferment on a group of applicants indicated by the title of the Act, believed to number about 50. Finally the British Nationality (Hong Kong) Act 1997 provided for the registration as British citizens of a number of inhabitants of Hong Kong, believed to number between 5,000 and 8,000, who, because of their non-Chinese ethnic origins did not acquire Chinese nationality under the terms of the Joint Declaration. It was argued that the United Kingdom owed a particular obligation to them because they were largely descendants of people who had settled in Hong Kong in the service of the Crown as soldiers and civil servants from other parts of the Empire, particularly India.

III. ALIENS AND CITIZENSHIP OF THE UNION

23–018   Until the Immigration Act 1971 the law distinguished between British subjects and aliens (subject to the special situation of citizens of the Republic of Ireland).[43] The Immigration Act 1971 introduced a new distinction between patrials (with the right of entry and abode) and non-patrials. Since the coming into effect of the British Nationality Act 1981 that terminology has been abandoned and the appropriate term for persons not coming within the terms of the British Nationality Act 1981 is again alien. Where, however, a non-British citizen or subject is a national of a member state of the European Community his rights in the United Kingdom fall to be treated under Community law. The importance of such rights as those of freedom of movement within the Community led to the introduction of the concept of Citizenship of the Union in the Maastricht Treaty (Article 17(1)[8]).

Aliens
23–019   Under the medieval common law aliens had practically no public or private rights. The rules were gradually relaxed by statute and a more liberal attitude on the part of the common law courts. By the end of the sixteenth century it was recognised that aliens in the King's dominions owed a temporary and local allegiance. Friendly aliens could bring personal actions such as trespass and debt, and could own personal property, including leaseholds.

At common law an alien probably had no right to enter this country.[44] The Crown probably had no prerogative power to send an alien (other than an enemy alien) compulsorily out of the realm,[45] but since the eighteenth century[46] the government has sought statutory powers to do so.

---

[43] The Ireland Act 1949, s.2 provided that citizens of the Republic of Ireland were not to be regarded as aliens. S.5(1) provided for the retention of British nationality (with certain exceptions) by persons born in Eire, or the Irish Free State, before 1922 (the date of the Anglo-Irish Treaty) who were British subjects immediately before 1949.

[44] *Musgrove v. Chun Teeong Toy* [1891] A.C. 272; criticised, Thornberry (1963) 12 I.C.L.Q. 422. But see *Schmidt v. Secretary of State for Home Affairs* [1969] 2 Ch. 149, 168, *per* Lord Denning M.R. Nothing in the Immigration Act 1971 impairs any prerogative powers possessed by the Crown in relation to aliens (s.33(5)). This saving applies *only* to aliens and hence is not applicable to British Overseas Citizens: *R. v. Immigration Appeal Tribunal, ex p. Secretary of State for the Home Department* [1990] 1 W.L.R. 1126.

[45] Forsyth, *Cases and Opinions on Constitutional Law* (1869) p. 181; Holdsworth, *History of English Law*, Vol. X, pp. 393–400. *cf.* dictum of Lord Atkinson in *Johnstone v. Pedlar* [1921] A.C. 262, 283.

[46] Aliens Act 1793.

Friendly aliens, i.e. citizens of countries with which the Crown is not at war,[47] have long had the right to contract, to own and dispose of personal property, and to bring and defend actions. They may now own and dispose of real property. Resident aliens owe allegiance to the Crown, and are subject to the general civil and criminal law.[48] They do not enjoy the parliamentary or local government franchise,[49] they may not sit in either House of Parliament[50] or hold any public office; but they may be employed in any civil capacity under the Crown (a) outside the United Kingdom, or (b) under a certificate issued by a Minister with Treasury approval. Aliens are subject to restrictions with regard to employment in the armed forces, the Civil Service in this country, and the merchant navy; jury service; the ownership of British ships; holding a pilot's certificate; change of name; and taking part in certain industrial activities.[51]

Enemy aliens,[52] *i.e.* nationals of countries with which the Crown is at war, **23–020** were at one time virtually rightless, unless exceptionally they were here with the licence of the King. In course of time it came to be seen that what mattered so far as commerce was concerned was to prevent any trade with the enemy country, regardless of what persons were carrying it on. And so an "enemy" came to mean any person (whether a British subject or not) who voluntarily resided or carried on business in an enemy country.[53] An enemy alien in this sense cannot enter into contracts by English law, and contracts entered into with him before the war are suspended for the duration of the war. "Enemy character" is largely of importance in relation to corporations, and in relation to offences under the Trading with the Enemy Acts.

An enemy alien cannot bring an action in the British courts; nor, if he was plaintiff in an action begun before the war, can he appeal during the war; for the enemy cannot be given the advantage of enforcing his rights by the assistance of the Sovereign with whom he is at war. On the other hand an enemy alien can be sued during the war, as that permits British subjects or friendly aliens to enforce their rights with the assistance of the Sovereign against the enemy; and if he is

---

[47] "Friendly" aliens may in some context include nationals of countries with which the Crown is at war, but who have come to reside or are allowed to remain here by the Sovereign's licence: *Wells v. Williams* (1697) 1 Ld.Raym. 282. The Sovereign's licence, express or implied, gives the protection of the law and the courts: *Sylvester's Case* (1702) 7 Mod. 150. A licence is commonly implied by the fact that an alien has registered and has been allowed to remain: *Thurn and Taxis (Princess) v. Moffitt* [1915] 1 Ch. 58; *Schaffenius v. Goldberg* [1916] 1 K.B. 284. See further, W. E. Davies, *The English Law relating to Aliens* (1931), Chap. 1.

[48] See also the Aliens Restriction (Amendment) Act 1919, s.3 which makes it an offence punishable by 10 years imprisonment for an alien to attempt or do any act calculated to cause sedition or disaffection among the civilian population; and by three months imprisonment if he promotes or attempts to promote industrial unrest in any industry in which he has not been bona fide engaged in the United Kingdom for the previous two years.

[49] But see for Citizens of the Union *post* para. 23–022.

[50] Act of Settlement 1700.

[51] See generally British Nationality and Status of Aliens Act 1914; Aliens Restriction (Amendment) Act 1919; Aliens Employment Act 1955. But see also *post*, para. 23–022 for Citizens of the Union.

[52] See Lord McNair and A.D. Watts, *Legal Effects of War* (4th ed., 1966) McNair, *Legal Effects of War* (3rd ed.).

[53] *Wells v. Williams* (1697) 1 Ld.Raym. 282; *The Hoop* (1799) 1 C.Rob. 196; *Janson v. Driefontein Consolidated Mines* [1902] A.C. 484. For the position of corporations, see *Daimler Co. v. Continental Tyre and Rubber Co* [1916] 1 A.C. 307; as to firms, see *Rodriguez v. Speyer Bros.* [1919] A.C. 59. Territory occupied by the enemy is regarded as enemy territory: *Sovfracht (V.O.) v. Van Udens Scheepvaart en Agentur Maatschappij (N.V. Babr.)* [1943] A.C. 203.

sued justice demands that he be allowed to appear and defend. Further, if he is unsuccessful as defendant he may appeal, for he is entitled to have the case decided according to law and therefore to have the error of a court of first instance rectified (*Porter v. Freudenberg*[54]). The Crown has the prerogative of confiscating enemy property, but if it is taken it is usually handed over to a Custodian during the war.[55]

23–021 With regard to the control of aliens for the security of the realm in time of war, the original distinction between enemy and friendly aliens is commonly used. Wartime legislation and emergency powers during both the two world wars gave the Crown very extensive powers of control over enemy aliens in this sense. The legislation expressly preserved the Crown's prerogative in relation to enemy aliens. At common law their licence to remain at large may be revoked at any time at the complete discretion of the Crown, and they can be interned[56] or deported.[57] The internment of an enemy alien is an act of state, and he has no right to apply for a writ of habeas corpus against the executive to challenge the Crown's power to intern or deport (*R. v. Bottrill, ex p. Kuechenmeister*[58]). In the last case it was discussed, but not decided, whether an interned enemy alien is in the position of a prisoner of war. Internment, however, does not revoke the licence to bring civil actions in the courts, or, probably, to commence habeas corpus proceedings against private persons.[59]

Citizenship of the Union[60]

23–022 In Chapter 6 we saw the impact on domestic law of the right of freedom of movement of workers under Article 39[48] of the Community Treaty. The *Factortame* litigation emphasised the importance of non-discrimination between community nationals: Article 43[52]. The Maastricht Treaty took further the recognition of individual rights arising from being a national of a member state and recognised a new Citizenship of the Union: Article 17(1)[8]. It also recognised new rights for such citizens, in particular the right to vote and stand as a candidate in local elections to the European Parliament in the State in which he resides.

IV. IMMIGRATION, ASYLUM AND DEPORTATION

23–023 The restriction on entry to the United Kingdom by legislation has a long history.[61] Since 1962 when Parliament passed the Commonwealth Immigrants

---

[54] [1915] 1 K.B. 857, CA *per* Lord Reading C.J. See also *Eichengruen v. Mond* [1940] 1 Ch. 785; *cf. Weber's Trustees v. Riemer*, 1947 S.L.T. 295 (counterclaim not permissible).

[55] See *e.g. Administrator of Austrian Property v. Russian Bank for Foreign Trade* (1931) 48 T.L.R. 37; *Bank voor Handel en Scheepvaart N.V. v. Administrator of Hungarian Property* (1954) A.C. 584.

[56] *R. v. Commandant of Knockaloe Camp* (1917) 117 L.T. 627; *ex p. Liebmann* [1916] 1 K.B. 268; *ex p. Weber* [1916] A.C. 421.

[57] *Netz v. Chuter Ede* [1946] Ch. 224; *Att.-Gen. for Canada v. Cain* [1906] A.C. 542, PC.

[58] [1947] K.B. 41, CA.

[59] *Ibid. per* Asquith L.I.

[60] See further, Wyatt and Dashwood, *op.cit.* pp. 494–497.

[61] V. Beavan, *The Development of British Immigration Law* (Croom Helm, 1986). See, too, A Dummett and A. Nicol, *op. cit.* Modern legislation may be regarded as beginning with the Aliens Act 1905 which followed a growth in the number of refugees fleeing, particularly from Russia and Poland, in the last decades of the nineteenth century.

Act restrictions have also applied to many categories of people falling within in the widest sense of the terms, British subjects of Commonwealth citizens. The period following the enactment of the Immigration Act 1971 has seen continuing legislative activity and constant litigation.[62] At the same time as Parliament has sought to restrict immigration the United Kingdom has become a party to the Geneva Convention relating to the Status of Refugees which seeks to protect those seeking asylum from persecution and prevent the deportation of refugees to countries where they face a well-founded fear of persecution.[63] The provisions of immigration law are also now subject to review in the courts in the light of the Human Rights Act 1998[64] and, in the case of citizens of the Union, in the light of Community law.[65]

In this immensely complex area it will not be possible here to do more than indicate in outline some of the more important issues raised by the legislation and the response of the courts to challenges to the legality of ministerial decisions.

Immigration

The detailed rules governing immigration and deportation are to be found in the Immigration Act 1971 (as amended) and the Immigration Rules made under section 3(2) of that Act. The content of the Act and the Rules, the application of the law and the role of the courts in reviewing the decisions of immigration officials and the Home Secretary have all been matters of controversy. To the individuals involved hardly any matter could be of greater moment than whether they are to be allowed entry to a particular country where, for one reason or another, they wish to live or whether, having settled in the United Kingdom they are to be required to leave. The legislation is couched in the widest terms, conferring extensive discretionary powers. The reluctance of Parliament to fetter the executive (or of the executive to be fettered) can hardly be better shown than by the fact that the Immigration Rules are not in the strict sense, delegated legislation which clarify and restrict the wider provisions of a statute. Section 3(2) speaks of "statements of the rules . . . laid down by [the Secretary of State] as to the practice to be followed in the administration of this Act."[66] A typical judicial comment on the status of the Rules is that of Lord Bridge in *R. v. Immigration Appeal Tribunal ex p. Singh*.[67]

23–024

"The rules do not purport to enact a precise code having statutory force. They are discursive in style, in part merely explanatory and, on their fact, frequently

---

[62] S. Legomsky, *Immigration and the Judiciary* (Oxford, 1987) provides a useful but now somewhat outdated survey.

[63] Convention and Protocol Relating to the Status of Refugees (1951, Cmd 9171) and (1967 Cmnd 3906); Asylum and Immigration Appeals Act 1993.

[64] And see the explicit reference to the Human Rights Act 1998 in the Immigration and Asylum Act 1999, s.65.

[65] *e.g. Van Duyn v. Home Office* [1974] E.C.R. 1337; [1975] 1 C.M.L.R. 1; *R. v. Bouchereau* [1978] Q.B. 732; *R. v. Secretary of State for the Home Department, ex p. Santillo* [1981] Q.B. 778; *R. v. Secretary of State for the Home Department, ex p. Dannenberg* [1984] Q.B. 766 *ante* para. 6–035. See Immigration Act 1988, s.7 *post* para. 23–026.

[66] The rules must be laid before Parliament and, if disapproved by either House the Home Secretary shall make such changes as seem required. Four sets of rules were made initially, dealing with Commonwealth citizens (H.C. 79 and H.C. 80), and EEC and non-Commonwealth nationals (H.C. 81 and H.C. 82) (the 1973 Rules). A revised version was produced in 1980: H.C. (1979–1980) No. 394 (Statement of Change in Immigration Rules). The current rules are H.C. 1984 No. 395, as amended, Cm. 4851 (2000).

[67] [1986] 1 W.L.R. 910, 917. See further, *post*, para. 29–004.

offer no more than broad guidance as to how discretion is to be exercised in different typical situations. In so far as they lay down principles to be applied, they generally do so in loose and imprecise terms."

They nonetheless have legal status to the extent that section 19 requires an adjudicator to allow an appeal against a decision that was "not in accordance with the law or with any immigration rules applicable."

Right of abode

23–025   Section 1 of the 1971 Act provides that all persons who have "the right of abode" under section 2 are free to live in, and to come and go into and from, the United Kingdom. Persons not having that right may live, work and settle in the United Kingdom by permission and subject to regulation and control; and those who were settled here when the Act came into force are treated as if they had been given definite leave to enter or remain. The Act does not control local journeys between the United Kingdom, the Isle of Man, the Channel Islands and the Republic of Ireland ("the common travel area"), subject to section 10 (*infra*).

Section 2, as amended by the British Nationality Act 1981, section 39 provides that a person has the right of abode in the United Kingdom if he is

(i) a British citizen; or

(ii) a Commonwealth citizen who satisfies certain requirements set out in the Section which in effect preserve for their lifetimes the right of abode possessed by certain Commonwealth citizens before the enactment of the 1981 Act.[68]

British citizen is used under the Act to include both categories of persons (section 2(2) as amended).

Regulation and control

23–026   Section 3 makes general provisions for regulation and control. Persons who are not British citizens require leave to enter or remain, which may be given for a limited or indefinite period, and may be subject to conditions restricting employment and occupation or requiring registration with the police.

The Immigration and Asylum Act 1999 amends section 3, allowing, for example, leave to enter to be granted before a person arrives in the United Kingdom.

---

[68] s.2(1)(d). He is a Commonwealth citizen born to or legally adopted by a parent who at the time of the birth or adoption had citizenship of the United Kingdom and Colonies by his birth in the United Kingdom or in any of the Islands.

(2) A woman is under this Act also to have the right of abode in the United Kingdom if she is a Commonwealth citizen and either—

(a) is the wife of any such citizen of the United Kingdom and Colonies as is mentioned in subsection (1)(a), (b) or (c) above or any such Commonwealth citizen as is mentioned in subsection (1)(d); or

(b) has at any time been the wife—

(i) of a person then being such a citizen of the United Kingdom and Colonies or Commonwealth citizen; or

(ii) of a British subject who but for his death would on the date of commencement of the British Nationality Act 1948 have been such a citizen of the United Kingdom and Colonies as is mentioned in subsection (1)(a) or (b).

Anyone claiming to be entitled to enter the United Kingdom by virtue of having the right of abode has the burden of proving the necessary status (section 3(8)).

As amended by section 3 of the Immigration Act 1988, section 3(9) of the 1971 Act provides that such proof can only be established by possession of a United Kingdom passport describing the holder as a British citizen or as a citizen of the United Kingdom and Colonies having the right of abode in the United Kingdom; or, a certificate of entitlement certifying that he has such a right of abode.[69]

The Immigration Act 1988, section 7 provides that anyone entering or remaining in the United Kingdom by virtue of an enforceable Community right or any provision made under section 2(2) of the European Communities Act 1972 does not require leave under section 3 of the 1971 Act.[70]

Crews of ships or aircraft may enter for limited periods without leave. Diplomats and their families and members of home, Commonwealth and visiting forces are exempt from control (section 8, as amended by the Immigration and Asylum Act 1999). Provision may be made by Order in Council with regard to persons entering otherwise than by ship or aircraft[71] *e.g.* by land from the Republic of Ireland. Such provisions may exclude the Republic of Ireland from the common travel area (section 10).

Refusal of leave

Persons who fail to satisfy immigration officials that they fulfil the requirements of the Immigration Rules will normally be refused leave to enter the United Kingdom. Applicants may be refused leave if they seek entry for a purpose not covered by the Rules.[72] Applicants who prima facie satisfy the requirements may be refused entry if already subject to a deportation order or if they have been convicted of an extraditable offence or on medical grounds.[73] Leave may also be refused because in the view of the Home Secretary an individual's exclusion is conducive to the public good.[74] This last reason for refusal confers a very wide discretion on the Home Secretary.[75]

23–027

Illegal entrants

An illegal entrant is defined by section 33(1) of the Immigration Act 1971 as "a person unlawfully entering or seeking to enter in breach of a deportation order or of the immigration laws, and includes also a person who has so entered."

A criminal offence is committed under section 24 if an immigrant enters the country illegally. An illegal entrant can be removed from the United Kingdom before he is entitled to appeal against the order. If he wishes to appeal he must do so from outside the United Kingdom (section 16 and Schedule 2). (In some circumstances the decision to remove an individual on the ground that he is an

23–028

---

[69] See *R. v. Secretary of State for the Home Department, ex p. Minta, The Times*, June 24, 1991. (British citizen's right to enter UK after holiday in Belgium challenged: he had travelled on a British Visitor's Passport).

[70] See the Immigration (European Economic Area) Regulations which apply not only to nationals of the European Union but also to those of members states of the EEA which are not members of the Union. See similarly the Immigration and Asylum Act 1999, s.90.

[71] By swimming the Channel?

[72] H.C. 395 para. 320(1).

[73] H.C. 395 para. 320(2) and (7).

[74] H.C. 395 para. 320(6).

[75] *cf. Schmidt v. Secretary of State for Home Affairs* [1969] 2 Ch. 149.

illegal entrant may be open to judicial review, as we shall see). For the purposes of the British Nationality Act 1981, an illegal entrant cannot claim to be "settled" in the United Kingdom for the purposes of that Act.

The meaning of "in breach of a deportation order" is clear but the Courts have found great uncertainty in the meaning of "in breach of the immigration laws". The law seems now to be settled that an immigrant is an illegal entrant not merely if he has evaded the immigration authorities in his entry but if he has obtained leave to enter by fraud or deception. There is no general duty of candour on an applicant to draw every fact to the attention of the immigration authorities which they might, had they known, have regarded as material; *R. v. Secretary of State for the Home Department, ex p. Khawaja*.[76]

The definition of section 33(1) has retrospective effect and applies to immigrants who had unlawfully entered the United Kingdom before the 1971 Act came into effect: *R. v. Governor of Pentonville Prison ex p. Azam*.[77]

23–029   The House of Lords in *Khawaja (supra)* not merely restricted the previously wide definition of illegal entrant but also extended judicial control over the removal of illegal entrants by holding that whether a person is an illegal entrant is a fact to be established to the satisfaction of the court: it is not sufficient that the immigration authorities regard him as such.[78]

An entrant who has relied in good faith on documents issued by British officials in error or for some improper motive is not an illegal entrant.[79] The prospect of such a person being branded as a criminal filled Sir Thomas Bingham M.R. with horror.[80]

Removal of persons unlawfully in the United Kingdom
23–030   Section 10 of the Immigration and Asylum Act 1999 contains a new and important power to order the removal from the United Kingdom of (i) any person who is in breach of the terms of a limited leave to enter or remain or remains beyond the time limited by the leave (ii) any person who obtained leave to remain by deception or (iii) directions have been given for the removal under the section of a person to whose family he belongs.

The power is exercisable by any immigration officer, as opposed to the power of deportation which is exercisable by the Secretary of State.

The statute envisages (section 66) that anyone falling within section 10 will have to pursue a right of appeal from the country to which they are returned unless the appeal is based on the human rights' provisions of section 65 or the Convention on Refugees (section 69(5)). A challenge to the removal order may be available by judicial review.

Asylum
23–031   One of the most controversial issues in the law of immigration in the last decade has been the position of immigrants claiming to be refugees from

---

[76] [1984] A.C. 74, HL; reversing *R. v. Secretary of State for the Home Department, ex p. Zamir* [1980] A.C. 930.
[77] [1974] A.C. 18.
[78] *i.e.* the question of status is a jurisdictional fact which must exist before the power of removal can be validly exercised, not a matter within the judgment or discretion of the relevant official or minister: see *post*, Chap. 31.
[79] *R. v. Secretary of State for the Home Department, ex p. Ku* [1995] Q.B. 364, CA.
[80] At p. 374.

persecution within the terms of the United Nations Convention relating to the Status of Refugees to which the United Kingdom is a party.

The Asylum and Immigration Appeals Act 1993, section 2 recognises the United Kingdom's obligations under the Convention by providing that nothing in the immigration rules shall lay down any practice which would be contrary to the Convention. Section 2 of the Asylum and Immigration Act 1996, however, allowed the Secretary of State to remove from the United Kingdom a person who had made a claim for asylum within the terms of the Convention provided that he is to be removed to another country (falling within subsection 3) of which he was not a national where he would not be treated in a way inconsistent with the Convention nor sent on to a third country otherwise than in accordance with the Convention. Subsection 3 applied to any country of the European Union or any country designated for the purposes of the subsection by statutory instrument. In *R. v. Home Secretary, ex p. Adan*[81] the Court of Appeal held that it could review the Secretary of State's decision to return an applicant to member states of the European Union to establish whether, in the view of the Court, the practice of those states was consistent with the true interpretation of the Convention. In the view of the Court the practice in France and Germany was not so consistent. The Secretary of State fared equally badly in attempting to designate Pakistan (*inter alia*) as a "safe country". The Court of Appeal held that it was entitled to review the minister's decision, despite its approval by Parliament, on the ground of irrationality.[82]

The Immigration And Asylum Act 1999 contains new provisions for removal to member states of the European Union (section 11) or to other "safe" third countries (section 12). Section 11 dispenses with the need for ministerial certification. Removal is subject to an appeal under section 65 (human rights) unless the Secretary of State has issued a certificate under section 72(2)(a) that the appeal is manifestly unfounded. Section 121)(a) and (b) provide for removal to member states not falling within section 11 (because they are not parties to the "standing arrangements" referred to in that section) or to other states designated by order. Section 12(4) and (5) provide for removal to countries not falling within section 12(1)(a) and (b) where the Secretary of State has issued a certificate that the person's life and liberty is not a risk by reason of his race, religion, etc. and that the third country would not send him to another country in breach of the Refugee Convention. In the case of countries falling in this second category (but not in the case of those falling within section 11 and section 12(1)(a) and (b)) there is a right of appeal to an adjudicator while still in the United Kingdom under section 71. In the latter cases there is a right of appeal under section 65 but it is not exercisable in the United Kingdom if the Secretary of State has certified that it is manifestly unfounded. It remains to be seen whether these sections have defeated the ability of the courts to intervene.

To fall within the Convention the applicant must show that owing to a well **23–032** founded fear of being persecuted for reasons of race, religion, nationality, membership of a particular social group or political opinion he is outside the country of his nationality and is unable or unwilling, owing to such fear, to avail himself of the protection of that country. The basis for the existence of a well founded fear is to be determined by the Secretary of State who has to conclude

---

[81] [1999] 3 W.L.R. 1274, CA.
[82] *R (Javed) v. Secretary of State for the Home Department, The Times*, May 24, 2001, The Asylum (Designated Countries of Destination and Designated Safe Third Countries) Order 1996; *post* para. 29–021.

that there is no real and substantial danger before he can order an applicant's return: *R. v. Secretary of State for the Home Department, ex p. Sivakumaran.*[83] The fear has to exist at the time of the proceedings; an "historic fear" which explains why the applicant originally left his country is not sufficient: *Adan v. Secretary of State for the Home Department.*[84] Fear of "persecution" in the form of violence from private citizens—such as skinheads—does not constitute persecution within the meaning of the Convention unless it could be shown that the State was unable or unwilling to offer protection to individuals at risk from such violence: *Horvath v. Secretary of State for the Home Department.*[85] The meaning of "social group" was considered by the House of Lords in *R. v. Immigration Appeal Tribunal, ex p. Shah.*[86] Two women applied for asylum on the ground that they feared persecution if they were returned to Pakistan as women who had been falsely accused of adultery and abandoned by their husbands. The House of Lords held that they belonged to a particular social group by virtue of the fact that the law in Pakistan discriminated against women as a group or, more specifically, according to Lord Steyn and Lord Hutton, the applicants belonged to a group identified as women suspected of adultery and lacking protection from the state.

The Convention does not protect persons accused of having committed serious non-political crimes in the country from which they have fled. The meaning of non-political crime was considered by the House of Lords in *T. v. Secretary of State for the Home Department*[87] where it upheld the decision of the Secretary of State to refuse asylum to T who had been involved in a bomb attack on Algiers airport in which 10 people died. Lord Mustill found the identifying of non-political crime in terrorism, a criminal act directed against a state, intended or calculated to create a state of terror in the minds of people. Lord Slynn thought some crimes, including the one in which T was involved, were so obviously beyond the pale that there was no need to pursue difficult questions of drawing the line generally between political and non-political crimes. Lord Lloyd (with whom Lord Keith and Lord Browne-Wilkinson concurred) suggested that to be political a crime had to have a political purpose and to have a close and direct link to the purpose. The bombing of the airport failed to satisfy his second requirement.

23–033   Parliament and ministers, by delegated legislation, have sought by various means to discourage the arrival in the United Kingdom of immigrants claiming to be entitled to asylum under the Convention. The Immigration (Carriers' Liability) Act 1987, for example, made the owners of aircraft or ships liable to fines for bringing to the United Kingdom anyone who was unable to produce to an immigration officer a valid passport or other document satisfactorily establishing his identity and nationality or citizenship. In 1996 the Secretary of State attempted to restrict the rights to social security benefits of various classes of asylum seekers by regulations made under the Social Security Contributions and Benefits Act 1992. The Court of Appeal held in *R. v. Secretary of State for Social*

---

[83] [1988] 1 A.C. 958, HL.

[84] [1999] 1 A.C. 293, HL (Civil war in Somalia: applicants at no greater risk than others involved in the fighting).

[85] [2000] 3 W.L.R. 379, HL (Applicants, Roma or Gypsies, failed to show that the authorities of Slovakia offered insufficient protection against racially motivated violence from other citizens).

[86] [1999] 2 A.C. 692.

[87] [1996] A.C. 742, HL. The House reviewed the authorities on the meaning of a crime of a political character in the law of extradition: see *post* para. 23–044.

Security, ex p. Joint Council for the Welfare of Immigrants[88] that the regulations were *ultra vires* because they amounted to rendering nugatory the rights of asylum seekers under the Asylum and Immigration Appeals Act 1993. General enabling words such as those in the Social Security Act 1992 could not extend to the making of delegated legislation which took away statutory rights conferred by another Act.

The Immigration and Asylum Act 1999 represents the most recent comprehensive attempt to build on these earlier efforts to reduce the attractions to would-be immigrants of attempting to enter the United Kingdom. In addition to provisions which have been considered earlier,[89] Part II creates new offences of carrying clandestine entrants (section 32), gives powers to detain vehicles used in such carrying and to sell them (sections 37 and 42; Schedule 1). Part V might be regarded as helping immigrants in that it is restricts the giving of advice on immigration law to qualified persons (section 84), and establishes an Immigration Services Commissioner to promote good practice by those who provide immigration advice or services (section 83). Appeals from decisions of the Commissioner lie to the Immigration Services Tribunal (section 87). Part VI regulates the provision of support for asylum seekers. The Secretary of State may provide support for destitute asylum seekers and their dependents under section 95. The Act envisages the provision of accommodation with the assistance of local authorities (sections 99 to 100), and gives the Secretary of State the power to designate "reception zones" (section 101), if local authorities fail to co-operate. Section 115 provides for the withdrawal of the social security benefits listed in subsection 1 from persons subject to immigration control. Part VIII contains elaborate provisions to put the running of detention centres on a statutory footing and Part VII inserts into the Immigration Act 1971 a number of sections giving the police and immigration officers powers of arrest, search, entry and search of premises, and the seizing of material. All these powers must, in the modern manner, be exercised according to such codes of practice as may be specified under section 145 and (apart from section 65 of the Act which refers to the Human Rights Acts 1998) are open to challenge on the ground of infringing the terms of the European Convention on Human Rights.

Deportation

The Home Secretary—as opposed to immigration officials—may order the **23–034** deportation of persons lacking the right of abode[90] under the Immigration Act 1971, section 3(5), as amended by the Immigration and Asylum Act 1999, Schedule 14.

The power arises where the Secretary of State believes (i) the deportation of an individual is conducive to the public good[91]; or (ii) another person to whose family he belongs is deported; or (iv) being seventeen or over he is convicted of an offence punishable with imprisonment and the court recommends him for deportation.[92] A deportation order is an order requiring a person to leave and

[88] [1997] 1 W.L.R. 275, CA; *post*, para. 29–013.

[89] *ante*, para. 23–26 and para. 23–030

[90] Subject to exceptions under section 7 in favour of Commonwealth citizens and citizens of the Republic of Ireland who satisfy specified residence tests.

[91] Those deported on this ground include Rudi Dutschke, the German political activist, in 1970, and Mark Hosenball and Philip Agee in 1977: see *R. v. Secretary of State for the Home Department, ex p. Hosenball* [1977] 1 W.L.R. 766, CA.

[92] Guidelines to be followed by courts in exercising this power were laid down in *R. v. Nazari* [1980] 1 W.L.R. 1366, CA.

prohibiting him from entering the United Kingdom (section 5). The Home Secretary has a discretionary executive power to make such an order,[93] and according to domestic law is not bound to afford the deportee a hearing before making an order.[94] Whether or not that remains the position, Article 5(4) of the European Convention guarantees a right to challenge the lawfulness of arrest or detention in a court, a provision which has already affected United Kingdom deportation law.[95] A bona fide order of deportation for the public good may be made to send an alien back to his own country, even though that country has requested his surrender for a criminal offence that is not extraditable.[96]

Decisions to deport are not necessarily taken by the Secretary of State personally. Under the *Carltona*[97] principle a decision may properly be taken by a senior civil servant: *R. v. Secretary of State for the Home Department, ex p. Oladehinde*.[98]

Section 3(6) authorises courts to recommend deportation after conviction of an offence punishable with imprisonment. The deportation order is made by the Home Secretary under section 5.

Appeals and Judicial Review

23–035   Part IV of the Immigration and Asylum Act 1999 establishes a comprehensive system for appeals in immigration matters, apart from those raising issues of national security which fall within the Special Immigration Appeals Commission Act 1997, as amended by the Immigration and Asylum Act 1999. Although Judicial Review is considered later, in Chapter 23, its importance in immigration matters justifies a specific reference to it here.

Appeals

23–036   The Immigration and Asylum Act 1999 continues the system of appeals to Adjudicators (Section 57 and Schedule 3) from whom appeal lies to the Immigration Appeal Tribunal (section 56 and Schedule 2), not to be confused with the Immigration Services Tribunal established under Part V.

Appeals lie against decisions that an applicant requires leave to enter the United Kingdom or refusal of leave (Section 59)[99] or against decisions which are alleged to be in breach of the right of asylum under the Convention on the Status of Refugees (Section 69). In the case of decisions to deport there are two possibilities. Section 63 provides for an appeal to an adjudicator where the deportation is on the grounds of the public good or as a consequence of a recommendation by a court under section 3(6) of the Immigration Act 1971.

---

[93] *ex p. Venicoff* [1920] 3 K.B. 72. *cf. R. v. Chiswick Police Superintendent, ex p. Sacksteder* [1918] 1 K.B. 578.

[94] *R. v. Governor of Brixton Prison, ex p. Soblen* [1963] 2 Q.B. 243, CA, *per* Lord Denning M.R. There is nothing in the 1971 Act to change the law on this point. In certain cases a statutory right of appeal is provided, see *post* para. 23–036.

[95] The Special Immigration Appeals Commission Act 1997 was passed following *Chahal v. UK* (1997) 23 E.H.R.R. 413 where the Court cited Art. 5 and Art. 13; *post* para. 23–036. Art. 8 may also be relevant. Immigration and Deportation issues do not as a general rule fall within Art. 6.

[96] *R. v. Governor of Brixton Prison, ex p. Soblen* [1963] 2 Q.B. 243, CA. The action of the Home Secretary was criticised as "disguised extradition"; P. O'Higgins, "Disguised Extradition: the Soblen Case" (1964) 27 M.L.R. 521; and see C. H. R. Thornberry, "Dr Soblen and the Alien Law of the United Kingdom" (1963) 12 I.C.L.Q. 414 *post*, para. 23–041.

[97] *Carltona Ltd v. Commission of Works* [1943] 2 All E.R. 560, CA.

[98] [1991] A.C. 254, HL.

[99] Section 60 restricts the right to appeal against a decision that leave to enter is required to appellants who possess the documents defined in the Immigration Act 1971, s.3; *ante* para. 23–026.

Where, however, deportation has been decided on as being in the interests of national security or foreign relations or for other reasons of a political nature appeal lies to the Special Immigration Appeals Commission established by the Special Immigration Appeals Commission Act 1997, as amended by the Immigration and Asylum Act 1999, Schedule 14. Before the establishment of the Commission such cases were referred to a non-statutory panel of advisers who made a report to the Secretary of State who was not bound to accept their advice. In *Chahal v. United Kingdom*[1] the Court of Human Rights held that such a panel was not a court within Article 5(4) and its existence and non-binding advice did not constitute an effective remedy within Article 13.

The Chairman and members of the Commission are appointed by the Lord **23–037** Chancellor and is duly constituted to hear an appeal if it consists of three member, one of whom holds, or has held, high judicial office (within the meaning of the Appellate Jurisdiction Act 1876) and one is or has been appointed as chief adjudicator under the Immigration Act 1971 or is a member of the Immigration Appeal Tribunal. Section 4 gives binding effect to the Commission's decisions and section 5(2) provides for a right of legal representation—both provisions intended to rectify the shortcomings in the earlier procedure identified in *Chahal*. In the light of possibly delicate (or serious) issues raised in these cases section 5(3) recognises the possibility of proceedings taking place in the absence of the appellant and his legal representative.

Finally in an attempt to prevent the duplication of appeals sections 74 to 78 provide a "One Stop" procedure which is intended to ensure that all possible grounds of appeal can be dealt with in one set of proceedings. Thus, in cases falling within section 74 an applicant who wishes to appeal against a refusal of leave to enter may have to disclose whether he also wishes to claim a right of asylum or that his rights under the Human Rights Act 1998 have been breached. To discourage appeals which are bound to fail, section 79 entitles the Immigration Appeal Tribunal to impose a penalty in cases where it considers an appeal has no merits.

Judicial Review

Although the Immigration Act 1971 does not provide for *appeal* to the High **23–038** Court, decisions of immigration officials and tribunals, and of the Home Secretary may be open to *review* on the grounds discussed later in Chapter 32. Thus a decision can be examined to see if the facts precedent to the valid exercise of a statutory power exist: is the applicant an illegal entrant?[2] A decision can be quashed if it is based on an error of law.[3] In *R. v. Immigration Appeal Tribunal, ex p. Begum*[4] Simon Brown J. quashed a decision on this ground, holding that the tribunal ought not to have applied a Rule in the Immigration Rules which was so unreasonable that it was invalid. Immigration officials must act fairly[5] and the Home Secretary must not, having created a "legitimate expectation" that he

---

[1] (1997) 23 E.H.R.R. 413.

[2] *R. v. Secretary of State for the Home Department ex p. Khawaja* [1984] A.C. 74.

[3] *R. v. Chief Immigration Officer, Gatwick Airport, ex p. Kharrazi* [1980] 1 W.L.R. 1396, CA; *R. v. Immigration Appeal Tribunal ex p. Singh* [1986] 1 W.L.R. 910, HL.

[4] *The Times*, July 24, 1986; applying to the Rules the test applicable to by-laws (*Kruse v. Johnson* [1898] 2 Q.B. 91), on the basis that the Rules were not delegated legislation in the normal sense; *post*, para. 29–004.

[5] *Re H.K.* [1967] 2 Q.B. 617.

would reach a decision on the basis of certain grounds, take into account other considerations.[6]

Judicial review is, however, a discretionary procedure. It should not be used as a means to avoid recourse to statutory procedures which are available under the Act. Normally the appropriate way to challenge a decision by an immigration officer is by the appellate process laid down in the 1971 Act: *R. v. Secretary of State for the Home Department, ex p. Swati*.[7]

23–039   On the other hand the Courts may refuse to interfere because the dispute does not involve a justiciable issue. For example, the special voucher scheme under which British Overseas citizens may be admitted to the United Kingdom has been held by the House of Lords to operate outside the Immigration Act 1971 and not to give rise to enforceable legal rights.[8] Whether an applicant was a refugee and therefore entitled to asylum was similarly regarded as non-justiciable by the Court of Appeal in *R. v. Secretary of State for the Home Department, ex p. Budaycay* but the House of Lords held that while the question of refugee status was for the Home Secretary to determine, the Courts could intervene if in doing so he had acted unlawfully or irrationally.[9] Lord Templeman, in words he repeated in *R. v. Secretary of State for the Home Department, ex p. Sivakumaran*[10] said:

"Applications for leave to enter and remain do not in general raise justiciable issues. Decisions under the Act are administrative and discretionary rather than judicial and imperative. Such decisions may involve the immigration authorities in pursuing inquiries abroad, in consulting official and unofficial organisations and in making value judgments. The only power of the court is to quash or grant other effective relief in judicial review proceedings in respect of any decision under the Act of 1971 which is made in breach of the provisions of the Act or the rules thereunder or which is the result of procedural impropriety or unfairness or is otherwise unlawful . . . where the result of a flawed decision may imperil life or liberty a special responsibility lies on the court in the examination of the decision-making process."

23–040   In the area of immigration law the remedy which is particularly important is that of habeas corpus; the writ by which an immigrant can challenge the legality of his detention before he is returned to the country from which he came or is deported to a third state which is prepared to accept him. The origin of the writ is discussed later in Chapter 24. It is in the sphere of immigration law that it has been most invoked in recent times. Dicta and decisions before the decision of the House of Lords in *R. v. Secretary of State for the Home Department, ex p. Khawaja*[11] had cast doubt on the efficacy of habeas corpus in immigration cases. In *Khawaja*, however, the House of Lords emphasised that once the applicant has established a prima facie case the burden of justifying the legality of any restraint of liberty lies on the executive. Lord Bridge said that the House should "regard

---

[6] *R. v. Secretary of State for the Home Department ex p. Asif Khan* [1984] 1 W.L.R. 537. See too *R. (Zeqiri) v. Secretary of State for the Home Department, The Times* March 16, 2001, CA (Legitimate expectation that all members of class would be treated in same manner as that member whose case had been submitted to courts for judicial determination).

[7] [1986] 1 W.L.R. 477, CA.

[8] *R. v. Entry Clearance Officer, ex p. Amin* [1983] 2 A.C. 818.

[9] [1987] 2 A.C. 514.

[10] [1988] 1 A.C. 958, 996.

[11] [1984] A.C. 74.

with extreme jealousy any claim by the executive to imprison a citizen without trial and allow it only if it is clearly justified by the statutory language relied on. The fact that, in the case we are considering detention is preliminary and incidental to expulsion from the country . . . strengthens rather than weaken the case for a robust exercise of the judicial function in safeguarding the citizen's rights".[12]

Habeas corpus, although not available as of right may not be refused *merely* because of the existence of an alternative remedy.[13]

In later cases the Court of Appeal expressed greater doubt about the usefulness of habeas corpus in immigration and deportation cases on the ground that the scope of judicial review had extended to a point at which it provided a more appropriate and effective remedy.[14]

V. Extradition

Introduction

Extradition may be used in a wide sense to refer to any surrender of a **23–041** criminal—suspected or convicted—from one jurisdiction to another. In a narrow sense it may be used to refer to surrender under the Extradition Act 1989, as opposed to surrender under the Backing of Warrants (Republic of Ireland) Act 1965. (Inside the United Kingdom a warrant issued in any part of the Kingdom may be executed in any other: Criminal Law Act 1977, s.38). The increased ease of travel between countries, and more recently the growth of violent terrorist crimes, have emphasised the importance of effective arrangements for the extradition of criminals (and have case doubt on the sanctity of the asylum formerly given to the perpetrators of political offences).

Extradition is not, unlike deportation, a punishment or sanction but part of the procedure of enforcing the criminal law and on that ground the English courts have rejected the argument that in the case of EEC nationals the process may be a violation of Article 39[48].[15]

An attempt by the executive to use deportation to return an individual to another state in circumstances not falling within the terms of the Extradition Act would, as was seen in the previous part of this chapter, be an abuse of power. Although such a challenge failed on the facts in the domestic case of *Soblen*,[16] a successful challenge in a similar situation in France resulted in the European Court of Human Rights holding that the applicant's detention was unlawful because it was not "with a view to deportation" within Article 5(1)(f) but

---

[12] p. 122. Also, see C. Vincenzi, "Aliens and the Judicial Review of Immigration Law" [1985] P.L. 93.

[13] *R. v. Governor of Pentonville Prison, ex p. Azam* [1974] A.C. 18, 32; *Quigley v. Chief Constable, Royal Ulster Constabulary* [1983] N.I. 238, 239; *post* para. 24–037.

[14] *R. v. Secretary of State for the Home Department, ex p. Cheblak* [1991] 1 W.L.R. 890, CA; *R. v. Secretary of State for the Home Department, ex p. Muboyayi* [1992] Q.B. 244, CA; *post* para. 24–034, n.83.

[15] *R. v. Governor of Pentonville Prison, ex p. Budlong* [1980] 1 W.L.R. 1110, DC; *R. v. Governor of Pentonville Prison, ex p. Healy, The Times*, May 11, 1984, DC (Proceedings under Backing of Warrants (Republic of Ireland) 1965 Act).

[16] *R. v. Governor of Brixton Prison, ex p. Soblen* [1963] 2 Q.B. 243, CA. "The law of extradition is one thing; the law of deportation is another"; *per* Lord Denning M.R. at p. 299.

disguised extradition designed to circumvent the refusal of the French courts to order his extradition: *Bonzano v. France*.[17]

Extradition Act 1989

23–042   The law of extradition is currently to be found in the Extradition Act 1989 which consolidates a number of earlier statutes dealing with extradition[18] and the provisions of the Fugitive Offenders Act 1967 which governed the procedure for the return of wanted persons between members of the Commonwealth.[19] The Act also amends the earlier law to give effect to recommendations of the Law Commission and the Scottish Law Commission.[20]

Section 1 provides three procedures for dealing with the extradition of a person *accused* of an *extradition crime* or unlawfully at large after the conviction of an *extradition crime*. These are (1) the new procedure established by Part III of the 1989 Act; (2) the procedure contained in Schedule 1 of the 1989 Act which applies to cases falling within the Extradition Act 1870; (3) the procedure for dealing with the return to a Commonwealth country.

23–043   Normally a person accused will be a person charged with an offence under the law of the requesting state. In *Re Ismail*,[21] however, the House of Lords held that "accused" was not a term of art. The court should take "a cosmopolitan approach" and give the word a purposive interpretation.[22] Their Lordships held that the term was wide enough to extend to a person against whom a warrant had been issued in Germany alleging that he was involved in criminal fraud and requiring him to give evidence in pre-trial inquiries.

Extradition Crime is defined for the purposes of the Act (apart from cases falling within Schedule 1) generally by reference to conduct punishable by imprisonment under the law of the requesting state and the United Kingdom of not less than 12 months. Formerly under the Extradition Act 1870 crimes were only extraditable offences if listed in Schedule 1 of that Act,[23] as amended from time to time.[24] The relevant date for determining whether the conduct if it had been committed in the United Kingdom would be criminal is the date of the occurrence of the facts alleged to have occurred in the requesting state, not the date of the request for extradition. In the view of the House of Lords in *R. v. Bow*

---

[17] (1987) 9 E.H.R.R. 297.

[18] There is no prerogative power to seize an alien in this country and hand him over to a foreign state: Forsyth, *Cases and Opinions on Constitutional Law*, pp. 369–370; *cf. East India Co v. Campbell* (1749) Ves.Sen. 246; *Mure v. Kaye* (1811) 4 Taunt. 43. See *Diamond v. Minter* [1941] 1 All E.R. 390.

[19] The Fugitive Offenders Act 1967 replaced the earlier Fugitive Offenders Act 1881. It was based on an agreement between the law ministers of 20 Commonwealth countries. It contained a number of improvements on the Extradition Act 1870 which have been carried forward into the Extradition Act 1989.

[20] For the interpretation of consolidation Acts, see F. Bennion, *Statutory Interpretation* (3rd ed., 1997, Butterworths), pp. 462–465. The courts will, of course, refer where appropriate to case law on the earlier legislation.

[21] [1999] 1 A.C. 320.

[22] *per* Lord Steyn at p. 500.

[23] According to Lord Diplock in *Government of Denmark v. Nielsen* [1984] A.C. 606, 615 the relevant crimes were described "in general terms and popular language".

[24] Additions were made, *e.g.* by the Genocide Act 1969, the Internationally Protected Persons Act 1978, the Suppression of Terrorism Act 1978 and the Aviation Security Act 1982. See *R. v. Bow Street Metropolitan Stipendiary Magistrate, ex p. Government of USA* [2000] 2 A.C. 216, HL. (Computer Misuse Act 1990, s.15: provision that crimes within the Act were extradition crimes impliedly amended Order in Council made under the Extradition Act 1870).

Street Metropolitan Stipendiary Magistrate, ex p. Pinochet (No. 3)[25] such was clearly the rule under the Extradition Act 1870 and despite the ambiguous wording of section 2 of the 1989 Act there was no reason to believe Parliament intended to change that rule.

Section 6 of the Extradition Act 1989 preserves the traditional rule that a **23–044** person is not to be surrendered for "an offence of a political character". The difficulty of defining political character is illustrated by a number of cases which were considered by the House of Lords in the context of the law of asylum in the case considered earlier, *T. v. Immigration Officer.*[26] Traditionally the case law assumed that the classification of an offence as political required the existence of a struggle between two parties over the government of the country in question. Thus a killing of a member of government forces by a member of an insurgent group might well be "political": *Re Castioni*[27] whereas the indiscriminate killing of members of the public by anarchists is not "political": *Re Meunier.*[28] In *Schtraks v. Government of Israel,*[29] where the charges involved were perjury and child-stealing, the case had become a political issue in Israel but that did not make it an offence of a political character. The idea behind the latter phrase, said Viscount Radcliffe, is that the fugitive is at odds with the state that applies for his extradition on some issue connected with the political control or government of the country. On the other hand in *ex p. Kolyczynski,*[30] where the member of a Polish trawler had taken charge of a ship, putting the master under restraint, and steered her into an English port because they feared they would be punished for their political opinions if they returned to Poland, they were successful in their application for habeas corpus, the Divisional Court holding that the offences were committed in order to escape from political tyranny. In *R. v. Governor of Winson Green, ex p. Littlejohn*[31] Widgery C.J., after reviewing the earlier authorities, said, "An offence may be of a political character either because the wrongdoer had some direct ulterior motive of a political kind when he committed the offence, or because the requesting state is anxious to obtain possession of the wrongdoer's person in order to punish him for his politics rather than for the simple criminal offence referred to in the extradition proceedings." An offence which might otherwise be of a political character will fall outside section 3 if it is committed not in the state against whose government it is directed but in the

---

[25] [2000] 1 A.C. 147, HL. The references in their Lordships' speeches to "double criminality" are, in the context, directed to the issue of the criminality of the conduct of the accused under United Kingdom law. They can hardly be intended to revive the doctrine of double criminality in the sense in which it was rejected in *Re Nielsen* [1984] A.C. 6060, HL and *U.S. v. McCaffery* [1984] 1 W.L.R. 867, HL: the duty of the English court is to satisfy itself that the conduct if committed in England would have been a crime by domestic law, not to examine the substantive law of the requesting state to establish whether its terms are in substantial agreement with those of the relevant, hypothetical, domestic offence. *Re Nielsen* was distinguished in *Government of Canada v. Aronson* [1990] 1 A.C. 579 on the different wording of the Fugitive Offenders Act 1967, s.3(1)(c), but the Extradition Act 1989 applies the one test of hypothetical conduct criminal by domestic law, subject to a "double punishability" requirement.

[26] [1996] A.C. 742, HL: *ante* para. 23–032.

[27] [1891] 1 Q.B. 149.

[28] [1894] 2 Q.B. 415.

[29] [1964] A.C. 556, HL. See C. F. Amerasinghe, "The *Schtraks* Case, defining Political Offences and Extradition" (1965) 28 M.L.R. 27.

[30] *R. v. Brixton Prison Governor, ex p. Kolczynski* [1955] 1 Q.B. 540.

[31] [1975] 1 W.L.R. 893, DC.

territory of a third state which is the state requesting extradition.[32] The concern which was earlier felt for offering asylum to political refugees has in recent years been replaced by a desire to ensure that terrorists cannot escape justice by claiming that status for themselves. Modern statutes have indirectly dealt with the problem by conferring power on United Kingdom courts to deal with violent crimes committed abroad which are in many cases likely to be the work of terrorists.[33] In order to facilitate the surrender of wanted criminals successive statutes, such as the Suppression of Terrorism Act 1978, provided that specific crimes were not to be regarded as being political offences. The Extradition Act 1989 continues this practice and provides for extradition for offences against a list of international conventions (section 22)[34] charges of genocide (section 23) and offences under the Suppression of Terrorism Act 1978 (section 24).

23–045   On the other hand, in addition to the plea of "offence of a political character", (section 6(1)(a)) section 6 also provides that a person is not to be extradited if:

(b) the offence is one under military law which is not also an offence under the general criminal law;

(c) the request for his return (though purporting to be made on account of an extradition crime) is in fact made for the purpose of prosecuting or punishing him on account of his race, religion, nationality or political opinions.

(d) he might, if returned, be prejudiced at his trial, or punished, detained or restricted in his personal liberty by reason of his race, religion, nationality or political opinions.[35]

Where an applicant fails to establish that he falls within any of the provisions of section 6, the Secretary of State has a discretion under section 12 not to order his return if he thinks it would be unjust or oppressive to do so.[36]

Before a State can seek to rely on the provisions of the Extradition Act 1989 it must comply with one of the three procedures envisaged by section 1 of the Act. The first of these is the existence of an extradition arrangements within section 3. This may take the form of a bilateral or multilateral treaty, for example the European Convention on Extradition.[37] In the case of Commonwealth countries (which are not signatories to the Convention) section 5 provides for their designation by Order in Council. No treaty is required, thus continuing the

---

[32] *Cheng v. Governor of Pentonville Prison* [1973] A.C. 931. (Appellant convicted in New York of an attempted murder there of visiting member of the ruling Taiwan regime; appellant, member of organisation dedicated to the overthrow of the regime; alleged crime not "of a political character".)

[33] *e.g.* Internationally Protected Persons Act 1978; Suppression of Terrorism Act 1978; Taking of Hostages Act 1982; Criminal Justice Act 1988, s.134(1) (Torture).

[34] Including the UN Convention Against Torture: see *R. v. Bow Street Metropolitan Stipendiary Magistrate, ex p. Pinochet (No. 3)* [2000]. 2 A.C. 147, HL.

[35] Section 25 contains further specific protection in the case of offences under the Taking of Hostages Act 1982.

[36] *Atkinson v. United States Government* [1971] A.C. 197, HL; *Royal Government of Greece v. Brixton Prison Governor* [1971] A.C. 250, HL.

[37] For the purposes of the Act, commonwealth signatories of the Convention are regarded as foreign states: s.3(2).

system which applied under the Fugitive Offenders Act 1967.[38] Designation is dependant on the relevant country adopting extradition legislation in parallel terms to the British. Thirdly, section 1 of the 1989 Act continues in existence, via Schedule 1, extradition arrangements made under section 2 of the Extradition Act 1870. In cases arising under Schedule 1 the definition of extradition crime will depend on the terms of the relevant Order in Council, as subsequently amended.[39]

Extradition is a judicial procedure which begins once the Secretary of State has agreed to a request for proceedings to begin.[40] The Extradition Act 1989 provides for proceedings to be heard before the chief metropolitan magistrate (or designated metropolitan magistrate) or the Sheriff of Lothian and the Borders.[41] In the absence of authorisation from the Secretary of State a metropolitan magistrate or sheriff may issue a provisional warrant (section 8(1)(b)).

23–046

Under the former law the requesting state had to satisfy the magistrate that there existed a *prima facie* case, justifying committal for trial under English law.[42] Section 9 of the 1989 Act, however, provides for the making of extradition arrangements under which there is no need to furnish evidence justifying committal to the court. This brings English (and Scottish) law into harmony with the provisions of the European Convention on Extradition. In *Re Evans*[43] the House of Lords upheld the refusal of the magistrate to allow the applicant to lead evidence to prove that be could not be convicted in Sweden of the offence with which he was charged. The magistrate's only concern is whether the conduct alleged could constitute an extraditable offence if committed within the United Kingdom: questions of evidence are for the foreign court.[44] Similarly, the magistrate or sheriff faced with a request for the return of a convicted prisoner within the terms of the Act is not entitled to examine an allegation of abuse of process.[45]

If a magistrate or sheriff commits the defendant for surrender he must inform him of his right to apply for habeas corpus or an application for review of the order of committal, as the case may be (section 11).[46] A person committed to be surrendered cannot be returned to the requesting state until the expiration of 15 days from the making of the order. Apart from the general law relating to habeas

23–047

---

[38] A State remains a designated Commonwealth country even after leaving the Commonwealth until its name is removed from the Order in Council designating it: *R. v. Brixton Prison Governor, ex p. Kahan* [1989] Q.B. 716, DC (Fiji).

[39] See *R. v. Bow Street Metropolitan Stipendiary Magistrate, ex p. Government of U.S.A.* [2000] 2 A.C. 216, HL; *supra*, n.24. See too *In Re Burke* [2001] 1 A.C. 422, HL. (Meaning in Order in Council of the phrase "sentence imposed").

[40] s.7; Sched. 1, para. 4.

[41] The earlier legislation confined all extradition proceedings to the metropolitan magistrates except in two cases: (1) Under s.16 of the Extradition Act 1870 where the crime for which extradition was sought was committed on board a ship which docked at a Scottish port; (2) under the Extradition Act 1985 if the removal to London of a prisoner arrested under the 1870 Act would be prejudicial to his life or health. See W. Finnie, "The Procedure of Extradition from Scotland" [1983] S.L.T. News 25 and 41.

[42] See, for example, *R. v. Governor of Pentonville Prison, ex p. Alves* [1993] A.C. 284, HL (Extradition to Sweden under Schedule 1 of the 1989 Act).

[43] [1994] 1 W.L.R. 1006, HL.

[44] And see *supra* n.25.

[45] *R. v. Governor of Pentonville, ex p. Sinclair* [1991] 2 A.C. 64, HL.

[46] A further example of the remedying of an oversight in the Extradition Act 1870: *Wan Ping Nam v. West Federal Minister of Justice, Secretary of State for Scotland and Lord Advocate*, 1972 S.C. 43, JC. (Absence of Habeas Corpus in Scots law made good by exercise of nobile officium of the High Court).

corpus, section 11(3) expressly gives the High Court (or the High Court of Justiciary) the power to free the applicant it would be unjust or oppressive to return him in all the circumstances, having regard to the trivial nature of the offence or the passage of time since the date of the alleged offence or escape from detention.[47] The Court has no inherent jurisdiction to entertain an application for habeas corpus in relation to extradition proceedings in circumstances falling outside the provisions of section 11(3): *Re Schmidt*.[48]

If a person has been committed for return to the requesting state and any application for habeas corpus has been unsuccessful the Secretary of State may make an order for his extradition under section 12 which again confers on the minister a discretion in similar terms to that conferred on the Court by section 11. Section 12 expressly directs attention to the possibility of the prisoner facing the death penalty. Apart from other considerations, to return a wanted person in such circumstances could now be open to challenge under the Human Rights Act 1998 in the light of *Soering v. United Kingdom*.[49]

Backing of warrants

23–048   The surrender of wanted criminals between the Republic of Ireland and the United Kingdom is governed by the Backing of Warrants (Republic of Ireland) Act 1965[50] and the Criminal Jurisdiction Act 1975. By section 1(1) of the 1965 Act a warrant issued in the Republic of Ireland by a judicial authority shall, subject to the provisions of the Act, be indorsed by a justice of the peace upon police application. Subsection (2) provides that an Irish warrant for the arrest of an accused person cannot be indorsed unless it is issued (a) in respect of an indictable offence, or (b) in respect of an offence punishable on summary conviction with imprisonment for six months and the requirements of the subsection relating to service or failure to appear before the irish court is satisfied. The endorsement is a formal process, the English (or Scottish) judge is not concerned with the existence of evidence to support the warrant.[51] Subsection (3) provides that an Irish warrant for the arrest of a person convicted of any offence against the laws of the Republic shall not be endorsed unless the purpose of the arrest is to enable him to be brought before a court of the Republic for sentence in respect of the conviction. In *Re Lawlor*[52] habeas corpus was granted to release a prisoner arrested on an Irish warrant where the Divisional Court was satisfied that it had been issued not to secure the return of the applicant to sentence him for an offence of which he had been earlier convicted but to ensure his availability as a witness at a murder trial.

Section 2 provides that after being brought before a magistrates' court on an endorsed warrant the court shall order his delivery to the Republican authorities unless (a) the offence specified does not correspond to any offence under the law of the relevant part of the United Kingdom which is an indictable offence, or is punishable on summary conviction with imprisonment for six months, or (b) is

---

[47] For an unsuccessful attempt to rely on the similar provisions of the Fugitive Offenders Act 1967, relating to unfairness arising from delay, see *Oskar v. Government of the Commonwealth of Australia* [1988] A.C. 366, HL.
[48] [1995] 1 A.C. 339, HL.
[49] (1989) 11 E.H.R.R. 439. See too *Chahal v. United Kingdom* (1996) 23 E.H.R.R. 413; *ante* para. 22–033.
[50] See "Anglo-Irish Extradition," (1967) 2 Irish Jurist 43; (1966) 29 M.L.R. 186.
[51] *Keane v. Governor of Brixton Prison* [1972] A.C. 204; *R. v. Governor of Risley Remand Centre, ex p. Marks* [1984] Crim.L.R. 238, DC (Similar rule applicable to return of convicted prisoner).
[52] (1977) 66 Cr.App.R. 75, DC.

of a political character[53] or an offence under military law which is not also an offence under the general criminal law, or (c) an offence under an enactment relating to taxes, duties or exchange control, or (d) there are *substantial grounds* for believing that if returned to the Republic the prisoner will be prosecuted or detained for another offence within category (b). The Suppression of Terrorism Act 1978 added to section 2 of the 1965 Act similar words to those quoted earlier in relation to section 6 of the Extradition Act 1989 to give added protection against the risk of prosecution on grounds of race, religion, etc.

A defendant who cannot bring himself within section 3 cannot resist extradition proceedings on the ground that he is liable on his return to be prosecuted for a non-political crime but a different crime from that for which his return has been sought: the Act leaves no room for the application of the international law rule of specialty: Re *McFadden*.[54]

23–049

Nor can a claim of abuse of process be raised to challenge a warrant being enforced under the 1965 Act which clearly intended to provide an expeditious procedure for returning wanted persons to the Republic of Ireland, subject only to the precise and limited protection against oppressive claims provided by the wording of the Act: *R. v. Governor of Belmarsh Prison, ex p. Gilligan*.[55]

The Criminal Jurisdiction Act 1975[56] sought to avoid the difficulties inherent in the surrender of wanted criminals from one jurisdiction in Ireland to the other by conferring extra territorial jurisdiction on the courts of Northern Ireland in the case of certain crimes. Any act committed in the Republic of Ireland which, if committed in Northern Ireland, would constitute one of the crimes listed in Schedule 1 (serious crimes of violence against the person, damage to property by fire, offences involving explosives and fire arms) will constitute a crime by the law of Northern Ireland. The Act also creates a new offence of hijacking a vehicle or ship anywhere in Northern Ireland or the Republic of Ireland which is triable in Northern Ireland. Consequential amendments are made to the Backing of Warrants (Republic of Ireland) Act 1965 to prevent the enforcement of warrants issued in the Republic against offenders who are or have been convicted or acquitted of an extra-territorial offence in Northern Ireland.

---

[53] For an unsuccessful attempt to rely on this provision see *R. v. Governor of Durham Prison, ex p. Carlisle* [1979] Crim.L.R. 175, DC (Detention in England under Prevention of Terrorism (Temporary Provisions) Act 1974 which defined terrorism as use of violence for political ends: Irish warrant issued for offences relating to explosions).

[54] *The Times*, March 13, 1982.

[55] [1999] 3 W.L.R. 1244, HL.

[56] See Report of the Law Enforcement Commission (Cmnd. 5627). There is corresponding legislation in the Republic of Ireland.

CHAPTER 24

FREEDOM OF PERSON AND PROPERTY[1]

I. FREEDOM OF THE PERSON

General principles

24–001   "The right to personal liberty as understood in England," says Dicey,[2] "means in substance a person's right not to be subjected to imprisonment, arrest, or other physical coercion in any manner that does not admit of legal justification." It is "one of the pillars of liberty," said Lord Atkin in *Liversidge v. Anderson*,[3] that "in English law every imprisonment is *prima facie* unlawful, and that it is for a person directing imprisonment to justify his act." Today the justification for imprisonment or other type of detention must also be in accordance with the E.C.H.R., as must the treatment of those imprisoned or detained. The Convention rights most likely to arise in this context are: "the right to liberty and security of person" (Article 5); "right to life" (Article 2); the right to "a fair and public hearing" in the determination of civil rights and criminal charges (Article 6)[4]; the right to "respect for private and family life, home and correspondence" (Article 8); the prohibition of discrimination (Article 14). When determining the scope of a statute restricting personal liberty, a court will have to interpret the law to comply with the Convention rights, "so far as it is possible to do so" (Human Rights Act 1998, s.3). In addition police officers are "public authorities" for the purpose of section 6(1) of the Human Rights Act 1998, and as such it is unlawful for them to act in a way incompatible with a Convention right. All those who are empowered to interfere with personal liberty, and the courts who are called upon to adjudicate on such matters, must in particular consider the E.C.H.R. requirement of "proportionality". This means that even justified actions have to be proportionate to the threat or problem they seek to prevent.[5]

The justification for detention or imprisonment is usually that the person is arrested and detained pending trial in court on a charge of crime, or after trial by a court of competent jurisdiction he has been convicted and sentenced to imprisonment or some other kind of detention provided by statute. Other kinds of lawful detention are committal for contempt of court[6] or Parliament,[7] custody pending deportation or extradition,[8] children in need of care and protection,[9] patients under Mental Health and Public Health Acts, and imprisonment for

---

[1] See D. Feldman, *Civil Liberties and Human Rights in England and Wales* (2nd ed., 2001); H. Fenwich: *Civil Rights* (2000).
[2] Dicey, *Law of the Constitution* (10th ed., E. C. S. Wade, 1959) pp. 207–208.
[3] [1942] A.C. 206, HL.
[4] See Andrew Ashworth, "Article 6 and the Fairness of Trials", [1999] Crim.L.R. 261.
[5] See further Chap. 22
[6] See *ante* Chap. 20.
[7] See *ante* Chap. 13.
[8] See *post* Chap. 23.
[9] Children Act 1989, Pt V.

failing to make certain payments in spite of having had the means to do so.[10] Preventive detention may take place under statutory war time regulations and anti-terrorist legislation. Detention for limited periods is also now permitted under the Police and Criminal Evidence Act 1984 (PACE Act), and under the Terrorism legislation.[11] All these types of detention must be considered in the light of Article 5 E.C.H.R., and in particular Article 5(1) which provides an exhaustive definition of the circumstances in which a person may be deprived of his liberty. In addition, to comply with Article 5 the detention procedure must be in accordance with municipal law and with the E.C.H.R. It will be for the relevant British court to consider these issues.

A restriction on liberty that falls short of detention or imprisonment is pro-   **24–002** vided by Part 1 Chapter 3 of the Criminal Justice and Police Act 2001 (CJP Act 2001). This gives a court the power in certain circumstances to make overseas travel restriction orders on those convicted of one of a list of drug trafficking offences.

For wrongful deprivation of liberty the following remedies are available in English law: (i) civil proceedings for damages in respect of malicious prosecution, false imprisonment or assault; (ii) criminal prosecution for assault, battery, or in respect of false imprisonment itself; (iii) application for a writ of habeas corpus[12] to obtain release; (iv) appeal against conviction or sentence to a higher court; (v) in appropriate cases an order of certiorari or prohibition.[13]

Personal liberty is, however, increasingly seen as not being confined to freedom from physical restraint. Modern methods of surveillance enable telephone calls to be intercepted or private conversations to be overheard.[14] The use of computers has led to concern about the storing of information about individuals and the use of that information by government agencies, the police or private commercial organisations. These and similar matters are discussed later.[15]

Police powers

Before 1984 the powers of the police derived from the common law and   **24–003** statute. The former were open to criticism for their uncertainty, the latter for varying in many cases from force to force, depending on the existence of local Acts of Parliament. Police methods used in investigating crimes had come under critical scrutiny in the report on the *Confait* Case.[16] In 1977 the government set up a Royal Commission on Criminal Procedure which reported in 1981.[17] The

---

[10] In *Benham v. United Kingdom* (1996) 22 E.H.R.R., the applicant had been imprisoned for non payment of the community charge (a civil matter). The E.Ct.H.R. held that under E.C.H.R. law he had been charged with a criminal offence (the Convention organs apply an autonomous approach to what is "criminal"), and the protection of Art. 6 applied, entitling him to legal aid.

[11] Prevention of Terrorism (Temporary Provisions) Act 1984, as re-enacted in the Terrorism Act 2000. In *Brogan v. United Kingdom* (1988) 11 E.H.R.R. 117, the E.Ct.H.R. held that detention under the 1984 Act was incompatible with Art. 5(3); the Government's response was to derogate from this article. S. 16 of the Human Rights Act 1998 expressly retains this derogation, but provides that it will cease to have effect after five years unless expressly extended by the Secretary of State.

[12] *post* para. 24–033.

[13] *post* Chap. 32.

[14] The Regulation of Investigatory Powers Act 2000 was passed, *inter alia*, to ensure that certain surveillance methods used by the police and other law enforcement agencies were compatible compatibility with the E.C.H.R. and the E.C. Telecoms Data Protection Directive (97/66/E.C.). See also the Data Protection Act 1998.

[15] *post*, Chap. 26.

[16] Fisher Report on the *Confait* Case, H.C. 338 (1977–78).

[17] Cmnd. 8092.

Report was followed by two Acts, the Prosecution of Offences Act 1985[18] and the PACE Act.[19] The latter Act attempted to strike a balance between the freedom of the citizen and the powers of the police. The powers of the police were increased but their exercise was subject to the restrictions contained in the Act. The PACE Act also changed laws of evidence and procedure and provided for the introduction of Codes of Practice (COP) (section 66,67)[20] to guide the police in the exercise of their powers. A further spate of miscarriages of justice cases, many of which involved allegations of police malpractice, resulted in the establishment of a Royal Commission on Criminal Justice which reported in 1993.[21] Some of its recommendations were included in the Criminal Justice and Public Order Act 1994[22] and the Criminal Procedure and Investigations Act 1996. In addition the Police Act 1997 and the Regulation of Investigatory Powers Act 2000 *inter alia* provide statutory authority for certain types of police surveillance operations, and the CJP Act 2001 gives the police additional powers to seize from premises and the person.[23] The PACE Act does not then provide an exhaustive code of police powers.

Stop and Search

24–004   The introduction of a generalised right to stop persons and vehicles was a particularly controversial provision of the PACE Act.[24] The value of stopping and searching as a crime prevention measure has been doubted and it is argued to have an adverse effect on public-police relations. Article 14 of the E.C.H.R. could be used to challenge a police force which used stop and search powers in a way which disproportionately affects ethnic minorities.[25]

Section 1 confers a power to detain and search on a constable in a place to which the public has access or in any other place "to which people have ready access at the time when he proposes to exercise the power but which is not a dwelling" (section 1(1)). The power extends to (i) persons and vehicles, (ii) to search for stolen or prohibited articles or prohibited blades,[26] (iii) which he has reasonable grounds to suspect that he will find. Prohibited articles are offensive weapons[27] or articles made or adapted for use in burglary, theft and other defined crimes. The police also have a power to search any person on school grounds if there is reasonable grounds to suspect he is in possession of any offensive

---

[18] *ante* para. 20–014.

[19] Michael Zander, *The Police and Criminal Evidence Act 1984* (2nd ed., 1996); K. Lidstone and C. Palmer, *The Investigation of Crime* (2nd ed., 1996). The PACE Act, with some modifications, was extended to Northern Ireland in 1989.

[20] There are currently five Codes of Practice: COP A, Stop and Search; COP B, Search of Premises and Seizure of Property; COP C, Detention, Treatment and Questioning; COP D, Identification; COP E, Tape-recording of interviews of suspects.

[21] Cm. 2263.

[22] Some of the provisions contained in this Act were contrary to the advise of the Royal Commission.

[23] Replacing the Interception of Communications Act 1985, and amending the Intelligence Services Act 1994 and Part III of the Police Act 1997.

[24] In addition all forces have powers to stop and search under a variety of other statutes such as the Misuse of Drugs Act 1971, s.23(2); for a full list see Annex A, COP A. These additional powers are also subject to the safeguards in s.2 PACE Act, and COP A applies to most of them.

[25] M. Fitzgerald, *Ethnic Minorities and the Criminal Justice System*, R.C.C.J. Research Study 20, (1993).

[26] s.139 of the Criminal Justice Act 1988, s.1(8A) of PACE.

[27] s.1(9)(a) "Offensive Weapon" means any article—
  (a) made or adapted for use for causing injury to persons; or
  (b) intended by the person having it with him for such use by him or some other person.

weapon or article with a blade or point.[28] The main guarantee that the power conferred by section 1 will not be abused is the requirement of reasonable grounds that a prohibited article or blade will be found. The Code of Practice on Powers of Stop and Search, emphasises that reasonable grounds require a foundation in fact, as opposed to mere suspicion, a hunch which cannot be explained or justified. It specifically excludes factors such as colour, manner of dress or hairstyle as the basis for reasonable suspicion. Procedural safeguards are contained in section 2 which, for instance, requires that a constable not in uniform should produce documentary evidence that he is a constable. In any case the constable must give his name and that of the station to which he is attached and the object of the search. Section 3 requires the making of a written record of searches carried out unless it is not practicable to do so; the person detained is entitled to a copy of the search record. A search to which a person voluntarily consents is outside the provisions of sections 1, 2, and 3 of the PACE Act, and is not governed by COP A.

A power to stop vehicles in a particular locality is conferred by section 4 for the purposes set out in the section, for example to ascertain whether a vehicle is carrying a person who has committed an offence, other than a road traffic offence[29] or a vehicles excise offence; or a person who is unlawfully at large. Such checks must, except as a matter of urgency, be authorised by an officer of at least the rank of superintendent. Again there must be reasonable grounds to believe that one of the requirements of the section has been satisfied.

Section 5 requires the inclusion in the annual reports of chief officers' statistics **24–005** relating to the exercise of search powers under sections 1 and 4. This is intended to facilitate supervision over the exercise of these powers by police authorities and the Inspectors of Constabulary.

Additional powers to stop and search in anticipation of violence are found in section 60 of the Criminal Justice and Public Order Act 1994 (CJPO).[30] This section applies when a senior officer reasonably believes that incidents of serious violence may take place in his police area, or that persons are carrying dangerous instruments or offensive weapons in that area. He may in these circumstances authorise in writing the stopping and searching of persons and vehicles within that locality for up to 24 hours.[31] The officer who conducts the stop and search is not required to have any reasonable suspicion that offensive weapons or dangerous instruments will be found. The Crime and Disorder Act 1998 s.25 further amends section 60 by giving the officer a power to require the removal of masks or other items used to conceal identity, and to seize such items.[32] A power similar to section 60 aimed at preventing certain types of acts of terrorism is found in the Terrorism Act 2000 ss.44–46, with the additional requirement that authorisations have to be confirmed by the Secretary of State within 48 hours of their being made.[33] All these provisions, since they do not require reasonable suspicion by the detaining police officer, could be in breach of Article 5(1)(c) of the E.C.H.R.

---

[28] s.139B of the Criminal Justice Act 1988, as amended by the Offensive Weapons Act 1996, s.4.
[29] See s.163 of the Road Traffic Act 1988.
[30] As amended by s.8 of the Knifes Act 1997.
[31] May be extended by a further 24 hours.
[32] There is no power to search for such items.
[33] Re-enacting ss. 13A and B of the Prevention of Terrorism (Temporary Provisions) Act 1989.

Arrest

24–006   Arrest is the restraint of a man's person or liberty, obliging him to be obedient to the law. Arrest commonly involves actual physical seizure (apprehension) of a person, using no more force than reasonably necessary, or a token restraint of a person's liberty indicating its compulsory nature.[34] The common law allows a person to use a reasonable amount of force to resist unlawful arrest without warrant, whether by a police officer or private citizen; but it is inadvisable to resist arrest by a police constable as the arrest may turn out to be lawful and resistance therefore an offence.

24–007   *(a) By warrant* No man may be arrested or imprisoned except under due process of law (Petition of Right 1627[35]). Where a person is suspected of having committed a serious indictable offence, the police may apply to a magistrate for a warrant for his arrest.[36] That warrant can only be granted on sworn information. Sufficient particulars of the charge must be specified in the warrant in non-technical language. A "general warrant," *i.e.* one which does not name the person to be arrested, is illegal.[37] In minor cases a summons is usually applied for.[38]

24–008   *(b) Without warrant* A common law power to arrest without warrant still exists for every citizen where a breach of the peace has been committed or threatened.[39] This power is of particular use to the police in public order situations, as it permits an arrest to prevent harm or violence, something not possible by statute.[40] In *Steel v. United Kingdom*,[41] the E.Ct.H.R. decided that breach of the peace was an "offence" in E.C.H.R. terms[42] and in consequence the arrestee had all the rights under Articles 5 and 6. It also accepted that the exercise of such a power is in compliance with the E.C.H.R. where someone's behaviour if it persisted, might provoke others to violence, but not otherwise. In *Foulkes v. Chief Constable of the Merseyside Police*[43] the Court of Appeal held that the police should only arrest in the clearest of circumstances where apparently lawful conduct gave rise to an apprehension of a breach of the peace. It may also be used to arrest for assault, and for assaulting or obstructing a police constable in the execution of his duty, offences for which a statutory power of arrest is limited to situations where the general arrest conditions (see below) are satisfied.

---

[34] Not every deprivation of liberty (detention) constitutes an arrest, which can only be effected in exercise of an asserted authority: *R. v. Brown* [1977] R.T.R. 160, CA.

[35] Relying on Magna Carta (9 Hen. III, c. 29.).

[36] Magistrates Court Act 1980, s.1. The increased powers of arrest without warrant found in PACE have further decreased the use of arrest warrants.

[37] See *Leach v. Money*, (1756) 3 Burr. 1962, 1984; 19 St.Tr. 1001; *Wilkes v. Lord Halifax* (1769) 19 St.Tr. 1407.

[38] Magistrates' Courts Act 1980, s.1(4).

[39] *R. v. Howell* [1981] 3 All E.R. 383, [1982] Q.B. 416. PACE s.26(5) expressly retains this power.

[40] However the police must have regard to Art. 10 E.C.H.R. and the right to freedom of expression when exercising this power.

[41] (1998) 28 E.H.R.R. 603, the E.Ct.H.R. found that despite inconsistent English decisions on the definition of breach of the peace, the law was sufficiently precise to comply with Art. 5(1)(c).

[42] Breach of the peace is not an offence in English law, *R. v. County Quarter Sessions Appeals Committee, ex p. M.P.C.* [1948] 1 K.B. 260.

[43] [1998] 3 All E.R. 705. See also *Bibby v. Chief Constable of Essex Police* (2000) 164 J.P. 297, where the Court of Appeal referred to the "now exceptional" common law powers of arrest, and provided guidelines.

The majority of the police powers to arrest without warrant are found in the PACE Act which provides a potential power to arrest for every criminal offence. There are two categories of offences in respect of which there is a power to arrest without warrant (sections 24 and 25); in addition there are preserved powers of arrest (section 26) and a variety of post PACE Act statutes providing summary powers of arrest for newly created offences which would not come under section 24 and in respect of which section 25 is considered inappropriate.[44]

The power to arrest without warrant in section 24 is in respect of an arrestable **24–009** offence[45] which is:

    (i) any offence for which the sentence is fixed by law: that is murder and treason;

    (ii) offences for which a person over 21 may be sentenced on first conviction to five years imprisonment;

    (iii) various listed statutory offences.[46]

Any person may arrest without warrant any person who is in the act of committing such an offence or whom he has reasonable grounds for suspecting to be committing such offence[47]; or anyone who has committed such an offence or whom he has reasonable grounds for suspecting to have committed such an offence. In addition a constable may, if he has reasonable grounds for suspecting an offence has been committed, arrest any person whom he has reasonable grounds for suspecting to be guilty of the offence.[48] He may also arrest anyone about to commit an arrestable offence or anyone whom he has reasonable grounds for suspecting to be about to commit an arrestable offence.[49] The powers conferred by the section extend also to conspiring to commit an arrestable offence, to attempting to commit and to inciting, aiding, abetting, counselling or procuring the commission of such an offence.

Section 25 provides a further power of arrest without warrant in the case of non-arrestable offences where one of the "general arrest conditions" in the section exists. A constable has the power under the section if he has reasonable ground for suspecting the commission of a non-arrestable offence and it appears to him that the service of a summons is impracticable for one of the reasons stated: for example that the name of the person concerned cannot be ascertained;

---

[44] *e.g.* a variety of offences under the Public Order Act 1986 and the C.J.P.O. Act 1994.

[45] Arrestable offence is to be distinguished from serious arrestable offence, defined in s.116; the police have additional powers in this type of offence: *infra.*

[46] Which are added to from time to time, for *e.g.* the new offence of "stalking" in the Protection from Harassment Act 1997 is an arrestable offence. The list was significantly extended by the Criminal Justice and Public Order Act 1994 and the Offensive Weapons Act 1996.

[47] For a consideration of the meaning of "reasonable grounds for suspecting", but in a different statute see *O'Hara v. Chief Constable of the Royal Ulster Constabulary* [1997] 1 All E.R. 129, HL. The E.C.H.R. requires objective grounds for such a suspicion.

[48] This reflects the changed role of arrest from a means of bringing an offender before a court, to an investigative tool for removing a suspect into the police station for questioning, *Mohammed-Holgate v. Duke* [1984] A.C. 437, HL.

[49] The extended statutory powers of the constable reflect the old common law—and are a reminder of the danger of the citizen taking upon himself the right of arrest: *Walters v. W. H. Smith & Son Ltd* [1914] 1 K.B. 595, CA; in *R. v. Self* (1992) 95 Cr. App.R. 42 the Court of Appeal confirmed that the citizen's power of arrest in s.24(5) was dependent on an arrestable offence having been committed.

that arrest is necessary to prevent the person causing himself or other physical harm, or to prevent the commission of an offence against public decency.

24–010   Section 26 rather confusingly repeals earlier statutory provisions authorising arrest without warrant but, by subsection (2), preserves a power to arrest without warrant in a variety of statutes listed in schedule 2.

In the effecting of an arrest section 3 of the Criminal Law Act 1967 provides that any person may use such force as is reasonable in the circumstances in the prevention of crime, or in effecting or assisting in the lawful arrest of offenders or suspected offenders and section 117 of the PACE Act provides that a constable may use reasonable force in the exercise of any power conferred by the Act. What will amount to reasonable force will have to be considered in the light of the E.C.H.R., which provides for the use of force "which is no more than absolutely necessary" (Article 2(2)). In addition Article 3, which prohibits "inhuman or degrading treatment" may mean that force can only be used in response to the detainee's conduct and should be in proportion to that conduct.[50]

The requirements of a valid arrest are defined in section 28. When a person is arrested otherwise than by being informed that he is under arrest, the arrest is not lawful unless the person arrested is informed as soon as practicable that he is under arrest. Where the arrest is by a constable the person arrested must be informed of his arrest even if the fact must be obvious. Whether a person has been told is a matter of fact: polite words of request, inviting a person to go to a police station, may fail to convey that he is being arrested.[51] The ground for the arrest must also be made clear at the time of the arrest or as soon as practicable after the arrest.[52] Again, in the case of arrest by a constable, this requirement must be complied with, even if the ground for arrest is obvious.

24–011   When a police officer has grounds to suspect a person of committing an offence, the suspect must be cautioned[53]; at the latest this will be at the time of arrest. The form of caution is: "You do not have to say anything. But it may harm your defence if you do not mention when questioned something which you later rely on in court. Anything you do say may be given in evidence." This has particular significance in the light of sections 34–39 of the CJPO Act 1994 which allow a court or jury in certain circumstances to draw inferences from an accused's silence, or his failure to give an explanation for, *e.g.* objects found with him or marks on him at the time of arrest.[54]

If an arrest takes place other than at a police station then the constable who makes the arrest, or to whom another person[55] transfers the custody of the arrested person, must take the arrested person to a designated police station as soon as practicable (section 30). (A designated station is defined by section 35(1); *infra.*) In these circumstances a constable may search an arrested person

---

[50] See *Ribbitsch v. Austria* (1996) 8 E.H.R.R. 45.

[51] *Alderson v. Booth* [1969] 2 Q.B. 216, DC, a case under the previous law.

[52] *D.P.P. v. Hawking* [1988] 1 W.L.R. 1166, although the defendant should have been informed of the ground of his arrest when it became practicable, this did not retrospectively make the arrest unlawful; however a claim for false imprisonment could succeed in respect the time when no reasons were given, but could have been given.

[53] COP C para. 10.

[54] *post* para. 24–017.

[55] See *John Lewis & Co Ltd v. Tims* [1952] A.C. 676, HL, the appellants were not liable for false imprisonment when, before handing the respondent over to the police, their private detectives took her to an office in order that the circumstances of her arrest might be explained to the managing director and to obtain authority to prosecute for theft.

if he has reasonable grounds for believing that the arrested person may present a danger to himself or others. The arrested person may also be searched for anything which might be used by the person to assist him to escape or which might be evidence relating to an offence.[56] Premises in which a person was arrested, or was immediately before his arrest (section 32(2)(b)) may similarly be searched. Again reasonable grounds for believing evidence may be found are required and in the case of a search of premises, a search is permitted only to the extent that it is reasonably required for the purpose of discovering the evidence. Additional powers to enter and search certain premises after the arrest of a person for an arrestable offence are found in section 18.[57]

Detention

Police have no power to detain (apart from exceptional anti-terrorist and emergency legislation) for questioning a person whom they have not arrested. Section 29 of the PACE Act recognises this common law principle. However, the PACE Act by permitting arrest on reasonable suspicion[58] recognises that the police station is the venue for the investigation of most serious offences and in Parts IV and V and COPC, attempt to regulate the treatment and questioning of those in police detention.   **24–012**

Persons may not be detained for longer than six hours at a police station which is not a designated police station (sections 30 and 35). At each designated station there must be one or more custody officers whose duty is to ensure that the requirements of Parts IV and V of the PACE Act are complied with. The PACE Act seeks to protect detained persons by separating the custodial and investigative powers of the police. It is the duty of the custody officer to decide whether there is sufficient evidence to charge an arrested person or, if not, whether to detain or release him. Where the custody officer decides there is not such evidence, there is a presumption that the arrestee is released, either with or without bail (section 37(2)). The custody officer may only authorise detention without charge if he has reasonable grounds for believing that it is "necessary to secure evidence relating to an offence for which he is under arrest, or to obtain such evidence by questioning him" (section 37(2)).[59] Detention must be reviewed at regular intervals by a custody officer, (if the person has been arrested and charged), or by a review officer (who must be at least the rank of inspector) if the person has been arrested but not charged (section 40). A review may be carried out by telephone where it is not reasonably practicable for an inspector to be present (section 40A as inserted by the CJP Act 2001). A general maximum period of detention without charge of 24 hours is established by section 41. An officer of the rank of superintendent or above may authorise a further period of detention up to 36 hours in the case of a serious arrestable offence (section 42).[60] An extension can be granted by magistrates for a maximum of 36 hours; and

---

[56] s.32(4) of the PACE Act limits the search to the removal of coat, jacket and gloves; but search of the mouth is permitted by s.59(2) of the CJPO Act which amends s.32(4).

[57] *post*, para. 24–044.

[58] *ante*, para. 24–009.

[59] In practice it appears that the police routinely authorise detention without an examination of the sufficiency of the evidence; I. McKenzie, R. Morgan and R. Reiner, "Helping the Police with their Inquiries: The Necessity Principle and Voluntary Attendance at the Police Station", [1990] Crim. L.R. 22.

[60] s.116 (as amended) creates several categories of serious arrestable offences.

further extensions to a maximum of 96 hours (section 43).[61] It is probable that these procedures and safeguards satisfy the E.C.H.R.

24–013　*Treatment and questioning* (Part V of the PACE Act) If detention has been authorised, the custody officer must start the written custody records of the detention, tell the arrestee of the grounds for the detention and inform him of his "rights"—to inform a third party of his detention (section 56), to free private legal advice (section 58) and to consult the COP.[62] The physical arrangements for the detention of persons at police stations are provided for in COP C and special provisions are made in respect of certain vulnerable groups (*e.g.* children and young persons, the intoxicated, the ill).[63] The main purpose of detention in a police station is to interview a suspect, and the PACE Act requires records to be kept of interviews, but does not require them to be tape recorded although it is general practice to do so, and COP E sets out guidance on this.[64]

Searches in Detention A power of search is conferred by section 54 and a right to retain any object which might be used by the person in custody to injure himself or aid his escape. Items may also be retained if the officer has reasonable grounds for believing that they may be evidence relating to an offence. The decision to search must be made in each instance in the light of the facts, and the detained person should be told the reasons for any seizure, unless it is impracticable to do so (section 54(5)).

24–014　Section 55 (as amended by CJP Act 2001) allows an inspector to authorise an "intimate search," that is a physical examination of a person's bodily orifices (section 65).[65] He must have reasonable grounds for believing that the person arrested and detained has concealed about him (i) anything which he might use to cause physical injury to himself or others and which he might so use while in police detention or the custody of a court; or (ii) a Class "A" drug which he was in possession of, with criminal intent, before arrest. Normally such a search must be conducted by a medically qualified person but a constable (of the appropriate sex) may carry out a search for an object within (i) if the inspector does not think an examination by a medically qualified person is practicable. Controls on this power of search are found in section 55 and COP A. Section 117 provides that constables carrying out searches under the section are entitled to use reasonable force, but it is arguable that in certain circumstances this could constitute "inhuman or degrading treatment" contrary to Article 3 E.C.H.R., or an interference with private life contrary to Article 8.

---

[61] In *Roberts v. Chief Constable of Cheshire Police* [1999] 2 All E.R. 326, the Court of Appeal held that a person was unlawfully detained once the time for the review of his detention had passed until such time as a lawful review was conducted, and in consequence such detention was the tort of false imprisonment.

[62] Research suggests that there has been an improvement in the way Custody Offices perform this task, compared to the early days of the PACE Act; D. Brown, T. Ellis, K. Larscombe, *Changing the Code: Police Detention under the Revised PACE Codes of Practice*, Home Office Research Study No. 129 (1993).

[63] There is doubt as to how effective these provisions have been, see C. Palmer, "Still Vulnerable after all these years", [1996] Crim.L.R. 633.

[64] Interviews with terrorist suspects and those suspected of Official Secrets offences do not have to be tape recorded.

[65] As amended by s.59(1) of the Criminal Justice Public Order Act 1994 to exclude the mouth from the definition of bodily orifices, enabling the police to search on arrest a suspect's mouth for, *e.g.* drugs.

The PACE Act[66] allows for the taking of intimate bodily samples (blood, semen or any other tissue fluid, urine, saliva or pubic hair, a dental impression or a swab from a body orifice other than the mouth (sections 62 and 65), and non-intimate samples: hair other than pubic hair; a sample taken from a nail or from under a nail; a swab taken from any part of a person's body including the mouth but not any other body orifice; saliva; a footprint or similar impression of any part of a person's body other than a part of his hand (sections 63 and 65). In addition the CJPO Act 1994 amended the PACE Act to provide a power for the police to obtain intimate and non-intimate body from those not in police detention.[67] All the powers to obtain samples are in respect of recordable offences[68]—a wider category than the "serious arrestable offences" as originally found in the PACE Act.

An intimate sample, whether from those who are or are not in police detention, can only be taken with consent. A court may, however, draw such inferences from a refusal to consent without good cause, as appear proper (section 62(10)). It could be questioned whether compelling a suspect to consent to the taking of a bodily sample (an interference with private life) or risk adverse inferences falls within the exceptions to Article 8 of the E.C.H.R.[69] Before a person is asked to provide an intimate sample an inspector has to authorise the taking of the sample on the basis that he has reasonable grounds for suspecting the person to be involved in a recordable offence and reasonable grounds to believe that the sample would confirm or disprove that involvement. The new power to obtain intimate samples from those not in detention (section 62(1A)) is in respect of those from whom at least two non-intimate samples have already been obtained and which were found to be insufficient. Intimate samples may only be taken by a medical practitioner or a registered nurse (section 62 as amended by the CJP Act 2001), and proper records must be kept.

Non-intimate samples may be taken with the suspect's consent, or by the **24–015** authorisation of an inspector who has to have reasonable grounds for suspecting the person's involvement in a recordable offence and reasonable grounds for believing that the sample will tend to confirm or disprove his involvement. In certain circumstances the non-consensual taking of a non-intimate sample could breach Articles 3 and 8 of the E.C.H.R. The power can be used in respect of those in police detention, and those who have been charged with a recordable offence and have not given a non-intimate sample or where the sample given was insufficient or unsuitable. In addition there is a power to obtain such samples from those convicted of recordable offences (section 63B) or detained following an acquittal on grounds of insanity (section 63C). The new provisions for the collection of non-intimate samples will assist the establishment of a DNA database similar to that which exists for fingerprints.

A detained person's fingerprints may, under section 61 (as amended by the CJP Act 2001) may be taken without his consent if (i) an inspector so authorises and he has reasonable grounds for suspecting the person's involvement in a criminal

---

[66] As amended by the CJPO Act 1994, which takes account of advances in D.N.A. technology.

[67] In *Saunders v. United Kingdom* (1997) 23 E.H.R.R. 313, the E.Ct.H.R. accepted that the use in evidence of fingerprints, intimate and non-intimate samples did not infringe the privilege against self-incrimination enshrined in Art. 6.

[68] s.27(4) of the PACE Act. These are offences listed in the National Police Records (Recordable Offences) Regulations 1985 and are generally those punishable by imprisonment.

[69] Particularly since the power to do so is in respect of "recordable offences" which covers some non-serious offences. *Saunders v. UK* (1997) 23 E.H.R.R. 313, suggests that such powers do not infringe Art. 6; however British courts could take a different view.

offence and that his fingerprints will tend to confirm or disprove his involvement or (ii) he has been charged with a recordable offence or he has been warned that he may be so charged.

In the case of the three preceding sections, where the person detained is under the age of 14 the consent required is that of the parent or guardian; between 14 and 17 both the person detained and his parent or guardian must consent.

Access to Legal Advice[70]

24–016   Suspects have a statutory right to consult a solicitor privately at any time,[71] and must be permitted to do so as soon as practicable (section 58(1)(2).[72] Delay (of a maximum of 36 hours) is only permitted if authorised by an officer of at least the rank of superintendent and only in respect of serious arrestable offences where he has reasonable grounds for believing that interference with the course of justice is likely (section 58(8)).[73] There has been an increase in the percentage of suspects requesting legal advise, from 24 per cent in the early days to 40 per cent in 1996.[74] The quality of the legal advise offered to suspects has given rise to concern,[75] and the Law Society introduced an "accreditation scheme" in an attempt to deal with this. The prospect of "adverse inferences" from an accused's failure to mention certain fact when questioned after caution[76] make the presence of a solicitor at interview particularly important. The E.Ct.H.R. has in effect suggested that the exclusion of a lawyer from the questioning of a suspect in these circumstances could be a violation of Article 6.[77]

Right to Silence[78]

24–017   The CJPO Act 1994 has affected the use that can be made of an accused's silence in the face of police questioning; it does not remove that right. Section 34(2) allows a court or jury to draw "such inferences as appear proper" from an accused's failure to mention, when questioned under caution or on being charged with an offence, any fact on which he subsequently relies on in his defence, provided that it is one which in the circumstances he could reasonably have been expected to have mentioned. Future use of section 34 must be in the light of

---

[70] Andrew Sanders and Lee Bridges, "The Right to Legal Advice", Chap. 4 in *Miscarriages of Justice* (Clive Walker and Keith Starmer eds, 1999).

[71] This is also an aspect of Art. 6 E.C.H.R.; the failure of some police stations to provide for telephone advise to be in private could infringe this article; but see *R. (on the application of M) v. Commissioner of Police for the Metropolis The Times*, August 17, 2001.

[72] There is still a common law right to see a solicitor as soon as reasonably practicable, *R. v. Chief Constable of South Wales ex p. Merrick* [1994] Crim.L.R. 852.

[73] *R. v. Samuel* (1988) 87 Cr.App. R. 232, in the absence of persuasive evidence of the existence of circumstances justifying delay the conviction was quashed. To deny a suspect a solicitor could be in breach of Art. 6 E.C.H.R., although the E.Ct.H.R. has accepted that restricting the right for good cause is permissable.

[74] T. Bucke and D. Brown, *In Police Custody: Police Powers and Suspects' Rights under the Revised PACE Codes of Practice*, Home Office Research Study 174 (1997). This, and other research, found great variations between police stations.

[75] J. Baldwin, *The Role of Legal Representatives at Police Stations*, R.C.C.J. Research Study No. 3 (1992).

[76] s.34 CJPO Act 1994.

[77] *Murray v. United Kingdom* (1990) 22 E.H.R.R. 29. However, in the light of other factors Murray's trial was not unfair; the lack of legal advise was not crucial on the facts of the case. As a consequence of this decision, ss.34–37 of the CJPO Act 1994 (below), were amended by s.58 of the Youth and Criminal Evidence Act 1999 to prohibit "adverse inferences" if the suspect had not had an opportunity to consult a solicitor.

[78] In *Smith v. Director of the Serious Fraud Office* [1992] 3 All E.R. 456, Lord Mustill identified six legal meanings for the term, only one of which has been affected by CJPO Act.

Condron v. United Kingdom.[79] In *Condron* the E.Ct.H.R. did not say that section 34 was in breach of the E.C.H.R. but said that it was essential to a fair trial that the judge should direct the jury not to draw an adverse inference if they were satisfied that the defendant had remained silent on his solicitor's advise, and there was a sound reason for this advise.[80] The E.Ct.H.R. has also stated that the powers of compulsory questioning under threat of punishment provided in the Companies Act 1985 are in breach of Article 6.[81] The decisions of the E.Ct.H.R. have implication for the interpretation of three other sections of the CJPO Act which allow inferences to be drawn.[82]

Admissibility of Confessions and Evidence[83]

Section 78[84] gives courts a discretion to refuse to admit evidence if it appears **24–018** that "having regard to all the circumstances, including the circumstances in which the evidence was obtained, the admission of the evidence would have such an adverse effect on the fairness of the proceedings that the court ought not to admit it." This could include breaches of the PACE Act or the COP. When exercising its exclusionary discretion under section 78, courts should give additional weight to the breach of a E.C.H.R. right as it is a "constitutional right".[85] The E.Ct.H.R. has permitted the use of unlawfully obtained evidence, its practice had been to assess whether the trial as a whole was fair, taking into account the way the evidence was obtained, and its impact at the trial.[86] However, in *Teixiera de Castro v. Portugal*[87] the E.Ct.H.R. suggested that where certain improprieties such as entrapment were used, then even to exclude the evidence would be insufficient; the prosecution should not have been brought in the first place.

Section 76 provides for the exclusion of improperly obtained confessions[88]; if the defendant represents to the court that a confession was so obtained, then it is for the prosecution to prove beyond reasonable doubt that this was not the case,[89] Evidence obtained by torture or maltreatment is inadmissible under the E.C.H.R.

---

[79] [2000] Crim.L.R. 679.

[80] The Court of Appeal in *R. v. Condron* [1997] 1 W.L.R. 827, had suggested that such a direction was "desirable". See also *R. v. Argent* [1997] 2 Cr.App.R. 27; *R. v. Roble* [1997] Crim. L.R. 449. See, R. Munday, "Inferences from Silence and European Human Rights Law", [1996] Crim.L.R. 370.

[81] *Saunders v. United Kingdom* (1997) 23 E.H.R.R. 313. Section 59 of and Sched. 3 to the Youth and Criminal Evidence Act 1999 provides for the inadmissibility in criminal proceedings of answers and statements given under compulsion.

[82] s.35 (failure of an accused to give evidence in court); s.36 (failure to give an explanation for objects, marks, etc. found on him or in his possession); and s.37 (failure to account for his presence at particular place or at a particular time).

[83] For further details see P. Mirfield, *Silence, Confessions and Improperly Obtained Evidence* (1997).

[84] See A. Choo and S. Nash, "What's the matter with s.78?", [1999] Crim.L.R. 929.

[85] See Lord Steyn in *Mohammed v. The State* [1999] 2 A.C. 111, PC.

[86] *Schenk v. Switzerland* (1988) 13 E.H.R.R. 242, subsequently in *Teixeria de Castro v. Portugal* (1999) 28 E.H.H.R. 1, a more interventionist approach was taken; in *Kahn v. United Kingdom* [2000] Crim.L.R. 684, a Chamber of the Court found no breach of Art. 6 despite a breach of Art. 8.

[87] (1998) 28 E.H.R.R. 101. See *Attorney-General's Reference No. 3 of 2000* [2001] Crim.L.R. 647, where the Court of Appeal distinguished *Teixiera*, the case is to go to the House of Lords.

[88] s.77 requires a jury to be given an additional warning before convicting a mentally handicapped person on the basis of a confession.

[89] *R. v. Paris, Abdullahi and Miller* (1993) 97 Cr.App.R. 99, illustrates the use of s.76, the advantages and limitations of tape recording interviews, and the inadequacy of some legal advisers. It is also one of only two cases where s.76 has been successfully invoked, see H. Fenwick, *Civil Rights* (2000) at p. 204.

Assaulting and obstructing a constable[90]

24–019   Section 89 of the Police Act 1996 (re-enacting section 51 of the Police Act 1964)[91] provides that it is an offence to assault a constable (or a person assisting him) in the execution of his duty, punishable on summary conviction with a term of imprisonment not exceeding six months or a fine not exceeding level 5 or both. Section 89(2) provides that it is an offence to resist or wilfully obstruct a constable (or a person assisting him) in the execution of his duty, punishable with a term of imprisonment not exceeding one month or a fine not exceeding level 3 or both.[92]

The importance of these provisions in a chapter on the freedom of the individual is that it is often through litigation arising under this section or its predecessors, that the scope of the powers and duties of the police are elucidated. A policeman, as we have seen, cannot normally detain without arresting: if he does so he is acting outside his powers. But is it an unlawful detention to tap a person on his shoulder and request him to stop and answer a question?[93] The limits of a statutory power to detain may well arise in proceedings under section 89.[94] The meaning of such phrases as "reasonable grounds"[95] and "reasonable force"[96] when used in the PACE Act and the distinction, if any, between "believing" and "suspecting"[97] are likely to be raised in this indirect way by prosecutions and appeals in respect of these offences. The freedom of the individual may be affected by the extent to which the courts are willing to recognise a discretion in constables to take decisions which they regard as necessary to prevent disorder,[98] or to keep traffic moving.[99] In doing so they will have to satisfied that the police officer's actions are proportionate to the harm he seeks to prevent. Equally important is the meaning the courts give to "obstruction," a word which could properly be confined to physical opposition but, on the other hand, has, in English courts, been extended to, for example, taking action which ensures that the criminal law is not broken so that the police find themselves, on arriving at what they expected to be the scene of a crime, unable to arrest anyone—other than the person who gave the warning of their coming.[1] In future all these issues will have to be considered in the light of the E.C.H.R.

---

[90] J. C. Smith and B. Hogan, *Criminal Law* (9th ed., J.C. Smith, 1999) Chap. 13.

[91] Most of the cases cited are on the 1964 Act.

[92] By s.89(3) this section also applies to a Northern Irish or Scottish constable who is executing a warrant or otherwise acting in England or Wales under a statutory power to do so.

[93] *Donnelly v. Jackman* [1970] 1 W.L.R. 562, DC (Action of constable within execution of duty). Courts are careful to distinguish between a touch to draw someone's attention and to apprehend or detain: *Collins v. Wilcock* [1984] 1 W.L.R. 1172, DC; see also *Mepstead v. D.P.P.* [1996] Crim.L.R. 111, but *cf. Bentley v. Brudzinski* (1982) 75 Cr.App.R. 217, DC.

[94] *e.g. Pedro v. Diss* [1981] 2 All E.R. 59, DC (Prisoner entitled to resist detention because PC had not told him, as the Court held he was bound to, that he was detaining him under statutory powers: Metropolitan Police Act 1839, s.66).

[95] *e.g.* s.1(3); s.25(1); s.32(1); s.54(4); s.55. *cf. Brazil v. Chief Constable of Surrey* [1983] 1 W.L.R. 1155, CA ("reasonable cause": Misuse of Drugs Act 1971 s.23(2): issue raised but not necessary to be determined by Court); *R. v. Forde* [1985] Crim.L.R., DC.

[96] s.117.

[97] Contrast s.1(3) and s.1(4); s.25(1) and s.32(1); s.61(4)(a) and (b).

[98] *post* Chap. 26, para. 27–008.

[99] *Johnson v. Phillips* [1976] 1 W.L.R. 65 (obstruction to refuse to drive wrong way down a one way street when directed to do so by a constable). See U. Ross, "Two Cases on Obstructing a Constable," (1977) Crim.L.R. 187.

[1] *Green v. Moore* [1982] Q.B. 1044 (DC); *Moore v. Green* [1983] 1 All E.R. 663 (After-hours drinking at Castle Hotel, Chepstow).

Assaulting

The elements of assault are those required normally under the cri
is no defence that the person accused was unaware that he was
constable.[2] However if the defendant honestly (but mistakenly) bel
was acting in self defence or in prevention of a crime, he may have
the basis that he did not intend to use *unlawful* force.[3]

Obstructing

In *Hinchliffe v. Sheldon*,[4] Lord Goddard L.C.J., defined obstructing as "mak- **24–021**
ing it more difficult for the police to carry out their duties." Such a wide
definition would require citizens to carry out willingly police constables' instructions (unless they had, correctly, determined that they fell outside the execution
of the constables' duties) and to co-operate fully in the investigation of crimes (so
that much of the Police and Criminal Evidence Act 1984 would be unnecessary).
It cannot be the criminal offence of obstructing a constable to do what one is
entitled to do, namely refuse to answer questions. In *Rice v. Connolly*[5] the
Divisional Court reached that conclusion by reliance on the wording of section
51(3) (now section 89(2) of the 1996 Act), "to . . . wilfully obstruct." It could
not, according to Lord Parker L.C.J. be wilful to do that which one had a legal
excuse to do, refuse to answer questions. In *Green v. D.P.P.*[6] it was similarly held
that to tell another not to answer questions was not an obstruction. Most of the
cases on obstruction have involved a physical element. A positive act, such as
drinking a quantity of alcohol to prevent the effective administration of a
breathalyser test, may be more likely to be regarded as an obstruction than a mere
refusal to act: *Dibble v. Ingleton*.[7] On the other hand a refusal to obey a
constable's instruction which is given with a view to avoiding a breach of the
peace[8] or to protect life[9] may constitute an obstruction.

A number of cases have considered the *mens rea* required before the offence
of obstruction is committed. In *Willmott v. Atack*[10] it was held that physically
obstructing a constable who was attempting to arrest someone did not constitute
an offence under section 51(3) (now section 89(2) of the 1996 Act) when the
intention had been to help the police. Croom Johnson J. paraphrased "wilfully"
as meaning "done with the idea of some form of hostility to the police." But
interference with a policeman who is attempting to arrest someone on the ground
that the wrong person is being arrested, constitutes wilfully obstructing: *Hill v.
Ellis*.[11] Both decisions were considered in *Lewis v. Cox*[12] where the Divisional

---

[2] *R. v. Forbes* (1865) 10 Cox C.C. 362. Proposals to reform the law on offences against the person
would require proof that the defendant knew or was reckless that the victim was a police officer: Law
Commission Consultation Paper No. 122 (1992).
[3] On the application of *R. v. Williams (Gladstone)* [1987] 3 All E.R. 411, which was applied by the
Court of Appeal in *Blackburn v. Bowering* [1994] 3 All E.R. 380, a case on assaulting an officer of
the court in the execution of his duty.
[4] [1955] 1 W.L.R. 1207.
[5] [1966] 2 Q.B. 414, DC. It is difficult to see how, as a matter of law, liability can be affected by
whether the refusal to answer questions is politely worded or accompanied by obscenities: *quaere
Ricketts v. Cox* (1981) 74 Cr.App.R. 298, DC.
[6] (1991) 155 J.P. 816.
[7] [1972] 1 Q.B. 480, DC.
[8] *post* para. 27–008.
[9] *Johnson v. Phillips* [1976] 1 W.L.R. 65.
[10] [1977] Q.B. 498, DC.
[11] [1983] Q.B. 680, DC.
[12] [1985] Q.B. 509, DC.

Court held that justices had erred in refusing to convict an accused who had opened the door of a police vehicle to ask a drunk who had been put inside the vehicle where he was being taken. A constable closed the door and warned the accused not to interfere. The latter, however, again opened the door and so prevented the vehicle from being driven away. The court held that the offence of wilful obstruction was committed by doing an act which interfered with the execution by the police of their duty, knowing or intending that it would interfere. Motive was irrelevant and the court found the use of such phrases as "hostility to the police" or "aimed at the police" unhelpful.[13] Unlike under section 89(1), it would be possible for defendant to argue that he honestly believed that the person he obstructed was not a constable, and in consequence his obstruction was not wilful.

Execution of duty

24–022   A constable is not acting within the execution of his duty when he does something which he has no right to do at law, for example, to attempt to detain someone whom he has not arrested,[14] to search someone whom he has no right to search,[15] to use force to take a person's fingerprints when not entitled to do so,[16] to attempt to enter premises with an invalid search warrant,[17] or to trespass on property.[18] In all these circumstances the citizen is entitled to refuse to co-operate with the instructions of a constable and, if necessary, to use reasonable force to resist unlawful demands.

Where, however, a constable is doing what he is legally entitled to do then he is acting within the execution of his duty, although a jurist might prefer to say that he was acting within the scope of his lawful powers. To resist arrest where a constable is entitled to arrest, for example for an apprehended breach of the peace,[19] or to refuse to keep a vehicle stationary as required under legislation to enable a constable to make inquiries under the relevant Act[20] are examples of assaulting or obstructing a constable in the execution of his duty. Although any touching of a person however slight may amount to a battery, a broad exception exists to this principle to allow, as Goff L.J. put it, "for the exigencies of everyday life",[21] which applies to police constable as well as other citizens. It will be a question of fact in each case whether the physical contact by the constable, "has in the circumstances gone beyond generally accepted standards

---

[13] The Court did not attempt to cast doubt on *Willmott v. Atack, supra.* which may perhaps be explained as being correctly decided on the ground that the accused did not intend to obstruct or realise that he was obstructing whereas in *Hill v. Ellis*, whatever his motive, the accused did intend to prevent the effecting of an arrest.

[14] *Collins v. Wilcock* [1984] 1 W.L.R. 1172; *Bentley v. Brudzinski* (1982) 75 Cr.App.R. 217; a police officer who took hold of someone's arm in the mistaken belief that she had been arrested by a colleague, was acting outside the execution of his duty, *Kerr v. D.P.P.* [1995] Crim.L.R. 394.

[15] *Lindley v. Rutter* [1981] Q.B. 128, DC; *Brazil v. Chief Constable of Surrey* [1983] 1 W.L.R. 1155, CA; *R. v. Eeet* [1983] Crim.L.R. 806, Crown Ct. *Cf. McBean v. Parker* [1983] Crim.L.R. 399, DC.

[16] *R. v. Jones (Yvonne)* (1978) 67 Cr.App.R. 166, CA.

[17] *Syce v. Harrison* [1980] Crim.L.R. 649, DC.

[18] *McLorie v. Oxford* [1982] Q.B. 1290, DC; *R. v. McKenzie and Davis* [1979] Crim.L.R. 174, Crown Ct. Whether a P.C. is trespassing or not may be a difficult question: *Robson v. Hallett* [1967] 2 Q.B. 939.

[19] *R. v. Howell (Errol)* [1982] Q.B. 416. See *post* para. 27–008 for the implications of the E.C.H.R. on this power. *Foulkes v. Chief Constable for Merseyside* [1998] 3 All E.R. 705, CA: power to arrest for an apprehended breach of the peace is "exceptional".

[20] *Lodwick v. Sanders* [1985] 1 W.L.R. 382, DC.

[21] *Collins v. Wilcock* [1984] 3 All E.R. 374, DC.

of conduct". For a police officer to take a man's arm to draw attention to what was being said to him, but without intending to arrest or detain him could, if it lasted no longer than reasonably necessary, still be within the execution of the police officer's duty.[22] To be within the execution of his duty a police officer does not have to be doing something which he is compelled by law to do, provided he is doing something that is within his legal powers, *e.g.* to keep the peace.[23] It is also part of the duty of the police to take steps to apprehend the perpetrators of crimes which they have reason are likely to be committed. In *Green v. Moore*[24] the warning of a licensee that police officers were keeping watch on his premises with a view to securing evidence that he and his customers were breaking the licensing laws was held to be an obstruction of police officers in the execution of their duty.

It should finally be noted that there is no power to arrest without warrant for an offence under section 89 unless a breach of peace has occurred or is reasonably apprehended: *Wershof v. Commissioner of the Police for the Metropolis*.[25] In the case of assaulting or resisting a constable a breach of the peace is almost inevitably involved. In many cases of obstruction it is difficult to believe that there can be any real risk of a breach of the peace. It may also be possible to rely on the power to arrest under the "general arrest conditions" (section 25 of the PACE Act), but the police officer must first indicate to the suspect the nature of the offence he suspects has been committed.[26]

Bail

Article 5 and 6 of the E.C.H.R. are relevant to bail proceedings, and the courts and police now have a duty to interpret the Bail Act 1976, as far as possible, to comply with these rights. Article 5(3) provides that anyone who has been lawfully arrested is entitled to "trial within a reasonable time, or to release pending trial," this in effect creates a presumption in favour of granting bail[27]; where bail is denied it must be justified by relevant and sufficient reasons based on the facts in the particular case.[28] Section 56 of the Crime and Disorder Act 1998 amends section 25 of the Criminal Justice and Public Order Act 1994, which had restricted the right to bail; although it is still not certain that the law on bail complies with Art. 5(3).[29]   **24–023**

In many cases a person who has been arrested may be released on bail pending trial. Initially a justice of the peace on issuing a warrant for arrest may grant bail by endorsing a direction to that effect and subject to the terms of section 117 of the Magistrates' Courts Act 1980, as amended by the PACE Act, s.47(8). Section   **24–024**

---

[22] *Mepstead v. D.P.P.* [1996] Crim.L.R. 111.

[23] *Coffin v. Smith* [1980] 71 Cr.App.R. 221, DC, where the police were found to be acting within their duty when they attended a youth club to ensure that no disorder occurred during a social function.

[24] [1982] Q.B. 1044, DC. See too *Moore v. Green* [1983] 1 All E.R. 663, DC. Contrast *Bastable v. Little* [1907] 1 K.B. 59 described by Donaldson L.J. in *Green v. Moore* as "a very curious decision based upon a highly eccentric view of the facts."

[25] (1978) 68 Cr.App.R. 82.

[26] *Nicholas v. Parsonage* [1987] R.T.R. 199.

[27] *Neumeister v. Austria* (1968) 1 E.H.R.R. 91.

[28] *e.g.* that the accused could interfere with the course of justice, *Wemhoff v. Germany* (1968) 1 E.H.R.R. 155; or for the preservation of public order, *Letellier v. France* (1991) 14 E.H.R.R. 83.

[29] See Philip Leach, [1999] Crim.L.R. 300. Section 56 was enacted in anticipation of the decision of the E.Ct.H.R. in *Caballero v. United Kingdom* (2000) 30 E.H.R.R. 643. The Law Commission Paper, *Bail and the Human Rights Act 1998*, No. 157 (1999), suggests that further amendments to s.25 are required.

38 of the PACE Act[30] regulates the granting of bail by the custody officer where a person arrested without a warrant or arrested under a warrant not endorsed for bail, is charged with an offence.[31] Section 38 provides for release from detention, either on bail or without bail, unless one of the conditions in that section is not complied with,[32] for example the name and address of the person charged cannot be ascertained or the custody officer has reasonable grounds for believing that the detention of the person arrested is necessary for his own protection or to prevent him causing physical injury to any other person. In the case of a person arrested and charged with an imprisonable offence if the custody officer has reasonable grounds to believe that detention is necessary to prevent the arrestee from committing an offence he may authorise detention rather than release. In exercising his powers under section 38 the custody officer is to have regard to the same conditions as a court when deciding whether to withhold bail under the Bail Act 1976.[33] Periodic reviews of the detention of those arrested and charged, similar to those outlined earlier in respect of those arrested and detained are required (section 40). At the end of each period defined in the Act the person must be released on bail unless a further period of detention can be justified. If the custody officer grants police bail he may do so unconditionally or subject to conditions, *e.g.* that the defendant does not interfere with witnesses, or go to a named place.[34] The police may vary the conditions, and the defendant may apply to the Magistrates' Court to have the conditions removed or varied, but in doing so he runs that risk of having more onerous conditions imposed or a decision taken to withhold bail.[35]

Where a person charged appears before magistrates or the Crown Court in connection with criminal proceedings the Bail Act 1976 s.4 confers a general right to bail.[36] The main exceptions to the right of bail of a person accused or convicted of an imprisonable offence are if the court is satisfied "that there are substantial grounds for believing[37] that the defendant if released on bail would: (a) fail to surrender to custody[38]; (b) commit an offence while on bail, or (c) interfere with witnesses."[39] Sections 25 and 26 of the CJPO Act 1994 restrict a court's power to remand on bail two categories of defendant: (i) those charged with murder, manslaughter, rape or attempted rape and who already have a conviction for such an offence; (ii) those charged with an indictable offence which it appears to the court was committed when he was on bail from an

---

[30] As amended by the CJPO Act 1994.

[31] For the requirements where the custody officer decides that he does not have sufficient evidence to charge the person arrested see *ante* para. 24–012.

[32] There are special rules for arrested juveniles, PACE Act, s.38(6), as amended by CJPO Act 1994.

[33] See below.

[34] See s.27 of the CJPO Act 1994, amending the Bail Act 1976. Early research suggests that although this provision has been used, there has also been a significant reduction in unconditional bail; J. Raine and M. Wilson, "Police Bail with Conditions", (1997) 37 B.J. Crim. 593.

[35] s.43B of the Magistrates' Court 1980 as amended by CJPO Act 1994.

[36] A person charged with treason can only be granted bail by order of a judge of the High Court or the Secretary of State, Magistrates' Court Act 1980, s.41.

[37] The onus is on the prosecution to establish those grounds, but only on the balance of probabilities, *Governor of Canterbury Prison, ex p. Craig* [1991] 2 Q.B. 195; this could be contrary to the E.C.H.R.

[38] The E.C.H.R. has been interpreted to require the release on bail of an accused who can provide sufficient surety to ensure his appearance at court; *Neumeister v. Austria* A/8 (1968) 1 E.H.R.R. 55, *Letellier v. France* A/207 (1991) 14 E.H.R.R. 83.

[39] Bail Act 1976, Sched. 1, Pt I, as amended.

existing charge. In the case of the first of these exceptions the original wording which gave the court no discretion in such cases has been altered to allow a court to grant bail if satisfied that "there are exceptional circumstances which justify it." In deciding whether or not to refuse bail the court is to have regard to for *e.g.* the nature and seriousness of the offence, the character, antecedents associations and community ties of the defendant.[40] A Magistrates' Court or Crown Court must give reasons for refusing bail or imposing conditions on bail (section 5(3)), the court must also give reasons if, despite representations to the contrary by the prosecution, it grants bail.[41] To meet the requirements of procedural fairness in Article 6 E.C.H.R., reasons for refusing bail will have to be detailed. A person refused bail may apply to the Crown Court or to the High Court to a judge in chambers, and he must be informed of his right. There is no right for an accused to make repeated bail applications to magistrates where bail has been refused. However, the court has a duty to consider bail in relation to every person with the presumptive right to bail who has been remanded in custody, whenever they appear in court. This appears to allow a defendant at his first hearing after the initial hearing at which bail was refused, to put forward arguments that had been used before, as well as new arguments.[42] The Bail (Amendment) Act 1993, s.1 gives the prosecution the right to appeal to the Crown Court against a decision by the magistrates to grant bail, but only with respect to relatively serious offences.[43] Section 5B of the Bail Act[44] allows the prosecution to apply to court to have the granting of bail or the conditions imposed on bail reconsidered in the light of new information which casts doubt on the earlier decision. This power is restricted to offences which are indictable or triable either way. Bail may also be granted by the higher courts in the course of their proceedings or pending an appeal. It is a criminal offence to fail without reasonable cause to surrender to custody at the time and place appointed (section 6).

Bail can be fixed at any amount, but the Bill of Rights 1688 provides that the **24–025** bail shall not be "excessive." In such cases as theft, fraud or smuggling, the amount of money involved may be very large, with a corresponding danger that the accused may leave the country. If the accused objects to the amount of bail he may appeal to a judge, or in appropriate cases may apply for a writ of habeas corpus.[45]

The exercise by justices of their power to grant bail is subject to judicial review by the High Court on the grounds discussed in Chapter 32. In particular they must consider each application on its merits and not in the light of a predetermined policy. In *R. v. Mansfield Justices, ex p. Sharkey*[46] certiorari was sought to quash grants of bail, made subject to the condition that the applicants,

---

[40] s.9, Sched. 1, Pt I.

[41] The requirement to give reasons was introduced in the Criminal Justice Act, s.153 in respect of charges of murder, manslaughter and rape. The CJP Act 2001, s.129, requires reasons to be given, whatever the charge.

[42] The actual meaning of Part IIA of Sched. 1 of the Bail Act (added by the Criminal Justice Act 1988) is unclear.

[43] Guidance issued to the C.P.S. suggests that this power will not be used very frequently.

[44] As inserted by CJPO Act 1994.

[45] *Ex p. Thomas* [1956] Crim.L.R. 119, DC. *cf. R. v. Governor of Brixton Prison, ex p. Goswami, The Times*, December 22, 1966; in *Neumeister v. Austria (No. 1)* A/8 (1968 E.H.R.R. the E.Ct.H.R. stated that the amount of bail had to be set by reference to the accused and his assets, and not by reference to the amount of loss imputed to him.

[46] [1985] Q.B. 613, DC.

who had been charged with public order offences and obstructing police officers, did not visit any premises for the purposes of picketing or demonstrating in connection with the 1984–85 miners' strike, other than peacefully to picket at their own places of work. The Divisional Court held that provided the magistrates perceived a real and not a fanciful risk of an offence being committed, they were entitled to impose conditions on bail. In the light of their knowledge of local conditions, outlined graphically in Lord Lane L.C.J.'s judgment, they were justified in concluding that there was such a real risk.[47]

Binding over

24–026   The power of magistrates to make a binding over order is a form of preventive justice, that is a power to subject to restriction someone who has not necessarily committed a criminal offence. A binding-over order requires that a person should enter into a recognisance (a bond whereby he binds himself under a penalty) with or without sureties (other persons who will vouch for him under penalty) to keep the peace or to be of good behaviour or both for a certain period. If that person commits a breach of the order, he and his sureties are liable to forfeit the whole or part of the sums in which they are bound. There is no legal limit to the amount of the recognisances or of the sureties, or to the period of the order (which is commonly twelve months). If the person concerned refuses to enter into a recognisance, or if he is unwilling or unable to find satisfactory sureties, the magistrates may commit him to prison for not more than six months or until he sooner complies with the order.[48] The power to bind over to keep the peace is probably of common law origin, and may have been exercised by the Conservators of the Peace. The power to bind over to be of good behaviour towards the Queen and her people is ascribed to the Justices of the Peace Act 1361.

Under the Magistrates' Courts Act 1980, s.115, the power on the complaint of any person to bind over another person to keep the peace or to be of good behaviour towards the complainant, must be exercised on complaint.

24–027   The power of the courts to bind someone over to keep the peace has been considered by the Law Commission and the E.Ct.H.R. The Law Commission considered the power unreasonable and vague and doubted whether it complied with the E.C.H.R.[49] However in *Steel v. United Kingdom*[50] the E.C.t.H.R. upheld the general compatibility of the powers to bind over with Articles 5 and 10 of the E.C.H.R. However in the case of three of the applicants their actions in handing out leaflets and holding a banner were "entirely peaceful", in consequence the police had insufficient grounds for fearing a breach of the peace, and the restrictions placed on their freedom of expression (Article 10) were disproportionate to the prevention of disorder. In deciding whether to make a binding over order magistrates will now have to have regard to the right of freedom of

---

[47] For a critical note see A. L. Newbold, "Picketing Miners and the Courts", [1985] P.L. 30.

[48] In *Lansbury v. Riley* [1914] 3 K.B. 229, DC, George Lansbury M.P., who incited suffragettes to militant action, was bound over to be of good behaviour in the sum of £1,000 with two sureties of £500 each; as he was unable or unwilling to find the sureties he was committed to prison for three months. It remains to be seen how long a period of detention will be allowed before it would be regarded as "disproportionate" to the danger being averted (Art. 10(2) E.C.H.R.). In *Steel v. United Kingdom* (1998) 28 E.H.R.R. 603, it was only by a slender majority that a period of imprisonment of 28 days was held not to be disproportionate.

[49] *Criminal Law: Binding Over: the Issues* (1994) Law.Com. No. 222.

[50] *op. cit.*

expression when taking decisions about breach of the peace. A further restriction on the powers of a court to bind someone over was imposed by the E.Ct.H.R. in *Hashman and Harrup v. United Kingdom*.[51] The behaviour of the defendants was found by Crown Court not to amount to a breach of the peace, but to be *contra bonos mores*, that is behaviour seen as "wrong rather than right in the judgment of the majority of contemporary fellow citizens"; the defendants were accordingly bound over. The E.Ct.H.R. found that the concept of *contra bonos mores* was inadequately defined for the purposes of Article 10(2) and in consequence the decision to bind the defendants over was contrary to the E.C.H.R. It is unlikely that courts will in future use this power.

The Court has a duty to warn a complainant or witness before binding him over, giving him an opportunity to say why he should not be bound over. A binding-over order is not a conviction and therefore at common law there was no appeal, but a statutory right of appeal was given in 1956.[52]

Other types of deprivation of liberty of the person

Detention on medical grounds

An exception to the right to liberty and security of the person in Article 5 of the E.C.H.R, is where, in accordance with a procedure prescribed by law the detention is "for the prevention of the spreading of infectious diseases, of persons of unsound mind, alcoholics or drug addicts or vagrants" (Article 5(e)). These people are those who "have to be considered as occasionally dangerous for public safety . . . (and in) their own interests."[53] The test of proportionality would seem to require a high standard of justification on the basis of something more than status alone, before such people can be compulsorily detained. In the case of those of unsound mind, objective medical evidence showing a medical disorder of a kind warranting compulsory confinement is required.[54] The conditions of confinement and the provision of suitable treatment are governed by Article 3 E.C.H.R. **24–028**

Various statutes authorise the detention of individuals on medical grounds whether in their own interests or those of the community at large. The National Assistance Act 1948, s.47 empowers a court to order, on the report of a designated medical officer, the compulsory removal to hospital or other place of persons who (a) are suffering from grave chronic disease or being aged, infirm or physically incapacitated are living in insanitary conditions, and (b) are unable to devote to themselves and are not receiving from other persons proper care and attention.

The Public Health (Control of Disease) Act 1984 provides for the compulsory removal to, and detention in, hospital of any person suffering from a notifiable disease (that is cholera, plague, relapsing fever, small-pox and typhus—section 10) by order of a justice of the peace (sections 37 and 38). The Secretary of State (by section 13) and local authorities (by section 16) have power to extend the compulsory detention provisions of the Act to other diseases. **24–029**

---

[51] (2000) 30 E.H.R.R. 241.
[52] Magistrates' Courts (Appeals from Binding-Over Orders) Act 1956.
[53] *Guzzardi v. Italy* (1980) 13 E.H.R.R. 333.
[54] *Winterwerp v. The Netherlands* [1979] 2 E.H.R.R. 387.

The provisions which occasion most controversy, however, are those relating to the detention[55] and treatment of people suffering from mental ill-health currently to be found in the Mental Health Act 1983.[56] These affect large numbers of individuals; involve, in many cases, prolonged periods of incarceration and the administration of treatments, to which the recipients may not have consented, which in some cases may have the most far reaching and irreversible mental and physical effects, without any guarantee of achieving their desired aims. The patient may, moreover, dispute that he or she is mentally ill or that compulsory detention or treatment is necessary. The Mental Health Act 1983 authorises admission for assessment and detention for treatment, in a mental hospital, against the wishes of a patient, where two registered medical practitioners so recommend (sections 2 and 3).

An accused person may be remanded to a hospital by order of the Crown Court or a magistrates' court for a report on his mental condition (section 35). The Crown Court, on the evidence of two registered medical practitioners, may remand an accused person to hospital for treatment (section 36). On conviction the Crown Court and magistrates' courts have power to commit the prisoner to a hospital (section 38) and in the case of the Crown Court to make a restriction order which prevents the prisoner (or patient) from being released except after an order of a Mental Health Review Tribunal or the Secretary of State (section 41). A restriction order can only be made where it appears to the Court that it is necessary for the protection of the public from serious harm in the light of the nature of the offence, the antecedents of the offender and the risk of his committing further offences if set at large. In the case of a prisoner serving a sentence of imprisonment the Secretary of State may on the advice of two registered medical practitioners direct that he be removed to a hospital (section 47).

24–030   A patient who believes that he is entitled to be discharged from a hospital where he is being detained may apply to a Mental Health Review Tribunal which has powers to order conditional or unconditional discharges of patients (sections 73 and 74 (restricted patients)).[57] The right of persons detained under the Mental Health Act 1983 to bring proceedings in relation to acts done under the legislation is curtailed by section 139. Subsection (1) provides that no one shall be liable for acts done under the Act on the ground of want of jurisdiction or any other ground unless the act was done in bad faith or without reasonable care. Any civil proceedings in relation to acts done under the mental health legislation require the leave of the High Court and criminal proceedings require the consent

---

[55] In *R. v. Broadmoor Special Hospital Authority, ex p. S and others*, DC, *The Times* November 5, 1997, it was accepted that a general power to conduct routine and random searches without consent of patients detained under the 1983 Act, was implied by the duty to maintain a safe and therapeutic environment. The precise policy had to satisfy the *Wednesbury* reasonableness test in each institution; it will also now have to satisfy in particular Article 5 E.C.H.R.

[56] Brenda M. Hoggett, *Mental Health Law* (4th ed., 1996). See *Reform of the Mental Health Act 1983*, Cm. 4480 (2000).

[57] The continued detention of a person found to be no longer suffering from mental illness, pending placement in a hostel, was held in *Johnson v. United Kingdom* (1999) 27 E.H.R.R. 296 to be a breach of Art. 5 E.C.H.R. See *R. (H) v. Mental Health Review Tribunal, North and East London Division* [2001] H.R.L.R. 752, where it was held that to require a patient to prove that he should no longer be detained was incompatible with Art. 5. A remedial order under the HRA (see para. 22–050) was made.

of the Director of Public Prosecutions except in the case of proceedings against the Secretary of State or a health authority.

The legality of detention under these sections is open to challenge by an application for a writ of habeas corpus or by an application for judicial review.

Detention following conviction[58]

"A convicted prisoner . . . retains all civil rights which are not taken away expressly or by necessary implication": *Raymond v. Honey*.[59] Examples of rights being taken away expressly are the right to vote (Representation of the People Act 1983, s.3(1)), disqualification of those imprisoned indefinitely or for more that one year from membership of the House of Commons (Representation of the People Act 1981, s.1), and those with recent or serious criminal convictions are disqualification from jury service (Juries Act 1974, s.1, Sched. 1, Part II).

24–031

A prisoner may be released before the end of the sentence laid down by the court which convicted him if the requirements of the Criminal Justice Act 1991, which provides arrangements for Parole Boards and the early release of prisoners, are satisfied.[60]

The right of which a prisoner is most obviously deprived is that of freedom of movement. Once sentenced he is liable to be detained in prison until the expiration of his sentence, subject to the control of the Secretary of State within the limits laid down by the Prison Act 1952 and the Prison Rules made under that Act. Section 12 gives the Secretary wide powers to commit prisoners to, and remove them from, such prisons as he may direct. Attempts to question the Home Secretary's wide powers of control with regard to the place of detention initially met with little success. An action claiming that the conditions of detention constituted false imprisonment failed in *Williams v. Home Office (No. 2)*[61] where Tudor Evans J. and, on appeal, Brightman L.J. expressed the view that, even if the detention were in breach of Prison Rules that would not in itself give rise to a cause of action. In *R. v. Secretary of State for the Home Department, ex p. McAvoy*,[62] Webster J. refused to interfere with a decision of the Home Secretary to remove the applicant, who was detained in custody pending trial, from one prison to another. The learned judge noted that although the power granted under section 12 was very wide, decisions under the section were "reviewable in principle" and the court could interfere if the Secretary of State could be shown to have misdirected himself in law. In *R. v. Deputy Governor of Parkhurst Prison ex p. Hague*[63] it was accepted that operational or managerial decisions affecting the transfer and segregation of prisoners were amenable to judicial review. It was also accepted that the broad terms of section 12 would always provide a complete answer to any claim for false imprisonment against the governor or anyone acting on his authority.

---

[58] See Livingstone and Owen, *Prison Law* (2nd ed., 1998).

[59] [1983] A.C. 1, 10, *per* Lord Wilberforce.

[60] The Crime (Sentences) Act 1997 makes changes to the early release provisions of the 1991 Act, but only a few of its provisions (those on prisoners sentenced to life imprisonment) have been brought into effect.

[61] [1981] 1 All E.R. 1211; [1982] 2 All E.R. 564, CA.

[62] [1984] 1 W.L.R. 1408.

[63] [1992] 1 A.C. 58, HL, 102, CA; see also *R. v. Home Secretary, ex p. Leech* [1994] Q.B. 198, CA.

24–032   Section 47 authorises the Secretary of State to make rules for "the classification, treatment, employment, discipline and control of" prisoners. The validity of such rules is open to challenge on the ground that they are *ultra vires, i.e.* beyond the limits of the power delegated to the minister by Parliament.[64] In *R. v. Secretary of State for the Home Department, ex p. Anderson*[65] a restriction on visits by a legal adviser to a prisoner contemplating legal proceedings in respect of complaints about treatment in prison which he had not also made through the internal prison procedure was held to be *ultra vires* because it conflicted with the right of unimpeded access to the courts, a right so fundamental that it could only be taken away by express language. As a result of this decision[66] and several decisions by the E.Ct.H.R.[67] the rules on prisoners' correspondence, lawyers' visits and written access to the courts were modified. In *R. v. Secretary of State for the Home Department ex p. Simms*[68] the House of Lords held that the Home Secretary's policy which indiscriminately banned oral interviews between prisoners and journalists was unlawful in so far as it undermined a prisoner's right of free speech. The Human Rights Act 1998 will enable the courts to consider a new ground of challenge to prison rules and administrative orders: incompatibility with the E.C.H.R.

The above are examples of how a change in judicial attitudes in the last 20 years,[69] both in the United Kingdom and in Strasburg, has had an effect on prison life. Further examples can be seen in the area of prison discipline[70] and the procedures for deciding on the release of mandatory and discretionary life sentence prisoners.[71] In other areas such as administration and prison management the courts have not intervened,[72] but changes have been made as a result of reports such as that by Lord Woolf. One of these was the establishment of the office of a Prisons Ombudsman in 1994. This officer is independent of the Prison Service and reports directly to the Home Secretary. His function is to investigate

---

[64] *post*, Chap. 32.

[65] [1984] Q.B. 778, DC.

[66] See too *R. v. Secretary of State for the Home Department, ex p. Leech* [1994] Q.B. 198, CA.

[67] *Golder v. UK* (1975) 1 E.H.R.R. 524; *Silver v. UK* (1980) 3 E.H.R.R. 475; *Campbell and Fell v. UK* (1985) 7 E.H.R.R. 165; [1984] P.L. 341; *Campbell v. UK* (1993) 15 E.H.R.R. 137.

[68] [2000] 2 A.C. 115. See also *R. v. Secretary of State for the Home Department, ex p. Daley* [2001] 2 W.L.R 1622, where the House of Lords held that a policy of examining prisoners' correspondence was in breach of Art. 8.

[69] Richardson and Sunkin, "Judicial Review: Questions of Impact" [1996] P.L. 79.

[70] In *R. v. Board of Visitors of Hull Prison, ex p. St Germain* [1979] Q.B. 425, CA, the Court of Appeal allowed judicial review of the disciplinary functions of the Board of Visitors (abolished in 1992). In *Leech v. Deputy Governor, Parkhurst Prison* [1988] 1 A.C. 533 the House of Lords accepted that judicial review could also apply to governor's disciplinary hearings. Partly as a consequence of these decisions, procedural changes were made to disciplinary hearings. The Woolf Report, *Prison Disturbances: April 1990*, Cm. 1456 (1991) resulted in further changes to prison discipline.

[71] *Weeks v. United Kingdom* (1988) 10 E.H.R.R. 293; *Thynne, Wilson and Gunnell v. United Kingdom* (1991) 13 E.H.R.R. 666; *Hussain v. United Kingdom (1996)* (1996) 22 E.H.R.R. 1. These decisions on the treatment of those subjects to a discretionary life sentence resulted in the Criminal Justice Act 1991. Decision of English courts in *R. v. Home Secretary, ex p. Doody and others* [1993] 1 All E.R. 577; *R. v. Home Secretary ex p. Pierson* [1997] 3 All E.R. 577; and *R. v. Home Secretary ex p. Thompson and Venables* [1997] 2 All E.R. 97 have had a similar result for those subject to a mandatory life sentence; see Crime (Sentences) Act 1997.

[72] It may be in the light of the Human Rights Act that judges will have to rethink this and be willing to undertake "a more searching judicial examination of the validity of prison regulations and practices." Livingstone and Owen, *Prison Law*, at p. 469.

complaints from prisoners and make recommendations to the Director General of the Prison Service.

Detention under the Immigration Act 1971[73]

The majority of those so detained are held in Immigration Detention Centres, but a substantial minority, mainly asylum seekers are in prison service establishments. The powers to detain apply both on arrival in the United Kingdom and after a person has spent some time there. The 1971 Act does not provide any time limit for detention, but it was said in *R. v. Governor of Durham Prison, ex p. Singh*[74] to be limited to the period reasonably necessary for the purpose for which it is given. Prolonged detention could be in breach of Article 5(1)(f) of the E.C.H.R. The procedure for review of detention is complex, and it has been doubted whether the law conforms with Article 5(4) of the E.C.H.R.[75]

24–033

Writ of habeas corpus[76]

The legality of any form of detention may be challenged at common law by an application for the writ of habeas corpus. In origin this writ, which is found in Edward I's reign, was merely a command by the court to someone to bring before itself persons whose presence was necessary to some judicial proceedings. In other words, it was "originally intended not to get people out of prison but to put them in it."[77] Habeas corpus[78] was a "prerogative" writ, that is, one issued by the King against his officers to compel them to exercise their functions properly. In the form habeas corpus *ad subjiciendum* (the form now commonly used)[79] it came to be available, under certain conditions, to private individuals. In the seventeenth century members of the parliamentary opposition imprisoned by command of the King availed themselves of the writ to seek release (*e.g.* Darnel's Case),[80] and it is from this application that originated its constitutional importance as the classic common law guarantee of personal liberty. The practical importance of habeas corpus as providing a speedy judicial remedy for the determination of an applicant's claim to freedom has been asserted frequently by judges and writers.[81] Nonetheless, the effectiveness of the remedy depends in many instances on the width of the statutory power under which a public authority may be acting and the willingness of the courts to examine the legality of decisions made in reliance on wide-ranging statutory provisions.[82] It has been

24–034

---

[73] As amended by the Immigration and Asylum Act 1999.

[74] [1984] 1 W.L.R. 704.

[75] Livingstone and Owen, *op. cit.* at p. 442. This remains the case even after the reform of the appeals system by Part IV of the Immigration and Asylum Act 1999.

[76] See R. J. Sharpe, *The Law of Habeas Corpus* (Oxford, 1976). William F. Duker, *A Constitutional History of Habeas Corpus* (1982); D. Clark and G. McCoy, *The Most Fundamental Right* (2000).

[77] Jenks, "The Story of Habeas Corpus," (1902) 18 L.Q.R. 64, 65.

[78] Habeas corpus = have (*i.e.* bring) the body [of X before the court].

[79] For a decision on the form *ad respondendum* see *R. v. Governor of Brixton Prison, ex p. Walsh* [1985] A.C. 154, HL.

[80] (1627) *The Five Knights' Case*, 3 St.Tr. 1; Holdsworth, *History of English Law*, Vol. VI, pp. 32–37. The Petition of Right 1627 declared that the orders of the Sovereign were not to be sufficient justification for the imprisonment of his subjects.

[81] *Greene v. Secretary of State for Home Affairs* [1942] A.C. 284, 302 *per* Lord Wright, quoted in *Phillip v. D.P.P. of Trinidad and Tobago* [1992] 1 A.C. 545 at PC 558 *per* Lord Ackner; Dicey, *The Law and the Constitution*, p. 199. "Probably the most sacred cow in the British Constitution"; *Linnet v. Coles* [1987] Q.B. 555 at 561 *per* Lawton L.J.

[82] De Smith, Woolf and Jowell, *Judicial Review of Administrative Action* (5th ed. 1995) p. 248. For the future, the courts' powers of intervention may be increased by reliance on Art. 5 of the E.C.H.R

suggested that the need for the "blunter remedy" of habeas corpus has diminished as judicial review has developed into an ever more flexible jurisdiction.[83] Procedural reform of the writ may be appropriate[84] but it is important not to lose sight of substantive differences between habeas corpus and remedies under judicial review. The latter are discretionary and the court may refuse relief on practical grounds[85]; habeas corpus is a writ of right, granted *ex debito justitiae*.[86]

Habeas corpus is available against any person who is suspected of detaining another unlawfully, and not merely against prison governors, the police or other public officers whose duties normally include arrest and detention. Habeas corpus was used in the eighteenth and early nineteenth centuries to set free slaves brought into this country by their owners, or who had escaped for protection to British warships, during the period when slavery was still lawful in parts of the British Empire and in other countries.[87] Habeas corpus is available to question detention by the police,[88] detention pending deportation[89] and for breach of immigration regulations,[90] and also during proceedings under legislation relating to extradition[91] and fugitive offenders.[92] It is also available to challenge the legality of detention under Mental Health legislation.[93] Two areas of uncertainty are detention by order of the House of Commons,[94] and decisions of military courts in times of martial law.[95]

For constitutional purposes the special significance of this remedy is that it is available against Crown servants acting in the name of the Crown.[96] Thus in *Home Secretary v. O'Brien*[97] the writ was issued against the Home Secretary,

---

[83] *R. v. Oldham Justices ex p. Cawley* [1997] Q.B. 1 at 16 DC *per* Simon Brown L.J. See too *R. v. Secretary of State for the Home Department ex p. Cheblak* [1991] 1 W.L.R. 890, CA; *R. v. Secretary of State for the Home Department ex p. Muboyayi* [1992] Q.B. 244; A. P. Le Sueur, "Should the Writ of Habeas Corpus be Abolished?" [1992] P.L. 13; M. Shrimpton, "In Defence of Habeas Corpus" [1993] P.L. 24; Simon Brown L.J., "Habeas Corpus—A New Chapter" [2000] P.L. 31.

[84] Law. Com. No. 226 (1994) Part XI.

[85] See Chap. 32.

[86] *Phillip v. D.P.P. of Trinidad and Tobago* [1992] 1 A.C. 545, PC.

[87] *Somersett v. Steuart* (1772) 20 St.Tr. 1 (Lord Mansfield C.J.): Somersett was later appointed wharfmaster of the new settlement of Sierra Leone (E. Fiddes in (1934) 50 L.Q.R. 1, 459); *Forbes v. Cochrane* (1824) 2 B. & C. 448; *The Slave Grace* (1827) 2 Hag.Adm. 94 (Lord Stowell); *cf. Hottentot Venus' Case* (1810) 13 East 195.

[88] *R. v. Holmes, ex p. Sherman* [1981] 2 All E.R. 612.

[89] *R. v. Home Secretary, ex p. Soblen* [1963] 1 Q.B. 829, CA; *R. v. Durham Prison Governor, ex p. Singh*, [1984] 1 W.L.R. 704; *R. v. Secretary of State for the Home Department ex p. Cheblak* [191] 1 W.L.R. 890.

[90] *R. v. Governor of Brixton Prison, ex p. Ahsan* [1969] 2 Q.B. 222, DC; *R. v. Governor of Richmond Remand Centre, ex p. Ashgar* [1971] 1 W.L.R. 129, DC; *R. v. Governor of Risley Remand Centre, ex p. Hassan* [1976] 1 W.L.R. 971, DC.

[91] *Re Castioni* [1891] 1 Q.B. 149; *R. v. Governor of Brixton Prison, ex p. Cabon-Waterfield* [1960] 2 Q.B. 498, DC; *Re Schmidt* [1995] 1 A.C. 339, HL.

[92] *R. v. Brixton Prison Governor, ex p. Naranjan Singh* [1962] 1 Q.B. 211, DC; *R. v. Brixton Prison Governor, ex p. Sadri* [1962] 1 W.L.R. 1304, DC; *Zacharia v. Republic of Cyprus* [1963] A.C. 634, HL; *R. v. Governor of Pentonville Prison ex p. Osman (No. 3)* [1990] 1 All E.R. 999.

[93] *R. v. Board of Control, ex p. Rutty* [1956] 2 Q.B. 109; *R. v. Managers of South Western Hospital ex p. M* [1993] Q.B. 683; *Re S.-C. (Mental Patient: Habeas Corpus)* [1996] Q.B. 599, CA; *R. v. Bournwood Community and Mental Health N.H.S. Trust ex p. L* [1999] 1 A.C. 458, HL.

[94] *ante* Chap. 13.

[95] *ante*, para. 19–033.

[96] *cf.* Mandamus which is not available against the Crown or a servant of the Crown to enforce a duty owed to the Crown: *post* para. 32–008: injunction and specific performance not available; Crown Proceedings Act 1947, s.21(1); *post*, para. 33–017.

[97] [1923] A.C. 603, HL.

who had ordered the detention of an Irishman in England during the Irish "troubles."

Habeas corpus cannot be granted to a person who is serving a sentence passed by a court of competent jurisdiction,[98] unless, probably, the Divisional Court is satisfied that the prisoner is being detained after the term of his sentence has expired.[99] The Divisional Court does not sit as a court of appeal on an application for habeas corpus, and it will not rehear matters decided by the judicial authority,[1] but it may consider whether that judicial authority had any evidence which would justify its assumption of jurisdiction.[2]

Habeas Corpus Act 1679

The passing of this Act, followed the case of Jenkes[3] who, after being arrested **24–035** for delivering a speech urging the summoning of Parliament, was kept in prison for several months without bail. The Act applied only to persons imprisoned (not after conviction by a court) for "criminal or supposed criminal matters". If the applicant showed that there was any ground for supposing that the prisoner was wrongfully imprisoned, the writ would be issued requiring the person detaining the prisoner to bring him before the court and to inform it of the grounds of his detention. If it is appeared that the prisoner was confined without lawful authority, the court would release him; otherwise it would release him on bail, or make provision for his speedy trial.

The Habeas Corpus Act 1679 imposed heavy penalties for not making due returns to the writ, not delivering to the prisoner promptly a true copy of the warrant of commitment, or shifting the custody of the prisoner from one place to another, or sending prisoners out of England. The obligation to hear applications for habeas corpus was laid on the Lord Chancellor and judges of the King's Bench, Common Pleas, Exchequer and Chancery. It appears that under section 9, judges of the Supreme Court are still liable to a penalty of £500 for wrongfully refusing to issue a writ of habeas corpus in the case of a person in custody on a criminal charge, but it is uncertain whether this applies only in vacation.

Habeas Corpus Act 1816

This Act provided that the Act of 1679 (with certain improvements) should **24–036** extend to detention otherwise than on a charge of crime.[4] The judges were required, on complaint made to them by or on behalf of the person in custody showing a prima facie ground for the complaint, to issue a writ of habeas corpus *ad subjiciendum*; and in cases to which the Act applied they might inquire into the truth of the return to the writ. Any person disobeying a writ sued out under this Act is guilty of contempt of court and becomes liable to imprisonment.

---

[98] *Re Wring, Re Cook* (Practice Note) [1960] 1 W.L.R. 138, DC. For a recent illustration see *R. v. Oldham Justices ex p. Cawley* [1997] Q.B. 1, DC.

[99] *Re Featherstone* (1953) 37 Cr.App.R. 146, *per* Lord Goddard C.J.

[1] *Ex p. Hinds* [1961] 1 W.L.R. 325, DC; affirmed by the House of Lords in *Re Hinds, The Times*, February 15, 1961.

[2] *R. v. Board of Control, ex p. Rutty* [1956] 2 Q.B. 109.

[3] (1676) 6 St.Tr. 1190. For an account of the passing of this Act, see Holdsworth, *History of English Law*, Vol. IX, pp. 112–117. The Bill is said by Bishop Burnett to have been saved at one stage by a teller counting one fat peer as ten.

[4] Except in the case of persons imprisoned for debt or on process in a civil action. These kinds of imprisonment (except for certain debts due to the Crown and judgment debts where the debtor has had the money to pay) were abolished by the Debtors Act 1869.

Lord Scarman, in *R. v. Home Secretary, ex p. Khawaja*[5] referred to "The great statute of 1816" which, he said, was "the beginning of the modern jurisprudence the effect of which" is that the courts will determine for themselves the existence of the facts which the executive cites as justifying its decision, for example that a person detained is an illegal immigrant.

Modern procedure on habeas corpus

24–037   Habeas corpus is a writ of right, but not of course, that is a prima facie case must be shown before it will issue. Otherwise as Lord Goddard C.J. said, all the prisoners of England could delay or even defeat justice.[6] It will not be refused *merely* because another remedy is available.[7] No application will be heard in person save for some exceptional reason.[8] The procedure is governed by schedule 1 of the Civil Procedure Rules which gives continuing effect to the provisions of the former Order 54 of the Rules of the Supreme Court.

Proceedings in criminal causes or matters are generally heard by a Divisional Court of the Queen's Bench Division; in civil cases by a single judge. Exceptionally, application may be made to a single judge of any division in court. In vacation, or at any time when no judge is sitting in court (*e.g.* at weekends or at night), application may be made to a judge sitting otherwise than in court, *e.g.* in vacation to a judge in chambers; at other times in an emergency, anywhere.[9] Application is to be *ex parte* (*i.e.* without notice to the other side) in the first instance, and on affidavit. The affidavit is made by the person restrained, or by someone on his behalf if he is incapable, setting out the nature of the restraint. The application is usually adjourned in order that notice may be given to the respondent. On the hearing of the application the court or judge may order that the person restrained be released. Such order is a sufficient warrant for his release, so that there is no need to issue the actual writ.

There is still power to order the immediate issue of the writ,[10] though this is rarely done. Where the writ is issued it is accompanied by a notice that in default of obedience proceedings for contempt of court against the party disobeying will be taken. The return to the writ must contain a copy of all the causes of the prisoner's detention. Argument then takes place on the return to the writ.

The Administration of Justice Act 1960, s.14, provides that on a criminal application for habeas corpus an order for release may be refused only by a Divisional Court of the Queen's Bench Division, even where the original application is made to a single judge, *e.g.* in vacation.

Habeas corpus is a remedy designed to facilitate the release of persons detained unlawfully, not to punish the person detaining and it is not, therefore,

---

[5] [1984] A.C. 74, HL. See *R. v. Brixton Prison Governor, ex p. Ahsan* [1969] 2 Q.B. 222, DC; *Re Shahid Iqbal* [1979] Q.B. 264, DC; [1979] 1 W.L.R. 425, CA; *Re Quigley* [1983] N.I. 245.
[6] *Re Corke* [1954] 1 W.L.R. 899.
[7] *Quigley v. Chief Constable, Royal Ulster Constabulary* [1983] N.I. 238, 239, *per* Lord Lowry, L.C.J. Dicta suggesting a discretion in the court to refuse the writ are to be found in *Re Keenan* [1972] 1 Q.B. 533, CA.
[8] *Re Greene* (1941) 57 T.L.R. 533. For informal applications by prisoners, see *Re Wring, Re Cook* [1960] 1 All E.R. 536 *per* Lord Parker C.J.; C. Drewry, S. Hughes and A. Shaw, "Informal Applications for the Writ of Habeas Corpus" [1977] P.L. 149.
[9] In the *Soblen* case, application was made to the chambers judge at his home in the middle of the night, and the order signed on the dining-room table: *R. v. Home Secretary, ex p. Soblen, The Times*, July 27, 1962.
[10] Even on an *ex parte* application.

issued after the detention complained of has come to an end: *Barnardo v. Ford.*[11]

Usually the question at issue is the legality of an admitted detention but the writ is available where it is the fact of detention that is in dispute: *Quigley v. Chief Constable, Royal Ulster Constabulary.*[12]

Successive applications

Before 1876 an application for habeas corpus could be made to each of the Courts of Queen's Bench, Common Pleas, Exchequer and Chancery.[13] After the Judicature Acts 1873–75 had amalgamated these courts into one High Court, there were dicta in the House of Lords and the Privy Council to the effect that Parliament could not have intended impliedly to restrict the rights of the subject in the vital matter of personal liberty, and that there was therefore a right to apply not only to each Division of the High Court but to each High Court judge individually.[14] In *Re Hastings*,[15] however, a series of decisions showed that two differently constituted Queen's Bench Divisional Courts, as well as the Chancery Division, were all parts of the same High Court for this as for other purposes, and therefore the decision of any one Division was the decision of the whole court.

24–038

The Administration of Justice Act 1960, s.14, now provides that no second criminal or civil application may be made on the same grounds, whether to the same or any other court or judge, unless fresh evidence is adduced[16]; and no such application may be made in any case to the Lord Chancellor. Whether successive applications may be made in vacation is still not certain.[17]

Appeal

An incidental effect of the Judicature Acts 1873–75 was that in non-criminal matters the persons detained might appeal to the Court of Appeal and thence to the House of Lords against a refusal to issue the writ or to discharge him under the writ.[18] On the other hand, a prisoner had no appeal against refusal to issue the writ in a criminal cause or matter, *i.e.* a matter of which the direct outcome might be his trial and possible punishment for an illegal act by a court claiming jurisdiction in that regard (*Amand v. Home Secretary and Minister of Defence of the Royal Netherlands Government*[19]). The person detaining had no appeal

24–039

---

[11] [1892] A.C. 326, HL; *Re Nicola Raine, The Times*, May 5, 1982, DC.

[12] [1983] N.I. 238. See subsequently, *Re Quigley* [1983] N.I. 245. (Was Mrs Quigley detained at a secret address against her will by the R.U.C., or was she willingly living under police protection to avoid intimidation by terrorists).

[13] Lord Goddard. "A Note on Habeas Corpus", (1949) 65 L.Q.R. 30; *cf.* D. M. Gordon, "The Unruly Writ of Habeas Corpus", (1963) 26 M.L.R. 520.

[14] *Cox v. Hakes* (1890) 15 App.Cas. 506, HL, *per* Lord Halsbury L.C.; *Eshugbayi (Eleko) v. Government of Nigeria (Officer Administering)* [1928] A.C. 459, PC, *per* Lord Hailsham L.C.; and see [1931] A.C. 662; *Home Secretary v. O'Brien* [1923] A.C. 603, HL, *per* Lord Birkenhead L.C. These dicta were disapproved *obiter* by the Irish Supreme Court in *The State (Dowling) v. Kingston (No. 2)* [1937] I.R. 699; see R. F. V. Heuston, "Habeas Corpus Procedure" (1950) 66 L.Q.R. 79.

[15] *Re Hastings (No. 1)* [1958] 1 W.L.R. 372, DC; *(No. 2)* [1959] 1 Q.B. 358, DC; *(No. 3)* [1959] 1 All E.R. 698, DC; [1959] Ch. 368, CA.

[16] The ingenuity of Mr Osman, detained under the Fugitive Offenders Act 1967, enabled him nonetheless to bring nine applications for the writ.

[17] Heuston, *Essays in Constitutional Law* (2nd ed. 1964), p. 127.

[18] *ex p. Woodhall* (1888) 20 Q.B.D. 832, CA; see *per* Lindley L.J. at p. 838.

[19] [1943] A.C. 147, HL, *per* Viscount Simon L.C.

against an order of the High Court discharging a prisoner from custody under the writ of habeas corpus (*Cox v. Hakes*[20]).

The Administration of Justice Act 1960, s.15, provides that an appeal shall lie in criminal as well as civil applications for habeas corpus, and that the appeal may be brought against an order for release as well as against the refusal of such an order.[21] In civil cases appeal lies through the Court of Appeal to the House of Lords. In criminal cases the appeal lies direct from the Divisional Court to the House of Lords.[22]

A Divisional Court which has granted an application for habeas corpus in a criminal case can order the applicant's detention or release on bail pending an appeal; but if no such order is made (*i.e.* if he has been released without bail) he may not be detained again if the appeal in the House of Lords goes against him. Where an application for habeas corpus has been granted in a civil case, the applicant may not in any event be detained again if the appeal goes against him, the right of appeal in such cases being to enable questions of law to be settled by the House of Lords.

Habeas Corpus to places overseas

24–040   The old rule, as stated by Lord Mansfield, was that a writ of habeas corpus could be issued out of England to any part of the dominions of the King of England. The writ did not lie to Scotland or the Electorate of Hanover.[23] It did, however, lie to the Isle of Man[24] and the Channel Islands.[25]

The Habeas Corpus Act 1862,[26] provides that no writ of habeas corpus shall issue out of England into any "colony or foreign dominion of the Crown" where a court has been established with authority to issue the writ and to ensure due execution thereof.[27] English Courts have no jurisdiction to issue habeas corpus on behalf of persons detained in Northern Ireland. In *Re Keenan*[28] the Court of Appeal held that the effect of the Habeas Corpus Act (Ireland) 1782 was to confer exclusive jurisdiction on the Irish Courts and nothing in the subsequent constitutional history of Ireland had affected that position.

It is doubtful whether habeas corpus can be issued to bring before the Queen's Bench Division an alien in a British ship on the high seas.[29]

---

[20] (1890) 15 App.Cas. 506, HL.

[21] See *e.g. R. v. Metropolitan Police Commissioner, ex p. Hammond* [1965] A.C. 810, HL.

[22] Administration of Justice Act 1960, s.1.

[23] *R. v. Cowle* (1759) 2 Burr., 834, 855–856.

[24] *Re Crawford* (1849) 13 Q.B. 613.

[25] *Carus Wilson's Case* (1845) 7 Q.B. 984.

[26] The Act was passed as a result of the case of *ex p. Anderson* (1861) 3 El & El 487 in which the British and Foreign Anti-Slavery Committee successfully applied to the Court of Queen's Bench for habeas corpus on behalf of Anderson, a negro slave who, after killing Seneca T. P. Diggs in defence of his freedom, had escaped from the United States into the colony of Upper Canada where he was arrested. The court, however, indicated that it thought the issue of the writ to a self-governing colony was inconvenient, unnecessary and *infra dignitatem*. (In subsequent proceedings in Canada it was held that there was no evidence for a charge of murder according to the law of Canada: hence the attempt to extradite him to the United States failed.) For a full account of the facts see Annual Register, 1861, pp. 520–528.

[27] The meaning of the Act is far from clear; see, for example, *ex parte Mwenya* [1960] 1 Q.B. 214 and notes in (1960) 76 L.Q.R. 25; (1960) 76 L.Q.R. 211.

[28] [1972] 1 Q.B. 533. *cf.* D. E. C. Yale, "Habeas Corpus—Ireland—jurisdiction," (1972) 30 C.L.J. 4.

[29] *R. v. Secretary of State for Foreign Affairs, ex p. Greenberg* [1947] 2 All E.R. 550.

II. FREEDOM OF PROPERTY

The Englishman's castle

In the absence of a legal right to privacy in British law, the prevention and **24–041**
regulation of state interference with a person's possessions and private life at
common law has been on the basis of the protection of property rights; the
Human Rights Act 1998 will cause this to change. "The house of every one is to
him as is his castle and fortress, as well for his defence against injury and
violence, as for his repose," it was said in *Seymayne's Case*[30]: "if thieves come
to a man's house to rob him, or murder him, and the owner or his servants kill
any of the thieves in defence of himself and his house, it is not felony, and he
shall lose nothing. So it is held every one may assemble his friends and
neighbours to defend his house against violence . . . because *domus sua cuique
est tutissimum refugium*." "By the laws of England," said Lord Camden C.J. in
Entick v. Carrington,[31] "every invasion of private property, be it ever so minute,
is a trespass. No man can set his foot upon my ground without my licence. . . .
If he admits the fact, he is bound to show by way of justification, that some
positive law has empowered or excused him." More recently Donaldson L.J. has
said, "That 'An Englishman's home is his castle' is one of the few principles of
law known to every citizen and was affirmed as early as 1604 in *Seymayne's Case*
. . . and reaffirmed as recently as 1980 in *Morris v. Beardmore* [1981] A.C. 446.
The rule is, of course, subject to exceptions, but they are few and it is for the
police to justify a forcible entry."[32] In *O'Loughlin v. Chief Constable of Essex*[33]
the Court of Appeal stated that the principle required police officers who wished
to *use to* enter premises by virtue of section 17 of the PACE Act, to first inform
the occupier of the correct legal reason why entry was required, before being
entitled to use force to obtain entry.[34]

Prior to the Human Rights Act, an action for trespass was the remedy for
unlawful police interference; the police had to justify the entry after the event.
The Human Rights Act will in effect require the police before entry to be satisfied
that there is a legal power to do so. In *R. v. Khan*[35] the House of Lords accepted
that police had trespassed to enable them to install a listening devise to record a
conversation between the defendant and another person. In installing such a
devise the police had complied with non-statutory Home Office guidelines, and
the House of Lords accepted that the trial judge had been right not to exclude the
evidence so obtained, despite probable breaches of Article 8. The E.Ct.H.R.
found that Article 8 had been breached, since in the absence of a statutory
scheme to regulate such activities, the interference with the applicant's right to
respect for his private life was not in accordance with the law; however he had
not been deprived of his right to a fair trial.[36] In anticipation of this decision, the

[30] (1603) 5 Co.Rep. 91, 91b. The maximum was anticipated by Staunford, Plees del Coron (1567)
"ma meason est a moy come mon castel." *Cf.* D.2.4.21: *de domo sua nemo extrahi debet.* "A man's
home is looked upon as his castle"; Hawkins, *Pleas of the Crown*, Bk 1. C. 28, s.10; quoted by Cave
J. in *Beatty v. Gillbanks* (1882) 15 Cox C.C. 138.
[31] (1765) 19 St.Tr. 1029, 1066.
[32] *McLorie v. Oxford* [1982] Q.B. 1290.
[33] [1998] 1 W.L.R. 374.
[34] Unless the circumstances made this impossible, impracticable or undesirable.
[35] [1997] A.C. 558.
[36] [2000] Crim.L.R. 684. This aspect of the decision was surprising since the evidence obtained
through the listening devise was the sole or main evidence against the applicant.

Police Act 1997 Part III[37] established a statutory system with respect to types of police surveillance involving unlawful conduct. Judicial supervision is required before warrants in respect of certain categories of crime only (sections 91 and 97); the absence of such supervision for all categories of crime could amount to a breach of Article 8 E.C.H.R.

24–042   Article 8 is of particular application to powers of entry, search and seizure. However, the lengthy list of limitations to this right in Article 8(2) means that a challenge to such powers will be difficult, provided that the exercise of a power is proportionate to its purpose.

Trespass, even to a dwelling house, is not a crime at common law; however by statute it may be a crime in certain circumstances.[38] The Criminal Law Act 1977[39] makes it an offence for a person (not being a displaced residential occupier or a protected intending occupier[40]) without lawful authority to use or threaten violence for the purpose of securing entry into premises on which to his knowledge someone is present who is opposed to the entry (section 6). Section 7, dealing with adverse occupation of residential premises, affects squatters. A person who is on premises as a trespasser, after having entered as a trespasser, is guilty of an offence if he fails to leave the premises on being required to do so by or on behalf of a displaced residential occupier or a protected intending occupier. The purpose of section 7 is to give a residential occupier or an intended residential occupier a faster means of recovering his premises from trespassers than by the use of a civil remedy. It is also an offence to trespass on premises with a weapon of offence (section 8) and to enter or to be on premises of a diplomatic or consular mission as a trespasser (section 9).

Police Powers of entry and search[41]

24–043   The powers of police officers to enter premises to arrest or search are governed by statute. Part II of the PACE Act lays down general rules while various statutes confer specific powers in particular circumstances. Code of Practice B provides additional guidance on search and seizure. There is no COP governing the entry of premises by police, but the Court of Appeal has applied, by analogy, COP B to entry.[42]

The PACE Act abolished common law powers to enter premises without a warrant with the exception of any power of entry to deal with or prevent a breach of peace (section 17(5) and (6)). Before exercising this power of entry the police must have a genuine belief that there is a "real and imminent risk of a breach of the peace occurring", but the breach need not be of a particular type.[43] The power

---

[37] As amended by the Regulation of Investigatory Powers Act 2000 *post*, Chap. 26.
[38] See *post* para. 27–014 for discussion of s.61 of the Criminal Justice and Public Order Act 1994. Trespass may also be a criminal offence by virtue of byelaws made, for example, by the British Railways Board: Transport Act 1962, s.67 (as amended).
[39] As amended or substituted by ss.72–74 of the CJPO Act 1994.
[40] As defined by s.12A of the 1977 Act, which includes an owner or tenant who requires the premises for his own residential occupation, *e.g.* a recent purchaser, a person who has been authorised to occupy a council house, or a returning holiday-maker.
[41] R. Stone, *Entry Search and Seizure* (3rd ed., 1997).
[42] *O'Loughlin v. Chief Constable of Essex* [1998] 1 W.L.R. 374.
[43] *McLeod v. Metropolitan Police Commissioner* [1994] 4 All E.R. 553, CA. In *McLeod v. United Kingdom* (1999) 27 E.H.R.R. the E.Ct.H.R. accepted that the power to enter to prevent a breach of the peace was sufficiently accessible and foreseeable in English law but, on the facts, the actions of the police were disproportionate to the legitimate aim of keeping the peace and therefore there was a breach of Art. 8.

of entry applies not only to public meetings on private premises, as established in *Thomas v. Sawkins*,[44] but also to private residences.[45]

Section 17 of the PACE Act authorises a constable to enter (if necessary using reasonable force, section 117) and search any premises for the purpose of (i) executing a warrant of arrest issued in connection with or arising out of criminal proceedings; (ii) arresting a person for an arrestable offence; (iii) arresting a person for certain statutory public order offences or sections 6 to 8 or 10 of the Criminal Law Act 1977; (iv) recapturing a person unlawfully at large whom he is pursuing[46]; or (v) saving life or limb or preventing serious damage to property. Except in the case of (v) the constable must have reasonable grounds for believing that the person he is seeking is on the premises. The power of search conferred by section 17 is only a power to the extent that is reasonably required for the purpose for which the power of entry is exercised (section 17(4)).

The powers conferred by the section are without prejudice to any existing under other statutes. Various Acts confer specific powers of entry to ensure that their terms are being complied with. The Misuse of Drugs Act 1971, s.23(1) for example empowers police to enter the premises of producers and suppliers of controlled drugs and examine books and documents relating to dealings in such drugs and inspect stocks of such drugs.[47]

Entry and search after arrest

Where a person has been arrested for an arrestable offence away from his own **24–044** premises, then section 18(1)(a) allows a constable to enter and search any premises[48] occupied by or controlled by the person arrested.[49] The constable must have reasonable grounds for suspecting that there is on the premises evidence other than items subject to legal privilege[50] that relates to the offence for which the person has been arrested or to some other arrestable offence "connected with or similar to that offence" (section 1(8)(b). Anything which the constable is entitled to search for may, if found, be seized and retained. The power (as in section 17) is exercisable only to the extent reasonably required for the purpose of the section. As a general rule a search under section 18 must be authorised in writing by an officer of the rank of inspector or above. A constable may, however, search without authorisation before taking a person to a police station "if the presence of that person at a place other than a police station is necessary for the effective investigation of the offence" (section 18(5)(b). Whatever the exact meaning of these words they seem to confer a power to search if the constable thinks it necessary.

Section 32 deals with the power to search the premises which were either the venue of the arrest or from where the suspect had left shortly before being

[44] [1935] 2 K.B. 249.

[45] *McLeod v. M.P.C. op. cit.*

[46] In *D'Souza v. D.P.P.* [1992] 4 All E.R. 545, the House of Lords held that there had to be evidence of actual pursuit by the police of a person unlawfully at large before they could enter premises under s.17(1)(b). In this case the person concerned had left a psychiatric hospital; in the case of escaped convicts it is arguable that they are regarded as being pursued at all times.

[47] See also Gaming Act 1968, s.43(2); Road Traffic Act 1988, s.6; Deer Act 1991 s.12.

[48] Defined in s.23 to include "any place".

[49] This is in addition to the common law powers to enter and search: *Cowan v. Condon* [2000] 1 W.L.R. 254, CA.

[50] Defined in s.10 to mean communications between a professional legal adviser and his client and items enclosed with or referred to in such communications when in the possession of a person entitled to possession of them but not including items held with the intention of furthering a criminal purpose.

arrested. A search may only be made for evidence relating to the offence for which the suspect was arrested (section 32(2)(b)), and only to the "extent that it is reasonably required for the purpose of discovering . . . such evidence" (section 32(3)), and the police officer must have reasonable grounds for believing that there is relevant evidence on the premises (section 32(6)).[51]

Seizure of articles[52]

24–045   Section 18(2) allows the police to seize anything for which they are entitled to search under that section. Section 19 confers a wide power to seize articles found by a constable who is lawfully on premises.[53] It is not necessary that they relate to the offences for which the owner or occupier has been arrested, or other or similar offences committed by the owner or occupier or that they implicate third parties in the offence for which the search was being conducted. Any article (other than one protected by legal privilege, section 19(6)) may be seized if the constable has reasonable grounds for believing that it has been obtained in consequence of the commission of an offence or that it is evidence in relation to an offence which he is investigating or any other offence. In both cases the right to seize is conditional on a belief that seizure is necessary to prevent the item being concealed, lost, altered or destroyed or (in the case of articles in the first category) damaged.

Section 21 provides in the case of articles seized under any of the provisions of the PACE Act or any other enactment, the right to be furnished with details of articles seized and subsequent access to them, under police supervision, and/or photocopies or copies of the article. Section 22 recognises and regulates the right of police to retain for as long as necessary articles which they have seized.

Search Warrants

24–046   It is a principle of the common law that a general warrant to search premises, *i.e.* one in which either the person or the property is not specified is illegal; any invasion of property without a legal power is trespass.[54] At common law the only type of warrant that could be issued was to search for stolen goods. Gradually there was a piecemeal development of statutory warrant powers to allow for warrants to be obtained from magistrates to search for prohibited goods such as dangerous drugs, stolen goods, forged documents, firearms, etc., and to search for evidence of specific statutory offences such as criminal damage, breaches of the Official Secrets Act and illegal gaming. However before the PACE Act there were no general statutory provisions governing the grant of search warrants.

The pre-existing statutory powers to obtain a search warrant remain *post* the PACE Act. Section 8 of the PACE Act entitles a justice of the peace to grant a

---

[51] Further requirements for a search under s.32 are found in COP B, para. 5. Despite the wide statutory powers to search it has been estimated that more that half of all searches are conducted by the police with the consent of the person entitled to grant entry to the premises; COP B, para. 4 provides guidance on this. Where entry is by consent the legal controls laid down by PACE can be by-passed.

[52] See also COP B, para. 6, and s.51 CJP Act 2001; see below para. 24–046.

[53] Even if the search and therefore the seizure is unlawful, the articles may still be admissible in evidence, subject to s.78 PACE. See below para. 24–046 for additional powers to seize provided by the CJP Act 2001.

[54] *Wilkes v. Wood* (1763) 19 St.Tr. 1153, where John Wilkes recovered £1,000 damages for trespass against Wood, an Under-Secretary of State, for entering his house and seizing his papers under a warrant to arrest the (unnamed) authors, printers and publishers of No. 45 of the North Briton. See also *Entick v. Carrington* (1765) 19 St.Tr. 1029 where Lord Camden L.J. delivered a powerful judgment against the legality of general warrants.

search warrant on the application of a constable when the justice is satisfied that there are reasonable grounds for believing that a serious arrestable offence[55] has been committed and that there is material on the premises described in the application which is likely to be of substantial value to the investigation of the offence. The material must be likely to be relevant evidence (*i.e.* legally admissible) and not consist of items subject to legal privilege, excluded materials or special procedure material. The magistrate must also be satisfied that it is not practicable to communicate with any person entitled to grant entry to the premises; or that, if practicable it is not practicable to communicate with any person entitled to grant access to evidence; or that entry to the premises will not be granted unless a warrant is produced; or that the purpose of a search may be frustrated or seriously prejudiced unless a constable arriving at the premises can secure immediate entry.[56] It is important that the magistrate is satisfied that the requirements of section 8 have been fulfilled, if not he should not issue the warrant.[57] A constable may seize and retain anything for which a search has been authorised under section 8. In *R. v. Chesterfield Justices ex p. Bramley*[58] it was held that the police could not seize a large collection of material to sift through it elsewhere to decide if some material within that collection came within the scope of the search warrant.[59] The law was changed by the CJP Act 2001. This allows the police, and other law enforcement agencies, to remove material from premises when it is not "reasonable practicable" to determine on the premises whether the material concerned could lawfully be seized. The power extends to the seizure and removal of computer discs and hard drives.

Three types of materials are expressly excluded from the power to obtain a **24–047** search warrant under section 8. The scope of items subject to legal privilege is defined in section 10.[60] Items held with the intention of furthering a criminal purpose are not subject to legal privilege (section 10(2)), the "intention" can be that of a client or a third party.[61] Excluded material is defined in section 11. It includes personal records acquired in the course of any business or occupation which are held in confidence, medical samples taken for medical purposes held in confidence and journalistic materials held in confidence. Special procedure material is, in effect, confidential papers which fall outside the scope of excluded materials because they are not personal records as defined in section 12 and journalistic material not held in confidence. Into the latter category would fall, for example, photographs taken by newspaper photographers during riots. Section 9 and schedule 1 allow the police to apply to a circuit judge to authorise access to

---

[55] s.116.
[56] s.8(3) of PACE Act.
[57] In *R. v. Guildhall Magistrates' Court, ex p. Primlaks Holding Co* [1989] 2 W.L.R. 841, the Divisional Court quashed two warrants on the basis that there were no grounds upon which the magistrate, properly directing himself, could reasonably have believed that the correspondence cited in the warrant, was neither subject to legal privilege nor special procedure material.
[58] [2000] Q.B. 576.
[59] Pt 2 and Scheds. 1 and 2. Provision is made for the retention and return of such property, and for a procedure whereby anyone with a relevant interest in the seized property can apply to the "appropriate judicial authority" for its return.
[60] In *R. v. Chesterfield Justices, ex p. Bramley* [2000] Q.B. 576, the DC laid down guidelines for cases where legal privilege was at risk.
[61] *R. v. Central Criminal Court, ex p. Francis and Francis* [1989] A.C. 346, where the "intention" was that of a relative of the solicitor's client. The case was on the powers under the Drug Trafficking Offences Act 1986, but the definition of items subject to legal privilege is the same as in PACE.

special procedure materials, and (in more limited circumstances) excluded materials.[62] The type of material to which the police require access is often of evidential value and held by third parties on a confidential basis.[63] This type of information is of particular importance in relation to fraud, terrorism, and drug offences; it may also be relevant in respect of the recent powers of the courts to confiscate from convicted defendants the proceeds of certain offences. In addition to section 9 of the PACE Act, several subsequent statutes[64] have created broadly similar powers to enable the police (or in certain circumstances customs and excise officials) to gain access to certain types of confidential materials. In all cases there are rules and safeguards laid down by statute, and a failure to observe these can result in the quashing of the order.[65]

General provisions, applicable to the enforcement of search warrants under any enactment are contained in sections 15 and 16 and COP B.[66] Section 15 requires a degree of particularity in specifying the grounds on which an application is made, the premises to be entered and the articles or persons to be sought.[67] A warrant shall authorise entry on one occasion only and which has to be made within one month from the date of issue of the warrant (section 16). Entry must be at a reasonable hour, unless it appears to the constable executing the warrant that the purpose of the search would be frustrated by an entry at a reasonable hour.

24–048   The variety of statutory provisions enabling the police to obtain permission to enter private premises have altered the law in favour of the public interest in crime detection and away from the common law notion of protection for private property. It is important that the police and the courts observe the safeguards provided in these enactments, and by the E.C.H.R. The courts should not be too easily persuaded by police claims that the requirements of the statutes are satisfied. The E.C.H.R. requires that any interference with an individual's private life (Article 8) or an individual's freedom of association (Article 11) has to be "necessary in a democratic society in the interests of public safety . . . or the protection of the rights and freedoms of others." This means that the interference has to be proportionate to the legitimate aim which the authority is seeking to enforce. The E.Ct.H.R. has said that it is not enough that search warrants have prior judicial authority; the warrant must not be too broad and should be

---

[62] s.9 cannot be used for items subject to legal professional privilege, but statutes passed since PACE do not necessarily have this limitation, *cf.* s.24 of the Public Order Act 1986.

[63] s.9(1) also entitles a police officer to ask the holder of such material to produce it, if he does there is no need to use Sched. 1: *R v. Singleton* [1995] 1 Cr.App.R. 431, where as part of a murder investigation a dentist had voluntarily handed over the accused's dental records.

[64] Powers are to found in: Criminal Justice Act 1988 (as amended by the Proceeds of Crime Act 1995), Terrorism Act 2000 and the Drug Trafficking Act 1994.

[65] *R. v. Southwark Crown Court, ex p. Bowles* [1998] 2 W.L.R. 715, HL: an order for the production of documents made under s.93H of the Criminal Justice Act 1988 could only be granted if the "dominant purpose" of the application was to assist in the recovery of the proceeds of the conduct of crime, and not to investigate criminal offences; *R. v. Central Criminal Court, ex p. Adegbesan* [1986] 1 W.L.R. 1292, DC. Order under s.9 of PACE quashed on the basis of insufficient detail of the relevant special procedure material.

[66] *R. v. Chief Constable of the Warwickshire Constabulary and another, ex p. Fitzpatrick and others* [1998] 2 All E.R. 65, on the relationship between s.8 and ss.15, 16.

[67] *R. v. Reading Justices, ex p. South Western Meat Ltd* [1992] Crim.L.R. 672, where it was held that since a defective warrant was invalid under s.15(1), the entry and search were unlawful and the court ordered the return of the documents which had been seized.

proportionate to the purpose of preventing crime and protecting the rights of others.[68]

Special powers of entry without a search warrant

24–049

The Terrorism Act 2000,[69] allows a senior police officer in specified circumstances to establish a police cordon around an area in connection with a terrorism investigation. Where such a cordon is in place, the police can search premises within the cordon without a warrant for materials connected with that investigation. A more extensive power to enter without a warrant to carry out installations for surveillance is found in Part III of the Police Act 1997.[70] Authorisation for such activities lies with the chief officer of police, and the Directors General of the National Crime Squad and the National Criminal Intelligence Service. Section 93 provides the criteria for granting such authorisation. The exercise of these powers is subject to the supervision, and to some extent control, of special Commissioners who are appointed from the ranks of senior judges (section 91). The width of these powers and the limitations in judicial supervision are likely to give rise to an early challenge under Article 8 E.C.H.R.

Customs, revenue and other officials

24–050

The powers of entry and seizure provided in Part II of the PACE Act relate only to the police. Other officials such as the Commissioners of Customs and Excise, the Inland Revenue and a wide range of inspectors and officers employed by local authorities, public utilities and government departments, have specific statutory power to enter and to inspect or search. These powers are governed by the terms of the empowering statute, but if such an entry is a search, then it appears that COP B has to be applied.[71]

The Customs and Excise Management Act 1979 confers power to board ships, aircraft and vehicles to "rummage and search" in connection with the preventing of smuggling (section 27). Officers may require information about goods being imported or exported and inspect documents relating to such goods (section 77). A right of entry on premises concerned with trading in alcohol is conferred by section 112 and a power to break open any part of such premises in order to look for any "secret pipe or other means of conveyance, cock vessel or utensil" (section 113). Without prejudice to specific powers, section 161 confers a general power to search in connection with offences against the law relating to Customs and Excise on any customs officer having with him a writ of assistance. Such a writ, which is issued by the High Court, has been described as, in effect, a general search warrant. Writs of assistance are made out at the beginning of each reign and are effective throughout the reign and for six months thereafter. It is questionable whether such writs are compatible with the E.C.H.R. By virtue of regulations made under section 114 of the PACE Act, Customs and Excise officers have the same power as the police to obtain a search warrant to search for evidence of a serious arrestable offence. All powers of entry under a search

---

[68] *Funcke v. France* A 256–A (1993); *Neimietz v. Germany* A 251–B (1992) 16 E.H.R.R. 97, where there was a warrant, but there was no special procedure safeguards for the searching of lawyers' premises.

[69] ss.33–36 and Sched. 5 para. 3, re-enacting the powers given to the police by the CJPO Act 1994.

[70] Prior to the enactment of Part III such activities were carried out under Home Office guidelines, an inadequate legal basis under the E.C.H.R. (see *post*, paras 26–017 to 26–018). Since 1994 MI 5 and MI 6 have such powers by statute, but only in furtherance of a warrant issued by the Home Secretary.

[71] *Dudley Metropolitan Borough Council v. Debenhams plc* (1994) 159 J.P. 18, DC.

warrant are subject to the PACE Act, ss.9, 15 and 16. Powers of entry without a warrant under the PACE Act, ss.17, 18, and 32 also apply to the Customs and Excise.

Under Schedule 11 of the Value Added Tax Act 1994 the Commissioners have further powers to enter premises, seize documents or other articles and search persons. The rules in relation to these powers are closer to those of the Inland Revenue that to other customs and excise powers.

24–051   The Inland Revenue has extensive powers to enter and search premises under section 20C of the Taxes Management Act 1970, which allows a circuit court judge to issue a warrant for the search and seizure of documents. Concern about the width of this power as highlighted in the case of *R. v. Inland Revenue Commissioners, ex p. Rossminster Ltd*[72] led to a minor amendment in 1989 which requires the judge to be satisfied that there are reasonable grounds for suspecting the commission of a *serious* offence involving fraud relating to tax matters and that evidence of the offence is to be found on premises specified. In addition the judge must now be satisfied that the issue of the warrant is compatible with the E.C.H.R. On entering premises with a warrant the officer may seize and remove anything whatsoever which he has reasonable cause to believe may be required as evidence for the purpose of proceedings in connection with the suspected offence of *serious* fraud. The appropriate procedure to challenge the legality of the seizure of documents by the Revenue is by means of an action for damages for trespass. This requires the Revenue to establish reasonable cause for believing that the documents which they removed constituted evidence of serious fraud. Sections 149, 150 of the Finance Act 2000 provide new powers to enable the Inland Revenue when conducting a criminal investigation to obtain access to documents held by a third party, such as a solicitor. An application for a production order has to be made to a judge; the third party may appear at the hearing.

Many statutes confer powers of entry and search on public officials, attached to various government departments, public utilities, regulatory bodies and local authorities. There is no consistency with regard to the persons authorised, the nature of the authorising document, length of notice, or whether notice is to be given to the owner or the occupier. The statute usually prescribes that the official must produce his written authority to any person who reasonably requires to see it.[73] If the conditions of entry prescribed by statute are not strictly fulfilled the owner is entitled to oppose entry. "When the sanitary inspector of the council arrived," said Lord Goddard C.J. in *Stroud v. Bradbury*,[74] "the appellant obstructed him with all the rights of a free-born Englishman whose premises are being invaded and defied him with a clothes prop and a spade. He was entitled to do that unless the sanitary inspector had a right to enter."

Examples of statutory powers of entry are afforded by the Building Act 1984, s.95 (authorised officer of local authority entitled to enter any premises at all reasonable hours to ascertain whether there has been any breach of building

---

[72] [1980] A.C. 952, HL. Partly because of concern at the powers of the Revenue Departments, the Committee on Enforcement Powers of the Revenue Departments, chaired by Lord Keith of Kinkel was established. It produced four volumes of reports: (1983) Cmnd. 8822 (2 vols.); (1984) Cmnd. 9120; (1985) Cmnd. 9440.

[73] *Grove v. Eastern Gas Board* [1952] 1 K.B. 77, CA, *Re* Gas Act 1948. Rights of entry for gas and electricity suppliers are regulated by the Rights of Entry (Gas and Electricity Boards) Act 1954, as amended by the Gas Act 1972, 1986, 1995 and the Electricity Act 1989.

[74] [1952] 2 All E.R. 76, DC (Public Health Act 1936).

regulations: access to premises other than factories or workplaces requires 24 hours' notice); the Health and Safety at Work etc. Act 1974, s.20 (inspectors entitled to enter premises to ensure compliance with the provisions of the Act); the Milk (Cessation of Production) Act 1985, s.2 (authorised official of Ministry of Agriculture entitled to enter land to establish whether a person has ceased to produce milk after receipt of a cessation payment under the Act) and the Local Government (Miscellaneous Provisions) Act 1982, s.17 (authorised officer of local authority entitled to enter premises if he has reason to suspect that unregistered person is engaging in acupuncture, tattooing, ear-piercing or electrolysis) and s.27 (power to enter to repair drains).

Search orders[75]

The Courts themselves have added to the number of persons entitled to enter premises and search for and seize items by the introduction of what was originally known as an Anton Piller order, after the leading case of *Anton Piller K.G. v. Manufacturing Process Ltd*[76] Further decisions have refined the principle which in that case received the approval of the Court of Appeal. In particular *Universal Thermosensors Ltd v. Hibben*[77] reviewed and tightened the procedures for these orders. In theory a defendant is requested to consent to admit the plaintiff to his premises to conduct a search: to refuse consent would, however, be contempt of court. The order, which is like a civil search warrant, is made without warning to the defendant, where the plaintiff can satisfy the court that he has a strong prima facie case, that there is a risk of serious damage to him from the alleged wrongdoing, that the defendants have possession of incriminating documents or other items of evidential value and there is a real possibility that they may be destroyed before proceedings *inter partes* can take place. The jurisdiction originated in the field of intellectual property law but is not confined to that area of the law. Uncertainty concerning the powers of a court to make such orders has been resolved by section 7 of the Civil Procedure Act 1997.[78]

24–052

Liability to taxation

Since the Bill of Rights (1688) it has been firmly established that taxation may only be imposed by authority of an Act of Parliament (*Att.-Gen. v. Wilts United Dairies*).[79] This is done by Parliament either directly, as in the case of income tax, customs and excise duties, capital gains and transfer taxes, or indirectly through the delegation of power to local authorities to levy council tax. Inland Revenue officials have an extensive power to "discover" what is not there and to assess taxpayers on that, in order to induce the latter to disclose what is there. The European Commission on Human Rights has accepted that ordinary measures to enforce tax payments do not involve the determination of a criminal charge within Article 6; the result may be different if heavy penalties could be imposed.[80]

24–053

[75] See Stone *op. cit.* Chap. 10.
[76] [1976] Ch. 55. For a consideration of the constitutional implications see M. Dockray, "Liberty to Rummage—A Search Warrant in Civil Proceedings?", [1977] P.L. 369. See also A. Staines, "Protection of Intellectual Property Rights", (1983) 46 M.L.R. 274.
[77] [1992] 3 All E.R. 257, and see Practice Direction [1996] 1 W.L.R. 552, which governs the proper manner for the execution of the order.
[78] In *Chappell v. United Kingdom* (1989) 12 E.H.R.R. 1 the E.Ct.H.R. held that the exercise of an *Anton Piller* order did not infringe Art. 8.
[79] (1921) 91 L.J.K.B. 897; (1921) 37 T.L.R. 844.
[80] *Abas v. the Netherlands* [1997] E.H.R.L.R. 418; *Bendenoun v. France* (1994) 18 E.H.R.R. 54.

Statutory restrictions on freedom of property

24–054   Parliament authorises and controls the compulsory acquisition of land by the Crown for defence purposes[81]; and by various Ministers, local authorities and public corporations under a great variety of statutes. A compulsory purchase by a local authority or public corporation must be confirmed by a Minister.[82] Statutes prescribe both the procedure of compulsory acquisition and the method of assessing compensation. There is no right to compensation except by statute[83]; but there is a strong presumption that if a statute authorises the compulsory acquisition of property, the owner is entitled to reasonable compensation: *Newcastle Breweries v. The King*.[84]

Article 1 of the First Protocol to the E.C.H.R. recognises the right to peaceful enjoyment of property and the right not to be deprived of it except in the public interest and subject to the conditions provided for by law and by the general principles of international law.[85] This right and those found in Articles 6, 7, and 8, could be relied on in challenging aspects of the various statutory proceeds of crime provisions which provide for the making of restraint, forfeiture or confiscations orders against defendants.[86] Far reaching proposals have been made which, if implemented, would extend the existing powers of the state to confiscate proceeds of crime, provide for civil forfeiture and for the taxation of unspecified profit.[87]

---

[81] *cf. Att.-Gen. v. De Keyser's Royal Hotel Ltd* [1920] A.C. 508, HL.

[82] The powers of Ministers to approve a compulsory purchase or to decide an appeal on a controversial planning appeal were challenged as a breach of Art. 6 E.C.H.R.: in *R. (Alconbury Ltd) v. Secretary of State for the Environment, Transport and the Regions* [2001] W.L.R. 1389, HL, it was held that decisions taken by the Minister were not incompatible with Art. 6 provided (as was the case) that they were subject to review by an independent tribunal.

[83] *Sisters of Charity of Rockingham v. The King* [1922] 2 A.C. 315, 322, PC, *per* Lord Parmoor.

[84] [1920] 1 K.B. 584; *Att.-Gen. v. De Keyser's Royal Hotel Ltd* [1920] A.C. 508, HL; *Manitoba Fisheries Ltd v. The Queen* (1978) 88 D.L.R. (3d) 462.

[85] This article has been unsuccessfully used to challenge the adequacy of statutory compensation in *Lithgow v. UK* (1986) 8 E.H.R.R. 329, *James v. UK* (1986) 8 E.H.R.R. 123.

[86] *e.g.* under the Drug Trafficking Act 1994, the Criminal Justice Act 1988, and the Terrorism Act 2000. See Evan Bell, "The E.C.H.R. and the Proceeds of Crime Legislation", [2000] Crim.L.R. 783.

[87] *Recovering the Proceeds of Crime*, Home Office (2000).

CHAPTER 25

FREEDOM OF EXPRESSION[1]

Introduction

Freedom of expression is generally recognised as having particular impor-   **25–001**
tance, but what is meant by such freedom? It must no doubt include writings and
words meant to influence political views, for example, the desirability of proportional representation as a method of electing members of the House of Commons.
But does freedom of expression include symbolic gestures intended to convey a
political message: the wearing of a particular coloured shirt to indicate support
for a political party; the vulgar sign in the presence of royalty intended to indicate
a profound conviction of the need for a republican form of government? There
may be doubts too about whether the right is confined to communicating political
ideas, and what is meant by communication? Does the freedom to publish books
criticising Marxism extend to the freedom to publish books criticising conventional views on matrimony or sexual mores in general? Are collections of
pornographic photographs (assuming agreement could be reached on the meaning of pornographic) also expressions of views about morality which are therefore entitled to claim the protection of the law?

While agreeing on the importance of the freedom of expression there may be
doubts about the propriety of limiting that freedom to achieve other ends, for
example to protect the young from corruption or to prevent public disorder. The
extent to which such limitations are thought appropriate is likely to depend on
why freedom of expression is believed to be important. Some may wish to argue
that restrictions on free expression may prevent society from ascertaining the
truth on matters of debate.[2] Others may see freedom to speak, write and read as
an aspect of each individual's right to moral independence.[3]

In many countries freedom of expression is constitutionally guaranteed,[4] but
until the enactment of the Human Rights Act 1998, in the United Kingdom
freedom of expression was, like other freedoms, residual and subject to limitation
by common law and statute. The United Kingdom Parliament and the courts had
no constitutional rights to concern them when dealing with issues of freedom of
expression. Several decision by the House of Lords illustrate the lack of influence
of the principle of freedom of expression. In *Attorney-General v. The Guardian*
Lord Bridge in his dissent stated that the majority opinion had undermined his

---

[1] Dicey, *Law of the Constitution* (10th ed. 1959), Chap. 6; E. Barendt, *Freedom of Speech* (1985); D. G. T. Williams, *Not in the Public Interest*; A. Boyle, "Freedom of Expression as a Public Interest in English Law" [1982] P.L. 574; Beatson and Cripps (eds), *Freedom of Expression and Freedom of Information* (2000); David Feldman *Civil Liberties and Human Rights in England and Wales* 2nd ed., (2001).

[2] "The ultimate good desired is better reached by free trade in ideas ... the best test of truth is the power of the thought to get itself accepted in the competition of the market"; *per* Mr Justice Holmes (dissenting) *Abrams v. U.S.*, 250 U.S. 616, 630 (1919); J.S. Mill, *On Liberty*, Chap. 2.

[3] "Our society—unlike most in the world—presupposes that freedom and liberty are in a frame of reference that makes the individual, not government the keeper of his tastes beliefs and ideas"; *per* Mr Justice Douglas (dissenting) *Paris Adult Theatre v. Slaton*, 413 U.S. 49, 73 (1973). R. Dworkin, "Is there a right to pornography," (1981) O.J.L.S. 177.

[4] For *e.g.*, the First Amendment to the Constitution of the United States provides that no law shall be made "abridging the freedom of speech or of the press".

confidence in the capacity of the common law to safeguard freedom of speech.[5] A difference in view can also be seen in comparing the majority and minority opinions in *Home Office v. Harman* where the majority held it to be contempt for a solicitor to allow a journalist to have access to documents which had been produced on discovery and read out in court. Lord Diplock for the majority said that the case was "*not* about freedom of speech, freedom of the press, openness of justice or documents coming into the public domain . . . (it) *is* about an aspect of the law of discovery of documents.[6] In *R. v. Secretary of State for the Home Office, ex p. Brind*[7] where, although the statutory authority under which the Minister acted was in very general terms, the House of Lords found the legislation to be unambiguous and refused to have regard to the general principle of freedom of speech.[8] However, in more recent cases there has been a greater willing by the Lords to recognise the importance of freedom of expression, but often as an aspect of the common law rather than by virtue of the E.C.H.R. In *Derbyshire County Council v. Times Newspapers*[9] there was specific reference to freedom of expression as an important legal principle which was vital to a democratic system of government,[10] and in *R. v. Secretary of State for the Home Department, ex p. Simms*[11] Lord Steyn said of the wish of a prisoner to challenge his conviction that it was, "not easy to conceive of a more important function which free speech might fulfil."

25–002　　Parliament, as will be obvious in this and succeeding chapters placed no particular value on free speech in competition with the claims, real or alleged, of public order, or national security. In the area of censorship on grounds of obscenity it was willing to legislate hastily and with little thought, at the instigation of the latest pressure groups.

Parliament, the courts and all public authorities will now have to take account of Article 10 of the European Convention, and various restrictions on freedom of expression may require reinterpretation in the light of that article. Article 10(1) recognises the right to freedom of expression, including the right to hold opinions and to receive and impart information and ideas without interference by public authority. It goes on to state:

> "This Article shall not prevent States from requiring the licensing of broadcasting, television or cinema enterprises.
> (2) The exercise of these freedoms since it carries with it duties and responsibilities, may be subject to such formalities, conditions, restrictions or penalties as are prescribed by law and are necessary in a democratic society, in the interests of national security, territorial integrity or public safety, for the prevention of disorder or crime, for the protection of the reputation or rights of others, for preventing the disclosure of information received in confidence, or for maintaining the authority and impartiality of the judiciary."

---

[5] [1987] 1 W.L.R. 1248 at 1286, *cf.* Lord Brandon (in the majority) at p. 1287–8 and see *post* para. 25–020.

[6] [1983] 1 A.C. 280 at 299; *cf.* Lord Scarman (dissenting) at p. 311.

[7] [1991] 1 A.C. 696.

[8] See also *Attorney-General v. Jonathan Cape Ltd* [1976] Q.B. 752 and *post* para. 25–020; *Whitehouse v. Gay News Ltd and Lemon* [1979] A.C. 617 and *post* para. 25–007.

[9] [1993] A.C. 534, and see Barendt, "Libel and Freedom of Speech in English Law", [1993] P.L. 449; see also *Reynolds v. Times Newspapers* [1999] 4 All E.R. 609, [2000] 2 A.C. 127.

[10] See also *Verrall v. Great Yarmouth B.C.* [1981] Q.B. 202.

[11] [2000] A.C. 115.

The approach of the E.C.H.R. to this article is to regard the right to freedom of expression as a right that is subject to a number of exceptions which must be narrowly interpreted and the necessity for the restrictions must be convincingly established. Unlike British courts it does not decide cases by trying to balance freedom of expression against other "rights": freedom of expression takes priority.[12] The Court has accepted that Member States have a margin of appreciation in assessing whether restrictions are "necessary".[13] This has been used to give stronger protection to political and journalist expression than to blasphemy[14] or obscenity.[15] The Court has stated that freedom of expression is "one of the essential foundations of a democratic society",[16] which entails giving discussion of political and governmental affairs particularly protection, an important aspect of which is the freedom of the press. The principle of freedom of expression has been said by the Court to apply as much to "'information' or 'ideals' that are favourably received or regarded as inoffensive or as a matter of indifference, but also to those that offend, shock or disturb the State or any sector of the population."[17]

This chapter will consider a series of limitations on freedom of expression, and examine freedom of expression in the context of the media. The following chapter will consider freedom of expression as an aspect of the right to know, and will look at the ways in which a variety of statutes, mostly passed since 1997, regulate both the State's right to know and the individual's right to privacy. It will also consider ways in which the State guards its secrets, and provides for freedom of information for the citizen.

I. DEFAMATION, LIBEL AND BLASPHEMY

Defamation

Unlike most of the restrictions on free speech considered later in this chapter which are concerned with conflicts between the citizen and the state, defamation is concerned with a conflict between citizens or between a citizen and a private organisation such as a newspaper.[18] In this area there may be conflicts between the rights of the person allegedly defamed and that of free speech or press freedom on the part of the alleged defamer. Although the E.C.H.R. does not recognise a right to a reputation, Article 10(2) recognises that there may be restrictions on freedom of expression "for the protection of the reputation or rights of others".

25–003

---

[12] *Sunday Times v. United Kingdom* (1979) 2 E.H.R.R. 245 at 281.

[13] Although the Court has indicated that the Convention organs can give a final ruling on whether a restriction is compatible with freedom of expression as protected by Art. 10; *Sunday Times v. United Kingdom (No. 2)* (1992) 14 E.H.R.R. 229, para. 50, and cited by the European Commission in its opinion in *Goodwin v. United Kingdom* (1996) 22 E.H.R.R. 123.

[14] *Lemon v. United Kingdom* (1982) 24 E.H.R.R. C.D. 75.

[15] *Handyside v. United Kingdom* (1976) 1 E.H.R.R. 737; see also *Wingrove v. United Kingdom* (1996) 24 E.H.R.R. 1.

[16] *Lingen v. Austria* (1986) 8 E.H.R.R. 407.

[17] *Handyside v. United Kingdom* [1976] 1 E.H.R.R. 737, para. 49.

[18] In *Derbyshire C.C. v. Times Newspapers Ltd* [1993] A.C. 543, HL it was unanimously held that to allow civil actions for defamation by the *institutions* of central or local government would be an undesirable fetter on the freedom of expression; individual members of such institutions are entitled to sue.

Defamatory matter is matter which exposes the person about whom it is published to hatred, ridicule or contempt, or which causes him to be shunned or avoided.[19] Such matter if in writing, printing or some other permanent medium,[20] is a libel, if in spoken words or significant gestures, a slander. Where the defendant had no intention of referring to the plaintiff, he may make an offer of amends involving the publication of a correction and apology, which (if accepted) stays the action.[21]

Communications made on certain occasions enjoy *absolute privilege*, either at common law or by statute, that is to say, no proceedings can be brought in respect of them. These occasions include: judicial proceedings and statements made in the course of litigation by judges, counsel and witnesses[22]; words uttered in the course of debates or proceedings in Parliament[23]; state communications, which include communications about state business made by persons in government service[24]; proceedings at a court-martial, and reports made in pursuance of military duty[25]; fair, accurate and contemporaneous reports (which are neither blasphamous nor indecent) in newspapers, or broadcasts from the United Kingdom of proceedings publicly heard before a court in the United Kingdom exercising judicial authority,[26] and certain other supra-national tribunals[27]; reports and other documents published by order of either House of Parliament,[28] the Parliamentary Commissioner's report to Parliament, communications by the Commissioner and M.P.s, and communications by the Commissioner or M.P.s to complainants.[29]

Communications on certain other occasions enjoy *qualified privilege*, that is to say, they are protected in the absence of actual malice or "malice in fact," *i.e.* spite, fraud or some other indirect motive of which the law disapproves.

25–004   Schedule 1 to the Defamation Act 1996 confers the protection of qualified privilege upon a wide range of reports. The 1996 Act is based on the structure of the previous law, but it expands the range of protected reports and makes some changes of detail. In particular, the privilege afforded by the law is no longer confined to reports in the news media. The reports and other statements privileged by Schedule 1 are divided into two categories: Part I covers those categories which are privileged "without explanation or contradiction", Part II applies to those which are privileged "subject to explanation or contradiction." With respect to those matters which fall into Part II, the defence of qualified

---

[19] *Capital and Counties Bank v. Henty* (1882) 7 App.Cas. 741, 771, *per* Lord Blackburn; *cf. Sim v. Stretch* (1936) 53 T.L.R. 669.

[20] A defamatory talking film is libel; *Youssoupoff v. Metro-Goldwyn-Mayer Pictures Ltd* (1934) 50 T.L.R. 581; so is a defamatory radio or television broadcast: Broadcasting Act 1990, s.166. Similarly public theatrical performances: Theatres Act 1968, s.4.

[21] Defamation Act, 1996, s.4. This had its origin in the Defamation Act 1952, the 1996 Act extends and simplifies the circumstances in which an offer of amends may be made.

[22] *Royal Aquarium Society v. Parkinson* [1892] 1 Q.B. 431. The exception extends to certain tribunals possessing similar attributes to a court: *Trapp v. Mackie* [1979] 1 W.L.R. 177, HL. *cf. Hasselblad (G.B.) Ltd v. Orbinson* [1985] Q.B. 475, CA.

[23] Article 9 of the Bill of Rights 1688, but see s.13 of the Defamation Act 1996 for the possibility of waiving this privilege; see *ante*, para. 13–015.

[24] *Isaacs & Sons v. Cook* [1952] 2 K.B. 391; but see *Szalatnay-Stacho v. Fink* [1947] K.B. 1.

[25] *Dawkins v. Lord Rokeby* (1875) L.R. 7 H.L. 744.

[26] *cf.* an administrative tribunal, *Collins v. H. Whiteway & Co* [1927] 2 K.B. 378.

[27] Defamation Act 1996, s.14 replacing a similar provision in the Law of Libel Amendment Act 1888. The previous law on the meaning of "fair and accurate" is likely to continue to apply: *Kimber v. Press Association* (1893) 62 L.J.Q.B. 152; *McCarey v. Associated Newspapers Ltd* [1964] 1 W.L.R. 855.

[28] Parliamentary Papers Act 1840, ss.1, 2.

[29] Parliamentary Commissioner Act 1967, s.10.

privilege is lost if, in effect, the defendant has not allowed the claimant a right of reply (section 15(2)).

The occasions covered by Part I include the following: fair and accurate reports of proceedings in public of a legislature[30] anywhere in the world (para. 1)[31]; fair and accurate reports, contemporaneous or not, of proceedings in public before a court anywhere in the world (para. 2)[32]; fair and accurate reports of proceedings in public of a person appointed to hold a public inquiry by a government or legislature anywhere in the world (para. 3); fair and accurate reports of proceedings anywhere in the world of an international organisation or conference (para. 4); a fair and accurate copy of, or extract from, any register or other document required by law to be open to public inspection (para. 5)[33]; a notice or advertisement published by or on authority of a court or judge or officer of a court, anywhere in the world (para. 6); a fair and accurate copy of, or extract from, matter published by or on the authority of a government or legislature anywhere in the world (para. 7).[34]

The statements privileged subject to explanation or contradiction provided by **25–005** Part II include the following: a fair and accurate copy of, or extract from, a notice or other matter issued for the information of the public by or on behalf of a legislature in any Member State of the European Union, the European Parliament, the government of a Member State, the European Commission, an international organisation or conference (para. 9); a fair and accurate report of proceedings at any public meeting held in a Member State (para. 12)[35]; a fair and accurate report of proceedings at a general meeting of a United Kingdom public company (para. 13); a fair and accurate report of the findings or decisions of any of a variety of arts, trade sport or charitable associations (para. 14).

Qualified privilege at common law confers protection on statements made by one person about a third party, where the person making the statement has a duty to communicate the matter and the recipient has an interest in receiving the information. The common law was concerned with providing protection with respect to specific communications to specific people. In *Reynolds v. Times Newspapers*[36] the House of Lords was invited to create a new category of qualified privilege: political information. Mr Reynolds, a former Prime Minister of Ireland sued the *Sunday Times* in respect of an article in which it suggested that he had misled the Irish Parliament and lied to Cabinet colleagues. The jury found that although the statements were defamatory and untrue, the paper had not acted maliciously in publishing them. The House of Lords refused to create a new category of qualified privilege, but recognised that the existing law on

---

[30] The European Parliament is expressly included.

[31] The protection recognised to exist at common law in *Wason v. Walter* (1868) L.R. 4 Q.B. 73, is in consequence practically redundant; it is arguable that the common law is wider than the Defamation Act, in that the latter does not apply to the publication of any matter which is not of public concern and is not for the public benefit (s.15(3)).

[32] This appears to make the common law protection of qualified privilege for non-contemporaneous reports and reports of foreign proceedings, redundant.

[33] Previously covered by the common law.

[34] This is also covered by s.3 of the Parliamentary Papers Act 1840, but s.3 is not redundant as it applies more widely than with respect to defamatory words.

[35] A public meeting is defined in para. 12(2). It is a question of law for the judge whether or not a meeting is a public meeting, see *McCartan Turkington Breen v. Times Newspapers Ltd* [2000] 4 All E.R. 913, [2001] 2 A.C. 277 (a meeting was public not private if the organisers opened it to the public, or by issuing a general invitation to the press manifested an intention that the proceedings of the meeting would be communicated to a wider public).

[36] *op. cit.* note 9.

qualified privilege applied to "matters of serious public concern", and laid down a non-exhaustive list of factors which would be relevant in deciding whether a particular communication would attract this type of qualified privilege. Applying these factors it did not accept that the *Sunday Times* could rely on the defence. It is probable that this decision gives adequate protection to freedom of expression as recognised by Article 10 and the E.Ct.H.R. case law; but *Reynolds* is much more restrictive and uncertain in its development of the law than is the position in other countries where politicians will only succeed in actions for defamation where malice can be established.

Libel

Criminal libel

25–006
Defamation is usually treated as a civil wrong, and as such it belongs to the law of tort. Slander is not a crime merely as defamation, but is only a crime if the words are also treasonable or seditious, etc. Libel may be a crime if it is likely to cause a breach of the peace or would seriously affect the reputation of the person defamed.[37] No prosecution for criminal libel against the proprietor, publisher or editor of a newspaper may be brought without the leave of a judge in chambers.[38] Leave was given by Wien J. in *Goldsmith v. Pressdram Ltd*[39] where a magazine had, in the view of the judge, engaged in a campaign of vilification for month after month against a person occupying a position of considerable public importance.[40]

Truth is normally a defence to a civil action for libel, for a person cannot lose a reputation which he has not got or does not deserve. In criminal libel truth is not a defence at common law. By section 6 of the Libel Act 1843 ("Lord Campbell's Act"), however, it is a defence to a prosecution for criminal libel if the accused can prove not only that the matter published was true in substance but also that the publication was for the public good. Truth, of course, is no defence if the matter is also seditious, etc.[41] Prosecutions for criminal libel are rare.

Blasphemy

25–007
"Every publication is said to be blasphemous which contains any contemptuous, reviling, scurrilous or ludicrous matter relating to God, Jesus Christ or the Bible, or the formularies of the Church of England as by law established. It is not blasphemous to speak or publish opinions hostile to the Christian religion or to deny the existence of God, if the publication is couched in decent and temperate language. The test to be applied is as to the manner in which the doctrines are advocated and not as to the substance of the doctrines themselves."[42] The

[37] *R. v. Wicks* [1936] 1 All E.R. 384, 386, *per* du Parcq. J.; *Goldsmith v. Pressdram Ltd* [1977] Q.B. 83; *R. v. Wells St. Stipendiary Magistrate, ex p. Deakin* [1980] A.C. 477 (HL); *Desmond v. Thorne* [1983] 1 W.L.R. 163.
[38] Law of Libel Amendment Act 1888, s.8. In *R. v. Wells St. Stipendiary Magistrate, ex. p. Deakin* [1980] A.C. 477, HL the House of Lords expressed concern at this involvement of judges, and suggested that the bringing of proceedings should in require the leave of the Attorney-General or the Director of Public Prosecutions.
[39] [1977] Q.B. 83. The action was subsequently settled.
[40] *cf. Desmond v. Thorne* [1983] 1 W.L.R. 163 where leave was refused as a prosecution would not be in the public interest.
[41] See Law Comm. No. 149 (1985) Cmnd. 9618, for proposals for reform.
[42] Sir J. F. Stephen, *Digest of Criminal Law* (9th ed.), p. 163.

common law misdemeanour of blasphemous words or writing seems to have been first recognised by the King's Bench in *R. v. Attwood*.[43] In the earlier cases blasphemy was virtually equivalent to a kind of seditious libel. After the decision of the House of Lords in *Bowman v. Secular Society*[44] that an attack on or denial of the truth of Christianity, unaccompanied by vilification, ridicule or irrelevance, was not contrary to the law, it came to be assumed that the gist of the offence of blasphemy lay in a tendency to cause a breach of the peace and prosecutions were rare.[45] In *R. v. Lemon*,[46] the question directly before the House of Lords was the *mens rea* requisite to establish liability for blasphemy. A majority of the House held that it was sufficient for the prosecution to prove that publication was intended and that the matter published was blasphemous, that is calculated to shock or outrage the feelings of ordinary Christians. Lord Scarman, one of the majority, and Lord Edmund Davies, one of the dissentients, expressly said that they did not regard the likelihood of a breach of the peace as being of the essence of the offence. The true test was the likelihood of outrage and insult.

Lord Scarman suggested that the offence of blasphemy ought to be extended to protect all religious beliefs. The Law Commission, on the other hand, came to the conclusion that the crime of blasphemy should be abolished, and that a new offence which extended to religions other than Christianity should not be enacted.[47] In *R. v. Chief Metropolitan Magistrate, ex p. Choudhury*[48] the Divisional Court upheld the decision of the Magistrate that the law of blasphemy only applied to attacks on Christianity, and that the religion of Islam was not protected.[49]

The E.Ct.H.R. has considered the relationship between freedom of expression (Article 10) and protection of religion (Article 9), and has accepted that a state may repress certain types of conduct incompatible with respect for the freedom of thought, conscience and religion of others.[50] It accepted in *Wingrove v. United Kingdom*[51] that there was no breach of Article 10 by the refusal to award the applicant's video work a classification certificate on the ground that it was blasphemous. The court accepted that: "English law of blasphemy does not prohibit the expression, in any form, of views hostile to the Christian religion. Nor can it be said that opinions which are offensive to Christians necessarily fall within its ambit . . . it is the manner in which the views are advocated rather than the views themselves which the law seeks to control."[52] The E.Ct.H.R. was not prepared to accept that restrictions on the propagation of material on the ground that it is blasphemous was unnecessary in a democratic society, but it indicated that it could revisit this matter in the light of future developments on the law of blasphemy in member states.

25–008

---

[43] (1617) Cro.Jac.421. See G. D. Nokes, *History of the Crime of Blasphemy* (1928), pp. 21 *et seq.*

[44] [1917] A.C. 406, HL.

[45] *R. v. Gott* (1922) 16 Cr.App.R. 87, CA.

[46] [1979] A.C. 617, a private prosecution brought against the editor and publishers of *Gay News*. An application to the European Commission of Human Rights was rejected as manifestly ill-founded: (1983) 5 E.H.R.R. 123.

[47] *Offences against Religion and Public Worship* Law Commission Report No. 145 (1985).

[48] [1991] 1 Q.B. 429.

[49] In *Choudhury v. United Kingdom*, application 17439/90, the European Commission rejected a complaint by the plaintiff on the failure of the law of blasphemy to protect Muslims, on the basis that Art. 9 could not be used to create positive obligations on States to protect religious sensibilities.

[50] In *Lemon v. United Kingdom* (1982) 24 E.H.R.R. C.D. 75, the Commission accepted that the law of blasphemy was an acceptable means of protecting the Art.9 rights of Christians.

[51] (1997) 24 E.H.R.R. 1.

[52] *ibid.* at para. 60.

II. OFFENCES AGAINST THE STATE, PUBLIC ORDER[53]

Sediton

25–009   The law of sedition is largely an historic survival, except in its more precise, statutory forms. The word "sedition" covers three indictable but non-arrestable common law offences: the publication of a seditious libel,[54] the uttering of seditious words, and conspiracy to do an act in furtherance of a seditious intention.[55] A seditious intention is necessary for all three offences. It is an intention to bring into hatred or contempt, or to excite disaffection against, the person of the Sovereign, or the government and Constitution of the United Kingdom as by law established, or either House of Parliament or the administration of justice, or to excite Her Majesty's subjects or attempt, otherwise than by lawful means, the alteration of any matter in Church or state by law established, or to raise discontent or disaffection among Her Majesty's subjects, or to promote feelings of ill will or hostility between different classes of her subjects (*R. v. Burns,* per Cave J.[56]). A qualification to the potential width of this definition was provided in *R. v. Chief Metropolitan Magistrate, ex p. Choudhury,*[57] where it was held that there had to be an intention to incite violence or create public disturbance or disorder against His Majesty or the institutions of government. Proof of an intention to promote feelings of ill-will or hostility between different classes of subjects was not sufficient.[58] It is not seditious to show the government has been mistaken, or to point out defects in the Constitution, or to excite people to attempt by lawful means the alteration of the law relating to Church or state, or to point out (with a view to their removal) matters which produce feelings of hatred or ill will between classes of Her Majesty's subjects.

In addition to a seditious intent, it must be established that the words have a tendency to incite public disorder. The truth of a statement is no defence to a criminal charge if it is seditious.[59]

It is doubtful if any useful purpose is served by the retention of a crime of sedition, for few if any acts which might be regarded as constituting sedition do not also fall within the scope of other common law or statutory offences.[60]

Incitement to mutiny or disaffection. By the Incitement to Mutiny Act 1797, passed after the naval mutiny at the Nore, persons maliciously endeavouring to seduce British soldiers or sailors from their duty and allegiance, or to commit an act of mutiny or traitorous practice, are to be guilty of an offence, and may receive a maximum punishment of imprisonment for life.

---

[53] See *post*, Chap. 26 for Official Secrets Act, and Chap. 27 for public order offences.
[54] Prosecutions for seditious libel were frequent during the late eighteenth century, at the instance either of the government or the House of Commons: *Wilkes v. Wood* (1763) 19 St. Tr. 1153, *Leach v. Money* (1765) 3 Burr. 1692, 1742, 19 St. Tr. 1001. Until Fox's Libel Act 1792, it was for the judge, not the jury to decide whether a libel was seditious; see Stephen *History of the Criminal Law*, Vol. II.
[55] Stephen, *History of the Criminal Law*, Vol. II, Chap. 24.
[56] 16 Cox. 355; approving Stephen, *Digest of the Criminal Law* (see 8th ed., art. 114).
[57] [1991] 1 Q.B. 429.
[58] The Divisional Court upheld the decision of the magistrate that Salman Rushdie's Book, *Satanic Verses*, was not a seditious libel.
[59] *R. v. Burdett* (1821) 4 B. & Ald. 314.
[60] See the Law Commission Working Paper No. 74 (1977), which was never implemented.

The Aliens Restriction (Amendment) Act 1919, s.3 creates an offen
causing or attempting to cause sedition or disaffection.

The Incitement to Disaffection Act 1934 makes it an offence for any person
maliciously and advisedly to endeavour to seduce any member of Her Majesty's
forces from his duty or allegiance[61] to Her Majesty (section 1); or to be in
possession, with intent to commit, abet, counsel or procure the commission of an
offence under section 1, of any document such that dissemination of copies
among members of the forces would be an offence against section 1 (section 2).
The Act enables a Judge of the High Court, if satisfied by sworn information that
an offence has been committed, and that evidence thereof is to be found on
premises named in the information, to grant a search warrant to the police on
their application therefor. A prosecution under this Act requires the consent of
the Director of Public Prosecutions.[62]

Incitement to racial hatred[63]

Until 1965 those who incited racial hatred could only be prosecuted for **25–010**
common law offences, such as sedition. The inadequacy of this situation resulted
in the introduction of a specific offence of incitement to racial hatred in the Race
Relation Act 1965. A variety of offences connected with incitement to racial
hatred are now contained in Part III of the Public Order Act 1986. Section 17
defines "racial hatred"[64] as hatred against a group of persons in Great Britain
defined by reference to colour, race, nationality (including citizenship) or ethnic
or national origin.[65] Section 18 makes it an offence to use threatening, abusive or
insulting words or behaviour, or to display written material possessing those
characteristics with intent to stir up racial hatred or in circumstances where racial
hatred is likely to be stirred up. An offence under the section can be committed
in public or private but in the latter case there is no offence where the words were
used or the material displayed in a dwelling house and were not heard or seen by
anyone outside the dwelling. It is a defence to show that the accused was inside
a dwelling at the time of an alleged offence and that he had no reason to believe
that persons outside the dwelling would hear or see the words or material. A
person who is not shown to have intended to stir up racial hatred is not guilty of
an offence under the section if he did not intend his words or behaviour to be, and
was not aware that it might be, threatening, abusive or insulting (section 18(5)).
Section 19 creates an offence of publishing and distributing written material
which is threatening, abusive or insulting.[66] Sections 20, 21 and 22 make similar
provisions in the case of the public performance of plays, the distributing or
showing or playing of recordings of visual images or sounds and the broadcasting
of threatening, abusive or insulting[67] visual images or sounds. The possession of
threatening, abusive or insulting written material or records with a view to

---

[61] *R. v. Arrowsmith* [1975] Q.B. 678.

[62] A similar offence with respect to the police is found in the Police Act 1997, s.91.

[63] R. Cotterell, "Prosecuting Incitement to Racial Hatred", [1982] P.L. 378; Wolffe "Value in
Conflict: Incitement to Racial Hatred and the Public Order Act 1986," [1987] P.L. 85.

[64] Only in Northern Ireland is there an offence of incitement to religious hatred.

[65] Incitement to religious hatred is not covered by Part III, but in *Mandla v. Lee* [1983] 2 A.C. 548,
it was held that the word "ethnic" was to be interpreted relatively widely, and in consequence Sikhs,
although originally a religious community, now constituted an ethnic group.

[66] Now an arrestable offence in s.24(2) PACE Act 1984, as inserted by s.155 Criminal Justice and
Public Order Act 1994.

[67] For a discussion of the meaning of these words see *post,* para. 27–023.

e an offence by section 23. Nothing in Part III of the Act accurate reports of proceedings in Parliament (section 26(1)) ate reports of judicial proceedings, if published contempora- as reasonably practicable and lawful (section 26(2)). tended the law on incitement to racial hatred to cover offences ction 28); provide entry and search powers in respect of a ction 23 (section 24) and a power to order forfeiture of written iction (section 25). Prosecutions in England and Wales may by or with the consent of the Attorney-General (section 27(1)).

Restrictions on the expression of racist ideas are legitimate under Article 10(2) of the E.C.H.R. as being for the protection of the rights of others. In addition, Article 17 provides that the Convention does not imply "for any State, group or person any right to engage in any activity aimed at the destruction of any of the rights and freedoms (set out in the Convention)".

Terrorism[68]

25–011 The Terrorism Act 2000 has the potential to restrict the freedom of expression of a wide variety of groups. Section 1 of 2000 Act defines terrorism extremely widely with the potential to cover the criminal activities of for example, animal and environmental groups.[69] The Secretary of State has power by order to proscribe any organisation that he believes to be concerned in terrorism (section 3(4)(5) and Schedule 2). A proscribed organisation is subject to a range of proscription-related offences. If animal rights and environmental groups that could fall under the new definition of terrorism are proscribed, this would limit the activities of such groups, and in particular limit their right to free expression. The Secretary of State in deciding whether to proscribe such groups should take account of Articles 10 and 11 of the E.C.H.R.

Journalists investigating the activities of groups concerned with terrorism as defined by the Act could be at risk of prosecution under section 19. This section makes it an offence not to disclose information where someone knows or believes that a person has committed a range of offences such as fund-raising for the purposes of terrorism and using money for the purposes of terrorism. The defence in section 19(3)—of having a reasonable excuse for not making the disclosure—should be interpreted in the context of E.C.H.R. rights, particularly where the investigation is into the activities of, for *e.g.*, animal rights groups.

III. CONTEMPT OF COURT[70]

25–012 The law on contempt of court can conflict with freedom of expression, and in particular with the requirement of a free press.[71] The reform of the aspects of the common law on contempt of court by the Contempt of Court Act 1981, was in response to the decision of the E.C.H.R. in *Sunday Times v. United Kingdom*,[72]

---

[68] See para. 19–050 and para. 27–039.
[69] See para. 27–039.
[70] C. J. Miller, *Contempt of Court* (3rd ed., 2000); Arlidge, Eady and Smith, *Contempt of Court* (2nd ed., 1999).
[71] *post*, para. 25–018.
[72] [1979] 2 E.H.R.R. 245.

which had found the law on contempt to be in breach of Article 10. The case arose out of a campaign by the *Sunday Times* on behalf of the victims of Thalidomide in connection with their action against the manufacturers of the drug. The *Sunday Times* was prevented by an injunction from publishing an article at a time when writs had been issued and the parties were attempting to reach a settlement. The speeches in the House of Lords upholding the injunction had suggested that any public comment directed to a litigant would constitute contempt, irrespective of the intentions of the publisher[73]: the strict liability rule.

Unintentional interference by prejudicial publications

The Contempt of Court Act 1981 attempts in a number of sections to clarify **25–013** and limit the rule of strict liability exemplified in the *Sunday Times* case, so far as that rule relates to "particular proceedings" (section 1). The rule is to apply only to a publication which creates a substantial risk that the course of justice will be seriously impeded or prejudiced (section 2) and at the time of the publication proceedings are "active", a term which is defined with particularity in Schedule 1. Substantial has been explained by the Court of Appeal as meaning "not insubstantial" or "not minimal"; it does not mean "weighty"[74]; this interpretation may require reconsideration in the light of Article 10 E.C.H.R.[75] The requirement that there is a serious impediment or prejudice to the course of justice indicates that a publication should only be regarded as contempt where the outcome of a legal action is likely to be affected. Where there is a series of articles—even in the same newspaper—each publication must be considered in its own right when determining whether section 2 has been satisfied: *Attorney-General v. M.G.N. Ltd.*[76] In this case Schiemann L.J. set out 10 principles to further explain the application of the strict liability rule in section 2. Section 3 provides a defence where the publisher, having taken all reasonable care, did not know proceedings were active.

Section 5 exempts from the strict liability rule a publication which discusses, or is part of a discussion, in good faith of public affairs or other matters of general interest if the risk of prejudice to particular legal proceedings is merely incidental. Once the defence has raised the issue of public interest, it is for the prosecution to prove that the risk of prejudice to the proceedings resulting from a discussion in good faith of matters of general public interest was not merely incidental to the discussion. Section 7 requires the consent of the Attorney-General or the motion of a court having the appropriate jurisdiction for the institution of proceedings under the strict liability rule. In *Peacock v. London Weekend Television Ltd*[77] the Court of Appeal held that section 7 did not prevent interested parties from applying for an interlocutory injunction to restrain a *threatened* contempt. Section 7 merely relates to the punishment of a contempt which has been committed.

---

[73] *Attorney-General v. Times Newspapers* [1974] A.C. 273.
[74] *Att.-Gen. v. News Group Newspapers Ltd* [1986] 3 W.L.R. 365, CA. Publication repeating materials the subject of pending libel proceedings which were unlikely to come to trial for a further 10 months: risk of prejudice not sufficiently serious to oust rule that injunction not normally available to restrain publication of libellous material before trial where defendant intends to plead justification. See also *Att.-Gen. v. ITN* [1995] 2 All E.R. 370.
[75] But see *Attorney-General v. Guardian Newspapers Ltd* [1999] E.M.L.R. 904; *Attorney-General v. Unger* [1998] 1 Cr.App. R. 308. Arlidge, Eady and Smith, *op. cit.* (1999), Chap. 4.
[76] [1997] 1 All E.R. 456.
[77] (1985) 150 J.P. 71.

The effect of section 2 and section 5 were considered by the House of Lords in *Attorney-General v. English*.[78] A doctor had been charged with murdering a handicapped baby, by directing a course of treatment which inevitably resulted in the baby's death. After the trial had begun a newspaper published an article in support of a "pro-life" candidate in a Parliamentary by-election. The article discussed in general terms the sanctity of life and the morality of attempting to ensure that only healthy babies survived birth. The House of Lords took the view that the article did create a substantial risk of seriously prejudicing the criminal trial within section 2(2) but was not a contempt of court because it clearly fell within section 5 as a comment in good faith on a matter of public interest.[79] To ensure compliance with the E.C.H.R. section 5 should be interpreted in a liberal way, giving proper regard to freedom of expression and the importance of the press in a democracy.

Deliberate interference with particular proceedings

25–014   Any act intended to interfere with the outcome of particular proceedings, such as attempts to bribe or intimidate judges, jurors or witnesses, or in any other way to impede or prejudice the administration of justice, may constitute common law contempt which was preserved by section 6(c) of the 1981 Act. This type of contempt extends also to attempting to deter litigants from exercising their legal rights or impeding their access to the courts. To hold a litigant up to public obloquy, for example, with the object of coercing him into compromising an action is a contempt of court: *Attorney-General v. Times Newspapers*.[80] Since the 1981 Act the common law has been used even where there were no active proceedings, as in *Attorney-General v. News Group Newspapers*[81] where the *Sun* newspaper supported financially and in its publications the private prosecution of a doctor for the rape of an eight year old girl. Articles published before the prosecution had become active were found to have incurred a real risk of prejudicing the trial of the doctor. In some cases either common law intentional contempt or strict liability contempt could apply[82]; if the former is used then the statutory defences available under the 1981 Act are not available. In *Attorney-General v. Punch Ltd*[83] the Court of Appeal held that where a court restrained by injunction the publication of specified material, a third party who with knowledge of the order, published the specified material, only committed a common law contempt if he thereby knowingly defeated the purpose for which the order was made.

Reporting of Judicial Proceedings

25–015   Section 4 of the Contempt of Court Act provides that a person is not guilty of contempt of court under the strict liability rule in respect of a fair and accurate report of legal proceedings held in public[84] published contemporaneously and in

---

[78] [1983] 1 A.C. 116.
[79] See also *Att.-Gen. v. Times Newspapers Ltd, The Times*, February 12, 1983, DC (Newspaper articles relating to Fagan, the intruder in the Queen's bedroom).
[80] [1974] A.C. 273.
[81] [1988] 2 All E.R. 906.
[82] *Att.-Gen. v. Hislop* [1991] 1 Q.B. 514.
[83] *The Times*, March 30, 2001, [2001] 2 All E.R. 655.
[84] *R. v. Rhuddlan Justices, ex p. H.T.V. Ltd* [1986] Crim.L.R. 329. (Arrest not within "legal proceedings held in public" and justices could not prohibit the publication of a film of a prisoner's arrest until the completion of his trial. Appropriate remedy for prisoner, if he objected to the film being shown was to apply to the High Court for an injunction).

good faith. To avoid a substantial risk of prejudice to the administration of justice in proceedings before it or other proceedings, pending or imminent, the Court may restrain the publication of any report of the proceedings or of any part of them for such period as it thinks necessary for that purpose.[85] The press and other news media should normally be allowed to make representations to the court before such an order is made.[86] Such orders should not be made lightly.[87] To breach such an order is civil contempt of court; there is no need to show a risk of prejudice to proceedings. It is questionable whether such an approach is proportionate to the legitimate aim of an order, or takes adequate account of the free press requirements of the E.C.H.R.[88]

Contempt and refusal to reveal sources of information

Section 10 of the Contempt of Court Act recognises the need to give journal-   **25–016** ists some protection from revealing in judicial proceedings the sources of their information.[89] It provides that no court may require a person to disclose the source of information contained in a publication for which he is responsible unless it is established to the satisfaction of the court that disclosure is necessary in the interests of justice or national security or for the prevention of disorder or crime. Several cases have interpreted this section, mainly in a restrictive way and in favour of the disclosure of sources. This is an example of a situation where the courts, in the light of the Human Rights Act 1998 and E.Ct.H.R. cases on freedom of expression, may have to reconsider the interpretation of a section of a statute. There are important differences in the approach of the E.Ct.H.R. and British courts: the latter sees the need to establish a balance between freedom of expression and justice or national security etc., and decides accordingly. The former places freedom of expression above the other considerations which are not rights, but exceptions to the right to freedom of expression which have to be interpreted narrowly.[90] In addition the E.Ct.H.R. regards a free press as such an important part of the democratic process that it is unwilling to give much weight to the margin of appreciation doctrine in cases involving press freedom.[91]

In *Secretary of State for Defence v. Guardian Newspapers*[92] the House of Lords held that the protection given by section 10 existed even where delivery was sought of a document which was the property of the plaintiff; and that the word "necessary" imposed a strict test which was not to be equated with convenient or expedient. However, the majority of the House accepted that an affidavit sworn by the respondent civil servant was sufficient to establish that it was necessary in the interests of national security to identify the person who copied the document and sent it to the *Guardian*. Subsequent cases have also indicated a willingness by the courts to be satisfied on the facts that disclosure was necessary for one of the reasons set out in the section without taking adequate account of the importance of a free press as an aspect of freedom of

---

[85] *Practice Direction (Contempt: Reporting Restrictions)* [1982] 1 W.L.R. 1475, CA.
[86] *R. v. Clerkenwell Magistrates' Court, ex p. Telegraph plc* [1993] 2 All E.R. 183.
[87] *Re Central Independent Television plc* [1991] 1 All E.R. 347; *cf. R. v. Beck, ex p. Daily Telegraph* [1993] 2 All E.R. 177.
[88] There are a variety of other provisions which restrict the reporting of court proceedings, see C. J. Miller *op. cit.* Chap. 10.
[89] There was no such privilege at common law: *Att.-General v. Clough* [1963] 1 Q.B. 773; *British Steel Corp. v. Granada Television Ltd* [1981] A.C. 1096.
[90] See *Sunday Times v. United Kingdom* (1979) 2 E.H.R.R. 245, at p. 281.
[91] See A. T. H. Smith, "The Press, the Courts and the Constitution," (1999) 52 C.L.P. 126.
[92] [1985] A.C. 339.

expression.[93] In *X Ltd v. Morgan Grampian (Publishers) Ltd*[94] a journalist had obtained from an informant confidential and sensitive information about the financial position of X Ltd which he had planned to use in a publication. X Ltd, having become aware of the planned publication, obtained an injunction restraining it, and an order that, in the interests of justice, the journalist should disclose his notes to enable them to identify the source of the information. The House of Lords upheld the order on the basis that it was necessary in the interests of justice for a company to be able to take remedial action against the source of a leaked document, for example by terminating his employment.

25–017   The journalist brought an action in the E.Ct.H.R. on the basis that the order to disclose his source was a breach of Article 10. The Court concluded that although the court order was in pursuit of the legitimate aim of protecting the rights of X Ltd, the order was not necessary in a democratic society, as the likely damage to X's interests did not outweigh the need to protect the press as the guardian of the public interest.[95] It was influenced in this decision by the fact that the injunction prohibiting publication of the information achieved X Ltd's objective of preserving its confidentiality. This decision appears to require courts in the application of section 10, to give precedence to the protection of sources and to be satisfied that to require a journalist to reveal his sources is proportionate to the ends being pursued, no matter how legitimate these ends may be. Although there are subsequent cases where the courts have refused to order disclosure, this has been on the basis of English cases, and not in consequence of an application of Article 10 as applied in *Goodwin*.[96] In *Camelot Group plc v. Centaur Ltd*[97] the Court of Appeal strangely concluded that the tests applied by the E.Ct.H.R. and the House of Lords were substantially the same, the only difference was in their assessments of the facts. In deciding to order the return of documents which would enable Camelot to identify the person who had leaked them, the court held that the interest of justice prevailed over the protection of sources. It distinguished *Goodwin* on the facts, and failed adequately to consider whether the disclosure of such documents would have a "chilling effect on the free flow of information."[98]

IV. LIBERTY OF THE PRESS

25–018   "The Press" generally covers printed matter of all kinds, and not merely newspapers and periodicals. "The liberty of the press," says Blackstone,[99] "consists in laying no previous restraints upon publications, and not in freedom from censure for criminal matter when published." This liberty, said Lord Mansfield in *Dean of St Asaph's Case*,[1] consists in "printing without any

[93] *Re an Inquiry under the Company Securities (Insider Dealings) Act 1985* [1988] 1 A.C. 660.
[94] [1991] 1 A.C. 1. See, T. R. S. Allan, "Disclosure of Journalists' Sources, Civil Disobedience and the Rule of Law", [1991] C.L.J. 131.
[95] *Goodwin v. United Kingdom* (1996) 22 E.H.R.R. 123.
[96] See *Sanders v. Punch* [1998] 1 W.L.R. 986; *John v. Express Newspapers* [2000] 3 All E.R. 257.
[97] [1999] Q.B. 124, CA.
[98] *Goodwin v. United Kingdom* at para. 39.
[99] Bl.Comm. IV, 151. He adds that "to censure the licentiousness, is to maintain the liberty, of the press": ibid. p. 153. And see *R. v. Burdett* (1820) 4 B. & Ald. 95, *per* Best J.: "Where vituperation begins, the liberty of the press ends."
[1] *R. v. Shipley* (1783) 21 St.Tr. 847, 1040; *ante*, p. 535. *Cf. British Steel Corporation v. Granada Television* [1981] A.C. 1096, 1168 *per* Lord Wilberforce.

previous licence, subject to the consequences of law." "The liberty of the press," said Alexander Hamilton,[2] "is the right to publish with impunity, truth, with good motives, for justifiable ends though reflecting on government, magistracy, or individuals." It has existed in this country since the end of the seventeenth century.

Soon after the introduction of the art of printing in the fifteenth century, a series of proclamations began to be issued to restrict and control printing, in addition to the law of treason, sedition, heresy and blasphemy. In England the printing of books in the early period was confined to the members of the Stationers' Company in London and to the Universities of Oxford and Cambridge.[3] Throughout most of the sixteenth and seventeenth centuries all printing required a licence. By an assumption of the prerogative of the Crown as *custos morum* in the late Tudor and early Stuart periods, secular printing was controlled by the Star Chamber and theological printing by the High Commission. Soon after the abolition of these bodies in 1641, a licence to print was required by the Licensing Act 1662. Several Licensing Acts followed, but the last expired in 1695. The Commons refused to renew it, not so much out of respect for freedom of expression but rather because experience showed that licensing did not succeed in its object. Since 1695, then, the press has been governed by the ordinary law of sedition and libel. No prosecution for criminal libel against the proprietor, publisher or editor of a newspaper may be brought without the order of a judge in chambers.[4] A curious survival from the time of the Napoleonic Wars is the requirement that every newspaper (and other printed object) shall bear the name and address on it of the printer concerned.[5] The Newspaper Libel and Registration Act 1881 establishes a register of proprietors of newspapers (section 8) and requires printers to make annual returns of the titles and proprietors of newspapers which they have printed.

The previous section on contempt of court considered a particular aspect of a free press, the following paragraphs will consider two other aspects of a free press that also require reconsideration in the light of the E.C.H.R: privacy and breach of confidence.

Privacy and the press

Press invasion of privacy has been of concern for some years, and the system of press self-regulation has been inadequate to protect the privacy of members of the public.[6] The lack of a right to privacy in English law[7] and the potential for the development of such a right as a consequence of the Human Rights Act 1998, have implications for press freedom. A balance will have to be found between Article 8 of the E.C.H.R. which protects the right to private and family life, home and correspondence, and freedom of expression as provided by Article 10. It remains to be seen how the British courts will respond to new opportunities for protecting privacy provided by the HRA, but in doing so they are required by section 12 to have particular regard to the importance of the E.C.H.R. right to

25–019

---

[2] In *People v. Croswell* (1804) 3 Johns (N.Y.) 337.

[3] For the history of the law of the Press, see Holdsworth, *History of English Law*, Vol. VI, pp. 360–378.

[4] Law of Libel Amendment Act 1888, s.8; *ante*, para. 25–006.

[5] Newspapers, Printers and Reading Rooms Repeal Act 1869 is the current legislation: see C. Manchester, (1982) 2 Leg.Stud. 180.

[6] See *post* para. 25–023 for discussion of the Press Complaints Commission.

[7] *Kaye v. Robertson* [1991] F.S.R. 62.

freedom of expression. Early cases indicate that in cases concerning the press and the publication of information, the courts are expanding the breach of confidence doctrine to accommodate the protection of privacy.[8] However, this development will not assist with physical intrusion and the acquisition of information such as occurred in *Kaye v. Robinson*[9] where a journalist and a photographer entered the hospital room of the claimant, a well known actor recovering from an accident, interviewed and photographed him when he was in no position to give his consent.

Confidentiality and public interest

25–020   The law of confidential information originally provided a protection for aspects of family life and for commercial secrets, but has been extended to apply also to protect government secrets. The principle was recognised, although held not to be applicable on the facts, in relation to the confidentiality of cabinet discussions in *Attorney-General v. Jonathan Cape Ltd.*[10] This opened the way for governments to seek injunctions to prevent the publication of government secrets, reaching a climax with the *Spycatcher* cases. *Spycatcher* was the title of a book written by Peter Wright to be published in Australia about his experiences as a former member of M.I.5. The Attorney-General sought an injunction in Australia to prevent its publication on the basis of that Mr Wright had obtained his information in confidence as a member of M.I.5, and that the public interest was in the protection of the secrecy of the Security Services. Pending a full hearing undertakings were given not to publish extracts from the book.[11] Several English papers reported the Australian legal proceedings including in their accounts allegations made in the book by Mr Wright, and the *Sunday Times* started a serialisation of the book, which by then was about to be published in the United States. These publications led to a series of actions both against the newspapers for contempt of court,[12] and by the Attorney-General seeking inter-locutory injunctions to restrain further publication of extracts from *Spycatcher*. Although by 1987 the book had been published in the United States and was available in the United Kingdom, interlocutory injunctions against several news-papers were upheld by the House of Lords pending a full trial. The majority opinion of the House of Lords in *Attorney-General v. Guardian Newspapers Ltd*[13] was on the ground that wider dissemination of the *Spycatcher* revelations could do further harm.[14] When the case came to full trial the Attorney-General's claim for permanent injunctions was refused. The case went to the House of Lords which held that since the contents of the book were in the public domain, no further damage could be done to the public interest.[15] The decision of the House of Lords confirmed that the press could be restrained by injunction from

---

[8] *Douglas and Others v. Hello! Ltd*, *The Times*, January 16, 2001, [2001] 2 All E.R 289; *Venables and Another v. News Group Newspapers and Others* [2001] 1 All E.R. 908. This development was suggested *obiter* by Laws J. in *Hellewell v. Chief Constable of Derbyshire* [1995] 1 W.L.R. 804.
[9] [1991] F.S.R. 62.
[10] [1976] Q.B. 752.
[11] The Australian courts eventually refused to restrain publication.
[12] *Attorney-General v. Newspaper Publishing plc* [1988] Ch. 333; *Attorney-General v. Times News-papers Ltd* [1992] 1 A.C. 191.
[13] [1987] 1 W.L.R. 1248.
[14] See the powerful dissenting opinion of Lord Bridge.
[15] *A-G v. Guardian Newspapers Ltd (No. 2)* [1990] 1 A.C. 109, Lord Griffith dissenting; the *Sunday Times* was liable for breach of confidence for its initial attempt to serialise the book, and was required to make an account of profits to the Crown.

publishing government secrets, provided that newspaper knew that the information was confidential and that some harm to the public interest would result from the publication.

In deciding whether to grant an injunction to restrain a breach of confidence, the courts have to consider where the public interest lies: it may lie in the publication of the information obtained in breach of confidence.[16] In *Lion Laboratories Ltd v. Evans*[17] disclosure of a confidential memorandum relating to the efficiency of a computerised instrument for measuring the level of alcohol in blood was held to be justified because of the public's entitlement to information which raised doubts about a device which was providing the evidence on which people were being convicted. The Court of Appeal, therefore, discharged the injunction granted at first instance against the *Daily Express*. In this case the defence of public interest was allowed even though there was no "iniquity" revealed by the confidential information. However, if there are other more beneficial ways to disclose confidential information which it may be in the public interest to disclose, other than the media, this could influence the court in its decision to grant an injunction.[18] In *X v. Y*[19] it was held that the public interest in allowing a newspaper to publish the names of practising doctors who were suffering from AIDs did not take precedence over the public interest in the confidentiality of medical records.

The use of injunctions to restrain a breach of confidence must now be in accordance with the E.C.H.R. Some guidance on the approach to take is provided by the E.Ct.H.R. decision in the action brought against the United Kingdom by the newspapers involved in the *Spycatcher* litigation.[20] The Court started from the basis that the injunctions were a restriction of free speech under Article 10, the main questions were therefore whether the restriction of freedom of expression imposed by the injunction had a legitimate aim under Article 10(2) and if so whether it was necessary in a democratic society. It accepted that an injunction was justified in the interests of national security and to maintain the judicial process by protecting confidential information pending trial of the full action. However, with respect to whether the injunctions were necessary, the Court distinguished between the period until July 1987 and subsequently. In the first period the reasons for the restriction on freedom of speech were sufficient to justify the restriction and proportionate to the aims. However, once the book was published in the United States, its confidential nature was destroyed, and the previous objectives were no longer sufficient to justify continuing the restrictions, to do so would prevent the press from informing the public about matters of legitimate public concern.

25–021

Section 12 of the Human Rights Act also provides guidance. Except in exceptional circumstances interlocutory injunctions are not to be granted without notice to the other side, and they should not be granted unless the court is satisfied that the applicant is likely to succeed on the merits at the trial. In deciding whether to grant relief, a court has to have special regard to the

---

[16] There is a distinction between what is interesting to the public and what is in the public interest, see *British Steel Corporation v. Granada Television Ltd* [1981] A.C. 1096 at p. 1168.

[17] [1985] Q.B. 526, CA.

[18] *Francome v. Mirror Group Newspapers* [1984] 2 All E.R. 408.

[19] [1988] 2 All E.R. 648.

[20] *Observer and Guardian v. United Kingdom* (1992) 14 E.H.R.R. 153, *Sunday Times v. United Kingdom* (1992) 14 E.H.R.R. 229.

E.C.H.R. right to freedom of expression. Where proceedings relate to journalistic, literary or artistic material, particular regard must be had to the extent to which the material is, or is about to become available to the public; the extent to which publication would be in the public interest; and any relevant privacy code (section 12(4)).

Disclosure of sources of information
25–022   The effect of section 10 of the Contempt of Court Act 1981 was discussed above.[21] Protection is given by the provisions of the Police and Criminal Evidence Act 1984 to journalistic material in relation to police powers to search premises and seize evidence found there.[22] The offence in section 19 of the Terrorism Act 2000[23] could be used to prosecute journalists who fail to report to the police matters concerning terrorism obtained by them in an interview. Assurances were given that the protection of sources was likely to fall within the defence of "reasonable excuse" in section 19(3).[24]

Press Complaints Commission
25–023   Unlike television and radio, the press is supervised through self-regulation, by the Press Complaints Commission (PCC). This is a non-statutory body established in 1991 to replace the Press Council, which had been widely criticised as slow, bureaucratic and partisan. It had also failed to prevent press intrusion into peoples' private lives, and failed to improve public recourse against the press.[25] The Press Complaints Commission was said to be a last chance for the press to prove that voluntary self regulation could work.[26] The PCC has an independent chairman and 15 other members, 10 of whom are from the newspaper industry. It publishes, monitors and implements a Code of Practice for the guidance of the press and the public. A review of the first two years of the new body was unenthusiastic, and recommended the establishment of a statutory body with powers to fine newspapers for breaches of the Code of Practice and to award compensation to aggrieved parties, it also proposed some new criminal offences and a new tort of infringement of privacy.[27] No changes were made in the law, but there is some evidence that the PCC has taken it role more seriously. However, it has limited powers, and no legal powers to enforce its adjudications. Self-regulation of the press has persisted because of the reluctance of governments to be seen to be interfering with free speech.

The PCC is a public authority under section 6 of the Human Rights Act 1998, and as such could be subject to litigation if it fails to properly protect private and family life as required by Article 8 of the E.C.H.R. Press concern that Article 8 could endanger freedom of the press and that the judges could use it to create a right to privacy,[28] lead to the inclusion of section 12 in the HRA.[29] It is arguable

---

[21] *ante*, para. 25–016.

[22] *ante*, para. 24–047.

[23] *ante*, para. 25–011.

[24] H.L. Deb., Vol. 613, col. 653; Vol. 614, col. 187. To provided reasonable excuse as a *defence* to revealing a source is not necessarily in accordance with the E.Ct.H.R. decision in *Goodwin v. United Kingdom* (1996) 22 E.H.R.R. 123, see *ante*, para. 25–017.

[25] *Report of the Committee on Privacy and Related Matters*, Cm. 1102, 1990 (Calcutt Report).

[26] Calcutt Report para. 14.38.

[27] Sir David Calcutt, *Review of Press Self-Regulation*, Cm. 2135 (1993). See also *Privacy and Media Intrusion*, H.C. 291 (1992–93).

[28] See *Spencer v. United Kingdom* [1998] 25 E.H.R.R. C.D. 105.

[29] *ante*, para. 22–018.

that the failure of the common law to recognise a right to privacy has been responsible for the pusillanimous attitude taken by the PCC and its predecessor to invasions of privacy.

V. Obscenity, Indecency and Censorship

Obscene publications

In early times, jurisdiction over obscenity was exercised by the ecclesiastical courts as a matter of morals; but this jurisdiction was taken over by the common law courts in *Curl's Case*,[30] where the misdemeanour of obscene libel was recognised. The Obscene Publications Act 1857 also empowered magistrates to authorise the seizure and destruction of obscene articles kept for sale or other purpose of gain. The test of obscenity for the purpose of both the misdemeanour and a destruction order was that laid down by Cockburn C.J. in *R. v. Hicklin*[31]:

    " . . . I think the test of obscenity is this, whether the tendency of the matter charged as obscenity is to deprave and corrupt those whose minds are open to such immoral influences, and into whose hands a publication of this sort may fall."

In the following paragraphs a variety of statutes concerned with obscenity and indecency will be considered. These by their very nature restrict freedom of expression, and will now have to be interpreted so far as it is possible, in accordance with E.C.H.R. rights. However, the E.C.H.R. allows for restraint on freedom of speech on the grounds of the protection of morality (Article 10(2)). In *Handyside v. United Kingdom*[32] the E.Ct.H.R. accepted that the Obscene Publications Act 1959 Act was within the Convention, and that in this area domestic legislators have a wide margin of appreciation in securing the freedoms guaranteed under the E.C.H.R.

25–024

The Obscene Publications Act 1959

This Act created the statutory offence of publishing[33] obscene matter,[34] which superseded the common law misdemeanour, and repealed and replaced the Act of 1857 as regards the seizure and forfeiture of obscene matter. The test of obscenity for the purposes of the Act is whether the effect "is, if taken as a whole, such as to tend to deprave and corrupt persons who are likely, having regard to all relevant circumstances, to read, see or hear the matter contained or embodied in it." The tendency to deprave and corrupt, instead of being a presumed consequence of obscenity, has become the test of obscenity and what has to be

25–025

---

[30] (1727) Stra. 788.
[31] (1868) L.R. 3 Q.B. 360, 371.
[32] (1976) 1 E.H.R.R. 737.
[33] As amended by the Broadcasting Act 1990, s.162(1)(b) and by the Criminal Justice and Public Order Act 1994, sched. 9, to include broadcasting and electronic transmission within the term "publication".
[34] The Criminal Justice and Public Order Act 1994 made the offences in s.1 of the 1959 Act arrestable offences, and classified them as serious arrestable offences.

proved.[35] The question is not whether an item can be described by terms regarded as synonyms of obscene, for example, filthy, shocking, repulsive, lewd, but whether it has a tendency to deprave and corrupt: *R. v. Anderson; R. v. Oz Publications Ltd.*[36] Thus it could be argued that the very degree of lewdness of a book might be such that, far from depraving it would produce feelings of horror and revulsion and so morally improve the reader: *R. v. Calder and Boyars Ltd.*[37] The depraving and corruption to which the statute refers has been held to extend beyond the sexual sphere to, for example, corrupting by advocating the illicit use of drugs: *Calder (John) Publications Ltd v. Powell.*[38] Whether an item is obscene is a question of fact for the jury on which expert evidence is inadmissible except in the case of material aimed at young children where the jury may require the help of psychiatric experts.[39]

An item is not obscene for the purposes of the 1959 Act if it is likely to corrupt only a minute number of people exposed to its influence, a "lunatic fringe of readers." On the other hand an item likely to corrupt a significant proportion of people exposed to it would be obscene.[40] Where it can be established that the particular persons to whom an item has been published (for example by sale) are not capable of being depraved by the item, it cannot be obscene under the 1959 Act.[41] That absurdity in the earlier legislation was remedied by creating a new offence of having an obscene article for publication for gain; Obscene Publications Act 1964, s.1 which provides that the question whether the article is obscene shall be determined by reference to such publication for gain of the article as in the circumstances it may reasonably be inferred the person charged had in contemplation and to any further publication that could reasonably be expected to follow from it.

25–026　　It is a defence under Section 4 of the 1959 Act[42] to prove that publication "is justified as being for the public good on the ground that it is in the interests of science, literature, art or learning,[43] or of other objects of general concern." The Act of 1959 also declares that, contrary to the former practice, the opinion of experts may be admitted either to establish or to negative this defence.[44]

For the purposes of the Act an "article" includes matter to be read or looked at, a sound record, film, or thing intended to be used for the reproduction or manufacture of obscene articles, *e.g.* a photographic negative, or cinematograph exhibition. A video cassette[45] and a computer disc[46] have been held to be within the Act.

---

[35] *D.P.P. v. Whyte* [1972] A.C. 849, in which the House of Lords held that middle-aged men who are already addicts of pornography are capable of being further depraved and corrupted.

[36] [1972] 1 Q.B. 304, CA.

[37] [1969] 1 Q.B. 151, CA.

[38] [1965] 1 Q.B. 509.

[39] *D.P.P. v. A. and B.C. Chewing Gum Ltd* [1968] 1 Q.B. 159, DC. Similarly in cases of obscenity involving drug use: jury not qualified to assess effect of drugs and of methods of using them recommended in book: *R. v. Skirving; R. v. Grossman* [1985] Q.B. 819, CA.

[40] *R. v. Calders and Boyars Ltd, supra.*

[41] *R. v. Clayton and Halsey* [1963] 1 Q.B. 163 (the case of the incorruptible police officers).

[42] As amended by the Criminal Law Act 1977, s.53.

[43] "Learning" is a noun, meaning "product of scholarship"; it is not a verb meaning teaching or educating: *Att.-Gen.'s Reference (No. 3 of 1977)* [1978] 1 W.L.R. 1123, CA.

[44] But evidence of supposed therapeutic benefit is inadmissible: *R. v. Staniforth; R. v. Jordan* [1977] A.C. 699, HL.

[45] *A.-G's Reference (No. 5 of 1980)*, [1980] 3 All E.R. 816.

[46] *R. v. Fellows and Arnold* [1997] 1 Cr. App. Rep. 244.

As will be seen later in this chapter, films are to some extent treated differently from items such as books and magazines.

Forfeiture

Where a person has been convicted of publishing (or having for gain for **25–027** publication) obscene articles, the court shall order the forfeiture of these articles. In addition when criminal proceedings have not been started, the police may take legal action against obscene articles by way of forfeiture. Under section 3 of the Obscene Publications Act 1959 a justice of the peace may issue a warrant empowering a constable to enter and search any premises, stall or vehicle, and to seize and remove any articles which he has reason to believe to be obscene articles kept for publication for gain. When the owner of the premises or user of the stall or vehicle has been summoned to appear to show cause why the articles should not be forfeited, the magistrates' court may order the articles to be forfeited if it is satisfied that they were obscene articles kept for publication for gain. The owner, author or maker may also appear to show cause against forfeiture. The defence of "public good" may be set up, and the opinion of experts may be admitted on either side. Appeal against a forfeiture order lies to the Crown Court or by case stated to the High Court.

Obscene Libel

The Obscene Publications Act 1959 does not expressly abolish the common **25–028** law misdemeanour of obscene libel but provides in section 2(4) that a person publishing an article shall not be proceeded against for an offence at common law consisting of the publication of any matter contained or embodied in the article where it is of the essence of the offence that the matter is obscene. In *Shaw v. Director of Public Prosecutions*[47] the House of Lords held that the section did not prevent the bringing of proceedings for a common law conspiracy to corrupt public morals or outrage public decency by the publication of an obscene article since the essence of the offence was the agreement not the publication.

Indecency

A number of statutes refer to "indecency" by which is meant a lower degree **25–029** of moral depravity than connoted by obscenity. From the point of view of the prosecutor this renders his task easier, particularly because the evidence of experts is not relevant. The Post Office Act 1953 section 11 makes it an offence to " . . . send or attempt to send or procure to be sent a postal packet which: (b) encloses any indecent or obscene print, painting, photograph, lithograph, engraving, cinematograph film, book, card or written communication, or any indecent or obscene article whether similar to the above or not . . . ."

In *R. v. Anderson; R. v. Oz Publications Ltd*[48] the defendants, although acquitted under the 1959 Act were convicted under the Post Office Act. Articles imported into the country are liable to be forfeited if they are "indecent or obscene." Thus books which, if published in England and prosecuted under the

---

[47] [1962] A.C. 220. See too *Knuller Publishing Printing and Promotions v. D.P.P.* [1973] A.C. 435. The conspiracies recognised by the House of Lords in these decisions are preserved in existence by the Criminal Law Act 1977, s.5(3). These offences would be unlikely to survive challenges under the E.C.H.R.
[48] [1972] 1 Q.B. 304, CA.

1959 Act, might be shown to be works of art or literature by expert evidence, are liable if published abroad to be seized by zealous customs officers.[49]

The Telecommunications Act 1984, s.43(1)(a) provides the offence of grossly offensive, indecent or obscene telephone calls. This offence is capable of applying to the sending of indecent matter in digital format from one computer to another over public telephone lines.[50]

25–030   The taking, distributing, publishing or possessing of indecent photographs or pseudo-photographs of children under the age of 16 is prohibited by the Protection of Children Act 1978. This statute is not aimed, as is much of the law considered in this section, at censorship because of the supposed deleterious effect on the users of obscene materials but at the easily identifiable harm to children who are involved in the taking of indecent photographs. The problems caused by digital technology have been addressed in the 1994 amendments to this Act.[51]

A further means of restricting access to indecent materials is by imposing controls. The public display of indecent matter is prohibited by the Indecent Displays (Control) Act 1981, an Act which is designed to prevent people from being brought into unwelcome proximity with indecent matter. The Act does not attempt to define indecent. Matter is defined as "anything capable of being displayed, except that it does not include an actual human body or any part thereof" (section 1(5)). The Act does not apply to television broadcasts, displays inside art galleries or museums, displays inside buildings owned by the Crown or local authorities, theatrical performances or cinematograph exhibitions. The effect of the exemption in the cases other than that of television broadcasts, is that the buildings concerned do not have to carry a statutory warning that indecent matter may be exhibited inside—as would a shop displaying such matter.

Section 3 of the Local Government (Miscellaneous Provisions) Act 1982 empowers a local authority to establish a licensing scheme for sex establishments in its area. This has been used particularly in respect of "sex shops"; the law is not concerned with the effect of the material sold, but on whether material is sold that falls within the definition of a "sex article" (Sched. 3). If a licence is granted, the shop will be subjected to conditions on displays, opening hours etc.

Reform

25–031   Attempts to reform the law relating to obscene publications raise difficult questions about what the purpose of the law is and what the justifications are for the criminal law interfering with the freedom of rational adults.

At present the law is explicable only on the basis that censorship is aimed at the minds of the people reading the books or viewing the films. There may be an argument that pornography ultimately leads to criminal acts against others but that is not the justification for the law at present.[52] Should the law concern itself with whether someone wishes to read Shakespeare or pornography?[53] To some

---

[49] Customs Consolidation Act 1876 s.42; Customs and Excise Management Act 1979, s.49; C. Manchester, "Customs Control of Obscene Literature" [1981] Crim.L.Rev. 531. Such control in the case of books is not contrary to E.C. law: *ante*, para. 6–036.

[50] The penalties for this offence were increased by s.92 of the Criminal Justice and Public Order Act 1994.

[51] As amended by s.84 of the Criminal Justice and Public Order Act 1994; see *R. v. Bowden* [2000] 2 All E.R. 418; *R. v. Atkins* [2000] 2 All E.R. 425.

[52] As shown by *D.P.P. v. Whyte* [1972] A.C. 849.

[53] Assuming pornography can be identified. Are the novels of Genet works of genius or the obscene products of a perverted mind, or both?

extent it seems that the law (or some law) against obscenity is justified on the ground that people are disgusted at the thought that other members of the community are reading pornography. But to base criminal laws on disgust alone is at best dangerous and at worst a denial of individuals' rights.

Comprehensive proposals for reform in this area of the law were made by the Williams Committee on Obscenity and Film Censorship,[54] but no action was taken on the report.

Regulating the media and entertainment

In addition to controlling the availability of obscene or indecent material by criminalisation, it is possible to control its availability by pre-censorship.   **25–032**

Broadcasting, cinema and videos

There is an extensive variation in the means whereby the different types of   **25–033**
media are regulated. Broadcasters are subject to very little official censorship, reliance is made on self-regulation. Films and videos are subject to a variety of self-regulation but with increasing statutory involvement. All are subject to a system of licensing, which is permissable under Article 10(1) of the E.C.H.R. but only with respect to the technical means of broadcasting and not the content. If a licence imposes non-technical conditions on a broadcaster, these are permissable only if they can be justified under Article 10(2).[55] Legislation such as the Obscene Publications Act 1959 now applies to all types of the media, though it was not always the case.[56]

Broadcasting[57]

It is, perhaps, not surprising that the content of programmes broadcast by radio   **25–034**
and television can generate particularly heated controversies about freedom of expression. A visit to a theatre is a deliberate choice; radio and television are already in the house. To the person who objects to a film it can be said that it is not necessary to go to the cinema to see it. The person who objects to a television programme is entitled on the contrary, to argue that he has to pay a licence to have a set; his views on what is suitable for showing have therefore, some weight.

Licensing and regulation of all television services, except for those run by the BBC, are the responsibility of the Independent Television Commission (ITC). The Radio Authority (RA) has a similar role with respect to radio. The legal restrictions relating to the contents of programmes is broadly similar in the case of the BBC, the ITC and the RA.[58] In the case of the BBC they are to be found in current BBC agreement[59] and in the case of the ITC and the RA in the

---

[54] Cmnd. 7772 (1979).

[55] *Brind v. United Kingdom* (1994) 77-A D.R. 42, where restrictions on the reporting of terrorists were held to be legitimate and proportionate.

[56] It was not until 1977 that it was applied to films, and 1990 when it was applied to broadcasting.

[57] T. Gibbons, *Regulating The Media* (1998).

[58] The ITC was established by s.1 of the Broadcasting Act 1990 (replacing the Independent Broadcasting Commission and the Cable Authority) to licence and regulate non BBC television services, including all satellite and cable services. The Broadcasting Act 1996 extends its functions to licensing multiplex and digital programme services. The R.A. was established to supervise sound programmes.

[59] Cm. 3152 (1996); revised BBC Charter Cm. 3248 (1996).

Broadcasting Act 1990.[60] Programmes must not offend against good taste or decency or be likely to encourage or incite to crime or to lead to disorder or to be offensive to public feeling. Codes must regulate the showing of violence. The use of subliminal images (those shown for so brief a period of time that the brain is influenced without the person concerned realising the fact) is specifically forbidden by section 6(1)(e) of the 1990 Act.[61] Other requirements relate to the provision of accurate and impartial news features and due impartiality on the part of persons providing programmes on matters of political or industrial controversy or current public policy.[62] The ITC is also required to draw up a code providing guidance with respect to the showing of violence, and the control of advertising, particularly with respect to the avoidance of advertisements directed towards a political end.

25–035   The courts regard the duty relating to the type of programmes which may not be broadcast as ultimately, enforceable by judicial action but they have also made it equally clear that they would not attempt to substitute their aesthetic judgments for those of the properly constituted broadcasting authorities: *Attorney-General, ex rel. McWhirter v. I.B.A.*[63]; *R. v. I.B.A., ex p. Whitehouse.*[64]

There is provision in both the BBC's Charter and Agreement and in the legislation governing commercial broadcasting, for direct interference by government.[65] Broadcasters can be required to refrain from broadcasting or transmitting any matter or matter of any class specified in a notice issued by the Secretary of State. In 1988 the Secretary of State issued a ban on the broadcasting of direct statements by members of terrorist organisations and other parties connected with Northern Ireland.[66] Ministers also have a power to require the broadcasting of any announcement.[67]

The Broadcasting Standards Commission

25–036   This was established by section 264 of the Broadcasting Act 1996 and constitutes a merger of the Broadcasting Standards Council (BSC) and the Broadcasting Complaints Commission.[68] The BSC consists of up to 15 members appointed by the Secretary of State; it is directed to make an annual report to the Secretary of State who shall, after considering it, lay it before both Houses of Parliament.

The legislation maintains a distinction between the BSC's complaints functions relating to privacy and fairness,[69] and its complaints functions with respect to standards of decency. With respect to the first of these functions the BSC's jurisdiction is limited in several ways (section 111), including a limitation on

---

[60] ss.6 and 84 respectively in the 1990 Act.
[61] Breach of the prohibition is not a criminal offence; *R. v. Horseferry Road Justices, ex p. I.B.A.* [1986] 3 W.L.R. 132, DC.
[62] s.6(1)(b),(c) of the 1990 Act, BBC Agreement cl.5. See Gibbons *op. cit.* pp. 94–124.
[63] [1973] Q.B. 269, CA.
[64] *The Times*, April 14, 1984, DC.
[65] Clause 8.2 of the 1996 Agreement, and ss.10(3),(4), 94(3),(4) of the Broadcasting Act 1990.
[66] See H.C.Deb. Vol. 138, col. 885, October 19, 1988. The ban was unsuccessfully challenged by journalists (not the broadcasters) in *R. v. Secretary of State for the Home Department, ex p. Brind* [1991] 1 A.C. 696.
[67] Clause 8.1 of the BBC agreement, and ss.10(1) and (2) and 94(1) and (2) of the 1990 Act.
[68] There had been confusion about the roles of the two bodies, and the Complaints Commission had been perceived as weak, see Cm. 2621 (1994) and H.C. 77 (1993–94). The first attempt to establish a statutory independent broadcasting body was in 1980.
[69] These will be personalised complaints and should be considered independently of considerations of programme-making.

those who have standing to complain.[70] However, in *R. v. Broadcasting Standards Commission, ex p. BBC*[71] the Court of Appeal agreed that the BSC was entitled to consider a complaint of unwarranted infringement of privacy by a company in connection with secret filming in a place to which the public had access. The sanctions available to the BSC are fairly ineffectual (sections 119 and 120).

The role of the BSC with respect to complaints on standards is connected with its duty to publish a code giving guidance on programme standards for the avoidance of "(a) unjust or unfair treatment in programmes . . . , or (b) unwarranted infringement of privacy in, or in connection with the obtaining of materials included in such programmes" (section 107). This section goes further than the previous law[72] in its requirement that the BSC articulates principles of fairness and decency. Section 108[73] requires a further code giving general guidance on the portrayal of violence and sexual conduct and on standards of taste and decency in programmes. The BSC is required to monitor and report on programmes to which section 108 applies. Where a complaint on standards is made to the BSC it does not have to hold a hearing; the adjudications that are made are concerned with the general issue of whether the broadcasters has complied with the BSC code and the broadcaster's own code. The only sanction is to require the broadcaster against whom the complaint was made to publish the complaint and the findings.

The theatre

Under the Theatres Act 1843 there was a censorship by the Lord Chamberlain **25–037** of the public performance of stage plays written after 1843. The Theatres Act 1968 abolished this censorship and repealed the Act of 1843. The 1968 Act, in effect, applies to theatrical performances (other than those given on a domestic occasion in a private dwelling (section 7(1)). It is an offence to present or direct the performance of a play which is obscene, that is if taken as a whole its effect was such as to tend to deprave and corrupt persons who were likely, having regard to all relevant circumstances, to attend it (section 2).

Like the 1959 Act, a defence of justification on the ground of public good is recognised (section 3). Again, following the earlier precedent, section 1(4) provides that prosecutions cannot be brought in respect of a performance within the Act for any common law offence of indecency or for various statutory offences. The 1968 Act goes further than its predecessor and provides that no person shall be proceeded against for an offence at common law of conspiring to corrupt public morals, or to do any act contrary to public morals or decency, in respect of an agreement to present or give a performance of a play, or to cause anything to be said or done in the course of such a performance.

By section 8 proceedings in England may not be commenced under the Act without the leave of the Attorney-General.[74] Theatrical performances are subject to the law against incitement to racial hatred by virtue of the Public Order Act 1986, s.20).

---

[70] *R. v. Broadcasting Complaints Commission ex p. BBC* [1995] E.M.L.R. 241.
[71] [2000] 3 W.L.R. 1327.
[72] s.152 Broadcasting Act 1990.
[73] Re-enacting s.152 of the 1990 Act.
[74] But see *Whitehouse v. Bogdanov, The Times*, March 19, 1982, for a way round the intention of the Act.

The cinema

25–038   The Cinematograph Act 1909 required a licence from the county council or the county borough council for the exhibition of inflammable films.[75] This was a safety measure, but local authorities soon began to refuse to license films which they thought offended public morals, a practice that was declared to be lawful.[76] The film industry thereupon set up its own unofficial body, now known as the British Board of Film Classification,[77] to certify and classify films intended for public exhibition.

The Cinemas Act 1985[78] makes local authorities responsible for the licensing of premises in which films are to be shown to the public. Local authorities have no duty to censor films, except in the case of children (section 1(3)), although they have a power to impose conditions which relate to the admission of adults (section 2(2)). They may, however, be liable if the terms of a licence allows the showing of films which are contrary to the law. They cannot delegate their responsibilities to the Board of Film Classification[79] but they may properly rely on its advice and require cinemas to which they grant licences not to show films which have not been approved by the Board.[80] The Home Office issues model licensing conditions which are used by most local authorities.

The Obscene Publications Act 1959 did not originally apply to public exhibitions of films, which were thus left subject to common law offences relating to indecency.[81] The Criminal Law Act 1977 amended the 1959 Act to bring the showing of films within the protection of that Act and further provided that no prosecution can be brought without the consent of the Director of Public Prosecutions, where the article is a moving picture film not less than 16mm. wide and publication of it took place or could reasonably be expected to take place only in the course of a cinematograph exhibition. Nor can any prosecution be brought for any common law offence or any conspiracy to corrupt public morals.

It is clearly illogical that a system of censorship should evolve out of legislation concerned with public safety. Decisions of the Board of Censors in earlier years showed British prudery at its worst. If there is to be censorship it is arguable that the responsibility must be that of a state organisation.[82]

Video recordings

25–039   Video works and recordings[83] are subject to a scheme of statutory censorship, introduced by the Video Recordings Act 1984[84] which creates an offence of supplying an uncensored video unless the video or the supply fall within the exempting provisions of the Act. The penalties for offences under the Act were increased by section 88 of the CJPO Act 1994.

---

[75] Extended to non-inflammable films by the Cinematograph Act 1952. Exemption from licensing requirements on the part of private cinema clubs, run for profit, was removed by the Cinematograph (Amendment) Act 1982.
[76] *London County Council v. Bermondsey Bioscope Ltd* [1911] 1 K.B. 445.
[77] Formerly known as the British Board of Film Censors.
[78] Consolidating earlier legislation.
[79] *Ellis v. Dubowski* [1921] 3 K.B. 621.
[80] *R. v. Greater London Council, ex p. Blackburn* [1976] 1 W.L.R. 550.
[81] *R. v. Greater London Council, ex p. Blackburn, supra.*
[82] See the recommendations by the Williams' Committee (1979) Cmnd. 7772.
[83] As defined by s.1 of the Video Recording Act 1984, as amended by the Criminal Justice and Public Order Act 1994 (CJPO Act) to include "any other device capable of storing data electronically".
[84] For a criticism of the Act and its procedure through Parliament as a private member's bill, see Neville March Hunnings, "Video Censorship" [1985] P.L. 214.

Classification certificates indicate whether a video is suitable for general viewing or only by persons over the age (not being over 18) specified on the certificate. In the latter case a further restriction may require that supplies of the video may only take place in licensed sex shops (section 7).

Elaborate provisions deal with the definitions of "exempted works" and "exempted supplies;" these provisions were amended by the CJPO Act. Section 2(1) exempts from the necessity to be classified (i) videos which are designed to inform educate or instruct; concerned with sport, religion or music; and (ii) video games. But no video in these categories is exempt if to a significant extent it depicts human sexual activities, torture, human genital organs and other listed activities and functions. To this list was added "techniques likely to be useful in the commission of offences." The definition of exempted supply is even longer and, for example, includes supplying videos for medical training; thus non-exempt videos under section 2(2) may be the subject of exempt supplies.

The Secretary of State acting under section 4 designated the British Board of Film Classification (BBFC) as the "designated authority" to classify video recordings. The 1984 Act did not lay down any detailed criteria for the BBFC to apply, other than to have regard to the likelihood of the video being viewed in the home. Section 90 of the CJPO Act 1994 inserts section 4A which requires the "designated authority" when deciding on classifications of videos to have special regard to any harm that may be caused to potential viewers,[85] or through their behaviour, to society by the manner in which the work deals with: criminal behaviour, illegal drugs, violent behaviour or incidents, horrific behaviour or incidents, or human sexual behaviour.

---

[85] Which is defined in s.4A(2) as "any person (including a child or young person) who is likely to view the video in question if a (particular classification) . . . were issued."

CHAPTER 26

FREEDOM OF EXPRESSION: OFFICIAL SECRECY AND THE RIGHT
TO KNOW

26–001   This chapter considers as an aspect of freedom of expression the right to seek and receive information and ideas: the right to know. Whereas Parliament and the courts operate openly, it is a characteristic of the third branch of government, the executive, that it operates in secret. The right to know has become more significant with the increase in government activities in the last 100 years. There are a variety of justifications for this right: it is an aspect of democracy that citizens should have information about the workings of government to enable them exercise their democratic responsibilities; the knowledge that information is liable to be made public should encourage a high standard of decision-making and discourage maladministration and fraud, and in consequence better government; some information is of personal concern to individuals who may wish to know of its existence and be satisfied of its accuracy. However, the right to know can never be absolute. It frequently has to be balanced against other public interests such as national security, the need to protect dealings with other countries and a desire for efficient government. Not only may the availability of information be restricted on these grounds, to reveal information that falls within them may be a criminal offence.

The first section of this chapter considers the ability of governments to prevent certain types of information being made available to citizens by the use of legislation and practice on official secrets.

The second section considers a different aspect of State interest, the interest of the State in the secret surveillance of the activities of individuals. Here it is the State which wants information and it is the individual who requires protection from such State interference. That is not to say that such activities should never be allowed, but they should only be permitted if conducted in clearly defined circumstances, for specific purposes and be independently regulated.

26–002   The final section considers how and when a citizen may have access to information held about himself by organisations such as banks, doctors, local authorities and government departments. It also looks more widely at something that the law and practice in both the above sections in effect prevent, namely the right to obtain information about the workings of government. The notion of open government has in the past been something that was available by consent of Ministers rather than by statutory right; this section will consider the extent to which this has changed under the Freedom of Information Act 2000. A final aspect of freedom of information is the Public Interest Disclosure Act 1998, which gives some protection to workers who, in the public interest, reveal information.

I. OFFICIAL SECRETS[1]

The Official Secrets Act 1911

The Bill that became the Official Secrets Act 1911 was introduced into the **26–003**
House of Lords after the Agadir crisis.[2] The Bill had been carefully considered
for some time in the Department but passed through Parliament with scarcely any
debate. Section 1(1) makes it an offence if any person "for any purpose prejudicial to the safety or interests of the State" (a) approaches or enters a prohibited
place[3]; or (b) makes a sketch or plan, etc. calculated or intended to be, or which
might be useful to an enemy; or (c) obtains, publishes or communicates to any
other person any sketch, etc. document or information which is calculated to be
or might be or is intended to be useful to an enemy.[4] Purpose prejudicial to the
safety or interests of the State may be inferred from the circumstances; and if the
accused acted without lawful authority in communicating information relating to
a prohibited place[5] he is presumed to have acted for a prejudicial purpose (section
1(2)). The prejudicial purpose refers to the intention of the accused, not the actual
or potential effect of his conduct. Section 1 is not limited to time of war: an
enemy may be actual or potential.

In *Chandler v. Director of Public Prosecutions*[6] members of an anti-nuclear
weapons group, the Committee of 100, were convicted under section 1 for
entering a RAF station, which was a prohibited place. Their intention was to sit
in front of aircraft so as to prevent them from taking off; their ultimate object
being to bring about nuclear disarmament, which they considered would be
beneficial to this country. The House of Lords, unanimously upholding their
convictions, held: first, that the section (in spite of the marginal note: ("Penalties
for spying") covered sabotage[7]; secondly, that the question whether the purpose
of the accused was "prejudicial to the safety or interests of the State" was a
question for the jury. "Purpose" meant direct purpose or object, not indirect
purpose or motive, and the accused might not give evidence as to the latter.
Ministers could not assert their opinion as to what was or was not prejudicial to
the interests of the State, though an officer of the Crown could give evidence
about what were the interests of the Crown and as to the airfield being part of the
defence system maintained for the protection of the realm.

---

[1] See D. G. T. Williams, *Not in the Public Interest* (1965); K. Robertson, *Public Secrets: A Study in
the Development of Governmental Secrecy* (1982).
[2] Germany's action in sending a gunboat to the port of Agadir, with a promise to assist the Moroccans
against France, nearly precipitated a European war.
[3] As defined in s.3 to include any defence works, arsenal, naval or air force station, camp, ship or
aircraft belonging to or occupied by the Crown.
[4] *R. v. Britten* [1969] 1 W.L.R. 151, CA; deterrent sentences may be appropriate.
[5] Which includes any defence works, arsenal, naval or air force station, camp, ship or aircraft
belonging to or occupied by the Crown (s.3).
[6] [1964] A.C. 763.
[7] This part of the decision was right according to the method of interpretation used by the courts at
the time, but it was inconsistent with statements made by Ministers in parliamentary debates on
Official Secrets Bills to the effect that s.1 of the 1911 Act was intended to be restricted to espionage:
Donald Thompson, "The Committee of 100 and the Official Secrets Act 1911", [1963] P.L. 201. In
the light of *Pepper v. Hart* [1993] A.C. 593, it is likely that a court today would come to a different
conclusion as to whether such activities came within s.1.

Their Lordships had difficulty with the meaning of "the State," an unusual expression in English law in relation to internal affairs.[8] Lord Reid said, "the State" did not mean the Government or the Executive, but meant perhaps the country, the realm or the organised community. Viscount Radcliffe in the context of this case spoke of the defence of the realm. According to Lord Hodson the organised State comprised those persons who dwelt therein and whose safety was to be considered. For Lord Devlin the State meant the organs of government of a national community, which in respect of the armed forces meant the Crown. It is suggested that the difficulty lies largely in the fact that the Government as the only agent legally capable of speaking for the Crown is liable to be confused, by itself and others, with the Government as a group of party politicians. The phrase "in the interests of the State" also occurred in section 2, where someone prosecuted for disclosing information contrary to that section, could attempt to prove that the disclosure was made on that basis. In *R. v. Ponting*[9] in directing the jury on the meaning of "the interest of the State", McCowan J. followed what had been suggested by Lord Pearce in *Chandler* and said that the expression meant the policies of the State laid down for it by the recognised organs of government and authority. This direction in effect neutralised Ponting's argument that he had acted in the interests of the State as an institution as distinct from the government of the day.[10]

Section 2 of the 1911 Act created what became known as a "catch all" provision. The wording created over 2000 different ways in which a person could face a prosecution under this section. The nub of the offence was the unauthorised communication to another of information gained in the service of the Crown or the receipt of such information. The information did not have to be important, harmful to the state or secret. No *mens rea* was required. Section 2 had long been widely criticised and several official reports had recommended its repeal and replacement[11]; this finally happened with the enactment of the Official Secrets Act 1989.[12]

The Official Secrets Act 1920

26–004   This was passed after experience of security problems during the First World War and was designed to enact for peace time the content of certain Defence of the Realm Regulations. Section 1(1) provides a variety of offences in connection with wearing an unauthorised uniform, impersonating a government official for the purpose of gaining admission to a prohibited place, and unlawfully retaining official documents for a purpose prejudicial to the safety or interests of the State. These and other offences such as obstructing or interfering with a military or police guard "in the vicinity of" a prohibited place are not ones that are of concern to freedom of expression. Section 7 provides that it is an offence to

---

[8] The term the State has been interpreted by the courts in different ways depending on the context, see, *e.g. Foster v. British Gas plc* [1991] 2 A.C. 306, with respect to the meaning of the state in E.C. law.

[9] [1985] Crim. L.R. 318.

[10] Ponting, a civil servant, had been charged with communicating confidential documents to another person contrary to s.2(1) of the 1911 Act (since repealed); despite the weight of the evidence against him and the nature of the direction to the jury, Ponting was acquitted.

[11] *Departmental Committee on Section 2 of the Official Secrets Act 1911* (1972) Cmnd. 5104; *Reform of Section 2 of the Official Secrets Act 1911* (1978) Cmnd. 7285; *Freedom of Information* (1979) Cmnd. 7520; *Reform of Section 2 of the Official Secrets Act 1911* (1988) Cm. 408.

[12] The failure of the prosecution of Clive Ponting, despite a clear indication by the trial judge to convict, probably spurred the government into reform.

attempt to commit any offence under the 1911 Act or the 1920 Act or[13] to do any act preparatory to the commission of an offence under either Act. Thus preparatory acts which are not even attempts may be punishable.[14] It suffices for a conviction, to show merely that the accused realised that a substantive offence might possibly follow the preparatory act, not that it must or probably would follow.[15] The effect of section 7 is to extend the scope of the 1911 and 1920 Acts and to make it easier to prove attempts to commit offences under these statutes, than elsewhere in the criminal law.

Prosecution under the Acts requires the consent of the Attorney-General or Lord Advocate.

The Official Secrets Act 1989[16]

This Act replaced the widely drawn section 2 of the 1911 Act by creating **26–005** specific categories of official information, and providing offences in connection with disclosing information, documents or other articles in respect of each category. Although the 1989 Act decriminalised certain types of disclosure, it did not in fact radically change the scope of official secrecy, as these categories are themselves widely drawn. For virtually all the categories the prosecution has to prove that the disclosure was damaging, the definition of which differs for each category. In addition, for all the offences the disclosure has to be "without lawful authority." Section 7 provides circumstances when a disclosure may be authorised, which differ depending on the identity of the person making the disclosure. An authorised disclosure by a Crown servant is one "made in accordance with his official duty"; by a government contractor it is one made "in accordance with an official authorisation" or "for the purposes of the functions for which he is a government contractor and without contravening an official restriction"; for any other person it is one made to a Crown servant for the purposes of his functions as a Crown servant, or made with official authorisation. It is also a defence for the discloser to show that "he believed that he had lawful authority to make the disclosure in question and had no reasonable cause to believe otherwise" (section 7(4)). Where the offences apply to Crown servants, government contractors, or members of the security and intelligence services, as the case may be, they do so with respect to past and present members of those groups. Sections 2, 3 and 4 apply only to Crown servants and government contractors. No prosecutions under the Act may be brought without the consent of the Attorney-General (section 9).

Security and intelligence[17] (section 1)

Section 1(1) provides that it is an offence for any person who is or who has **26–006** been a member of the security or intelligence services[18] to disclose, without lawful authority, any information, document or other article "relating to security or intelligence which is or has been in his possession by virtue of his position as a member of any of those services or in the course of his work (having been notified that section 1(1) applies to him.)". There is no requirement for section

---

[13] *R. v. Oakes* [1959] 2 Q.B. 350.

[14] *cf.* s.1(1) of the Criminal Attempts Act 1981.

[15] *R. v. Bingham* [1973] Q.B. 870, CA.

[16] See S. Palmer, "The Government Proposals for Reforming s.2 of the Official Secrets Act 1911" [1988] P.L. 523; "Tightening Secrecy Law", [1990] P.L. 243.

[17] *i.e.* M.I.5, M.I.6, see s.1(9).

[18] Or someone notified by a Minister that because of his work he is subject to s.1(1) s.1(6).

1(1) that the disclosure should be damaging (*cf.* section 1(3) and ss.2–6), all information no matter how innocuous is covered. Section 1(3) creates a similar separate offence in respect of Crown servants or government contractors.[19] However, here the disclosure has to be damaging, which is defined as causing damage to any aspect of the work of the security and intelligence services (section 1(4)(a)); or, if it would be likely to cause such damage (section 1(4)(b)). It is not necessary to show that the actual document disclosed would cause damage provided the document is part of a class of information, document etc. the unauthorised disclosure of which is likely to cause damage as defined in section 1(4)(a). Section 1(5) provides defences of innocent disclosure. The person concerned has to prove that at the time of the alleged offence "he did not know, and had no reasonable cause to believe", that the unauthorised disclosure related to security or intelligence, or, in the case of an offence under section 1(3), that the disclosure would be damaging.

Defence[20] (section 2)

26–007   The meaning of defence includes defence policy and other matters relating in general to the armed forces such as weapons, stores and plans for supplies and services in time of war (section 2(4)). A disclosure is damaging under this section if the information either causes or is likely to cause any of the following results: "(a) it damages the capability of . . . the armed forces . . . to carry out their tasks or leads to loss of life or injury to members of those forces or serious damage to (their) equipment or installations; or (b) . . . it endangers the interests of the United Kingdom abroad, seriously obstructs the promotion or protection . . . of those interests or endangers the safety of British citizens abroad" (section 2(2)).[21] The definition of damaging in this section is clearly very wide, and it is questionable whether it is sufficiently precise to satisfy the requirements of the E.C.H.R.

International relations (section 3)

26–008   This section is concerned with (a) information relating to international relations or (b) confidential information which was obtained from a State (other than the United Kingdom) or an international organisation, and which the Crown servant or government contractor has obtained by virtue of his position as such. The test of damaging is the same as that in section 2(2)(b); but where the information was confidential, or obtained by virtue of the position of the discloser as a Crown servant or government contractor, then the fact that it was confidential or the nature of its contents may be sufficient in itself to show that it was damaging for the purpose of the section.[22]

Crime and special investigation powers (section 4)

26–009   This section applies to information the disclosure of which would, or would be likely to result in the commission of an offence; facilitate an escape from legal custody or prejudice the safekeeping of those in such custody; impede the prevention, detection, apprehension or prosecution of suspected offenders (section 4(2)). Section 4 also applies to information obtained by virtue of the

---

[19] Again, it imposes a lifetime obligation on these people to refrain from breaching s.1(3). Wide definitions of both terms are found in s.12.

[20] Defined in s.2(4).

[21] s.2(3) provides a similar defence to that provided in s.1(5).

[22] s.3(4) provides a similar defence to that provided in s.1(5).

authority of an interception warrant under section 5 of the Regulation of Investigatory Powers Act 2000. There is no requirement of damage in this section, the section penalises disclosures which have one of the above results.[23]

Additional provisions

The above offences are directed at a variety of public officials. Sections 5 and 6 are concerned with stopping other people, or organisations such as the press, from disclosing certain types of information. Although these sections were intended to apply to the press in the same way as to any individual, they should now be interpreted in the light of the E.C.H.R. and the recognition by the E.Ct.H.R. that the press has a special position as guardian of the public interest.[24] **26–010**

Section 5 provides that it is an offence for the recipient of any information which falls within the categories outlined above, to further disclose that information. It will have to be proved that the discloser knew or had reasonable cause to believe that the information concerned was protected by the Act. In the case of information which falls under sections 1 to 3, it will have to be established that the disclosure was "damaging", a term that should now be interpreted narrowly by the courts in the light of Article 10 E.C.H.R. and section 12 of the Human Rights Act 1998, particularly where the disclosure is by the press.

Section 6 provides that it is an offence to disclose information relating to security, intelligence, defence or international relations which has been communicated in confidence to another State and has come into the discloser's possession without that State's authority. Unlike the previous sections of the Act, there is a defence of "prior disclosure" (section 6(3)). Section 8 imposes a duty on Crown servants and government contractors to safeguard any information etc. to which they have access where its disclosure would be contrary to the Act. It is an offence for example to retain such information contrary to his official duty or to fail to take such care as would prevent the unauthorised disclosure or such information (section 8(1)).

"D.A." Notices[25]

Closely connected with the topic of the scope of the Official Secrets Acts is that of "Defence Advisory" (DA) Notices, which may, according to taste, be represented as a further form of control over the publication of information which government departments do not wish to be publicised, as guide-lines for self-censorship or as a safety valve against the rigours of the Official Secrets Acts. Since 1912 there has been an official Defence, Press and Broadcasting Committee consisting of civil servants in defence departments and representatives of the press and broadcasting, whose purpose is to indicate to the press and broadcasting authorities when they may safely commit an offence against the Official Secrets Acts without risk of being prosecuted. A DA notice asks editors and publishers not to publish certain specified items of defence information, the publication of which would be prejudicial to the national interest. It is true that some of these items might not be covered by the Acts, but on the other hand much defence information that is strictly speaking secret is communicated to the **26–011**

---

[23] Section 4(4) provides a similar defence to that provided in s.1(5).

[24] *Observer and Guardian v. United Kingdom* (1992) 14 E.H.R.R. 153, para. 59.

[25] Until 1992 known as "D" Notices, see J. Jaconelli, "The D Notice System", [1982] P.L. 37; H.C. 773 (1979–80); *The Protection of Military Information*, Cmnd. 9112 (1983). See D. Fairley, "D-Notices, Official Secrets and the Law", (1990) 10 O.J.L.S. 430.

press for background knowledge, and prosecution is unlikely if it was in a DA notice.[26]

Breach of Confidence

26–012　In addition to the use of the criminal law to protect state secrets, governments have also used the civil law to impose prior restraint on the disclosure of certain information, on the basis that to prosecute after the event is inadequate if secret information has already entered the public domain. This is done by attempting to obtain an injunction for breach of confidence and was discussed in Chapter 25.[27]

II. State Surveillance

26–013　States have been involved in the surveillance of their subjects and aliens for centuries. In the last 20 years the means to do this have become more sophisticated and more successful. In addition the police and other law enforcement agencies have been encouraged to move towards proactive, intelligence-led policing, both to discover potential criminal activity and as evidence in the prosecution of those involved in know criminal activity. There is also the ability to record and store for future use information obtained by, for, *e.g.* CCTV, much of which will include information about individuals and events that are not covered by the criminal law.

This is an area where a balance has to be found between State interest and individual privacy. It is concerned with the right to informational autonomy, the right to control what information is available about oneself. It is also concerned with the need of the State to protect itself and its citizens and by definition democracy. In this field the E.C.H.R. has been most influential and the E.Ct.H.R. in its jurisprudence has given extensive guidance on the balance between individual privacy and State interests. Interference by the State with a person's private life, home or correspondence must be justified by one of the exceptions in Article 8(2) and must be the minimum necessary to obtain one of the stated legitimate aims. In addition the legitimate aim must be adequately prescribed by law, and necessary in a democratic society—or proportional to the end to be achieved. This is an area where although the E.Ct.H.R. has accepted that states have a "margin of appreciation" in respect of the checks and balances in force to oversee and monitor such activities, it has laid down minimum requirements.

The need for the United Kingdom to comply with the E.C.H.R. has resulted in legislative reform. Until the enactment of a variety of statutes, surveillance was regulated by administrative guidelines, and relied on the common law approach that anything could be done that was not prohibited. Such an approach was clearly not in accordance with the rights based approach of the E.C.H.R. The bodies involved in such activities include the Security Services, that is M.I.5 and M.I.6, Government Communications Headquarters (GCHQ) and the various police forces. Until the enactment of the Security Services Act 1989, and the Intelligence Services Act 1994, M.I.5, M.I.6 and GCHQ were unregulated by

---

[26] However, "compliance with the DA Notice system does not relieve the editor of responsibilities under the Official Secrets Acts." para. 4 of the memorandum issued by the Defence Press and Broadcasting Advisory Committee (1993).

[27] *ante*, para. 25–020.

law. The law to be discussed below is mainly concerned with the regulation of surveillance by the police, although certain aspects of the regulation of the powers of MI5 and MI6 and GCHQ are also covered. These bodies still obtain many of their powers under the 1994 Act. Despite reform in 1997 and 2000, the law on surveillance remains confused.

Interception of Communications

Until 1985, the legal basis for the right to intercept communications, whether **26–014** with or without warrant, could be found, if at all in the royal prerogative. In 1985 the Interception of Communications Act was enacted to provide a regulatory regime for the interception of communications in the course of their transmission by post or by means of a public telecommunications system.[28] The majority of this Act has been replaced by Part I of the Regulation of Investigatory Powers Act 2000 (RIP Act). There were several reasons for its replacement.[29] At the time of the 1985 Act there was only the public telecommunications system, to this there has been added a growing private communications system, which the 1985 Act failed to cover. This meant that to intercept such communications was "not in accordance with the law."[30] Advances in technology also meant that data held by communication service providers relating to the use of the communications service by customers could be of use for law enforcement purposes, but although there was statutory provision for the voluntary disclosure of such information, powers of compulsory disclosure were limited. Finally there was a general need to ensure compliance with the E.C.H.R. The scheme for interception of communications has been described as an improvement on the 1985 scheme, but as will be seen, defects remain.[31]

Section 1 of RIP Act, which virtually reproduces section 1 of the 1985 Act, creates an offence of unlawfully intercepting a communication sent by post or by a public or private telecommunications system[32] (*e.g.* a hotel network). Section 1(3) creates a tort of unlawful interception which applies to an interception expressly or impliedly permitted by the person with the right to control a private telecommunication system, but without being authorised under the RIP Act.[33] An interception has lawful authority if it falls within sections 3, 4, or 5; an interception which is lawful under these sections is lawful for all purposes, which means that it will be a defence to an action under the HRA Act 1998. Section 3 provides for a variety of consensual interceptions without a warrant *e.g.* the use of an answerphone to record a message, or where the communication is subject to surveillance under Part II of the RIP Act. Section 4 enables certain interceptions to be lawfully conducted without a warrant if they are carried out in accordance with regulations made under section 4 (*e.g.* to enable businesses to

---

[28] In 1957 a report by a Committee of Privy Councillors, Cmnd. 283, had recommended legislation to regulate and limit the interception of communications; Sir Robert Megarry V.-C. in *Malone v. Metropolitan Police Commissioner* [1979] Ch. 344, described it as a subject "which cries out for legislation." It was the decision of the E.Ct.H.R. in *Malone v. United Kingdom* (1985) 7 E.H.R.R. 14 that the lack of legal controls over the issuing of warrants to tap telephones amounted to a breach of Art. 8, which resulted in the 1985 Act.

[29] See Cm. 4368 (1999).

[30] See *Halford v. United Kingdom* (1997) 24 E.H.R.R. 523. In *R. v. Effick* [1995] 1 A.C. 309, it was held that since the calls taped were made on a cordless telephone s.1 did not apply.

[31] See Akdeniz, Taylor and Walker, "Regulation of Investigatory Powers Act 2000 (1): Big Brother.gov.uk: State surveillance in the age of information and rights", [2001] Crim.L.R. 73.

[32] See s.2 for the definition of these and other terms.

[33] Such conduct is not a criminal offence (s.1(6)).

monitor certain business communications),[34] or under other specified legislation which includes legislation relating to prisons and hospitals which provide high security psychiatric services.

26–015   Section 5 provides for interceptions under warrant issued by the Home Secretary[35] for a variety of purposes connected with the interception of postal or telecommunications, and it is very similar to section 2 of the 1985 Act. Section 6 lists those who can apply for such a warrant, which includes the Director-General of M.I.5, the Chief of M.I.6 and the chief constables of the Scottish and Northern Irish police forces. Chief Constables in England and Wales must make applications through the National Criminal Intelligence Service. Before the Home Secretary can issue a warrant he must be satisfied that it is necessary: in the interests of national security; for preventing or detecting serious crime[36]; to safeguard the economic well-being of the United Kingdom[37]; to give effect to any international mutual assistance agreement to prevent or detect serious crime. Although these grounds are similar to the exceptions to a right to private life found in Article 8 E.C.H.R., they may not be clearly enough defined to be "in accordance with the law". The Home Secretary must be satisfied that the conduct authorised by the warrant is proportionate to what is sought to be achieved by that conduct. The statutory requirements of "necessary" and "proportionate" were inserted to ensure that the powers under section 5 were exercised in accordance with the E.C.H.R. A warrant is valid for three months (subject to renewal); one issued in the interests of national security or to safeguard the economic well-being of the United Kingdom can be renewed for up to six months, other warrants can only be renewed for up to three months; in all cases warrants can be repeatedly renewed. Sections 11 and 12 enable communications service providers to be required to assist the interception process, with the prospect for additional requirements to provide technical assistance being imposed by further regulations—the State is to make a fair contribution to the costs involved (section 14). Sections 15–18 provide general safeguards for the use of interception material.[38]

The supervision of the new interceptions scheme is considered below.[39]

Acquisition and disclosure of communications data

26–016   Communications data, or "traffic" data is information that relates to the use that may be made of a communication; it exists independently of the content of the communication, *e.g.* the details of a telephone number dialled, the location of the person making a call by mobile telephone, the address on a postal item. Authorisation to obtain such data from postal or telecommunications operators can be given by a designated official within the police, the intelligences services, the Inland Revenue, etc. (section 25). The official concerned must be satisfied that it is necessary to obtain such data on grounds laid down in section 22(2). The

---

[34] The Telecommunications (Lawful Business Practice) (Interception of Communications) Regulations 2000, see H. Milgate, 150 N.L.J. 1862.

[35] In exceptional circumstances a senior official may sign a warrant (s.6), but such a warrant is only valid for a maximum of five working days, after which it must be renewed by the Home Secretary (s.9).

[36] See s.81.

[37] This will only apply if the information sought relates to the acts or intentions of those outside the British Isles (s.5(5)).

[38] See P. Mirfield, "Regulation of Investigatory Powers Act 2000 (2): Evidential Aspects", [2001] Crim. L.R. 91.

[39] *post*, para. 26–022.

grounds specified are wider than those provided in section 5, for *e.g.* they include: preventing or detecting crime or preventing disorder, in the interests of public safety or protecting public health, in connection with a variety of revenue matters. Before issuing a notice authorising the disclosure of such data, the official must be satisfied that obtaining the data in question by the conduct authorised is proportionate to what is sought to be achieved.[40] When an authorisation is given, the operator concerned can be compelled (if necessary by civil proceedings) to obtain or disclose the data.[41]

The controls over the acquisition and disclosure of communications data are less onerous than those for the interception of communications; this is on the basis that they involve a less serious invasion of privacy,[42] but it is possible that there are inadequate for E.C.H.R. purposes. In certain circumstances there will be recourse to the Interception of Communications Tribunal.

Surveillance by technical devises and covert human intelligence sources

Until the enactment of Part III of the Police Act 1997 the use or installation of **26–017** bugging devises, video surveillance and vehicle tracking apparatus and the jamming of private communications systems was governed by a Home Office Circular sent to chief constables. In *R. v. Khan* Lord Nolan described the lack of a statutory regime for such operations as "astonishing".[43] In anticipation of an adverse ruling by the E.Ct.H.R,[44] Part III of the Police Act provided for surveillance conducted by entry onto, or interference with property which would otherwise amount to for *e.g.* trespass or criminal damage.[45] This still left several types of covert surveillance not subject to statutory authorisation *viz.*: directed surveillance, intrusive surveillance and the use and conduct of covert human intelligence sources. These are now regulated under Part II of the RIP Act. In consequence the law on surveillance is complicated and there are fine distinctions between the various types of surveillance and the ways of authorising them. It is arguable that the law on this area is not sufficiently ascertainable to satisfy the E.C.H.R.[46] Other general concerns are the wide use of executive decision-making to further implement the law, the lack of judicial supervision, and the fact that someone who has been subject to any of these types of surveillance is not entitled to be told this even after the event.

The placing of technical equipment in property

The legal framework to authorise covert entry upon and interference with **26–018** property by the police and other law enforcement agencies[47] is in Part III of the Police Act 1997. Section 92 provides that no entry on, or interference with property or wireless telegraphy is unlawful if authorised under Part III of Act. Authorisation can be given by an authorising officer *viz.*: chief constables and the Commissioner of the Metropolitan Police; the Directors General of the National

---

[40] s.23 specifies the form the authorisation must take.
[41] There is provision for the payment of "appropriate contributions" to the operators as compensation for the cost involved in complying with notices (s.24).
[42] See *Malone v. United Kingdom* (1985) 7 E.H.R.R. 14.
[43] [1996] 3 W.L.R. 162 at p. 175; see also H.C. 18 (1994–95), where the Home Affairs Select Committee recommended a statutory basis for such activities.
[44] *Khan v. United Kingdom* [2000] Crim.L.R. where a breach of Art. 8 was found.
[45] In the case of, for example jamming communication systems or other unlawful interference with wireless telegraphy, it would be an offence under the Wireless Telegraphy Act 1949, 1967.
[46] See JUSTICE, *Under Surveillance* (1998), p. 19.
[47] *e.g.* National Criminal Intelligence Service, National Crime Squad, Customs and Excise.

Criminal Intelligence Service and the National Crime Squad, a designated customs officer (section 93(5)).[48] Before authorisation is given the authorising officer has to believe that the proposed action is necessary in that it is likely to be of substantial value in the prevention or detection of serious crime (defined in section 93(4)) and that it cannot be reasonably undertaken by other means (section 93(2)). The formalities for authorisation, and for renewal or cancellation, are similar to those for the interception of communications (sections 95 and 96). Under section 91, Commissioners—who must be judges of a degree of seniority as defined in the Act—are appointed for a variety of purposes.[49] One of these is to consider and, if appropriate, approve certain authorisations, e.g. in sensitive situations such as private residences, offices, hotel bedrooms; or where material would be found which is legally privileged, or is confidential, personal or journalistic information (sections 97 to 100). This limited involvement of the Commissioners provides an element of independent scrutiny with respect to matters where there is the potential for the greatest invasion of privacy[50]; however there is a potential conflict between this role of the Commissioners and their other role of hearing complaints.[51]

Further details on the implementation of Part III is provided in a Code of Practice issued by the Home Office, a quasi-legislative procedure which may not be sufficient for E.C.H.R. purposes. Originally this was issued under the 1997 Act, but it is now issued under section 71 of the RIP Act. The COP issued have all been extremely detailed and appear to limit the wide discretion allowed to the authorisation agents under the 1997 Act. In this way they appear to help ensure that the exercise of the powers under the 1997 Act are in accordance with the E.C.H.R. requirements such as proportionality and that account is taken of privacy requirements. However breach of the COP is only a disciplinary offence, and it is questionable how far such Codes can actually limit the wide discretionary powers provided in the Act.

An important exception to Part III is where the police or other agencies have the consent of e.g. the owner to place a devise on premises; this fails to have regard to the privacy rights of those who are subjected to surveillance. This type of surveillance is subject to a voluntary COP drawn up by the Association of Chief Police Officers (ACPO); it is doubtful if this procedure is compatible with the E.C.H.R.

Directed surveillance, intrusive surveillance and the conduct and use of covert human intelligence sources

26–019　Not all listening devises require installation on property, some can operate at long distance or are operated on microwave technology. Such devises were not covered by the 1997 Act, nor were they regulated by any other law. A further area unregulated by law was the use of informers[52] and undercover police officers—human intelligence sources.[53] These are all forms of covert surveillance, and to leave them unregulated could have led to challenges under the HRA 1998, hence

---

[48] There are special provision for dealing with applications for authorisations when an authorisation officer is not available (s.94).

[49] See s.91 and *post* para. 26–022.

[50] This may be sufficient to satisfy the requirements laid down by the E.Ct.H.R. in *Funke v. France* (1993) 16 E.H.R.R. 297.

[51] *post* para. 26–023. In *Piersack v. Belgium* (1983) 5 E.H.R.R. it was stated that the same body should not both permit and sanction activities.

[52] There were ACPO guidelines.

[53] See *Texeira de Castro v. Portugal* (1999) 28 E.H.R.R. 101.

the provisions in the RIP Act. Section 27 provides that these types of activities, if authorised under the Act, will be lawful for all purposes. However, the RIP Act does not require the police, etc., to obtain authorisation before carrying out any of these activities, and since the very nature of these operations is secret and may never come to light, the authorisation procedure could be ignored—with the risk that if it did come to light it would be open to challenge.

Directed surveillance is defined as covert surveillance which is not intrusive, and is undertaken for the purpose of a specific investigation or operation, which is likely to result in the obtaining of private information about a person and is not an immediate response to events or circumstances (section 26(2)).

Intrusive surveillance is covert surveillance carried out by an individual on residential premises or in a private vehicle, or which involves the use of a surveillance devise in respect of such premises or vehicle (section 26(3)).[54] The fine distinctions which are drawn between the two types of surveillance are further explained in the COP issued under section 71. There is also the potential for overlap between intrusive surveillance and section 97 of the Police Act 1997. In consequence the law in this area may not be sufficiently "accessible" for E.C.H.R. purposes. Questionably, directed surveillance is regarded as less intrusive than intrusive surveillance, and there is a different authorisation procedure for the two types of surveillance.

The RIP Act provides a broadly similar scheme for the authorisation of directed surveillance (section 28) and the conduct and use of human intelligence sources (section 29). Authorisations for either of these activities can be given by persons designated by Order to do so; these are people within the relevant public authority, in other words only internal authorisation is required, and it is for a Government Minister to decide who is a designated person.[55] The relevant public authorities are listed in Schedule 1 and include the various police forces, the intelligence services, the armed forces, and a variety of government departments and other bodies; again these can be added to by the Home Secretary. The criteria for authorisation are similar to those for the acquisition of communication data[56] (section 28(3), section 29(3)), and can be added to by Order by the Home Secretary. Before authorising either of these activities the person designated must believe that the authorisation is necessary on one of the grounds specified and that the proposed activity is proportionate to what it seeks to achieve (section 28(2), section 29(2)).

The authorisation scheme for intrusive surveillance differs depending upon whether it is a police or customs authorisation or one concerning the intelligence services, Ministry of Defence or H.M.'s Forces. An application for authorisation for intrusive surveillance by the police and Customs and Excise is to be made to a *senior* authorising officer[57]; other authorities have to apply to the Home Secretary. As before those entitled to give authorisation have to be satisfied that the proposed activity is necessary and proportional. The criteria for necessary are

---

[54] The Home Secretary may by Order alter or add to the definitions of surveillance, subject to the affirmative procedure in Parliament (s.47).

[55] See ss.33, 34 for the rules for authorisation.

[56] s.22(2), *ante* para. 26–015.

[57] As defined by s.32(6), which includes police chief constables and the equivalent in a variety of non-Home Office forces.

more limited than for directed surveillance, but similar to those for the interception of communications. They are: in the interests of national security, to prevent or detect serious crime; in the interests of the economic well-being of the United Kingdom (section 32(3)). Where it is the Ministry of Defence or a member of the forces who is seeking authorisation, only the first two criteria apply (section 41). Where an authorising officer grants a police or customs authorisation, he must give notice of this to a Surveillance Commissioner,[58] who must approve the authorisation before it can take effect (sections 35, 36 and 37). A decision by a Surveillance Commissioner not to approve intrusive surveillance may be appealed to the Chief Surveillance Commissioner. Where authorisation is given by the Home Secretary there is no need to have it approved by a Surveillance Commissioner. There are additional rules for authorisations granted by the Home Secretary to the intelligence services (sections 42 and 44).

Investigation of electronic data protected by encryption

26–020   This creates a power to demand that a person in possession of encrypted materials either disclose the information in an intelligible form or disclose the key to that material (sections 50 to 52). Refusal to do so is a criminal offence, and it is for the person to whom a notice is addressed to show that the key is not in their possession: a reverse onus requirement that may fall foul of Article 6 of the E.C.H.R. (section 53).

Scrutiny and supervision of the operation of the various Acts

26–021   The 1985 Act had established a Commissioner to keep the working of that Act under review, and a tribunal to act as a complaints mechanism for those who suspected that their telephones or mail were subject to unlawful interference; similar Commissioners and tribunals were statutorily established in 1989 and 1994 in respect of surveillance by M.I.5 and M.I.6 respectively, and in 1997 with respect to police surveillance. The RIP Act replaces the scheme established in 1985, and makes changes to the other schemes.

26–022   Section 57 of the RIP Act provides for the appointment by the Prime Minister of an *Interception of Communications Commissioner* (who must be a judge), and who has a duty to keep the warrant procedure under review[59] and assist the Tribunal. The powers of the Commissioner under the 1985 Act were limited, and continue to be limited under the RIP Act.[60] However, in common with the other Commissioners (below), he is a public authority for the purposes of the HRA 1998 and as such will have to ensure that in granting warrants proper account has been taken of the E.C.H.R. and in particular Article 8. As before a range of people involved with the interception of communications are required to disclose or provide him with information to enable him to carry out his duties. Previously the Commissioner had no staff, and section 58(7) provides for the Secretary of State to agree to the appointment of staff. The Commissioner makes an annual report to the Prime Minister which is to be laid before Parliament (section 58). In the past reports have been brief and there continues to be provision for them

---

[58] below, para. 26–023. Special provision is made for "urgent" situations.

[59] He receives a list of warrants; the previous Commissioner found no instances of a warrant being issued unjustifiably.

[60] It is made clear that it is not a function of the Commissioner (and the other Commissioners provided for in the Act) to keep under review the exercise by the Secretary of State of his power to make subordinate legislation.

to be censored by the Prime Minister in certain circumstances; there is no Select Committee to monitor surveillance, and it may be concluded that parliamentary scrutiny is minimal.

Section 59 establishes the *Intelligence Services Commissioner*, who replaces the Commissioners established under the 1989 Act and the 1994 Act. His function is to keep the warrant procedure and relevant activities (apart from interception of communications) of the security services, officials of the armed forces and of the Ministry of Defence[61] under review. This includes review of their powers and duties under Parts II and III of the RIP Act, that is surveillance and covert human intelligence sources and the investigation of electronic data protected by encryption. He also makes an annual report to Parliament. The Intelligence and Security Committee in the House of Commons oversees the expenditure, administration and policy of M.I.5, M.I.6 and GCHQ, but not operational matters.

Surveillance Commissioners including a Chief Surveillance Commissioner, were **26–023** established by section 91 of the 1997 Act. Their functions are: to keep under review the scheme of authorisations for covert entry upon and interference with property by the police and others, to approve (or not) "sensitive" authorisations to enter property etc.[62] Section 62 of the RIP Act extends the function of the Chief Commissioner to enable him to review the use of Parts I and II of that Act. The appointment of Assistant Surveillance Commissioners is provided for by section 63, reflecting the increased oversight role for the Commissioners. The provisions relating to the appointment, etc. of these various Commissioners are broadly similar to the Interception of Communications Commissioner (RIP Act, ss.59, 60, Police Act, s.91).

A *Tribunal* is established by the RIP Act to hear complaints and other proceedings specified in the Act. This replaces the Tribunal set up under the 1985 Act and takes over the complaints jurisdiction of the Tribunals set up under the 1989 and 1994 Acts and the complaints function of the Surveillance Commissioners under the 1997 Act. The members of the Tribunal must have held high judicial office or similar. The Tribunal has three main functions.[63]

(i) It is the forum for dealing with actions which challenge the compatibility of the actions of the intelligence services and other agencies with the E.C.H.R. under section 7(1)(a) of the HRA 1998. This means that challenges to telephone tapping etc. which raise questions of, for example the right to privacy, can not be raised in a court. This procedure may not satisfy the fair trial requirements of Article 6 particularly if the Secretary of State in making rules for the Tribunal exercises some of the powers available to him. These powers include allowing it to sit in secret; prevent it from giving reasons for its decisions; take decisions in the absence of any person, including the complainant (sections 66 and 69). Where the Tribunal is exercising this first function, there is no provision for appeal, another possible breach of Article 6.

---

[61] Other than in Northern Ireland (s.59); s.61 provides for the appointment of a Investigatory Powers Commissioner for Northern Ireland.

[62] *ante* para. 26–018.

[63] The Home Secretary may allocate it additional functions (s.65(2)(d)).

(ii) It is the forum for complaints in connection with conduct in connection with for example interception warrants, entry or interference with property.

(iii) To consider and determine any reference to them by any person that he has suffered any detriment as a consequence of any prohibition of restriction under section 17. Section 17 excludes from legal proceedings the use of materials intercepted by virtue of telephone tapping etc.

The Tribunal, like its predecessor, is to exercise a form of judicial review (section 67). Whether it will exercise its jurisdiction in a manner sufficient to satisfy Article 6 will depend in part on its procedural rules. The Tribunal may only state that a determination has or has not been made in favour of the applicant or complainant, as before this will not enable it to reveal, for example whether or not there has been an interception and if so whether it was authorised. The Tribunal does not give reasons for its decision, and there is an attempt in section 67(8) to prevent appeal or review except as provided by the Home Secretary. The obligation on the Home Secretary to do so is limited to complaints under (ii) above, and with respect to any new jurisdiction he has given the Tribunal. Doubts have been cast on official assurances that the Tribunal is E.C.H.R. compliant.[64]

III. Freedom of Information and Open Government[65]

26–024   Although the common law recognised freedom of expression, it did so as a negative liberty, it did not develop a concept of freedom of information.[66] Indeed by virtue of doctrines such as Crown privilege and confidentiality the common law acted to prevent open government and preserve secrecy.[67] This can be contrasted with the position in the United States where the First Amendment's guarantee of free speech was interpreted to include access to information and the notion of open government.[68] International treaties such as the United Nations Covenant on Civil and Political Rights in Article 19(2), expressly recognises the connection between freedom of expression and the right to seek and receive information and ideas; Article 10 of the E.C.H.R. does so by implication. The ethos of secrecy has been seen as an important aspect of government in the United Kingdom, something that would only change if required to do so by legislation.[69] This section will first consider a variety of statutory reforms that

---

[64] See Akdeniz, Taylor and Walker *op. cit.*

[65] Beatson and Cripps (eds), *Freedom of Expression and Freedom of Information* (2000); R. Austin, Chap. 12, "Freedom of Information, the Constitutional Impact" in Jowell and Oliver, *The Changing Constitution* (4th ed., 2000); P. Birkinshaw, *Freedom of Information: The Law, the Practice and the Ideal* (3rd edn., 2001).

[66] See the Hon. Sir Anthony Mason, "The Relationship Between Freedom of Expression and Freedom of Information", Chap. 13 in *Freedom of Expression and Freedom of Information* (2000), and Sir Stephen Sedley, "Information as a Human Right", Chap. 14 *op. cit.*

[67] A change in approach in the common law can be seen in *Conway v. Rimmer* [1968] A.C. 910 and *Attorney General v. Guardian Newspapers Ltd (No. 2)* [1990] 1 A.C. 1010.

[68] *New York Times Co v. United States* 403 U.S. 713 (1971); but see also the Freedom of Information Act 1966.

[69] See the remarks by Sir Richard Scott in his *Report into the Export of Defence Equipment and Dual-Use Goods to Iraq* H.C. 115, vol. iv (1995–96).

aimed to make official information more widely available, but only in limited specified circumstances, before considering the more general attempt to do so in the Freedom of Information Act 2000.

The Data Protection Act 1998

An aspect of the right to know is the right of an individual to know what **26–025** information is held about him on government records. This is reflected in the Data Protection Act 1998 which replaces the 1984 Act of the same name and was passed to implement European Council Directive 95/46. Although the 1998 Act addresses some of the flaws in the previous legislation, it retains the core structure of the 1984 Act. It is notable that in passing both Acts there was little official recognition that this legislation was concerned with human rights. The 1998 Act is likely to be relied on in preference to reliance on the rights given to individuals to have access their health and medical records provided by the Access to Personal Files Act 1987 and the Access to Health Records Act 1990.

Data protection legislation is designed to provide protection for privacy in relation to personal information. The data covered by the Act was been widened by the 1998 Act to include not just information stored electronically, but also to certain paper records (section 1). The definition of data was amended by the Freedom of Information Act 2000 to extend to all data held by a public authority. This enables data subjects[70] to have access to personal data held about them by public authorities by way of the Data Protection Act rather than the Freedom of Information Act. Those who hold data covered by the Act are subject to a system of compulsory notification and registration and have to comply with the eight data protection principles laid down in Schedule 1. The idea of these principles is to limit the use which can be made of personal information and to regulate the control of such information by requiring it, *e.g.* to be obtained lawfully and fairly and to be relevant and accurate. Additional protections are provided for sensitive data, which includes information about a person's race or ethnic origins, physical or mental health or condition (section 2). An Information Commissioner[71] has extensive regulatory powers to enforce the data protection principles, appeals against her decision can be made to the Information Tribunal. An individual who suffers damage or distress by reason of the contravention of the Act can seek damages (section 13). This provides a possibility for an action against the press for the misuse of data information which causes distress (subject to section 32).

The 1998 Act provides certain rights for those to whom the information **26–026** relates: the *data subject*. The data subject is entitled to be told whether information about him is being processed, and if so he is entitled to have a more extensive range of information about this data than was the case under the 1984 Act (section 7). He has additional rights including, in certain circumstances, the right to prevent processing of data likely to cause damage or distress (section 10), to prevent processing for the purpose of direct marketing (section 11) and to go to court to obtain an order for the rectification, blocking, erasing or destruction of inaccurate data (section 14).

The Data Protection Act has the potential to apply widely to all types of bodies who control data within the meaning of the Act. Not surprisingly extensive

---

[70] See below para. 26–026.
[71] The name given to the Data Protection Commissioner by the Freedom of Information Act 2000, in consequence the supervision and enforcement both Acts are by the same person.

exemptions to the Act are found in Part IV, and the Secretary of State has significant powers to exempt classes of personal data from the Act. The exclusions from the Act include data processed for the following purposes: safeguarding national security (section 28); prevention or detection of crime and the collection of taxes (section 29); in connection with health, education and social work (section 30); regulatory functions over a variety of areas *e.g.* financial services, charities, fair trading, health and safety at work (section 31); research, history and statistics (section 33). Section 3 of the Act provided for an exemption for "special purposes", this is further explained by section 32, which exempts data which is processed *only* for the purposes of journalism, art or literature. The majority of the exemptions are connected with the working of government, and as such they enable the government to maintain secrecy.

Environmental Information Regulations 1992 (as amended 1998)

26–027 These regulations which provide a right of access to environmental information held by public authorities required revision to implement the Aarhus Convention 1998, and section 74 of the Freedom of Information Act 2000 makes provision for this. The eventual regulations will provide a code for access to environmental information, and are likely to follow the pattern of the Freedom of Information Act 2000.

Local Government

26–028 The Local Government (Access to Information) Act 1985 imposed a statutory duty on local authorities to disclose information. The Local Government Act 2000, s.22 extends this openness to local authority executives. Certain information is exempted, and all other information held by local authorities is covered by the Freedom of Information Act.[72]

The Freedom of Information Act 2000

26–029 So far as the general right to official information was concerned, the previous Conservation Government issued the *Code of Practice on Access to Government Information*[73] in 1994 (revised in 1997). This was a non-statutory and little publicised document which although it required government departments to make official information available, this was not a legally enforceable obligation; the notion of open government represented by the Code was one which provided more transparency in the working of government, but was based on the grace and favour of government and not on a statutory right. In addition the Code provided an extensive list of class based exemptions, further restricting its usefulness. Its operation was supervised by the Parliamentary Commissioner for Administration.[74]

The Labour Government elected in 1997 had a manifesto commitment to introduce a Freedom of Information Act which would differ from the existing Code by giving rights of access to information, imposing duties on those holding information to make information available and having a formal means of enforcement and appeal. The Bill which formed the basis of the Freedom of Information Act 2000 had a long gestation period.[75] The 2000 Act applies to

---

[72] See S.I. 2000 No. 3272.
[73] See Cm. 2290.
[74] *post* para. 34–006.
[75] See the White Paper Cm. 3818 (1997); a consultation document and draft Bill, Cm. 4355, which departed from many of the more liberal aspects of the 1997 White Paper; and pre-legislative scrutiny by committees in both Houses H.C. 570 (1998–99), H.L. 97 (1998–99).

United Kingdom public authorities and regional public authorities in England, Wales and Northern Ireland. It does not apply to such public authorities in Scotland. In March 2001 the Scottish Executive published for consultation a draft Freedom of Information Act which, if enacted, will be in many respects more liberal than the 2000 Act.[76]

Section 1 of the Freedom of Information Act provides a general right of access to information held by public authorities[77] which includes government departments, local authorities, health authorities, maintained schools, the British Council, the Sentencing Advisory Panel and a wide variety of bodies listed in Schedule 1, which can be amended by the Secretary of State. This right has two aspects: the right to know whether or not the information requested exists and the right to be given the information if it is held. The right is backed up by imposing duties on public authorities to comply with these rights. However the rights and duties are subject to a variety of limitations and exemptions.

The first type of limitation is relatively uncontroversial and is based on the need to make the Act workable, it is not concerned with the substance of the information requested. It allows a public authority to refuse a request for example because further information is required to enable it to comply (section 1(3)); the cost of compliance would exceed "the appropriate limit"; (found in detailed regulations) (section 12); the request is "vexatious" or is a repeated request for the same information (section 14).

The second types of restriction is more controversial and is based on the content of the information requested. Part II of the Act creates 23 exemptions, which can be applied to limit either of the rights created by section 1; however, they do not necessarily apply in the same way to the duty to confirm or deny the existence of the information as they apply to the duty to release the information. Eight of these exemptions are in whole or in part absolute *viz.*: the information is accessible by other means (section 21); the information deals with security matters (section 23); court records (section 32); Parliamentary privilege (section 34); information held by either House of Parliament which would prejudice effective conduct of public affairs (section 36); personal information concerning the applicant (section 40); confidential information (section 41); information whose disclosure is prohibited by statute, court order or European Community law (section 44).[78] The fact that one of these absolute exemptions applies does not necessarily mean that disclosure is not required, only that it is not required under the Freedom of Information Act. The exceptions to the common law duty of confidence may enable information that falls under section 41 to be disclosed by other means and information covered by section 40 may be available by virtue of the Data Protection Act 1998.[79]

The remaining exemptions are subject to a public interest test: the relevant public authority has to decide whether the public interest in disclosure is outweighed by the public interest in concealment (section 2). The exemptions subject to a public interest test are: information intended for future publication

26–030

---

[76] See http://www.scotland.gov.uk/news/2001/03. In July 1999 a non-statutory Code of Practice on Access to Scottish Executive information was published which will remain in force until the new Act is enacted.

[77] Defined in s.3, and listed in sched. 1. See too s.7 which controversially allows the Secretary of State an extensive power by order to create additional limitations on the type of information which s.1 requires public authorities to disclose, thereby further limiting the application of the Act.

[78] There are about 400 such provisions.

[79] *ante* para. 26–025.

(section 22); national security (section 24)[80]; defence (section 26); international relations (section 27); relations within the United Kingdom (section 28); the economy (section 29); investigations and proceedings conducted by public authorities, *e.g.* investigating or prosecuting criminal offences (section 30); law enforcement (section 31); audit functions (section 33); information relating to the formulation of government policy, Ministerial communications etc. (section 35); communications with the Queen (section 37); health and safety (section 38); environmental information (section 39); personal information with respect to a third party (section 40); legal professional privilege (section 42); commercial interests (section 43). Most of the sections provide the "prejudice" test to help determine where the public interest lies. Such a test should require the prejudice to be real and substantial.[81] Exactly what interest or interests have to be prejudiced is defined vaguely in some of the sections, *e.g.* sections 27 and 28, which has the potential to limit the right to disclosure. Section 35 does not require the application of a prejudice test, the exemption is very wide and could result in a great deal of information about government being exempt from disclosure.

It is questionable whether the Act with its extensive exemptions will ensure that there is more open government, there is plenty of opportunity provided by the Act to foster continued secrecy in government.

The implementation and enforcement of the Act

26–031   Section 18 of the Act renames the Data Protection Commissioner as the Information Commissioner, and the Data Protection Tribunal as the Information Tribunal. The Commissioner and the Tribunal have important roles in enforcing and promoting the Act. To ensure that the Act is working properly, power to issue codes of practice are given to the Home Secretary and the Lord Chancellor who, in advance of making such codes, have to consult the Commissioner (sections 45 and 46). Public authorities have a duty to adopt, implement, operate and keep under review publication schemes (section 19). Such schemes first have to be approved by the Commissioner, who in addition may approve model schemes for public authorities not wishing to devise their own schemes (section 20). Publication schemes have to specify the classes of information which the public authority publishes or intends to publish, specify the manner in which information is to be published, and indicate whether a charge will be made for access to such material. One of the advantages of a publication scheme for a public authority is that information that has been, or is going to be, published falls within sections 21 and 22, and may provide a statutory justification for refusing access.

The Commissioner has a general duty to promote good practice and general compliance with the Act by public authorities. This includes giving advise on how to handle requests for information, the management of records and the handling of complaints. If it appears to the Commissioner that a public authority is not complying with good practice, she may make recommendations specifying the steps to be taken to rectify the position (section 48). The Commissioner is required to make an annual report to Parliament on the exercise of her functions under the Act (section 49).

---

[80] s.24 does not cover all aspects of national security, information that does not fall within s.23 is covered by s.24. For both sections certificates signed by senior Government Ministers are required to certify that the relevant section applies (s.25); for limited review of such certificates by the Tribunal, see s.60.

[81] The draft FOI Act (Scotland) provides the test of "substantial prejudice".

In addition to supervisory functions the Commissioner has enforcement functions (Part IV). Someone who has had a request for information refused can apply to the Commissioner for a decision that an application for access to information has not be dealt with by a public authority in accordance with the requirements of the Act. The Commissioner may only decline such a request in limited circumstances such as undue delay by the complainant or a failure by the complainant to exhaust the internal complaints procedures provided by the public authority (section 50(2)). To enable her to reach a decision on the merits of a complaint the Commissioner may serve the public authority with an information notice (section 51), backed up if necessary by a power to obtain from a circuit judge a warrant to enter and search the premises of a public authority (section 55 and Schedule 3). If the Commissioner is satisfied that the public authority was in breach of the Act, then she may issue a decision notice specifying the steps the public authority must take to comply with the Act, or an enforcement notice requiring it within a specified time scale to comply with the Act (section 52). A limitation to these powers is found in section 53, which allows the Government in certain circumstances to nullify a decision or an enforcement notice served on a government department, the National Assembly of Wales or other public authorities so designated by a Minister. The Commissioner's decisions are treated as court orders and can be enforced by proceedings for contempt of court (section 54).

Appeals from the Commissioner are to the Information Tribunal, and can be made by the applicant or the public authority (Part V). The Tribunal has wide powers, it can review any findings of fact made by the Commissioner, and in addition to quashing the Commissioner's decision, it can substitute its own decision. An appeal from the Tribunal to the High Court can only be made on a point of law (section 59).

The Public Interest Disclosure Act 1998[82]

The Public Interest Disclosure Act (PIDA) rectifies the position whereby **26–032** workers who disclosed information in the public interest had no statutory protection from victimisation by their employers. The workers covered by the Act are broadly those defined by section 43 of the Employment Rights Act 1996 (ERA). Not all workers are covered, *e.g.* the police service and the security service are excluded, but Crown servants are included. The PIDA makes a distinction between "protected" and "qualifying" disclosures, and inserts new provisions into the ERA to provide for the relevant protections. A protected disclosure is a qualifying disclosure which falls within section 43C to 43H of the ERA. This includes disclosures which, in the reasonable belief of the worker, show that a criminal offence has been committed; that a person has failed in a legal obligation; that the health or safety of an individual is endangered; that the environment is likely to be damaged, etc. If a disclosure falls within the definition of a qualified disclosure, to be a protected disclosure it must also fall under sections 43C to 43H. These include disclosures: made in good faith to the discloser's employer; made in the course of obtaining legal advise; made in good faith to a proscribed person such as the Chief Executive of the Criminal Cases Review Commission, the Health and Safety Executive and the Environment Agency; made in good faith, and with respect to something of an exceptionally serious

---

[82] Yvonne Cripps, Chap. 17, "The Public Interest Disclosure Act 1999", in Beatson and Cripps, *op. cit.*

nature, in certain circumstances to someone other than the discloser's employer. An employee's dismissal or redundancy is unfair if the principle reason for it was a protected disclosure (sections 103A and 105(6A) of the ERA). In 1999 regulations were introduced whereby there is no longer an upper limit on the compensation available to an employee dismissed primarily for making a protected disclosure. This Act, together with the Freedom of Information Act, could prevent important information about disasters such as rail and sea accidents, and environmental pollution and financial mismanagement being hidden. The PIDA, by protecting workers from retaliation from employers who are keen to prevent the public from being aware of important information, is another aspect of a move towards more open government.

CHAPTER 27

FREEDOM OF ASSEMBLY AND ASSOCIATION[1]

Introduction

These freedoms, which are closely associated with freedom of speech, include: **27–001** (a) taking part in public meetings, processions and demonstrations; and (b) forming and belonging to political parties, trade unions, societies and other organisations. Under English law, until the coming into force of the Human Rights Act 1998, these were by and large liberties rather than rights in the strict sense, and were residual.[2] A wide variety of statutory provisions applied (and still apply) to regulate and in some cases limit these liberties. However the courts have interpreted some of these limitations in the light of a common law principle in favour of freedom of assembly.[3] In certain limited circumstances only does statue law recognise positive rights to freedom of assembly and freedom of speech.

The European Convention on Human Rights recognises a right to freedom of peaceful assembly and association (Article 11) and a right to free expression (Article 10). Both these articles permit restrictions on these freedoms, but only in so far as is provided in the articles themselves, and the E.Ct.H.R. has adopted a strict approach to the restrictions found in both Article 10(2) and Article 11(2). In future statutory and common law restrictions on freedom of assembly and association will have to be interpreted and applied so as to comply with the E.C.H.R.,[4] and it should be born in mind that all legal provisions discussed in this Chapter are potentially open to question. Articles 10 and 11 require any limitation on the right stated to be: (i) prescribed by law, and (ii) necessary in a democratic society. Each article specifies its particular requirements for (ii), which, in addition, must be "proportionate to the legitimate aim pursued"[5]; in other words, even when the State is acting in accordance with a legitimate aim in its restriction to a Convention right, the State must demonstrate that the restriction is strictly necessary to achieve that aim.[6]

---

[1] Robertson, *Freedom, the Individual and the law* (3rd ed., 1995); R. Card, *Public Order Law* (2000).

[2] For the position at common law see Dicey, *Law of the Constitution* (10th ed.) Chap. 7; also David Williams, *Keeping the Peace: The Police and Public Order* (1967); L. Radzinowicz, *History of English Criminal Law*, Vol. 4 (1968) especially Chap. 4.

[3] See for, *e.g. Burden v. Rigler* [1911] 1 K.B. 337, *Hirst and Agu v. Chief Constable of West Yorkshire* 85 Cr. App. R. 143, *D.P.P. v. Jones* [1999] 2 All E.R. 257, HL, [1999] 2 A.C. 240; but *cf. Arrowsmith v. Jenkins* [1963] 2 Q.B. 561. See also the dictum of Lord Denning *Hubbard v. Pitt* [1976] Q.B. 142 "so long as good order is maintained, the right to demonstrate must be preserved". In his report *The Red Lion Square Disorders of June 15*, 1975 Cmnd. 5919, Scarman L.J (as he then was) suggested that there was a right to demonstrate subject only to limits required by the need for good order and the passage of traffic. K. J. Keith, "The Right to Protest", in *Essays on Human Rights* (ed. Keith, N.Z., 1968), p. 49; O. Hood Phillips, "A Right to Demonstrate?" (1970) 86 L.Q.R. 1,

[4] See Mead, "The Human Rights Act—A Panacea for Peaceful Public Protest?" [1998] J.Civ.Lib. 206; Fenwick, "The Right to Protest, the Human Rights Act and the Margin of Appreciation", (1999) 62 M.L.R. 491.

[5] *Handyside v. United Kingdom* (1979–80) 1 E.H.R.R. 737.

[6] In *Steel v. UK* (1998) 28 E.H.R.R. 603 the E.Ct.H.R. suggests that the punishment of peaceful protesters is disproportionate to the aim of the maintenance of public order.

Articles 10 and 11 are likely to provide fertile grounds for argument in the fields of freedom of assembly and association.

I. FREEDOM OF ASSEMBLY

Public meetings, assemblies and demonstrations

27–002   The common practice of holding public meetings dates from the habit of promoting meetings to discuss and present petitions to Parliament in the late eighteenth and early nineteenth centuries, the popular interest in parliamentary affairs being no doubt stimulated, first, by a more widespread dissemination of newspapers, and then by the extension of the franchise. The restrictive legislation of that period shows that the executive was concerned with criticism of the government, whereas the later statutes are intended mainly to prevent outbreaks of disorder (although the Public Order Act 1986 and subsequent legislation go beyond this). Today public meetings, assemblies and processions are still of importance in context of demonstrations on matters as diverse as animal rights, capitalism, gay rights and the status of Tibet. In addition there has been the use of mass picketing at the scenes of industrial disputes and problems surrounding groups of people attending sporting events. Although a wide variety of laws and offences will apply to all types of meetings, assemblies and demonstrations, account will have to be taken to ensure that the application of law in question is in accordance with Articles 10 and 11 E.C.H.R., this means that a different view could be taken of the application of, for example section 4 of the Public Order Act 1986, to a football supporter and an animal rights protester.

A "*public meeting*" may be defined as a meeting held for the purpose of discussing or expressing views on matters of public interest, and which the public or any section thereof is invited to attend. A public meeting may be held either on private premises or in a public place. "Private premises" are premises to which the public have access only by permission of the owner or occupier. A "public place" includes any highway or any other premises or place (such as a public park, sea beach or public road) to which the public have or are permitted to have access, whether on payment or otherwise,[7] or by virtue of express or implied permission. The Public Order Act 1986, s.14[8] enables conditions to be imposed in certain circumstances, on a "public assembly" which is defined in section 16.

There is a general liberty to promote or take part in a public meeting on private premises, subject to infringement of particular legal rules. It is doubtful whether there is such a general liberty to promote or take part in a public meeting in a public place without the licence of the owners (often the local authority[9]), since this will almost invariably involve trespass to land as well as in many cases an obstruction or a public nuisance, although a public meeting in a public place is not necessarily unlawful.[10]

---

[7] Definitions adapted from Public Order Acts and Criminal Justice Act 1972.

[8] *post* para. 27–012.

[9] It may be arguable that, with the entry into force of the Human Rights Act 1998, there is a duty on public authorities to provide a place for public assemble.

[10] *cf.* A. L. Goodhart, "Public Meetings and Processions", (1937) 6 C.L.J. 161. See also E. C. S. Wade, "The Law of Public Meetings", (1938) 2 M.L.R. 177; E. R. Ivamy, "The Right of Public Meeting", (1949) C.L.P. 183. For a consideration of the laws that could be infringed by the holding of public meetings or demonstrations see *post* para. 27–011 *et seq.*

The place of assembly

Public meetings in private premises or places

The owner or occupier of private premises, for example, the hirer of a hall, may hold a public meeting there or licence others to do so. The organiser of the meeting may exclude or eject trespassers, after first asking them to leave; if they refuse he may use reasonable force, although he may not arrest or detain them. A qualification to this right of the occupier or licensee is found in the common law power of the police to enter such premises to deal with or prevent a breach of the peace,[11] as recognised in *Thomas v. Sawkins*.[12] This case has been criticised as it recognised a police power not only to enter private premises to quell an existing breach of the peace, but also to do so where there were reasonable grounds for believing that a breach of the peace was imminent. The E.Ct.H.R. has accepted that this is a legitimate aim within the E.C.H.R.[13] It would appear that the power to enter to deal with or prevent a breach of the peace may apply also to private meetings on private premises.[14] In addition, the police have particular powers to deal with certain types of noisy, nocturnal, open air gatherings.[15] Section 14 of the Public Order Act 1986 is not applicable to indoor meetings.

Public meetings in public places

There is no general obligation on state authorities to provide places for public **27–004** assemblies or for the exercise of free speech,[16] nor is there any common law right to use a common,[17] the foreshore,[18] public parks,[19] gardens or town halls as venues. There is rather more latitude towards public meetings in public parks and gardens, which are intended for recreation and exercise, than to such meetings on the highway. By-laws made by local authorities usually require the written permission of the council for holding a meeting on grounds, such as a square or park, belonging to the local authority as the highway authority or otherwise.[20] Permission may be refused if a breach of the peace is apprehended. By-laws may create minor offences triable summarily in the magistrates' courts.

---

[11] This power is expressly preserved in s.17 of the PACE Act 1984.

[12] [1935] 2 K.B. 434.

[13] *McLeod v. United Kingdom* 27 E.H.R.R. 493. This case was concerned with entry to a private house, and it was held that in those circumstances the means employed by the police were disproportionate to the ends. The court also accepted that the concept of breach of the peace had been sufficiently clarified by the English courts over the last 20 years for it to be regarded as defined with sufficient precision for the purposes of the E.C.H.R.

[14] *McLeod v. Commissioner of the Metropolis* [1994] 4 All E.R. 553, CA, but subject to the comments of the E.Ct.H.R. in *McLeod v. United Kingdom op. cit.*

[15] s. 63–66, C.J.P.O. Act 1994, see *post* para. 27–013.

[16] Unless this is implied in Arts. 10, 11 E.C.H.R.

[17] *De Morgan v. Metropolitan Board of Works* (1880) 5 Q.B.D. 155.

[18] *Brighton Corporation v. Packham* (1908) 72 J.P. 318.

[19] *Bailey v. Williamson* (1873) L.R. 8 Q.B. 118, (Hyde Park); *R. v. Cunninghame Graham and Burns* (1888) 16 Cox C.C. 420, (Trafalgar Square).

[20] Trafalgar Square and Hyde Park are also subject to restrictions under the Royal and Other Parks and Gardens Regulations 1988. Regulations were first issued in 1892 by Asquith (Home Secretary), who had defended Cunninghame Graham when at the Bar: Roy Jenkins, *Asquith*, pp. 64–65. In *Rai and Others v. United Kingdom* (1995) 82-A D.R. 134, the European Commission was satisfied that a ban on meetings in Trafalgar Square on issues related to Northern Ireland was permitted within Art. 11(2). The fact that other central locations were available for such meetings was crucial to the decision.

way is not necessarily unlawful.[21] The highway is in ...nembers of the public have a right to pass and repass . It had been accepted that this applied at common law . ancillary extensions as looking at shop windows, and ...as. In *Jones v. D.P.P.*[22] Lords Irvine, Hutton and Clyde held ...of passage should go beyond the rubric of "incidental or ...age and repassage, which placed "unrealistic and unwarranted ...ommonplace day to day activities."[23] The majority of the House of ...ed that the public's common law right to use the highway included reasonable, peaceful, non-obstructive temporary assembly or demon- which included "handing out leaflets, collecting money for charity, sing... carols . . . having a picnic or reading a book."[24] To exceed the common law right to use the highway is technically the tort of trespass against the owner of the surface of the highway, which is usually the local highway authority.[25] To trespass repeatedly might amount to nuisance, public or private.[26] There is also the possibility of the offences of obstructing the highway,[27] aggravated trespass,[28] and trespassory assemblies.[29] In addition sections 12 and 14 of the Public Order Act 1986 impose certain requirements on the holding of processions and meetings, which if breached could lead to prosecution.[30] The Protection of Harassment Act 1997 is sufficiently wide in its terms to allow, for example, injunctions to be granted to prevent protesters gathering on the highway outside the homes or premises of those involved in animal experiments.[31] To breach an injunction could result in an award of damages. The Criminal Justice and Police Act 2001, s.42 gives the police a power to direct persons reasonably believed to be harassing a person in his home to leave the vicinity of residential premises. Knowingly to disobey such a direction is a summary offence.

27–005 Special regulations may apply to meetings and processions in the vicinity of Parliament. At the commencement of the session each House, by order, gives directions that the Commissioner of Metropolitan Police shall keep, during the session, the streets leading to the Houses of Parliament free and open, and that no obstruction shall be permitted to hinder the passage of the Lords or Members.[32]

---

[21] In *Burden v. Rigler* [1911] 1 K.B. 337, DC, it was held that where R and others had disturbed a political meeting on the highway, they could be convicted of disorderly conduct at a lawful public meeting, contrary to the Public Meeting Act 1908.

[22] [1999] 2 A.C. 240.

[23] *per* Lord Irvine at p. 256.

[24] *per* Lord Irving at p. 255. Lords Slynn and Hope dissented, they adhered to the traditional view that the public's right to use the highway was as a highway. The wider interpretation of the common law put forward by the majority is in accordance with the requirements of Art. 11 E.C.H.R.

[25] *Tunbridge Wells Corporation v. Baird* [1896] A.C. 434; *Llandudno U.D.C. v. Woods* [1899] 2 Ch. 705. Technical trespasses are in practice tolerated, and even if pursued are unlikely to attract more than a nominal penalty.

[26] *post* para. 27–031.

[27] Highways Act 1980, s.137, *post* para. 27–028.

[28] Criminal Justice and Public Order Act 1994, ss.68, 69, *post* para. 27–014.

[29] s.14A of the Public Order Act 1986, *post* para. 27–012; *D.P.P. v. Jones* was concerned with a trespassory assembly.

[30] *post* para. 27–015 *et seq.*

[31] Obviously Art. 11 E.C.H.R. should be considered before an injunction is granted in respect of a public protest.

[32] The Metropolitan Police Commissioner gives effect to this order by issuing directions specifying the streets concerned, Metropolitan Police Act 1839, s.52. A failure to comply with the regulations can result in prosecution and a fine; *Papworth v. Coventry* [1967] 1 W.L.R. 663, DC.

There are limited exceptions to the position that there is no right to hold public meetings in public places. A statutory right is given to candidates at general and local elections to hold a public meeting in furtherance of his candidature. This places an obligation on local authorities to provide a place for such meetings.[33] The Education (No. 2) Act 1986 places an obligation on university, polytechnics and colleges to ensure freedom of speech within the law, and to ensure that the use of premises is not denied to any person or group on the grounds connected with a person or body's beliefs, views, policies or objectives.[34]

Restrictions on meetings, assemblies and demonstrations

27–006

Freedom of assembly is restricted in several ways: the police have common law powers to preserve the peace, which may be used to prevent or disperse assemblies and demonstrations; there are the provisions in the Public Order Act 1986 and Criminal Justice and Public Order Act 1994 which (i) seek to regulate various types and assemblies and processions and (ii) provide a variety of offences that could apply to those who take part on meetings and demonstrations; there are a number of statutory offences (which were not necessarily specifically enacted to regulate public assembly) and common law rules that could be infringed. Meetings addressed by members of "proscribed organisations", picketing and sporting events also give rise to issues connected with free assembly, and these will be considered later.

Common law powers to prevent and provide for the dispersal of meetings, assemblies and demonstrations

27–007

The executive have no power to prohibit a meeting beforehand, unless it is to be on government property. The police, however, have a primary duty to preserve the peace, or more accurately to prevent a breach of the peace.[35] In the past the police have used their powers to keep the peace to prevent people reaching demonstrations, to prevent a meeting from starting, or to order it to disperse at any time after it has started. These powers are backed up by the power to arrest without warrant for breach of the peace; the possibility of a later charge of obstructing a police officer in the execution of his duty,[36] if the police order is disregarded; and the use of the power to seek a binding over order.[37] The use of these powers will now have to be tempered in the light of Articles 10 and 11 E.C.H.R.

Definition of breach of the peace

27–008

It is clearly in the public interest that the public peace is preserved, but in preserving the peace there is a danger that freedom of expression and freedom of assembly may be compromised. What amounts to a breach of the peace has only been clarified by the courts over the last 20 years and the E.Ct.H.R. has accepted that it is sufficiently certain to comply with the requirement "prescribed by law" as required by Article 10(2).[38]

---

[33] Representation of the People Act 1983, ss.95–97.
[34] See *R. v. University of Liverpool, ex p. Caesar-Gordon* [1991] 1 Q.B. 124.
[35] See *Coffin v. Smith* (1980) 71 Cr.App.Rep. 221 " . . . a police officer's duty is to be a keeper of the peace and to take all necessary steps with that in view" *per* Donaldson L.J.
[36] Police Act 1996, s.89, see *ante*. para. 24–019 *et seq*. There is a power to arrest without warrant if the obstruction causes or is likely to cause a breach of the peace, or if the general arrest conditions set out in s.25(3) of PACE Act 1984 apply.
[37] *ante*. para. 24–026, Art. 11 has resulted in restrictions on this power.
[38] *McLeod v. United Kingdom* 27 E.H.R.R. 493.

In *R. Howell*[39] Watkins L.J. suggested that:

"there is likely to be a breach of the peace whenever harm is actually done or is likely to be done to a person or in his presence his property or a person is in fear of being so harmed through an assault, an affray, a riot unlawful assembly or other disturbance."[40]

However, in the same year Lord Denning, in a differently constituted Court of Appeal, defined breach of the peace more broadly to include conduct which did not involve violence or a treat of violence.[41] Subsequent cases have followed *Howell*,[42] and the E.Ct.H.R. has accepted that: "breach of the peace is committed only when an individual causes harm, or appears likely to cause harm, to persons or property, or acts in a manner the natural consequences of which would be to provoke violence in others."[43]

This raises a particular problem, namely where a person's or a group's activities are lawful, but those actions provoke others to commit a breach of the peace. The leading case in English law, *Beatty v. Gillbanks*,[44] established that the unlawful must yield to the lawful, and that those who organised assemblies could not be responsible for breaches of the peace by those opposed to them. Subsequent cases qualified this principle,[45] but more recently, and clearly influenced by the requirements of the E.C.H.R.,[46] the courts have been more inclined to return to the principle established in *Beatty v. Gillbanks*.

27–009   In *Foulkes v. Chief Constable of the Merseyside Police*[47] Beldam L.J. accepted that: "the common law power of a police constable to arrest where no actual breach of the peace had taken place but where he apprehends that such a breach may be caused by apparently lawful conduct is exceptional". This comment was influenced by the availability in the Public Order Act 1986 of a variety of offences with powers of arrest without warrant.[48] Beldam L.J. considered that the power to arrest those whose behaviour was lawful but provocative was limited to those cases where there was a real and present threat to a serious or imminent breach of the peace. In *Nicol and Selvanayagam v. D.P.P.*[49] protesters threw sticks into the water and took other action in an attempt to stop a fishing competition. Although the protesters were doing nothing unlawful *per se*, the Divisional Court accepted that their conduct was unreasonable and if they had

---

[39] [1982] Q.B. 416.

[40] *infra* p. 427.

[41] *R v. Chief Constable of Devon and Cornwall, ex p. Central Electricity Generating Board* [1982] Q.B. 458.

[42] *Percy v. D.P.P.* [1995] 1 W.L.R. 1382, [1995] 3 All E.R. 124; *Nicol and Selvanayagam v. D.P.P.* [1996] 160 J.P. 155.

[43] *McLeod v. UK* at p. 511.

[44] (1882) 9 Q.B. 308.

[45] As have the statutory powers to regulate meetings and processions, see *post* para. 27–011 *et seq.*

[46] The E.Ct.H.R. has held that a State may have a positive obligation to protect participants in a peaceful demonstration from disruption by counter demonstrators, *Plattform Ärzte für das Leben v. Austria* (1988) 13 E.H.R.R. 204.

[47] [1998] 3 All E.R. 705, CA.

[48] *e.g. Wise v. Dunning* [1902] 1 K.B. 167, where the conduct of the defendant would now be covered by the Public Order Act 1986. Also *O'Kelly v. Harvey* (1883) 14 L.R.Ir. 105, the decision that a police officer may disperse a public meeting if he believed that there would be a breach of the peace and that there was no other way of preventing it, would be unlikely to stand today in the light of the variety of statutory powers available to the police.

[49] (1966) 160 J.P. 155.

not been restrained the anglers would have been provoked into violence. implication is that lawful conduct that is reasonable can not be regarded as giving rise to a risk of a breach of the peace even if others are provoked to violence. A decision that behaviour is lawful but unreasonable, because those being protested against are unduly sensitive, could result in an action which could restrict freedom to protest. In *Redmond-Bate v. D.P.P.*[50] Sedley L.J. held that: "Free speech included not only the inoffensive but the irritating, the contentious, the eccentric, the heretical, the unwelcome and the provocative provided it did not tend to provoke violence." The fact that a crowd, some of whom were hostile to the speaker, had gathered did not entitle the police to request the defendant to stop preaching, and when she would not do so, to arrest her in apprehension of a breach of the peace. In consequence by refusing to comply with the police officer's instruction she was not guilty of obstructing a police officer in the execution of his duty.[51]

The question whether there has been a reasonable apprehension of a breach of the peace is an objective one, and the court must be satisfied that there existed "proved facts from which a constable could reasonably have anticipated such a breach."[52] In the past the courts have been reluctant to interfere with a police officer's assessment of a situation, but the obligations under the E.C.H.R. may result in a greater willingness by the courts to assess the reasonableness of a police officer's decision. Likewise the police will have to take account of the freedom to protest and freedom to speak when deciding whether there is a reasonable apprehension of a breach of the peace.

In addition to the need for reasonable grounds for an apprehension of a breach **27–010** of the peace (as defined above), the risk of the breach of the peace has to be imminent. In the past the police, supported by the courts, have taken a generous view of what is imminent. Relying on their powers to prevent a reasonably apprehended breach of the peace, during the miners' strike 1984/85 the police used road blocks to prevent pickets reaching proposed picket sites.[53] In *Moss v. McLachlan*[54] four would-be picketers ignored police requests to turn back and attempted to force their way through a police cordon which was on a road between one and a half and four miles from likely picket sites. Their subsequent conviction for obstruction of the police was upheld by the Divisional Court, on the ground that there was ample evidence to justify the police view that there was a real possibility of a breach of the peace at the sites of the proposed picketing. The unwillingness of the court to examine the reasonableness of the police view and the rather generous interpretation of imminent in the context of someone behaving lawfully, may need reconsideration in the light of Article 11. In *Peterkin v. Chief Constable of Cheshire*,[55] the County Court did not accept that

---

[50] *The Times*, July 28, 1999 [2000] H.R.L.R. 249.
[51] But *cf. Percy v. D.P.P. op. cit.* note 42, where the Divisional Court accepted that conduct not of itself unlawful could amount to breach of the peace if the words provoked violence in others even where those others had attended in order to cause trouble; see also *Wise v. Dunning* [1902] 1 K.B. 218, *Duncan v. Jones* [1936] 1 K.B. 218.
[52] *Piddington v. Bates* [1961] 1 W.L.R. 162 at p. 169. In *Moss v. McLachlan* [1985] I.R.L.R. 7.7, DC, it was held that in deciding whether or not there was a reasonable apprehension of a breach of the peace, the police were entitled to take into account their knowledge of the course of the dispute at a nearby colliery, see *below*.
[53] The setting up of road blocks is now governed by s.4 of the Police and Criminal Evidence Act 1984.
[54] [1985] I.R.L.R. 77, DC.
[55] *The Times*, November 16, 1999.

,ed an imminent threat of breach of the peace when a hunt
:d on a country lane half a mile from where a hunt was due

· Act 1986[56]

.er Act 1986, as amended by the Criminal Justice and Public
JPO Act 1994), provides a variety of powers to regulate public
rocessions.

Assemv̲̲ᷚ

27–012   *Conditions* can be imposed by virtue of section 14, on a public assembly of 20
or more people held in a public place which is wholly or partly open to the air
(section 16). However there is no power to ban such assemblies, and there is no
need to give advance notice of a proposed assembly to the police.[57] Before
conditions may be imposed the senior officer of police (section 14(2), having
regard to the time, place and circumstances of either an existing or proposed
assembly, must reasonably believe that either: "(a) it may result in serious public
disorder, serious damage to property or serious disruption to the life of the
community, or (b) the purpose of the persons organising it is the intimidation of
others with a view to compelling them not to do an act they have a right to do,
or to do an act they have a right not to do."[58] (section 14(1)). If the senior police
officer has a reasonable belief as outlined above, he may then give such directions: "as appear to him necessary to prevent such disorder, damage, disruption
or intimidation." The directions which may be imposed on the organiser of the
assembly, or those taking part, are with regard to the place of the assembly, its
maximum duration, or the maximum number of persons who may take part
(section 14(1)). Anyone who organises or takes part in a public assembly and
knowingly fails to comply with a condition imposed commits a summary
offence.[59] In both cases it is a defence for the accused to prove that his failure to
comply with the condition arose from circumstances beyond his control (section
14(4)(5)). A constable in uniform may arrest without warrant anyone he reasonably suspects is committing an offence under section 14.

Assemblies cannot be banned, but by virtue of the Criminal Justice and Public
Order Act 1994 section 70 which inserts sections 14A, 14B and 14C into the
1986 Act, in certain circumstances *trespassory public assemblies* can be banned.
Section 14A was enacted to deal with gatherings of new age travellers at places
like Stonehenge, but its provisions could also be used in respect of other types of
trespassory assemblies that fall within the requirements of the section. Section
14A enables the chief officer of police to apply to the council[60] or district for an
order[61] prohibiting, for up to four days, all *trespassory* assemblies in a specified

---

[56] For the background to the 1986 Act see the Home Office, *Review of the Public Order Act and
Related Legislation*, Cmnd. 7891 (1980), and the Law Commission Working Paper No. 82 (1982) and
Report No. 123 (1983); the Scarman Report on the Brixton riots (1981) Cmnd. 8427 See generally,
Richard Card, *Public Order Law* (2000), A. T. H. Smith, *Offences against Public Order* (1987).

[57] Where the police want to impose conditions on a proposed assembly, they must do so in writing
(s.14(3)).

[58] For a discussion of these criteria and the possibility of judicial review see the section on public
processions, *post*, para. 27–015.

[59] It is also an offence to incite another not to comply with a condition imposed on an assembly
(s.14(6)).

[60] In the case of the London police forces the application is made to the Home Secretary.

[61] The Home Secretary has to consent to such an order, and can modify a proposed order
(s.14A(2)).

area.[62] The chief officer has reasonably to believe that an assembly of 20 or more people is to be held in any district at a place on land to which the public has no right of access or only a limited right of access, that it is likely to be held without the permission of the owner or in such a way that it will exceed the permission or the public's right of access, and that it may result:

"(i) in serious disruption to the life of the community, or

(ii) where the land, or a building or monument on it, is of historical, architectural, archaeological or scientific importance, in significant damage to the land, building or monument." (section 14A(1))

An application can only be made with respect to land in the "open air" (section 14A(9)),[63] and land includes land forming part of the highway, enabling an order to be sought in respect of an assembly on the highway if the conditions provided in section 14A(1) are satisfied. Before such an order is made the relevant authority should be mindful of its obligations under the Human Rights Act 1998 and the limitations imposed by Article 11(2) of the E.C.H.R.

Once such an order is made, it is an offence to organise an assembly which a **27–013** person knows is prohibited under section 14A, to take part in such an assembly or to incite another to do so, (section 14B).[64] Section 14C give a police constable in uniform power to stop and redirect anyone who is within the area to which the order applies and who is reasonably believed to be on his way to an assembly within that area and which the police officer believes is likely to be an assembly prohibited by the order. A failure to comply with such an order may be an offence.[65]

A particular type of assembly recognised by the CJPO Act 1994 is the *"rave"*, defined in section 63 as: "a gathering on land in the open air of 100 or more persons (whether or not trespassers) at which amplified music is played through the night . . . and is such as, by reason of its loudness and duration and time at which it is played, is likely to cause serious distress to the inhabitants of the locality." Sections 63–66 provide a variety of powers to direct those reasonably believed to be planning a rave, those waiting for a rave to begin to, and those taking part in a rave, to desist; those who refuse a police direction may be guilty of an offence.[66]

Power to remove trespassers Section 61 of CJPO Act 1994 provides for the **27–014** criminalisation of trespass in certain circumstances. A senior police officer may give a direction to trespassers to leave land and to remove any vehicles or other property they have with them on the land provided that the officer reasonably believes that:

a) two or more persons are trespassing on land;

---

[62] s.14A(6).

[63] *cf.* s.14 where the assembly can be wholly or partly in the open air.

[64] A police officer in uniform has a power to arrest without warrant anyone whom he reasonably suspect to be committing an offence under s.14B.

[65] See *D.P.P. v. Jones op. cit.*

[66] Art. 11 is less likely to be of application here; in *Anderson and Others v. United Kingdom* [1998] E.H.R.L.R. 218 it was accepted by the European Commission on Human Rights that the right under Art. 11 does not include a right to gather for purely social purposes.

b) that those so present have the common purpose of residing on the land for any period;

c) that reasonable steps have been taken by or on behalf of the occupier to ask the trespassers to leave;

d) that either (i) any of the trespassers has caused damage to land or property or used threatening, abusive or insulting words or behaviour to the occupier of the land or others connected with him or (ii) the trespassers have brought more than six vehicles on to the land.

A failure to comply with such a direction is a summary offence. Although section 61 was aimed at "new age travellers", it could apply to other types of trespassers, including those demonstrating or picketing on private land.[67]

The offence of *aggravated trespass* is provided in section of the 68 CJPO Act 1994, and applies where a person trespasses on land in the open air and, in relation to any lawful activity which persons are engaging in or are about to engage in on that or adjoining land, does there anything which is intended by him to have the effect:

a) of intimidating those persons or any of them so as to deter them or any of them from engaging in that activity or

b) of obstructing that activity or

c) of disrupting that activity.

A police officer who has a reasonable belief that aggravated trespass under section 68 is, has been or is intended to be committed, may direct those concerned to leave; a failure to do so may amount to an offence (section 69).

These offences have been used successfully against anti-hunt protesters.[68]

Public Processions[69]

27–015   A public procession is defined by section 16 of the Public Order Act 1986 as a procession in a public place. A procession has been described as a meeting on the move, and many processions are in fact preliminary to the holding of a meeting.

Written advance notice is required by section 11 to be given of a public procession[70] intended to demonstrate support for or opposition to the views or actions of any person or body of persons; to publicise a cause or campaign; or to commemorate an event must be delivered to the relevant police station, not less

---

[67] The predecessor to s.61 was s.39 of the Public Order Act 1986, but because of problems with its interpretation and application, it was repealed and replaced by s.61.

[68] *Winder v. D.P.P.* (1996) 160 J.P. 713, DC, *Capon v. D.P.P.* (unreported) discussed by David Mead in [1998] Crim.L.R. 870. Both cases indicate a willing by the courts to broaden the interpretation of these sections to increase police discretion and limit freedom to protest.

[69] There are significant differences in Northern Ireland and Scotland on public order law in general and on processions in particular. See Brigid Hatfield, "Order in the Law of Public Order?", (1987) 38 N.I.L.Q. 86; The Public Processions (Northern Ireland) Act 1998 provided a new legal framework for the regulation of processions in Northern Ireland, including the establishment of a Parades Commission to take decisions on proposed parades; and see Imelda McAulay, "Reforming the law on contentious parades in Northern Ireland", [1998] P.L. 44.

[70] s.16, which also defines "public place", but does not stipulated the number of persons needed for a procession to be a public procession.

than six clear days before the date of the intended procession. Where this is not "reasonably practicable," then delivery should be as soon as delivery is reasonably practicable. The notice must specify the date, time and route of the proposed procession, and the name and address of the organiser (section 11(3)). Each of the persons organising a procession for which proper notice has not been given, or in respect of which the date, time or route differs from that given in the notice, is guilty of an offence.[71] To allow for processions in response to an unexpected event, the above provisions will not apply if it is "not reasonably practicable to give advance notice of the procession" (section 11(1)). The requirement of notice does not apply to processions commonly or customarily held in an area, and funeral processions organised by a funeral director acting in the normal course of his business (section 11(2)). The police do not have to consent to a procession, the notice requirement is to forewarn the police.[72]

Before the senior police officer[73] can impose *conditions* on an actual or proposed procession he must have regard to the time, place, circumstance and route or proposed route of the procession (section 12). In the light of these if he reasonably believes that either

"(a)   it may result in serious public disorder, serious damage to property or serious disruption to the life of the community, or

(b)   the purpose of the persons organising it is the intimidation of others with a view to compelling them not to do an act they have a right to do, or to do an act they have a right not to do,"

then he may give directions[74] to the organisers or participants imposing conditions on the procession. The requirement of serious disruption to the life of the community is capable of wide interpretation, while the intimidation provision does not necessarily require any connection with public disorder. A wide discretion is given to the police as to the conditions which are imposed since the section provides that he may impose "such conditions as appear to him necessary to prevent such disorder, damage, disruption or intimidation, including conditions as to the route of the procession or prohibiting it from entering any public place specified in the directions" (section 12(1)). To organise or take part in a procession and knowingly to fail to comply with a condition is an offence.

However, it is a defence to prove that the failure arose from circumstances **27–016** beyond the control of the accused (section 12(4)(5)). It is also an offence to incite another not to comply with a condition imposed on a procession (section 12(6)). A constable in uniform may arrest without warrant anyone he reasonably suspects is committing any of the above offences.

The police decision to impose conditions on a procession could be subject to judicial review.[75] This could be on one of two grounds. First that there was no basis for the police officer's reasonable belief that the procession would result in

---

[71] For possible defences, where the burden of proof is on the defendant, see s.11(8) and (9).

[72] s.11 does not apply to Scotland which is regulated by the Civic Government (Scotland) Act 1982, ss.62 and 65.

[73] Defined in s.12(2). In relation to a procession being held or a procession intended to be held where persons are assembling with a view to taking part in it, it means the most senior in rank of the police officers present at the scene. In the case of a proposed procession, it means the chief officer of police, who may delegate his functions to a deputy or assistant chief constable (s.15).

[74] Directions in respect of a proposed procession must be in writing (s.12(3)).

[75] See B. Hadfield, "Public Order Police Powers and Judicial Review", [1993] P.L. 915.

serious public disorder, serious damage to property or serious disruption to the life of the community. This could include a challenge to the meaning of, for example, "serious disruption to the life of the community." Secondly, that even if there was a basis for the police officer's beliefs, the conditions imposed were not necessary to prevent disorder, damage, disruption or intimidation. Given that section 12(1) provides that the police officer may give such directions as appear to him necessary, until the coming into force of the Human Rights Act it would have proved difficult to challenge the legality of directions given, except on the ground that they are totally unreasonable. However, an argument based on a breach of Article 11 E.C.H.R. could be raised on the ground that the conditions imposed did not fall within the restrictions permitted under Article 11(2). It may also be possible in certain circumstances to seek judicial review of a decision *not* to impose conditions.[76]

In certain circumstances processions may be *prohibited* (section 13). Where the senior police officer reasonably believes that, because of particular circumstances existing in any district or part of a district, the powers under section 12 will be insufficient to prevent the holding of a public procession from resulting in "serious public disorder," then he shall apply to the council of the district for an order prohibiting for up to three months, the holding of all public processions or of any class of public processions so specified, in the district or part of the district (section 13(1)). On receiving such an application, the council may, with the consent of the Secretary of State, make an order either in the terms of the application or with such modifications as may be approved by the Secretary of State (section 13(2)). Where the area concerned is the City of London, or the metropolitan police district, then the power to seek an order is given to the Commissioner of Police for the City of London or the Commissioner of Police of the Metropolis, who may, with the consent of the Secretary of State, make a similar order to that outlined above. It is an offence to organise, take part, or incite another to take part in a prohibited procession (section 13(7)(8)(9)), and all three offences are arrestable without warrant by a constable in uniform (section 13(10)).

27–017   Orders prohibiting processions may also be subject to judicial review. Section 13 is worded in terms of the "reasonable belief" of the senior police officer, which could provide some prospect of a successful application for judicial review. In the past courts have been unwilling to interfere with the exercise of discretion granted to senior police officers.[77] However, it is clear that under Article 11 of E.C.H.R., orders banning marches can only be justified in extreme circumstances.[78]

Public Order Offences[79]

27–018   In addition to regulating marches and assemblies, the Public Order Act 1986 made extensive reforms to a variety of public order offences. The Criminal Justice and Public Order Act 1994 amended and added to the 1986 Act and introduced additional public order offences.

---

[76] *Re Murphy* [1991] 5 N.I.J.B. 72, QBD and 88, CA.
[77] *Kent v. Metropolitan Police Commissioner, The Times,* May 15, 1981.
[78] *Christians against Racism and Fascism v. United Kingdom* (1980) 21 D.R. 138.
[79] See Richard Card, *ante.*

Riot (section 1, Public Order Act 1986)

The problems encountered by the police in bringing successful prosecutions **27–019** for the common law offence of riot in the wake of the 1984–85 miners' dispute was one of the reasons for the 1986 reforms. Until 1984–85, most of the cases on riot arose out of the Riot (Damage) Act 1886, which provides that where premises are injured or the property therein is destroyed or stolen by any persons "riotously and tumultuously assembled", compensation to the persons aggrieved is to be paid out of the local police fund.[80] It is not necessary for someone to have been prosecuted and convicted for riot before a claim for compensation can be brought.

The offence of riot is the most serious of the public order offences. It is triable only on indictment and punishable by imprisonment for up to 10 years or a fine or both. The consent of the Director of Public Prosecutions is required before a prosecution for riot, or incitement to riot, can be instituted (section 7(1)). The minimum number required for riot is 12 persons present together who use or threaten unlawful violence for a common purpose. Those involved do not have to form a cohesive group or use or threaten violence simultaneously (section 1(2)). Only those who use unlawful violence in the prescribed circumstances are guilty of riot. Provided at least one person is so liable, the other members of the group, if they have the appropriate *mens rea*, may be guilty of aiding and abetting riot[81] or of a lesser offence, such as violent disorder. Violence for this offence, and for the offences of violent disorder (section 2) and using threatening abusive or insulting words or behaviour (section 4), means any violent conduct towards property or persons, whether or not damage or injury is caused or intended (section 8). For this offence, and for the offences of violent disorder, affray and threatening, abusive or insulting behaviour, the definition of the offence is in terms of unlawful violence.[82] The definition of violence concentrates on the conduct rather than the consequences of the violence and section 8 provides that violence: "is not restricted to conduct causing or intended to cause injury or damage but includes any other violent conduct". To assist in proving a common purpose, it is provided that: "the common purpose may be inferred from conduct" (section 1(3)).[83] The conduct of the "persons who are present together" must be such as could cause a person of reasonable fitness present at the scene to fear for his personal safety. For this offence, as with those of violent disorder (section 2) and affray (section 3) no person of reasonable firmness need actually be, or be likely to be, present at the scene. In common with all the offences in Part I, riot may be committed in private as well as in public places (section 1(5)).[84] It must be proved that a person accused of riot either intended to use violence or was aware that his conduct may be violent (section 6(1)).[85] For the purpose of the

---

[80] See for example, *Ford v. Metropolitan Police District Receiver* [1921] 2 K.B. 344.

[81] *R. v. Jefferson* 99 Cr.App. Rep. 13, CA.

[82] Violence justified on the grounds of, for example, reasonable force in self-defence, is not unlawful; *R. Rothwell* [1993] Crim. L.R. 626, CA.

[83] For example by making the same gestures, or as in *op. cit.* celebrating England's victory over Egypt in a football match.

[84] Since the offences in Pt I can be committed in a public or a private place (subject to certain exceptions for private dwellings), there is no need for a definition of public place in this Part.

[85] For all offences in Pt I of the Act a provision is made with regard to those who are intoxicated. A person whose awareness is impaired by intoxication, whether by drink, drugs or other means, shall be taken to be aware of "that of which he would be aware if not intoxicated, unless he shows either that his intoxication was not self-induced or that it was caused solely by the taking . . . of a substance in the course of medical treatment," (s.6(5)).

Riot (Damages) Act 1886,[86] "riotous" and "riotously" are to be construed in accordance with section 1 (s.10(1)).[87] Riot is an arrestable offence by virtue of section 24 of the Police and Criminal Evidence Act 1984.

Violent disorder (section 2, Public Order Act 1986)[88]

27–020   This is a wide offence covering both the actual use of violence and the threat of violence. The offence requires that three or more persons present together use or threaten unlawful violence and that their conduct, taken together, would cause a (hypothetical) person of reasonable fitness present at the scene to fear for his personal safety. There is no need for a common purpose on the part of the three or more persons,[89] which marks an important distinction between this offence and riot and may explain why violent disorder a more frequent charge than that of riot. Nor is it necessary for violent disorder that the persons concerned used or threatened unlawful violence simultaneously (section 2(2)). The *mens rea* is an intent to use or threaten violence or an awareness that conduct may be violent or threaten violence (section 6(2)). The offence of violent disorder is triable either way, and is an arrestable offence by virtue of section 24 of the Police and Criminal Evidence Act 1984.[90] The offence of violent disorder may be used in respect of behaviour that would not give rise to serious public order problems.

Affray (section 3, Public Order Act 1986)[91]

27–021   Section 3 provides that a person is guilty of affray if he uses or threatens unlawful violence towards another and his conduct is such as would cause a (hypothetical) person of reasonable firmness present at the scene to fear for his personal safety (section 3(1)). Where two or more persons use or threaten the unlawful violence, it is the conduct of them taken together that must be considered for the purpose of section 3(1) (section 3(2)). The threat of unlawful violence must be a physical threat and cannot be made by the use of words alone (section 3(3)).[92] In this section, unlike sections 1 and 2, violence does not include violent conduct towards property (section 8). The provision that affray may be committed in private as well as public (section 3(5)), and that no person of reasonable firmness need actually be, or be likely to be, present at the scene, means that a fight in a private house could amount to the public order offence of affray. The *mens rea* is the same as for the offence of violent disorder (section 6(2)), and a constable may arrest without warrant anyone he reasonably suspects is committing affray (section 3(6)).[93] This is a more limited power of arrest than

---

[86] Also the Merchant Shipping Act 1894, s.515.

[87] Any enactment in force before s.10 came into effect, which contained the word "riot" or cognate expressions, which would have been construed in accordance with the common law offence of riot, is to be construed in accordance with s.1 (s.10(3)).

[88] For elements which this offence has in common with riot, see earlier section.

[89] *R. v. Mahroof* (1988) 88 Cr.App.R. 317; it was held in *R. v. Hebron* [1989] Crim.L.Rev. that being present at the scene of a fight where bottles were being thrown at the police and threats being made, was sufficient.

[90] The penalties on conviction on indictment are up to five years imprisonment, or a fine or both; on summary conviction up to six months imprisonment or a fine not exceeding the statutory maximum.

[91] For elements which this offence has in common with riot, see earlier section. The meaning of this section was considered by the House of Lords in *I v. D.P.P.* [2001] 2 W.L.R. 765.

[92] In *R. v. Dixon* [1993] Crim.L.R. 579, it was held that where the defendant set his dog on police officers with the words, "Go on, go on", the dog was being used as a weapon, and the conduct amounted to affray.

[93] The mode of trial and punishment is the same as for violent disorder, except that on conviction on indictment the maximum term of imprisonment is three years (s.3(7)).

that which applies to sections 1 and 2 by virtue of section 24 of the Police and Criminal Evidence Act 1984. It is likely that the common law power to arrest without warrant for an actual or threatened breach of the peace will be available in circumstances which would amount to an offence under sections 1, 2, or 3.

Threatening, Abusive, Insulting Words or Behaviour; Disorderly Conduct

Three offences, found in the 1986 Act, cover a variety of words or behaviour **27–022** and have several elements in common. The most serious offence is section 4, which has similarities with section 5 of the Public Order Act 1936 (which was repealed in 1986). Section 4A was inserted by section 154 of the Criminal Justice and Public Order Act 1994; although section 5 is the least serious of the three offences, it is one of the most controversial sections in the 1986 Act. Section 31 of the Crime and Disorder Act 1998 provides three separate offences which apply if an offence committed under sections 4, 4A or 5, is "racially aggravated".[94]

Threatening, abusive or insulting words or behaviour (section 4)

There are two alternative limbs to section 4. The accused must either **27–023**

(a) use towards another person threatening, abusive or insulting words or behaviour, or

(b) distribute or display to another person any writing, sign or other visible representation which is threatening, abusive or insulting.

In either case, the accused must do so with an "intent to cause that person to believe that immediate unlawful violence will be used against him or another by any person, or to provoke the immediate use of unlawful violence by that person or another, or whereby that person is likely to believe that such violence will be used or it is likely that such violence will be provoked" (section 4(1)). This list of possible consequences of the accused's words or behaviour covers a wide spectrum, and makes section 4 potentially far reaching. In considering the "likely" effect of the accused's conduct, the existing law, whereby the accused must "take his audience as he finds them,"[95] may continue to apply, although considerations of Article 10 and 11 E.C.H.R. may result in a different conclusion.

The words "threatening, abusive or insulting" appeared in section 5 of the 1936 Act, and it is likely that the cases interpreting them apply to sections 4, 4A and 5.[96] In *Cozens v. Brutus*[97] it was held that "insulting" must be given its ordinary meaning: "it is a question of fact in each case and not a question of

---

[94] For the definition of "racially aggravated" see s.28 of the Crime and Disorder Act 1998; a racially aggravated offence under the Crime and Disorder Act is punishable more severely than an offence under the Public Order Act, see s.31(4),(5). The offences of riot, violent disorder and affray are not covered by the 1998 Act, since the penalties for these offences were considered adequate.

[95] *Jordan v. Burgoyne* [1963] 2 Q.B. 744, DC, and see A. T. H. Smith [1987] Crim.L.R. 156 at p. 164 for an argument to the contrary.

[96] For example *Simcock v. Rhodes* (1977) Cr.App.Rep. 192, DC; *Jordan v. Burgoyne* [1963] Q.B. 744 (DC). The words "threatening abusive or insulting" are also constituents of ss.18(1), 19(1), 20(1), 21(1), 23(1) of the 1986 Act.

[97] [1973] A.C. 854, HL (anti-apartheid demonstration on Wimbledon tennis court; spectators angered, but not insulted). *cf. Masterson v. Holden* [1986] 1 W.L.R. 1017, DC. (Overt homosexual conduct in Oxford St. at 1.55 a.m. Justices "most likely to know what is insulting behaviour" at that hour in that place).

law." Provided the conduct is "threatening, abusive or insulting", it is not necessary that anyone who witnessed it felt threatened etc.[98]

The accused has to be shown to:

(i) intend, or be aware that his words or behaviour towards another person is threatening, abusive or insulting (s.6(3)); and

(ii) (a) that he intended to cause another person to believe that immediate unlawful violence will be used against him or another; or

   (b) that he intended to provoke the immediate use of violence by another person, or

   (c) that another person was "likely to believe that such violence[99] will be used or it is likely that such violence will be provoked" (s.4(1)).

27–024   Section 4 requires the threatening, abusive or insulting words or behaviour to be used towards another person, or distributed or displayed to another. In *Atkins v. D.P.P.*[1] where the accused's threats were made with respect to a third party who was not present at the time, there was no offence. In *Horseferry Road Stipendiary Magistrate, ex p. Siadatan*[2] the Court of Appeal upheld a refusal by a magistrate to issue a summons against Penguin Books Ltd for an offence under section 4 in respect of the publication of a book by Salman Rushdie which was regarded as offensive by most Muslims, on the basis that there was insufficient evidence of a threat of *immediate* unlawful violence. It suggested that immediate did not mean instantaneous, but that it had to be likely that: "violence will result within a relatively short period of time without any other intervening occurrence."

An offence under section 4 (and sections 4A and 5) can be committed in a private as well as in a public place, but excluding, in effect, domestic disputes (sections 4(2), 4A(2) and 5(2)). A constable may arrest without warrant anyone he reasonably suspects is committing an offence under section 4 (section 4(3)). For this offence, and the offence under section 5, the police could also, in certain circumstances, rely on their common law powers of arrest without warrant in connection with a breach of the peace; and their powers under section 25 of the Police and Criminal Evidence Act 1984. Offences under this section are triable summarily only.[3]

Harassment, alarm or distress (sections 4A and 5)

27–025   Two further summary offences, covering harassment alarm or distress were introduced to deal with the types of antisocial behaviour prevalent in particular in inner city areas, but which did not fall under section 4. Such behaviour is frequently directed at vulnerable groups such as the elderly and ethnic minority groups. Section 4A was introduced to fill a perceived gap in the law and provide for a similar, but more serious offence than that found in section 5.[4]

---

[98] *Parkin v. Norman* [1983] Q.B. 92, *Marsh v. Arscott* (1983) 75 Cr.App.Rep. 211, DC.

[99] Which must be *immediate* unlawful violence, see below.

[1] (1989) 89 Cr.App.R. 199, DC.

[2] [1991] 1 Q.B. 260.

[3] The penalties are imprisonment for up to six months or a fine not exceeding level 5 on the standard scale, or both. Where a person has been tried on indictment for violent disorder or affray, and found not guilty, the jury may, as an alternative, find him guilty of an offence under s.4 (s.7(3)).

[4] The origin of this offence was a report from the Home Affairs Select Committee H.C. 27 (1993–94) which suggested a new offence of racially motivated violence; the Home Secretary rejected these calls, but instead introduced s.4A which is more general.

Both sections are concerned with a person who either "a) uses threatening, abusive or insulting words or behaviour, or disorderly behaviour or b) displays any writing, sign or other visible representation which is threatening, abusive or insulting", (sections 4A(1) and 5(1)). In neither case need the words or behaviour be directed toward another. The discussion of the meaning of "threatening, abusive and insulting", in section 4 apply here also.[5] "Disorderly" is only found in sections 4A and 5, it is not defined and whether or not the words or behaviour are disorderly is a question of fact: no element of violence is required.[6] Nor are the words "harassment, alarm or distress" (found only in sections 4A and 5), defined; they are also questions of fact. Both offences can be committed in a "public or private place" which in the context of sections 4A and 5 have the same meaning as in section 4 (sections 4A(2) and 5(2)). There are additional defences available under sections 4A and 5 that are not available under section 4, in each case the onus of proof is on the accused. These are that he had no reason to believe that there was anyone with hearing in sight who was likely to be caused harassment, alarm or distress; that he was inside a dwelling and had no reason to believe that his words, behaviour, writing, etc. would be heard or seen by a person outside that or any other dwelling; that his conduct was reasonable[7] (sections 4A(3) and 5(3)).

For an offence under *section 4A*[8] the prosecution does not have to show that **27–026** the defendant's threatening etc words, behaviour or display were directed towards another person.[9] The differences between this offence and section 5 are that the prosecution must show that the defendant intended to cause harassment, alarm or distress and that an actual victim (not necessarily the one intended) suffered accordingly.[10] The reluctance of such victims to go to court and give evidence may reduce the effectiveness of this offence. The power of arrest and penalty is the same as that for section 4.

An offence under *section 5* is committed in respect of the same type of words, behaviour[11] or display as that found in section 4A, and it must be "within the hearing or sight of a person[12] likely to be caused harassment, alarm or distress thereby" (section 5(1)). There is no need for actual harassment, alarm or distress, it is sufficient that the words or behaviour are likely to cause that person harassment, alarm or distress.[13] The accused must either intend or be aware that his words, behaviour, writing, etc. is threatening, abusive or insulting or he intends or is aware that his behaviour is or may be disorderly (section 6(4)). If a person engages in "offensive conduct", which means conduct which a police officer reasonably suspects to constitute an offence under section 5 (section 5(5)), and the police officer's warning to stop such conduct is ignored, then the police

---

[5] *ante.*
[6] *Chambers v. D.P.P.* [1995] Crim.L.R. 896.
[7] An objective test. In determining this, account may be taken of all the circumstances, including the reasons for the defendant's conduct: *Morrow v. D.P.P.* [1994] Crim.L.R. 58, DC.
[8] The penalties for this offence are the same as for s.4.
[9] *cf.* s.5 below.
[10] Unlike ss.4 and 5, s.4A does not specifically require the prosecution to show that the defendant intended that his words, behaviour etc. to be threatening etc, or be aware that this was the case; it is assumed that this is also required for s.4A.
[11] In *Vignon v. D.P.P.* [1997] Crim.L.R. 289, DC, it was accepted that it was open to the magistrates to find that installing a hidden video camera in a changing room fell within the behaviour prohibited by s.5.
[12] Which has been held to include a police officer: *D.P.P. v. Orum* [1989] 1 W.L.R. 88.
[13] Which can include alarm etc about the safety of a third party, *Lodge v. D.P.P., The Times*, October 26, 1988, DC.

officer who gave the warning, or another police officer,[14] may arrest that person without warrant. The power to arrest is essentially a preventative measure.[15] This is potentially a very wide offence and its use, application and interpretation has been controversial.[16] The Human Rights Act 1998 may provide scope for argument as to its application.

Some general statutory offences and common law provisions

27–027   There are a variety of offences which could apply in public order situations, and which were enacted without any consideration of the need to provide for freedom of assembly. Should any dispute arise today, then a court should attempt to interpret and apply them "as far as it is possible to do so" in a way which is compatible with Convention rights (section 3(1) of the HRA Act 1998). A public authority which seeks to rely on or apply the provisions of these statutes should bear in mind its obligation in section 6 of the HRA Act.[17]

Highways Act 1980

27–028   Wilful obstruction of the highway without lawful authority or excuse is a summary offence under the Highways Act 1980, s.137. There is a power of arrest without warrant under the general arrest conditions provided by the Police and Criminal Evidence Act 1984, s.25. It is not necessary for the prosecution to prove that anyone was actually obstructed, nor is it a good defence that there was a way round the obstruction, or that there was no intention to obstruct,[18] although these facts may go to mitigation. The courts have for some time looked at this offence in the wider context of freedom of assembly.

In *Hirst v. Chief Constable of Yorkshire*[19] the Divisional Court considered this section and suggested that in deciding whether there was an obstruction it should be asked whether what was being done was incidental to the right of passing and repassing. If not, than there was an obstruction, but it would not amount to an offence if it was a reasonable obstruction. In considering this question Otton J. suggested that account should be taken of the fact that the defendants were exercising rights of assembly and demonstration. In *D.P.P. v. Jones*[20] Lords Irvine and Hutton referred to the right to peaceful assembly on the highway[21]; Lord Hutton suggested that this right would be unduly restricted if it could not in some circumstances be exercised on the public highway.

The Public Meeting Act 1908

27–029   The offences created by this Act are ones designed to protect free speech and public protest, but they have been used very little. Under this Act, as amended by the Public Order Act 1936, disorderly conduct designed to break up a lawful

---

[14] The Public Order (Amendment) Act 1996 was passed to cure a defect in the original s.5 highlighted in *D.P.P. v. Hancock and Tuttle* [1995] Crim.L.R. 139, whereby the constable who effected the arrest had to be the constable who had administered the warning.

[15] The penalty is a fine not exceeding level 3 on the standard scale.

[16] See Andrew Ashworth, "Criminalising Disrespect", [1995] Crim.L.R. 98.

[17] *ante*, para. 22–016.

[18] *Arrowsmith v. Jenkins* [1963] 2 Q.B. 561, DC. This was in fact under the similar provision in the 1959 Highways Act.

[19] (1986) 85 Cr.App.R. 143.

[20] [1999] 2 A.C. 240.

[21] The case was not on s.137; Lord Clyde did not go as far as Lords Irvine and Hutton in recognising a common law right to assemble on the highway, and Lords Slynn and Hope dissented from this proposition.

public meeting is a summary offence. However, the fact that a mee the highway is not enough in itself to make the meeting unlawful fc of the Public Meeting Act 1908, in the absence of some other ele obstruction.[22] Under the Act of 1908, as amended, if a constab suspects any person of committing an offence under that Act he ma) by the chairman of the meeting, require the person to give his name If the person refuses to give his name and address, or gives a fal address, he is guilty of an offence. The constable may arrest withouι warrant if the person refuses to give his name and address, or if the constable reasonably suspects him of giving a false name and address.[23]

Obstructing or assaulting a police officer in the execution of his duty[24]

Cases such as *Duncan v. Jones*[25] demonstrated how these offences which were **27–030** intended to be defensive or preventive weapons became used by the police as offensive or punitive weapons.[26] The Human Rights Act will require a reconsideration of this approach in the context of public protest.[27]

Miscellaneous Offences and Torts

A wide variety of offences and torts could be committed by those taking part **27–031** in assemblies, processions and demonstrations. These include incitement to racial hatred,[28] sedition,[29] and offences connected with the possession of an offensive weapon in any public place.[30] In addition there are general laws governing criminal damage, the possession of firearms and explosives, and offences against the person. A public procession may easily involve the common law offence of public nuisance. A public nuisance will be caused if the user of the highway, although reasonable from the point of view of those taking part in the procession, is not reasonable from the point of view of the public. This question depends on the circumstances of the case, and may be affected by the numbers taking part, the occasion, duration, place and hour, and also whether the obstruction is trivial, casual, temporary and without wrongful intent.[31] The tort of *nuisance* may also apply. Unreasonable interference with the rights of others to use the highway could be a species of the tort of private nuisance, which may give rise to an action for damages or the granting of an injunction.[32] In the light of Article 11 of E.C.H.R. it is suggested that nuisance, whether public or private, which has been little used in the context of assemblies and processions, is unlikely to be relied upon in the future.

---

[22] *Burden v. Rigler* [1911] 1 K.B. 337, DC.

[23] See Police and Criminal Evidence Act 1984, s.25, s.26 and sched. 7.

[24] See *ante* para. 24–019 *et seq.*

[25] [1931] 1 K.B. 218.

[26] E. C. S. Wade, "Police Powers and Public Meetings", (1937) 6 C.L.J. 175; T. C. Daintith, "Disobeying a Policeman-A Fresh Look at *Duncan v. Jones*" [1966] P.L. 248.

[27] See *Redman-Bate v. D.P.P., The Times*, July 28, 1999, [2000] H.R.L.R. 249.

[28] *ante*, para. 25–010.

[29] *ante*, para. 25–009.

[30] Prevention of Crime Act 1953, as amended by the Public Order Act 1986, the Criminal Justice Act 1988 as amended by the Offensive Weapons Act 1996.

[31] *Lowdens v. Keaveney* [1903] Ir.R. 82; *R. v. Clark* [1964] 2 Q.B. 315, CCA where a conviction for incitement to commit nuisance was quashed because the jury had not been directed to consider whether or not there was a reasonable use of the highway.

[32] *Thomas v. N.U.M.* [1985] I.R.L.R. 136, at p. 149. See Hazel Carty [1985] P.L. 542. *News Group Newspapers Ltd and others v. S.O.G.A.T. '82* [1986] I.R.L.R. 336. *Hunter v. Canary Wharf Ltd* [1997] A.C. 655.

Meetings addressed by a member of a proscribed organisation

The Terrorism Act 2000, section 12 makes it an offence to organise or to speak at a meeting in the knowledge that the meeting is to be addressed by a person who belongs or professes to belong to a proscribed organisation.[33] A meeting for the purposes of this clause is a gathering of three or more persons, whether or not the public is admitted. It is not necessary that the speaker or organiser supports the proscribed organisation, or any form of terrorism. It is questionable whether section 12 is compatible with Articles 10 and 11 of E.C.H.R.

Picketing[34]

27–033
The word picket is used to describe those who gather outside a particular place with the aim of persuading others not to enter. Although usually connected with industrial disputes, this is not necessarily the case.[35] There is no legal right to picket as such, but "peaceful picketing" in industrial disputes has long been recognised as being lawful. There is therefore a statutory freedom or liberty to picket peacefully in certain circumstance. The present law is contained in the Trade Union and Labour Relations (Consolidation) Act 1992 (TULRA), s.220. This provides that:

> "It shall be lawful for a person in contemplation or furtherance of a trade dispute to attend—
>
> > (a) at or near his own place of work, or (b) if he is an official of a trade union, at or near the place of work of a member of that union whom he is accompanying and whom he represents,
>
> for the purpose only of peacefully obtaining or communicating information, or peacefully persuading any person to work or abstain from working."

The immunity given by this section is to attend at or near certain places for particular purposes, so that such attendance does not of itself constitute the torts of trespass[36] or nuisance, or the criminal offences of obstructing the highway or "watching or besetting."[37] However, this may not be the case where mass picketing (*infra*) is involved. The immunity given to those covered by section 220 is in respect only of peaceful picketing, which means without causing a breach of the peace.[38] It is also only in respect of the attendance of pickets for the purposes set out in the section, and if the attendance of the pickets is for any other purpose the immunity is lost.[39] The predecessor to section 220 was described in *Broome v. D.P.P.*[40] as giving a narrow but real immunity, which gives: "no protection in relation to anything the pickets may say or do whilst they are

---

[33] As defined by the Terrorism Act 2000, section 3.

[34] Originally a military term for a small detachment of troops, from the French *piquet*.

[35] *e.g.* consumer picketing and see *D.P.P. v. Fidler* [1992] 1 W.L.R. 91 where a group of people assembled outside an abortion clinic with the aim of dissuading women from entering.

[36] The application of the law of trespass to picketing should now be considered in the light of *Jones v. D.P.P. ante*, which could allow pickets to claim that a peaceful, non-obstructive picket line was not trespass to the highway. s.42 of the Criminal Justice and Police Act 2001 (*ante*, para. 27–004) is expressly stated not to apply to lawful picketing under TULRA.

[37] s.241 TULRA 1992, re-enacting s.7 of the Conspiracy and Protection of Property Act 1875 *infra*.

[38] *e.g. Piddington v. Bates* [1961] 1 W.L.R. 162, DC.

[39] *e.g. Tynan v. Balmer* [1967] 1 Q.B. 91, DC.

[40] [1974] A.C. 587.

attending if what they say or do is itself unlawful."[41] Any pickets who are not covered by the terms of section 220, run the risk of committing the same range of criminal offences and torts as any other demonstrator. In addition they can be sued for certain industrial torts, such as inducement to breach of contract or prosecuted for one of the offences in section 241 of the TULRA[42] which include: intimidating any other person with a view to compelling[43] him to abstain from doing any act which such other person has a legal right to do; and watching and besetting the place where another person works, with the same view.[44]

Mass picketing

Although mass picketing is not unlawful under section 220, the greater the **27–034** number of pickets involved, the easier it will be to infer a purpose other than that of peacefully obtaining or communicating information. In *Broome v. D.P.P.* Lord Reid said that in a case of mass picketing "it would not be difficult to infer as matter of fact that pickets who assemble in unreasonably large numbers do have the purpose of preventing free passage"[45]—in other words a purpose outside the limits of section 220. In *Thomas v. N.U.M. (South Wales Area) and others*[46] Scott J. suggested that: "mass picketing—by which I understand to be meant picketing so as by sheer weight of numbers to block the entrance to premises or to prevent the entry thereto of vehicles or people— . . . is clearly both common law nuisance and an offence under section 7 of the (Conspiracy and Protection of Property Act)".[47] Although there is no statutory limit to the number of pickets, the Code of Practice on Picketing,[48] while recognising this,[49] goes on to suggest that: "pickets and their organisers should ensure that in general the number of pickets does not exceed six at any entrance to a workplace; frequently a smaller number will be appropriate."[50] Scott J. in *Thomas v. N.U.M.* was clearly influenced by this guidance since the injunction granted was to restrain the organisation of picketing at colliery gates by more than six persons.[51] The suggested limit of six pickets may need to be read in the light of Article 11 of the E.C.H.R., since the peacefulness or otherwise of a picket line should depend on the attitude of the pickets and not on an arbitrary number of pickets. It may be that the provision on numbers could be regarded as necessary in a democratic society to preserve public order.

Breach of the peace[52]

The most important powers relied on by the police in connection with the maintenance of public order at picket lines are those connected with breach of the

[41] *ibid., per* Lord Salmon at p. 603.
[42] See Francis Bennion, "Mass Picketing and the 1875 Act", [1985] Crim.L.Rev. 64, which discusses the use made of the predecessor to s.241 during the 1984/85 miners' dispute.
[43] In *D.P.P. v. Fidler* [1992] 1 W.L.R. 91 it was held that watching and besetting for the purpose of persuasion as opposed to coercion did not fall within the section.
[44] The Protection from Harassment Act 1997 is sufficiently wide to apply to the mere presence of pickets, if they cause alarm or distress to any person on more than one occasion.
[45] *ante*, at p. 598.
[46] [1985] I.R.L.R. 1365.
[47] *ibid.*, at p. 153.
[48] Originally published in 1980. The present revised and reissued version (May 1992) is in force as if made under s.203 of the TULRA 1992.
[49] para. 47.
[50] para. 51.
[51] See also *News Group Newspapers Ltd v. S.O.G.A.T. '82* [1986] I.R.L.R. 337.
[52] *ante*, para. 27–008.

peace. These powers, backed up by the offences of obstructing and assaulting a police officer in the execution of his duty,[53] and obstructing the highway, have enabled the police to limit both the number of pickets,[54] and their activities.[55] The restrictions now recognised as applying to police powers to keep the peace apply to the use of these powers in the context of picketing.

Public Order Act 1986

27–035   Various aspects of this Act have significance for the legality of picketing and associated activities. All the offences in Part I[56] could be used in respect of non peaceful picketing. Of particular significance are the offences of violent disorder (section 2), threatening behaviour (section 4), intentional harassment (section 4A), and disorderly behaviour (section 5). The most important section so far as picketing is concerned is section 14,[57] which enables the police to impose conditions on an open air assembly of more than 20 persons in a public place. This allows the police to limit the location, duration or size of a picket. Although the extensive common law powers of the police in effect enable them to impose such restrictions on pickets, it is only where it is necessary to do so to keep the peace. Section 14 extends the grounds upon which the police may impose conditions on assemblies to include a reasonable belief that the assembly will result in "serious disruption to the life of the community" or where there is a reasonable belief that: "the purpose of the persons organising (the assembly) is the intimidation of others with a view to compelling them not to do an act they have a right to do, or to do an act they have a right not to do." The powers available to the police to seek to ban trespassory assemblies (sections 14A, 14B and 14C) could be used in the event of a long strike, such as that of the miners in 1984/85. The general requirement to give advance notice of public processions (section 11) is likely to limit the possibility of mobile demonstrations in the course of industrial disputes.

Sporting events

27–036   The levels of violence and general public order problems at sporting events, and in particular at football matches, led to the enactment of specific legislation. The Criminal Justice (Scotland) Act 1980 and the Sporting Events (Control of Alcohol, etc.) Act 1985 both aimed to reduce the perceived cause of the problems by creating offences in connection with the carrying of alcohol on coaches, trains, and vehicles adapted to carry more than eight persons (section 1A) where the principal purpose of the journey is to go to or from a "designated sporting event".[58] Both Acts provide for offences connected with drunkenness at desig-nated sports grounds, and regulate the sale and supply of alcohol within sports grounds. Additional offences were introduced by the Football (Offences) Act 1991 with respect to misbehaviour at a "designated football match". These include offences of throwing objects (section 2),[59] chanting of an indecent or racist nature (section 3), and pitch invasion (section 4).

[53] *ante*, para. 24–019 *et seq.*
[54] *Piddington v. Bates* [1960] 1 W.L.R., DC.
[55] *Tynan v. Balmer* [1967] 1 Q.B. 91, DC.
[56] *ante*, para. 27–011 *et seq.*
[57] *ante*, para. 27–012 *et seq.*
[58] This can include not only particular sporting events, but also classes of such events, and can be made in respect of events outside Great Britain.
[59] s.8 of the Public Order Act 1987 could also apply to throwing objects, but it would be more difficult for the prosecution to prove.

Banning orders

Part IV of the Public Order Act, (as amended by the
Disorder) Act 1999 and the Football (Disorder) Act 200(
whereby a person who appears before a court for a
threatened violence to person or property committed
prescribed football match, may be subjected to a domest
30). Such an order precludes the person concerned
matches for a specified period. There is provision in se(
of State, by order, to extend these orders to other s[
banning orders can only be made with respect to match
The Football Spectators Act 1989, as amended, allows a court to make a
international banning order to prevent those convicted of the offences specified
in Schedule 1 of the Act, from attending football matches outside England and
Wales.[60] Additions powers are available under the 2000 Act to enable the police,
in specified circumstances, to prevent people from leaving the country while they
seek a banning order, and to allow the police to detain a person for up to six hours
while they make further inquiries before seeking a banning order.

II. FREEDOM OF ASSOCIATION

Article 10 on free speech and Article 11 of E.C.H.R. are relevant here. Article **27–038**
11 recognises the right to form and join a trade union, and imposes an obligation
on States to "both permit and make possible" the freedom for individual trade
unionist to protect their rights.[61] Restrictions on these rights are permissable if
they fall within Articles 10(2) or 11(2). These have been interpreted to allow, for
example, special restrictions on the political activities of civil servants and local
government officers.[62] Apart from certain restrictions on these groups and also on
the police and members of the armed forces, there are relatively few legal
restrictions on the freedom to form and join associations for political or other
purposes; those that exist are concerned mostly with terrorism or other types of
violence.[63]

Proscribed organisations

The Terrorism Act 2000[64] reforms andextends existing counter-terrorism legis- **27–039**
lation and put it on a permanent basis.[65] Part II deals with proscribed organisations, the law on which is now the same throughout the United Kingdom. Section

---

[60] An international football banning order can also be made in respect of offences of another country
which correspond to those found in Sched. 1; corresponding offences under *inter alia* Scottish, Irish,
French and Italian law have been listed in an Order in Council.

[61] *National Union of Belgian Police v. Belgium* (1975) 1 E.H.R.R. 578.

[62] *Council for Civil Service Unions v. United Kingdom* (1988) 10 E.H.R.R. 269; *Ahmed and Others
v. United Kingdom* (2000) 29 E.H.R.R. 1.

[63] Other limitations are that the association does not involve a criminal conspiracy, Criminal Law Act
1977, s.1, or a civil conspiracy (which is a tort).

[64] The Act is based on proposals made in Lord Lloyd of Berwick's *Inquiry into Legislation against
terrorism* Cm. 3420 (1996), and the Government's response in *Legislation against terrorism*, Cm.
4178 (1998).

[65] It replaces the Prevention of Terrorism (Temporary Provisions) Act 1989, the Northern Ireland
(Emergency Provision) Act 1996 and ss.1–4 of the Criminal Justice (Terrorism and Conspiracy) Act
1998.

s a power to proscribe organisations, which are concerned in inter-
or domestic terrorism[66]; sections 11 and 12 provides for offences in
ction with membership (or professed membership) of proscribed organisa-
ns,[67] including the promotion of such organisations and of meetings in support
of them. The 2000 Act provides for the establishment of the *Proscribed Organisations Appeal Committee*, to hear cases where the Secretary of State has refused
to de-proscribe an organisation. Human rights issues could be raised with respect
to the compatibility of future banning orders, particularly if the body concerned
claims to be a political party.

It is an offence under section 13 for a person in a public place to wear any item
of dress or to wear, carry or display any article in such a way or in such
circumstances as to arouse reasonable apprehension that he is a member or
supporter of a proscribed organisation.

The wearing of "political" uniforms

27–040   It is an offence under section 1 of the Public Order Act 1936[68] to wear in any
public place or at any public meeting a uniform signifying association with any
political organisation or with the promotion of any political object. The Home
Secretary may give permission for the wearing of such uniform on a ceremonial
or other special occasion. The consent of the Attorney-General is necessary for
the continuance of a prosecution after a person has been charged in court. In
O'Moran v. D.P.P.[69] men wearing dark glasses, black or blue berets and dark
clothing when escorting the coffin of a fellow supporter of the IRA in a funeral
procession in London, were held to be wearing a uniform for this purpose.

The statutes against liveries and maintenance passed in Tudor times were
repealed in the nineteenth century as being no longer necessary. In the years
between the wars, however, the growth of militant fascist, communist and other
extreme organisations led, or threatened to lead, to serious public disorder.
Section 2 of the Public Order Act 1936 therefore enacted that if members or
adherents of any association of persons are:

"(a)   organised or trained or equipped for the purpose of enabling them to be
       employed in usurping the functions of the police or of the armed forces
       of the Crown: or

 (b)   organised and trained or organised and equipped either for the purpose
       of enabling them to be employed for the use or display of physical force
       in promoting any political object or in such manner as to arouse reason-
       able apprehension that they are organised and either trained or equipped
       for that purpose,"

then any person who takes part in the control or management of the association
or in so organising or training its members or adherents, is guilty of an offence
punishable by fine and imprisonment. The consent of the Attorney-General is

---

[66] Terrorism as defined in section 1 adopts a wider definition than under the previous legislation.
[67] Under the previous law there were separate proscription regimes for Great Britain and Northern
Ireland. sched. 2 of the 2000 Act lists all organisations currently proscribed as being proscribed
throughout the United Kingdom. The Home Secretary has power to add to or remove names from this
list, and it is likely that organisations connected with international terrorism will be added to the
list.
[68] Which applies to Scotland.
[69] [1975] Q.B. 864, DC.

necessary before initiating a prosecution under this section. A person charged with taking part in the control or management of such an association may plead that he neither consented to nor connived at the unlawful organisation, training or equipment.[70]

---

[70] In *R. v. Jordan and Tyndall* [1963] Crim.L.R. 124. The Court of Appeal held that the fact that there was no evidence of actual attacks or plans for attacks on opponents did not necessarily remove grounds for "reasonable apprehension of that purpose".

PART VI

ADMINISTRATIVE LAW

The preceding chapters, with the exception of that on the European Communities, have all been concerned with areas of law that would have been known to Blackstone. The centre of political power may have shifted over the centuries but in legal theory the legislature (Parliament) and the executive (the Crown) are the bodies known to the common law from time immemorial. The armed forces and the police nowadays derive their existence and powers from statute but both discharge the primary duty of any state, to protect the lives and property of its citizens from attack whether from enemies abroad or criminals at home. The acquisition of nationality and the control of aliens are equally areas of law as old as the constitution even if they are nowadays based on statute. In the nineteenth century, however, the State began to recognise new obligations. To carry them out it created organisations of a kind unknown in earlier times and gave to them powers which were similarly unknown formerly. It is with these new developments that the following chapters are concerned. The chapter on Crown Proceedings may seem to be out of place in such a discussion. Crown Proceedings is a subject which has its origins in the beginnings of the Constitution but its modern importance is not in connection with the position of the monarch in her private capacity but with the position of the government and the many public bodies which can claim, in the eyes of the law, to form part of "the Crown." Moreover, despite the long history of the law relating to the unique legal position of the Crown, the current law is explicable only in the light of the Crown Proceedings Act 1947.

It is the law relating to these new developments that can conveniently be described as Administrative Law, to which must be added the law relating to the control of the exercise of these statutory powers by the courts, Judicial Review. Here also, the origins of the law stretch back into history but the link between the control exercised by the Court of King's Bench over justices of the peace in the eighteenth century and the review of the legality of decisions of local authorities and other public bodies is little more than a formal one.

In a book dealing with both constitutional and administrative law it is not necessary to attempt to define with any particularity where the line between the two should be drawn. For practical purposes the fore-going general description of the contents of the following chapters could be said to suffice. It may seem strange that writers and judges[2] had disputed with vigour the very existence of administrative law and the desirability of the adoption of administrative law (if such a subject does exist) into the law of the United Kingdom. To a large extent the dispute is, or was, one of words. If, by administrative law, is meant a system of rules applicable to public bodies which are enforced in special courts, the United Kingdom did not recognise administrative law in 1885[3] and it does not do so now. If by administrative law is meant that the ordinary courts possess a power of review over the legality of administrative acts then clearly the United Kingdom does recognise administrative law and presumably in that sense Dicey

---

[1] Sir William Wade and C. Forsyth, *Administrative Law* (8th ed., Oxford 2000); P. P. Craig, *Administrative Law* (4th ed., Sweet & Maxwell, 1999).
[2] *Supra* p. 32.
[3] The date of the first edition of Dicey's *The Law of the Constitution*.

would approve.[4] The dispute may also be a political one, disguised as a question about law. The statement that a country does not, or should not, have a body of administrative law may conceal the writer's political view that the State ought not to have the types of organisation and undertake the types of activities which typically are regarded as falling within the scope of administrative law.

Since the decision of the House of Lords in *O'Reilly v. Mackman*[5] the courts have begun to use a new terminology in which they distinguish between private law and public law. The latter, vague phrase is sufficiently wide to cover both constitutional and administrative law. Indeed in those jurisdictions where the distinction, borrowed from Roman law,[6] has long been followed public law includes criminal law—although it may be doubted whether the House of Lords had that area of law in mind. Lord Wilberforce has warned of the danger of using, except as convenient shorthand, terms taken from other legal systems where they belong and applying them out of context.[7] Certainly the discovery of public law and, even more, of public law rights, unknown to private law, as a consequence of procedural reforms,[8] designed to rationalise the remedies available where public bodies have acted unlawfully, was somewhat surprising. The availability of remedies to litigants in cases where formerly the courts could not interfere may, at least to the litigants concerned, seem to be proof of the merits of the new distinction between private and public law.[9] On the other hand, it can be argued that by the adoption of the terminology the courts have, in effect, given themselves an almost unlimited power to decide when to strike down decisions of public bodies, untrammelled by earlier rules and precedents. Despite the general terms in which the House of Lords has in the last few years referred to public law it is difficult to believe that in effect it can mean more than administrative law. It can hardly be thought, for example, that by reference to public law, the courts would claim the right (which they have carefully denied themselves in the past) to scrutinise the proceedings of Parliament or to set limits to the legislative competence of Parliament.[10] Nor is it likely that the actions of the government in the sphere of foreign affairs are now susceptible to judicial review.[11]

The growth of administrative law[12]

Almost 100 years ago Maitland pointed out that, at first sight, Parliament in the eighteenth century got through more work than it did in the nineteenth. But, on

---

[4] It is in this sense that the judges have congratulated themselves on creating a body of administrative law: *Breen v. A.E.U.* [1971] 2 Q.B. 175, *per* Lord Denning M.R., *Mahon v. Air New Zealand* [1984] A.C. 808, 816 *per* Lord Diplock.

[5] [1983] 2 A.C. 237.

[6] In the Institutes public law is defined as "*quod ad statum rei Romanae spectat*" while private law is "*quod ad singulorum utilitatem pertinet*": I.1.1.4. In the Digest Ulpian describes public law as that which "*in sacris, in sacerdotibus, in magistratibus consistat*": D.1.1.1.2.

[7] *Davy v. Spelthorne B.C.* [1984] A.C. 262. See too Parker L.J. in *Wandsworth L.B.C. v. Winder* [1983] 3 W.L.R. 563, CA; affirmed HL [1985] A.C. 461.

[8] *post* para. 32–001.

[9] In practice the individual litigant may be more impressed by the risk of an action failing because it was begun by what turned out to be the wrong procedure: see the criticisms of H.W.R.W. "Public Law, Private Law and Judicial Review," (1983) 99 L.Q.R. 166, and the rebuttal of those criticisms by Woolf L.J., "Public Law-Private Law: Why the Divide? A Personal View," [1986] P.L. 220; *post* para. 3–011.

[10] *ante* para. 32–012.

[11] *cf. Ex p. Molyneaux* [1986] 1 W.L.R. 332 *ante*.

[12] A. V. Dicey, *Law and Public Opinion During the Nineteenth Century* (2nd ed., 1914, reprinted 1962); H. W. Arthurs, *Without the Law* (1985).

inspection, a volume of statutes from that earlier period contained little that in subsequent ages would be regarded as legislation. Many Acts, public as well as private, dealt with individual cases rather than attempted to lay down general rules. The public acts for 1786, for example, included

> "an act for establishing a workhouse at Havering, an act to enable the king to license a playhouse at Margate, an act for erecting a house of correction in Middlesex, an act for incorporating the Clyde Marine Society, an act for paving the town of Cheltenham, an act for widening the roads in the borough of Bodmin. Fully half of the public acts are of this petty local character. Then as to the private acts, these deal with particular persons: an act for naturalizing Andreas Emmerich, an act for enabling Cornelius Salvidge to take the surname of Tutton, an act for rectifying mistakes in the marriage settlement of Lord and Lady Camelford, an act to enable the guardians of William Frye to grant leases, an act to dissolve the marriage between Jonathan Twiss and Francis Dorrill. Then there are almost countless acts for enclosing this, that and the other common. One is inclined to call the last century the century of *privilegia*. It seems afraid to rise to the dignity of a general proposition; it will not say, 'All commons may be enclosed according to these general rules,' 'All aliens may become naturalized if they fulfil these or those conditions,' 'All boroughs shall have these powers for widening their roads,' 'All marriages may be dissolved if the wife's adultery be proved.' No, it deals with this common and that marriage."[13]

In the nineteenth century, however, soon after the Reform Act of 1832 Parliament began, in Maitland's words again:

> "to legislate with remarkable vigour, to overhaul the whole law of the country—criminal law, property law, the law of procedure, every department of the law—but about the same time it gives up the attempt to govern the country, to say what commons shall be enclosed, what roads shall be widened, what boroughs shall have paid constables and so forth. It begins to lay down general rules about these matters and to entrust their working partly to officials, to secretaries of state, to boards of commissioners, who for this purpose are endowed with new statutory powers, partly to the law courts."[14]

In this outburst of legislative activity is to be found the origins of that area of law now generally regarded as administrative law.

Maitland attributed Parliament's anxiety in the eighteenth century *to govern* the country by deciding individual cases itself to jealousy of the Crown. Memories of the power of the monarch were too recent; by the nineteenth century that fear had receded. But, at least equally important, was the transformation wrought by the Industrial Revolution. Without that Bentham, Brougham and others might have called for reform in vain or, if it came, it would have taken a different form; "Watt and Stephenson were much more responsible for undermining the dominantly feudal legal system expounded by Blackstone, than Bentham and

---

[13] F. W. Maitland, *Constitutional History of England* (1908) p. 383.
[14] *op. cit.* p. 384.

Brougham."[15] The concentration of people in large cities presented new problems in sanitation, public health and housing. Working conditions in mines and factories produced calls for legal regulation. The construction of canals and railways was possible only because Parliament was prepared to grant to the companies powers to acquire land compulsorily where the owners refused to sell. Education came to be seen as a concern of the government in the public interest as well as for the benefit of individual citizens. In this century the State has further concerned itself with making provision for a wide range of financial payments to the elderly, the unemployed and others in need. From compulsory purchase the legislature has progressed to attempting generally to control the use to which land is put through various Town and Country Planning Acts. From detailed legislation restricting and regulating the activities of money-lenders and hire purchase companies the legislature has proceeded to make general provision for the protection of consumers when obtaining credit in one form or another.[16]

The consequences of these legislative developments from 1832 onwards largely form the subject matter of the succeeding chapters of this Part. Parliament has entrusted the carrying out of legislation to bodies of various kinds, whether elected local authorities or non-elected public corporations of widely differing composition and constitution. These bodies may be under duties to provide services or have powers to ensure compliance with statutory standards. Duties and powers, too, may be conferred on individual ministers. Legislation cast in wide, general terms and often dealing with highly technical subject matter requires more detailed implementation by rules and regulations, usually but not always made by ministers (Chapter 29). Disputes relating to the provision of services and the regulation of activities may be best dealt with by particular tribunals established outside the structure of the civil and criminal courts (Chapter 30). The increase in the powers of ministers and the proliferation of bodies with the legal ability to affect the rights and duties of citizens (and public bodies) has led to the recognition of the need for procedures to deal with grievances of various kinds relating to the working of the administration (Chapter 34). Where it is alleged that the administration has acted in such a way that it has exceeded its legal powers the appropriate remedy is recourse to the Courts (Chapters 31 and 32). Finally something must be said about the cases and circumstances in which the rights and duties of public officials and bodies under the general law may differ from those of the private citizen (Chapter 33).

---

[15] Mr Justice Frankfurter, "Foreword to a Discussion of Current Developments in Administrative Law," (1937–8) 47 Yale L.J. 515, quoted H. W. Arthurs, *op. cit.* p. 34.
[16] Consumer Credit Act 1974: a statute of 193 sections and 5 Schedules which nonetheless can be described as "merely a blueprint for the system of regulation and licensing which it establishes"; Guest and Lloyd, *Current Law Statutes Annotated.*

CHAPTER 28

PUBLIC CORPORATIONS AND REGULATORY BODIES[1]

I. NATURE AND PURPOSE OF PUBLIC CORPORATIONS[2]

In addition to the central government departments under the direct control of **28–001** Ministers of the Crown, and the local government authorities elected by the local electors, public affairs in Great Britain are administered by or with the aid of various public bodies.

Once Parliament had begun in the nineteenth century, in Maitland's words to legislate instead of trying to govern,[3] it became necessary to establish bodies to carry out the purposes of legislation themselves or to supervise and regulate other bodies. Particularly since the end of the Second World War, Parliament has established public bodies to provide commercial services which had formerly been provided by private companies and local authorities. The increasing acceptance of responsibility by the State for matters cultural, environmental and artistic is shown by the establishment of Councils and Commissions. Racial harmony and sexual equality are seen to be best fostered by establishing Commissions. Tourism, the interests of Consumers, the supervision of Gaming, the encouragement of Design are all appropriate matters for a board or committee. The more important of these bodies are created by statute or royal charter.[4] They all possess a considerable, although varying, degree of independence from ministerial and therefore parliamentary control. To the extent that they are all directly responsible neither to Parliament nor to local authorities they can be said to belong to the class of Quangos, an acronym which can be translated either to mean quasi autonomous non-governmental organisation or quasi autonomous national government organisations.[5] Whether such a classification, which can include at one extreme Boards of nationalised industries and at the other the National Association of Youth Clubs, is of great value may be doubted. In this

---

[1] *Government Enterprise* (ed. W. Friedmann and J. F. Garner, 1970); J. A. G. Griffith and H. Street, *Principles of Administrative Law* (5th ed., 1973), Chap. 7; W. A. Robson, *Nationalised Industry and Public Ownership* (2nd ed., 1962); Herbert Morrison, *Government and Parliament* (1954), Chap. 12; Sir Arthur Street, "Quasi-Government Bodies since 1918", in *British Government since 1918* (by Sir G. Campion and Others); *Public Enterprise* (ed. Robson); D. N. Chester, *The Nationalised Industries: A Statutory Analysis* (Institute of Public Administration, 2nd ed., 1951); *The Nationalised Industries* (Cmnd. 7131, 1978); T. Prosser, *Nationalised Industries and Public Control* (1986).

[2] The term was first used in the Report of the Crawford Committee on Broadcasting in 1926 (Cmnd. 2599).

[3] *ante*, Introduction. The Poor Law Commissioners had been followed by the Inclosure Commissioners (1844), the Railway Commission (1846) and the General Board of Health (1848). This century saw, *inter alia*, the Port of London Authority (1908) and the London Passenger Transport Board (1933).

[4] Other methods include, royal warrant, treasury minute, registration under the Companies Act or as a charitable trust.

[5] P. Holland, *Quango, Quango, Quango* (1978). *What's Wrong With Quangos?* (Outer Circle Policy Unit 1979). The vagueness of the term "quango" is obvious from the differences in the lists of such organisations in these two publications. See also *Report on Non Departmental Public Bodies* (1980, Cmnd. 7797).

chapter the main attention will be devoted to public authorities or public corpora-tions[6] in a rather narrower sense, with particular emphasis on nationalised industries and bodies of constitutional significance, whether, strictly speaking, corporations or not.

It is difficult to generalise about these public corporations. A possible classifi-cation is as follows:

(i) Managerial—industrial or commercial

28–002   Executive bodies set up to manage nationalised industries or branches of commerce, *e.g.* National Coal Board; British Railways Board; British Steel Corporation; Central Electricity Generating Board, Electricity Council and area electricity boards; South of Scotland Electricity Board, North of Scotland Hydro-electricity Board; Post Office; Bank of England; United Kingdom Atomic Energy Authority.

After the Second World War nationalisation usually took the form of the compulsory acquisition of the assets of existing private undertakings and the vesting of them in a public corporation.[7] From the time of Disraeli's purchase of shares in the Suez Canal Company the government had been aware of the possibility of establishing public control of a private undertaking through owner-ship of its shares. A similar procedure ensured government control of the Cable and Wireless Co. In 1938 a small government holding was established and in 1946 all the shares of the company were transferred into the ownership of named civil servants.[8] In 1971 Rolls Royce was rescued from financial collapse by the purchase of its shares by a new company created by statute[9] and in 1975 legislation enabled the government to buy the shares of British Leyland when it, too, faced financial disaster.[10]

The Bank of England, established by statute and Royal Charter in 1694[11] was similarly brought into public control by the transfer of its stock to Treasury ownership.[12] As we saw in Chapter 11, the Bank of England Act 1998 has transferred to the Bank independent responsibility for the setting of interest rates in the context of the economic policies of Her Majesty's Government. In relation to its regulatory responsibilities the Bank was liable to be sued for misfeasance in public office.[13]

Among the public corporations providing commercial services the Post Office occupies a unique position. Historically, it originated as a department of State

---

[6] There is no consistency of usage in statutes; the Post Office, for example, was "a public authority"; Post Office Act 1969. The British Telecommunications Act 1981, however, created "a public cor-poration."

[7] Coal Industry Nationalisation Act 1946; Transport Act 1947; Electricity Act 1947; Gas Act 1948, as amended by the Gas Act 1972; Airways Corporations Act 1949 (see now Civil Aviation Act 1980). A late example of this type of nationalisation is provided by the Aircraft and Shipbuilding Industries Act 1977 (British Aerospace and British Shipbuilders).

[8] Cable and Wireless Act 1946. Similarly in 1914 the government acquired a majority shareholding in Anglo Persian Oil Co.

[9] Rolls-Royce (Purchase) Act 1971.

[10] British Leyland Act 1975.

[11] The Bank obtained the exclusive right of issuing bank notes in England and Wales by the Bank Charter Act 1844, s.11. Existing rights were preserved. The last private bank with the right to issue notes was Messrs. Fox, Fowler & Co of Wellington, Somerset, who merged with Lloyds in 1921.

[12] Bank of England Act 1946; a new Charter was granted: Cmd 6752.

[13] *Three Rivers District Council v. Governor and Company of the Bank of England, The Times,* March 23, 2001, HL; *post* para. 32–021. Under the Bank of England Act 1998, the Bank no longer has regulatory responsibilities.

providing an essential service to the Crown. The opening of its services to the public was a device to raise money. Blackstone discussed "the post office or duty for the carriage of letters" in that part of the Commentaries devoted to the King's Revenue. "There cannot," he said, "be devised a more eligible method ... of raising money upon the subject [than by a duty on letters]; for therein both the government and the people find a mutual benefit. The government acquires a large revenue; and the people do their business with greater ease, expedition, and cheapness, than they would be able to do if no such tax (and of course no such office) existed."[14] In the nineteenth century telegraphs and telephones were added to its monopoly. In 1967 a government White Paper recommended turning the Post Office into a public corporation in order that it could be run on commercial lines, bringing to its business a structure and method drawing on the best modern practice.[15] The legislation which followed that report preserved for the Post Office its remarkable immunity from actions in tort which had been explicable when it was part of the Crown in earlier centuries and had even survived the passing of the Crown Proceedings Act 1947.[16] Nor has it ever been suggested that the new status of the Post Office affects the long established rule that there is no contractual relationship between the Post Office and the sender of a letter or parcel.[17] As will be seen below the Post Office not merely has the longest history of modern commercial public corporations but has also been involved in the latest stage in the history of such bodies, privatisation.

(ii) Managerial—social services

Executive bodies set up to manage social services, *e.g.* development corpora-   **28–003**
tions for the various new towns,[18] the New Towns Commission[19] and the Urban Development Corporations[20]; National Health Service bodies[21]; British Broadcasting Corporation; Water Authorities.

The British Broadcasting Corporation is unusual in having been created by royal charter and in deriving its income from a licence fee levied on the holders of (formerly) wireless and (now) television sets. Its first charter was granted in 1926; the current charter was granted in 1996.[22] Because of the way the BBC has operated since its foundation it is thought of as providing a social service but broadcasting can be regarded as a commercial undertaking, which is the case with the services falling under the control of the Independent Television Commission.[23]

The Water Authorities similarly tend to be thought of as providing a public service although they charge for their services. The Water Act 1973 removed

---

[14] *Bl. Comm.* i. 323. "A branch of the revenue"; *Whitfield v. Le Despencer* (1778) 2 Cowp. 754, 764 *per* Lord Mansfield.
[15] *Reorganisation of the Post Office* (Cmnd. 3233, 1967).
[16] Crown Proceedings Act 1947, s.9; Post Office Act 1969, s.29; *American Express v. British Airways Board* [1983] 1 W.L.R. 701.
[17] *Triefus Co Ltd v. Post Office* [1957] 2 Q.B. 352, CA. See [1972] P.L. 97. See too its statutory privileges, *e.g.* the Telegraph Act 1878; *Post Office v. Mears Construction* [1979] 2 All E.R. 814.
[18] New Towns Act 1946; New Towns Act 1965.
[19] New Towns Act 1981; New Towns and Urban Development Corporations Act 1985.
[20] Local Government, Planning and Land Act 1980.
[21] National Health Service Act 1977; National Health Service and Community Care Act 1990. See C. Webster, *The National Health Service—A Political History* (Oxford, 1998) and G. Rivett, *From Cradle to Grave—Fifty Years of the NHS* (King's Fund, 1998).
[22] Cm 3248.
[23] See T. Prosser, *Law and the Regulators* (Oxford, 1997) Chap. 9.

responsibility for the supply of water from local authorities and statutory under-takers and transferred it to the new regional authorities which were also to be responsible for water resources generally—conservation, sewage disposal, pollution and drainage.[24]

(iii) Regulatory and advisory

28–004   (a) Bodies set up to regulate private enterprise in certain fields, *e.g.* the Civil Aviation Authority[25]; the Director General of Fair Trading, and the Health and Safety at Work Commission and Executive.

The office of Director General of Fair Trading was created by the Fair Trading Act 1973. The Consumer Credit Act 1974 confers on the Director General a wide range of duties and powers which exemplify strikingly the devices to which Parliament has recourse to ensure the effective operation of much modern legislation. It is the duty of the Director General:

(a) to administer the licensing system set up by the Consumer Credit Act;

(b) to exercise the adjudicating functions conferred on him by the Act in relation to the issue, renewal, variation, suspension and revocation of licences, and other matters;

(c) generally to superintend the working and enforcement of the Act, and regulations made under it; and

(d) where necessary or expedient, himself to take steps to enforce the Act, and regulations so made.

The Director is also required to keep under review and from time to time advise the Secretary of State about—

(a) social and commercial developments in the United Kingdom and elsewhere relating to the provision of credit or bailment or (in Scotland) hiring of goods to individuals, and related activities; and

(b) the working and enforcement of this Act and orders and regulations made under it (section 1).

28–005   In addition, he is to arrange for the dissemination of such information and advice as it may appear to him expedient to give to the public about the operation of the Act, the credit facilities available and other matters within the scope of his functions (section 4). The Director is also a tribunal, for the purposes of the Tribunal and Inquiries Act 1992, with regard to the exercise of his licensing functions (section 3).

Possibly one of the most important and certainly most controversial regulatory authorities to be established is the Financial Services Authority, created by section 1 of the Financial Services and Markets Act 2000. It assumes responsibility for the work of nine self regulatory bodies recognised by the Secretary of State under the terms of the Financial Services Act 1986.

Serious concerns have been voiced about the compatibility of the powers of the Authority with the terms of the Convention on Human Rights. In substance,

---

[24] H. M. Purdue, "The Implications of the Constitution and Functions of Regional Water Authorities" [1979] P.L. 119. For the current legislation, see below at para. 28–013.
[25] Civil Aviation Act 1982. And see the Transport Act 2000.

for example, some of its powers are criminal but its procedures do not necessarily comply with those required of criminal procedures by the Convention. It is empowered to fine anyone engaging in market abuse (section 123) but the definition of market abuse in section 118 is remarkably vague, even when supplemented by any Code issued under section 119. In addition to its vagueness it applies to anyone, not merely those who, in other circumstances, fall within the regulatory power of the Authority. The general duties of the Authority are defined by section 2 of the Act in terms which it would be impossible to paraphrase:

"In discharging its general functions the Authority must, so far as is reasonably possible, act in a way—

(a) which is compatible with the regulatory objectives; and
(b) which the Authority considers most appropriate for the purpose of meeting those objectives.

(2) The regulatory objectives are—

(a) market confidence;
(b) public awareness;
(c) the protection of consumers; and
(d) the reduction of financial crime.

(3) In discharging its general functions the Authority must have regard to—

(a) the need to use its resources in the most efficient and economic way;
(b) the responsibilities of those who manage the affairs of authorised persons;
(c) the principle that a burden or restriction which is imposed on a person, or on the carrying on of an activity, which are expected to result from the imposition of that burden or restriction;
(d) the desirability of facilitating innovation in connection with regulated activities;
(e) the international character of financial services and markets and the desirability of maintaining the competitive position of the United Kingdom;
(f) the need to minimise the adverse effects on competition that may arise from anything done in the discharge of those functions;
(g) the desirability of facilitating competition between those who are subject to any form of regulation by the Authority."

The Health and Safety Commission and the Health and Safety Executive are **28–006** bodies corporate established by the Health and Safety at Work etc. Act 1974 to further the purposes of the Act (sections 10 and 11). In addition to very general statements of their responsibilities for advising, monitoring and overseeing various sections deal with specific matters; for example, section 16 provides for the approval by the Commission of Codes of Practice issued under the Act. Section 18 imposes on the Executive the duty of making adequate arrangements for the enforcement of the provisions of the Act, except to the extent that other authorities have specific responsibilities.

(b) Bodies set up to advise Ministers and other authorities with regard to the exercise of their powers and responsibilities, *e.g.* the Police Council,[26] the Nature

---

[26] Police Act 1964, s.45(4).

Conservancy Council,[27] renamed English Nature by the Countryside and Rights of Way Act 2000, s.73), the various advisory bodies established under the Environment Act 1995. The Audit Commission, established by the Local Government Finance Act 1982[28] is an advisory body in so far as it is required to make recommendations for improving economy, efficiency and effectiveness in the provision of local government services and to report on the impact of such services of statutory provisions and directions given by ministers (sections 26 and 27). As the body responsible for organising the auditing of local government accounts it can perhaps be regarded as a regulatory or managerial body (section 12). The Human Fertilisation and Embryology Act 1990 established the Human Fertilisation and Embryology Authority which, in the areas indicated by its name, must keep developments under review and advise the Secretary of State (section 8). It also has the responsibility of licensing research activities through a number of committees (section 9).

(c) Miscellaneous Bodies. Two important bodies with powers of advising, monitoring and enforcing legislation are the Commission for Racial Equality and the Equal Opportunities Commission, both of which were established by statute to operate in areas formerly falling outside the direct concern of the law.[29] The Commonwealth Development Corporation was established "to assist overseas countries . . . in the development of their economies."[30] The National Biological Standards Board is a body corporate which is responsible for the establishment of standards for, the provision of standard preparations of, and the testing of biological substances.[31] The Learning and Skills Council for England[32] was established to secure the provision of proper facilities for education (other than higher) for persons between 16 and 19. (It also has responsibilities for those over 19). The Crown Agents were constituted as a body corporate by the Crown Agents Act 1979 and their full title (Crown Agents for Overseas Governments and Administrations) explains their role: to act as agents on behalf of governments and public authorities specified in Schedule 3 of the Act.[33]

II. LEGAL POSITION OF PUBLIC CORPORATIONS[34]

28–007   The main constitutional problems relate to the legal status of those public corporations that manage some nationalised industry or branch of commerce or public service, especially their liability in contract and tort, and the question of parliamentary supervision. The latter is discussed in Part IV below.

---

[27] Wildlife and Countryside Act 1981, s.24.

[28] See now the Audit Commission Act 1998, as amended by the Local Government Act 2000, s.90.

[29] Race Relations Act 1976; Race Relations (Amendment) Act 2000; Sex Discrimination Act 1975.

[30] Commonwealth Development Corporation Act 1978; Commonwealth Development Corporation Act 1996.

[31] Biological Standards Act 1975.

[32] Learning and Skills Act 2000.

[33] For the Agents' subsequent history, see *post*, Part III and the Crown Agents Act 1995.

[34] Glanville Williams, *Crown Proceedings* (1948), pp. 4–8, 21–28, 30–37, 85; J. A. G. Griffith, "Public Corporations as Crown Servants" 9 U.T.L.J. 169; H. Street, *Government Liability* (1953), pp. 28–36; W. Friedmann, "The New Public Corporations and the Law" (1947) 10 M.L.R. 233–254, 377–395; W. A. Robson, "The Public Corporations in Britain Today" (1959) 63 Harv. Law Rev. 1321–1348.

Appointment and powers

To ascertain the legal position of any public corporation it is necessary first of all to look at the particular Act of Parliament that created it, for no two of them are alike. It is generally provided that they are bodies corporate, with perpetual succession and a common seal and power to hold land. The chairmen and other members of the boards are appointed and may be removed by the competent Minister or by the Crown. Their members do not have to be representative of any particular interests. Their salaries are generally fixed by the Minister with the approval of the Treasury. The large number of appointments to be made, subject to no effective form of control, has placed in the hands of ministers a power of patronage undreamed of even in the eighteenth century. As there are no shareholders to exercise any control over the board, the Acts provide that the Minister may set up advisory committees or councils to advise him.

28–008

The powers of a public corporation are set out in the constituent Act. They are subject to judicial determination by the doctrine of *ultra vires* (*Smith v. London Transport Executive*[35]), but their powers in some cases are very wide. There is generally no legal means by which these bodies may be compelled by private citizens to exercise their functions. The Minister might be able to apply for mandamus or a declaration in some cases, unless this is expressly excluded by statute. The Transport Act 1962, s.3(1), provided that it should be the "duty" of the Railways Board to provide railway services, and in connection therewith such other services and facilities as might appear to the Board to be expedient; but section 3(4) went on to say that no such duty or liability should be enforceable by judicial proceedings. A similar provision was contained in the Post Office Act 1969, s.9(4).[36] Exceptionally, the Transport Act 1968, s.106(1), allowed any person to apply to the court for an order requiring the Waterways Board to maintain commercial and cruising waterways for public use. Usually nationalisation statutes provided that the Minister may give directions "of a general character" in the public interest.[37] In some cases he has power to give specific directions, *e.g.* to the former National Enterprise Board.[38] In the cases of the BBC and the IBA the Home Secretary has powers to give directions requiring that an announcement be broadcast, or requiring that those bodies refrain from broadcasting particular items.[39] This issue will be considered below in connection with privatisation. A Minister cannot give a direction which contradicts the provisions of the Act of Parliament under which he is purporting to act.[39a]

Liability to judicial proceedings

The question whether a public corporation is a servant or agent of the Crown is of considerable legal importance. If it is a servant or agent of the Crown, civil proceedings would be governed by the Crown Proceedings Act 1947 (unless it was set up by a later statute expressly or impliedly inconsistent with the Act), and the action (if available) would have to be brought by or against the authorised

28–009

---

[35] [1951] A.C. 555, HL; and see *post*, Chap. 31.
[36] See *Harold Stephen & Co v. The Post Office* [1977] 1 W.L.R. 1172, CA.
[37] *e.g.* Coal Industry Nationalisation Act 1946, s.3(1).
[38] Industry Act 1975, s.7(1); *Booth & Co. v. N.E.B.* [1978] 3 All E.R. 624.
[39] Broadcasting Act 1981, s.29. See *R. v. Secretary of State for the Home Department, ex p. Brind* [1991] 1 A.C. 696, HL, *ante* para. 22–011 and para. 25–035.
[39a] *Laker Airways Ltd v. Department of Trade* [1977] Q.B. 643, CA.

department or the Attorney-General. The corporation would also have the advantage of the Crown privileges relating to injunction, execution and interrogatories,[40] and would not be bound by Acts of Parliament (including rates and taxes) unless expressly or by necessary implication.[41] And this might well affect the position of individual members of the board and its employees.

If the corporation is not a servant or agent of the Crown, the Crown Proceedings Act does not apply: it would be liable in the ordinary way in contract and tort; its staff would be employees of the corporation and not Crown servants; and proceedings by or against it (in so far as not expressly excluded or limited by the statute) would be in the name of the corporation (*Mersey Docks and Harbour Board v. Gibbs*[42]).

Where the statute is not explicit

28–010   Most of the earlier Acts creating public corporations were not explicit on the question whether the corporation was a servant or agent of the Crown. In so far as such Acts have not been replaced by later legislation, if the matter should come before the court it would be a question of interpretation.

In *Tamlin v. Hannaford*[43] the Court of Appeal held that the British Transport Commission[44] was not a servant or agent of the Crown. The question in issue was whether a house which had been leased from the Great Western Railway was withdrawn from the protection of the Rent Restriction Acts by reason of its being vested in the British Transport Commission under the Transport Act 1947.[45] In considering whether any subordinate body is entitled to the Crown privilege of not being bound by a statute unless Parliament shows an intention that it should be bound, said Denning L.J. in delivering the judgment of the Court, the question is not so much whether it is an "emanation of the Crown"[46] but whether it is properly to be regarded as a servant or agent of the Crown.[47] This depended on the true construction of the Transport Act 1947, especially the powers of the Minister in relation to the Commission.[48] When Parliament intends that a new corporation should act on behalf of the Crown, it usually says so expressly.[49] In the absence of express provision the proper inference, in the case (at any rate) of a commercial corporation, is that it acts on its own behalf.

It is probable that none of the industrial or commercial corporations created after the Second World War is a servant or agent of the Crown. None of them is in the list of "authorised departments" issued by the Treasury under the Crown Proceedings Act 1947, s.17, although this is not conclusive as proceedings may

[40] *post*, Chap. 33.

[41] *ante*, para. 15–019.

[42] (1866) L.R. 1 HL 93; *Gallagher v. Post Office* [1970] 1 All E.R. 712; *Westwood v. Post Office, The Times*, November 24, 1972, CA.

[43] [1951] 1 K.B. 18. And see *British Broadcasting Corporation v. Johns* [1965] Ch. 32; *Mellinger v. New Brunswick Development Corporation* [1971] 1 W.L.R. 604; *Trendtex Trading Corporation v. Central Bank of Nigeria* [1977] Q.B. 529.

[44] Predecessor of the British Railways Board.

[45] *cf.* Crown Lessees (Protection of Sub-Tenants) Act 1952, which extended to sub-tenants of Crown lands the benefit of the Rent Restriction Acts.

[46] *cf. Gilbert v. Trinity House Corporation* (1886) 17 Q.B.D. 795.

[47] *International Ry v. Niagara Parks Commission* [1941] A.C. 328, PC.

[48] See *Central Control Board (Liquor Traffic) v. Cannon Brewery Co* [1918] 2 Ch. 123; [1919] A.C. 757.

[49] *e.g.* Central Land Board (now dissolved); Town and Country Planning Act 1947; *Glasgow Corporation v. Central Land Board*, 1956 S.L.T. 41. Also the former National Assistance Board and Land Commission.

be taken under that Act against the Attorney-General. Many proceedings have been brought by and against industrial corporations in their own names without the question being raised in court.[50]

Where the statute is explicit
The National Health Service Act 1946, s.13, expressly stated that a regional **28–011** hospital board, notwithstanding that it exercised functions on behalf of the Minister, should be entitled to enforce rights and be liable for liabilities (including liability in tort) as if it were acting as a principal: proceedings were to be brought by or against the board in its own name, and it was not entitled to the privileges of the Crown in respect of discovery or production of documents. Similar principles applied to a hospital management committee, although it exercised its functions on behalf of the regional hospital board.[51] On the other hand, the Crown might claim privilege in respect of its documents; and it was held in *Nottingham Area No. 1 Hospital Management Committee v. Owen*[52] that a hospital vested in the Minister of Health under the Act of 1946 was "premises occupied for the public service of the Crown" under the Public Health Act 1936, and that the justices had therefore no jurisdiction to make an order under that Act to abate a nuisance constituted by a smoking chimney.

Later Acts constituting public corporations have been explicit on the point, at least in cases where there might be doubt, as in the case of corporations that own or occupy land or have taken over functions formerly exercised by a Minister. Thus the Atomic Energy Authority Act 1954 provided that land occupied by the Authority was deemed for rating purposes to be occupied by the Crown for public purposes; otherwise the Authority was not to enjoy Crown privileges. The Electricity Act 1957, s.38, stated: "It is hereby declared for the avoidance of doubt that neither the Electricity Council nor the Generating Board nor any of the Area Boards are to be treated as the servant or agent of the Crown or as enjoying any status, immunity or privilege of the Crown, and no property of the Council or any of those Boards is to be regarded as property of, or held on behalf of, the Crown." Similar provision was made by the New Towns Act 1965, s.35(3), with regard to the Commission for the New Towns.[53]

The Crown Agents Act 1979, s.1(5) provides that the Crown Agents, "despite their name" are not to be regarded as servants of the Crown nor as agents except to the extent that they so act by virtue of any provision in the Act authorising them to do so.

Conversely, the Postal Services Act 2000, s.1 and the Utilities Act 2000, s.1, both provide explicitly that the functions of the Postal Services Commission and the Gas and Electricity Markets Authority are to be performed on behalf of the Crown.

Post office
The purpose of the Post Office Act 1969 was that the Post Office should cease **28–012** to be a government department and should become an independent corporation, and the Act was, of course, quite explicit on this point. The functions and powers formerly exercised by the Postmaster-General as a Minister of the Crown were

---

[50] *e.g. National Coal Board v. Galley* [1958] 1 W.L.R. 16.
[51] *Bullard v. Croyden Hospital Group Management Committee* [1953] 1 Q.B. 511.
[52] [1958] 1 Q.B. 50, DC. And see *Pfizer v. Ministry of Health* [1965] A.C. 512.
[53] New Towns Act 1981, s.35.

transferred to the new corporation. The postal service as we saw above is a public service derived from a prerogative monopoly of the Crown.[54] As a public corporation it retained immunity from actions in tort which even other government departments lost under the Crown Proceedings Act 1947.[55] Section 29 of the Post Office Act provided that, subject to section 30, no proceedings in tort lie against the Post Office for any loss or damage arising out of the postal or telecommunication service. The Post Office was exempt, for example, from liability for loss of or damage to unregistered postal packets, and for defamation published by telegram, telephone or postmark.[56] The section further provided that (contrary to common law) no individual—whether officer, servant, agent or independent contractor of the Post Office—was subject, except at the suit of the Post Office, to any civil liability for any loss or damage from which the Post Office is exempt. The question whether, despite this wide measure of immunity, the Post Office might, in some circumstances, be liable as a bailee was raised but not answered in *Stephen & Co v. The Post Office*.[57] Section 30 of the Post Office Act provided that the Post Office was liable for the loss of, or damage to, a *registered inland*[58] *postal packet* due to the wrongful act, neglect or default of an officer, servant or agent of the Post Office while dealing with the packet; proceedings had to be brought within 12 months instead of the usual six years.

As we shall see in Part III the Post Office has been turned into a company by the Postal Services Act 2000. The substance of sections 29 and 30 are preserved by sections 90 and 91 of the new Act but they are now described as attaching to the "universal service provider", that is any organisation licensed under the Act to provide a universal post service as defined in section 4(1). The provisions relating to registered inland packets are similarly preserved (sections 91 and 92) but the Secretary of State, after consulting the Postal Services Commission and the Consumer Council for Postal Services may amend the terms of those sections (section 93).

III. Privatisation

28–013 The Conservative Government which was elected in 1979 began a programme of divesting itself of control of nationalised industries by turning them into companies in which the shares are owned by member of the public and in some cases selling to the public shares which the government owned in a company. The objects and motives of the programme were varied and probably conflicting and

---

[54] In *Malins v. Post Office* [1975] I.C.R. 60. Thesiger J. held that, at least in the case of employees engaged prior to the 1969 Act, the Post Office had inherited the right of the Crown to dismiss at will or upon reasonable notice, whatever the terms of the servant's contract.

[55] *post*, Chap. 33.

[56] *Boakes v. Postmaster-General, The Times*, October 27, 1962, CA: postmark, "Remember that Road Accidents are Caused by People Like You."

[57] [1977] 1 W.L.R. 1172, CA. (Mandatory injunction to order Post Office to deliver up postal packets in its possession, detained as a result of industrial action, refused.)

[58] *i.e.* posted in the United Kingdom, the Isle of Man or the Channel Islands for delivery therein.

inconsistent.[59] Little thought was given to the long term consequences of establishing systems of control by regulators with statutory powers to fix prices and licence companies. The concept of privatisation has been embraced world-wide, while remaining in fashion with the current Labour government. The European Union committed itself to competition in fields previously in the hands of state monopolies, in particular telecommunications, transport, postal services and energy at the Lisbon Summit in 2000. (By the time of the Stockholm meeting in 2001 it had become clear that France was not, in fact, prepared to open its public services to foreign competition.)

The first method of privatisation is exemplified by the case of British Telecommunications. The British Telecommunications Act 1981 established a public corporation whose duty was to provide throughout the British Islands such telephone services as satisfy all reasonable demands for them except to the extent that provision was, in the corporation's opinion, impracticable or not reasonably practicable (section 3). The Telecommunications Act 1984 abolished British Telecommunications' monopoly in the field of telecommunications and provided that on a date nominated by the Secretary of State all the assets of the corporation should vest in a company nominated by the minister (section 60). Subsequently shares in the company were offered for public sale. Similar arrangements were made in relation to British Airways by the Civil Aviation Act 1980, in relation to British Aerospace by the British Aerospace Act 1980 and in relation to British Gas by the Gas Act 1986. Electricity was similarly privatised by the Electricity Act 1989, Water by the Water Act 1989,[60] the railway system by the Railways Act 1993, as amended by the Transport Act 2000 and the coal industry by the Coal Industry Act 1994.[61]

The political controversy involved in any suggestion of privatising the Post **28–014** Office is avoided by the Postal Services Act 2000 which, as will be seen, subjects the Post Office to the legal regime common to privatised industries. The Post Office becomes, by section 62, a company subject to the Companies Act 1985 but the shares will be held by the Secretary of State.

The method of privatisation by disposing of shares held by the government in an existing company is illustrated by the case of Cable and Wireless Ltd.[62]

It is not necessary, of course, to sell all the shares in a company. In the case of the National Air Traffic Services, for instance, which had been formed as a company by the Conservative Government in 1996, the Transport Act 2000, s.41 provides for the sale of 51 per cent of the shares and the retention by the government of 49 per cent plus a controlling "golden share".[63] This arrangement,

---

[59] The motives behind privatisation are largely responsible for the development of Next Step Agencies and the process of contracting out of services: Local Government Act 1988 (but see now Local Government Act 1999) and the Deregulation and Contracting Out Act 1994. See P. P. Craig, *Administrative Law* (4th ed., Sweet & Maxwell, 1999) Chap. 5.

[60] Followed by a consolidating statute, the Water Industry Act 1991, and more recently by the Water Industry Act 1999.

[61] Other examples include the Ordnance Factories and Military Services Act 1984; Airports Act 1986; Ports Act 1991. The Crown Agents Act 1995 seems to be a typical privatisation statute but the government gave assurances during the passage of the legislation that the shares would not be offered for sale on the open market but would be transferred to an independent foundation, established as a company by guarantee.

[62] British Telecommunications Act 1981, s.79. Other examples are the sale of Amersham International and British Nuclear Fuels (Atomic Energy (Miscellaneous Provisions) Act 1981 and of Rolls Royce, originally bought in 1971, Jaguar Motors and British Petroleum.

[63] C. Graham and T. Prosser, "Golden Shares: Industrial Policy by Stealth?" [1988] P.L. 413.

while not amounting to privatisation, enables the government to draw on private finance through a relationship called PPP, Public-private Partnership.

A common feature of the scheme for privatising the basic utilities—such as gas or water—is the creation for each industry of a statutory regulator[64] known by an appropriate ugly acronym, for example OFTEL or OFWAT. Each regulator is empowered to license suppliers in the relevant market and to regulate the prices which may be charged for the product.

The Telecommunications Act 1984 established the precedent of licensing and regulation by a Director General in charge of an office—in that case OFTEL. The Utilities Act 2000 in providing a unified regulatory regime for gas and electricity departed from that precedent by replacing the two Directors with a body corporate, the Gas and Electricity Markets Authority (GEMA). Similarly the regulatory body in the case of postal services is a body corporate—the Postal Services Commission (section 1). In both cases the statutes provide that the relevant bodies exercise their functions on behalf of the Crown.

28–015   The regulator has the power to issue licences to applicants in each area and to attach conditions to them. He is also, very importantly, entitled to fix the prices suppliers may charge within limits set by a formula. In exercising these powers regulators can be faced with conflicting considerations. The Utilities Act 2000 indicates clearly that in exercising their powers the principal objective of the Secretary of State and the authority is to protect the interests of the consumer[65] and to promote effective competition (sections 9 and 13). These considerations, while admirable, may nonetheless point in different ways, whether in relation to fixing a price or attaching conditions to a licence. The Postal Services Commission must exercise its powers in the manner it considers best calculated to ensure the provision of a universal postal service (section 3). The requirements of a universal postal service are defined in section 4.

Although the regulators are clearly intended to act independently in the exercise of their statutory powers, ministers are entitled to issue directions to them in specific circumstances. Thus both the Telecommunications Act (section 94) and the Postal Services Act (section 101) authorise the Secretary of State to give to the relevant bodies such directions as appear to him to be requisite in the interests of national security or relations with a foreign government. He may also give a direction requiring such persons "to do, or not to do, a particular thing specified in the direction". Any direction given under the section will be laid before each House of Parliament unless the Secretary of State is of opinion that disclosure of the direction is against the interests of national security or relations with a foreign government or the commercial interests of any person. On those grounds the Secretary of State may also forbid any person to reveal that he has received a direction.[66]

The Railways Act 1993 entitles the Secretary of State to give directions in the case of "hostilities, severe international tension or great national emergency (section 118). More mundanely he can also give directions to require railway

---

[64] T. Prosser, *Law and Regulators* (Oxford, 1997); "Regulation, Markets and Legitimacy", Chap. 5 of *The Changing Constitution* (eds J. Jowell and D. Oliver) (4th ed., Oxford, 2000); C. Graham *Regulating Public Utilities* (art, 2000); J. Froud, R. Boden, A. Ogus and P. Stubbs, *Controlling the Regulators* (Macmillan 1998); A. McHarg, *Accountability and the Public/Private Distinction* (Oxford, 2000); P. P. Craig, *op. cit.* Chap. 11.

[65] The need for provision to secure protection for the interests of the consumer was recognised by the Citizens Charter and found early expression in the Competition and Service (Utilities) Act 1992.

[66] Similarly the Water Industry Act 1991, s.208 which also includes "mitigating the effects of any civil emergency".

operators to take steps to ensure that the users of railway services are protected from violence (section 119).

IV. REGULATING THE REGULATORS

In the era from the end of the Second World War to the late 1970s the basic **28–016** industries and utilities were, as we have seen, nationalised and subject to a much greater, general control by ministers than is the case now under typical privatisation statutes. In the earlier era the question was seen as one of accountability of ministers to Parliament for nationalised industries. It was not a question that was satisfactorily answered.[67] Ministers, for instance, could be asked questions about the exercise of their statutory powers to give directions to the board of a nationalised industry.[68] But experience showed that in practice they often exerted unofficial pressure in the form of "requests"[69] which could not form the subject matter of questions in the House. Ministers often refused to answer questions on the ground that they related to matters of day to day administration of the industry.

From 1956 to 1979 there was a Select Committee on Nationalised Industries which had power: to examine the Reports and Accounts of the nationalised industries established by Statute whose controlling Boards are appointed by Ministers of the Crown and whose annual receipts are not wholly or mainly derived from moneys provided by Parliament or advanced from the Exchequer". This Committee was very active and issued a number of reports, several of which were critical of the role Ministers played in the running of nationalised industries.[70] The reform of the Select Committee system in 1979 resulted in the abolition of this committee,[71] only a few years before the abolition of the nationalised industries themselves. In the case of privatised industries minister have, as we have seen, only limited powers to give directions. The regulators are appointed for a fixed term and only removable for incapacity or misbehaviour. But it cannot be pretended that there is no political concern in the functioning of the industries they regulate—whether from the disconnection of water supplies of customers who cannot pay their bills or the safety of passengers travelling on the railway system.

A suggestion that a Select Committee be established with responsibility for **28–017** privatised utilities and industries (on the analogy of the Select Committee on Nationalised Industries) was rejected by the Trade and Industry Committee.[72]

---

[67] See Sir Ivor Jennings, *Parliament* (2nd ed., 1957), Chap. 10; Herbert Morrison, *Government and Parliament* (1954), Chap. 12; W. A. Robson, *Nationalised Industry and Public Ownership*, Chaps 7, 8–10; *Report from the Select Committee on Nationalised Industries* (1952) H.C. No. 332, 1, pp. 130–133; A. H. Hanson, *Parliament and Public Ownership* (Hansard Society, 1961). See too works cited *ante*, para. 28–001 n.1.

[68] *ante*, para. 12–024.

[69] D. Coombs, "The Scrutiny of Ministers' Powers by the Select Committee on Nationalised Industries", [1965] P.L. 9; H. W. R. Wade, "Anglo-American Administrative Law: Some Reflections", (1965) 81 L.Q.R. 357, 361–363.

[70] See, *e.g.* Second Report from the Select Committee on Nationalised Industries, *The British Steel Corporation*, H.C. 26 (1977–78) and Fourth Report from the Select Committee, *British Waterways Board*, H.C. 239 (1977–78).

[71] For the present system, see *ante*, para. 11–016 and para. 12–029.

[72] HCSO (1996–97) paras 15–16.

The Public Accounts Committee has undertaken a general survey of the regulatory framework of the electricity, gas, telecommunications and water industries, and specific investigations into individual regulators.[73] Individual industries fall within the areas of responsibilities of particular select committees but there may be issues which cross departmental boundaries.

In an era of judicial activism recourse to the courts[74] might be thought to offer a means of challenging decisions of the regulators or, where relevant, ministers. Actions for breach of statutory duty cannot be regarded as a realistic possibility in the light of abstract language of the relevant provisions and the complete absence of any suggestion that a duty is owed to any particular class of litigant.[75] Judicial review in theory must be available where regulators can be argued to have exercised their powers irrationally or unlawfully.[76] Finally there is always the possibility of invoking the Human Rights Act 1998.

[73] See *Graham op. cit.* p. 76.
[74] *post*, Chap. 31.
[75] *post*, para. 32–021.
[76] *Mercury Communications Ltd v. Director General of Telecommunications* [1996] 1 W.L.R. 48, HL merely unhelpfully decided that a dispute about the terms of a licence did not have to be made the subject of an application for judicial review.

CHAPTER 29

DELEGATED LEGISLATION[1]

In this chapter it is proposed to discuss delegated legislation in the sense in **29–001** which that phrase is commonly used to refer to regulations and rules made under powers delegated by Parliament to Ministers, local authorities and other bodies. The logical distinction between Acts of Parliament (primary legislation) and delegated (or secondary) legislation is not always as clear as would be expected. The distinction has been blurred by the Human Rights Act 1998 which includes in the definition of primary legislation Measures (see below), and a range of Orders in Council made under statute (section 21(1)). The term "Acts" is not legislatively defined and it is not made clear whether the Acts made by the Scottish Parliament and Northern Ireland Assembly are a species of primary or delegated legislation.[2] Legislation by the Queen and Commons under the Parliament Acts 1911 and 1949 may arguably be regarded as a special kind of delegated legislation.[3]

I. NATURE AND PURPOSE OF DELEGATED LEGISLATION

The delegation of law-making power by Parliament to other persons or bodies **29–002** is no new practice, although it has greatly increased in frequency and importance in the nineteenth and twentieth centuries, and will continue to increase in this century.[4] In the period between the Wars the growth of delegated legislative powers was a matter of controversy among writers on the newly emerging subject of administrative law. There has been no diminution in resort to such powers since 1945 but widespread use of them has continues to be accepted,

---

[1] *Report of the Committee on Ministers' Powers ("Donoughmore Committee")* (1932) Cmd. 4060; Sir Carlton Allen, *Law and Orders* (3rd ed., 1965); Wade and Forsyth, *Administrative Law* (8th ed., 2000), (Sir William Wade and Christopher Forsyth eds.), Chap. 23; J. A. G. Griffith, "The Constitutional Significance of Delegated Legislation in England", (1950) 48 *Michigan Law Review* 1079; G. Ganz, "Delegated Legislation: A Necessary Evil or a Constitutional Outrage?", Chap. 3 in *The Constitution After Scott* (Adam Tomkins ed., 1998).

[2] See Noreen Burrows, *Devolution* (2000), pp. 56–68. The Human Rights Act 1998 defines subordinate legislation for the purpose of that Act as including Acts from the Scottish Parliament and Northern Ireland Assembly (s.21). This was necessary to enable judicial control to be exercised over such legislation in the light of the prohibition in the Scotland Act and the Northern Ireland Act on either body legislating contrary to the E.C.H.R.

[3] *ante*, para. 4–035.

[4] About 1,500 general statutory instruments are laid before Parliament each year. There has been a growth not only in terms of the number of general statutory instruments, but also in terms of their length. See evidence submitted by the Clerk of the House to the Procedure Committee H.C. 48 (1999–2000), pp. 26–27.

despite recent events such as those commented on in the Scott Report.[5] Indeed new types of delegated legislation have been devised.[6]

The judicial control of delegated legislation, exercised mainly under the doctrine of *ultra vires*, is discussed later in Chapter 31.

The executive has no inherent power, as it has in France, to issue ordinances or decrees filling out the details of statutes. The authority of an Act of Parliament is necessary: *Case of Proclamations*[7] When the government commands a majority in Parliament it can procure from Parliament any powers it thinks it needs.

We consider in this section the nature and purpose of delegated legislation, and in the next section the parliamentary safeguards that have been provided.

Forms of delegated legislation

29–003   Delegated legislation takes various forms and assumes a variety of names. The primary classification is according to the person or body which has the legislative power, of which for present purposes the chief are:

    (i) *The Queen in Council*—power to issue Statutory Orders in Council, *e.g.* under the Emergency Powers Act 1920. This kind of delegated legislation has the most dignified and "national" character.

    (ii) *Ministers and other heads of government departments*—power to issue departmental or ministerial regulations, rules, orders, etc. These are extremely numerous, and legislation made under them is much greater in bulk year by year than Acts of Parliament.

    (iii) *Local Authorities*—power to make byelaws for their areas under the Local Government Act 1972 s.235(1), and other Acts.

    (iv) *Public bodies*—power conferred by their constituent Acts to make byelaws and other regulations for the purposes for which they were created.[8]

    (v) *Rule Committees*—power to make rules for procedure in court, *e.g.* Civil Procedure Rule Committee (Civil Procedure Act 1997 s.1)[9]; Crown Court Rule Committee (Supreme Court Act 1981, s.86); and judges or committees with power to make rules of procedure relating to family proceedings, bankruptcy, etc.

    (vi) *Measures*—under the Church of England (Assembly) Powers Act 1919 delegated legislation relating to the Church of England is framed by the General Synod of the Church and presented for Royal Assent after

---

[5] *Report of the Inquiry into the Export of Defence Equipment and Dual-Use Goods to Iraq and Related Prosecutions* H.C. 115 (1995–96).

[6] See *post* paras 29–030 *et seq.* In addition from 1974 to 2000 the government of Northern Ireland was, exceptionally, conducted through the form of delegated legislation under the Northern Ireland Act 1974; although such legislation was subject to more parliamentary control than most delegated legislation, it was still of a minimal degree. For powers devolved to the National Assembly for Wales to make subordinate legislation, see *ante* Chap. 5.

[7] (1610) 32 Co.Rep. 74; (1610) 2 St.Tr. 723. The exception is the prerogative of the Crown to legislate by Order in Council, *ante*, Chap. 15 and *post*, Chap. 35.

[8] *e.g.* Internal Drainage Boards (Land Drainage Act 1991, s.66); Nature Conservancy Councils (Wildlife and Countryside Act 1981, s.37); Strategic Rail Authority (Transport Act 2000, s.201).

[9] Replacing the Supreme Court and County Court Rule Committees, for its composition see s.2. The rules made by the Committee have to be laid before Parliament and are subject to the negative procedure.

approval by both Houses of Parliament. A Measure may amend or repeal the whole or any part of any Act of Parliament, including the 1919 Act.[10]

(vii) *Special Procedure Orders* under the Statutory Orders (Special Procedure) Acts 1945 and 1965 are now rare, and have been replaced by Orders under the Transport and Works Act 1992.[11]

Quasi legislation[12]

In addition to delegated legislation, of various kinds, statutes increasingly provide for the making of "Codes of Practice" which have legal effect to the extent that their terms are usually laid before Parliament and must be taken into account by tribunals and courts where they are relevant to proceedings. Breach of their provisions is not in itself unlawful but may be evidence of failure to behave according to a requisite standard, whether that of the careful driver or the reasonable employer.[13] Differing views were initially expressed about the legal status of the immigration rules made under the Immigration Act 1971[14] but there can now be no doubt that they form a kind of "quasi-law", to be interpreted in a less technical way than statutes and delegated legislation.[15] The growing resort to informal legislation of various kinds is open to question on grounds of inadequate Parliamentary control and a large degree of immunity from judicial control.[16] Indirectly, however, informal legislation may be challenged in the courts. For example, a minister entrusted with a discretion by statute cannot fetter that discretion[17] but must in each case consider the relevant merits before reaching a decision. Hence if a minister issues a circular declaring how he is going to deal with individual cases in advance, a particular decision may be attacked on the ground that the minister had prejudged the issue.[18] Moreover, in

29–004

---

[10] *e.g.* Synodical Government Measure 1969 which amended the 1919 Act. A Measure to amend the procedure for the appointment of Bishops was rejected by the House of Commons in July 1984.

[11] See Chap. 10 para. 11–036.

[12] G. Ganz, *Quasi-legislation: Recent Developments in Secondary Legislation* (1987).

[13] Road Traffic Act 1988, s.38 (The Highway Code); Employment Protection Act 1975, s.6; Police and Criminal Evidence Act 1984, ss.66–67, see *ante* para. 24–003; the Police Act 1976 provides that the Secretary of State may issue "guidance" relating to the investigation of complaints (s.83), and in relation to the conduct of disciplinary hearings (s.87). Failure to observe such guidance "shall be admissible in evidence on any appeal". (s.83). Under the Health and Safety at Work, etc. Act 1974 the Health and Safety Commission may approve and issue Codes of Practice with the consent of the Secretary of State under ss.16 and 17. There is no requirement of laying before Parliament.

[14] In *R. v. Chief Immigration Officer, Heathrow Airport, ex p. Salamat Bibi* [1976] 1 W.L.R. 979, Roskill L.J. thought the rules had the force of delegated legislation. In *R. v. Secretary of State for the Home Department, ex p. Hosenball* [1977] 1 W.L.R. 766, Lord Denning M.R. described the rules as "rules of practice laid down for the guidance of immigration officers and tribunals". Geoffrey Lane L.J. said: "These rules are very difficult to categorise or classify. They are in a class of their own."

[15] *R. v. Immigration Appeal Tribunal, ex p. Alexander* [1982] 1 W.L.R. 1076, 1080 *per* Lord Roskill; *R. v. Immigration Appeal Tribunal, ex p. Bakhtaur Singh* [1986] 1 W.L.R. 910, 917, *per* Lord Bridge who cited with approval the dictum of Geoffrey Lane L.J. in *ex p. Hosenball, supra*. See similarly *R. v. Secretary of State for the Home Department, ex p. Swati* [1986] 1 All E.R. 717, 719, *per* Sir John Donaldson, M.R. "documents called House of Commons Statements". See also *R. v. Immigration Appeal Tribunal, ex p. Begum, The Times*, July 24, 1986.

[16] R. Baldwin and J. Houghton, "Circular Arguments: The Status and Legitimacy of Administrative Rules", [1986] P.L. 239.

[17] *post*, para. 31–010.

[18] *R. v. Secretary of State for the Home Department, ex p. Bennett, The Times*, August 18, 1986, CA.

Gillick v. West Norfolk Area Health Authority[19] the House of Lords recognised that its own earlier decision in *Royal College of Nursing v. Department of Health and Social Security*[20] involved the existence of a jurisdiction in the courts to declare that advice contained in a public document, even if non-statutory in form, was erroneous in law. Such a jurisdiction, according to Lord Bridge, was no doubt "salutary and indeed a necessary one in certain circumstances" but it should be exercised sparingly. The number of cases, his Lordship thought, where a non-statutory publication by a department raised "a clearly defined issue of law, unclouded by political, social or moral overtones, [would] be rare."

Statutory Instruments

29–005   The Statutory Instruments Act 1946, which is mainly concerned with the publication[21] of the more important kinds of delegated legislation, provides in section 1 that where by that Act or any subsequent Act power to make, confirm or approve orders, rules, regulations or other subordinate legislation is conferred on the Crown in Council or any Minister or government department, then *if the power is expressed to be exercisable by Order in Council or by Statutory Instrument*, as the case may be, any document by which that power is exercised shall be known as a "Statutory Instrument". The expression is also important in connection with laying before Parliament[22] and the work of the scrutiny committees.[23] The term "Statutory Instrument" also extends to any legislative instrument made after January 1, 1948, in exercise of a power conferred before that date to make "Statutory Rules" within the meaning of the (repealed) Rules Publication Act 1893.[24]

The reasons for delegated legislation

29–006   In spite of much criticism it has been generally accepted since the report of the Committee on Ministers' Powers in 1932 that delegated legislation has come to stay in our legal system, and that there are the following legitimate reasons for its use:

(i) *Pressure on parliamentary time*

29–007   Parliament in its legislative work—especially in the House of Commons— barely has time to discuss essential principles. Much time can be saved, and amendments to Acts of Parliament obviated, by delegating the consideration of procedure and subordinate matters to Ministers and their departments.

(ii) *Technicality of subject-matter*

29–008   The subject-matter of modern legislation is often highly technical. Technical matters, as distinct from broad policy, are not susceptible to discussion in Parliament and therefore cannot readily be included in a Bill. Delegation to Ministers enables them to consult expert advisers and interested parties while the regulations are still in the draft stage. Under the Building Act 1984, for example,

---

[19] [1981] A.C. 800.
[20] [1986] A.C. 112.
[21] *post*, para. 29–036.
[22] *post*, para. 29–019.
[23] *post*, para. 19–024.
[24] See Statutory Instruments Regulations 1947 (S.I. 1948 No. 1) which, broadly provides, *inter alia*, that every instrument of a *legislative* character made by a rule-making authority (which includes Her Majesty in Council and any Government Department) shall be a Statutory Instrument if made after January 1, 1948.

the Secretary of State is given wide powers to make regulations relating to the design and construction of buildings in order to secure the health, safety and welfare of persons, to conserve energy and to prevent waste and contamination of water (section 1). In making such regulations he is to take the advice of the Buildings Regulations Advisory Committee and to consult other bodies and representatives of the interests concerned (section 14).

(iii) *Flexibility*

In large and complex measures it is not possible to foresee all the contingencies and local conditions for which provision will have to be made, and it would be difficult to settle all the administrative machinery in time for insertion in the Bill. Delegated legislation provides a degree of flexibility, as changes can be made from time to time in the light of experience without the necessity for a series of amending Acts, *e.g.* under Road Traffic and Social Security legislation. It can also allows for experimentation, as in Town and Country Planning Acts, and for adjusting financial provisions in consequence of, *e.g.* changes in the value of money, as in the level of fines[25] or expenditure on elections.[26]

29–009

(iv) *Emergency powers*

In emergencies, such as war, serious strikes and economic crises, there would often not be time to pass Acts of Parliament, even if (as may not be the case) Parliament is sitting. Within limits unlawful acts can be done bone fide on the authority of the government in the expectation of later being legalised by an Act of Indemnity, but this is clearly not a desirable proceeding. Hence the emergency powers delegated by the Defence of the Realm Acts 1914–15 and the Emergency Powers (Defence) Act 1939–40 in two world wars, and the permanent peacetime provisions of the Emergency Powers Act 1920.

29–010

The Scott Report was a salutary reminder that emergency powers initially granted for a limited period may continue long after the justifying emergency has ceased.[27]

Concerns with certain types of delegated powers

(i) *Usurping the role of Parliament*

The Committee on Ministers to Powers recommended that enabling or skeleton legislation, that is legislation which contains only basic principles and which leaves the details to be provided by delegated legislation, should be exceptional.[28] Such legislation shifts the balance of power between Parliament and the Executive. The increase in this type of legislation, and in particular legislation which delegated extensive and contentious powers to Ministers to make or change policy, was one of the reasons for the creation in 1992 of the House of Lords Delegated Powers Scrutiny Committee.[29] One of the functions of this Committee is to report on whether Bills inappropriately delegate legislative powers. Examples of Acts which delegate powers in relation to matters of

29–011

[25] Magistrates' Court Act 1980 s.143, as amended, Criminal Justice Act 1982 s.38.
[26] Parliamentary Parties Elections and Referendums Act 2000, s.155.
[27] H.C. 115 (1995–96) C1.1–1.65; Civil servants and Ministers were happy to rely on the Import, Export and Customs Powers (Defence) Act 1939 until its allegedly temporary provisions were regularized in the Import and Export Control Act 1990.
[28] Cmd. 4060 (1932) p. 31.
[29] Since 1994 known as the Delegated Powers and Deregulation Committee.

principle are the Education (Student Loans) Act 1990, the Child Support Act 1991 and the Jobseekers Act 1995. It was on the recommendation of this Committee that the Pollution Prevention and Control Bill 1999 was re-written.[30]

Major policy changes may be required by European Directives which can be implemented by delegated legislation under the authority of the European Communities Act 1972 s.2 and Schedule 2, *e.g.* Equal Pay and Working Time Regulations.

(ii) *Imposition of taxation or incurring of expenditure*

29–012   Only if an Act of Parliament makes specific provision can taxation be imposed by delegated legislation.[31] Section 2 of the Emergency Powers (Defence) Act 1939 provided that the Treasury might by order impose, in connection with any scheme of control authorised by Defence Regulations (themselves delegated legislation), such charges as might be specified in the order. The Excise Duties (Surcharges or Rebates Act 1979 (as amended) allows for excise duties to be amended by delegated legislation, and the Value Added Tax Act 1994 s.2 contains a power to vary that tax by delegated legislation by 25 per cent. Certain taxes may be collected for a limited period by resolution of the Commons under the Provisional Collection of Taxes Act 1968.[32] The first exercise of the power provided by section 82 of the Welfare Reform and Pensions Act 1999, whereby Ministers can place a Report before the House seeking approval of expenditure on new services in advance of the Royal Assent to the Bill creating those services, was criticised by the Social Security Committee.[33]

(iii) *Power to modify or adapt the enabling Act or other Acts of Parliament: "Henry VIII clauses"*[34]

29–013   Parliament sometimes delegates to a Minister the power of modifying the enabling Act so far as may appear to him to be necessary for the purpose of bringing the Act into operation. Such provisions are usually transitional.

More controversially power may be given to a Minister to modify or adapt other Acts of Parliament by delegated legislation, for example, by the Local Government Act 1972, s.254(2) which allows the Secretary of State or appropriate Minister to amend, repeal of revoke any provision of any Act passed before 1st April 1974.[35] The growth in the inclusion of such provisions in legislation, with variable degrees of Parliamentary control over the making of delegated legislation which amends primary legislation, was another reason for the establishment of the Delegated Powers Scrutiny Committee in the House of Lords.[36] Exceptional examples of this type of provision are found in the European Communities Act 1972 s.2(2),[37] Part I of the Deregulation and Contracting

---

[30] See too HL 11 (1993–94) on the Education Bill.

[31] See *Att.-Gen. v. Wilts United Dairies* (1922) 91 L.J.K.B. 897; (1921) T.L.R. 884; Art. 4 Bill of Rights 1688; *cf. McCarthy and Stone Development Ltd v. Richmond-on-Thames L.B.C.* [1992] 2 A.C. 48.

[32] *ante*, para. 12–014.

[33] See H.C. 180 (1999–2000).

[34] This name arose by a far-fetched analogy to the Statute of Proclamations 1539 (repealed in 1547), which gave the king a limited power to legislate by proclamation.

[35] See also the Sex Discrimination Act 1975 and Courts and Legal Services Act 1990.

[36] See Memorandum by Lord Alexander to the Procedure Committee H.C. 152 (1995–96), pp. 58–61.

[37] *ante*, para. 6–018.

Out Act 1994,[38] and the Human Rights Act 1998, s.10(2). The alternative to such powers would often involve the drafting and passing of large numbers of amending Acts.[39]

The courts are aware of the constitutional significance of such powers and have indicated that a power to modify the provisions of a statute by delegated legislation should be narrowly and strictly construed.[40]

(iv) *Powers excluded from the jurisdiction of the courts*

The right of the citizen to ask the court to declare delegated legislation *ultra vires* may be expressly excluded by Parliament,[41] although it is not clear precisely what words in an Act will be held to have this effect.[42] The Committee on Ministers' Powers regarded such a provision as generally objectionable, and only justifiable in very exceptional cases, *viz.* in emergency legislation and in cases where finality is desirable, *e.g.* Regulations under the Foreign Marriage Act 1892, on which the validity of marriages may depend. In these non-emergency cases, where property or status may be affected, the Committee suggested that the regulations should be open to challenge for a short initial period. **29–014**

(v) *Sub-delegation*

The power of delegated legislation vested in one authority is itself sometimes delegated to another authority, and this sub-delegation may go through several stages in a hierarchy of law-making authorities. Thus section 1(3) of the Emergency Powers (Defence) Act 1939, which gave power to issue Defence Regulations by Order in Council, stated that Defence Regulations might empower any authorities or persons to make orders, rules and by-laws for any of the purposes for which Defence Regulations might themselves be made. Ministerial orders were issued under the Regulations, directions under these orders, and licences under these directions. **29–015**

Sub-delegation is only lawful if expressly or impliedly authorised by the enabling Act, for the prima facie principle is *delegatus non potest delegare*,[43] which is discussed more fully later. The requirement of authorisation applies throughout the hierarchy of rules, as does the doctrine of *ultra vires* below the enabling Act itself. Although it is said that sub-delegation should not usually be required except in emergencies, the Pollution Prevention and Control Act 1999 (implementing an E.C. Directive) contains powers to sub-delegate.

(vi) *Failure to exercise an enabling power*

This can arise either as a failure to use powers laid down in a statute to further implement the legislation, or a failure to bring some or all of a statute into force. Generally the courts have regarded the non-use of enabling powers as a political matter for Parliament. In *R. v. Secretary of State for the Home Department, ex p.* **29–016**

---

[38] *post*, para. 29–031.
[39] See V. Korah, "Counter Inflation Legislation. Whither Parliamentary Sovereignty?" (1976) 92 L.Q.R. 42.
[40] See *R. v. Secretary of State for Social Security, ex p. Britnell* [1991] 1 W.L.R. 198; *R. v. Secretary of State for Social Security, ex p. Joint Council for the Welfare of Immigrants* [1997] 1 W.L.R. 275; *Hyde Park Residence Ltd v. Secretary of State for the Environment, Transport and the Regions and Another, The Times,* March 14, 2000.
[41] *cf. Chester v. Bateson* [1920] 1 K.B. 829.
[42] See *post*, para. 32–016 *et seq.*
[43] *post*, para. 31–019.

Fire Brigades Union[44] the opinion of the majority of the House of Lords was that the formula "this Act shall come into force on such day as the Secretary of State may by order made by statutory instrument appoint" did not impose a legally enforceable duty on the Secretary of State to bring the Act into force. However he had a duty to keep under consideration whether or not to bring it into force. There is merit in the provision found in an unsuccessful Private Members Bill—the Parliamentary Government Bill 1999—to the effect that any provision of an enactment which is not commenced within five years of the passing of the Act should cease to have effect.

II. PARLIAMENTARY SAFEGUARDS FOR DELEGATED LEGISLATION[45]

29–017   Apart from the common law jurisdiction of the courts to prevent a power of delegated legislation from being exceeded by declaring its exercise void as *ultra vires* in cases that may be brought before them,[46] Parliament provides a number of safeguards—of varying degrees of efficacy—to secure the proper use of the power. No attempt has been made in this country to establish a uniform code of procedure for the making and testing of delegated legislation, such as has been provided in somewhat different circumstances[47] by the American Administrative Procedure Act 1946. Several reports have concluded that there are defects in the system for considering delegated legislation and recommended reforms, which by and large await implementation.[48] As will be seen, the enactment of the Deregulation and Contracting Out Act 1994 resulted in additional parliamentary procedures in respect of the making of deregulation orders, but this amounts to a tiny fraction of the total number of Statutory Instruments.

1. At the pre-legislative stage

29–018   The *Delegated Powers and Deregulation Committee* in the House of Lords,[49] in addition to its work on Deregulation Orders,[50] considers almost all bills, including draft bills and government amendments to bills, before they reach their committee stage in the Lords. It reports on whether "the provisions of any bill inappropriately delegate legislative power or whether they subject the exercise of

[44] [1995] 2 A.C. 513.

[45] Report of Committee on Ministers' Powers (1932) Cmd. 4060, pp. 41–48, 64–70; J. E. Kersell, *Parliamentary Supervision of Delegated Legislation*; Erskine May, *Parliamentary Practice* (22nd ed.), Chap. 23; Report from the Select Committee on Procedure (1977–1978) H.C. 588; J. D. Hayhurst and Peter Wallington, "Parliamentary Scrutiny of Delegated Legislation", [1988] P.L. 547;

[46] *post*, Chap. 31.

[47] See B. Schwartz and H. W. R. Wade Q.C., *Legal Control of Government* (1972) App. I; Louis Jaffe, "The American Administrative Procedure Act", [1956] P.L. 218.

[48] See *Report from Joint Committee on Delegated Legislation* (1971–1972) H.L. 184 and H.C. 475; Fourth Report from the Procedure Committee, *Delegated Legislation*, H.C. 152 (1995–96); First Report from the Procedure Committee, *Delegated Legislation*, H.C. 48 (1999–2000); the Royal Commission on the Reform of the House of Lords Cm. 4534 (2000), in Chap. 7 set out proposals for reform of the system of scrutinising statutory instruments.

[49] This was established in 1992 as the Delegated Powers Scrutiny Committee, its name and functions were altered following the enactment of the Deregulation and Contracting Out Act 1994. For an account of the work of this committee see: C. Himsworth, "The Delegated Powers Scrutiny Committee", [1995] P.L. 34; Phillipa Tudor, "Secondary Legislation: Second Class or Crucial?", (2000) 21 Statute Law Rev. 149.

[50] *post* para. 29–032.

legislative power to an inappropriate degree of parliamentary scrutiny." The Committee has paid special attention to Henry VIII clauses and skeleton legislation.[51] This Committee is not concerned with the merits of a bill, only with powers delegated by a bill. The relevant government department has to provide a memorandum on a bill explaining and justifying the degree of delegation found in it. Although the Committee's role is only to advise the House and it has no powers to amend bills, most of its recommendations have been accepted by Government and the necessary amendments made to bills.[52]

2. Laying before Parliament

There is no general Act which requires delegated legislation to be laid before   **29–019**
Parliament. Even the Statutory Instruments Act 1946 does not require all Statutory Instruments to be so laid. The enabling Act has to be examined in each case. Enabling Acts now usually, but not invariably, require Statutory Instruments to be laid. Laying is usually before both Houses, except as regards financial matters when it is before the Commons only.[53] Conversely, statutes may require the laying before Parliament of delegated legislation which does not fall within the Statutory Instruments Act; for example, Immigration Rules made under section 3 of the Immigration Act 1971 or Recommendations for the Welfare of Livestock under section 3 of the Agriculture (Miscellaneous Provisions) Act 1968.

There is no uniformity in the requirements as to laying, most instruments are subject to the negative procedure, some to the affirmative procedure. The Minister who introduces the enabling Act decides what method of laying (if any) shall be prescribed. There are no rules, and it has been said of the distinction that it is: "grounded as often as not on the fortuitous outcome of past debate on the parent legislation. Some affirmatives are of relatively little significance; some negatives are of great importance."[54] Since 1992, the Delegated Powers and Deregulation Committee has helped to ensure that there is greater consistency of approach.

The requirements as to laying may take any of the following forms:

(a) *"Negative parliamentary procedure"*
    (i) To be laid before Parliament with immediate effect, but *subject* to annul-   **29–020**
ment (by Order in Council) following a resolution of either House (*"negative resolution"*), usually without prejudice to the validity of anything done thereunder before annulment. This is the commonest form. Before 1948 there was no uniform period for the passing of negative resolutions, but section 5 of the Statutory Instruments Act 1946 prescribes a period of 40 days after laying excluding any time during which Parliament is dissolved or prorogued or both Houses are adjourned (section 7). Where an instrument is subject to negative resolution, unless a member of the Commons moves a "prayer" for its annulment it will not be debated. Even if such a Motion is tabled the government may ignore the Motion, allow it to be debated in a Standing Committee on Delegated Legislation or on the Floor of the House. The latter is rare. It is by agreement

---

[51] *ante* para. 29–011 and 29–013.
[52] See evidence to the Procedure Committee H.C. 152 (1995–96), pp. 58–64, and evidence to the Procedure Committee H.C. 48 (1999–2000), p. 20.
[53] "Parliament" in s.4 of the Rates Act 1984 was held to mean the House of Commons alone for the purpose of laying in *R. v. Secretary of State for the Environment ex p. Greenwich L.B.C., The Times,* December 19, 1985, CA.
[54] Memorandum submitted by the Clerk of the House to the Procedure Committee H.C. 152 (1995–96), p. 47.

between the Party Whips that an instrument "prayed against" is referred to a Standing Committee. The Procedure Committee has suggested that where at least 20 members have signed a prayer seeking the annulment of an instrument, a member should be allowed at the start of public business to move that the matter should be referred to a Standing Committee,[55] and that "praying time" should be extended from 40 to 60 days. In practice instruments have seldom been annulled,[56] because the Minister could count on the government's majority. Even if the Government were "caught napping", the Minister could introduce another instrument in identical terms. There has not been enough time in recent years for members to debate prayers for annulment. In any event no amendment of the instrument is possible, although as a result of criticism the Minister may withdraw it and submit another in a modified form.

(ii) To be laid *in draft* before Parliament, but subject to a resolution that no further proceedings be taken. An adverse resolution may be passed by either House within 40 days (Statutory Instrument Act 1946, s.6), which stops further progress on that draft but does not prevent fresh drafts being laid. Prison Rules are made in this way.

(b) *"Affirmative parliamentary procedure"*

29–021   (i) To be laid before Parliament, either in draft or when made, but not to take effect until approved by *affirmative resolution* in each House, which is normally required to be passed within 28 days (excluding any time when Parliament is dissolved or prorogued or both Houses are adjourned). This requires the Government to find time in each House, and unlike the negative procedure it at least allows some form of Parliamentary scrutiny. Since 1995 all affirmative instruments are automatically referred to a Standing Committee on Delegated Legislation unless the Government decides that they should be debated on the Floor of the House. The debate in the Committee is limited to one and a half hours and is on a formal and unamendable Motion, there is no provision for amendment of an Order. A formal approval motion is then put before the House without debate, even if the Order has not been approved by the Committee. If an Order has been "de-referred" to the Floor of the House, it will be debated on a formal and unamendable Motion to approve it; there is a limitation of one and a half hours on such debates. It is rare for such Motions to be defeated if the Government has a majority in the Commons; the House of Lords rejected the Draft Greater London Authority (Expenses) Order in February 2000.[57]

The fact that an Order has been debated in and approved by Parliament does not prevent a court reviewing delegated legislation on the grounds of illegality, procedural impropriet; or *Wednesbury* unreasonableness. In *R. (on the application of Javed) v. Secretary of State for the Home Department*[58] the Court of Appeal held that it was entitled to review the legality of the Asylum (Designated Countries of Destination and Designated Safe Third Countries) Order 1996 in

---

[55] H.C. 152 (1995–96), para. 27.

[56] In 1969 the Government was unwilling to implement recommendations from the Boundary Commission, but to comply with the letter of the law the necessary draft Orders were laid before Parliament, the Minister successfully moving that they should not be approved. In February 2000, the House of Lords rejected the Greater London Authority Election Rules.

[57] In October 1994 the House of Lords had agreed to a Motion in which it affirmed its right to vote on any subordinate legislation, H.L. Deb., Vol. 558, col. 356, October 20, 1994.

[58] *The Times*, May 24, 2001, [2001] 3 W.L.R. 323; see Wade and Forsyth, *op. cit.* n. 1 at p. 26, and *Stockdale v. Hansard* (1839) 9 Ad. & E. 1.

designating Pakistan as a country in which there was no serious risk of persecution, on the basis that the applicants had established that among women in Pakistan there was risk of persecution.[59] The Court did not accept that in the short debates in Parliament, in which the position of women was not mentioned, that there had been a sufficient evaluation to enable a decision to be made that the Secretary of State could legally include Pakistan in the Order.

(ii) Sometimes an instrument is to be laid before Parliament with immediate effect, but will cease to have effect unless approved by resolution within the prescribed period. This method combines prompt operation with parliamentary control, *e.g.* regulations made under the Emergency Powers Act 1920.

(c) *To be laid without further provision for control*
    This method is now very uncommon. It is used where Parliament contemplates **29–022** that a Minister should take some action, and merely demands to be kept informed of the action taken, *e.g.* the postponing order under the New Valuation Lists (Postponement) Act 1952. No resolution is necessary for the instrument to take effect. Where an instrument is merely laid before the House, it is usually impracticable to find time during the ordinary business of the Commons to move an address for its annulment, and if it is raised on the motion for adjournment no division is allowed. Questions may be asked about regulations lying on the table of the House. The Scott Report was critical of the fact that Orders made under the Import and Export Control Act 1990 were subject to no Parliamentary control.[60]
    The procedure of the two Houses and the time available—especially in the Commons—are not adequate to take full advantage of the opportunity for control offered by the laying of regulations before Parliament.
    Local instruments, dealing with such matters as local authorities' powers, are far more numerous than general instruments. They are registered, but Parliament is usually not concerned with control or even information, and they are seldom required to be laid before Parliament.

Legal effect of the requirement of laying
    The legal effect of the requirement that instruments are to be laid before **29–023** Parliament is uncertain. Is it "mandatory" (imperative), so that the instrument is invalid if the requirement is not fulfilled; or merely "directory", imposing on a public officer a duty of imperfect obligation, but not affecting validity?[61] It seems that so far as concerns instruments subject to negative resolution, and probably also those subject to affirmative resolution, the requirement is directory.[62] There is no penalty specified if the requirement is not observed. In 1944 it was

---

[59] The court cited *R. v. Immigration Appeals Tribunal, ex p. Shah* [1999] 2 A.C. 692, where on the facts it was established that there was a risk of persecution against women in Pakistan.
[60] H.C. 115 (1995–96), Vol. I, C 1.80–1.121.
[61] *post*, para. 31–005.
[62] It was so held by the West Indian Court of Appeal in *Springer v. Doorly* (1950) L.R.B.G. 10; (1950) L.Q.R. 299. The regulations in that case were to be laid "as soon as possible". And see *Bailey v. Williamson* (1873) L.R. 8 Q.B. 118, *Starey v. Graham* [1899] 1 Q.B. 406, 412; A.I.L. Campbell, "Laying and Delegated Legislation", [1983] P.L. 43. However, in *R. v. Secretary of State for Social Services, ex p. London Borough of Camden and another* [1987] 2 All E.R. 560, it was held that: regulations which were not to be made until a draft had been approved by both Houses of Parliament did not come into force in the absence of such approval; the requirement of laying did not extend to documents referred to, but not embodied in, the regulations.

discovered that the Home Secretary had for three years overlooked the requirement that National Fire Service Regulations should be laid before Parliament "as soon as may be" after they were made.[63] An Indemnity Act[64] was therefore passed indemnifying the Home Secretary against "all consequences whatsoever, if any" incurred by this failure.

Section 4(1) of the Statutory Instruments Act 1946 provides that where any Statutory Instrument is required to be laid before Parliament after being made, a copy of the instrument shall be laid before each House before the instrument comes into operation, except in cases of urgency notified to the Lord Chancellor and the Speaker of the Commons.[65]

What constitutes "laying before the House" is for each House to decide. The Laying of Documents before Parliament (Interpretation) Act 1948 defined statutory references to "laying" as taking such action as is directed by virtue of any Standing Order or Sessional Order or other direction or practice of either House to constitute laying, even though it involves action taken when the House is not sitting.[66]

3. Scrutinising committees[67]

Joint Select Committee on Statutory Instruments

29–024   Since 1973, a Joint Committee of both Houses has scrutinised statutory instruments[68] which are required to be laid before both Houses of Parliament—and, in the case of general statutory instruments, whether or not they are required to be laid.

Its terms of reference are to consider whether the special attention of the House should be drawn to any instrument on any of the following grounds, that:

(i) it imposes a charges on the public revenues, or requires the payment of a fee to a public authority for services or a licence;

(ii) it is made in pursuance of an Act specifically excluding it from challenge in the courts;

(iii) it purports to have retrospective effect, where the parent Act confers no such authority;

(iv) there appears to have been unjustifiable delay in its publication, or in laying it before Parliament;

---

[63] Fire Services (Emergency Provisions) Act 1941.

[64] National Fire Service Regulations (Indemnity) Act 1944. See also Price Control and other Orders (Indemnity) Act 1951 and the Town and Country Planning Regulations (London) Indemnity Act 1971. *cf.* Documentary Evidence Act 1868. Sir Carleton Allen, *op. cit.* p. 146, remarked that the Home Secretary in 1944 "lost a unique opportunity of studying the prison system from the inside."

[65] Sections 4 and 5 do not apply to order which are subject to special parliamentary procedure or to any other instrument which is required to be laid before Parliament before it comes into operation (s.7(3)).

[66] Rules presented to Parliament in a command paper are "laid before Parliament": *R. v. Immigration Appeal Tribunal, ex p. Joyles* [1972] 1 W.L.R. 1390, DC.

[67] See para. 6–029 for an account of the committees concerned with the implementation of secondary European Community law.

[68] Including draft statutory instruments and those implementing European Community Directives, but excluding deregulation orders, which are considered by the Deregulation Committee, and Church of England measures, which are considered by the Ecclesiastical Committee.

(v) there appears to have been unjustifiable delay in notifying the Speaker where, on the ground of urgency, the instrument came into operation before being laid before Parliament;

(vi) there appears to be a doubt whether it is *intra vires* or it appears to make some unusual or unexpected use of the powers conferred by the statute under which it is made;

(vii) for any special reason its form or purport calls for elucidation;

(viii) the drafting appears to be defective;

or on any other ground which does not impinge on its merits or on the policy behind it.

The work of the committee is one which depends on specialist legal skills. **29–025** Although it has the assistance of Counsel to the Speaker and of Counsel to the Lord Chairman of Committees, it was said of it that it can only hope to perform the role of a lay jury, lacking the skills for the job in hand.[69] The Joint Committee may require the government department concerned to explain, either by memorandum or witness, any instrument under consideration; and the Committee is instructed, before drawing the special attention of the House to any instrument, to afford the department concerned an opportunity of furnishing an explanation. The Committee is concerned with matters of *form*, as set out in its terms of reference. It is not concerned with policy, which is a matter for Parliament. The practice has developed of electing a member of the Opposition as chairman of the Scrutiny Committee, who would not be embarrassed by conflicting loyalties if the Committee criticises departmental action.

The increase in the volume of delegated legislation has put pressure on this committee. Between one and five per cent of Statutory Instruments are reported by the Joint Committee as falling within one of the grounds outlined above. The House of Lords is prohibited by Standing Order No. 70 from considering an instrument requiring affirmative resolution before the Joint Committee has reported. There is no such limitation in the Commons, and instruments have been debated by in the House on in committee before the Joint Committee has reported.[70]

Select Committee on Statutory Instruments

This is composed of the Commons Members of the Joint Committee on **29–026** Statutory Instruments, and it fulfils the same function as the Joint Committee in respect of those instruments that have to be laid only before the Commons.

Standing Committees on Delegated Legislation

As was seen above, most House of Commons debates on statutory instruments **29–027** are held in Standing Committees rather than on the Floor of the House. The Standing Committee to which an instrument is committed is required only to consider it on a motion: "That the committee has considered the instrument (or draft instrument)". The Chairman of the Committee reports the Statutory Instrument to the House irrespective of whether or not the motion has been agreed; a vote against the Motion by the Committee has no procedural significance,

---

[69] Evidence to the Procedure Committee H.C. 152 (1995–96), p. 28.
[70] Suggestions for such a S.O. in the House of Commons have been made by the Joint Committee and the Procedure Committee.

although it may result in a Instrument being debated on the Floor of the House. This means of sifting Statutory Instruments has been criticised, and it has been proposed that the Committee should be able to consider substantive motions, *e.g.* that the instrument be approved, or be annulled as well as being able to take note of the Instrument.[71] In addition the existing procedure makes no distinction between those Statutory Instruments that are complex and those that are not. It has been proposed that a Sifting Committee[72] should be established to scrutinise all Statutory Instruments subject to negative procedure, and to identify those of sufficient political importance to merit debate, and to refer such Instruments to a Standing Committee on Delegated Legislation. Since such a reform would require more time, and it was recommended that the period of 40 days for considerations of Statutory Instruments subject to negative procedure should be extended to 60 days.

Reform

29–028   There has long been concern as to the inadequacy of the arrangements for scrutinising delegated legislation.[73] The increase in the use of delegated legislation has compounded this problem. Proposals for reform were made by the Procedure Committee in 1996 and 2000, and by the Royal Commission on the Reform of the House of Lords.[74] In addition to proposals already discussed other suggestions include the creation of a new category of "super affirmative instruments" which would require scrutiny by the relevant departmental Select Committee[75] before being laid in draft before each House, a procedure similar to that for Deregulation Orders.[76] This procedure would be used for instruments of particular significance and complexity, and would enable more effective parliamentary input than that exists at present for affirmative instruments. The Royal Commission on the House of Lords approved the reforms suggested by the Procedure Committee. It was in favour of going further and proposed that the reformed House of Lords should have an enhanced role in scrutinising delegated legislation. Its proposals included giving it a formal power to delay delegated legislation, and the provision of more opportunities for Committees in the Lords to consider delegated legislation in draft form. None of the reports favoured allowing either House to amend Statutory Instruments once they had been formally laid before Parliament.

4. Special types of Delegated Legislation

29–030   There are several types of delegated legislation introduced in recent years which have resulted in more extensive controls with respect to how they are made than those outlined above.

---

[71] See H.C. 152 (1995–96).

[72] H.C. 152 (1995–96); the Royal Commission on the House of Lords Cm. 4534 (2000) suggested a Joint Sifting Committee; the Procedure Committee has also accepted this as a viable alternative to a Commons' committee, H.C. 48 (1998–99).

[73] Starting with the Committee on Ministers Powers. Cmd. 4060 (1932).

[74] H.C. 152 (1995–96), H.C. 48 (1999–2000), Cm. 4534 (2000); see also the Hansard Society Report, *Making the Law* (1992). For an earlier unimplemented Report from the Procedure Committee see H.C. 588 (1977–78).

[75] *ante*, para. 12–027 *et seq.*

[76] *post* para. 29–031.

Deregulation orders[77]

Part I of the Deregulation and Contracting Out Act 1994 gave Ministers broad   **29–031**
powers to amend or repeal *any* Act of Parliament passed up to the end of the
1993–94 Session in order to remove or reduce a statutory burden on a trade,
business, profession or individual, provided that it could be achieved "without
removing any necessary protection" (section 1(1)). The purpose of this legislation was to remove from businesses the costs of complying with outdated and
unnecessary legislation, and to do so by means of secondary, rather than primary,
legislation. The powers in the 1994 Act to amend or repeal an Act of Parliament
by delegated legislation, known as Henry VIII clauses, are in consequence
subject to a complex parliamentary procedure designed to provide exceptional
safeguards.

There are three stages to the making of a deregulation order:

(i) Before making a deregulation order the Minister has to consult "such
organisations as appear to him to be representative of interests substantially
affected by his proposals." The government department concerned must take
account of the responses to its consultations, which could result in the proposal
being abandoned, amended or pursued instead by primary legislation.[78] There is
no time limit for this stage.

(ii) A proposal containing the draft Order is laid before Parliament. The   **29–032**
proposal must include details of, *e.g.* the burden to be removed, the savings that
would result from the removal of the burden, the protections that exist, the
consultations made. The proposal is considered concurrently by the House of
Commons Deregulation Committee,[79] and in the House of Lords by the Select
Committee on Delegated Powers and Deregulation.[80] Each committee has to
report to the appropriate House within 60 days of the proposal being made that
the proposal is an appropriate use of the power given by the 1994 Act without
amendment; or that it is an appropriate use of the power but requires amendment;
or that no draft Order should be laid. In the latter case the relevant department
should be given warning of the decision. Each committee applies broadly similar
criteria when considering a proposal.[81] The most important are: the appropriateness of the proposal; the incidence, identification and magnitude of the burden;
the adequacy of the consultation[82]; whether there is adequate protection for those
affected by the legislation to be amended or repealed. In reaching its decision
each committee may take oral and written evidence, and the two committees
have a working relationship with one another.

(iii) At the end of the 60 day period the Minister may lay the draft Order for
approval by each House. He is required when doing so to have regard to the
Committees' Reports and to lay with the draft Order details of any representations made by the Committees and any changes made to the Order. He does not
have to make any changes. Each Committee will consider the draft Order once
more. Final draft Orders are subject to the affirmative procedure, and the
Commons Committee will recommend what form this should take. It may
propose approval either without a debate, or after a debate (limited to one and a

---

[77] David Miers, "The Deregulation Procedure: An Expanding Role", [1999] P.L. 477.
[78] See H.C. 311 (1994–95).
[79] Established for this purpose in 1994.
[80] *ante*, para. 11–030.
[81] See S.O. No. 124A (House of Commons), the House of Lords has not formulated its de-regulation
procedure in a S.O.
[82] See H.C. 817 (1995–96).

half hours). If the Committee recommends that the draft Order should not be approved the Government has to table a Motion to disagree with the Committee's Report, which may be debated for up to three hours. If the House approves the motion, then the question on the draft Order is immediately put to the House. The House of Lords generally debates all such Orders. In the light of the Committees' Reports the Minister may decide not to lay the Draft Order.

The most extensive use made of deregulation orders was from 1995–97, since when it has been relatively little used.[83] The new procedures for the approval of deregulation orders have been judged a success; it subjects the making of this type of delegated legislation to a much greater degree of scrutiny than is the norm for delegated legislation.

Regulatory Reform Orders[84]

29–033   The procedure established above was seen as a basis for further expanding the power to make law by Order, and resulted in the enactment of the Regulatory Reform Act 2001. However this Act is concerned with amending primary legislation to *impose* new burdens or *increase* existing burdens, provided the Order has also the effect of removing or reducing a burden (section 1(3)). The Act has the potential to apply much more widely than the 1994 Act, as its provisions can be applied in respect of any legislation imposing burdens on a person "in the carrying on of any activity". This will include businesses, charities, and the public sector. The procedure for making Regulatory Reform Orders is very similar to that for Deregulation Orders, with the same stages as outlined above; the wider powers available to Ministers under the 2001 Act is reflected in additional requirements with respect to making explanatory information available to Parliament. If used extensively there will be implications for the workload of the relevant committees in each House, and additional resources will be required if these committees are to continue to perform to a high standard. For, *e.g.* an early proposal is to reform the fire safety regime—currently spread over 120 pieces of primary legislation and a similar number of Statutory Instruments—a major task.

Remedial Orders under the Human Rights Act 1998[85]

29–034   Section 10 and Schedule 2 of the Human Rights provides for a "fast track" procedure for the amendment of legislation which has been declared incompatible by a court by virtue of section 4, or in the light of a E.Ct.H.R. decision against the United Kingdom. This procedure can only be used if a Minister considers that there are "compelling reasons for proceeding under (section 10)". A remedial order can be far reaching, *e.g.* it may amend any primary legislation, or be retrospective. It must be laid in draft before Parliament for 60 days with

---

[83] See Report from the Deregulation Committee, *The Future of the Deregulation Procedure*, H.C. 709 (1997–98), Select Committee on Delegated Powers and Deregulation, *Special Report*, HL 158 (1997–98).

[84] For the background see *The Publication of the Draft Regulatory Reform Bill*, Cm. 4713 (2000); *Report on the Regulatory Reform Bill*, Select Committee on Delegated Powers and Deregulation HL 61 (1999–2000), *Second Report on the Regulatory Reform Bill*, HL 8 (2000–01). David Miers, "Regulatory Reform Orders: A new weapon in the armoury of law reform," (2001) 21 Public Money and Management, para. 29–034.

[85] See Wade and Forsyth *op. cit.*, n. 1 pp. 190–1, where this procedure is considered in the light of constitutional principle. The first such order was made as a consequence of the decision of the Court of Appeal in *R. (H.) v. Mental Health Review Tribunal, North and East London Division* [2001] H.R.L.R. 752, and see *post*, para. 24–029.

an explanatory statement and approved by each House. An Order can be made without such approval if the Minister declared that because of the urgency of the matter it is necessary to make the order without a draft being so approved. In these circumstances additional requirements apply, in any event the Order will cease to have effect if not approved by resolutions of both Houses.

5. Other controls in Parliament

(a) Motions of censure on the Minister responsible for the instrument.   **29–035**

(b) Debate and possibly motion.

(c) Questions to Ministers. In either House questions may be asked about instruments lying on the table, but no debate is allowed on a question.

6. Publication

The Rules Publication Act 1893, s.1 requires antecedent publicity for limited   **29–036** classes of statutory rules. Subsequent publication was provided for by section 3, which required all statutory rules made after 1893 to be sent forthwith after they were made to the Queen's printer.

The Statutory Instruments Act 1946 repealed the Rules Publication Act 1893 and generalised the procedure for subsequent publication; but it made no provision for antecedent publicity, the reason given being that the practice of informal consultation with outside interests had become general. Immediately after the making of any "Statutory Instrument" as defined in section 1,[86] it is to be sent to the Queen's printer and numbered, and copies shall "as soon as possible" be printed and sold (section 2). The Stationery Office is to publish lists showing the date on which every Statutory Instrument printed and sold by the Queen's printer was first *issued* by that office; and in any legal proceedings a copy of any list so published purporting to bear the imprint of the Queen's printer shall be received in evidence of the date on which any Statutory Instrument was first issued by the Stationery Office (section 3(1)).

Delegated legislation generally comes into operation when it is made, unless some other date is specified therein. Failure to comply with any requirement for publication will not normally affect the validity of the instrument concerned.[87] The Statutory Instruments Act 1946, s.3(2), however, provides that where any person is charged with an offence under a Statutory Instrument, it shall be a defence to prove that the instrument had not been "issued" by the Stationery Office at the date of the alleged contravention, unless it is proved that at that date reasonable steps had been taken for the purpose of bringing the purport of the instrument to the notice of the public, or of persons likely to be affected by it, or of the person charged.[88]

---

[86] *ante*, para. 29–005.

[87] *Jones v. Robson* [1901] 1 Q.B. 680; but *cf. Johnson v. Sargant* [1918] 1 K.B. 101; Lanham, (1974) 37 M.L.R. 510 [1983] P.L. 395. Publication may be a prerequisite of validity in a case such as that of the immigration rules, which are defined by the Immigration Appeals Act 1969, s.24(2) as "rules ... which have been published and laid before Parliament". An Act of Parliament comes into operation on the date on which it receives the Royal Assent (printed beneath the title), unless some other date is specified: Acts of Parliament (Commencement) Act 1793; *R. v. Smith* [1910] 1 K.B. 17.

[88] The 1946 Act was amended by the Statutory Instruments (Production and Sale) Act 1996 to allow for the printing and sale of Statutory Instruments under the authority of HMSO; see Ganz *op. cit.* n. 1 at pp. 78–79.

29–037   Where any Statutory Instrument is required to be laid before Parliament after being made, copies sold by the Queen's printer must show the date on which it came or will come into operation; and either the date on which copies were laid before Parliament or a statement that such copies are to be laid before Parliament (section 4(2)).

The Treasury, with the concurrence of the Lord Chancellor and the Speaker of the Commons, is empowered to make regulations for the purposes of the Act, including the numbering, printing and publication of Statutory Instruments, and the exemption of any classes of Statutory Instrument from the requirement of being printed and sold (section 8). The Statutory Instruments Regulation 1947 made thereunder are contained in S.I. 1948 No. 1, which begins the printed series of *Statutory Instruments* that replaces the previous *Statutory Rules and Orders*.

The Regulations exempt from the printing requirement Statutory Instruments which are local, or are otherwise regularly printed as a series (Reg. 5); or temporary (Reg. 6); contain bulky Schedules (Reg. 7); or where it would be contrary to the public interest that they should be printed before coming into operation (Reg. 8). Such exemption requires the certificate of the "responsible authority", *i.e.* the authority that makes the instrument. In *Simmonds v. Newell*[89] a conviction for the offence of selling in contravention of an Iron and Steel Prices Order was quashed by the Divisional Court, because the Schedules had not been printed and no certificate had been issued under Regulation 7 exempting from printing, and presumably reasonable steps had not been taken under section 3(2). Parker J. said it was not necessary to decide whether a Statutory Instrument is wholly invalid if it is required by section 2 to be printed and it is not printed, or whether section 3(2) provides a defence whether the Statutory Instrument is required to be printed or not. In *R. v. Sheer Metalcraft*,[90] a prosecution for buying in contravention of an Iron and Steel Price Order, the Schedules had not been printed and no certificate of exemption had been issued; but the jury found the accused guilty, because sufficient steps had been taken to bring the Schedules to their notice. Streatfield J. told the jury that a Statutory Instrument is "made" (*i.e.* effective) when it is made by the Minister and (presumably, where laying is required) laid before Parliament: whether a Statutory Instrument has been "issued" *i.e.* printed) is a different question, which can be raised as a defence under section 3(2). The neglect to print or to certify exemption from printing did not make the order invalid, and it was admissible in evidence.

7. Prior consultation[91]

29–038   Acts of Parliament delegating legislative power sometimes provide that the Minister may, or shall, consult interested bodies or an advisory committee before issuing regulations.[92] The interested bodies may be specified in the Act or left to the Minister's discretion. The Minister is not usually bound to accept such advice. Thus the Minister must consult the Council on Tribunals before making

---

[89] [1953] 1 W.L.R. 846; *sub nom. Defiant Cycle Co v. Newell* [1953] 2 All E.R. 38.
[90] [1954] 1 Q.B. 586.
[91] See J. F. Garner, "Consultation in Subordinate Legislation" [1964] P.L. 105; A. D. Jergensen, "The Legal Requirements of Consultation", [1978] P.L. 290.
[92] *e.g.* Building Act 1984, s.14. The Health and Safety Commission is required similarly to consult before drafting Codes of Practice under the Health and Safety at Work etc. Act 1984: see s.16. The Deregulation and Contracting Out Act 1994 and the Regulatory Reform Act 2001 make extensive and detailed provisions for consultation, see *ante* para. 29–033.

procedural rules for tribunals that come under its supervision; and the Lord Chancellor must consult the Council before making procedural rules for statutory inquiries.[93] In *R. v. Secretary of State for Health, ex p. United States Tobacco International Inc.*[94] it was held that in carrying out his duty to consult the Secretary of State had to act in accordance with the rules of natural justice. What was required for this would depend on the facts of each case. It was on the recommendation of the House of Lords Delegated Powers Scrutiny Committee that a requirement was imposed on the Minister to consult the Social Security Advisory Committee before making exercising his powers to make delegated legislation under the Social Security (Incapacity for Work) Act 1994. This Committee also ensured that the Pollution Prevention and Control Act 1999 imposed wider consultation requirements on the Minister than at first envisaged in the Bill. In some cases a draft scheme is to be prepared by the interested body (*e.g.* a local authority), and confirmed or approved by the Minister. Exceptionally, the Minister is required to submit draft regulations to an advisory committee, without being bound to accept their suggested amendments. Apart from such statutory provisions, the practice of consultation has become generally established.

---

[93] Tribunals and Inquiries Act 1971, ss.10 and 11.
[94] [1992] Q.B. 353, DC.

CHAPTER 30

ADMINISTRATIVE JURISDICTION[1]

Introduction

30–001   "Administrative jurisdiction" or "administrative justice" is a name given to various ways of deciding disputes outside the ordinary courts. It is not possible to define precisely what bodies constitute the "ordinary courts," although that expression is used in the Tribunals and Inquiries Act 1992. There are some bodies that might be placed under the heading either of ordinary courts or of special tribunals. Guidance cannot be found in the name of a body; the Employment Appeal Tribunal, for example, is a superior court of record[2] while it was doubted whether a local valuation court was really a court.[3] Certain matters involving calculations of figures or scientific problems, such as the assessment of rates and taxes, local audit, patents, inventions and performing rights, have been considered by Parliament unsuitable for the ordinary courts. Then there has been a great increase of governmental activity, both central and local, under statutory powers in the late nineteenth, twentieth and twenty-first centuries, and a number of social services are provided in the Welfare State. Under both these heads there are complex systems of regulation and control, such as national insurance, pensions, the health service, education, public transport, the regulation of agriculture, rent control, housing and redevelopment, town and country planning and the consequent compulsory acquisition of land. It is inevitable that disputes should arise, or conflicts of rights and interests between the individual citizen and the central or local government authority. The ordinary courts are appropriate for the decision of purely legal rights; but in many[4] of the kinds of cases of which we are speaking, the question in issue is not one of purely legal rights but a conflict between private and public interests, bound up in a greater or lesser degree with ministerial policy as outlined by statute.

30–002   The "administrative justice" we are considering in this chapter must be distinguished from that distinct system of administrative law known in legal systems which have developed under the influence of French law where a separate body of administrative courts or tribunals exercise the jurisdiction which in the common law system belongs to the High Court exercising its supervisory jurisdiction by way of judicial review. Those systems, too, have specialised tribunals for dealing with particular categories of dispute but questions of the

---

[1] *Report of Committee on Administrative Tribunals and Enquiries* ("Franks Committee") (1957) Cmnd. 218; *Memoranda submitted by Government Departments* (6 vols., H.M.S.O. 1956); *Minutes of Evidence* (H.M.S.O. 1956–1957); *Report of the Committee on Ministers' Powers* (1932) Cmd. 4060, s.III.
    Sir Carleton Allen, *Administrative Jurisdiction* (reprinted from [1956] P.L. 13–109); W. A. Robson, *Justice and Administrative Law* (3rd ed., 1951); *Towards Administrative Justice* (Michigan, 1963); Harry Street, *Justice in the Welfare State* (2nd ed., 1975); G. Ganz, *Administrative Procedures* (1974). H. W. R. Wade and C. F. Forsyth, *Administrative Law* (8th ed., Oxford, 2000); M. Harris and M. Partington, *Administrative Justice in the 21st Century* (Hart, 1999).
[2] Employment Tribunals Act 1996, s.20.
[3] *Att.-Gen. v. BBC* [1981] A.C. 303; *ante*, para. 20–007.
[4] But not all: Employment Tribunals deal with disputes between private employers and employees.

legality of government actions are decided according to principles of administrative law in administrative courts.[5]

The subject covered in this chapter under the title of administrative justice is one particularly likely to be affected by the Human Rights Act 1998.

Reference was made in Chapter 22 to examples, even before the Human Rights Act 1998 came into force, of changes necessitated to tribunals as a result of decisions of the European Court of Human Rights.[6] Since the Act came into effect the Employment Appeal Tribunal has held that new procedures for appointing lay members to employment tribunals guaranteed their independence in a way which made the tribunals "Convention compliant".[7] The House of Lords has rejected a claim that the powers of the Secretary of State under the Town and Country Planning Act 1990, the Transport and Works Act 1992, the Highways Act 1980 and the Acquisition of Land Act 1981 to make decisions on planning applications and orders are incompatible with Article 6 (determination by an independent and impartial tribunal of civil rights and obligations).[8] There remains, however, considerable scope for litigation in this area in relation to the independence and impartiality of existing tribunals and in some cases of the absence of bodies entitled to make binding decisions or otherwise provide effective remedies.[9] (Article 13)

The Lord Chancellor announced, in May 2000, the establishment of a Review of Tribunals, a body to be chaired by Sir Andrew Leggatt, a former Lord Justice of Appeal. Its task will involve recommending "a coherent structure for the delivery of administrative justice".

Where Parliament does not consider the ordinary courts suitable for the decision of such disputes, especially at first instance, it prescribes at least three other methods of deciding them: **30–003**

   (i) administrative tribunals;

   (ii) ministerial decision after statutory inquiry[10];

   (iii) ministerial decision, in which the Minister uses his discretion without any prescribed procedure.[11]

The Franks Committee (1957)[12] regarded both tribunals and other administrative procedures as essential to our society. Preference should be given, however, to entrusting adjudication to the ordinary courts rather than to tribunals, unless there are clearly special reasons which make a tribunal more appropriate. Similarly, a tribunal is to be preferred to a Minister, but it is not always possible to express policy in the form of regulations capable of being administered by an

---

[5] L. N. Brown and J. S. Bell, *French Administrative Law* (5th ed., Oxford, 1998); J. W. Allison, *A Continental Distinction in The Common Law* (Revised ed., Oxford, 2000).

[6] *e.g.* Mental Health Review Tribunals: *X v. United Kingdom* (1981) 4 E.H.R.R. 188 led to amendments contained in the Mental Health Act 1983. Immigration: *Chahal v. United Kingdom* (1996) 23 E.H.R.R. 413 led to the Special Immigration Appeals Commission Act 1997.

[7] *Scanfuture UK Ltd v. Secretary of State for Trade and Industry, The Times*, April 26, 2001.

[8] *R. (Alconbury Developments Ltd) v. Secretary of State for the Environment, Transport and the Regions* [2000] 2 W.L.R. 1389, HL.

[9] On the extent to which the United Kingdom Courts can take account of Article 13, see *ante* para. 22–017 and para. 22–043.

[10] *post*, para. 30–024.

[11] *post*, para. 30–024.

[12] (1957) Cmnd. 218, paras 406–408; see *post*, para. 30–018 and para. 34–002. *cf. Report of the Committee on Ministers' Powers* (1932) Cmd. 4060, pp. 115–118.

independent tribunal. The Franks Committee examined the working of administrative law in other countries, notably the United States and France; but concluded that, although there are advantages in comparative study, each country must work out for itself, within the framework of its own institutions and way of life, the proper balance between public and private interest.

I. Tribunals[13]

30–004   These are independent statutory tribunals whose function is judicial. The tribunals are so varied in composition, method of appointment, functions and procedure, and in their relation to Ministers on the one hand and the ordinary courts on the other, that a satisfactory formal classification is impossible.

Reasons for creating special tribunals[14]

30–005   The reasons why Parliament increasingly confers powers of adjudication on special tribunals rather than on the ordinary courts may be stated positively as showing the greater suitability of such tribunals, or negatively as showing the inadequacy of the ordinary courts for the particular kind of work that has to be done. In the following summary we choose mainly the former method.

(i) *Expert knowledge*

30–006   Many of the questions that have to be decided under modern social legislation call for an expert knowledge of matters falling outside the training of the lawyer; also an understanding of the policy of the legislature and experience of administration. They are not primarily legal questions, although at some stage a judicial habit of mind may be required. Members of the Lands Tribunal, for example, may be lawyers or persons experienced in questions relating to valuation of land.[15] Mental Health Review Tribunals include legal, medical and lay members.[16] Employment Tribunals normally include one member representing associations of workers and one representing employers' associations.[17]

(ii) *Cheapness*

30–007   The vast number of questions that arise from day to day, affecting the interests of thousands of people, must be disposed of much more cheaply than can be done in the stately and costly courts of law. The speed and informality mentioned below contribute to the relative cheapness of administrative justice.

(iii) *Speed*

30–008   Again, if these multitudinous questions are to be disposed of without the delay that would clog the administrative machine and work great hardship on interested parties, institutions must be devised and procedure adopted that will dispatch the

[13] Exhaustive information down to 1957 is contained in the *Memoranda submitted by Government Departments* to the Franks Committee. See also R. E. Wraith and D. G. Hutchesson, *Administrative Tribunals* (1973); J. A. Farmer, *Tribunals and Government* (1974); H. Street, *Justice in the Welfare State* (2nd ed., 1975); J. Fulbrook, *Administrative Justice and the Unemployed* (1978).
[14] S. H. Legomsky, *Specialized Justice* (1990, Oxford).
[15] Lands Tribunal Act 1949.
[16] Mental Health Act 1983.
[17] Employment Tribunals Act 1996.

business much more speedily than the ordinary courts can do. Indeed, the courts would not have time to take over this work, in addition to what they already have, without being entirely reconstituted and so losing their present identity.

(iv) *Flexibility*

Although every body of men that has to make decisions evolves in course of   **30–009**
time general working principles, and government departments tend to follow their own precedents, the new tribunals are not hampered by the rigid doctrine of binding precedent adhered to by the courts.[18] They thus have greater freedom to develop new branches of law on the basis of modern social legislation and suitable to the needs of the Welfare State, as in times past the Court of Chancery developed Equity.[19] This does not mean that the decisions of tribunals are entirely capricious and unpredictable: there is a growing practice for some of them to publish selected decisions.

(v) *Informality*

Tribunals are not bound by such complex rules of procedure or such stringent   **30–010**
rules of evidence as prevail in the ordinary courts.[20] They may admit hearsay evidence[21]; they must observe the rules of natural justice but there is not necessarily a right in all cases to cross examine witnesses.[22] Unlike the judges of the ordinary courts, members of tribunals are entitled to rely in deciding cases not merely on the evidence before them but on their professional or industrial knowledge relating to the subject matter of the dispute before them. To hold otherwise would, of course, reduce if not completely destroy the value of choosing members of tribunals by reference to their special knowledge. They may rely on "their cumulative knowledge and experience of the matter in hand."[23] A doctor, for example, may advise other members of a tribunal from his personal experience of the weight to be given to evidence relating to medical matters.[24]

Examples of statutory tribunals

In many important areas of everyday life matters affecting a large part of the   **30–011**
population are subject to the jurisdiction of statutory tribunals—for example social security benefits of all kinds, employment law, questions of discrimination, immigration, education, mental health. Most tribunals are of recent origin but some have a long history. The General Commissioners of Income Tax date back to 1798.

A common structure, particularly in the case of tribunals of modern origin which deal with large numbers of cases and sit throughout the United Kingdom, is a tribunal of three; a legally qualified Chairman and two members chosen

[18] *Merchandise Transport v. B.T.C.* [1962] 2 Q.B. 173.
[19] *cf. James v. Minister of Pensions* [1947] K.B. 867 (Denning J.).
[20] *R. v. Deputy Industrial Injuries Commissioner, ex p. Moore* [1965] 1 Q.B. 456.
[21] *Miller (T.A.) v. Ministry of Housing and Local Government* [1968] 1 W.L.R. 992, CA.
[22] *R. v. Newmarket Assessment Committee, ex p. Allen Newport Ltd* [1945] 2 All E.R. 371, 373; *R. v. Deputy Industrial Injuries Commissioner, ex p. Moore (supra)*; *Nicholson v. Secretary of State for Energy* (1977) 76 L.G.R. 693; decisions recognising in the circumstances a right to cross examine. *Contra, Kavanagh v. Chief Constable of Devon and Cornwall* [1974] Q.B. 624.
[23] *Metropolitan Properties v. Lannon* [1969] 1 Q.B. 577, 603 *per* Edmund-Davies L.J. (Rent Assessment Committee).
[24] *R. v. Medical Appeal Tribunal, ex p. Hubble* [1958] 2 Q.B. 228, 240 *per* Diplock J., affirmed [1959] 2 Q.B. 408. See also *Dugdale v. Kraft Foods Ltd* [1977] I.C.R. 48 (E.A.T.).

because of their expertise in the relevant field and representing "both sides" where that can be said to be applicable, for example in employment tribunals. In other cases, for example the Lands Tribunal, there is a small number of members from whom a tribunal is constituted when required. In the particular instance of the Lands Tribunal one member of the panel sitting alone constitutes the Tribunal.

Social security

30–012 There is an elaborate arrangement of tribunals in this wide and important area which covers entitlement to benefits and payments of various kinds.[25] Appeals lie to an Appeals Tribunal. Each tribunal normally consists of a legally qualified Chairman and two members chosen from a panel of persons having knowledge or experience of conditions in the area and being representative of persons working and living in the area but may be constituted by a sole member.[26] The system of tribunals as a whole is under the control of a President who is responsible for superintending the general working of the tribunals.

Appeal lies, subject in some cases to leave, to Commissioners. An appeal is normally heard by one Commissioner. The Chief Commissioner decides which decisions shall be reported.

Employment tribunals[27]

30–013 This is another important body of tribunals, sitting throughout the United Kingdom, with a wide and varied jurisdiction. Established in 1965 to deal with claims relating to redundancy payments they subsequently acquired jurisdiction over unfair dismissals, discrimination claims under the Sex Discrimination and Race Relations legislation and appeals against improvement and prohibition notices served under the Health and Safety at Work, etc. Act 1974. The tribunals are under the supervision of a President. Each tribunal consists of a legally qualified chairman and two laymen, one chosen from a list prepared in consultation with employers' representatives, the other from a list prepared in consultation with trades unions. The Employment Rights (Resolution of Disputes) Act 1998, however, provides for a number of situations where the Chairman may sit alone.[28]

A special feature of Industrial Tribunals is that appeal lies to the Employment Appeal Tribunal which consists of a High Court Judge and two lay members.[29]

Immigration

30–014 The provision for hearing appeals relating to immigration by Immigration Adjudicators and the Immigration Appeal Tribunal has been outlined earlier in Chapter 23.

---

[25] Social Security Administration Act 1992; Social Security Act 1998; M. Adler, "Lay tribunal members and administrative justice" [1999] P.L. 616.
[26] See Adler, n. 25 *supra*.
[27] Employment Tribunals Act 1996.
[28] Rules for appointing lay members held to be compatible with Convention on Human Rights in *Scanfuture UK Ltd v. Secretary of State for Trade and Industry, The Times*, April 26, 2001, EAT.
[29] The court is unusual in having a jurisdiction which extends to both Scotland and England: Employment Tribunals Act 1996, s.20.

Mental health review tribunals

These important bodies and the difficult jurisdiction which they have to **30–015**
exercise have been discussed in Chapter 24.[30]

Taxation

Appeals against assessments to income tax lie in some cases to General **30–016**
Commissioners, in some to Special Commissioners. The former are appointed by
the Lord Chancellor and are residents with knowledge of the area in which they
sit.[31] Usually two Commissioners hear an appeal which is conducted informally.
Special Commissioners[32] are appointed by the Treasury. They are senior civil
servants; hearings are in London, sometimes before two, sometimes one Commissioner.

Value Added Tax is collected by the Customs and Excise. Appeals are heard
by Value Added Tax Tribunals which are under the supervision of a President.
Each tribunal consists of a Chairman, appointed by the Lord Chancellor, and one
or two laymen chosen from a panel nominated by the Treasury. (The Chairman
may sit alone).[33]

Miscellaneous

Further examples which illustrate the width of matters referred to administrative tribunals of various kinds might include Commons Commissioners,[34]
the Foreign Compensation Commission,[35] the Independent Schools Tribunal,[36]
the Special Educational Needs Tribunal[37] the Conveyancing Appeals Tribunal[38]
and the Plant Varieties and Seeds Tribunal.[39] The Wireless Telegraphy Appeal
Tribunal, established by the Wireless Telegraphy Act 1949 is unusual in that it is
believed never to have heard an appeal. More recent examples include the
Tribunal established by the Regulation of Investigatory Powers Act 2000, the
Financial Services and Markets Tribunal established by the Financial Services
and Markets Act 2000 and the Adjudication Panels set up by the Local Government Act 2000 from which members will be selected to form Case Tribunals to
investigate complaints of unethical behaviour in local government. The Director
General of Fair Trading is regarded as a tribunal for the purposes of the
adjudicatory powers which he exercises under the Fair Trading Act 1973,
the Consumer Credit Act 1974 and the Estate Agents Act 1979. Appeals from the
Director General lie to the Competition Commission, established by the Competition Act 1998. The Freedom of Information Act 2000 gives adjudicative
powers to the Information Commissioner (formerly the Data Protection Commissioner) with appeals to the Information Tribunal (formerly the Data Protection
Tribunal). The Financial Services and Markets Act 2000, section 132 establishes

---

[30] See J. Peay, *Tribunals on Trial* (Oxford, 1989).
[31] Taxes Management Act 1970, s.2.
[32] Taxes Management Act 1970, s.4.
[33] Value Added Tax Act 1994, s.82 and sched. 12.
[34] Commons Registration Act 1965.
[35] Foreign Compensation Acts 1950 and 1969.
[36] Education Act 1996, s.476.
[37] Education Act 1996, s.333. The School Standards and Framework Act 1998 established Exclusion
appeal panels (sched. 18) and Admission Appeal Panels (scheds 24 and 25).
[38] Courts and Legal Services Act 1990, s.41.
[39] Plant Varieties Act 1997.

a Tribunal to which appeal lies from decisions of the Financial Services Authority.[40] Appeal from the tribunal lies to the Court of Appeal or Court of Session.

Tribunals of Inquiry, established under the Tribunals of Inquiry (Evidence) Act 1921 belong in a class of their own and are discussed earlier in Part I of Chapter 7.

Domestic tribunals

30–017   Some disciplinary bodies set up for professional or other associations are established by statute, often with appeal to the courts, and therefore find a place here since bodies exercising statutory powers against individuals will normally be regarded as operating in the area of public law.[41]

The supervisory jurisdiction of the High Court[42] is exercised over statutory domestic tribunals in a similar way to that over administrative tribunals, in that they must observe the principles of natural justice; and this supervisory jurisdiction over them provides useful precedents for administrative law.[43] However, whereas excess of jurisdiction renders a statutory tribunal liable to damages, excess of jurisdiction by a non-statutory tribunal does not, unless there is a breach of contract or malice.[44] Proceedings against non-statutory domestic tribunals may be commenced in the normal way. In addition to damages, where appropriate, declarations and injunctions are available but not certiorari and prohibition.[45]

Disciplinary committees have been created by statute for a large number of professions to hear complaints of misconduct and with power to strike members off the register. The Medical Act 1983, for example, establishes a Professional Conduct Committee with power to remove a doctor's name from the register of medical practitioners, either for a fixed period or indefinitely, on proof of conviction of a criminal offence or of serious professional misconduct. Appeal lies to the Privy Council.[46] Architects, Farriers and Pharmacists, on the other hand, may appeal from professional bodies to the High Court.[47]

---

[40] *ante* para. 28–005.

[41] *R. v. General Medical Council ex p. Gee* [1986] 1 W.L.R. 226; affirmed [1986] 1 W.L.R. 1247, CA.

[42] *post*, Chap. 32.

[43] Lord Justice Morris, "The Courts and Domestic Tribunals" (1953) 69 L.Q.R. 318; D. Lloyd, "The Disciplinary Powers of Professional Bodies" (1950) 13 M.L.R. 281 and (1952) 15 M.L.R. 413; J. D. B. Mitchell, "Domestic Tribunals and the Courts" (1956) 2 *British Journal of Administrative Law* 80; J. Gareth Miller, "The Disciplinary Jurisdiction of Professional Tribunals" (1962) 25 M.L.R. 531; *Report of Departmental Committee on Powers of Subpoena of Disciplinary Tribunals* (1960) Cmnd. 1033.

[44] *Byrne v. Kinematograph Renters Association* [1958] 1 W.L.R. 762.

[45] Now, the remedies of a prohibiting or quashing order. *R. v. National Joint Council for the Craft of Dental Technicians ex p. Neate* [1953] 1 Q.B. 704, DC. *Post*, p. 687.

[46] Medical Act 1983, s.36 and s.40. Similarly, Dentists Act 1984 s.27 and s.29. Appeal also lies to the Privy Council under the Veterinary Surgeons Act 1966. The Health Act 1999, s.60 and Sched. 3 contain wide powers for the amendment of legislation regulating the medical and associated professions.

[47] Architects (Registration) Act 1931; Farriers (Registration) Act 1975 and Farriers (Registration) (Amendment) Act 1977; Pharmacy Act 1954; Medicines Act 1968. Appeals by doctors, dentists and veterinary surgeons and practitioners from decisions of the tribunal established under the Misuse of Drugs Act 1971 lie to the High Court.

Tribunals and Inquiries Act 1992

A Committee on Administrative Tribunals and Inquiries under the chairman- **30–018**
ship of Sir Oliver Franks (later Lord Franks) was appointed by the Lord Chancellor: "To consider and make recommendations on: (a) The constitution and
working of tribunals other than the ordinary courts of law, constituted under any
Act of Parliament by a Minister of the Crown or for the purposes of a Minister's
functions. (b) The working of such administrative procedures as include the
holding of an inquiry or hearing by or on behalf of a Minister on an appeal or as
the result of objections or representations, and in particular the procedure for the
compulsory purchase of land." The Committee reported in 1957.[48]

The purpose of Parliament in providing that certain decisions should not be left
to the ordinary courts but should be subject to special procedures, said the
Committee, must have been to promote good administration; and the general
characteristics that should mark these special procedures are "openness, fairness
and impartiality." It was not possible to define the principles on which it had been
decided that some adjudications should be made by tribunals and others by
Ministers: the distinction was a fact that had to be accepted. Tribunals should be
regarded as machinery provided by Parliament for adjudication, rather than (as
the Committee on Ministers' Powers had suggested in 1932) as part of the
machinery of administration.

The Government accepted most of the recommendations of the Franks Committee in the Tribunals and Inquiries Act 1958. Certain reforms could be introduced by administrative directions to government departments or local
authorities. The most important innovation made by the Act was the creation of
a Council on Tribunals.[49] (The composition and work of the Council is considered in Chapter 34.) The Act also made further provision as to the appointment, qualifications and removal of the chairman and members, and as to the
procedure, of certain tribunals; it provided for appeals to the courts from certain
tribunals; it required the giving of reasons for certain decisions of tribunals and
Ministers; and it extended the supervisory powers of the High Court. The Act
was amended in 1959[50] and 1966,[51] and the law was consolidated by the
Tribunals and Inquiries Act 1971 and again by the Tribunal and Inquiries Act
1992.

Appointment of members of tribunals

The chairmen of some tribunals are appointed by the Lord Chancellor, and the **30–019**
chairmen of certain other tribunals are selected by the appropriate Minister from
a panel of persons appointed by the Lord Chancellor[52] (section 6).

The Council on Tribunals may make to the appropriate Minister general
recommendations as to the appointment of members of the tribunals specified in
Schedule 1 (*i.e.* those under the supervision of the Council), and also of the
relevant panels, and the Minister "shall have regard" to such recommendations.

---

[48] (1957) Cmnd. 218.

[49] The idea appears to have originated with Professor W. A. Robson, who proposed a "Standing
Council on Administrative Tribunals" (see Franks Report, *Minutes of Evidence*, p. 496), in addition
to an Administrative Appeal Tribunal. It was reinforced by H. W. R. Wade's proposal for an
"Administrative Court" (*ibid.* pp. 551–555).

[50] Town and Country Planning Act 1959, s.33 (provision of rules of procedure for statutory
inquiries).

[51] Tribunals and Inquiries Act 1966 (provision of rules of procedure for discretionary inquiries).

[52] Or the Lord President of the Court of Session or the Lord Chief Justice of Northern Ireland.

A Minister may not, with certain exceptions, terminate the appointment of a member of a tribunal specified in Schedule 1, or of a relevant panel, without the consent of the Lord Chancellor (section 7).

Procedure

30–020   The Minister must consult the Council on Tribunals before making or approving procedural rules for the tribunals that come under its supervision. There are now no restrictions on legal representation before most statutory tribunals.[53] Legal aid is not available except before the Lands Tribunal, the Employment Appeal Tribunal, Mental Health Review Tribunals and the Commons Commissioners. In the case of other tribunals, however, legal advice is available. In many cases litigants will in fact have the help of their unions or similar bodies.[54] Presumably, too, the right which the Court of Appeal recognised in *McKenzie v. McKenzie*[55] for a litigant to be accompanied by a friend to assist by taking notes and giving advice applies to tribunals as much as to the ordinary courts.

Appeals from tribunals

30–021   A party to proceedings before most statutory tribunals, who is dissatisfied with the tribunal's decision on a point of law, may either appeal to the High Court or require the tribunal to state a case for the opinion of the High Court. Appeal lies by leave of the High Court or of the Court of Appeal to the Court of Appeal,[56] and thence to the House of Lords (section 11).

The scope of this right depends on the view of the courts on what constitutes a point of law as opposed to a question of fact. Whether or not the facts were as alleged by an applicant is a matter for the tribunal. Whether those facts in the light of the appropriate rules of law give rise, for example, to a contract of employment is a matter of applying the law to the facts. If a court does not wish to interfere it can call that second stage too a question of fact. If it does wish to interfere it can conclude that it raised a point of law because no reasonable tribunal could have reached such a conclusion unless it had made an error in understanding or applying the law.[57]

Supervisory powers of superior courts

30–022   Any provision in an Act passed *before* August 1, 1958, that any order or determination shall not be called into question in any court, or any similar provision which excludes any of the powers of the High Court, shall not prevent the removal of the proceedings into the High Court by order of certiorari or prejudice the powers of the High Court to make orders of mandamus (section 12).[58] It does not, however, affect statutory provisions prescribing a special time limit within which applications to the High Court must be made.

---

[53] An exception is provided by tribunals which deal with complaints against National Health Service practitioners: Health and Social Security Act 1984, s.5 and Sched. 3.
[54] See the explicit recognition of this likelihood in the Employment Tribunals Act 1996, s.6(1). *Bache v. Essex County Council, The Times* February 2, 2000, CA.
[55] [1971] p. 33.
[56] The Court of Session takes the place of the High Court and the Court of Appeal in relation to proceedings in Scotland.
[57] *post* para. 32–015.
[58] These are now the remedies of a mandatory or quashing order. There is a corresponding provision in relation to Scotland.

Reasons to be given for decisions

Where a tribunal which comes under the supervision of the Council gives a **30–023** decision, it is the duty of the tribunal to furnish a written or oral statement of the reasons for the decision *if requested to do so* by persons concerned. (s.10) The statement may be refused, or the specification of the reasons restricted, on the grounds of national security. Such a statement forms part of the decision and must be incorporated in the record, so that the order will be a "speaking order" for the purposes of certiorari (or quashing order).[59]

The courts have held that the reasons given must be "proper, adequate reasons" which are intelligible and deal with the substantial points which had been raised.[60]

II. MINISTERIAL DECISIONS AND INQUIRIES

Parliament often provides that, before a decision is made by a Minister or other **30–024** public authority which affects the rights of citizens, an inquiry must be held at which those whose interests are concerned may state their objections to the action proposed before a final decision is made. Inquiries are usually prescribed by statute before land is compulsorily acquired for such purposes as town development, slum clearance, the building of housing estates, schools and hospitals, and road improvement; and also before town and country planning schemes are confirmed. Inquiries may also be prescribed in relation to the provision of social services, and for other schemes of control. Most inquiries are arranged by the Ministry for the purposes of its own housing and planning cases and those of local authorities. The procedure provides a framework for a fair hearing in the weighing of the proposals of a public authority against the interests of persons affected by them. The Minister is not bound by the recommendations of the Inspector who holds the inquiry: he must, on the contrary form his own independent decision.[61] An important exception, however, is provided by the power in the Town and Country Planning Act, 1990, Sched. 6 to delegate the power in certain classes of planning appeals to an inspector. In such cases his decision is final.[62]

Some Ministers have the power—often without appeal—to make decisions directly affecting the rights of individuals or other public authorities. This power of decision may be either original or appellate. In either case it may involve a dispute between a public authority and an individual or between two public (often local) authorities. The power is in a greater or less degree discretionary, usually there is no kind of appeal from it, and in the cases we are now considering no public inquiry or other form of procedure is prescribed by statute. Normally, therefore, citizens can only complain about these decisions through

---

[59] *post,* para. 32–004.
[60] *Re Poser and Mills' Arbitration* [1964] 2 Q.B. 467. For other statutory provisions requiring the giving of reasons for decisions see *Iveagh (Earl) v. Minister of Housing and Local Government* [1964] 1 Q.B. 395; *Givaudan & Co v. Minister of Housing and Local Government* [1967] 1 W.L.R. 250; *Elliott v. Southwark L.B.C.* [1976] 1 W.L.R. 499; *French Kier Developments v. Secretary of State for the Environment* [1977] 1 All E.R. 296.
[61] *Nelsovil Ltd v. Minister of Housing and Local Government* [1962] 1 W.L.R. 404.
[62] S.I. 1981 No. 804; S.I. 1995 No. 2259.

such political means as letters to Members of Parliament, questions in the House and motions in debates on the adjournment.

Examples are the Home Secretary's power to hear appeals from police officers against dismissal or reduction in pay, and his powers relating to prison administration; and the judicial functions of various Ministers in relation to such matters as bankruptcy, weights and measures, registration of business names and trademarks and licensing of road transport.

The Minister *may* hold an inquiry in many of these cases but in such cases the parties concerned will lack the rights which they have where an inquiry must be held.[63]

Inquiries[64]

30–025   A typical provision requiring the holding of an Inquiry is to be found in the Acquisition of Land Act 1981. The Act lays down general procedural rules to be observed before compulsory purchase powers conferred by various statutes can be exercised. Section 13 of the 1981 Act provides that if any objection has been made to a proposed compulsory purchase order the Minister shall before confirming the order either cause a public local inquiry to be held or afford to any objector a hearing. Little can be learned from the Act of any rules relating to the holding of such an inquiry or who might hold it. Section 35 of the Town and Country Planning Act 1990 similarly requires the minister, before confirming a structure plan proposed for a planning authority for the development of its area, to afford to any objectors "an opportunity of appearing before and being heard by a person appointed by him for the purpose." Sections 16 and 106 of the Highways Act 1980 require the holding of inquiries and, in some instances, section 16 requires an inquiry under the Statutory Orders (Special Procedure) Act 1945.

Procedure

30–026   The Franks Committee made a number of recommendations relating to procedure at inquiries and, in particular, advocated the adoption of statutory rules to regulate procedure.

The Lord Chancellor was given statutory power to make rules for procedure, after consultation with the Council of Tribunals, by the Town and Country Planning Act 1959, s.33: see now the Tribunals and Inquiries Act 1992, s.9. In due course rules were made for many of the more important types of inquiry[65] and are usually followed by analogy in cases where strictly they do not apply. The rules relate to the notice to be given to persons entitled to appear before the inquiry; the right to representation and the right to call evidence and cross examine. The rules define the right to appear by reference to people whose legal rights are effected by the scheme or proposal. Within limits Inspectors allow parties to appear who may not be within the terms of the rules and there is judicial support for the view that a local inquiry is open to anyone living in the locality.[66]

---

[63] *Essex County Council v. Ministry of Housing and Local Government* (1967) 18 P. & C.R. 531 (Stansted Airport Inquiry).

[64] R. E. Wraith and G. B. Lamb, *Public Inquiries as an Instrument of Government* (1971).

[65] Compulsory Purchase by Public Authorities (Inquiries Procedure) Rules 1976, S.I. 1976 No. 746. Town and Country Planning (Inquiries Procedure) (England) Rules 2000 S.I. 2000 No. 1624. Highways (Inquiries Procedure) Rules 1976, S.I. 1976 No. 721.

[66] *Wednesbury Corporation v. Ministry of Housing and Local Government* (No. 2) [1966] 2 Q.B. 275, 302 *per* Diplock L.J.

Apart from express procedural rules an inspector must observe the rules of natural justice (or act fairly or not behave with procedural impropriety[67]). Hence he must not receive evidence from one party in the absence of another[68] or base his report on considerations which the objectors had not known were in his mind so that they had had no chance to deal with them.[69]

Fairness and the general nature of local inquiries were considered by the House of Lords in *Bushell v. Secretary of State for the Environment*,[70] an inquiry held under the Highways Act 1959, before the Highways Inquiries Rules had come into force. The House of Lords, Lord Edmund-Davies dissenting, upheld the refusal of the inspector to allow cross-examination of the department's expert witnesses on the reliability and statistical validity of the methods of traffic prediction used by the department to produce its estimates of future traffic needs. Lord Diplock, whose speech contains the lengthiest analysis of the role of the inspector, preferred to use the word "fair" to describe the procedure required to be followed by the inspector; natural justice was too liable to connote "the procedure followed by English courts of law." What is fair is to be determined in the light of the nature of the subject matter of the inquiry and of the practical realities as to the way in which administrative decisions forming judgments based on technical considerations are reached. A refusal to permit cross-examination is not *per se* unfair. In *Bushell* the method of computing traffic flow was not a topic suitable for investigation by individual inspectors at individual inquiries, unlike the route of a particular stretch of motorway. It was more akin to a question of policy—should motorways be built at all?—which is a matter for Parliament, not local inquiries.[71]

Since the coming into force of the Human Rights Act 1998 questions of procedure may now be open to challenge by reference to Article 6 of the Convention.

The Inspector's Report

Inspectors were, until recently, largely, full time members of the departments **30–027** for which they hold inquiries. Although this could give rise to some doubt about their independence and impartiality the Franks Committee emphasised that it had received "virtually no criticism of the qualifications of inspectors or of the manner in which they conduct enquiries." Nonetheless the Committee finally decided to recommend that inspectors should be put under the control of the Lord Chancellor rather than being employed as full-time members of particular departments or being appointed from time to time by a department to conduct a particular inquiry. That recommendation was not accepted by the Government. However, the Departments of the Environment and Transport did agree that highway inquiries should in future be conducted by inspectors nominated by the Lord Chancellor.[72]

---

[67] *post*, para. 31–013 *et seq.*
[68] *Hibernian Property Co Ltd v. Secretary of State for the Environment* (1973) 27 P. & C.R. 197.
[69] *Fairmount Investments v. Secretary of State for the Environment* [1976] 1 W.L.R. 1255, HL.
[70] [1981] A.C. 75. See too *R. v. Secretary of State for Transport, ex p. Gwent County Council* [1987] 1 All E.R. 161.
[71] The extent to which policy is a proper issue to be raised at an inquiry may depend on whether it is a "local inquiry" or a more far ranging inquiry, in which policy questions are inevitably involved, such as that into proposals to build an airport at Stansted or a nuclear reactor at Sizewell: M. Purdue, R. Kemp and T. O'Riordan, "The Government at the Sizewell B Inquiry" [1985] P.L. 475.
[72] Report on the Review of Highway Inquiry Procedures, Cmnd. 7133 (1978).

Even as formerly organised the hearing of inquiries was probably consistent with Article 6 of the Convention on Human Rights because the availability of judicial review provided the necessary guarantee of an impartial, independent hearing: *Bryan v. UK*.[73]

The independence and impartiality of Inspectors has, however, been strengthened by the establishment as an executive agency of a Planning Inspectorate.

Another important aspect of public confidence in the operation of inquiries is the right to know the contents of the inspector's report. There is likely to be suspicion about a system which grants a hearing and requires ministers in some cases to reopen inquiries or allow further representations, if the report at the centre of the procedure is withheld from the parties. The courts gave no right to see the report but the Franks Committee recommended publication on the ground that "fair play for the citizen" required that he should know what the inspector said to the minister. This recommendation has been accepted and is specifically included in the statutory rules of procedure governing various classes of inquiries. The report is not, however, made available until the minister has made his decision.

The role of the Minister

30–028   Once the inspector has concluded his hearing and produced his report the rights of the ministers and objectors are now largely governed by statutory rules. The Franks Committee had been concerned about the extent to which a minister might take into account new evidence received after an inquiry had concluded. The committee suggested a distinction between new factual evidence and advice on policy, which the Government accepted. A minister is, in many cases, now required to notify all the parties concerned if (i) he intends to differ from an inspector on a finding of fact or (ii) he is likely to disagree with the inspector's recommendations because he has taken into consideration new evidence (which includes expert evidence on a matter of fact) or any new issue of fact (which does not include questions of government policy). Where the minister is differing on a finding of fact the parties have 21 days in which to make written representations. In the other cases the parties have 21 days within which to ask for the reopening of the inquiry. An example of the rules being successfully invoked to invalidate a ministerial decision is to be found in *French Kier Developments Ltd v. Secretary of State for the Environment*.[74] In making his report, an inspector disregarded a document put before him but the minister relied on that document to justify a refusal to accept the inspector's recommendations. Willis J. held that to attach any weight to the contents of the document in the circumstances amounted to the taking into consideration of new evidence and the parties should therefore have had the opportunity to reopen the inquiry. The difficulty which may arise in interpreting the new rules is illustrated by *Murphy (J.) and Sons Ltd v. Secretary of State for the Environment*.[75] An inspector had recommended against allowing a site to be developed for residential use because of the amount of noise coming from the plaintiff company's adjoining premises. The minister, however, granted permission for the development and the plaintiff's company claimed that, in doing so, he had differed from the inspector on a finding of fact. Ackner J. held that the minister had not differed from the inspector on a finding of fact but from the inspector's expression of opinion on the planning merits,

[73] (1995) 21 E.H.R.R. 342.
[74] [1977] 1 All E.R. 296.
[75] 1973 1 W.L.R. 560.

which did not give the plaintiff the right to make further representations.[76] In the case of inquiries governed by these or similar rules the right to make further representations or to reopen the inquiry only arises if the minister differs from his inspector.

In *Bushell v. Secretary of State for the Environment*[77] the House of Lords emphasised that, whatever the restrictions on the minister in reaching his decision, he is perfectly entitled to consult his departmental officials and obtain from them the best advice that he can: "Once he has reached his decision he must be prepared to disclose his reasons for it, because the Tribunals and Inquiries Act 1971 so requires; but he is, in my view, under no obligation to disclose to objectors and give them an opportunity of commenting on advice, expert or otherwise, which he receives from his department in the course of making up his mind. If he thinks that to do so will be helpful to him in reaching the right decision in the public interest he may, of course, do so; but if he does not think it will be helpful—and this is for him to decide—failure to do so cannot in my view be treated as a denial of natural justice to the objectors."[78]

---

[76] See *Lord Luke of Pavenham v. Minister of Housing and Local Government* [1968] 1 Q.B. 172.
[77] [1981] A.C. 75.
[78] At p. 102 *per* Lord Diplock.

CHAPTER 31

JUDICIAL CONTROL OF PUBLIC AUTHORITIES: I. LIABILITY[1]

31–001   We consider in this chapter the general principles in accordance with which the courts control the exercise of powers by public authorities. The remedies available for this purpose are dealt with in the next chapter, and civil proceedings by and against the Crown in Chapter 33. In the terminology of Lord Diplock in *O'Reilly v. Mackman*[2] Part I of this chapter deals with judicial control through Public Law while Part II deals with control through the mechanism of Private Law.

I. PUBLIC LAW: EXCESS OR ABUSE OF POWERS

Judicial control of powers

31–002   The exercise by public bodies of powers conferred on them by statute or by the common law[3] may be open to review in the courts on a number of grounds. As a general principle it can be said that the courts do not concern themselves with the wisdom of a particular decision; they cannot, as it is said, examine the merits. They can, however, examine whether a public body has exceeded the powers given to it so that its decision is *ultra vires,* or whether the procedure followed in reaching a decision was flawed by a failure to observe the principles of natural justice. A decision may also be open to review because it is one that no reasonable body could have reached: the *Wednesbury*[4] principle. For present purposes it is unnecessary to consider whether all these grounds should be regarded as aspects of the *ultra vires* doctrine.[5] In the following pages the various bases for judicial review will be examined by reference to the traditional terminology which formerly was to be found in the case law. Reference must, however, be made to Lord Diplock's new terminology which has begun to appear in judgments and which, as will be seen, may be of importance if it extends the scope of judicial review. In the *GCHQ* case Lord Diplock said:

> "Judicial review has I think developed to a stage today when . . . one can conveniently classify under three heads the grounds upon which administrative action is subject to control by judicial review. The first ground I would call

---

[1] See de Smith, Woolf and Jowell, *Judicial Review of Administrative Action* (5th ed., 1995).
[2] [1983] 2 A.C. 237.
[3] *Council of Civil Service Unions v. Minister for the Civil Service* [1985] A.C. 374.
[4] *Associated Provincial Picture Houses v. Wednesbury Corporation* [1948] 1 K.B. 223; *post,* para. 31–011.
[5] Lord Diplock described review on the *Wednesbury* grounds of unreasonableness as involving a type of *ultra vires: British Airways v. Laker Airways* [1985] A.C. 58. For judicial doubt that *ultra vires* is the underlying basis of judicial review, see Sir John Laws, "Illegality, the problem of Jurisdiction" in *Judicial Review* (ed. Supperstone and Goudie, 1992); "Lord Woolf; Droit-Public-English Style", [1995] P.L. 57. See further C. Forsyth, "Of Fig Leaves and Fairy Tales", [1996] Camb. L.J. 122. J. Jowell, "Of Vires and Vacuums" [1999] P.L. 448. See also *Judicial Review and the Constitution* (ed. C. Forsyth, Hart, 2000).

'*illegality*,' the second '*irrationality*,' and the third '*procedural impropriety*.' That is not to say that further development on a case by case basis may not in course of time add further grounds."[6]

Within a year that classification had been described as "a valuable and already 'classical' but certainly not exhaustive analysis of the grounds upon which courts will embark on the judicial review of an administrative power exercised by a public officer."[7]

The Human Rights Act 1998 has introduced a new ground of challenge, that a public authority has acted in breach of a convention right, which may be regarded as a specific example of illegality.[8]

Ultra Vires rule

A Minister, a local authority and any public body may only validly exercise **31–003** powers within the limits conferred on them by common law or statute. A decision may fall outside those powers and so be *ultra vires* because the body concerned has attempted to deal with a matter outside the range of the power conferred on it—substantive *ultra vires*—or because it has failed, in reaching its decision, to follow a prescribed procedure—procedural *ultra vires*.

In so far as the common law powers of public authorities are part of the royal prerogative the jurisdiction of the courts over them was asserted in such cases as the *Case of Monopolies*[9] the *Case of Proclamations*[10] and *The Zamora*.[11] In the *GCHQ* Case the House of Lords clearly affirmed that the exercise of prerogative powers is subject to judicial review, although that case was concerned with natural justice (or procedural impropriety), where the powers relate to matters which are "justiciable."[12]

As regards the innumerable statutory powers, the question is one of interpretation of the statute concerned. The acts of a competent authority must fall within the four corners of the powers given by the legislature.[13] The court must examine the nature, objects and scheme of the legislation, and in the light of that examination must consider what is the exact area over which powers are given by the section under which the competent authority purports to act.[14]

In *Attorney-General v. Fulham Corporation*,[15] for example it was held that a **31–004** local authority which had power under the Baths and Wash-houses Acts 1846 to 1878 to establish baths, wash-houses and open bathing places was not entitled to carry on the business of a laundry, and was acting *ultra vires* in washing or partly

---

[6] *Council of Civil Service Unions v. Minister for the Civil Service* [1985] A.C. 374, 410. One development to which Lord Diplock referred specifically was the possible recognition of the principle known to the European Court of Justice as proportionality: see, for example, *R. v. Intervention Board for Agricultural Produce, ex p. E.D. & F. Man (Sugar) Ltd* [1986] 2 All E.R. 115. See further, *R. v. Secretary of State for Transport, ex p. Pegasus Holdings (London) Ltd* [1988] 1 W.L.R. 990; *R. v. Secretary of State for the Home Department, ex p. Brind* [1991] 1 A.C. 696.
[7] *R. v. Secretary of State for the Environment, ex p. Nottinghamshire C.C.* [1986] A.C. 240, *per* Lord Simon.
[8] See *ante* para. 22–016.
[9] (1602) 11 Co.Rep. 84b.
[10] (1610) 12 Co.Rep. 74.
[11] [1916] 2 A.C. 77.
[12] *C.C.S.U. v. Minister for the Civil Service* [1985] A.C. 374; *ante*, para. 15–004.
[13] *per* Lord Greene M.R. in *Carltona Ltd v. Commissioners of Works* [1943] 2 All E.R. 560, 564.
[14] *per* Sachs J., in *Commissioners of Customs and Excise v. Cure and Deeley Ltd* [1962] 1 Q.B. 340.
[15] [1921] 1 Ch. 440.

washing customers' clothes as distinct from providing facilities for persons to wash their own clothes.

A more controversial and difficult example is provided by *Bromley L.B.C. v. G.L.C.*[16] where the legality of a grant by the G.L.C. to the London Transport Executive was challenged on a number of grounds. The House of Lords held, *inter alia*, that the grant was *ultra vires* because the authority did not have the power to make grants to the Transport Executive merely for the purpose of reducing fares. In *Re Westminster City Council*[17] the House of Lords held that attempts by the G.L.C. in the last months of its existence to provide funding for future years for the Inner London Education Authority and an array of voluntary bodies was *ultra vires*.

Delay in exercising a statutory power, if contrary to express or implied requirements in the relevant Act, may invalidate the decision on the ground of *ultra vires*.[18]

Legislative Powers

31–005   Delegated legislation has been held void on the ground of *ultra vires* in a number of cases. In *Chester v. Bateson*,[19] it was held that a regulation made by the Minister under the Defence of the Realm Act 1914 was *ultra vires* in that it made it an offence to take, without the consent of the Minister, any proceedings in the courts for the recovery of possession of houses occupied by workmen employed on war production in special areas so long as they continued to pay their rent and to observe the other conditions of the tenancy. In *Commissioners of Customs and Excise v. Cure and Deeley*[20] a purchase tax regulation which provided that if any person furnished an incomplete return the Commissioners might determine the amount of tax appearing to them to be due and demand payment thereof, which amount should be deemed to be proper tax due unless within seven days it was shown *to the satisfaction of the Commissioners* that some other amount was due, was held *ultra vires* the Finance (No. 2) Act 1940.

---

[16] [1983] A.C. 768; "An ultra vires case which involved difficult questions of construction of some obscurely worded statutory provisions"; *Pickwell v. Camden L.B.C.* [1983] 1 All E.R. 602, 628 *per* Ormrod L.J.

[17] [1983] 1 A.C. 768. In the case of the voluntary bodies the House, in reaching its conclusion, had to distinguish its own previous decision in *Manchester C.C. v. Greater Manchester C.C.* (1980) 78 L.G.R. 560; something which Lord Bridge found himself unable to do.

[18] *Simpsons Motor Sales (London) Ltd v. Hendon Corporation* [1963] Ch. 57, 82–83 *per* Upjohn L.J.; cited and approved [1964] A.C. 1088, 1117; *Collector of Land Revenue South West District Penang v. Kam Giu Paik* [1986] 1 W.L.R. 412, PC.

[19] [1920] 1 K.B. 829, DC. Applied to invalidate a Home Office standing order restricting access to solicitors by prisoners in *R. v. Secretary of State for the Home Dept., ex p. Anderson* [1984] Q.B. 778, DC. And see *Att.-Gen. v. Wilts United Dairies* (1921) 91 L.J.K.B. 897; (1921) 37 T.L.R. 884, HL, no authority to impose charges; *Utah Construction & Engineering Pty Ltd v. Pataky* [1966] A.C. 629, PC, power to make regulations relating to "the manner of carrying out excavation work" did not extend to imposing an absolute duty of care on employers; *Hotel and Catering Industry Training Board v. Automobile Proprietary* [1969] 1 W.L.R. 697; [1969] 2 All E.R. 582, HL, power to establish training boards for persons "in any activities of industry or commerce" did not extend to persons employed by private clubs. For an unsuccessful attempt to claim that regulations were *ultra vires* because of vagueness and arbitrariness see *McEldowney v. Forde* [1971] A.C. 632, HL; discussed, D. N. MacCormick, "Delegated Legislation and Civil Liberty" (1970) 86 L.Q.R. 171.

[20] [1962] 1 Q.B. 340. The Purchase Tax Act 1963, s.27(2), later provided that where a person did not keep proper accounts and the Commissioners estimated the amount of tax due, the amount should be recoverable unless *in any action relating thereto* the person liable proved the amount properly due and that amount was less than the amount estimated. For a more recent example see *R. v. Customs and Excise Commissioners, ex p. Hedges & Butler Ltd* [1986] 2 All E.R. 164.

In *Daymond v. Plymouth C.C.*[21] the House of Lords held that a power to fix such charges as a water authority might "think fit" did not authorise the making of an Order levying charges for sewage services on the occupiers of properties which were not connected to public sewers.

The fact that a rule has been laid before the Houses and not been annulled does not bar review by the courts,[22] and it should be immaterial that a Statutory Instrument has been affirmed by a resolution of both Houses.[23]

Where the enabling Act prescribes a particular *procedure* for the exercise of a power, the exercise of the power may be void if that procedure is not followed.[24] In *Agricultural Horticultural and Forestry Industry Training Board v. Aylesbury Mushrooms Ltd*[25] the Minister purported to make an industrial training order under the Industrial Training Act 1964, s.1(4) which required him, before making an order to "consult any organisation," appearing to him to be representative of substantial numbers of employers engaged in the activities concerned. ... " Donaldson J. held that failure to consult the body representing mushroom growers rendered the order in question invalid as against mushroom growers.

31–006

In considering the effect of procedural irregularities the Courts distinguish between mandatory requirements, breach of which results in invalidity, and directory requirements, breach of which does not result in invalidity. The more important the requirement, the more likely it is that it will be held to be mandatory. To attempt to deduce clear principles from the case law is, however, impossible.[26] Moreover, even where the court holds that a mandatory requirement has not been complied with, relief may be withheld.[27]

Byelaws are *ultra vires* if they are repugnant to the general law; but it is not easy to decide in what circumstances a byelaw will be held invalid on that ground. It obviously must not be contrary to statute, although it can, of course, forbid what would otherwise be lawful at common law. In *Powell v. May*[28] a

[21] [1976] A.C. 609. See now Water Charges Act 1976; *South West Water Authority v. Rumbles* [1984] 1 W.L.R. 800, CA.

[22] *Mackay v. Marks* [1916] 2 I.R. 241; *Institute of Patents Agents v. Lockwood* [1894] A.C. 347, 366; *Hoffman La Roche v. Secretary of State for Trade and Industry* [1975] A.C. 295; *Laker Airways Ltd v. Department of Trade* [1977] Q.B. 643, CA; *cf. Bowles v. Bank of England* [1913] 1 Ch. 57.

[23] But see the reluctance of the House of Lords to examine the *reasonableness* of guidance given by a minister which had in accordance with statute been submitted for Parliamentary approval—and duly approved: *R. v. Secretary of State for the Environment, ex p. Nottinghamshire C.C.* [1986] A.C. 240.

[24] See *R. v. Minister of Health, ex p. Yaffe* [1930] 2 K.B. 98 (failure to follow appropriate procedure at local inquiry invalidated subsequent Ministerial order). *Cf. Minister of Health v. The King (on the prosecution of Yaffe)* [1931] A.C. 494, where the House of Lords approved the principle laid down by the Court of Appeal but upheld the scheme.

[25] [1972] 1 W.L.R. 190. See too *R. v. Secretary of State for Transport, ex p. Philippine Airlines, The Times*, October 17 (1984), CA. For an unsuccessful attempt to invoke procedural *ultra vires* see *Port Louis Corporation v. Att.-Gen. of Mauritius* [1965] A.C. 1111, PC. See too *R. v. Post Office, ex p. Association of Scientific, Technical and Managerial Staffs* [1981] I.C.R. 76, CA; *R. v. Secretary of State for Trade and Industry, ex p. Ian Kynaston Ford* (1985) 4 Tr. L. 150.

[26] For discussions of the distinction see *Coney v. Choyce* [1975] 1 All E.R. 979; *London & Clydeside Estates Ltd v. Aberdeen D.C.* [1980] 1 W.L.R. 182, HL; *R. v. St Edmundsbury B.C., ex p. Investors Ltd* [1985] 1 W.L.R. 1168; *Steeples v. Derbyshire C.C.* [1984] 3 All E.R. 468; *Walsh v. Barlow* [1985] 1 W.L.R. 90; *Secretary of State for Trade and Industry v. Langridge* [1991] Ch. 402, CA; *Wang v. C.I.R.* [1994] 1 W.L.R. 1286, PC.

[27] *R. v. Secretary of State for Social Services ex p. Association of Metropolitan Authorities* [1986] 1 W.L.R. 1.

[28] [1946] K.B. 330. And see *Thomas v. Sutters* [1900] 1 Ch. 10; *White v. Morley* [1899] 2 Q.B. 30; *Gentel v. Rapps* [1902] 1 K.B. 160, 166; *R. and W. Paul Ltd v. Wheat Commission* [1917] A.C. 139.

byelaw made by a county council forbidding generally any person to frequent or use any street or other public place for the purpose of bookmaking or betting or wagering, was held invalid as being repugnant to the Street Betting Act 1906 and the Betting and Lotteries Act 1934, which would have allowed the appellant bookmaker certain defences.

Where a statutory instrument or byelaw contains *ultra vires* provisions it may be possible to sever the offending portions and preserve other parts of the instrument or byelaw which fall within the powers conferred by Parliament.[29]

Judicial Powers

31–007   A tribunal or other body with a limited jurisdiction acts *ultra vires* if it purports to decide a case falling outside its jurisdiction. Thus a rent tribunal which is given power to fix the rent of a dwelling house cannot make an order relating to premises which are let for business purposes.[30] If such a tribunal erroneously concludes that the facts of a case fall within its jurisdiction its decision is *ultra vires* and can be set aside by the courts. Facts which must exist if a tribunal is to exercise its jurisdiction validly are known as *jurisdictional facts*. On matters which do not go to jurisdiction the tribunal may err without exceeding its jurisdiction. No satisfactory test has ever been suggested to distinguish jurisdictional from non-jurisdictional facts but there is no doubt that the courts use the distinction as the basis for exercising their supervisory control.

Since *Anisminic Ltd v. Foreign Compensation Commission*[31] it has also been the law that a tribunal acting within its jurisdictional limits may act *ultra vires* if it errs in applying the relevant law to the facts. Prior to that case it had been believed that errors of law made after embarking on consideration of a matter within a tribunal's jurisdiction could not deprive it of jurisdiction.[32] Such errors were only open to review if they were apparent from the formal statement of the tribunal's decision: error of law on the fact of the record.[33] It is not yet clear whether *Anisminic* has established that every error of law amounts to an excess of jurisdiction, in which case error of law on the face of the record no longer has any significance. In the case of tribunals, as distinguished from courts of limited jurisdiction (such as county courts) there is support for the wide view of *Anisminic* in *Re Racal Communications*.[34] On the other hand the Privy Council in *South East Asia Fire Bricks Sdn. Bhd. v. Non-Metallic Mineral Products Manufacturing Employees Union*[35] has affirmed the continued distinction between jurisdictional and non-jurisdictional errors.

---

[29] *Dunkley v. Evans* [1981] 1 W.L.R. 1522, DC; *D.P.P. v. Hutchinson* [1990] 2 A.C. 783, HL.

[30] *R. v. Hackney, Islington and Stoke Newington Rent Tribunal ex p. Keats* [1951] 2 K.B. 15n. See too *White and Collins v. Minister of Health* [1939] 2 K.B. 838; *supra*, para. 23–038 *et seq* for immigration cases.

[31] [1969] 2 A.C. 147.

[32] A view often expressed in the words of Lord Sumner in *R. v. Nat Bell Liquors Ltd* [1922] A.C. 128, 151, PC.

[33] This head of review raises the difficult matter of distinguishing between questions of law and questions of fact. C. T. Emery and B. Smythe, "Error of Law in Administrative Law" (1984) 100 L.Q.R. 612; J. Beatson, "The Scope of Judicial Review for Error of Law" (1984) 4 O.J.L.S. 22; G. Pitt, "Law, Fact and Casual Workers" (1985) 101 L.Q.R. 217; *post*, para. 32–015.

[34] [1981] A.C. 374. See too *R. v. Hull University Visitor, ex p. Page* [1993] A.C. 682, 707. *De Smith op. cit.* 244–249.

[35] [1981] A.C. 363. The Privy Council preferred the dissent of Geoffrey Lane L.J. in *Pearlman v. Harrow School Governers* [1979] Q.B. 56 to the view expressed in that case by Lord Denning M.R.

The possible extension of review beyond errors of law to questions of fact has been raised by the House of Lords in *R. v. Criminal Injuries Board, ex p. A.*[36]

Abuse of power

Statutes often confer upon ministers, local authorities and other public bodies **31–008** discretionary powers, for example in the area of planning law or when a trade or occupation is subject to a system of licensing. The courts, in the absence of a statutory right of appeal, cannot review the correctness of a decision made in the exercise of such a discretionary power. They may, however, interfere where the power has been improperly exercised so that the person exercising the power has acted in a way not intended by Parliament. Abuse of power, in this sense, includes exercising a power for an unauthorised purpose,[37] disregarding relevant considerations in reaching a decision[38] or taking into account irrelevant considerations.[39]

Even where a discretion seems unfettered the courts will interfere where it has been exercised in a way which thwarts or frustrates the objects of the Act conferring the power: *Padfield v. Minister of Agriculture, Fisheries and Food.*[40] A Minister possessing an apparently unlimited power to revoke licences has been held not to be entitled to use that power to revoke licences bought before the date of an announced increase in licence fees.[41]

It cannot be assumed merely from a Minister's refusal to give reasons for the way he has exercised a discretionary power that he has reached his decision by taking into account factors which he ought to have ignored or that he has disregarded factors which he ought to have regarded as relevant.[42]

Abuse of power may be either in good faith or in bad faith. An authority acts **31–009** in bad faith if it acts dishonestly, in order to achieve an object other than that for which it believes the power has been given; or maliciously, if it acts out of personal animosity. Thus a local authority which has the power of compulsory acquisition of land for civic extensions or improvements would not be entitled to acquire compulsorily if its purpose were merely to reap the benefit of enhanced values (*Municipal Council of Sydney v. Campbell*[43]); nor may an education authority which has power to dismiss teachers on educational grounds dismiss them in order to effect economy (*Hanson v. Radcliffe Urban District Council*[44]). The court may infer the purpose for which the enabling Act granted the power,

---

[36] [1999] 2 A.C. 330, HL.

[37] *e.g. R. v. Leigh* [1897] 1 Q.B. 132; power to require pensioner to present himself for medical examination was used to attempt to secure L's return to the United Kingdom to subject him to the jurisdiction of the Bankruptcy Court. See too *Webb v. Minister of Housing and Local Government* [1965] 1 W.L.R. 755; *Westminster Bank v. Minister of Housing and Local Government* [1971] A.C. 508; H. W. R. Wade (1970) 86 L.Q.R. 165; *R. v. Hillingdon L.B.C., ex p. Royco Homes* [1974] Q.B. 720.

[38] *R. v. Greater Birmingham Appeal Tribunal, ex p. Simper* [1974] Q.B. 543; *Grunwick Processing Laboratories v. A.C.A.S.* [1978] A.C. 655.

[39] *Short v. Poole Corporation* [1926] Ch. 66; *dictum* that the red hair of a teacher clearly irrelevant to consideration of exercise by a local authority of its powers and duties in connection with maintaining "efficient" schools. *Bromley L.B.C. v. G.L.C.* [1983] A.C. 768. (G.L.C. improperly influenced by terms of political manifesto).

[40] [1968] A.C. 997, *post*, p. 689.

[41] *Congreve v. Home Office* [1976] Q.B. 629. For a critical comment see G. Ganz, [1976] P.L. 14.

[42] *Gouriet v. Union of Post Office Workers* [1978] A.C. 435; *British Airways v. Laker Airways* [1985] A.C. 58.

[43] [1925] A.C. 338.

[44] [1922] 2 Ch. 490.

and hold that the power has been abused, *e.g.* where a local authority referred tenancies in bulk to a rent tribunal so as in effect to turn the tribunal into a general rent-fixing agency (*R. v. Paddington Rent Tribunal, ex p. Bell Properties Ltd*[45]). The High Court can control the exercise of statutory powers if they are being exercised otherwise than in accordance with the purpose for which they were conferred. Thus a compulsory purchase order made in 1951 in order to provide a car park was set aside as it was based on a notice to treat served in 1939 for the purpose of widening the street and creating a market hall (*Grice v. Dudley Corporation*[46]).

The question is complicated where a power is exercised both for an authorised and an unauthorised purpose.[47] The courts on the whole have tried to find the true purpose for which the power was exercised. Thus in *Westminster Corporation v. L. & N. W. Ry.*,[48] where the local authority had power to construct underground public conveniences, the court considered whether this was the true purpose which the Corporation sought to affect in acquiring land compulsorily, or whether it was merely a colourable device to enable it to make a subway for pedestrians. Where a public body has exercised a power to achieve a legitimate purpose, the fact that incidentally it achieves another purpose of its own which is not a relevant objective in the eyes of the law does not invalidate the decision. But where the purpose of the exercise is improper it is irrelevant that a legitimate purpose is also served. In *R. v. ILEA, ex p. Westminster C.C.*[49] Glidewell J. had to consider the legality of the expenditure of funds by ILEA under the Local Government Act 1972, s.142 which authorises expenditure on the publication of "information on matters relating to local government." The learned judge concluded that the publication of certain facts by ILEA was intended not merely to inform but to persuade the public to accept ILEA's views about the wisdom of the Government's education policies. The expenditure was held to be unlawful; persuasion not information had been the true purpose of the authority; its decision had been materially affected by its wish to pursue an unauthorised objective. The courts tend to avoid the question of motive, which seems to be immaterial if the purpose is within the statute (*Robins & Son Ltd v. Minister of Health*[50]), for they must not usurp the discretion given to administrative authorities.

31–010   A difficulty which has arisen in a number of cases is the extent to which a body exercising a discretionary power has the right in reaching decisions in individual cases to have regard to a general policy which it has formulated. Clearly, licensing justices who refuse all applications for licences because they have a policy of attempting to stop the sale of alcohol are not exercising the discretion vested in them.[51] But concern about drunkenness and hooliganism in the late evening may justify a general policy of not granting late licences provided that

[45] [1949] 1 K.B. 606.
[46] [1958] Ch. 339. And see *Webb v. Minister of Housing and Local Government* [1965] 1 W.L.R. 755; [1965] 2 All E.R. 195, CA, *supra.*
[47] See *e.g. Earl Fitzwilliam's Wentworth Estate Co v. Minister of Town and Country Planning* [1951] 2 K.B. 284, CA; [1952] A.C. 362, HL.
[48] [1905] A.C. 426.
[49] [1986] 1 W.L.R. 28. See also *R. v. Broadcasting Complaints Commission, ex p. Owen* [1985] Q.B. 1153, 1177 *per* May L.J.; decision lawful even although reached in reliance on a reason bad in law if Commission would have reached the same decision in reliance on other valid reasons.
[50] [1939] 1 K.B. 537.
[51] *R. v. L.C.C., ex p. Corrie* [1918] 1 K.B. 68. See too *Sagnata Investments v. Norwich Corporation* [1971] 2 Q.B. 614.

each application is genuinely considered on its merits.[52] In the words of Ackner L.J. in *R. v. Secretary of State for the Environment, ex p. Brent L.B.C.*[53] it is not necessary that each case must be approached with an open mind in the sense of an empty mind but the mind of the person exercising the discretion "must be kept 'ajar.' "

Unreasonableness

The requirement that public bodies vested with statutory powers must exercise them reasonably was asserted by Lord Macnaghten in *Westminster Corporation v. London and North Western Railway.*[54] Modern discussions of unreasonableness in the field of judicial review almost inevitably, however, start from the judgment of Lord Greene, M.R. in *Associated Provincial Picture Houses Ltd v. Wednesbury Corporation.*[55] The Master of the Rolls cited various defects which might render a decision "unreasonable," of the kind discussed in the previous pages. He went on, however, to envisage the possibility of a decision being open to challenge on the ground that it is unreasonable in the sense that, in the view of the court, it was a decision which no reasonable body could reach. Lord Greene's judgment has been frequently quoted in subsequent cases and is so well known that later judges often refer to "the *Wednesbury* principle" without any further explanation. In *Secretary of State for Education and Science v. Tameside Metropolitan Borough Council*[56] the House of Lords referred to Lord Greene's judgment in the *Wednesbury* case and Lord Diplock said,

31–011

"In public law 'unreasonable' as descriptive of the way in which a public authority has purported to exercise a discretion vested in it by statute has become a term of legal art. To fall within this expression it must be conduct which no sensible authority acting with due appreciation of its responsibilities would have decided to adopt."

Because of the frequent citation of Lord Greene's words it is important, as judges have emphasised, not to treat them as a legislative text, not to take them out of context and to read the whole of the judgment since at different places the principle of unreasonableness is defined (or described) in different terms.[57]

Usually where an administrative decision has been quashed on the ground of unreasonableness at least one of the specific vitiating factors already discussed has been held to have been present. Is, however, unreasonableness merely a short hand way of referring to those factors or does it go beyond them? While there is no clear judicial authority the current tendency of the courts to widen the scope of judicial review suggests that it would be unsafe to assert that unreasonableness must be confined to the former of the two meanings, *i.e.* a synonym for the

31–012

---

[52] *R. v. Torbay Licensing Justices, ex p. White* [1980] 2 All E.R. 25. See too *Docherty v. South Tyneside Borough, The Times*, July 3, 1982; *R. v. Secretary of State for the Home Dept., ex p. Bennett, The Times*, August 18, 1986, CA. The leading authority for the legality of the adoption in principle of a policy is *British Oxygen v. Board of Trade* [1971] A.C. 616, HL.

[53] [1982] Q.B. 593, DC.

[54] [1905] A.C. 426.

[55] [1948] 1 K.B. 223. (Condition attached to licence for opening of cinema on Sunday that no child under the age of 15 should be admitted not unreasonable).

[56] [1977] A.C. 1014. See *post*, para. 32–020.

[57] *Pickwell v. Camden L.B.C.* [1983] Q.B. 962, *per* Ormrod L.J.; *R. v. Chief Registrar of Friendly Societies, ex p. New Cross Bldg. Society* [1984] 2 W.L.R. 370, *per* Griffiths L.J.; *R. v. Home Secretary, ex p. Benwell* [1984] 3 W.L.R. 843, 855 *per* Hodgson J.

various specific issues discussed earlier. The argument for the widest possible meaning is strengthened—or at least not weakened—by Lord Diplock's choice in the *GCHQ* case of the term irrationality to refer to cases falling within the *Wednesbury* principle.[58] He went on to explain that head of review as applying to "a decision which is so outrageous in its defiance of logic or of accepted moral standards that no sensible person who had applied his mind to the question to be decided could have arrived at it."

Byelaws may be held void for unreasonableness. In *Kruse v. Johnson*[59] Lord Russell of Killowen C.J. said that local byelaws are not unreasonable merely because particular judges may think that they go farther than is necessary or convenient; but a court might hold them unreasonable if they were found to be partial or unequal in their operation between classes, or if they were manifestly unjust, disclosed bad faith, or involved such oppressive or gratuitous interference with the rights of those subject to them as could find no justification in the minds of reasonable men. Applying this test, the court held that the byelaw in question, which authorised a householder or police constable to request a person to desist from playing a musical instrument within fifty yards of any dwelling house, was not unreasonable.

In subsequent cases the courts have emphasised the heavy burden lying on anyone who challenges the reasonableness of a byelaw.[60]

It is doubtful whether the principle laid down in *Kruse v. Johnson* applies to delegated legislation[61] although it might be open to argument that a particular rule or regulation is so unreasonable that it must be beyond the limits envisaged by Parliament. The special status of Immigration Rules made under the Immigration Act 1971[62] has been held to justify the courts applying to them the test of reasonableness as laid down in *Kruse v. Johnson*.[63]

Natural justice: procedural impropriety[64]

31–013   Natural justice, at least as that phrase is normally used by lawyers, refers principally to two fundamental principles of procedure: that whoever takes a decision should be impartial, having no personal interest in the outcome of the case (*nemo judex in re sua*) and that a decision should not be taken until the person affected by it has had an opportunity to state his case (*audi alteram partem*). Natural justice may sometimes be used in a wider sense to refer to a

---

[58] *ante*, para. 31–011
[59] [1898] 2 Q.B. 91. "The judgment in *Kruse v. Johnson* has been quoted so frequently in subsequent cases that it has almost been erected into a sacred text"; *Belfast Corporation v. Daly* [1963] N.I. 78, 88, *per* Black L.J. For byelaws made by non-elected bodies see *Cinnamond v. British Airports Authority* [1980] 1 W.L.R. 582; *British Airways Authority, v. Ashton* [1983] 3 All E.R. 6; *R. v. British Airways Authority, ex p. Wheatley* [1983] R.T.R. 466, CA.
[60] *Burnley B.C. v. England* (1978) 76 L.G.R. 393; 77 L.G.R. 227; *Startin v. Solihull M.B.C.* [1979] R.T.R. 228.
[61] *Sparks v. Edward Ash Ltd* [1943] 1 K.B. 222, CA; *Taylor v. Brighton B.C.* [1947] K.B. 737, CA. In *Maynard v. Osmond* [1977] Q.B. 240 the Court of Appeal rejected a claim that a ministerial regulation was unreasonable; hence the question of invalidity on that ground did not arise. See further A Wharam, "Judicial Control of Delegated Legislation: the Test of Reasonableness" (1973) 36 M.L.R. 611; J. P. Casey, "Ministerial Orders and Review for Unreasonableness" [1978] P.L. 130.
[62] *ante*, para. 23–024 and para. 29–004.
[63] *R. v. Immigration Appeal Tribunal, ex p. Begum*, The Times, July 24, 1986.
[64] D. J. Hewitt, *Natural Justice* (1972); Paul Jackson, *Natural Justice* (2nd ed., 1979); H. H. Marshall, *Natural Justice* (1959); G. P. Flick, *Natural Justice: Principles and Practical Application* (2nd ed., 1984).

number of fundamental principles which are said to underlie the common law[65] but in these pages attention will be directed to natural justice in its narrower sense.

The principles of natural justice were originally applied to the process by which courts themselves made their decisions. A breach of natural justice was one of the grounds on which the decision of a lower court could be upset by a higher court. In the course of time these principles came to be applied to administrative authorities.

There is authority for regarding the requirements of "natural justice" as a special part of the *ultra vires* rule, on the ground that a decision made contrary to the principles of natural justice, when the rights of particular individuals are adversely affected, is no decision within the terms of the enabling Act.[66]

1. A man may not be a judge in his own cause[67]

The law relating to disqualification for bias—or the appearance of bias— **31–014** extends beyond the ground covered by the maxim that a man may not be a judge in his own cause to cover any circumstances where the facts may lead to a real likelihood of bias. Previous case law must now be read in the light of the decision of the House of Lords in *R. v. Bow Street Metropolitan Stipendiary Magistrate, ex p. Pinochet Ugarte (No. 2)*[68] and of the Court of Appeal in *Locabail (UK) Ltd v. Bayfield Properties Ltd*.[69] Formerly the distinction was drawn between financial interest, where it was said that any interest, however small, entailed automatic disqualification on the ground of bias[70] and allegations of bias on other grounds where it was necessary to demonstrate the requisite degree of likelihood or danger of bias. In *Pinochet (No. 2), however*, the House of Lords explained that financial interest was only one way in which a judge might be regarded as being personally involved in the case before him. A similar, automatic disqualification would arise wherever a judge had a strong personal interest in the case before him.

Not every financial interest leads to automatic disqualification. An interest can be disregarded if it is *de minimis* or nominal and indirect.[71]

Cases not involving automatic disqualification may arise where a judge is said to have preconceived notions on the merits of a claim, acquaintance with one of the parties or for any reason has given cause to doubt his ability to determine the case before him with judicial impartiality. No doubt to discourage future litigation the Court of Appeal in *Locabail (UK) Ltd* expressly stated that it could not envisage circumstances in which a challenge on the ground of partiality could

---

[65] *Ong Ah Chuan v. Public Prosecutor* [1981] A.C. 648.
[66] *Spackman v. Plumstead District Board of Works* (1885) 10 App.Cas. 229, *per* Lord Selbourne L.C.; *Errington v. Minister of Health* [1935] 1 K.B. 249, 268, *per* Greer L.J., and p. 279, *per* Maugham L.J. *cf. General Medical Council v. Spackman* [1943] A.C. 627, 640, *per* Lord Wright; *White v. Kuzych* [1951] A.C. 585 (P.C.) *per* Viscount Simon at p. 600.
[67] See D. E. C. Yale, "*Iudex propria causa*, an historical excursus" (1974) 33 C.L.J. 80.
[68] [2000] 1 A.C. 119.
[69] [2000] Q.B. 451, CA.
[70] *Dimes v. Proprietors of Grand Junction Canal* (1852) 3 H.L. Cas. 759. (Decree of Lord Cottenham L.C. set aside when it was discovered that he was a shareholder in the company involved in the litigation before him.)
[71] *Locabail (UK) Ltd v. Bayfield Properties Ltd, supra. R. v. Mulvihill* [1990] 1 W.L.R. 438, CA (Judge not disqualified from presiding at trial of person accused of robbing a branch of a bank of which the judge was a shareholder).

succeed which was based on the religion, ethnic national origin, gender, age, class, means or sexual orientation of the judge. Nor, ordinarily, could an objection be based on the judge's social or educational or service or employment background or history.[72]

In cases alleging non-automatic bias the claimant must satisfy the court that the facts establish a real danger of bias: *R. v. Gough*.[73] The court will not set aside a decision on the basis of "mere vague suspicions of whimsical, capricious and unreasonable people ... mere flimsy elusive morbid suspicions."[74]

31–015   In some cases a decision may be quashed not because of the likelihood or reasonable suspicion of bias but on the principle enunciated by Lord Hewart C.J. in *The King v. Sussex Justices, ex p. McCarthy*.[75] The conviction of McCarthy for a motoring offence was quashed because the clerk to the justices, a member of a firm of solicitors who were to represent the plaintiff in civil proceedings arising out of the collision in connection with which McCarthy was charged, retired with the justices, although in fact he did not give them any advice on the conviction. Lord Hewart L.C.J. said in that case: "A long line of cases shows that it is not merely of some importance, but is of fundamental importance that justice should not only be done but should manifestly and undoubtedly be seen to be done." Where a social worker involved in adoption proceedings retired with the justices their determination was quashed because justice had not been seen to be done.[76]

2. *"Audi alteram partem"*

31–016   Each party must have reasonable notice of the case he has to meet; and he must be given an opportunity of stating his case, and answering (if he can) any arguments put forward against it. In criminal cases this elementary principle of justice is expressed in the saying that "no one ought to be condemned unheard." As was quaintly stated in *Dr Bentley's Case* (1723)[77]: "Even God himself did not pass sentence upon Adam before he was called upon to make his defence."

The maxim *audi alteram partem*, where it applies, does not mean that a person is entitled to be heard orally.[78] Nor does the maxim necessarily mean that a person has the right to have his case determined by the person who heard the evidence at first instance. Thus in *Local Government Board v. Arlidge*[79] the House of Lords refused a house owner's application to quash a decision of the Local Government Board confirming a closing order made by a borough council, although he had not been told which members of the Board gave the decision,

---

[72] p. 480.
[73] [1993] A.C. 646.
[74] *R. v. Queen's County JJ.* [1908] 2 I.R. 285, 294 *per* Lord O'Brien C.J.
[75] [1924] 1 K.B. 256, 259. *R. v. Lower Munslow Justices, ex p. Pudge* [1950] 2 All E.R. 756. See also *R. v. East Kerrier Justices, ex p. Mundy* [1952] 2 Q.B. 719; *Practice Note (Justices' Clerks)* [1953] 1 W.L.R. 1416; [1953] 2 All E.R. 1306; *Metropolitan Properties v. Lannon* [1969] 1 Q.B. 577; *R. v. Altrincham Justices, ex p. Pennington* [1975] Q.B. 549.
[76] *Re B (Adoption by Parents)* [1975] Fam. 127.
[77] *R. v. Chancellor of Cambridge University* (1716) 1 Str. 557. R. F. V. Heuston has pointed out that divine punishment may be administered without a preliminary hearing: *Belshazzar's Feast, Dan v: Essays in Constitutional Law* (2nd ed., 1964) p. 185.
[78] *Board of Education v. Rice* [1911] A.C. 179 HL, *per* Lord Loreburn L.C. And see *Lloyd v. McMahon* [1987] A.C. 625, HL; *R. v. Army Board, ex p. Anderson* [1992] Q.B. 169.
[79] [1915] A.C. 120.

and had not been given an oral hearing by the Board or allowed to see the report of the inspector. It would, in the view of the House of Lords, be unrealistic and impracticable to expect a large department of state to deal with each case before it in the way in which a court might be expected to.[80] Natural justice requires adequate warning of a hearing and details of the charges to be met in order to allow a party to prepare his case properly.[81] Legal representation is not necessarily essential to a fair hearing. None the less the gravity of a charge, or the consequences of an adverse decision, may require a tribunal to allow legal representation. The question must turn, in each case, on the exercise by the tribunal concerned of a genuine discretion as opposed to the application of an inflexible rule.[82] Nor does natural justice require that reasons for decisions should be given.[83] The giving of reasons, however, may be required by resort to the concert of fairness.[84]

The importance of natural justice in administrative law lies in the wide range **31–017** of administrative powers which must be exercised in accordance with the two principles discussed in the previous pages. In *Board of Education v. Rice*[85] Lord Loreburn said that to "act in good faith and fairly listen to both sides ... is a duty lying upon everyone who decides anything." Throughout succeeding years in this century, however, the courts took a more cautious view and only required public bodies to observe the rules of natural justice when they were acting "judicially," a concept which was interpreted restrictively. A decisive change in judicial attitude occurred in *Ridge v. Baldwin*.[86] Under the Municipal Corporations Act 1882, s.191(4) a Watch Committee was empowered at any time to suspend or dismiss any borough constable whom the Committee thought to have been negligent in the discharge of his duty or otherwise unfit to carry out his duty. The Chief Constable of Brighton had been acquitted at the Old Bailey on charges of corruption, but the judge in the trial of two of his subordinates cast aspersions on his leadership of the force, and remarked that a new chief constable was needed. The Watch Committee then dismissed him for neglect of duty, but without formulating any specific charge or giving him an opportunity to be heard except that his solicitor addressed the Committee at one of two meetings. The House of Lords, reversing a unanimous Court of Appeal, gave judgment for the Chief Constable. Their Lordships held that the rules of natural justice applied, so that the Watch Committee ought to have informed him of the charges and given him an opportunity to be heard. Merely to describe a statutory function as "administrative," "judicial," "quasi-judicial," said Lord Reid, is not in itself enough to settle the requirements of natural justice. Where officials and others

---

[80] But see *post* para. 31–019 on sub-delegation. The question, in the case of statutory bodies, is one of statutory interpretation.

[81] *Sloan v. General Medical Council* [1970] 1 W.L.R. 1130; *R. v. Thames Magistrates' Court, ex p. Polemis* [1974] 1 W.L.R. 1371.

[82] *R. v. Board of Visitors of H.M. Prison, The Maze, ex. p. Hone* [1988] A.C. 379, HL.

[83] *R. v. Gaming Board for Great Britain, ex p. Benaim* [1970] 2 Q.B. 417, CA.

[84] *R. v. Home Secretary, ex p. Doody* [1994] 1 A.C. 531, HL. See too *R. v. Secretary of State for the Home Department, ex p. Fayed* [1998] 1 W.L.R. 763, CA. The uncertain scope of this requirement is clear from the decision in *R. v. Higher Education Funding Council, ex p. Institute of Dental Surgery* [1994] 1 W.L.R. 242. In further consideration of the requirement the Privy Council drew attention for the future to the importance of Art. 6(1) of the E.C.H.R: *Stefan v. G.M.C.* [1999] 1 W.L.R. 1293.

[85] [1911] A.C. 179, 182.

[86] [1964] A.C. 40.

have power to make decisions affecting the rights of individuals, the rules of natural justice must be observed.

31–018   In *Schmidt v. Secretary of State for Home Affairs*[87] Lord Denning M.R. extended the scope of natural justice to decisions involving *legitimate expectations*. In subsequent cases the House of Lords has contrasted legitimate expectations in the sphere of public law with rights in the private sphere.[88] A legitimate expectation can arise from past conduct, *e.g.* regularly granting a hearing before issuing licences,[89] or an assurance, *e.g.* that any illegal immigrant who gives himself up to the authorities will not be deported without being given a hearing.[90] There seems no reason why a legitimate expectation cannot exist in the private sphere. A non-statutory body which governs a sport may be bound to grant a hearing to an applicant for a licence if it has done so in the past: *McInnes v. Onslow Fane*.[91] Whether a legitimate expectation exists is a question for the court to determine. The hope of a prisoner that the existing rules for granting parole will not be altered does not amount to a legitimate expectation that the Secretary of State will not change them in the exercise of his statutory powers: *In Re Findlay*.[92] An expectation created by an assurance can be terminated by notice.[93]

Particularly in the context of legitimate expectations the courts, following the lead of Lord Diplock in the *GCHQ* case,[94] increasingly refer to *procedural impropriety* rather than breach of natural justice. It has been objected that it is "hard on that old faithful friend [Natural Justice] which has rendered such signal service, if it is now to be cast aside."[95] The new phrase, however, seems to provide grounds of review going beyond what traditionally had been regarded as constituting breaches of natural justice. Lord Diplock in the *GCHQ* case included within procedural impropriety breach of statutory rules of procedure which did not necessarily amount to a breach of natural justice. Later cases suggest the phrase can cover various forms of "unfairness," such as going back on an

---

[87] [1969] 2 Ch. 149, 170. In *Kioa v. West* (1985) 62 A.L.R. 321 Brennan J. said the seed planted by Lord Denning in *Schmidt* had subsequently grown luxuriantly. (The judgments in *Kioa v. West* offer exhaustive analyses of the concept of legitimate expectation.) See further, P. Cane, "Natural Justice and Legitimate Expectation" (1980) 54 A.L.J. 546; S. Churches, "Justice and Executive Discretion in Australia" [1980] P.L. 397; K. Mackie, "Expectations and Natural Justice" (1985) 59 A.L.J. 33.

[88] *O'Reilly v. Mackman* [1983] 2 A.C. 237; *Council of Civil Service Unions v. Minister for the Civil Service* [1985] A.C. 374.

[89] *O'Reilly v. Mackman, supra* (Hearings normally granted to prisoners before revoking remission—to which there is no right—for misconduct); *Council of Civil Service Unions v. Minister for Civil Service supra, per* Lord Diplock; *R. v. Wear Valley D.C., ex p. Binks* [1985] 2 All E.R. 699; noted (1986) 102 L.Q.R. 24.

[90] *Att.-Gen. of Hong Kong v. Ng Yuen Shiu* (1983) 2 A.C. 629, PC; noted (1983) 99 L.Q.R. 499; *R. v. Liverpool Corporation, ex p. Liverpool Taxi Fleet Operations' Association* [1972] 2 Q.B. 299.

[91] [1978] 1 W.L.R. 1520.

[92] [1985] A.C. 319. Followed, *R. v. Minister of Defence, ex p. Walker* [2000] 1 W.L.R. 806. "The ministry was entitled to change its policy: see *In Re Finlay, per* Lord Hoffmann at p. 815. See also *R. v. Secretary of State for the Home Dept, ex p. Hindley* [2001] 1 A.C. 410, HL. Nor can landowners rely on the more generous terms of treaty when land is compulsorily acquired under the less generous terms of legislation: an "elementary fallacy" that treaties give rise to rights enforceable in British courts: *Winfat Enterprise HK Co Ltd v. Att.-Gen. of Hong Kong* [1985] A.C. 733. (The full background is to be found in [1983] H.K.L.R. 211; [1984] H.K.L.R. 32.)

[93] *Hughes v. D.H.S.S.* [1985] A.C. 776.

[94] *Council of Civil Service Unions v. Minister for the Civil Service, supra.*

[95] H. W. R. Wade, (1985) 101 L.Q.R. 153, 155. Lord Scarman described the new terminology as "a humdrum modernism for breach of natural justice"; [1990] P.L. 490.

assurance,[96] giving misleading advice on the grounds on which a minister exercises his discretion[97] or the unreasonable manner in which a decision is reached.[98] In this "developing field of law"[99] the courts are now prepared to talk of substantive legitimate expectations where public bodies might have so acted that it would be unfair to go back on the decision challenged.

Sub-delegation of powers[1]

The prima facie rule is that a person or body to whom powers are entrusted **31–019** may not delegate them to another, *delegatus non potest delegare*[2]—unless expressly or impliedly authorised to do so.[3] Thus in *Allingham v. Minister of Agriculture*[4] a Divisional Court held that the Bedfordshire War Agricultural Committee, to which the Minister of Agriculture had validly delegated his power under Defence Regulations to give directions with respect to the cultivation of land, and which had decided that sugar beet should be grown on eight acres of the appellant's land, had no power to delegate to their executive officer the power to specify the particular field to be cultivated. On the other hand, in *Smith v. London Transport Executive*[5] the Executive was validly acting as delegate of the British Transport Commission in operating a bus service. Certain powers, such as that conferred by Defence Regulations on the Home Secretary to intern persons of hostile origin or association,[6] must be exercised by the Minister personally; but generally it is contemplated that a Minister may authorise civil servants in his department to perform routine administrative functions on his behalf.[7] This is not delegation in the strict sense, for the act of the official is really the act of the Minister, who retains control and responsibility. In *Woollett v. Minister of Agriculture and Fisheries*,[8] where members of an agricultural land tribunal were to be appointed by the Minister, it was held that they could be appointed by X on behalf of the Minister, but not by X in his capacity as the secretary of the tribunal. In *Vine v. National Dock Labour Board*,[9] where the Board had purported to delegate its disciplinary powers to a committee, the House of Lords said that both the nature of the duty and the character of the person to whom it is entrusted have to be considered. Judicial authority cannot normally be sub-delegated; administrative powers sometimes may but often may not be sub-delegated; as regards

---

[96] *R. v. I.R.C., ex p. Preston* [1985] A.C. 835.

[97] *R. v. Home Secretary, ex p. Asif Khan* [1984] 1 W.L.R. 1337. ("Bad and grossly unfair administration . . . positively cruel"; *per* Parker L.J. at p. 1348).

[98] *Wheeler v. Leicester City Council* [1985] A.C. 1054.

[99] *R. v. North and East Devon Health Authority, ex p. Coughlan* [2001] Q.B. 213, 242 *per* Lord Woolf M.R. See Søren Schønberg, *Legitimate Expectations in Administrative Law* (Oxford, 2000).

[1] See D. Lanham, "Delegation and the Alter Ego Principle," (1984) 100 L.Q.R. 587.

[2] *Delegata potestas non potest delegari*: 2 Co.Inst. 597.

[3] Building Act 1984, s.13, for example, expressly provides that the Secretary of State may delegate to "a person or body" his powers under s.12 to approve particular building materials as satisfying statutory requirements.

[4] [1948] 1 All E.R. 780, DC. And see *Ellis v. Dubowski* [1921] 3 K.B. 621.

[5] [1951] A.C. 555, HL.

[6] See *Liversidge v. Anderson* [1942] A.C. 206, HL.

[7] *Carltona Ltd v. Commissioners of Works* [1943] 2 All E.R. 560 (requisitioning of land); *R. v. Skinner* [1968] 2 Q.B. 700, CA (approval of breathalyser); *Re Golden Chemical Products Ltd* [1976] Ch. 300 (presentation of winding-up petition under s.35 of the Companies Act 1967); *R. v. Secretary of State for the Home Department ex p. Oladehinde* [1991] 1 A.C. 254, HL. (Home Secretary entitled to authorise senior officials in his department to make decisions to depart on his behalf.)

[8] [1955] 1 Q.B. 103.

[9] [1957] A.C. 488; approving *Barnard v. National Dock Labour Board* [1953] 2 Q.B. 18, CA.

the disciplinary powers in this case, whether called judicial or quasi-judicial, their Lordships held that they could not be sub-delegated.[10]

When a power has been validly delegated by one authority to another, the exercise of the power by the latter must be within the power delegated by the former,[11] and any conditions attached to the delegation must be complied with.[12]

Estoppel

31–020   The converse of the problem discussed in the preceding sections is that which arises where an individual maintains that a public body's exercise of a statutory power is valid while the authority concerned seeks to challenge its validity. A dispute of this nature raises the question of the extent to which the doctrine of estoppel is applicable to public authorities.[13] It might seem unjust that a citizen who has erected a building in the belief, induced by an official of a planning authority, that everything was in order should have to demolish that building because the authority alleges that the official had no power to grant permission.[14] On the other hand, to apply the doctrine of estoppel to public bodies might be thought to destroy the *ultra vires* doctrine by allowing them to extend their powers by making representations which would bind them by estoppel.[15] Recent developments in judicial review have suggested a solution to the dilemma. For a public body to attempt to go back on a decision which it has made might be "unfair" and judicial review would be available where the action in question would have been equivalent to a breach of a representation giving rise to an estoppel in the case of a private individual: *R. v. Inland Revenue Commissioners, ex p. Preston.*[16] Another way of reaching a similar result is to say that the re-opening of a decision is "unreasonable" or "irrational": *R. v. West Glamorgan C.C., ex p. Gherssary.*[17] The limits to this new approach are, at present, unclear. It could hardly be applied where a public body had attempted to do what it had no power to do at all.[18] In some cases it might be reasonable (or rational or fair) for a public body to go back on its previous decision after informing the person

---

[10] See also *Re S (A Barrister)* [1970] 1 Q.B. 160; *R. v. Race Relations Board, ex p. Selvarajan* [1975] 1 W.L.R. 1686; Paul Jackson (1974) 90 L.Q.R. 158; (1975) 91 L.Q.R. 469. For valid subdelegation of an administrative power see *Meaden v. Wood, The Times*, April 30, 1985, DC (Home Secretary as police authority, entitled to delegate regulation of street collections under statutory powers to Commissioner of Metropolitan Police).

[11] *Smith v. London Transport Executive, ante.*

[12] *Blackpool Corporation v. Locker* [1948] 1 K.B. 349, CA: Minister delegated to local authorities power to requisition houses, subject to making provision for disposal of furniture; requisition *ultra vires* because conditions not complied with.

[13] For the position of the Crown, see *post*, para. 33–016.

[14] *Wells v. Minister of Housing and Local Government* [1967] 1 W.L.R. 1000; *Lever Finance v. Westminster L.B.C.* [1971] 1 Q.B. 222. See also *H.T.V. v. Price Commission* [1976] I.C.R. 170; *Re Liverpool Taxi Owners Association* [1972] 2 Q.B. 299.

[15] *Minister of Agriculture and Fisheries v. Mathews* [1950] 1 K.B. 148; *Rhyl U.D.C. v. Rhyl Amusements* [1959] 1 W.L.R. 465; *Southend-on-Sea Corporation v. Hodgson (Wickford)* [1962] 1 Q.B. 416, DC; *Western Fish Products Ltd v. Penwith D.C.* [1981] 2 All E.R. 204; (1978) 77 L.G.R. 185, CA; *Rootkin v. Kent C.C.* [1981] 1 W.L.R. 1186, CA. See further P. P. Craig, "Representations by Public Bodies" (1977) 93 L.Q.R. 398; G. Ganz, "Estoppel and *Res Judicata* in Administrative Law" [1965] P.L. 237; M. A. Fazal, "Reliability of Official Acts and Advice" [1972] P.L. 43.

[16] [1985] A.C. 835, HL.

[17] *The Times*, December 18, 1985.

[18] *e.g.* purporting to create a lease when the authority concerned had no power to do so: *Minister of Agriculture and Fisheries v. Mathews, supra.*

affected of its wish to do so and affording a full hearing before reaching a new conclusion.

II. Private Law: Ordinary Judicial Control

Where a tort or breach of contract has been committed by a public authority,   **31–021**
its liability may be said to be prima facie the same as that of a private individual. The authority is moreover responsible for the torts and contracts of its employees and agents in the same way as an ordinary individual or corporation. This presumption, however, is subject to certain important qualifications. The great difference between public authorities and private individuals is that the former have so many and various *powers* conferred on them which ordinary individuals or corporations do not have, and which may cause harm to private citizens but the proper exercise of which does not entitle an injured person to a right of action. Local authorities, for example, have power to order houses to be demolished, to acquire land compulsorily, and to do works which would ordinarily constitute nuisances. These powers are given because the authority is acting on behalf of the public, and where public and private interests conflict, policy generally requires that the former must prevail.

On the other hand, public authorities are mostly the creations of statute, and have only such powers as are expressly conferred by statute. The citizen may therefore find that a contract which he thought he had entered into is void as being beyond the power of the authority to make.

Further, when the citizen has a remedy he may find that it does not lie against the public authority, but only against the person who appeared to be (but who in law was not) the servant of that authority.

Lastly, the fact that a public authority has failed to perform some duty does not necessarily mean that a citizen can take proceedings against it either to compel it to perform the duty or for damages for failing to do so.

Liability in contract

Statutory public authorities, such as local authorities and public corporations,   **31–022**
have a general power to make contracts in the discharge of their functions. They may have specific contractual powers as well. If a public authority enters into a contract in relation to some matter that is beyond its powers—a question of statutory interpretation—the contract is *ultra vires* and void.[19] For *intra vires* contracts, public authorities are generally liable in the ordinary way, *e.g.* a contract by a local authority to sell coke (*Bradford Corporation v. Myers*[20]).

Some countries, such as France, have a theory of "administrative contracts," whereby many of the contracts made by public authorities are governed by different rules from private-law contracts.[21] English law has no theory of "administrative" or "public" contracts, but a public authority cannot by contract bind itself not to exercise powers conferred on it by statute (*Ayr Harbour*

[19] *Rhyl U.D.C. v. Rhyl Amusements* [1959] 1 W.L.R. 465; [1959] 1 All E.R. 257. But see *ante*, para. 31–020 as to the effect of estoppel.
[20] [1916] 1 A.C. 242, HL.
[21] H. Street, *Governmental Liability*, pp. 81–84; L. N. Brown and J. Bell, *French Administrative Law* (5th ed., 1998), Chap. 8. French public authorities may also enter into private-law contracts, *e.g.* a commercial lease.

Trustees v. Oswald[22]). The exact scope of this principle is not clear. It has been suggested that the underlying principle is that of governmental effectiveness, so that "no contract would be enforced in any case where some essential governmental activity would be thereby rendered impossible or seriously impeded."[23] Such a contract, it is suggested, is not void if it is the kind of contract that the authority has power to make, but it is not specifically enforceable. This leaves open the question of compensation to the other contracting party, which is due in justice but for which the common law does not seem to make provision. If this suggestion is sound, it applies to public authorities generally the principle of Crown contracts stated in the *Amphitrite* case.[24]

Agreements between public bodies and private individuals which appear to possess the characteristics of a contract may be held not to constitute a contract when the agreement is one where the terms are determined by statute.[25]

Liability for nuisance

31–023   There is a presumption that statutory powers are not intended to be exercised in such a way as to cause a nuisance, *e.g.* that the power of a local authority to build hospitals does not authorise the erection of a small-pox hospital in a residential area. If the power is *imperative, i.e.* imposes a duty to perform some act in a certain manner, so that it appears expressly or by necessary implication that it cannot be performed without causing a nuisance, then a nuisance may be committed[26] but if the power is expressly or impliedly *permissive, i.e.* the performance of the act is merely rendered not illegal in itself, then ways and means must be found to prevent its causing a nuisance. The burden of proving that the power is imperative rests on the party purporting to act thereunder (*Metropolitan Asylum District v. Hill*[27]). Similar considerations arise where fumes from a power station injure neighbouring property (*Corporation of Manchester v. Farnworth*[28]).

A nuisance may be caused either by an act or an omission, so that where this tort is committed the distinction between misfeasance and non-feasance, is irrelevant (*Pride of Derby Angling Association Ltd v. British Celanese Ltd*[29]).

---

[22] (1883) 8 App.Cas. 623, HL, *per* Lord Blackburn at p. 634. And see *York Corporation v. Henry Leetham & Son* [1924] 1 Ch. 557; *Birkdale District Electricity Supply Co v. Southport Corporation* [1926] A.C. 355, *per* Lord Birkenhead at p. 364; *William Cory & Son Ltd v. City of London Corporation* [1951] 1 K.B. 8; *Dowty Boulton Paul v. Wolverhampton Corporation* [1971] 1 W.L.R. 204; *Triggs v. Staines U.D.C.* [1969] 1 Ch. 10; *Leicester (Earl of) v. Wells-next-the-Sea U.D.C.* [1973] Ch. 110; *Cudgen Rutile (No. 2) Ltd v. Chalk* [1975] A.C. 520; *Royal Borough of Windsor and Maidenhead v. Brandrose Investments* [1983] 1 W.L.R. 509.

[23] J. D. B. Mitchell, *The Contracts of Public Authorities* (1954), p. 7. And see Mitchell, "Limitations on the Contractual Liability of Public Authorities" (1950) 13 M.L.R. 318, 455; "Theory of Public Contract Law" (1951) 63 Jur.Rev. 60.

[24] *Rederiaktiebolaget Amphitrite v. The King* [1921] 2 K.B. 500; *post*, para. 33–006.

[25] *W. v. Essex C.C.* [1999] Fam. 90, CA, following *Norweb Plc v. Dixon* [1995] 1 W.L.R. 636. See further [1972] P.L. 97.

[26] See *Department of Transport v. N. W. Water Authority* [1984] A.C. 336, HL; *Allen v. Gulf Oil Refining Ltd* [1981] A.C. 1001, HL.

[27] (1881) 6 App. Cas. 193, HL. *cf. Hammersmith and City Ry v. Brand* (1869) L.R. 4 H.L. 171; *Edgington v. Swindon Corporation* [1939] 1 K.B. 86; *Marriage v. East Norfolk Rivers Catchment Board* [1950] 1 K.B. 284.

[28] [1930] A.C. 171, HL. See also *R. v. Epping (Waltham Abbey), ex p. Burlinson* [1947] 2 All E.R. 537, DC.

[29] [1953] Ch. 149, CA.

Liability for negligence

Even where a statutory power is bound to interfere with private rights to some **31–024** extent, the power must be exercised with due care towards those likely to be affected. The leading case is the decision of the House of Lords concerning one of the first large public corporations, *Mersey Docks and Harbour Board v. Gibbs*,[30] where the Board was held liable to the owners of a ship and her cargo for damage caused by its negligence in leaving a mud bank at the entrance to the docks.[31]

So local authorities have been held liable for damage caused by negligence due to leaving a heap of stones unlighted on the highway (*Foreman v. Corporation of Canterbury*[32]), due to failing to detect a leak in the water supply system (*Corporation of Manchester v. Markland*[33]), and to carelessly inserting or failing to maintain a traffic stud (*Skilton v. Epsom and Ewell Urban District Council*[34]).

Nonetheless, the application of the law of negligence to public bodies can give rise to particular problems. Thus the status of the defendant as a public body may be a relevant consideration in determining whether it would be "fair, just and reasonable" to impose a duty of care.[35] In the case of actions against the police the courts have progressed from refusing to find a duty of care to individual citizens owed by police investigating crimes[36] to the existence of an immunity from action in such circumstances.[37] (Further litigation is likely in these areas, following the Human Rights Act and the decision of the European Court on Human Rights in *Osman v. United Kingdom*[38]).

The difficulty of establishing negligence against public authorities is illustrated by *Stovin v. Wise*[39] where a road accident had occurred as the result of a highway authority's failure to remove, under its statutory powers, a large bank of earth which obscured the view of users of the highway. The speech of Lord Hoffmann, speaking for the three law lords constituting the majority, expressed serious doubts about imposing liability in negligence on a public body for failure to *exercise* a statutory power, as opposed to cases involving damage arising from a defective use of a statutory power.[40]

---

[30] (1866) L.R. 1 H.L. 93. And see *Geddis v. Proprietors of the Bann Reservoir* (1878) 3 App. Cas. 430.

[31] *post*, para. 32–021.

[32] (1871) L.R. 6 Q.B. 214.

[33] [1934] 2 K.B. 101.

[34] [1937] 1 K.B. 112.

[35] *Caparo Industries plc v. Dickman* [1990] 2 A.C. 605, HL; *X (Minors) v. Bedfordshire C.C.* [1995] 2 A.C. 633, HL; *Barrett v. Enfield L.B.C.* [1999] 3 W.L.R. 79, HL; [1999] L.G.R. 473.

[36] *Hill v. Chief Constable of West Yorkshire* [1989] A.C. 53, HL. (The Yorkshire Ripper: no duty owed to relatives of victims of the killer.)

[37] *Ancell v. McDermott* [1993] 4 All E.R. 355, CA. (No liability to road user injured by hazardous conditions when the police had failed to place warning signs, although aware of danger); *Osman v. Ferguson* [1993] 4 All E.R. 344, CA. (Action alleging negligent failure to protect young boy from injury at hands of man known to the police to be obsessed with the boy, struck out.) Contrast *Swinney v. Chief Constable of Northumbria Police* [1996] 3 All E.R. 449, CA. (Action for failing to protect confidentiality of police informant: CA refused to strike out claim in negligence.)

[38] [1999] Fam.Law 86. See *Barrett*, *supra* n. 35, *per* Lord Browne-Wilkinson at pp. 84–85.

[39] [1996] 2 A.C. 923, HL.

[40] The *East Suffolk Catchment Board v. Kent* [1941] A.C. 74, HL returns to judicial favour after a period in the wilderness following *Anns v. Merton L.B.C.* [1978] A.C. 728, HL. For a critical comment on *Stovin*, see R. A. Buckley, "Negligence in the Public Sphere: Is Clarity Possible?" (2000) 51 N.I.L.Q. 25. See also, S. H. Bailey and M. J. Bowman, "Public Authority Negligence Revisited", (2000) 59 Camb L.J. 85.

Failure to perform statutory duties

31–025   Whether a public authority is liable for damages to a private individual for injury caused by the failure to perform a statutory duty, depends on the facts of the case and the interpretation of the statute imposing the duty. The plaintiff has to show that the duty was owed to himself and not merely to the public generally, that Parliament intended to confer on members of the class to which he belongs a private right of action, that the damage he suffered was caused directly by the breach of duty, and that the damage was of the kind contemplated by the statute.[41] The provision of some other remedy, such as complaint to the Minister, will often be held to exclude an action for damages. The House of Lords reviewed the earlier authorities in *X (Minors) v. Bedfordshire C.C.*[42] where Lord Browne-Wilkinson said that the principles applicable in determining whether such statutory cause of action exists are now well established, "although the application of those principles in any particular case remains difficult."[43]

Authorities such as Coke, Hawkins and Blackstone asserted that failure to perform a statutory duty constituted an indictable misdemeanour. Disobedience to the words of a statute constituted a form of contempt, punishable by the King's justices. This doctrine of contempt of statute was held by the Divisional Court in *R. v. Horseferry Road Justices, ex p. Independent Broadcasting Authority*[44] to be no more than a rule of statutory construction. In modern statutes, at any rate, very clear words would be required before the court would hold that a breach of statutory duty constituted a crime.

---

[41] *Groves v. Lord Wimborne* [1898] 2 Q.B. 402, 415, *per* Vaughan Williams L.J.; *Cutler v. Wandsworth Stadium Ltd* [1949] A.C. 398. *cf. Gorris v. Scott* (1874) L.R. 9 Exch. 125.

[42] [1995] 2 A.C. 633, HL.

[43] At p. 731.

[44] [1986] 3 W.L.R. 132; claim that I.B.A. had failed to carry out its duty under Broadcasting Act 1981, s.4(3) to prevent transmission of images for such a short duration that they could influence television viewers without their realising what had been done. The complainant alleged that during a programme called "Spitting Image" an image of his face had been briefly transmitted superimposed on the body of a naked woman.

Chapter 32

JUDICIAL CONTROL OF PUBLIC AUTHORITIES: II. REMEDIES

The legality of acts and decisions of public bodies may be challenged directly **32–001**
by recourse to the supervisory jurisdiction of the High Court, that is by seeking
to show that a decision has been vitiated by one or more of the factors considered
in the previous chapter such as unreasonableness or breach of natural justice. The
challenge may, however, arise in the course of an action in tort or contract or
criminal proceedings. The owner of property may, for example, after it has been
demolished by a local authority bring an action in trespass which, if he is to be
successful, involves establishing that the decision to demolish lacked legal
authority because it had been reached without giving him a hearing.[1] A tenant
who believes that his local authority has unlawfully increased his rent may refuse
to pay the increase and when, sued for possession, raise the invalidity of the
decision as a defence.[2] Yet another possibility is to seek an injunction to restrain
a public body from acting unlawfully[3] or a declaration that it has so acted.[4] Until
recent reforms in the law of remedies the choice of the remedy was in the hands
of the individual claiming to be aggrieved. In 1977, however, a new procedure—
application for judicial review—was introduced by adding a new Order 53 to the
Rules of the Supreme Court and subsequently given statutory recognition by the
Supreme Court Act 1981, section 31. Judicial interpretation of the new procedure
established a distinction, as we have seen earlier, between public and private law
rights and duties. In the former case a plaintiff had to proceed by way of an
application for judicial review; he could no longer choose to challenge the act of
a public body in the course of litigation begun in the normal way by writ. In
certain cases, discussed later in Part III of this chapter, decisions of ministers and
tribunals are subject to statutory rights of appeal.

Following more recent changes to civil procedure and the adoption of new
Civil Procedure Rules (CPR) Order 53 became, from October 2, 2000, Part 54 of
the new rules. As will become obvious throughout this chapter, there have been
a number of changes in wording, new names, for example, being given to old
remedies.[5]

I. SUPERVISORY JURISDICTION OF THE HIGH COURT

"Prerogative writs" were writs brought by the King against the officers to **32–002**
compel them to exercise their functions properly or to prevent them from abusing
their powers. They could be issued at various periods of their history either out

---

[1] *Cooper v. Wandsworth Board of Works* (1863) 14 C.B.(N.S.) 180.
[2] *Wandsworth London Borough Council v. Winder* [1965] A.C. 461.
[3] *e.g. Boyce v. Paddington Corporation* [1903] 1 Ch. 109, CA.
[4] *e.g. Vine v. National Dock Labour Board* [1957] A.C. 488, HL.
[5] M. Fordham, "Judicial review: the new rules" [2001] P.L. 4; T. Cornford and M. Sunkin, "The Bowman Report" [2001] P.L. 11.

of the Court of King's Bench or the Court of Chancery, or both. The term "prerogative writ" was applied to habeas corpus in the reign of James I; but it is not until Lord Mansfield[6] and Blackstone that we find it grouped with certiorari, prohibition and mandamus as "prerogative writs" because they were not directed immediately to the tribunal or person concerned but were supposed to issue from the King to a royal officer, such as the sheriff.[7] The chief prerogative writs were habeas corpus, prohibition, certiorari, mandamus and *quo warranto*; but of these only the first remains as a writ,[8] the last has been abolished, and the others are now orders.[9] Part 54 now speaks of the remedies of mandatory, prohibiting or quashing orders. The old names, however, cannot be abandoned because they are embedded in hundreds of years of case law.

Before the reforms of 1977 litigants who resorted to the supervisory jurisdiction of the High Court had to choose which order they wished to seek. A prerogative order could not be sought together with or as an alternative to other remedies such as damages or an injunction. The ambit of certiorari and prohibition was limited to bodies performing judicial functions, a concept of uncertain width. Other characteristics (and defects) of the orders led litigants increasingly to prefer the remedies of the injunction and the declaration.[10] Following various proposals for reform,[11] the Rules of the Supreme Court were amended in 1977 to provide a procedure known as the application for judicial review which enables a litigant to seek relief while leaving to the court the decision as to which particular remedy is appropriate.[12]

32–003   A litigant may proceed by way of a claim for judicial review where the remedy sought is (i) an order of certiorari, prohibition or mandamus or (b) a declaration or injunction. The latter remedies may be granted on an application for judicial relief if the court considers it just and convenient to do so having regard (a) to the nature of the matters in respect of which relief may be granted by way of certiorari, prohibition or mandamus, and (ii) the nature of the persons and bodies against which relief may be granted by such orders. An application for judicial review cannot be made without the leave of the Court. The first request for leave can be dealt with by a judge on the basis of the written application and he need not sit in open court. If leave is refused a second application may be made to a judge sitting in open court (or in certain cases to a Divisional Court of the Queen's Bench). A claim for damages may be included in a claim for judicial review. Where the court considers that the proceedings should have been commenced by writ it may order them to continue as if so commenced.[13] To be entitled to seek judicial review the claimant must have what the court considers

---

[6] *R. v. Cowle* (1759) 2 Burr. 834, 835.

[7] For an account of their origin and development, see S. A. de Smith, "The Prerogative Writs" (1951) 11 C.L.J. 40; D. C. M. Yardley, "The Scope of the Prerogative Orders in Administrative Law" (1957–1958) 12 N.I.L.Q. 78; de Smith, *Judicial Review of Administrative Action*, Appendix 1.

[8] For habeas corpus, see *ante*, para. 24–034 *et seq.*

[9] Administration of Justice (Miscellaneous Provisions) Acts 1933 and 1938.

[10] See G. J. Borrie, "The Advantages of the Declaratory Judgment in Administrative Law," (1955) 18 M.L.R. 138.

[11] *Remedies in Administrative Law: Law Com. Report No. 73.* Cmnd. 6407 (1976). See H. W. R. Wade, "Remedies in Administrative Law," (1976) 92 L.Q.R. 334.

[12] See now also Supreme Court Act 1981, s.31.

[13] There is no provision for the converse situation but Woolf L.J. has said that there is no obstacle in an appropriate case for the court to give leave then and there in an action before it begun by writ: "Public Law—Private Law: Why the Divide" [1986] P.L. 220, 232.

to be a "sufficient interest" in the matter to which the application relates. An application, or claim in the new terminology, for judicial review must normally be brought within three months of the decision complained of,[14] but the court has a discretion to allow applications outside the time limit.[15]

A. The Remedies

Order 53 and Section 31 of the Supreme Court Act 1981 did not introduce new remedies but a new, general procedure for applying for a group of remedies. Hence the old law relating to the scope of the individual remedies remains relevant, except where changed by the reforms.[16] Part 54 similarly has not affected the substantive law.

1. Certiorari (Quashing Order)[17]

This is an order issued to an "inferior court" or a person or body exercising what the High Court regards as a "judicial" or "quasi-judicial" function, to have the record of the proceedings removed into the High Court for review, and (if bad) to be quashed.

32–004

What is an "inferior court" for this purpose, or whether a person or body exercises powers of a "judicial" or "quasi-judicial" nature, is a question for the High Court to decide. The former *locus classicus* was the dictum of Atkin L.J. in *R. v. Electricity Commissioners*[18]: "Whenever any body of persons having legal authority to determine questions affecting the rights of subjects, and having the duty to act judicially, act in excess of their legal authority, they are subject to the controlling jurisdiction of the King's Bench Division, exercised in these writs" (*i.e.* certiorari and prohibition). It was made clear in *Ridge v. Baldwin*[19] (a declaratory action) that authority to determine questions affecting the rights of subjects and the duty to act judicially are not two separate requirements: the latter is not additional to the former. Certiorari has been held to lie against a county court judge, a coroner, the Patents Appeal Tribunal, the Medical Appeal Tribunal, a local valuation court, rent tribunals, a Minister holding a public inquiry and a

---

[14] The apparently inconsistent provisions of 0.53 r.4 and s.31(6) Supreme Court Act 1981 were reconciled in *R. v. Dairy Produce Tribunal ex p. Caswell* [1990] 2 A.C. 738, HL. It is not thought that Pt 54 has effected any change in the position.

[15] *R. v. Criminal Injuries Board ex p. A* [1992] 2 A.C. 330, HL (Leave granted after delay of 10 months: delay not in itself ground for refusing relief at substantive hearing).

[16] For example a generalised test of "sufficient interest" has replaced the former rules relating to *locus standi; post* para. 32–010.

[17] The former writ of certiorari appears first to have been used against the Commissioners of Sewers charged by a statute of 1531 to see to the repair of sea walls, but most of the earlier cases were against justices. For the history, see Holdsworth, *History of English Law*, Vol. X, pp. 199–206; D. C. M. Yardley, "The Grounds for Certiorari and Prohibition" (1959) 37 Can.Bar Rev. 294; and *R. v. Northumberland Compensation Appeal Tribunal ex p. Shaw* [1951] 1 K.B. 711, *per* Lord Goddard L.C.J.; [1952] 1 K.B. 338 *per* Denning L.J.

[18] [1924] 1 K.B. 171.

[19] [1964] A.C. 40, *per* Lord Reid; *cf. per* Lord Hewart C.J. in *R. v. Legislative Committee of the Church Assembly ex p. Haynes-Smith* [1928] 1 K.B. 411. Atkin L.J.'s dictum is too wide as regards certiorari and ecclesiastical law; *post,* para. 32–005, n.38.

local election court.[20] By statute, certiorari lies to the Crown Court except in relation to that Court's jurisdiction in matters relating to trials on indictment.[21] In *Board of Education v. Rice*[22] certiorari and mandamus were granted against the Board of Education because, in a dispute between the managers of a school and the local education authority, they had not decided the question which the statute directed them to decide. In *R. v. Manchester Legal Aid Committee ex p. Brand*[23] Parker J. concluded that a legal aid committee, being unconcerned with questions of policy and having to decide wholly on the facts of a particular case solely on the evidence before them, "must act judicially, not judiciously," and was therefore subject to certiorari.

Scope of certiorari

32–005   The grounds on which certiorari lies are:

(i) *Want or excess of jurisdiction* For this reason certiorari was granted against a licensing authority which had given permission to open a cinema on Sunday, whereas this was prohibited by statute[24]; and against a legal aid committee which had granted a legal aid certificate to a trustee in bankruptcy on the basis of the means of the bankrupt instead of the means of the trustee (*R. v. Manchester Legal Aid Committee, ante*[25]).

(ii) *Denial of natural justice*[26] Certiorari has been issued at the instance of a ratepayer to quash the decision of a rural district council permitting a certain development of land, since one of the councillors who voted on the resolution was interested in the use of the land[27]; and to quash a decision of the General Medical Council removing a doctor's name from the medical register, because the Council had refused to hear certain evidence which it ought to have heard (*General Medical Council v. Spackman*[28]). In *R. v. Barnsley M.B.C. ex p. Hook*[29] the Court of Appeal granted certiorari to quash a decision of a committee of the defendant corporation on the ground of bias.

(iii) *Error on the face of the record* It was commonly thought at one time that certiorari was limited to cases of jurisdiction and natural justice, but the Court of Appeal held in *R. v. Northumberland Compensation Appeal Tribunal ex p.*

---

[20] *R. v. Worthington-Evans ex p. Madan* [1959] 2 Q.B. 145, DC; *R. v. Hurst (Judge), ex p. Smith* [1960] 2 Q.B. 133, DC; *Pearlmath v. Keepers and Governors of Harrow School* [1979] Q.B. 56; *R. v. Greater Manchester Coroner ex p. Tal* [1985] Q.B. 67, DC; *Baldwin and Francis Ltd v. Patents Appeal Tribunal* [1959] A.C. 663, HL; *R. v. Medical Appeal Tribunal ex p. Gilmore* [1957] 1 Q.B. 574, CA; *R. v. East Norfolk Local Valuation Court* [1951] 1 All E.R. 743; *R. v. Fulham Rent Tribunal* [1951] 2 K.B. 1; *R. v. Paddington Rent Tribunal ex p. Bell Properties* [1949] 1 K.B. 666; *Errington v. Minister of Health* [1935] 1 K.B. 249; *K. v. Cripps ex p. Muldoon* [1984] Q.B. 686, CA.
[21] Supreme Court Act 1981, s.29(3); *re Smalley* [1985] A.C. 622, HL; *R. v. Central Criminal Court ex p. Raymond* [1966] 1 W.L.R. 710, DC. See also, *R. v. D.P.P. ex p. Kebilene* [2000] 2 A.C. 362, HL.
[22] [1911] A.C. 179, HL.
[23] [1952] 2 Q.B. 413, DC.
[24] *The King v. London County Council ex p. Entertainments Protection Association* [1931] 2 K.B. 215.
[25] [1952] 2 Q.B. 413. See also *R. v. Fulham Rent Tribunal* [1951] 2 K.B. 1, on review of jurisdictional facts.
[26] For the principles of natural justice, see *ante*, para. 31–010 *et seq.*
[27] *The King v. Hendon Rural District Council, ex p. Charley* [1933] 2 K.B. 696.
[28] [1943] A.C. 627, HL.
[29] [1976] 1 W.L.R. 1052.

Shaw[30] that this remedy is also available where an interior tribunal has issued a "speaking order" (*i.e.* an order showing the reasons on which it is based), and an error of law appears on its face. In that case the applicant complained that the tribunal had made an error in computing the compensation to which he was entitled by statute for loss of employment on the nationalisation of the health service. The award set out the manner in which the sum was computed, and this enabled the court to hold that the computation was not in accordance with the statutory regulations and that the decision must be quashed. Error on the face of the record renders a decision voidable. There was usually no obligation on a tribunal to make a "speaking" or reasoned order before the Tribunals and Inquiries Act 1958, replaced by section 10 of the 1992 Act.[31]

"Record" was defined by Denning L.J. (as he then was) in *Ex p. Shaw* as including the document initiating the proceedings, the pleadings, if any, and the adjudication but not the evidence and not the reasons for the decision unless incorporated into adjudication by the tribunal. In *Baldwin & Francis v. Patents Appeal Tribunal*[32] Lord Denning said the record also included all documents which appear from the formal order of the tribunal to constitute the basis of its decision. In *R. v. Southampton Justices ex p. Green*[33] the Court of Appeal held that affidavits from justices as to their reasons for a decision constituted part of the record and revealed an error of law on the face of the record.

A record may be written or oral under section 10 of the Tribunal and Inquiries Act 1992. The courts cited that section to justify a liberal approach to the meaning of "record" in cases outside the scope of the Act: *R. v. Knightsbridge Crown Court ex p. International Sporting Club (London) Ltd.*[34] Following Order 53 and *O'Reilly v. Mackman* the court should not, according to Woolf J. "be shackled and prevented from doing justice by restrictive historical decisions."[35]

32–006

Following *Anisminic*, however, this learning, at least in English courts, is of historic interest only and all errors of law, whether on the record or not are likely to be treated as going to jurisdiction.[36]

Certiorari does not lie to review subordinate legislation.[37] It does not lie against ecclesiastical courts, because ecclesiastical law is a different system of law from that administered in the High Court,[38] or against voluntary (*i.e.* non-

---

[30] [1952] 1 K.B. 338; confirming Divisional Court at [1951] 1 K.B. 711; following *Walsall Overseers v. London and North Western Ry* (1879) 4 App.Cas. 30, HL and *R. v. Nat Bell Liquors Ltd* [1922] 2 A.C. 128, HC.
And see *R. v. Patents Appeal Tribunal ex p. Swift & Co* [1962] 2 Q.B. 647, DC; *R. v. Medical Appeal Tribunal ex p. Gilmore* [1957] 1 Q.B. 574, DC, *per* Denning L.J.

[31] *ante*, para. 30–023.

[32] [1959] A.C. 663; the other members of the House expressly refused to consider what documents, if any, other than the actual order of the tribunal, constituted the record. Lord Denning's definition was followed in *Ex p. Swift, ante. cf. Belsfield Court Construction Co. v. Pywell* [1970] 2 Q.B. 47; pleadings not part of arbitrator's award.

[33] [1976] 1 Q.B. 11.

[34] [1982] Q.B. 304, DC (Quashing of oral judgment).

[35] *R. v. Knightsbridge Crown Court ex p. The Aspinall Curzon Ltd, The Times*, December 16, 1982. (Affidavit evidence could be treated as part of the record.)

[36] *R. v. Greater Manchester Coroner ex p. Tal* [1985] Q.B. 67.

[37] *R. v. Legislative Committee of the Church Assembly ex p. Haynes-Smith* [1928] 1 K.B. 411.

[38] *The King v. Chancellor of St. Eamunasoury and Ipswich Diocese* [1948] 1 K.B. 195. *cf.* prohibition.

statutory) domestic tribunals,[39] nor does it lie for dismissal of a person under an ordinary contract of employment.[40]

2. Prohibition (Prohibiting Order)

32–007   The former writ of prohibition issued out of the King's Bench or other superior court directing the judge and parties to a suit in any inferior court to cease from the prosecution thereof on the ground that the cause did not belong to that jurisdiction.[41] The penalty for disobedience is committal for contempt. It was mainly by this writ that the common law courts in earlier days contested the jurisdiction of the Admiralty and ecclesiastical courts.

The order of prohibition issues to *prevent* an inferior court or tribunal from exceeding or continuing to exceed its jurisdiction or infringing the rules of natural justice. Prohibition is governed by similar principles to certiorari, except that it does not lie when once a final decision has been given. It will issue to prevent magistrates exceeding their jurisdiction[42] and to prevent a Board of Prison Visitors from hearing a charge which they were not entitled to deal with.[43] In *R. v. Liverpool Corporation ex p. Liverpool Taxi Fleet Operators' Association*[44] it was granted to prohibit a local authority from acting on a resolution with regard to the number of taxicab licences to be issued, without first hearing representations on behalf of interested persons.

Prohibition has been granted against Electricity Commissioners to prevent them from holding an inquiry with a view to bringing into force an *ultra vires* scheme for the supply of electricity (*R. v. Electricity Commissioners*[45]); and against Income Tax Commissioners, an assessment committee and rent tribunals.[46] But it was decided in *The King v. Legislative Committee of the Church Assembly ex p. Haynes-Smith*,[47] where application was made for an order to prohibit the Church Assembly from proceeding further with the Prayer Book Measure 1927, that it would not issue against a legislative or deliberative body. Nor will prohibition be issued to a military tribunal administering martial law (*Re Clifford and O'Sullivan*[48]).

[39] *R. v. National Joint Council for the Craft of Dental Technicians ex p. Neste* [1953] 1 Q.B. 704, DC; *R. v. Post Office ex p. Byrne* [1975] I.C.R. 221. This limit on the availability of certiorari was overlooked by the Divisional Court in *R. v. Aston University Senate ex p. Roffrey* [1969] 2 Q.B. 538; criticised on that ground, *Herring v. Templeman* [1973] 3 All E.R. 569, 585 *per* Russell L.J. *cf. R. v. Criminal Injuries Compensation Board, ex p. Lain* [1967] 2 Q.B. 864, CA; certiorari may be issued against a public body set up by prerogative as part of an administrative scheme approved by both Houses and financed by parliamentary funds. See also *R. v. Panel on Takeovers and Mergers ex p. Datafin* [1987] Q.B. 815.
[40] *Vidyodaya University of Ceylon v. Silve* [1965] 1 W.L.R. 77; [1964] 3 All E.R. 865, PC: dismissal of university professor. The remedy is an action for damages if the dismissal was in breach of contract.
[41] Bl.Comm. iii, 105. See D. C. M. Yardley, "The Grounds for Certiorari and Prohibition" (1959) 37 Can.Bar Rev. 294.
[42] *e.g. R. v. Horseferry Road Justices ex p. L.B.A.* [1986] 3 W.L.R. 132.
[43] *R. v. Board of Visitors of Dartmoor Prison ex p. Smith* [1986] 3 W.L.R. 61, CA.
[44] [1972] 2 Q.B. 299, CA.
[45] [1929] 1 K.B. 171, *per* Atkin L.J. Certiorari was refused in that case.
[46] *Kensington Income Tax Commissioners v. Aramayo* [1916] 1 A.C. 215; *R. v. North Worcestershire Assessment Committee ex p. Hadley* [1929] 2 K.B. 397; *R. v. Tottenham and District Rent Tribunal ex p. Northfield* [1957] 1 Q.B. 103.
[47] [1928] 1 K.B. 411. The House of Commons rejected the Prayer Book Measure.
[48] [1921] 2 A.C. 570, HL.

Where a final decision has been made by the inferior court prohibition is **32–008** obviously useless, but certiorari is available to enable the High Court to review and, if necessary, to quash the decision. Thus prohibition was the appropriate remedy to prevent the Minister of Health from proceeding to confirm an *ultra vires* housing scheme (*R. v. Minister of Health ex p. Davis*[49]), but certiorari was appropriate when an *ultra vires* scheme had already been approved by the Minister (*Minister of Health v. R. ex p. Yaffe*[50]). Certiorari and prohibition may be granted together, for example, to quash a decision already made by a rent tribunal and to prevent it continuing to exceed or abuse its jurisdiction (*R. v. Paddington Rent Tribunal, ex p. Bell Properties Ltd*[51]).

Prohibition and mandamus were issued together in *R. v. Kent Police Authority ex p. Godden*[52] where, on the compulsory retirement of a police chief inspector on the ground that he was permanently disabled, it was held that the chief inspector's medical advisers were entitled to see all the material placed before the medical practitioner appointed to make the decision about disablement.

Since the introduction of Order 53 there is little significance in any distinction between prohibition and the injunction in cases relating to public law.

3. Mandamus (Mandatory Order)

The order of mandamus may be issued to any person or body (not necessarily **32–009** an inferior court) commanding him or them to carry out some public duty.

Mandamus has been issued to compel the hearing of an appeal by a statutory tribunal,[53] the determination of a dispute between a local education authority and school managers (*Board of Education v. Rice*[54]), to procure the production of a local authority's accounts for inspection,[55] against a returning officer to declare a councillor elected,[56] against an electoral registration officer to correct the register of electors[57] against a county court judge to make a legal aid order,[58] and against the Board of Trade requiring them to investigate the affairs of the applicant company under the Companies Act.[59] Mandamus was not granted to compel the College of Physicians to admit an applicant (*R. v. Askew*[60]), to order a magistrate to hear a case covered by parliamentary privilege,[61] or to compel the Chairman of Convocation of London University to call a meeting, as the matter could have been put to the Visitor (*R. v. Dunsheath ex p. Meredith*[62]).

Mandamus is not available against the Crown itself, nor against a servant of the Crown to enforce a duty owed exclusively to the Crown (*R. v. Secretary of*

---

[49] [1929] 1 K.B. 619.
[50] [1931] A.C. 494.
[51] [1939] 1 K.B. 666.
[52] [1951] 2 Q.B. 662, CA.
[53] *The King v. Housing Tribunal* [1920] 2 K.B. 334.
[54] [1911] A.C. 179.
[55] *R. v. Bedwellty U.D.C., ex p. Price* [1934] 1 K.B. 333.
[56] *R. v. Soothill ex p. Ashdown, The Times*, April 2, 1955.
[57] *R. v. Calderwood ex p. Manchester Corporation, The Times*, February 27, 1974.
[58] *R. v. Judge Fraser Harris ex p. The Law Society* [1955] 1 Q.B. 287.
[59] *R. v. Board of Trade ex p. St. Martin's Preserving Co.* [1965] 1 Q.B. 603, DC.
[60] (1768) 4 Burr. 2186.
[61] *R. v. Graham-Campbell, ex p. Herbert* [1935] 1 K.B. 594; *cf. R. v. Ogden ex p. Long Ashton R.D.C.* [1963] 1 W.L.R. 274; [1963] 1 All E.R. 574, DC.
[62] [1931] 1 K.B. 127. And see *Sammy v. Birkbeck College, The Times*, November 3, 1964, and May 20, 1965, CA (mandamus refused).

State for War,[63] *The Queen v. Lords of the Treasury*[64]), because a third party cannot require an agent to perform a duty which he owes solely to his principal. But mandamus may be issued against Ministers or other Crown servants to enforce a statutory duty owed to the applicant as well as to the Crown (*The Queen v. Special Commissioners for Income Tax*[65]). In *Padfield v. Minister of Agriculture, Fisheries and Food*[66] the House of Lords held that where a minister had by statute an unfettered discretion whether or not to refer a complaint to a committee, he must consider only relevant matters and exclude irrelevant, ones, and that even where he gave no reasons for not referring the matter to the committee he should be required by mandamus to consider the complaint lawfully.

4. Injunction and Declaration

32–010   Where the right claimed by a litigant is a public law right these remedies must be sought by means of an application for judicial review.[67] The substantive rules relating to these remedies are discussed later in Part V which deals with private law remedies.

An injunction is a court order requiring the defendant to do or refrain from doing an act while a declaration (or declaratory judgment) declares what the law is. Although, as will be seen in Part V, the declaratory judgment is not available to answer hypothetical questions, recent developments in the public law sphere establish that it is not confined to disputes relating to decisions of public bodies. In appropriate cases the court has jurisdiction to declare that a ministerial circular is or is not based on a mistaken view of the law[68] or that an intended payment by a local authority, if made, would be *intra vires*.[69] The prospect of obtaining a declaration that an intended course of action would or would not be criminal is extremely remote.[70]

B. Sufficient Interest

32–011   A claimant for judicial review must satisfy the court that he has a sufficient interest in the matter to which the application relates.[71] This general requirement replaces the rules relating to locus standi which formerly applied to each individual remedy. Then, as now, a member of the public had no right to impugn the legality of a decision taken by a public body unless he could establish an individual right or claim of some kind. The test to be satisfied was defined (or

---

[63] [1891] 2 Q.B. 326.
[64] (1872) L.R. 7 Q.B. 387. See E. C. S. Wade, "The Courts and the Administrative Process" (1947) 63 L.Q.R. 164.
[65] (1889) 21 Q.B.D. 313. And see *R. v. Board of Trade ex p. St. Martin's Preserving Co, supra.*
[66] [1968] A.C. 997.
[67] *O'Reilly v. Mackman* [1983] 2 A.C. 237 was an unsuccessful attempt to obtain a declaration without using the procedure of judicial review; *Cocks v. Thanet DC* [1983] 2 A.C. 286, an unsuccessful attempt to obtain an injunction.
[68] *Gillick v. West Norfolk and Wisbech Area Health Authority* [1986] A.C. 112.
[69] *R. v. Bromley L.B.C. ex p. Lambeth L.B.C., The Times*, June 16, 1984.
[70] *Imperial Tobacco Ltd v. Att.-Gen.* [1980] 1 W.L.R. 322, HL.
[71] Supreme Court Act 1981, s.31(3).

described) in varying terms in relation to particular remedies. It was possible for an applicant to satisfy the requirement of locus standi in relation to one remedy but not to another.[72]

The meaning of "sufficient interest" was considered by the House of Lords in *R. v. Inland Revenue Commissioners ex p. National Federation of Self Employed and Small Businesses Ltd.*[73] In line with the current judicial approach to judicial review sufficient interest was given the widest possible meaning while reserving to the court a discretion in particular cases to refuse a hearing or deny a remedy. The House of Lords was reluctant to separate locus standi from the facts and merits of an application. The requirement of standing should, it seems, be looked at twice: first when the applicant applies for leave to seek judicial review. At that stage the court is concerned to do no more than "prevent abuse by busybodies, cranks, and other mischief-makers."[74] If leave is granted, the court may, when the merits of the case are clear to it, revise its initial judgment and conclude that the applicant lacks the necessary interest. The application before the House had been made by an association of taxpayers who wished to challenge the legality of a compromise which the Inland Revenue had made with a group of print-workers who had been defrauding the revenue. The House of Lords held that while it had been correct to grant leave to apply for review, the applicants, on the facts, lacked sufficient interest to challenge the legality of the compromise. The assessment of one taxpayer is no concern of another; indeed, each individual's tax liability is a confidential matter. The Inland Revenue was reasonably trying to carry out its duty to collect taxes. Dicta did envisage the possibility of cases of sufficient gravity where taxpayers might have *locus standi.*[75] The House distinguished the position of the taxpayer from that of the ratepayer. In the latter case assessments of property are a public matter and there is a common fund so that each ratepayer's contribution is affected by the assessment of his neighbour.[76] An individual taxpayer, by contrast, seeking to challenge decisions of the revenue authorities in relation to his own affairs has, without doubt, sufficient interest.[77] In *R. v. H.M. Treasury ex p. Smedley*[78] a taxpayer challenged the legality of a draft Order in Council laid by the Treasury before Parliament.[79] The Court of Appeal decided the substantive question against Smedley and therefore did not have to express a concluded view on whether he has a sufficient interest to apply for judicial review. Slade L.J. emphasised the width of the test laid down in the *Inland Revenue* case, *supra* and indicated that the court would hear an application provided it was satisfied that it was not "of a frivolous nature."

This wide approach to the meaning of sufficient interest has been followed in subsequent cases and, in particular, the courts have recognised that pressure

[72] *e.g. Gregory v. Camden L.B.C.* [1966] 1 W.L.R. 899. But see now *Steeples v. Derbyshire C.C.* [1985] 1 W.L.R. 256.
[73] [1982] A.C. 617.
[74] At p. 653, *per* Lord Scarman.
[75] *e.g.* Allegations of large scale fraud and corruption on the part of the revenue.
[76] So ultimately is each taxpayer's liability affected by his neighbour's contribution. In *Arsenal Football Club Ltd v. Ende* [1979] A.C. 1. (the correctness of which the House was concerned to uphold) the plaintiff was not applying under p. 53 but as a "person aggrieved" under the General Rate Act 1967, s.69; see *post*, para. 32–015.
[77] *e.g. R. v. Special Commissioners ex p. Stipplechoice Ltd* [1985] 2 All E.R. 465, CA.
[78] [1965] Q.B. 857.
[79] *ante* para. 6–016.

groups and organisations of various kinds may have sufficient interest to eluci-
date the law.[80]

C. The Scope of Judicial Review

32–012   Judicial review is a procedure available only in disputes raising questions of
public law. The court must before an application can succeed be satisfied that the
respondent is a public authority and that the right at issue is a public right.

Although the courts have not attempted to define what is meant by public
authority guidance can be gained from the cases cited in the preceding pages in
relation to the particular remedies. Generally it might be said that judicial review
is available against any minister or body exercising common law or statutory
powers which affects the rights of individuals unless there is a reason to the
contrary.[81] Thus it will be available not merely against departments of central and
local government but also against the General Medical Council because of its
statutory powers of control over the medical profession,[82] and against Boards of
Prison Visitors.[83] The new procedure does not, however, give the High Court a
jurisdiction which it formerly lacked. Decisions of superior courts are not,
therefore, subject to review.[84] Nor is an organisation necessarily a public authority because it has been created by statute. The question is whether the powers it
is exercising are of a public law or governmental kind. A commercial decision,
for example, by a nationalised industry is unlikely to be subject to judicial
review: *R. v. National Coal Board ex p. National Union of Mineworkers*.[85]

In the leading case of *R. v. Panel on Takeovers and Mergers ex p. Datafin*[86] the
Court of Appeal held that judicial review was available against a body exercising
what might be called *de facto* powers, without a common law or statutory basis
when its decisions had wide ranging significance and, in the absence of such a
body, Parliament would have had to legislate to establish a body having statutory
powers.[87]

D. The Availability of Other Remedies

32–013   The availability of another remedy may be relevant in one of two ways to an
application for judicial review.

---

[80] *R. v. Secretary of State for Social Services ex p. Child Poverty Action Group* [1989] 1 All E.R.
1047; *R. v. Secretary of State for Foreign and Commonwealth Affairs ex p. World Development
Movement* [1995] 1 W.L.R. 386.
[81] *R. v. Secretary of State for the Home Department ex p. McAvoy* [1984] 1 W.L.R. 1408; no judicial
review of decision taken for "operational and security reasons."
[82] *R. v. G.M.C. ex p. Gee* [1986] 1 W.L.R. 226. Domestic Tribunals exercising a jurisdiction based on
contract are outside p. 53: *Law v. National Greyhound Racing Club Ltd* [1983] 1 W.L.R. 1302,
CA.
[83] e.g. *R. v. Board of Visitors of Dartmoor Prison ex p. Smith* [1986] 3 W.L.R. 61, CA.
[84] The Crown Court is subject to review except with regard to "matters relating to trial on indictment"; Supreme Court Act 1981 s.29(3); In re *Smalley* [1985] A.C. 622, HL; *R. v. Central Criminal
Court ex p. Raymond* [1986] 1 W.L.R. 710, DC.
[85] *The Times*, March 8, 1986.
[86] [1987] Q.B. 815. Contrast the old law on certiorari: *ex p. Neate, ante* para. 32–005.
[87] See further *R. v. Disciplinary Committee of the Jockey Club ex p. Aga Khan* [1993] 1 W.L.R.
909.

First, the court may decide that the alternative remedy is the exclusive remedy provided by law and there is no jurisdiction to grant review.[88] A recent, unsuccessful, attempt on this ground to deny jurisdiction to the court is to be found in *R. v. Secretary of State for the Environment ex p. Ward*.[89] Section 9 of the Caravan Sites Act 1968 entitled the minister to give directions to local authorities requiring them to provide caravan sites in accordance with their statutory duties: "any such directions shall be enforceable, on the application of the Minister, by mandamus." A local authority was unwilling to carry out its duty and the Secretary of State was unwilling to seek mandamus against them. The applicant, a gypsy, sought judicial review against the local authority and the Secretary of State. Woolf J. held that section 9 did not preclude an application for judicial review although it would have precluded any private law application by an individual litigant.

Secondly, more commonly the existence of an alternative remedy is a factor to be taken into account by the court in deciding whether, in its discretion, to grant relief.

"Judicial review should not be granted where an alternative remedy is available."[90] The courts are particularly reluctant to intervene where Parliament has provided a comprehensive appellate system, for example, in the field of social services: *R. v. Secretary of State for Social Services ex p. Connolly*.[91] Similarly in relation to immigration the Court of Appeal emphasised the undesirability of granting leave to seek judicial review before applicants had exhausted their statutory rights under the Immigration Act 1971: *R. v. Secretary of State for the Home Department ex p. Swati*.[92] On the other hand, an application may be granted if there are special circumstances such as the inordinate delay in the domestic disciplinary process in *R. v. Chief Constable of the Merseyside Police ex p. Calveley*.[93]

E. DISCRETIONARY

32–014 Judicial review is a procedure in which the court has a discretion whether to grant relief at two stages. First, the claimant must obtain leave to apply. At that stage he must, as we have seen, demonstrate *prima facie* a sufficient interest to be allowed to proceed. He must also give some reason for believing that there is ground for challenging the decision of which he complains and, if there is an alternative remedy available, suggest why that should not prevent leave being granted. It was because the applicant failed to satisfy both these preliminary hurdles that the Court of Appeal refused leave to apply for judicial review of an

---

[88] *Barraclough v. Brown* [1897] A.C. 615; *Pasmore v. Oswaldtwistle Urban District Council* [1898] A.C. 387.
[89] [1984] 1 W.L.R. 834; distinguishing *Kensington and Chelsea L.B.C. v. Wells* (1973) 72 L.G.R. 289, CA. See generally, *Pyx Granite Co v. Ministry of Housing* [1960] A.C. 260.
[90] *R. v. Inland Revenue Commissioners ex p. Preston* [1985] A.C. 835, 852 *per* Lord Templeman.
[91] [1986] 1 W.L.R. 421.
[92] [1986] 1 W.L.R. 477; See too *R. v. Chief Adjudication Officer ex p. Bland*, *The Times*, February 6, 1985, DC.
[93] [1986] Q.B. 424, CA. The judgments contain a useful survey of earlier authorities. See also, *Harley Developments v. Commission of Inland Revenue* [1996] 1 W.L.R. 727, PC.

immigration officer's decision in *R. v. Secretary of State for the Home Department ex p. Swati*.[94] The House of Lords has emphasised the need to have some
ground to believe that a decision is subsequently open to challenge before
granting leave in *R. v. Secretary of State for the Environment ex p. Puhlhofer*.[95]
The applicants had been granted leave to challenge a decision of the Hillingdon
Council under the Housing (Homeless Persons) Act 1977.[96] The House held that
the Council had correctly decided that the applicants were not homeless. It also
indicated, however, concern that leave to apply should not be given too easily in
future cases. Lord Brightman said that he was

"troubled at the prolific use of judicial review for the purpose of challenging
the performance by local authorities of their functions under the 1977 Act.
Parliament intended the local authority to be the judge of fact. The Act
abounds with the formula when, or if, the housing authority are satisfied as to
this, or that, or have reason to believe this, or that. Although the action or
inaction of a local authority is clearly susceptible to judicial review where they
have misconstrued the Act, or abused their powers or otherwise acted perversely, I think that great restraint should be exercised in giving leave to
proceed by judicial review. The plight of the homeless is a desperate one, and
the plight of the applicants in the present case commands the deepest sym-
pathy. But it is not, in my opinion, appropriate that the remedy of judicial
review, which is a discretionary remedy, should be made use of to monitor the
actions of local authorities under the Act save in the exceptional case. . . .
Where the existence or non-existence of a fact is left to the judgment and
discretion of a public body and that fact involves a broad spectrum ranging
from the obvious to the debatable to the just conceivable, it is the duty of the
court to leave the decision of that fact to the public body to whom Parliament
has entrusted the decision-making power save in a case where it is obvious that
the public body, consciously or unconsciously, are acting perversely."

32–015   In *R. v. Monopolies and Mergers Commission ex p. Argyll Group plc*[97] the
Court of Appeal held that a judge had been right to refuse leave to seek judicial
review of a decision taken by the Chairman of the Commission. The decision, in
the view of the Court, was outside his statutory powers but equally the Court had
no doubt that the Commission itself, which did have the power to decide, would
have come to the same conclusion.

Secondly, where leave has been granted and the application for relief has been
successful the court still has a discretion with regard to the granting of remedies.
The nude sunbathers in *Glynn v. Keele University*,[98] for example, failed to obtain
an injunction because of their own behaviour and because, even after a hearing,
a similar decision would have been reached. The Court may be concerned about
the inconvenience and upheaval that would be caused if it quashed a statutory
instrument in reliance on which parties had been acting.[99] In *R. v. Secretary of*

---

[94] [1986] 1 W.L.R. 477.
[95] [1986] A.C. 484.
[96] See now Housing Act 1985, ss.58–78. *Cocks v. Thanet DC* [1983] 2 A.C. 286, *supra* para. 32–009
had established that decisions under the Act required to be challenged by judicial review.
[97] [1986] 1 W.L.R. 763.
[98] [1971] 1 W.L.R. 487.
[99] *R. v. Secretary of State for Social Services ex p. Association of Metropolitan Authorities* [1986] 1
W.L.R. 1.

State for the Environment ex p. Ward,[1] Woolf J. refused to grant mandamus against the Secretary of State because it could not be said that he had acted improperly or irrationally in reaching the decision which he had and interference would, in the light of the complicated situation, be premature. The learned judge quashed the decisions of the council which had been challenged (by certiorari) but refused to issue injunctions ordering them what to do next.

II. STATUTORY RIGHTS OF APPEAL

A right of appeal on a question of law may lie to the High Court from the **32–016** decision of a tribunal or Minister. The Tribunals and Inquiries Act 1958, s.9 (now s.11 of the 1992 Act) introduced a general right of appeal from a wide range of tribunals listed in Schedule 1 to the Act.[2] In addition rights of appeal are contained in many other statutes. The Acquisition of Land Act 1981 for example provides that any person who wishes to challenge the validity of a compulsory purchase order on the ground that it is *ultra vires* the Act may apply to the High Court.[3] The Town and Country Planning Act 1990 provides for appeals to the High Court against decisions of the Secretary of State (ss.289, 290).

Appeals to the ordinary courts may be by an indirect route as for example, in the case of appeals under the Lands Tribunal Act 1949 to the Lands Tribunal, from which an appeal on a point of law lies to the Court of Appeal.

As in the cases discussed in the preceding section an applicant must show that he has the necessary *locus standi* or, in the commonly used statutory words, is a person aggrieved. In *Ex p. Sidebotham*[4] James L.J. said: "A 'person aggrieved' must be a man who has suffered a legal grievance, a man against whom a decision has been pronounced which has wrongfully deprived him of something or wrongfully refused him something, or wrongfully affected his title to something." In line with that narrow approach it was held that a landowner had no *locus standi* to appeal against planning permission granted to a neighbouring landowner.[5] In *Arsenal Football Club v. Ende*[6] the House of Lords adopted a more generous approach and held that a ratepayer was entitled to challenge the valuation of any property in his rating area whether or not he could show that the decision challenged had a demonstrable effect on his pocket, rights or interests.

An applicant must also show that his appeal relates to a question of law as opposed to a question of fact, a distinction which it is not always easy to draw.[7] Whether A threw soup over B is clearly a question of fact. A tribunal may, however, in the light of a number of facts relating to the terms and conditions of A's work, have to decide whether A is an employee of B or an independent contractor or whether indeed there is any form of legal relationship between the two at all. If the courts wish to extend their appellate jurisdiction over a particular

---

[1] [1984] 1 W.L.R. 834.

[2] *ante*, para. 30–021.

[3] See *Smith v. East Elloe Rural District Council* [1956] A.C. 736; discussed *post*, para. 32–016.

[4] (1880) 14 Ch.D. 458, 465.

[5] *Buxton v. Minister of Housing and Local Government* [1961] 1 Q.B. 278.

[6] [1979] A.C. 1. In *Steeples v. Derbyshire L.C.* [1985] 1 W.L.R. 256 Webster J. said that it would "make an ass of the law" to require in other contexts a stricter test of *locus standi*; than that required by Order 53 (Now CPR, Pt 54).

[7] See articles cited *ante*, para. 31–007, n. 33.

type of tribunal they can categorise problems involving the classification of facts—was A an employee—as questions of law.[8] If they wish to avoid interfering with a tribunal's exercise of its jurisdiction they can treat such questions as matters of fact.[9] Or, as a compromise they can say that a question of law arises only when a decision on the application of the law to the facts is such that no tribunal properly instructed could have reached that conclusion.[10]

III. EXCLUSION OR RESTRICTION OF THE JURISDICTION OF THE COURTS

32–017   Statutes have purported or appeared to exclude judicial review by the courts by the use of various drafting formulae, though with scant success. The Tribunals and Inquiries Act 1992, s.12 (replacing the Act of 1958, s.11) now provides that any provision in an Act passed before August 1, 1958, that any order or determination shall not be called in question in any event, or any provision in such an Act which by similar words excludes any of the powers of the High Court, shall not prevent the use of the remedies of certiorari or mandamus except in the case of Acts making special provision for applications to the High Court within a limited time.

It was held by the Court of Appeal in *R. v. Medical Appeal Tribunal ex p. Gilmore*[11] that a formula like "any such order or decision shall be final" does not bar certiorari: it makes the decision final on the facts, but not final on the law. The formula that an order or rules made "shall have effect as if enacted in this Act" has dicta of the House of Lords both for and against the exclusion of judicial control.[12]

A different kind of provision is that found in some Acts concerning planning and the compulsory acquisition of land, which set a *time limit* (commonly six weeks) in which the validity of the order may be challenged in the High Court, and specifying the permitted grounds of complaint as (a) *ultra vires* or (b) non-compliance with the statutory procedure, and stating that subject to these provisions the order may not be questioned in any legal proceedings. The main purpose of such provision is to limit the time within which an order or decision may be questioned in the courts, so as to ensure that the *title* to land acquired by a public authority for building, etc. should not remain uncertain after a short time. In *Smith v. East Elloe Rural District Council*[13] the House of Lords held, by a majority of three to two, that after the six weeks' period a compulsory purchase order could not be challenged even on the ground that it had been procured by

---

[8] *Davies v. Presbyterian Church of Wales* [1986] 1 W.L.R. 323, HL (Question whether minister was employee of his church a question of law.)

[9] *O'Kelly v. Trust House Forte plc* [1984] Q.B. 90.

[10] *Edward v. Bairstow* [1956] A.C. 14.

[11] [1957] 1 Q.B. 575, CA. See also *South East Anglia Fire Bricks v. Non-Metallic Mineral Products Manufacturing Employees Union* [1981] A.C. 363.

[12] *Institute of Patent Agents v. Leshwood* [1894] A.C. 347, *obiter dicta* that judicial review was excluded; *Minister of Health v. R. ex p. Yaffe* [1931] A.C. 494, *obiter dicta* that judicial review was not excluded; see *R. v. Minister of Health ex p. Yaffe* [1930] 2 K.B. 98, CA.

[13] [1956] A.C. 736. The plaintiff had previously obtained damages against the council and contractors for trespass, as the continuance of wartime requisition was done in bad faith; *Smith v. East Elloe R.D.C.* [1952] *Current Property Law*. In subsequent proceedings by the plaintiff against the clerk and a representative of the Ministry for damages for conspiracy to injure, Diplock J. held that there was no conspiracy, that damages had already been recovered for trespass, and his Lordship was not satisfied that the clerk had in fact acted in bad faith: *Smith v. Pyewell, The Times*, April 29, 1959.

bad faith. It was not necessary to decide whether the order could be challenged for bad faith within six weeks. Of the minority who thought the order could be challenged for bad faith after six weeks, Lord Reid thought this was not excluded by the statute and Lord Somervell thought such remedy lay under general principle. The majority decision was much criticised as offending against the principles of natural justice; but although justice may require compensation for loss brought about by fraud, that does not necessarily mean that an order on which title to land is based should be upset.

The question was considered by the House of Lords in *Anisminic v. Foreign Compensation Commission*[14] The Foreign Compensation Act 1950, s.4, provided that "the determination by the Commission of any application made to them under this Act shall not be called in question in any court of law"; but the House of Lords (reversing the Court of Appeal) held by four to one that this provision did not prevent the court from making a declaration that the Commission's determination was a nullity. Lord Reid said: "It is one thing to question a determination which does exist: it is quite another thing to say that there is nothing to be questioned. . . . It is a well established principle that a provision ousting the ordinary jurisdiction of the court must be construed strictly. . . . No case has been cited in which any other form of words limiting the jurisdiction of the court has been held to protect a nullity. . . . Undoubtedly such a provision protects every determination which is not a nullity." Cases where the decision of a tribunal may be a nullity are: where it had no jurisdiction to enter into the inquiry; where it gave its decision in bad faith; where it made a decision which it had no power to make; where it failed to comply with the requirements of natural justice; where in good faith it decided the wrong question; and where it failed to take account of something of which it was required to take account, or based its decision on a matter which it ought not to have taken into account. Something much more specific than this Act would be required if it is to be held that Parliament intended to exclude the court's jurisdiction on any of these grounds. **32–018**

The *East Elloe* case (*ante*) was distinguished in the *Anisminic* case. Lord Reid did not regard the former case (in which he had dissented) as very satisfactory. It is not certain, he said, whether the plaintiff was claiming that the authority which made the order had itself acted in bad faith, in which case the order would be a nullity; or whether she was alleging that the clerk had fraudulently misled the council and the Ministry, in which case the result would be quite different.

In *R. v. Secretary of State for the Environment ex p. Ostler*[15] the Court of Appeal held, for a variety of reasons, that *East Elloe* had not been overruled by *Anisminic* and was applicable to a case involving a six week time limit under the Highways Act 1959. *Anisminic* was distinguished as applying only where there is a complete ouster of the courts' jurisdiction as opposed to an ouster after a time **32–019**

---

[14] [1969] 2 A.C. 147. Browne J.'s judgment at first instance, which was upheld by the House of Lords, is reported at [1969] 2 A.C. 223. See H. W. R. Wade, "Constitutional and Administrative Aspects of the *Anisminic* Case" (1969) 85 L.Q.R. 198; B. C. Gould, "Anisminic and Jurisdictional Review" [1970] P.L. 258; D. M. Gordon, "What did the Anisminic Case decide?" (1971) 34 M.L.R. 1; note by 5. A. de Smith in [1969] C.L.J. 161.

cf. Foreign Compensation Act 1969, s.3: No determination by the Commission may be called in question in any court of law, except (a) case stated on question of law to Court of Appeal concerning jurisdiction or interpretation of Order in Council and (b) proceedings on ground that determination is contrary to natural justice.

[15] [1977] Q.B. 122.

limit[16]; that it dealt with a determination by a judicial body whereas *East Elloe* dealt with an order of an administrative character; that it dealt with an actual decision whereas *East Elloe* dealt with the validity of the process by which the decision was reached; that it dealt with the ultimate question of jurisdiction as opposed to an attack on the validity of an order made within jurisdiction; and, finally that it dealt with the ultimate question of the payment of compensation as opposed to the validity of a compulsory purchase order.[17]

An exclusion clause which seems to have been drafted with the intention of defeating the reasoning in *Anisminic* is to be found in the Interception of Communications Act 1985. Section 7 "establishes a tribunal to investigate complaints relating to the interception of communications under the Act." Subsection (8) provides that "the decisions of the Tribunal (*including any decisions as to their jurisdiction*) shall not be subject to appeal or liable to be questioned in any court." (Italics added.) An exclusion clause of rather doubtful effect is to be found in the British Nationality Act 1981 s.44. Subsection (1) directs that any discretion vested by or under the Act in the Secretary of State shall be exercised without regard to the race, colour or religion of any person who may be affected by its exercise. Subsection (2) then provides that the Secretary of State shall not be required to give any reason for any decision made under his discretionary powers and any such decision "shall not be subject to appeal to, or review in, any court." Then subsection (3), apparently inconsistently provides that "Nothing in this section affects the jurisdiction of any court to entertain proceedings of any description concerning the rights of any person under any provision of this Act". Has subsection (1) given applicants a right not to be discriminated against?

32–020   In various contexts statutes[18] may provide that the issuing of a certificate is conclusive evidence that the requirements of an Act have been complied with[19] or that certain facts have occurred. In an earlier chapter reference was made to the conclusive effect of the Speaker's certificate issued under the Parliament Act 1911.[20] In the following chapter it will be seen that a Secretary of State may issue conclusive certificates under sections 10 and 40 of the Crown Proceedings Act 1947.[21] Such a form of ouster clause leaves little scope for judicial review, unless the validity of the certificate itself is attacked, for example on the ground of forgery. In *R. v. Registrar of Companies, ex p. Central Bank of India*[22] the Court of Appeal refused to inquire into whether the requirements of the Companies Act 1948 had been complied with in the light of a certificate that they had, such certificate being "conclusive evidence" under the Act. Lawton L.J. said that Parliament, by making the certificate conclusive evidence had excluded not the jurisdiction of the court but the admission of evidence.

32–021   Apart from directly excluding judicial review statutes may restrict the jurisdiction of the courts by conferring powers on ministers in subjective terms: the

[16] *per* Lord Denning, citing H. W. R. Wade, *Administrative Law* (3rd ed.), pp. 151–153. See (4th ed.) pp. 579–582.
[17] See J. Alder, "Time Limit Clauses and Judicial Review—*Smith v. East Elloe Revisited*" (1975) 38 M.L.R. 274; J. Alder, "Time Limit Clauses and Conceptualism, A Reply," (1960) 43 M.L.R. 670; L. H. Leigh, "Time Limit Clauses and Jurisdictional Error," [1980] P.L. 34.
[18] The courts themselves have recognised the conclusive effect of certificates in the sphere of foreign affairs; *ante* para. 15–023.
[19] *e.g. Ex p. Ringer* (1909) 25 T.L.R. 718, DC.
[20] *ante* para. 8–036.
[21] *post* para. 33–033 and para. 33–012.
[22] [1986] Q.B. 1114 The current legislative provision is s.401 of the Companies Act 1985.

minister may act "if satisfied." In such cases the courts may accept that they can only enquire if the minister was satisfied, not if he had reasonable grounds to be so.[23] Lord Salmon accurately, if unhelpfully, summarised the case law when he said, "[Those words] *may* confer an absolute discretion on the Executive. Sometimes they do, but sometimes they do not."[24] The courts have had to consider the scope of its jurisdiction where statutes use subjective language in two cases in the controversial area of relations between central and local government. The Education Act 1944, section 68 provides that the Secretary of State may give directions to a local education authority if he is satisfied that it had acted or was proposing to act "unreasonably." In *Secretary of State for Education and Science v. Tameside Metropolitan Borough Council*[25] the House of Lords held that the section required the existence of certain facts, *i.e.* those from which a properly directed minister could conclude the existence of unreasonableness in the *Wednesbury* sense. The evaluation of the facts was a matter for the subjective judgment of the minister; their existence was a matter for the court. (The House held that no facts existed from which an inference of unreasonableness could be drawn.) In *R. v. Secretary of State for the Environment ex p. Norwich County Council*[26] the Council challenged the legality of the Secretary of State using his default powers under the Housing Act 1980 s.23(1) which provided that the Secretary of State could give notice of his intention to exercise his statutory powers "where it appears . . . that tenants . . . have or may have difficulty in exercising the right to buy effectively and expeditiously."[27] The Court of Appeal held that no question of unreasonableness on the part of the Council was involved: unlike the *Tameside* case that word had not been used in the statute. Thus the power of the Minister was wider in the *Norwich* case. The Court held that in exercising his power he must act fairly and reasonably. On the facts he had done so since there was overwhelming evidence that tenants were having difficulty in exercising their rights.

The widest ministerial discretion of all, and the most complete exclusion of judicial control, occurs where the courts conclude that a particular issue is "non-justiciable." We have seen earlier that the courts are willing to recognise that Acts of State may be acts over which they have no jurisdiction[28] and in the GCHQ case, while asserting the right of review over powers derived from the Royal Prerogative, the House of Lords admitted that the exercise of certain prerogative powers would continue to fall outside the scope of judicial review.[29]

IV. PRIVATE LAW REMEDIES AGAINST PUBLIC AUTHORITIES

1. Action for damages

When an injury is done to a citizen's person or property by a public authority acting *ultra vires* or in abuse of power, an action for damages may be brought in   **32–022**

[23] See *ante*, para. 19–043.
[24] *Att.-Gen of St. Christopher, Nevis and Anguilla v. Reynolds* [1980] A.C. 637, PC.
[25] [1977] A.C. 1014. See too *Secretary of State for Employment v. ASLEF* (No. 2) [1972] 2 Q.B. 455.
[26] [1982] Q.B. 808.
[27] See now Housing Act 1985, s.164.
[28] *Nissan v. Att.-Gen.* [1970] A.C. 179.
[29] *Council of Civil Service Unions v. Minister for the Civil Service* [1985] A.C. 374.

circumstances where an action would lie against a private individual. The actions most commonly brought are for trespass,[30] false imprisonment,[31] negligence,[32] and nuisance.[33] It has been suggested that in cases not falling within the limits of established torts there may be a liability in damages for malicious use of statutory powers.[34]

If a public authority commits a breach of contract which it was within the powers of the authority to make, an action for damages will lie.[35]

2. Injunction and specific performance

32–023   Where a public authority threatens to do or to continue to do some unlawful act, such as a nuisance, an action may be brought for an injunction to restrain the authority from doing or continuing to do so. The breach of an injunction amounts to contempt of court. An injunction was originally an equitable remedy. It may be sought in addition to or instead of damages, but will only be granted at the discretion of the court exercised judicially and in the type of cases in which it would lie against a private individual. In *Pride of Derby Angling Association v. British Celanese Ltd*[36] an injunction was granted against the Derby Corporation and the British Electricity Authority to restrain them from continuing a nuisance by polluting a river. Although injunction is discretionary and will not be granted if, for example, damages would be a sufficient remedy, yet there is a prima facie right to an injunction if the defendant threatens to continue the nuisance.

Injunction is the appropriate method for questioning the right of a person to hold a particular office.[37] Proceedings in such a case must be brought by an application for judicial review.[38]

Where an act done by a public authority affects the public generally, the Attorney-General may sue for an injunction on behalf of the public. In some cases he may allow his name to be used at the request ("on the relation") of some individual ("the relator") who is substantially the party affected. This is called a "relator action."[39] A citizen may claim an injunction against a public authority in his own name only where, in addition to the threatened breach of a public right, either some private right of his is affected or he will suffer some damage peculiar to himself (*Boyce v. Paddington Borough Council*[40]; *Gouriet v. Union of Post Office Workers*[41]).

An action for specific performance of a contract may be brought against a public authority in similar circumstances to those in which specific performance

---

[30] *Cooper v. Wandsworth Board of Works* (1863) 14 C.B. (N.S.) 180; *ante* para. 32–001.
[31] *Percy v. Glasgow Corporation* [1922] A.C. 299.
[32] *Mersey Docks and Harbour Board v. Gibbs* (1866) L.R. 1 H.L. 93, *ante*, para. 31–024; *Davy v. Spelthorne B.C.* [1984] A.C. 262, HL; private law action for damages available even though negligence alleged occurred in connection with exercise of statutory powers.
[33] *Metropolitan Asylum District v. Hill* (1881) 6 App.Cas. 193.
[34] *Dunlop v. Woollahra Municipal Council* [1982] A.C. 158, PC; *Racz v. Home Office* [1994] 2 A.C. 45, HL; *Three Rivers D.C. v. Bank of England* [2000] 2 W.L.R 1220, HL.
[35] *Armour v. Liverpool Corporation* [1939] Ch. 422.
[36] [1953] Ch. 149, CA.
[37] Supreme Court Act 1981, s.30. Until its abolition by the Administration of Justice Act (Miscellaneous Provisions) 1938 the procedure in such cases had been by way of *Quo Warranto*.
[38] Supreme Court Act 1981, s.31(1)(c).
[39] *Att.-Gen. v. Wimbledon House Estate Co* [1904] 2 Ch. 34; *Att.-Gen. v. Bastow* [1957] 1 Q.B. 514; *Att.-Gen v. Smith* [1958] 2 Q.B. 173.
[40] [1903] 1 Ch. 109.
[41] [1978] A.C. 435.

would be granted against an ordinary corporation or private individual.[42] The contract must, of course, be one of the kind that is on principle enforceable against government authorities.[43]

3. Action for a declaration[44]

An action for a declaration asks for a "declaration of right." It may be brought **32–024** in the High Court even though no damages or other relief is claimed. The claim is often brought together with a claim for an injunction, and similar rules apply with regard to suing in the plaintiff's own name or at his relation by the Attorney-General.[45] There must be a justiciable issue,[46] and this remedy cannot be brought in order to ask hypothetical questions.[47] The Court, in its discretion, will not grant a declaration unless the remedy would be of real value to the plaintiff.[48] The Court will not grant declarations "which are academic and of no practical value."[49] A declaratory judgment cannot be directly enforced, but it may be assumed that a public authority will observe the law when the High Court declares what it is.

The action for a declaration has been used to test the validity of delegated legislation, and the *vires* of decisions of tribunals whether statutory or voluntary.[50] But a declaratory judgment cannot quash a decision, and the remedy may not be appropriate where the decision was within jurisdiction but there is error on the face of the record.[51] Since the adoption of the application for judicial review it will not, of course, be possible to apply for a declaration by writ if the issue is one of public law.[52]

---

[42] *Crook v. Corporation of Seaford* (1871) L.R. 6 Ch. 551; *cf. Crampton v. Varna Ry* (1872) 7 Ch.App. 562.

[43] See *ante*, para. 31–021.

[44] I. Zamir, *The Declaratory Judgment* (2nd ed., 1993, Lord Woolf and J. Woolf, eds.); E. Borchard, *Declaratory Judgments* (2nd ed., 1941), especially pp. 875–926.

[45] *ante*, para. 18–011.

[46] *Cox v. Green* [1966] Ch. 216; a question of professional etiquette is not justiciable. But *cf. Pharmaceutical Society of Great Britain v. Dickson* [1970] A.C. 403.

[47] *Re Barnato, Ioel v. Sanger* [1949] Ch. 258. *Mellstram v. Garner* [1970] 1 W.L.R. 603. *cf. Hampshire County Council v. Shonleigh Nominees* [1970] 1 W.L.R. 865.

[48] *Bennett v. Chappell* [1966] Ch. 391, CA.

[49] *Williams v. Home Office (No. 2)* [1981] 1 All E.R. 1211, 1248 *per* Tudor Evans J. (Appeal dismissed on procedural grounds: [1982] 2 All E.R. 564, CA.)

[50] *Davis v. Carew-Pole* [1956] 1 W.L.R. 833; [1956] 2 All E.R. 524; *Ceylon University v. Fernando* [1960] 1 All E.R. 631, PC.

[51] *Punton v. Ministry of Pensions and National Insurance (No. 2)* [1964] 1 W.L.R. 226; CA decision of National Insurance Commissioner. But see P. Cane, "A Fresh Look at Punton's Case," (1980) 43 M.L.R. 266.

[52] Even before the decision in *O'Reilly v. Mackman* [1983] 2 A.C. 237 the courts could, and did, refuse to hear applications for declarations where they thought that the procedure under Order 53 would be more appropriate: *e.g. Bousfield v. North Yorkshire C.C.* [1982] 44 P. & C.R. 203; *sub nom Re Tillmire Common*, [1982] 2 All E.R. 615. (Dillon J. refused to hear a summons for a declaration that a decision of a Commissioner under the Commons Registration Act 1965 was voidable for error of law on the face: proceedings in the Chancery Division were "misconceived and an abuse of process.")

Chapter 33

CROWN PROCEEDINGS

I. Liability of the Crown

Introduction[1]

33–001   Two ancient and fundamental rules of English constitutional law were abolished by the Crown Proceedings Act 1947. The first, that proceedings against the Crown for breach of contract or restitution of property could only be taken after obtaining a *fiat* by the inconvenient procedure of petition of right, was due to the principle that the King could not be impleaded in his own courts.[2] The second, that the Crown could not be proceeded against at all in tort, was due to the same principle coupled with the doctrine that "the King could do no wrong." No action lay at common law against the Sovereign personally, whether for public or private acts. Also—contrary to the law of agency and of master and servant—no action lay against the Sovereign for breach of contract or torts committed by Ministers, other officers or departments acting as servants or agents of the Crown. In certain cases, however, a petition of right would lie. The maxim "the King can do no wrong" meant not only that the King could not be made liable by action, but also that wrong could not be imputed to the King, and therefore he could not be said to have authorised another to commit a wrong. This ruled out the maxim *qui facit per alium facit per se* where the Crown was the employer. As there is no concept of the state in English law, and as government departments are merely groups of Crown servants, this meant that the citizen could not claim satisfaction out of public funds for torts committed by the Crown.

The immunity of the Crown at common law, subject to the limited and inconvenient procedure by petition of right, became increasingly serious in modern times owing to the growth of state activity, for the Crown had become the largest employer, contractor and occupier of property in the country. The grievance that it was necessary to apply to the Home Secretary for a *fiat* before bringing a petition of right was more a matter of form than of substance, for in practice the Attorney-General always recommended that the *fiat* should be granted where there was any sort of prima facie case against the Crown. On the other hand, the personal liability incurred by Crown servants for torts committed in their official capacity often failed to satisfy injured parties, who might not even know which individual was responsible; while the practice whereby the Treasury, in what it considered appropriate cases, paid ex gratia compensation where

---

[1] Gleeson E. Robinson, *Public Authorities and Legal Liability* (1925); G. S. Robertson, *Civil Proceedings by and against the Crown* (1908). For the history, see Holdsworth, *History of English Law*, Vol. IX, pp. 7–45; "The History of Remedies against the Crown" (1922) 38 L.Q.R. 141, 280.

[2] A privilege probably peculiar to the Sovereign and not an incident of feudal lordship. The immunity of the ordinary lord from actions in his own courts is anyway doubtful: Paul Jackson, "Sovereign Immunity: A Feudal Privilege?" (1975) 91 L.Q.R. 171; S. F. C. Milsom, *The Legal Framework of English Feudalism* (1976), pp. 80 *et seq.*

Crown servants were unsuccessful defendants was illogical, arbitrary and probably unlawful.

Matters came to a head at the end of the Second World War in two cases of **33–002** persons injured by the condition of premises occupied by the Crown. In *Adams v. Naylor*[3] two boys pursued a ball into a minefield which was negligently marked and fenced. One of the boys was killed, the other injured. An action was brought against an officer of the Royal Engineers, whose name had been supplied by the War Department as the responsible officer. It was not known who was personally responsible for the state of affairs at the time of the accident, and the House of Lords criticised *obiter*[4] the practice of government departments putting up "nominated" or "nominal" defendants as whipping-boys. Soon afterwards the Court of Appeal in *Royster v. Cavey*[5] felt constrained to follow the considered dicta of the House of Lords, where an employee in a Ministry of Supply ordnance factory, who had received personal injuries while so employed, wished to bring an action for negligence at common law and for breach of statutory duty under the Factories Act 1937. The plaintiff was supplied by the Treasury Solicitor with the name of the superintendent of the factory, but the latter had no connection with the factory at the time of the accident. The court held that it had no jurisdiction to try an action against him, as he was neither the occupier of the factory nor the plaintiff's employer.[6]

A comprehensive Crown Proceedings Bill[7] was then introduced by the Lord Chancellor, Viscount Jowitt. The Bill was privately examined by an informal committee of Law Lords and others, presided over by Viscount Simon, while the Lord Chancellor consulted all the other available judges. Lord Jowitt could therefore fairly claim that the Bill received "the unanimous approval of the entire Bench of Judges."

Crown Proceedings Act 1947[8]

The main objects of the Act were, as far as practicable, to make the Crown **33–003** liable in tort in the same way as a private person, and to reform the rules of procedure governing civil litigation by and against the Crown, especially by allowing an action without a *fiat* where the petition of right previously lay. The Act adopts the Anglo-American principle of treating the state (or "the Crown") for the purpose of litigation as nearly as possible in the same way as a private citizen, instead of borrowing the Continental idea of a separate system of

---

[3] [1946] A.C. 543.

[4] The case was decided on the Personal Injuries (Emergency Provisions) Act 1939.

[5] [1947] 1 K.B. 204. For a more recent attempt to resurrect John Doe as a defendant in an action against a government department see *Barnett v. French* [1981] 1 W.L.R. 848; "On the Demise of John Doe," (1983) 99 L.Q.R. 341. For the statutory solution to the problem see Regd. Traffic Regulation Act 1984, s.130.

[6] *Lane v. Cotton* (1701) 1 Ld.Raym. 646.

[7] Based partly on a draft Bill of 1927 (Cmd. 2842) prepared by a committee under two earlier Lord Chancellors, Birkenhead and Haldane. The delay was due largely to the misgivings of the Service Departments and the Post Office (then a government department).

[8] R. McM. Bell, *Crown Proceedings* (1948); J. R. Bickford Smith, *The Crown Proceedings Act, 1947* (1948); Glanville L. Williams, *Crown Proceedings* (1948); Sir Carleton Allen, *Law and Orders* (3rd ed., 1965), Chap. 10; H. Street, "Crown Proceedings Act, 1947" (1948) 11 M.L.R. 129–142; Sir Thomas Barnes, "The Crown Proceedings Act, 1947" (1948) 26 Can.Bar Rev. 387; G. H. Treitel, "Crown Proceedings: Some Recent Developments" [1957] P.L. 321.

For comparative surveys, see H. Street, *Governmental Liability* (1953); B. Schwartz and H. W. R. Wade, *Legal Control of Government* (1972); L. Neville Brown and J. Bell, *French Administrative Law* (5th ed., 1998); P. W. Hogg, *Liability of the Crown* (2nd ed., 1989).

administrative law. The effect is to bring English constitutional law nearer in one way to the conception of "the rule of law" than it was when Dicey wrote.

Part V applies the Act with appropriate modifications to Scotland,[9] and section 53 provided for the extension of the Act by Order in Council to Northern Ireland with any necessary modifications.

The Act is only concerned with the liability of the Crown in respect of the government in the United Kingdom (section 40(2)). A certificate of a Secretary of State to the effect that any alleged liability of the Crown arises otherwise than in respect of Her Majesty's Government in the United Kingdom shall, for the purposes of the Act be conclusive as to the matter certified (section 40(3)).[10] As a result of such a certificate being issued, Sir Robert Megarry V.-C. held that he had no jurisdiction under the Act to hear a case relating to alleged tortious acts committed by British forces in Berlin.[11] (Apart from the Act no proceedings lay because the Crown is not otherwise liable in tort and the Attorney-General could not be sued because he has no responsibilities or functions outside England, Wales and Northern Ireland.)[12]

Right to sue the Crown in contract, etc.

33–004

"Section 1. Where any person has a claim against the Crown after the commencement of this Act, and, if this Act had not been passed, the claim might have been enforced, subject to the grant of His Majesty's fiat, by petition of right, or might have been enforced by a proceeding provided by any statutory provision repealed by this Act, then, subject to the provisions of this Act, the claim may be enforced as of right, and without the fiat of His Majesty, by proceedings taken against the Crown for that purpose in accordance with the provisions of this Act."

This section gives the individual a right to sue the Crown without any *fiat* in cases where, if the Act had not been passed, he could (i) bring a petition of right or (ii) take any proceedings under special statutory provisions repealed by the Act, *e.g.* War Department Stores Act 1867. Proceedings by way of petition of right were abolished by section 13.

Most of the actions in contract brought against the Crown since the Act came into force have been settled out of court. Disputes over building contracts with the government usually go to arbitration.

Section 1 did not create a new cause of action, and so the limitations on the scope of the former petition of right continue to apply to this right of action.

Scope of petition of right[13]

33–005

The theory of the petition of right was that as the King was the fountain of justice, he would cause justice to be done as soon as the matter was brought to

---

[9] J. R. Bickford Smith, *The Crown Proceedings Act, 1947* (1948), pp. 49–58 (by K. W. B. Middleton); Fraser, *Outline of Constitutional Law* (2nd ed.), Chap. 11; J. D. B. Mitchell, *Constitutional Law* (2nd ed., 1968), Chap. 17.

[10] *R. v. Secretary of State for Foreign and Commonwealth Affairs ex p. Trawnik, The Times*, April 18, 1985, DC (Certificate not reviewable unless a nullity, *i.e.* not a genuine certificate, or on its face it had been issued outside the statutory power. The Court "would not use the *Anisminic* principle to trespass on the royal prerogative.")

[11] *Trawnik v. Lennax* [1965] 1 W.L.R. 532.

[12] So held by the Court of Appeal, reversing the Vice Chancellor on this second point: [1985] 1 W.L.R. 544.

[13] Clode, *Petition of Right* (1887); Holdsworth, *History of English Law*, Vol. IX, 7–45.

his notice. Petition of right lay first for the recovery of land of which the Crown had wrongly taken or retained possession, and for the recovery of chattels real and probably chattels personal. It also apparently lay for certain cases of damage caused by undue user of Crown property, such as the wrongful assertion of an easement causing damage.[14] When the law of contract developed, a petition of right came to be granted for breach of contract, at first for debt or liquidated damages (*e.g.* on a contract for goods supplied), and later for unliquidated damages.[15] In *Thomas v. The Queen*[16] it was held that Thomas, an engineer, was entitled to bring a petition of right claiming a reward and his expenses in respect of an artillery invention in accordance with an agreement with the Secretary of State for War. The remedy was also available to recover liquidated or unliquidated sums due under a statute where no other remedy was provided (*Attorney-General v. De Keyser's Royal Hotel Ltd*[17]) and was probably available in quasi-contract.[18]

There were four limitations or exceptions to the availability of a petition of right:

(i) Owing to the prerogative immunity in tort, a petition of right did not lie for a pure tort, that is, a tort unconnected with the wrongful taking of property, such as negligence or trespass. Thus in *Viscount Canterbury v. Attorney-General*,[19] an ex-Speaker failed in his claim for compensation from the Crown for damage done to his furniture by the negligence of certain Crown servants who, by burning an excessive quantity of old Exchequer tallies, caused a fire which destroyed the Houses of Parliament in 1834. Similarly, in *Tobin v. The Queen*[20] the owners of a ship trading in palm oil off the coast of Africa failed in their claim for compensation from the Crown for the destruction of the ship and cargo by the captain of *H.M.S. Espoir*, who had falsely assumed that she was engaged in the slave trade which he had statutory authority to suppress. The same rule would apply to false imprisonment, conversion and libel.

(ii) Contracts of service with members of the armed forces are controlled by the prerogative.[21] The position of civilian officers and civil servants is in some respects not free from doubt.[22]

(iii) Contracts that fetter future executive action. During the First World War **33–006** the Swedish (neutral) owners of *S.S. Amphitrite* were induced to send the ship to a British port by a letter from the British Legation at Stockholm stating that she would be released if she proceeded to the United Kingdom with a cargo of approved goods. The ship did so but was nevertheless refused a clearance, and

---

[14] *Tobin v. The Queen* (1864) 16 C.B.(N.S.) 310, *per* Erle C.J. at pp. 363–365.

[15] *The Bankers' Case* (1700) 14 St.Tr. 1.

[16] (1875) L.R. 10 Q.B. 31.

[17] [1920] A.C. 508, HL. And see *Commercial and Estates Co of Egypt v. Board of Trade* [1925] 1 K.B. 271 (angary; compensation payable by international law).

[18] *cf. Brocklebank Ltd v. R.* [1925] 1 K.B. 52. Since the Crown Proceedings Act, if not before, the question of waiver of tort is irrelevant. See further, Street, *Governmental Liability*, pp. 125–127; A. W. Mewett, "The Quasi-Contractual Liability of Governments" (1959–60) 13 U.T.L.J. 56.

[19] (1843) 1 Phillips 306; (1843) 12 L.J.Ch. 281.

[20] (1864) C.B.(N.S.) 310; *ante*. The judgment of Erle C.J. suggests that an action would have lain against the captain.

[21] *ante*, para. 19–005. And see Z. Cowen, "The Armed Forces of the Crown" (1950) 66 L.Q.R. 478.

[22] *ante*, para. 18–026.

the owners brought a petition of right for damages for breach of contract: *Rederiaktiebolaget Amphitrite v. The King.*[23] Rowlatt J. gave judgment for the Crown, on the ground that there was no enforceable contract. "It is not competent for the Government," said his Lordship, "by enforceable contract to fetter its future executive action, which must necessarily be determined by the needs of the community when the question arises. It cannot by contract hamper its freedom of action in matters which concern the welfare of the State." The judgment was an unconsidered one and no authorities were cited, but it is generally taken as an authority for the principle stated above. On the facts of the case it would have been sufficient to hold that the letter from the British Legation was merely an expression of present intention of what the government would do, and that the Crown did not intend to enter into contractual relations.[24] Rowlatt J. distinguished "commercial" contracts, on which the Crown can be made liable. Otherwise the limits of the supposed rule are uncertain,[25] and in fact no subsequent English decision has been based on it.[26] The common law makes no provision for compensation in such cases.

(iv) *Contracts dependent on grant from Parliament.* In *Churchward v. R.*[27] Churchward contracted with the Admiralty Commissioners to maintain a mail service between Dover and the Continent for eleven years, expressly in consideration of an annual sum to be provided by Parliament. The Admiralty terminated the contract in the fourth year, and the Appropriation Act of that year provided that no part of the sum appropriated towards the post office packet service should be paid to Churchward after a certain date. Churchward naturally failed in his petition of right for breach of contract, but dicta in that case have led to the view that the provision of funds by Parliament is an implied precedent condition for the liability of the Crown on its contracts, and even for the validity of Crown contracts.[28] There is no good reason, however, why funds should be antecedently or specifically appropriated by Parliament in order that the Crown may make contracts through responsible Crown servants in the course of their

---

[23] [1921] 3 K.B. 500.

[24] This reasoning was approved by Denning J. in *Robertson v. Minister of Pensions* [1949] 1 K.B. 227, 231. And see *Australian Woollen Mills Ltd v. Commonwealth of Australia* [1956] 1 W.L.R. 11; [1955] 3 All E.R. 711, PC.

[25] See Holdsworth in (1929) 45 L.Q.R. 166 for a strong criticism of the rule. According to one view, the *Amphitrite* case, if kept within due limits, supports the general principle of "governmental effectiveness": J. D. B. Mitchell, *The Contracts of Public Authorities*, pp. 27, 52 *cf.* Street, *op. cit.* p. 98.

[26] *cf. The Steaua Romana* [1944] p. 43. The *Amphitrite* case was followed by the High Court of Southern Rhodesia in *Waterfalls Town Management Board v. Minister of Housing* [1956] Rhod. and Ny. L.R. 691. It was not referred to in *Board of Trade v. Temperley Steam Shipping Co* (1927) 27 Ll.L.R. 230 where the Court of Appeal held that the implied obligation of a party to a contract not to interfere with the performance of the contract did not apply to prevent a Crown servant exercising his statutory powers so as to interfere with a contract to which the Crown was a party. It was referred to by Devlin L.J. in *Crown Land Commissioners v. Page* [1960] 2 Q.B. 274, where it was held that the Crown as lessor was not prevented by implied covenant for quiet enjoyment from exercising a statutory power to requisition from one of its tenants, and in *Dowty Boulton Paul Ltd v. Wolverhampton Corporation* [1971] 1 W.L.R. 204 where, however, Pennycuick V.-C., in interlocutory proceedings, thought that it would not avail to release the Corporation from contractual liabilities. See further *Cudgen Rutile (No. 2) Ltd v. Chalk* [1975] A.C. 520, PC; C. Turpin, *Government Contracts* (1972), pp. 19–25; Rogerson, "On the Fettering of Public Powers" (1971) P.L. 288; *ante*, para. 31–022.

[27] (1865) L.R. 1 Q.B. 173; 6 B. & S. 807.

[28] (1865) L.R. 1 Q.B. 173, 209, *per* Shee J.; *cf. per* Cockburn C.J. at pp. 200–201.

official duties. Enforceability, on the other hand, is a different matter from validity, and the other party cannot obtain satisfaction from the Crown if parliamentary funds are not available when the time arrives for payment.[29]

The Petitions of Right Act 1860 provided a simpler procedure than that which existed at common law, following complaints by Army contractors during the Crimean War about the difficulty of recovering debts from the War Department. **33–007**

A Crown servant is not personally liable at common law for the breach of a contract entered into by him in his official capacity. Thus in *Macbeath v. Haldimand*[30] the King's Bench held General Haldimand, Governor of Quebec, not liable for stores ordered by him from Macbeath for the Fort of Michilimakinac. The plaintiff knew that the goods were for government use, and that the defendant was not contracting personally. Thus stated, it is merely an application of the general law of agency. It is now clear that a petition of right would have lain before 1948 in the circumstances of this case.[31]

There were some statutory exceptions. Parliament occasionally used language referring to the bringing of actions by or against a government department or Minister in his official capacity, with or without incorporating that department or Minister. The effect of such language and the extent (if any) of liability to be sued depended on the interpretation of the words used in the particular statute. The matter was reviewed by the Court of Appeal in *Minister of Supply v. British Thomson-Houston Co.*,[32] where it was held that the War Department Stores Act 1867 rendered the Minister of Supply liable to be sued on official contracts concerning military stores. The Ministry of Transport Act 1919 expressly made the Minister officially liable in tort as well as contract.

Liability of the Crown in tort

"Section 2(1). Subject to the provisions of this Act, the Crown shall be subject to all those liabilities in tort to which, if it were a private person of full age and capacity, it would be subject: **33–008**

(a) in respect of torts committed by its servants or agents;

(b) in respect of any breach of those duties which a person owes to his servants or agents at common law by reason of being their employer; and

(c) in respect of any breach of the duties attaching at common law to the ownership, occupation, possession or control of property . . . "

---

[29] *Commercial Cable Co v. Government of Newfoundland* [1916] 2 A.C. 610, 617, PC *per* Viscount Haldane; *Mackay v. Att.-Gen. for British Columbia* [1922] 1 A.C. 457, 461, *per* Viscount Haldane; *Commonwealth of Australia v. Kidman* (1926) 32 A.L.R. 1, 2–3, PC *per* Viscount Haldane; *New South Wales v. Bardolph* (1934) 52 C.L.R. 455, 474, *per* Evatt J.: and see *per* Dixon J. *cf. Att.-Gen. v. Great Southern and Western Ry of Ireland* [1925] A.C. 754, 773, 779, HL. See further, Colin Turpin, *op. cit.*

[30] (1786) 1 T.R. 172.

[31] *Thomas v. R.* (1875) L.R. 10 Q.B. 31. Few petitions of right on contracts were brought from the time of the Restoration, when the Sovereign came to rely almost entirely on parliamentary grants to finance the government of the country, until the Crimean War.

[32] [1943] K.B. 478.

This is the most important section, which provided the *raison d'être* of the Act. The marginal note reads: "Liability of the Crown in tort," but the Act does not make the Crown liable generally in tort: subsection (1) makes the Crown liable in three classes of case:

(a) *Vicarious liability to third parties for torts,* such as negligence or trespass committed by servants in the course of their employment, and for the authorised or ratified torts of independent contractors.

At common law actions in tort could not be brought against government departments, for they are not legal entities but consist of a number of individual Crown servants. Nor could the injured party sue the head of the department or other superior officer of the Crown servant who committed the tort, because they are fellow servants of the Crown and do not stand to each other in the relation of master and servant[33]; unless the superior officer actually ordered or directed the commission of the tort, in which case it would also be his act.[34] The general rule was therefore that the action had to be brought against the actual wrongdoer or wrongdoers, and it had to be brought against them personally and not as servants or agents of the Crown or of the department, nor as a department. Thus in *Raleigh v. Goschen*[35] an action for trespass to land brought against Goschen (First Lord of the Admiralty), the Lords Commissioners of the Admiralty and the Director-General of Naval Works was dismissed on the ground that it should have been brought against the engineer employed by the Admiralty and/or the two marines who actually committed the trespass with him, and/or against such (if any) of the defendants personally as had actually ordered or directed the trespass.

33–009   A proviso to section 2(1) adds that the Crown shall not be liable unless, apart from the Act, an action in tort would have lain against the servant or agent. This may be intended to preserve such defences as act of state or acting under prerogative or statutory powers (which in any case is provided for by section 11); but is has the effect of exempting the Crown in any exceptional cases which might arise where an ordinary employer might be held liable even though the servant who actually committed the tort could not for some reason be sued.[36]

In *Dorset Yacht Co Ltd v. Home Office,*[37] where the plaintiff's yacht was damaged by Borstal trainees who had escaped from a nearby camp where they were under the control of Borstal officers, the House of Lords held as a preliminary issue that the Home Office owed a duty of care to the plaintiffs capable of giving rise to liability in damages if negligence could be proved. Lord Denning M.R. in the Court of Appeal said that the Crown would be similarly liable if it

---

[33] *Bainbridge v. Postmaster-General* [1906] 1 K.B. 178; *Town Investments v. Department of the Environment* [1978] A.C. 359, HL.

[34] *Lane v. Cotton* (1701) Ld.Raym. 646.

[35] [1898] 1 Ch. 73: the Admiralty wanted the land at Dartmouth in order to build a naval college. See also *Madrazo v. Willes* (1820) 3 B. & Ald. 353, and *Walker v. Baird* [1892] A.C. 491 (naval captains liable for wrongful damage to property inflicted in the supposed course of duty).

[36] *e.g. Smith v. Moss* [1940] 1 K.B. 424. And see *Twine v. Bean's Express Ltd* [1946] 1 All E.R. 202, 204.

[37] [1970] A.C. 1004. In *Greenwell v. Prison Commissioners* (1951) 101 L.J. 486; (1952) 68 L.Q.R. 18 the plaintiffs obtained damages in a county court for damage to their vehicle caused by boys who had escaped from an "open" Borstal. See C. J. Hamson, "Escaping Borstal Boys and the Immunity of Office" (1969) 27 C.L.J. 273. See too *Writtle (Vicar of) v. Essex C.C.* (1979) 77 L.G.R. 656 (The case of the infant arsonist). The limitations to *Dorset Yackt* in the context of general principles of tortious liability are discussed in *King v. Liverpool C.C.* [1986] 1 W.L.R. 890, CA.

negligently permitted prisoners to escape and they commit foreseeable damage.[38]

The tortious acts of prison staff to prisoners may also give rise to cases of vicarious liability.[39]

(b) *Breach of common law duties owed by an employer to his employees, viz.* to supply proper plant, to provide a safe system of working and to select fit and competent fellow-servants.[40]

(c) *Common law liability attaching to the ownership, occupation, possession or* **33–010** *control of property.* This would include liability for nuisance; the rule in *Rylands v. Fletcher*[41]; liability for dangerous chattels, etc. The right to sue under section 2 is implied, for *ubi jus ibi remedium.*[42]

Section 2(2) provides that, in those cases where the crown is bound by *statutory duties* which are also binding on persons other than the Crown and its officers, the Crown shall be liable in tort for breach of such statutory duties if private persons are so liable.[43] In order to make the Crown liable under this subsection it must be shown, first, that the Crown is *bound* by the statute, the presumption against this[44] being preserved by section 40(2); secondly, that other persons (including local authorities or public corporations) are also bound by the statute; and thirdly, that other persons can be made liable in tort for such breach.

Where functions are conferred by law directly on an officer of the Crown, he is regarded for the purpose of this section as if he were acting as an agent under instructions from the Crown (subs.(3)). The Crown has the benefit of any statute regulating or limiting the liability of a government department or Crown officer (subs.(4)).

Subsection 5 excludes proceedings against the Crown for acts done by any person "while discharging or purporting to discharge any responsibilities of a judicial nature vested in him, or any responsibilities which he has in connection with the execution of judicial process".[45] Thus if judges, magistrates or constables exceed the limits of their immunity, they do not—even if they are regarded as Crown servants or agents[46]—render the Crown liable for torts committed while discharging or purporting to discharge their judicial functions. An initial decision that a claimant is or is not entitled to a social security benefit

---

[38] See *Greenwell v. Prison Commissioners, ante.*

[39] *Morgan v. Att.-Gen.* [1965] N.Z.L.R. 134; *Ferguson v. Home Office, The Times,* October 8, 1977. A claim in negligence failed in *Ellis v. Home Office* [1953] 2 Q.B. 135 where the Home Secretary successfully claimed that Crown Privilege entitled the withholding of documents vital to the plaintiff's case. A claim alleging assault and trespass against a prison doctor failed in *Freeman v. Home Office (No. 2)* [1984] Q.B. 524.

[40] *Joseph v. Ministry of Defence, The Times,* March 4, 1980, CA. (Unsuccessful claim by employee of Ministry of Defence for illness allegedly caused by breach of employer's duty.)

[41] (1866) L.R. 1 Ex. 265; (1868) L.R. 3 H.L. 330.

[42] *Ashby v. White* (1703) 1 Smith L.C. (13th ed.), p. 251; 2 Ld.Raym. 320, 938.

[43] *cf. Royster v. Capey* [1947] K.B. 204; *Cooper v. Hawkins* [1904] 2 K.B. 164.

[44] *ante,* para. 15–019.

[45] See A. Rubinstein, "Liability in Tort of Judicial Officers" (1963) 15 U.T.L.J. 317.

[46] *cf.* Holdsworth, "The Constitutional Position of the Judges" (1932) 48 L.Q.R. 25–26; *Lewis v. Cattle* [1938] 2 K.B. 454 (police constable).

is, on the other hand, an administrative not a judicial function. A judicial element would arise at the appeal stage, heard before a tribunal.[47]

Officers (*i.e.* Ministers and other servants: section 38(2)) who may render the Crown liable under section 2 are limited to those appointed directly or indirectly by the Crown and paid wholly out of the Consolidated Fund or moneys provided by Parliament, or holding an office which would normally be so paid (subs.(6)). This provision, which is narrower than the vague common law definition of a Crown servant,[48] covers unpaid temporary civil servants, but not police or other public officers forming part of the government of the country who are appointed or paid by local or other public authorities.[49]

33–011   Many actions against the Crown in tort have been commenced in the High Court and county court, but most have been settled.[50] A number of writs have been in running-down cases, involving the negligence of drivers of government-owned vehicles.[51]

Where the Crown is liable under Part I of the Act, section 4 applies to the Crown the law relating to indemnity and contribution between tortfeasors and contributory negligence.[52] It is presumed that the Crown is bound by certain statutes reforming the law of tort, whether passed before or after the Crown Proceedings Act, even though the intention to bind the Crown does not appear either in the Crown Proceedings Act or expressly or by necessary implication in such statutes themselves. Section 10 of the Crown Proceedings Act (*infra*) seems to imply that the Fatal Accidents Act 1846 (compensation for dependants of deceased) and the Law Reform (Miscellaneous Provisions) Act 1934, s.1 (survival of causes of action on death) apply to the Crown.[53] But nothing is said about the Crown, for instance, in the Defamation Act 1952, which Act put the defendant in a better position than he was at common law.[54]

Section 3 makes the Crown liable if it authorises a servant or agent to infringe a patent, trademark or design or copyright.[55] The statutory right of the Crown is

---

[47] *Jones v. Dept of Employment* [1989] Q.B.I., CA. *Welsh v. Chief Constable of Merseyside Police* [1993] 1 All E.R. 692 (Failure to pass on information to court by CPS: not a judicial act within s.2(5)).

[48] *Bank voor Handel en Scheevbaart N.V. v. Administrator of Hungarian Property* [1954] A.C. 584, HL. See also *Ranaweera v. Ramachandran* [1970] A.C. 962, PC at 972–973, *per* Lord Diplock.

[49] See now Police Act 1996, s.88 for vicarious liability of Chief Constables; *ante* para. 21–011. For a successful claim in negligence see *Rigby v. Chief Constable of Northamptonshire* [1985] 1 W.L.R. 1242. *Stanbury v. Exeter Corporation* [1905] 2 K.B. 838 (agricultural inspector); *Tamtin v. Hannaford* [1950] 1 K.B. 18 (British Transport Commission).

[50] See, *e.g. Churchill v. Foot, The Times*, January 28, 1968; *Freshwater Biological Association v. Ministry of Defence, The Times*, December 14, 1970.

[51] In *Browning v. War Office* [1963] 1 Q.B. 750, CA, where a member of the United States Air Force was injured through the negligence of a driver of a British army lorry, the question in issue was the measure of damages. See also *Brazier v. Ministry of Defence* [1965] 1 Lloyd's Rep. 26; *The Tramontana II v. Ministry of Defence and Martin* [1969] 2 Lloyd's Rep. 94; *Bright v. Att.-Gen.* [1971] 2 Lloyd's Rep. 68, CA.

[52] In particular, the Law Reform (Married Women and Tortfeasors) Act 1935 and the Law Reform (Contributory Negligence) Act 1945.

[53] In *Levine v. Morris* [1970] 1 W.L.R. 71, CA the personal representatives of a man killed in a motor accident successfully sued the Ministry of Transport as well as a private driver for negligence.

[54] See G. H. Treitel, "Crown Proceedings: Some Recent Developments" [1957] P.L. 321, 322–326.

[55] The infringement of a patent copyright is not properly classified as a tort, but it was held in *Feather v. Reg.* (1865) 6 B. & S. 257 that a petition of right was not appropriate.

preserved to use patents on paying compensation assessed by the Treasury,[56] as are rights of the Crown under the Atomic Energy Act 1946.

There are certain matters where the analogy between the Crown and the subject breaks down, for in these spheres the functions of the Crown involve responsibility of a kind which no subject undertakes. Examples are the defence of the realm and the maintenance of the armed forces.[57]

Provisions relating to the armed forces

Section 10(1) of the 1947 Act provided that members of the armed forces **33–012** could not bring actions in tort against other members of the armed forces or the Crown in relation to injuries or death arising from anything suffered while on duty as a member of the armed forces or (whether on duty or not) while on any land or premises or vehicle for the time being used for the purposes of the armed forces, provided that the Secretary of State certified that the injury or death would be attributable to armed service for the purposes of the awarding of a pension. Section 10(2) in similar terms excluded liability on the part of the Crown for injuries or death arising from the nature or condition of any land, premises or vehicles being used for the purposes of the armed forces.

Apart from the question whether a pension could provide comparable compensation to that obtainable in an action in tort, the courts held that the immunity conferred on the Crown operated if a certificate were issued, even if a pension were not subsequently paid.[58]

Increasing dissatisfaction with the provisions of section 10 led to litigation and some judicial ingenuity in construing the section.[59] A lengthy Parliamentary campaign finally led to the enactment of a Bill, introduced by Mr Winston Churchill, as the Crown Proceedings (Armed Forces) Act 1987.

Section 1 of the 1987 Act repeals section 10 but section 2 empowers the **33–013** Secretary of State to revive section 10 when there is imminent national danger or a great emergency has arisen or for the purposes of warlike activities outside the United Kingdom or other operations in connection with warlike activity.

After the repeal of section 10 a member of the armed forces who wishes to sue for injuries sustained in military service must of course succeed in showing that the act complained of was negligent. Sir Hartley Shawcross, in the Second Reading of the 1947 Bill, had pointed out that service life inevitably involves highly dangerous activities which, if done by private citizens would be extremely blameworthy. The difficulty facing such a litigant, at least in relation to activities occurring in the heat of battle is illustrated by *Mulcahy v. Ministry of Defence*.[60] The Court of Appeal struck out an action based on injuries allegedly suffered when the plaintiff was "in a war zone taking part in warlike operations . . . a member of a gun crew . . . engaged in firing shells on enemy targets". The Court held that in such circumstances it would not be fair just and reasonable to impose on the Crown a duty to maintain a safe system of work. Reference was also made

---

[56] Since the Patent Act 1907 patents are effective against the Crown, but the Crown has a right to use patents on paying compensation. See *Pfixer Corporation v. Ministry of Health* [1965] A.C. 512, HL, use of patented drugs by hospital under National Health Service. See now, Patents and Design Act 1977, ss.55–59.

[57] Also formerly the Post Office, *ante*, para. 28–012.

[58] *Adams v. War Office* [1955] 1 W.L.R. 1116.

[59] *Bell v. Secretary of State for Defence* [1986] Q.R. 322, CA; disapproved, *Pearce v. Secretary of State for Defence* [1988] A.C. 755. See too, *Brown v. Lord Advocate* 1984 S.L.T. 146.

[60] [1996] Q.B. 732, CA.

to *Burmah Oil Co v. Lord Advocate*[61] and *Shaw Savill & Albion Co v. Commonwealth*[62] as justifying the immunity of the Crown from liability. In more mundane circumstances, the widow of a deceased sailor who asphyxiated on his vomit when drunk, failed to establish a duty of care owed by senior officers to prevent servicemen drinking to excess: *Barrett v. Ministry of Defence.*[63]

Acts done under prerogative or statutory powers

33–014 Section 11 states that nothing in the above provisions shall extinguish or abridge the prerogative or statutory powers of the Crown: in particular, the powers exercisable by the Crown, whether in peace or war, for the defence of the realm or the training or maintenance of the armed forces. Among prerogative powers not mentioned are those relating to the treatment of aliens, the employment of Crown servants and the principle of the *Amphitrite* case.[64] Statutory powers would include the billeting of soldiers.

A Secretary of State, "if satisfied" as to the facts, may issue a conclusive certificate that the act was necessarily done in the exercise of the prerogative, for example that it was necessary for the sake of practice to fire guns that have broken windows or kept people awake at night. It remains the function of the court to decide whether, and to what extent, the alleged prerogative exists.[65] This section is of fundamental importance for the word "prerogative" has a very wide range.

No such certificate may be made in the case of statutory powers, and indeed their express preservation was not necessary.

The Queen in her private capacity

33–015 The Act does not apply to proceedings by or against, nor does it authorise proceedings in tort to be brought against, the Queen in her private capacity (section 40(1)), or in right of the Duchy of Lancaster or Cornwall (section 38(3)). This preserves the Queen's personal immunity in tort; but it is uncertain whether for breach of contract (*e.g.* sale of groceries to Buckingham Palace) or wrongful detention of property by the Queen personally the subject can still proceed under the Petitions of Right Act 1860, or whether he is thrown back on the ancient common law petition of right.[66] There are in fact no reported instances of petitions of right against a Sovereign in his private capacity, but the doubt as to procedure is inconvenient as Her Majesty might legitimately wish to deny liability or dispute the amount.

Estoppel

33–016 The arguments for and against applying the doctrine of estoppel to public bodies generally have been discussed earlier.[67] The same arguments apply to the Crown in its public capacity and there is judicial authority for the view that the

---

[61] [1965] A.C. 75, HL.

[62] (1940) 66 C.L.R. 344. See Hogg, *op. cit.* 135 *et. seq.*

[63] [1995] 1 W.L.R. 1217, CA. (Duty of care, however, arose on taking responsibility for deceased once he had lost consciousness. Damages recoverable reduced by two-thirds to reflect deceased's contributory negligence.)

[64] *Rederiaktiebolaget Amphitrite v. The King* [1921] 3 K.B. 500; *ante*, para. 33–006.

[65] *Case of Monopolies* (1602) 11 Co.Rep. 84b; *Case of Proclamations* (1610) 12 Co.Rep. 74; *Att.-Gen. v. De Keyser's Royal Hotel Ltd* [1920] A.C. 506, HL; *Burmah Oil Co v. Lord Advocate* [1965] A.C. 75, HL.

[66] See *post*, para. 33–019.

[67] *ante*, para. 31–020.

same answer applies to the Crown.[68] In *Laker Airways Ltd v. Department of Trade*[69] Lord Denning M.R. said, "The underlying principle is that the Crown cannot be estopped from exercising its powers, whether given in a statute or by common law, when it is doing so in the proper exercise of its duty to act for the public good, even though this may work some injustice or unfairness to a private individual. ... It can, however, be estopped when it is not properly exercising its powers, but is misusing them; and it does misuse them if it exercises them in circumstances which work injustice or unfairness to the individual without any countervailing benefit for the public."[70]

II. Civil Proceedings by and Against the Crown[71]

Jurisdiction and procedure

The Crown Proceedings Act 1947 provides that the civil proceedings[72] by and against the Crown which are allowed by Part I of the Act shall be heard in the High Court (section 13) or the county court (section 15) as in actions between subjects and in accordance with rules of court, and similar principles apply to appeals (section 22).

33–017

The Treasury is required to publish a list of authorised government departments, and proceedings are to be instituted by or against the appropriate department, or—if there is, or appears to be, no appropriate department—the Attorney-General (section 17). It will be noticed that proceedings under the Act are not taken by or against either the Queen or the ministerial head of the department.

Section 21 of the Crown Proceedings Act prohibits the granting of an injunction or specific performance against the Crown or against an officer of the Crown if the effect of the order would be to give any relief against the Crown which could not have been obtained directly in proceedings against the Crown. The meaning of the section was subjected to elaborate (but probably not final) analysis in *Re M*.[73] The Secretary of State, Kenneth Baker, had rejected a claim to asylum by M who was subsequently deported from the United Kingdom in

---

[68] *e.g. Robertson v. Minister of Pensions* [1949] 1 K.B. 227; In *Re 56 Denton Road Twickenham* [1953] Ch. 51. But see *Howell v. Falmouth Boat Construction Co Ltd* [1951] A.C. 837, 845 *per* Lord Simonds. The application of estoppel by representation was discussed, but not decided, in *Territorial and Auxiliary Forces Association v. Nichols* [1944] 1 K.B. 35, CA.

[69] [1977] Q.B. 643.

[70] See further, H. Street, *Governmental Liability* (1953), p. 156; P. W. Hogg, *Liability of the Crown* (2nd ed., 1989), p. 189. There seems to be no doubt that the Crown is bound by equitable proprietary estoppel: *Plimmer v. Mayor of Wellington* (1884) 9 App.Cas. 699; *Att.-Gen. to Prince of Wales v. Collom* [1916] 2 K.B. 193.

[71] R. M. Bell, *Crown Proceedings* (1948); J. R. Bickford Smith, *The Crown Proceedings Act 1947* (1948); Glanville L. Williams, *Crown Proceedings* (1948); Carleton Allen, *Law and Orders* (3rd ed.), Chap. 10; S. A. de Smith, *Judicial Review of Administrative Action* (2nd ed., 1968); H. Street, *Governmental Liability* (1953).

[72] The Act does not apply to criminal or Prize proceedings; nor does it affect proceedings on the Crown side of the Queen's Bench Division, *e.g.* habeas corpus, certiorari, prohibition and mandamus (s.38(2)).

[73] [1994] 1 A.C. 377.

circumstances which were alleged to constitute a contempt of court by the Home Secretary. The Court of Appeal held that the Home Secretary had been guilty of contempt in defying an injunction issued by the High Court. In the House of Lords it was argued that contempt proceedings do not lie against the Crown, a department of state or a minister of the Crown acting in his capacity as such. That in turn involved a consideration of the jurisdiction of the court to issue injunctions against those parties. Lord Woolf, in the leading speech, emphasised the personal liability of ministers for acts constituting private law wrongs, as a consequence of the constitutional principle that the Crown can do no wrong.[74] Nothing in the section took away existing rights: it was part of legislation intended to make it easier for proceedings to be brought against the Crown.[75] Thus, at most section 21 appears to prevent injunctions being granted against "the Crown" where that term is used in a general sense, which in the case of statutory duties is unlikely to occur. In public law proceedings under the Supreme Court Act 1981, s.31 Lord Woolf demonstrated again that injunctions were available against ministers contrary to the view mistakenly expressed by Lord Bridge in *R. v. Secretary of State for Transport ex p. Factortame Ltd.*[76]

The availability of the declaration against the Crown in the sense of ministers and departments has been established since *Dyson v. Attorney-General.*[77]

33–018   If the Crown seeks an injunction it may, since 1947, be required to give an undertaking in damages as a condition of its being granted, as in the case of a private litigant. Where the injunction is sought, not to enforce a proprietary of contractual right of the Crown, but to restrain a breach of the law in the public interest the court has a discretion not to require such an undertaking.[78]

The remedies provided by the Act do not limit the discretion of the Court to grant mandamus in cases where that might have been granted before the commencement of the Act, *i.e.* (semble) where a duty is owed to a citizen.[79]

An action may be brought against the Attorney-General or (since the Crown Proceedings Act) against the appropriate authorised department, asking the court to declare what the law is on a given point where the Crown or servants of the Crown threaten to do something which is thought to be illegal. This remedy against the Crown originated in the Court of Exchequer.[80] In *Dyson v. Attorney-General*[81] the Court of Appeal held that this was a proper procedure where the plaintiff contended that a threat by the Inland Revenue Commissioners to impose a pecuniary penalty for neglecting to make certain returns within a specified time

---

[74] *Feather v. The Queen* (1865) 6 B. & S. 257, 296 *per* Cockburn C.J.
[75] See similarly, *British Medical Association v. Greater Glasgow Health Board* [1989] A.C. 1211, HL. In the view of Lord Woolf, *Merricks v. Heathcoat-Amory* [1955] Ch. 567, where an injunction to prevent a minister laying draft regulations before Parliament was refused, was correctly decided but dicta of Upjohn J. suggesting an injunction could never be obtained against a minister in his official capacity were incorrect.
[76] [1990] 2 A.C. 85. See Wade, "Injunctive Relief against the Crown" (1991) 107 L.Q.R. 4.
[77] [1991] 1 K.B. 410.
[78] *Hoffman La Roche & Co v. Secretary of State for Trade and Industry* [1975] A.C. 295; *Kirklees M.B.C. v. Wickes Building Supplies Ltd* [1993] A.C. 227.
[79] See *Padfield v. Minister of Agriculture, Fisheries and Food* [1968] A.C. 997; *ante*, para. 32–008.
[80] *Pawlett v. Att.-Gen.* (1668) Hardr. 465. See *Tito v. Waddell (No. 2)* [1977] Ch. 106, 256.
[81] [1911] 1 K.B. 410; discussed by the House of Lords in *Gouriet v. Union of Post Office Workers* [1978] A.C. 435. See also *Hodge v. Att.-Gen.* (1839) 3 Y. & Co.Ex. 342; *Esquimalt and Nenaimo Ry v. Wilson* [1920] A.C. 358, PC.

was illegal and *ultra vires* the Finance Act 1910.[82] The action cannot be brought where a petition of right was formerly appropriate, *e.g.* for a money claim against the Treasury.[83]

Certain existing procedures which were already working satisfactorily were retained, *e.g.* relator actions, and proceedings by or against the Public Trustee, Charity Commissioners and Registrar of the Land Registry (section 23). Proceedings against the Crown by petition of right and *monstrans de droit* were abolished, and the Petitions of Right Act 1860 was wholly repealed.[84]

Statutes relating to the limitation of actions now generally bind the Crown.[85]

Proceedings against the Sovereign in her private capacity

The Petitions of Right Act 1860 contemplated that petitions of right could be **33–019** brought against the Sovereign in her private capacity, for section 14 distinguished these from petitions relating to any public matter. In the case of public matters the Treasury were authorised to pay out of moneys legally applicable thereto or voted by Parliament for that purpose, while in the case of private matters the amount to which the suppliant was entitled was to be found out of such moneys as Her Majesty should be graciously pleased to direct. At first sight section 29(1) and the Second Schedule to the Crown Proceedings Act appear to repeal the Petitions of Right Act completely; and as section 40(1) of all the Crown Proceedings Act provides that "nothing in this Act shall apply to proceedings by or against, or authorise proceedings in tort to be brought against, His Majesty in His private capacity," it would seem that a citizen in proceeding against the Queen in her private capacity (*e.g.* for groceries supplied to her at Buckingham Palace), is thrown back on the old common law procedure by petition of right—for it cannot be contemplated that the Act intended to render the subject altogether remediless in such cases. On the other hand, the saving clause in section 40(1) above and the expression "subject to the provisions of this Act" in sections 1 and 13 could be held to mean that neither the abolition of petitions of right nor the repeal of the petitions of Right Act applies to proceedings against Her Majesty in her private

[82] See also *Gillick v. West Norfolk and Wisbeck Area Health Authority* [1986] A.C. 112; *ante* para. 32–009.
[83] *Bombay and Persia Steam Navigation Co v. Maclay* [1920] 3 K.B. 402, 408. Nor can the court make an interim (interlocutory) declaration against the Crown in such cases: *Underhill v. Ministry of Food* [1950] 1 All E.R. 591. CPR r.25(1)(6) seems to envisage a general power to award interim declarations but the rule may be *ultra vires* in the light of *Riverside Mental Health NSA Trust v. Fox* [1999] F.L.R. 614, CA (Interim declaration, "a creature unknown to English law"). See further *Civil Procedure* (The White Book) Vol. 1 (Spring 2001), para. 25.113. An interim injunction may, of course, be available since *R. v. Secretary of State for Transport ex p. Factortame (No. 2)* [1991] A.C. 603, HL.
[84] *cf. Franklin v. Att.-Gen.* [1974] Q.B. 185 where claims to interest on Rhodesian government stock under the Colonial Stock Act 1877 were brought under the old common law procedure governing petitions of right. See also *Franklin v. Att.-Gen. (No. 2)* [1974] Q.B. 205, CA; *Barclays Bank v. The Queen* [1974] Q.B. 823.
The following proceedings by the Crown were also abolished: Latin and English informations; writs of *capies ad respondendum, subpoena ad respondendum*, and appraisement; writs of *scire facies*; writs of extent and of *diem clausit extremum*; and writs of summons under Pt V of the Crown Suits Act 1865.
[85] Limitation Act 1980, s.37. But special periods may apply to claims by the Crown, *e.g.* to recover land or foreshore: Limitation Act 1980, Sched. 1, Pt II.

capacity. The latter is probably the better interpretation, although the draftsman has gone a clumsy way about it.[86]

Judgments and execution

33–020   The Crown is put in the same position as subjects with regard to interest on debts, damages and costs (section 24). The Act requires the appropriate department to pay any damages and costs certified in the order of the court; but no execution can be levied against the Crown,[87] and no person is individually liable under any order for payment by the Crown (section 25).[88] On the other hand, the Crown relinquished its former prerogative modes of execution; and it lost its special rights to imprison for debt, except in two cases where the person would already have had the money, *viz.* failure to pay death duties or purchase tax (section 26).[89] The procedure for enforcing payment of fines, *e.g.* for smuggling, is retained.

Creditors are entitled to attach moneys owing to their debtors by the Crown in the same way as if the Crown were a subject, except for (a) wages and salaries payable by any officer of the Crown and (b) any money which by law is exempted from being taken in execution or assigned (section 27).

Discovery and interrogatories

33–021   The Crown Proceedings Act allowed the court for the first time to require the Crown, *in civil proceedings to which the Crown is a party,* to make discovery of documents and to answer interrogatories (section 28(1)). Discovery (as formerly known) is the disclosure which one party to an action commenced by writ is generally required to make to the other party of relevant documents which are, or have been, in his possession, custody or power. In exceptional cases a court order for discovery is necessary. Certain documents are privileged from production.[90] Interrogatories are written questions relevant to the action which a party may administer to his opponent to be answered on affidavit. Leave of the Master is required, and privilege may be claimed on the same grounds as in discovery of documents.

Crown Privilege and Public Interest Immunity

33–022   The proviso to section 28(1) preserves the rule—*applying also to actions to which the Crown is not a party,* and covering the trial as well as interlocutory proceedings—which authorises or requires the withholding of any document or the refusal to answer any question on the ground that the disclosure of the document or the answering of the question would be *injurious to the public interest.* The objection to such disclosure or answer is usually made by the head of the department concerned.

Subsection (2) goes further by providing that any rules of court made for the purpose of section 28 shall secure that the *existence* of a document will not be disclosed if, in the opinion of a Minister of the Crown, it would be injurious to

---

[86] See further D. B. Murray, "When is a repeal not a repeal?" (1953) 16 M.L.R. 50.
[87] *Wick and Dennis' Case* (1589) 1 Leo. 190.
[88] It is still possible, however, to sue a Crown servant personally for damages in a case like *Raleigh v. Goschen* [1898] 1 Ch. 73 (*ante,* para. 33–008) although there does not seem to be much point in doing so.
[89] The provision relating to purchase tax was repealed by the Finance Act 1972, s.54(8) and Sched. 28, Pt II.
[90] See further CPR 31 and CPR Sched. 1, RSCO 77, r.12(2).

the public interest[91] to disclose the existence thereof. This exception was necessary because the general rules of court require that the documents which the party objects to producing should be set out in the affidavit of documents, and the Crown may wish to claim privilege for the fact that a document exists.

At the time of the passing of the 1947 Act, and for many years afterwards, it was believed to be the law in England, as the result of dicta in *Duncan v. Cammell, Laird*, that the Crown possessed a right to withhold documents on the grounds of public interest in a wide range of cases without such right being, in any real sense, subject to judicial control.[92] However, after criticism of this wide view of "Crown Privilege" in a number of decisions in the Court of Appeal,[93] the House of Lords restated the Law in *Conway v. Rimmer*[94] where it held that the right to determine what the public interest requires is that of the court which is entitled to call for the documents, and decide after inspecting them whether an order for their production to the other party ought to be made. *Duncan v. Cammell, Laird* was not followed, and may be said to have been overruled so far as concerns the inspection by the court of documents in a civil case for which the Crown claims privilege. Otherwise the main effect of *Conway v. Rimmer* was to narrow the ratio of *Duncan v. Cammell, Laird* by holding that Viscount Simon's dicta were too wide, although the actual decision was, on the facts, undoubtedly right.

Lord Reid later in *Conway v. Rimmer* announced that he had examined the documents, and could find nothing in any of them the disclosure closure of which would be prejudicial to the proper administration of the local constabulary or to the general public interest. He was therefore of the opinion that they must be made available in the litigation.[95]   **33–023**

Subsequent decisions of the House of Lords have established that the phrase "Crown Privilege," used to describe the withholding of documents on the ground of public interest, is a misnomer for two reasons. First, because the Crown does not have the choice whether or not to withhold the documents in question. Non-production is *required* by the public interest and is a matter which may be raised

---

[91] The Memorandum accompanying the Crown Proceedings Bill specified "defence, foreign affairs, and related matters." On the second reading, suggestions that "public security," "public safety" or "defence of the realm" should be substituted for "public interest" were not accepted by the government.

For the appalling case of *Odlum v. Stratton* (1946), see Allen, *Law and Orders* (3rd ed.), App. 2.

[92] [1942] A.C. 624. The dependants of sailors who were drowned in a new British submarine, *Thetis*, which sank on her trials just before the beginning of the Second World War had brought an action against the builders of *Thetis*. War had begun when the litigation commenced and the House of Lords upheld the First Lord of the Admiralty's objection to the production of plans of the submarine which were in the possession of the contractors. Captain H. P. K. Oram, one of the four survivors of the disaster, died in June 1986, aged 92.

[93] *Merricks v. Nott-Bower* [1965] 1 Q.B. 57; *Re Grosvenor Hotel, London (No. 2)* [1965] Ch. 1210; *Wednesbury Borough Council v. Ministry of Housing and Local Government* [1965] 1 W.L.R. 261; [1965] 1 All E.R. 186.

[94] [1968] A.C. 910, citing Scottish, Australian and American cases. In *Glasgow Corporation v. Central Land Board*, 1956 S.C., HL 1 the House of Lords had held that *Duncan v. Cammell, Laird* did not represent Scots Law. In *Conway* a former probationary police constable, suing his former superintendent for malicious prosecution, sought production of reports made on him during his probation.

[95] *Conway v. Rimmer* (Note) [1968] A.C. 996; [1968] 2 All E.R. 304n. (Nevertheless, the plaintiff eventually lost his action for malicious prosecution because he failed to prove want of reasonable cause: *The Times*, December 17, 1969.) See also *Norwich Pharmacal Co v. Customs and Excise Commissioners* [1974] A.C. 133; Tapper (1974) 37 M.L.R. 92.

by any party to the litigation or by the court itself.[96] Second, public interest as a ground for non-disclosure of documents is not confined to the functioning of departments or organs of the central government. In so holding, the House of Lords, in *D. v. N.S.P.C.C.*,[97] allowed the respondent society to withhold the sources of information which it received of an alleged instance of cruelty to children.

33–024   The right (or duty) to withhold documents in the public interest is now generally described as *Public Interest Immunity.* Lord Scarman, however, sounded a warning note in *Science Research Council v. Nasse*[98] when he said,

> "I regret the passing of the currently rejected term 'Crown Privilege'. It at least emphasised the very restricted area of public interest immunity . . . [which] exists to protect from disclosure only information the secrecy of which is essential to the proper working of the government of the state. Defence, foreign relations, the inner workings of government at the highest level . . . and the prosecution process in its pre-trial stage are the sensitive areas where the Crown must have the immunity of the government of the nation is to be effectually carried on. We are in the realm of public law, not private right."

Lord Scarman regarded the *N.S.P.C.C.* case as exceptional, turning on the special position of the Society in enforcing the provisions of the Children and Young Persons Act 1969 which was comparable with that of a prosecuting authority in criminal proceedings.

In deciding whether to allow documents to be withheld the courts now try to weigh in the balance the public interest of the nation or the public service in non-disclosure against the public interest of justice in the production of the documents. The balancing of the conflicting claims involved in a claim of privilege will inevitably lead to different conclusions in different cases depending on the weight particular judges give, for example, to the need to protect confidential information or facilitate inquiries into allegations of misconduct. Thus the House of Lords upheld the refusal of an order of discovery in *Lonrho Ltd v. Shell Petroleum*[99] on the ground of the need to guarantee to informants complete confidentiality if a government inquiry were to have any likelihood of success in discovering the truth.

33–025   The difficulty in balancing the conflicting interests and, perhaps, changing judicial attitudes can be seen from various cases concerning documents arising in the course of investigations and complaints relating to allegations of police behavior. In *R. v. Chief Constable of West Midlands Police ex p. Wiley*[1] the House of Lords refused to extend immunity to documents arising out of complaints to the Police Complaints Authority on the ground that they belonged to a class of document the production of which was contrary to the public

---

[96] *Rogers v. Home Secretary* [1973] A.C. 388; applied, *R. v. Cheltenham Justices* [1977] 1 W.L.R. 95; *Crompton (Alfred) Amusement Machines v. Customs and Excise Commissioners (No. 2)* [1974] A.C. 405; *Air Canada v. Secretary of State (No. 2)* [1983] 2 A.C. 394; *cf. Medway v. Doublelock Ltd* [1978] 1 W.L.R. 710.

[97] [1978] A.C. 171.

[98] [1980] A.C. 1028, 1087.

[99] [1980] 1 W.L.R. 627. ("The circumstances which have given rise to the disputes about discovery are quite exceptional; they are unlikely to recur in any other case and, for that reason, they do not in my view provide a suitable occasion for any general disquisition by this House upon the principles of law applicable to the discovery of documents"; *per* Lord Diplock at p. 632.)

[1] [1995] 1 A.C. 274.

interest, overruling a number of earlier authorities.[2] Lord Woolf suggested that in civil litigation the question of the right to require production of documents could often be settled by reference to Order 24 r. 8 (now CPR 31.17) which limits the right to discovery to cases where it is necessary for disposing of a case.

Following the *N.S.P.C.C.* case the confidential nature of information has been recognised as justifying a claim to public interest immunity in *Gaskin v. Liverpool C.C.*[3] but not in *R. v. Bournemouth Justices ex p. Grey*[4] where information obtained by an adoption society in relation to the child of an unmarried couple was held admissible in affiliation proceedings between the same couple. Hodgson J. pointed out that in the *N.S.P.C.C.* case and *Gaskin* the objections to production had not been taken, as here, by a private person, the social worker employed by the agency, but by a public body with statutory duties. In *Campbell v. Thameside M.B.C.*[5] the Court of Appeal held that a teacher who had been attacked by a pupil was entitled, in an action in negligence against the local authority, to see reports made to the authority by psychologists which, she alleged, showed that the pupil was known to be violent. The importance of the documents to the teacher's case and the nature of the action justified distinguishing cases involving issues of wardship, child care and adoption where discovery had been refused. In *Williams v. Home Office*[6] McNeill J. ordered production of Home Office documents relating to the establishment of "control units" in prisons to deal with difficult prisoners because of the importance of the issues involved.

The Courts will not order disclosure where it is sought by a plaintiff who is engaged on a "fishing expedition," hoping to find in documents in the defendant's possession information which might support a case against them for which he has no other evidence.[7] In *Air Canada v. Secretary of State for Trade (No. 2)*[8] the House of Lords refused to inspect documents for which public interest immunity had been claimed when the plaintiff had failed to show that there were reasonable grounds for believing that they contained information likely to help their case or damage their adversary's. **33–026**

A claim to disclosure will also fail if the action to which it is incidental must for some reason be struck out as, for example, in *Buttes Gas and Oil Co v. Hammer (No. 3)*[9] where the House of Lords granted an order staying all proceedings between the parties because they amounted to an attempt to require the courts to adjudicate on transactions between foreign sovereign states. Such matters fall outside the jurisdiction of the English courts.

It now seems that there are no *classes* of document, for example Cabinet minutes or papers, which are always immune from production. In *Burmah Oil Co Ltd v. Bank of England*[10] the appellant company sought discovery of various documents despite a detailed affidavit by the Chief Secretary to the Treasury

[2] *Neilson v. Laugharne* [1981] 1 Q.B. 736, CA; *Makanjuola v. M.P.C.* [1992] 3 All E.R. 617, CA.
[3] [1980] 1 W.L.R. 1549 (Child care service records) Lord Denning M.R. described the plaintiff as "a psychiatric case, mentally-disturbed and quite useless to society." For the plaintiff's side of the story, see James MacVeigh, *Gaskin* (1982). A right of access to information concerning his childhood in care was upheld by the European Court of Human Rights: *Gaskin v. United Kingdom* (1990) 12 E.H.R.R. 36.
[4] *The Times*, May 31, 1986.
[5] [1982] Q.B. 1065.
[6] [1981] 1 All E.R. 1151.
[7] *Gaskin v. Liverpool Corporation* [1980] 1 W.L.R. 1549.
[8] [1983] 2 A.C. 394; T. S. R. Allen, "Abuse of Power and Public Interest Immunity: Justice, Rights and Truth" (1985) 101 L.Q.R. 200.
[9] [1982] A.C. 888.
[10] [1980] A.C. 1090.

objecting to their production on the ground of public interest. The documents included memoranda of meetings attended by Ministers but did not include Cabinet papers. The House of Lords ultimately agreed, after inspecting the documents, that production should not be ordered because disclosure of their contents was not necessary for disposing fairly of the company's case. The importance of the case lies, however, in dicta which suggest that there is no *class* of document which is, in all circumstances, immune from discovery.[11] In each case a claim to immunity must be based on the *contents* of the documents involved.

Despite the new judicial attitude to claims to public interest immunity a claim based on the ground of national security is still unlikely to be questioned.[12]

33–027   The claim of "Public Interest Immunity" is the personal responsibility of the ministerial head of the department, although if it does not appear that he has himself considered the documents he may be given an opportunity to swear a further affidavit.[13] Where the documents are those of a former government the affidavit may properly be sworn by a senior civil servant because "a powerful convention prevents ministers having access to papers of their predecessors."[14]

A claim to public interest immunity raises particularly acute issues in criminal proceedings. As in the *Matrix Churchill* trial, considered at length in the Scott Report,[15] immunity may be claimed by a minister but in many other cases claims may arise at the level of the police, for example, to protect the identity of informants or the secrets of other information gathering procedures.

33–028   The *Matrix Churchill* trial arose out of prosecutions on charges of illegal export of arms to Iraq. Ministers certified that the public interest required the withholding of documents which the accused claimed to be relevant to their defence, the trial judge decided to examine the documents and rejected the claim to immunity. On the basis of the documents the accused were acquitted. It subsequently emerged that one minister who had been unhappy about signing the claim to immunity had been advised that he had no discretion to consider what the public interest required.[16] Exposure of what had happened and criticisms voiced in the Scott Report led to the Attorney General announcing in December 1996 that in future public interest immunity would only be claimed where it was believed that disclosure would cause "real harm" to the public interest.[17]

Apart from the specific doctrine of public interest immunity the more general law relating to the rights of the accused with regard to access to material and information in the hands of the prosecution is placed on a statutory footing by the Criminal Procedures and Investigations Act 1996.

---

[11] Lord Wilberforce at p. 1113; Lord Edmund-Davies at p. 1127; Lord Keith of Kinkel at p. 1134; Lord Scarman at p. 1144. The opposite view is expressed by Lord Salmon at p. 1121; J. Hannan, "Inspection of Cabinet Documents—To Yield or Not to Yield" (1982) 45 M.L.R. 471. See also Lord Fraser in *Air Canada v. Secretary of State for Trade* (No. 2), *supra.*

[12] *Balfour v. Foreign and Commonwealth Office* [1994] 1 W.L.R. 681, CA (Unfair dismissal claim by member of diplomatic service. Court refused to Inspect documents for which minister claimed privilege on ground of national security).

[13] *Re Grosvenor Hotel (No. 1)* [1964] Ch. 464, CA.

[14] *Air Canada v. Secretary of State for Trade, supra, per* Lord Wilberforce at p. 437.

[15] 1996, H.C. 115; *supra* para. 17–018 and para. 19–046.

[16] A view based on a dictum of Bingham L.J. in *Makanjuola v. M.P.C.* [1992] 3 All E.R. 617 which Lord Woolf in *Wiley* suggested had been taken further than the Lord Justice intended.

[17] For a critical comment see Supperstone and Coppel, "A New Approach to Public Interest Immunity" [1997] P.L. 211.

CHAPTER 34

NON-JUDICIAL REMEDIES

Introduction
 People may wish to resort to non-judicial remedies where they have a griev-   **34–001**
ance to complain of, or a wrong to be righted, for various reasons and in many
different circumstances. Where there is a dispute about the law the courts may
provide an effective remedy. But even in such cases the Courts may show a
reluctance to intervene in disputes concerning the legality of acts of the executive. It is notable that both the Council on Tribunals and the Parliamentary
Commissioner were established before the upsurge in judicial activism of the late
1960s and 1970s.[1] In many cases, however, complainants may be unhappy about
the way a decision was reached, delays and rudeness on the parts of public
officials, for example. There may be no doubt about what the law is: it may,
however, be thought that the law should be changed. In some cases people may
simply want information; why, for example, did a patient fail to recover after an
operation. A decision may be thought to have been reached on a mistaken view
of the facts; a complainant may want to be able to produce new evidence or to
have an opportunity to rebut conclusions reached by a public official. In the
following Parts of this chapter we shall examine the Council on Tribunals and the
Parliamentary Commissioner for Administration and other Commissioners with
specialised jurisdictions. Other statutory non-judicial remedies which have been
discussed in earlier chapters include the Police Complaints Authority[2] and the
Broadcasting Standards Commission.[3]
 Apart from procedures and bodies established to deal with complaints relating
to specific types of problems, Members of Parliament discharge an important role
in offering a means of redress for grievances of every kind.[4] Constituents may,
and do, write to their M.P.'s about grievances for which they have found no
remedy elsewhere. In some cases it may be appropriate to pass the complaint to
the Parliamentary Commissioner for Administration (*infra*, Part II). In others the
appropriate action may be a letter to a minister or some public body or a question
in the House. The importance of this aspect of the work of M.P.'s has grown
steadily in the last thirty years.

I. THE COUNCIL ON TRIBUNALS[5]

 The Franks Report[6] recommended the creation of a Council on Tribunals to   **34–002**
exercise various functions in relation to Statutory Tribunals. The Council was

[1] See Chap 32.
[2] para. 21–021.
[3] para. 25–036.
[4] Alan C. Page, "M.P.s and the Redress of Grievances" [1985] P.L. 1.
[5] *Council on Tribunals: Special Report on Functions* (1980) Cmnd. 7805; D. C. M. Yardley, "The Functions of the Council on Tribunals," [1980] Jo. Soc. Wel. Law 265; D. G. T. Williams, "The Council on Tribunals: The First Twenty Five Years" [1984] P.L. 73; A. W. Bradley, "The Council on Tribunals: Time for a Broader Role?" [1991] P.L. 6.
[6] (1967) Cmnd. 218.

established by the Tribunals and Inquiries Act 1958 and continues in existence by section 1 of the Tribunals and Inquiries Act 1992. The functions of the Council are

(a) to keep under review the constitution and working of the tribunals specified in Schedule 1,[7] and from time to time to report on their constitution and working;

(b) to consider and report on such particular matters as may be referred to the Council with respect to "tribunals other than the ordinary courts of law," whether or not specified in Schedule 1; and

(c) to consider and report on such matters as may be referred, or as the Council may determine to be of special importance, with respect to administrative procedures involving the holding by a Minister of a statutory inquiry.

The Council consists of 10 to 16 members including the Parliamentary Commissioner for Administration. There is a Scottish Committee of the Council, consisting of two or three members of the Council and three or four other persons appointed by the Secretary of State. The chairmen of the Council and of the Scottish Committee are paid a salary, and the other members may be paid fees.

The Council reports to, and receives references from, the Lord Chancellor and the Secretary of State. The Council is required to make an annual report on its proceedings, and the Lord Chancellor and the Secretary of State are to lay the annual report before Parliament, with such comments (if any) as they think fit.

Work of the Council on Tribunals

34–003   There are more than 2,000 tribunals under the supervision of the Council. The Council not only acts as a "watchdog" but also as a focus of information. It keeps under review the constitution and working of tribunals. With regard to statutory inquiries its function is to consider and report on such matters as may be referred to it by the Lord Chancellor or the Secretary of State, or as the Council may determine to be of special importance. It does not recommend the kinds of person who should be appointed to conduct inquiries. Complaints are digested by a complaints committee. The Council's powers are not executive but advisory, and it does not act as a court of appeal from tribunals. Nor does it seek to impose uniformity on all tribunals.

Although the work of the Council is mainly of a routine nature it has also become involved in controversial cases of notoriety which illustrate the Council's strengths and weaknesses.

The *Chalk Pit* case[8] was the subject of a special report to the Lord Chancellor. Major Buxton, a landowner, complained to the Council[9] about the decision of a Minister to allow a firm to use a gravel pit adjoining his piggeries for the production of chalk. The inspector who conducted the inquiry reported that the production of chalk would result in dust being blown onto adjoining land, with serious detriment to animals and crops. Major Buxton alleged that the Minister

---

[7] Other tribunals may be added by Statutory Instrument.
[8] See Griffith and Street, *A Casebook of Administrative Law* (1964) pp. 142–174.
[9] He had been unsuccessful in the courts as he was not a "person aggrieved": *Buxton v. Minister of Housing and Local Government* [1961] 1 Q.B. 278; *ante*, para. 32–015.

consulted the Minister of Agriculture privately between the end of the inquiry and the announcement of his decision, thus stultifying the inquiry. The Council made a report to the Lord Chancellor on the problem of handling new factual evidence noted by Ministers after statutory inquiries; with the result that a Statutory Instrument was later issued directing a Minister to re-open an inquiry on request if he disagrees with the inspector on receiving new evidence (including expert opinion) or has considered a new issue of fact not raised at the inquiry.

The *Packington Estate* case, on which the Council also produced a special **34–004** report, was interesting not only for the light it threw on the way the Minister of Housing and Local Government (Richard Crossman) dealt with an application by a local authority for planning permission but also for what it revealed of the importance one Minister, at least, attached to the work of the Council. Although the Ministry had agreed to meet members of the Council to discuss the complaints of local landowners about the procedure being followed, the Minister sent a letter to the local authority granting planning permission two days before the date arranged for the meeting with the Council—a procedure which might fairly be described as "a deliberate and blatant attempt to stultify the activities of an independent statutory body established to act as a watchdog. . . . " [10]

Annual reports show that the Council is consulted on rules of procedure for a number of tribunals and for Inquiries. It has made representations about accommodation, public hearings and legal aid. The Council is also consulted on Bills affecting existing or creating new tribunals. Where, however, its views are rejected there is no procedure for making this publicly known.

II. PARLIAMENTARY COMMISSIONER FOR ADMINISTRATION [11] AND OTHERS

Maladministration

Neither courts nor tribunals can offer a remedy when private citizens complain **34–005** that public authorities, although they have acted within the law, have failed to observe the proper standards of administrative conduct. It is faults of this kind which are often described as *maladministration*. Mr Crossman, in the debate on the Parliamentary Commissioner Bill, gave as examples of such conduct "bias, neglect, inattention, delay, incompetence, ineptitude, perversity, turpitude, arbitrariness and so on." [12] An example is the *Crichel Down* case,[13] where a landowner complained that the Ministry of Agriculture had refused to hand back to

[10] [1966] P.L. 1, 6.

[11] *The Parliamentary Commissioner for Administration* (1965), Cmnd. 2767; *The Citizen and the Administration*, Part III. A report by *Justice* (Whyatt Report, 1961); *The Ombudsman: Citizen's Defender*, ed. D. C. Rowst (2nd ed., 1968); *Our Fettered Ombudsman, A report by Justice* (1977); Sir Edmund Compton, "Parliamentary Commissioner for Administration" (1969) 10 J.S.P.T.L. 106; Paul Jackson, "The Work of the Parliamentary Commissioner for Administration" [1971] P.L. 39; Sir Alan Marre, "Some Thoughts on the Role of the Parliamentary Commissioner for Administration" (1972) 3 *Cambrian Law Rev.* 54; Sir Cecil Clothier, "The Value of an Ombudsman," [1986] P.L. 204; G. Marshall, *Constitutional Conventions* (1984) Chap. V: F. Stacey, *Ombudsmen Compared* (1978): R. Gregory and P. G. Hutchesson, *The Parliamentary Ombudsman* (1975); P. Giddings, "The Parliamentary Ombudsman: a successful alternative", Chap. VIII of *The Law and Parliament* (eds. D. Oliver and G. Drewry, Butterworths 1998).

[12] 734 H.C. Deb., col. 51.

[13] (1954) Cmd. 9176; C. J. Hamson, "The Real Lesson of Crichel Down" (1954) 32 *Public Administration* 383. *cf.* R. M. Jackson, "Judicial Review of Legislative Policy" (1955) 18 M.L.R. 571.

him after the war part of his land which had been requisitioned during the war and was no longer required by the Ministry for the purposes for which it had been requisitioned. In this particular case the Minister was induced by the outcry to hold a departmental inquiry, which criticised the conduct of certain officials in the Ministry, with the result that the officials were moved to different work and the Minister (although not personally involved) resigned his office. The citizen's only remedies at that time were for his Member of Parliament to ask a question in the House, to raise the matter in the debate on the adjournment or in debates on supply, to correspond with the Minister or to persuade the Minister to hold an *ad hoc* inquiry.

Parliamentary Commissioner for Administration

34–006   For some years there had been discussion on the suggestion[14] that a Parliamentary Commissioner, with an independent status like that of the Comptroller and Auditor-General, should be appointed for this country, whose functions would be similar to those of the Ombudsman known to Scandinavian countries and then recently introduced into New Zealand. Hesitation in the past was due largely to the fear that the appointment of such an independent official would interfere with ministerial responsibility, which is stronger here than in Scandanavia; and to a less extent to the fact that it was difficult to foresee how much work would fall to a Commissioner in a country with a population much greater than that of any of the Scandinavian countries or New Zealand. In 1967 the Parliamentary Commissioner Act was passed.[15]

Appointment

34–007   The Parliamentary Commissioner Act 1967 provides for a Parliamentary Commissioner of Administration to be appointed by letters patent. In 1977 the Government agreed that in future before an appointment was made it would consult the Chairman of the Select Committee on the Parliamentary Commissioner of Administration (see *infra*). His salary is charged on the Consolidated Fund.[16] He may be removed on an address from both Houses, and he is excluded from membership of the Commons. He is an *ex officio* member of the Council on Tribunals, whose functions (as in cases like the *Chalk Pit* case) overlap his own, and in some cases the citizen may choose whether to complain to the Commissioner or the Council. He is also a member of the Commissions for Local Administration (*infra*).

Investigation of complaints

34–008   A person who thinks he has suffered injustice as a result of malad-ministration by a department or authority of the central government may complain to a

---

[14] The suggestion for an Inspector-General of Administration was originally made by Professor F. H. Lawson in [1957] P.L. 92–95. The Government turned down the suggestion for a Parliamentary Commissioner in 1961: 640 H.C. Deb., cols 1693–1756.

[15] For the geographical spread of the institution in the last few years see *Our Fettered Ombudsman*, A report by *Justice* (1977), App. A. For a comparison of the Parliamentary Commissioner and the French *médiateur* see L. Neville Brown and P. Lavirotte (1974) 90 L.Q.R. 211; L. Neville Brown and J. Bell, *French Administrative Law* (5th ed., 1998). See too Colin T. Reid, "The Ombudsman's Cousin: The Procuracy in Socialist States" [1986] P.L. 311.

[16] See further, Parliamentary and other Pensions and Salaries Act 1976, s.6.

member of the House of Commons in writing within twelve months from first having notice of the matter. The Commissioner has a discretion whether or not to conduct an investigation.[17] An investigation is conducted in private. The principal officer of the department or authority concerned must be given an opportunity to comment on the allegation. The complainant has no right to appear, but the Commissioner may see him if he thinks fit. The Commissioner has the same powers as the High Court to require a Minister, civil servant or other persons to furnish information or produce documents, excluding proceedings or papers of the Cabinet or a Cabinet committee. There is no Crown privilege[18] at the investigation stage; but a Minister may claim Crown privilege in respect of the *publication* or passing on of documents or information if their disclosure would in his opinion be prejudicial to the safety of the state or otherwise contrary to the public interest. The Official Secrets Act would prevent the Commissioner from including such information in his reports.

Departments and authorities covered

The departments and authorities in respect of whom the Commissioner may investigate complaints are set out in Schedule 2. They include most of the central government departments, but do not cover local authorities, public corporations, the police or the National Health Service. The list may be added to or reduced by Order in Council, the instrument being subject to annulment by resolution of either House.   **34–009**

Matters excluded from investigation are set out in Schedule 3. The excluded matters are within the functions of the departments listed in Schedule 2, *viz.*: foreign relations; action taken outside the United Kingdom (except by consular officials)[19]; the government of Her Majesty's overseas dominions; extradition, fugitive offenders investigation of crime,[20] and security of the state (including passports); civil or criminal proceedings in any court, court-martial or international tribunal; the prerogative of mercy; medical matters; commercial contracts; personnel matters of the armed forces, civil service, teachers or police; the grant of honours, and royal charters. This list may be reduced by Order in Council.

Devolution

The Scotland Act 1998 section 91 requires the Scottish Parliament to make provision for dealing with complaints relating to maladministration arising from the exercise of devolved powers. The Parliamentary Commissioner retains his jurisdiction over complaints relating to maladministration in areas of reserved matters wherever they arise. The Government of Wales Act 1998, s.111 appoints a Welsh Administration Ombudsman to deal with maladministration arising from the actions of the new executive.   **34–010**

The jurisdiction of the Parliamentary Commissioner extends to Northern Ireland in the case of complaints relating to actions of the United Kingdom

---

[17] *Re Fletcher's Application* [1970] 2 All E.R. 527n. (CA. Leave to appeal refused by HL); mandamus does not lie.
[18] *ante*, para. 33–022. For the position of the Local Commissioners, see *post*, para. 34–016.
[19] Parliamentary Commissioner (Consular Complaints) Act 1981.
[20] *i.e.* by or on behalf of the Home Office.

Government Legislation by the Northern Ireland Parliament introduced a Parliamentary Commissioner for Northern Ireland and a Commissioner for Complaints to whom the public had a right of direct access.[21] The latter Commissioner has jurisdiction over personnel matters, which reflects one of the reasons for the creation of the office, a wish to provide a remedy for allegations of discrimination in employment. A person whom the Commissioner finds to have suffered injustice as the result of maladministration may apply to court for damages and the Commissioner may request the Attorney-General to apply for an injunction or other relief where he concludes that a public body is likely to continue in a course of maladministration.

Reports by Commissioner

34–011   Where the Commissioner conducts or decides not to conduct an investigation he must send a report to the member concerned; and when he conducts an investigation he must send a report to the principal officer of the department concerned. If he thinks injustice has been caused, and that it has not been or will not be remedied, he may lay a special report before each House.

The Commissioner must lay a general report annually before each House on the performance of his functions, and he may lay special reports from time to time.

The Commissioner's reports show annually a large percentage—often over 50—of complaints that fall outside his jurisdiction. The proportion of cases investigated in which maladministration is found has risen year by year which suggests more thorough investigations as his staff have become more experienced and, perhaps, a widening view of what constitutes maladministration. One of the most controversial findings of maladministration was made in his Third Report on the *Sachsenhausen* Case.[22] The Commissioner concluded that the Foreign Office had, in determining whether a number of applicants were entitled to be compensated as inmates of German concentration camps as opposed to ordinary prison camps failed to attach due weight to various pieces of evidence. The Foreign Secretary finally accepted the Commissioner's report, while commenting,

> "When the Ombudsman has made enough decisions perhaps we shall have an Ombudsman to look at the Ombudsman's decisions and if he gets 100 per cent. right I shall be surprised."[23]

The *Barlow Clowes Affair*[24] concerned large numbers of investors who lost considerable sums of money which they had entrusted to the firm of Barlow Clowes claimed that the Department of Trade and Industry had been guilty of

---

[21] Parliamentary Commissioner (Northern Ireland) Act 1969; Commissioner for Complaints (Northern Ireland) Act 1969; K. P. Poole, "The Northern Ireland Commissioners for Complaints" [1972] P.L. 131. See the Commissioner for Complaints (Northern Ireland) Order 1996; Northern Ireland Act 1998, s.78.

[22] (1967–68) H.C. 54. See G. F. Fry, "The Sachsenhausen Concentration Camp Case and the Convention of Ministerial Responsibility" [1970] P.L. 336.

[23] Hansard, H.C. Deb, Feb. 5, 1968.

[24] R. Gregory and G. Drewery, "Barlow Clowes and the Ombudsman" [1991] P.L. 192 and 408.

maladministration in exercising its regulatory powers in relation to Barlow Clowes. The Commissioner found that there had been maladministration and, although the government refused to accept his findings it nonetheless agreed to pay £150m in compensation.[25]

Considerable sums were also obtained for poultry farmers whose birds had been killed following fears about salmonella in eggs. It subsequently emerged that the Ministry of Agriculture had paid compensation at a lower rate than the farmers were entitled to under statutory rules.[26]

More recently the Commissioner exposed maladministration in the DSS and the Benefits Agency when they gave misleading advice about the law relating to the rights of widows and widowers in connection with the SERPS pension scheme. Their rights had been curtailed by the Social Security Act 1986 but official leaflets continued to refer to the more generous rules under earlier legislation. The Commissioner was satisfied that the Departmental response offered a global solution which was fair and satisfactory.[27]

Select Committee on the Parliamentary Commissioner for Administration[28]

A Select Committee of the Commons was set up to deal with complaints by Members of Parliament who think the Commissioner has failed to deal properly with complaints forwarded by them, to consider what remedial action has been taken by the departments, and to recommend changes in the law. The Select Committee does not act as a court of appeal from the Commissioner's findings. In its first two annual reports the Committee criticised the narrow way in which the Commissioner was interpreting his jurisdiction.[29] It recommended an extension of the Commissioner's powers to cases where the departmental procedure for reviewing a rule, or the grounds for maintaining it, could be shown to be defective. The Committee has more than once recommended that the Commissioner should have power to investigate personnel matters and staffing within the Civil Service. In 1984 the Committee recommended that the Commissioner's jurisdiction should be extended to a number of Quangos a proposal which, for once the government was prepared to accept.[30]

34–012

Judicial Review

Although there is no jurisdiction to order the Commissioner to undertake an investigation,[31] there is jurisdiction to intervene where he has undertaken an

34–013

---

[25] *i.e.* from the pockets of tax payers who had been too cautious or too poor to invest in Barlow Clowes.

[26] (1992–93) H.C. 519; H.C. 593.

[27] (1999–2000) H.C. 305; (2000–01) H.C. 271. The original reduction will be phased in over a period of years.

[28] R. Gregory, "The Select Committee on the Parliamentary Commissioner for Administration" [1982] P.L. 49.

[29] (1967–68) H.C. 258; (1967–68) H.C. 350. See Geoffrey Marshall in *The Commons in Transition* (ed. A. H. Hanson and B. Crick, 1970), Chap. 6.

[30] A list of 50 bodies, including the Commission for Racial Equality, the Equal Opportunities Commission, the Arts Council, the Research Councils, Developments Corporations and such other less well known bodies as the Red Deer Commission and The Commissioners of Northern Lighthouses. See H.C. 619, 1983–4; Parliamentary and Health Service Commissioners Act 1987.

[31] *Re Fletcher's Application* [1970] 2 All E.R. 527, CA; *ante* para. 34–008.

investigation[32] and has failed to exercise his discretion in accordance with the standards set by the courts in reviewing the exercise of discretionary powers.[33]

Reform

34–014   To the extent that, in many cases, the Parliamentary Commissioner has achieved redress for individuals where otherwise they would have been left without a remedy, his office must be regarded as fulfilling a useful function. In a number of ways, however, that usefulness might, it is thought, be increased. To allow complaints to be made directly to the Commissioner rather than through Members of Parliament, and to give greater publicity to his activities might help to raise the public standing of the office.

The rule that complaints can only be made through a member has to some extent been circumvented by the practice of forwarding complaints sent to the Commissioner to the complainant's member and seeking his agreement to the Commissioner dealing with it. The exclusion from his jurisdiction of personnel matters in the civil service and the commercial and contractual dealings of the Government has been regularly criticised by the Commissioner and the Select Committee and by Justice.[34] The Government, however, so far remains unmoved.[35]

Health Service Commissioners[36]

34–015   The solution adopted in the Parliamentary Commissioner Act 1967 for dealing with complaints against the administration has been extended by subsequent legislation to the National Health Service. Three Health Service Commissioners for England, Wales and Scotland were established in 1972 and 1973.[37] Since their inception all three posts have been held by the Parliamentary Commissioner for Administration. With some slight variation between the 1972 and 1973 Acts, the Health Service Commissioners may investigate alleged instances of maladministration arising out of the provision of medical services under the National Health Services by a wide range of boards and authorities. Until the legislation of 1996 no action taken solely as a result of a clinical judgment could be investigated. Complaints may be made directly by a person aggrieved and need not be forwarded by a Member of Parliament.

Reports on maladministration within the Health Services have dealt with individual complaints relating to delays in admission to hospital, failure to indicate to patients that they may refuse to be examined in the presence of medical students and allegations of operations carried out without consent, as well as more general matters such as the failure of health departments to issue adequate warnings to doctors and parents on the dangers of whooping cough vaccine.[38]

---

[32] *R. v. Parliamentary Commissioner for Administration ex p. Dyer* [1994] 1 W.L.R. 621, CA; *R. v. Parliamentary Commissioner ex p. Balchin* [1997] C.O.D. 146.

[33] *ante*, para. 31–008.

[34] *Our Fettered Ombudsman* (1977).

[35] Cmnd. 8274 (1981).

[36] P. Giddings, "The Health Service Ombudsman after twenty five years and The Health Service Ombudsman: reports on clinical failings," [1999] P.L. 200 and 589.

[37] National Health Service (Scotland) Act 1972; National Health Service Re-organisation Act 1973. The current legislation is the Health Service Commissioners Act 1993, as amended by the Health Services Commissioners (Amendment) Act 1996 and the Health Service Commissioners (Amendment) Act 2000.

[38] Parliamentary Commissioner for Administration, 6th report, *Whooping Cough Vaccine* (1977).

Commissions for local administration[39]

The Ombudsman system was extended to local government by the Local Government Act 1974 which established two Commissions for Local Administration, one for England and one for Wales.[40] The Parliamentary Commissioner is a member of each of the Commissions. The jurisdiction of the Commissions extends to local authorities, police authorities, other than the Secretary of State, and other public bodies. Complaints of maladministration must be referred to the commissioner responsible for the area in question through a member of the authority against which the complaint is made. If, however, a member refuses to refer a complaint the local commissioner may proceed to investigate it—as happened, for example, in *R. v. Local Commissioner for Administration for the North and East Area of England ex p. Bradford Metropolitan City Council.*[41] The requirement of an initial reference to a member of a local authority is justified on the ground that it affords the authority an initial opportunity to remedy an alleged wrong before a commissioner becomes involved. It is also said to protect the commissioners from being overwhelmed by unsubstantial complaints. The Act expressly provides that a local commissioner cannot question the merits of a decision taken without maladministration (section 34(3)). In the *Bradford* Case (*supra*) Lord Denning M.R. said, "Parliament did not define 'maladministration.' It deliberately left it to the ombudsman himself to interpret the word as best he could: and to do it by building up a body of case law on the subject." His Lordship then quoted the list of examples given by Mr Crossman. It was, he added, "a long and interesting list, clearly open-ended, covering the *manner* in which a decision is reached or discretion is exercised: but excluding the merits of the decision itself or of the discretion itself." A Commissioner cannot deal with a complaint relating to any action in respect of which the person aggrieved has a right of appeal or review, whether to the Courts or to a Minister, or any other remedy by way of legal proceedings unless the commissioner is satisfied that it would be unreasonable to expect resort to be had to that right or remedy.

34–016

Initially the effectiveness of local commissioners was limited by the interpretation put by the Courts on section 32(3) of the 1974 Act which allowed local authorities to withhold documents on the ground of public interest.[42] That shortcoming has been remedied by amending legislation.[43] A second weakness (shared by other Commissioners, with the exception of the Commissioner for Complaints in Northern Ireland) is that they have no power to remedy injustices caused by maladministration. Local authorities are merely required to consider any reports submitted to them and notify the appropriate commissioner what action, if any, they propose to take. In a number of cases where commissioners found maladministration local authorities have refused to take any action.[44]

34–017

---

[39] D. Foulkes, "The Work of the Local Commissioner for Wales" [1978] P.L. 264; D. C. M. Yardley, "Local Ombudsmen in England" [1983] P.L. 522; *The Local Ombudsman—a review of the first five years* (Justice Report, 1980).

[40] The Local Government (Scotland) Act 1975 similarly established a Commissioner for Local Administration in Scotland. In Northern Ireland local government is within the jurisdiction of the Commissioner for Complaints. Under the Local Government Act 2000 the power to investigate unethical behaviour which in England is vested in the Standards Board is, in the case of Wales, vested in the Commission for Local Administration, ss.68–74.

[41] [1979] Q.B. 287, CA.

[42] *Re a Complaint against Liverpool City Council* [1977] 1 W.L.R. 995, DC.

[43] Local Government Planning and Land Act 1980, s.184.

[44] 92 cases (out of 1,500) over 10 years.

The Local Government Act 2000, section 92 extends provisions for dealing with maladministration by all owing local authorities to make a payment or provide some other benefit to a person whom they think has been or may have been adversely affected by any action taken by them or on their behalf which may have amounted to maladministration. Thus a complainant may be compensated without approaching the commissions for local administration. The power, here, to compensate relates to being "adversely affected" whereas the commission's jurisdiction relates to "injustice" caused by maladministration, presumably a stricter requirement than that of being adversely affected.

Conclusion

34–018
There can be no doubt of the continuing popularity of the Ombudsman concept. It is offered as a solution to every problem. The banks and insurance companies have, for instance, introduced their own voluntary systems of dealing with complaints by an Ombudsman.

Statutory ombudsmen have been created to deal with complaints in various areas relating to financial services, now under the one umbrella of the Financial Services and Markets Act 2000. The Courts and Legal Services Act 1990 created two ombudsmen, a Conveyancing Ombudsman to deal with complaints about licensed conveyancers and a Legal Services Ombudsman to deal with complaints relating to legal professional bodies. The Pensions Ombudsman created by the Social Security Act 1990 is in fact a tribunal with a power to make legally binding decisions and is subject to the jurisdiction of the Council on Tribunals.[45] The very word is used indiscriminately to describe almost anyone with a power to investigate complaints—for example the non-statutory Independent Complaints Adjudicator to whom prisoners may complain is often so called.[46] To the widespread national adoption of the concept[47] can now be added its adoption by the European Union. The Treaty of Maastricht provided for the appointment of an Ombudsman by the European Parliament: Article 195 [138e]. Citizenship of the Union includes the right to raise complaints with the Ombudsman: Article 21 [8d].

But it should not be overlooked how firmly governments resist attempts to extend the jurisdiction of the Parliamentary Commissioner into the very areas where it might be thought that he could be effective. It is difficult to avoid the feeling that the "filtering" or "screening" of complaints by members of Parliament and councillors has little to do with concern for the best interests of the complainants. Nor should it be forgotten that the provision of a remedy may be a poor substitute for the elimination of a problem.

---

[45] A. T. Brady [1991] P.L. 7. Pensions Schemes Act 1993, ss.145–151.
[46] *ante*, para. 24–032. A distinct appointment from that of Chief Inspector of Prisons, the first two holders of which office, Judge Stephen Tumin and Sir David Ramsbotham, caused successive governments embarrassment by their damning reports of conditions in prisons.
[47] *ante* para. 34–006 n. 15.

Part VII

The Commonwealth

CHAPTER 35

DEPENDENT TERRITORIES[1]

I. The British Islands

The British Islands consist of the United Kingdom, the Isle of Man and the Channel Islands.[2] The Isle of Man and the Channel Islands are neither part of the United Kingdom nor are they colonies; but they are part of Her Majesty's dominions, and persons born in them are British citizens by birth. For the purposes of the British Nationality Act 1981 they are treated as part of the United Kingdom.

35–001

The United Kingdom's ratification of the European Convention on Human Rights in 1951 extended to the Channel Islands and the Isle Man. The unwillingness of the Isle of Man to abandon corporal punishment of juvenile offenders despite the decision of the Human Rights Court in *Tyler v. United Kingdom*[3] led to the abolition of the right of individual petition in the case of the island.

The inclusion of the Channel Islands and the Isle of Man in the EEC presented constitutional, administrative and economic difficulties. Accordingly, after consultation with them, the United Kingdom sought for the islands arrangements short of full membership, and proposed a form of association under Article 238 of the Treaty of Rome, now Article 310.

Isle of Man[4]

The Isle of Man was formerly under the suzerainty of the Kings of Norway and Scotland, but Kings of England exercised some degree of control over the island after 1290 (Edward I), and the island finally came into the allegiance of the English Crown in 1399 (Henry IV). It was held more or less independently[5] by the Stanley family (Earls of Derby) as Lords of Man under letters patent until 1736, when it passed to the Duke of Atholl. The Crown bought out the Duke's regalities and customs rights in 1765.[6] To these were added the ecclesiastical patronage and other general manorial rights in 1825.[7] The island has retained its ancient internal constitution as modified by statute,[8] and has legislative autonomy

35–002

---

[1] The title to this Chapter is used as a convenient description for a number of territories of different legal status, despite the Government's decision to refer for the future to the remaining colonies as overseas territories rather than dependent territories.

[2] Interpretation Act 1978, s.5 and Sched. 1.

[3] (1978) 2 E.H.R.R.I. See *supra* para. 23–032.

[4] See *The British Commonwealth: Development of its Laws and Constitutions: 1 The United Kingdom*, pp. 485 *et seq.* (by D. C. Holland); *Report of the Commission on the Isle of Man Constitution* (1959) (Chairman, Lord MacDermott); *Report of the Joint Working Party on the Constitutional Relationship between the Isle of Man and the United Kingdom* (1969); *Royal Commission on the Constitution 1969–1973* (Kilbrandon) (1973) Cmnd. 5460, I. Part XI; G. Kinley, "The Isle of Man," *Guardian Gazette*, January 25, 1978.

[5] Although appeal lay to the Privy Council: *Christian v. Corrin* (1716) 1 P.Wms. 329.

[6] Isle of Man Purchase Act 1765.

[7] Duke of Atholl's Rights, Isle of Man, Act 1825.

[8] *e.g.* Isle of Man Constitution Acts 1961 to 1971, passed by the Manx legislature largely to implement recommendations of the MacDermott Commission (1959).

in most respects. The island is, however, in strict theory subject to the authority of the United Kingdom Parliament, although Westminster legislation extending to the Isle of Man is, in practice, restricted to such matters as defence, postal services, wireless telegraphy, copy-right, merchant shipping and civil aviation.[9] Not being part of the United Kingdom[10] it is not bound by Acts of Parliament except where it is included either expressly or by necessary implication.[11] Statutes may be extended to the Island by Order in Council.

The legislature is known as the Court of Tynwald.[12] Legislation may be initiated in either branch of the legislature (Legislative Council and House of Keys,[13] and is debated in each branch separately, although there are provisions for conferences. Bills are signed in Tynwald at joint sittings of the branches: they require the confirmation of the Sovereign in Council and a declaration of the Royal Assent in Tynwald.[14]

The Queen's representative is the Lieutenant-Governor. A confidential Executive Council was set up in 1961 to advise the Lieutenant-Governor on matters of principle, policy and legislation. The Home Secretary is the main channel of communication between the United Kingdom and the Isle of Man, and advises the Lieutenant-Governor.

The island has its own system of courts. Manx land law is largely Norse in origin and is unique. Appeal lies to the Judicial Committee of the Privy Council from the Staff of Government Division.[15]

The Channel Islands[16]

35–003   The Channel Islands formed part of the Duchy of Normandy, and remained to the King of England when the rest of Normandy reverted to France in the thirteenth century. They are not part of the United Kingdom.[17] The common law

[9] For a recent example see the Isle of Man Act 1979 which deals *inter alia* with law relating to customs and excise. Over 700 statutes which had been repealed in the United Kingdom but, due to oversight, not in the Isle of Man were repealed by the Statute Law Revision (Isle of Man) Act 1991.

[10] *Davison v. Farmer* (1851) 6 Ex. 242.

[11] *Sodor and Man (Bishop) v. Derby (Earl)* [1751] 2 Ves.Sen. 337.

[12] Probably derived from Norse *Thing-vollr* or *Thing-Wald* = Parliament field or meeting-place of the assembly.

[13] The original of the term "Keys" is obscure: it is perhaps a corruption of a Manx Gaelic expression meaning "the twenty-four." The earliest use of the word "Keys" seems to have been in 1585.

[14] Before the Acts of Tynwald (Emergency Promulgation) Act 1916, Acts had to be promulgated in English and Manx at Tynwald Hill, St John's, before they became law. Since the Act (s.3) they cease to have force if they are not promulgated in the customary manner within 12 months. The Royal assent was signified in 1982 by the Lieutenant Governor instead of the Queen in Council as previously.

[15] For the history of appeals, see J. H. Smith, *Appeals to the Privy Council from the American Plantations*, pp. 171–174. For an example, see *Frankland v. The Queen* [1987] A.C. 576, PC.

[16] See L. A. Sheridan, *The British Commonwealth: Development of its Laws and Constitutions: 1 The United Kingdom*, pp. 1141 *et seq. Royal Commission on the Constitution 1969–1973* (Kilbrandon), (1973) Cmnd. 5460, I. Pt. XI; *Report of Committee of Privy Council on Proposed Reforms in the Channel Islands* (1947) Cmd. 7074; F. De L. Bois, "Parliamentary Supremacy in the Channel Islands" [1983] P.L. 385. J. H. Le Patoured, *The Medieval Administration of the Channel Islands, 1199–1399: Minquiers and Ecrehos Case*, I.C.J. Reports (1953) p. 47.

[17] *Navigators and General Insurance Co v. Ringrose* [1962] 1 W.L.R. 173; [1962] 1 All E.R. 97, CA: (commercial document); *Rover International Ltd v. Cannon Films Sales Ltd* [1987] 1 W.L.R. 1597 at 1603 ("beyond the seas" for the purpose of the Rules of the Supreme Court made under the Civil Evidence Act 1968). In *Re a Debtor ex p. Viscount of the Royal Court of Jersey* [1981] Ch. 384, Goulding J. held that the Royal Court of Jersey is a "British Court elsewhere" for the purpose of the Bankruptcy Act 1914, s.122. In *Chloride Ltd v. F & W Freight Ltd* [1989] 1 W.L.R. 823 the Court of Appeal held that a contract of carriage of goods between Manchester and Jersey was not a contract

of the Channel Islands is still the ancient custom of the Duchy, the principal authority being *Le Grand Coustumier du Pays et Duché de Normandie* which was compiled in the thirteenth century.

The islanders, though loyal to the Crown, affect to recognise the Sovereign only in right of the Duchy of Normandy, and they deny the right of the United Kingdom Parliament or the Queen in Council to legislate for them without the consent of the States (the legislatures) confirmed by registration in the local Royal Court.[18] There is no real doubt of the legislative competence of Parliament, which legislates for the islands in such matters as customs and excise, the armed forces, extradition, fisheries, telegraphs, Post Office, copyright, merchant shipping and civil aviation; but the efficacy of legislation by prerogative Orders in Council is uncertain. In practice, the consent of the States (legislatures) is obtained and the Act or Order is registered, the islanders asserting—contrary to the British view—that it is the local registration which gives it legal effect. Statutes may be extended to the Islands by Order in Council.

The Crown appoints a Lieutenant-Governor for each of the Bailiwicks of Jersey and Guernsey,[19] who summon the States and have powers, subject to the Home Secretary and the Secretary of State for Defence, in relation to the preservation of peace and defence. The Home Secretary was traditionally the channel of communication between the Channel Islands and the Crown, a role recently transferred to the Lord Chancellor's Department.

Appeal lies as of right in civil cases from the courts of Jersey and Guernsey to the Judicial Committee of the Privy Council.[20] There is no appeal to the Judicial Committee as of right in criminal cases; but it was held in *Renouf v. Attorney-General for Jersey*[21] that the prerogative power to grant special leave to appeal had never been relinquished, although special leave would only be granted where there was a grave miscarriage of justice.

Both the Isle of Man and the Channel Islands were named in a report published in June 2000 by the Organisation for Economic Co-operation and Development among a group of 35 tax havens which are alleged to harm international trade and investment by offering shelter to tax dodgers. The United Kingdom government welcomed the report but it is not clear what power it has to force changes.

II. TERRITORIES OF THE COMMONWEALTH[22]

The British Empire

This name has now fallen into disuse. For a long time it was employed to mean all territories over which the Crown exercised or claimed some degree of control,   **35–004**

of carriage between two countries for the purposes of the international convention to which effect was given in the United Kingdom by the Carriage of Goods by Road Act 1965. To hold otherwise would make nonsense of the Convention; it was "not helpful" to look at the general law to decide the question: *per* Dillon L.J. at 827.

[18] See further R. E. M., "*The Jersey Incident of 1889: Re Daniel*" (1984) 100 L.Q.R. 41.

[19] Alderney and Sark are dependencies of Guernsey. See A. R. de Carteret, *The Story of Sark* (1956).

[20] For the early history of appeals, see J. H. Smith, *op. cit.* pp. 4 *et seq.*, 63 *et seq.*

[21] [1936] A.C. 445. For later cases, see *Quin v. The King, The Times*, November 8, 1951; *Manley-Casimir v. Att.-Gen. for Jersey, The Times*, February 12, 1965 (Jersey law and practice apply); *Vaudin v. Hamon* [1974] A.C. 569 (application of *La Charte aux Normans* 1314 to law of property in Sark).

[22] See further on general matters, Sir William Dale; *The Modern Commonwealth* (1983), Sir Kenneth Roberts-Wray, *Commonwealth and Colonial Law* (1966) Chaps 1 and 2; S. A. de Smith, *The*

viz. the British Islands (including the United Kingdom), British India, British colonies, protectorates, and those self-governing colonies which in the early part of this century came to be known as the Dominions. The expression probably included protected states but not mandated (later trust) territories.

The sixteenth and seventeenth centuries saw some colonial expansion, mainly for the purpose of trade. English colonial expansion was the result of private enterprise and not government policy. If British subjects took possession of territory by settlement, the authority of the Crown extended to them; if they took by conquest, they acquired for the Crown.[23] The earliest colonial constitutions were letters patent to a proprietor or company, authorising him or it to trade and exercise jurisdiction within the area. "Royal" colonies, in which the direct governmental authority was the Crown, came later, the first being Virginia in 1624. It was clear that Parliament had jurisdiction in settled colonies, and the common law extended to settlers all the constitutional rights of Englishmen. The prerogative was more extensive in conquered colonies, which in the first instance the King could govern as he pleased, but the King could not without Parliament take away constitutional rights that he had granted.[24] Central political control over the colonies was vested in the Privy Council, which formed committees for trade and plantations. Parliament interfered chiefly in revenue matters and the passing of Acts of trade and navigation.

With the American declaration of independence in 1776 Britain lost 13 North American colonies. She learned by this experience, and retained and developed "the second British empire," which expression covers the period from the loss of the American colonies to the development of colonial self-government in the middle of the nineteenth century. The main common law principles relating to colonial government were established by the middle of the eighteenth century in such cases as *Campbell v. Hall.*[25]

The expression "the third British Empire" is sometimes used to describe the period of the development of self-government in certain colonies, *e.g.* in Canada, Australia and New Zealand, from the middle of the nineteenth century to the formal recognition of Dominion status by the Statute of Westminster 1931; and the name "fourth British Empire" has been given to the looser association of the Commonwealth since the end of the Second World War.[26]

Her Majesty's dominions

35–005   These are all territories under the sovereignty of the Crown. A synonym sometimes used is "British territory." The expression would not ordinarily include protectorates[27] or trust territories, although it might do so for the purposes of particular statute.[28]

Vocabulary of Commonwealth Relations (1954). There are statutory definitions for particular purposes of some of the expressions used in this section.

[23] *Campbell v. Hall* (1774) 1 Cowp. 204; (1774) 20 St.Tr. 287, 322–323.

[24] *Calvin's Case* (1609) 7 Co.Rep. 1 at f. 17b. Later this was taken to mean, when representative institutions had been granted.

[25] (1774) 1 Cowp. 204.

[26] *post*, Chap. 36.

[27] *cf.* Roberts-Wray, *op. cit.* p. 23, where sovereignty in the sense of ownership is distinguished from sovereignty in the sense of governmental power. In the latter sense, the Crown may be said to have sovereignty in protectorates.

[28] *e.g.* reciprocal enforcement of foreign judgments.

At common law it was said that the Crown was one and indivisible throughout the Sovereign's dominions, and the King was everywhere present in his dominions.[29] Thus in *Williams v. Howarth*[30] the Privy Council held that the debt due from the Government of New South Wales in respect of the pay of a soldier who had fought in the Boer War (when New South Wales was a colony) was discharged by the payment of a smaller amount from the Imperial Government. But in *R. v. Secretary of State for Foreign and Commonwealth Affairs ex p. Indian Association of Alberta*,[31] the Court of Appeal held that the doctrine of the indivisibility of the Crown no longer represented the law, and hence an English Court could not grant to the Indian peoples of Canada a declaration relating to the treaty obligations entered into by the Crown. In each of its realms the Crown is now answerable only for obligations relating to that realm. Lord Denning M.R. thought that while it had been "a settled doctrine of constitutional law that the Crown was one and indivisible" in the eighteenth and nineteenth centuries,[32] a change had occurred in "the first half of this century—not by statute—but by constitutional usage and practice."[33] The Master of the Rolls referred in particular to the definition of the status of the relationship of the United Kingdom and the Dominions adopted in 1926 at the Imperial Conference. Kerr and May L.JJ. traced the recognition of the divisibility of the Crown to the nineteenth century. In support of their view they relied on the decision of Page-Wood V.-C. in *Re Holmes*[34] that a petition of right relating to land in Canada could not be heard in an English court.

British possessions
They are any parts of Her Majesty's dominions exclusive of the United Kingdom.[35]   **35–006**

British colonies
These are any parts of Her Majesty's dominions excluding the British Islands,   **35–007** and excluding independent members of the Commonwealth, their provinces and states.[36] Formerly persons born in a British colony were citizens of the United Kingdom and Colonies by birth. After the coming into effect of the British Nationality Act 1981 such persons become British Dependent Territories citizens or British Overseas citizens.[37] Acquisition of British Dependent Territories citizenship by birth after the commencement of the 1981 Act is limited to the children of a parent already possessing that citizenship or being settled in a

---

[29] See *Amalgamated Society of Engineers v. Adelaide Steamship Co.* (1920) 28 C.L.R. 129; *Re Bateman's Trusts* (1873) L.R. 15 Eq. 355; *Re Oriental Bank Corpn. ex p. The Crown* (1884) 28 Ch.D. 643. *cf. post*, para. 36–022.

[30] [1905] A.C. 551. See H. V. Evatt, *The Royal Prerogative* (1987) Chap. 9.

[31] [1982] Q.B. 892, CA; pet. dis. 937 [not for] "any technical or procedural grounds [but because of] the accumulated reasons given in the judgment of the Court of Appeal": *per* Lord Diplock. See further, Paul Jackson, "The Crown: Some Recent Proceedings" (1982) 7 *Holdsworth Law Rev.* 91.

[32] At p. 911 and p. 917.

[33] At p. 916.

[34] (1861) 2 John & H. 527. See also *Att.-Gen. v. Great Southern and Western Ry Co of Ireland* [1925] A.C. 754; *R. v. Secretary of State for the Home Department ex p. Bhurosah* [1968] 1 Q.B. 266; *Mellenger v. New Brunswick Corpn.* [1971] 1 W.L.R. 604.

[35] Interpretation Act 1978, s.5 and Sched. 1.

[36] *ibid.*

[37] ss.23 and 26.

dependent territory.[38] Inhabitants of Gibraltar[39] and the Falkland Islands[40] are, exceptionally, entitled to British citizenship.

British protectorates

35–008   These were territories under the protection of the Crown. They were not British territory, and did not form part of Her Majesty's dominions. The Crown was responsible for their defence and external affairs. Internally some were administered in a similar way to colonies ("protectorates" in the strict sense).[41] These are now all independent. Others were administered, with varying degrees of British supervision, by their native rulers ("protected states").[42] They are specified in the British Protectorates, Protected States and Protected Persons Order 1982.[43] Their inhabitants, if they have not acquired the citizenship of an independent Commonwealth country have the status of British Protected Persons.[44]

British trust territories

35–009   These were former mandated territories whose administration was entrusted to the Crown by the allied and associated powers in 1919 to be executed on behalf of the League of Nations. After the last war they were administered under the name of trust territories by the United Kingdom or other Commonwealth governments on behalf of the Crown in accordance with the Charter of the United Nations. Trust territories were not British territory, and did not form part of Her Majesty's dominions.[45] All have now acquired independence. Their inhabitants, unless they have acquired the citizenship of an independent Commonwealth country may have the status of British Protected Persons.[46]

Dependent territories

35–010   This was a non-technical term which came into use to refer to all territories in the Commonwealth which were not independent. It is a convenient way of referring to colonies, protectorates, protected states and trust territories. It has received statutory recognition in the British Nationality Act 1981, s.50(1).[47]

---

[38] s.15. See similar restrictions on acquisition of British citizenship: *ante* para. 23–007. Restoration of British citizen was promised in a White Paper (Cm 4264) in 1998: *post* para. 35–032.

[39] British Nationality Act 1981, s.5.

[40] British Nationality (Falkland Islands) Act 1983.

[41] Where the Crown had acquired jurisdiction in a foreign country by treaty, grant or other lawful means, this jurisdiction was exercised under the Foreign Jurisdiction Act 1890 (replacing the Foreign Jurisdiction Act 1843); see *R. v. Ketter* [1940] 1 K.B. 787; *Nyali Ltd v. Att.-Gen.* [1956] 1 Q.B. 1, CA; *Ex p. Mwenya* [1960] 1 Q.B. 241, CA. See further Hall, *Foreign Jurisdiction of the British Crown;* Jenkyns, *British Rule and Jurisdiction beyond the Seas.*

[42] *Mighell v. Sultan of Johore* [1894] 1 Q.B. 149; *Duff Development Co v. Kelentan Government* [1924] A.C. 797, HL; *Sultan of Johore v. Abubakar Tunku Aris Bendahar* [1952] A.C. 318.

[43] No. 1070, made under the British Nationality Act 1981; amended by British Nationality (Brunel) Order 1983, No. 1699.

[44] British Nationality Act 1981, s.38 and s.50(1).

[45] H. Duncan Hall, *Mandates, Dependencies and Trusteeship*; Clive Parry. "The Legal Nature of Trusteeship Agreements" (1950) B.Y.I.L. 164.

[46] Note 44, *ante.*

[47] Sched. 6 lists as British Dependent Territories: Anguilla, Bermuda, British Antarctic Territory, British Indian Ocean Territory, Cayman Islands, Falkland Islands and Dependencies, Gibraltar, Hong Kong, Montserrat, Pitcairn, Henderson, Ducie and Oeno Islands, St Helena and Dependencies, The Sovereign Base Areas of Akrotiri and Dhekelia (as defined in the Cyprus Act 1960, s.2(1)), Turks and Caicos Islands and Virgin Islands.

Dependencies

This too was not a technical term.[48] It was sometimes used in the same sense **35–011** as "dependent territories" (*ante*), but was not popular there. It is better applied to miscellaneous territories, such as a territory dependent placed under the authority of another (*e.g.* Ascension Island and Tristan da Cunha as dependencies of St. Helena); British possessions which are so small as to be virtually unadministered (*e.g.* the Great and Little Basses and Minicoy); and similar outposts under the jurisdiction of independent members of the Commonwealth. It has received formal recognition by its use in the British Nationality Act 1981.

The Commonwealth

In 1884 Lord Rosebery said in a speech in Australia that "the Empire is a **35–012** Commonwealth of Nations."[49] The name "British Empire" began to fall into disfavour between the Wars in those countries that were acquiring independence, and "the British Commonwealth of Nations"[50] or "British Commonwealth"[51] came into use, either as synonymous with the whole British Empire, or as referring to the independent parts as in "the British Empire and Commonwealth." The "British Commonwealth" then ousted "the British Empire" almost completely in popular usage. The Asian and African members, however, preferred "the Commonwealth"[52] simply and this last name on account of its shortness has come into general favour, except perhaps in the Commonwealth of Australia where it is ambiguous. The term now usually includes dependent territories as well as independent members.

Independent members of the Commonwealth[53]

This expression covers—in addition to the United Kingdom—those countries **35–013** still in the Commonwealth whose "Dominion status" was recognised by the Statute of Westminster 1931 (now Canada,[54] the Commonwealth of Australia[55] and New Zealand); and those former dependent territories that have since been granted independence by special statutes, *e.g.* India, Sri Lanka (Ceylon), Ghana (Gold Coast) and Nigeria, and whose membership has been agreed by the other members of the Commonwealth. Sometimes they are called "members of the Commonwealth" or "Commonwealth countries." Citizens of these countries are Commonwealth citizens under the British Nationality Act 1981, section 3.

It also now includes Mozambique and Cameroon which joined the Commonwealth in 1995 without any former links with the Crown.

---

[48] *Re Maryon-Wilson's Estate* [1912] 1 Ch. 55, 66, *per* Farwell L.J.; *Re Brassey's Settlement* [1955] 1 W.L.R. 192; [1955] 1 All E.R. 577.

[49] "I say that these are no longer colonies in the ordinary sense of the term, but I claim that this is a nation. . . . There is no need for any nation, however great, leaving the Empire, because the Empire is a Commonwealth of Nations": Robert Rhodes James, *Rosebery* (1963), p. 196. Lloyd George also used this expression at the Imperial War Cabinet in 1917.

[50] Anglo-Irish Treaty 1921.

[51] J. X. Merriman (Prime Minister of Cape Colony) in the 1880s: General Smuts at the Imperial War Conference 1917.

[52] Nehru, 1948.

[53] See *post*, Chap. 36.

[54] The provinces of Canada and the states of Australia are *sui generis*: see *Mellenger v. New Brunswick Development Corporation* [1971] 1 W.L.R. 604, CA; *cf.* Canada Act 1982 and Australia Act 1986.

[55] *ibid.*

III. BRITISH COLONIES[56]

Introduction

35–014 The Crown is immediately related to a colony[57] as Sovereign. Colonies are under the sovereignty of the Crown both in the sense of governmental power and in the sense of ownership or belonging.[58] The duty of the Crown to afford protection to citizens of colonies is one of imperfect obligation and is unenforceable in the courts.[59]

The constitution of a colony is contained in several documents. The basic instrument is usually an Order in Council or letters patent, but sometimes an Act of Parliament. This provides for the government of the colony, and generally includes provisions relating to the composition and powers of the legislative and executive councils and the superior courts. Letters patent constitute the office of Governor and define his duties and powers. Royal instructions, issued from time to time by the Secretary of State, prescribe the manner in which the Governor is to exercise his functions. A Royal Commission appoints the Governor for the time being.

The central purpose of British colonial policy at the end of the last war was stated to be to guide the colonial territories to responsible self-government within the Commonwealth in conditions that ensure to the people both a fair standard of living and freedom from oppression from any quarter. The Secretary of State is ultimately responsible for their government, but this is discharged by a Governor or Administrator working through the civil service. The remaining dependent territories are now few. They include the colonies of Gibraltar,[60] the Falkland Islands,[61] St Helena[62] in the South Atlantic, Pitcairn[63] in the Pacific, and several

---

[56] Dale, *op. cit.* pp. 305 *et seq.* Sir Kenneth Roberts-Wray, *Commonwealth and Colonial Law* (1966); *Changing Law in Developing Countries* (ed. J. N. D. Anderson, 1963); Sir Hilary Blood, *The Smaller Territories* (1958); Sir Ivor Jennings, *The Approach to Self-Government* (1956); Sir Keith Hancock, *Colonial Self-Government* (1956); O. Hood Phillips, "The Making of a Colonial Constitution" (1955) 71 L.Q.R. 51.

For the history, see Holdsworth, *History of English Law*, Vol. XI pp. 35–139, 229–267; A. B. Keith, *Responsible Government in the Dominions* (2nd ed., 1928); C. E. Carrington, *The British Overseas* (1950); Sir Alan Burns, *In Defence of Colonies; John Bowle, The Imperial Achievement* (1974); W. D. McIntyre, *The Commonwealth of Nations: Origin and Impact* (1977). See also *Forsyth's Cases and Opinions on Constitutional Law* (1869); *Opinions on Imperial Constitutional Law*, ed., D. P. O'Connell and A. Riordan (Melbourne, 1971). For future developments, see *Partnership for Progress and Prosperity: Britain and Overseas Territories* (1988, Cm. 4264).

[57] *ante*, para. 35–007.

[58] See, *e.g. Tito v. Waddell (No. 2)* [1977] Ch. 106 (Megarry V.-C.); obligation of Crown in respect of extraction of phosphates in Ocean Island was governmental, not fiduciary; *Buck v. Att.-Gen.* [1965] Ch. 745, CA: if Crown were a trustee of certain lands in Sierra Leone, such trust could not be enforced in English courts.

[59] *Mutasa v. Att.-Gen.* [1980] Q.B. 114.

[60] Ceded by Spain under the Treaty of Utrecht in 1713. Spain for some years has been agitating for its return.

[61] Sovereignty long disputed by Argentina. The British Government insists that the United Kingdom title is derived from early settlement, reinforced by formal claims in the name of the Crown, and completed by open, continuous, effective and peaceful possession, occupation and administration of the islands since 1833 (save for the 10 weeks of forcible Argentine occupation in 1982). Further, the exercise of sovereignty has consistently been shown to accord with the wishes of the islanders: *Fifth Report from Foreign Affairs Committee*, Session 1983–84; *Falkland Islands: Observations by Her Majesty's Government* (H.M.S.O., 1985).

[62] Settled in 1659; recaptured from the Dutch after short interruption in 1673.

[63] Settled in 1790 by mutineers from *H.M.S. Bounty*.

Caribbean islands acquired in various ways.[64] The total population of all these territories is in the region of 189,000—ranging from over 60,000 in Bermuda to 54 in Pitcairn.

Hong Kong

By contrast, the former colony of Hong Kong had a population of around six **35–015** million. The territory consisted of land ceded by China in 1842 and 1860 and partly of land leased in 1898 for 99 Years. With the approaching end of the lease negotiations began between China and the United Kingdom over the future of the colony. The agreement between the two states was given effect in the United Kingdom by the Hong Kong Act 1985 under which British sovereignty over the entire territory would end on July 1, 1997.[65] A new type of citizenship—British National (Overseas)—was created for the inhabitants. This citizenship gave no right of abode but it did confer a right to a British passport. Subsequent unease at the plight of certain groups of residents in Hong Kong after the handing-over to China and pressure exerted particularly in the House of Lords led to three further statutes. The British Nationality (Hong Kong) Act 1990 authorised the Secretary of State to register up to 50,000 persons and their dependents as British citizens, on the recommendation of the Governor of Hong Kong. It was hoped, or believed, that the security of possessing British citizenship would encourage this group (whose presence was important for the territory's economic development) to stay in Hong Kong. The Hong Kong (War Wives and Widows) Act 1996 conferred British citizenship on a group of women believed to number between 50 and 60 by virtue of having been married to a husband whose war service would have entitled her to residence in the United Kingdom if still so married. Finally the British Nationality (Hong Kong) Act 1997 conferred British nationality on those British National (Overseas) citizens who failed to acquire Chinese nationality because of their non-Chinese ethnic origins. This group was estimated to number between 5000 and 8000 and it was argued that a moral obligation was owed to them because they were largely descendants of people who had settled in Hong Kong in the service of the Crown as soldiers and civil servants from other parts of what was then the Empire, particularly from India.

In pursuance of the dual policy of political advancement and economic development, the United Kingdom Parliament has provided large sums of capital for economic development and social welfare in the colonies and other dependent territories. Political changes in the direction of self-government or independence have indeed been so rapid in recent years that they have outstripped economic and social development; and the constitutions of particular territories are nowadays so transitory that it is impracticable to describe them here individually.

Colonies may be classified according to the manner in which they were acquired, which may have been: (i) by *settlement* in territory where there was no population or indigenous peoples, or (ii) by *conquest or cession* of territory having an organised society. (The terms of any treaty of cession do not give the inhabitants of a colony rights which are enforceable in the local courts or by the

---

[64] The surviving colonies are described in H. Ritchie, *The Last Pink Bits* (1997).
[65] Reports on the implementation of the Sino British Joint Declaration that led to the present arrangement (One country, Two systems) are made at six monthly intervals to Parliament by the Secretary of State: *e.g.* Cm. 5067, covering July-December 2000.

Privy Council.[66]) This distinction, which came to be recognised in the seventeenth century,[67] affects the constitutional position of the colony, especially the legislative power. It also determines the system of private law that prevails in a given colony. But both the private and the public law are subject to legislative changes, so that this distinction is now largely of historical interest.

A more modern classification is that into (i) colonies *possessing responsible government* (commonly called "self-governing colonies"), and (ii) colonies *not possessing responsible government* ("non-self-governing colonies," formerly known as "Crown colonies"). This distinction rests on whether or not the executive is responsible for most purposes to the colonial legislature (to the lower House if that legislature is bicameral). Any remaining non-self-governing territories would be those with very small populations.

Settled colonies[68]

35–016   Settlement might be by: (i) occupation by British settlers under the authorisation of the Crown, *e.g.* Canada (excluding Quebec and Ontario), the Australian colonies[69] and some of the West Indies; (ii) recognition by the Crown, as British territory, of unauthorised settlements by British subjects, *e.g.* British Honduras, the Pitcairn Islands and Tristan da Cunha; or (iii) formal annexation of uninhabited islands or uninhabitable Arctic or Antarctic areas, *e.g.* some of the Pacific Islands, the Isles of Northern Canada, the Ross Dependency of New Zealand, the Falkland Islands and the British Antarctic Territory.

British settlers took with them the common law of England[70] and the statute law as existing at the time of settlement. Subsequent Acts of Parliament did not apply to the colony unless they were expressed to apply to that colony or to colonies generally.[71] The law, whether enacted or unenacted, that the settlers carried with them was only such as was applicable to their new situation and suitable to the condition of a young colony.[72]

Conquered and ceded colonies[73]

35–017   Cession was usually the result of conquest. The varieties of acquisition by these two means were: (i) conquest only; (ii) conquest on terms of surrender; (iii) cession by treaty with a civilised state, *e.g.* Grenada; (iv) voluntary cession by the inhabitants, *e.g.* Malta, Fiji. The Privy Council in *Sammut v. Strickland*[74] said that colonies acquired by voluntary cession, or by cession after conquest,

---

[66] *Winfat Enterprise (H.K.) Co. Ltd v. Att.-Gen. of Hong Kong* [1985] A.C. 733, PC.

[67] See, *e.g. Calvin's Case* (1709) 7 Co.Rep. 1; *Blankard v. Galdy* (1693) 2 Salk. 411.

[68] As this topic is now mainly of historical interest, no distinction is made in the examples given between existing colonies and territories that have acquired independence since the last war.

[69] Penal settlements may have constituted a separate kind of colony: see *per* Eggleston J. in *Newbery v. The Queen* [1965] 7 F.L.R. 34, 39; and see (1965) 11 A.L.J. 409 *et seq.*

[70] *Pictou Municipality v. Geldert* [1893] A.C. 524. *Tito v. Waddell (No. 2)* [1977] Ch. 106, 132, *per* Sir Robert Megarry V.-C. "The English concept of perpetuities arrived at Ocean Island with the flag, a blessing that the Banabans may not then have appreciated"; (*ibid.* at p. 220).

[71] *Memorandum* (1722) 2 P.Wms. 74; *New Zealand Loan Co. v. Morrison* [1898] A.C. 349.

[72] *Whicker v. Hume* (1858) 7 H.L.C. 124, 161, *per* Lord Cranworth. In settled colonies where there was a small indigenous population, the native law might still be applied to the natives, *e.g.* the Maoris of New Zealand: see *Hoani Te Heuheu Tukino v. Aotea District Maori Land Board* [1941] A.C. 308, PC. New Zealand should perhaps be regarded as having been voluntarily ceded by the inhabitants.

[73] As this topic is now mainly of historical interest, no distinction is made here between existing colonies and territories that have acquired independence since the last war.

[74] [1938] A.C. 678.

were in the same position in British constitutional law as colonies acquired by conquest merely.

In conquered or ceded colonies the existing legal system was retained unless and until it was altered or abrogated by the Crown (*Campbell v. Hall per* Lord Mansfield C.J.[75]). The legal system might, for example, be Roman-Dutch law, customary French law, the Code Napoléon, Hindu law, Mohammedan (Islamic) law or native African custom. Existing laws were abrogated if they were: (i) contrary to Acts of Parliament, whether general or particular, extending to the colony[76]; (ii) contrary to British constitutional principles[77]; or (iii) repugnant to the fundamental religious or ethical principles of Europeans.[78]

English law was introduced by Act of Parliament or local legislation into some colonies acquired by conquest or cession. This refers to the common law and statute law as they existed at the date of the application of English law to the colony or at some specified date.[79]

Legislation by the United Kingdom Parliament

There has never been any real doubt in British constitutional law about the competence of Parliament to legislate for the colonies, nor, in view of the doctrine of the supremacy of Parliament, are there any legal restrictions on this power. From the middle of the nineteenth century, however, there was a convention against Parliament legislating without their consent for the self-governing colonies that became Dominions in 1931.[80] A similar convention came to apply in the present century to a newer group of self-governing colonies, including Southern Rhodesia, Malta and the Gold Coast (now Ghana). Any doubt there may have been as to how far Acts of Parliament passed after the foundation of a given colony applied to that colony were set at rest by section 1 of the Colonial Laws Validity Act 1865, which states that "an act of Parliament, or any provision thereof, shall ... be said to extend to any Colony when it is made applicable to such Colony by the *express words or necessary intendment* of any Act of Parliament."

35–018

Where parliamentary authority is necessary or desirable for legislation in respect of colonies, Parliament usually prefers to authorise the issue of Orders in Council by the Crown. British Acts are used for matters of general concern, such as Admiralty jurisdiction, aerial navigation, armed forces, copyright, currency, extradition, foreign enlistment, fugitive offenders, international treaties, merchant shipping, nationality and citizenship, official secrets, reciprocal enforcement of judgments, and territorial waters jurisdiction; and also for constitutional changes such as grant of independence or where more than one colony are concerned.

---

[75] (1774) 1 Cowp. 204 (Grenada); following *Calvin's Case* (1609) 7 Co.Rep. 1 and *Blankard v. Galdy* (1693) 2 Salk. 411.

[76] *Campbell v. Hall* (1774) *ante.*

[77] *Union Government Minister of Lands v. Whittaker's Estate* [1916] App.D.(S.A.) 203.

[78] *Calvin's Case* (1609) 7 Co.Rep. Ia 17; *Blankard v. Galdy* (1693) 2 Salk. 411; *Memorandum* (1722) 2 P.Wms. 75; *Campbell v. Hall, supra.* And see *R. v. Picton* (1804–10) 30 St.Tr. 225, 529, 883–955 (torture in Trinidad); *Fabrigas v. Mostyn* 20 St.Tr. 175, 181; (1773) 1 Cowp. 161 (Minorca); *Khoo Hooi Leong v. Khoo Chong Yeoh* [1930] A.C. 346, PC (legitimacy of children of second wife).

[79] *Att.-Gen. v. Stewart* (1815) 2 Mer. 143, 160; *R. v. Vaughan* (1769) 4 Burr. 2494.

[80] *post*, Chap. 36.

Legislation by the Crown

35–019   This may take the form of Orders in Council, proclamations or letters patent. Here it is necessary to distinguish between settled colonies on the one hand and conquered or ceded colonies on the other.

For settled colonies

35–020   The prerogatives of the Crown, and the rights and immunities of British subjects, in colonies established by occupancy and settlement are similar to those that obtain in this country (*Kielley v. Carson*[81]). The Crown may constitute the office of Governor, and an Executive Council; appoint a Governor and issue royal instructions to him; establish courts of justice; and provide for the summoning of a legislature[82] with power to legislate and tax. In this way constitutions were first granted to Bermuda (1620) and most of the early American colonies. Any other form of constitution was thought to require at common law an Act of Parliament, as with the Australian colonies in the early nineteenth century. Apart from its constituent power, the Crown could not at common law legislate for settled colonies.[83]

As the Crown had no direct lawmaking power at common law, legislation by the Imperial Parliament was also necessary to empower the Crown to make laws for such sparsely populated settlements as the Falkland Islands and those on the West Coast of Africa. General statutory powers, exercisable by Order in Council, were given to the Crown for this purpose by the British Settlements Act 1887.[84] The Act applied in effect to settled colonies that had not already been granted representative institutions, such as the Straits Settlements.[85]

For conquered or ceded colonies

35–021   The Crown has a prerogative (common law) power to legislate for conquered or ceded colonies, exercisable by Order in Council, proclamation or letters patent. This includes the power to establish any kind of constitution. When a representative legislature[86] has been granted to a colony, the prerogative power to legislate cannot be exercised while such grant is in force, as that would be repugnant to the grant, unless (as is now almost invariably the case) such power is expressly reserved in the grant.[87] Where the power to amend a colonial constitution by prerogative is reserved, it may be exercised retrospectively.[88] If, however, the representative government is *revoked*, whether by Imperial Act or by a valid exercise of the prerogative (*i.e.* in the latter case, where power to revoke was reserved), the prerogative power to legislate revives, even though such power of resumption has not been expressly reserved.[89]

---

[81] (1842) 4 Moo.P.C. 63, 84–85 (Newfoundland).

[82] Roberts-Wray, *op. cit.* p. 152, points out that there is little judicial authority for the common opinion that would limit the prerogative to the setting up of a *representative* legislature.

[83] *Re Lord Bishop of Natal* (1865) 3 Moo.P.C.(N.S.) 115, 148, *per* Lord Chelmsford L.C.

[84] Consolidating the Settlements of Coast of Africa and Falkland Islands Act 1843 and the West coast of Africa and Falkland Islands Act 1860, and amended in 1945.

[85] Singapore, Penang and Malacca.

[86] A representative legislature is defined for the purposes of the Colonial Laws Validity Act 1865 as a colonial legislature comprising a legislative body of which (at least) one-half are elected by the inhabitants of the colony.

[87] *Campbell v. Hall* (1774), 1 Cowp. 204; Lofft 655; 20 St.Tr. 239 (K.B., *per* Lord Mansfield C.J.); duty on sugar exported from Grenada, a colony ceded by France.

[88] *Abeyesekara v. Jayatilake* [1932] A.C. 260, PC.

[89] *Sammut v. Strickland* [1938] A.C. 678, PC; imposition of customs duties in Malta, a ceded colony, whose representative institutions had been revoked by Act of Parliament. And see *Newbery v. The*

Powers of colonial legislatures

Colonial legislatures are subordinate lawmaking bodies, and their powers **35–022** depend on the statute, Orders in Council or letters patent granting them. They are invariably given a general power to make laws "for the peace, order and good government" of the colony. A colonial legislature is restricted as to the area of its powers, but within that area it is unrestricted and does not act as an agent or delegate.[90] No decision on the validity of colonial legislation appears to have turned on this expression, and the courts have never analysed the words. The expression is tautologous because "peace" and "order" come under "government," and "good" is not justiciable.[91] Such restrictions as there are on the making of laws with extraterritorial operation[92] are a deduction from the power to make laws "for" the territory, or perhaps for the government "of" the territory.[93]

Colonial Laws Validity Act 1865

The early common law rule was the rather vague one that a colonial Act was **35–023** invalid if repugnant to English law, and so some of the colonial constitutions that were enacted before 1865 provided that the legislative assembly should not pass legislation repugnant to (*i.e.* inconsistent with) the law of England. A controversy arose in the early 1860s when Boothby J. of South Australia passed adverse judgments on certain Acts passed by the South Australian legislature. Some he held contrary to English law, and others invalid because the Governor had not reserved them for the royal pleasure. The two Houses of the South Australian Parliament passed addresses asking for his removal. The matter went, in accordance with constitutional practice, to the Secretary of State for the Colonies, who asked the Law Officers (Sir Roundell Palmer and Sir Robert Collier) to advise. Their opinion was that the colonial Acts were invalid if contrary to United Kingdom Acts; that royal instructions to reserve assent to certain classes of Bills were instructions to the Governor only, not affecting the validity of such Acts if he gave his assent; but that, as regards repugnance to English law, a distinction was to be drawn between the "fundamental" principles and the non-fundamental rules of English law.[94] Such a distinction, if it ever existed, was complicated and no longer practicable.

The result was the passing of the Colonial Laws Validity Act 1865, which

---

Queen [1965] 7 F.L.R. 34: power of Crown to place Norfolk Island under authority of Australia: Norfolk Island was occupied by the inhabitants of Pitcairn Island, who were descended from the mutineers of the *Bounty*.

[90] *Hodge v. R.* (1883) 9 App.Cas. 117, 131 (Ontario); *Powell v. Apollo Candle Co* (1885) 10 App.Cas. 282 (New South Wales); *Bribery Commissioner v. Ranasinghe* [1964] A.C. 172 (PC), *per* Lord Pearce.

[91] *cf. Riel v. R.* (1880) 10 App.Cas. 675 (Canada); *D'Emden v. Pedder* (1904) 1 C.L.R. 91, 109 (Tasmania); *Croft v. Dunphy* [1933] A.C. 156 (Canada); *R. v. Fineberg* [1968] N.Z.L.R. 443 (New Zealand).

[92] *post*, para. 35–026.

[93] See Roberts-Wray, *op. cit.* 369–370.

[94] Keith, *Responsible Government in the Dominions*, I, pp. 339–341. D. P. O'Connell and A. Riordan, *Opinions on Imperial Constitutional Law* (1971), Section IV. Addresses to remove Boothby J. were presented in 1862 and 1866, but the Law Officers did not advise his removal, especially as some of the Acts held invalid by him were so. In 1867 he was removed by the Governor in Council under the Colonial Leave of Absence Act 1782: Keith, *op. cit.* II, pp. 1072–1073.

applied to all Her Majesty's dominions except the Channel Islands, the Isle of Man and India.[95] The Act was intended to be declaratory.

The Colonial Laws Validity Act 1865, s.2, provides that: "Any Colonial Law which is or shall be in any respect repugnant to the provisions of any *Act of Parliament* extending to the Colony to which such Law may relate, or repugnant to any Order or Regulation made under authority of such Act of Parliament, or having in the Colony the force and effect of such Act, shall be read subject to such Act, Order or Regulation, and shall, *to the extent of such repugnancy, but not otherwise*, be and remain absolutely void and inoperative."

Section 3 provides that: "No Colonial Law shall be or be deemed to have been void or inoperative on the ground of repugnancy to the Law of England unless the same shall be repugnant to the provisions of some such Act of Parliament, Order or Regulation as aforesaid."

A "colonial law" is defined in section 1 as including laws made for a colony by the Queen in Council (whether statutory or prerogative) as well as by the colonial legislature. It will be seen from the words we have put in italics in section 2, that a colonial law is only void for repugnancy if it is repugnant to an Act of Parliament or statutory order, etc. made thereunder, and that it is only void to the extent of such repugnancy. Section 3 makes the matter quite clear by expressing it in a different way.[96]

The validity of colonial laws may be tested in actions brought before the courts of the colony, and on appeal to the Privy Council.[97]

35–024   Section 4 provides that: "No Colonial Law, passed with the concurrence of or assented to by the Governor of any Colony, or to be hereafter so passed or assented to, shall be or be deemed to have been void or inoperative by reason only of any Instructions with reference to such law or the subject thereof which may have been given to such Governor by or on behalf of Her Majesty, by any Instrument other than the Letters Patent or Instrument authorising such Governor to concur in passing or to assent to Laws for the peace, order and good government of such Colony, even though such Instructions may be referred to in such Letters Patent or last-mentioned Instrument." Thus failure to observe royal instructions does not invalidate the Governor's assent to a Bill unless such instructions are actually embodied—not merely referred to—in the principal instrument defining his general legislative authority, so as in effect to form part of the constitution of the colony. Apart from this exception, the Governor's failure to regard royal instructions is a matter between him and the Crown, which—though it might result in his recall—does not affect the validity of colonial laws assented to by him.

Section 5 of the Colonial Laws Validity Act 1865 provides that: "*Every Colonial Legislature* shall have, and be deemed at all times to have had, full power within its jurisdiction to establish *Courts of Judicature*, and to abolish and reconstitute the same, and to alter the constitution thereof, and to make provision for the administration of justice therein." Such laws must be passed in the

---

[95] Similar principles applied to India. The Act still applies to the Australian States, although they are no longer colonies.

[96] See *Phillips v. Eyre* (1870) L.R. 6 Q.B. 1.

[97] A colonial legislature may debate, pass and present a Bill to the Governor—without being impeded by declaration or injunction—although it would, if enacted, be void under the Colonial Laws Validity Act as being repugnant to United Kingdom statute; *Rediffusion (H.K.) Ltd v. Att.-Gen. of Hong Kong* [1970] A.C. 1136, PC. See O. Hood Phillips, "Judicial Intervention in the Legislative Process" (1971) 87 L.Q.R. 321.

appropriate manner and form, as mentioned below in connection with constitutional amendments.

Section 5 of the Act further provides that: "Every *Representative* Legislature shall, in respect to the Colony under its jurisdiction, have, and be deemed at all times to have had, full power to make laws respecting the *constitution, powers and procedure of such Legislature*; provided that such Laws shall have been passed *in such manner and form* as may from time to time be required by any Act of Parliament, Letters Patent, Order in Council, or *Colonial Law* for the time being in force in the said Colony." This part of section 5 applies to a *representative* legislature, which is defined in section 1 of the Act as being "any Colonial Legislature which shall comprise a Legislative Body of which [at least] one half are elected by the inhabitants of the Colony." The expression "constitution" here refers to the composition of the legislature, not the general constitution of the colony. It was held by the Privy Council in *Att.-Gen. for New South Wales v. Trethowan*[98] that a representative colonial legislature can bind its successors. In that case an Act passed by the legislature of New South Wales[99] in 1929 providing that no Bill to abolish the Legislative Council (the upper house) should be presented to the Governor for his assent unless it had been approved by a referendum, and that this provision should apply to any Bill repealing or amending the Act, was effective after a change of government in 1930 to present the abolition of the Legislative Council without a referendum having been held.

Such a colonial legislature probably has to remain representative.[1] It cannot enlarge its own powers so as to make a unilateral declaration of independence. In *Madzimbamuto v. Lardner-Burke*,[2] an appeal from Southern Rhodesia, (a self-governing colony since 1923), after the Unilateral Declaration of Independence (UDI), the Privy Council stated that: (i) The nature of the sovereignty of the Queen in the United Kingdom Parliament over a British colony must be determined by the constitutional law of the United Kingdom; (ii) the Queen in the United Kingdom Parliament was still sovereign in Southern Rhodesia at the relevant time (1965), and therefore the Southern Rhodesia Act 1965 and Orders in Council passed thereunder were of full legal effect in Southern Rhodesia; and the convention under which the United Kingdom Parliament did not legislate without the consent of the Government of Southern Rhodesia, although important as a convention, had no effect in limiting the powers of the United Kingdom Parliament.

A colonial statute by describing itself as a Constitution Act does not *ipso facto* require any special procedure for its amendment. Thus it was held by the Judicial Committee in *McCawley v. The King*[3] that the Constitution Act 1867, passed by

35–025

[98] [1932] A.C. 526; *ante*, para. 4–032. And see *Att.-Gen. (N.S.W.) v. Trethowan* (1931) 44 C.L.R. 394 (High Ct. Austr.) *per* Dixon J., at pp. 425–427; Mr Justice Owen Dixon, "The Law and the Constitution" (1935) 51 L.Q.R. 590, 602–604.

[99] Not a colony then, but still subject to the Colonial Laws Validity Act 1865.

[1] *Taylor v. Att.-Gen. (Queensland)* (1917) 23 C.L.R. 457, 477, *per* Gavan Duffy and Rich JJ.

[2] [1969] 1 A.C. 645. Lord Pearce based his dissenting opinion on the doctrine of "necessity"; *cf. per* Sir Jocelyn Simon P., in *Adams v. Adams (Att.-Gen. intervening)* [1971] P. 188; validity of English woman's divorce in Rhodesia after U.D.I. See Roberts-Wray, *op. cit.* pp. 991–993; L. H. Leigh, "Rhodesia after UDI" [1966] P.L. 148; "Rhodesian Crisis—Criminal Liabilities" by B. A. Hepple, P. O'Higgins and C. C. Turpin [1966] Crim.L.R. 5, and O. Hood Phillips, *ibid.* p. 68. See also Leslie Wolf-Phillips, *Constitutional Legitimacy: a study of the doctrine of necessity.* (Third World Foundation, 1979) pp. 45–69; P. Mirfield, "When is a Judge not a Judge" [1978] P.L. 42.

Southern Rhodesia became the independent Republic of Zimbabwe by the Zimbabwe Act 1979.

[3] [1920] A.C. 691, *per* Lord Birkenhead L.C. See Mr Justice Owen Dixon, "The Law and the Constitution" (1935) 51 L.Q.R. 590, 602–604.

the Queensland legislature under the authority of an Imperial Act, could be amended in the ordinary way and did not require a special Amendment Bill, since it did not prescribe any specific manner or form. The constitutions of the Australian states (formerly colonies) were in this sense "uncontrolled" and not "controlled."

Extra-territorial legislation[4]

35–026   The power of a colonial legislature extends to the making of laws for the peace, order and good government *of the colony*, including its territorial waters. Special powers to legislate beyond these limits are conferred by the United Kingdom Parliament in such matters as defence and merchant shipping. Whether, apart from any special powers expressly conferred by Imperial Act, a colonial law purporting to have extra-territorial effect is for that reason necessarily void is uncertain. The Colonial Laws Validity Act 1865 does not deal with this question. There are dicta by the Privy Council in *Macleod v. Attorney-General for New South Wales*[5] and other cases[6] to the effect that such legislation is void; but some of the later cases, notably *Croft v. Dunphy*[7] throw doubt on the principle thought to have been established in *Macleod's* case.[8]

These Privy Council cases concerned Canada, Australia and New Zealand when they were self-governing colonies progressing towards independence. A similar latitude was allowed to the Indian legislature under the Government of India Act 1935 in *Wallace v. Commissioners of Income Tax, Bombay*,[9] where an Act imposing income tax on income accruing to any company if the greater part of its income arose in British India, was held validly to extend to a company registered in the United Kingdom, apparently on the principle that a subordinate legislature may legislate with extra-territorial effect if there is a sufficient "territorial connection" with the person affected or with a thing in which he is concerned. As regards a person, the territorial connection would extend at least to his presence, residence, domicile or carrying on of business in the legislating territory, but not to the ownership of shares in a foreign company which carried on only part of its business in that country.

---

[4] See D. P. O'Connell, "The Doctrine of Colonial Extra-Territorial Legislative Incompetence" (1959) 75 L.Q.R. 318; *cf.* Sir John Salmond, "The Limitations of Colonial Legislative Power" (1917) 33 L.Q.R. 117. The question remained of importance also with regard to the Australian states: D. P. O'Connell, "Problems of Australian Coastal Jurisdiction" (1958) 34 B.Y.I.L. 199, 248 *et seq.*

[5] [1891] A.C. 455: New South Wales Act penalising bigamy, "whosoever" and "whatsoever."

[6] *e.g. Ashbury v. Ellis* [1893] A.C. 339 (New Zealand Act allowing judicial proceedings where defendant outside the jurisdiction); *Peninsular and Oriental Steam Navigation Co v. Kingston* [1903] A.C. 471 (Australian Act penalising the breaking of customs seals on the high seas); *Att.-Gen. for Canada v. Cain* [1906] A.C. 542 (Canadian Act impliedly authorising restraint of alien immigrant outside territorial limits).

[7] [1933] A.C. 156: Canadian Act (passed before the Statute of Westminster) defining Canadian territorial waters in case of vessels registered in Canada as extending to twelve marine miles, at a time when according to the English law view of international law territorial waters extended only to three marine miles. Lord Sankey L.C. in *British Coal Corporation v. The King* [1935] A.C. 500, PC referred to the doctrine forbidding extra-territorial legislation as "a doctrine of somewhat obscure extent."

[8] In *R. v. Lander* [1919] N.Z.L.R. 305, the Court of Appeal of New Zealand (Stout C.J. dissenting) followed *Macleod v. Att.-Gen. for New South Wales* in the case of a British subject who, while a member of the New Zealand Expeditionary Force, committed bigamy in England. See D. P. O'Connell, "The Doctrine of Colonial Extra-Territorial Legislative Incompetence" (1959) 79 L.Q.R. 318; O'Connell and Riordan, *op. cit.* section V.

[9] (1948) 75 I.A. 86, PC; *per* Lord Uthwatt.

The Report of the Inter-Imperial Relations Committee of the Imperial Conference, 1926,[10] referred to "the difference between the legislative competence of the Parliament of Westminster and of the Dominion Parliaments, in that Acts passed by the latter operate, *as a general rule*, only within the territorial area of the Dominion concerned." The Report of the Conference on the Operation of Dominion Legislation (1929)[11] said: "It would not seem to be possible in the present state of the authorities to come to definite conclusions regarding the competence of Dominion Parliaments to give their legislation extra-territorial operation."

Rejection, reservation and disallowance

A colonial Governor, as representative of the Queen and a constituent part of the colonial legislature, has power to *refuse his assent to Bills* submitted to him by the legislature, or may in some cases return Bills to the legislature with proposed amendments. The classes of cases in which the Governor should refuse his assent are commonly set out in his instructions.   **35–027**

A colonial Governor has power to *reserve* Bills submitted to him by the colonial legislature, by withholding his assent until Her Majesty's pleasure be taken thereon. The exercise of this power by the Governor may, according to royal instructions, be either obligatory in the case of certain topics, or discretionary in all cases. Her Majesty's pleasure would be made known on the advice of the Secretary of State.[12]

The Crown, acting on the advice of the Secretary of State, has the power to *disallow* or annul a colonial Act. The power exists at common law, but is embodied in most constituent Acts—especially in non-self-governing colonies—usually with a time limit of one or two years. Modern means of speedy communication have deprived this power of its former usefulness. Its continued existence is inconvenient, as lawyers and others in the colony cannot be certain until the prescribed period has elapsed whether the ordinance will continue in force. The power would rarely, if ever, be exercised in relation to a colony possessing fully responsible government unless general Commonwealth interests were involved.

Composition of colonial legislatures

There have been colonies with no legislative body, the sole lawmaking power in the colony being vested in the Governor or High Commissioner. Where there is a legislative body—as there will be nowadays if there is a substantial population—it may be composed in varying proportions of one or more of the following elements: *ex officio* members, *i.e.* senior executive officers who are members by virtue of their office; nominated members, official or unofficial, appointed by the Crown or the Governor; elected members, chosen by an electorate whose franchise varies from colony to colony.   **35–028**

There have been almost as many varieties of colonial legislatures as of colonies, and their constitutions have been subject to frequent change. Post-war constitution-making tendencies prior to full self-government have been to confer Legislative Councils on colonies that had no legislative body; to turn official

[10] Cmd. 2768.
[11] Cmd. 3479. Hence section 3 of the Statute of Westminster 1931, relating to the Dominions.
[12] For the Governor's converse "reserved power" of certifying laws against the will of the legislature, see *post*, para. 35–029.

majorities into unofficial majorities, elected minorities into elected majorities, and Assemblies with elected majorities into Assemblies wholly elected; to substitute universal adult suffrage (with racial quotas in mixed populations) for property or educational franchise qualifications; and to confer some degree of responsible government, especially as regards internal affairs, on colonies with wholly or mainly elected Assemblies.

The powers of the Governor

35–029   Executive government in the colonies is carried on in the name of the Crown by Governors.[13] Governors are appointed by the Crown on the advice of the Secretary of State; and they are responsible to the Crown, although in most colonies the executive depends on the local legislature for supply. The powers of Governors vary; but generally they are empowered by their commission, to appoint members of the Legislative and Executive Councils; to issue writs for the election of members to representative bodies, and to summon or dissolve such bodies; to appoint and dismiss Ministers (if any); to appoint officials; to assent or refuse assent to Bills, or to reserve them for the Crown's assent[14]; to authorise the expenditure of public funds; to remit penalties and pardon offenders.[15] If there is no representative government, they initiate taxation and appropriation measures and usually other Bills.

Where the legislature is representative but the colony is not self-governing, the Governor usually has a *reserved power* (commonly known as his "reserve power" or power of "certification"[16]), if he considers it expedient in the interests of public order, public faith or good government that a Bill introduced into the legislature but not passed by it within a reasonable time shall have effect, to declare that such Bill shall have effect as if it had been passed by the legislature. "Public order," etc. is defined to include the responsibility of the colony as a territory within the Commonwealth, and all matters pertaining to public officers. The Governor is required to report to a Secretary of State any such declaration and the reasons therefor, together with any written objections by members of the legislature.

In addition to these powers, commonly granted by the instruments appointing them, Governors have extensive and detailed authority conferred on them by various statutes in respect of customs, defence works, naturalisation of aliens, and many other matters.

The prerogative powers in relation to foreign affairs, war and peace are not delegated to the Governor of a colony.[17] "The prerogative of the Queen, when it has not been expressly limited by local law or statute," it has been stated,[18] "is as extensive in Her Majesty's colonial possessions as in Great Britain."

---

[13] In some colonies the representative of the Crown is called Lieutenant-Governor or High Commissioner, but for the present purposes it is convenient to describe them all as Governors.

[14] *ante*, para. 35–027.

[15] On this last point, see O. R. Marshall, "The Prerogative of Mercy" [1948] C.L.P. 104, 116–126; Roberts-Wray, *op. cit.* pp. 341 *et seq.* There is statutory authority for the removal of persons sentenced to imprisonment from a colony to the United Kingdom: Colonial Prisoners Removal Act 1884.

[16] No certificate is in fact issued.

[17] See J. E. S. Fawcett, "Treaty Relations of British Overseas Territories" [1949] B.Y.I.L. 86.

[18] *per* Lord Watson in *Liquidators of Maritime Bank of Canada v. Receiver-General of New Brunswick* [1892] A.C. 441.

Executive council and ministers

Executive Councils consisted at first of officials serving in this capacity *ex* **35–030**
officio or nominated by the Governor. At an early stage of development, nominated unofficial members are introduced. The unofficial element grows, and nomination may be made on the recommendation of the Legislative Council. The functions of an Executive Council in non-self-governing colonies (formerly known as "Crown colonies") is advisory only. The Governor may be required to consult the Council on certain matters, but he is not bound by its advice. When the legislature becomes representative (*i.e.* has an elected majority) the unofficial members of the Executive Council will probably be members of the legislature and leaders of opinion there, so that the Governor will try to avoid acting against their unanimous advice.

The introduction of the ministerial system is the next stage[19] in the development of a colony towards self-government. Departments are assigned by the Governor to unofficial members of the Executive Council as Ministers, who are also elected members of the legislature. The Governor is now instructed to act normally on the advice of the Executive Council, and the elected Ministers will by convention depend on the confidence of the legislature. Certain departments are retained by officials, including defence and external affairs. Finance will tend to be among those departments entrusted to Ministers. The Attorney-General's department and internal security may be retained by officials for a time. The Governor's reserved power in matters involving public order, public faith and good government[20] will be available in an emergency. The leader of the majority in the elected House may now be styled Chief Minister.

Development of internal self-government[21]

The last transitional stage before independence within (or outside) the Com- **35–031**
monwealth is usually internal self-government, the United Kingdom retaining control only over defence and external affairs,[22] and the power to suspend the constitution in an emergency, for which the Secretary of State remains responsible to Parliament. All the other departments are now administered by elected Ministers holding the confidence of the legislature. A Public Service Commission and a Judicial Service Commission will be set up, and provision made for the independence of the judiciary, the Auditor-General and the Director of Public Prosecutions.

The Executive Council now becomes the Council of Ministers or Cabinet, operating as far as possible the conventions of the British Cabinet system, and the Chief Minister is styled Prime Minister. At some stage the Governor no longer summons or presides over the Executive Council.

The description given above must be taken merely as typical. It may not exactly fit any particular territory. These developments in executive government should be considered alongside the typical development of colonial legislatures[23] in order to obtain a general picture of the growth of internal self-government in

[19] Sometimes a "membership system" has intervened, responsibility for certain government departments being assigned to unelected members of the Executive Council.
[20] *ante*, para. 35–029.
[21] See further, S. A. de Smith, *The New Commonwealth and its Constitutions* (1964) Chap. 2.
[22] Responsibility for defence and external affairs may be entrusted to a United Kingdom Commissioner, as in the pre-independence constitutions of Singapore and Malta. Also, a limited treaty-making power may be delegated under the authority of statute to a self-governing colony.
[23] *ante*, para. 35–028.

dependent territories since the Second World War. The chief remaining limitations are the subordination of the colonial legislature to the United Kingdom Parliament, and the lack of international personality.[24]

Future Developments

35–032   A review of the status of the 13 remaining colonies took place, following the volcanic eruption in Montserrat in 1997 when it was complained that the United Kingdom had failed to offer speedy or effective help. A White Paper[25] recommended referring to the 13 areas as "British Overseas Territories", with their own minister in the Foreign Office. An Overseas Territories Council will be established which will meet before each Commonwealth summit.

It is envisaged that British citizenship will be restored to the territories[26] which were deprived of it by the British Nationality Act.

On the other hand the United Kingdom government expects the Overseas Territories to bring their laws into line with the European Convention on Human Rights and, in particular wishes to see the abolition of laws permitting capital punishment and corporal punishment, and of laws prohibiting homosexual acts. Steps must also be taken to ensure effective financial regulation and prevent the use of the Territories for money laundering.

---

[24] The pre-independence constitutions of Singapore and Malta, although they retained the legal status of colonies, gave them the name of "States"; see O. Hood Phillips, "The Constitution of the State of Singapore" [1960] P.L. 50.

[25] *Partnership for Progress and Prosperity: Britain and the Overseas Territories* (1998, Cm. 4264).

[26] Gibraltar and the Falklands already possess British citizenship: *ante* para. 23–009 and para. 23–010.

CHAPTER 36

INDEPENDENCE WITHIN THE COMMONWEALTH

1. THE DOMINIONS AND THE STATUTE OF WESTMINSTER

Development of Dominion status[1]

The development of responsible government in the colonies originated in the   **36–001**
report sent from North America by Lord Durham in 1839 to the British Government. Upper and Lower Canada already had representative assemblies. The gist of Lord Durham's Report was that it was a necessary consequence of the grant of representative institutions that the Governor should entrust the administration to such men as could command a majority. In other words, responsible Cabinet government should be introduced, and this could be effected simply by a change in the Governor's instructions. Responsible government was accordingly introduced into the united colonies of Ontario and Quebec under Lord Elgin in 1848. Full autonomy in internal affairs was gradually supplemented by a degree of autonomy in external affairs. The British North America Act 1867 implied the existence of responsible government in the new federal Dominion of Canada. The same principles came to be extended to Newfoundland, the Australian colonies (now states), New Zealand and the South African colonies during the latter part of the nineteenth century, to the federal Commonwealth of Australia in 1900, the Union of South Africa in 1909 and the Irish Free State when granted Dominion status in 1922. The autonomy of the Dominions received further impetus by the recognition of Canada, Australia, New Zealand and South Africa as separate members of the League of Nations after the 1914–18 war.

The Balfour Declaration of 1926[2] described the position and mutual relations of the United Kingdom and the Dominions at that time as:

> "autonomous Communities within the British Empire, equal in status, in no way subordinate one to another in any aspect of their domestic or external affairs, though united by a common allegiance to the Crown, and freely associated as members of the British Commonwealth of Nations."

The principles of equality and similarity appropriate to status, however, did not universally extend to function, *e.g.* diplomacy and defence. The Crown was the symbol of the free association of the members of what was then called the British Commonwealth of Nations, and they were united by a common allegiance to the Crown, based on the common status of British subjects. It was resolved at the

---

[1] A. B. Keith, *Responsible Government in the Dominions* (2nd ed., 1928); *The Dominions as Sovereign States* (1938); *Speeches and Documents on the British Dominions, 1918–1931*; Dawson, *The Development of Dominion Status, 1900–1936*; R. T. E. Latham, "The Law and the Commonwealth," in Hancock, *Survey of Commonwealth Affairs*, 1 (1937), pp. 595 *et seq.; The Round Table*, No. 240 (Diamond Jubilee Special number, 1970). H. Duncan Hall, *Commonwealth: A History of the British Commonwealth of Nations* (1971); N. Mansergh, *The Commonwealth Experience* (1982); H. H. Marshall, *From Dependence to Statehood.*
[2] *Report of Imperial Conference, 1926*, Cmd. 1768. This has nothing to do with Balfour's statement about Zionism.

Imperial Conference of 1926[3] that a treaty applying only to one part of the Empire should be made on the advice of the government of that part, and should be stated to be made by the Sovereign on behalf of that part. Dominions might have their own seals for authenticating treaties if they wished. The mutual relations among the self-governing members of the Commonwealth were regarded as being governed, not by international law, but largely by conventions whose character was something between international law and constitutional law (the "*inter se* doctrine").[4]

36–002   The principle that a Dominion might exchange diplomatic representatives with a foreign country was recognised in 1920 in the case of Canada and the United States. The Dominions had come to possess their own armed forces. Although a Dominion could not be compelled without its consent to give active assistance in a war in which the Crown was engaged, it was not generally admitted before 1939 that a Dominion could remain technically neutral in such a war.

The Imperial Conferences of 1926 and 1930[5] resolved that the Sovereign should act on the direct advice of the Dominion Ministers in relation to the appointment of the Governor-General, who was the representative of the Sovereign and not of the British Government. The power of reserving Bills of a Dominion legislature, which had been rarely exercised, ought not to be exercised against the wishes of that Dominion. The power of disallowing Dominion legislation was by convention not exercised.

Conventions were formulated that any alteration in the law touching the succession to the Throne or the Royal Style and Titles should require the assent of the Parliaments of all the Dominions as well as of the Parliament of the United Kingdom[6]; and that laws thereafter made by the United Kingdom Parliament should not extend to any of the Dominions as part of the law of that Dominion otherwise than at the request and with the consent of that Dominion.[7] Further, uniformity of legislation as between the United Kingdom and the Dominions in such matters as the law of prize, fugitive offenders and extradition, could best be secured by the enactment of reciprocal statutes based on consultation and agreement.[8]

The Statute of Westminster 1931[9]

36–003   The Statute of Westminster[10] dealt only with *legislative* powers, and not exhaustively with them. The chief matters with regard to which legislation of the United Kingdom Parliament was required in order to reconcile the law relating to legislative powers with the conventional status of the Dominions were: (i) the operation of the Colonial Laws Validity Act 1865, which nullified Dominion

---

[3] *ante.*
[4] See J. E. S. Fawcett, *The British Commonwealth in International Law* (1963), Chap. 15; *The Inter Se Doctrine of Commonwealth Relations* (1958); R. Y. Jennings. "The Commonwealth and International Law" (1953) B.Y.I.L. 320; *cf.* R. T. E. Latham, "The Law and the Commonwealth" in Hancock's *Survey of British Commonwealth Affairs*, Vol. I, pp. 602 *et seq.*
[5] Cmd. 3717.
[6] *Report of the Conference on the Operation of Dominion Legislation*, 1929, Cmd. 3479.
[7] (1930) Cmd. 3717.
[8] (1926) Cmd. 2768; (1949) Cmd. 3479.
[9] K. C. Wheare, *The Statute of Westminster and Dominion Status* (5th ed.); *Constitutional Structure of the Commonwealth* (1960) Chap. 2. See also Sir Ivor Jennings. *op. cit.* Beaglehole (ed.), *New Zealand and the Statute of Westminster*; W. P. M. Kennedy, "The Imperial Conferences, 1926–1930: The Statute of Westminster" (1932) 48 L.Q.R. 191.
[10] The title of the Statute was suggested by Sir Maurice Gwyer, then Treasury Solicitor and a member of the Conference on the Operation of Dominion Legislation, and later Chief Justice of India.

legislation repugnant to United Kingdom statute law; (ii) the doubtful rule that the Dominions could not pass legislation having extra-territorial effect; and (iii) the legally unfettered power of the United Kingdom Parliament to legislate for the Dominions. Attention was drawn to these matters by the Imperial Conference, 1926.[11] They were fully considered by the Conference on the Operation of Dominion Legislation, 1929,[12] whose resolutions were adopted by the Imperial Conference, 1930.[13] They determine the contents of the most important sections of the Statute of Westminster, which was passed by the Imperial Parliament in 1931 on the recommendation of the Imperial Conference, 1930, after the communication of resolutions of the Parliaments of the six Dominions.

The preamble recites: (i) the fact that the Imperial Conferences of 1926 and 1930 concurred in making certain declarations and resolutions; (ii) the convention relating to the law touching the succession to the Throne and the Royal Style and Titles; (iii) the convention with regard to legislation by the United Kingdom Parliament for the Dominions; (iv) that "it is necessary for the ratifying, confirming and establishing of certain of the said declarations and resolutions of the said Conferences that a law be made and enacted in due form by authority of the Parliament of the United Kingdom"; and (v) the request and consent of each of the six Dominions to the passing of the statute.

The expression "Dominion" in section 1 was defined as meaning any of the following: Canada, the Commonwealth of Australia, New Zealand, the Union of South Africa,[14] the Irish Free State,[15] and Newfoundland.[16] Section 11 provided that, notwithstanding the Interpretation Act 1889, the expression "colony" should not, in any subsequent Act of the United Kingdom Parliament, include a Dominion or any province or state forming part of a Dominion.[17]

Repugnance of Dominion legislation to United Kingdom statutes

36–004

Section 2 provides as follows:

"(1) *The Colonial Laws Validity Act 1865 shall not apply to any law made after the commencement of this Act by the Parliament of a Dominion.*

(2) No law and no provision of any law made after the commencement of this Act by the Parliament of a Dominion shall be void or inoperative on the ground that it is repugnant to the law of England, or to the provisions of any existing or future Act of Parliament of the United Kingdom, or to any order, rule or regulation made under any such Act, and the powers of the Parliament of a Dominion shall include the power to amend or repeal any such Act, order, rule or regulation in so far as the same is part of the law of the Dominion."

---

[11] Cmd. 2768.
[12] Cmd. 3479.
[13] Cmd. 3717. These Reports have been referred to by the Judicial Committee; see W. Ivor Jennings, "The Statute of Westminster and Appeals to the Privy Council" (1936) 52 L.Q.R. 173, 175–177.
[14] South Africa became a republic and seceded from the Commonwealth in 1961. The provisions of the Statute of Westminster as affecting South Africa had been enacted as part of the law of the Union by the Status of the Union Act 1934.
[15] The Irish Free State, called Eire after 1937, seceded from the Commonwealth in 1949, and now calls herself the Republic of Ireland. See Republic of Ireland Act 1948 (Ir.); Ireland Act 1949 (UK); *Re Article 26 of the Constitution and the Criminal Law (Jurisdiction) Bill, 1975* [1977] I.R. 129.
[16] The Statute never came into operation as regards Newfoundland, which is now a province of Canada.
[17] See now, Interpretation Act 1978, s.5 and Sched. 1. s.11 of the Statute of Westminster was repealed by section 25 of the Interpretation Act 1978.

Subsection (2) was inserted in case the mere repeal of the Colonial Laws Validity Act[18] as affecting the Dominions should leave them in the position in which they would have been at common law before 1865. It applies only to Dominion legislation passed after the commencement of the Statute, but any void Act previously passed could be given validity by re-enactment. It covers "any existing or future Act" of the United Kingdom Parliament, but it is doubtful whether it extends to the amendment or repeal of the statute itself.

Extraterritorial operation of Dominion legislation

36–005   Section 3 states: "It is hereby declared and enacted that the Parliament of a Dominion has full power to make laws having extraterritorial operation." This set at rest, so far as Dominion legislation was concerned, any doubts that might have existed as a result of the dicta in *Macleod v. Attorney-General for New South Wales*.[19] In practice, territorial limitations on the operation of legislation of all legislatures are quite common, and arise from the express terms of statutes or from rules of construction applied by the courts as to the presumed intention of the legislature, regard being had to the comity of nations and other considerations. What this section was designed to get rid of was any constitutional limitations there may have been which placed Acts of Dominion Parliaments in a different position in this respect from Acts of the Imperial Parliament. It did not mean that a Dominion could alter the law of the United Kingdom or of other Dominions or of foreign countries, but that it could pass legislation (for example) in criminal matters, "which attaches significance for courts within the jurisdiction of facts and events occurring outside the jurisdiction."[20]

Extension of United Kingdom legislation to the Dominions

36–006   Section 4 provides as follows: "*No Act of Parliament of the United Kingdom passed after the commencement of this Act shall extend, or be deemed to extend, to a Dominion as part of the law of that Dominion, unless it is expressly declared in that Act that that Dominion has requested, and consented to, the enactment thereof.*"

The request and consent required is that of the *government* of the Dominion concerned, except that in the case of Australia section 9(3) required also the request and consent of the Commonwealth Parliament as the Senate might not be in agreement with the government. Actual request and consent are not required: merely an express declaration of request and consent in the United Kingdom Act would be sufficient.[21] The significance of the words "as part of the law of that Dominion" has been discussed in Chapter 4 concerning the legislative power of the United Kingdom Parliament. Whether the Courts of a Dominion would enforce a United Kingdom Act which was clearly inconsistent with section 4, is another matter. Dixon C.J. said in *Copyright Owners Reproduction Society v. E.M.I. (Australia) Pty Ltd*[22] that there was a strong presumption that the United Kingdom Parliament would not legislate for a Dominion without its consent even before 1931, and there is therefore a rule of construction in the Australian High Court that, in the absence of evidence of such consent, a United Kingdom Act is not intended to apply to that country. The preamble to His Majesty's Declaration

---

[18] *ante*, para. 35–023.
[19] [1891] A.C. 455. See *ante*, para. 35–026.
[20] Wheare, *The Statute of Westminster and Dominion Status*, p. 167.
[21] *Manuel v. Att.-Gen.* [1983] Ch. 77, 106, *per* Slade L.J.
[22] (1958) 100 C.L.R. 597; (1958) 32 A.L.J.R. 306.

of Abdication Act 1936[23] recited that "the Dominion of Canada, pursuant to the provisions of section 4 of the Statute of Westminster 1931, has requested and consented to the enactment of this Act, and the Commonwealth of Australia, the Dominion of New Zealand, and the Union of South Africa have assented thereto." The Abdication Act made an alteration in the law touching the succession to the Throne which could, with the necessary consents, have been made to extend to the Dominions.

The Statute of Westminster did not recite or provide that the United Kingdom Parliament *would* legislate for a Dominion whenever it requested and consented. A general convention probably existed or developed to that effect, though the matter could have raised difficulties with regard to federal Dominions such as Canada and Australia.

Application to Canada[24]

Canada was the only Dominion that had no power to amend its Constitution   **36–007**
Act. This limitation is to be accounted for partly by the relatively early date of the British North America Act 1867 and partly by the federal nature of its Constitution. When the Conference on the Operation of Dominion Legislation reported in 1929 the provinces had not been consulted about the proposed Imperial Act, and the Report of the Imperial Conference, 1930, shows that certain of the provinces protested against the proposed legislation—in particular, section 2—until they had had an opportunity to determine whether their rights would be adversely affected. The saving clause relating to legislation by the Canadian Parliament (section 7) reads: "(1) Nothing in this Act shall be deemed to apply to the repeal, amendment or alteration of the British North America Acts 1867 and 1930, or any order, rule or regulation made thereunder . . .(3) The powers conferred by this Act upon the Parliament of Canada . . .shall be restricted to the enactment of laws in relation to matters within the competence of the Parliament of Canada . . ." If Canada wished for constitutional amendments, or to have constituent power, it was free—(*semble*) subject to consultation with the provinces—to ask the United Kingdom Parliament to pass the necessary legislation. This in fact occurred when the British North America (No. 2) Act 1949 conferred on the Canadian Parliament a power of constitutional amendment by means of ordinary legislation, with certain important exceptions such as matters assigned exclusively to the provincial legislatures.

The "patriation" of the Canadian Constitution[25]

For more than 20 years successive Canadian Prime Ministers tried to bring   **36–008**
about the "patriation" of the Canadian Constitution by obtaining agreement among the Provinces, which did not want to lose control over natural resources in their territories, to a formula for constitutional amendment. The Canadian Supreme Court gave an advisory opinion that there was no legal requirement for the Provinces to be consulted before the Queen was requested to lay before the

---

[23] N. Mansergh, *Documents and Speeches on British Commonwealth Affairs*, 1931–52, I, pp. 179 *et seq.*; *Survey of British Commonwealth Affairs*, 1931–39, pp. 41–46; R. T. E. Latham, Appendix to "The Law and the Commonwealth"; K. H. Bailey in *Politics*, March and June 1938; Wheare, *op. cit.* pp. 278–290.
[24] P. Hogg, *Constitutional Law of Canada: Canada Act 1982* (1982). B. Laskin, *Canadian Constitutional Law.*
[25] D. C. M. Yardley, "The Patriation of the Canadian Constitution," (1982) 7 *Holdsworth Law Rev.* 84; G. Marshall, *Constitutional Conventions* (1984) Chap. XI.

United Kingdom Parliament a Bill to amend the Canadian Constitution where provincial rights or the relations between the Federation and the Provinces would be affected, but the majority thought that convention required there to be at least a substantial measure of provincial agreement.[26] While the Canada Bill was before the United Kingdom Parliament an unsuccessful attempt was made to obtain a declaration from the English courts that, in view of treaties made with the Indians by George III, Indian rights ought to be excluded from the effects of the proposed legislation. The English Court of Appeal held that the obligations of the Crown to the Indian peoples were now those of the Crown in right of Canada and not in right of the United Kingdom.[27]

The Preamble to the Canada Act 1982 recites that Canada (*i.e.* The Canadian Government) requested and consented to its enactment by the United Kingdom Parliament, and that the Canadian Parliament submitted an address to Her Majesty requesting her to cause a Bill to be laid before the United Kingdom Parliament for that purpose. Section 1 enacts the draft (Canadian) Constitution Act 1982, set out in Schedule B. Section 2 provides that no Act of the United Kingdom Parliament passed after the Constitution Act 1982 comes into force shall extend to Canada as part of its law, and section 4 of the Statute of Westminster is repealed so far as Canada is concerned. The Constitution Act provides a complicated procedure for amendment by the Canadian Parliament of the Canadian Constitution, including the federal distribution of powers. A Charter of Rights and Freedoms, applicable to the legislatures and governments of the Federation and the Provinces, is contained in Part I. This Charter, unlike the Canadian Bill of Rights of 1960, is judicially enforceable, though federal or provincial legislation may expressly override the four "fundamental freedoms."[28] The Constitution, which includes the Canada Act 1982, the Constitution Act 1982 and the scheduled "Constitution Acts" (including the series of British North America Acts) is to be the supreme law of Canada.[29]

The Queen in person signed the Proclamation in Ottawa inaugurating the new Canadian Constitution.

Application to Australia[30]

36–009   Sections 2–6[31] of the Statute of Westminster were adoptive with respect to Australia, and Australia adopted them after Japan entered the war in 1942, as from the commencement of the war with Germany.[32]

---

[26] *Re Amendment of the Constitution of Canada* (1961) 125 D.L.R. (3d) 1. See *First Report from the Foreign Affairs Committee, Session 1980–81: British North America Acts: The Role of Parliament*, H.C. 42 (Kershaw); *Second Report on the British North America Acts; the Role of Parliament* (1961). See also O. Hood Phillipe, "Constitutional Conventions in the Supreme Court of Canada" (1982) 98 L.Q.R. 194; *cf.* Rodney Brazier and St. John Robilliard, "Constitutional Conventions. The Canadian Supreme Court's View Reviewed" [1982] P.L. 28.

[27] *Manuel v. Att.-Gen.* [1983] Ch. 77, CA; *Noltcho v. Att.-Gen.* [1983] Ch. 77 at 89 (Megarry V.-C.), following *R. v. Secretary of State for Foreign and Commonwealth Affairs ex p. Indian Association of Alberta* [1982] Q.B. 892, CA; (pet. dis.) 937, HL.

[28] See *Canadian Charter of Rights and Freedoms*, eds., Tanapolsky and Baudouin (Toronto, 1982); G. L. Peiria, "Legal Protection of Human Rights: The contemporary Canadian experience" (1985) 5 L.S. 261.

[29] See further, Peter Hogg, *The Canada Act 1982 Annotated* (Toronto, 1983).

[30] W. A. Wynes, *Legislative, Executive and Judicial Powers in Australia*; C. Howard, *Australian Federal Constitutional Law*; L. Zines, *The High Court and the Constitution* (Sydney 1981); G. Winterton, *Parliament, the Executive and the Governor-General* (Melbourne, 1983).

[31] s.5 concerned merchant shipping and s.6 Admiralty courts.

[32] Not from the passing of the Statute of Westminster: *Ex p. Bennett; Re Cunningham* (1967) 86 W.N. (Pt 2) (N.S.W.) 323.

The Commonwealth of Australia Constitution Act 1900 provides the legal basis of federation under the Crown, which the recital states was intended to be indissoluble. Sections 1–8 of the Act, which involve the federal principle, make no provision for their amendment by the Australian Parliament.[33] The *Constitution*, which is contained in section 9 of the Constitution *Act*, can be altered by the Commonwealth Parliament, but only after a referendum.[34] This position was reserved by sections 8 and 9(1) of the Statute of Westminster, which provided that: "8. Nothing in this Act shall be deemed to confer any power to repeal or alter the Constitution or the Constitution Act of the Commonwealth of Australia ... otherwise than in accordance with the law existing before the commencement of this Act. 9. (1) Nothing in this Act shall be deemed to authorise the Parliament of the Commonwealth of Australia to make laws on any matter within the authority of the States of Australia, not being a matter within the authority of the Parliament or Government of the Commonwealth of Australia."[35]

Australia Act 1986

36–010   The provisions of the virtually identical Australia Acts passed by the United Kingdom and Commonwealth[36] Parliaments in 1986 were agreed to by the Queen, the Commonwealth Government, all the State Governments and the United Kingdom Government after extensive consultations between the Commonwealth and State Governments over a period of several years. The Commonwealth Parliament enacted its Act under section 51 (xxxviii) of the Constitution. The legislation was designed to remove the residual constitutional links between Australia and the United Kingdom Parliament, Government and judicial system, but the position of the Queen as Queen of Australia is not changed.

The preamble to the United Kingdom Act recites that the Parliament and Government of the Commonwealth of Australia have, with the concurrence of the States of Australia, requested and consented to the enactment of an Act of the United Kingdom Parliament in the terms therein set forth (thus fulfilling the requirements of sections 4 and 9(3) of the Statute of Westminster).

The Act deals first with legislative powers by providing that no future Act of Parliament of the United Kingdom shall extend, or be deemed to extend, to the Commonwealth or a State or Territory of Australia as part of its law (section 1). It goes on to deal with State legislation by declaring that the legislative powers of the Parliament of each State include full power to make laws for the peace, order and good government of that State having extra-territorial operation (following section 3 of the Statute of Westminster), and that the legislative powers of each State include all legislative powers that the United Kingdom Parliament might have exercised for that State before the commencement of the Act, but not including the capacity to engage in relations with countries outside Australia

[33] See G. Sawer, "The British Connection" (1973) 47 A.L.J. 113.
[34] The proposed amendment must be approved not only by a majority of all the votes, but also by a majority of the votes in a majority of the states; and any amendment diminishing the proportionate representation of a State in the House of Representatives requires the approval of the majority of voters in that State: Constitution of the Commonwealth s.128.
[35] The constitutions of the Australian states, though written (based largely on United Kingdom statutes), are largely flexible (subject to retaining such fundamentals as the monarchy); see *McCawley v. The King* [1920] A.C. 591, PC; R. D. Lumb, *The Constitutions of the Australian States* (2nd ed., Brisbane, 1965).
[36] "The Commonwealth" in the context of the Australia Act means the Commonwealth of Australia.

(section 2). The provisions of the Colonial Laws Validity Act 1865 so far as they applied to State Parliaments are repealed (section 3, modelled on section 2 of the Statute of Westminster applying to Commonwealth legislation); but the removal of restrictions on State Parliaments does not affect the Statute of Westminster, the Commonwealth Constitution Act or the Commonwealth Constitution (section 5). Certain restrictions on merchant shipping legislation[37] by State Parliaments are repealed (section 4, corresponding to section 5 of the Statute of Westminster applying to Commonwealth Acts). State legislation respecting the constitution, powers and procedure of the State Parliament must be made in the manner and form (if any) required from time to time by the law of that State (section 6, continuing the effect of section 5 of the Colonial Laws Validity Act).

36–011   The Act then deals with executive powers and functions. Instead of the Queen being formally advised on State matters as hitherto by United Kingdom ministers following recommendations from State Premiers to the Foreign and Commonwealth Office, it is provided that Her Majesty's representative in each State shall be the Governor and all the Queen's powers and functions in respect of a State shall be exercisable only by him, except that the appointment and dismissal of the Governor will be done on the advice of the State Premier. While Her Majesty is personally present in a State, however, she may, following mutual and prior agreement, exercise any of her State functions on the advice of the State Premier (section 7). Any powers to disallow, suspend, reserve or withhold assent to Acts or Bills of State Parliaments are abolished (sections 8 and 9); and the United Kingdom Government will have no responsibility for the government of any State (section 10).

All appeals from Australian courts[38] to the Privy Council, whether under statute or prerogative, are terminated, thus making the High Court of Australia the final court of appeal from Australian courts (section 11).

Sections 4, 9(2) and (3) and 10(2) of the Statute of Westminster,[39] in so far as they were part of the law of the Commonwealth or of a State or Territory, are repealed (section 12). This Act or the Statute of Westminster in so far as it is part of the law of the Commonwealth or of a State or Territory, may be repealed or amended only by a Commonwealth Act passed at the request or with the concurrence of all the State Parliaments (section 15).[40]

There was no need for honours, which are awarded by virtue of the prerogative, to be dealt with in the Act; but the Queen has agreed, with the approval of the United Kingdom and Australian Governments, that the Premier of any State whose Government wishes to do so may make recommendations direct to Her Majesty for awards of Imperial Honours.

Application to New Zealand
36–012   Sections 2–6[41] of the Statute of Westminster were adoptive with respect to New Zealand, which adopted them after the last war without retrospective effect.

---

[37] Merchant Shipping Act 1894, ss.735 and 736.

[38] "Australian courts" in this Act do not include the High Court of Australia, from which all appeals to the Privy Council had already been abolished, subject to s.74 of the Constitution (*Inter se* questions certified by the High Court) which had no longer any practical operation: *Kirmani v. Captain Cook Critises Pty Ltd (No. 2), ex p. Att.-Gen. of Queensland* (1984) 50 A.L.R. 108.

[39] *ante,* para. 36–003.

[40] This does not apply to a repeal of amendment made in exercise of powers conferred on the Commonwealth Parliament by any future amendment of the Constitution.

[41] See note 31 *supra.*

The Constitution of New Zealand was to a very considerable extent alterable by the Parliament of New Zealand; but the powers of alteration conferred by the Constitution Acts were subject to certain qualifications, and it was a matter of doubt whether those qualifications had been removed by section 5 of the Colonial Laws Validity Act. As in the case of Canada and Australia, it was for New Zealand to make representations to the Imperial Parliament if it wished for further constituent power. Section 8 of the Statute of Westminster therefore provided that: "Nothing in this Act shall be deemed to confer any power to repeal or alter ... the Constitution Act of the Dominion of New Zealand otherwise than in accordance with the law existing before the commencement of this Act." When New Zealand adopted sections 2–6 in 1947 she asked for and obtained an Imperial Act that gave her complete constituent powers.[42]

In *Fitzgerald v. Muldoon*[43] Wild C.J. adopted Dicey's definition of sovereignty in relation to the New Zealand Parliament.

In reliance on its powers and with no need for resort to Westminster, unlike Australia and Canada, the New Zealand Parliament enacted, in 1996, the Constitution Act which sets out the basic principles of the New Zealand constitution. Section 15(1) recognises that the Parliament of New Zealand has full power to make laws; section 15(2) provides that no Act of the United Kingdom Parliament passed after the commencement of the Act will extend to New Zealand and section 25 provides that the Statute of Westminster is to cease to have effect as part of The Law of New Zealand.[44] In 1990 the legislature also enacted a Bill of Rights but in neither case is the legislation entrenched.

II. THE COMMONWEALTH AT THE PRESENT DAY[45]

Grant of independence[46]

Whereas the grant to British dependent territories of responsible self-government within the Commonwealth, or of independence, is a matter for the United Kingdom Government and the territory concerned, the question of the admission of a territory to full membership of the Commonwealth is one on which all existing members are consulted. From the Indian Independence Act and the   **36–013**

---

[42] New Zealand Constitution (Amendment) Act 1947. See J. C. Beaglehole (ed.), *New Zealand and the Statute of Westminster* (1944); A. E. Currie. *New Zealand and the Statute of Westminster*, 1931 (1944); J. L. Robson (ed.), *New Zealand, Development of its Laws and Constitution* (2nd ed., 1967); New Zealand Constitution Amendment Act 1973 (N.Z.); (extraterritorial legislation).

[43] [1976] 2 N.Z.L.R. 615, 622.

[44] I. S. Dickinson, "Up-dating the New Zealand Constitution", [1988] P.L. 193.

[45] Sir William Dale, *The Modern Commonwealth* (1983); Sir Kenneth Roberts-Wray, *Commonwealth and Colonial Law* (1966) K. C. Wheare, *The Constitutional Structure of the Commonwealth* (1960); S. A. de Smith, *The New Commonwealth and its Constitutions* (1964); *The Vocabulary of Commonwealth Relations* (1954). Heather J. Harvey, *Consultation and Co-operation in the Commonwealth* (1952); J. E. S. Fawcett, *The British Commonwealth in International Law* (1963); *Changing Law in Developing Countries* (ed. J. N. D. Anderson, 1963); *Parliament as an Export* (ed. Sir Alan Burns, (1966); V. Bogdanor *The Monarchy and the Constitution* (1995) Chap. 10; Wolf-Phillips, "Post-Independence Constitutional Change in the Commonwealth" (1970) XVII *Political Studies*, p. 18.

[46] The gradual acquisition of independence by Canada, Australia and New Zealand is described in the previous section.

Ceylon Independence Act of 1947,[47] the grant of independence has been effected by Act of Parliament.[48] Independence involves, first, the acquisition of international personality which is recognised by other countries. It leads to application, sponsored by the United Kingdom, for membership of the United Nations, which is invariably accepted. Independence also gives rise to complex problems of state succession.[49] Secondly, independence involves the freedom of the country concerned from dependence on the Parliament and Government of the United Kingdom.

Independence Acts

36–014   The Independence Act will therefore remove, in the manner of sections 2, 3 and 4 of the Statute of Westminster,[50] the three legislative limitations of repugnancy, extra-territoriality and the powers of the United Kingdom Parliament. The doctrine of repugnancy[51] is abolished by a provision on the lines of section 2 of the Statute of Westminster, whereby no future law made by the Parliament of the territory concerned shall be void on the ground that it is repugnant to any existing or future Act of Parliament. This would probably include the Independence Act itself, even if it is not specifically mentioned. Section 3 of the Statute of Westminster, authorising legislation with extra-territorial operation, was needed in relation to the Dominions in 1931, as that Statute did not make a definite break between dependence and independence: it was a statutory declaration of existing facts that had been brought about by gradual evolution. In the post-war Independence Acts this provision may not be necessary as the power of extra-territorial legislation is probably implied by independence, but it may be inserted *ex abundante cautela.*

The provision that future Acts of the United Kingdom shall not apply to the country concerned has been modelled on section 4 of the Statute of Westminster. That section was followed closely in the case of Ceylon (now Sri Lanka) and Ghana (formerly the Gold Coast). The Indian Independence Act, however, omitted the "request and consent" and substituted "unless it is expressly extended thereto" by a law of the Indian legislature. The Nigerian, Sierra Leone and later Acts merely omit the contingency that they might request and consent to United Kingdom legislation.

36–015   The powers of disallowance and reservation and the reserved power of certification were abolished by the Indian Independence Act 1947. The power of disallowance survived in theory in relation to Canada until 1982 and Australia until 1986 and has not been formally abolished in relation to New Zealand, but by convention it was never exercised after they became "self-governing". In other cases of independence these extraneous powers will have been abolished by amendment to the pre-independence constitution.

Independence in the case of former colonies, *e.g.* Ghana, Nigeria and Malta, which involves the transfer of sovereignty to territories that previously had no

---

[47] Sri Lanka (Ceylon) adopted an autochthonous republican Constitution in 1972. The Constitution of 1978 provides for an executive President: see M. J. A. Cooray, *Judicial Role under the Constitutions of Ceylon/Sri Lanka* (Colombo, 1982).

[48] The Ireland Act 1949 recognised a *fait accompli.*

[49] See Roberts-Wray, *op. cit.* pp. 267–269; Fawcett, *op. cit.* Chap. 18. And see *The Effect of Independence on Treaties* (International Law Association, 1966).

[50] *ante,* para. 36–004 *et seq.*

[51] Colonial Laws Validity Act 1865, s.2.

international personality, is usually described in the Act as "fully responsible status" within the Commonwealth. Protectorates (*e.g.* Uganda) and trust territories (*e.g.* Tanganyika, now part of Tanzania) were not within Her Majesty's dominions, and therefore Independence Acts have technically annexed them to the Crown in order that on the withdrawal of protection they might be granted independence within the Commonwealth. In the case of trust territories this process required the approval of the United Nations. The independent Federation of Malaya (now Malaysia) was formed by agreement between the United Kingdom and the rulers of the protected Malay states, prior approval having been given by Act of Parliament.

The Statute of Westminster did not deal with executive powers, because their exercise was adequately governed by constitutional conventions, and the Statute was not intended at the time it was passed actually to confer independence.[52] The Indian Independence Act 1947 provided that the United Kingdom Government should cease to be responsible for the government of India, and this has been followed in Acts granting independence to former colonies. Acts conferring independence on protectorates either do the same or provide that Her Majesty shall cease to have jurisdiction over the territory.

There is usually an Agreement between the United Kingdom and the territory **36–016** concerned that the latter shall succeed to the rights and obligations affecting it arising out of international agreements.[53] Other countries appear to accept this. Sometimes the grant of independence has been accompanied by an Agreement with the United Kingdom on external affairs, defence and public officers. This was so, for example, with Ceylon,[54] Malaya, Nigeria, Singapore and Malta.[55]

It is also necessary for Parliament to pass an Act continuing the law of the United Kingdom in force here in relation to the territory so far as it is applicable to its new constitutional status,[56] and to modify certain existing Acts of Parliament, *e.g.* British Nationality Acts (countries whose nationals are Commonwealth citizens), the Army and Air Force and Naval Discipline Acts (Commonwealth forces); and Acts relating to visiting forces and diplomatic immunities.[57]

A special kind of non-colonial though dependent status was devised for certain small islands in the Caribbean by the West Indies Act 1967[58] following the break-up of the Federation of the West Indies in 1962 and the independence of Jamaica and Trinidad and Tobago. The islands concerned were to be "States in association with the United Kingdom". The United Kingdom retained responsibility for defence, external affairs and citizenship, while the Associated States each had control of internal affairs including constitutional amendments, the Colonial Laws Validity Act ceasing for these purposes to apply to them. The association

---

[52] But see now: *Noltcho v. Att.-Gen.* [1983] Ch. 77, 89 *per* Sir Robert Megarry V.-C., following *R. v. Secretary of State for Foreign and Commonwealth Affairs ex p. Indian Association of Alberta* [1982] Q.B. 892, CA; (pet.dis) 937, HL.

[53] *e.g.* Cmnd. 2633 (Malta).

[54] Sir Ivor Jennings, *The Constitution of Ceylon* (3rd ed., 1953); "The Making of a Dominion Constitution" (1949) 65 L.Q.R. 456.

[55] Cmnd. 2423; Cmnd. 2410.

[56] *e.g.* Ghana (Consequential Provisions) Act 1960.

[57] The latest is the Brunei and Maldives Act 1985.

[58] *Constitutional Proposals for Antigua, St Kitts, Nevis, Anguilla, Dominica, St Lucia, St Vincent, Grenada* (1965) Cmnd. 2865; *Report of Antigua Constitutional Conference 1966*, Cmnd. 2963.

could be terminated by either side. This "Caribbean Arrangement" did not last long, and one by one the Associated States were granted independence.[59]

Independence constitutions

36–017   The constitution of the newly-independent country will have been drafted by agreement between the Secretary of State and the local party in power, sometimes in consultation with opposition or minority parties. It is often contained in a statutory Order in Council separate from the Independence Act, as this is a quicker and more flexible way of getting parliamentary approval. When the constitution has come into operation in what is now an independent country, provisions made thereunder by Order in Council cannot be challenged in the English courts.[60]

In addition to Canada and Australia, a number of post-war constitutions of Commonwealth members have some kind of federal form. These include India, Nigeria,[61] Malaysia, Uganda and Kenya.

Fundamental rights in the Commonwealth, though traceable ultimately to natural law and influenced in their formulation by the European and other regional conventions had their immediate origin in the principles of English law. The earliest example in the Commonwealth of a Bill of Rights in the modern sense is the Constitution of Tonga of 1875, which was probably inspired by Methodist missionaries. Most of the post-war constitutions include an entrenched declaration of fundamental rights, with power of judicial review.[62] The first was the Indian Constitution,[63] which came into force in 1950. The Nigerian declaration of fundamental rights (1960) formed the model for several later formulations in other Commonwealth countries, being derived not only from those in the Constitutions of Pakistan (1956) and Malaya (1957), which themselves borrowed extensively from India, but also from the European Convention.

36–018   Amendment of the constitutions of Commonwealth countries usually requires some special procedure at least for altering provisions relating to a federal distribution of powers, fundamental rights, and communal or minority guarantees. In *Bribery Commissioner v. Ranasinghe*,[64] an appeal from Ceylon, the Privy Council said: "a legislature has no power to ignore the conditions of lawmaking that are imposed by the instrument which itself regulates the power to make law. This restriction exists independently of the question whether a legislature is sovereign". These special provisions, however, may later be repealed by means of their own special procedure, as was done in the case of Ghana.

Commonwealth countries, a little time after achieving independence, often wish to base a revised constitution on a local *grundnorm*: they assert the principle of constitutional "autochthony", that is, that their constitution is sprung from their native soil and not derived from a United Kingdom statute. Strictly,

---

[59] See Sir Fred Phillips, *West Indian Constitutions: Post-Independence Reform* (1985).
[60] *Buck v. Att.-Gen.* [1965] Ch. 745, CA, affirming Wilberforce J. [1964] 3 W.L.R. 850. And see *Manuel v. Att.-Gen.; Noltcho v. Att.-Gen.* [1983] Ch. 77; applying *R. v. Secretary of State for Foreign and Commonwealth Affairs ex p. Indian Association of Alberta* [1982] Q.B. 892, CA, and *Buck v. Att.-Gen. supra.*
[61] The Nigerian Federation, which has gone through a number of changes since independence, was said to be unique in that it was not formed from units that were previously separate countries. The divisions were mainly tribal.
[62] Dale *op. cit.* Ch. 12; see Sir K. Roberts-Wray, "Human Rights in the Commonwealth" (1968) 17 I.C.L.Q. 908.
[63] H. M. Seervai, *Constitutional Law of India* Vol. 1 (3rd ed., Bombay, 1983).
[64] [1965] A.C. 172.

autochthony requires a breach in legal continuity, an actual or technical revolution.[65] A complete breach in legal continuity is attended by some risk if the local courts are independent and impartial. The notion of autochthony is hardly applicable at any rate to Canada, Australia or New Zealand.[66]

Dependent peoples usually want at first to adopt British methods of parliamentary and Cabinet government, adapted to suit local conditions. The main constitutional conventions are commonly formulated or incorporated by reference. The balance of power between conflicting ethnic, religious, linguistic or regional interests needs to be settled before independence.[67] An independent country should be economically viable. It must provide for its own defence and the handling of external affairs. The governmental structure should not be too complex in relation to the population. Literacy is not essential for the franchise. Capable leaders can usually be found to fill the ministerial posts; but beyond this there is the urgent need for an honest and efficient civil service. The dearth of administrators is largely a question of education, and the main obstacle in the way of providing education is the cost.

The desire for independence is itself stimulated by British political ideas, and nationalism marks the later stage in the development of a dependent territory. There is in effect only one party, whose aim is to end "colonialism"; but the British political system presupposes two main parties or groups, one being an effective opposition capable of providing an alternative government. The one-party principle may be introduced before long, especially after the country has become a republic with a strong Presidential system.[68] Thus the "Westminster model"[69] of parliamentary democracy was soon abandoned in Pakistan and Ghana, and later in Nigeria, Uganda, and a number of other Commonwealth countries.

Full membership of the Commonwealth

The Commonwealth was based on conventions which grew out of practice, **36–019** relating largely to the acquisition and discontinuance of membership. Although it is not an international person it has become an association of an international kind, for it has developed an organisation, acquired a headquarters and developed the beginnings of a constitution, including instruments agreed by Heads of Government such as the London Declaration of 1949 (Head of the Commonwealth), the Agreed Memorandum on the Commonwealth Secretariat of 1965, the Singapore Declaration of 1971 (description of the association, its membership and objectives), the Lusaka Declaration of 1979 (human rights) and the Harare Declaration of 1991 (the promotion of democracy one of the aims of the

[65] Wheare, *The Constitutional Structure of the Commonwealth*, Chap. 4; *cf.* Kenneth Robinson, "Constitutional Autochthony in Ghana" (1961) 1 *Journal of Commonwealth Political Studies*, 41; "Constitutional Autochthony and the Transfer of Power," in *Essays in Imperial Government* (ed. Robinson and Madden, 1963), p. 249; The Canadian Constitution of 1982 was as nearly autochthonous as practicable.

[66] Roberts-Wray, *op. cit.* pp. 289–295; *ante*, pp. 751–756.

[67] See S. A. de Smith, "Mauritius: Constitutionalism in a Plural Society" (1968) 31 M.L.R. 601; Claire Palley, "Constitutional Devices in multi-racial and multi-religious societies" (1969) 19 N.I.L.Q. 377.

[68] See N. O. Nwabueze, *Presidentialism in Commonwealth Africa* (1974). One-party republics in the Commonwealth at present are Bangladesh, Kenya, Malawi, Seychelles, Sierra Leone, Tanzania and Zambia. Zimbabwe looks like going the same way.

[69] See *per* Lord Diplock in *Hinds v. The Queen* [1977] A.C. 195, TC; D. C. M. Yardley, "The Effectiveness of the Westminster Model of Constitution," *Year Book of World Affairs 1977*, Vol. 31, p. 342.

Commonwealth).[70] Other agreements are the Gleneagles Agreement of 1977 (apartheid in sport) and the Melbourne Declaration of 1981 (economic aid to developing countries). These instruments, however, can hardly be said to create legal, as opposed to political and moral, obligations.

In order that a country may be admitted to full membership of the Commonwealth it must be: (i) independent; (ii) willing to recognise the Queen as Head of the Commonwealth; and (iii) willing to co-operate. The Singapore Declaration begins by describing the Commonwealth of Nations as a voluntary association of independent sovereign states, each responsible for its own policies, consulting and co-operating in the common interests of their peoples and in the promotion of international understanding and world peace. Membership of the Commonwealth, it continues, is compatible with the freedom of member Governments to be non-aligned or to belong to any other grouping, association or alliance. Under the Harare Declaration a committee known as the Commonwealth Ministerial Action Group was established to monitor compliance with the terms of the Declaration.[71]

36–020   The decision to grant independence, as has been said, is made by the United Kingdom.[72] Then, if the government of the country concerned so wishes, the United Kingdom invites the governments of the other full members of the Commonwealth, because they have equality of status, to agree to the full membership of that country. If they, or a majority of them, did not agree, the country concerned would become independent within the Commonwealth, but it would not be a *full* member. On the other hand, there appears to be no rule that the members must be unanimous: a minority probably cannot prevent its becoming a full member although they might ignore it or even secede.

To be admitted to the Commonwealth it is not necessary that the applicant state had, before independence, been a Crown territory. Mozambique and Cameroon which joined the Commonwealth in 1995 are examples.[73]

The number of independent members of the Commonwealth is now 53.

While both sentiment and self-interest may be said to operate in keeping the older Dominions in the Commonwealth, self-interest predominates in determining new countries to join the Commonwealth; although even in them sentiment is not absent, especially among administrators, lawyers and educated persons generally. The advantages of the association to new members include continued financial aid; the secondment of skilled personnel, such as administrators and teachers; mutual trade; and co-operation of many kinds, such as the provision of diplomatic information and help in time of trouble. There are also unofficial links such as are formed by associations of Members of Parliament, lawyers, doctors, scientists and technologists. No disadvantages or limitations are involved in membership.

It has been recognised since the last war that an independent member may leave the Commonwealth by voluntary secession. Secession, to be fully effective, requires not only local legislation but also an act of the United Kingdom Parliament for such purposes as amending legislation relating to nationality. The

---

[70] Dale, *op. cit.* Ch. 2; "Is the Commonwealth an international organisation"? (1982) 31 I.C.L.Q. 451.

[71] Pakistan was not expelled from the Commonwealth following the military coup in October 1999 but developments are being kept under review.

[72] Or Australia, etc., in relation to dependencies of other Commonwealth countries.

[73] Cyprus entered the Commonwealth six months after the termination of its colonial status in order to emphasise the voluntary nature of its membership.

secession of Eire in 1948 was recognised by the other members,[74] that of South Africa in 1962[75] and that of (West) Pakistan in 1972.[76]

Pakistan was re-admitted to the Commonwealth in 1989[77] and South Africa in 1994.[78]

Following a coup in 1987 and the declaration of a republic, the membership of Fiji was treated as having "lapsed".

The Monarchy in the Commonwealth[79]

The symbol of Commonwealth association is the Queen and Head of the Commonwealth. The Queen has adopted a personal flag—initial E and Crown within a chaplet or roses—for use where the royal standard (especially associated with the United Kingdom) is inappropriate.

The convention recited in the preamble to the Statute of Westminster[80] still requires that an alteration by the United Kingdom Parliament in the law touching *the succession to the Throne* should have the assent of the Parliaments of all the Dominions (or realms owing allegiance to the Crown).[81] They would presumably also need to pass their own legislation in order to make such an alteration in the law effective in their own countries. It is suggested that the republics and separate monarchies (such as Malaysia) in the Commonwealth need only be informed of the change made in the law identifying the Head of the Commonwealth, although as a matter of courtesy they would probably be kept informed of any preliminary discussions.

On the other hand, as regards a change made by one member in *the Royal Style and Titles* used by that member—at least within the bounds set by recent precedent—it seems that convention since 1952 no longer requires the assent of any of the other members. On the accession of Queen Elizabeth II in February 1952 proclamations of the Royal Style and Titles were issued in the independent countries of the Commonwealth which, except in the case of New Zealand, differed from that issued in the United Kingdom. Later that year discussions were held among the members, and it was agreed that each one should adopt a title to suit its own circumstances but including a common element. As a result Canada, Australia and New Zealand in 1953 adopted the same royal titles as the United Kingdom, but incorporated a specific reference to their own territory, thus: "Elizabeth II, by the Grace of God of the United Kingdom, Canada [Australia, New Zealand] and Her other Realms and Territories, Queen, Head of the

36–021

---

[74] Ireland Act 1949: but the Republic of Ireland is not to be regarded as a foreign country nor are its citizens to be regarded as aliens in the United Kingdom.

[75] South Africa Act 1962: South Africa became a foreign country, and its citizens became aliens unless they were also citizens of the United Kingdom and Colonies or of some other Commonwealth country.

[76] Pakistan Acts 1973 and 1974; *R. v. Chief Immigration Officer, Heathrow Airport, ex p. Salamat Bibi* [1976] 1 W.L.R. 979, CA. The former East Pakistan (renamed Bangladesh) remained in the Commonwealth: Bangladesh Act 1973. Burma (1947), Somaliland (1960), Southern Cameroons (1961) and Aden (1971) left the Commonwealth on obtaining independence.

[77] Pakistan Act 1990.

[78] South Africa Act 1995.

[79] Dale, *op. cit.*, pp. 35–39. Sir Ivor Jennings, *Constitutional Laws of the Commonwealth* (3rd ed.), Vol. I pp. 18–25; J. E. S. Fawcatt *The British Commonwealth in International Law* pp. 79–85; D. P. O'Connell, "The Crown in the British Commonwealth" (1957) 61 I.C.L.Q. 103.

[80] *ante*, para. 36–003.

[81] Suppose they do not all agree?

Commonwealth, Defender of the Faith."[82] In the republics and separate monarchies (e.g. Malaysia) the Queen is recognised only as Head of the Commonwealth.[83]

36–022   The Queen is a part of the legislature in each of her realms, and the government of each is carried on in her name on the advice of the Ministers in that country. The extent to which prerogative powers in relation to external affairs were transferred to the Governor-General in the former Dominions varied.[84]

Her Majesty during her tours of the Commonwealth has personally opened sessions of Commonwealth Parliaments, presided over Executive Councils and meetings of the Privy Council, administered the oath of office to Ministers and signed letters of credence of Commonwealth ambassadors.

Following the dismissal of the Australian Prime Minister (Mr Gough Whitlam) and the appointment of the Leader of the Opposition (Mr Fraser) as caretaker Prime Minister by the Governor-General (Sir John Kerr) in 1975, the Speaker of the House of Representatives wrote to the Queen asking her to intervene. Her Majesty replied; "The written Constitution, and accepted constitutional conventions, preclude the Queen from intervening personally in those functions [given to the Governor-General by the Constitution] once the Governor-General has been appointed, and from interfering with His Excellency's tenure of office except upon advice from the Australian Prime Minister." It is not clear who advised Her Majesty on that occasion, or who drafted her letter.[85]

Some controversy arose early in 1984 out of the Queen's Christmas broadcast to the Commonwealth (in which Her Majesty spoke of her recent visit to India and her meeting with Mrs Gandhi, the Indian Prime Minister) over the question whether convention requires the Head of the Commonwealth to take advice from ministers of the United Kingdom or of the Commonwealth countries concerned, or whether she may act without such advice. Statements were made by both Buckingham Palace and Mrs Thatcher, the Prime Minister, in the House of Commons to the effect that as Head of the Commonwealth the Queen may act without formal advice, and these statements were consistent with the opinion expressed by a former legal adviser to the Commonwealth Office.[86]

36–023   That does not, however, mean that she may, as Head of the Commonwealth, differ publicly from the views of the Government on a matter on which the Government has formed a particular view. In July 1986 there was speculation in a newspaper article that the Queen, as Head of the Commonwealth, did not agree with the Prime Minister on the wisdom of applying (or not applying) economic sanctions against South Africa.[87] Whatever the truth of that story, it would

---

[82] All the overseas countries described her as "Elizabeth the Second," although she was the first Elizabeth to reign over them as distinct Kingdoms: cf. MacCormick v. Lord Advocate, 1953 S.C. 396 (Scotland). In 1973 Her Majesty personally signed an Australian Act giving her the title of Queen of Australia, instead of Queen of the United Kingdom and Australia.

[83] post, para. 36–024.

[84] Further prerogative powers, extending to war and peace, were transferred at the beginning of 1978 to the Governor-General of Canada. cf. now, Canada Act 1982 and Australia Act 1986, ante.

[85] See D. P. O'Connell, "The Dissolution of the Australian Parliament: 11 November, 1975," (1976) 57 The Parliamentarian, p. 1; and letter from D. P. O'Connell and J. M. Finnis to The Times, November 25, 1975.

[86] Sir William Dale, letter to Daily Telegraph January 31, 1984. cf. Mr Enoch Powell, M.R.: "ministerial advice that ministerial advice is not requisite is also ministerial advice": letter to The Times, January 26, 1984. See further, R. W. Blackburn, "The Queen and Ministerial Responsibility" [1985] P.L. 361.

[87] The Sunday Times, July 20, 1986, ante, para. 17–024.

obviously be constitutionally improper for the Queen to express in public a view which was contrary to that of Her Ministers as the United Kingdom on a matter concerning the policy of the United Kingdom.

"The Crown" usually means the central government,[88] and as there are as many independent governments as there are independent countries of the Commonwealth, "the Crown" in any of these will usually mean the government of that country. This is especially so where statute has expressly or impliedly designated a particular fund to meet a debt.[89] Further, disputes between member nations of the Commonwealth are possible, such as the dispute between India and Pakistan on the status of Kashmir. The Crown may at the same time be at war in respect of some Commonwealth territories and at peace in respect of others. In the Second World War not only did some Commonwealth countries make separate declarations of war against Germany and Japan, but Eire remained neutral throughout. Since the war the members of the Commonwealth have not pursued a common foreign policy. They differed, for example, over the Suez Canal intervention in 1956 and on the question of recognising Communist China. Some have entered into regional treaties with non-members to the exclusion of other members.

The conclusion is that the common law doctrine of the indivisibility of the Crown[90] has been modified, from the English law point of view, by legislation and constitutional convention. The Queen holds several offices as Head of State. The legal systems of other Commonwealth countries generally regard the Crown as divisible, but within the federations it is indivisible for certain purposes. In international law the Crown is clearly divisible. Some writers would describe the relation of the Crown to the various realms in the Commonwealth as a new kind of personal union, but no formula yet devised is adequate to cover all the facts.

Republics in the Commonwealth

The India (Consequential Provisions) Act 1949[91] recognised that India[92] was **36–024** a republic while remaining a member of the Commonwealth. Since its new Constitution came into force in 1950, India no longer owes allegiance to the Crown. The Queen is not Queen of India, but India recognises the Crown as the Head of the Commonwealth with which it is associated and of which it is a full member. The desire of India to remain a full member of the Commonwealth after the coming into force of her republican Constitution was discussed at a meeting of Commonwealth Prime Ministers in 1949, which issued a declaration[93] to the effect that the Governments of the other Commonwealth countries, the basis of whose membership of the Commonwealth was not thereby changed, accepted and recognised India's continuing membership. This declaration modified the Balfour declaration of 1926,[94] and dropped the term "British" as applied to the

---

[88] *ante*, para. 15–007.
[89] *Att.-Gen. v. Great Southern and Western Ry of Ireland* [1925] A.C. 754.
[90] *ante*, para. 35–005.
[91] And see Statute Law (Repeals) Act 1976, Pt VII.
[92] *i.e.* the former British India excluding Pakistan, but including most of the former Indian states.
[93] For the negotiations leading to this declaration, including recognition by India of the King as "Head of the Commonwealth," see J. W. Wheeler-Bennett, *King George VI*, pp. 719–731.
[94] *ante*, para. 36–001.

Commonwealth. A similar process was gone through in 1956 in relation to Pakistan which has since left the Commonwealth.[95]

The existence of republics within the Commonwealth marks the end of that "common allegiance" which featured so prominently in the Balfour declaration; but the concept of allegiance, now divorced from British nationality, appears to have no legal significance except in the law of treason.

Citizenship[96]

36–025   As has been seen in Chapter 23, there is no longer a common code of British nationality. The first sign of divergence was the Canadian Nationals Act 1921, and crisis came with the Canadian Citizenship Act 1946. This led to a conference of legal experts on Commonwealth nationality and citizenship in 1947. Their proposal was that the United Kingdom and the other Commonwealth countries should each define their own citizenship, and that the citizens of the various Commonwealth countries should be recognised in every part of the Commonwealth as "British subjects" or "Commonwealth citizens."

This "common clause" was adopted by the United Kingdom, Canada, Australia and New Zealand. It does not necessarily mean, however, that British citizens (formerly citizens of the United Kingdom and Colonies) have in those other three countries the same citizenship and political rights as their citizens have in the United Kingdom.[97] Other Commonwealth countries recognise "Commonwealth citizens" in various ways.

Consultation and co-operation

36–026   After the Imperial Conference of 1937 the practice of holding more or less regular Imperial Conferences, with fixed agenda and full published reports, was discontinued. There have since been ad hoc meetings of Commonwealth heads of government to review the state of the war and to discuss post-war settlements; to discuss international relations, economic affairs and defence; to answer the question of India's continued membership of the Commonwealth after adopting a republican constitution; to discuss South Africa; to discuss the Common Market; the world political situation; the progress of British territories towards independence, and membership of the Commonwealth; the means of promoting closer co-operation between the peoples of the Commonwealth; world economic affairs; disarmament; trade and immigration. Meetings of all the member states are now held biennially.

There have also been other Conferences from time to time below heads of government level, for example, the British Commonwealth Conference on Nationality and Citizenship, 1947; and the Conference of Commonwealth Foreign Ministers at Colombo in 1950, which recommended the establishment of a Commonwealth Consultative Committee to plan developments for South and South-East Asia ("the Colombo Plan").

Since the war, treaty relations among members of the Commonwealth no longer appear to differ from those existing between other states. In the absence of any provision to the contrary, they would be governed by international law. When members of the Commonwealth have accepted the compulsory jurisdiction

---

[95] The number of republics (with either constitutional or executive Presidents) within the Commonwealth currently stands at 31, compared with 16 Realms acknowledging the Queen as Head of State and 6 indigenous monarchies.

[96] Dale, *op. cit.* pp. 187–189.

[97] *ante* para. 23–025 for the application of the Immigration Act 1971 to Commonwealth citizens.

of the International Court of Justice, they have tended to reserve disputes with Commonwealth countries. The United Kingdom no longer excludes such disputes arising after 1968. No formal machinery had been devised for settling disputes between members of the Commonwealth. An advisory opinion of the Privy Council has been sought twice in disputes between Commonwealth members.[98] Settlement through the machinery of the United Nations has also been resorted to twice: between India and South Africa in 1946 over the treatment of Indians in the latter country, and between India and Pakistan over the future status of Kashmir in 1954.

Commonwealth High Commissioners in the United Kingdom now take precedence with ambassadors of foreign states and are accorded the title of "Excellency." Republican members of the Commonwealth may send ambassadors rather than High Commissioners to other Commonwealth countries. These representatives of Commonwealth governments in the United Kingdom were granted immunities similar to those of foreign diplomatic representatives in 1952.[99]   **36–027**

Consultation, exchange of information and co-operation among Commonwealth countries are found mainly in the fields of external affairs, defence, finance and economics, education and law. There is also a fair degree of mutual help. The obligation to consult, however, is not clearly defined, and consultation tends to be a one-way traffic. The United Kingdom would not change any law affecting citizens of Commonwealth countries, such as the Fugitive Offenders Acts, without consulting the other members, and in this case probably trying to effect reciprocal arrangements. The principle obtains of non-intervention in each other's domestic affairs. Apart from express agreements, no positive obligations are involved in Commonwealth membership. Generally, there is no definite Commonwealth policy. In particular, there is no common foreign policy. The experience of Eire in the last war shows that a member of the Commonwealth— even one of the Queen's realms (as Eire was then)—may remain neutral in a war in which the Crown is engaged. Eire's neutrality was recognised by the enemy belligerents, and by the neutral countries.

The media for consultation include the Crown and the Governors-General, meetings of Prime Ministers, other Ministers and officials, the exchange of High Commissioners or Ambassadors, and regular communication between the Foreign and Commonwealth Office and the Departments of External Affairs of Commonwealth countries.[1]   **36–028**

There are also a number of official organs for co-operation covering such matters as agriculture and forestry, education, air transport, economics, scientific liaison, shipping, statistics and telecommunications. Assistance of various kinds is provided by the Commonwealth Development Corporation.[2] Collective defence has been a major preoccupation both in war and peace, but the recent tendency is for regional international arrangements such as the North Atlantic Treaty Organisation. The Commonwealth Foundation administers a fund for increasing interchanges between Commonwealth organisations in professional

---

[98] *Re Cape Breton* (1846) 5 Moo.P.C. 259 (annexation of Cape Breton to Nova Scotia); *Re Labrador Boundary Dispute* (1927) 137 L.T. 187.
[99] Diplomatic Immunities (Commonwealth Countries and Republic of Ireland) Act 1952; Diplomatic Privileges Act 1964; *ante*, para. 15–033.
[1] The United Kingdom temporarily broke off diplomatic relations with Uganda in 1976, British interests being looked after by France.
[2] Commonwealth Development Corporation Acts, 1978 and 1982. The Commonwealth Development Corporation Act 1999 provides for the privatisation of the corporation.

fields. The Foundation is an autonomous body, maintaining a close liaison with the Commonwealth Secretariat, and is financed by contributions from Commonwealth governments.

The Commonwealth Secretariat[3]

36–029   The Commonwealth Secretariat, established in 1965 as a visible symbol of the spirit of co-operation animating the Commonwealth, is at the service of all Commonwealth governments. The Secretariat derives its functions from the authority of Commonwealth heads of government, and the Secretary-General has access to heads of government. The Secretariat has no executive functions. Among its chief purposes are to disseminate factual information to all member countries on matters of common concern; to assist existing agencies in the promotion of Commonwealth links; and to help to co-ordinate preparations for future meetings of Commonwealth heads of government and of other Commonwealth Ministers.

The Commonwealth Secretariat Act 1966 provides that the Secretariat shall have the legal capacity of a body corporate, and it and its staff have the privileges and immunities conferred by the Schedule. The certificate of a Secretary of State is conclusive as to any relevant fact.

---

[3] Cmnd. 2713, *Agreed Memorandum on the Commonwealth Secretariat; The Commonwealth Relations Office Year Book 1966*, Chap. 3; Margaret Doxey, "The Commonwealth Secretariat," *Year Book of World Affairs 1976*, p. 69.

CHAPTER 37

APPEALS TO THE PRIVY COUNCIL[1]

I. Appeals from Dependent Territories

The abolition of the jurisdiction of the Council in the seventeenth century did **37–001**
not extend to appeals from overseas territories, *e.g.* the Channel Islands, the Isle
of Man, colonies ("plantations"), and later India. The remaining jurisdiction
rested on the prerogative of the King as the fountain or reservoir of justice; but
its exercise came to be regulated by the Judicial Committee Acts of 1833 and
1844, which created the judicial Committee of the Privy Council to hear all Privy
Council appeals.[2] The Crown has the prerogative to determine what is the
jurisdiction of the Judicial Committee.[3] The Colonial Courts of Admiralty Act
1890 provided for the continued hearing of appeals by the Privy Council from
courts in any British possession invested with Admiralty jurisdiction where there
was no right of appeal to a local court or on appeal from a local court. There is
power to make rules of court.

Privy Council Precedents
A Privy Council decision (technically an opinion) is binding on the courts of **37–002**
the country from which the appeal came. The Judicial Committee said in the
Bakhshuwen case[4] that decisions of the Board on Islamic law in appeals from
India bound the Court of Appeal for Eastern Africa, and there are older dicta to
the effect that the Boards' decisions are binding throughout the Privy Council's
overseas jurisdiction[5] but the statement should probably be restricted, first to
cases where the relevant parts of the legal systems concerned are the same and,
secondly to appeals from dependent territories. Decisions of the House of Lords
on United Kingdom legislation which has been adopted in similar terms in a
colony should be treated by colonial courts as binding, according to the Board in
Delasala v. Delasala,[6] although in juristic theory such decisions are persuasive
only.

---

[1] N. Bentwich, *Privy Council Practice* (3rd ed., 1937); Sir Kenneth Roberts-Wray, *Commonwealth
and Colonial Law*, pp. 433–463; Sir William Dale, *The Modern Commonwealth* pp. 128–129; Loren
P. Beth, "The Judicial Committee: Its Development, Organisation and Procedure" [1975] P.L. 219;
E. McWhinney, *Judicial Review in the English-Speaking World.* For the early history, see J. H. Smith,
Appeals to the Privy Council from the American Plantations (1965); P. A. Howell, *The Judicial
Committee of the Privy Council 1833–1876.*
[2] *ante*, para. 16–010.
[3] *Australian Consolidated Press v. Uren* [1969] 1 A.C. 590, PC.
[4] *Fatuma Bin Salim Bakhshowen v. Mohamed Bin Salim Bakhshuwen* [1952] A.C. 1; *Australian
Consolidated Press v. Uren, supra.* In *Frankland v. The Queen* [1987] A.C. 576, on an appeal from
the Isle of Man concerning the common law *mens rea* of murder the Privy Council took the view that
decisions of the House of Lords were persuasive only. See H. H. Marshall, "The Binding Effect of
Decisions of the Judicial Committee of the Privy Council" (1968) 17 I.C.L.Q. 743; G. W. Bartholo-
mew in (1952) 1 I.C.L.Q. 392; Roberts-Wray, *op. cit.* pp. 572–575.
[5] *e.g. Robins v. National Trust Co* [1927] A.C. 515.
[6] [1980] A.C. 546. Decisions of the Council reflect differing views: see J. W. Harris, "The Privy
Council and the Common Law" (1990) 106 L.Q.R. 574; *post* para. 37–010.

Appeals lie from the Channel Islands, the Isle of Man and the colonies, and by virtue of the Foreign Jurisdiction Act 1890 they formerly lay from protectorates, protected states and British trust territories.

Appeals to the Judicial Committee from overseas territories fall into two main classes:

(1) Appeals by "right of grant."

(2) Appeals by "special leave" of the Privy Council.

1. Appeals by "right of grant"

37–003   These are called appeals "by right of grant" because the limits are defined by Imperial Act, Order in Council or local statute, although fundamentally the appeal is founded on "the prerogative right and, on all proper occasions, the duty, of the Queen in Council to exercise an appellate jurisdiction" (*R. v. Bertrand*[7]). They fall into two groups: (a) appeals "as of right" in the narrow sense, and (b) appeals at the discretion of the local court. In so far as these appeals rest on Act of Parliament or Order issued thereunder, they cannot be limited or abolished by the colonial legislature.[8] Leave to appeal to the Privy Council must be obtained from the local court, usually the Supreme Court of the territory. Neither group of appeals by right of grant now in fact includes criminal cases.[9]

(a) *Appeals "as of right"*

37–004   Although this kind of appeal is called "as of right," application for leave to appeal has to be made to the local court; but the latter must grant leave to appeal if certain conditions are fulfilled. These conditions vary in different territories, although there is now a fair degree of uniformity. Generally speaking, an appeal lies "as of right" where the decision complained of is a final judgment, the subject-matter involved is worth a specified minimum sum, and the appellant fulfils the prescribed conditions, *e.g.* as to the time within which application is to be made.[10]

(b) *Appeals at the discretion of the local court*

37–005   If these conditions are not fulfilled, *e.g.* because the sum involved is below the prescribed minimum or the judgment is not a final one, the local court may have a discretion to grant leave to appeal if it considers that the question is one which by reason of its great general or public importance or otherwise ought to be submitted to Her Majesty in Council. It commonly requires security for costs.

2. Appeals by "special leave" of the Privy Council

37–006   These are sometimes still called "prerogative" appeals, although they are now regulated by the Judicial Committee Act 1844. The Judicial Committee may grant special leave to appeal where:

---

[7] (1867) L.R. 1 P.C. 520.
[8] Colonial Laws Validity Act 1865, s.2.
[9] *Falkland Islands Co v. R.* (1863) 1 Moo.P.C.(N.S.) 299; and see *Chung Chuck v. The King* [1930] A.C. 244.
[10] *Royal Hong Kong Jockey Club v. Miers* [1983] 1 W.L.R. 1049.

(i) there is no grant of the right of appeal from the court; or

(ii) the local court has no power to grant leave to appeal in the particular case, that is, generally in criminal cases; or

(iii) the local court has power to grant leave to appeal in the particular case, but has refused leave[11]; or

(iv) appeal lies directly to the Privy Council under the Judicial Committee Act 1844 from a court which is not a court of final appeal.

The power to grant special leave to appeal cannot be limited or abolished by the legislature of a dependent territory except under the authority of an Act of Parliament, first, because that would be repugnant to the Judicial Committee Acts of 1833 and 1844 and therefore void under the Colonial laws Validity Act 1865; and, secondly, because it could only be effective if construed as having an extraterritorial operation, and a colonial Act cannot in general have extraterritorial operation. The decision of the Privy Council in *Nadan v. The King*[12] was explained in this way in *British Coal Corporation v. The King*,[13] although it would have been sufficient to base it on repugnancy to Imperial statute.

Special leave to appeal may be granted in criminal cases as well as civil cases, but different principles are applied.

(a) *Civil cases*

The Judicial Committee will grant special leave to appeal in civil cases only **37–007** "where the case is of gravity involving a matter of public interest or some important question of law, or affecting property of considerable amount, or where the case is otherwise of some public importance or of a very substantial character."[14] Thus special leave was granted where the question was whether gold and silver minerals discovered in British Columbia in the nineteenth century were vested in the Crown as represented by the Government of Canada or that of British Columbia.[15] Special leave has been granted on important questions of law even though the amount involved was below the prescribed minimum for an appeal by right of grant[16]; in constitutional cases such as the interpretation of a colonial Act[17]; where the revenue rights of the Crown are concerned[18]; and where the colonial court acted without jurisdiction.[19] Cases where special leave is likely to be granted although the matter is not of great public importance include questions affecting status, the validity of marriage, the legitimacy of children and injury to character or professional reputation.[20]

---

[11] *Davis v. Shaughnessy* [1932] A.C. 106.

[12] [1926] A.C. 482.

[13] [1935] A.C. 500, PC; and see *Att.-Gen. for Ontario v. Att.-Gen. for Canada* [1947] A.C. 127, PC.

[14] *Prince v. Gagnon* (1882) 8 App.Cas. 103, 105; *Caldwell v. McLaren* (1883) 9 App.Cas. 295.

[15] *Att.-Gen. of British Columbia v. Att.-Gen. of Canada* (1889) 14 App.Cas. 295.

[16] *Sun Fire Office v. Hart* (1889) 14 App.Cas. 98.

[17] *Ex p. Gregory* [1901] A.C. 128.

[18] *Re Att.-Gen. of Victoria* (1866) 3 Moo.P.C.(N.S.) 527.

[19] *The Queen v. Price* (1854) 8 Moo.P.C. 203.

[20] *e.g. Le Mesurier v. Le Mesurier* [1895] A.C. 517; *Att.-Gen. of the Gambia v. N'Jie* [1961] A.C. 617. And see *Re Dillet, infra*.

On the other hand, special leave will not be granted to determine merely abstract right, or purely hypothetical questions; or in election petitions; nor generally on questions of fact.

(b) *Criminal cases*

37–008   In *Re Dillet*[21] Lord Blackburn said of appeals in criminal cases: "the rule has been repeatedly laid down, and has been invariably followed, that Her Majesty will not review or interfere with the course of criminal proceedings, unless it is shown that, by a disregard of the forms of legal process, or by some violation of the principles of natural justice, or otherwise, substantial and grave injustice has been done." These principles were restated by the Board in 1914 in *Arnold v. The King-Emperor*.[22] "It is not guided by its own doubts of the appellant's innocence or suspicion of his guilt. It will not interfere with the course of the criminal law unless there has been such an interference with the elementary rights of an accused as has placed him outside of the pale of regular law, or unless, within that pale, there has been a violation of the natural principles of justice so demonstratively manifest as to convince their Lordships, first, that the result arrived at was opposite to the result which their Lordships would themselves have reached, and, secondly, that the same opposite result would have been reached by the local tribunal also if the alleged defect or misdirection had been avoided."[23] It may be noted that these principles were laid down at a time when there was no system of criminal appeals in this country. They have, however, continued to be applied in more recent times: *Ragho Prasad v. The Queen*.[24]

Where the Privy Council has jurisdiction, whether civil or criminal, it may hear an appeal from either party. Thus in *Attorney-General of Ceylon v. K. D. J. Perera*[25] the Judicial Committee allowed an appeal by the Crown against the decision of the Court of Criminal Appeal of Ceylon ordering a new trial (not an acquittal) of a person who had been convicted of murder by the court of first instance.

The Judicial Committee follow the usual practice of appellate courts in not granting leave to appeal in criminal cases on questions of fact. A misdirection to the jury is not by itself a sufficient ground for interference if either the local Appeal Court or the Judicial Committee itself is satisfied that the facts nevertheless indicate the guilt of the accused. Appeals will not be heard from a military tribunal administering martial law (*Tilonko v. Attorney-General of Natal*[26]), or from courts-martial administering military law.[27] The petitioner will generally be expected to have availed himself of any right of appeal to the local courts before approaching the Privy Council.[28]

---

[21] (1887) 12 App.Cas. 459; Chief Justice of colony acted in effect as prosecutor, witness and judge. See too, *Ibrahim v. The King* [1914] A.C. 599, 614 *per* Lord Sumner: the *locus classicus* according to Lord Hailsham, *Badry v. D.P.P.* [1983] 2 A.C. 297, 302.

[22] [1914] A.C. 644.

[23] See, *e.g. Chang Hang Kiu v. Piggot* [1909] A.C. 312 (grossly improper procedure), *Knowles v. The King* [1930] A.C. 366 (jury in murder trial not told they could return verdict of manslaughter); *Ras Behari Lal v. The King-Emperor* (1933) 60 Ind.App. 354 (juryman had insufficient knowledge of English).

[24] [1953] A.C. 200; following *R. v. Bertrand* (1867) L.R. 1 P.C. 520; *Buxoo v. The Queen* [1998] 1 W.L.R. 820, following *Badry supra.*

[25] *Attygale v. The King* [1936] A.C. 338.

[26] [1907] A.C. 93, 461.

[27] *Mohammad Yakub Khan v. R.* (1947) 63 T.L.R. 94.

[28] *Kenyatta v. R.* [1954] 1 W.L.R. 1053.

II. Appeals from Independent Commonwealth Countries

Appeals and the Statute of Westminster

Immediately before the passing of the Statute of Westminster 1931, appeal lay   **37–009**
by *right of grant* from the Court of Appeal of New Zealand, and in some cases
directly from the Supreme Court of New Zealand with the leave of that court.
Appeal by right of grant also lay from the superior courts of the Canadian
provinces, and (in relation to their state jurisdiction) from the Supreme Courts of
the Australian states. As has been pointed out, such right of appeal could be
altered or abolished by a Dominion legislature, subject to the provisions of the
Colonial Laws Validity Act 1865.[29]

Before the passing of the Statute of Westminster the Dominions could not
restrict or abolish the jurisdiction of the Privy Council to grant *special leave* to
appeal: (i) by reason of the Colonial Laws Validity Act 1865, s.2, because the
jurisdiction of the Judicial Committee rested on—or was regulated by—the
Judicial Committee Acts 1833 and 1844; and (ii) because they could not legislate
with extraterritorial effect, except for the peace, order and good government of
their territory (*Nadan v. The King*[30]).

The general principles on which special leave from the Dominions was at that
time granted were explained by Viscount Haldane in *Hull v. McKenna*.[31] Generally, he said, the jurisdiction of Dominion courts should be regarded as final:
only in exceptional cases would the Judicial Committee use its discretion to grant
leave to appeal. Leave was very sparingly granted in criminal cases. Otherwise,
leave was more freely granted in *inter se* disputes from federal Dominions
(except in so far as limited by statute in the case of Australia) and from India than
in cases from unitary dominions. This practice followed the wishes of the various
Dominions themselves.

The question of appeals to the Judicial Committee was discussed by the   **37–010**
Imperial Conference of 1926, but no proposal was made beyond recording the
understanding that "it was no part of the policy of His Majesty's Government in
Great Britain that questions affecting judicial appeals should be determined
otherwise than in accordance with the wishes of the part of the Empire primarily
affected." The Imperial Conference, 1930, did not agree on any solution to the
question of appeals from the Dominions to the Privy Council, and it seems fairly
clear that the Statute of Westminster 1931 was not intended to affect them.

After the passing of that Statute, however, the Judicial Committee held that
sections 2 and 3 enabled the Dominions to which the Statute applied to abolish
all appeals to the Privy Council, criminal[32] and civil,[33] including appeals by
special leave. The same consequence followed without any doubt from the Indian
Independence Act 1947 and subsequent Independence Acts affecting other territories. Since the legislature of an independent Commonwealth country may at
any time modify or terminate appeals to the Privy Council, said Viscount

---

[29] Though it was doubtful whether the Australian Parliament could abolish such appeals from the
States even with their concurrence.
[30] [1926] A.C. 482, PC: Canada.
[31] Reported in [1926] Ir.R. 402: the first appeal from the Irish Free State.
[32] *British Coal Corporation v. The King* [1935] A.C. 500. See W. Ivor Jennings, "The Statute of
Westminster and Appeals" (1936) 52 L.Q.R. 173.
[33] *Att.-Gen. for Ontario v. Att.-Gen. for Canada* [1947] A.C. 127. See C. G. Pierson, *Canada and the
Privy Council* (1960).

Radcliffe in *Ibralebbe v. The Queen*,[34] true independence is not in any way compromised by continuance of such appeals.

In *De Morgan v. Director-General of Social Welfare*,[35] the Judicial Committee, on appeal from New Zealand, held that the right of appeal could be excluded not merely by express statutory words but also by necessary intendment.

Privy Council precedents

37–011   The courts of an independent Commonwealth country are probably not bound by Privy Council decisions on appeal from another country, even where the laws in force in the countries concerned are similar. The attainment of independence, involving an independent legal system and the voluntary nature of the retention of appeals to the Privy Council, may be said to sever the previously undivided jurisdiction of the Privy Council.[36] Such decisions, on the other hand, would be strongly persuasive, apart from the probability that the Privy Council would decide the question in the same way.

The Privy Council has expressed conflicting views on whether the courts of Commonwealth countries (and the Council itself) are bound by decisions of the House of Lords. In *Australian Consolidated Press Ltd v. Uren*[37] it held that the High Court of Australia was not bound by *Rookes v. Barnard*.[38] In *Abbott v. The Queen*[39] it refused to follow *Lynch v. D.P.P. for Northern Ireland*.[40] The Privy Council, on the other hand, attributed binding effect to decisions of the House of Lords in *Hart v. O'Connor*[41] and *Tai Hing Cotton Mill Ltd v. Liu Chong Hing Bank Ltd*.[42]

Waning jurisdiction of the Privy Council[43]

37–012   Appeals to the Privy Council, as we have seen, have now been abolished by the "older" Commonwealth countries of Canada[44] and Australia.[45] Such appeals may be abolished by the legislation establishing the constitution of a newly independent Commonwealth country,[46] but they are usually retained at least for

---

[34] [1964] A.C. 900, PC. And see *Geelong Harbour Trust Commrs v. Gibbs* [1974] A.C. 810; the Privy Council does not think it proper to interfere with matters of legal policy, *e.g.* whether or not to follow a previous decision of the courts of the country concerned, as opposed to substantive law.

[35] [1998] A.C. 275, PC (Power of PC to entertain appeals was no longer wholly prerogative but, in essence, statutory. Earlier authorities had failed to take account of impact of Judicial Committee Acts 1833 and 1844). *Walker v. The Queen* [1994] 2 A.C. 3644, PC. See too *Dow Jones (Asia) Inc. v. A.G. of Singapore* [1989] 1 W.L.R. 1308 for example of purely statutory right of appeal.

[36] There are dicta to the effect that the Judicial Committee is part of the hierarchy of each system of courts from which appeal l'es, *e.g. British Coal Corporation v. The King* [1935] A.C. 500, 52, *cf. ante*, para. 37–002.

[37] [1969] 1 A.C. 590, PC.

[38] [1972] 2 A.C. 1027, HL.

[39] [1977] A.C. 755, PC.

[40] [1975] A.C. 653, HL See also *Frankland v. The Queen* [1987] A.C. 576, PC.

[41] [1985] A.C. 1000.

[42] [1986] A.C. 80. See further J. W. Harris, cited *supra*, n. 6.

[43] See H. H. Marshall, "The Judicial Committee of the Privy Council; a Waning Jurisdiction" (1964) 13 I.C.L.Q. 697; Enid M. Campbell, "The Decline of the Jurisdiction of the Judicial Committee of the Privy Council" (1959) 33 A.L.J. 196; Lord Normand, "The Judicial Committee of the Privy Council" [1950] C.L.P. 1.

[44] *ante*, n. 32 and n. 33.

[45] *ante*, para. 36–011.

[46] *cf. Ibralebbe v. The Queen* [1964] A.C. 900 (PC); attainment of independence of itself does not abrogate jurisdiction of Privy Council.

a time on attainment of independence. The tendency has been to abolish the Privy Council's jurisdiction, however, on assuming republican status, as with India, Pakistan, Cyprus,[47] Ghana, Nigeria, Sri Lanka and Malta.

From the New Zealand Court of Appeal appeal lies in most cases, and in exceptional cases directly from the Supreme Court.[48] The abolition of the right of appeal is, however, regularly suggested.

As Malaysia (formerly Malaya) became a monarchy not owing allegiance to the Queen, an arrangement was made whereby the Head of State should refer appeals, or applications for special leave to appeal, to the Judicial Committee in certain cases; the opinion of the Judicial Committee being then reported direct to the Head of State.[49] The Judicial Committee thus became part of the judicial system of Malaysia. Another device has been to make appeals lie from a republic to the Judicial Committee itself, and not to the Queen in Council.[50]

Despite its waning jurisdiction the Privy Council has in recent years dealt with   **37–013** a variety of interesting and often controversial issues. In a succession of cases it has recognised that "less rigidity" and "greater generosity" are required in interpreting constitutions than statutes.[51] In *A.G. of Trinidad and Tobago v. Whiterman*[52] Lord Keith said that "the language of a constitution falls to be construed not in a narrow and legalistic way, but broadly and purposively so as to give effect to its spirit and this is particularly true of those provisions which are concerned with the protection of human rights." The Privy Council applied that approach in holding that a constitutional right to legal representation would be nullified without the implication of a right to be informed of the constitutional guarantee. As was seen earlier,[53] the Privy Council has interpreted constitutions on the assumption that they are based, or should be based, on the separation of powers.[54] In *Browne v. The Queen*[55] a sentence of detention during the Governor General's pleasure (passed under legislative powers) was held to be unconstitutional because the Governor General was part of the executive; questions of

---

[47] Except appeals from the Senior Judges' Court of the Sovereign Base Areas.

[48] *e.g. Lee v. Lee's Air Farming Ltd* [1961] A.C. 12; *Boots Chemists (New Zealand) v. Chemists Service Guild of New Zealand* [1968] A.C. 457. In *Thomas v. The Queen* [1980] A.C. 125 the Judicial Committee held that no appeal lay from an "opinion" given by the New Zealand Court of Appeal on a reference to the Court by the Governor General under s.406(6) of the Crimes Act 1961 which allows the Governor General, if he desires the assistance of the Court, to refer a point for the Court's opinion. Recent examples include *Cussons (New Zealand) Ppty Ltd v. Unilever plc* [1998] A.C. 328 (trademarks); *Countrywide Banking Corpn v. Dean* [1998] A.C. 338 (insolvency); *Commissioner of Inland Revenue v. Wattie* [1999] 1 W.L.R. 873 (revenue); *A.G. of New Zealand v. Horton* [1999] 1 W.L.R. 1195 (compulsory purchase).

[49] Agreement of 1958. See *Hussien (Shaabin Bin) v. Kam (Chong Fook)* [1970] A.C. 492; *Ningkan (Stephen Kalong) v. Government of Malaysia* [1970] A.C. 379; *Teh Cheng Poh v. Public Prosecutor, Malaysia* [1980] A.C. 458. Following the abolition of the right of appeal by Malaysian legislation, the relevant UK legislation was repealed by the Statute Law (Repeals) Act 1989: Federation of Malaya Independence Act 1957, s.3 and Malaysia Act 1963, s.5.

[50] *e.g.* Malawi Independence Act 1964, s.5; Kenya Independence Act 1963, s.6. These provisions are no longer in force.

[51] *Minister of Home Affairs v. Fisher* [1980] A.C. 637; *Société United Docks v. Govt of Mauritius* [1985] A.C. 585.

[52] [1991] 2 A.C. 240, 247. See also *A.G. of Hong Kong v. Lee Kwong-Kut* [1993] A.C. 951, *per* Lord Woolf; *Ming Pao Newspapers v. A.G. of Hong Kong* [1996] A.C. 907, 917 *per* Lord Jauncey.

[53] *Supra* para. 2–021.

[54] *Liyanage v. R.* [1967] 1 A.C. 259; *Hinds v. R.* [1977] A.C. 195; *A.G. of Fiji v. D.P.P.* [1983] 2 A.C. 672; *John v. D.P.P.* [1985] 1 W.L.R. 657.

[55] [2000] 1 A.C. 45.

punishment were for the judiciary.[56] Fundamental rights before the Board have included the right to bail[57]; the right of a detained person to communicate with a lawyer[58] the right to a fair hearing of a criminal charge within a reasonable time[59] the right to legal representation[60]; the right not to be deprived of property without compensation[61]; the right to freedom of expression[62] and the inviolability of premises against unlawful search.[63] The extent to which a constitutional presumption of innocence is compatible with imposing the burden of proof relating to particular issues on a defendant was considered in *A.G. of Hong Kong v. Lee Kwong-Kut*.[64] In *Matadeen v. Pointu*[65] the Privy Council refused to find a general principle of equality of treatment in the constitution of Mauritius and held that individuals were protected against discrimination only on the specific grounds laid down in the constitution. The most controversial aspect of the Council's work has come to be its role in relation to appeals concerning the death penalty. It has clearly established that capital punishment is not, in itself, unconstitutional as a "cruel and unusual punishment".[66] But in *Pratt v. A.G. for Jamaica*[67] it was held that unconscionable delay in carrying out a sentence of death may make the punishment "cruel". In *Thomas v. Baptiste*[68] it was stated that the prison conditions in which a condemned prisoner is kept may themselves constitute cruel and unusual treatment but do not of themselves render the carrying out of the death sentence, cruel or unusual. "It would be otherwise if the man were kept in solitary confinement or shackled or flogged or tortured . . . A state which imposes such punishments forfeits its right to carry out the death

---

[56] Applying *Hinds v. The Queen, supra* and *R. v. Secretary of State for the Home Department ex p. Venables* [1998] A.C. 407. See also *Ali v. The Queen* [1992] 2 A.C. 93. (Provision that D.P.P. could choose to direct that offence be heard before a court which could, on conviction, only impose death penalty, unconstitutional).

[57] *Attorney-General of the Gambia v. Jobe* [1984] A.C. 689. (Constitutionality of Special Criminal Court also in issue). For a critical note see, Barbara de Smith, "The Judicial Committee as a Constitutional Court" [1984] P.L. 557.

[58] *Thornhill v. Attorney-General of Trinidad and Tobago* [1981] A.C. 61.

[59] *Bell v. D.P.P.* [1985] A.C. 937 (Jamaica). In *D.P.P. v. Tokai* [1996] A.C. 856, on appeal from Trinidad and Tobago, the Privy Council refused to read into a constitutional provision guaranteeing a "right to a fair hearing in accordance with the principles of fundamental justice" a right to a trial within a reasonable time. Delay was a matter for the judge by virtue of his general jurisdiction to prevent abuse of process. See also *Charles v. The State* [2000] 1 W.L.R. 384.

[60] *Mitchell v. The Queen* [1999] 1 W.L.R. 1679. (Conviction quashed: trial continued without adjournment when defendant's counsel withdrew from the proceedings.) *Dunkley v. The Queen* [1995] 1 A.C. 419 applied. *Robinson v. The Queen* [1985] A.C. 956 and *Ricketts v. The Queen* [1998] 1 W.L.R. 1016, distinguished.

[61] *Société United Docks v. Govt. of Mauritius* [1985] A.C. 585; *Blomquist v. A.G. of Dominica* [1987] A.C. 489; *Morgan v. A.G. of Trinidad and Tobago* [1988] 1 W.L.R. 297; *Alleyne Forte v. A.G. Trinidad and Tobago* [1998] 1 W.L.R. 68.

[62] *De Freitas v. Permanent Secretary of Ministry of Agriculture, Fisheries, Lands and Housing* [1999] 1 A.C. 69.

[63] *A.G. of Jamaica v. Williams* [1998] A.C. 351.

[64] [1993] A.C. 951.

[65] [1999] 1 A.C. 98.

[66] *De Freitas v. Benny* [1976] A.C. 239. In *Boodram v. Baptiste* [1999] 1 W.L.R. 1709 the Privy Council emphasised that it was not deciding whether the death penalty was in itself unlawful. "The question for their Lordships Board is whether hanging today in Trinidad and Tobago is or is not a lawful method of execution." Held lawful because expressly authorised by legislation, subject to which the constitution took effect.

[67] [1994] 2 A.C. 1. (Delay of more than five years after sentence strong grounds for assuming "inhuman or degrading punishment".)

[68] [2000] 2 A.C. 1.

sentence in addition."[69] Pre-trial delay will not normally be taken into account in determining whether execution after a long period of detention amounts to cruel and unusual punishment.[70] In *Reckley v. Minister of Public Safety (No. 2)*[71] the Privy Council refused to interfere with the decision of the Committee which advised the Minister on the exercise of the prerogative of mercy. The prisoner had no right to make representations to the Committee or to know what material was before the Committee. Lord Goff repeated the words of Lord Diplock in *de Freitas v. Benny*,[72] "Mercy is not the subject of legal rights. It begins where legal rights end." *R. v. Secretary of State for the Home Department ex p. Bentley*[73] was distinguished on the ground that it dealt with an error of law by the Home Secretary, "an exceptional situation".

In *Lewis v. Attorney General of Jamaica*,[74] however, the Privy Council   **37–014** allowed the appeals of six men condemned to death and refused to follow a number of earlier, recent decisions of its own. The delays in carrying out the sentences varied from 4 years 11 months to 6 years 10 months. *Pratt* alone would have justified the decision to advise that the sentences should be commuted. The Privy Council, however, upheld two other, more controversial grounds of appeal. First, it held that although the merits of the decision of the Governor General on the exercise of the prerogative of mercy was not open to review, the procedure by which the Jamaican Privy Council reached its conclusion on its recommendation to the Governor General was open to review. The majority of the Privy Council refused to follow *Reckley v. Minister of Public Safety*.[75] Lord Slynn thought that there was not such a clear cut distinction as to procedural matters between mercy and legal rights as Lord Diplock's aphorism might indicate. Secondly, it held, refusing to follow *Fisher v. Minister of Public Safety and Immigration (No. 2)*[76] and *Higgs v. Minister of National Security*[77] that the right to the protection of the law "guaranteed under the constitution of Jamaica extended to protect the applicants rights under the United Nations Convention on Human Rights 1969 and the Inter-American Convention on Human Rights which Jamaica had ratified although it had not incorporated them into domestic law. The reasoning by which that conclusion was reached is thus explained by Lord Slynn:

> "It is of course well established that a ratified but unincorporated treaty, though it creates obligations for the state under international law, does not in the ordinary way create rights for individuals enforceable in domestic courts and this was the principle applied in the *Fisher (No. 2)* case. But even assuming that that applies to international treaties dealing with human rights, that is not the end of the matter. . . . In their Lordships' view when Jamaica acceded to the American Convention and to the International Covenant and allowed individual petitions the petitioner became entitled under the protection

[69] At p. 28 *per* Lord Millett.
[70] *Fisher v. Minister of Public Safety and Immigration* [1998] A.C. 673; *Thomas v. Baptiste, supra.*
[71] [1996] 1 A.C. 527.
[72] [1976] A.C. 239, 247.
[73] [1994] Q.B. 349.
[74] [2000] 3 W.L.R. 1785. "Whatever the humanitarian attractions of the opinion delivered by Lord Slynn, Lord Hoffmann" dissent is a devasting critique of the reasoning of the majority.
[75] *Supra*, n. 71.
[76] [2000] 1 A.C. 434.
[77] [2000] 2 A.C. 228.

of the law provision in section 13 to complete the human rights petition procedure and to obtain the reports of the human rights bodies for the Jamaican Privy Council to consider before it dealt with the application for mercy and to the staying of execution until those reports had been received and considered." (At p. 1811).

37–015 Thirdly, the Privy Council indicated that had it been necessary it would have held that the Jamaican courts should have investigated the allegations of harsh treatment to see whether they were such as to render the carrying out of the death sentence in itself cruel and unusual.

Unease has been expressed at this aspect of the work of the Privy Council[78] when capital punishment has been abolished in the United Kingdom and mens' lives may turn on a nice calculation of how many years and months they have spent in prison.

Suggested Commonwealth Court of Appeal[79]

37–016 We have noticed the tendency for Commonwealth countries to abolish appeals to the Privy Council on assuming republican status, if not before. This is no criticism of the objective impartiality of the Judicial Committee, as may be seen from the use made of that body as part of the machinery for the removal of judges in some independent Commonwealth countries. But the criticisms of the Judicial Committee as a court of appeal are that it appears to be virtually a British Court sitting in London (although in 1926 Viscount Haldane had already emphasised that the Judicial Committee sat in London purely for reasons of convenience: "[It is] not a body strictly speaking with any location"[80]); it cannot fully understand the background of the legal system it is applying; and its jurisdiction, based as it is largely on the prerogative to grant special leave to appeal to colonies, is inconsistent with independence, and especially with republican status. It is a harmless anomaly that the form of procedure is advisory rather than judicial; and this could be obviated by the method devised by Kenya and Malawi.[81]

The Commonwealth Prime Ministers' Conference in 1962 expressed the hope that the regular appointment of judges from other Commonwealth countries would strengthen the Judicial Committee and emphasise its importance as a Commonwealth link. Such appointments are made from time to time on a temporary basis. A later proposal, which had a good deal of support, was to set up a peripatetic Commonwealth Court composed of judges from various Commonwealth countries. Its jurisdiction would be twofold: (i) as a final court of appeal in certain cases from the courts of the Commonwealth countries, and (ii) to determine justiciable disputes between Commonwealth countries. Some would add the jurisdiction of a Supreme Court for the enforcement of a Commonwealth Bill of Rights.

37–017 Procedural problems would have to be solved. Should appeal to the Commonwealth Court always be as of right? If not, on what principles should leave to appeal be granted? And on what principles should decisions of the courts of Commonwealth countries be upset—for any error, or only for a gross miscarriage

---

[78] Lord Browne-Wilkinson, *The Lawyer* (1999), p. 22.
[79] See Gerald Gardiner and Andrew Martin, *Law Reform Now* (1963) p. 16; Nwabueze, *The Machinery of Justice in Nigeria* (1963) Chap. 10; H. H. Marshall, "A Commonwealth Court" (1965) *Round Table* No. 221, p. 6.
[80] *Hull v. M'Kenna* [1926] I.R. 402, 404.
[81] *Supra*, para. 37–012.

of justice? Questions such as these could no doubt be settled by legal experts without undue difficulty. But there are more formidable obstacles to be overcome. One is that the United Kingdom would be expected to abolish the appellate jurisdiction of the House of Lords[82] and to accept for herself the new Commonwealth Court as the final court of appeal, at least in some cases, from British courts. Another question is the composition of the court. How would the judges be selected? Would some countries be willing to spare senior judges for this purpose? Would the composition be scrutinised by the country visited? Would the country visited always supply one of its own judges? Lastly, the question of the expense of a court going on circuit round the world is usually raised in discussion of this proposal; and certainly the fares and subsistence allowances would amount to a significant item. On the other hand, we should also take into account the cost to litigants of the present system of appeals going to the Privy Council in London.

A Commonwealth Law Ministers' Meeting in 1966 under the chairmanship of Lord Gardiner, the Lord Chancellor, considered a proposal for a Commonwealth Court of Appeal. Some countries expressed their approval, but the majority have not shown themselves interested. Support came from the smaller Commonwealth countries that still used the Judicial Committee, but little has been heard of this suggestion recently.[83]

---

[82] The merger of the judicial functions of the House of Lords with those of the Privy Council was often discussed in the nineteenth century: Robert Stevens, "The Final Appeal: Reform of the House of Lords and Privy Council 1867–1876" (1964) 80 L.Q.R. 343.

[83] For a dispiriting survey of the role of the Judicial Committee and proposals for reform, see Robert Stevens, "The Role of the Judiciary: Lessons from the End of Empire" in *Essays for Patrick Atiyah*, (ed. Case and Stapleton 1991).

INDEX

ABDICATION,
  no precedent for, 14–005
ABUSE OF POWER,
  generally, 31–008—31–010
ACCESSION COUNCIL,
  composition of, 14–003
ACTE CLAIR,
  doctrine, 6–023
ACT OF PARLIAMENT,
  amendment, limits on, 4–002—4–004
  authentication, 4–026—4–027
  repeal, 4–002—4–004
  territorial application, 3–020—3–021
  Union, 4–005—4–010
    Ireland, 4–005
    Scotland, 4–006—4–010
ACT OF STATE,
  aliens, as to, 15–024
  British citizens, as to, 15–024—15–026
  Commonwealth citizens, as to,
    15–025—15–026
  definition, 15–021
  foreign states, as to, 15–022—15–023
  individuals, as to, 15–024—15–026
  protectorates, within, 15–024
  war, declaration of, 15–023
ADJOURNMENT,
  Parliament, of, 8–009
ADMINISTRATIVE AUTHORITIES,
  actions involving, 2–024
  powers, 2–023
  structure, 2–023
ADMINISTRATIVE FUNCTION,
  generally, 1–015
ADMINISTRATION OF JUSTICE,
  See JUSTICE, ADMINISTRATION OF
ADMINISTRATIVE JURISDICTION
  administrative law distinguished,
    30–002
  Franks Committee, 30–003, 30–028
  human rights and, 30–002
  inquiries, 30–025—30–028
  inspector,
    decisions, 30–026
    report of, 30–027
  meaning, 30–001
  Minister
    decisions, 30–024
    role of, 30–028
  tribunals, 30–004—30–023
  And see TRIBUNALS

ADMINISTRATIVE LAW
  constitutional law distinguished, 1–013,
    2–011
  development of, 2–024, intro to Pt. VI
  French, rule of law and,
    2–029—2–030, 2–031
  jurisdiction and,
    See ADMINISTRATIVE JURISDICTION
  no distinct system, 2–023—2–024
  public law, as, 1–014, 2–023
  public/private distinction, intro to Pt. VI
  rule of law and, 2–031
  system, 2–023—2–024
  topics covered, 2–023
ADMINISTRATIVE TRIBUNALS,
  jurisdiction, 2–023
  powers, 2–020
ADVISORY BODIES,
  See also Public corporations
  establishment, 28–004—28–006
AFFRAY,
  offence of, 27–021
ALIEN,
  Commons, disqualified from, 10–005
  enemy, 23–020—23–021
  EU citizenship and, 23–018—23–022
  friendly, 23–019
  generally, 23–019
  status of, 23–002, 23–005
ALLEGIANCE,
  relevance, 23–001
ANGLO-IRISH AGREEMENT,
  conclusion of, 5–008
ANGLO-IRISH INTER-GOVERNMENT
    COUNCIL,
  establishment of, 5–008
APPEAL,
  Appellate Jurisdiction Act, 9–097
  Courts-Martial Appeal Court, 19–013,
    19–014
  Habeas corpus cases, 24–039
  House of Lords as final, 9–044—9–051
  immigration matters, in,
    23–035—23–037
  lords of, 9–012, 9–041
  point of law, on,
    Court of Appeal, to, 10–062
    Court of First Instance, to, 6–009
    Court of Justice, to, 6–008
  tribunals, from, 30–020
  statutory rights of, 32–016,

APPLICATION FOR JUDICIAL REVIEW,
See JUDICIAL REVIEW
ARISTOTLE,
  functions of government, on, 1–015
  rule of law, on, 2–025
ARMED FORCES,
  actions for damages, 19–015—19–016
  appeals, 19–013, 19–014
  Commons, disqualify for, 10–007
  contract of service, 19–005
  Courts-Martial Appeal Court,19–013,
    19–014
  courts-martial system, 19–010—19–013
    reform of, 19–012
  Crown liability for, 33–012—33–014
  damages actions, 19–015—19–016
  detention, 19–012
  generally, 19–001
  human rights and, 19–012
  High Court jurisdiction, 19–014
  history, 19–002—19–003
  legal position, 19–004—19–008
  military law, 19–009
  Mutiny Acts, 19–002
  ordinary law, subject to, 19–005
  prerogative powers over, 15–013,
    19–004
  superior orders as defence,
    19–006—19–008
  visiting forces, 19–017—19–018
  war crimes, 19–008, 9–027
ARMY,
  See also ARMED FORCES
  generally, 19–002
ARREST,
  caution on, 24–011
  effecting, 24–010
  entry and search after, 24–044
  meaning, 24–006
  Parliamentary privilege and, 13–016
  place of, 24–011
  resistance to, 24–006
  search, and, 24–011
  terrorism, powers as to, 19–053.
    24–012
  valid, requirements for, 24–010
  warrant,
    with, 24–007
    without, 24–008—24–011
      arrestable offence, for,24–009
      non-arrestable offence, for, 24–009
ARRESTABLE OFFENCE
  types of, 24–009
ASSAULTING A CONSTABLE,
  defence, 24–020
  duty, in course of, 24–019, 27–030

ASSAULTING A CONSTABLE—cont.
  elements, 24–020
ASSEMBLY, FREEDOM OF,
  See also PUBLIC MEETINGS
  affray, 27–021
  aggravated trespass, 27–004, 27–014
  breach of the peace, 27–008—27–010
  by-laws and, 27–004
  common law powers, 27–007
  conditions, 27–012—27–013,
    27–015—27–016
  harassment/alarm/ distress, 27–025
  highway, obstructing, 27–004, 27–028
  Human Rights Act 1998, effect of,
    27–001
  E.C.H.R., and, 24–001
    See also EUROPEAN CONVENTION ON
      HUMAN RIGHTS
    effect of, 27–001
  offensive conduct, 27–022—27–026
  proscribed organisation,
    meetings addressed by, 27–006,
      27–032
  new age travellers, 27–014
  picketing, 27–006, 27–032—27–035
  place of, 27–003—27–005
  police powers, 27–003,
    27–006—27–007, 27–014
  prohibition order,
    application for, 27–012,
      27–016—27–017
    non-compliance, effect of, 27–013
  public meetings, 27–002—27–007
  Public Order Act 1986, 27–009,
    27–011—27–026, 27–035
    public order offences,
      27–018—27–026
    regulatory powers under,
      27–011—27–017
  public processions, 27–015—27–017
  raves, 27–013
  restrictions, 27–006
  rights, 27–001, 27–004, 27–005
  riot, 27–019
  sporting events, 27–006,
    27–036—27–037
  threatening/abusive/insulting acts,
    27–022—27–024
  trespassers,
    removal of, 27–014
  trespassory, 27–004, 27–012
  violent disorder, 27–020
ASSOCIATION, FREEDOM OF,
  E.C.H.R., effect of, 27–038
  political uniforms, wearing, 27–040
  proscribed organisations, 27–039

ATTAINDER,
Acts of, 8–006
ATTORNEY-GENERAL,
consent regime, 20–014
departments, 18–013
office, 18–010
powers, 5–023,
nolle prosequi, 2–020, 20–003
role, 18–011—18–012
AUDI ALTERAM PARTEM,
principles, 31–016—31–018
AUDIT,
Commission, establishment. 28–006
National, 12–017
AUSTIN,
doctrine of sovereignty, 3–001
AUSTRALIA,
citizenship, 36–026
constitution
amendment, 1–007
flexibility, 1–008
conventions in, 7–008
Dominion status of, 4–011, 4–013
Parliamentary supremacy, and,
4–032—4–033
Prime Minister, choice of, 17–032
Statute of Westminster and,
36–009—36–011
AUTHENTICATION,
Acts of Parliament, of, 4–026—4–027

BACKING OF WARRANTS,
generally, 23–048—23–049
BAIL,
amount of, 24–025
granting, 24–024
human rights and, 24–022
right to, 24–024
BALFOUR DECLARATION,
statement, 36–001
BALLOT,
secret, 2–016, 10–057
BANK OF ENGLAND,
responsibilities, 28–002
BELFAST AGREEMENT,
See also NORTHERN IRELAND
aspects of, 5–010
conclusion of, 5–009
BELGIUM,
administrative law in, 1–013, 2–031
constitution
amendment, 1–007
BILL OF RIGHTS,
dispensing and suspending powers,
3–005

BILL OF RIGHTS—*cont.*
English, 2–007
declaratory, mainly, 2–031
E.C. and, 4–017
taxation and, 3–009
U.S., 1–020
BILLS,
carry over of, 11–032
classification, 11–020—11–021
drafting, 11–019
Finance, 12–015
hybrid, 11–020—11–021
money,
See MONEY BILLS
private, 11–020
procedure on, 11–036—11–038
Private Members', 11–034—11–035
public, 11–020
amendments, selection of, 11–027
committee stage, 11–026
first reading, 11–024
introduction, 11–023
ordinary procedure on,
11–022—11–029
report stage, 11–028
second reading, 11–025
third reading, 11–029
BINDING OVER,
human rights and, 24–027
powers, 24–026—24–027
preventative justice, 24–026
BLACKSTONE,
allegiance, on, 23–001
exponents, 28–001
fundamental freedoms, on, 1–019
jury trial, on, 20–017
Parliamentary supremacy, on, 3–013,
4–003
royal prerogative, on, 15–003
separation of powers, on, 1–017
source of law, as, 2–010
Sovereign,
fountain of all justice, 20–002
treason, on, 14–013, 14–017
BLASPHEMY,
common law, at, 25–007
freedom of expression and, 25–008
BOOKS OF AUTHORITY,
source of constitutional law, as, 2–010
BOUNDARY COMMISSIONS,
Electoral Commission,
transfer of functions to, 10–043,
10–045
establishment, 10–044
functions, 10–044
independent, 2–016, 10–044

BOUNDARY COMMISSIONS—*cont.*
reports, 10–044
BRACTON,
rule of law, on, 2–025, 15–002
source of law, as, 2–010
BREACH OF THE PEACE,
apprehension of
reasonable grounds for, 27–009
common law powers, 27–009
definition, 27–008
police powers, 27–009
prevention, 27–007
risk, 27–010
BRITISH BROADCASTING CORPORATION,
operation, 28–003
BRITISH-IRISH COUNCIL,
creation of, 5–048
BRITISH-IRISH INTERGOVERNMENTAL
CONFERENCE,
focus, 5–048
BRITISH CITIZENSHIP,
Dependent Territories, 23–013
generally, 23–007
loss of, 23–010
naturalisation, by, 23–004, 23–008
overseas, 23–014
registration, by, 23–004, 23–009
resumption of, 23–012
BRITISH COLONIES,
ceded, 35–017, 35–021
classification, 35–015
composition, 35–007
conquered, 35–017, 35–021
constitution, 35–014
Crown's relationship with, 35–014
Executive councils, 35–030
extra-territorial legislation, 35–026
future developments, 35–032
governor,
powers, 35–029
representative of the Queen, 35–027
Hong Kong, 35–015
legislation for,
Crown, by, 35–019—35–021
U.K. Parliament, by, 35–018
legislatures of, 35–022
composition, 35–028
powers, 35–022—35–027
self-government in, 35–031
settled, 35–016, 35–020
BRITISH DEPENDENT TERRITORIES,
citizenship, 23–013
BRITISH EMPIRE,
history, 35–004
BRITISH ISLANDS,
composition, 35–001—35–003

BRITISH OVERSEAS,
citizenship, 23–014
BRITISH POSSESSIONS,
composition, 35–006
BRITISH PROTECTED PERSONS,
definition, 23–016
BRITISH PROTECTORATES,
composition, 35–008
BRITISH SUBJECTS,
See also NATIONALITY
status, 23–015
BRITISH TRUST TERRITORIES,
composition, 35–009
BROADCASTING,
content of programmes,
25–033—25–036
BRYCE,
constitution
types of, 1–007
BUDGET,
resolution, 12–014
BY-ELECTION,
dissolution of Parliament and, 8–020
generally, 10–050
BY-LAWS,
freedom of assembly and, 27–004
local authorities, by, 2–007, 27–004,
29–003

CABINET,
Act of Settlement and, 17–002
Civil Contingencies Unit, 19–028
collective responsibility,
17–010,17–021
committees, 17–011—17–012
composition, 17–007
confidentiality, 17–022—17–023
Control Policy Review Staff, 17–015
conventions as to, 7–015—7–018
dissolution and, 17–006
functions, 17–005—17–006
history, 17–001—17–004
inner, 17–013
Ministers
Lords, in 17–008
responsibility, 17–016—17–024
office, 17–014—17–015
origins in the Privy Council, 17–001
overlords experiment, 17–009
partial, 17–013
Prime Minister and,
See PRIME MINISTER
role, 2–020
shadow, 17–010
size, 17–009
Sovereign's influence, 17–024

CABINET—*cont.*
  system, 2–015
    conventions as to, 7–015—7–018
CANADA,
  citizenship law and, 23–003, 36–025
  constitutional conventions and, 7–006
  Dominion status of, 4–011
  Parliamentary supremacy and,
    4–012—4–013
  patriation of constitution, 36–008
  Statute of Westminster and, 36–007
  voting system, 10–058
CENSORSHIP,
  See also EXPRESSION, FREEDOM OF,
    OBSCENITY
  broadcasting, 25–033—25–036
  cinema, 25–038
  generally, 25–031
  press, 25–019, 25–023
  theatre, 25–037
  video recordings, 25–039
CENTRAL GOVERNMENT,
  Departments,
    See GOVERNMENT DEPARTMENTS
CERTIORARI,
  order, 32–004
  scope, 32–004—32–006
CEYLON,
  constitution, 2–020, 3–014
  independence, 4–014
CHAIRMAN OF WAYS AND MEANS,
  role, 10–022
CHANCELLOR OF THE EXCHEQUER,
  office of, 18–002
CHANNEL ISLANDS,
  British Isles, in, 35–003
CHILTERN HUNDREDS,
  role, 10–011
CINEMA,
  censorship, 25–038
CITIZENSHIP,
  See also NATIONALITY
  British, 23–007—23–014
  categories, 23–006
  commonwealth, 36–025
CITY OF LONDON,
  Corporation, 2–036
CIVIL CONTINGENCIES UNIT,
  establishment, 19–028
CIVIL LIST,
  generally, 15–013
CIVIL PROCEEDINGS,
  initiation of, 20–013
  limitation periods, 20–003
CIVIL SERVICE,
  Appeal Board, 18–029

CIVIL PROCEEDINGS—*cont.*
  arrears of pay, 18–027
  Codes, 18–029
  Commons, disqualifies for, 10–007
  confidentiality and, 18–030
  constitutional role, 18–029
  contractual relations with Crown,
    18–028
  Crown Service, 18–025
  dismissal from, 18–026, 18–028
  employment
    conditions, 18–029
    disputes, 18–028, 18–029
    royal prerogative, governed by,
      18–026
  freedom of expression, right to,
    restrictions on, 18–031
  generally, 18–021
  impartiality, 18–029
  legal status, 18–026—18–028
  management, 18–022
  Minister, 18–022
  Next Steps Agencies, 18–023—18–024
  organisation, 18–022
  political activities, 18–031
  recruitment, 18–022
  role, 18–022
  Scotland, in, 18–022
  secretariat of departments, 18–021
  structure, 18–022
  Wales, in, 18–022
  who constitutes, 18–025
CLERK,
  House of Commons, to, 10–020
  Parliament, to, 9–019
CLOSURE MOTION,
  device of, 11–012
CODES OF PRACTICE,
  provisions as to, 29–004
COKE,
  administration of justice, on, 20–002
  Magna Carta, on, 1–019
  martial law, on, 19–034
  non–performance of statutory duty, on,
    31–015
  Parliament as court, on, 8–001
  Parliamentary privilege, on, 13–02
  Parliamentary supremacy, on, 2–025,
    3–103, 4–002
  Privy Council, on, 16–002
  Treason Act 1495, on, 4–002
  source of law, as, 2–010
COLLECTIVE RESPONSIBILITY,
  Cabinet, of, 17–010, 17–021
COLONIAL LAWS VALIDITY ACT 1865,
  provisions, 35–023—35–025

Colonies, British,
  See British Colonies
Commission for Racial Equality,
  establishment, 28–006
Commissions for Local
    Administration,
  role, 34–016—34–017
Commons, House of,
  See House of Commons
Commonwealth,
  See also Nationality
  Australia in, 36–009—36–010
  Canada in, 36–007—36–008
  citizenship, 23–005, 36–025
  consultation and co–operation,
    36–026—36–028
  conventions as to, 7–019
  Crown in, 36–023
  Development Corporation, 28–006,
    36–028
  Dominion status, 36–001—36–002,
    36–003
  full membership, 36–019—36–020
  independence and, 36–013—36–018
  independent members, 36–013
  monarchy in, 36–021—36–023
  New Zealand in, 36–012
  origins of name, 35–012
  republics in, 36–024
  Secretariat, 36–029
  Statute of Westminster,
    36–003—36–012
  territories of, 35–004—35–013
Community Law,
  See European Community Law
Competition,
  free, 6–037
Comptroller and Auditor General,
  role, 12–018—12–019
Conciliabulum,
  Cabinet origins, 17–001
Confidence,
  breach of,
    doctrine, expanding, 25–019
    restraining, 25–020—25–021,
      26–012
  Cabinet papers, of, 17–022—17–023
  Civil Service and, 18–030
  common law duty, 26–030
  vote of, 8–019—8–020
Conseil Constitutionnel,
  Establishment, 1–011
Communications,
  data
    acquisition, 26–016

Communications—*cont.*
  data—*cont.*
    disclosure, 26–016
    interception of,
      provision for, 26–014—26–015
      supervision, 26–021—26–023
Conseil d'Etat,
  establishment, 1–013
Constituencies,
  See also Elections
  boundaries and, 10–044
  spending, 10–050
  third party spending. 10–051
Constitutional Adjudication,
  federal states, in, 1–010
Constitutional Conventions,
  Australia, in, 7–008
  Cabinet system, forming, 7–007,
    7–015—7–017
  Canada, in, 7–006, 7–008
  classification of, 7–014—7–019
  Commons/Lords relations, regulating,
    7–018
  Commonwealth relations, regulating,
    7–019
  courts do not enforce, 7–003
  custom distinguished, 7–001
  definition, 7–001
  Dicey on, 2–029, 7–001,
    7–012—7–013
  doctrines distinguished, 7–004
  establishment, 7–010
  evolution of state and, 7–009
  fact distinguished, 7–002
  growth and transformation, 7–007
  habit distinguished, 7–002
  importance, 2–017
  Jennings on, 7–003, 7–006, 7–010
  judicial recognition, 7–005—7–007
  judicial rules of practice distinguished,
    7–002
  laws distinguished, 1–003, 2–017,
    7–003
  legislation and, 7–007
  local government, in, 7–014
  Lords/Commons relations, regulating,
    7–018
  matters of, 2–015
  ministerial responsibility, as to, 7–017
  next step agencies, impact on,
    18–024
  Mitchell on, 7–003
  nature of, 7–001—7–007
  non-political rules, 7–002
  observation of, reasons for,
    7–011—7–013

CONSTITUTIONAL CONVENTIONS—*cont.*
practice distinguished, 7–002
proceedings in Parliament, regulating,
7–018
principles distinguished, 7–004
privilege distinguished, 2–017
public opinion and, 7–012
purpose of, 7–008—7–009
recognition by judiciary, 7–005—7–007
Royal Assent and, 7–010
royal prerogative, exercise of,
7–015—7–017
rules enforced by Parliament
distinguished, 7–004
statute and, 7–007
traditions distinguished, 7–004
United States, in, 7–007
unwritten laws, distinguished, 7–001
usage distinguished, 7–002
CONSTITUTIONAL COURTS,
establishment, 1–010
CONSTITUTIONAL LAW,
See also CONSTITUTIONS, UNITED
KINGDOM CONSTITUTION
administrative law distinguished,
1–013, 2–011
amendment, 1–007—1–008
fundamental rights and, 1–019
generally, 1–001
heads of state and government,
distinguishes, 14–001
next steps agencies, issues raised by,
18–024
public law, as, 1–014
scope, 1–012
separation of powers and, 1–017
topics covered, 2–023
CONSTITUTIONAL MONARCHY,
elements of, 2–013, 7–009
CONSTITUTIONS,
See also CONSTITUTIONAL LAW,
UNITED KINGDOM
CONSTITUTION
amendment, 1–007
flexible, 1–007—1–008
U.K., 2–011
fundamental laws and, 1–009—1–011
independence, 36–017—36–018
judicial review of legislation and,
1–009—1–011
meaning, 1–005
rigid, 1–007—1–008
framing, 1–009
subdivision, 1–008
U.K., 2–011
scope of, 1–012—1–020

CONSTITUTIONS—*cont.*
state, of a, 1–005
supreme, 4–001
term, use of, 1–005
unwritten, 1–006, 1–008
U.K.
See UNITED KINGDOM CONSTITUTION
written, 1–006, 1–008
effect of, 1–013, 4–001
CONTEMPT OF COURT,
appeal, rights of, 20–044
civil, 20–045—20–045
criminal distinguished, 20–044
Official Solicitor, role of, 20–046
punishment, 20–045
criminal, 20–047—20–054
civil distinguished, 20–044
enforcement of, 20–044
face of the court, in the, 20–050
freedom of expression and,
25–012—25–023
human rights and, 20–043, 20–047,
20–048
interference,
deliberate,
particular proceedings, with,
20–051, 25–014
justice, with, 20–048
unintentional,
prejudicial publications, by,
20–052, 25–013
jurisdiction to punish, 20–053
law as to, 20–043
legal aid, availability of, 20–044
misleading term, 20–043
punishment, 20–045, 20–053
refusal to reveal sources of
information, 25–016—25–018
reporting of judicial proceedings,
25–015
scandalising the court, 20–047
Scotland, in, 20–043, 20–044
sources of information,
disclosure of, 25–016—25–018,
25–022
victimising witnesses, 20–049
CONTEMPT OF PARLIAMENT,
bribery, 13–009
CONTRACT,
Crown, 33–004
CONTROL POLICY REVIEW STAFF,
appointment, 17–015
CONVENTION,
constitutional, 2–015, 2–017
See also CONSTITUTIONAL
CONVENTIONS

CONVENTION—*cont.*
custom distinguished, 7–001
Dicey on, 2–029, 7–001,
7–012—7–013
unwritten law distinguished, 7–001
CORONATION,
procedure, 14–004
CORPORATIONS, PUBLIC,
See PUBLIC CORPORATIONS
CORRUPT AND ILLEGAL PRACTICES,
Commons, disqualify for, 10–005
generally, 10–061
COUNCIL ON TRIBUNALS,
creation, 30–018
function, 34–002—34–003
COURT OF SESSION,
Act of Union and, 4–007
jurisdiction, 2–011
COURTS,
See also ADMINISTRATION OF JUSTICE,
JUDICIARY
administration, 18–009
civil rights and, 22–001
contempt of,
See also CONTEMPT OF COURT
English system, 20–009
executive powers, 2–020
jurisdiction excluded, 32–017—32–021
meaning, 20–007
Northern Irish system, 20–010
proceedings, initiation of,
20–012—20–016
Scottish system, 20–011
U.K. system, 20–008—20–011
COURTS-MARTIAL,
appeals, 19–013
reform, 19–012
system, 19–010—19–013
CRIMES,
Commons, disqualifying from, 10–005
special investigation powers and,
26–009
war,
See WAR CRIMES
CRIMINAL PROCEEDINGS,
initiation of, 20–014—20–016
legal aid for, 20–016
limitation periods 20–003
CROMWELL,
Instrument of Government 1653, 2–006
CROWN,
See also CROWN PROCEEDINGS, ROYAL
PREROGATIVE, SOVEREIGN
armed forces, liability for,
33–012—33–014
bona vacantia, 15–013

CROWN—*cont.*
colony, 35–016
Commonwealth context, in, 36–023
demise of the, 8–014
Estate, 15–013
function of the, 1–004, 2–020
liability, 33–001
meaning, 15–007
privilege, 33–022—33–028
public corporations and,
28–009—28–012
rule of law and, 2–030
time does not run against, 20–003
CROWN PROCEEDINGS,
Act 1947, 33–003
armed forces and, 33–012—33–014
contract, in cases of, 33–004
Crown privilege, 33–022—33–028
discovery, 33–021
estoppel and, 33–016
history, 33–001—33–002
interrogatories, 33–021
judgments and execution, 33–020
jurisdiction, 33–017—33–018
petition of right, scope of,
33–005—33–007
prerogative acts and, 33–014
procedure, 33–017—33–018
public interest immunity,
33–022—33–028
Queen in private capacity, 33–015,
33–019
statutory powers and, 33–014
tort, in cases of, 33–008—33–011
CROWN PROSECUTION SERVICE,
conduct of proceedings, 20–015
Director of Public Prosecutions,
20–014
establishment, 18–013,
powers, 20–014
CURIA REGIS
See also PRIVY COUNCIL
precursor of Parliament, 8–001, 16–001
CUSTOM
source of constitutional law, as, 2–009
CYPRUS, REPUBLIC OF,
constitution
amendment, 1–008
review, 1–011

DAMAGES,
action for,
public authorities and, 32–022
DA NOTICE,
D Notice, replacing, 26–011

DATA,
  definition, 26–025
  protection of
    Act 1998, 26–025—26–026
    encryption by, 26–020
DEBATES,
  basis for, 6–033
  generally, 12–027—12–028
  limiting and organising,
    11–011—11–014
  rules, 11–007—11–010
DECLARATION,
  action for, 32–023
  remedy, as, 32–010
DEFAMATION,
  freedom of expression and,
    25–003—25–005
DEFENCE,
  Advisory (DA) notice, 26–011
  information as to, 26–010
  meaning, 26–007
  Ministry of, 18–003, 18–020
DELEGATED LEGISLATION,
  authority, 29–002
  Codes of Practice, 29–004
  concerns with certain types,
    29–011—29–016
  consultation, 29–038
  European secondary legislation, 6–027
  expenditure, incurring, 29–012
  forms of, 29–003
  growth of, 29–002
  Human Rights Act 1998, effect of,
    29–001
  judicial control, 29–002
  laying before Parliament,
    29–019—29–023
  nature and purpose, 29–002—29–016
  Parliamentary safeguards,
    29–017—29–036
  Parliament's role, usurping, 29–011
  powers, 2–020
    adapt legislation, to, 29–013
    concerns over, 29–011—29–016
    enabling,
      failure to exercise, effect of,
        29–016
    jurisdiction of courts, excluded from,
      29–014
    modify legislation, to, 29–013
    primary legislation distinguished,
      29–001
    publication, 29–036—29–037
    quasi legislation, 29–004
    reasons for, 29–006—29–010

DELEGATED LEGISLATION—cont.
  scrutinising committees,
    29–024—29–029
  special types of, 29–030—29–035
  Statutory Instruments, 29–005
  sub–delegation, 29–015
  taxation, imposing, 29–012
  ultra vires, 29–002, 31–005—31–007
DELEGATUS NON POTEST DELEGARE,
  rule, 31–019
DEMONSTRATIONS,
  See ASSEMBLY, FREEDOM OF, PUBLIC
    MEETINGS
DEPARTMENTS OF GOVERNMENT,
  See GOVERNMENT DEPARTMENTS
DEPENDENCIES,
  administration of, 15–013
  term, 35–011
DEPENDENT TERRITORIES,
  term, 35–010
DEPORTATION,
  confessions, admissibility of, 24–018
  detention with a view to, 23–041
  evidence, admissibility of, 24–018
  Home Secretary's powers, 23–035
  order,
    appeal against, 23–036
    breach of, meaning, 23–028
    making, 23–035
DETENTION,
  access to legal advice, 24–016
  armed forces, 19–012
  conviction, following, 24–031—24–032
  habeas corpus and
    See HABEAS CORPUS
  Immigration Act 1971, under, 24–033
  justification for, 24–001
  medical grounds, on, 24–028—24–030
    See also MENTAL HEALTH ACT
  police, by, 24–012—24–17
  procedure, 24–001
  right to silence, 24–017
  searches in, 24–013—24–016
    intimate, 24–014
    non-intimate, 24–015
  silence, right to, 24–017
  treatment and questioning, 24–013
DEVOLUTION,
  administrative, 5–004
  achievements, 5–050
  Attorney-General's role, 5–023
  background, 5–007
  Cabinet style of government, 5–017
  decentralisation distinguished, 5–002
  effect of, 2–001
  funding, 5–018

DEVOLUTION—*cont.*
England, in, 5–042—5–046
future of, 5–050
generally, 5–001
Guidance Notes, 5–047
human rights and, 5–016
impetus for, 5–006
intra-governmental relations and, 5–047
issues, 5–015
Joint Ministerial Committee, 5–047
Kilbrandon Commission, 5–005, 5–042
Lord Chancellor's role, 2–021
Members' interests, conduct and privileges, 5–019
Memorandum of Understanding, 5–047
nationalism, growth of, 5–004
nature of, 5–002
Northern Ireland, in, 5–008—5–010, 5–029—5–035, 5–050
schemes, generally, 5–012—5–019
Scotland, in, 5–004, 5–020—5–028, 5–050
Secretaries of State, role of, 5–014
term 5–002
Wales, in, 2–002, 5–004, 5–036—5–041, 5–050
DICEY,
administrative law, on, 2–024
civil rights, on, 22–001
conventions, on, 2–029, 7–001, 7–012—7–013
definitions, 1–007, 1–008, 1–009
dismissal of a government, on, 8–024
influence of, 2–023
martial law, on, 19–024
Parliamentary supremacy, on, 2–029, 3–103, 4–003, 22–001
personal liberty, on, 24–001
Royal prerogative, on, 15–003, 15–016
rule of law, on, 2–029—2–032, 15–016
DIPLOMATIC PRIVILEGE,
generally, 15–032—15–033
DIRECTIVE PRINCIPLES OF STATE POLICY,
morally binding, 1–011
DIRECTIVES (EC LAW),
direct effect, 4–016, 6–013—6–014
DIRECTOR OF PUBLIC PROSECUTIONS,
role, 20–014
DISCLAIMER,
peerage, of, 9–005
DISCOVERY,
Crown Proceedings and, 33–021
DISCRIMINATION,
Commission for Racial Equality and, 28–006

DISCRIMINATION—*cont.*
Equal Opportunities Commission, 28–006
DISPENSING,
powers, 3–004—3–006
DISSOLUTION OF PARLIAMENT,
by-election defeats and, 8–020
Cabinet and, 17–006
confidence, vote of, and, 8–019—8–020
conventions governing, 8–019
defeats in the House of Commons and, 8–019—8–021
exceptional situations, 8–022—8–028
general election defeat, on, 8–018
generally, 8–009, 8–013, 8–015
legal position, 8–018
prerogative of, 8–018—8–028
Prime Minister's right to, 8–018—8–021
series of, 8–026
Sovereign, by the, 8–022
dismissal of a ministry, 8–024
refusal of, 8–025—8–026
with or against advice, 8–023
DOMESTIC TRIBUNALS,
supervision, 30–017
DOMINION,
definition, 4–011, 36–003
legislation, 36–004—36–005
extraterritorial operation of, 36–005
U.K. statutes, repugnance to, 36–004
status, 4–011—4–014, 36–001—36–002
DOMINIONS, HER MAJESTY'S,
composition, 35–005
Statute of Westminster, and, 4–011—4–015, 36–001—36–012
DOWNING STREET DECLARATION
Northern Ireland, on, 5–009
DROIT ADMINISTRATIF,
equality before the law and, 2–029—2–030
establishment, 1–013
misunderstanding of, 2–023
protection of the individual, 2–031
DUCHY OF LANCASTER,
Chancellor of, 8–002

EIRE,
See IRELAND, REPUBLIC OF
ELECTIONS,
See also FRANCHISE
appeal on question of law, 10–062
ballot, 10–057
by-, 10–050

ELECTIONS—*cont.*
campaigns, 10–046—10–049
constituency expenditure,
10–050—10–051
national expenditure,
10–052—10–054
law reforms, 10–037—10–041
candidates, 10–047—10–048
selection procedure, 10–059
conduct of, 10–046
corrupt and illegal practices, 10–061
disputed, 10–061
Election court, 10–062
electoral agents, 10–048
Electoral Commission,
10–042—10–045
See also ELECTORAL COMMISSION
expenses, 10–049—10–054
meaning, 10–050
regulation,
constituency spending,
10–050—10–051
generally, 10–049
national campaign spending,
10–052—10–054
third party spending, 10–051,
10–054
European, 6–019—6–020, 9–026
local government, 10–059
media and, 10–055—10–056
referendums, 10–063
returning and registration officers,
10–036
voting system, 6–019—6–020, 9–026,
10–042, 10–058—10–060
alternative proposals, 10–060
E.C.H.R. on, 22–049
ELECTORAL COMMISSION,
appointment, 10–42
boundaries, 10–044
constituencies, 10–044
establishment, 10–042, 10–043
desirability, 10–037
functions, 10–043, 10–045
referendums, supervision of, 10–063
registers of, 10–041
EMERGENCY POWERS,
Act 1920, 19–026—19–027
Act 1963, 19–028
common law, 19–019—19–025
delegated legislation and, 29–012
Energy Act 1976, 19–029
First World War, during, 19–031
Northern Ireland, in, 19–030
martial law, 19–023—19–025

EMERGENCY POWERS—*cont.*
personal freedom and,
19–034—19–036
public order, maintaining,
19–019—19–022
Second World War, during,
19–032—19–034
statutory, 19–026—19–037
peacetime, in, 19–026—19–030
wartime, 19–031—19–037
terrorism,
See TERRORISM
EMPLOYMENT,
tribunal, 30–002
ENFORCEABLE COMMUNITY RIGHTS,
See also EUROPEAN COMMUNITIES,
EUROPEAN COMMUNITIES ACT,
EUROPEAN COMMUNITY LAW
generally, 4–016, 6–017, 6–022
ENGLAND,
devolution in, 5–042
government offices, 5–044
Grand Committee, 5–046
Regional Development Agencies,
creation of, 5–043
provision for, 5–042
representation at Westminster, 5–045
ENVIRONMENT TRANSPORT AND REGIONS,
department of, 18–003, 18–020
EQUAL OPPORTUNITIES COMMISSION,
establishment, 28–006
EQUALITY,
rule of law and, 2–029
ESTIMATES,
government departments' expenditure,
12–006—12–009
ESTOPPEL,
application,
Crown, 33–016
public bodies, 31–020
EUROPEAN ATOMIC ENERGY COMMUNITY,
creation of, 6–001
EUROPEAN COAL AND STEEL COMMUNITY,
creation of, 6–001
EUROPEAN COMMISSION,
composition, 6–007
role of, 6–007
EUROPEAN COMMUNITIES,
See also EUROPEAN COMMUNITIES ACT,
EUROPEAN COMMUNITY LAW,
EUROPEAN COURT OF JUSTICE
accession to, 6–001
aims of, 6–001, 6–014
definition, 6–016
elections, 6–019—6–020

EUROPEAN COMMUNITIES—*cont.*
　enforceable Community rights, 4–016,
　　4–017, 6–017, 6–019, 6–022
　existence of, 6–001
　institutions, 6–003—6–010
　Parliamentary supremacy and,
　　4–017—4–019
　scrutiny reserve, 6–028
　Single European Act 1986 and, 6–002
　Treaties,
　　ancillary, 6–016
　　definition, 6–016
　　additions, 6–016
　Treaty of Amsterdam 1999 and, 6–002,
　　6–027
　Treaty of European Union 1993 and,
　　6–002, 6–027
　U.K. legislation on, 6–015—6–021
EUROPEAN COMMUNITIES ACT 1972,
　ancillary legislation, 6–015
　conflicts with U.K. law, 4–020—4–023
　courts' view of, 4–021—4–023
　definitions, 6–016
　devolution and, 5–015, 5–021, 5–030
　directives and, 4–016
　effect. 4–016, 6–015
　enforceable Community right, 4–016,
　　4–017, 6–017, 6–019, 6–022
　European Court of Justice,
　　reference to, under, 4–016, 6–017,
　　　6–018, 6–019, 6–023—6–026
　House of Lords view of, 4–023
　generally, 4–016
　monist nature of, 6–002
　provisions, of, 4–016, 6–016—6–018
　purpose of, 4–016
　Regulations and, 4–016
　secondary legislation, 6–027
　authorised by, 4–016
　section 2, 4–016, 6–017—6–018,
　　6–022, 6–038
　sovereignty, transfer of by,
　　4–017—4–019
　statesmen's view of, 4–019
　subordinate legislation, power to make,
　　6–018
　supremacy of Community law, 4–021
　Union Acts, whether contrary to,
　　4–007, 6–038
　withdrawal, 4–030
EUROPEAN COMMUNITY,
　See also EUROPEAN ASSEMBLY,
　　EUROPEAN COMMUNITIES ACT,
　　EUROPEAN COMMUNITY LAW

EUROPEAN COMMUNITY LAW,
　See also EUROPEAN ASSEMBLY,
　　EUROPEAN COMMUNITIES ACT,
　　EUROPEAN COMMUNITIES,
　　EUROPEAN COURT OF JUSTICE
　acte clair doctrine, 6–023
　breach of Community rights, effect of,
　　6–038—6–038
　competition in, free, 6–037
　conflicting with U.K. law,
　　4–020—4–023
　devolution and, 5–015, 5–021, 5–030,
　　5–048
　direct applicability, 6–012—6–014,
　　6–021
　direct effect, 6–012—6–013
　directives, 4–016
　　effectiveness of, 6–012—6–014
　　enforceable Community rights in,
　　　4–016
　discrimination and, 6–038
　effect of, 22–014
　equal treatment in, 6–038, 6–039
　European Convention on Human
　　Rights and, 4–024, 6–039—6–040
　free competition in, 6–037
　freedom of movement, 6–035
　free movement of goods, 6–036
　general principles of law,
　　6–039—6–040
　goods, free movement of, 6–036
　horizontal effectiveness, 6–012, 6–013
　impact of, 6–035—6–040
　indirect applicability, 6–013
　interpretation, 6–014
　movement, freedom of, 6–035
　national legislation
　　compatibility of, 6–014
　preliminary rulings, 6–023—6–026
　　U.K. courts, in, 6–025—6–026
　reference to European Court,
　　6–023—6–026
　　U.K. courts, from, 6–025—6–026
　regulations 4–016, 6–012
　secondary legislation, 6–027
　sex discrimination and, 6–038
　scrutiny reserve, 6–028
　sources, 6–011
　supremacy of 4–021, 4–023,
　　6–012—6–014
　vertical effectiveness, 6–012, 6–013
　U.K. law,
　　interpretation of, 6–014
　　source of, as, 6–021

EUROPEAN CONVENTION ON HUMAN RIGHTS AND FUNDAMENTAL FREEDOMS,
assembly and association, freedom of, 27–001, 27–038
devolution and, 5–015 5–021, 5–030
domestic law, as to, 4–024, 22–002, 22–014
E.C. and, 6–039—6–040
effect of, 1–020, 4–024
enforcement, 22–005
expression, freedom of, 25–001—25–002, 25–008
fair trial, right to, 20–012
Human Rights Act, before, 22–007—22–013
Isle of Man and, 35–001
judicial approach to, 22–007—22–008
personal freedom, 24–001
principles, 2–028, 6–001
property, freedom of, 24–054
ratification, 6–001, 22–005
reforms to, 22–006
reliance on, European Court, in, 22–012—22–013
religion, protection of, 25–008
rights guaranteed by, 22–028—22–049
statutory interpretation, as aid to, 22–009—22–011
EUROPEAN COUNCIL,
Council of Ministers distinguished, 6–005
establishment, 6–003
EUROPEAN COUNCIL OF MINISTERS,
composition, 6–005
decisions, 6–005—6–006
European Council distinguished, 6–005
EUROPEAN COURT OF AUDITORS,
composition, 6–010
role, 6–010
EUROPEAN COURT OF FIRST INSTANCE,
appeal to, 6–009
composition, 6–008, 6–009
establishment, 6–008
jurisdiction, 6–008, 6–009
reference to, 6–009
EUROPEAN COURT OF HUMAN RIGHTS,
cases against the U.K., 22–012—22–013
EUROPEAN COURT OF JUSTICE,
See also EUROPEAN COMMUNITIES, EUROPEAN COMMUNITY LAW
acte clair doctrine, 6–023
appeal to, 6–008
composition, 6–008, 6–009
duties, discharge of, 6–011
enforceable Community rights, 4–016

EUROPEAN COURT OF JUSTICE—cont.
European Communities Act and, 4–016
jurisdiction, 6–008—6–009, 6–023
preliminary rulings, 6–009
references to, 4–016, 6–017, 6–018, 6–019, 6–023—6–026
U.K. courts, from, 6–025—6–026
supremacy of, 4–023
EUROPEAN ECONOMIC COMMUNITY,
establishment of, 6–001
European Community, renamed, 6–002
EUROPEAN PARLIAMENT,
composition, 6–004
elections to, 6–019—6–020, 9–026, 10–059
powers, 6–004
EUROPEAN UNION,
citizenship of, effect of, 23–022
creation of, 6–001, 6–002
institutions, 6–003—6–010
Treaty on, 6–003
EXECUTIVE COUNCILS,
colonial, 35–030, 35–031
EXECUTIVE FUNCTION,
generally, 1–015
EXPENDITURE, PUBLIC,
See also NATIONAL FINANCE
Committee of Public Accounts, 12–017, 12–020
generally, 12–005—12–006
legality of, 12–017
survey, 12–006, 12–007
EXPRESSION, FREEDOM OF,
See also EUROPEAN CONVENTION ON HUMAN RIGHTS
blasphemy, 25–007—25–008
broadcasting, 25–033—25–036
cinema, 25–038
common law, at, 26–024
confidentiality, and, 25–020—25–021
constitutionally guaranteed, 25–001
contempt of court and, 20–047, 25–012—25–017
defamation and, 25–003—25–005
human rights and, 25–001—25–002, 25–003, 25–008
incitement to racial hatred, 25–010
indecency and, 25–029—25–030
libel, 25–006
limitations, 25–003—25–039
meaning, 25–001
media, regulating, 25–032—25–039
obscenity and, 25–024—25–031
See also OBSCENITY
official secrecy and, 26–001—26–032
See also OFFICIAL SECRETS

EXPRESSION, FREEDOM OF—*cont.*
  pre-censorship, 25–032
  press, liberty of, 25–018—25–023
  Press Complaints Commission, 25–023
  public interest, 25–023
  sedition, 25–009
  terrorism, 25–011
  theatre, 25–037
  video-recordings, 25–039
EXTRADITION,
  Act 1989, 23–042—23–047
    procedure under, 23–046—23–047
    reliance on, 23–045
  crime, defined, 23–043, 23–045
  exemption, 23–044—23–045
  generally, 23–041
  habeas corpus and, 23–047
  Ireland, to, 23–048—23–049
  person accused, meaning, 23–043
  political character
    definition, 23–044
    offences of, 23–044, 23–045
  procedure, 23–046—23–047

FAIR TRADING,
  director-general of, 28–004—28–005
  tribunal, as, 30–016
FALKLAND ISLANDS,
  nationality, 23–010
FILM,
  censorship, 25–038
FINANCE,
  Bill, 12–003
  national,
    See NATIONAL FINANCE
FINANCIAL SERVICES AUTHORITY,
  appeal from, 30–016
  establishment, 28–005
FIRST LORD OF THE TREASURY,
  role, 17–025
FOREIGN AND COMMONWEALTH OFFICE,
  role, 18–015
FOUNTAIN OF HONOUR,
  Sovereign as, 15–015
FRANCE,
  administrative law in, 1–013, 2–023,
    2–029—2–030, 2–031
  constitution in, 1–006
    amendment, 1–007
    organic laws, promulgation of,
      1–011
  Declaration of the Rights of Man,
    1–020
FRANCHISE,
  See also ELECTIONS
  custody, persons remanded in, 10–032

FRANCHISE—*cont.*
  disqualification, 10–35
  electoral register, 10–027
  history, 10–025
  local government, 10–059
  mental patients, 10–031
  overseas electors, 10–030
  persons remanded in custody, 10–032
  qualifications, 10–026—10–035
  residence, 10–028
    notional, 10–033
  service voters, 10–029
  voters, classes of, 10–029—10–023
  voting, manner of, 10–034
FRANKS COMMITTEE,
  recommendations, 30–003, 30–018,
    30–026, 30–027
FREEDOM,
  assembly, freedom of,
    See ASSEMBLY, FREEDOM OF
  association, 27–038—27–030
  expression, of,
    See EXPRESSION, FREEDOM OF
  information, of,
    See INFORMATION
  person, of the,
    See PERSONAL FREEDOM
  press, of the, 25–018—25–023
  property,
    See PROPERTY, FREEDOM OF
  speech
    See EXPRESSION, FREEDOM OF
FUGITIVE OFFENDERS,
  Act, 1967, 23–042
FUNDAMENTAL LAW,
  judicial review of legislation and,
    1–009—1–011
  Parliamentary supremacy as,
    1–019—1–020
FUNDAMENTAL RIGHTS,
  formulation of, 1–019—1–020

GERMAN FEDERAL REPUBLIC,
  constitution
    amendment, 1–008
    review, 1–011
GHANA,
  Independence, 4–014
GOVERNMENT,
  collective responsibility,
    17–020—17–021
  departments, powers, 2–020
  functions of, 1–015—1–016
  information, access to,
    26–029—26–030

GOVERNMENT—*cont.*
  individual responsibility of,
    17–016—17–019
  local,
    see LOCAL GOVERNMENT
  open, notion of, 26–002
  parliamentary, 2–014
  presidential, 17–035
  representative, 2–016
  responsible, 2–015, 2–017
GOVERNMENT DEPARTMENTS,
  See also CIVIL SERVICE
  Agriculture, Fishers and Food, Ministry
    of, 18–003, 18–020
  Culture, Media and Sport, 18–020
  Defence, 18–003, 18–020
  Education and Employment,
  Environment, Transport and Regions,
    18–003, 18–020
  Foreign and Commonwealth
    Office,18–015
  International Development, 18–020
  functions, transfer of, 18–003, 18–020
  head of, 18–005
  Health, 18–020
  historical origins, 18–001—18–003
  Home Office, 18–014
  Law Officers', 18–010—18–013
  Lord Chancellor's, 18–009
  ministers,
    number of, 10–004, 10–010, 18–004
  Northern Ireland Office, 18–019
  offices of state, 18–001—18–003
  organisation, 18–005—18–006
  Parliamentary Secretaries, 18–006
  Privy Council Office, 18–016, 18–020
  Secretaries of State,
    number of, 18–003
    office, 18–001
    role, 18–005
  Scottish Office, 18–017
  Social Security, 18–020
  statutory creation, 18–003
  Trade and Industry, 18–003
  Treasury, 18–007—18–008
    See also TREASURY
  Welsh Office, 18–018
GOVERNORS, COLONIAL,
  role, 35–028
  powers, 35–029
GREAT COUNCIL,
  House of Lords' origin in, 9–002
GREAT SEAL,
  custody of 18–001

GUILLOTINE,
  motion, 11–014

HABEAS CORPUS,
  Act 1679, 24–035
  Act 1816, 24–036
  appeals, 24–039
  availability, 24–034
  immigration cases, in, 23–040
  origins, 24–034
  places overseas, to, 24–040
  procedure on, 24–037
  purpose, 24–037
  successive applications, 24–038
  writ of right, 24–034
HEALTH AND SAFETY,
  work, at, 28–006
HEALTH SERVICE COMMISSIONERS,
  establishment, 34–015
HELIGOLAND,
  cession, 4–014
HIGH COURT,
  See also JUDICIAL REVIEW
  supervisory jurisdiction, 30–017,
    30–022, 32–002
HIGH COURT OF PARLIAMENT,
  court, meaning, 8–001
  history, 8–001—8–002
HIGHER LAW,
  Parliamentary supremacy and,
    3–011—3–012, 4–001
HIGHWAY,
  obstruction, 27–028
HOME OFFICE,
  functions, 18–014
  powers, 2–020, 23–034
HOME SECRETARY,
  rules, 24–032
HONG KONG,
  Parliamentary supremacy in, 4–033
HOUGHTON COMMITTEE,
  report of the, 2–016
HOUSE OF COMMONS,
  See also LEGISLATION, NATIONAL
    FINANCE, PARLIAMENTARY
    PROCEDURE
  Act of Settlement, 10–003
  administration, scrutiny of the,
    12–021—12–033
  affirmation and oath, 10–002
  age limits for membership, 10–005
  aliens, disqualified, 10–005
  armed forces disqualified, 10–007
  bankruptcy disqualifies, 10–005
  casual vacancies, 13–017
  Chairman of Ways and Means, 10–022

HOUSE OF COMMONS—*cont.*
Chiltern Hundreds and, 10–011
civil service disqualified, 10–007
clergy disqualified, 10–005
Clerk of, 10–020
commission members disqualified,
    10–007
committees of, 11–016
composition, right to determine,
    13–017
confidence, vote of, 8–019—8–020
corrupt and illegal practices
    disqualifying, 10–005
crimes disqualifying, 10–005
Disqualification Acts, 10–004,
    10–007—10–014
disqualification from membership,
    10–002—10–014
    effect of, 10–012
    Privy Council, jurisdiction of,
        10–013
elections to, 10–025—10–063
    See also ELECTIONS
E.U. law, scrutiny of,
    committee, by, 6–029—6–031
    debate, by, 6–034
Father of, 10–016
foreign legislators disqualified, 10–007
franchise, 10–025—10–036
    See also FRANCHISE
government contractors, 10–004
history, 10–001—10–004
judiciary disqualified, 10–007
legislation
    See LEGISLATION
Lords,
    conflict with, 8–029—8–039
    See also PARLIAMENT ACTS
    relations with, 7–018
membership, 10–001—10–024
    interests and conduct, 5–019,
        13–028—13–034
mental illness disqualifies, 10–005
ministers,
        number limited, 10–004, 10–010,
            18–004
        responsibility to Parliament, 2–015
            17–016—17–021
oath and affirmation, 10–002
obligation to accept office,
    relaxation, 10–014
office of profit under the Crown,
    10–003, 10–007, 10–011
payment of members, 10–015
peers and peeresses disqualified,
    10–005

HOUSE OF COMMONS—*cont.*
pensions
    Crown, from, and 10–003
    Members, to, 10–015
police forces disqualified, 10–007
privileges,
    See also PARLIAMENTARY PRIVILEGE
    generally, 13–004—13–024
Privy Council, jurisdiction over
    qualification, 10–013
procedure in, 11–001—11–029,
    11–031—11–038
    See also PARLIAMENTARY PROCEDURE
register of members' interests
    establishment, 5–019, 13–029
    purpose, 13–034
    unenforceable, 13–029
role, 2–020
Roman Catholic Relief Act, 10–002
scrutiny reserve. 6–028
Serjeant-at-Arms, 10–021
Speaker, 10–016—10–019
    See also SPEAKER OF THE HOUSE OF
        COMMONS
specified officers disqualified, 10–007
staff, 10–023
treason disqualifies, 10–005
tribunal members disqualified, 10–007
whips, 10–024
women, admission of, 10–002
HOUSE OF LORDS,
    See also LEGISLATION, PARLIAMENTARY
        PROCEDURE
abolition of competent, 3–019
Act 1999, 9–035
Appellate Committee,
    Constitutional Court, as, 9–052
Appellate Jurisdiction Act, 9–097
Appointments Commission, 9–011
    reformed second chamber, of, 9–039
attendance, Standing Orders as to,
    9–014
Chairman of Committees, 9–018
Clerk of the Parliaments, 9–019
Committee on Lords Interests, 13–035
Commons,
    conflict with, 8–029—8–039
    See also PARLIAMENT ACTS
    relations with, 7–018
composition, 3–019, 9–001,
    9–007—9–019
    reformed second chamber, of, 9–038
        appointed members, 9–039
        existing life peers, 9–042
        generally, 9–038

HOUSE OF LORDS—*cont.*
composition—*cont.*
　reformed second chamber, of—*cont.*
　　Lords of Appeal in Ordinary,
　　　9–042
　　regional members, 9–040
　　religious representation, 9–040
　　transitional, 9–007, 9–009, 9–035
　Court of Appeal, as final,
　　9–044—9–051, 20–008
　delaying power,
　　exercise, 9–024
　　reduction, 8–032
　disqualification from membership,
　　9–013
　E.U. law, scrutiny of,
　　committee, by, 6–029, 6–032
　　debate, by, 6–034
　functions, 9–020—9–033
　　delay of legislation, 9–024—9–027
　　general debate, 9–031
　　pre-legislative scrutiny, 9–021
　　private bills,
　　　initiation of, 9–028
　　　scrutiny of, 9–028
　　public bills,
　　　initiation of, 9–028
　　　revision of, 9–022—9–023
　　reformed second chamber, of, 9–037
　　scrutiny
　　　delegated legislation, of, 9–029
　　　E.U. matters, of, 9–030
　　　Executive, of the, 9–030
　　Select Committees, 9–033
　Gentlemen Usher of the Black Rod,
　　9–019
　general debate, 9–031
　hereditary peerages,
　　disclaimer of, 9–005
　　elected, 9–009
　　exclusion of holders of, 9–003
　history, 9–002
　Judicial Committee,
　　Constitutional Court, as, 9–052
　legislation,
　　delaying, 9–024—9–027
　　delegated, scrutinising, 9–029
　　initiating, 9–028
　　revising, 9–022—9–023
　　scrutinising delegated, 9–029
　Lord Chancellor in, 9–015—9–018,
　　9–050, 18–009
　Lords of Appeal in Ordinary, 9–012,
　　9–041
　Lords Spiritual, 9–008
　limitation of powers, 2–016

HOUSE OF LORDS—*cont.*
　Money Bills,
　　See MONEY BILLS
　officers, 9–015—9–019
　peerage
　　claims, 9–004
　　future of the, 9–006
　　hereditary, 9–003, 9–005, 9–009
　　life, 9–010, 9–042
　　personal privileges, 13–027
　　powers, 9–020—9–033
　　privileges, 13–026—13–027
　　procedure in, 11–030
　　recent development, 9–003
　　reform, 9–034—9–043
　　　history, 9–034
　　　Parliament Acts and, 8–032, 8–034
　　　Royal Commission
　　　　recommendations,
　　　　　9–036—9–042
　　　two stages, 9–035
　　register of interests, 13–035
　　resources,
　　　reformed second chamber, of, 9–043
　　role, 2–020
　　　reformed second chamber, of, 9–037
　　Royal Commission on,
　　　establishment, 9–001, 9–035
　　　recommendations, 9–036—9–042
　　　terms of reference, 9–036
　　Scottish courts, appeals to and from,
　　　9–051, 20–008
　　scrutiny
　　　delegated legislation, 9–029
　　　E.U. matters, 9–030
　　　Executive, of the, 9–030
　　　reserve, 6–028
　　Select Committees, 9–032–9–033
　　Sergjeant-at-Arms, 9–019
　　Speaker, 9–015, 18–009
　　Standing Orders on attendance, 9–014
　　transitional, 9–007, 9–009, 9–035
HUMAN RIGHTS,
　See also HUMAN RIGHTS ACT 1998
　European Convention on,
　　See EUROPEAN CONVENTION ON
　　　HUMAN RIGHTS
　Civil servants role, 18–031
　devolved bodies and, 5–016
　fundamental rights, 1–019—1–020
　international covenants, 22–004
　Lord Chancellor's role, 18–009
　U.K. Constitution and, 2–034
HUMAN RIGHTS ACT, 1998,
　application, 22–050—22–055

HUMAN RIGHTS ACT, 1998—*cont.*
  enactment, 22–003
    effect of, 1–019
  entry into force, 6–001
  Convention rights, 22–028—22–049
  scheme of, 22–015—22–027
HYBRID BILLS,
  nature of, 11–020—11–021

ILLEGAL ENTRANT,
  definition, 23–029
IMMIGRATION,
  Act 1971, 23–024—23–029
    detention under, 24–033
  Act 1988, 23–026
  appeals, 23–035—23–037
    one-stop procedure, 23–037
  asylum, 23–031—23–034
    statutory provisions, 23–031
  Asylum Act 1999, and, 23–031
  amendments, 23–026
  appeals system, establishing,
    23–035—23—036
  deportation, 23–034
  E.U. nationals, 23–026
  history, 23–023
  human rights and, 23–023, 23–037
  illegal entrants, 23–028—23–030
    laws, in breach of,
      meaning, 23–029
  judicial review, 23–038—23–040
  leave to enter,
    refusal of, 23–027
    requirement for, 23–026
  Refugee Convention, 23–031—23–033
  regulation and control, 23–026
    exemptions from, 23–026
  remedies, 23–038—23–040
    effective, 23–036
  removal of persons unlawfully in U.K.,
    23–030
  right of abode, 23–025
  rules, 23–024
  Special Appeals Commission,
    23–037—23–037
  tribunal, 30–014
IMMUNITY,
  Crown, of, 33–001
  diplomatic, 15–032—15–033
  judicial, 2–019, 20–041—20–042
  public interest
    See PUBLIC INTEREST IMMUNITY
IMPEACHMENT,
  judicial proceedings, 8–004—8–005

INCITEMENT,
  disaffection, to, 25–009
  mutiny, to, 25–009
  racial hatred, to, 25–010
INDECENCY,
  See also OBSCENITY
  offence of, 25–029—25–030
INDEPENDENCE,
  Acts, 4–014—4–015, 36–014—36–015
  constitutions, 36–016—36–017
  grant of,
    Parliamentary supremacy and,
      4–011—4–105
INDEPENDENT TELEVISION COMMISSION,
  role, 28–003
INDIA,
  constitution in, 1–011, 2–032
  responsible Parliamentary government,
    2–015
  voting system, 10–058
INITIATIVE,
  law-making method, as, 1–105
INFORMATION,
  access to,
    environmental, 26–027
    generally, 26–024
    government, 26–029—26–031
    local government, 26–028
    personal, 26–025—26–026
  availability of, 26–001
  breach of confidence, 26–012
  Commission, 26–031, 30–016
  data protection, 26–025—26–026
  disclosure in the public interest,
    26–032
  freedom of, 26–002
    Act 2000, 26–029—26–030
      enforcement, 26–031
      implementation, 26–031
    concept, 26–024
    open government and,
      26–024—26–032
  local government, 26–028
  official secrets, 26–003—26–012
    See also OFFICIAL SECRETS
  public interest disclosure, 26–032
  right to seek and receive, 26–001
  State interference, 26–001.
    26–0013—26–023
  Tribunal, 26–031
INJUNCTION,
  remedy, as, 32–010, 32–023
INLAND REVENUE,
  concessions, 3–006
INNER CABINET,
  role, 17–013

INQUIRIES,
Inspector's report, 30–027
Ministerial decisions and,
30–024—30–028
procedure, 30–026
provisions for, 30–025
role of Minister, 30–028
INSPECTORS,
inquiry, 30–027
INSTRUMENT OF GOVERNMENT,
Cromwell's, 2–006
INTELLIGENCE SERVICES,
See SECURITY SERVICES
Commissioner, 26–021—26–022
Tribunal, 26–023
INTERCEPTION OF COMMUNICATIONS,
See COMMUNICATIONS
INTERNATIONAL,
covenants, 22–004
law, primacy of, 4–001
relations, information as to, 26–008,
26–010
INTERROGATORIES,
Crown Proceedings and, 33–021
IRELAND, NORTHERN,
See NORTHERN IRELAND
IRELAND, REPUBLIC OF,
Acts of Union and, 4–005
British nationality, retention of, 23–018
constitution in, 1–010, 1–011, 2–032
entry without leave, 23–026
extradition arrangements with,
23–048—23–049
Northern Irish problems, as to, 5–008
secession from Commonwealth, 4–005
Statute of Westminster 1931, 4–011
ISLE OF MAN,
British Isles, in, 35–001—35–002
E.C.H.R. and, 35–001
tax haven, as, 35–003
ISRAEL,
constitution in, 1–006
ITALY,
constitution
review, 1–011

JENNINGS, SIR IVOR,
administrative law defined, 1–013
conventions, on, 7–003, 7–006, 7–010,
8–027
JUDICIAL COMMITTEE OF THE PRIVY
COUNCIL,
appeals to,
right of grant, 37–003—37–005
discretion of local court, at,
37–005

JUDICIAL COMMITTEE OF THE PRIVY
COUNCIL—*cont.*
appeals to—*cont.*
right of grant—*cont.*
right, as of, 37–004
special leave, by, 37–006—37–008
civil, 37–007
criminal, 37–008
Statute of Westminster and, 37–010
Channel Islands, from, 35–003
Commonwealth Court of Appeal,
proposed, 37–016
composition, 16–010
death penalty overseas, as to, 16–012
devolution and, 16–012
history, 16–009
human rights and, 37–013—37–015
Isle of Man, from, 35–002
jurisdiction, 2–020, 5–015, 5–040,
9–052, 10–013, 16–011, 20–008
new role, 16–012
precedents, 37–011
procedure, 16–013
special reference, 16–014
Statute of Westminster and, 37–010
warning jurisdiction of, 37–012
JUDICIAL FUNCTION,
generally, 1–015
Parliament, of, 8–003
JUDICIAL PRECEDENT,
source of constitutional law, as, 2–008
JUDICIAL REVIEW,
See also PUBLIC AUTHORITIES
abuse of power, 31–008—31–010
administrative action, of,
See also PUBLIC AUTHORITIES
alternative remedies, effect of, 32–013
application for, 32–001—32–015
audi alteram partem, 31–016—31–019
delegatus non potest delegare, 31–019
discretionary procedure, 23–038,
32–014
estoppel, 31–020
grounds, 31–002
immigration matters, of,
23–038—23–039
jurisdiction of courts excluded,
32–017—32–021
legislation, of, 1–009—1–011, 2–020
legitimate expectations, 31–018
natural justice, 31–013—31–018
nemo judex in re sua, 31–014—31–015
non-justiciability and, 32–021
Parliamentary Commissioner for
Administration, of, 34–013

JUDICIAL REVIEW—*cont.*
  procedural impropriety,
    31–013—31–018
  public processions, decisions as to,
    27–016, 27–017
  remedies, 32–001—32–023
    availability of other, effect of,
      32–013
    certiorari, 32–003—32–006
    declaration, 32–010
    injunction, 32–010
    mandamus, 32–009
    prohibition, 32–007—32–008
  scope, 32–012
  Speaker's decision, of, refused, 10–019
  sub-delegation of powers, 31–019
  sufficient interest, 32–011
  ultra vires rule, 31–003—31–007
  unreasonableness, 31–011—31–012
JUDICIARY,
  See also ADMINISTRATION OF JUSTICE
  administration, 20–034
  advice to executive, 20–032—20–033
  appointment system, 20–006, 20–026
    conditions, 20–034
    reform to, 20–027—20–028
    terms, 20–034
  circuit,20–030
  Commons, disqualified from, 10–007,
    20–037
  discipline, 20–031
  district, 20–030
  duties, 2–021, 20–026,
    20–032—20–033
  executive,
    no general duty to advise,
      20–032—20–033
  human rights and, 20–028, 20–031,
    20–033, 20–039
  immunity of, 2–019, 20–041—20–042
  impartiality, 20–036—20–040
  independence of, 2–018—2–019,
    20–025—20–035
    generally, 20–025
  justice of the peace, 20–030
  Lord Chancellor and, 9–017—9–018,
    20–026—20–028
  natural justice, 20–038
  non-judicial duties of, 20–033
  oath, 20–026
  proceedings of, publicity, 20–040
  removal of, 2–018, 20–029
  resignation, 20–031
  retirement, 20–029
  salaries of, 2–019, 20–029
  sentencing, 20–035

JUDICIARY—*cont.*
  superior, 20–029
  tenure, 20–029—20–030
  training, 20–031
JURISDICTION, ADMINISTRATIVE,
  See ADMINISTRATIVE JURISDICTION
JURISPRUDENCE,
  generally, 1–002—1–003
JURY,
  challenge, 20–020—20–023
  impartiality, 20–020—20–023
  reform proposals, 20–024
  service, 20–019
  trial by, 20–017—20–024
    civil cases, in, 20–018
    coroner's cases, in, 20–018
    criminal cases, in 20–017
    generally, 20–017
  vetting, 20–020—20–023
JUSTICE, ADMINISTRATION OF,
  See also JUDICIARY
  appointment of judges, 20–006, 0–026
  civil proceedings, 20–013
  contempt of court,
    See also CONTEMPT OF COURT
  courts, 20–007—20–011
    See also COURTS
  criminal proceedings, 20–014—20–016
    legal aid, 20–016
  Crown, position of, 20–002—20–005
  generally, 20–001
  jury trial and, 20–017—20–023
  nolle prosequi, 20–003
  prerogative and, 20–002—20–005
  proceedings,
    civil, 20–013
    criminal, 20–014—20–016
    initiation of, 20–012
    legal aid, 20–016
    publicity of, 20–040
  publicity of proceedings, 20–040
JUSTICES OF THE PEACE,
  appointment, 20–026
  ex-officio, 20–026
  removal, 20–030
  role, 20–009
JUSTICIARY, HIGH COURT OF,
  Act of Union and, 4–007

KILBRANDON COMMISSION,
  See also DEVOLUTION
  reports, 5–005, 5–042

LAW,
  constitutional,
    See CONSTITUTIONAL LAW

LAW—*cont.*
  constitutional—*cont.*
    generally, 1–001
  custom of Parliament, and, 1–002,
    2–009
  definition, 1–002—1–003
  enforcement, 1–002
  fundamental, 1–009—1–011
  international,
    See INTERNATIONAL LAW
  meaning, 1–002—1–003
  morality and, 1–003
  natural justice principles, 6–039
  organic, 1–006
  Queen, not enforceable against, 1–002
  state, 1–004
LAW COMMISSIONS,
  Act, 9–017
LAW OFFICERS,
  departments, 18–010
LAYMEN,
  part played by, 20–009
LEARNING AND SKILLS COUNCIL,
  establishment, 28–006
LEGAL AID,
  civil proceedings, in, 20–013
  criminal proceedings, in, 20–016
LEGAL RULES,
  private morality distinguished, 1–003
  public morality distinguished, 1–003
LEGAL SECRETARIAT,
  composition, 18–013
LEGAL SERVICES COMMISSION,
  establishment, 20–013, 20–016
LEGISLATION,
  See also BILLS, PARLIAMENT ACTS,
    PARLIAMENTARY PROCEDURE
  carry over of bills, 11–032
  classification, 11–020—11–021
  compatibility with E.C.H.R., 4–024
  delegated,
    See DELEGATED LEGISLATION
  devolution, 5–005—5–006,
    5–020—5–041
  Dominions, extended to, 36–006
  drafting, 11–019
  hybrid bills, 11–020—11–021
  judicial review of, 1–009
  manner and form, 4–025—4–037
  primary defined, 29–001
  private bills, 11–020
  Private Members' Bills,
    11–034—11–035
  procedure on, 11–018—11–038
    generally, 11–018
    Lords, in the, 11–030

LEGISLATION—*cont.*
  procedure on—*cont.*
    ordinary on public bills,
      11–022—11–029
    private bills, 11–036—11–038
  public bills, 11–020
  Royal Assent, 11–031
  scrutiny, 11–033
  sovereign, by, 3–002—3–012
  subject matter of, 4–002—4–024
  subordinate,
    See DELEGATED LEGISLATION
LEGISLATIVE FUNCTIONS,
  generally, 1–015
LEGISLATURES, COLONIAL,
  composition, 35–028
  powers, 35–022—35–027
LEGITIMATE EXPECTATIONS,
  natural justice and, 31–018
LIBEL,
  criminal, 25–006
  obscene, 25–028
LOCAL GOVERNMENT,
  access to information, 26–028
  history of, 2–035
  inauguration, 2–036
  Ombudsmen, 34–016—34–017
  powers, 2–020
  structure, 2–035
LOCKE,
  functions of government, on, 1–105
  fundamental rights, on, 1–019
  separation of powers, on, 1–017
LONDON,
  City of London Corporation, 2–036
    police, 21–002, 21–012
  directly elected mayor, 2–037
  government of, 2–036
    City, outside the, 2–037
    standards, raising, 2–037
    elections for, 10–059
  Lord Mayor and aldermen
    appointment, 20–026
  policing, 21–002, 21–003
    accountability, 21–004
    authorities, 21–013
    Commissioner of Metropolitan
      Police,
    appointment, 21–014
LORD ADVOCATE,
  office, 18–010
LORD CHANCELLOR,
  circuit judges, as to, 20–030
  department, 18–009
  office, history of, 18–001—18–002

LORD CHANCELLOR—*cont.*
role of, 2–020, 20–026—20–027
devolution issues, in, 2–021
House of Lords, in, 9–015—9–018
scrutiny, under, 18–009
tribunals, functions as to, 30–019
LORD PRESIDENT OF THE COUNCIL,
duties, 18–002, 18–016
LORD PRIVY SEAL,
duties, 18–002, 18–020
office, 18–001
LORDS OF APPEAL,
in ordinary, 9–012, 9–041
security of tenure, 2–018

MAGNA CARTA,
nature of, 2–007
MAGNUM CONCILIUM,
House of Lords' origin in, 9–002
MAITLAND,
martial law, on, 19–009
Parliament, on, 28–001
MALADMINISTRATON,
See OMBUDSMEN
MANDAMUS,
order, 32–008
MANDATE,
doctrine of, 3–023
MANIFESTOES,
party, 3–023
MARTIAL LAW,
English law, whether known to,
19–034—19–035
Maitland on, 19–010
MEETING, PUBLIC,
See ASSEMBLY, FREEDOM OF, PUBLIC
MEETING
MENTAL HEALTH ACT,
detention under, 24–029—24–030
Mental Health Review Tribunal,
24–030
restriction order, 24–029
rights under, 24–030
MERCY,
prerogative of, 2–020, 20–004
MILITARY FORCES,
See ARMED FORCES
MILITARY LAW,
generally, 19–008
MINISTERS,
appointment and dismissal,
prerogative powers, 15–013
Code of conduct, 17–017, 17–018
delegated legislation, 29–003
functions, 2–019

MINISTERS—*cont.*
number limited, 10–004, 10–010,
18–004
powers, 2–020
responsible to Parliament, 2–015,
17–016—17–021
next steps agencies, impact of,
18–024
role, 2–020
MITCHELL,
conventions, on , 7–003
MONARCHY,
See also PREROGATIVE, ROYAL,
SOVEREIGN
Commonwealth and, 36–021—36–023
constitutional, 2–013, 7–009
limited, 2–013, 2–017
title to the throne, 14–002
MONEY BILLS,
See also PARLIAMENT ACTS
delay by Lords of one month, 8–034
early conflicts, 8–029
enactment without Lords' consent,
8–034
meaning, 8–034
Parliament Act 1911 and,
8–030—8–031, 8–034
rejection of, 8–029
unaffected by Parliament Act 1949,
8–033
MONOPOLIES,
grant of, 3–007
MONTESQUIEU,
functions of government, on, 1–015
political liberty, on, 1–017
separation of powers, on, 2–022
MONTFORT, SIMON DE,
founder of House of Commons,
10–001
MUTINY ACT,
effect of, 19–002

NATIONAL ASSEMBLY FOR WALES,
See WALES
NATIONAL FINANCE,
annual cycle, 12–004
Bank of England, 12–016
budget resolutions, 12–014
Committee of Public Accounts,
12–017, 12–020
Comptroller and Auditor General,
12–018—12–019
Consolidated Fund
Acts, 12–009
services, 12–005
Contingencies Fund, 12–010

NATIONAL FINANCE—*cont.*
Crown and Commons,
12–002—12–003
Departmental Select Committees, role,
12–011
estimates, 12–006—12–009
consideration of, 12–008
Finance Bill, 12–015
public expenditure, 12–005—12–006
legality of, securing, 12–017
survey, 12–006, 12–007
public revenue, 12–012
regulation of, 12–001
supply,
business, 12–008
guillotine, 12–009
services, 12–005
ways and means business, 12–013
NATIONAL HEALTH SERVICE,
Act 1946, 28–11
bodies, 28–003
NATIONALITY,
Act of 1914, 23–002
Act of 1948, 23–003—23–004
Act of 1981, 23–005
aliens, 23–019
enemy, 23–020—23–021
citizenship of the E.U., and, 23–018
allegiance and, 23–001
British citizenship,
acquisition, 23–004, 23–007
legal rights conferred, 23–007
loss of, 23–011
naturalisation, by, 23–004, 23–008
registration, by, 23–004, 23–009
resumption of, 23–012
British Dependent Territories
citizenship, 23–013
British National (Overseas), 23–017
British Overseas citizenship, 23–014
British Protected Persons,
status, 23–016
British subjects,
status, 23–003, 23–005, 23–015
Canada and, 23–003
citizen of U.K. and colonies,
23–003—3–005
concept, 23–001
Commonwealth citizen,
23–003, 23–005
E.U. citizens, 23–022
Falkland Islanders, of, 23–010
Hong Kong inhabitants, of, 23–017
immigration controls, 23–026—23–033
See also IMMIGRATION
Irish citizens, 23–018

NATIONALITY—*cont.*
patriality and, 23–018
NATURALISATION,
citizenship, by, 23–004, 23–008
NATURAL JUSTICE,
denial, 32–004
principles, 6–039, 31–003—31–018
NATURAL LAW,
no judicial decision in favour, 4–001
NEMO JUDEX IN RE SUA,
doctrine, 31–013, 31–014—31–015
NEW ZEALAND,
citizenship, 32–026
constitution in, 1–006
Dominion status of, 4–011
Parliamentary supremacy in, 4–031
Prime Minister, 17–032
Statute of Westminster and, 36–012
voting system, 10–058
NEXT STEPS AGENCIES,
Constitutional issues, 18–024
development, 18–023
financing, 18–023
NIGERIA,
Independence, 4–014
NOLLE PROSEQUI,
Attorney General, by, 2–020, 20–003
NORTHERN IRELAND,
Anglo-Irish agreement, 5–008
Assembly
Code of Conduct, 5–019, 5–032
committees, election of, 5–033
creation of, 5–010—5–011
elections for, 5–011
functions, 5–030, 5–032, 5–035
legislative,
competence, 5–030
pledge of office, 5–035
primary legislation, 5–034
procedure, 5–034
powers, 5–030
scrutiny functions, 5–035
secondary legislation, 5–034
Belfast Agreement,
aspects of, 5–010
conclusion of, 5–009
implementation of, 5–011
North/South Ministerial Council,
5–047
referendum on, 5–010
British-Irish Council, 5–048
constitutional status, 2–004—2–005,
4–005
courts of, 2–004, 20–010
devolution for,
background to, 5–029

NORTHERN IRELAND—*cont.*
　devolution for—*cont.*
　　electoral system, 5–013
　　funding, 5–018
　　government, Cabinet style, 5–017
　　human rights and, 5–016, 5–030
　　institutional framework for, 5–010
　　issues, 5–015
　　Order, 5–011
　　members' interests, conduct and
　　　privileges, 5–019, 5–032, 5–035
　　provisions for, generally, 5–012
　　subordination to Westminster, 5–014
　　suspension of, 5–011
　Downing Street Declaration, 5–009
　emergency legislation in, 19–029
　Executive,
　　appointment, 5–031
　　Code of Conduct, 5–019, 5–032
　　composition, 5–031
　　dismissal, 5–031
　　functions, 5–030, 5–032
　government, 5–003
　Grand Committee, 5–046
　Office, 18–019
　ombudsmen, 34–017
　Parliamentary Commission, 34–010
NORTHERN IRELAND ASSEMBLY,
　See NORTHERN IRELAND

OBSCENITY,
　defence to, 25–026
　forfeiture of articles, 25–027
　history, 25–024
　indecency and, 25–029—25–030
　obscene libel, 25–028
　Obscene Publications Act 1959,
　　25–025
　reform of law, 25–031
　statutory offence, 25–025
　test of, 25–024
OBSTRUCTING A CONSTABLE,
　definition, 24–021
　generally, 24–019
　mens rea required, 24–021
OFFENCES AGAINST THE STATE,
　incitement,
　　mutiny or disaffection, 25–009
　　racial hatred, to, 25–010
　official secrets and,
　　See OFFICIAL SECRETS
　public order, 25–009—25–011
　sedition, 25–009
　terrorism, 25–011
　　See TERRORISM

OFFENCES AGAINST THE STATE—*cont.*
　treason,
　　See TREASON
OFFICES OF STATE,
　See also GOVERNMENT DEPARTMENTS
　generally, 18–001—18–003
OFFICIAL SECRETS,
　Act 1911, 26–003
　Act 1920, 26–004
　Act 1989, 26–005
　categories of, 26–005—26–010
　　crime, 26–009
　　defence, 27–007
　　international relations, 26–008
　　security and intelligence, 26–006
　　special investigation powers, 26–009
　Chandler v. DPP, 26–003
　confidence, breach of, 26–012
　DA notices, 26–011
　disclosure, 26–010
　freedom of information,
　　See also INFORMATION, FREEDOM OF
　　open government, and, 26–002,
　　　26–024—26–032
　generally, 26–001
　press, position of, 26–010
　prohibited place, 26–003
　purpose, meaning, 26–003
　State,
　　See also STATE
　　meaning, 26–003
　　surveillance, 26–001,
　　　26–013—26–023
OMBUDSMEN,
　appointment, 34–007, 34–016, 34–015,
　　34–017
　Commissions for local administration,
　　34–016—34–017
　devolution, effect of, 34–010
　generally, 34–001
　Health Service Commissioners, 34–015
　investigation of complaints, 34–008
　judicial review, 34–013
　jurisdiction, 34–009
　local government, 34–016—34–017
　maladministration, 34–005
　Northern Ireland, in, 34–010
　Parliamentary Commissioner for
　　Administration, 34–001, 34–006
　private sector, 34–018
　reform, 34–014
　reports, 34–011
　Select Committee on, 34–012
　Scotland, in, 34–010
　Wales, in, 34–010

OPPOSITION,
Leader of the, 2–016
ORDER IN COUNCIL,
nature of, 16–005
OVERLORDS,
experiment, 17–009

PARDON,
prerogative of, 20–005
PARLIAMENT,
See also HOUSE OF COMMONS, HOUSE
OF LORDS, PARLIAMENTARY
PROCEDURE, PARLIAMENTARY
SUPREMACY
Acts of,
See ACTS OF PARLIAMENT
adjournment of, 8–009
Attainder, Acts of, 8–006
bribery of members, 13–009
Coke on, 8–001
Commons and Lords in conflict,
8–029—8–039
See also PARLIAMENT ACTS
Curia Regis, descended from, 8–001
composition, alterable, 3–019
contempt of, 13–009
delegated legislation, control of,
29–017—29–038
demise of the Crown and, 8–014
dissolution, 8–009, 8–013, 8–015
See also DISSOLUTION OF
PARLIAMENT
prerogative of, 8–018—8–028
duration of, 8–009, 8–013—8–014
emergence, 3–002
frequency of, 8–013—8–014
High Court of, 8–001—8–039
history, 8–001—8–008
houses, division into, 10–001
impeachment, 8–004—8–005
Inquiry, Committees and Tribunals of,
8–007
judicial functions, 8–003—8–006
law and custom, 1–002, 4–030, 13–002
Lords and Commons in conflict,
8–029—8–039
meaning, 4–031
meeting, 8–009—8–017
new, of, 8–016
ministerial responsibility, 2–015,
17–016—17–021
next steps agencies, impact of,
18–014
Money Bills
See MONEY BILLS

PARLIAMENT—cont.
privileges of,
See PARLIAMENTARY PRIVILEGE
proceedings in, 13–006—13–008
prorogation of, 8–009, 8–012
public corporations, regulating,
28–016—28–017
questions in, 12–022—12–026
recess, 8–012
Reform Bill, 8–029
Royal Assent in, 8–011, 8–012
Royal prerogative in, 8–010—8–012
Sayles on, 8–002
Scottish,
See SCOTLAND
secondary Community legislation, role
in making, 6–027
session, beginning of new, 8–017
Sovereign's presence in, 8–010
summons of new, 8–015
supremacy of, 2–006, 2–012, 2–020
PARLIAMENT ACTS,
Acts passed under, 9–025—9–026
amendments, effect of, 4–037
delaying power of the Lords under,
8–034, 8–038
purpose, 8–033
delegated legislative procedure, 4–035
duration of Parliament, 8–013
events leading to 1911 Act,
8–030—8–031, 9–034
events leasing to 1949 Act,
8–032—8–033, 9–034
excluded measures, 8–036, 8–037
House of Lords,
reform of, 8–032, 8–034
without consent of, 4–036
Money Bills and, 8–034
Parliamentary supremacy and,
4–035—4–037
provisions, 8–034—8–036
reforms proposed
1968, in, 8–038
2000, in, 8–039
retroactive effect of, 8–033
Speaker's certificate, 8–034, 8–035,
8–036
validity of 1949 Act doubted, 4–035
Wakeham report, 8–039
PARLIAMENT ROLLS,
source of Parliament Acts, 4–026
PARLIAMENTARY COMMISSIONER FOR
ADMINISTRATION,
See OMBUDSMEN
PARLIAMENTARY GOVERNMENT,
responsible, 2–014—2–016, 2–017

PARLIAMENTARY PRIVILEGE,
advocacy, prohibition on paid,
13–018,13–029, 13–033
arrest, freedom from, 13–016
breach of, 13–021
penalties, 13–024—13–025
procedure on complaint of, 13–023
bribery a contempt, 13–009
broadcasting, 13–013
Code of Conduct, 13–029, 13–032
Coke on, 13–002
Committees,
Members' Interests, on, 13–028,
13–029
Privileges, of, 13–028, 13–029
Standards in Public Life,
establishment, 13–028
replacement of former
Committees, 13–029
role, 13–031, 13–028
Commons, of, 13–004—13–025
composition of, right to determine,
13–017
contempt,
examples, 13–021
meaning, 13–020
penalties, 13–024—13–025
procedure on complaint of, 13–023
types, 13–022
courts and Parliament, 13–003
Defamation Act 1996, s. 13, 13–015
freedom of speech and debate,
13–005—13–015
human rights, effect on, 13–003
Lords, of, 13–026—13–027
members' conduct and interests,
13–028—13–035
misconduct cases, 13–031
register of, 13–029, 13–034
Parliament's disciplinary and penal
powers, 13–020—13–025
nature, 13–001—13–003
Parliamentary Commissioner for
Standards,
appointment, 13–029, 13–030
register, 13–029, 13–034
role, 13–030
Parliamentary papers, publication of,
13–011—13–012
proceedings in Parliament,
13–006—13–008
exclusive right to regulate,
13–018—13–019, 13–028
precincts and criminal acts, 13–007
reports of, use of, in court
proceedings, 13–014

PARLIAMENTARY PRIVILEGE—cont.
proceedings in Parliament—cont.
statutory definition, 13–008
register of members' interests, 13–029,
13–034
reporting Parliament,
13–011—13–012
strangers, exclusion of, 13–010
PARLIAMENTARY PROCEDURE,
business, order of, 11–006
closure motion, 11–012
committees, 11–016
Commons, in the, 11–006—11–017
content, 11–002
debates, 12–027—12–028
basis for, 6–033
limiting and organising,
11–011—11–014
rules, 11–007—11–010
divisions, 11–010
finance,
See NATIONAL FINANCE
generally, 11–001
guillotine, 11–014
history, 11–003
legislation,
procedure on, 11–018—11–038
programming, 11–013
nature, 11–001—11–005
questions in Parliament,
12–022—12–026
scrutiny of administration,
12–021—12–033
Select Committees, 12–028—12–033
sources, 11–004—11–005
suspension of members, 11–009
urgency motions, 11–008
Westminster Hall sittings, 11–017
working methods, 11–016
PARLIAMENTARY SOVEREIGNTY,
See PARLIAMENTARY SUPREMACY
PARLIAMENTARY SUPREMACY,
amendment of Acts, 4–002—4–004
areas covered, 3–020—3–021
Australia, in, 4–032—4–033
authentication of Acts, 4–026—4–027
Blackstone on, 3–012, 3–013, 4–003
Ceylon, in, 3–014, 4–034
Coke on, 2–005, 3–003, 3–011, 3–013.,
4–002
composition of Parliament, 3–019
limit on, as, 4–030
contrary arguments, 4–030—4–034
devolution and, 5–014, 5–040
Dicey on, 2–029, 3–013, 4–003,
22–003

PARLIAMENTARY SUPREMACY—*cont.*
dispensing power and, 3–004—3–006
doctrine, 2–021, 2–025, 2–031
establishment of, 3–001
European Communities Act 1972 and,
    4–016—4–024
form and manner of legislation,
    4–025—4–037
fundamental law, as, 3–014—3–015
higher law and, 3–011—3–012, 4–001
history of, 3–001—3–012
Hong Kong, in, 4–033
House of Lords, abolition of, 3–019
independence,
    Acts and, 4–014—4–015
    Grant of, 4–011—4–015
inland revenue concessions and, 3–006
international law and, 3–026—3–02,
    4–001
Irish union and, 4–005
judiciary and, 3–011—3–012
King's legislative powers,
    3–002—3–010
    dispensing powers, 3–004—3–006
    monopolies, 3–007
    judiciary and, 3–011—3–012
    proclamations, 3–003
    subject matter, examples of,
        3–018—3–021
    suspending powers, 3–004—3–006
    taxation, 3–008—3–010
legislation,
    amendment of, 4–002—4–004
    manner and form of, and,
        4–025—4–039
    repeal of, 4–002—4–004
    subject matter of, and,
        4–002—4–024
legislative, 2–012, 3–015
    definition, 3–013
    devolution and, 5–015
    effect of, 2–034
    meaning, 3–013
    principles, 3–014
    rule of law inconsistent with, 2–032
limits to, theories of, 3–012
mandate, doctrine of the, and, 3–023
manifestoes and, 3–023
meaning of, 3–013
modern cases recognising,
    4–015—4–017
nature of, 3–013—3–028
New Zealand, in, 4–031
organised interests and, 3–025
Parliament Acts and, 4–035—4–037
persons covered, 3–020—3021

PARLIAMENTARY SUPREMACY—*cont.*
political opinion as limit on, 3–023
practical limits to, 3–022—3–028
pressure groups and, 3–025
private Acts, applies to, 3–016
procedure,
    substance of legislation
        distinguished, 4–028—4–030
proclamations and, 3–011
public opinion and, 3–024
redefinition of Parliament as limit on,
    4–030—4–031
Regency Acts, 4–038
repeal of Acts, 4–004—4–004
retrospective legislation, 3–018
Scottish Union and, 4–006—4–010
self-limitation, problem of, 4–001
    conclusions, 4–039
ship-money and, 3–009
South Africa, 3–014
subject matter of legislation and,
    4–002—4–024
substance of legislation
    procedure of legislation
        distinguished, 4–028—4–030
suspending power and, 3–004—3–006
taxation and, 3–008—3–010
territorial application, 3–020—3–021
Trethowan's case, 4–032—4–033
Union Acts and, 4–005—4–010
unwritten rule, 2–006
Westminster, statute of, 4–011
withdrawal from E.C. and, 4–030
PARTIAL CABINET,
nature of, 37–013
PARTIES,
political,
See POLITICAL PARTIES
PASSPORT,
issue of, 15–027
Office, 18–015
PEERAGE,
See HOUSE OF LORDS
PERSONAL FREEDOM,
admissibility of confessions and
    evidence, 24–018
arrest and, 24–006—24–011
    warrant, by, 24–007
    without warrant, 24–008—24–011
assaulting a constable and,
    24–019—24–020
bail, 24–023—24–025
binding over, 24–026—24–027
detention by police and,
    24–012—24–015

PERSONAL FREEDOM—*cont.*
    E.C.H.R. and, 24–001
    And see European Convention on
        Human Rights
    general principles, 24–001—24–002
    habeas corpus
        See HABEAS CORPUS
    Human Rights Act, effect of, 24–001
    legal advice, access to, 24–016
    obstructing a constable and, 24–019,
        24–021
    physical restraint, not confined to,
        24–002
        See also PRIVACY
    police powers and, 24–003—24–022
    prisoners' rights, 24–031
    privacy and,
        See PRIVACY
    religion, freedom of, 25–028
    search in detention, 24–014—24–015
    silence, right to, 24–017
    stop and search powers,
        24–004—24–005
    remedies for wrongful deprivation,
        24–002
PETITION OF RIGHT,
    Act 1628, 3–008, 19–033
    scope, 33–005—33–007
PICKETING,
    breach of peace and, 27–034
    mass, 27–034
    meaning, 27–033
    Public Order Act 1986, 27–035
POLICE,
    accountability, 21–012—21–020
    act 1997, 26–017—26–020
    administration
        development, 21–003—21–004
        local basis, on, 21–001
    assaulting, 24–019—24–020
    authorities, 21–013
        Home Secretary, report to, 21–014
        statutory obligations, 21–014
    Chief Constable,
        appointment, 21–013
        functions, 21–015
    Commons, disqualified from, 10–007
    complaints against, 21–021—21–023
    centralising, 21–005
    detention, 24–012—24–018
        access to legal advice, 24–016
        confessions, admissibility of, 24–018
        evidence, admissibility of, 24–018
        silence, right to, 24–017
    discipline, 21–024
    discretion, 21–007—21–008

POLICE—*cont.*
    duty, 21–007—21–008
        execution of, 24–022
    entry powers, 24–043—24–049
    functions, 21–006
    history, 21–002—21–004
    legal status of, 21–009—21–010
    liability and, 21–011
    Metropolitan, 21–003, 21–004
        Commissioner, 21–014
        Police Authority, establishment
            21–004
    obstructing, 24–019, 24–021
    powers,
        arrest, 24–006—24–011
        detention, 24–012—24–015
        entry and search, 24–043—24–049
        freedom of the person and,
            24–003—24–022
        public order,
            See ASSEMBLY, FREEDOM OF
    public accountability, 21–020
    Royal Commissions,
        establishment, 21–003,
        recommendations, 21–003—21–005
    search powers, 24–043—24–049
        statutory, 24–003
        stop and search, 24–004—24–005
    Secretary of State
        functions, 21–016—21–019
        powers, 21–01 6—21–019
        surveillance,26–013—26–021
        See also STATE
    vicarious liability and, 21–011
POLITICAL PARTIES,
    development of, 2–016
    funding, 10–037—10–040
    law reform as to, 10–037—10–041
    manifestoes and, 3–023
    registration, 10–038, 10–041
    role, 10–038
    short money to, 10–040
POLITICAL SYSTEM,
    forms of, 2–016
POST OFFICE,
    status, 28–002, 28–012
PREROGATIVE,
    orders, certiorari, 32–003—32–036
        generally, 32–002
        mandamus, 32–009
        prohibition, 32–007—32–008
    powers, 33–014
    royal
        See ROYAL PREROGATIVE

PRESBYTERIAN CHURCH IN SCOTLAND,
  Parliamentary supremacy and,
    4–008—4–009
PRESS,
  freedom of, 25–018—25–023
    religion, protection of, and, 25–008
  guardian of public interest, 26–010
  self-regulation, 25–019, 25–023
PRESS COMPLAINTS COMMISSION,
  establishment, 25–023
PRESSURE GROUPS,
  consultation with, 3–025
PRESUMPTION,
  interpretation, of, 3–012
PREVENTION OF TERRORISM,
  See TERRORISM
PRIME MINISTER,
  choice of, 17–028—17–032
  Civil Service, head of, 18–008, 18–022
  deputy, 17–030
  dissolve Parliament, right to,
    8–018—8–021
  First Lord of the Treasury, 17–025
  functions, 17–026—17–027
  formal position of, 17–025
  history of office, 17–025
  Intelligence Service and, 17–026
  legal,
    existence, 7–015
    powers, 17–025
  Lords, in, 17–033
  office at No. 10, 17–015
  Prime Ministerial government,
    17–034—17–035
PRISONERS,
  Commons, disqualified from, 10–005,
    24–031
  early release, 24–031
  freedom of movement, 24–031
  human rights and, 22–032, 22–050,
    22–054, 24–032
  jury service, disqualified from, 24–031
  rights, 24–031
    voting, 24–031
  rules, 24–032
PRISONS OMBUDSMAN,
  establishment, 24–032
PRIVACY,
  absence of legal right to, 24–041
  human rights and, 24–041
  Interception of Communications Act
    1985, 26–014—26–015
  press, and, 25–019
  religion, freedom of, 25–028

PRIVATE LAW,
  actions involving administrative bodies,
    2–024
  public law distinguished, 1–014
PRIVATE MEMBERS' BILLS,
  generally, 11–034—11–035
  procedure, 11–036—11–038
PRIVATISATION,
  generally, 28–013—28–015
PRIVILEGE,
  diplomatic, 15–032—15–033
  Parliamentary
    See PARLIAMENTARY PRIVILEGE
  sovereign, 15–032
PRIVY COUNCIL,
  Cabinet origins in the, 17–001
  committees, 16–008
  Commons, disqualification jurisdiction
    for, 10–013
  composition, 16–003
  functions, 16–004—15–006
  history, 16–001—16–002
  judicial committee of
    See JUDICIAL COMMITTEE OF THE
      PRIVY COUNCIL
  meetings, 16–007
  Office, 18–016
  Orders in Council, 16–005
    Arts Minister in, 18–020
  proclamations, 16–005
PROCEDURAL IMPROPRIETY,
  natural justice and, 31–013—31–018
PROCESSIONS,
  See PUBLIC PROCESSIONS
PROCLAMATIONS,
  case of, 3–003, 15–002, 29–002, 22–011
  nature of, 16–005
  prerogative limited by law, 15–019
  statute of, 3–003
PROHIBITION,
  order, 32–007—32–008
PROPERTY, FREEDOM OF,
  Customs and Excise powers,
    24–050—24–054
  E.C.H.R. on, 24–054
    See also EUROPEAN CONVENTION ON
      HUMAN RIGHTS
  Englishman's home is his castle,
    24–041—24–042
  entry and search powers,
    24–043—24–049
    special, 24–049
  forcible entry, 24–042
  human rights and, 24–041—24–042
  Inland Revenue, powers,
    24–050—24–054

PROPERTY, FREEDOM OF—*cont.*
search
  orders, 24–052
  warrants, 24–046—24–049
seizure of articles, 24–045
statutory restrictions on, 24–054
taxation, liability to, 24–053
trespass not a crime, 24–042
PROROGATION,
prerogative, exercise of, 8–012
PUBLIC ACCOUNTS COMMITTEE,
role, 12–017, 12–020
scrutiny by, 12–017
PUBLIC AUTHORITIES,
See also JUDICIAL REVIEW
appeals from, statutory, 32–016
damages action against, 32–022
declaration, action for, 32–024
injunction against, 32–023
judicial control
  powers, of, 31–002—31–020
  private law, 31–021—31–025
  public law, 31–002—31–020
  remedies, 32–001—32–024
liability,
  contract, 31–022
  generally, 31–021
  negligence, 31–024
  nuisance, 31–023
  statutory duties, non–performance of,
    31–025
private law remedies against,
  32–022—32–024
specific performance against, 32–023
statutory rights of appeal, 32–016
PUBLIC CORPORATIONS,
advisory, 28–004—28–006
appointment, 28–008
classification, 28–002—28–006
Crown, relationship with,
  28–009—28–011
judicial proceedings and,
  28–009—28–011
legal position, 28–007—28–012
managerial, 28–002
  industrial/commercial, 28–002
  social services, 28–003
nature, 28–001—28–006
National Health Service, 28–011
origins, 28–001
Post Office, 28–012
powers, 28–008 privatisation,
  28–013—28–015
purpose, 28–001—28–006
regulatory, 28–004—28–006
  regulating the, 28–016—28–017

PUBLIC INTEREST,
confidentiality and, 25–020—25–021
disclosure of information, in, 26–031
immunity, 33–022—33–028
publication in, 25–026
right to know, balanced against,
  26–001
test, 26–030
PUBLIC LAW,
actions involving administrative bodies,
  2–024
private law distinguished, 1–014
PUBLIC MEETING,
See also ASSEMBLY, FREEDOM OF
conditions on, 27–006
definition, 27–002
disorderly conduct,
  break up, designed to, 27–029
dispersal, 27–007—27–010
highway, on, 27–004. 27–028
history, 27–002
  Parliament, near, 27–005
practice, 27–002
prevention, 27–007—27–010
private places, in, 27–003
  definition, 27–002
proscribed organisation, addressed by,
  27–032
public places, in, 27–004
  definition, 27–002
restrictions on, 27–006
right to hold, no,
  exceptions, 27–005
PUBLIC ORDER,
See also ASSEMBLY, FREEDOM OF
common law emergency powers,
  19–019—19–022
PUBLIC ORDER OFFENCES,
affray, 27–021
assaulting a police officer, 27–030
disorderly conduct, 27–025
  lawful public meeting, designed to
    break up, 27–029
highway, obstruction of, 27–028
incitement to racial hatred, 27–031
  See also INCITEMENT TO RACIAL
    HATRED
nuisance, 27–031
person, against the, 27–031
police officer, obstruction of, 27–030
possession
  firearms and explosives, 27–031
  offensive weapon in public place,
    27–031
public nuisance, 27–031
reforms to, 27–018

PUBLIC ORDER OFFENCES—*cont.*
  riot, 27–019
  sedition, 27–031
    And see SEDITION
  statutory, 27–027—27–037
    threatening, abusive, insulting words/
      behaviour, 27–022—27–026
  violent disorder, 27–020
PUBLIC PROCESSIONS,
  conditions, 27–015
    judicial review of, 27–016
  definition, 27–015
  prohibition, 27–016
    judicial review of, 27–017

QUEEN,
  See SOVEREIGN

RACIAL HATRED,
  definition, 25–010
  incitement to, 25–010
REFERENCE TO EUROPEAN COURT OF
    JUSTICE,
  See EUROPEAN COMMUNITY LAW,
    PRELIMINARY RULINGS
REFERENDA,
  E.C. membership, on, 4–019
  law-making method, as, 1–015
  use of, 10–063
REFORM BILL,
  effect of, 8–029
REGENCY ACTS,
  Parliamentary supremacy and, 4–038
  provisions, 14–008—14–00—14–010
REGIONAL DEVELOPMENT,
  agencies,
    creation of, 5–042
    purpose of, 5–042
  Regional Chambers, as to, 5–043
  first step towards, 5–042
  Government Offices, 5–044
REGISTRATION,
  citizenship, by, 23–004, 23–009
REGULATIONS (E.C.),
  directly applicable, 6–012
  making of, 4–018
  secondary legislation as, 4–016
REGULATORY BODIES,
  See also PUBLIC CORPORATIONS
  generally, 8–016—28–017
RELIGION,
  freedom of, 25–028
REPRESENTATIVE GOVERNMENT,
  nature of, 2–016
REPUBLIC OF IRELAND,
  See IRELAND, REPUBLIC OF

RESPONSIBLE GOVERNMENT,
  Parliamentary, 2–014—2–015
RESPONSIBILITY, MINISTERIAL,
  generally, 2–015, 17–016—17–021
  Next steps, impact of, 18–024
REVENUE,
  prerogative powers, 15–013
  public, 12–012
RIGHT, PETITION OF,
  Act 1628, 3–008, 19–033
  scope, 33–005—33–007
RIGHTS,
  bill of,
    See BILL OF RIGHTS
  fundamental, 1–019—1–020
  Universal Declaration of, 1–020
RIOT,
  generally, 27–019
ROMAN LAW,
  influence of, 1–014
ROYAL AIR FORCE,
  See also ARMED FORCES
  generally, 19–002, 19–003
ROYAL ASSENT,
  constitutional convention,
    refusal of, whether, 7–010
  Parliament, in, 8–011
  procedure, 11–031
ROYAL FAMILY,
  husband of Queen Regnant, 14–007
  marriages of, 14–007
  princes and princess, 14–007
  Prince of Wales, 14–007
  Sovereign, 14–007
ROYAL NAVY,
  See also ARMED FORCES
  generally, 19–003
ROYAL PREROGATIVE,
  See also ACT OF STATE
  administration of justice, 20–002
  appointment and dismissal of
    Ministers, 15–013
  armed services, over, 15–013
  Civil Service, operation and control,
    18–022
  classification of, 15–007—15–009
  conventions as to, 7–015—7–017
  custom of, 2–009, 2–013
  defence matters, in, 15–016–15–017
  dependencies, to administer, 15–013
  diplomatic representation,
    15–032—15–033
  discretionary nature, 15–004 –15–005
  dismissal of a Ministry, 8–024
  dissolution of Parliament,
    See DISSOLUTION OF PARLIAMENT

ROYAL PREROGATIVE—*cont.*
  domestic affairs, in, 15–012—15–020
  ecclesiastical, 15–014
  emergencies, in, 15–016—15–017
  executive, 15–012—15–017
  foreign affairs, in, 15–021—15–033
  fountain of honour, 15–015
  history, 15–002—15–006
  judicial, 15–018
  legally vested in the Sovereign, 15–006
  legislative, 15–019—15–020
  liability for exercise, 33–014—33–015
  meaning, 15–001
  mercy, of, 20–004
    exercise of, 2–020
  Ministry, dismissal of, 8–024
  miscellaneous, 15–015
  nature, generally, 15–001—15–011
  pardon, of, 20–005
  passports, to issue, 15–027
  Parliament, in, 8–010
  personal, 15–007, 15–009
  political, 15–007
  refuse to dissolve Parliament, to,
    8–025—8–026
  residual nature, 15–004
  revenue, over, 15–013
  Sovereign immunity, 15–032—15–033
  statute,
    Crown, not binding on, 15–019
    effect of, 15–010
    relationship between, 15–011
  territory, to cede, 15–031
  treaties, to make, 15–028—15–031
RULE OF LAW,
  arbitrary power, excludes, 2–029
  binding nature of, 2–029
  Delhi Declaration on, 2–028
  Dicey on, 2–029—2–032
  discretionary powers and, 2–030
  equality before the law, 2–029—2–030
  extra-legal devices, 2–027
  formal characteristics of rules and,
    2–028
  historical meaning of, 2–025—2–027
  judge–made nature of law and
  lawful authority for its actions,
    requires, 2–026—2–027
  limited legislative power,
    2–026—2–027
  political beliefs and, 2–028
  significance, 2–033
  substantive element, 2–028
  term, as a, 2–025—2–027

SAYLES,
  Parliament, on, 8–002
SCANDALISING THE COURT,
  effect of, 20–047
SCOTLAND,
  Act of Union 4–006—4–010
  Advocate-General, 18–010
  administrative devolution for, 5–004
  Church of, 4–007—4–008
  constitutional status, 2–003
  Court of Sessions, 20–011
  devolution to,
    background to, 5–007
    electoral system, 5–013
    funding, 5–018
    future of, 5–050
    government Cabinet style, 5–017
    human rights and, 5–016, 5–021
    impetus to introduce, 5–006
    issues, 5–015
    members' interests, conduct and
      privileges, 5–019, 5–028
    statutory provisions for,
      generally, 5–012
      subordination to Westminster,
        5–014, 5–023
  E.C. law, compatibility with, 5–021
  Executive,
    appointment, 5–022
    composition, 5–022
    dismissal, 5–022
    establishment of, 5–020, 5–022
    functions, 5–021, 5–023
    legislative competence, 5–021
    Sovereign's powers, 5–023
  Grand Committee, 5–046
  House of Commons,
    reduction of seats in, 5–045
  House of Lords,
    appeals to and from, 9–051, 20–008
  nationalism in, 5–005—5–006
  Parliament,
    Code of Conduct, 5–028
    committees, establishment of, 5–024
    control of, 5–022
    election to, 5–022, 5–028, 10–059
    establishment of, 5–020
    functions, 5–021, 5–028
    legislative
      competence, 5–021
      procedures, 5–025—5–028
    maladministration, as to, 34–010
    primary legislation, 5–026
    secondary legislation, 5–027
    scrutiny functions, 5–028
    Sovereign's powers, 5–023

SCOTLAND—*cont.*
  Parliament—*cont.*
    power to make laws, 5–021
    Roman law in, 1–014
    Scottish Office, 18–017
    Solicitor-General, 18–010
    U.K. powers to make laws for, 4–010,
      5–021
SCOTTISH CONSTITUTIONAL CONVENTION,
  devolution, in favour of, 5–007
SEARCH,
  arrest, following, 24–044
  emergency powers, 19–033—19–034
  orders, 24–052
  police powers, 24–043—24–049
  property, of, 24–044
  warrants, 24–046—24–049
    special powers of entry without,
      24–049
SECRET BALLOT,
  existence of, 2–016
SECRETARY OF STATE,
  Culture, Media and Sport, for, 18–020
  Home Office, 21–016—21–019,
    23–034
  Northern Ireland, for, 2–005, 18–019
  number of, 18–003
  office of, 18–001
  role, 18–005
  Scotland, for, 18–017,
  Trade and Industry, 18–003
  Wales, for, 18–018
SECURITY SERVICES,
  accountability, 19–040
  Directors, 19–039
  information as to, 26–010
  location, 19–038
  non-statutory basis, 19–038
  official secrets and, 26–006, 26–010
  origin, 19–038
  Parliamentary accountability, 19–040
  publicity, 19–039
  responsibilities, 19–038
  statutory basis, 19–038
SEDITION,
  law of, 25–009
  meaning, 25–009
SELECT COMMITTEES,
  departmental,
    role, 12–011
      work, 12–033
  functions, 12–029
  Parliamentary Commissioner for
    Administration, on, 34–012
  powers, 12–030 –12–031

SELECT COMMITTEES—*cont.*
  statutory instruments, on,
    29–024—29–026
  Treasury, 12–011
  work of departmental, 12–033
SEPARATION OF POWERS,
  concept
    importance, 2–022
    reliance on, 2–021
  doctrine of, 1–017—1–018, 2–032
  English Constitution, in the, 2–021
SERIOUS FRAUD OFFICE,
  establishment, 18–013
SEX DISCRIMINATION,
  E.C. law, in, 6–038
SHIP MONEY,
  revenue, as, 3–009
SINGLE EUROPEAN ACT,
  entry into force, 6–002
SOCIAL SECURITY,
  tribunal, 30–012
SOLICITOR-GENERAL,
  England and Wales, for, 18–010
SOUTH AFRICA,
  constitution, 3–014
  Dominion status, former, 4–011
SOVEREIGN,
  See also MONARCHY, ROYAL
    PREROGATIVE
  abdication, 14–005
  accession, 14–003
  Cabinet, influence on, 17–024
  conventions concerning role of,
    7–015—7–017
  coronation, 14–004
  Crown liability and, 33–015, 33–019
  duties, 14–007
  functions, 2–019
  honour, fountain of all, 15–015
  immunity, 15–032
  justice, fountain of all, 20–002
  law-maker, as, 3–002—3–010, 20–002
  Parliament, presence in, 8–010
  Prime Minister, choice of,
    17–028—17–032
  Private Secretary of, 14–011
  Regency Acts, 14–008
  Royal family, 14–007
  style and titles, 14–006
  treason against,
    And see TREASON
    14–012—14–023
  under 18, 14–010
SOVEREIGNTY OF PARLIAMENT,
  See PARLIAMENTARY SUPREMACY

SPEAKER OF THE HOUSE OF COMMONS,
  election, 8–016, 10–016
  Electoral Commission, appointment of,
    10–042
  functions, 1–002, 10–017—10–019
  history, 10–016
  judicial review of decision, 10–019
  mental illness of MP and, 10–005
  Money Bills, certification of, 8–034,
    10–018
  Parliament Acts,
    certificates by, under, 8–035
    duties under, 10–018
  Parliamentary elections, 10–017
  re-election, 10–016
  remuneration, 10–019
  representative of House of Commons,
    10–017
  retirement,10–019
  rulings from the Chair, 10–018
  Sovereign consents to choice, 10–016
SPECIAL APPEALS COMMISSION,
  composition, 23–037
  establishment, 23–036
  procedure, 23–037
SPECIFIC PERFORMANCE,
  action for, 32–022
SPEECH, FREEDOM OF,
  See EXPRESSION, FREEDOM OF
SPORTING EVENTS,
  banning order, 27–037
  public order and, 27–036—27–037
STANDARDS IN PUBLIC LIFE,
  Commission on
      establishment, 13–028
      role 13–028–13–029, 13–031,
        13–034
  Commissioner of, 13–030
  Committee on, 10–037
STATE,
  constitution, 1–005
    See also CONSTITUTION
  definition, 1–004
  immunity, 15–032—15–033
  offences against,
    See OFFENCES AGAINST THE STATE
  Official Secrets Act, meaning in,
    26–003
  surveillance, 26–013—26–023
    challenge, actions of, 26–023
    Commissioners, 26–021—26–022
    communications data, as to, 26–016
    covert human intelligence sources,
      by, 26–017, 26–019
    directed, 26–019
      authorisation, 26–019

STATE—cont.
  surveillance—cont.
    directed—cont.
      definition, 26–019
    electronic data, investigation of,
      26–020
    generally, 26–013
    human rights and, 26–013
    interception of communications,
      legislation, 26–014—26–015
      supervision of, 26–021—26–023
    intrusive, 26–019
      authorisation, 26–019
      definition, 26–019
    legislation,
      operation of, 26–021—26–023
    technical devices, by, 26–017
      placing of, 26–018
    Tribunal, 26–023
STATUTE,
  law, 2–006
  Parliamentary supremacy and,
    See PARLIAMENTARY SUPREMACY
  proclamations, case of, 3–003, 22–011
  rolls, 4–026
  source of constitutional law, as, 2–007
  Westminster, of,
    See STATUTE OF WESTMINSTER
STATUTE OF WESTMINSTER,
  Australia, as to, 36–009—36–011
  Canada, as to, 36–007—36–008
  effect of, 4–011—4–013
  generally, 7–019, 36–003—36–006
  grants of independence, 4–011—4–013
  New Zealand, as to, 36–012
  Privy Council, appeals to, and,
    37–009—37–010
  royal style and titles, alteration to,
    14–006
STATUTORY INSTRUMENT,
  appeal rights, 32–016
  provisions as to, 29–005
STOP AND SEARCH,
  powers, 24–004—24–005
    emergency, 19–033—19–034
SUBORDINATE LEGISLATION,
  See DELEGATED LEGISLATION
SUPERVISORY JURISDICTION OF HIGH
  COURT,
  See also JUDICIAL REVIEW
  generally, 30–017, 30–022, 32–002
SUPPLY,
  See also NATIONAL FINANCE
  business, 12–008
  wartime, 19–037

SUPREMACY OF PARLIAMENT,
See PARLIAMENTARY SUPREMACY
SURVEILLANCE COMMISSIONS,
establishment, 26–023
SUSPENDING POWER,
exercise of, 3–004—3–006
SWITZERLAND,
constitution in, 1–006
adjudication, 1–010
amendment , 1–007

TAXATION,
Parliamentary supremacy and,
3–008—3–010
tribunal, 30–016
TERRORISM,
burden of proof, 19–046
courts' powers, 19–044
defence to, 19–046
definitions, 25–011, 19–042—19–043
extra-territorial jurisdiction, 19–041
freedom of expression and, 25–011
human rights and, 19–041, 19–042,
19–045
international, 19–041
legislation against, 10–041
Northern Ireland affairs and, 19–042
offences,
criminal, 19–044
defence to, 19–046
specific, 19–045
types, 19–043,
police powers, 19–044
proscribed organisations,
19–043—19–044
recent phenomenon, 19–041
statutory provisions, 19–043—19–046
TEXT BOOKS,
source of law, as, 2–010
THEATRE,
censorship, 25–037
TORT,
Crown liability for, 33–008—33–011
public authorities, 31–013—31–025
TREASON,
adhering to Sovereign's enemies,
14–015—14–016
alarming/injuring Sovereign, 14–022
allegiance, breach of, 14–012, 14–018
Chancellor, slaying, 14–017
Commons, disqualifies for, 10–005
compassing/imagining Sovereign's
death, 14–013
constructive, 14–018
felony, 14–021

TREASON—cont.
generally, 14–012
levying war, 14–014
misprision of, 14–020
punishment for, 14–019
reform proposals, 14–023
succession, depriving/hindering next,
14–018
trial for, 14–019
TREASURY,
composition, 18–007
responsibilities, 18–008
role, 18–007
Select Committee, 12–011
Solicitor, 18–013
TREATIES,
expressly made,
Parliament, subject to confirmation
of, 15–029
law, alteration to, involving, 15–029
maritime boundaries,
cession and delimitation of, 15–031
power to make, 15–028
private rights, affecting, 15–030
taxation, alteration to, involving,
15–029
TRESPASS,
action for,
remedy for police interference, as,
24–041
freedom of assembly and, 27–004,
27–012
TRIAL,
jury, by, 20–017—20–024
right to a fair, 20–012
TRIBUNALS,
appeals from, 30–020
appointment of members, 30–004,
30–019
Commons, members disqualified from,
10–007
composition, 30–004
creation, reasons for, 30–005—30–010
Council on,
consultation, 30–020
establishment, 30–018
decisions, reasons for, 30–023
Director–general of Fair Trading,
30–016
domestic, 30–017
employment, 30–00230–013
examples of statutory, 30–011—30–016
functions, 30–004
immigration, 30–014
information, 30–016

TRIBUNALS—*cont.*
  Inquiries Act 1992 and,
      30–018—30–022
  inquiry, of, 30–016
  mental health review, 30–015
  procedure, 30–004, 30–020
  professional disciplinary, 30–017
  reasons,
      creation, for, 30–005—30–010
      decisions, for, 30–023
  review, 30–002
  social security, 30–012
  supervision, 30–017, 30–022
  taxation, 30–016
TRUST TERRITORIES BRITISH,
  independence, 35–009

ULTRA VIRES,
  judicial acts, 31–007
  legislation, 31–005—31–006
  local government, 2–035
  rule, 31–003—31–007
UNION,
  Ireland, with, 2–004—2–005, 4–005
  Scotland, with, 2–003, 4–006—4–010
  Wales, 2–002
UNITED KINGDOM CONSTITUTION,
  administrative law and, 2–023—2–024
  books of authority as source, 2–010
      custom, 2–009
  conventions and,
      See also CONSTITUTIONAL
          CONVENTIONS
      importance of, 2–017
  custom as source of, 2–009
  flexible nature, 2–011
  general characteristics, 2–001—2–037
  human rights and, 2–034
  individual rights under,
      22–002—22–003
  judicial precedents as source, 2–008
  judiciary, position of, 2–018—2–019
  laws, 2–006
  legislative supremacy of Parliament,
      2–012
  monarchy, position of, 2–013
  Parliamentary government in, 2–016
  Parliamentary sovereignty in
      See also PARLIAMENTARY
          SUPREMACY
      generally, 2–012
  representative government in, 2–016
  responsible government in,
      2–014—2–015
  rule of law in,
      See also RULE OF LAW

UNITED KINGDOM CONSTITUTION—*cont.*
  rule of law in—*cont.*
      generally, 2–025—2–033
      separation of powers in, 2–020—2–022
      sources of, 2–007—2–010
      sovereignty of Parliament, 2–012
      statutes as source, 2–007
          Acts of Parliament, 2–007
          delegated legislation, 2–007
          subordinate legislation, 2–007
      unitary, 2–001—2–005, 5–001
      unwritten, 2–006—2–010
UNITED NATIONS,
  Universal Declaration of Human
      Rights, 1–020, 22–004
UNITED STATES,
  Bill of Rights, 1–020
  constitution in, 1–006, 1–010
      amendment, 1–007
  expression, freedom of, in, 26–024
  independence, 4–014
  presidential system, 2–015
  separation of powers in, 1–018
  voting system, 10–058
UNIVERSAL ADULT SUFFRAGE,
  existence of, 2–016
UNIVERSAL DECLARATION OF HUMAN
      RIGHTS,
  adoption of, 1–020
  human rights elaborated in, 22–004
  principles, 2–028

VOTING,
  See ELECTIONS, FRANCHISE

WALES,
  administrative devolution for, 5–004
  constitutional status, 2–002
  devolution for,
      background, 5–007
      electoral system, 5–013
      E.C. law and, 5–037
      funding, 5–018
      future of, 5–050
      government, Cabinet style, 5–017
      human rights and, 5–016, 5–037
      impetus to introduce, 5–006
      issues, 5–015
      members' interests, conduct and
          privileges, 5–019
      provisions for, generally, 5–012
      subordination to Westminster, 5–014
  Executive Committee,
      composition, 5–040
      functions, 5–040
  Grand Committee, 5–046

WALES—*cont.*
National Assembly, 5–036
  Accountability, 5–040
  committees,
    roles, 5–041
    structure, 5–039
  control of, 5–041
  elections, 5–036, 10–059
  establishment, 5–036, 5–038
  functions, 5–037—5–038
  legislative competence, 5–037
  powers, 5–037
nationalism in, 5–005—5–006
Welsh Office, 18–018
WAR CRIMES,
Act 1991, 9–026
liability, 19–007
WAYS AND MEANS,
business, 12–013

WARRANT,
backing of, 23–048—23–049
arrest by, 24–007
arrest without, 24–008—24–011
WEST LOTHIAN QUESTION,
possible solutions, 5–042, 5–045
WESTMINSTER, STATUTE OF,
See STATUTE OF WESTMINSTER
WHIPS,
role, 10–024
WITENAGEMOT,
precursor of Parliament, 8–001, 9–002
WRITS,
certiorari, 32–004—32–007
declaration, 32–010
habeas corpus,
  See HABEAS CORPUS
injunction, 32–010
mandamus, 32–009
prerogative, 32–002
prohibition, 32–007—32–008